Footprint Scotland Handbook

The travel guide

Alan Murphy

*For my part, I travel not to go anywhere,
but to go. I travel for travel's sake. The
great affair is to move.*

Robert Louis Stevenson

Scotland Handbook
Second edition
© Footprint Handbooks Ltd 2002

Published by Footprint Handbooks
6 Riverside Court
Lower Bristol Road
Bath BA2 3DZ. England
T +44 (0)1225 469141
F +44 (0)1225 469461
Email discover@footprintbooks.com
Web www.footprintbooks.com

ISBN 1 903471 29 X
CIP DATA: A catalogue record for this
book is available from the British Library

Distributed in the USA by
Publishers Group West

® Footprint Handbooks and the
Footprint mark are a registered
trademark of Footprint Handbooks Ltd.

Credits

Series editors
Patrick Dawson and Rachel Fielding

Editorial
Editor: Catherine Charles
Maps: Sarah Sorensen

Production
Typesetting: Mark Thomas, Emma
Bryers, Leona Bailey, and Jo Morgan
Maps: Robert Lunn, Claire Benison and
Maxine Foster
Colour maps: Kevin Feeney

Cover: Camilla Ford

Design
Mytton Williams

Photography
Front cover: gettyone Stone
Back cover: Scotland in Focus
Inside colour section: gettyone Stone;
James Davis Travel Photography;
Scotland in Focus; Robert Harding
Picture Library; ImageState.

Print
Manufactured in Italy by LEGOPRINT

Scotland

Shetland Islands
Unst
Yell
Fetlar
Mainland
Lerwick

N

0 km 40
0 miles 40

See colour maps at back of book

Ben Nevis	Natural feature
Callanish	Archaeological feature
Loch Ness	Water feature

North Sea

Orkney Islands
Westray
Rousay
Sanday
Eday
Stronsay
Mainland
Shapinay
Maes Howe ⁖
Kirkwall
Hoy
South Ronaldsay
Pentland Firth

Cape Wrath
Durness
Thurso
John o'Groats
Wick

Kinlochbervie

Lewis
Callanish ⁖
Stornaway

Outer Hebrides
Harris
Tarbert

Ullapool
Dornoch

The Minch
Moray Firth

North Uist
Benbecula
The Little Minch
South Uist
Portree
Skye
Kyle of Localsh
Black Isle
Inverness
Strathspey

Barra
Armadale
Aviemore
Loch Ness

Rum
Mallaig
Fort Augustus
Grampian Mountains
Braemar
Aberdeen

Inner Hebrides
Eigg
Fort William
▲ Ben Nevis
● Glencoe
Pitlochry

Coll
Tiree
Tobermory
Mull
Oban
Dundee
Perth
St Andrews

Atlantic Ocean
Fingal's cave ●
Iona
Inveraray
Loch Lomond
Callander
Firth of Forth

Colonsay
Jura
Kilmartin Glen ⁖
Stirling

Islay
Bute
□ **Glasgow**
□ **EDINBURGH**

Arran
Campbeltown
Brodick

NORTHERN IRELAND
ENGLAND

Contents

Front cover Tradition reflected in modernity in Glasgow, Scotland's largest city

Previous page Autumn carpets the Scottish countryside in a thousand luminous hues, from lustrous gold to blazing orange

Opposite page A field of foxgloves in Glen Rosa, on the Isle of Arran

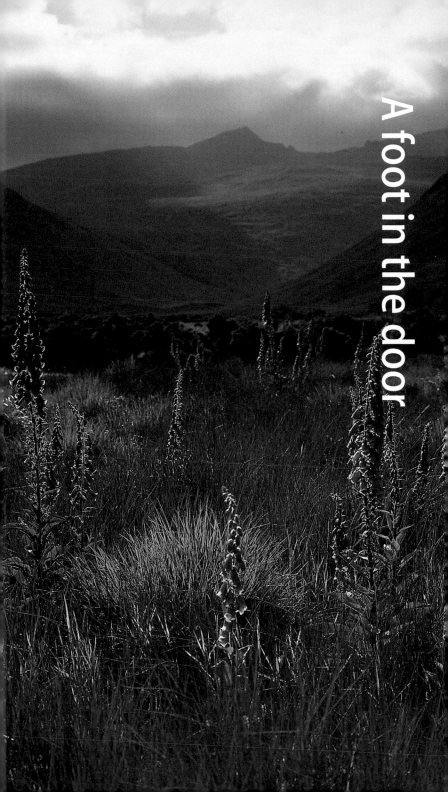

A foot in the door

Right The glories of the Scottish Highlands are made all the more rewarding by the absence of other people, as here in Glen Garry
Below The view from Calton Hill to the Edinburgh Castle. Scotland's capital is one of the great European cities, matching even Paris, Prague or Rome in grandeur

Above The Clyde Auditorium, better known as the 'Armadillo', from Bell's Bridge over the River Clyde, Glasgow
Right Statue of Alexander Selkirk, the real-life Robinson Crusoe, who hailed from the East Neuk of Fife

Introduction

Heard the one about the Scottish boomerang? It never comes back, it just talks constantly about coming back. This pretty much sums up the Scots' attitude to their own country. They may not necessarily live there, but they still take an inordinate amount of pride in their homeland. Every self-respecting Scot comes over all proprietorial when introducing the glories of their country to a loved one or friend for the first time. So much so, you'd think they'd designed the whole place themselves, as if the jaw-dropping scenery of Wester Ross, say, or the Trossachs, was some kind of DIY makeover: "Oh, yes, we got rid of that awful woodchip and planted the hillsides in Caledonian pine forest. The native woodland look is so new millennium".

Mist opportunities

The Scots have every right to be proud. When the rain stops falling and the mist clears there is no more beautiful place on Earth. If there is a heaven, then it must look like this, but let's hope the petrol's cheaper. About the only thing Scotland doesn't have going for it is a dependable climate. If you want to lie on a beach all day soaking up rays, then you really ought to go somewhere else. Ironically though, many of the country's greatest attractions are made even more appealing by the notoriously fickle weather conditions. And that's not just the whisky talking. Take all those medieval castles, for instance. Soaked in the blood of centuries and scarred from countless battles and feuds, these ruins are at their brooding best when shrouded in mist. The myriad prehistoric standing stones, burial chambers and brochs (ancient high-rise houses) are evocative enough places when the sun is shining, but under a bruised sky they take on a tangibly sinister feel, which only enhances their strange other-worldliness.

Haute culture

Scotland also boasts two world-class cities: Edinburgh and Glasgow. Few urban places make such a strong impression on the visitor as Scotland's capital. It is, without doubt, one of the most beautiful and elegant cities in Europe with a grandeur that matches anything Prague, Vienna or Rome has to offer – hence its traditional tag, 'the Athens of the North'. In keeping with its status as one of the great European cities, Edinburgh's many excellent museums and art galleries boast the finest collections outside London, and every August the city plays host to the biggest arts festival on the planet. Edinburgh during its festival has been described as "the cultural hub of the world".

Style and substance

If Edinburgh's tourist trappings become too much, take a trip to Glasgow, Scotland's largest city, which has long been ignored by visitors in favour of its great rival. A decade ago, much to Edinburgh's chagrin, Glasgow was chosen as European City of Culture, and has never looked back since. The Kelvingrove and Burrell galleries boast two of the finest art collections in Britain, and Glasgow is also home to both Scottish opera and Scottish ballet, as well as having some of the most exciting theatre companies in the country. In 1999, it received another top accolade: City of Architecture and Design. Now, the many Victorian architectural treasures of the "Second City of the Empire" are being given the attention they deserve, and can stand alongside the internationally-acclaimed creations of Charles Rennie Mackintosh. The city has other attractions. It has a thriving continental-style café culture, many stylish bars and bistros and was recently voted the UK's top city outside London for the choice and quality of its restaurants. But it is the people of Glasgow who really set it apart. Its atmosphere is infused with those vital ingredients missing from so many large urban centres – warmth and humour. Glasgow is without doubt the friendliest of Britain's large cities.

Room to roam

Scotland is one of the least densely populated countries in Europe. Not much smaller than its southern neighbour, England, it has only one tenth of its population – and most of them are crammed into the narrow central belt. This leaves two-thirds of the country unspoiled. The Scottish Highlands are one of Europe's last great wildernesses: one of the few places in this increasingly cluttered continent where you can really get away from it all. Okay, so you can't depend on the weather, but there's an old hikers' adage that states that there's no such thing as bad weather, only inadequate clothing, which pretty much sums up the kind of attitude you'll need to enjoy the great outdoors in this part of the world.

Take the high road Scotland's greatest appeal is to those who love the outdoor life. There are mountains galore to climb or ski down, lochs to fish and wildlife to watch, or you can just sit back and take in all that stunning scenery. In the Highlands in particular, there are countless opportunities to leave civilization a long way behind. You could explore Scotland's long distance footpaths which snake through some of the country's finest scenery. These include the West Highland Way which starts in Glasgow and ends at Fort William, the less well known Speyside Way, which passes through the heart of whisky country, and the Southern Upland Way, which runs from coast to coast through Dumfries and Galloway and the Borders. The more adventurous can try their hand (or feet) at 'Munro Bagging', which is not some dubious public school practice but the name given to the popular pursuit of climbing Scotland's 284 mountains higher than 3,000 feet. This offers the chance to explore wild areas of unparalleled beauty such as Glen Coe, Torridon, Kintail or the Cairngorms. In winter, the snow turns the Munros into major expeditions, but also brings the opportunity for downhill skiing. Resorts such as Glenshee, the Nevis Range, Glencoe, the Lecht and the Cairngorms are open from December to April and on a good day offer some superb skiing.

Caledonian McStrange The Scottish mainland is surrounded by hundreds of islands, each one with its own distinct history and culture. Crossing to these islands doesn't just feel like a different country, it can feel like you're entering another time zone. Where else could you find a police station using gerbils as paper shredders, or the swings in the playground padlocked to ensure strict observance of the Sabbath? Lying off the west coast are the Hebridean islands, home of the Gaelic culture, where the road signs include English spellings almost as an afterthought and the local people speak Gaelic as their native tongue.

Northern exposure Off the northern tip of the mainland is Orkney, an archipelago of 70 islands, which has spawned some of Scotland's greatest writers. No surprising perhaps, given that Orkney has such an eventful history. The islands were ruled by the Vikings for 650 years until the 15th century and despite their remote location, played a dramatic role at the end of the First World War when the German fleet was scuttled in Scapa Flow. But if you think Orkney seems remote, then you ain't seen nothing yet. The Shetland Isles are so far north they can only be included on maps as an inset. In fact, they still don't seem a part of Britain: the nearest mainland town is Bergen, in Norway, and Norwegian is taught in the schools.

Previous pages The perenially photogenic harbour at Crail, in Fife

Right The mystical Eildon Hills, near the Borders town of Melrose, are said to be the resting place of King Arthur and his knights
Below Lone Bothy by Ben Arkle, in Sutherland. Now that's what I call isolated
Next pages Glencoe is a mecca for climbers and hikers. Here, two hardy souls traverse the Aonach Eagach ridge

Above Och aye, the coo! These hairy beasts will always have a place in the hearts of visitors
Right The Trotternish Peninsula, Isle of Skye

Scotched myths

There's a lot more to Scotland than bagpipes and whisky. Forget the clichéd images of *Brigadoon* and *Braveheart*, the dreadfully twee tartan tat and Celtic kitsch that, sadly, still exists in the 21st century and is too often passed off as a genuine Scottish experience. This is one of the most fasinating countries in Europe and shouldn't need to try and fool visitors with tired old myths in order to sell itself as a world-class tourist destination.

Gullible travels The biggest myth of all, of course, is the one concerning a certain monster. You don't need a PhD in ecology to be able to see that a single member of any species isn't going to get very far on its own. In order to survive from the Jurassic to the present day it would have to be in the company of other members of its species. Quite aside from the fact that Loch Ness is too cold and devoid of life to support a population of plesiosaurs, as reptiles they would need to break the water's surface at least every few minutes. So, why is it that on every day of the tourist season, coach after coach arrives in the lay-bys beside Loch Ness, a piper hurriedly stuffs his fags in his sporran and starts playing his pipes, and a bunch of eager, camera-toting visitors scan the placid waters in the hope of seeing a dinosaur? Great piles of 'Nessie' soft toys grace the shelves of Visitor Centre gift shops, along with the obligatory 'see you, Jimmy' wigs and bunnets, tins of shortbread and butterscotch and those scary, tartan-clad dolls with the fluttering eyelashes. It's all about as authentic as Idi Amin's claim to the Scottish throne and as depressing as a wet weekend in Wolverhampton.

The reel McCoy Another myth, that's more difficult to dispel, is that the Scots see life through a whisky-induced haze. This may be a bit of an exaggeration, but it cannot be denied that there's nothing the Scots love more than a good party, preferably involving lots of alcohol, singing and dancing. Music and dancing is an intrinsic part of Highland culture and you're never too far from a ceilidh (pronounced 'kay-lee'), a kind of Highland knees-up, which is somewhere between a barn dance and a rugby scrum. One of the most unforgettable experiences of a Highland holiday is to find yourself in a pub in the the middle of nowhere, consuming copious quantities of whisky with the locals and then being hurled by a bunch of total strangers around the room, to the accompaniment of a fiddle and accordian. By the time you reach the top of the nearest mountain the next day, you'll have forgotten all about the hangover.

Game on You'd have to be very unlucky not to experience at least one local festival. The calendar is bursting with them. Many have their roots in pagan ceremonies, others, such as *Up Helly-Aa* on Shetland, are of Viking origin, while some are downright crazy, like the *Jedburgh Hand Ba'* game – a weird mixture of basketball, rugby and mud-wrestling. Amongst the most colourful events are the Highland Games, traditional gatherings involving dancing, massed pipes and various sporting competitions. Much of the time is taken up by large, hairy men in kilts throwing around heavy objects of varying size and shape, but there are also track events and the prestigious individual piper's competition. There are over a hundred of these gatherings held in towns and villages up and down the country during the summer months.

Left Urquhart Castle overlooks Loch Ness, home to one of Scotland's greatest myths
Below The Orkney islands contain many of Scotland's most impressive archaeological sites, including the Stenness Stone.
Next page In winter Scotland's landscapes take on a different appearance and altogether new appeal

Left The clearest expression of Scottish culture comes through music, and a spontaneous outburst of furious playing can be expected at any time
Above The Glenfiddich distillery in Dufftown, self-proclaimed 'Malt Whisky Capital of the World'

Essentials

2

18

Essentials

Planning your trip

Where to go

Scotland is a small country but there's a lot to see and trying to cram everything into a first visit can be very frustrating. There are many, many places of great natural beauty and the country's long, turbulent history has left a rich heritage of medieval castles, cathedrals, palaces, abbeys and historic towns and cities. So, where do you begin?

Those arriving by air will start in **Edinburgh**, the capital, or **Glasgow**, Scotland's largest city. Edinburgh is one of the world's truly great cities and deserves at least a few days to explore its castle, palace, medieval streets, fine Georgian architecture, art galleries and museums, and enjoy its liberal licensing laws. Glasgow is less than an hour from Edinburgh and though it lacks the capital's tourist credentials, it is worth a visit for its elegant Victorian architecture, the genius of Charles Rennie Mackintosh – Scotland's very own Gaudí – and its friendly and quick-witted citizens.

If you only have a week and you want to see some Highland scenery, you can head straight for the hills from Glasgow and Edinburgh. A short distance north of Glasgow is **Loch Lomond**, gateway to the Western Highlands and a beautiful introduction to the spectacular sights which lie in wait farther north. From Loch Lomond you should head north through **Glencoe**, one of the main highlights of a visit to Scotland, to **Fort William**, the main tourist centre for the Western Highlands. From Fort William there are two routes to another of Scotland's most popular attractions, the **Isle of Skye**. The quickest route is by road and bridge, via **Kyle of Lochalsh**, but by far the most romantic and scenic route is by **train** from Fort William to **Mallaig**, and by **ferry** from there to **Armadale**. You should then leave at least three days to explore the island, or more if you plan to do any **walking**. | **One week trip**

Alternatively, or if you have more time at your disposal, it's only a short drive north from Edinburgh to **Perthshire**. Though not as dramatic as the northwest, the mountains, rivers, lochs and glens of the Perthshire Highlands are very beautiful and easily accessed. If you also want a slice of history thrown in, then you could make a round trip from **Perth** to the historic town of **Stirling**, with its important castle, and return via **Callander** and the **Trossachs**. Also near Perth is the medieval town of **St Andrews**, home of Scotland's oldest university and the world's most famous golf course. From St Andrews, it's an easy day trip to the charming fishing villages of the **East Neuk of Fife**. | **Two/three week trip**

An alternative to Fort William and Skye, or in addition if you have more time, would be to head from Glasgow or Edinburgh to **Oban**, the main ferry port of the west coast, and make the short trip to the beguiling **Isle of Mull**, which tends to be attract fewer visitors than Skye in the summer months, and from where you can pop across to its divine neighbour, **Iona**, or explore the amazing Fingal's Cave on **Staffa**. Or you could head south from Oban, through **Argyll**, with its many **prehistoric sites**, and take a ferry to the little-visited islands of **Islay**, famous for its **malt whiskies**, and **Jura**. Both are great places for **walking** holidays. Also within reach of Argyll, or Ayrshire, is the island of **Arran**, described as 'Scotland in miniature' and ideal for walking or **cycling**.

If you have three or four weeks at your disposal then you can make the stunningly beautiful trip north from Kyle of Lochalsh, along the coast to **Ullapool**. Most visitors don't make it north of Ullapool but those who do are rewarded with the most spectacular landscapes of the northwest. You can sail from Ullapool across to the **Outer Hebrides**, a long, narrow archipelago stretching from **Lewis** and **Harris** in the north to **Barra** in the south. But note that most of the islands are fiercely religious and | **Three/four weeks**

Getting off the beaten track

It is easy enough to visit the main towns and tourist sights by bus or train, but getting off the beaten track without your own transport requires careful planning and an intimate knowledge of rural bus timetables. Even if you're driving, getting around the remote Highlands and Islands can be a time-consuming business as much of this region is accessed only by a *sparse network of tortuous, twisting, single-track roads. Be sure to allow plenty of time for getting around the Highlands and Islands, especially for the countless impromptu stops you'll be making to admire the views, and book ferries in advance during the busy summer season. All this is covered in greater detail in 'Getting around' (see page 43).*

transport is non-existent on a Sunday. Alternatively, you could include a trip to the **Orkney Islands**, with their many Stone Age ruins, or the culturally-distinct **Shetland Isles**, which are so far north of the mainland that they can only be included on maps as an inset.

When to go

The **high season** is from May to September, and this is when Scotland receives the vast majority of visitors. Though the weather tends to be better during the summer months, prices for accommodation are higher in the high season and hotels and guesthouses in the most popular places need to be booked in advance. It's also a good idea to make reservations - at this time - on ferries to the islands, especially to Skye and Mull. A major advantage to visiting in the summer months is the long hours of daylight, especially farther north, where the sun doesn't set till around 2200 or later in June and July.

During the **low season**, from October to Easter, many tourist sights are closed, and travelling around the Highlands and Islands can be difficult as public transport services are limited. Many of the smaller tourist offices are also closed during the low season. Though some hotels and guesthouses close during the low season, the majority are now open all year round, as are most restaurants. Taking everything into consideration, May and September are probably the best months to visit Scotland, though Glasgow and Edinburgh are worth visiting at any time of the year.

Climate

For a seven-day weather forecast service, call Weather Check, T0891-3331111 plus 101 for the northwest, 102 for the northeast, and 103 for Glasgow, Edinburgh and southern Scotland

The Scottish climate is notoriously unpredictable, especially on the west coast, where a bright, sunny morning can turn into a downpour in the time it takes to butter your toast. Predicting the weather is not an exact science and tables of statistics are most likely a waste of time. There's an old saying in Scotland that if you don't like the weather, then wait 20 minutes, and this just about sums up the climate. The west coast receives far more rain than the rest of the country and the east coast gets more sunshine. The west coast is also milder in the winter due to the relatively warm waters of the Gulf Stream. Winters in the north can be very harsh, especially in the mountains and glens, making hiking conditions treacherous. Winter storms also make it difficult to travel around the islands as ferry services are often cancelled. Generally speaking, May to September are the warmest months, with an average summer high of around 18-19°C and, though they are often the driest months, you can expect rain at any time of the year, even in high summer. So, you'll need to come prepared, and remember the old hikers' adage that there's no such thing as bad weather, only inadequate clothing.

Tours and tour operators

There are many companies offering general interest or special interest tours of Scotland. Travel agents will have details, or you can check the small advertisements in the travel sections of newspapers, or contact the *British Tourist Authority* or *Scottish Tourist Board* for a list of operators (see boxes for contact details).

A great and cheap way to get around Scotland is on one of the **jump-on-jump-off** backpacker bus tours. These leave from Edinburgh daily, except Sunday, and stop off at independent hostels in Perth, Pitlochry, Inverness, Loch Ness, Isle of Skye, Fort William, Glencoe, Oban and Glasgow. You can hop on and off whenever you please, and you don't need to stay at any of the hostels. Prices range from around £55 to £85 for a complete circuit. The main operators are *Haggis Backpackers*, 11 Blackfriars Street, Edinburgh EH1 1NB, T0131-5579393, www.haggis-backpackers.com; *Go Blue Banana*, T0131-5562000, www.gobluebanana.com; and *Macbackpackers*, T0131-5589900, www.macbackpackers.com *Haggis Backpackers* also run trips from London to Edinburgh, calling in at several tourist sights in England en route. These companies also run excellent-value Highland tours, leaving from Edinburgh. Prices start at £75 for three days, up to around £139 for six days. Prices do not include accommodation or food. Several other companies run similar tours, including *Rabbie's Trail Burners*, 207 High Street, Edinburgh, T0131-2263133; www.rabbies.com

Bus tours

Bespoke *Cycle Tours*, The Bothy, Camusdarach, Arisaig, Inverness-shire, PH39 4NT, T01687-450272, www.scotland-info.co.uk/tours *Scottish Border Trails*, Venlaw High Rd, Peebles, EH45 8RL, T01721-722934, arthur@trails.scotborders.co.uk *Scottish Cycle Safaris*, 29 Blackfriars St, Edinburgh, EH1 1NH, T0131-5565560. *Scottish Cycling Holidays*, 87 Perth St, Blairgowrie, Perthshire, PH10 6DT, T01250-876100, www.sol.co.uk/s/scotcycl/

Cycling tours

Two recommended British companies aimed at the more mature traveller are *Saga Holidays*, Saga Building, Middelburg Square, Folkestone, Kent CT20 1AZ, T0800-300500; and *Shearings Holidays*, Miry Lane, Wigan, Lancs WN3 4AG, T01942-824824. Saga also operates in the USA, 222 Berkeley Street, Boston, MA 02116; and in Australia, Level 1, 10-14 Paul Street, Milsons Point, Sydney 2061. Other tour operators in the USA are *Abercrombie & Kent*, T1-800-3237308, www.abercrombiekent.com; *Especially Britian*, T1-800-8690538; *Prestige Tours*, T1-800-8907375; *Sterling Tours*, T1-800-7274359, www.sterlingtours.com; and *Cross-Culture*, 52 High Point Dr, Amherst MA01002-1224, T800-4911148, www.crosscultureinc.com

General sightseeing tours

   Timberbush Tours, 555 Castlehill, Edinburgh, EH1 2ND, T0131-2266066, www.timberbush-tours.co.uk Run a variety of 1-2 day guided tours around the country in mini-coaches, from £21 to £58. For something a wee bit different there's the wonderfully quirky *Classique Tours*, T0141-8894050, www.classiquetours .co.uk 5-day tours start at £275 and their 7-day Grand Hebridean Tour is £485.

Golfing tours are organized from the USA by *Golf International Inc*, T1-800- 8331389; and *Jerry Quinlan's Celtic Golf*, T1-800-5356148, www.jqcelticgolf.com

Golf tours

In Britain *Assynt Guided Holidays*, Birchbank, Knockan, Elphin, Sutherland, T/F01854-666215. *Avalon Trekking Scotland*, Bowerswell Lane, Kinnoull, Perth, PH2 7DL, T/F01738-624194. *C-N-Do Scotland*, Unit 32, STEP, Stirling, FK7 7RP, T/F 01786-445703, www.btinternet.com/-cndo.scotland. *Glen Coe Mountain Sport*, 37 Park Rd, Ballachulish, Glen Coe, Argyll, PA39 4JB, T01855-811472, www. glencoe-mountain-sport.co.uk. *Lomond Walking Holidays*, 34c James St, Riverside,

Walking tours

Essentials

British Tourist Authority offices overseas

The BTA represents the STB abroad. More information can be obtained from their website (www.bta.org.uk), or from the offices listed below:
Australia *Level 16, The Gateway, 1 Macquarie Pl, Circular Quay, Sydney NSW 2000, T02-93774400, F02-93774499.*
Belgium and Luxembourg *306 Av Louise, 1050 Brussels, T2-6463510, F2-6463986.*
Canada *111 Avenue Rd, Suite 450, Toronto, Ontario MR5 3J8, T416-9256326, F416-9612175.*
Denmark *Montergade 3, 1116 Copenhagen K, T33-339188, F33-140136.*
France *Maison de la Grande-Bretagne, 19 Rue des Mathurins, 75009 Paris, T1-44515620, F1-44515621.*

Germany, Austria and Switzerland *Taunustrasse 52-60, 60329 Frankfurt, T69-2380711.*
Ireland *18/19 College Green, Dublin 2, T1-6708000, F1-6708244.*
Italy *Corso Vittorio Emanuele II No 337, 00186 Rome, T6-68806821, F6-6879095.*
Netherlands *Stadhouderskade 2 (5e), 1054 ES Amsterdam, T20-6855051, F20-6186868.*
New Zealand *17th Floor, Fay Richwhite Building, 151 Queen St, Auckland 1, T09-3031446, F09-3776965.*
South Africa *Lancaster Gate, Hyde Park Lane, Hyde Park 2196, Johannesburg, T011-3250342.*
USA *7th Flr, 551 Fifth Av, New York, NY 10176-0799, T212-986-2200/ 1-800-GO-2-BRITAIN.*
10880 Wilshire Blvd, Suite 570, Los Angeles, CA 90024, T310-4702782.

Stirling, FK8 1UG, T/F01786-447752, www.biggar-net.co.uk/lomond. *North-West Frontiers*, 18A Braes, Ullapool, IV26 28Z, T/F01854-612628, www.nwfrontiers.com. *Ossian Guides*, Sanna, Newtonmore, Inverness-shire, PH20 1DG, T/F01540-673402. *Rua Reidh Lighthouse*, Melvaig, Gairloch, Wester Ross, T/F01445-771263, ruareidh@netcomuk.co.uk. *Scottish Border Trails*, Drummore, Peebles, EH45 8RL, T01721-720336.

In North America *Above the Clouds Trekking*, T800-2334499, www.gorp.com /abvclds.htm. *British Coastal Trails*, T800-4731210, www.bctwalk.com. **Himalayan Travel**, T800-2252380, www.gorp.com/himtravel.htm

In Australia and New Zealand *Adventure Specialists*, 69 Liverpool St, Sydney, T02-92612927. *Adventure Travel Company*, 164 Parnell Rd, Parnell, East Auckland, T09-3799755. New Zealand agents for Peregrine Adventures. *Peregrine Adventures*, 258 Lonsdale St, Melbourne, T03-96638611, www.peregrine.net.au; also branches in Brisbane, Sydney, Adelaide and Perth.

Finding out more

The best way of finding out more information for your trip to Scotland is to contact the **British Tourist Authority** (BTA) in your country or write (or email) direct to the head office of the **Scottish Tourist Board** (STB). (See boxes above for contact details). The BTA and STB can provide a wealth of free literature and information such as maps, city guides, events calendars and accommodation brochures. Travellers with special needs should also contact their nearest BTA office. If you want more detailed information on a particular area, you should contact the **area tourist boards**.

Useful websites The official Scottish Tourist Board site and the various area tourist board sites infor- mation on accommodation, transport and tourist sights as well as outdoor activities such as walking, skiing, fishing etc. **www.britannia.com** is a huge UK travel site. Click

Scottish Tourist Boards

Scottish Tourist Board Central Information Department 23 Ravelston Terr, Edinburgh EH4 3EU, T0131-3322433, www.visitscotland.com
In London 19 Cockspur St, London SW1 5BL, T020-7930 2812.

Area Tourist Boards

Aberdeen & Grampian Tourist Board 27 Albyn Pl, Aberdeen AB10 1YL, T01224-632727, www.castlesandwhisky.co.uk
Angus & City of Dundee Tourist Board, 7-21 Castle St, Dundee DD1 3AA, T01382-527527, www.angusanddundee.co.uk
Argyll, the Isles, Loch Lomond, Stirling & Trossachs Tourist Board 7 Alexandra Par, Dunoon, Argyll PA23 8AB, T01369-701000, www.scottish.heartlands.org
Ayrshire & Arran Tourist Board Burns House, Burns Statue Sq, Ayr KA7 1UP, T01292-288688, www.ayrshire-arran.com
Dumfries & Galloway Tourist Board 64 Whitesands, Dumfries DG1 2RS, T01387-253862, www.galloway.co.uk

Edinburgh & Lothians Tourist Board 3 Princes St, Edinburgh EH2 2QP, T0131-4733800, www.edinburgh.org
Greater Glasgow & Clyde Valley Tourist Board 11 George Sq, Glasgow, G2 1DY, T0141-2044400, seeglasgow.com
The Highlands of Scotland Tourist Board Peffery House, Strathpeffer IV14 9HA, T01479-810363, UK T0870-5143070, www.host.co.uk
Kingdom of Fife Tourist Board Tourist Information Centre, 70 Market St, St Andrews KY16 9NU, T01334-470021, www.standrews.com
Orkney Tourist Board 6 Broad St, Kirkwall, Orkney KW15 1NX, T01856-872856, www.visitorkney.com
Perthshire Tourist Board Lower City Mills, West Mill St, Perth PH1 5QP, T01738-627958, www.perthshire.co.uk
Scottish Borders Tourist Board Tourist Information Centre, Murray's Green, Jedburgh TD8 6BE, T01835-863435, www.scot-borders.co.uk
Shetland Islands Tourism Market Cross, Lerwick, Shetland ZE1 0LU, T01595-693434, www.visitshetland.com
Western Isles Tourist Board 26 Cromwell St, Stornoway, Isle of Lewis HS1 2DD, T01851-703088, www.witb.co.uk

---

on 'Scotland guide' for a massive selection of subjects plus links to various sites including newspapers. Also useful is **www.bbc.co.uk** the UK's most popular site with an excellent what's on guide.

www.electricscotland.com Massive directory with lots of information on clans, travel etc. In-depth history pages.
www.scotland.gov.uk Updates on government affairs in Scotland.
www.scottish.parliament.uk Easy to use guide to the Scottish Parliament.
www.geo.ed.ac.uk/home/scotland/scotland/html Background information on history, politics and geography.
www.scotland.net Scotland online: with good information on golf, walking and climbing and also features **www.travelscotland.co.uk** Run in conjunction with STB, with magazine-style features and reviews.
www.scotland-info.co.uk Good for local information on hotels, shops and restaurants.
www.aboutscotland.co.uk Useful for accommodation.
www.walkscotland.com Suggested walks, contacts and practical information for hikers and climbers.
www.golfscotland.co.uk Everything you need to know on golf in Scotland.

www.ski.scotland.net Information on ski conditions at all centres, updated daily.
www.born2ski.com and **www.ifyouski.com** Both sites have Scotland pages with useful ratings.
www.ceolas.org Celtic music site with lots of information and sounds.
www.scotchwhisky.net Everything you ever wnater to know about the "water of life".
www.go-edinburgh.co.uk the official site for the all the Edinburgh festivals.
www.edinburghevents.com Lists everything taking place in the capital.
www.clyde-valley.com/glasgow Covers all Glasgow sights and updated regularly.
www.hebrides.com Comprehensive site for the islands.

Language

Though the vast majority of Scots speak English, to the untutored ear the Scottish dialect can be hard to understand, as many words and expressions are derived not from English but from **Lowland Scots**, or *lallans*, which is now recognized as a separate language as opposed to simply a regional dialect. In the Highlands and Islands, the accent is very clear and easy to understand. In fact, it is said that people from Inverness speak the clearest English in the UK.

In Orkney more people speak Cantonese than Gaelic

Scotland's oldest surviving language is **Scottish Gaelic** *(Gaidhlig, pronounced 'Gallic')*. Often referred to as the national language, it has been spoken the longest. Introduced to the country by Irish immigrants in the third and fourth centuries, its use soon spread and became well established. The language is spoken by about 85,000 people in Scotland (about 2% of the population). This is in the *Gaidhealtachd*, the Gaelic-speaking areas of the Outer Hebrides, parts of Skye, and a few of the smaller Hebridean islands. Gaelic is one of the Celtic languages, which has included Irish Gaelic, Manx, Welsh, Cornish and Breton. Today only Scottish and Irish Gaelic, Welsh and Breton survive.

Some road signs in the Highlands and Islands are in Gaelic

Those wishing to **teach themselves Gaelic** could start with the BBC *CanSeo* cassette and book. A good phrasebook *is Everyday Gaelic* by Morag MacNeill (Gairm). Also, the Celtic Heritage Centre, based on Arran, has a great store of Gaelic and Celtic information and documents; they publish a quarterly newsletter. Macbain's *Etymological Dictionary of the Gaelic language* contains a wealth of words and information.

Disabled travellers

For travellers with disabilities visiting Scotland independently can be a difficult business. While most theatres, cinemas and modern tourist attractions are accessible to wheelchairs, **accommodation** is more problematic. Many large, new hotels do have disabled suites, but will charge more, and most B&Bs, guesthouses and smaller hotels are not designed to cater for people with disabilities. **Public transport** is just as bad, though newer buses have lower steps for easier access and some *ScotRail* intercity services now accommodate wheelchair-users in comfort. Taxis, as opposed to minicabs, all carry wheelchair ramps, and if a driver says he or she can't take a wheelchair, it's because they're too lazy to fetch the ramp.

Wheelchair users, and blind or partially sighted people are automatically given 30-50% discount on train fares, and those with other disabilities are eligible for the **Disabled Person's Railcard**, which costs £14 per year and gives a third off most tickets. There are no reductions on buses, however.

Information & organizations

If you are disabled you should contact the travel officer of your national support organization. They can provide literature or put you in touch with travel agents specializing

British embassies abroad

Australia High Commission: Commonwealth Av, Yarralumla, Canberra, ACT 2600, T02-62706666, www.uk.emb.gov.au

Canada High Commission: 80 Elgin St, Ottowa, K1P 5K7, T613-2371530, www.bis-canada.org

France 9 Av Hoche, 8e, Paris, T01-42663810.

Germany Friedrich-Ebert-Allee 77, 53113, Bonn, T0228-234061.

Ireland 29 Merrion Rd, Ballsbridge, Dublin 4, T01-2053700.

Israel 192 Hayarkon St, Tel Aviv, T3-7251222, www.britemb.org.il/

Netherlands Koningslaan 44, 1075AE Amsterdam, T20-6764343.

New Zealand High Commission: 44 Hill St, Wellington, T04-4726049, www.brithighcomm.org.nz

South Africa High Commission: 91 Parliament St, Cape Town 8001, T21-4617220.

USA 3100 Massachusetts Av NW, Washington DC 20008, T202-4621340, www.britain-info.org

in tours for the disabled. The Scottish Tourist Board produces a guide, *Accessible Scotland*, for disabled travellers, and many local tourist offices can provide accessibility details for their area. For more information, contact **Disability Scotland**, Princes House, 5 Shandwick Place, Edinburgh EH2 4RG, T0131-2298632. The **Royal Association for Disability and Rehabilitation** (RADAR), Unit 12, City Forum, 250 City Road, London, EC1V 8AF, T020-72503222, www.radar.org.uk, is a good source of advice and information, and produces an annual guide on travelling in the UK (£7.50 including P&P). The **Holiday Care Service**, 2nd floor, Imperial Building, Victoria Road, Horley, Surrey RH6 7PZ, T-1293-774535, provides free lists of accessible accommodation and travel in the UK.

Gay and lesbian travellers

Scotland is generally tolerant of homosexuality, though overt displays of affection outside 'gay' venues are not advised. Edinburgh in particular has a flourishing gay scene and is a relatively easy place for gay travellers to feel safe and comfortable. Don't assume that because men are wearing skirts in the Highlands that people take a relaxed attitude to homosexuality. The same prejudices apply as elsewhere in rural parts of the UK. There are no towns in the Highlands large enough to support an active gay scene.

Gay Scotland magazine, T0131-5572625, is a good source of information. For more information contact the **Gay Switchboard**, T0131-5564049, or the **Lesbian Line**, T0131-5570751. Details of gay pubs and clubs are given for Glasgow (on page 234) and Edinburgh (on page130). For a good selection of gay events and venues, check out **www.whatsonwhen.com** or the UK gay-scene index at **www.queenscene.com** which has information on clubs, gay groups, accommodation, events, HIV/AIDS and cultural and ethical issues. Other good sites include: **www.gaybritain.co.uk**; **www.gaytravel.co.uk**; **www.rainbownetwork.com**; and **www.gaypride.co.uk**

Student travellers

There are various official youth/student ID cards available. The most useful is the **International Student ID Card** (ISIC). For a mere £6 the ISIC card gains you access to the exclusive world of student travel with a series of discounts, including most forms of local transport, up to 30% off international airfares, cheap or free admission to museums, theatres and other attractions, and cheap meals in some restaurants. There's also free or discounted internet access, and a website where you can check the latest student travel deals (www.usitworld.com). You'll also receive the ISIC handbook, which ensures you get the most out of services available. ISIC cards are available at student travel centres (see page 15, 32 and 33). US and Canadian citizens are also entitled to emergency medical coverage, and there's a 24-hour hotline to call in the event of medical, legal or financial emergencies.

If you're aged under 26 but not a student, you can apply for a **Federation of International Youth Travel Organisations** (FIYTO) card, or a **Euro 26 Card**, which give you much the same discounts. If you're 25 or younger you can qualify for a **Go-25 Card**, which gives you the same benefits as an ISIC card. These discount cards are issued by student travel agencies (see pages above) and hostelling organizations (see page 41).

Studying in Scotland If you want to study in Scotland you must first prove you can support and accommodate yourself without working and without recourse to public support. Your studies should take up at least 15 hours a week for a minimum of six months. Once you are studying, you are allowed to do 20 hours of casual work per week in the term time and you can work full-time during the holidays. In **North America** full-time students can obtain temporary work or study permits through the **Council of International Education Exchange** (CIEE), 205 E 42nd Street, New York, NY 10017, T212-8222600, www.ciee.org For more details, contact your nearest British embassy, consulate or high commission, or the Foreign and Commonwealth Office in London, T020-7270 1500.

Travel with children

Flying with kids
Visit:
www.babygoes2.com

Inform the airline in advance that you're travelling with a baby or toddler, and check out the facilities when booking as these vary with each aircraft. British Airways now has a special seat for under 2s; check which aircraft have been fitted with them when booking. Pushchairs can be taken on as hand luggage or stored in the hold. Skycots are available on long-haul flights. Take snacks and toys for in-flight entertainment, and remember that swallowing food or drinks during take-off and landing will help prevent ear problems.

Eating out Eating out with children in Scotland can be a frustrating experience, and some establishments are downright unhelpful. Furthermore, the attitude to breastfeeding in public is still some way behind the rest of Europe. In major towns and cities Italian restaurants are often more child-friendly. In more remote areas, however, most people are helpful and friendly.

Women travellers

Single women should beware of the devastating Celtic charm

Travelling in Scotland is neither easier nor more difficult for women than travelling in other other parts of the UK. Generally speaking, Scots are friendly and courteous and even lone women travellers should experience nothing unpleasant. In the main cities and larger towns, the usual precautions need to be taken and you should avoid walking in quiet, unlit streets and parks at night. More specific warnings are given in the Edinburgh and Glasgow chapters.

Working in Scotland

Pick up a copy of What Scotland, a free guide for independent travellers living and working in Scotland; T020-7384 9330

Citizens of **European Union** (EU) countries can live and work in Britain freely without a visa, but **non-EU residents** need a permit to work legally. This can be difficult to obtain without the backing of an established company or employer in the UK. Also, visitors from Commonwealth countries who are aged between 17 and 27 may apply for a working holiday-maker's visa which permits them to stay in the UK for up to two years and work on a casual basis (ie non-career oriented). These certificates are only available

Overseas consulates in Scotland

The following consulates are all in
Edinburgh (Phone code: 0131):
Australia 37 George St, T6243333.
Canada 30 Lothian Rd, T2204333.
Denmark 4 Royal Terr, T5564263.
France 11 Randolph Cres, T2257954.
Germany 16 Eglinton Cres, T3372323.
Italy 32 Melville St, T2263631.
Japan 2 Melville Cres, T2254777.
Netherlands 53 George St, T2203226.
Spain 63 North Castle St, T2203226.

Sweden 22 Hanover St, T2206050.
Switzerland 66 Hanover Pl, T2265660.
USA 3 Regent Terr, T5568315.

The following consulates are in Glasgow
(Phone code: 0141):
Germany 158 West Regent St, T2210304.
Italy 24 St Enoch Square, T2263000.
Norway 80 Oswald St, T2041353.
Spain 389 Argyle St, T2216943.
Sweden 16 Robertson St, T2217845.

Essentials

from British embassies and consulates abroad, and you must have proof of a valid return or onward ticket, as well as means of support during your stay. **Commonwealth** citizens with a parent or grandparent born in the UK can apply for a **Certificate of Entitlement to the Right of Abode**, allowing them to work in Britain.

An option for citizens of some **non-commonwealth** countries is to visit on an 'au pair' placement in order to learn English by living with an English-speaking family for a maximum of two years. Au pairs must be aged between 17 and 27, and come from one of the following countries: Andorra, Bosnia-Herzegovina, Croatia, Cyprus, Czech Republic, The Faroes, Greenland, Hungary, Macedonia, Malta, Monaco, San Marino, Slovak Republic, Slovenia, Switzerland or Turkey. This can be a good way to learn English, but check out the precise conditions of your placement before taking it up.

Before you travel

Getting in

Visas regulations are subject to change, so it is essential to check with your local British embassy, high commission or consulate before leaving home. Citizens of all European countries – except Albania, Bosnia, Bulgaria, Macedonia, Romania, Slovakia, Yugoslavia and all former Soviet republics (other than the Baltic states) – require only a passport to enter Britain and can generally stay for up to three months. Citizens of Australia, Canada, New Zealand, South Africa or the USA can stay for up to six months, providing they have a return ticket and sufficient funds to cover their stay. Citizens of most other countries require a visa from the commission or consular office in the country of application. **Visas**

The **Foreign Office's website** (www.fco.gov.uk) provides details of British immigration and visa requirements. Also the **Immigration Advisory Service** (IAS) offers free and confidential advice to anyone applying for entry clearance into the UK: County House, 190 Great Dover Street, London SE1 4YB, T020-73576917, www.vois.org.uk

For **visa extensions** contact the Home Office, Immigration and Nationality Department, Lunar House, Wellesley Road, Croydon, London CR9, T020-86860688, before your existing visa expires. Citizens of **Australia**, **Canada**, **New Zealand**, **South Africa** or the **USA** wishing to stay longer than six months will need an Entry Clearance Certificate from the British High Commission in their country. For more details, contact your nearest British embassy, consulate or high commission, or the Foreign and Commonwealth Office in London, T020-72701500.

Customs regulations & tax	Visitors from EU countries do not have to make a declaration to customs on entry into the UK. The limits for **duty-paid goods** from within the EU are 800 cigarettes, or 1kg of tobacco, 10 litres of spirits, 20 litres of fortified wine, 90 litres of wine and 110 litres of beer. There is no longer any duty-free shopping. Visitors from non-EU countries are allowed to import 200 cigarettes, or 250g of tobacco, two litres of wine, and two litres of fortified wine or one litre of spirits. There are various import restrictions, most of which should not affect the average tourist. There are tight **quarantine restrictions** which apply to animals brought from overseas (except for Ireland).

For more information on British import regulations, contact HM Customs and Excise, Dorset House, Stamford Street, London, SE1 9PJ, T020-79283344, www.hmce. gov.uk

Many goods in Britain are subject to a **Value Added Tax** (VAT) of 17.5%, with the major exception of books and food. Visitors from non-EU countries can save money through the Retail Export Scheme, which allows a refund of VAT on goods to be taken out of the country. Note that not all shops are participants in the scheme and that VAT cannot be reclaimed on hotel bills or other services.

What to take

You'll be able to find everything you could possibly need for your trip in Scottish cities, so you can pack light and buy stuff as you go along. Given the climate, however, you should bring warm and waterproof clothing, whatever the time of year. Also bring light clothes in the summer, preferably long-sleeved to protect you from the midges.

If you're planning on doing some hill-walking you should come properly prepared, as the weather can change rapidly in the mountains (for more details, see page 60). It's worth treating your boots with a waterproofing agent as some of the trails cross boggy ground.

A **sleeping bag** is useful in hostels. A **sleeping sheet** with a pillow cover is needed for staying in **Scottish Youth Hostel Association** (SYHA) hostels to save you the cost of having to hire one. A padlock can also be handy for locking your bag if it has to be stored in a hostel for any length of time. Other useful items include an alarm clock (for those early ferry departures), an adaptor plug for electrical appliances, an elastic clothes line and, if you're hill-walking or camping, a Swiss Army knife, torch (flashlight) and compass.

Insurance	It's a good idea to take out some form of travel insurance, wherever you're travelling from. This should cover you for theft or loss of possessions and money, the cost of all medical and dental treatment, cancellation of flights, delays in travel arrangements, accidents, missed departures, lost baggage, lost passport, and personal liability and legal expenses.

There are a variety of policies to choose from, so it's best to shop around to get the best price. Your travel agent can also advise you on the best deals available. *STA Travel* and other reputable student travel organizations often offer good-value travel policies. Travellers from North America can try the *International Student Insurance Service* (ISIS), which is available through *STA Travel*, T1-800-7770112, www.sta-travel.com Some other recommended travel insurance companies in North America include *Travel Guard*, T1-800-8261300, www.noelgroup.com; *Access America*, T1-800-2848300; *Travel Insurance Services* (1-800-9371387); *Travel Assistance International*, T1-800-8212828; and *Council Travel*, 1-888-COUNCIL, www.counciltravel.com Another company worth calling for a quote is *Columbus Direct*, T020-7375 0011. **Older travellers** should note that some companies won't cover people over 65 years old, or may charge high premiums. The best policies for older travellers are offered by *Age Concern* (T01883-346964).

Points to note: you should always read the small print carefully. Some policies exclude 'dangerous activities' such as scuba diving, skiing, horse riding or even trekking. Not all policies cover ambulance, helicopter rescue or emergency flights home. Find out if your policy pays medical expenses direct to the hospital or doctor, or if you have to pay and then claim the money back later. If the latter applies, make sure you keep all records. Whatever your policy, if you are unfortunate enough to have something stolen, make sure you get a copy of the police report, as you will need this to substantiate your claim.

Money

The British currency is the pound sterling (£), divided into 100 pence (p). Coins come in denominations of 1p, 2p, 5p, 10p, 20p, 50p, £1 and £2. *Bank of England* banknotes are legal tender in Scotland, in addition to those issued by the *Bank of Scotland*, *Royal Bank of Scotland* and *Clydesdale Bank*. These Scottish banknotes (bills) come in denominations of £5, £10, £20, £50 and £100 and are legal tender in the rest of Britain, though some shopkeepers south of the border may be reluctant to accept them.

Some retail outlets and visitor attractions will accept euros; check with the Scottish Tourist Board for latest news.

Banks

Most towns and villages in Scotland have a branch of at least one of the big four High Street banks – *Bank of Scotland*, *Royal Bank of Scotland*, *Clydesdale* and *TSB Scotland*. In small and remote places, and on some islands, there may only be a mobile bank which runs to a set timetable. This timetable will be available from the local post office.

Bank opening hours are Monday-Friday from 0930 to between 1600 and 1700. Some larger branches may also be open later on Thursdays and on Saturday mornings. Banks are usually the best places to change money and cheques. Outside banking hours you'll have to use **bureaux de change**, which can be found in most city centres and also at the main airports and train stations. Note that some *bureaux* charge high commissions for changing cheques. Those at international airports, however, often charge less than banks and will change pound sterling cheques for free. Avoid changing money or cheques in hotels, as the rates are usually very poor.

Credit cards & ATMs

Most hotels, shops and restaurants in Scotland accept the major credit cards (*Access/MasterCard*, *Visa* and *Amex*), though some places may charge for using them. They may be less useful in more remote rural areas and smaller establishments such as B&Bs which will often only accept cash. You can withdraw cash from selected banks and ATMs (or cashpoints as they are called in Britain) with your cash card. Your bank or credit card company will give you a list of locations where you can use your card.

Visa card holders can use the *Bank of Scotland*, Clydesdale Bank, *Royal Bank of Scotland* and *TSB* ATMs; *Access/MasterCard* holders can use the *Royal Bank* and *Clydesdale*; *Amex* card holders can use the *Bank of Scotland*.

If you have an account with a High Street bank in England or Wales, you can use your cashpoint card in Scotland. Bank of Scotland and *Royal Bank* take *Lloyds* and *Barclays* cash cards; *Clydesdale* takes *HSBC/Midland* and *National Westminster* cards. *Bank of Scotland*, *Clydesdale* and most building society cashpoints are part of the Link network and accept all affiliated cards.

Travellers' cheques

The safest way to carry money is in travellers' cheques. These are available for a small commission from all major banks. *American Express (Amex)*, *Visa* and *Thomas Cook* cheques are widely accepted and are the most commonly issued by banks. You'll normally have to pay commission again when you cash each cheque. This will usually be one percent, or a flat rate. No commission is payable on *Amex* cheques cashed at *Amex* offices. Make sure to keep a record of the cheque numbers and the cheques you've

Essentials

Flights from Britain and Ireland

Flights to Glasgow and Edinburgh
Aer Lingus *from Dublin, Cork, Donegal and Shannon.* **British Airways** *from London Heathrow and Gatwick, Birmingham, Belfast City and International, Bristol, Cardiff, Manchester and Southampton (also from Londonderry to Glasgow).* **British European** *from Birmingham (also from London City, Cork and Shannon to Glasgow).* **British Midland** *from London Heathrow, East Midlands, Jersey (to Glasgow), Leeds/Bradford and Manchester.* **Eastern Airways** *from Norwich to Edinburgh.* **easyJet** *from London Luton and Belfast International.* **Go** *from London Stansted, Belfast International, Bristol and Dublin.* **KLM AirUK** *from London Stansted and City.* **Manx Airlines** *from Isle of Man to Glasgow.* **Ryanair** *from London Stansted and Dublin to*

Glasgow Prestwick. **Scot Airways** *from London City.*

Flights to Aberdeen **British Airways** *from London Heathrow and Gatwick, Belfast International, Birmingham, Leeds/Bradford, Manchester and Newcastle.* **British European** *from London City.* **British Midland** *from Manchester.* **Eastern Airways** *from East Midlands, Humberside, Norwich and Teeside.* **easyJet** *from London Luton.* **KLM Air UK** *from London City.*

Flights to Dundee **Scot Airways** *from London City.*

Flights to Inverness **British Airways** *from London Gatwick.* **easyJet** *from London Luton.*

Flights to Wick **Eastern Airways** *from Newcastle.*

---

cashed separate from the cheques themselves, so that you can get a full refund of all uncashed cheques should you lose them. It's best to bring sterling cheques to avoid changing currencies twice. Also note that in Britain travellers' cheques are rarely accepted outside banks, so you'll need to cash them in advance and keep a good supply of ready cash.

Money transfers If you need money urgently, the quickest way to have it sent to you is to have it **wired** to the nearest bank via **Western Union** (T0800-833833) or **Moneygram** (T0800-894887). Charges are on a sliding scale; ie it will cost proportionately less to wire out more money. Money can also be wired by **Thomas Cook** or **American Express**, though this may take a day or two, or transferred via a bank draft, but this can take up to a week.

Cost of living/ travelling Scotland can be an expensive place to visit, though there is plenty of budget accommodation available and backpackers will be able to keep their costs down. Edinburgh is the most expensive city, and prices are also higher in more remote parts of the Highlands and Islands. Petrol in particular is very expensive in the Highlands and Islands, where it can cost up to 10p per litre more than in the central Lowlands. Accommodation and restaurant prices also tend to be higher in more popular destinations and during the busy summer months.

The minimum daily budget required, if you're staying in hostels or cheap B&Bs, cycling or hitching, and cooking your own meals, will be around £25 per person per day. If you start using public transport and eating out occasionally that will rise to around £30-40. Those staying in slightly more upmarket B&Bs or guesthouses, eating out every evening at pubs or modest restaurants and visiting tourist attractions, such as castles or museums, can expect to pay around £40-50 per day. If you also want to hire a car and use ferries to visit the islands, and eat well, then costs will rise considerably and you'll be looking at at least £75 per person per day. Single travellers will have to pay more than half the cost of a double room in most places, and should budget on spending around 60% of what a couple would spend.

Airlines in Britain and Ireland

*Aer Lingus, Ireland T01-8444777; UK
T0645-737747, www.aerlingus.ie*
British Airways, *T08457-733377,
www.britishairways.com*
British European, *T08705-676676.*
British Midland, *T0870-6070555,
www.iflybritishmidland.com*
Eastern Airways, *T01955-603914.*

*easyJet , T0870-6000000,
www.easyjet.com*
Go, T0845-6054321, www.go-fly.com
KLM UK, *T08705-074074, www.klm.com*
Manx Airlines, *T08457-256256.*
Ryanair , *T08701-569569; Ireland
T01-6097800, www.ryanair.com*
Scot Airways, *T0870-6060707.*

Discount travel agents in Britain and Ireland

Council Travel, *28a Poland St, London,
W1V 3DB, T020-74377767,
www.destinations-group.com.*
STA Travel, *27 Forrest Rd, Edinburgh,
T0131-2267747; 86 Old Brompton Rd,
London, SW7 3LH, T020-73616161,
www.statravel.co.uk. They have other
branches in London, as well as in Brighton,
Bristol, Cambridge, Leeds, Manchester,
Newcastle-upon-Tyne and Oxford and on
many university campuses. Specialists in
low-cost student/youth flights and tours,*

also good for student IDs and insurance.
Trailfinders, *194 Kensington High St,
London W8 6FT, T020-79383939.*
USIT Campus, *53 Forrest Rd, Edinburgh,
T0131-2256111; 52 Grosvenor Gdns,
London SW1 0AG, T020-77303402,
www.usitcampus.com   Student/youth
travel specialists with branches also in
Belfast, Brighton, Bristol, Cambridge,
Manchester and Oxford. The main
Ireland branch is at 19 Aston Quay,
Dublin 2, T01-6021777.*

Getting there

Air

Generally speaking, the cheapest and quickest way to travel to Scotland from out-side the UK is by air. There are good links to Edinburgh and Glasgow, with direct flights from many European cities, and direct flights from North America to Glasgow. There are also flights from a few European cities to Aberdeen and Inverness. There are no direct flights from North America to Edinburgh; these are usually routed via London or Dublin. There are also daily flights from Ireland and regular flights to most Scottish airports from other parts of the UK. There are no direct flights to Scotland from Australia, New Zealand, South Africa or Japan. You will have to get a connection from London.

Those wishing to visit England as well should note that it is generally cheaper to fly to Scotland from the rest of Britain if you use an Airpass bought in your own coun-try. This is offered by **British Airways** and **British Midland.** Airpasses are valid only with an international scheduled flight ticket.

Airlines flying from North America

Air Canada, T1-800-7763000,
www.aircanada.ca
American Airlines, T1-800-4337300,
www.americanair.com
Continental Airlines, T1-800-2310856,
www.flycontinental.com
Delta Airlines, T1-800-2414141,
www.delta-air.com
Icelandair, T1-800-2235500,

www.icelandair.com
Northwest Airlines, T1-800-4474747,
www.nwa.com
TWA, T1-800-2212000, www.twa.com.
United Airlines, T1-800-5382929,
www.ual.com
Virgin Atlantic Airways, T1-800-8628621,
www.fly.virgin.com

Discount travel agents in North America

Air Brokers International, 323 Geary St,
Suite 411, San Francisco, CA94102,
T1-800-8833273, www.airbrokers.com.
Consolidator and specialist in RTW and
Circle Pacific tickets.
Council Travel, 205 E 42nd St, New York,
NY 10017, T1-888-COUNCIL,
www.counciltravel.com. Student/budget
agency with branches in many other US
cities.
Discount Airfares Worldwide On-Line,
www.etn.nl/discount.htm. A hub of
consolidator and discount agent links.
*International Travel Network/Airlines of
the Web*, www.itn.net/airlines. Online air

travel information and reservations.
STA Travel, 5900 Wiltshire Blvd, Suite 2110,
Los Angeles, CA 90036, T1-800-7770112,
www.sta-travel.com. Discount
student/youth travel discount company
with branches in New York, San Francisco,
Boston, Miami, Chicago, Seattle and
Washington DC.
Travel CUTS, 187 College St, Toronto, ON
M5T 1P7, T1-800-6672887,
www.travelcuts.com. Specialist in student
discount fares, IDs and other travel services.
Branches in other Canadian cities.
Travelocity, www.travelocity.com. Online
consolidator.

Buying a ticket
Also worth trying are:
www.expedia.co.uk
www.lastminute.com
www.cheapflights.co.uk
www.e-bookers.com
www.deckchair.com
www.flynow.com
www.dialaflight.co.uk

There is a mind-boggling number of outlets for buying your plane ticket, and finding the best deal can be a confusing business. **Fares** will depend on the season. Ticket prices to Scotland are highest from around early June to mid-September, which is the tourist high season. Fares drop in the months either side of the peak season – mid-September to early November and mid-April to early June. They are cheapest in the low season, from November to April, when very few visitors are willing to brave the Scottish winter. The exception is during Christmas and New Year when seats are at a premium and prices rise sharply. It's also worth noting that flying at the weekend is normally more expensive.

It is always worth spending a bit of time researching the various options available and starting early, as some of the cheapest tickets have to be bought months in advance and the most popular flights sell out quickly. One of the best ways of finding a good deal is to use the internet. There are a number of sites where you can check out prices and even book tickets. You can search in the travel sections of your web browser or try the sites of the discount travel companies and agents listed in this section.

Cheap flight tickets fall into two categories: official and unofficial. Official tickets are called budget fares, Apex, super-Apex, advance-purchase tickets, or whatever a particu-lar airline chooses to call them. Unofficial tickets are discounted tickets which are released by airlines through selected travel agents. They are not sold directly by airlines. Discounted tickets are usually as low or lower than the official budget-price tickets.

Return tickets are usually a lot cheaper than buying two one-way tickets. **Round-the-World** (RTW) tickets can also be a real bargain, and may even work out

Airlines flying from Australia and New Zealand

Air France, T02-93211030 (Sydney), www.airfrance.com
Air New Zealand, T09-3573000, www.airnz.co.nz
British Airways, T02-92583200 (Sydney); T09-3568690 (Auckland), www.british-airways.com
Cathay Pacific, T02-99315500 (Sydney), www.cathaypacific.com
Gulf Air, T02-92442199 (Sydney).
Japanese Airlines (JAL), T02-92721111 (Sydney); T09-3799906 (Auckland).
Korean Air, Australia, T02-9262 6000

(Sydney); T09-3073687 (Auckland).
Qantas, www.qantas.com.au
Singapore Airlines, T02-93500100 (Sydney); T09-3793209 (Auckland).
South African Airways, T02-92234448 (Sydney), www.saa.co.za
Thai Airways, T02-92511922 (Sydney); T09-3773886 (Auckland), www.thaiair.com
United Airlines, T02-92924111 (Sydney); T09-3793800 (Auckland), www.ual.com
Virgin Atlantic, Australia, T02-93526199, www.flyvirgin.com/atlantic/

Discount travel agents in Australia and New Zealand

Flight Centres, 82 Elizabeth St, Sydney, T13-1600; 205 Queen St, Auckland, T09-3096171. Also branches in other towns and cities.
STA Travel, T1300-360960, www.statravelaus.com.au, 702 Harris St, Ultimo, Sydney, and 256 Flinders St, Melbourne. In New Zealand: 10 High St,

Auckland, T09-3666673. Also in major towns and cities and university campuses.
Travel.com.au, 80 Clarence St, Sydney, T02-92901500, www.travel.com.au
UK Flight Shop, 7 Macquarie Pl, Sydney, T02-92474833, www.ukflightshop.com.au Also branches in Melbourne and Perth.

---

cheaper than a return fare. RTW prices start at around £900 (US$1,500), depending on the season. Note that it's easy to include London on a Round-the-World itinerary, but a stop in Scotland may be harder to arrange and may involve backtracking. It may be cheaper and easier to buy the London to Scotland leg separately or to travel overland to Scotland from London.

When trying to find the best deal, make sure you check the route, the duration of the journey, stopovers allowed, any travel restrictions such as minimum and maximum periods away, and cancellation penalties. Many of the cheapest flights are sold by small agencies, most of whom are honest and reliable, but there may be some risks involved with buying tickets at rock-bottom prices. You should avoid paying too much money in advance, and you could check with the airline directly to make sure you have a reservation. You may be safer choosing a better-known travel agent, such as *STA*, which has offices worldwide, or *Trailfinders* in the UK, or *Council Travel* in the USA. These and other reputable discount companies and agents are listed above.

There are direct flights to Scotland's three main airports – Glasgow, Edinburgh and Aberdeen – almost hourly from **London** Heathrow, Gatwick, Stansted and Luton airports. There are also daily flights from provincial UK airports and from **Dublin**. To fly on to the smaller airports, you'll need to change planes (see page 44 for more details on domestic flights). The cheapest flights leave from London Luton or Stansted, plus a few provincial airports, with *Ryanair*, *easyJet* and *Go*. If you book on-line, fares can be as little as £5 one-way during promotions, but usually you can expect to fly for under £50 return. These tickets are often subject to rigid restrictions, but the savings can make the extra effort worthwhile. Cheaper tickets usually have to be bought at least a week in advance, apply to only a few midweek flights, and must include a Saturday night stayover. They

Flights from Britain, Ireland & Europe
Full details of flights from Britain and Ireland are given in the box on page 30

are also non-refundable, or only partly refundable, and non-transferable. A standard flexible and refundable fare from London to Glasgow or Edinburgh will cost at least £150-200 return.

Specialist agencies such as *Usit Campus* or *STA* (see above) offer Domestic Air Passes on *British Airways* flights to travellers under 26 years old. These give you substantial discounts on 'Hopper' flights to Inverness and the Hebrides.

There are direct flights to Edinburgh and Glasgow from **Amsterdam**, **Brussels**, **Copenhagen**, **Frankfurt**, **Madrid**, **Paris** and **Zurich**. Also to Glasgow from **Gothenberg** and Edinburgh from **Zurich**. There are also direct flights to Aberdeen from **Amsterdam**, **Copenhagen** and **Stavangar**, and to Inverness from **Amsterdam** and **Zurich**. Discount charter flights are often available to young travellers aged under 26 and holders of ISIC cards through the large student travel agencies listed above. The London listings magazine *Time Out* is a good place to look for cheap fares, as well as free magazines such as *TNT* which you can find outside train and tube stations in London.

Flights from North America There are direct flights to Glasgow from **New York Newark** (*Continental*), **Chicago** (*American Airlines*) and **Toronto** (*Air Canada*). There are also flights from many other US and Canadian cities via London with the Transatlantic carriers listed on page 32. Icelandair flies to Glasgow via Reykjavik from **Boston**, **Halifax**, **Minneapolis**, **New York**, **Orlando** and **Washington**. *Northwest Airlines* flies via Amsterdam to Glasgow, Edinburgh and Aberdeen from **Detroit**, **Memphis** and **Minneapolis**, with onward flights operated by *KLM UK*. Because of the much larger number of flights to

Getting there

Railcards

There are a variety of railcards which give discounts on fares for certain groups. Cards are valid for one year and most are available from main stations. You need two passport photos and proof of age or status.

Young Person's Railcard: for those aged 16-25 or full-time students in the UK. Costs £18 and gives 33% discount on most train tickets and some ferry services.

Senior Citizen's Railcard: for those aged over 60. Same price and discount as above.

Disabled Person's Railcard: costs £14 and gives 33% discount to a disabled person and one other. Pick up application form from stations and send it to: Disabled Person's Railcard Office, PO Box 1YT, Newcastle-upon-Tyne, NE99 1YT. It may take up to 21 days to process, so apply in advance.

Family Railcard: costs £20 and gives 33% discount on most tickets (20% on others) for up to four adults travelling together, and 81% discount for up to four children.

London, it is generally cheaper to fly there first and get an onward flight (see above for the best deals).

For low season Apex fares expect to pay around US$400-600 from New York and other East Coast cities, and around US$500-700 from the West Coast. Prices rise to around US$700-900 from New York, and up to US$1,000 from the West Coast in the summer months. Low season Apex fares from Toronto and Montreal cost around CAN$600-700, and from Vancouver around CAN$800-900, rising to $750-950 and $950-1150 respectively during the summer.

There are no direct flights to Scotland from Australia or New Zealand. You will have to get an onward flight from London. The cheapest scheduled flights to London are **via Asia** with *Gulf Air* or *Thai Airways*. They charge A$1300-1500 in low season and up to A$1800 in high season, and involve a transfer en route. Flights via **Africa** start at around $2000 and are yet more expensive via **North America**. Flights to and from Perth via Africa or Asia are a few hundred dollars cheaper.

The cheapest deal currently on offer is with *Britannia Airways/Airtours'* charter flights from Australia or New Zealand to London Gatwick or Manchester via Singapore and Bahrain. It's a 'no-frills' service which only runs between November and March. Fares start at around $1100 in low season and up to $1750 in high season. For more details contact the *UK Flight Shop* (see above).

The cheapest scheduled flights from **New Zealand** are with *Korean Air, Thai Airways* or *JAL*, all of whom fly via their home cities for around NZ$2000-2300. The most direct route is via North America with *United Airlines*, via Chicago or Los Angeles. Fares range from around NZ$2800 in low season to NZ$3200 in high season. *Britannia Airways'* charter flights from Auckland cost from around NZ$1600 in low season to NZ$2100 in high season.

A **Round-the-World** (RTW) ticket may work out just as cheap as a return ticket. Good deals are offered by *Qantas/British Airways*. As with North America, it may be cheaper to buy the London to Scotland leg of the trip separately.

Flights from Australia & New Zealand

Road

Road links to Scotland are excellent, and a number of companies offer express coach services day and night. This is the cheapest form of travel to Scotland. The two main operators between England and Scotland are *National Express*, T08705-808080, www.gobycoach.com, and its sister company *Scottish Citylink*, T08705-505050, www.city.link.co.uk There are direct buses from most British cities to **Edinburgh,**

Bus & coach
For details of the various discount passes available, see page 44

Glasgow, **Aberdeen** and **Inverness**. Tickets can be bought at bus stations or from a huge number of agents throughout the country. Fares from London to Glasgow and Edinburgh with *National Express* are between £30 and £40 for an economy advance return. Fares to Aberdeen and Inverness are a little higher. The London to Glasgow/Edinburgh journey takes around eight hours, while it takes around 11-12 hours for the trip to Aberdeen and Inverness.

Car
See page 45 for more details of driving conditions in Scotland and for information on hiring vehicles

There are two main routes to Scotland from the south. In the east the A1 runs to Edinburgh and in the west the M6 and A74(M) runs to Glasgow. The journey north from London to either city takes around eight to 10 hours. The A74(M) route to Glasgow is dual carriageway all the way. A slower and more scenic route is to head off the A1 and take the A68 through the Borders to Edinburgh. There's an *Autoshuttle Express* service to transport your car overnight between England and Scotland and vice versa while you travel by rail or air. For further information T08705-133714; reservations T08705-502309.

Sea

The only direct route to Scotland from Europe is on the *Smyril Line* (Aberdeen T01224-572615; Faroe Islands T01-5900) service to **Lerwick** (Shetland) from Norway (Bergen), Iceland (Seydisfjordur) and the Faroe Islands (Torshavn). It sails from mid-May to early September only once a week and takes 12 hours. A sleeping berth one way from Norway and Faroe Islands costs £63 in high season. You then have to get from Lerwick to Aberdeen. *P&O Scottish Ferries* (T10224-572615) sail Monday-Friday from Lerwick to Aberdeen (14 hours; £55 per passenger in high season)

Ferries from Northern Ireland

Larne to Cairnryan: *P&O Irish Sea*, T0870-2424777, www.poirishsea.com, has several crossings daily to Cairnryan. The journey takes one hour. **Belfast to Stranraer:** *Stena Line,* T0870-707070, www.stenaline.co.uk, run numerous ferries (three hours) and high-speed catamarans (1½ hours). **Belfast to Troon:** *Seacat Scotland* run daily services (2½ hours; £250 for two adults and a car), T08705-523523, www.seacat.co.uk

Train

There are fast and frequent rail services from London and other main towns and cities in England to Glasgow, Edinburgh, Aberdeen and Inverness. Two companies operate direct services from London to Scotland: *GNER* trains leave from Kings' Cross and run up the east coast to Edinburgh, Aberdeen and Inverness; and *Virgin* trains leave from Euston and run up the west coast to Glasgow. Journey time from London is about 4½ hours to Edinburgh, five hours to Glasgow, seven hours to Aberdeen and eight hours to Inverness. *Scotrail* operate the **Caledonian Sleeper** service if you wish to travel overnight from London Euston to Aberdeen, Edinburgh, Glasgow, Inverness and Fort William. This runs nightly from Sunday to Friday.

Eurostar, T08705-186186, www.eurostar.com, operates high-speed trains through the Channel Tunnel to London Waterloo from Paris (three hours), Brussels (two hours 40 minutes) and Lille (two hours). You then have to change trains, and stations, for the onward journey north to Scotland. If you're driving from continental Europe you could take **Le Shuttle**, which runs 24 hours a day, 365 days a year, and takes you and your car from Calais to Folkestone in 35-45 minutes. Fares range from £84 to £165 per carload, depending on how far in advance you book or when you travel (T08705-353535 for bookings).

Touching down

Electricity The current in Britain is 240V AC. Plugs have three square pins and adapters are widely available.

Emergencies For **police**, **fire brigade**, **ambulance** and, in certain areas, **mountain rescue** or **coastguard**, dial 999.

Laundry Most towns have coin-operated launderettes. The average cost for a wash and tumble dry is about £3. A service wash, where someone will do your washing for you, costs around £4-5. In more remote areas, you'll have to rely on hostel and campsite facilities.

Time Greenwich Mean Time (GMT) is used from late October to late March, after which time the clocks go forward an hour to British Summer Time (BST). GMT is five hours ahead of US Eastern Standard Time and 10 hours behind Australian Eastern Standard Time.

Toilets Public toilets are found at all train and bus stations and motorway service stations. They may charge 20p, but are generally clean, with disabled and baby-changing facilities. Those in town centres are often pretty grim.

Weights and measures Imperial and metric systems are both currently in use. Distances on roads are measured in miles and yards, drinks are poured in pints and gills, but generally, nowadays, the metric system is used elsewhere.

Essentials

Enquiries

National Rail Enquiries, T08457-484950, www.railtrack.co.uk, for information on rail services and fares. For advance credit/debit card bookings, T08457-550033. *GNER*, T08457-225225, www.gner.co.uk; *Virgin*, T08457-222333; *ScotRail*, T08457-550033, www.scotrail.co.uk

Fares

For details of various discount rail passes and rail services within Scotland, see 'Getting around' (page 47)

To describe the system of rail ticket pricing as complicated is a huge understatement and impossible to explain here. There are many and various discounted fares, but restrictions are often prohibitive, which explains the long queues and delays at ticket counters in railway stations. The cheapest ticket is a **Super Apex**, which must be booked at least two weeks in advance, though this is not available on all journeys. Next cheapest is an **Apex** ticket which has to be booked at least seven days before travelling. Other discount tickets include a **Saver** return, which can be used on all trains, and a **Super Saver**, which costs slightly less but cannot be used on a Friday or during peak times. For example, a *GNER* London-Edinburgh **Saver** return costs £82.50, while an **Apex** is £51. A standard return with *Scotrail* on this route is £65. All discount tickets should be booked as quickly as possible as they are often sold out weeks, or even months, in advance, especially Apex and Super Apex tickets. The latter tickets guarantee seat reservations, but Saver and Super Saver tickets do not. These can be secured by paying an extra £1. A **Caledonian Sleeper Apex** return ticket from London to Edinburgh or Glasgow costs £89, while an open return is £125.

Touching down

Scottish airports

Glasgow, T0141-8871111. Terminal facilities include car hire, bank ATMs, currency exchange, left luggage, tourist information, T8484440, and shops, restaurants and bars. There's also a Travel Centre, T8484330, in the UK Arrivals concourse (open daily 0800-2200 in summer and till 1800 in winter), and a Thomas Cook Hotel & Travel Reservations desk in the International Arrivals concourse, T8877220. **Edinburgh**, T0131-3331000. Edinburgh airport has all facilities, including a tourist information

For details of flights to the airports listed here, see box on page 30. For all UK airports, visit www.baa.co.uk

Essentials

The Countryside Code

- *Drive carefully and behave courteously to other motorists and cyclists on narrow, winding island roads. Park vehicles where they will not be a hazard or disruption to other motorists, residents or businesses*
- *Keep to public paths through farmland to minimise crop damage, and avoid 'short-cuts' on steep terrain to prevent soil erosion and damage to natural vegetation*
- *Litter is an eye-sore, harmful to farm animals, wildlife and the water supply – leave no waste and take all your rubbish home*
- *Protect wildlife, plants and trees*
- *Respect ancient monuments, buildings and sites of religious importance – do not vandalise or cause graffiti*
- *Many of the abandoned crofts are derelict and dangerous – keep out for your own safety*
- *Avoid damaging crops, walls, fences and farm equipment and fasten all gates*
- *Do not collect wildflowers, seabird eggs or historical artefacts for souvenirs*
- *Avoid pollution of water supplies - there are few toilets outside of villages so when walking in the countryside bury human waste and toilet paper in the*

- *ground and at least 30 metres from water courses*
- *Guard against all risk of fire from matches, cigarettes, cooking stoves and campfires*
- *Keep dogs under careful control, especially when near to sheep at lambing-time, seabird nesting sites at cliff edges and avoid dog-fouling in public places*
- *Respect the peace, solitude and tranquillity of the islands for others to enjoy – keep noise to a minimum*
- *The landscape can be spectacular but dangerous – take particular care along precipitous cliff edges, hilltops and slippery coastal rocks*
- *Stay away from working areas on the moors and hills during grouse-shooting, lambing season, deer culling and heather burning, and respect other locally or nationally imposed access restrictions*
- *Report any damage or environmental concerns to the landowner or the Scottish Environment Protection Agency (SEPA) in Stornoway (T01851-706477)*
- *Be adequately prepared when you walk in the hills – check the weather forecast, carry warm, waterproof clothing and adequate food and water supplies, and know how to use a map and compass*

desk, currency exchange, ATMs, restaurants and bars (first floor) and shops (ground floor and first floor). For car hire, Avis, Budget, Europcar, Hertz and National car hire desks are located in the terminal in the main UK arrivals area. Scotland's other main airports are **Aberdeen**, T01224-722331, **Inverness**, T01463-232471, **Prestwick**, T01292-511006, **Dundee**, T01382-643242, and **Wick**, T01955-602215.

Airport tax All air tickets are subject to a passenger service charge and airport tax. For economy fare flights within the UK and from EU countries the tax is £5. For all other flights it is £20. Taxes on first-or club-class flights are £10 for UK and EU and £40 for other destinations. The service charge varies from one airport to another.

Tourist information

Tourist offices – called Tourist Information Centres (TICs) – can be found in most Scottish towns. Their addresses, phone numbers and opening hours are listed in the relevant sections of this book. Opening hours vary depending on the time of year, and many of the smaller offices are closed during the winter months. All tourist offices provide information on accommodation, public transport, local attractions and restaurants, as well as selling books, local guides, maps and souvenirs. Many also have free street plans and leaflets describing local walks. They can also book accommodation for you (see page 40), for a small fee. Addresses of the main office of the *Scottish Tourist Board* and the *Area Tourist Boards* are given on page 23.

Most of Scotland's tourist attractions, apart from the large museums and art galleries in the main cities, are open only from Easter to October. Full details of opening hours and admission charges are given in the relevant sections of this guide.

Museums, galleries & monuments

Over 100 of the country's most prestigious sights, and 185,000 acres of beautiful countryside, are cared for by the **National Trust for Scotland** (NTS), 26-31 Charlotte Square, Edinburgh EH2 4ET, T0131-2439300, www.nts.org.uk National Trust properties are indicated in this guide as 'NTS', and entry charges and opening hours are given for each property. If you're going to be visiting several sights during your stay, then it's worth taking annual membership. This costs £28, £12 if you're aged under 26 and £47 for a family, and gives free access to all NTS and NT properties. The *National Trust Touring Pass* costs £18 per adult and £28 for a family, and gives free admission to its properties for seven days. A 14-day pass costs £26 and £44 respectively. YHA and HI members and student-card holders get 50% discount on NTS admission charges.

Historic Scotland (HS), Longmore House, Salisbury Place, Edinburgh EH9 1SH, T0131-6688800, www.historic-scotland.gov.uk, manages more than 330 of Scotland's most important castles, monuments and other historic sites. Historic Scotland properties are indicated as 'HS', and admission charges and opening hours are also given in this guide. Historic Scotland offer an *Explorer Ticket* which allows free entry to 70 of their properties including Edinburgh and Stirling castles. It costs £17 per adult and £35 for a family for seven days, and £22/£42 for 14 days. It can save a lot of money, as entry to Edinburgh Castle alone is £7.50 per adult.

Many other historic buildings are owned by local authorities, and admission is cheap, or in many cases free. Most municipal **art galleries and museums** are free, as well as most state-owned museums, including those in Edinburgh and Glasgow. Most fee-paying attractions give a discount or concession for senior citizens, the unemployed, full-time students and children under 16 (those under five are admitted free everywhere). Proof of age or status must be shown. Many of Scotland's **stately homes** are still owned and occupied by the landed gentry, and admission charges are usually between £4 and £6.

Local customs and laws

Visitors will generally find their Scottish hosts to be friendly and obliging. In fact, the level of hospitality should be a significant part of the enjoyment of your trip. Those visiting the Outer Hebrides, however, need to be aware of the strict observance of the Sabbath on those islands.

Tipping in Scotland is at the customer's discretion. In a restaurant you should leave a tip of 10-15% if you are satisfied with the service. If the bill already includes a service charge, you needn't add a further tip. Tipping is not normal in pubs or bars. Taxi drivers will expect a tip for longer journeys, usually of around 10%; and most hairdressers will also expect a tip. As in most other countries, porters, bellboys and waiters in more upmarket hotels rely on tips to supplement their meagre wages.

Tipping

Responsible tourism

Sustainable or eco-tourism has been described as: "...ethical, considerate or informed tourism where visitors can enjoy the natural, historical and social heritage of an area

Essentials

Essentials

Accommodation price codes

Accommodation prices in this book are graded with the letters below and are based on the cost per person for two people sharing a double room with en suite bathroom during the high season. Cheaper rooms with shared bathrooms are available in many hotels, guesthouses and B&Bs. Many places, particularly larger hotels, offer substantial discounts during the low season and at weekends. All places *listed are recommended as providing good quality and value within their respective price category. Note that price codes for youth hostels are not given in the accommodation listings, as they all cost under £15 per person per night.*

L £80 plus   *A £66-80*
B £46-65   *C £36-45*
D £26-35   *E £16-25*
F £15 and under

without causing adverse environmental, socio-economic or cultural impacts that compromise the long-term ability of that area and its people to provide a recreational resource for future generations and an income for themselves…"

The Highlands and Islands of Scotland are beautiful, dramatic and wild, but also a living, working landscape and a fragile and vulnerable place. By observing the simple guidelines outlined on the previous page and behaving responsibly, you can help to minimise your impact and protect the natural and cultural heritage of this unique island environment so that it can continue to be appreciated by other visitors.

For further information on what action is being taken either in Scotland, throughout UK or across the world to control against the negative aspects of tourism on the natural environment and traditional cultures, contact **Tourism Concern** in London (T020-77533330) or the **Tourism and Environment Forum** (www.greentourism.org.uk).

Safety

For more information on mountain safety, see page 60   Though Scottish cities have their fair share of crime, much of it is drug-related and confined to the more deprived peripheral areas. However, visitors to Scotland should take heed of the usual advice and avoid wandering around unlit city centre streets or parks alone at night. The major saftey issue when visiting the Highlands and more remote parts relates to the unpredictable weather conditions. Everyone should be aware of the need for caution and proper preparation when walking or climbing in the mountains.

Where to stay

Places to sleep are identified by a ■ symbol on maps   Accommodation in Scotland will be your greatest expense. It ranges from hostels and cheaper Bed and Breakfasts (B&Bs) to upmarket hotels, many of which are converted castles and country mansions. If you'd like to stay in a Scottish castle as a paying guest of the owner, contact *Scotts Castle Holidays*, T0131-2297111, www.scottscastles.com

Tourist Information Centres will help find accommodation for you. They can recommend a place within your particular budget and give you the number to phone up and book yourself, or will book a room for you. Some offices charge a small fee (usually £1) for booking a room, while others ask you to pay a deposit of 10% which is deducted from your first night's bill. Most tourist offices also offer a **Book-a-Bed-Ahead** service, which reserves accommodation for you at your next destination. This costs £3 per booking and is particularly useful in July and August, or if you'll be arriving in a town late. Addresses of the main office of the Area Tourist Boards are given on page 23.

Youth Hostel Associations

Australia *Australian Youth Hostels Association, 422 Kent St, Sydney, T02-92611111.*
Canada *Hostelling International Canada, Room 400, 205 Catherine St, Ottawa, ON K2P 1C3, T800-6635777.*
England & Wales *Youth Hostel Association (YHA), Trevelyan House, 8 St Stephen's Hill, St Albans, Herts AL1 2DY, T01727-855215, www.yha/england/wales/org.uk*
France *FUAJ, 7 Rue Pajol, 75018 Paris, T1-44 898727 .*
Germany *Deutsches Jugendherbergswerk, Hauptverband, Postfach 1455, 32704 Detmold, T5231-74010.*

Ireland *An Oige, 61 Muntjoy St, Dublin 7, T01-8304555, www.irelandyha.org*
New Zealand *Youth Hostels Association of New Zealand, PO Box 436, Christchurch 1, T03-379970.*
Northern Ireland *Youth Hostel Association of Northern Ireland, 22 Donegal Rd, Belfast, BT12 5JN, T01232-324733.*
Scotland *Scottish Youth Hostel Association (SYHA), 7 Glebe Cres, Stirling FK8 2JA, T01786-451181, www.syha.org.uk*
USA *Hostelling International-American Youth Hostels (HI-AYH), 733 15th St NW, Suite 840, PO Box 37613, Washington DC 20005, T202-7836161, www.hostels.com*

Note that single rooms are in short supply and many places are reluctant to let a double room to one person, even when they're not busy. Single rooms are usually more than the cost per person for a double room and in some cases cost the same as two people sharing a double room.

Hotels, guesthouses and B&Bs

Area tourist boards publish accommodation lists which include campsites, hostels, self-catering accommodation and STB-approved hotels, guesthouses and B&Bs. Places participating in the STB system will have a plaque displayed outside which shows their grading, determined by a number of stars ranging from one to five. These reflect the level of facilities, as well as the quality of hospitality and service. However, do not assume that a B&B, guesthouse or hotel is no good because it is not listed by the tourist board. They simply don't want to pay to be included in the system, and some of them may offer better value.

At the top end of the scale, there are some fabulously luxurious hotels, often in spec- **Hotels**
tacular locations. Many of them are converted baronial mansions or castles and offer a chance to enjoy a taste of aristocratic grandeur and style. At the lower end of the scale, there is often little to choose between cheaper hotels and guesthouses or B&Bs. The latter often offer higher standards of comfort and a more personal service, but many smaller hotels are really just guesthouses, and are often family-run and every bit as friendly. Note that some hotels, especially in town centres or in fishing ports, may also be rather noisy, as the bar can often be the social hub. Rooms in most mid-range to expensive hotels almost always have bathrooms en suite. Many upmarket hotels offer excellent room-only deals in the low season.

Guesthouses are often large, converted family homes with up to five or six rooms. They **Guesthouses**
tend to be slightly more expensive than B&Bs and, though they are often less personal, usually provide better facilities, such as en suite bathroom, colour TV in each room and private parking. In many instances they are more like small budget hotels. Many guesthouses offer evening meals, though this may have to be requested in advance.

Bed & breakfasts B&Bs provide the cheapest private accommodation. At the bottom end of the scale you can get a bedroom in a private house, a shared bathroom and a huge cooked breakfast for around £15-20 per person per night. Small B&Bs may only have one or two rooms to let, so it's important to **book in advance** during the summer season and on the islands where accommodation options are more limited. More upmarket B&Bs have en suite bathrooms and TVs in each room and usually charge from £20-25 per person per night. In general, B&Bs are more hospitable, informal, friendlier and offer better value than hotels. Many B&B owners, particularly in the Highlands and Islands, are a great source of local knowledge and can even provide OS maps for local walks. B&Bs in the Outer Hebrides also offer dinner, bed and breakfast, which is useful as eating options are limited, especially on a Sunday.

Some places, especially in ferry ports, charge room-only rates, which are slightly cheaper and allow you to get up in time to catch an early morning ferry. However, this means that you miss out on a huge **cooked breakfast**. If you're travelling on a tight budget, you can eat as much as you can at breakfast time and save on lunch as you won't need to eat again until evening. This is particularly useful if you're heading into the hills, as you won't have to carry so much food. Many B&B owners will even make up a packed lunch for you at a small extra cost.

Hostels

For those travelling on a tight budget, there is a large network of hostels offering cheap accommodation. These are also popular centres for backpackers and provide a great opportunity for meeting fellow travellers. Hostels have kitchen facilities for self-catering, and some include a continental breakfast in the price or provide cheap breakfasts and evening meals. **Advance booking** is recommended at all times, and particularly from May to September and on public holidays, and a credit card is often useful.

Scottish Youth Hostel Association (SYHA) The SYHA is separate from the YHA in England and Wales. It has a network of over 80 hostels which are often better and cheaper than those in other countries. They offer bunk-bed accommodation in single-sex dormitories or smaller rooms, kitchen and laundry facilities. Prices range from £6-8 for the cheapest up to £11-13 for for the most expensive. Prices are cheaper for juniors (under 18s). Those in large towns and cities and main tourist centres are more expensive. The average cost is £8-10 per person per night. Though some rural hostels are still strict on discipline and impose a 2300 curfew, those in larger towns and cities tend to be more relaxed and doors are closed as late as 0200. Some larger hostels provide breakfasts for around £2.50 and three-course evening meals for around £4-5.

The SYHA produces a handbook (free with membership) giving details of all their youth hostels, including transport links. This can be useful as some hostels are difficult to get to without your own transport. You should always phone ahead, as many hostels are closed during the day. Phone numbers are listed in this guide. Many hostels are closed during the winter. Details are given in the *SYHA Handbook*.

For Scottish residents, adult membership costs £6, and can be obtained at the SYHA National Office (see box for address), or at the first SYHA hostel you stay at. SYHA membership gives automatic membership of *Hostelling International* (HI). Youth hostel members are entitled to half-price entry to all National Trust for Scotland properties. The SYHA also offers an **Explore Scotland** and **Scottish Wayfarer** ticket, which can save a lot of money on transport and accommodation, especially if you're not a student (see page 41).

Independent hostels The *Independent Backpackers Hostels of Scotland* is an association of nearly 100 independent hostels/bunkhouses throughout Scotland. They charge between £6 and £15 per person per night, though the average is around £8-10. They tend to be more laid-back, with fewer rules and no curfew, and no membership is required. They all have dormitories, hot showers and self-catering kitchens. Some include continental breakfast, or provide cheap breakfasts. All these hostels are listed in the *Independent Hostel Guide*, which is available from tourist offices, or send an A5 SAE to: Pete Thomas, Croft Bunkhouse & Bothies, Portnalong, Isle of Skye, IV47 8SL. They also have a website, www.hostel-scotland.co.uk

Camping, self-catering and campus accommodation

There are hundreds of campsites around Scotland. They are mostly geared to caravans, and vary greatly in quality and level of facilities. The most expensive sites, which charge up to £10 to pitch a tent, are usually well-equipped. Sites are usually only open from April to October. If you plan to do a lot of camping, you should buy *Scotland: Camping & Caravan Parks* (£3.95), available from most tourist offices. It lists around 150 camping and caravan parks graded by the STB.

Camping

North Americans planning on camping should invest in an **international camping carnet**, which is available from home motoring organizations, or from *Family Campers and RVers* (FCRV), 4804 Transit Road, Building 2, Depew, NY 14043 (T1-800-2459755). It gives you discounts at member sites.

There is plenty of STB-approved self-catering accommodation available, ranging from remote farmhouse cottages to city-centre apartments. The minimum stay is usually one week in the summer peak season, or three days or less at other times of the year. Expect to pay at least £150 per week for a two-bedroom cottage in the winter, rising to £250 in the high season. Places in the city range from around £200 to over £700 per week. A good source of self-catering accommodation is the STB's guide (£5.95), which lists over 1,200 properties and is available from any tourist office.

Self-catering

The *National Trust for Scotland* owns many historic properties which are available for self-catering holidays. Prices start at around £250 per week in high season. Contact them at 5 Charlotte Square, Edinburgh EH2 4DU, T0131-2265922. For something a bit different, *Highland Hideaways* has a range of more individual self-catering properties, mainly in the Highlands and Islands. For a free brochure write to them at 5-7 Stafford Street, Oban, Argyll PA34 5NJ, T01631-526056.

Many Scottish universities open their halls of residence to visitors during the summer vacation (late June to September), and some also during the Easter and Christmas breaks. Many rooms are basic and small with shared bathrooms, but there are also more comfortable rooms with private bathrooms, twin and family units, and self-contained apartments and shared houses. Full board, half board, B&B and self-catering options are all available. Prices for bed and breakfast tend to be roughly the same as most B&Bs, but self-catering can cost as little as £50 per person per week. Local tourist offices have information, or contact the *British Universities Accommodation Consortium*, T0115-9504571, for a brochure. Details are given in this guide under the relevant travel section.

Campus accommodation

Getting around

Public transport is generally good and efficient. With a combination of buses, trains, ferries, walking, hiring a bike, plenty of time and careful planning, you can get almost anywhere. Most places in the Central Lowlands, between Glasgow, Edinburgh and Dundee, are easily reached by bus and train. Services in the north and south of

Scotland are less efficient and it can be a slow and difficult process getting to more remote parts of the Highlands and Islands and Argyll. Public transport can also be expensive, but there's a whole raft of discount passes and tickets which can save you a lot of money. Hiring a car can work out as a more economical, and certainly more flexible, option, especially for more than two people travelling together. It will also enable you to get off the beaten track and see more of the country.

Maps You'll find a good selection of maps of Scotland in many bookshops and at the main tourist offices. **Road atlases** can be bought at most service stations. The best of these are the large-format ones produced by the *AA*, *Collins* and *Ordnance Survey* which cover all of Britain at a scale of around three miles to one inch and include plans of the major towns and cities. The *Michelin* and *Bartholomew* fold-out maps are also excellent, as are the official regional tourist maps published by *Estate Publications*, which are ideal for driving and which are available from most tourist offices.

The best detailed maps for walking are the *Ordnance Survey* maps, which are unsurpassed for accuracy and clarity. These are available at different scales. The *Landranger* series at 1:50,000 (1¼ inches to a mile) covers the whole of Britain and is good for most walkers. The new *Explorer* and *Outdoor Leisure* series are 1:25,000 and offer better value for walkers and cyclists. An excellent source of maps is *Stanfords* at 12-14 Longacre, London WC2E 9LP.

Air

There is no departure tax on flights form Highlands and Islands airports

As well as the main airports of Glasgow, Edinburgh and Aberdeen, Scotland has many small airports, many of them on islands (one of them, on Barra, uses the beach as an airstrip). Internal flights are expensive, however, and not really necessary in such a small country, unless you are short of time and want to visit the Outer Hebrides or Orkney and Shetland. For example a return flight from Edinburgh or Glasgow to Shetland costs over £250. There are discounted tickets available, such as Apex fares, which must be booked at least 14 days in advance, and special offers on some services. *BA's* **Highland Rover** costs £189 and allows you to take any five flights within seven days (except inter-island flights within Orkney or Shetland).

The majority of flights are operated by *British Airways/Loganair*, T08457-733377, www.british-airways.com. For inter-island flights in Shetland, you should book direct through *Loganair*, T01595-840246. Other carriers are *British Midland*, T08457-554554, www.iflybritishmidland.com. For information on flight schedules, call the airports listed on page 37, or *British Airways*. The *British Airports Authority* (BAA) publishes a free *Scheduled Flight Guide*.

Road

Bus & coach
Budget backpacker tours can be a cheap way of getting to and around Scotland (see page 21)

Travelling around Scotland by bus takes longer than the train but is much cheaper. There are numerous local bus companies, but the main operator is *Scottish Citylink*, T08705-505050, www.citylink.demon.co.uk, part of the *National Express* group. Bus services between towns and cities are good, but far less frequent in more remote rural areas. Note that long-distance express buses are called coaches.

Passes and discounts There are a number of discount and flexible tickets for bus/coach travel in Scotland. Full-time students, or those aged under 25 or over 50, can buy a *National Express* **Coach Card** or *Scottish Citylink* **Smart Card** for £9, both of which are valid for one year and get you a 30% discount on all *National Express* and *Scottish Citylink* fares within the UK. A **Family Card** costs £18 and allows two children to travel free with two adults, though children normally travel for half price.

The **Tourist Trail Pass** offers unlimited travel on all *Scottish Citylink* and *National Express* services throughout Britain. Passes cost from £49 for two days' travel out of three, up to £190 for 14 days' travel out of 30. They can be bought from major travel agents, at Gatwick and Heathrow airports, as well as from bus stations in Scottish towns and cities. The *National Express* **Explorer Pass** offers unlimited travel within a specified period on *Scottish Citylink* buses. It is available to overseas visitors but must be bought outside Britain. It costs £59 for three days' travel within a five-day period, £110 for seven days in a 21-day period, and £170 for 14 days in a 30-day period. Smart Card and Discount Coach Card holders can get a 30% discount on these prices. In **North America** these passes are available from *British Travel International*, T1-800-3276097, www.britishtravel.com, or from *US National Express*, T502-2981395.

The SYHA sells its own **Explore Scotland** bus pass, which allows free travel on *Citylink* services. It costs £155 for five days and £250 for eight days, and includes seven nights' hostel accommodation, free SYHA membership and free entry to many *Historic Scotland* properties. They also sell a **Scottish Wayfarer** ticket which is similar but also includes rail travel, *CalMac* ferries and discounts on many *P&O Ferries*. It costs £160 for four days, £270 for eight days, and £299 for 12 days.

Postbus services Many rural areas, particularly in the Highlands and Islands, can only be reached by Royal Mail postbuses. These are minibuses that follow postal delivery routes and carry up to 14 fare-paying passengers. They set off early in the morning from the main post office and follow a circuitous route as they deliver and collect mail in the most far-flung places. They are often very slow on the outward morning routes but quicker on the return routes in the afternoons. It can be a slow method of getting around, but you get to see some of the country's most spectacular scenery, and it is useful for walkers and those trying to reach remote hostels or B&Bs. There's a restricted service on Saturdays and none on Sundays. A free booklet of routes and timetables is usually available from local Tourist Information Centres. For more information on postbuses call the **Royal Mail** in Edinburgh, T0131-2287407.

Car Travelling with your own private transport is the ideal way to explore the country. This allows you to cover a lot of ground in a short space of time and to reach remote places. The main disadvantages are traffic congestion and parking, but this is only a problem in the main cities and on the motorways in the central belt. Roads in Scotland are generally a lot less busy than those in England, and driving is relatively stress-free, especially on the B-roads and minor roads. In remote parts of the country, in the Highlands and Islands in particular, many roads are **single track**, with passing places indicated by a diamond-shaped signpost. These should also be used to allow traffic behind you to overtake. Remember that you may want to take your time to enjoy the stupendous views all around you, but the driver behind may be a local doctor in a hurry. Don't park in passing places. A major driving hazard on single track roads are the huge numbers of sheep wandering around, blissfully unaware of your presence. When confronted by a flock of sheep, slow down and gently edge your way past. Be particularly careful at night, as many of them sleep by the side of the road (counting cars perhaps). Also note that petrol in the Highlands and Islands is a lot more expensive than in other parts of the UK, and that petrol stations and garages are few and far between.

Rules and regulations To drive in Scotland you must have a current driving licence. Foreign nationals also need an **international driving permit**, available from state and national motoring organizations for a small fee. Those importing their own vehicle should also have their vehicle registration or ownership document. Make sure you're adequately insured. In all of the UK you **drive on the left. Speed limits** are 30 miles per hour (mph) in built-up areas, 70 mph on motorways and dual carriageways, and 60 mph on most other roads.

Essentials

Essentials

Car hire companies

Britain/Europe *Arnold Clark,*
T0131-2284747 (Edinburgh);
T0141-3399886 (Glasgow). Avis,
T08705-900500; Budget, T0800-181181;
easyCar, www.easycar.com; EuroDollar,
T01895-233300; Europcar, T08457-222525;
First European, T0131-3353411
(Edinburgh), T0141-8861072), Glasgow.
Hertz, T08705-996699; Holiday Autos,
T8705-300400, www.holidayautos.com;
Melvilles, T0131-3375333 (Edinburgh),
T0141-3395757 (Glasgow); National Car
Rental, T08705-365365; Thrifty,
T0131-3371319 (Edinburgh),
T0141-4454440 (Glasgow).

North America *Alamo, T800-5229696,*
www.goalamo.com; Avis, T800-3311084,
www.avis.com; Budget, T800-5270700,
www.budgetrentacar.com; Dollar,
T800-4216868, www.dollar.com;
Hertz, T800-6543001, www.hertz.com;
Holiday Autos , T800-4227737,
www.holiday/colauto.com; National,
T800-CAR-RENT, www.nationalcar.com;
Thrifty, T800-3672277, www.thrifty.com
Australia *Avis, T1800-225533; Budget,*
T1300-362848; Hertz, T1800-550067.
New Zealand *Avis, T09-5262847;*
Budget, T09-3752222; Hertz,
T09-3676350.

Motoring organizations It's advisable to join one of the main UK motoring organizations during your visit for their **24-hour breakdown assistance**. The two main ones in Britain are the **Automobile Association** (*AA*), T0800-448866, www.theaa.co.uk, and the **Royal Automobile Club** (*RAC*), T0800-550550, rac.co.uk One year's membership of the *AA* starts at £46 and £39 for the *RAC*. They also provide many other services, including a reciprocal agreement for free assistance with many overseas motoring organizations. Check to see if your organization is included. Both companies can also extend their cover to include Europe. Their **emergency numbers** are: *AA* T0800-887766; *RAC* T0800-828282. You can call these numbers even if you're not a member, but you'll have to a pay a large fee. In remote areas you may have to wait a long time for assistance. Also note that in the Highlands and Islands you may be stranded for ages waiting for spare parts to arrive.

Motorcycle hire is very expensive, ranging from around £200 up to £350 per week

Car hire This can be expensive in Scotland and you may be better off making arrangements in your home country for a fly/drive deal through one of the main multi-national companies. The minimum you can expect to pay is around £150-180 per week for a small car. Local hire companies often offer better deals than the larger multi-nationals, though *easycar* offer the best rates at around £10 per day. They are based at Glasgow airport and there are plans to open a branch in Edinburgh (check their website for latest information). Some companies such as *Melvilles* offer the flexibility of picking up in Glasgow and leaving in Edinburgh, and vice versa. Most companies prefer payment with a credit card, otherwise you'll have to leave a large deposit (£100 or more). You'll need a full driver's licence (one or two years) and be aged over 21 (23 in some cases).

Hitching As in the rest of the UK, hitching is never entirely safe, and is certainly not advised for anyone travelling alone, particularly women travellers. Those prepared to take the risk should not find it too difficult to get a lift, especially in the Highlands and Islands, where people are far more willing to stop for you. Bear in mind, though, that you will probably have to wait a while even to see a vehicle in remote parts.

Sea

There are around 60 or so inhabited islands off the coast of Scotland, and nearly 50 of them can be reached by a scheduled ferry service. Most ferries carry vehicles and can

Ferry companies

Caledonian MacBrayne, *The Ferry Terminal, Gourock, PA19 1QP, T01475-650100, Reservations T08705-650000, reservations@calmac.co.uk, www.calmac.co.uk.*
John O' Groats Ferries, *T01955-611353.*

Orkney Ferries, *Shore St, Kirkwall, KW15 1LG, T01856-872044, www.orkneyislands.com*
P&O Scottish Ferries, *PO Box 5, Jamieson's Quay, Aberdeen AB11 5NP, T01224-572615, www.poscottishferries.co.uk.*
Western Ferries, *T0141-3329766.*

be booked in advance. If you're travelling to the islands by car, it's a good idea to book ferries in advance whatever the time of year, particularly to the more popular islands.

The majority of ferry services on the west coast are operated by *Caledonian MacBrayne*, or *CalMac* as they're more commonly known. They sail from **Oban**, **Mallaig** and **Ullapool** to over 20 islands in the **Inner** and **Outer Hebrides**. They also run services on the **Firth of Clyde**. Fares are expensive, especially with a car, but if you're planning on using ferries a lot, you can save a lot of money with an **Island Hopscotch** ticket, which offers reduced fares on 17 set routes. The ticket is valid for one month and you need to follow your set itinerary, though this can be changed en route without too much fuss. For more details and some sample fares, see under the relevant destination. A more flexible option is the **Island Rover**, which offers unlimited travel on *CalMac* ferries for a set period, though you still need to make reservations. An eight-day pass costs £43 per passenger and £210 for a car, and a 15-day pass costs £63 per passenger and £315 for a car. *CalMac* schedules are complicated, but fares and frequency of sailings are given under each relevant destination in this guide. *Western Ferries* runs services between **Gourock** and **Dunoon** and **Islay** and **Jura**.

P&O Scottish Ferries run car ferries to **Orkney** and **Shetland**. Ferries to Orkney depart from **Aberdeen** once or twice weekly and take eight to 10 hours, or from **Scrabster**, near Thurso, a few times daily and take two hours. Fares from Aberdeen are about £80-85 return for passengers and £140 for a car; from Scrabster it costs £30-35 per passenger and £80-85 for a car. There's also a passenger ferry from **John O' Groats** to Orkney which sails daily during the summer only (May-September) and is run by *John O' Groats Ferries* (see page 47).

P&O Ferries run an overnight ferry from **Aberdeen** to **Shetland** daily except Saturday during the summer months. The journey takes 14-20 hours. Fares are around £115-120 per passenger and £180 for a car. You should also book in advance on these routes if you're travelling by car.

The **Orkney** islands are linked by services run by *Orkney Ferries*, T01856-872044, while **Shetland's** inter-island ferries are run by *Shetland Islands Council*, T01806-244234. There are also numerous small operators offering day-trips to various islands. Details of these are given in the relevant chapters.

Train

The rail network in Scotland is limited and train travel is comparatively expensive, but trains are a fast and effective way to get around and also provide some beautifully scenic journeys. The West Highland line to Fort William and Mallaig and the journey from Inverness to Kyle of Lochalsh are amongst the most beautiful rail journeys in the world and well worth doing. Services in the central belt, between Glasgow, Edinburgh, Stirling, Perth, Dundee and Aberdeen are fast and frequent, and there are frequent trains to and from Inverness.

Details of the different rail passes and railcards available are on the next page; details of the different types of tickets are on page 36

Discount rail passes

Eurorail passes are not recognized in Britain, but **ScotRail** offers a couple of worthwhile travel passes. The most flexible is the **Freedom of Scotland Travelpass**, which gives unlimited rail travel within Scotland. It is also valid on all **CalMac** ferries on the west coast, many **Citylink** bus services in the Highlands, some regional buses, and Glasgow Underground. It also gives 33% discount on **P&O Ferries** from Scrabster to Orkney and 20% discount on **P&O Ferries** from Aberdeen to Orkney and Shetland. It costs £69 for four days' travel out of eight consecutive days, £99 for any eight out of 15 consecutive days, and £119 for any 12 out of 15 consecutive days. The **Highland Rover** is more limited. It allows unlimited rail travel in the Highlands region, plus the West Highland line from Glasgow, and travel between Aberdeen and Aviemore. It also allows free travel on **Citylink** buses between Oban, Fort William and Inverness. It costs £49 for any four out of eight consecutive days. The **Festival Cities Rover** covers the central region and costs £29 for any three out of seven days. Holders of **Senior Citizen's** or **Young Person's Railcard** get a 30% discount on these passes.

ScotRail operates most train services. For information on fares and timetables, contact **National Rail Enquiries**, T0345-484950, open 24 hours. You can buy train tickets at the stations, from major travel agents, or over the phone with a credit/debit card. For advance credit/debit card bookings call T0345-550033, or www.scotrail.co.uk. For busy long-distance routes it's best to reserve a seat. Seat reservations to Edinburgh, Glasgow, Aberdeen or Inverness are included in the price of the ticket when you book in advance. If the ticket office is closed, there's usually a machine on the platform. If this isn't working, you can buy your ticket on the train.

Cyclists should note that though train companies have a more relaxed attitude to taking bikes on trains, reservations for bikes (£3.50) are still required on some services.

Keeping in touch

Communications

Internet It is now de rigeur amongst travellers to get an email address you can access through the internet, such as hotmail or yahoo. As in many places, internet access in Scotland is extensive and often easier and more reliable than the phone. Every major town now has at least one internet café, with more springing up daily. Email works out much, much cheaper than phoning home and is also useful for booking hotels and tours and for checking out information on the web. Many hotels now have internet and many hostels also offer internet access to their guests. Websites and email addresses are listed where appropriate in this guide. The Scottish Tourist Board and area tourist boards have their own websites and these are given on page 23. **Cybercafés** are also listed under each relevant section. Most of these can be found in Edinburgh and Glasgow. In the absence of any cybercafés listed under a particular town try the public library for internet access or ask at the tourist office.

Post Most **post offices** are open Monday-Friday 0900 to 1730 and Saturday 0900 to 1230 or 1300. Smaller sub-post offices are closed for an hour at lunch (1300-1400) and many of them operate out of a shop. Post offices keep the same half-day closing times as shops.

Stamps can be bought at post offices, but also from vending machines outside, and also at many newsagents. A first-class letter to anywhere in the UK costs 27p and should arrive the following day, while second-class letters cost 19p and take between two to four days. Airmail letters of less than 20g cost 37p to Europe. To the USA and Australia costs 45p for 10g and 65p for 20g. For more information about *Royal Mail* postal services, call T08457-740740 or www.royalmail.com

Most public **payphones** are operated by *British Telecom* (*BT*) and are fairly widespread in towns and cities, though less so in rural areas. *BT* payphones take either coins (20p, 50p and £1) or **phonecards**, which are available at newsagents and post offices displaying the *BT* logo. These cards come in denominations of £2, £3, £5 and £10. Some payphones also accept credit cards.

Telephone
Operator: T100
International operator: T155
Directory enquiries: T192
Overseas directory enquiries: T153

For most countries (including Europe, USA and Canada) calls are cheapest between 1800 and 0800 Monday-Friday and all day Saturday and Sunday. For Australia and New Zealand it's cheapest to call from 1430 to 1930 and from midnight to 0700 every day.

Phone codes for towns and cities are given in the margin by the town's heading throughout this book. You don't need to use the area code if calling from the same area. Any number prefixed by 0800 or 0500 is free to the caller; 08457 numbers are charged at local rates and 08705 numbers at the national rate.

To **call Scotland** from overseas, dial 011 from USA and Canada, 0011 from Australia and 00 from New Zealand, followed by 44, then the area code, minus the first zero, then the number.

To **call overseas from Scotland** dial 00 followed by the country code. Country codes include: **Australia** 61; **Ireland** 353; **New Zealand** 64; **South Africa** 27; **USA** and **Canada** 1.

Media

The main British daily and Sunday newspapers are widely available in Scotland and some of them publish special Scottish editions, among them the *Scottish Daily Mail*, *Scottish Daily Express* and Rupert Murdoch's notorious scandal sheet, *The Sun*.

Newspapers & magazines

The **Scottish press** produces two main 'quality' newspapers, the liberal-leaning *The Scotsman*, published in Edinburgh, and *The Herald*, published in Glasgow, which is the oldest daily newspaper in the English-speaking world, dating from 1783. The biggest-selling daily is the *Daily Record*, a tabloid paper (or red top as they are known). The Sunday equivalents of the dailies are *Scotland on Sunday* from the *Scotsman* stable, the *Sunday Herald* and the *Sunday Mail*, published by the *Daily Record*. Provincial newspapers are widely read in Scotland. The two biggest-selling titles are the parochial *Press and Journal* from Aberdeen and *The Courier & Advertiser*, published by Dundee's giant DC Thomson group, who also produce *The Beano* and *Dandy* kids' comics. DC Thomson publish Scotland's most successful Sunday newspaper, the *Sunday Post*, famous for its *Oor Wullie* and *Broons* cartoon charaters. In the Highlands the main papers are the weekly *Oban Times* and the radical, crusading *West Highland Free Press* published on Skye. Visitors to Glasgow and Edinburgh should buy a copy of the fortnightly listings magazine, *The List*, with lively features and previews, and reviews of all events in both cities.

Foreign newspapers and magazines, including *USA Today* and the *International Herald Tribune*, are available in larger newsagents, especially in central Edinburgh and Glasgow. *Time* and *Newsweek* are also available in larger newsagents and bookstores.

There are five main **television channels** in Scotland; the publicly funded *BBC 1* and *2*, and the independent commercial stations, *Channel 4*, *Channel 5* and *ITV*. The *ITV* network in Scotland is formed by *STV*, which serves central Scotland and parts of the West Highlands,

TV & radio

the Aberdeen-based *Grampian TV* which produces a lot of Gaelic programmes, and *Border TV* which covers Dumfries and Galloway and northwest England.

The BBC network also broadcasts several **radio channels**, most of which are based in London. These include: *Radio 1* aimed at a young audience; *Radio 2* targeting a more mature audience; *Radio 3* which plays mostly classical music; *Radio 4* which is talk-based and features arts, drama and current affairs; and *Radio 5 Live* which is a mix of sport and news. *Radio Scotland* (92-95FM, 810MW) provides a Scottish-based diet of news, sport, current affairs, travel and music. It also provides a Gaelic network in the northwest, and local programmes in Orkney and Shetland. There are also a large number of local **commercial radio stations**, stretching from Shetland in the north to the Borders. The local Glasgow station is *Clyde 1* (102.5FM), while in Edinburgh it is *Radio Forth* (97.3FM).

Food and drink

Places to eat are marked on maps in this book with the ● symbol — While Scotland's national drink is loved the world over, Scottish cooking hasn't exactly had a good press over the years. This is perhaps not too surprising, as the national dish, **haggis**, consists of a stomach stuffed with diced innards and served with mashed tatties (potatoes) and neeps (turnips). Not a great start. And things got even worse when the Scots discovered the notorious deep-fried Mars bar.

But Scottish cuisine has undergone a dramatic transformation in recent years and Scotland now boasts some of the most talented chefs, creating some of the best food in Britain. The heart of Scottish cooking is local produce, which includes the finest fish, shellfish, game, lamb, beef and vegetables, and a vast selection of traditionally made cheeses. What makes Scottish cooking so special is ready access to these foods. What could be better than enjoying an aperitif whilst watching your dinner being delivered by a local fisherman, knowing that an hour later you'll be enjoying the most delicious seafood?

Modern Scottish cuisine is now a feature of many of the top restaurants in the country. This generally means the use of local ingredients with foreign-influenced culinary styles, in particular French. **International cuisine** is also now a major feature on menus all over the country, influenced by the rise of Indian and Chinese restaurants in recent decades. Indeed, so prevalent are exotic Asian and Oriental flavours that curry has now replaced fish and chips (fish supper) as the nation's favourite food.

Anyone staying at a hotel, guesthouse or B&B will experience the hearty **Scottish breakfast**, which includes bacon, egg, sausage and black pudding (a type of sausage made with blood), all washed down with copious quantities of tea, Scotland's staple drink. Although coffee is readily available everywhere, do not expect *cappuccinos* and *café lattes*: filter coffee is the staple 'tea-substitue' in most hotels and B&Bs. You may also be served kippers (smoked herring) or **porridge**, an erstwhile Scottish staple, which is now eaten by few people. Porridge is made with oatmeal and has the consistency of Italian polenta. It is traditionally eaten with salt, though heretics are offered sugar instead. **Oatcakes** (oatmeal biscuits) may also be on offer, as well as potato scones, baps (bread rolls), bannocks (a sort of large oatcake) or butteries (butter-laden bread similar to a croissant). These local baked goodies can be spread with marmalade, brought to the world's breakfast tables by the city of Dundee (see page 387).

After such a huge cooked breakfast you probably won't feel like eating again until dinner, or **tea**, taken between 1700 and 1800, and a national institution consisting of a cooked main course (usually fish and chips) and a *smorgesbord* of scones and cakes, washed down with more pots of tea.

Scottish dishes — Fish, meat and game form the base of many of the country's finest dishes. Scottish **beef**, particularly Aberdeen Angus, is the most famous in the world and has escaped

Eating categories

Essentials

*In this book places to eat are divided into three categories: **expensive** (over £20 a head); **mid-range** (£10-20 a head); and **cheap** (under £10 a head). These prices are based on a two-course meal (main course plus starter or dessert) without drinks. We have tried to include an equal number of choices in each category, though this is not always possible. All places listed are recommended as offering relatively good value, quality and standards of service within their respective price category.*

the worst of the recent BSE scares. This will, or should, usually be hung for at least four weeks and sliced thick. **Game** is also a regular feature of Scottish menus, though it can be expensive (dear), especially **venison** (deer), but delicious and low in cholesterol. **Pheasant** and **hare** are also tasty, but **grouse** is, quite frankly, overrated.

Fish and **seafood** are fresh and plentiful, and if you're travelling around the northwest coast you must not miss the chance to savour local mussels, prawns, oysters, scallops, langoustines, lobster or crab. **Salmon** is, of course, the most famous of Scottish fish, but you're more likely to be served the fish-farmed variety than 'wild' salmon, which has a more delicate flavour. Trout is also farmed extensively, but the standard of both remains high. **Kippers** are also a favourite delicacy, the best of which come from Loch Fyne or the Achiltibuie smokery (see page 260). **Arbroath smokies** (smoked haddock) are a tasty alternative.

Haggis has made something of a comeback, and small portions are often served as starters in fashionable restaurants. Haggis is traditionally eaten on *Burns Night* (25 January) in celebration of the great poet's birthday, when it is piped to the table and then slashed open with a sword at the end of a recital of Robert Burns' 'Address to the Haggis'. Other national favourites feature names to relish: **cock-a-leekie** is a soup made from chicken, leeks and prunes; **cullen skink** (my own favourite) is a delicious concoction of smoked haddock and potatoes; while at the other end of the scale of appeal is **hugga-muggie**, a Shetland dish using fish's stomach. There's also the delightfully named **crappit heids** (haddock heads stuffed with lobster) and **partan bree** (a soup made form giant crab's claws, cooked with rice). Rather more mundane is the ubiquitous **Scotch broth**, made with mutton stock, vegetables, barley, lentils and split peas, and **stovies**, which is a mash of potato, onion and minced beef.

Waist-expanding **puddings** or desserts are a very important part of Scottish cooking and often smothered in butterscotch sauce or syrup in order to satisfy a sweet-toothed nation. There is a huge variety, including **cranachan**, a mouth- watering mix of toasted oatmeal steeped in whisky, cream and fresh raspberries, and **Atholl Brose**, a similar confection of oatmeal, whisky and cream.

Eaten before pudding, in the French style, or afterwards, are Scotland's many home-produced **cheeses**, which have made a successful comeback in the face of mass-produced varieties. Amongst the tastiest examples are **Lanark Blue**, made from unpasteurized ewe's milk and similar to Roquefort, and **Teviotdale** and **Bonchester**, which both come from the Borders. Many of the finest cheeses are produced on the islands, especially Arran, Mull, Islay and Orkney. **Caboc** is a creamy soft cheese rolled in oatmeal and is made in the Highlands.

There are places to suit every taste and budget. In Edinburgh and Glasgow in particular you'll find a vast selection of eating places, including **Indian**, **Chinese**, **Italian** and **French** restaurants, as well as **Thai**, **Japanese**, **Mexican**, **Spanish** and, of course **Scottish**. More and more restaurants, however, are moving away from national culinary boundaries and offering a wide range of **international** dishes and flavours, so you'll often find **Latin American**, **Oriental** and **Pacific Rim** dishes all on the same menu. This

Where to eat

Which whisky?

*Opinions vary as to what are the best single malts and as to when you should drink them. As a rough guide, I would recommend a Speyside malt such as Glenmorangie or Glenlivet **before dinner** and one of the Islay malts – Ardbeg, Bowmore, Bunnahabhain (pronounced 'bun-a-haven'), Lagavulin, or the very*

*wonderful Laphroaig (pronounced 'la-froig') – **after dinner**.*

If the Islays are not to your taste, then you could try instead Highland Park from Orkney or perhaps Tamdhu or Aberlour from Speyside. Those eternal favourites, Glenfiddich and The Macallan, can be enjoyed at any time.

---

is particularly the case in the many continental-style **bistros**, **brasseries** and **café-bars**, which now offer a more informal alternative to traditional restaurants. It is becoming increasingly irrelevant to talk of a particular nationality of cooking, and for this reason places to eat in this guide are grouped according to price and location instead. Not surprisingly, other parts of Scotland do not offer the same choice as Edinburgh and Glasgow, two cities with the greatest selection of places to eat in the UK outside London. **Vegetarians** are increasingly well catered for, especially in the large cities, where exclusively vegetarian/vegan restaurants and cafés are often the cheapest places to eat. Outside the cities, vegetarian restaurants are thin on the ground, though better-quality eating places will normally offer a reasonable vegetarian selection.

For a **cheap** meal, you're best bet is a **pub**, **hotel bar** or **café**, where you can have a one-course meal for around £5 or less, though don't expect gourmet food. The best value is often at lunch time, when many restaurants offer three-course **set lunches** or business lunches for less than £10. You'll need a pretty huge appetite to feel like eating a three-course lunch after your gigantic cooked breakfast, however. Also good value are the **pre-theatre dinners** offered by many restaurants in the larger towns and cities (you don't need to have a theatre ticket to take advantage). These are usually available from around 1730-1800 till 1900-1930, so you could get away with just a sandwich for lunch.

The biggest problem with eating out in Scotland, as in the rest of the UK, is the ludicrously limited serving hours in most pubs and hotels. These places only serve food between 1230 and 1400 and 1700 and 1900, seemingly ignorant of the eating habits of foreign visitors, or those who would prefer a bit more flexibility during their holiday. In small places especially it can be difficult finding food outside these strictly enforced times. Places which serve food all day till 2100 or later are restaurants, fast-food outlets and the many chic bistros and café-bars, which can be found not only in the main cities but increasingly in smaller towns. The latter often offer very good value and above-average quality.

Those who prefer to eat to live, rather than the other way round, need never spend more than £5-6 for lunch and £7-10 for dinner, excluding drinks. It is generally not difficult to find a **cheap** meal, though on many of the islands and in parts of the northwest Highlands, there is less choice and prices tend to be higher. Also, if you're on a tight budget avoid those restaurants at visitor centres or other such tourist traps, as they tend to charge exorbitant prices for very average food. At the other end of the scale, there are many excellent **restaurants**. Outside Edinburgh and Glasgow, these are often found in hotels, where you can enjoy the finest of Scottish cuisine, often with a continental influence. You can expect to pay from around £25 a head up to £40 or £50 in the very top establishments.

Essentials

How malt whisky is made

Malt whisky is made by first soaking dry barley in tanks of local water for two to three days. Then the barley is spread out on a concrete floor or placed in cylindrical drums and allowed to germinate for between eight and 12 days, after which it is dried in a kiln, heated by a peat fire. Next, the dried malt is ground and mixed with hot water in a huge circular vat called a 'mash tun'. A sugary liquid called 'wort' is then drawn from the porridge-like result and piped into huge containers where living yeast is stirred into the mix in order to convert the sugar in the wort into alcohol. After about 48 hours the 'wash' is transferred to copper pot stills and heated till the alcohol vaporizes and is then condensed by a cooling plant into distilled alcohol which is passed through a second still. Once distilled, the liquid is poured into oak casks and left to age for a minimum of three years, though a good malt will stay casked for at least eight years.

Drinks

Beer is the staple alcoholic drink in Scotland. The most popular type of beer is lager, but connoisseurs should sample one of the many excellent types of **heavy**, which is a thick, dark ale served at room temperature with a full, creamy head. Types of heavy are graded by the shilling, which indicates its strength; the higher the number the stronger the beer. The usual range is 60 to 80 shillings (written 80/-). The best ales are hand-pumped from the cask under pressure. Beer is served in pints, or half pints, and you'll pay between £1.50 and £2.50 for a pint, depending on the brew and location of the pub.

The market is dominated by the large brewers – *Youngers*, *McEwan's*, *Scottish & Newcastle* and *Tennet's*. They produce smooth, strong beers, but the country's best seller is, strangely enough, *Tartan Special*, which is weak and tasteless by comparison. For the best of Scottish beers, however, you should try one of the small **local breweries**. Edinburgh's *Caledonian* produces a wide range of excellent cask ales. Others worth trying are *Belhaven*, brewed in Dunbar near Edinburgh, *Maclays*, brewed in Alloa, and the very wonderful *Greenmantle*, brewed in the Borders.

No visit to Scotland would be complete without availing oneself of a 'wee dram'. There **Whisky** is no greater pleasure on an inclement Highland evening than enjoying a malt whisky in front of a roaring log fire whilst watching the rain outside pelt down relentlessly. The roots of Scotland's national drink (*uisge beatha*, or 'water of life' in Gaelic) go back to the late 15th century, but it wasn't until the invention of a patent still in the early 19th century that distilling began to develop from small family-run operations to the large manufacturing business it has become today. Now more than 700 million bottles a year are exported, mainly to the United States, France, Japan and Spain.

There are two types of whisky: **single malt**, made only from malted barley; and **grain**, which is made from malted barley together with unmalted barley, maize or other cereals, and is faster and cheaper to produce. Most of the popular brands are blends of both types of whisky – usually 60-70% grain to 30-40% malt. These **blended** whiskies account for over 90% of all sales worldwide, and most of the production of single malts is used to add flavour to a blended whisky. Amongst the best-known brands of blended whisky are *Johnnie Walker*, *Bells*, *Teachers* and *Famous Grouse*. There's not much between them in terms of flavour and they are usually drunk with a mixer, such as water or soda.

Single malts are a different matter altogether. Each is distinctive and should be drunk neat to appreciate fully its subtle flavours, though some belive that the addition of water helps free the flavours. Single malts vary enormously. Their distinctive flavours and aromas are derived from the peat used for drying, the water used for mashing, the type of oak cask used and the location of the distillery. Single malts fall into four groups: Highland, Lowland, Campbeltown and Islay. There are over 40 distilleries to choose from, most offering guided tours. The majority are located around Speyside, in the northeast. The region's many distilleries include that perennial favourite, *Glenfiddich*, which is sold in 185 countries. A recommended alternative is the produce of the beautiful and peaceful Isle of Islay, whose malts are lovingly described in terms of their peaty quality. Scots tend to favour the 10 year-old *Glenmorangie*, while the most popular in the USA is *The Macallan*.

Shopping

See also individual towns' Essentials sections for tips on local bargains

The shelves of gift shops in every tourist attraction from John O' Groats to Jedburgh are stuffed full of dreadful tartan tat such as 'See-you-Jimmy' wigs and bonnets, Loch Ness monster replicas and those scary-looking tartan dolls with flickering eyelashes. All very harmless (except for the dolls which give you nightmares), but not doing much for Scotland's image. But amongst all this tourist kitsch are many excellent high-quality goods on offer.

Scottish **textiles**, especially the tartan variety, are popular and worth buying. Everything from a travelling rug to your own kilt outfit. Shops up and down the country, and especially in Edinburgh and Inverness, can tell which clan your family belongs to and make you a kilt in that particular tartan. For the full outfit, including kilt, sporran, jacket, shoes and *skeann dhu* dagger, expect to pay in the region of £600, or more if you want more elaborate accessories. There are mill shops making tweeds and cloths in many parts of Scotland. Most are in the Borders, though it is not necessarily cheaper to buy at source. **Harris Tweed** is also a good buy and you can watch your cloth being woven on the Hebridean islands of Harris and Lewis.

Knitwear is also good value and sold throughout Scotland, though the cashmere industry in the Borders is suffering from high trade tariffs. Shetland is a good place to find high-quality wool products. Note that Aran jumpers are not from the island of Arran, but from Aran (with one 'r') in Ireland. **Jewellery** is another popular souvenir and there are many excellent craft shops throughout the Highlands and Islands making beautiful jewellery with Celtic designs. **Glassware** is also popular, particularly Edinburgh crystal and Caithness glass, as well as **pottery**.

Food is another good souvenir and not just the ubiquitous shortbread sold in tartan tins. If you haven't far to travel home, **smoked salmon**, or any other smoked product, is good value. One of the best places for food products is the island of **Arran**, where you can buy their delicious local mustards and preserves, smoked fish and game, and cheeses. And, of course, there's **whisky**. Most distilleries will refund the cost of their guided tour in the form of a discount voucher on a bottle of their brand whisky.

Shopping hours

Shop hours in Scotland are generally Monday to Saturday from 0900-1730 or 1800. In larger towns and cities, many shops also open on Sundays and late at night, usually on a Thursday and Friday. Large supermarkets and retail complexes found outside large towns are open till 2000 or later Monday-Saturday and till 1600 on Sunday. In the Highlands and Islands, few shops are open on Sunday, most notably in the Outer Hebrides where nothing is open on a Sunday. Also note that in many rural areas there is an early-closing day when shops close at 1300. This varies from region to region, but the most common day is Wednesday.

Entertainment and nightlife

Football (soccer) is Scotland's most popular spectator sport. The *Scottish Football League*, established in 1874, is the main competition, with three divisions of 10 teams and one of 12. Scottish football is dominated, and always has been, by the two main Glasgow teams, *Rangers* and *Celtic*, known collectively as the 'Old Firm', who regularly attract crowds of over 50,000. For a brief period in the 1980s this stranglehold was broken by *Aberdeen* and *Dundee United*, but events since have proved this an aberration rather than a trend. Money is the main reason for this and the Old Firm have seemingly endless pots of the stuff, which is why they have been able to fill their team with expensive foreign imports and win most of the domestic competitions. Though neither side has fared too well in European competition in recent years, Celtic were the first British side to win the European Cup, in 1967.

Spectator sports

Scotland's top 12 teams make up the Premier League, which has become a battle between the big two for the championship. Teams in the lower divisions mostly exist on a shoestring budget, though the other major competition, the Scottish FA Cup, still throws up occasional upsets, such as Celtic's defeat at the hands of lowly *Inverness Caledonian Thistle* in 1999. The domestic football **season** runs from early August to mid-May. Most matches are played on Saturdays at 1500, and there are often games through the week, on Tuesday and Wednesday evenings at 1930. There is usually a match on a Sunday afternoon, which is broadcast live on satellite TV. **Tickets** range from £10 up to £20 for big games.

The **national** team play at the recently renovated Hampden Park in Glasgow. Their passionate supporters, known as the 'Tartan Army', have gained something of an international reputation for their fun-loving attitude and self-deprecating humour in the face of defeat. This has stood them in good stead over the years for, despite qualifying for most World Cup Finals since 1974, Scotland have never managed to reach the second round, failing against such footballing giants as Iran and Costa Rica along the way.

Rugby Union Rugby is one of the major sports of the country but lags a long, long way behind football in terms of popularity. The national team plays at Murrayfield in Edinburgh, and during match weekends there's always a great atmosphere in the city. Every year, in February and March, Scotland takes part in the **Six Nations Championship**, along with the other home teams, plus France and Italy. The most important game, though, is the clash with the 'Auld enemy', England. Tickets for games are hard to come by, but you can contact the *Scottish Rugby Union* (*SRU*), T0131-3465000, for details of upcoming home fixtures and where to find tickets.

The club rugby scene is in a state of disarray, with many of the top players having moved to England or France. One area of the country where rugby is still strong is the Borders. The Borders town of Melrose is home of **seven-a-side rugby**, a variation of the 15-a-side game, and the **Melrose Sevens**, is the biggest tournament of the year in Scotland. The club rugby season runs from September to May.

Shinty (or *camanachd* in Gaelic) is an amateur sport similar to Ireland's hurling. It's a physical game played at a fast and furious pace, and is a bit like hockey, but with more blood. The game is played mostly in the Highlands, and the highlight of the season is the **Camanachd Cup Final**, which attracts a large crowd and is televised on STV.

Scotland has its own national ballet, opera and orchestra as well as many fine theatres up and down the country. Glasgow and Edinburgh have lively **club scenes**, but

Cultural events

you'll also find nightclubs outside the major cities. For a comprehensive guide to what's on in Glasgow and Edinburgh, look out for the fortnightly listings magazine *The List*. **Celtic culture** is alive and well in many parts, particularly in the Highlands and Islands, and you'll be able to hear traditional folk music in many pubs. At weekends you may also happen across a **ceilidh** in the local village hall or hotel. These traditional dances can be raucous affairs but great fun, even if you don't have a clue what you're doing. Ask for details at the local tourist office.

Pubs & bars As in the rest of Britain, **pubs** are the main focus of social life and entertainment for most Scots. These vary greatly, from traditional old inns full of character (and often full of characters) to chic and trendy bars where you can order *foccacia* bread with sundried tomatoes washed down with your bottle of continental lager whilst you dance to DJs. Most city pubs are owned by the large breweries and only serve their own particular beers. There is also a growing number of chain pubs appearing on the high streets of many towns. In remote parts of the Highlands and Islands the local hotel bar is often the only watering hole for miles around, and many pubs close for a couple of hours between 1400 and 1600, which can be very annoying on a wet afternoon. Pubs generally are open from 1100 till 2300 Monday-Saturday and Sunday from 1100-1200 till 2230. In towns and cities many pubs are open till 2400 or 0100 on Friday and Saturday nights, or even later in Edinburgh, which has more relaxed licensing laws.

Holidays and festivals

Bank holidays **New Year's Day** and **2 January**, **Good Friday** and **Easter Monday**, **May Day** (the first
Contact the relevant Monday in May), Victoria Day (the last Monday in May), 25 and 26 December (**Christ-**
Area Tourist Board for **mas Day, Boxing Day**). There are also local public holidays in spring and autumn.
more details Dates vary from place to place. Banks are closed during these holidays, and sights and shops may be affexcted to varying degrees.

Events There is a huge range of organized events held throughout Scotland every year,
Details of local ranging in size and spectacle from the Edinburgh Festival, the largest arts festival in
festivals are given in the world, to more obscure traditional events featuring ancient customs dating back
the Essentials sections many centuries. The Scottish Tourist Board (STB) publishes a comprehensive list,
of individual towns; *Events in Scotland*, twice a year. It's free and is available from the main tourist offices.
also visit The most popular tourist events are the **Highland Games** (or Gatherings), a series of
www.whatsonwhen competitions involving lots of kilts, bagpipes and caber-tossing, which are held across
.com the Highlands and Islands, the northeast and Argyll from **June to September**. The best known is the **Braemar Gathering** (see page 419), which is attended by various members of the Royal Family. Those at Oban and Dunoon are large events, but smaller gatherings are often more enjoyable and 'authentic'. **Folk festivals** are also great expressions of Celtic culture, and a list of the best and most popular is given on page 659.

Sport and special interest travel

Scotland is a great country for outdoor activities and many visitors come specifically to enjoy the magnificent scenery as they walk in the hills, cycle through forests, ski down mountains or head off in search of rare wildlife. The coastline, lochs and rivers are ideal for fishing and offer plenty of opportunities for a whole range of watersports, including windsurfing, sailing and scuba diving, and there are lots of beautiful beaches, especially on the northwest coast and the islands.

Calendar of events

New Year's Day *A variety of ancient local celebrations take place, including the Kirkwall Ba' Game, a mixture of football and mud wrestling.*

Up-Helly-Aa *Re-enactment of the ancient Viking fire festival held on Shetland on the last Tuesday in January (see page 624).*

Celtic Connections *Huge celebration of Celtic music from around the world, held in various venues throughout Glasgow over two weeks in January.*

Burns Night *Burns suppers held on 25th January all over the country to celebrate the poet's birthday. Lots of haggis, whisky and poetry recitals.*

Scottish Grand National *Held at Ayr racecourse in April.*

Rugby Sevens *Seven-a-side rugby tournament held throughout the Borders.*

Scottish FA Cup Final *Held at Hampden Park in Glasgow in May.*

The Highland Festival *Held over two weeks from late May till early June at venues throughout the Highland region. For details, T01463-719000, www.highlandfestival.org.uk*

Riding of the Marches *Horse riding, parades, brass bands etc commemorating the wars between the Scots and the English. Held in various towns in the Borders from June to August (see page 145).*

Royal Highland Show *Scotland's largest agricultural show, held at Ingliston, near Edinburgh, in June.*

International Jazz Festival *Held in Glasgow in July.*

T in the Park *Scotland's largest outdoor music festival featuring many of the best pop and rock bands. Held at Balado Airfield at Kinross in July.*

Edinburgh International and Fringe Festival *The greatest arts extravaganza on the planet, held over three weeks in August. At the same time is the*

Edinburgh Military Tattoo, *a massed pipe bands and military pageantry on the esplanade of Edinburgh Castle.*

World Pipe Band Championships *Held in Glasgow in August.*

Spirit of Speyside Whisky Festival *Held on Speyside in May.*

Braemar Highland Gathering *Attended by the Royal Family in September.*

National Mod *Competitive Gaelic music festival held at various locations in October (check with the Tourist Board).*

Tour of Mull Rally *The highlight of the Scottish rally season, run over the island's public roads (no wonder they're in such appalling condition) in October.*

Aberdeen Alternative Festival *The northeast's major arts and culture fest, held in October.*

Hogmanay *Old year's night, and the most important national celebration. Possible derivations of the word include Holag Monath, Anglo Saxon for 'holy month', and Hoog min dag, which is Dutch for 'great love day'. Edinburgh's huge street party is the largest such celebration in the northern hemisphere.*

Essentials

Hillwalking

Scotland is a walker's paradise. Throughout the country there are numerous marked trails, ranging from short walks to long-distance treks from one side of the country to the other. Whatever your taste or level of fitness and experience, you'll find plenty of opportunities to get off the beaten track and explore the countryside.

Walking routes are denoted in the text by this symbol in the margin

The best time for hiking in the mountains is usually from May to September, though in the more low-lying parts, April to October should be safe. Winter walking in the Highlands requires technical equipment such as ice axes and crampons and a lot of experience. July and August are the busiest times, though only the most popular routes, such as Ben Nevis, get really crowded. Another problem during these months

Essentials

Useful organizations

Forestry Commission, 231 Corstorphine Rd, Edinburgh EH12 7AT, T0131-3340303.
John Muir Trust, *41 Commercial St, Edinburgh EH6 6JD, T0131-5540114*
Scottish Natural Heritage, *12 Hope Terr,*

Edinburgh EH9 2AS, T0131-4474784, www.snh.org.uk
Woodland Trust, *Glenruthven Mill, Abbey Rd, Auchterarder, Perthshire PH3 1DP, T01764-662554*

are midges (see page 65). May to mid-June is probably the most pleasant time overall, as the weather can often be fine and the midges have yet to appear. September is also a good time, though it can be a lot colder.

Access Scotland has a long tradition of generally free responsible access to mountain and moorland. This free access, of course, relies on walkers behaving responsibly and recognizing that the countryside is a place of work as well as recreation. Most land in Scotland is privately owned and at certain times of the year, such as the main shooting seasons, walkers may be asked to respect certain restrictions on access. The main **deer stalking** season runs from mid-August to 20 October and the **grouse shooting** season is between 12 August (referred to as the 'Glorious Twelfth') and 10 December. For more information on this, see *Heading for the Scottish Hills* which is published by the Mountaineering Council of Scotland (see below) and the Scottish Landowners Federation and gives estate maps and telephone numbers to call for local advice. There may also be restricted access during the lambing season (March-May).

It is not an offence to walk over someone's land in Scotland but, especially during the stalking and shooting seasons, you may be asked to take a different route, though this rarely happens. At the time of writing there are two new national parks proposed; one is the Cairngorms National Park due to open in early 2003, and the other is Loch Lomond and Trossachs National Park, which is due to open in April 2002. Furthermore, there is free access at all times of the year to areas owned by the **National Trust for Scotland** (address on page 39). These areas include Torridon and Glencoe. There is also free access to most land owned by the **Forestry Commission**, and there is good public access to land owned by the **John Muir Trust**, **Scottish Natural Heritage**, the **Royal Society for the Protection of Birds** (address on page 64) and the **Woodland Trust**, though these areas are not marked on *Ordnance Survey* (OS) maps. Also not shown on OS maps are **Rights of Way**, which are signposted by the Scottish Rights of Way Society's green metal signs. The society publishes maps of rights of way, many of which follow ancient 'drove roads' through the hills.

Information & advice The **Scottish Tourist Board** is a useful source of information for walkers (address on page 23). Local tourist offices have details of interesting local walks. The organizations listed opposite are also useful sources of information.

Many walk descriptions and maps are given in this guidebook, but these should ideally be used in conjunction with a good map, such as the *Ordnance Survey* (OS) *Landranger* series. The relevant map numbers have been listed, where possible, with the route description. OS maps can be found at Tourist Information Centres and also at **outdoor shops**, which are usually staffed by experienced climbers and walkers who can give good advice about the right equipment. The best-equipped shops are *Tiso*, www.tiso.co.uk, who have branches in the main towns and cities; and *Nevisport* in Fort William. For a list of recommended **walking guidebooks and maps**, see page 65.

Munros, Corbetts and Grahams

There are 284 mountains over 3,000ft (914m) in Scotland, known as 'Munros', after Sir Hugh Munro, first president of the Scottish Mountaineering Club (SMC), who published the first comprehensive list of these mountains in 1891. In the 1920s a further list was published, of the 221 summits between 2,500 and 3,000ft, by J

Rooke Corbett, and these became known as 'Corbetts'. A third list, of summits between 2,000 and 2,500ft was compiled by Fiona Graham and published in 1992. This list was subsequently revised and corrected and now all peaks of between 2,000 and 2,500ft are called 'Grahams'.

Long distance walks

There is a network of long walking trails across Scotland which are carefully prepared to provide ideal walking conditions together with sufficient places for accommodation and supplies en route. These walks can be attempted in full, or sampled in part by less experienced walkers. Area tourist boards and local tourist offices can provide information and advice for their own particular sections. Two of the three main trails, the **Southern Upland Way** (see page 138) and the **Speyside Way** (see page 428) are covered in the relevant sections of this guide.

The best-known, and busiest, long distance trail is the **West Highland Way**, which runs for 95 miles from Milngavie (pronounced 'mull-guy'), just north of Glasgow, to Fort William. The route progresses steadily from the Lowlands, along the eastern shore of **Loch Lomond** and the traverse of the western edge of **Rannoch Moor**, to enter **Glencoe** at White Corries. It continues over the Devil's Staircase, past Kinlochleven, and through **Glen Nevis** to Fort William. Many walkers finish off with an ascent of **Ben Nevis** (4,406ft), the highest mountain in Britain (see page 472). **Further information**, including a trail leaflet with accommodation and facilities guide, is available from *West Highland Way Ranger Service*, Balloch Castle, Balloch, G53 8LX, T01389-758216.

There are several other long distance trails, including **St Cuthbert's Way** (see page 138) and the **Pilgrim's Way** in southern Scotland. Two trails which are not yet fully completed are the **Clyde Walkway**, which will eventually run from the heart of Glasgow to New Lanark, and the **Fife Coastal Path**, which will run for 60 miles along the Fife coastline, from North Queensferry, at the foot of the Forth Bridge, to the Tay Bridge at Dundee. The section from North Queensferry to Pittenweem (39 miles) is complete. Leaflets covering both trails are available from the Greater Glasgow and Clyde Valley and Fife area tourist boards (addresses on page 23).

Short walks

Many of the most popular short walks, including the ascent of Ben Nevis, are described in this guidebook. These range from gentle strolls through forest glades to strenuous hikes, steep hills and mountains, and also include some beautiful coastal trails. One of the most popular pastimes in Scotland is Munro-bagging (see page 59), which involves climbing as many peaks over 3,000ft as possible. The best area for this is the **Highlands**, which provide many challenging peaks, and it's possible to climb several in a day. Many of these hills are straightforward climbs, but many also require a high level of fitness and experience, and all require proper **clothing** (see next page). You should never attempt walks beyond your abilities.

Other good areas for walking include the **Isles of Arran**, **Mull**, **Islay** and **Skye**, **Perthshire**, **Stirling** and the **Trossachs** and **Galloway**. The mighty **Cairngorms** are better known as a winter ski area, but provide excellent year-round hillwalking and climbing. This is extremely wild terrain, however, and suitable only for experienced walkers. There are many opportunities for less experienced walkers in

Essentials

Essentials

Cycling organizations

Cyclists' Touring Club (CTC), Cotterell House, 69 Meadrow, Godalming, Surrey, GU7 3HS, T01483-417217, www.ctc.org.uk. The largest cycling organization in the UK, providing a wide range of services and information on transport, cycle hire and routes, from day rides to longer tours.
Forestry Enterprise, 21 Church St, Inverness, IV1 1EL, T01463-232811. Provides information on Scotland's extensive network of forest trails.

The Scottish Cyclists' Union (SCU), The Velodrome, Meadowbank Stadium, London Rd, Edinburgh, EH7 6AY, T0131-6520187, www.btinternet.com/~scottish.cycling Produces an annual handbook and calendar of events for road racing, time trialling and mountain biking.
SUSTRANS, 53 Cochrane St, Glasgow, G1 1HL, T0141-5720234, www.sustrans.co.uk Provides information on new cycle trails.

Rothiemurchus Estate and Glenmore Forest Park around **Aviemore**. Other areas which are best left to serious climbers are **Torridon**, **Kintail** and **Glencoe**, though the latter also offers a few more straightforward walks through spectacular scenery (see page 477).

Climbing

The Cairngorms and Cuillins on Skye offer the most challenging climbing in Scotland, as do Glencoe and Torridon. For a list of climbing guidebooks, see page 65. For more detailed information, contact the **Mountaineering Council of Scotland**, 4a St Catherine's Road, Perth, T01738-638227. A recommended rock climbing and mountaineering instructor is Gary Latter, Kinalty Cottage, By Kirriemuir, Angus, DD8 5LY, T01575-530308.

Mountain safety

A weather phone-line service is available from the following numbers: East Highlands T0891-333197; West Highlands T0891-333198

Visitors to Scotland should be aware of the need for caution and safety preparations when walking or climbing in the mountains. The nature of Scottish weather is such that a fine sunny day can turn into driving rain or snow in a matter of minutes. Remember that a blizzard can be raging on the summit when the car park at the foot of the mountain is bathed in sunshine. It is essential to get an up-to-date weather forecast before setting off on any walk or climb.

Whatever the time of year, or conditions when you set off, you should always carry or wear essential items of clothing. A basic list for summer conditions would be: **boots** with a good tread and ankle support and a thick pair of socks; **waterproof jacket and trousers**, even on a sunny day; **hat and gloves** are important if the weather turns bad; **warm trousers** should be worn or carried, tracksuit bottoms are okay if you also have waterproof trousers; **spare woolly jumper or fleece jacket** will provide an extra layer; **map and compass** are essential to carry and to know how to use. Other essentials are **food and drink**, a simple **first aid kit**, a **whistle** and a **torch**. A small 25-30 litre rucksack should be adequate for carrying the above items. Also remember to leave details of your route and expected time of return with someone, and remember to inform them on your return.

In the winter extra warm clothing is needed, as well as an **ice axe** and **crampons** (and the ability to use them). The skills required for moving over ice or snow should be practised with an experienced and qualified mountain guide/instructor.

Cycling and mountain biking

The bicycle was invented in Scotland, near Dumfries, so it seems appropriate that travelling by bike is one of the best ways to explore the country. Most towns and cities, however, are not particularly cycle-friendly. Very few have proper cycle routes, and there's the added problem of security. It's best to stick to rural backroads, especially unclassified roads and country lanes, which are not numbered but are signposted and marked on OS maps. There are also forest trails and dedicated routes along canal towpaths and disused railway tracks. The main problem in rural areas, though, is the availability of spare parts.

The **south of Scotland** is particularly good for cycle touring due to the quiet roads, gentle gradients and large number of B&Bs and pubs. The wild and remote **Highlands** are popular with cyclists, but this is also walking country, and cyclists should stick to tracks where a right to cycle exists and be considerate towards walkers. The *Forestry Commission* has 1150 miles of excellent off-road routes up and down the country. These are detailed in a series of *Cycling in the Forest* leaflets, which are available from Forestry Enterprise offices (see above) and from most tourist offices. These are best used by **mountain bikes** with multi gears, though easier routes can be attempted on hybrid or standard bikes.

You can cut down on the amount of pedalling you have to do by **transporting your bike** by train. Bikes can be taken free on most local rail services on a first come-first served basis (call *ScotRail* bookings, T08457-550033). On long-distance routes you'll have to make a reservation and pay a small charge (£3.50). Space is limited on trains so it's a good idea to book as far in advance as possible. **Bus and coach** companies will not carry bikes, unless they are dismantled and boxed. **Ferries** transport bikes for a small fee and **airlines** will often accept them as part of your baggage allowance. Check with the ferry company or airline about any restrictions.

Bike rental is available at cycle shops in most large towns, cities and tourist centres. Expect to pay from around £6 to £15 per day, or from £50 a week, plus a refundable deposit. There's also the option of a **cycling holiday package**, which includes transport of your luggage, prebooked accommodation, route instructions and food and backup support. A list of specialists is given above.

The STB publishes a free booklet, *Cycling in Scotland*, which is useful and suggests routes in various parts of the country, as well as accommodation and repair shops. Many area tourist boards also provide cycling guides for their own areas. A list of useful **cycle guides and books** is given on page 65.

Skiing

Conditions in Scotland are not as good or reliable as anywhere in the Alps, but on a clear, sunny day, and with good snow, you can enjoy some decent skiing. However, at weekends, in conditions like these, expect the slopes to be very busy. Scotland offers both **alpine** (downhill) and **nordic** (cross-country) skiing, as well as the increasingly popular **snowboarding**. The high season is from January to April, but it is possible to ski from as early as November to as late as May. Ski packages are available, but it's easy to arrange everything yourself and there's plentiful accommodation and facilities in and around the ski centres.

There are **five ski centres** in Scotland. The largest are **Glenshee**, which has the most extensive network of lifts and selection of runs, as well as snow machines, and **Cairngorm**, which has almost 30 runs spread over an extensive area. **Glencoe** is the oldest of the ski resorts, and the **Nevis Range**, at Aonach Mor near Fort William, has the highest ski runs and only gondola in Scotland, as well as a dry slope. **The Lecht** is the most remote centre, and is good for beginners and families and for nordic skiing. Access

Essentials

to all five centres is easiest by car. Each resort has a ski patrol and facilities for snowboarding.

Costs Ski equipment and clothing can be hired at all resorts, but lessons should be booked in advance. Prices vary from centre to centre, but on average expect to pay around £13 per day for hire of skis, sticks and boots, and around £12 per day for ski clothes. Snowboard hire is around £16-17 per day for board and boots. Lift passes cost around £18-20 per day, or £68-80 for five days. Ski lessons are around £18 for four hours. Packages including ski hire, tuition and lift pass cost from around £125 to £155 for five days. These prices are for adults; prices for juniors are less.

Information

Check out www.born2ski for everything from snow reports to apres ski ratings

Details for each of the five resorts, including phone numbers, are given in the appropriate place in the main text. For further general information contact the *Scottish Tourist Board* for its *Ski Scotland* brochure and accommodation list, or visit their website, www.ski.scotland.net, which is updated daily. Or you can contact the *Scottish National Ski Council*, T0131-3177280, www.snsc.demon.co.uk They produce a useful *Snowsport Scotland Handbook*.

The **Ski hotline** weather-report service gives the latest snow and weather conditions plus a five-day forecast. Phone: T0891-654 followed by: 655 for Cairngorm; 656 for Glenshee; 657 for The Lecht; 658 for Glencoe; 660 for Nevis Range; and 659 for cross country skiing.

Fishing

Scotland's rivers, streams, lochs and estuaries are among the cleanest waters in Europe and are filled with salmon, trout (sea, brown and rainbow) and pike. Not surprisingly, then, fishing (coarse, game and sea) is hugely popular in Scotland.

There is no close season for **coarse fishing** or **sea angling**. For **wild brown trout** the close season is early October to mid-March. The close season for **salmon** and **sea trout** varies from area to area and between net and rod fishing. It is generally from late August to early February for net fishing, and from early November to early February for rod fishing.

No licence is required to fish in Scotland, but most of the land and rivers are privately owned so you must obtain a **permit** from the owners or their agents. These are often readily available at the local fishing tackle shop and usually cost from around £15, though some rivers, such as the Tweed, can be far more expensive.

The STB's booklet *Fish Scotland* is a good introduction and a source of all kinds of information. It is available free from tourist offices, or by post (see page 23). Also contact the *Scottish Federation of Sea Anglers*, Brian Burn, Flat 2, 16 Bellevue Road, Ayr, KA7 2SA, T01292-264735; or *Scottish National Anglers Association*, David Wilkie, Administration Office, Caledonia House, South Gyle, Edinburgh, EH12 9DQ, T0131- 3398808.

Golf

To arrange golfing holidays visit scotland-golf-tours .co.uk

Scotland has over 400 golf courses, with more being built all the time, and, therefore has more courses per head of population than any other country in the world. Any decent sized town in Scotland will have a golf course nearby and most, if not all, are available for play. There are many public courses, which tend to be both cheap and extremely busy, often have excellent layouts. The majority of private clubs allow visitors, although many have restrictions as to what days these visitors can play. Weekends are usually reserved for club competitions for the members so it is best to try to play on a weekday. All private clubs have a dress code and it is inadvisable to turn up for a round in a collarless shirt and jeans. These minor caveats aside, you are more than likely to receive a warm and courteous welcome.

One of the unique attractions of golf in Scotland is the accessibility of its famous venues. The average football fan will never get the chance to play at Wembley Stadium, likewise the club tennis player is unlikely to play a few sets on the Centre Court at Wimbledon, but any golfer can, for example, play at Carnoustie or St Andrews. This represents a unique opportunity to follow in the footsteps of golf's legendary players and compare your own game, however unfavourably, with theirs. **Green fees** for one of the top championship courses will cost from around £40 upwards. Many clubs offer a daily or weekly ticket. A **Golf Pass Scotland** costs between £46 and £70 for five days (Monday-Friday), depending on the area. *Golf in Scotland* is a free brochure listing 400 courses and clubs with accommodation details. For a copy contact the *Scottish Tourist Board*. The *British Tourist Authority* (BTA) has a very useful *Golfing Holidays* booklet which provides details of golfing holidays and major golf tournaments in Britain. (BTA and STB address on page 23). For a list of recommended golf books, see page 65.

Wildlife watching

Almost anywhere around the northern coasts of Scotland there is a chance to see dolphins and occasionally porpoises, seals and whales. The most popular place to see **dolphins** is in the Moray Firth area which has a resident population of about 150, most frequently seen in the summer months. Other good places to catch glimpses of the creatures are at the entrance to the Caledonian Canal at Inverness, Nairn beach, Arderseir, Fort George, Fortrose and Cromarty. **Seals** can be seen in abundance. They can often be observed lolling about on sandbanks when the tide is out, and there are plenty of seal-spotting boat trips on offer from spring to autumn. **Otters** are more elusive. They tend to live on undisturbed remote stretches of the seashore or quiet areas of a river. If you are determined to spot the creatures, for further information contact *Skye Environmental Centre* (home to the *International Otter Survival Fund*), T01471-822487. **Whales**, Minke and Orcas, inhabit the Atlantic, Pentland Firth and the Moray Firth. Contact the **Highlands of Scotland Tourist Board**, T0870-5143070, www.highlandfreedom .com, for details of boat trips.

Birdwatching Scotland is great for birdwatching. Over 450 species have been recorded, including vast colonies of seabirds, birds of prey and many rare species. Among the best places in Scotland to see birds are **Handa Island** off the coast of Sutherland, and the **Treshnish Islands**, off Mull, where you'll see colonies of shags, razorbills, guillemots and puffins. Details of how to get there are given in the relevant sections. Other excellent places for birdwatching include **Caerlaverock** near Dumfries, the **Isle of May** off the coast of Fife, the **Bass Rock** off North Berwick, **Fowlsheugh** near Stonehaven, and **Loch Garten** by Boat of Garten, where you can see ospreys. Many of the Hebridean islands, such as **Islay** and **Mull**, are home to a rich variety of seabirds and you can also see golden eagles.

Orkney and **Shetland** are famous for their rich variety of birdlife and are home to large colonies of seabirds and migratory birds. There are puffins, kittiwakes, fulmars, shags, razorbills, guillemots and even auks.

Other outdoor activities

Diving There are thousands of dive sites around Scotland's shores, with a rich variety of marine life and plenty of wrecks to explore. The **West Coast** offers the best diving, as the water is warmed by the effects of the Gulf Stream and is not cold, even without a dry suit. Among the best sites are the **west coast of Harris**, the **Summer Isles** and the remote island of **St Kilda**. There are lots of wrecks in the **Sound of Mull**, and the chance to find a Spanish Galleon off **Tobermory**. **Scapa Flow** in Orkney is world-renowned as the

Useful organizations

*Further information can be obtained from the **Royal Society for the Protection of Birds**, 17 Regent Terr, Edinburgh EH7 5BT, T0131-5573136; the **Scottish Ornithologists Club**, 21 Regent Terr,*

*Edinburgh EH7 5BT, T0131-5566042; and the **Scottish Wildlife Trust**, Cramond House, Cramond Glebe Road, Edinburgh EH4 6NS, T0131-3127765, which owns and runs over 100 nature reserves.*

burial site of the German World War I fleet. On the **East Coast**, there is a great marine reserve off **St Abb's Head**, near Eyemouth, with some spectacular rock formations.

Contact **Scottish Sub Aqua Club**, 40 Bogmoor Place, Glasgow, G51 47Q, T0141-4251021; or **British Sub Aqua Club** (Scottish Federation), 67 Moredun Park, Gilmerton, Edinburgh EH17, T0131-6644381. A recommended dive operator is *Dive Scotland*, T0131-4412001, in Edinburgh.

Surfing Scotland has some of the best surfing beaches in Europe. But this is no Hawaii, with its sunbleached hair and bronzed bodies: surfing in Scotland is strictly for the hardy, with water temperatures rarely above 15°C and often as low as 7°C. A good wet suit is therefore essential. The waves, though, make up for the freezing waters and compare with those in Hawaii and Australia. The main season is September to December.

The best beaches on the **West Coast** are to be found at the northern tip of the **Isle of Lewis** and at **Machrihanish**, down near the Mull of Kintyre. On the **North Coast** the top spot is **Thurso**, especially at Dunnet Head to the east of town. Another recommended place is **Strathy Bay**, near Bettyhill, halfway between Thurso and Tongue. On the **East Coast** the best beaches are **Pease Bay**, south of Dunbar, near Cockburnspath on the A1, and **Nigg Bay**, just south of Aberdeen, between Montrose and Arbroath.

There is a bi-monthly surf magazine, *Surf*, which is a good source of information. Also try the surf shops, which sell equipment and provide information on the best breaks. **Glasgow**: *Clan*, 45 Hyndland Street, Partick, T0141-3396523; *Boardwise*, 1146 Argyle Street, T0141-3345559. **Edinburgh**: *Momentum*, 22 Bruntsfield Place, T0131-2296665. **Aberdeen**: *Granite Reef*, 45 Justice Street, T01224-621193.

Pony trekking & horse riding Pony Trekking is a long-established activity in Scotland and miles of beautiful coastline, lochsides, and moorland are accessible on horseback. There are numerous equestrian centres around the country catering to all levels of riders. The Scottish Tourist Board produces a *Trekking & Riding* brochure listing riding centres around the country, all of them approved by the *Trekking and Riding Society of Scotland* (*TRSS*) or the *British Horse Society* (*BHS*). Centres offer **pony trekking** (leisurely strolls at walking pace for novices), **hacks** (short rides at a fast pace for experienced riders) and **trail riding** (long distance rides at no more than a canter). The **Buccleuch Country Ride** is a four-day route through the Borders, using private tracks, open country and quiet bridleways. For more information, contact the *Scottish Borders Tourist Board*, T01835-863435. For general information contact the *TRSS*, Horse Trials Office, Blair Atholl, Perthshire, T01796-481543, or the *BHS*, British Equestrian Centre, Stoneleigh Park, Kenilworth, Warwicks CV8 2LR, T01203-414288.

Paragliding If you fancy getting high during your visit, you can try your hand at the exciting sport of paragliding. Courses and flights are offered by *Parapente Ecosse* in

The midge

The major problem facing visitors to the Highlands and Islands of Scotland during the summer months is Culicoides Impunctatus – or the midge, as it's more commonly known. These tiny flying creatures are savage and merciless in the extreme and hunt in huge packs. No sooner have you left your B&B for a pleasant evening stroll, than a cloud of these bloodthirsty little devils will attack from nowhere, getting into your eyes, ears, nose and mouth – and a few places you forgot you even had. The only way to avoid them is to take refuge indoors, or to hide in the nearest loch.

Midges are at their worst in the evening and in damp, shaded or overcast conditions, and between late May and September, but they don't like direct sunlight, heavy rain, smoke and wind. Make sure you're well covered up and wear light-coloured clothing (they're attracted to dark colours). Most effective is a midge net, if you don't mind everyone pointing and laughing at you. Insect repellents have some effect, particularly those with DEET, but herbal remedies such as bog myrtle, lavender, citronalla or eucalyptus are considered equally effective. Once you've been attacked the best treatments are antihistamine creams or dock leaves – and don't scratch the bites!

Essentials

Edinburgh, T0700-0782589, paraglide_scotland@compuserve.com; and *Flying Fever*, No 2 Coastguard House, Kildonan, Isle of Arran, T01770-820292, www.arran.uk.com/kildonan/flyingfever

Scotland's rivers, lochs and deeply indented coastline offer great opportunities for canoeing or kayaking. For information, contact the **Scottish Canoe Association**, Caledonia House, South Gyle, Edinburgh EH12 9DQ, T0131-3177314, www.scot-canoe. org. They organize tours, including introductory ones for beginners. Also try *Splash Rafting* of Aberfeldy, splashraft@compuserve.com

Canoeing

Curling is nothing to do with hairdressing, but is in fact a winter game which involves sliding smooth circular granite stones across the ice as close to the centre of a target as possible, while your team-mates use brooms to sweep away the loose white flakes (a bit like hairdressing, in fact). It is still occasionally played on frozen ponds but more commonly played in indoor ice rinks.

Curling

Health

No vaccinations are required for entry into Britain. Citizens of **EU** countries are entitled to free medical treatment at National Health Service hospitals on production of an E111 form. Also, Australia, New Zealand and several other non-EU European countries have reciprocal health-care arrangements with Britain.

Medical emergency: dial 999 or 112 (both free) for an ambulance

Citizens of other countries will have to pay for all medical services, except accident and emergency care given at Accident and Emergency (A&E) Units at most (but not all) National Health hospitals. Health insurance is therefore strongly advised for citizens of non-EU countries.

Pharmacists can dispense only a limited range of drugs without a doctor's prescription. Most are open for normal shop hours, though some are open late, especially in larger towns. Local newspapers will carry lists of which are open late.

Doctors' surgeries are usually open from around 0830-0900 till 1730-1800, though times vary. Outside surgery hours you can go to the casualty department of the local hospital for any complaint requiring urgent attention. For the address of the nearest hospital or doctors' surgery, T0800-665544.

You should encounter no major problems or irritations during your visit to Scotland. The only exceptions to this are the risk of **hypothermia** if you're walking in the mountains in difficult conditions (see page 60), and the dreaded **midge** (see box page 65).

Edinburgh

Edinburgh

Few cities make such a strong impression on the visitor as Edinburgh. Scotland's capital is without doubt one of the most beautiful and elegant cities in Europe. Its urban bits are separated by parks and gardens and, most stunning of all, cliffs and rocks and grassy hills – even a few dormant volcanoes! This is real nature rather than the manicured stuff, which is all you get in most other cities.

The views around Edinburgh have to be seen to be believed: down from the castle across the Georgian New Town; from the New Town out across the Firth of Forth; from Arthur's Seat across the surrounding moors; and the most dramatic cityscape in Europe, from Calton Hill down the length of Princes Street to the castle. Edinburgh is so spectacular that it has an almost unreal quality. The great novelist, Robert Louis Stevenson, who was born and bred here, described the city as a "profusion of eccentricities, this dream in masonry and living rock", and went on to express his astonishment that it was "not a dropscene in a theatre, but a city in the world of everyday reality".

Fittingly, such a spectacular setting provides the stage for the Edinburgh International Festival, the largest cultural event on the planet, held over three weeks in August and September. Also in keeping with its status as one of the great European cities, Edinburgh has many excellent museums and art galleries: the National Gallery of Scotland, the Scottish National Gallery of Modern Art and the Museum of Scotland all boast the finest collections outside London.

Edinburgh

Ins and outs

Getting there

Population: 440,000
Phone code: 0131
See also 'Transport',
on page 128

Air Edinburgh international airport, T3331000 general enquiries, T3443136 airport information, is 8 miles west of the city centre on the A8 Edinburgh-Glasgow road. The airport has all the usual facilities, including a tourist information desk, *bureau de change*, ATMs, bars and restaurants (on the first floor) and shops (ground floor and first floor). The tourist information desk, in the international arrivals area, will book accommodation and car hire. For **car hire**, *Avis*, *Budget*, *Europcar*, *Hertz* and *National* car hire desks are located in the terminal in the main UK arrivals area. For **flight information**, see page 29.

Two **bus** services, *Airline 100* (T5556363) and *Guide Friday* (T5562244) run between the airport and the main train station at Waverley Bridge. From Waverley Bridge, buses start at 0600 and then run every 15 mins between 0715 and 1955, and then every 30 mins till 2155. From the airport the first bus is at 0630, then every 15 mins till 2100, and then every 30 mins till 2230. The main pick up/drop off points in town are at the West End of Princes Street and Haymarket train station. Both services cost £3.30 single for adults; £3 for children. An open return fare is £5, £3 for children. Tickets can be bought from the driver, at the Tourist Information Centre or at the *Guide Friday* Tourism Centre (see Tours of Edinburgh, page 76). The journey time is 25 mins, though this will be longer during the rush hours. **By taxi** from the airport to the city centre will cost £15 in one of the white airport taxis, while a black taxi cab will cost around £12. Journey time is roughly 20 mins. The airport is easily reached by **car**. Parking costs £1.70 per hr short term, or £4.70 per day long term.

For details of rail links from London, see page 36

Train All trains to Edinburgh go to Waverley station, T5562477, off Waverley Bridge at the east end of Princes St. This is where the main ticket booking office is located. Note that during peak periods a wait of 30-40 mins is not unusual. Leave at least 10 mins to buy tickets for immediate travel at other times. Taxis collect passengers from the station concourse, but if the queue is depressingly long, there's another taxi rank on Waverley Bridge. All trains to the north and to the west coast, including Glasgow, also stop at Haymarket station. For timetable and ticket enquiries: T08457-484950.

Bus The city's new bus station is under construction so buses currently leave from St Andrews Sq (see 'New Town' map), only a few minutes' walk from Waverley station. This is the terminal for all coaches from England, from other towns and cities around Scotland and also for local services to outlying towns and villages. There are left luggage lockers on the south side of the square.

Getting around

Bicycle This is just about the best way to get around the city, despite the hilly terrain. Many of the main roads have cycle lanes and there are plenty of cycle routes around the town and out into the surrounding countryside. The local cycling association, **Spokes**, 232 Dalry Rd, T3132114, www.spokes.org.uk publishes a very good cycle map (£4.95, available at the TIC). For details of cycle hire companies see page 130. If you've brought your own bike and need spares, you'll find everything you'll need at *Edinburgh Bicycle Co-op*, 8 Alvanley Terr, T2281368; open Mon-Fri 1000-1900, Sat/Sun 1000-1800.

See also 'Transport' page 128

Bus Public transport is generally good and efficient. There are two main bus companies operate most services in and around the city: *Lothian Regional Transport* (*LRT*) use maroon and white double deckers, while *First Edinburgh* operate the same routes using green and yellow buses. They also run the so-called 'Barbie' buses, which are pink and more user-friendly for parents with kids and disabled passengers.

Things to do in Edinburgh

- Take a walk along the Water of Leith from the Scottish Gallery of Modern Art to the Botanic Gardens.
- Climb Arthur's Seat for the wonderful views then descend to the Sheep's Heid Inn in Duddingston village for lunch.
- Be very afraid...when you visit the haunted underground city vaults on one of the city's many ghost tours.
- Visit the state-of-the-art Museum of Scotland, then head round the corner to the ghoulishly entertaining Sir Jules Thorn Exhibition of the History of Surgery.
- Don't miss the Royal Yacht Britannia where you can take a peek at Queenie's bedroom and admire all that chintz.

Edinburgh

Car Edinburgh is one of the least car-friendly cities in Britain. The main routes into town have been turned into 'greenways', which give buses priority, and on-street parking is limited to 10 mins. The centre of town is a complicated system of one-way streets designed to ease congestion. The privatized traffic wardens are ruthless in their dedication to duty. Free parking in most of central Edinburgh is limited to resident-parking permit holders only, Mon-Fri 0830-1800, and the police have powers to tow away illegally parked cars. For details of car rental companies based in the city, see page 129.

On foot Although Greater Edinburgh occupies a large area relative to its population of less than half a million, most of what you'll want to see lies within the compact city centre which is easily explored on foot. The centre is clearly divided in two, with the main thoroughfare, Princes Street, and its gardens, running between them. The **Old Town** is a medieval maze of cobbled streets, wynds and closes on or around the Royal Mile, which runs from the castle down to the palace. The **New Town** is the symmetrical layout of wide streets lined with elegant Georgian buildings which runs north from Princes Street. Though most of the main sights are within walking distance of each other, Edinburgh is a hilly city and a full day's sightseeing can leave you exhausted.

An excellent way to see the sights and avoid wearing out shoe leather is to take one of the city bus tours (Guide Friday or LRT); see page 76

The city's main **Tourist Information Centre** is at 3 Princes St, on top of Waverley Market, T4733800, F4733881, www.edinburgh.org Open Apr and Oct Mon-Sat 0900-1800, Sun 1100-1800; May and Sep Mon-Sat 0900-1900, Sun 1100-1900; Jun Mon-Sat 0900-1900, Sun 1000-1900; Jul and Aug Mon-Sat 0900-2000, Sun 1000-2000; Nov-Mar Mon-Sat 0900-1800, Sun 1000-1800. It gets very busy during the peak season and at festival time, but has the full range of services, including currency exchange, and will book accommodation, provide travel information and book tickets for various events and excursions. They also stock a wide range of guides, maps and leaflets covering all of Scotland. There's also a tourist information desk at the **airport**, in the international arrivals area, T3332167. It's open Apr-Oct Mon-Sat 0830-2130, Sun 0930-2130; Nov-Mar Mon-Fri 0900-1800, Sat 0900-1700, Sun 0930-1700.

Information

Another useful tourist information resource is the **Backpackers Centre**, 6 Blackfriars St, T5579393 next to *Haggis Backpackers*. They provide information about hostels and tours and will book coach and ferry tickets.

The City Council has produced a free map of the different bus routes around Edinburgh. This is available from the TIC or from the **LRT ticket centres** at 31 Waverley Bridge, T2258616 (open Easter-Oct Mon-Sat 0800-1800, Sun 0900-1630; Nov-Easter Tue-Sat 0900-1630), or 27 Hanover St, T5556363 (open Mon-Sat 0830-1800). Both offices sell travel cards. Traveline runs a public-transport information service for

Edinburgh, East Lothian and Midlothian: T0800-232323 (local calls) or T2253858 (national calls), Mon-Fri 0830-2000. Their office is at 2 Cockburn St, near Waverley Station.

History

Edinburgh's early history begins on the Castle Rock, which was occupied in the Bronze and Iron Age. Following a brief visit by the Romans, the Angles of Northumbria came, saw, conquered and hung around for a while. In the 7th century, their king, Edwin, rebuilt the earlier fortress of Dun Eadain – the Fortress on the Slope – and changed its name to Edwin's Burgh.

The town only began to develop beyond the fortress during the 11th century; the pace of growth quickening when the new king, David I, moved his capital from Dunfermline to Edinburgh in 1124. Four years later he founded his abbey at Holyrood and the Burgh's continued progress was marked in 1329 by the granting of a charter by Robert the Bruce.

From the reign of James II to James IV (1437-1513) the city flourished. The first town wall was built in 1437 (the Wellhouse Tower at the northern foot of Castle Rock is the only remaining trace), followed by the construction of Holyrood Palace. This Renaissance period also saw much patronage of the arts and education, including the granting of a charter to the Royal College of Surgeons in 1506, and the establishment of Scotland's first printing press in 1508.

The Renaissance era was brought to a sudden end, however, by the disastrous defeat at Flodden in 1513, and there followed more than a century of darkness and despair. During the years of the "rough wooing", in 1544 and 1547, Henry VIII, never a man to cross, devastated the city. Edinburgh suffered further following the return of Mary, Queen of Scots from France, in 1561, in what were seven turbulent and tragic years. When Mary's son, James VI, became James I of England with the Union of Crowns in 1603, he moved his court to London and Edinburgh entered a period of obscurity.

Obscurity did not bring peace, however. The bitter and bloody religious struggle that began in Mary's short reign reached its climax in the 17th century. First, the National Covenant was signed at Greyfriars in 1638, then Cromwell occupied the city in 1650, and in the same year Montrose was executed. Meanwhile, witches continued to be burned on the castle esplanade and over 100 Covenanters were martyred in the Grassmarket.

At the beginning of the following century Edinburgh fared little better. Charles II had rebuilt Holyrood Palace during the Restoration but this proved a false dawn. With the Act of Union of 1707 the city became even less important as a capital. Then came an almost surreal moment, in 1745, with the Jacobite Rebellion, when the Young Pretender held court at Holyrood following his victory at Prestonpans, while the castle remained in government hands.

Towards the end of the 18th century the city's fortunes suddenly changed for the better with the florescence of the Arts and Sciences during the Scottish Enlightenment. Adam Smith, David Hume, Goldsmith, Sir Walter Scott, Robert Louis Stevenson and Allan Ramsay are only a few of the many prominent and brilliant names to feature during the 18th and 19th centuries. Also at this time, the city began to spread outside the confines of its cramped Castle Rock tenements. With the bridging of the Cowgate, building spread southwards beyond the Flodden Wall.

More significantly, the city extended northwards over the next 70 years or so with the building of the most distinguished and extensive area of Georgian architecture in Britain. Two of the most noteworthy landmark events of this period happened in 1818 and 1822. In 1818, Sir Walter Scott instigated a search of the castle for the Scottish regalia, which had been forgotten since 1707. Then, in 1822, he organized the highly successful visit by George IV, the first royal visitor for over a century. The royal visit not only breathed life back into Holyrood Palace, but also revived a feeling of national pride and brought to an end the prevailing mood of despair which had engulfed the nation after defeat at Culloden.

The Industrial Revolution was to affect Edinburgh less than any other city in Britain and it remained essentially professional rather than an industrial. But, though 20th-century development on the whole left the best areas of old and Georgian Edinburgh untouched, the city underwent massive urban expansion, swallowing up many smaller burghs, including the port of Leith.

Since the second world war Scotland's capital city has gained international recognition as the home of the **Edinburgh International Festival**, and now, at the beginning of the new millenium, is set to take its place on the European political stage with the building of the new **Scottish Parliament**.

Sights

The city centre is divided in two. North of Princes Street is the elegant neoclassical New Town, built in the late 18th and early 19th centuries to improve conditions in the city. South of Princes Street, across the beautiful Princes Street Gardens, is the Old Town, a rabbit warren of narrow alleys and closes, inhabited by the ghosts of Edinburgh's seamy past, and the inspiration for Stevenson's famous Dr Jeckyll and Mr Hyde. This medieval Manhattan of high-rise tenements runs from the castle down to the Palace of Holyroodhouse. Overlooking the palace is Edinburgh's largest and most impressive extinct volcano, Arthur's Seat, an authentic piece of mountain wilderness within a stone's throw of the city centre.

The best place to start a tour of Edinburgh is in the medieval Old Town, where you'll find most of the famous sights, from the **castle**, down through the **Royal Mile**, to the **Palace of Holyroodhouse**. South of the Royal Mile is the **Grassmarket**, the **Cowgate** and **Chambers Street**, site of the **University of Edinburgh** and two of the city's best museums, the **Royal Museum of Scotland** and the recently opened **Museum of Scotland**. The **New Town** also deserves some serious exploration, in particular the excellent **National Gallery**, **Royal Scottish Academy** and **National Portrait Gallery**. A bit further out from the centre are the **Royal Botanic Garden** and the **Gallery of Modern Art**. Though in theory you could 'do' the Old Town in a day, you really need several days to do it justice, and to leave yourself enough energy to explore the rest of the city. You should also leave enough time to enjoy the wild, open countryside of **Holyrood Park** and take a stroll up **Arthur's Seat**, from where you get stupendous views of the whole city and beyond.

The Old Town

The city skyline is dominated by the castle, Scotland's prime tourist attraction and the most visited sight in Britain outside London. The castle sits on top of an extinct volcano, protected on three sides by steep cliffs, and is well worth a visit, if only for the great views over the city from its battlements.

Edinburgh Castle

Edinburgh

Edinburgh

Edinburgh's Weather

To describe Edinburgh's weather as changeable would be a huge understatement. The popular refrain states that if you don't like the weather, then just wait 20 minutes. Perhaps Robert Louis Stevenson best summed up the climatic conditions in his home town, "The weather is raw and boisterous in winter, shifty and ungenial in summer, and downright meteorological purgatory in spring". So, before you leave your hotel or guesthouse, be sure to pack your rain jacket, sunglasses, sunblock, thermals, gloves, woolly hat and snow shoes – and maybe an ice axe and crampons in case you fancy a walk up Arthur's Seat.

Not surprisingly, such a strategic site has been the focus of much attention over the centuries. The Picts, Scots, British (Welsh) and Angles disputed ownership of the Castle Rock until the Scots finally came out on top. Edinburgh then went on to become established as Scotland's capital but, due to its proximity to England, was under constant threat of invasion from south of the border. Since 1174, when it was held by the English for 12 years, the castle defences have hardly had a moment's rest. In 1296 King Edward I occupied this prime piece of real estate, then, in 1314, the Earl of Moray famously climbed the north face and drove out the English incumbents to reinstate King Robert the Bruce. The castle has withstood many sieges since then – the longest from 1570 to 1573, in defence of Mary, Queen of Scots – but has also been breached on a few occasions. In 1650 it succumbed to Cromwell's New Model Army, and in 1689, when the Duke of Gordon tried, but failed, to hold out against the Protestant army of William of Orange.

Today, the castle is still 'invaded' on a regular basis, this time by crowds of a rather more benign nature, namely tourists. You can easily wander round the castle yourself, but for a more colourful introduction to its eventful past, you can join one of the first-rate guided tours.

The castle is entered from the top of the Royal Mile, via the **Esplanade**, which was built in the 18th and 19th centuries as a parade ground. During the Festival, the Esplanade is the setting for the Military Tattoo (see page 124) and from the south wall there are excellent views across to the Pentland Hills. Dotted around the Esplanade are various memorial plaques to members of the Scottish regiments who fell in overseas wars, and several military monuments, including one of Field Marshall Earl Haig, one of the city's most notorious sons, whose insane trench warfare strategy in the First World War led to such horrific casualties.

A drawbridge, the last ever built in Scotland, leads to the 19th-century **Gatehouse**, which is flanked by modern statues of Sir William Wallace and Robert the Bruce. The main path then leads steeply up, through the **Portcullis Gate**, to the **Argyll Battery** then the **Mill's Mount Battery**. Every day (except Sundays, Christmas Day and Good Friday) since 1851, the 'one o' clock gun' has been fired from the Mill's Mount Battery as a time-check for the city's office workers. From both batteries there are wonderful views across Princes Street, the New Town and the Firth of Forth.

The steep and winding road continues up past the **Governer's House** and the **New Barracks**, both built in the 18th century (many of the buildings within the castle walls date from the 18th century or later). Then the road turns once more, through Foog's Gate, to the summit of Castle Rock and **St Margaret's Chapel**, the oldest surviving building in the castle, and probably in the city itself. The tiny, simple yet beautiful building is said to have been

---

24 hours in Edinburgh

For those unlucky enough to have only a day to spend in Edinburgh, the following itinerary should give a taste of why it is the most visited British city outside London.

Start the day at the **Castle**, after which you'll need a breather and a well-earned coffee break at the **Elephant House**, on George IV Bridge. Afterwards, head across the road to the excellent **Museum of Scotland** in Chambers Street.

If you're feeling peckish, take a wee stroll down to **Black Bo's** on Blackfriars Street for a superb vegetarian lunch.

Then head down towards Princes Street and pop into the **National Gallery of Scotland**, the city's finest art gallery. If you've still got plenty of energy, head up The Mound and down the Royal Mile to the **Palace of Holyroodhouse**.

If the weather's fine, you may fancy a walk up to Calton Hill for the wonderful views, then head down to the nearby **Pivo Caffe** for a drink.

Then it's into a taxi and down to Leith for a superb seafood dinner at **Fishers**, followed by a nightcap or two in one of the harbourside bars .

---

built by Margaret herself, but the Norman style suggests it was constructed later, most likely as a memorial by her son, King David I. Following Cromwell's capture of the Castle in 1650, the chapel was used as an ammunition store, until Queen Victoria had it restored, and it was eventually rededicated in 1934. In front of the chapel is the **Half Moon Battery**, which offers the best panoramic views over the city.

South of the chapel is **Crown Square**, the most secure and most important section of the entire complex. The eastern side is taken up by the **Palace of Holyrood House**, begun in the 15th century and remodelled in the 16th century for Mary, Queen of Scot's. Above the main doorway are the initials of Mary and her husband Henry, Lord Darnley. Here, in 1566, Queen Mary gave birth to James VI, later to become James I of England. Rumour has it that her child was stillborn, and the newborn baby of a serving maid was put in its place, but like much else in Scottish history, the truth remains elusive.

Later, in 1617, the Palace buildings were extended with the addition of the **Crown Room**, where the **Honours of Scotland** are now displayed – the royal crown, the sceptre and the sword of state. There is no more potent symbol of Scottish nationhood than these magnificent crown jewels, which were last used for the coronation of Charles II in 1651, an event which incurred the wrath of one Oliver Cromwell, who made repeated but unsuccessful attempts to get rid of the jewels. Then, in 1707, the crown jewels were locked away in a chest and forgotten about. They were presumed lost for over a century, until Sir Walter Scott initiated a search and rediscovered them in 1818. The oldest of the Honours is the **sceptre**, bestowed on James IV by Pope Alexander VI and later remodelled for James V. The even more impressive **sword of state** was presented to James IV by Pope Julius II in 1507. The jewel-encrusted **crown** contains the circlet of gold with which Robert the Bruce was crowned at Scone in 1306, and was remade for James V in 1540. Also housed in the Crown Room is the recently-installed **Stone of Destiny** (see below), the seat on which the ancient kings of Scotland were crowned. However, no one knows whether this is, in fact, the real stone.

On the south side of the square is James IV's **Great Hall.** Once the seat of the Scottish Parliament and later used for state banquets, it now houses a display of arms and armour. On the west side of the square is the 18th-century **Queen Anne Barracks**, which now contains the **Scottish United Services**

Tours of Edinburgh

One of the best ways to see the city sights is to take a **guided bus tour** on board an open-top double decker bus. These depart from Waverley Bridge every 15 minutes, the first one leaving around 0900 and the last one between 1730 and 2000, depending on the time of year. The complete tour lasts an hour, stopping at the main tourist sights, but tickets are valid for the full day and you can hop on and off any of the company's buses at any of the stops. The **Guide Friday** tours are recommended and cost £8.50 per person (students £7/children £2.50); Guide Friday Tourism Centre, 133-135 Canongate, Royal Mile, T5562244, www.guidefriday.com **Lothian Regional Transport (LRT)** run similar guided bus tours; £7.50 (students £6/children £2.50). Tickets and further information from their city centre offices (see Ins and outs, page 70).

There are various **guided walking tours** of Edinburgh, which fall into roughly two categories: historical tours of the medieval closes and wynds of the Royal Mile during the day, and spooky, nocturnal tours of the city's dark and grisly past. Some of the latter tours include a visit to the 200 year-old haunted vaults hidden deep beneath the city streets. There are several versions of these tours, but two of the main operators are **Robin's Tours**, T/F5579933, whose tours leave from outside the TIC and **Mercat Tours**, T/F2256591, who leave from the Mercat Cross by St Giles Cathedral. Braver souls may wish to experience the **City of the Dead Haunted Graveyard Tour**, T0771-5422750, which leaves from the Mercat Cross nightly at 2030 and involves being locked in a haunted graveyard with the notorious Mackenzie poltergeist.

There are also guided walking tours of **Arthur's Seat** with **Geowalks**, T5555488, www.geowalks.demon.co.uk Most of these guided walking tours last around two hours and cost £5-7 per person.

During the Festival in August the **Edinburgh Voluntary Guides** take small group of tourists on **free guided tours** from the Castle Esplanade down to the Palace of Holyroodhouse. Just turn up at Cannonball House (by the entrance to the esplanade) between 1000 and 1100 and 1400 and 1500, or call T6647180.

Those who prefer a little libation with their guided tour should try the highly-acclaimed **Edinburgh Literary Pub Tour**, a witty exploration of the city's distinguished literary past, which starts at the Beehive Inn in the Grassmarket. The two-hour tour costs £7 per person (students £5). Tickets can be booked at the tourist office or direct from The **Scottish Literary Tour Company**, T2266665, www.scot-lit-tour.co.uk

Museum. On the north side stands the neo-Gothic **Scottish National Monument**, designed by Sir Robert Lorimer and a dignified testament to the many tens of thousands of Scottish soldiers killed in the First World War.

From the western end of Crown Square you can descend into the **Vaults**, a series of dark and dank chambers, once used as a prison for French captives during the Napoleonic Wars. One of the rooms contains **Mons Meg**, the massive iron cannon forged here in the reign of James IV (1488-1513). It was said to have had a range of nearly 1½ miles and was used for salutes on royal occasions. It was taken to the Tower of London in 1754, where it stayed until Sir Walter Scott persuaded George IV to return it during the latter's state visit to Scotland in 1822. ■ *Apr-Sep daily 0930-1800, Oct-Mar 0930-1700. Last admission 45 mins before closing. £7.50, £2 child, £5.50 concession. T2259846 (HS)*.

Royal Mile

Running through the heart of the medieval Old Town, from the castle down to the **Palace of Holyrood-house**, is the **Royal Mile**, where you'll find a greater concentration of historic buildings than almost anywhere else in Britain. This street was described by Daniel Defoe (who lived in Edinburgh at the beginning of the 18th century) as "perhaps the largest, longest and finest Street for buildings, and Number of Inhabitants, not in Britain only, but in the world". It is now also one of the busiest tourist thoroughfares in the world, especially during the Festival. Consequently, it's full of shops selling tacky souvenirs, but not even this can detract from its sheer magnificence.

The 1,984 yards of the Royal Mile, from the Castle Keep to the Palace, comprises four separate streets: (from top to bottom) **Castlehill**, **Lawnmarket**, the **High Street** and the **Canongate**. Branching out from these is a honeycomb of wynds and closes, entered via archways known as pends. A close is the entrance to a 'land' or high-rise tenement block, and wynds are the narrow and winding alleyways giving access to the main street. These were the scene of many important – and sinister – events over the centuries and are certainly worth exploring in detail.

Here, the city's aristocracy, gentry, merchants and commoners lived together, often in the same building, with the upper classes at the bottom and the *hoi polloi* at the top. Until the end of the 18th century, the Old Town was the hub of fashionable society. Indeed, such was the concentration of talent that John Amyat, the King's chemist, remarked that he could stand at the Mercat Cross and "in a few minutes take fifty men of genius by the hand".

At the turn of the 19th century the Old Town was gradually abandoned by the Great and the Good of Edinburgh, who moved lock, stock and barrel to the New Town in what was called 'The Great Flitting'. The Old Town deteriorated into an overcrowded slum. People would throw their refuse and sewage out of the tenement windows onto the street, shouting to the passers-by, below with the traditional warning of "Gardyloo" (from the French *garde a l'eau*). Not surprisingly, such a place of filth and squalor was highly vulnerable to epidemics and it is only in the past century that the Royal Mile has been cleaned and turned into one of the most fascinating and picturesque streets in the world.

The narrow uppermost part of the Royal Mile nearest the castle is known as **Castlehill** Castlehill. Just below the Castle Esplanade is an iron fountain which marks the spot where more than 300 Edinburgh women were burned as witches between 1479 and 1722. Behind the fountain rises Ramsay Gardens, a distinctive and picturesque late 19th-century apartment block which grew around the octagonal Goose Pie House, home of 18th-century poet Allan Ramsay, author of *The Gentle Shepherd*. These early apartments were designed by Sir Patrick Geddes, a pioneer of architectural conservation and town planning, who created them in an attempt to regenerate the Old Town.

At the corner of Castlehill and Castle Wynd is **Cannonball House**, which takes its name from a cannonball embedded in the west wall. According to legend, the cannonball was fired from the Castle during the '45 rebellion, but in fact it marks the high-water level of the city's first piped water supply in 1681. Next door is the **Scotch Whisky Heritage Centre**, 354 Castlehill, where you can find out everything you ever wanted to know about Scotland's national drink. The best part is the bond bar, where you can sample some of the vast range of malt whiskies on offer before buying a bottle in the gift shop.

■ *Daily Jun-Sep 0930-1800, Oct-May 1000-1730. £5.50, £2.75 children, £3.85 concession. T2200441, www.whisky-heritage.co.uk* Across the street is the **Edinburgh Old Town Weaving Company**, which has a real working mill where you can see tartan being woven and a small exhibition. ■ *Daily 0900-1730. Free entry to mill and a small charge for the exhibition. T2261555.*

A few doors further down, on the corner of Ramsay Lane, is the **Outlook Tower**, which has been one of the capital's top tourist attractions since a **camera obscura** was set up in the hexagonal tower by optician, Maria Theresa Short, in 1854. The device consists of a giant camera which sweeps around the city and beams the live images onto a tabletop screen, accompanied by a running commentary of the city's past. There's also an exhibition of photographs taken with a variety of home-made pinhole cameras and the rooftop viewing terrace offers fantastic views of the city. ■ *Daily Apr-Oct 0930-1800 (later in Jul/Aug), Nov-Mar 1000-1700. £4.25, £2.10 children, £3.10 concession. T2263709.*

A little further down, on the opposite side of the street is the **Tolbooth Kirk**, whose distinctive spire is the highest in the city and a distinctive feature of the Edinburgh skyline. The building was originally intended to house the General Assembly of the Church of Scotland, but they moved across the street in the 1850s. The Tolbooth Kirk was where the city's Gaelic speakers used to worship, until it was closed in 1981. It has recently been converted into **The Hub**, which houses the ticket centre for Edinburgh International Festival (see page 125). The Hub also stages various events and is home to the excellent *Café Hub* (see page 115). Opposite is the neo-Gothic **New College and**

Central Edinburgh

Assembly Hall. Built in 1859, it is the meeting place of the annual General Assembly of the Church of Scotland and is also used during the Festival to stage major drama productions.

The Tolbooth Kirk and Assembly Hall mark the top of the Lawnmarket, a much broader street named after the old linen market which used to be held here. At the northern end is **Milne's Court**, built in 1690 and skilfully renovated in 1971 as student residences. Next comes **James Court**, a very prestigious address, where the philosopher David Hume lived and where Boswell entertained Dr Johnson in 1773.

Lawnmarket

Back on the Lawnmarket itself, at number 477b, is **Gladstone's Land**, the most important surviving example of 17th-century tenement housing in the Old Town, where the cramped conditions meant that extension was only possible in depth or upwards. The magnificent six-storey building, completed in 1620, contains remarkable painted ceilings and was the home of an Edinburgh burgess, Thomas Gledstanes. The reconstructed shop booth on the ground floor has replicas of 17th-century goods and the first floor of the house has been refurbished as a typical Edinburgh home of the period. If you like what you see, then you can also stay here (see page 37). ■ *1 Apr-end-Oct Mon-Sat 1000-1700, Sun 1400-1700. £3.50, £2.50 concession. T2265856 (NTS).*

Further down Lawnmarket, steps lead down to Lady Stair's Close, where you'll find **Lady Stair's House**, another fine 17th-century house, though restored in pseudo-medieval style. It is now the home of the **Writer's Museum**, dedicated to the three giants of Scottish literature, Burns, Scott and Stevenson. ■ *Mon-Sat 1000-1700 and Sun 1400-1700 during the Festival only. Free. T5294901.*

Opposite Gladstone's Land is **Riddle's Court**, another of David Hume's residences. Here also is the late-16th-century house of Bailie McMorran, who was shot dead by pupils of the Royal High School during a riot in 1595 against the proposed reduction in school holidays. Further down the street on the same side is **Brodie's Close**, named after the father of one of Edinburgh's most nefarious characters, Deacon Brodie. He was an apparent pillar of the community by day and a burglar by night, until his eventual capture and hanging in 1788. Robert Louis Stevenson co-wrote a play about his life, which was to provide the inspiration for *Dr Jeckyll and Mr Hyde*.

Across George IV Bridge, at the top of the High Street, stands the **High Kirk of St Giles**, the only parish church of medieval Edinburgh and

High Street

Edinburgh

Stone of Destiny

Edinburgh Castle is the home of the famous Stone of Destiny, the subject of much controversy and rumour throughout the country's troubled past.

According to legend, the Stone of Destiny was the biblical 'Jacob's Pillow', on which Jacob dreamed of a ladder of angels leading from earth to heaven. The stone is said to have arrived in Scotland from the Holy Land, via Spain and Ireland. The king, Kenneth MacAlpin, moved it to Scone, near Perth, where the ancient coronation custom continued. Rumour has it that the supposed original, stolen by Edward I in 1296, which remained under lock and key in Westminster Abbey until 1996, is a poor substitute made of Perthshire sandstone, and that the real article was hidden, to reappear when Scotland regained her

sovereignty. Some say Bruce was crowned on it, after which it went with his great ally, Angus Og of the Isles, to Islay for safekeeping.

Students removed the stone from Westminster in 1950 and returned it, briefly, to Scotland. Thereafter, unfolds a farcical tale of substitutes, replicas, claims and counter-claims. Some say the real stone was discovered around 100 years ago buried in Macbeth's ruined fort on Dunsinnan. Could this be the hiding place chosen by the monks of Scone in 1296, or did Macbeth hide it centuries earlier? If the stone – returned so ceremoniously from Westminster to Scotland in 1996 in a vain attempt to restore flagging Tory fortunes north of the border – is a fake, where is the real one? Somebody knows and isn't telling.

the home of Presbyterianism, where the firebrand preacher John Knox launched the Scottish Reformation. The Kirk is mistakenly called St Giles Cathedral. This is because Charles I called it so when he introduced bishops into the Church of Scotland and the name stuck, even after Presbyterianism was re-established. The church was given a major face-lift in the 19th century, covering most of its Gothic exterior, but parts of the original medieval building still survive, most notably the late-15th-century crowned tower. The four huge octagonal pillars which support the central tower are thought to date back to the previous Norman church, built in 1120 and razed to the ground by English invaders in the late 14th century.

The church has had a colourful past ever since medieval times when the Scottish Parliament met here. It was the launchpad for the Scottish Reformation, as mentioned above, then, around the turn of the 16th century, it was divided up and used as law courts, the town clerk's office, a school and a prison. When the High Kirk returned to its religious function it was partitioned into four different churches, each serving its own congregation, finally being reunified after its Victorian restoration.

One of the most celebrated incidents in the church's history happened in 1637, when an attempt to read from the English prayer book so incensed Jenny Geddes, a humble stallholder, that she launched her stool at the bishop's head, shouting (according to tradition): "False thief, will ye no say mass about my lug?", which roughly translates as "stop saying mass or you're in big trouble, mate!". A plaque marks the spot where the stool landed and recounts the ensuing riot. Such disturbances led to the National Covenenant of 1638, establishing the Presbyterian Church of Scotland in defiance of Charles I. This in turn led to Civil War, during which many Covenanters were imprisoned in the church. Two of the most famous figures of the war, the royalist Marquis of Montrose and the convenanting Marquis of Argyll, were both executed outside the church and now lie entombed within its walls, facing each other from opposite aisles.

There have been many additions to the High Kirk since its restoration. One of these is the very beautiful **Thistle Chapel**, the Chapel of the Most Ancient and Most Noble Order of the Thistle (Scotland's foremost order of chivalry). It was designed by Sir Robert Lorimer and built in 1911. The elaborate ornamentation and fine carvings are exquisite (look out for the angel playing the bagpipes). There are also several Pre-Raphaelite stained-glass windows in the church, and above the west door is a memorial window to Robert Burns, rather surprising given that the great bard was hardly an upholder of Presbyterian values. There's a good café in the church crypt (see page 115). ■ *Easter-Sep Mon-Fri 0900-1900, Sat 0900-1700, Sun 1300-1700; Oct-Easter Mon-Sat 0900-1700, Sun 1300-1700. Free (donations welcome). T2259442.*

Outside the High Kirk of St Giles, on **Parliament Square**, is an imposing equestrian statue of King Charles II and, nearby, a flat stone bearing the legend 'I.K. 1572' marks the reputed burial place of John Knox. In front of the west door of the church is the site of the city Tolbooth, demolished in 1817. The Tolbooth entrance is marked by a heart-shaped pattern in the cobblestones, known as the **Heart of Midlothian**, and made famous by Sir Walter Scott in his eponymous novel. Should you see passers-by spitting on it, it's not a sign of disrespect, but supposed to bring good luck. Behind the church is the **Mercat Cross**, where public proclamations are traditionally read. The present cross is a replica, gifted to the city by the then prime-minister, W.E. Gladstone.

The rest of Parliament Square is formed by the Law Courts, Parliament House and the Signet Library. The **Law Courts**, where Sir Walter Scott practised as an advocate, were originally planned by Robert Adam (1728-1792), who contributed so much to the grace and elegance of the New Town, but due to lack of funds were built to designs by Robert Reid (1776-1856). On the west side of the square is the **Signet Library**, centre for the Society of Her Majesty's Writers to the Signet, an organization that originated from the 15th-century Keepers of the King's Seal, or signet. It boasts one of the finest neoclassical interiors in the city, but unfortunately can only seen by prior written application, except on very occasional open days. **Parliament House**, facing the south side of St Giles, was the meeting place of the Scots Parliament between 1639 and 1707. It is now used by the city's lawyers in between court sittings, but is readily accessible during the week. The most notable feature is the magnificent Parliament Hall with its wonderful 17th century hammerbeam roof.

On the opposite side of the High Street is **Edinburgh City Chambers**, designed by John Adam (brother of Robert) and built in 1761 as the Royal Exchange. However, it proved not to the liking of the city's traders, who preferred to conduct their business in the street, so in the early 19th century it became the headquarters of the city council. Beneath the city chambers is **Mary King's Close**, closed off for many years after the 1645 plague and now open to guided tours (see page 76). A little further down is **Anchor Close**, where the first editions of *Encyclopaedia Britannica* and of Robert Burns' poems were printed at the printing works of William Smellie.

Cockburn St leads down to Market St, home of the new Edinburgh Dungeon, an entertaining trawl through Scotland's more sinister past (open daily 1000-1800. £6.95, £4.95 child, £5.95 concession)

At the junction of the High Street and South Bridge is the **Tron Kirk**, founded in 1637, and now more famously known as a favourite Hogmanay rendezvous. The church was named after the Tron, a public weighing beam which stood close by and which was a popular place for merchants to sell their wares. If they were found guilty of selling short measures, they were nailed to the Tron by their ears. The church was built to accommodate the Presbyterian congregation ejected from St Giles during the latter's brief period as a cathedral and continued in use until it was closed in 1952. It now houses the Old Town tourist information centre, and recent excavations have revealed sections of Marlin's Wynd, which ran from the High Street down to the Cowgate.

Past the junction of the North and South Bridges, on the north side of the High Street, is **Carruber's Close**, where Sir James Simpson, the discoverer of chloroform, ran a medical dispensary in the 1860s. Above the entrance to **Paisley Close** is the bust of a boy saved from beneath the rubble when the tenement collapsed in 1861, killing 35 inhabitants, an incident which helped to hasten the much-needed improvement of the Old Town's buildings.

In Chalmers Close, just to the west, is **Trinity Apse**, a sad reminder of the Holy Trinity Church, one of Edinburgh's finest pieces of Gothic architecture, demolished in 1848 to make room for the railway line to Waverley. The stones from the original were carefully numbered for rebuilding on the present site, but pilfering depleted the stock so much that only the apse could be reconstructed, in 1852, on the present site. It is now a **Brass Rubbing Centre**, where you can make your own rubbings from the materials supplied. ■ *Apr-Sep Mon-Sat 1000-1700; also Sun 1200-1700 during the Festival only. Free. T5564364.*

On the opposite side of the High Street, in Hyndford's Close, is the **Museum of Childhood**, which is full of kids screaming with excitement at the vast collection of toys, dolls, games and books, and nostalgic adults yelling "I used to have one of those!". There's even a video history of the various Gerry Anderson TV puppet series such as *Thunderbirds* and *Fireball XL5*. The museum also covers the serious issues of childhood, such as health and education, but that doesn't spoil the sheer fun of the place. ■ *Mon-Sat 1000-1700 and Sun 1400-1700 during the Festival, free, T5294142.*

Almost directly opposite is the early 16th-century **Moubray House**, thought to be the oldest inhabited building in Edinburgh, but closed to the public. This is where Daniel Defoe was based when he came to Edinburgh in 1706 as an English agent to help negotiate the Act of Union. Next door is **John Knox's House**, one of the Royal Mile's most distinctive buildings and dating from the late 15th and 16th centuries. It's not known for sure whether or not the Calvinist preacher actually lived here, but the house did belong to James Mossman, goldsmith to Mary, Queen of Scots. Today, the house is a rather austere museum devoted to the life and career of John Knox. ■ *Mon-Sat 1000-1700 (in Aug also Sun 1200-1700). £2.25, £1.75 concession, £0.75 child. T5569579.*

Canongate

The High Street ends at the junction of St Mary's Street and Jeffrey Street, where the city's eastern gate, Netherbow Port, once stood. The remaining part of the Royal Mile, the Canongate, was a separate burgh for over 700 years, taking its name from the canons (priests) of Holyrood Abbey. As it was near the Palace of Holyroodhouse, the area developed as the court quarter with several fine residences being built there. Though the Canongate went into decline once the court moved to London in the early 17th century, it could still boast an impressive number of aristocrats among its inhabitants, even in the late 18th century.

The most lavish of Canongate's mansions is **Moray House**, built in 1628 for the daughter of Lord Darnley. Charles I visited here on several occasions and Cromwell used it as his headquarters in 1648. And if that weren't enough historical significance, in 1707 the Treaty of Union was signed in a summerhouse in the garden. More recently, the building has been used as the centre for Moray house College of Education, one of Scotland's leading teacher-training establishments. A little further east is the 16th century **Huntly House**, the city's main local history museum, but disappointing nevertheless. Among the highlights is the original copy of the National Covenant of 1638. ■ *Mon-Sat 1000-1700 and Sun 1400-1700 during the Festival. Free. T5294143.*

Opposite Huntly House is the late-16th-century **Canongate Tolbooth**, the original headquarters of the burgh administration, as well as the courthouse and burgh prison. It now houses **The People's Story**, a genuinely interesting museum which describes the life and work of the ordinary people of Edinburgh from the late 18th century to the present day. The museum is filled with the sights, sounds and smells of the past and includes, among others, reconstructions of a prison cell, a workshop and a pub. ■ *Mon-Sat 1000-1700 and Sun 1400-1700 during the Festival. Free. T5294057.* Next door to the Tolbooth is the **Canongate Kirk**, built in 1688 to house the congregation expelled from Holyrood Abbey when it was taken over by James VII (II of England) to be used as the chapel for the Order of the Thistle. More interesting, though, is the churchyard, burial place of many famous people. Among the list of notable names is Adam Smith, the father of political economy, who lived in Panmure House nearby, the philosopher Dugald Stewart and Robert Fergusson, arguably Edinburgh's greatest poet who died tragically at the

Royal Mile detail

6 Edinburgh Backpackers Hostel *A2*	**8** Creelers *A2*	**22** Biddy Mulligan's *B1*
7 High Street Hostel *B3*	**9** Dubh Prais *A3*	**23** Bliss *B3*
8 Ibis *B2*	**10** Elephant House *B1*	**24** Bow Bar *B1*
9 Royal Mile Backpackers *A3*	**11** Gordon's Trattoria *A2*	**25** Carwash *A1*
10 Thistle Inn *B1*	**12** Igg's *A3*	**26** City Café *B2*
	13 Jacksons *A2*	**27** EH1 *A2*
■ **Sleeping**	**14** Le Sept *B2*	**28** Jolly Judge *A1*
1 Bank *A3*	**15** Lower Aisle *A2*	**29** Living Room *B2*
2 Brodie's Backpacker Hostel *A3*	**16** Patisserie Florentin *A2*	**30** Three Sisters *B2*
3 Central Youth Hostel *B2*	**17** Polo Fusion *A1*	
4 Cowgate Tourist Hostel *B2*	**18** Viva Mexico *A2*	○ **Entertainment**
5 Crowne Plaza *A3*		**1** Gilded Balloon *B3*
	■ **Bars & pubs**	**2** Honeycomb *B3*
● **Eating**	**19** Attic *B2*	**3** Liquid Room *B1*
1 Bann's UK *B2*	**20** Bannerman's *B3*	**4** St Cecilia's Hall *B3*
2 Baracoa *B1*	**21** Bar Kohl *B1*	**5** Whistlebinkies *B3*
3 Barioja *A3*		
4 Black Bo's *B3*		
5 Bleu *B1*		
6 Byzantium *B1*		
7 Common Grounds *A1*		

tender age of 23 after being forced into the local madhouse during a bout of depression. Robert Burns, who was greatly inspired by Fergusson's poetry, donated the headstone in 1787, inscribed with his own personal tribute.

The last few yards of the Royal Mile, which forms the approach to the precincts of Holyrood Abbey and Palace, is known as the **Abbey Strand**. The strange little turreted 16th century building here is known as **Queen Mary's Bath House**, where, legend has it, Mary, Queen of Scots bathed in sweet white wine. However, it is more likely that it was a summer pavilion or dovecot. Opposite the main gates of the Palace of Holyroodhouse is the site of the new **Scottish Parliament** building, scheduled for completion in Atumn 2002. At present the parliament sits in the Church of Scotland headquarters on The Mound.

The Palace of Holyroodhouse

The palace began life as the abbey guest house, until James IV transformed it into a royal palace at the beginning of the 16th century. The only remaining part of the Renaissance palace is the northwest tower, built as the private apartments of his son James V. Most of the original building was damaged by fire in 1543 and further in 1650 during its occupation by Cromwell's troops, never the most considerate of guests.

The present palace largely dates from the late 17th century when the original was replaced by a larger building for the Restoration of Charles II, although the newly crowned monarch never actually set foot in the place. It was built in the style of a French chateau, around a large arcaded quadrangle and is an elegant, finely proportioned creation. Designed by William Bruce, it incorporates a castellated southwest tower that balances perfectly the northwest original.

Inside, the oldest part of Holyroodhouse is open to the public and is entered through the **Great Gallery**, which takes up the entire first floor of the north wing. Here, during the '45 rebellion, Bonnie Prince Charlie held court, and it is still used for big ceremonial occasions. The walls are adorned with over one hundred portraits of Scottish Kings, most of them mythical, beginning with 'Fergus I, BC 330' and ending with James VI. Commissioned from the Flemish artist, Jacobus de Wet, they have been described as "paltry daubings [...] painted either from the imagination, or porters hired to sit for the purpose". They certainly make for some amusing viewing.

The **Royal Apartments**, in the northwest tower, are mainly of note for their association with Mary, Queen of Scots and in particular for the queen's most infamous incident in the palace's long history. It was here that the queen witnessed the brutal murder, organized by her husband, Lord Darnley, of her much-favoured Italian private secretary, David Rizzio. He was stabbed 56 times, on a spot marked by a brass plaque and, until it was removed quite recently, by a distinctly unsubtle fake bloodstain.

The later parts of the palace, known as the **State Apartments**, are less interesting, though decorated in Adam Style, with magnificent white stucco ceilings, particularly the Throne Room and Dining room. These are associated with later monarchs, such as George IV, who paid a visit in 1822, dressed in flesh-coloured tights and the briefest of kilts, rather appropriately perhaps, given the length of time he actually spent here. But it was Queen Victoria and Prince Albert who returned the palace to royal favour, as a stopover on their way to and from Balmoral. This custom has been maintained by her successors and the present queen still spends a short while here every year at the end of June and beginning of July. ■ *1 Apr-31 Oct daily 0930-1800; 1 Nov-31 Mar 0930-1630 (by guided tour only). Closed to the public during state functions and during the annual royal visit in the last two weeks of Jun and first week in Jul. £6.50, £3.30 child, £5 concession, £16.50 family. T5561096, www.royal.gove.uk*

In the grounds of the palace are the ruins of Holyrood Abbey. According to legend King David I, son of Malcolm Canmore and St Margaret, was out hunting here one day in 1128, when he was charged by a huge stag and thrown from his horse. The stag then tried to gore him, and the king grabbed hold of its antlers to protect himself, only to find that he was instead holding a crucifix set between the horns. The stag then disappeared, leaving the crucifix in his hands. That night in a dream he was commanded to build a "house for Canons devoted to the Cross", and so he founded an Augustinian abbey of the Holy Rood (another word for Cross) on the site of his miraculous escape. The only surviving part of King David's Norman church is a doorway in the far southeastern corner. Most of the remains date from the early 13th century.

Holyrood Abbey

The abbey was, at its height, a building of great importance and splendour, and this is hinted at in the surviving parts of the west front. Much of it was destroyed, as were many of the county's finest ecclesiastical buildings, during the Reformation. During the reign of Charles I it was converted to the Chapel Royal and later to the Chapel of the Order of the Thistle, but it suffered severe damage once more, this time during the 1688 revolution. Some restoration work was attempted in the 18th century, but this only caused the roof to collapse in 1768, and since then the building has been left as a ruin. In the Royal Vault beneath the abbey are buried several Scottish Kings, including David II (son of Robert the Bruce), James II, James V and Lord Darnley, 'King Consort' to Mary, Queen of Scots.

Edinburgh is blessed with many magnificent green, open spaces, and none better than Holyrood Park (Queen's Park) – a 650-acre rugged wilderness of mountains, crags, lochs, moorland, marshes, fields and glens – all within walking distance of the city centre. This is one of the city's greatest assets, and it's easy to wander around till you're lost from the eyes and ears of civilization.

Arthur's Seat & Duddingston

The park's main feature, and the city's main landmark, is **Arthur's Seat**, the igneous core of another extinct volcano, and the highest of Edinburgh's hills (822ft). It is probably named after Arthur, Prince of Strathclyde, rather than King Arthur of legend, as many believe. Another dominating feature of the Edinburgh skyline is the precipitous **Salisbury Crags**, lying directly opposite the south gates of the palace.

The best walk in the city is to the summit of **Arthur's Seat**, from where you get the very best view of the city, as well as the Pentland Hills to the south, the Firth of Forth and of Fife to the north, and, on a clear day, to the Highland peaks, 70 or 80 miles away. The walk to the top is a popular one, and easier than it looks. If you want to avoid the crowds during summer, then make an early start before breakfast and watch the sun rise over East Lothian.

There are several different routes, all of which take less than an hour, but a good circular walk that takes in the wilder bits and the lochs, starts from **St Margaret's Loch**, little more than an artificial pond, at the far end of the park from the palace. To reach the loch, follow Queen's Drive east (left) from the palace for about two-thirds of a mile (1 km) and it's on the right. Leave the car park beside the loch and head around the loch up towards the 15th-century ruin of **St Anthony's Chapel**. Pass the ruined chapel on your right and after a few hundred yards you'll see the main summit towering above you on the right. Keeping the summit to your right, climb over a saddle which joins the path up from **Dunsapie Loch**, which you can see below you on the left, and continue up a rocky path to the top.

Dunsapie Loch is overshadowed by **Dunsapie Hill**, which makes a great place for an evening picnic and from here it's an easy drop down to

Duddingston Village, just outside the park boundary, and one of the most attractive and unspoilt of the old villages that have become part of the city suburbs. The village **Kirk** dates back to the 12th century and the *Sheep Heid Inn* (see page 120) is a great place to stop off for some liquid sustenance and a bite to eat. Adjoining the village, on the south side of Arthur's Seat, is **Duddingston Loch**, the largest of the park's lochs, which is a sanctuary for waterfowl. It can also be reached via Queen's Drive, heading right from the palace for about four miles.

There are other routes to the top of Arthur's Seat. One starts opposite the palace car park and winds up by the foot of Salisbury Crags, This is the **Radical Road**, built in 1820 and so called because Sir Walter Scott suggested it be constructed by a group of unemployed weavers from the west, who were believed to hold radical political views. This is where James Hutton is said to have dreamt up the idea of geology by looking at the rock formations. The road traverses the ridge below the crags and continues on grass through "Hunter's Bog" and up to the summit. You can also walk along the top of the crags, though there is no path.

South of the Royal Mile

Although the Royal Mile is the main tourist attraction, there are some interesting, and sometimes even quiet, corners of the Old Town to be found not so

Old Town

■ Sleeping	● Eating	6 Kebab Mahal C4
1 Apex International C2	1 Bookstop Café C3	7 Khushi's C4
2 Castle Rock Hostel B2	2 Clarinda's Tearoom A5	8 Librizzi's C4
3 Scotsman A3	3 Dial B3	9 Nicolsons C4
	4 Elephants & Bagels C3	10 Pancho Villa's A4
	5 Favorit C3	11 Petit Paris C2

very far away from the hordes, not to mention the Museum of Scotland, one of the city's 'must-see' attractions.

Holyrood Road runs from the palace back to the Old Town, running parallel to and south of the Canongate. Close to the palace is one of the city's newest attractions, and now one of its most popular, **Dynamic Earth**. This is one of many Millenium Projects funded by National Lottery funds and has proved one of the most successful. The visitor is taken on a fascinating journey of discovery from the very beginnings of time right through to the future. Using the state-of-the-art technology and special effects, you'll experience every environment on Earth and encounter many weird and wonderful creatures. An absolute must if you've kids in tow and you're guaranteed to find out things about our planet that you never knew. ■ *Apr-Oct daily 1000-1800; Nov-Mar Wed-Sun 1000-1700. £6.95, £3.95 child/concession, T5507800, www.dynamicearth.co.uk*

Holyrood Road continues west till it's crossed by the Pleasance and becomes the **Cowgate**, one of Edinburgh's oldest streets and once one of its finest. It runs almost parallel to the High Street, but on a much lower level, and when the South and George IV bridges were built over it, linking the Old and New Towns, it was half-buried below street level and reduced to a dark, desolate canyon of neglect and decay. In recent years the Cowgate has become one

Holyrood to the Cowgate

Edinburgh

Detailed map
A Royal Mile detail, page 83
Related maps
B New Town, page 92
C New Town: Calton Hill, page 96
D South Edinburgh, page 102
E West Edinburgh, page 100

12 Suruchi C4	● **Bars & pubs**	19 Royal Oak B4	4 La Belle Angele B3
13 Witchery by the Castle B2	14 Canon's Gait A4		5 McEwan Hall C3
	15 Doric Tavern A3	○ **Entertainment**	6 Pleasance Theatre B4
	16 Greyfriars Bobby C2	1 Bedlam Theatre C3	7 Reid Concert Hall C3
	17 Iguana C3	2 Club Mercado A3	
	18 Negociants C3	3 Festival Theatre C4	

of the city's best night-life streets, with many good pubs and clubs, but it attracts few tourists, and remains a spooky place to wander in alone after dark.

There are, however, a couple of very notable and very interesting buildings here. At the corner of Niddry Street is the exquisite **St Cecilia's Hall**, built in 1763 for the Edinburgh Musical Society. The interior, modelled on the opera house at Parma, is stunningly beautiful, with an oval music hall and concave elliptical ceiling. In the 18th century it was the city's main concert hall, and since its restoration in 1966 has again been used as a venue for concerts, especially during the Festival (see also 'Entertainment', on page 122). The Hall also houses the **Russell Collection** of early keyboard instruments for Edinburgh's University's Music Department. ■ *Wed and Sat 1400-1700. £3.*

Further west along the Cowgate is **Magdalen Chapel**, founded in 1541. The unremarkable façade is Victorian but the fine interior is Jacobean and worth a look, in particular to see the only pre-Reformation Scottish stained glass still in its original position. ■ *Mon-Fri 0930-1630; other times by arrangement, T2201450. Free.*

Grassmarket to George IV Bridge The Cowgate passes beneath George IV bridge to become the Grassmarket, a wide cobbled street closed in by tall tenements and dominated by the castle looming overhead. The Grassmarket, formerly the city's cattle market, has been the scene of some of the more notorious incidents in the city's often dark and grisly past. The public gallows were located here and over a hundred hanged Covenanters are commemorated with a cross at its east end. It was in the Grassmarket, in 1763, where Captain Porteous was lynched by an angry mob after he had ordered shots to be fired at them as they watched a public execution. At the west end, in a now vanished close, is where **Burke and Hare** lured their hapless murder victims, whose bodies they then sold to the city's medical schools. The gruesome business finally came to an end when Burke betrayed his partner in crime, who was duly executed in 1829. Today, the Grassmarket is one of the main nightlife centres, with lots of busy restaurants and bars lining its north side. One of these, the *White Hart Inn*, was patronized by Robert Burns.

At the northeastern corner of Grassmarket are the few remaining buildings of the old **West Bow**, which once zig-zagged up to the Royal Mile. It was swept away in the early 19th century and replaced by **Victoria Street**, an attractive two-tiered street with arcaded shops below and a pedestrian terrace above. This curves up from the Grassmarket to **George IV Bridge** and the **National Library of Scotland**, founded in 1682 and one of the largest public libraries in the UK. It holds a rich collection of early printed books and manuscripts, historical documents and the letters and papers of notable national literary figures, which are displayed for the public. ■ *Mon-Sat 1000-1700.*

Greyfriars & around At the southwestern end of George IV Bridge, at the top of Candlemaker Row, is the statue of **Greyfriars Bobby**, the faithful little Skye terrier who watched over the grave of his master John Gray, a shepherd from the Pentland Hills, for 14 years until his own death in 1872. During this time Bobby became something of a local celebrity and was cared for by locals who even gave him his own collar (now in the Huntly House Museum, see page 82), and every day, on hearing the one o'clock gun, he would go to the local pub (now named in his honour) to be fed. By the time of his death, his fame had spread to such an extent that Queen Victoria herself suggested that he be buried beside his master. The little statue, modelled from life and erected soon after his death, is one of the most popular, and sentimental, of Edinburgh's attractions, thanks to a number of tear-jerking movies of the wee dog's life.

The grave that Bobby watched over is the nearby **Greyfriars Kirkyard**, one of Edinburgh's most prestigious burial grounds. Here lie the poet Allan Ramsay, the architects John and Robert Adam, the philanthropist George Heriot (see below), James Douglas, Earl of Morton and Regent of Scotland during James VI's minority, and the poet Duncan Ban McIntyre (1724-1812) whose epic *Beinn Dorain* is considered one of the greatest poems in the Gaelic language.

Greyfriars also has its its sinister tales. Some of the memorials are protected with metal lattices. This was to defeat the efforts of body-snatchers. One woman was buried here while in a trance and awoke when body-snatchers tried to remove the rings from her fingers. Most notorious of all is the tale of George 'Bloody' Mackenzie, former Lord Advocate, who is interred here. Greyfriars is particularly associated with the long struggle to establish the Presbyterian church in Scotland. The kirkyard was the first place where the National Covenant was signed, on 28 February 1638. Later, in 1679, over 1,200 Covenanters were imprisoned by Mackenzie in a corner of the kirkyard for three months, and many died of exposure and starvation. The prison, known as the 'Black Mausoleum', behind the church on the left, is said to be haunted by Mackenzie's evil presence and is visited as part of one of the city's ghost tours (see page 76). **Greyfriars Kirk,** somewhat overshadowed by the graveyard, dates from 1620 and was the first church to be built in Edinburgh after the Reformation.

West of Greyfriars Kirkyard, and reached from Lauriston Place, is **George Heriot's Hospital School**, one of the finest pieces of Renaissance architecture in Scotland. It was founded as a school for the teaching of "puir fatherless bairns" in 1659 by 'Jinglin Geordie' Heriot, James VI's goldsmith, although it had previously been used as a hospital by Cromwell during the Civil War. It is now one of Edinburgh's most prestigious fee-paying schools. You can't go inside but you can wander round the quadrangle and admire the towers, turrets and carved doorways of this fine palatial building. West of George Heriot's, leading north off Lauriston Place, is the **Vennel**, a narrow passage of steps that descends to the Grassmarket. On the eastern side is the best surviving section of the **Flodden Wall**, the old city wall built in the wake of Scotland's disastrous defeat at Flodden in 1513.

Across the road from Greyfriars Bobby, running between George IV Bridge and South Bridge, is Chambers Street, home of two of the best museums in Scotland. On the corner of Chambers Street and George IV Bridge is the **Museum of Scotland**, a striking contemporary building housing a huge number of impressive Scottish collections which were transferred from the National Museum of Antiquities. The museum is a veritable treasure trove of intriguing and important artefacts, including Roman gold and silver, Pictish and Gaelic carved stones and medieval armour. One of the most popular exhibits is 'The Maiden', Edinburgh's once-busy guillotine. The Museum also contains an excellent rooftop restaurant, *The Tower* (see page 109). ■ *Mon-Sat 1000-1700 (Tue till 2000), Sun 1200-1700. Free. Full disabled access to all floors. Free guided tours at 1415 (and 1800 on Tue). T2474422, www.nms.ac.uk*

The Museums & around the University

Edinburgh

You can easily move between the two museums via covered walkways

Further east along Chambers Street, on the same side, is the **Royal Museum of Scotland**. The extensive and eclectic range of collections on display include everything from Classical Greek sculptures to stuffed elephants, from whale skeletons to Native North American totem poles. It's all here, beautifully-presented in a wonderful Victorian building, designed by Captain Francis Fowkes of the Royal Engineers (architect of the Royal Albert Hall in London) and built in 1888 in the style of an Italianate palace. Of particular note is the largely hands-on technology section which features a dazzling collection of machinery of the Industrial Revolution. The magnificent atrium soars high above and makes a very impressive entrance to what is probably the most complete museum in the country. To cap it all, there's a great café (see page 115). ■ *Same opening hours as the Museum of Scotland. T2257534.*

Alongside the Royal Museum is the earliest surviving part of the **University of Edinburgh**, the **Old College**, built between 1789 and 1834, whose main courtyard is reached through the massive arch on Nicolson Street. Edinburgh University is the largest in Scotland, founded in 1582 (the oldest is St Andrews). The finest section is the **upper library**, a magnificent architectural achievement, which is now used for mainly ceremonial occasions, but can be viewed by guided tour in summer. The upper museum hall, once housed the Royal Museum before it moved to its present site, and now is the home of the **Talbot Rice Gallery**, which features the University's collection of Renaissance European painting as well as several temporary exhibitions every year. ■ *Talbot Rice Gallery open Tue-Sat 1000-1700 (daily during the Fesitval). Free. T6502210. There are also free lunchtime guided tours of the Old College 19 Jul-28 Aug, Mon-Sat, starting at 1300 at the reception, T6506379. For more details T6502252.*

Almost opposite the Festival Theatre, at 18 Nicolson Street, is the Royal College of Surgeons, which houses the **Museum of Pathology and Anatomy**, a gruesome freak show of various diseased and abnormal body parts. ■ *Open only by booking well in advance and to groups of at least 12. T5271649.* Hidden behind the Royal College of Surgeons, at 19 Hill Square, is the **Sir Jules Thorn Exhibition of the History of Surgery and Dental Museum**, a bit of a mouthfull but a hidden gem which outlines the history of surgery in the city since the early 16th century. It's all a bit ghoulish but great for kids. ■ *Mon-Fri 1400-1600. Free. T5271600.*

The main University campus is further south, around **George Square**. Among the most notable buildings there is the Faculty of Music's **Reid Concert Hall** (see also page 122), built in 1858 in Italian Renaissance style. The University's chief ceremonial centre is the **McEwan Hall**, a huge Italian-style basilica completed in 1897.

The New Town

The neoclassical New Town, one of the boldest schemes of civic architecture in the history of Europe, is what makes Edinburgh a truly world-class city, every bit as impressive as Paris or Prague, Rome or Vienna. Built in a great burst of creativity between 1767 and 1840, it was the product of the Scottish Enlightenment. Even today, it is still inconceivable how, in the words of one historian, "a small, crowded, almost medieval town, the capital of a comparatively poor country, expanded in a short space of time, without foreign advice or foreign assistance, so as to become one of the enduringly beautiful cities of western Europe."

The New Town was essentially conceived by Edinburgh's forceful Lord Provost (Lord Mayor), **George Drummond**, who wanted his city to be a tribute to the Hanoverian-ruled United Kingdom, which he had helped create. His plan was to extend the city northwards onto a rectangular plateau known as Barefoot Parks, on the far side of the Nor' Loch (north loch) under the Castle Rock. Work began on draining the loch in 1759, to make way for Princes Street Gardens, and, five years later, construction began on the North Bridge, which would give access to the New Town. The following year a competition was announced for the plans and the winner was an unknown 22-year-old architect, **James Craig**. His design symbolized the union of Scotland and England, reflected in many of the street names. The grand central thoroughfare of the First New Town, as the area came to be known, is **George Street**, named in honour of the king. It links two great civic squares, **St Andrew** in the east and St George's (later to become Charlotte) in the west. On either side of George Street, and running parallel to it, are two long lanes, **Thistle Street** and **Rose Street**, symbolizing the national emblems of the two countries. Traversing George Street are **Hanover Street** and **Frederick Street**.

The grid-iron pattern is a model of unity, simplicity and regularity, but its overriding success is the use made of the available space. Princes Street and Queen Street are both singles terraces, facing respectively south to the Castle and north towards the Firth of Forth. The beautiful symmetry of the plan and great views on offer were exploited fully by architect Robert Adam, who contributed greatly to the later phases of the work with many elegant neoclassical buildings. The speed with which the New Town was built is astonishing, considering the quality of the building. By the end of the century most of George Street, Castle Street, Frederick Street and Princes Street was in place as well as **Register House**, the north side of **Charlotte Square**, the **Assembly Rooms and Music Hall**, and **St Andrew's Church**.

The southernmost terrace of the New Town plan was never intended to be the most important, but Princes Street has developed into the city's main thoroughfare and principal shopping street. It is also one of the most visually spectacular streets in the world, because the south side has remained undeveloped, allowing superb uninterrupted views of the Castle Rock, across the valley now occupied by Princes Street Gardens. The north side of the street has lost any semblance of style and is now an undistinguished jumble of modern architecture. Princes Street may be Edinburgh's equivalent of Oxford Street in London, but at least the magnificent view makes walking its length a more pleasant experience.

Princes Street to Queen Street

Everything worthwhile in Princes Street is on the south side, with a few notable exceptions. At the far northeast end of the street is **Register House** (1774-1834), one of Adam's most sumptuous and glorious buildings and now the headquarters of the Scottish Record Office, which stores historical and legal documents – including birth, marriage and death certificates, wills and census records – dating as far back as the 13th century. Unfortunately, the effect of such a superb building is somewhat marred by the **St James Centre**, a huge modern shopping complex that rears its ugly head behind and serves as an unhappy testament to the city's single greatest planning blunder.

Directly opposite is **North Bridge**, originally built in the 1760s as the main artery between the Old and New Towns and completely rebuilt in the late 19th century to span Waverley station. North Bridge runs between the city's main post office and the **Balmoral Hotel**, one of the most luxurious of the city's hotels and a major landmark. Beside the hotel, the **Waverley Market** is a tasteful modern shopping complex, sunk discreetly below street level, and in stark contrast to the St James Centre. The roof gives access to the Tourist Office and forms a nice open-air piazza.

Running along most of the south side of Princes Street are the sunken **Princes Street Gardens**, which were formed by the draining of Nor' Loch in the 1760s and are now a very pleasant place to sit and relax during the summer. Standing in East Princes Street Gardens, is the towering **Scott Monument**, over 200ft high and resembling a huge Gothic spaceship, and built in 1844 as a fitting tribute to one of Scotland's greatest literary figures. Beneath the archway is a statue of Sir Walter Scott, and there are also 64 statuettes of characters from his novels. The monument is open to the public, and a 287-step staircase climbs to a platform near the top of the spire, from where you get wonderful views. ■ *Mar-May and Oct Mon-Sat 0900-1800, Sun 1000-1800; Jun-Sep Mon-Sat 0900-2000, Sun 1000-1800; Nov-Feb 0900-1600. £2.50.* Opposite the Scott Monument is the other notable building on the north side of Princes Street, the elegant 19th-century department store, **Jenners**, Edinburgh's answer to Harrods.

A little further west, Princes Street gardens are divided in two by **The Mound**, a huge artificial slope that runs from George IV Bridge in the Old Town down to

■ Sleeping
1 17 Abercromby Place *A4*
2 Albany & Haldane's Restaurant *A5*
3 Balmoral *B6*
4 Frederick House *B3*
5 Princes Street Backpackers *B5*
6 Sibbett House *A4*

● Eating
1 A Room in the Town *A3*
2 à Table *A3*
3 Bar Napoli *B4*
4 California Coffee Company *B4*
5 Cosmo *B2*
6 Erawan Express *C2*
7 Erawan Oriental *B5*
8 Glass & Thompson *A4*
9 Henderson's Salad Table *B4*
10 Kweilin *A4*
11 Laigh Bake House *A4*

Princes Street, and was formed by dumping the earth excavated during the building of the New Town. At the junction of The Mound and Princes Street are two of Edinburgh's most impressive neoclassical public buildings, the **Royal Scottish Academy** and the **National Gallery of Scotland**, both designed by William Playfair between 1822 and 1845 in the style of Greek temples. The oldest of the two is the Royal Scottish Academy, which presents an annual exhibition by its members from April to July and special exhibitions during the Festival. To the rear of the RSA, the National Gallery of Scotland houses the largest permanent collection of Old Masters outside London, many of which are on loan from The Duke of Sutherland. There are paintings by Raphael, Rubens, El Greco, Titian, Goya, Vermeer and Rembrandt. Also featured are Gaugin, Cezanne, Renoir, Degas, Monet, Van Gogh and Turner, and the Scottish collection is unrivalled with important works by Raeburn, Ramsay, Wilkie and James Drummond. Around the galleries is a wide space which has long been used as Edinburgh's version of Hyde Park Corner. ■ *Mon-Sat 1000-1700, Sun 1200-1700. Free (charges sometimes for loan exhibitions). T6246200, www.natgalscot .ac.uk The RSA is closed for refurbishment and due to reopen in 2003.*

12 Le Café St Honoré B3	● **Pubs & bars**	23 Po-Na-Na B3	4 Stand Comedy Club A5
13 Librizzi's B3	18 Abbotsford B5	24 Rose Street Brewery B4	5 Venue B6
14 Mussel Inn B4	19 Bar 38 C2		
15 Rhodes & Co B5	20 Café Royal Bistro Bar,	○ **Entertainment**	*Related maps*
16 Siam Erawan A3	Circle Bar & Oyster Bar	1 Assembly Rooms B4	*A New Town:*
17 Tampopo &	B5	2 Hill Street Theatre B3	*Calton Hill, page 96*
Henderson's Bistro B4	21 Guildford Arms B5	3 Ross Open Air Theatre	*B Old Town, page 86*
	22 Kenilworth C3	C3	*C West Edinburgh,*
			page 100

On the other side of The Mound is **West Princes Street Gardens**, beautifully located right under the steep sides of Castle Rock. At the entrance is the world's oldest Floral Clock, which is laid out every year with over 20,000 plants. Further west is the **Ross Open Air Theatre**, used for various musical events, particularly during the Festival and at Hogmanay. Behind it a footbridge crosses the railway line and a path leads to the ruined **Wellhouse Tower**, one of the oldest buildings in the city, dating from the reign of David II (1329-71).

At the far western corner of Princes Street Gardens, below the junction of Princes Street and Lothian Road, is **St Cuthbert's Church and Churchyard**. This is the oldest church site in the city, dating back to the reign of Malcolm III, though the present church was mostly built in the 1890s. The churchyard is worth visiting and a peaceful refuge from the Princes Street traffic. Here lies Thomas de Quincey (1785-1859), author of *Confessions of an English Opium Eater*, a classic account of drug addiction in the early 19th century. De Quincey spent the last years of his life in Edinburgh, the city featured in Irvine Welch's late-20th-century tale of drug addiction, *Trainspotting*.

Running to the north and parallel to Princes Street is **George Street**, a bustling thoroughfare of upmarket shops, banks, offices and fashionable bars and restaurants. At the eastern end is **St Andrew Square**, which began life as a fashionable residential area. The most impressive building, on the eastern side of the square, is the headquarters of The Royal Bank of Scotland. This handsome 18th-century town house was originally the home of Sir Laurence Dundas, but was remodelled in the 1850s when the wonderful domed ceiling was added. The Royal Bank was only one of the many banks, insurance, business and legal firms to occupy premises here and it is now one of the wealthiest business squares in Europe. In the centre of the square is the massive 100 ft pillar, carrying the statue of the lawyer and statesman Henry Dundas, first Viscount Melville (1742-1811), chief ally of William Pitt the Younger and once described as the "absolute dictator of Scotland".

A few hundred yards along George Street the **Assembly Rooms and Music Hall** (1787) once the social hub of the New Town and now a major Fringe venue. Opposite is the oval-shaped St Andrew's Church, now known as the **Church of St Andrew and St George**. The church is famous as the scene of the 'Great Disruption' of 1843, when the Church of Scotland was split in two. The 'evangelicals', led by Thomas Chalmers, went on to form the Free Church of Scotland, which proclaimed a much stricter but more democratic form of Presbyterianism.

At the western end of the street is **Charlotte Square**, designed by Robert Adam in 1791 and considered by most to be his masterpiece. Like its counterpart, St Andrew Square, Charlotte Square was originally purely residential, but is now the heart of the city's financial community, home to bankers, investment-fund managers, stockbrokers, corporate lawyers, accountants and insurance executives. Charlotte Square has long been the most prestigious address in the city, particularly the **north side**, the oldest part and the best preserved. Number six is the official residence of the Secretary of State for Scotland. The upper floors of number seven are the official residence of the Moderator of the General Assembly of the Church of Scotland, while the lower floors are open to the public as the **Georgian House**, which gives a fascinating insight into how Edinburgh's gentry lived in the late 18th century. The house has been lovingly restored by the NTS and is crammed with period furniture and hung with fine paintings, including portraits by Ramsay and Raeburn. In the basement the wine cellar and kitchen are also authentically reconstructed. The National Trust for Scotland has its head offices on the south side at number 27. ■ *1 Mar-31 Oct Mon-Sat 1000-1700, Sun 1400-1700; Nov-Dec Mon-Sat 1100-1600, Sun 1400-1600. £5, £4 concession . T2263318.*

On the west side of the square is St George's Church, originally designed by Adam but following his death in 1792 the plans were abandoned on grounds of cost and the building you see today was built in 1811 by Robert Reid. In the 1960s it was refurbished as **West Register House** (part of the Scottish Record Office). It is open to the public and features displays of historical documents. ■ *Mon-Fri 1000-1600. Free.*

Parallel to George Street, and slightly downhill from it, is **Queen Street**, the most northerly terrace of James Craig's New Town plan, bordered by Queen Street Gardens to the north. This was a prime residential area of the New Town, with excellent views across the Firth of Forth towards Fife, and the air of exclusivity has been maintained, in that the gardens are accessible only to key holders who live nearby.

The only public building of interest here is the **Scottish National Portrait Gallery**, at the far eastern end of the street, a huge late-19th-century red sandstone building, modelled on the Doge's Palace in Venice. The gallery contains a huge range of pictures of notable Scots from the 16th century to the present day. It also has a good café (see page 116). ■ *Mon-Sat 1000-1700, Sun 1400-1700 (till 1800 and from 1100 on Sun during the festival. Free. T6246200.*

In the first few decades of the 19th century there were major extensions to the original New Town, spreading to the north, west and east, and all in keeping with the neoclassical theme. Perhaps the most interesting of the New Town extensions is the area around Calton Hill, another of Edinburgh's dead volcanoes, which grew beyond the east end of Princes Street.

Calton Hill

The slopes of Calton Hill are covered with many fine buildings, which probably earned Edinburgh the epithet 'Athens of the North'. You could take a circular route, clockwise right round the hill, starting from Leith Walk and heading along **Royal Terrace**, **Calton Terrace**, **Regent Terrace**, **Regent Road** and **Waterloo Place**, which leads into the east end of Princes Street. The best of the buildings are to be found in the magnificent sweep of Regent Terrace, hailed as the most beautiful of all Regency terraces in Britain, with fantastic views across to Arthur's Seat and Salisbury Crags.

On Regent Road, 200 yards east of the junction with Regent Terrace, is the former **Royal High School**, perhaps the finest of all Edinburgh's Greek temples. It was built in 1825-29 by Thomas Hamilton, a former pupil of the school and architect of the **Robert Burns Monument**, which stands on the opposite side of the road. The Royal High is the oldest school in Scotland, dating back to the 12th century (the previous premises were near the Cowgate in the Old Town), and its long list of famous former pupils includes Robert Adam, Sir Walter Scott and Alexander Graham Bell. The school moved premises in 1970, to the western outskirts of the city.

The High School had been proposed as the seat of the new Scottish Parliament back in the 1970s. It is now the Scottish HQ of the Crown Office

Further west on Regent Road, on the south side, is **St Andrews House**, a massive Art Deco structure housing government offices, built on the site of **Calton Jail**. Until 1864, public executions were carried out on top of the jail, watched by crowds who stood opposite on the slopes to the south of the City Observatory (see below). The only part of the jail that remains is the castellated **Governor's House**, which looks onto the **Old Calton Burial Ground**, on the south side of Waterloo Place. The slightly spooky cemetery contains Robert Adam's tower built for the great empiricist David Hume, Thomas

Hamilton's obelisk to the political martyrs of 1793 and a memorial to the Scottish-American soldiers who fought in the American Civil War, complete with a statue of Abraham Lincoln. You may come across a mausoleum to Robert Burns, but this is for the architect of the Nelson Monument and not to be confused with the poet Robert Burns.

Another of the absolute musts for visitors to Edinburgh is to climb to the top of **Calton Hill**, via the stairs at the east end of Waterloo Place. The views from the top are simply stunning, especially up the length of Princes Street and the sweep of the Forth Estuary. Calton Hill is also the site of anarchic pagan festivities at the feast of **Beltane** in May, and at night it's a popular cruising area for the nearby gay community. On the west side of the hill, overlooking the St James Centre, is the old **City Observatory**, built by Playfair in 1818 for his uncle, a renowned mathematician and philosopher. It was abandoned in 1895 when light pollution became too great and relocated to Blackford Hill (see page 103). The observatory equipment is still used by students and the small, domed pavilion now houses the **Edinburgh Experience**, a 20-minute

New Town: Calton Hill

Sleeping	Eating	Bars & pubs
1 Carlton Greens *D5*	1 Blue Moon *B1*	6 Barony Bar *B1*
2 Ecosse International *A3*	2 Lost Sock Diner *B1*	7 Baroque *C1*
3 Royal Terrace *C4*	3 Nexus Café *B1*	8 Basement *C1*
	4 Tapas Tree *C2*	9 Mathers *C1*
	5 Valvona & Crolla *B3*	10 Outhouse *C2*

3-D presentation of the city's history. ■ *Apr-Oct daily 1000-1700. £2, £1.20 child*. The observatory complex also contains the **Old Observatory**, a fantasy Gothic castle and the last surviving building of James Craig, the designer of the New Town.

Calton Hill is full of monuments of all shapes and sizes. Southwest of the observatory is the **Monument to Dugald Stewart** (1753-1828), a Playfair construction commemorating an obscure University professor. A little further south, overlooking Regent Road, is **Nelson's Monument**, a 108-ft tower built in 1816 to commemorate Nelson's victory at the Battle of Trafalgar. It's a strange-looking structure, built in the shape of an upturned telescope, and every day, at precisely one o' clock, a large ball is still dropped from the mast at the top to mark the time for ships in the Firth of Forth. It's worth climbing to the top of the monument, for the panoramic views are even better. ■ *Apr-Sep Mon 1300-1600, Tue-Sat 1000-1600; Oct-Mar Mon-Sat 1000-1500. £2.* Standing beside Nelson's monument is the **National Monument**, an over-ambitious project begun in 1822 by Playfair as a memorial to those who fell in the Napoleonic Wars. The intention was to build a replica of the Parthenon in Athens, incorporating catacombs for the burial of Scotland's greatest figures, but the money ran out and it never got further than what you can see today – 12 huge columns which have come to be known as 'Edinburgh's Disgrace'.

The Northern New Town

The earliest of the New Town extensions, begun in 1803, was the Northern New Town, which extends downhill from Queen Street Gardens, as far as Fettes Row to the north and bounded to the west by the Water of Leith and Broughton Street to the east. This area is the best preserved of the New Town extensions and has retained its residential character.

The latest, and finest, part of the northern development, begun in 1822, is the **Moray Estate**, to the east of Queensferry Street, designed by James Gillespie Graham, another of Edinburgh's architectural geniuses. This part of the New Town is characterized by gracious curves and circles, none finer than **Moray Place**, a magnificent twelve-sided circus. From Moray Place you can head east into **Heriot Row**, the southernmost avenue of the Northern New Town, where Robert Louis Stevenson spent most of his life (at number 17).

To the northwest, straddling both

11 Pivo Caffe *D2*
12 Planet Out *C2*

○ **Entertainment**
1 CC Blooms *C2*
2 Ego *C2*
3 Playhouse Theatre *C2*

Related maps
A Old Town, page 86
B New Town, page 92

Edinburgh

sides of the Water of Leith to the east of Dean Bridge, is the old village of **Stockbridge**, a fascinating bazaar of antique shops, second-hand bookstores and various other bohemian-type outlets (see page 125), with a fair number of good restaurants and bars . The residential streets on the far side of the river were developed by the painter Henry Raeburn. The most notable of these is **Ann Street**, named after Raeburn's wife and described by the poet Sir John Betjeman as "the most attractive street in Britain". It is now one of the most prestigious addresses in the city and is the only street in the New Town whose houses each have a front garden. Nearby is **Danube Street**, once home to Edinburgh's most notorious brothel, and now the epitome of middle-class decency.

The eastern 'boundary' of the Northern New Town is formed by **Broughton Street**, which, along with the area around the Playhouse Theatre, is the centre of the city's thriving gay scene (see page 130), with numerous bars, clubs, cafés and restaurants. On the corner of Broughton Street and East London Street, is **Mansfield Place Church**, a late-19th-century neo-Norman edifice, now famous as the site of an amazing scheme of Pre-Raphaelite murals by **Phoebe Traquair**, a leading light in the Scottish Arts and Crafts Movement. These murals were created by her over eight years (1893-1901), working alone seven days a week without pay. They have suffered badly due to years of neglect but will hopefully be restored in the near future. Her work can also be seen on the walls of the Song School at **St Mary's Cathedral** (see above).

Further north, beyond the northern boundary of the New Town and the Water of Leith, is the district of Inverleith, where you'll find Edinburgh's gorgeous **Royal Botanic Garden**, on Inverleith Row. Contained within its 72 acres is a mind-boggling variety of plants and trees, as well as walkways, ornamental gardens, various hothouses and huge open spaces, with not a dog poo in sight. Many of the exotic species you can see were discovered by Scottish collectors during their expeditions around the globe. There's an awful lot to enjoy, but particularly notable are the outdoor rock garden, the huge

A walk along the Water of Leith

One of the best ways to escape the traffic fumes is to take a stroll along the Water of Leith, Edinburgh's picturesque river, which can be walked beside for most of its length. The walkway runs from Roseburn, past the Gallery of Modern Art, through Dean Village, past the Royal Botanic Garden, then a short walk along the road at Canonmills before passing Warriston cemetery and on down to Leith docks.

Particularly charming is the walk upstream from Stockbridge, into the verdant gorge under the Dean Bridge, where the running water blocks out any traffic noise. At Dean Village you can either continue up the riverside towards the Gallery of Modern Art, or turn right, up the steep slope of Dean Path to Dean Cemetery.

Victorian Palm House, the amazing Glasshouse Experience and the new Chinese Garden, featuring the largest collection of Chinese wild plants outside China. At the southern end of the gardens, at the highest point, is **Inverleith House**, a fine Georgian mansion which stages a changing programme of exhibitions. The Terrace Café is a good place for lunch (see page 116), with stupendous views across the New Town to the castle. ■ *Nov-Feb daily from 1000-1600; till 1800 Mar-Apr and Sep-Oct; till 2000 May-Aug. Free, but voluntary donations welcome. Take buses 8, 17, 23 and 27 from city centre. T5527171.*

West Edinburgh

The western extension of the New Town followed a couple of years after the eastern extension and spread southwest from Shandwick Place, along West Maitland Street to **Haymarket**, whose railway station was built in 1840 as the original terminus of the line from Glasgow, before it was extended east to

Edinburgh

Waverley. It also spread northwest along Queensferry Street towards **Melville Street**, the most impressive thoroughfare in the West End. At its western end in Palmerston Place, is **St Mary's Cathedral**, the second-largest church in Scotland, designed by George Gilbert Scott in Gothic style, and featuring a set

West Edinburgh

Sleeping		Eating		7 Lune Town *C2*
1 Bonham *A1*		1 Atrium & blue *C4*		8 Ndbele *F5*
2 Caledonian *B4*		2 Bar Roma *A3*		9 Oriental Dining
3 Point *D5*		3 Indian Cavalry Club *C2*		Centre & Henry's
4 Simpsons *E5*		4 Indigo Yard *A3*		Cellar Bar *D4*
5 St Mary's Music School *C1*		5 Jasmine Chinese *C4*		10 Sukothai *E5*

Related maps
A Old Town, *page 86*
B New Town, *page 92*

N

0 metres 100

of murals by Phoebe Traquair (see previous page).

Queensferry Street follows the old coaching route to South Queensferry (see page 133) and soon reaches the wooded valley of the **Water of Leith**, the little river which flows from the Pentland Hills to the port of Leith where it enters the Firth of Forth. The road crosses the steep valley along the 100-ft-high **Dean Bridge**, a remarkable feat of engineering, built by Thomas Telford in the 1830s. At one time, the Water of Leith powered over 70 mills and below the bridge is **Dean Village**, a picturesque old milling community which has been revitalized with the conversion of some of the mills into designer flats. From here you can walk along the river into neighbouring Stockbridge, past **St Bernard's Well**, a mineral spring covered by a mock Doric temple. It has recently been restored and is sometimes open to the public, but take note that the waters were once described as having "a slight resemblance in flavour to the washings of a foul gun barrel".

At the north end of Dean Bridge, to the west of Trinity Church, is **Dean Cemetery**, one of Edinburgh's finest places of final rest. The cemetery houses the graves of the likes of architect William Playfair, pioneering photographer Octavius Hill, and Dr Joseph Bell, who is said to have been the flesh-and-blood inspiration for Arthur Conan Doyle's character Sherlock Holmes. It also contains many excellent examples of 19th-century sculpture.

About 10 minutes' walk from Dean Village, set in spacious wooded grounds along Belford Road, is the **Scottish National Gallery of Modern Art**, which is definitely worth visiting, even if you know *nada* about Dada. It opened to the public in 1984 as the first ever gallery in Britain devoted to 20th century art. The hugely-impressive permanent collection features everything from the Impressionists to Hockney and is now second in Britain

Edinburgh

**Map labels:**
George St
Rose Street North La
Rose St
Rose Street South La
Rose Street South La
Castle St
Street La
Princes St
Princes St Gardens
Castle
King's Stables Rd
OLD TOWN
Castle Terr
Johnston Terr
Castle Terr
Cornwall St
King's Stables Rd
Spittal St
King's Stables La
West Port
Bread St
Lady Lawson St
Fountainbridge
Riego St
High Riggs
Lauriston St
Edinburgh College of Art
Lauriston Pl
Chalmers
Lauriston Pk
Glen St
Lauriston Gdns
Brougham Pl
Panmure Pl
Drumdryan St
Brougham St
Home St
Tarvit St
Lonsdale Terr
Valleyfield St
Leven Terr
Leven St
Glengyle Terr

B

only to the Tate Museums in London. It is particularly strong on Expressionism, with works by Picasso, Cezanne, Matisse, Magritte, Mondrain, Henry Moore, Kandinsky, Klee, Giacometti and Sickert all displayed, among many other important names, including many contemporary Scottish artists. There are also frequent temporary exhibitions, and don't miss the excellent café, especially if the sun is shining (see page 116). Across the street is the new **Dean Gallery** (same opening hours as above and also free), featuring the work of Edinburgh-born artist Sir Eduardo Paolozzi. It also houses a major Dada and Surrealist collection and exhibitions of contemporary art. ■ *Both galleries open Mon-Sat 1000-1700, Sun 1400-1700. Free. A free bus leaves the National Gallery and visits the Portrait Gallery then these galleries. It leaves the National Gallery at 1100 and every hour on the hour till 1600. For more details T6246200.*

Three miles west of the city centre, is **Edinburgh's Zoo**, by far the largest in Scotland, set in 80 acres on the side of Corstorphine Hill. Whatever you think of zoos, this one is highly respected for its serious work as well as being an enormous amount of fun. There are over 1,000 animals from all over the world, but the zoo is best known for its penguins – the largest breeding colony of Antarctic penguins anywhere outside Antarctica itself. You can watch the famous penguin parade at 1400 daily (March-October weather permitting) and see them swimming underwater in the world's largest penguin pool. The latest attractions are the endangered Asiatic lions and the Magic Forest, full of marmosets and tamarins. There are also animal handling sessions, available at an extra £1 per person, and afternoon animal talks (ask for details at the zoo entrance). ■ *Apr-Sep daily 0900-1800; Oct-Mar 0900-1630. £7, £4 child. T3349171, www.edinburghzoo .org.uk, there are numerous buses from Haymarket and Princes St.*

South Edinburgh

■ Sleeping	● Eating	
1 Armadillo Guest House *A1*	1 Ann Purna *A4*	5 Engine Shed Café *A4*
2 Cruachan Guest House *A1*	2 Apartment *A1*	6 Favorit *A2*
3 Edinburgh First *B6*	3 California Coffee	7 Howies *A4, B1*
4 Prestonfield House *B6*	Company *A3/A4*	8 Isabel's Café *A4*
5 Town House *A1*	4 Dragon Way *B4*	9 Kaffe Politik *B2*
		10 Kalpna *A4*

South Edinburgh

The city also developed south from the Old Town, creating a district which became known as **Southside** and which today forms the heart of the University quarter. Beyond this area, and the open parkland of the **Meadows** and **Bruntsfield Links**, are the residential suburbs of **Merchiston, Marchmont, Newington** and **Morningside**. The latter has traditionally been the home of Edinburgh's elite, or 'crème de la crème', as Miss Jean Brodie might have put it in her Morningside accent, renowned for its "rifained zenzitivity".

To the south of Marchmont are the **Braid Hills**, which are mostly occupied by two golf courses, part of a great ring of golf courses that almost completely encircle the city. The hills are ideal for a Sunday walk. Beyond Morningside, Comiston Road leads south past **Blackford Hill** (539 ft), at the top of which stands the city's **Royal Observatory**. Visitors can find out all about the mysteries of the solar system, play with various hands-on exhibits and enjoy the panoramic views of the city. ■ *Mon-Sat 1000-1700, Sun 1200-1700. £3.50, £2.50child, £2 concession. T6688405. Take buses 40 or 41 from The Mound and get off at Blackford Av, or walk from Comiston Rd.* At the foot of Blackford Hill, on Blackford Glen Road, is the starting point for the **Hermitage of Braid** nature trail, a lovely gentle walk along the Braid Burn. The track is easy to follow and although the hill is within the city, there's a real sense of being out in the countryside. The path takes you to Hermitage House, an 18th-century mansion which now serves as an information centre. ■ *Mon-Fri 1000-1600, Sun (Apr-Sep only) 1100-1800.*

Edinburgh

11 Metropole *B4*	● **Bars & pubs**	○ **Entertainment**
12 Montpeliers *B1*	16 Bar Ce Lona *A4*	1 King's Theatre *A2*
13 Phenecia *A3*	17 Bennet's Bar *A2*	2 Queen's Hall *A4*
14 Susie's Diner *A4*	18 Pear Tree *A4*	
15 Wok Bar *A3*		

Related maps
A Old Town, page 86
B West Edinburgh, page 100

Leith and Newhaven

Leith is a good 20-min walk from the top of Leith Walk, or you can take one of the many buses which head that way. Near the top of Leith Walk is a statue of Sherlock Holmes, whose creator, Sir Arthur Conan Doyle, lived nearby

Leith Walk leads from Princes Street down to the port of **Leith**, which has a distinct flavour all of its own. There has been a settlement here for over 800 years and the harbour has been used commercially since Edward I captured Berwick for England in 1296. Leith became a burgh in its own right in 1833 and only became integrated into the city of Edinburgh in 1920. In its heyday, Leith was Scotland's major port. Ships exported coal, salt, fish, paper, leather and local ale and returned with grain, timber, wine and foreign delicacies, from Northern Europe and as far afield as North America and Australia

Up until the 1950s, Leith and nearby **Granton** supported large deep-sea fishing fleets and were landing thousands of whales every year. Between the two ports the shoreline was lined with shipyards, dry docks, breaking yards and repair yards. When the fishing and shipping trade decanted south, the heart was ripped out of Leith. Much of its old centre was replaced with grim housing schemes and the port area fell into decay. However, the old port's fortunes have changed in recent years and Leith has been turned around. Millions have been spent on restoring many of its fine historic buildings, and it is now one of the best parts of the city for eating and drinking, with scores of fashionable restaurants, bistros and bars (see pages 114 and 120). At the same time private developers have been converting old warehouses and office buildings into expensive dockside flats.

The old port still has its rough edges, and you'll need to be careful after dark, but it's worth a visit, especially **The Shore**, the road which follows the last stretch of the Water of Leith before it reaches the Firth of Forth. In the adjoining streets are some of the most notable buildings to have been given a face-lift, such as the old **Customs House** on Commercial Street, **Trinity House** on Kirkgate and the former **Town Hall** on Constitution Street. Set

Leith

● **Sleeping**
1 Malmaison *A3*

● **Eating**
1 Fishers *A2*

2 (fitz)henry *B2*
3 Martin Wishart *B2*
4 Shore *A2*
5 Skippers *A2*
6 Vintners Rooms *B2*

7 Waterfront *A2*

● **Pubs & bars**
8 Bar Java *B3*
9 King's Wark *B2*

Edinburgh

back from The Shore is **Lamb's House**, a well-preserved Renaissance house, which was the home of Andro Lamb, the merchant with whom Mary, Queen of Scots spent her first night on her return to Scotland in 1561. It is now used as an old people's day centre.

Leith's main attractions is the **Royal Yacht Britannia**, which is now moored at its own purpose-built Ocean Terminal, complete with swanky restaurants, bars and shops. The old ship is well worth visiting, despite the rather steep entrance charge, and a genuine and fascinating insight into the lives of the royals. It's like stepping into a 1950s time warp and you'll be amazed (or appalled) at the sheer ordinariness of it all. ■ *Mon-Fri 1030-1630, Sat/Sun 0930-1630; till 1930 fri-Sun in Aug. £7.75, £5.95 concession, £3.75 child. To pre-book tickets T5555566 (daily 0900-1730) or at the Tattoo Office, 32 Market St. Guide Friday and LRT buses (No X50) run a shuttle bus to and from Waverley Bridge every 20 mins from 1010 (0950 Sat/Sun Mar-Oct) till 1605 Mon-Fri and 1650 Sat/Sun (till 1910 Fri-Sun in Aug).*

A mile west of Leith is the little port of Newhaven, once a busy fishing community and one of the most colourful and interesting parts of Edinburgh. The fishing has now gone and though the little fishermen's cottages have been restored, there is no life left in the place, other than the occasional pleasure yacht in the harbour. The village's proud maritime past is told in the excellent **Newhaven Heritage Museum**, 24 Pier Place. The little, one-room museum has hands-on exhibits, a dressing-up box, evocative living history recordings and various activities for children. ■*Daily 1200-1700, free, T5514165, take bus 7, 10, 11 or 16 from Leith Walk.*

Newhaven
Next door to the museum is Harry Ramsden's fish & chip shop biut it's worth heading further west along the seafront to the Starbank Inn

Essentials

Sleeping

As you'd expect in Scotland's major tourist city, Edinburgh has a huge selection of places to stay, more than any other place in Britain outside London. Many of the **hotels** are concentrated in the New Town and the West End, particularly around Princes St, Calton Hill and the streets north of Haymarket station. There are also hundreds of **guest houses** and **B&Bs** dotted all over the city. There are several areas which have a particularly high concentration, all within about 2 miles of the centre and all on main bus routes, such as Bruntsfield and Mayfield, both south of the centre, Pilrig, east of the city centre heading towards Leith, and west from Haymarket along the Corstorphine Rd. Many hotels offer good deals during the low season, especially at weekends, and also offer a standby room rate throughout the year. This can save a lot of money but can also involve a lot of frustrating legwork.

There are also 4 official **SYHA hostels** and several **independent hostels**, most of which are convenient, and a couple of **campsites** which are not too far from the centre. Most of the universities and colleges offer **campus accommodation**, but this is neither cheap nor centrally located. Another option, if you're staying a week or more, is **self-catering**, which is cost-effective, or you can **rent** a room or flat (see page 108).

If you arrive in Edinburgh without a reservation, particularly during the festival, or at Hogmanay, the chances are you won't find a room anywhere near the centre. It pays to **book well in advance**. The **Tourist Information Centre** (see page 71) sends out its accommodation brochure for free so that you can book a place yourself, or their Central Reservations Service, T4733855, centres@eltb.org, will make a reservation for you, for a non-refundable fee of £5. *Thomas Cook* has a hotel reservation service which also

Edinburgh

charges £5 for bookings. They have three branches, at Waverley Steps, near the TIC, T5570905, at Waverley station, T5570034, and at the airport, T3335119. They are open 0700-2230 (bookhotel@cordex.co.uk).

Old Town **L-B** *Apex International Hotel*, 31-35 Grassmarket, T3003456, www.apexhotels .co.uk 168 rooms. Large, recently converted former University building in the heart of the Old Town. Good value, though top floor rooms with castle views are more expensive. **L** *Crowne Plaza Hotel*, 80 High St, T5579797, F5579789, www.crowneplazaed .co.yk 238 rooms. Slap bang in the heart of it all, halfway between the castle and Holyrood Palace. Parking, gym and indoor pool. **L** *Scotsman Hotel*, North Bridge, T5565565, www.scotsmanhotel.co.uk 68 rooms and suites. The former offices of the eponymous newspaper have been transformed into a 5-star hotel where guests can sleep in the newsroom and drink in the features department.

B *Bank Hotel*, 1 South Bridge, T5569043. 9 individually-themed rooms. Well-situated on the corner of the Royal Mile and good value. Lively bar downstairs (*Logie Baird's*). **B** *Hotel Ibis*, 6 Hunter Sq, T2407000, F2407007. 99 rooms. Part of the *Accor* group. Modern hotel handy for everything. Breakfast extra. Low-season discounts.

C-D *Thistle Inn*, 94 Grassmarket. T2202299. 29 rooms. Basic but close to the action and ideal for those who stay out late.

F *Brodie's Backpacker Hostel*, 12 High St, T5566770, F5588400. High-quality hostel with good range of facilities. Weekly rates of £60 per week. **E-F** *Central Youth Hostel*, 4 Robertson Close, Cowgate, open 1 Jul-1 Sep. For bookings, contact the Eglinton SYHA (T3371120, eglinton@syha.org.uk) **E** *Cowgate Tourist Hostel*, 94-116 Cowgate, Old Town, T/F2262153, F2267355. 42 rooms. **F** in low season. Basic but good facilities and location and no curfew. **E-F** *Edinburgh Backpackers Hostel*, 65 Cockburn St, T2201717, info@hoppo.com Just off the Royal Mile, therefore busy and noisy. No curfew. 97 beds in 10 dorms, 3 doubles and 1 triple. **F** *Castle Rock Hostel*, 15 Johnston Terr, T2259666, castle-rock@scotlands-top-hostels.com Prime location below the castle. Vast building with 150 beds in various dorms. Same group as the High St and Royal Mile Hostels. **F** *High Street Hostel*, 8 Blackfriars St, Old Town, T5573984, high-street@scotlands-top-hostels.com. Cheap, lively and right in the heart of things. No curfew. Long-established backpacker hang-out. Close by is its wee sister, **F** *Royal Mile Backpackers*, at 105 High St, Old Town, T5576120, which is also lively and great value. They also have hostels in Inverness, Fort William, Oban, Glasgow and on Skye.

New Town **L-B** *Albany Hotel*, 39-43 Albany St, T5560397, F5576633. 21 rooms. New Town Georgian elegance only a few minutes from Princes Street. Its excellent basement restaurant, *Haldane's* is listed on page 111. **L** *Balmoral Hotel*, 1 Princes St, T5562414, F5573747, www.rfhotels.com/balmoral 184 rooms. Located above Waverley station, this city landmark is superior in every sense. Its main restaurant, *The Grill*, is excellent and the brasserie, *Hadrian's*, is listed on page 111. **L** *Channings*, South Learmonth Gdns, T3152226/3323232, F3329631, reserve@ channings.co.uk. 48 rooms. Cosy and stylish sister hotel to *The Howard*. Formed from 5 traditional townhouses, with great views from the top floor. Its brasserie is also highly rated. **L** *The Howard*, 34 Great King St, T5573500, F5576515, reserve@thehoward.com. 15 rooms. Beautiful Georgian townhouse famous for its chintzy luxury. Its basement restaurant, *36*, is one of the city's finest and is listed under 'Eating'. **L** *Royal Terrace Hotel*, 18 Royal Terr, T5573222, F5575334. 110 rooms. Exquisitely furnished rooms, most with whirlpool spa. The last word in decadent over-indulgence.

B-D *Carlton Greens*, 2 Carlton Terr, T5566570, T5576680, www.british-trust-hotels. co.uk 26 en suite rooms. Georgian townhouse hotel on a quiet street at the bottom of Calton Hill. Good quality rooms at good value. **B-D** *Frederick House Hotel*, 42 Frederick St, T2261999, F6247064, www.townhousehotels.co.uk 45 en suite rooms. Newly refurbished townhouse in the heart of the town. Prices includes breakfast in *Café Rouge* opposite. **B** *17 Abercromby Place*, 17 Abercromby Pl, T5578036, F5583453. 9 rooms. Classic townhouse hotel and former home of renowned New Town architect, William Playfair. Sumptuous style and superb views.

C *Sibbett House*, 26 Northumberland St, T5561078. 5 rooms. Friendly, intimate Georgian townhouse that even includes the odd 'skirl o' the pipes' by the host. **C** *Stuart House*, 12 East Claremont St, T5579030, stuarto@globalnet.co.uk. 6 rooms. No smoking. Tastefully refurbished Georgian townhouse on the east side of the New Town.

D *Six*, Mary's Place, 6 Mary's Pl, Raeburn Pl, T3328965, sixmarysplace@ btinternet.com 8 rooms. Non-smoking guest house on busy Stockbridge main street. Friendly, informal atmosphere. Offers good vegetarian cooking. There are many good guesthouses off Leith Walk. These include: **D** *Ecosse Internatinal*, 15 McDonald Rd, T5564967. 5 rooms. Cosy guesthouse close to Broughton St. Their warm welcome includes a wee dram; **E** *Balquhidder Guest House*, 94 Pilrig St, T5543377. 5 rooms. Victorian former church manse with lots of character, 10-15 minutes' walk from Princes St.

There are 2 SYHA hostels, one at either end of Princes St: **F** *Princes Street Back-p*ackers, 5 West Register St, T5566984. Behind *Burger King* at the east end of Princes St near St Andrews Sq. Cheap, basic and very popular. Great value breakfast and free Sun dinner. The same people also run **F** *Princes Street West Backpackers*, 3-4 Queensferry St, West End, T/F2262939, princes.west@cabinet.co.uk. With bar, cable TV and email facilities. Also free Sun dinner and 7th consecutive night is free.

West Edinburgh

L *The Bonham*, 35 Drumsheugh Gdns, T2266050, F2266080, reserve@ thebonham.com 48 rooms. This trio of townhouses was turned into a hotel in 1998. Rooms are all decorated differently in trendy, yet elegant contemporary styles. The suites have lofty ceilings and the bath and 3-poster beds are so big you could get lost in them. The superb restaurant is listed on page 113. **L** *Caledonian Hotel*, Princes St, T4599988, F2258221. 246 rooms. Prestigious, luxurious and salubrious, this West End institution underwent a recent multi-million-pound refurbishment and now includes a sports club (open to the public). Its excellent and expensive main restaurant, *The Pompadour*, is still a great culinary experience but has lost something of its former glory.

B *Point Hotel*, 34 Bread St, T2215555, F2219929, www.point-hotel.co.uk 140 en suite rooms. This former Co-op department store has been stylishly refurbished and is now the height of contemporary chic and minimalist elegance. The suites are huge and some have jacuzzis. Handily placed for the castle and Royal Mile. Its bar and grill, *Mondobbo*, is equally stylish and is listed on page 120. **B** *Simpsons*, 79 Lauriston Pl, T6227979, F6227900, www.simpsons-hotel.com 58 en suite rooms. Former maternity hospital offering smart, comfortable and airy rooms. Breakfast not included but available at *Whereto?* café opposite.

C-D *West End Hotel*, 35 Palmerston Pl, T2253656, F2254393. 8 rooms. Good location and good value. Popular with visiting Highlanders and therefore a good selection of whiskies in the bar.

E-F *Belford Hostel*, 6-8 Douglas Gdns, T2216209 (bookings T0800-0966868), info@hoppo.com 98 beds in small dorms, also double rooms. About a mile from the West End near Dean Village and the Gallery of Modern Art. Plenty of entertainment and facilities and no curfew. It may be a converted church, but don't expect any quiet reflection. **F** *Eglinton Youth Hostel*, 18 Eglinton Cres, West End, T3371120. SYHA hostel in a quiet street about 1 mile west of the centre, near Haymarket train station. 160 beds, most in dorms but also 12 rooms for 4. Includes continental breakfast. Doors closed at 0200 and hostel closed in Dec.

Edinburgh

Edinburgh

South Edinburgh

L-A *Prestonfield House Hotel*, Priestfield Rd, Prestonfield, T6683346, F6683976. Magnificent 17th-century mansion with period features, set in its own 13 acres of gardens below Arthur's Seat with Highland cattle and peacocks strutting around. All this only five minutes from Princes Street. A new wing was added recently, increasing the number of rooms to 31. The expensive restaurant is not the best around by any means, but dining here is something special. **L-B** *The Bruntsfield Hotel*, 69 Bruntsfield Pl, T2291393, bruntsfield@queensferry- hotels.co.uk. 50 rooms. Large, comfortable hotel in a quiet area overlooking Bruntsfield Links, one mile south of Princes Street. Its restaurant, *The Potting Shed*, serves excellent modern Scottish cuisine.

C *Teviotdale House Hotel*, 53 Grange Loan, T6674376, teviotdale.house@ btinternet.com   7 rooms. No smoking. Quiet refinement, great value and wonderful breakfasts. **D** *Sherwood Guest House*, 42 Minto St, T6671200, sherwdedin @aol.com. 5 rooms. Non-smoking Georgian townhouse in a street full of guest houses and B&Bs. Minto Street continues into Mayfield Gdns, where there's also plenty of places to stay, including the very good **C-E** *International Guest House*, at number 37, T6672511, intergh@easynet.co.uk

D *The Town House*, 65 Gilmore Pl, T2291985, www.thetownhouse.com 5 rooms. No smoking. Very nice Victorian guest house in a street full of similar accommodation, such as **D-E** *Cruachan Guest House*, No 53, T/F2296219, janette@cruachan9. freeserve.co.uk and **D-E** *Armadillo Guest House*, No 12, T/F2296457.

F *Bruntsfield Youth Hostel*, 7 Bruntsfield Cres, T4472994. Reliable and well-run SYHA hostel in quiet area overlooking the links, but within easy reach of the centre (takes buses 11, 15 or 16 from south side of Princes St). Doors locked at 0200. Book ahead at peak times.

Leith & Newhaven

A *Malmaison Hotel*, 1 Tower Place, Leith, T4685000, F4685002, www.malmaison .com 60 rooms. Award-winning designer hotel in the hip waterfront quarter. Sleek sophistication and cool, contemporary chic. Its stylish brasserie and café-bar are firm favourites with local celebs (see page 115).

Campus accommodation

D *Heriot-Watt University Riccarton Campus*, T4513669, ecc@hw.ac.uk. 6 miles west of the city centre in Currie, open all year round. **A** *Edinburgh First*, 18 Holyrood Park Rd, T6512184, www.EdinburghFirst.com Open Mar-Apr and Jun-Sep. Main halls of residence less than 2 miles from the centre, near the Commonwealth Pool and Holyrood Park. Self-catering accommodation in 475 en suite rooms. **E** *Napier University*, 219 Colinton Rd, 4554621, F4554411. Open Jun-Sep. B&B and use of sports facilities. To get there take buses 23 and 27 from the Mound. They also have self-catering flats for rent (minimum 3 nights); for details T4554331. **E** *St Mary's Music School*, Coates Hall, 25 Grosvener Cres, T5387766, F4677289, info@st.marys.music.school.co.uk Open Jul-Aug only. Well-situated in the West End, not far from Haymarket station. Includes continental breakfast.

Camping

There are 2 good campsites a short bus ride from the centre. **F** *Edinburgh Caravan Club Site*, Marine Dr, T3126874. Open all year. Run by the Caravan Club of Great Britain, with good facilities. 5 miles northwest of the centre in Silverknowes. Take a 28 bus from town. **E-F** *Mortonhall Caravan Park*, 38 Mortonhall Gate, Frogston Rd East, T6641533, enquiries@mortonhallcp.demon.co.uk Open Mar-Oct. Well-equipped site about 6 miles southwest of town. From the city bypass take the Lothianburn or Straiton junction, or take a 7 or 11 bus from Princes Street.

Self-catering

For those spending several days in the city there's the alternative option of renting a self-catering apartment. Prices range from around £200 per week right up to £800 and above, depending on the type of accommodation, and there's usually a minimum stay of anything from two nights up to one week. For a detailed list of the various types of self-catering accommodation on offer, see the tourist office's accommodation brochure. **The National Trust for Scotland** also have a number of properties available for self-catering holidays, (for details see page 37).

Eating

In keeping with its growing reputation as one of the great European cities, Edinburgh's restaurant scene has undergone something of a transformation in recent years and the capital now boasts a wide range of places, to suit all tastes and budgets. The culinary scene has a distinctly cosmopolitan feel, with a large number of Italian, French, Mexican, Spanish, Indian, Thai and Chinese restaurants. There are also a growing number of eateries offering fusion cooking, which combines a range of international flavours. Scottish cuisine is also well represented, from traditional fare to more contemporary eclectic cuisine using various international influences, but all using the very best of Scottish ingredients such as game and seafood.

BYOB is a commonly used abbreviation meaning bring your own bottle

Fish and seafood lovers will not be disappointed and should head down to **Leith**, with its many stylish restaurants and bistros located around the refurbished dockside. **Vegetarians** are also well catered for, with a selection of good, economical places, particularly around the University. This is where you'll find the best-value eating in town, though the more tourist-oriented restaurants in the Old and New Towns offer good value two-course set menus at lunch-time. If you eat well at lunch and restrict yourself to a snack or light supper in the evening, then dining out in Edinburgh need not be expensive.

Most of the restaurants serve from 1200-1430 and 1800-2200 and are closed on Sundays, though times are listed below. If you don't want to be restricted by these eating times, then try some of the many excellent **bistros**, which are often better value and many of which serve food daily until around 0100. The city's countless bars also serve reasonably priced food, and the cheapest lunches are often found in the city cafés. Bars and cafes are listed in separate sections after Eating. Note that a seat in one of the more upmarket restaurants can be hard to come by during busy periods, such as the Festival, so it's best to book whenever possible.

Expensive *Iggs*, 15 Jeffrey St, T5578184. Superb Spanish restaurant which has recently expanded to include a new tapas bar, *Barioja*, next door. Serves the best tapas in town at lunch, then in the evening changes to a contemporary Scottish restaurant with a formidable reputation. Open Mon-Sat 1200-1430, 1800-2230. *Librizzi's*, 22a Nicolson St, T6681997. At the lower end of this category and great value. If you like Italian food, especially fish, there are few, if any, better places to eat. Open Mon-Sat 1200-1400, 1730-2300. *The Tower*, Museum of Scotland, Chambers St, T2253003. Still the place to be seen amongst the corporate set, and recent reports of pretentious service can't detract from superb Scottish menu and magnificent views across the city skyline from the rooftop terrace. No smoking. Open daily 1200-2300. *The Witchery by the Castle*, 352 Castlehill, T2255613. Dining doesn't get much more atmospheric than here in one of Edinburgh's finest, on the Royal Mile. Downstairs, in a converted schoolyard, is the impossibly romantic *Secret Garden*, a real hidden gem. Both restaurants share the same glorious Scottish menu. This was formerly a meeting place for Satanists, so go on, be a devil. Open daily 1200-1600, 1730-2330.

Old Town

Mid-range *Bann's UK*, 5 Hunter Sq, T2261112. Just off the Royal Mile by the Tron Kirk. A popular street performance place during the festival so perfect for an al fresco lunch. Busy but laid-back and offering an adventurous range of dishes. Great value. Open daily 1000-2300. **Black Bo's**, 57-61 Blackfriars St, T5576136. Vegetarian restaurant that is one of the city's truly great culinary experiences. So good even the most fanatical carnivore might even give up meat. Supremely imaginative use of various fruits gives the exotically delicious dishes a real splash of colour. Their lunch is superb value at under £10. The bar next door serves the same food. Open Mon-Sat 1200-1400, 1800-2230, Sun 1800-2230. **Bleu**, 36-38 Victoria St, T2261900. No traditional separate courses here, just a wide range of truly delicious French tapas dishes, guaranteed to set the taste buds tingling. There's another branch in Union St, opposite the Playhouse. Open daily 0900 till late. **Creelers**, 3 Hunter Sq, T2204447. Wonderfully fresh seafood and a great location beside the Tron church, with outdoor seating in the summer. You can push the boat out in the more formal restaurant at the rear or save your pennies in the busy bistro at the front, where the cheap 2-course lunch is great value. Open Mon-Thu 1200-1430, 1730-2230, Fri/Sat till 2300, Sun 1730-2230.

The Dial, 44-46 George IV Bridge, T2257179. Basement restaurant that is as notable for its cool design as for its top-notch modern Scottish cuisine. Menu features some old favourites as well as more unusual Caledonian culinary incarnations. Open Mon-Sat 1200-1500, 1800-2300, Sun 1200-1500, 1900-2300. **The Doric Tavern**, 15/16 Market St, T2251084. Very near Waverley station. Upstairs bistro offering great food and the perfect place to while away an entire afternoon without realizing the time. Open Mon-Sat 1200-0100, Sun 1230-0100. **Dubh Prais**, 123b High St, T5575732. Small basement restaurant in the heart of the Royal Mile offering the best of traditional Scottish cooking, as well as more contemporary innovations. Dinner is à la carte, but you can enjoy a two-course set lunch for a tenner. Open Tue-Sat 1200-1400, 1830-2230. **Le Sept**, 7 Old Fishmarket Close, T2255428. Down a steep, cobbled close off the High Street below St Giles. This lively little restaurant is famed for its superb crêpes but also has a 3-course set menu offering good French bistro-type food. Separate no smoking room. Open Mon-Thu 1200-1345, 1800-2200, Fri 1200-2300, Sat 1200-2230, Sun 1200-2130.

Nicolsons, 6a Nicolson St, T5574567. Large, airy bistro, done out in 1930s Art Deco style and attracting a hip crowd as well as the occasional Harry Potter aficionado (JK Rowling used to come here to write when it was a humble café). Mediterranean-style with a Far Eastern tinge. Open Mon-Fri 1200-1500, 1700-2300, Sat/Sun 1200-2400. **Pancho Villas**, 240 Canongate, T5574416. Ay, Chihuahua! If you want to stuff yourself on the finest Mexican food and have a fun time in the process, then look no further. Open Mon-Thu 1200-1430, 1800-2230, Fri 1200-2230, Sat 1200-2300, Sun 1800-2230. **Petit Paris**, 38-Vi40 Grassmarket, T2262442. Francophiles will fall in love with this place. Everything about it is French to the core, especially the superb food. BYOB Sun-Thu (£2 corkage). Open daily 1200-1500, 1730 till late. **Polo Fusion**, 503 The Lawnmarket, T6627722. Specializes in fusion cooking (some might say confusion), which is very much the flavour of the month. This combines different flavours and ingredients from around the globe to create wonderfully original tastes. Substantial portions and a lively atmosphere. Open Mon-Thu 1200-1400, 1800-2200, Fri/Sat till 2230. **Suruchi**, 14a Nicolson St, T5566583. Opposite the Festival Theatre and upstairs. A cut above the average curry house offering varied southern Indian cuisine with a strong vegetarian emphasis. Their set lunch and pre-theatre dinner are particularly good value. Menu is written in Scots, which some might find amusing and others simply tiresome. Open Mon-Sat 1200-1400, 1730-2330, Sun 1730-2330. **Viva Mexico**, 41 Cockburn St, T2265145. This Mexican restaurant has been around longer than most and it's easy to see why. Definitely one of the top two in town. Open Mon-Sat 1200-1430, 1830-2230, Sun 1830-2200.

Cheap **Baracoa**, 7 Victoria St, T2255846. Cuban bar/restaurant offering two-for-the-price-of-one meals before 1900 and various cheap drink deals. Fantastic value and a lively spot, especially early evening. Open daily 1100-0100. **Gordon's Trattoria**, 231

High St, T2257992. Great value Italian food, which is why it's so popular. Great for people-watching in summer when tables spill out onto the street. Open Sun-Thu 1200-2400, Fri and Sat till 0300. *Helio's Fountain*, 7 Grassmarket, T2297884. Small, self-service veggie café founded on Steiner principles. Good for an economical lunch or just a quiet break from the hustle and bustle. No smoking. Open Mon-Sat 1000-1800, Sun 1200-1700. *Kebab Mahal*, 7 Nicolson Square, T6675214. No frills halal café-takeaway serving good kebabs and curries for under a fiver. No alcohol served on premises. Open daily 1200-2400, Fri/Sat till 0200. *Khushi's*, 16 Drummond St, T5568996. The city's first ever Indian restaurant has been serving simple, tasty curries to poor students for many decades. Basic decor but great value. Several vegetarian options. BYOB and no corkage charge. Open Mon-Thu 1200-1430, 1700-2030, Fri/Sat till 2100.

Expensive *Café Royal Oyster Bar*, 17a West Register St, T5564124. An Edinburgh institution and much-loved by numerous celebrities. The ornate tiles and stained-glass windows create an atmosphere of Victorian elegance and opulence – just make sure you look at the prices! There are better seafood restaurants in town but none are as classy. Open daily 1200-1400, 1900-2200. The adjoining bar is just as impressive (see page 119). *Cosmo*, 58a North Castle St, T2266743. Elegant and expensive Italian restaurant that's superior in every sense. Excellent food (especially the fish), excellent wine list and excellent service. Popular with the city's more distinguished visitors (Sean C is shaid to have dined here). Booking essential. Open Mon-Fri 1230-1415, 1900-2245, Sat 1900-2200. *Duck's at Le Marche Noir*, 2-4 Eyre Pl, T5581608. Classic French provincial cooking (perhaps Edinburgh's finest) in sumptuous surroundings. Complemented by an extensive wine list. Open Mon-Fri 1200-1400, 1900-2200, Sat 1900-2230, Sun 1830-2130. *Haldane's*, 39 Albany St, T5568407. Smart Scottish country house cuisine in the centre of town. Excellent value set lunch. No smoking. Open Mon-Thu 1200-1400, 1800-2130, Fri till 2200, Sat 1800-2230, Sun 1800-2130. *Hadrian's*, 2 North Bridge (under the *Balmoral Hotel*), T5575000. Excellent modern Scottish cuisine with nouvelle-ish tendencies, soothing and well-designed modern surroundings. Superb value for money. Open daily 1200-1430, 1830-2230 (Sun 1230-1500). *Le Café Saint-Honoré*, 34 Thistle Street La, T2262211. Tucked away in a little side street, this place couldn't be any more French. An authentic corner of Paris in the heart of Scotland's capital. The food is seriously French, too, and seriously priced, but seriously wonderful. Seriously! Open Mon-Fri 1200-1415, 1900-2200, Sat 1900-2200 only. *36*, 36 Great King St, T556-3636. Basement restaurant of the *Howard Hotel* (see under 'Sleeping'). One of *the* places to eat in the capital. The very best of modern Scottish cuisine in contemporary, minimalist surroundings. Open Sun-Fri 1200-1400, 1900-2200, Sat 1900-2200. No smoking.

Mid-range *A Room in the Town*, 18 Howe St, T2258204. Excellent quality Scottish produce presented with flair and imagination in a friendly atmosphere. Exceptional value. BYOB. Open daily 1200-1500, 1730 till late. *Bell's Diner*, 7 St Stephen St, T2258116. The best burgers and steaks in town. This diner is popular with Stockbridge locals, students and tourists alike who come for its honest, filling and great value food in an informal atmosphere. Open Mon-Fri 1800-2300, Sat/Sun 1200-2300. *Blue Parrot Cantina*, 49 St Stephen St, T2252941. Set in the heart of quasi-bohemian Stockbridge, this is arguably the city's finest Mexican restaurant, offering a varied selection of dishes in a relaxed atmosphere. Open Mon-Fri and Sun 1700-2230, Sat 1300-2230. *Howies*, 4-6 Glanville Pl, T2255553. The newest addition to the *Howie's* range of bistros. Chic yet informal and with the same superb value Scottish menu.

Kweilin, 19-21 Dundas St, T5571875. A bit more expensive than other Chinese restaurants in town but backed up by some of the most imaginative Cantonese cooking

New Town

Edinburgh

around. Open Tue-Thu 1200-2245, Fri/Sat 1200-2315. *Loon Fung*, 2 Warriston Pl, T5561781. Still one of the great Oriental eating experiences in town, this Cantonese restaurant is an old favourite, with a wide selection of dim sum and seafood dishes. Open Mon-Thu 1200-2330, Fri 1200-0030, Sat 1400-0030, Sun 1400-2330. *The Lost Sock Diner*, 11 East London St, T5576097. Relaxed by day and buzzing by night, this bistro offers a huge range of dishes at unbeatable value. Open Mon 0900-1600, Tue-Sat 0900-2200, Sun 1000-1700. *Maison Hector*, 47-49 Deanhaugh St, T3325328. Described as Stockbridge's answer to Central Perk, this is one of Edinburgh's original bistros but still one of the best. Restaurant serves a fine Scottish/French menu while the café-bar area is just brill for weekend brunch. Open Mon-Wed 1100-2400, Thu/Fri till 0100, Sat 1030-0100, Sun 1030-2400. *The Mussel Inn*, 61-65 Rose St, T2255979. What could be better than a huge pot of steaming fresh mussels and a bowl of fantastic chips? Not much, judging by the popularity of this place, in the heart of pub-land. A must for seafood-lovers. Open Mon-Thu 1200-1500, 1800-2200, Fri/Sat 1100-2200. *Rhodes & Co*, 3-15 Rose St, T2209190. Recently opened by TV celebrity chef Gary Rhodes. Very retro (food and decor), serving British standards as you've never tasted before. Open Mon-Sat 1200-1430, 1800-2230, Sun 1200-1430.

Siam Erawan, 48 Howe St, T2263675. Edinburgh's original Thai restaurant and still the best. The cosy basement ambience encourages you to take your time. Open Mon-Sat 1200-1430, 1800-2300, Sun 1800-2230. They now have three other branches, which may or may not be as good: *Baan Erawan*, 14 South St Andrew St, T5568558; *Erawan Express*, 176 Rose St. T2200059; *Erawan Oriental*, 14 South St Andrew St, T5564242. *Tapas Olé*, 10 Eyre Pl, T5562754. Excellent tapas, friendly service and a good vibe. Good value lunch menu. There's a new branch in the Old Town, at 4a Forrest Rd, T2257069. Open daily 1100-2300. *Tapas Tree*, 1 Forth St, T5567718. This Spanish restaurant, has built up a reputation for excellent food and service. Their tapas are good value, particularly the lunch-time specials, and they even offer a vegetarian selection. Booking advised at weekends. Open daily 1100-2300.

Cheap *à table*, 4 Howe St, T2205335. Eating here is like sitting in someone's French farmhouse kitchen. There's one huge table in the middle where you're served with healthy continental dishes made from organic produce. Open Mon-Fri 0830-1730, Sat 1000-1800, Sun 1000-1600. *Bar Napoli*, 75 Hanover St, T2252600. Basic Italian which offers much the same as the others in the street but which has the added advantage of offering the best-value set lunch and it stays open late. Open Mon-Thu and Sun 1200-0200, Fri/Sat 1200-0400. *Henderson's Salad Table*, 94 Hanover St, T2252131. This basement vegetarian self-service restaurant is the oldest in the city and still one of the best. It can get very busy but manages to combine efficiency with comfort. Excellent value 2-course set lunch. Open Mon-Sat 0800-2230. Upstairs is their deli and takeaway, and round the corner, at 25 Thistle St, is *Henderson's Bistro*, T2252605, which provides the same excellent food but in more intimate surroundings, with table service and at only slightly higher prices. *Tampopo*, 25a Thistle St, T2205254. Japanese fast-food at its best. Always busy with takeaway trade, so if you're after a quick, healthy, tasty and economical snack, this is the place for you. Try the sushi. Open Mon 1200-1500, Tue-Sat 1200-1500, 1800-2100.

West Edinburgh **Expensive** *The Atrium*, 10 Cambridge St (same building as the Traverse Theatre), T2288882. Award-winning Scottish cooking in elegant modern surroundings. This outstanding restaurant is one of the best in town, but by no means the most expensive. Open Mon-Fri 1200-1430, 1800-2230, Sat 1800-2230. Upstairs is its stylish sister bistro, *blue*.

Mid-range *Bar Roma*, 39a Queensferry St, T2262977. Traditional Italian serving a huge variety of pasta and pizza to huge numbers of late-night revellers in a fun atmosphere. Open Mon-Thu and Sun 1200-2400, Fri/Sat till 0100. *blue*, 10 Cambridge St (upstairs from *The Atrium*), T2211222. The stylish and minimalist interior of this leading city bistro attracts the arty and media types as well as the more sober suits. Sister to the outstanding *Atrium*, so not surprisingly the food on offer is a substantial cut above the rest. Also a great place for a drink, its well-stocked bar boasts a satisfying selection of malts and excellent service. Open Tue-Sat 1200-0100, Sun and Mon till 1200. *Caledonian Alehouse & Bistro*, 1-3 Haymarket Terr, T3371006. Upstairs bistro offering genuine Scottish cuisine at decent prices. Set lunch is excellent value. Open Mon-Thu 1200-1500, 1800-2100, Fri/Sat till 2200, Sun 1800-2200 only. *Howie's*, 63 Dalry Rd, T3133334. Something of an Edinburgh institution, this chain of bistros hits the spot every time with imaginative Scottish food that is always tasty and great value (BYOB policy), in an informal atmosphere. The others are in the New Town and Southside. Open Mon 1800-2200, Tue-Sun 1200-1400, 1800-2200.

The Indian Cavalry Club, 3 Atholl Pl, T2283282. Classy and exclusive Indian in 'Last days of the Raj' style, and with a deserved reputation for outstanding food. Popular for business lunches, which are great value. Smart dress advised. Open daily 1200-1400, 1730-2330. *Indigo Yard*, 7 Charlotte La, T2205603. This converted and covered-over courtyard has been transformed into an immensely popular bar and restaurant. The menu is cosmopolitan (Thai, Mexican, French, Italian etc) and the food excellent. Serves lunch, dinner and late supper. See also 'Bars'. Open daily 0830-0100. *Jasmine Chinese Restaurant*, 32 Grindlay St, T2295757. Handy for the theatres and cinemas, this stylish and modern Chinese restaurant is better value than most and something a little bit different. Open Mon-Thu 1200-1400, 1700-2330, Fri till 0030, Sat 1400-0030, Sun 1400-2230. *Lune Town*, 38 William St, T2201688. Varied and exciting Chinese food served in a cosy, friendly atmosphere. Good dim sum and excellent value set lunch. Open Mon-Thu 1200-1430, 1800-2330, Fri till 2400, Sat 1500-2400, Sun 1600-2300. *Restaurant at the Bonham*, 35 Drumsheugh Gdns, T6239319. This is part of the eponymous hotel and every bit as stylish. Scottish cuisine with a Californian touch and better quality than you could expect at these prices. Open Mon-Fri 1200-1400, 1830-2130, Sat/Sun 1200-1400, 1830-2200. *Sukothai*, 23 Brougham Place, T2291537. This busy little Thai restaurant is very handy for theatres and cinemas so ideal for a quick pre-show bite. Their 'all-you-can-eat' Sun buffet is excellent value.

Cheap *La Cuisine D'Odile*, 13 Randolph Cres, T2255685. Hidden away in the French Institute, this is genuine quality French cuisine at amazingly low prices. Great views from the terrace in the summer. Open Tue-Sat 1200-1400 only. *Oriental Dining Centre*, 8-16 Morrison St, T2211288. Dim Sum bar (open daily 1200-0300), Noodle Shack (open Mon-Sat 1730-0200) and Chinese restaurant (daily 1200-2400) all rolled into one. Good vegetarian selection and fresh seafood daily. Jazz bar downstairs (see page 123).

Mid-range *Ann Purna*, 45 St Patrick's Sq, T6621807. Well-respected and popular vegetarian/vegan restaurant specializing in southern Indian and Gujerati cooking. Understated elegance and great value. No smoking. Open Mon-Fri 1200-1400, 1730-2300, Sat/Sun 1730-2300. *The Apartment*, 7-13 Barclay Pl, T2286456. Edinburgh's most talked-about new eating establishment. Hip and happening place where the portions are as big as the owner's personality. A truly different eating experience with dishes divided into 'CHLs' (Chunky Healthy Lines), 'Slabs', 'Fish Things' and 'Other Things'. All in all, a great night out. Open Mon-Fri 1800-2300, Sat/Sun 1200-1500, 1800-2300. *Buffalo Grill*, 12-14 Chapel St, T6677427. This is beef central. The steaks are high quality and limitless in this small and intimate diner decked out in Wild West style. It's not all burgers and steaks, but that's why people keep coming. Open Mon-Fri 1200-1400, 1800-2215 (Sat 1800-2215 only), Sun 1700-2000. *Dragon Way*, 74 South Clerk St, T6681328. If you can get past the completely OTT decor, the food in this Cantonese

South Edinburgh

restaurant is actually very good. Good value set lunch and dinners. Open Mon-Fri 1200-1430, 1700-2400, Sat 1700-2400 only, Sun 1800-2400.

Howie's, 75 St Leonards St, T6682917. Another branch of the highly-acclaimed Edinburgh bistro chain. Also at 208 Bruntsfield Pl, T2211777. (See under 'West End' above.) *Montpeliers*, 159-161 Bruntsfield Pl, T2293115. Bruntsfield's favourite bistro serves meals or snacks at pretty much any time of the day or night. Stylish and relaxed it's popular with locals for lunch and young trendies are attracted by their pitchers of cocktails at night. Open daily 0900-0100. *Mother India*, 10 Newington Rd, T6629020. Sister restaurant of the famous Glasgow establishment. Downstairs is more studenty and laid-back while upstairs is altogether more formal, but both offer excellent Punjabi cooking. Set lunch and pre-theatre dinner are great value. Open Mon-Sat 1700-2230 (Fri also 1200-1400), Sat till 2330, Sun 1500-2230. *Phenecia*, 55-57 West Nicolson St, T6624493. Spanish/North African dishes served in a relaxed atmosphere. Cheap lunches so it gets busy at lunch-times. BYOB policy makes it good value for dinner. Open Mon-Sat 1200-1400, 1800-2300, Sun 1800-2200.

Cheap *The Engine Shed Café*, 19 St Leonard's La, T6620040. Tucked away in a residential area off St Leonard's St, this small vegetarian café provides just about the best value lunch in town. Bread is baked on the premises and can be bought separately. Bakery and café provides work experience for adults with learning difficulties. No smoking. Open Mon-Thu 1030-1530, Fri till 1430, Sat till 1600, Sun 1100-1600. *Isabel's Café*, 83 Clerk St, T6624014. Tiny vegetarian restaurant at the back of the *Nature's Gate* health food shop. The vegetarian and vegan menu has non-dairy and non-wheat options. Ridiculously cheap meals and snacks served in a laid-back atmosphere. No smoking. Open Mon-Sat 1130-1830 (Tue and Sat till 1530). *Kalpna*, 2-3 St Patrick's Square, T6679890. This popular and imaginative Indian vegetarian is one of the best of its kind in the UK, using fantastically inventive and sophisticated sauces. Buffet lunch is a bargain at £4.50, but not quite the same as the full dinner experience. Don't leave town without trying it. No smoking. Open Mon-Fri 1200-1400, 1730-2300, Sat 1730-2300. *Susie's Diner*, 51-53 West Nicolson St, T6678729. Self-service vegetarian/vegan diner offering a broad range of dishes, including Mediterranean and Middle Eastern. Popular with students and lecturers from the nearby University. Also belly dancing nights and live music at weekends. Good food and atmosphere. Open Tue-Sat 0900-2100, Mon till 2000, Sun 1200-1900. *Wok Bar*, 30 Potterrow, T6678594. Thai, Japanese, Chinese and Malaysian favourites served in chic, contemporary surroundings. Open Mon-Wed 1100-2230, Thu-Sat till 2300, Sun 1200-2230.

Leith & **Expensive** *Fishers*, 1 The Shore, T5545666. This is one of Edinburgh's finest fish res-
Newhaven taurants, in an area packed full of them. It's housed in the tower at the end of The Shore. Open daily 1215-2230. *(fitz)henry*, 19 Shore Pl, T5556625. This stylish warehouse brasserie is one of only two city eateries to receive a Michelin Red M (the other is *The Atrium*) for its genuinely original and excellent Scottish cooking. Open Mon-Thu 1230-1430, 1830-2230, Fri/Sat till 2230. *Restaurant Martin Wishart*, 54 The Shore, T5533557. French-influenced cuisine at its finest from the renowned chef. Unfussy decor for a memorable meal. Open Tue-Fri 1200-1400, 1900-2200, Sat 1900-2200. *Skippers*, 1a Dock Pl, T5541018. Many in the know would say this is the best place to eat seafood in town. This nautical bistro is small and intimate, and very popular, so you'll need to book. Open Mon-Sat 1230-1400, 1900-2200. *The Vintners Rooms*, 87 Giles St, T5546767. These former wine vaults dating from the 17th century now house a restaurant and bar, both lit by candlelight and oozing historic charm and romance. The food is French provincial and excellent, as is the service. Meals in the bar at lunch-times are cheaper. Open Mon-Sat 1200-1400, 1900-2230.

Mid-range *Daruma-Ya*, 82 Commercial St, T5547660. Japanese cuisine in elegant 19th-century surroundings and served by friendly, helpful staff. Sounds an unlikely combination but check it out for yourself. Set lunches and dinners are great value. Open Mon 1830-late, Tue-Sat 1200-1400, 1830-late. *Malmaison Brasserie*, 1 Tower Pl, T468-5000. Attached to the acclaimed Malmaison Hotel (see 'Sleeping'). Excellent French brasserie food in stylish surroundings. Open Mon-Fri 0700-1000, 1200-1400, 1800-2230 (Sat from 0800, Sun till 2200). *The Shore*, 3-4 The Shore, T5535080. One of the city's best fish restaurants with a real fire and huge windows overlooking the Water of Leith. No smoking. You can eat from the restaurant menu in the adjoining bar. Open Mon-Sat 1100-2400, Sun 1230-2300. *Tinelli*, 139 Easter Rd, T6521932. This out of the way Italian is one of the city's best and well worth the effort of finding it. Genuine Italian cooking of the highest quality and fantastic value. It's small and gets busy so book ahead. Open Mon-Sat 1200-1430, 1830-2300. *Umberto's*, 2 Bonnington Rd La (off Broughton Rd), T5541314. Very good Italian food with a Scottish flavour at one of the most child-friendly restaurants in town. In the evening, you can pig out and eat and drink as much as you can for £15. Open Mon-Sat 1200-1430, 1700-2200, Sun 1200-1800. *The Waterfront*, 1c Dock Pl, T5547427. Great for fish or just for a relaxing drink. Seating in the conservatory or cosy booths. Open Mon-Thu 1200-2300, Fri/Sat till 2400, Sun 1230-2230.

Cafés

Sightseeing can be a tiring business in Edinburgh. Listed below are the pick of the city's coffee houses and tearooms, where you can recharge the batteries with that essential caffeine kick, or simply put your feet up and enjoy a nice cup of tea in pleasant surroundings. Many cafés also offer the best value for lunch or a snack. Look out for the *California Coffee Company*'s red police boxes which serve excellent 'coffee to go' with a personal touch: at St Patrick's Sq, Middle Meadow Walk/Teviot Pl, Hope Park Cres, George St near Hanover St, and Rose St East behind M&S

The Bookstop Café, 4 Teviot Pl, T2255298. Small and friendly bookshop and café where **Old Town** you can relax with a book and a good cup of coffee. And if you buy a book you get the coffee free! Popular with students and nurses from the local hospital. Also filled rolls made to order. Open Mon-Sat 1000-1930, Sun 1130-1930. *Café Couronne*, Royal Museum of Scotland, 2 Chambers St, T2474111. Elegant pâtisserie in the museum foyer serving good coffee and great cakes and pastries. No smoking. Open Mon-Sat 1000-1600, Sun 1200-1600. At the back of the museum, next to the Lumière cinema, is *Petite Couronne*, a self-service café-bar offering good value snacks. No smoking. Open Mon-Thu 1000-1630, Fri/Sat 1000-1630, 1700-2030, Sun 1200-1630, 1700-2030. *Café Hub*, Castle Hill, T4732015. Coffee drinking doesn't get any more stylishly laid-back than this. The food on offer is tasty, inventive and available all day and evening, and there's seating outside on the terrace in summer. The Hub plays host to the Festival Club, as well as housing the ticket centre for the International Festival (see page 125).No smoking. Open daily 0930-2300. *Café Lucia*, Festival Theatre, 13-29 Nicolson St, T6621112. Light, airy and contemporary café with a relaxed feel. Usual array of light snacks on offer. No smoking. Open from 1000 till half an hour after the show (from 1600 on Sun). *City Art Centre Café*, 1 Market St, T2203359. Good coffee and cakes and an affordable selection of main dishes in a spacious environment with helpful staff. No smoking. Open Mon-Sat 0830-1700, Sun (only during exhibitions) 1100-1700. *Clarinda's Tearoom*, 69 Canongate, T5571888. Cosy, traditional tearoom serving home-baked scones, shortbread and lots of waist-enhancing cakes. Good stopping-off point on the way to Holyrood Palace. No smoking. Open Mon-Sat 0900-1645, Sun 1000-1645. *Common Grounds* , 2-3 North Bank St, The Mound, T2261416.

Edinburgh

American-style café with a vast range of coffees and teas. A nice place to relax and take a break from shopping or sightseeing. Cakes, sandwiches and a vegetarian-friendly menu. Smoking only downstairs, where you can hear live music most nights.

Elephant House, 21 George IV Bridge, T2205355. Very studenty – a great place to linger over coffee and bagels or one of many cheap snacks and main courses. Mellow vibe and lots of elephants (on the walls, not at the tables). Café bar by evening with live music. Open Mon-Fri 0800-2300, Sat/Sun 1000-2300. *Elephants & Bagels*, 37 Marshal St, T6684404. Continuing the elephant theme, and lots more bagels from the same stable. Good coffee too. Open Mon-Fri 0800-1800, Sat/Sun 1000-1700. *Favorit*, 19-20 Teviot Place, T2206880. Café/bar/deli with an Italian-American look. A cool place to stop for a quick coffee and sandwich at any time of the day or night. Open daily 0830-0300. Also at 30-32 Leven St. *Fruitmarket Café*, Fruitmarket Gallery, 45 Market St, T2261843. One of the coolest cafés in town with windows large enough to guarantee being seen. A great place for a quick, cheap and tasty lunch, or just for coffee and chat. No smoking. Open Mon-Sat 1100-1700, Sun 1200-1700. *The Lower Aisle*, St Giles Cathedral, High St (entrance via Parliament Square), T2255147. This self-service café underneath the cathedral is popular with the legal profession. Good for a cheap light lunch. Open Mon-Fri 0930-1630, Sun 0900-1400. *Patisserie Florentin*, 8 St Giles St, T2256267. Large and lively place to stop for a coffee, a filled croissant and a generous slice of Edinburgh life. Open Sun-Fri 0700-2100, Sat 0700-2200.

New Town *Blue Moon*, 1 Barony St, T5562788. Gay café in the city's 'pink triangle'. Good selection of cakes, also snacks and meals. Gets busy later in the evening with pre-clubbers. Open Mon-Fri 1100-0030, Sat/Sun 0900-0030. *Cyberia*, 88 Hanover St, T2204403. One of the city's best internet cafés that's hugely popular with surfers and non-surfers alike. Open Mon-Sat 1000-2200, Sun 1200-1900 (see also page 129). *Glass & Thompson*, 2 Dundas St, T5570909. Coffee shop and deli with the emphasis on quality food. Popular with local residents who know a good thing when they see (and taste) it. Open Mon-Fri 0830-1830, Sat 0830-1730, Sun 1100-1630. *The Laigh Bake House*, 117a Hanover St, T2251552. Downstairs from the hustle and bustle is a quiet little corner of the Orkneys and Edinburgh's oldest coffee house. Nothing to disturb the peace and stillness save the ticking of the clock and the rustling of newspapers and the occasional squeal of delight from someone tasting the indescribably delicious hazelnut meringue gateau for the very first time. The food is made from purely organic ingredients. Open Mon-Sat 0830-1700. *The Queen Street Café*, The Scottish National Portrait Gallery, 1 Queen St, T5572844. The best scones and caramel shortcake in town, not to mention excellent value snacks and light meals, served in grand surroundings. No smoking. Open Mon-Sat 1000-1630, Sun 1400-1630. *Starbucks*, Waterstone's, 128 Princes St, T2263610. Features the usual wide range of coffees but the reason it merits inclusion is the wonderful view of the castle. Popular with browsers, shoppers and as a meeting point. No smoking. Open Mon-Sat 0800-2000, Sun 1030-1800. *Terrace Café*, Royal Botanic Garden, Inverleith Row, T5520616. Set in the grounds next to Inverleith House, this is little more than a school canteen, but the views of the castle, Old Town and Arthur's Seat take some beating. No smoking. Open daily 0930-1800. *Valvona & Crolla*, 19 Elm Row, T5566066. More authentically Italian than almost anything you'd find in New York. Great home cooking and the best cappuccino in town. Needless to say, somewhere this good is very, very popular. No smoking. Open Mon-Sat 0800-1700.

West Edinburgh *Cornerstone Café*, St John's Church, 3 Lothian Rd, T2290212. In the church vaults, a quiet refuge from the Princes Street traffic offering cheap and tasty vegetarian meals. *The Gallery Café*, The Scottish Gallery of Modern Art, 74 Belford Rd, T3328600. There are few better ways to spend a couple of hours on a sunny afternoon than to sit outside in the walled sculpture garden enjoying a coffee and cake, a light snack, or something more substantial washed down with a glass of wine. This is one of the city's great delights. Open Mon-Sat 1000-1630, Sun 1400-1630. *Ndbele*, 57 Home St, T2211141. A real taste of southern Africa in the Tollcross. Huge selection of sandwiches with some unusual fillings such as smoked ostrich. Nice, friendly atmosphere. Open daily 1000-2200. *Web 13*, 13 Bread St, T229-8883. Another internet café (see page 129) that's good enough to include here. A great place to hang out and surf, or just hang out and enjoy their good-value food. Open Mon-Fri 0900-2200, Sat 0900-2000, Sun 1100-2000.

South Edinburgh

Café Q, Queen's Hall, 87 Clerk St, T6683456. Spacious and peaceful. Good value, wholesome food that's strong on vegetarian choices. No smoking. Open Mon-Sat 0930-1700. *Kaffe Politik*, 146-148 Marchmont Rd, T4469873. Stylish surroundings, healthy, vegetable-based food, excellent home baking and good coffee. At its best on a lazy Sun, enjoying brunch with the newspaper. Open daily 1000-2200. *Metropole*, 33 Newington Rd, T6684999. Stylish and trendy converted bank boasting a wide range of teas and coffees and cappuccino to rival the best. Also a good range of snacks and sandwiches. No smoking. Open daily 0900-2200.

Bars and pubs

Edinburgh has more bars per square mile than any other European city. That may just be the drink talking, but the city does boast an inordinate amount of watering holes, from centuries-old pubs brimming with history, to the latest in contemporary chic. There's a bar for everyone in this town. And if that weren't enough, the city is blessed with liberal licensing laws, which are relaxed even further during the Festival in Aug and over Christmas and New Year. It is not a problem finding bars open till past midnight any night of the week and some are open till 0300 at weekends. Edinburgh may not be quite the city that never sleeps, but it's doing pretty well in the insomnia stakes.

A good area for bars is around the **Grassmarket**, in the Old Town, which gets very lively at weekends and is particularly popular with students, as are the bars in the **Southside**, near the University. There are also lots of bars around the **Tollcross**. Those looking for more hip and happening places should head for the cluster of cool bars around **Broughton Street**, at the east end of the New Town. This is in the 'pink triangle', the centre of the city's gay scene, though many of the bars are not exclusively gay. An area with a diverse mix of drinking holes is **Leith**. Here you'll find everything from the roughest spit-and-sawdust joints to the trendiest waterside warehouse conversions. Edinburgh's most famous drinking street is **Rose Street**, a narrow pedestrianized lane between Princes Street and George Street, but it has seen better days and only one or two of its many hostelries are worthy of note.

Edinburgh's' pre-club bars are mainly situated in the area between George IV Bridge and the High Street in the City Centre and at the area at the top of Leith Walk, formerly the 'Pink Triangle', see above. These are open from 1100-0100 Mon-Fri and 1230-0100 Sun. During the Festival and the Xmas/ New Year period all premises get the opportunity to open an extra 2 hours, so many stay open till 0300.

An excellent way to explore some of the city's more notable pubs is to take the **Edinburgh Literary Pub Tour** (see page 76). Or, if you want to investigate the strange smell that permeates the city, then head along to Edinburgh's own independent **Caledonian Brewery**, 42 Slateford Road, T6238066, where you can take a tour and see traditional techniques and equipment in use and sample some of their fine ales. Mon-Fri at 1100, 1230, 1400. £5. The other breweries are the giant Scottish and Newcastle, who produce *McEwan's* and *Younger's*, and the tiny Rose Street Brewery, which has its own pub.

Old Town *Bannerman's*, 212 Cowgate, T5563254. Huge, cavernous cellar-type pub that was once a real ale favourite but has now been taken over by young trendies. Still a good place to relax by the fire or have a big Sun fry-up. Open till 0100 daily. *Bar Kohl*, 54 George IV Bridge, T2256936. Small but very busy bar which trades on the divergent themes of flavoured Vodka and Gangsta Rap. The bar has over 50 different flavoured Vodkas and a mixed clientele of clubbers, drinkers and Ali-G types (due to the constant Hip-Hop played on the Stereo). Trendy bar with 250 types of vodka on offer. Open Mon-Sat till 0100. *Biddy Mulligan's*, 96 The Grassmarket, T2201246. One of the most popular bars on the Grassmarket drinking strip, and that's saying something. Packed with students during term time and huge groups of lads and lassies at weekends, when it tends to get raucous. Open daily till 0100. *Bliss*, 253 Cowgate. Formerly spit and sawdust bar now revamped and frequented by club goers. *The Bow Bar*, 80 West Bow (halfway down Victoria St), T2267667. No nonsense, no frills pub for real ale enthusiasts and those who long for the days before mobile phones and sun-dried tomatoes. A dependable pint in an ever changing world. Open Mon-Sat till 2330, Sun till 2300.

The Canon's Gait, 232 Canongate, T5564481. Worth a stop, especially around lunchtime for its excellent-value food. *Carwash*, 1-13 North Bank St, T2200054. Stepping inside is like reliving the Seventies, except that the prices have gone up. Makes you wish you'd packed the flares and permed wig. Open Mon-Sat 1200-0100, Sun 1800-0100. *Cellar No 1*, 1 Chambers St, T2204298. Basement cellar-bar that attracts a wide variety of people and gets lively at night. Good-value pub food and a good selection of wines. Features DJs Tue-Thu and live jazz Fri and Sat nights. Open Mon-Sat 1200-0100, Sun 1800-0100. *City Café*, 19 Blair St, T2200125. Style bar done out like an American diner with chrome-topped bar and booth seating. Still the busiest and most vibrant pre-club bar. Set on two floors with large bar area with pool tables to rear on top floor and smaller bar where funky House/Garage DJ's play at weekends. Open daily till 0100.

EH1, 197 High St, T2205277. Attracts workers from the High Street area during week and popular with tourists sitting in the sun. In the vicinity of the main clubs which are situated around the Cowgate/Royal Mile area and is a modern furbished bar with a small area at the back where DJ's play on Fri-Sat nights. Open daily 0930-0100. *Greyfriar's Bobby*, 24 Candlemaker Row, T2258328. Old-style bar named after the brave wee Skye Terrier who died waiting for a taxi to stop on a Sat night. Very popular with tourists and students, who come for the cheap bar meals. Open daily till 0100. *Iguana*, 41 Lothian St, T2204288. Next door to *Negociants*. Refurbished from old student haunt the Bristo Bar. Smart deco and DJ's Fri/Sat night. Large video screens. Can be too noisy to maintain any form of conversation. Popular with clubbers going to Potterrow which is a Student Venue. The food is excellent and the menu imaginative, but it gets busy at night, so book if you want to be sure of a table. Open daily 0900-0100.

Jolly Judge, 7 James Court, T2252669. Turn off the High Street just down from the castle, down a narrow close, then down the stairs to reach this cosy, intimate wee place. Live folk music and good-value bar food. Open Mon/Sun till 2300, Tue-Sat till 2400. *The Living Room*, 235 Cowgate, T2254628. Dark and dingy place that attracts the city's hipsters. If you don't like the music then you're probably too old. Open daily till 0100. *Negociants*, 45-47 Lothian St, T2256313. Is it a bar, is it a bistro? Both, actually. Great for a relaxing lunch-time beer or coffee and popular with students and professionals alike. At night it's a fave late-night watering hole with DJs and dancing downstairs. The menu is international in flavour, excellent value and available till 0230. Good place for a relaxing Sun brunch. Open daily 0900-0300. *The Royal Oak*, 1 Infirmary St. If it's a late-night session of traditional folk music you're after, then look no further. Every night at around 2200 there's a spontaneous outbreak of singing and fiddle playing, washed down with copious quantities of whisky and beer. Open daily till 0200. *The Three Sisters*, 139 Cowgate, T6226800. One of the city's liveliest pubs. Huge cavernous place divided into 3 themed sections. Courtyard out front gets very busy in summer. Dancing nightly upstairs. Open till 0100.

The Abbotsford, 3 Rose St, T2255276. Big, old reliable pub in a street that's largely lost **New Town** its drinking appeal. Good, solid pub lunches and a restaurant upstairs that's open in the evenings. Open Mon-Sat till 2300. *The Baillie Bar*, 2 St Stephen St, T2254673. Dark, smoky basement bar in bohemian Stockbridge. Attracts a more mature clientele (the *auld yins*, in other words). Serves above-average pub food. *Bar 38*, 126-128 George St, T2206180. Large, elaborately decorated and popular with the after-work, young professional crowd. And, yes, those toilets are worth checking out! Open Mon-Sat till 0100, Sun till 2400. *Barony Bar*, 81-85 Broughton St, T5570546. Stylish and lively place where you won't feel like you've gatecrashed your young nephew's party. Very busy at weekends. Good bar food. Open till 2400, weekends till 0030. *Baroque*, 39-41 Broughton St, T5570627. Brightly coloured décor that's not quite as loud as the young party lovers who frequent this popular bar. Usual range of trendy grub and a great selection of juices. Open daily till 0100. *The Basement*, 10-12a Broughton St, T5570097. This Broughton Street original feels like it's been around for ever and is just as hip and happening as ever. Good bistro food with a mainly Mexican flavour. Open daily 1200-2400.

Café Royal Circle Bar, 19 West Register St, T5564124. You can't help feeling spoiled in these elegant and civilized surroundings. Adjacent to the famous *Café Royal Oyster Bar* (see 'page 111). Treat yourself to the seafood menu while enjoying the sumptuous splendour. Open Mon-Wed 1100-2300, Thu till 2400, Fri/Sat till 0100, Sun till 2300. Next door upstairs is the *Café Royal Bistro Bar*, a big favourite with the rugger fraternity. *Cask and Barrel*, 115 Broughton St, T5563132. Set in the hip Broughton St part of the New Town, but very different from many of the other, more glamorous places. Real Ale, brass taps and wooden fittings, try the local Deuchar's IPA. *The Cumberland Bar*, 1 Cumberland Street, T5583134. Classic New Town bar that oozes refinement and respectability. Fine selection of real ales, a beer garden and some decent nosh. A good place to kick back and while away an hour or several. Open Mon-Wed till 2330, Thu-Sat till 2400, Sun till 2200. *The Guildford Arms*, 1 West Register St. Ornate Victorian bar with an excellent selection of good ales. Open Sun-Wed till 2300, Thu-Sat till 2400.

The Kenilworth, 152 Rose St, T2264385. Beautiful old bar serving good quality pub food. Special children's menu. Open Mon-Thu and Sun till 2300, Fri/Sat till 0100. *Mathers*, 25 Broughton St, T5566754. A welcome respite from the unremitting cool of this part of the city. Just a plain and simple bar serving good beer and unpretentious food in relaxed surroundings. Open Mon-Thu till 2400, Fri/Sat till 0030, Sun till 2300. *The Outhouse*, 12a Broughton St La, T5576668. Under the same management as *Ego* nightclub, small dark bar which is not very plush but does fill up quickly and has a good atmosphere. Open daily 1200-0100. *Pivo Caffé*, 2-6 Calton Rd, T5572925. At the top of Leith Walk opposite the St James Centre. Czech-themed bar offering a thick slice of Prague. Very good czech beer and huge portions of grub. Lively buzz in evenings when it's full of students on their way to *The Venue*. Open daily till 0100. *Po-Na-Na*, 43b Frederick St, T2262224. Done out like an Arabic souk with many nooks and crannies in which to get up to no good. Transforms into a club later on with much madness and mayhem. And it all goes on till 0300 every night. *Pop Rocket*, 2A Picardy Pl. Frequented by clubbers going to *Ego* and *The Venue*. Nice decor with 2 floors but is seldom busy after 2300 at weekends. *Rose Street Brewery*, 55 Rose St, T2201227. One of the best pubs in this street. Brews its own ales on the premises and these are on tap in the ground-floor bar. Food served upstairs in the restaurant. Open Mon-Thu till 2300, Fri/Sat till 2400.

Edinburgh

West Edinburgh *Bert's Bar*, 29-31 William St, T2255748. A better class of rugby bar which attracts the more refined aficionado as well as the occasional Charlotte Street mafioso. A pie and a pint doesn't get much better than this. Open Mon-Wed till 2300, Thu-Sat till 2400. *The Caley Sample Room*, 58 Angle Park Terr, T3371006. Sells the full range of ales from the nearby Caledonian Brewery. Popular with rugby and footie fans enjoying a pre- or post-match pint with their pie and chips (both Murrayfield rugby stadium and Tynecastle football ground are close by). *Filmhouse Café Bar*, 88 Lothian Rd, T2295932. Comfortable place to relax whether or not you're catching a movie. Busy at lunchtimes and evenings with a wide mix of people who come for coffee and chat or to enjoy the excellent-value vegetarian food. A good place for star-spotting during the film festival. Open Sun-Thu till 2330, Fri/Sat till 0030. *Mather's*, 1 Queensferry St. Good real ale pub with a gorgeous interior. Open Mon-Thu till 2400, Fri/Sat till 0100. *Mondobbo*, 34 Bread St, T2215555. Part of the supremely stylish *Point Hotel*, and don't it show. Popular with local office workers for a sophisticated light lunch or after work for happy-hour cocktails. Open Mon-Thu and Sun till 2400, Fri/Sat till 0100. *Traverse Bar Café*, Traverse Theatre, 10 Cambridge St, T2285383. Very stylish bar that's popular with luvvies, suits and students. Excellent and affordable food served at all times and regular special drinks offers. Open Mon till 2300, Tue-Thu and Sun till 2400, Fri/Sat till 0100.

South Edinburgh *Bar Ce Lona*, 2-8 West Crosscauseway, T6628860. Mediterranean-style bar with civilized table service and al fresco eating. Try their flavoured margaritas or enjoy brunch on a sunny Sun. Live bands and DJs at weekends. Open daily 1100-0100. *Bennet's Bar*, 8 Leven St, T2295143. Next to the King's Theatre. Marvel at the carved wooden gantry, the stained-glass windows, the huge mirrors, and the glass-topped tables with inlaid city maps while you enjoy a great pint of beer and perhaps some good old-fashioned (and cheap) food (served in the back room at lunch-times only). One of the city's finest traditional howffs. Open Mon-Wed till 2330, Thu-Sat till 0030, Sun till 2300. *The Canny Man's*, 237 Morningside Road. Part museum/part pub that's been serving good real ale and a vast smorgasbord of sandwiches in most interesting surroundings since Victoria was on the throne, and probably to the same bunch of regulars. A word of caution. If the publican doesn't like the look of you, you'll be out on yer ear. Open Mon-Sat till 2400, Sun till 2300. *The Pear Tree*, 38 West Nicolson St, T6677533. Near the University, so a favourite student haunt, this was once a focal point for the city's crusties but now the occasional suit can be spotted. Boasts Edinburgh's only decent-sized beer garden, which is not only packed in summer, but populated at other times of the year. Also serves amazingly cheap food. Open Mon-Wed and Sun till 2400, Thu-Sat till 0100. *Sheep Heid Inn*, 43 The Causeway, Duddingston, T6566951. An 18th- century coaching inn that makes a pleasant stop for a refreshing drink after a walk over Arthur's Seat. You could make a day of it and include Duddingston Loch and village and lunch here in the restaurant upstairs or in the bar. Either way it's good. In summer there's the added attraction of the open-air barbecue. Open Mon-Wed and Sun till 2300, Thu-Sat till 2400.

Leith & Newhaven Bar *Java*, 48-50 Constitution St, T4677527. Good little bar that opens early for breakfast and has a beer garden out back, also has rooms for B&B upstairs. Open Mon-Wed till 2400, Thu-Sun till 0100. *King's Wark*, 36 The Shore. T5549260. One of the oldest pubs in Leith, dating back to the early 17th century and it appears not to have changed much. Real historical atmosphere and some damned fine food to boot. Open Mon-Thu 1200-2300, Fri/Sat till 2400, Sun 1100-2300. The Pond, 2 Bath Rd, T4673825. A 5-min walk east of Commercial St. Very unusual decor to say the least. Open Mon-Thu 1600-0100, Fri-Sun 1400-0100. *Starbank Inn*, 64 Laverockbank Rd, Newhaven. On the seafront between Newhaven and Leith. Nice old pub where you can enjoy a good pint of real ale and the views across the Forth. Also does bar food. Open Sun-Wed till 2300, Thu-Sat till 2400.

Entertainment

As host of the World's premiere arts festival, Edinburgh is well endowed with various cultural venues. But don't be mistaken in thinking that when the Festival packs its bags and leaves in early Sep the city hibernates till Aug comes round again. The city's cultural scene is thriving throughout the year, catering equally well for the avid culture vulture or hedonistic night owl. The many fine **theatres** and **concert halls** have full and varied programmes. Club culture in the capital has improved greatly in the last few years and Edinburgh now boasts some of the UK's best club nights, many of which go on until 0400 or 0500. These change frequently but tend to use the same venues, which are listed below. Those who prefer their music live, can take advantage of the liberal licensing laws and check out **jazz**, **folk** and **rock** bands any night of the week in many of city's 700-plus bars. The main live music venues are listed below, but also see under 'Bars'. The city's vibrant **gay scene** has been centred around the Playhouse Theatre at the top of Leith Walk, the 'pink triangle', for many years. It has continued to develop around Broughton St, with new places constantly opening up, be they exclusively gay or gay-friendly. A large percentage of the city's trendiest bars, cafés and clubs can now be found on or around Broughton St, making Edinburgh an easy city for the gay tourist to visit.

For a full list of what's on, visit www. edinburghevents.com

To find out **what's on** in the city, pick up a copy of *The List*, the fortnightly listings magazine that tells you what's happening and where in both Edinburgh and Glasgow. Alternatively, the local evening paper, the *Edinburgh Evening News*, appears daily except Sun and gives details of what's going on the city on that day. Tickets and information on all events are available at the **Tourist Information Centre**. You can also find flyers (promotional leaflets) for various events at the main concert halls and theatres and in many of the bars and cafés in the centre of town.

Art galleries

Aside from the main galleries mentioned in the 'Sights' section, Edinburgh has several smaller spaces where the work of up-and-coming contemporary artists can be viewed. *City Art Centre*, 2 Market St, T5293993. Houses 6 exhibition galleries. Home to the city's collection of Scottish art, with works by Peploe, McTaggart, Ferguson and Eardley as well as more contemporary artists such as Blackadder and Paolozzi, as well as being one of the leading temporary exhibition spaces in the UK. Also has a café. Open Mon-Sat 1000-1700, Sun during the Festival only 1400-1700. Usually free, but charges for selected shows. *Edinburgh Printmakers Workshop and Gallery*, 23 Union St, off Leith Walk, T5572479. Exhibits a huge range of contemporary etchings, lithographs and screenprints. You can buy prints in the shop at reasonable prices and see the workshops. Open Tue-Sat 1000-1800. Free. *The Fruitmarket Gallery*, 45 Market St, T2252383. Near Waverley station. One of the country's major venues for exhibitions of national and international contemporary art. Also has a good bookshop and café. Open Mon-Sat 1100-1800, Sun 1200-1700. Free. *Stills Gallery*, 23 Cockburn St, T622-6200. Scotland's leading photographic gallery, with a good café. Open Tue-Sat 1000-1700. Free.

For information on the various art exhibitions presented throughout the city, access the Edinburgh Gallery Guide website at www.edinburgh-galleries.co.uk

Cinemas

The Cameo, 38 Home St, T2284141. In the Tollcross. 3 screens showing new arthouse releases and cult classics. Late showings at weekends and a good bar with video screen showing short films, comfy seating and snacks. Great place for movie buffs to hang out. Bar open Sun-Wed 1230-2300, Thu-Sat till 0100. *The Dominion*, 18 Newbattle Terr, T4474771. A nice old-fashioned cinema down in Morningside. 3 screens showing new releases. *Filmhouse*, 88 Lothian Rd, T2282688. Three screens showing a wide range of movies, including new arthouse releases, obscure foreign films and old classics. Good café-bar. Hosts the annual Film Festival, so you never know who you might bump into. *Odeon*, 7 Clerk St, T6670971. 5-screen complex showing mainstream releases. *UGC*

Edinburgh

Cinemas, Fountainpark, Dundee St, T0870-9020417. Vast 13-screen complex which also includes bars, restaurants, gym and nightclub.

Clubs
Consult The List for the latest information.

Most of the clubs listed are in the Old Town and most are open till 0300 (later during the Festival). All of the venues are open from between 1000-1030 to 0300 (Festival and Xmas/New Year till 0500). Standard charges are from £8-10 for members and £10-13 for non-members.

La Belle Angele, 11 Hasties Cl. Underground venue situated up one of the closes leading from the Cowgate. Alternates Sat between trance/house night 'Atomic Baby' and funky/deep house night 'Ultra Groove', flyers in most of the pre-club bars will let people know exactly what is on. *Club Mercado*, 36-39 Market St. There are 2 sides to this venue, on a Fri from 1700 onwards its TFI Friday night is the most popular post work venue for the city's office workers and half price drinks are served till 2000 to a backdrop of Wham, Abba, young secretaries and leering bosses. Not for the faint hearted. On Sat it is a club venue alternating between the funky/commercial 'Eye Candy' and the house night 'Blast'. Suns are fairly popular with the camp/kitsch night Tackno. *The Venue*, 17-23 Calton Rd. Situated at the east side of the city centre, recently refurbished and under new management it hosts nights such as 'Up' and 'Cerotonin'. *Studio 24*, 24-26 Calton Rd. At opposite end of the street to *The Venue*. Falling to pieces but nevertheless has good atmosphere and splits in to 2 separate venues (upstairs and downstairs) on fortnightly Sat for 'Oxygen' a gay friendly hard house night and 'Mingin' a very gay trance/techno night run by the 'Joy' team, the other weekends are usually rock nights for grungeys and goths or the occasional fetish/rubber night so check what's on before going.

Ego,14 Picardy Pl. Refurbished casino situated at top of Leith Walk, hosts various club nights, its biggest draws are the long running gay night 'Joy' which runs fortnightly on Sat and 'Vegas' which runs monthly and is frequented by twenty-to-thirty somethings who enjoy spending their Saturday nights dancing to Kenny Rogers, Neil Diamond and Johnny Cash. *The Honeycomb*, 15 Niddry St. Much-vaunted attempt to house an Edinburgh superclub, formerly known as 'The Vaults' allegedly £100 mn has been spent on its refurbishment and it hosts 'Sublime' the long running trance/house night, 'It' which is the premises own funky house night and the popular gay friendly nights 'Luvley' which runs the 3rd Sat of every month and 'Taste' which runs every Sun and remains the biggest Sun night Club in Edinburgh.

Comedy venues

Gilded Balloon Theatre, 233 Cowgate, T2262151. One of the main Fringe comedy venues, famous for its riotous *Late'n'Live* slot. Here you'll see some of the best, and occasionally some of the worst, young comedians on the circuit. It also puts on regular comedy shows throughout the year. *The Stand Comedy Club*, 5 York Pl, T5587272. Showcase for emerging comedy talent 7 nights a week. By day it's a popular café-bar serving budget lunches, and on Sun there's free comedy with your lunch. Open Mon-Thu 1200-2400, Fri 1200-1900, 1930-0100, Sat 1930-0100, Sun 1230-2400.

Concert halls
For details of current performances, see The List or Sat's Scotsman newspaper

Classical music played by one of the national orchestras can often be heard at the main civic concert hall, the *Usher Hall*, Lothian Rd and Grindlay St, T2281155. Smaller classical ensembles, as well as jazz, blues, folk, rock and pop groups, can be heard at *Queen's Hall*, 89 Clerk St, T6682019. Less frequent performances are also staged at *Reid Concert Hall*, Bristo Sq, T6504367, and the wonderful 18th century *St Cecilia's Hall*, Cowgate and Niddry St, T6502805.

Blue Moon Café (see 'Cafés' above). Gay-run but straight-friendly café that's always busy. *Café Kudos*, 22 Greenside Pl (at the front of the Playhouse Theatre), T5564349. Outside seating in summer. Popular with bright young things. Open daily till 0100. *CC Blooms*, 23 Greenside Place (next to the Playhouse), T5569331. Packed almost every night upstairs and downstairs on the dancefloor. This is where everyone ends up. Open daily till 0300. *New Town Bar*, 26 Dublin St, T5387775. Fairly mixed crowd upstairs. Downstairs is called *Intense* – appropriately named and full-on. Open daily till 0130, weekends till 0230. *Intense* open Thu-Sun. *Nexus Café*, 60 Broughton St, T478-7069. Comfortable and laid-back spot overlooking the garden behind the Gay and Lesbian Centre. Good all-day breakfasts (also vegetarian) and reasonably priced snacks. Good pre-club meeting place. Open daily 1100-2300. *Planet Out*, 6 Baxter's Pl, T5573379. Close to the *Playhouse*. Lively place in the heart of the action. Open daily till 0100.

Gay clubs & bars
There are many gay or gay-friendly cafés, bars and restaurants on Broughton St and several of these are listed elsewhere in the 'Eating', 'Cafés' and 'Bars' sections

Good places to catch up-and-coming young **indie bands** are *La Belle Angele*, *The Liquid Room* and *The Venue*, all of which are listed above under 'Clubs'. The Liquid Room has extablished itself as good place to see touring acts such as Moby and Mogwai. They also host the T on The Fringe music festival. The Attic, on the Cowgate (T2258382) has become the focal point for new talent. During the festival they host their own mini festival called Planet Pop. The Playhouse Theatre (see below) is a favourite with old codgers like Lou Reed and Van Morrison. And in more recent years, the *Ross Open Air Theatre* in Princes Street Gardens, T2204351, has been used for major music gigs at Hogmanay and during the Festival.

Live music venues

Live **jazz** can be heard in *Henry's Cellar Bar*, Morrison St, T2211228. Also know as the Jazz Joint, this tiny cellar bar shows a vast range of acts. You can also eat upstairs in the Oriental restaurants (see page113). Jazz can also be heard on Fri and Sat nights at *Cellar No 1* (see page 118). Occasional jazz concerts, as well as a growing number of top rock and pop gigs, also take place at the *Queen's Hall* (see above). One of the best places to hear authentic grassroots **folk music** is *The Royal Oak* (see under 'Bars'). Another good bet is the *Tron Ceilidh House*, 9 Hunter Square, behind the Tron Kirk, T2201550. Below the ground floor bar are two basement levels, with regular folk sessions and a comedy club. Open Sun-Thu till 2400, Fri/Sat till 0100. Nighthawks should head down to *Whistlebinkies*, Niddry St, T5575114, where you can listen to raucous folk till 0300. Two more popular folk venues are upstairs in the famous *Café Royal* in West Register Street (see under 'Bars') and the *West End Hotel* in Palmerston Place (see under 'Sleeping'). The *West End Hotel* is also a good place to find out where and when ceilidhs are taking place in the city.

Bedlam Theatre, 11b Bistro Pl, T2259893. Home of the University's Bedlam Theatre Company. A bit hit or miss but you can always grab a cheap and wholesome bite to eat in the café. *Festival Theatre*, Nicolson St, T5296000. The city's showcase theatre with a hugely varied programme including the world's leading companies. There's also an excellent café (see page 115). *Hill Street Theatre*, 19 Hill St, T2266522. Homely little venue that's one of the Festival Fringe stalwarts. *King's Theatre*, 2 Leven St, T2291201. Refurbished Edwardian theatre showing everything from Shakespeare to panto. *Netherbow Arts Centre*, 43 High St, T5569579. Home to the Scottish Storytelling Centre, with children's shows during the day and Scottish drama for adults in the evenings. *Playhouse Theatre*, 18-22 Greenside Pl, T5572950. Vast 3,000-seater theatre where you can catch all the glitzy West End productions as well as the occasional rock star. Used during the official Festival for dance and opera. *Pleasance Theatre*, 60 The Pleasance, T5566550. One of the top Fringe venues staging comedy and drama. The outdoor cobbled courtyard is a great place to hang out during the Festival for a bit star-spotting. *Royal Lyceum*, 30 Grindlay St, T2299697. Lovely old Victorian theatre staging mainstream drama all year round. *Theatre Workshop*, 34 Hamilton place, T2265425. Small, accessible and amenable theatre down in bohemian Stockbridge

Theatres

Edinburgh

Edinburgh

 Festival City

Every year Edinburgh plays host to the world's biggest arts festival when the capital bursts into life in a riot of entertainment unmatched anywhere. Edinburgh during its Festival has been variously described as "simply the best place on Earth" and "the cultural hub of the world". There's a unique buzz about the place as over a million tourists descend on the city to experience a mind-blowing variety of performances. Dance groups, opera and theatre companies, orchestras, string quartets, comedians and puppeteers play to audiences in concert halls, theatres, church halls, pubs, clubs, hotels, Masonic lodges and big tents all across the city. Meanwhile, outdoors, the streets, parks and squares are filled with fire-eaters, jugglers, clowns, musicians, trapeze artists and escapologists all vying for your attention and to relieve you of your small change. The best places to see the street performers are the Mound, the High Street and Rose Street.

The Edinburgh Festival is actually a collection of different festivals running alongside each other, from the end of July through to the beginning of September. The **International Festival** tends to be a fairly highbrow affair and features large-scale productions of opera, ballet, classical music, dance and theatre performed in the larger venues. It ends with an open air concert and spectacular fireworks display in Princes Street Gardens. The **Festival Fringe** began life in 1947 as an adjunct to the International, or "official" Festival, but has since grown so large it now overshadows its big brother and threatens to outgrow the city. Last year over 500 companies performed in nearly 200 venues; everything from the country's leading comedians at the Assembly Rooms to a group of existentialist students staging "Waiting for Godot" in Mandarin in a draughty church hall. Over the years the Fringe has been a major showcase for fresh talent and the likes of Billy Connolly, Maggie Smith, Emma Thompson, Rowan Atkinson and Harry Enfield all started out here. The Fringe continues to be the launching pad for many of our greatest actors, comedians, writers and directors as well as pushing back the boundaries of art and entertainment. A good opportunity to preview many of the Fringe performers for free is Fringe Sunday, which takes place in Holyrood Park, at the foot of the Royal Mile.

The **International Jazz and Blues Festival** kicks the whole thing off in July and features some of the world's leading performers, as well as many lesser known ones, playing in just about every pub in the city centre. The **International Film Festival** is the UK's most important film festival and screens many brilliant new movies long before they reach London and the rest of the country. It is also the longest continually running event of its kind in the world. The **International Book Festival**, meanwhile, may look like a just a bunch of tents in Charlotte Square, but the marquees are full of some of the biggest names in literature holding readings, discussions, interviews and a whole range of workshops for adults and children. Although it's a separate event, the **Military Tattoo**, set against the magnificent backdrop of Edinburgh Castle, is very much part of the Festival. It's an unashamedly kilt-and-bagpipes event, featuring Massed Pipes and Drums, display teams, dancers and bands from all over the world.

During the Festival, many of Edinburgh's tourist attractions have longer opening hours. Many of the main Festival venues are used throughout the year and are listed under **Entertainment** (page 55). For details of Festival dates and booking information see **Festival Information**.

with a reputation for innovative and daring productions. *Traverse Theatre*, 10 Cambridge St, T2281404. Internationally renowned theatre dedicated to encouraging the cream of new writing talent. Consistently good entertainment. Also blessed with the excellent restaurant, *The Atrium*, in the foyer and *blue* bistro upstairs (see 'Eating'), as well as a good bar (see 'Bars').

Festival Information

Edinburgh International Festival
11-31 August 2002. Box office: The Hub,
Castlehill, T4732000, www.eif.co.uk
Edinburgh Festival Fringe
4-26 August 2002. Box office: 180 High
Street, T2265257, www.edfringe.com
Edinburgh International Film Festival
Over 2 weeks in August. Box office:
Filmhouse, 88 Lothian Road, T2292550,
www.edfilmfest.org.uk
Edinburgh International Jazz & Blues
Festival
From end-July to early August. Box office:
29 St Stephen St, T2252202,
www.jazzmusic.co.uk
International Book Festival
2 weeks August. Box office: 137 Dundee St,

T2285444, www.edbookfest.co.uk
Edinburgh Military Tattoo
11-31 August. Box office: 32 Market St,
T2251188, www.edintattoo.co.uk
International Science Festival
2 weeks in early August. Box office:
Roxburgh's Court, off 323 High St,
T2605860, www.sciencefestival.co.uk
For full information about the International
Festival events, and for access to the
websites of all the Edinburgh Festivals visit
the official festival site:
www.go-edinburgh.co.uk
The free daily listings magazine, The Guide,
is a good way to find out what's on and
where. The List and The Scotsman also
give comprehensive coverage.

Festivals

Edinburgh not only hosts the world's greatest arts festival in Aug, but also stages several other notable events throughout the rest of the year. The most renowned of these is **Edinburgh's Hogmanay**, which has grown to become one of the world's major winter events and which was the largest Millenium celebration in the northern hemisphere. It starts on the 29 Dec with a torchlit procession through the city centre followed by four days of various events, including pop and rock concerts. The highlight is the giant street party on the 31st (which is for ticket holders only). Accommodation is always fully booked at this time. For information contact The Hub , or www. edinburghshogmanay.org

The **Folk Festival**, at the beginning of **Apr**, is a massive event and draws performers from near and far, T5543092. The **Scottish International Children's Festival** is the UK's largest performing arts festival for children and is held at the end of **May** (Box office: 45a George St, T2258050, www.imaginate.org.uk). At the end of **Jun** is the **Royal Highland Show**, at the Royal Highland Centre, Ingliston, T3356200. It's a sort of display of the best of rural Scotland, with pedigree livestock competitions, flower shows, craft fairs and showjumping, amongst other things. Also in Jun, usually in the 1st week, is the **Caledonian Beer Festival**, held at Edinburgh's own Caledonian Brewery on Slateford Road (see 'Bars', on page 117). The event features dozens of real ales, food and live music (mostly jazz) in the brewery's Festival Hall. See local press for details, or T3371286. The **Filmhouse** (see 'Cinemas', on page 121) also hosts a number of foreign film seasons, most notably French (in **Nov**) and Italian, in **Apr**. There's also a gay film season, in **Jun**. For details, T2282688.

Shopping

Edinburgh's shops are best known for traditional Scottish souvenirs and upmarket goods, food products in particular. The main shopping street is **Princes Street**, where you'll find all the main department stores such as *Debenhams, Frasers, BHS, Marks & Spencers*. Two independent department stores are *Jenners*, also on Princes Street, and *Aitken & Niven*, at 77-79 George St. **George Street** is the place to come for fashionistas

Edinburgh

as it's lined with chic clothes chops. Harvey Nicks is due to open in St Andrews Sq in 2002. Good places to look for second-hand and antique art, jewellery and books are around the **New Town** (St Stephen St, Northwest Circus Pl, Thistle St), **Broughton St**, **Victoria St** and the **Grassmarket**. Shopping hours are now more relaxed and many of the main city centre outlets are open till 1930-2000 on Thu and on Sun.

Antiques & junk *Byzantium*, 9 Victoria St, T2251768. Two floors of popular collectables from the 40s to the 70s, as well as antiques and hippy chic. Good place to browse, with a café on the third floor. Open Mon-Sat 1000-1730, and Sun during the Festival. *Just Junk*, 34 Broughton St, T5576353. Small, reasonably priced range of stuff from the 50s and 60s. Open Mon-Sat 1100-1800. *Utilities*, 87 Broughton St, T5574385. A real Aladdin's Cave where you could lose hours just browsing. Open Tue-Sat 1030-1830, Sun 1200-1600.

Books *James Thin*, 53-59 South Bridge, T5566743. This venerable Scottish chain has branches across the city and throughout the country, but this particular branch has a good second-hand department. Open Mon-Fri 0900-2200, Sat 0900-1730, Sun 1100-1700. *Waterstone's*, 128 Princes St (West End), T2262666. One of three city branches of this major chain, with a massive range of titles, well-informed staff and a pleasant second-floor café with fantastic views of the castle (see also 'Cafés'). Open Mon-Fri 0800-2100, Sat 0800-2000, Sun 1030-1800. Other branches at 13-14 Princes St, T5563034 and 83 George St, T2253436. *The Cook's Bookshop*, 118 West Bow, T2264445. Owned by celebrity chef Clarissa Dickson Wright with a wide selection of new and second-hand cookery books. Open Mon-Fri 1000-1700, Sat 1030-1700. *West Port Bookshop*, 145 West Port, T2294431. Wonderfully ramshackle, old-fashioned second-hand bookshop. Open Mon-Fri 1030-1730, Sat 1130-1700.

Clothes & shoes *Cruise*, 94 George St, T2263524 (also at 14 St Mary's St, T5562532). Expensive but high-quality range of designer clothes for men and women. Open Mon-Wed and Fri 1000-1800, Thu till 1900, Sat 0900-1800, Sun 1300-1700. *Smiths*, 124 High St, T2255927. Top British designer menswear. *Jenners* on Princes St stocks a wide range of men's designer labels. *Corniche*, 2 Jeffrey St, T5563707. Stocks all the top names in women's fashion. Open Mon-Sat 1000-1730. *Flip*, 59-61 South Bridge, T5564966. Edinburgh branch of the national chain of second-hand American retro clothing. Open Mon-Sat 0930-1730. *Hand in Hand*, 3 Northwest Circus Pl, T2263598. For second-hand women's clothes. *Schuh*, 6 Frederick St, T2200290, and 32 North Bridge, T2256552. The best for trendy footwear. *Barnets*, 7 High St, T5563577. For those who prefer a more classic shoe. **Shoe repairs** *Master Cobbler*, 5 Waverley Steps, T5573756. *Uppermost Shoe repairs*, 9 North Bridge Arcade, T2264584. *H Robertson*, 21a Castle St, T2263464.

On Goerge St you'll find Coast, French Connection, Karen Millen, Jigsaw & Escada

Food & drink There are more food outlets than any other type of shop in the capital, so you won't have trouble finding your haggis, whisky and shortbread. *Peckhams*, 155-159 Bruntsfield Pl, T2297054. Fine vintners and victualers that leave you salivating and a few quid lighter. This is where you can buy the famed MacSween haggis. Open daily till 2200. *The Scotch Whisky Heritage Centre*, 354 Castlehill (see also 'Sights'). Finding alcohol isn't a problem in Edinburgh, but here you can sample the stuff before parting with your cash. Open daily 0930-1800 (from 1230 on Sun). *Valvona & Crolla*, 19 Elm Row (see also 'Cafés'). Superb Italian deli importing fresh produce direct from Italy. Café at the back where you can linger and savour the delights on offer. Open Mon-Wed and Sat 0800-1800, Thu/Fri till 1930. *Royal Mile Whiskies*, 379 High St, T2253383. Over 300 types of whisky to choose from and all kinds of attractive gift packages. Open Mon-Sat 1000-1900, Sun 1200-1900. *Ian Mellis*, 30a Victoria St, T2266215. An overwhelming selection of cheeses, in every sense of the word. Open Mon-Sat 0930-1730, next door to *La Sologne*, a tempting patisserie. *Real Foods*, 37 Broughton St, T5571911. The best-stocked vegetarian and vegan grocery shop in town. Open Mon-Wed 0900-1830, Thu and Sat till 1730, Fri till 1900, Sun 1100-1700.

For tartan tack go to the top end of the Royal Mile. Those wishing to hire a kilt, or have one made, should try *McCalls of the Royal Mile*, at 11 High St, T5573979, or *Kinloch Anderson*, on the corner of Dock St and Commercial St, Leith, T5551390. There's also *Hector Russell*, on the High St and on Princes St. For woollens try *Judith Glue* – Orkney Island Knitwear, 64 High St, T5565443. Open Mon-Sat 0930-1800, Sun 1200-1700. Also *The Cashmere Store*, 2 St Giles St, T2254055, and *Number Two*, 2 St Stephen Place, T2256257. Those looking for something a bit different should check out *Round the World*, at 82 West Bow, T2257086, and 15 North West Circus Pl, T2257800, or *Eden*, at 37-39 Cockburn St, T2203372. There are a few interesting shops in Raeburn Place, such as *Blackadder Gallery*, at number 5, T3324605. For jewellery, try *Hamilton and Inches*, 87 George Street, T225 4898, open Mon-Fri 0930-1750, Sat 0930-1700.

Gifts & souvenirs

Avalanche, 17 West Nicolson St, T6682374, 63 Cockburn St, T2253939, and 28 Lady Lawson St, T2281939. Specializes in new and used vinyl and CDs. The Cockburn St branch is a good place to find out about clubs and gigs. Open daily 1000-1800. *Backbeat*, 31 East Crosscauseway, T6682666. Excellent second-hand record shop with a great selection of jazz, blues and soul. Open Mon-Sat 1000-1730. *Blackfriar's Folk Music Shop*, 49 Blackfriar's St (off the Royal Mile), T5573090. Wide range of traditional Scottish musical instruments. *FOPP*, 55 Cockburn St, T2200133. Another record shop on a street full of them. Good for mainstream, indie and dance music. Open Mon-Sat 0930-1900, Sun 1100-1800.

Music

Blacks Outdoor Leisure, 13-14 Elm Row, T5563491, and 24 Frederick St, T2258686. Good range of clothes and equipment for hikers, skiiers and ramblers. Open Mon-Wed and Fri 0900-1800, Thu 0930-1900, Sat 0900-1730. *Graham Tiso*, 13 Wellington Place and Rose St. Excellent for all kinds of outdoor clothing and sports equipment.

Outdoor & sports

Sports

There's indoor rock climbing at *Alien Rock*, Old St Andrew's Church, Pier Pl, Newhaven, T5527211. Climbing walls of various degrees of difficulty and a bouldering room.

Climbing

Edinburgh has 2 Scottish Premier League teams, who play at home on alternate Saturdays during the league season. Heart of Midlothian, or Hearts, play at Tyncastle, on the Gorgie Road about a mile west of Haymarket, and Hibernian (Hibs) play at Easter Road, east of the centre near Leith. Rivalry between the two is fierce, but thankfully free from the religious bigotry of their Glasgow counterparts.

Football

There are many fine golf courses around Edinburgh, especially along the coast of East Lothian, but most are private. Public courses in and around the city include the two at *Braid Hills*, T4476666, *Silverknowes*, T3363843, *Torphin Hill*, T4414061, and *Lothianburn*, T4452288. If you plan on playing a lot of golf, then you should buy the *Lothian and Edinburgh Golf Pass*, which costs £5 and allows you to play on 20 courses throughout the region at discounted rates. For details, contact the tourist board, T4733800, www.edinburgh.org/golf.

Golf

Edinburgh & Lasswade Riding Centre, Kevock Rd, Lasswade, T6637676. *Pentland Hills Icelandics*, Rodgersrigg Farm, Carlops (south of Hillend Ski Centre), Midlothian, T01968-661095. *Tower Farm Riding Stables*, 85 Liberton Drive, T6643375.

Horse riding

Rugby   Scotland's national side play at Murrayfield Stadium, a few miles west of the city centre and reached from Corstorphine Rd or Roseburn St. For tickets T3645000, though these are scarce for major internationals.

Skiing   *Midlothian Ski Centre*, at Hillend, take the A702 off the City Bypass at the Lothianburn exit, T4454433 (open Mon-Sat 0930-2100, Sun 0930-1900). Artificial ski slope for ski and snowboarding practice and instruction. Also downhill mountain bike trail and chairlift for those who want to admire the view.

Sports centres   Meadowbank Sports Centre, 139 London Rd, T6615351. The city's main venue for athletics meetings. Indoor and outdoor multi-sports complex with fitness room, squash courts, all weather pitches, velodrome and climbing wall. Open Mon 0930-2300, Tue-Sun 0900-2300. To get there, take bus no 15 or 26 from Princes St (north side) or a no 45 from the Mound. *Craiglockart Tennis and Sports Centre*, 177 Colinton Rd, T4430101. Indoor and outdoor tennis courts, squash, badminton, pulse-centre gym, fitness studio and free weights. Open Mon-Thu 0900-2300, Fri 1000-2300, Sat/Sun 0900-2230. Take bus no 10 from Princes St (south side) or no 27 from the Mound going south.

Swimming pools   *Ainslie Park Leisure Centre*, 92 Pilton Rd, T5512400. Swimming pool, sauna, steam room, spa, pulse-centre gym, fitness suite. Open Mon-Fri 1000-2200, Sat/Sun 1000-1800. Take bus no 28 or 29 from the Mound to Crewe Toll, or 27 to Ferry Road. *Leith Waterworld*, 377 Easter Road, T5556000. At the foot of Leith Walk. Good children's facilities. Open Mon-Fri 0900-1700, Sat/Sun 1000-1700 during school holidays. *Royal Commonwealth Pool*, Dalkeith Rd, T6677211. The biggest and most popular in the city, with a 50 m pool, flumes, diving pool, children's area, sauna and gym. Open Mon-Fri 0900-2100, Sat/Sun 1000-1600. To get there take a no 14, 21, 33, 82 or 83 bus south from North Bridge.

Transport

Long distance   **Air**   There are many flights to Edinburgh from all over Europe, Ireland and from around the UK. Flights from North America arrive via Glasgow. (For flight details, see page 70). There is one daily flight from Edinburgh to **Inverness**, which takes 45 mins.

Bus   There are numerous bus services from London and prices are very competitive. There are also links with other English cities, such as Newcastle, Manchester, Birmingham and York. (For details of these services, see page 70.) Buses leave from St Andrew Square bus station to most of the major towns in Scotland. Most west coast towns are reached via Glasgow. There are numerous buses to and from **Glasgow** (£5-7 return fare). There are also regular daily buses to: **Aberdeen** (4 hrs; £13-15 single); **Dundee** (2 hrs 10 mins, or 1 hr 25 mins direct; £6-7 single); **Perth** (1½ hrs, or 1 hr direct; £4-6 single); **Inverness** (4½ hrs, or 3 hrs 40 mins direct; £12-14 single), via Pitlochry and Aviemore. One of the main operators is *Scottish Citylink*, T08705-505050, with buses to virtually every major town in Scotland. For bus services to and from English towns and cities, contact *National Express*, T08705-808080, www.gobycoach.com

Train   There are regular daily services to and from London King's Cross. (For details of frequency and fares, see page 70.) *ScotRail* runs regular daily train services to **Inverness** (3¾ hrs), via **Stirling** (45 mins), **Perth** (1¼ hrs), **Pitlochry** and **Aviemore** (3 hrs). Also to **Aberdeen** (2¾ hrs), via **Kirkcaldy** and **Dundee** (1¾ hrs). There are trains every 30 mins to and from **Glasgow** (50 mins; £8-10 day return). There is also a regular service to **North Berwick** (35 mins).

Bus Buses are reasonably frequent during working hours from 0700, but after 1900 and on Sun they are much less so, with some routes stopping completely. Main city-centre bus stops have timetables on display and some have clear maps of the bus routes served by that stop and the fares, which are paid to the driver on all buses. Be warned that *LRT* buses are **exact fare only**, and drivers don't give change – ever. *First Edinburgh* services don't require the exact fare. Both offer saver tickets (£2.20, £1.50 child; £1.50 for adults after 0930 Mon-Fri and all day Sat/Sun). These can be bought from the driver and are valid on all buses except the Airlink, Britannia X50, night buses or tours. A 7-day card costs £10.50. **Night buses** run every hour from 0015 till 0315, leaving from Waverley Bridge. Contact *Traveline* or *LRT* for details.

Local
See also page 70

Taxi The council-imposed city taxi fares are not cheap, costing from around £3 for the shortest of trips up to around £6 from the centre to the outskirts. There are far more people wanting to get home late on Fri or Sat night than there are cabs on the streets, so be prepared to wait, walk or phone. Some of the larger 24-hr companies are: *Capital Castle Taxis*, T2282555; *Central Radio Taxis*, T2292468; *Edinburgh Taxis*, T2288989; *Radio Cabs*, T2259000.

Directory

Banks The major **Scottish banks** have branches throughout the city, those with cash dispensers (ATMs) in the centre of town are: *Bank of Scotland*, Canongate, Chambers St, George St, 141 Princes St, 38 St Andrews Sq, Shandwick Pl, The Mound (head office); *Royal Bank of Scotland*, George St, North Bridge, Princes St, St Andrews Sq; *Clydesdale Bank*, 29 George St, Hanover St, North Bridge. The major **English clearing banks** all have branches in the city, and are open Mon-Fri only (phone for opening times): *Barclays*, 1 St Andrew Sq, T0845-6000; *Lloyds/ TSB*, 113 George St, T2264021; *HSBC*, 76 Hanover St, T4653200; *NatWest*, 80 George St, T2266181. For **currency exchange**: *Thomas Cook*, 79a Princes St, T2204039. Open Mon-Fri 0900-1730, Sat 0900-1700. Also have other exchange bureaus in the main tourist office at Waverley Market (open Mon-Sat 0900-2000) and in the accommodation kiosk at Waverley station (see page 105). To change money outside office hours, try the upmarket hotels, though expect to pay a hefty commission. Also *American Express*, 139 Princes St, T2259179. Open Mon-Fri 0900-1730, Sat 0900-1600, Sun (Jul-Sep only) 1000-1600.

Car hire The main national car-hire companies can all be found at the airport. The following are local companies which may offer better deals: *Arnold Clark*, Lochrin Pl, T2284747; *Condor*, 45 Lochrin Pl, Tollcross, T2296333; *Lo-Cost*, 1a Wardlaw Terr (off Slateford Rd), T3132220; *Melville's*, 9 Clifton Terr, Haymarket, www.melvilles.co.uk. **Communications** Internet: there are cybercafés throughout the city, but two of the best are *Cyberia*, 88 Hanover St, T2204403, open Mon-Sat 1000-2200, Sun 1100-2000, prices from £2.50 per half hour (£2 concession) and *Web 13*, 13 Bread St, T2298883, open Mon-Fri 0900-2200, Sat 0900-2000, Sun 1100-2000, prices from £2.50 per half hour at peak times (1200-1700 Mon-Sat) and £3.50 at all other times. Both are also listed under 'Cafés' (see page 116). *Easy Everything*, Hanover Buildings, 58 Rose St, T2203580. Open 24 hrs and cheapest in town at £1 per hr. **Post office**: central offices at 8-10 St James Centre and 7 Hope St. There is a late collection from the post box at the Royal Mail head office, 10 Brunswick Rd (one third of the way down Leith Walk). A Poste Restante service is available at any post office, providing you have no permanent address in Edinburgh. Envelopes should be marked 'Poste Restante' in the top left corner with your name above the address of the office. **Consulates** See page 27.

See also page 46

Edinburgh

Cycle hire *Central Cycle Hire*, 13 Lochrin Pl, T2286333, F2283686. £15/day. Open Mon-Fri 0930-1800, Sat 0930-1730, Sun 1200-1700. *Edinburgh Cycle Hire*, 29 Blackfriars St, T5565560. £10-12/day. Open daily 0900-2100.

Disabled access and facilities Edinburgh is not the most accessible of cities, particularly around the Old Town. All cinemas and permanent theatres have full access. Guide dogs are welcome on public transport and at most Festival venues. The *Lothian Coalition for Disabled People*, T4752360, F4752392, publishes *Access in Lothian*, which they will send out on request. *Artlink*, T2293555, provide an arts access service to Edinburgh residents, so should be able to provide information and access hints. New black cabs can take wheelchairs and the taxi firms listed on page 129 all have facilities for disabled passengers. Full details of disabled access on public transport from *Traveline*, T0800-232323. The Fringe Office at 180 High St, T2265257, has a Disability Fact Sheet for further information and holds a list of contacts for each venue. **Drugs information** *Crew 2000* has a walk-in information shop at 32 Cockburn St, T2203404, where volunteers offer impartial information and advice on all aspects of using illicit and non-medical drugs. Open Mon-Wed, Fri and Sat 1300-1700, Thu 1600-2000.

Gay and Lesbian *Gay Men's Health*, T5589444; *Gay Switchboard*, T5564049; *Lesbian Line*, T5570751). **Genealogical research** *Scottish Genealogy Society Library & Family History Centre*, 15 Victoria Terr, T2203677. Open Tue and Thu 1030-1730, Wed 1030-2030, Sat 1000-1700. £5 per session for non-members. *Scottish Roots Ancestral Research Service*, 16 Forth St, T4778214. Open Mon-Fri 0900-1700 by appointment.

Medical services Edinburgh's 24-hr walk-in accident and emergency department is at *The Royal Infirmary of Edinburgh*, 1 Lauriston Place, T5361000. If it's not an emergency but you still need to see a doctor look in the *Yellow Pages*, or call the Primary Care department, T5369000. **Alternative medicine**: *Napiers Dispensary and Clinic*, 1 Teviot Pl, T2255542, and 35 Hamilton Pl, Stockbridge, T3752130. Open Mon 1000-1730, Tue-Sat 0900-1730. Health practitioners providing non-conventional remedies. **Chemist (Pharmacy)**: *Boots the Chemist*, 48 Shandwick Place, T2256757. Open Mon-Sat 0800-2100, Sun 1000-1700. In an emergency outisde these times, go to The Royal Infirmary. **Dental**: *Edinburgh Dental Institute*, Level 7, Lauriston Building, Lauriston Place, T5364931. Open Mon-Fri 0900-1500. They provide free walk-in emergency treatment though you still need to book an appointment. If it's not an emergency but you need to see a dentist, look in the *Yellow Pages* or call the Primary Care department, as above. **STDs/HIV/AIDS**: *The Genito-Urinary Medicine* (GUM) clinic is at Lauriston Building, Lauriston Pl (men T5362103; women T5362104). Open Mon-Fri 0830-1700, till 1830 on Thu. Free confidential advice and treatment on sexually transmitted and other diseases.

Laundry *Sundial Laundrettes* offer coin-operated or service washes, full laundry service, ironing, dry-cleaning and alterations. They have several branches at: 7 East London St, T5562743, next to the *Lost Sock Diner* (see 'Eating', page 112); 84 Dalry Rd, T5387002; 17 Roseneath St, T2292137; *Tarvit Laundrette*, 7 Tarvit St, T2296382. **Left luggage** Left-luggage lockers at Waverley train station, T5502031, by platform 11, open 0700-2300. Also at St Andrew Square bus station on platform A1 (24 hours) and at Edinburgh Airport, T3331000, in a portakabin next to the new extension, open 0600-2200. **Libraries** *Central Library*, George IV Bridge, T2255884. Open Mon-Fri 0900-2100, Sat 0900-1300. Excellent Scottish and local reference sections. *National Library of Scotland*, George IV Bridge, T2264531. Open Mon-Fri 0930-2030, Sat 0930-1300. Superb copyright library, for research purposes only. Reference facilities at

Walking in the Pentlands

*A relatively easy walk which provides great views and varied scenery starts at **Boghall Farm**, headquarters of the Pentlands Regional Park, on the A702 to Biggar. There are regular buses from the city centre, including the 4, 15 and 100. The circular walk covers five miles and takes around three hours. There's a map of the route in the car park at Boghall.*

Follow the Farm Trail signs from the corner of the car park, through the gates and along a fenced path. Cross the main track and follow the path past a pond and up Boghall Glen. Cross the burn by a footbridge and continue along the path. Follow the yellow arrows through a gate, up the side of a field and through another gate. Then head left to pick up the main track heading into the hills.

*Follow the track steadily upwards, passing through several gates. Then it curves right and climbs to **Windy Door Nick**, the pass between **Allermuir Hill** (91,618 ft) and **Caerketton Hill** (1,499 ft). Turn left and follow the clear path to the*

top of Allermuir Hill. The views from here, north to the Forth bridges and beyond, and south to the main Pentland ridge, are magnificent.

From here, retrace your steps to the Nick and continue up Caerketton Hill. The views from the top are equally good, and extend further east to Berwick Law and the Bass Rock. Head east from the summit. Stay by the fence to pass a large cairn, then descend steeply to a fence corner. On your left you can see the Hillend ski slope. At the fence corner, cross the stile and continue down to the wood. Turn right here and you'll see the yellow arrows again, taking you along the top edge of the wood. When the wood ends, walk through gorse to a stile, then across open ground past a large mast and back to the cottage.

*Three miles south of Boghall is the **Flotterstone Inn**, which does a decent pub lunch or evening meal from 1800-2000. This is also the starting point for further walks in the Pentlands, most notably the one to Glencorse.*

Edinburgh

the *Map Room*, 33 Salisbury Pl; open Mon-Fri 0930-1700, Sat 0930-1300. **Lost property** Property found and handed in to the police (including property found in taxis) is sent to the **Police HQ** at Fettes Av, T3113131. It can be collected Mon-Fri 0900-1700. There are lost-property departments at **Edinburgh Airport**, T3331000, and **Waverley train station**, T5502711. *Lothian Regional Transport* have a lost-property department at Shrub Place, about a third of the way down Leith Walk, on the left-hand side, T5544494. Open Mon-Fri 1000-1330.

Safety Edinburgh is, in general, a reasonably safe and civilized place, but some precautions should be taken. Some areas are best avoided for women walking alone at night. Lothian Road and the Grassmarket are not particularly dangerous but full of beer-soaked revellers who may prove irritating. The Meadows' walkways are lonely at night and potentially risky. The narrow, secluded wynds and closes of the High Street have also been the scenes of assaults in the past. The back streets of Leith are also best avoided at night as they are one of the city's most notorious red-light districts. If you are robbed or assaulted and need to report the crime, call 999. The police information centre is at 188 High St, T2266966, open daily 1000-2200. **Rape crisis centre**: T5569437.

Around Edinburgh

South of the Braid Hills, beyond the City Bypass, are Edinburgh's Pentland Hills, a serious range of hills, remote in parts, rising to almost 2,000 ft and which stretch around 16 miles from the outskirts of Edinburgh to

The Pentland Hills

Lanarkshire. The hills offer relatively painless climbs and you'll be rewarded with magnificent views once you reach the top.

On the northern slopes of the Pentlands is the village of **Swanston**, a huddle of 18th-century thatched, whitewashed cottages. The largest of these, Swanston Cottage, was the holiday home of the Stevenson family, where the sickly young Robert Louis spent his summers.

There are many paths up to the various Pentland summits and round the lochs and reservoirs. One of the many walks is described above, but if you want to explore more fully there are many books about the Pentlands, including *25 Walks in Edinburgh and Lothian* (HMSO, 1995). Ordnance Survey Landranger Map no 66 covers the area.

The main access is by the A702, which passes the *Midlothian Ski Centre* at **Hillend** (see also page 61). There's a marked walking trail up to the ski slope, or you can take the chair lift. At the top of the slope it's a short walk to **Caerketton Hill** for fantastic panormaic views of Edinburgh, the Firth of Forth and the hills of Fife and Stirlingshire.

Lauriston Castle, Cramond & Dalmeny

About five miles northwest of town is Lauriston Castle, a fine Edwardian country mansion set in lovely grounds overlooking the Firth of Forth. The original tower house is late 16th century, with many neo-Jacobean additions by William Burn in the 19th century. It was once the home of John Law, who founded the first bank in France and obtained sole trading rights in the Lower Mississippi, which he christened Louisiana in honour of the French King. The interior contains fine collections of period furniture and antiques. ■ *Apr-Oct Sat-Thu 1100-1300 and 1400-1700; Nov-Mar Sat/Sun 1400-1600. £4.50, concession £3. T3362060.*

One mile further west is the lovely little coastal village of **Cramond**, situated where the River Almond flows into the Forth. The 18th-century village of whitewashed houses is the site of an ancient Roman fort, a large part of which has been excavated. The most recent discovery was a magnificent sandstone sculpture of a lioness dating from the second century BC. In addition to being steeped in ancient history, Cramond boasts a pleasant promenade, a golf course and a lovely, wooded walk along the banks of the Almond river towards the 16th century **Old Cramond Brig**. And if that weren't enough to tempt you, there's also **Cramond Island**, which can be reached via a raised walkway when the tide is out. Just make sure you keep an eye on the time or you may find yourself stuck there for longer than you anticipated. Tide times are posted on the shore, and are also available from the Tourist Information Centre.

A local passenger ferry service still crosses the River Almond at Cramond. ■ *0900-1300 and 1400-1700 in summer, till 1600 in winter, closed Fri.* From the other side of the river it's a two-mile walk to **Dalmeny House**, the Earl of Rosebery's home for over 300 years. The present house, built in 1815 in Tudor Gothic, contains a superb collection of 18th-century French furniture, porcelain and tapestries and paintings, including portraits by Gainsborough, Raeburn, Reynolds and Lawrence. There is also a fascinating collection of Napoleon Bonaparte memorabilia, assembled by the fifth Earl of Rosebery, a former Prime Minister. ■ *Jul and Aug Sun 1300-1730, Mon and Tue 1200-1730 (last admission 1645). £4, £2 child. T3311888.* The house can also be reached via the village of **Dalmeny**, eight miles west of Edinburgh, on the A90 then B924. There's a bus service from St Andrew Square to Chapel Gate, one mile from the house, or you can take a train which stops at the village station. The main point of interest in the village is the wonderful 12th-century church.

Seven miles south of Edinburgh, in the county of **Midlothian**, just off the A701 to Penicuik, lies the little village of Roslin, home of the mysterious 15th-century **Rosslyn Chapel**. Perched above the North Esk, the magnificent and unique chapel has a richly carved interior full of Biblical representations and pagan and masonic symbols and has been described as "a fevered hallucination in stone". Foundations were laid in 1446 for a much larger church which was never built. What exists is the Lady Chapel, inspiration of Sir William Sinclair, who himself supervized masons brought from abroad who took 40 years to complete it to his design. According to legend, his grandfather, the adventurer Prince Henry of Orkney, set foot in the New World a century before Columbus. This is backed up by the carvings of various New World plants. One of the most fascinating sights in the church, and the most elaborate carving, is the **Prentice Pillar**. Legend has it that while the master mason was away in Rome making additional drawings to complete the pillar, an apprentice finished it for him. On the mason's return he murdered the apprentice in a fury.

Speculation as to the purpose of the chapel dwells on esoteric secrets and a plethora of recent books claims that the Holy Grail, supposedly brought from the East by the Knights Templar, is buried here. Whether or not you believe this, you'll still find its architecture and atmosphere fascinating. Once you've seen the chapel, there are some very pleasant walks in nearby Roslin Glen, from where you get great views of Roslin Castle. ■ *Mon-Sat 1000-1700, Sun 1200-1645. £4, £3.50 concession. T4402159, www.rosslynchapelt.org.uk Take one of the regular buses for Penicuik from St Andrews Sq.*

Roslin

Rosslyn Chapel is the most interesting sight in Midlothian, but there are a few other worthwhile places of interest, especially if you've got kids in tow. **Butterfly and Insect World** is part of **Dobbie's Garden World**, in **Lasswade**, near **Dalkeith**. This large glass enclosure has loads of butterflies fluttering around while you stroll past tropical plants and water features. There are also creepy crawlies, which are thankfully in individual cages in a separate area. There's also a café in the garden centre. ■ *Daily 0930-1730 (1000-1700 in winter). £3.95, £2.85 child. T6634932. To get there, leave the city bypass at the Gilmerton exit or Sheriffhall roundabout, or take buses 3, 80 or 80a.*

A mile or so south of Dalkeith is **Newtongrange**, a former mining village whose Lady Victoria Colliery closed in 1981 and has been transformed into the **Scottish Mining Mueum**. Here you can get some idea of what working conditions were like more than 1,500 ft below ground during the guided tour led by former miners, and you can see the massive steam engine, the largest in Scotland, which hauled men and coal up and down the pit shaft for 87 years. ■ *Mar-Oct daily 1000-1700. £4, £2.20 child . T6637519. There are regular buses from central Edinburgh (3, 30, 82).*

Other sights around Midlothian

Less than a mile from Dalmeny is the ancient town of South Queensferry, which gets its name from the 11th-century St Margaret, who used the town as the crossing point during her trips between her palaces in Edinburgh and Dunfermline, which was Scotland's capital at that time. The town's narrow main street is lined with picturesque old buildings, most striking of which is the row of two-tiered shops. If you fancy a drink, or a meal, or perhaps a bed for the night, try the historic *Hawes Inn*, which was featured in Stevenson's *Kidnapped*. The town is dominated by the two great bridges that tower overhead on either side, spanning the Firth of Forth at its narrowest point. The massive steel cantilevered **Forth Rail Bridge**, over a mile and a half long and 360 ft high and is a staggering monument to Victorian engineering. It was

South Queensferry

To get to South Queensferry from Edinburgh, take buses 43, X43, 47 or 47a from St Andrew Sq

built in 1883-90 and 60,000 tons of steel were used in its construction. Beside it, is the **Forth Road Bridge**, a suspension bridge built between 1958 and 1964, which ended the 900-year-old ferry crossing between South and North Queensferry. The Road Bridge is open to pedestrians and it's worth walking across for the views of the Rail Bridge.

From Hawes Pier, right underneath the Rail Bridge, you can take a variety of **pleasure boat cruises** on the Forth. *Jet Boat Tours* , T3314777, have cruises up the River Almond at Cramond, looking out for dolphins, seals and porpoises en route, as well as 'Bridge Tours' and 'Jet-Boat fun rides'. ■ *Prices are around £5-10 per person. Cruises run Apr/May/Sep/Oct weekends and public holidays 1000-1800; Jun-Aug daily 0930-2000.*

Inchcolm Abbey There are also Sealife Cruises on board the *Maid of the Forth*, T3314857, as well as Evening Cruises beneath the bridges with jazz and folk accompaniment. The most interesting cruise of all, and the most popular, is the cruise to the island of Inchcolm, whose beautiful ruined **abbey**, founded in 1123 by King Alexander I, is the best-preserved group of monastic buildings in Scotland. The oldest surviving building is the 13th-century octagonal chapter house. You can also climb the tower for great views of the island, which is populated by nesting seabirds and a colony of seals. ■ *Sailings from Easter to Oct. Evening jazz and ceilidh cruises throughout the summer on Fri, Sat and Sun evenings. £7.50, £5.75 concession, £3.60 child. T3314857.*

Hopetoun House Two miles west of South Queensferry is Hopetoun House, which thoroughly deserves its reputation as 'Scotland's finest stately home'. Set in 100 acres of magnificent parkland, including the Red Deer park, the house is the epitome of aristocratic grandeur and recently celebrated its 300th birthday. Hopetoun House is perhaps the finest example of the work of William Burn and William Adam. It is, in fact, two houses in one. The oldest part was designed by William Bruce and built between 1699 and 1707. In 1721 William Adam began enlarging the house by adding the facade, colonnades and grand State Apartments. It was built for the Earls of Hopetoun, later created Marquesses of Linlithgow and part of the house is still lived in by the Marquess of Linlithgow and his family. The house contains a large collection of art treasures and the grounds are also open to the public. You could come here and pretend you're a member of the aristocracy for the day, then go back to your tiny B&B and weep. ■ *Daily Apr-end of Sep, and every weekend in Oct, 1000-1730. £5.30, £2.70 child. T3312451, www.hopetounhouse.com*

Southern Scotland

4

Southern Scotland

The vast swathe of Southern Scotland covered in this chapter comprises East Lothian, the Scottish Borders, Dumfries and Galloway and Ayrshire. It's an area usually overlooked by those on their way to Glasgow, Edinburgh or further north, and consequently relatively free from the litter-strewn lay-bys and crowded beauty spots of more favoured parts.

Despite its proximity to the English border, the south of Scotland is in many ways at the very heart of the country. Under constant threat during the long wars with England, its people were at the front line in the defence of Scottish nationhood. It is therefore no coincidence that Scotland's two greatest literary figures, **Robert Burns** and **Sir Walter Scott**, were born and lived here.

Southern Scotland is divided neatly by the A74(M), the main route from England to Scotland. To the east of this line the main tourist focus is the Borders region, with its peaceful little mill towns, in particular the lovely little town of **Melrose**. To the north are the narrow ranges of the **Lammermuir**, **Moorfoot** and **Pentland Hills**. North of the Lammermuirs is **East Lothian**, with its sandy bays and rugged coastline.

The landscape becomes ever more wild and mountainous as you head west from the Tweed Valley across the **Southern Uplands**. The most spectacular scenery is west of Dumfries, in the **Galloway Forest Park**. The **Solway coast**, from Dumfries to the Mull of Galloway, is equally appealing. North of Galloway is the **Ayrshire** coast, lined with seaside resorts and some great golf courses, and best known for its associations with Robert Burns, especially Alloway, where he was born.

Ins and outs

Getting   **Bus** services are good around Ayrshire, East Lothian and between the main towns
around   in the Borders, and there are also regular services between Dumfries and Stranraer,
along the A75, but services to more remote parts are limited.

   Train services are limited to the line north from Berwick-upon-Tweed to Edinburgh on the east coast, and lines from Dumfries and Stranraer to Ayrshire in the
west, with links to Glasgow.

   Details of all **public transport services** are given under the relevant towns and
villages. Phone numbers of travel information lines and the main operators are also
given. Bus timetables are available at local tourist offices.

Walking   The south of Scotland is excellent walking country, and there are numerous
marked trails through the forests and hills and circular walks around the towns,
especially in the Tweed Valley. The tourist offices have leaflets detailing all the
main routes. There are also a number of Ranger-led walks, details of which are also
available at tourist offices.

   For the more ambitious hiker there are two long-distance trails. The 62-mile **St
Cuthbert's Way** is a cross-border trail which links several places associated with St
Cuthbert, who started his ministry at Melrose in the mid-seventh century and
ended it at Lindisfarne (Holy Island), on the Northumberland coast. The
waymarked route starts at **Melrose Abbey** and climbs across the Eildon Hills
before joining the River Tweed. Highlights include Dere Street, a Roman Road, the
Cheviot foothills, St Cuthbert's Cave and the causeway crossing to Lindisfarne.
They can also provide a trail pack which includes maps and route descriptions
(£13.50 including P&P).

   The most famous and demanding of walks is the 212-mile **Southern Upland
Way**, www.dumgal.gov.uk/southernuplandway, which runs from Portpatrick on
the west coast, near Stranraer, to Cockburnspath on the Berwickshire coast in the
east, south of Dunbar. The route passes through a great variety of scenery, from the
Rhinns of Galloway to the wild heartland of Southern Scotland to the gentler eastern Borders. The most picturesque sections are the beginning and the end, but in
between the highlights include Glen Trool, the Lowther Hills, St Mary's Loch and
the River Tweed. A route leaflet is available from the *Countryside Ranger Service*,
Scottish Borders Council, Harestanes Visitor Centre, Ancrum, Jedburgh TD8 6UQ,
T/F01835-830281. There is also a trail pack (£14.99), available from the Dumfries &
Galloway or Scottish Borders tourist boards.

Cycling   The quiet backroads of southern Scotland also make it ideal for exploring by bike,
especially the Tweed Valley, Galloway Forest Park and around The Machars peninsula. The **Tweed Cycleway** is a waymarked 90-mile route which follows minor
roads through the beautiful Tweed Valley, from Biggar to Berwick-upon-Tweed.
The tourist office provides a free guide, *Cycling in the Scottish Borders*, which features over 20 routes, including the Tweed Cycleway. Another route is the **Four
Abbeys Cycle Route**, a 55-mile circular tour which takes in Melrose, Dryburgh,
Jedburgh and Kelso. It is described in the *Four Abbeys Cycle Way* guide (£2 including P&P) available from Tourist Information Centres.

Things to do in Southern Scotland

- Take a trip back time with a visit to Traquair House, one of Scotland's great country houses.
- Take a walk on the magic side, in the enchanted Eildon Hills, which overlook the lovely borders town of Melrose.
- Lose your heart in romantic Sweetheart Abbey, on the beautiful Solway coast.
- Explore the wild and rugged Galloway Forest Park, where you can see red deer and even golden eagles.

East Lothian

East Lothian stretches east from Musselburgh, to the east of Edinburgh, along the coast to North Berwick and Dunbar. This is real golfing country, with a string of excellent courses running the length of the coast, and there are miles of sandy beaches. The East Lothian coast is also home to huge colonies of seabirds, especially on the Bass Rock, a dramatic volcanic islet off North Berwick. Inland is the attractive historic market town of Haddington, and further south the village of Gifford is the gateway to the Lammermuir Hills, which form the boundary with the Borders region and offer good walking opportunities.

There are good transport links with Edinburgh and most of the main sights can be visited in a few day trips from the capital. **Trains** from Edinburgh stop in Musselburgh, Prestonpans, North Berwick and Dunbar. There are also regular **buses** to all the main towns. For more information on East Lothian and for a free accommodation, contact **Edinburgh and Lothians Tourist Board** (T0131-4733800, F4733881, www.edinburgh.org), or East Lothian TICs in Musselburgh, North Berwick and Dunbar.

Ins & outs

For public transport information call Traveline (T0800-232323); see also page 70

Musselburgh to North Berwick

Six miles east of Edinburgh, across the River Esk, is the town of **Musselburgh**. It's a fairly humdrum place, but may be of interest to golfing enthusiasts as the original home of golf; Royal Musselbugh is one of the oldest clubs in the country. It is also a target for naturalists who come to see the huge populations of migrating waders, ducks and seabirds which flock to the mouth of the River Esk. Ice cream lovers may also be interested to note that *Luca's* on the High Street has most of the competition licked and is definitely worth a stop if you're passing by. There's also a **Tourist Information Centre**, just off the A1 at Old Craighall, T6536172. Open October-March Monday-Saturday 0900-1700; April/May Monday-Saturday 0900-1800; June/September Monday-Saturday 0900-1800, Sunday 1000-1500; July Monday-Saturday 0900-1900; August Monday-Saturday 0900-2000, Sunday 1000-1600.

Phone code: 0131
Colour map 6, grid A2

Ten miles east of Musselburgh is the conservation village of **Aberlady**, at the mouth of the River Peffer. A row of Georgian cottages lines the main street and there's a lovely old church which hints at Aberlady's erstwhile importance as a port. The old harbour is silted up and now forms part of the mudflats and salt marshes of the **Aberlady Bay Nature Reserve**, which is the home of numerous seabirds.

A couple of miles north of Aberlady is **Gullane**, a resort town with an exclusive air which is hopelessly devoted to **golf**. There are no fewer than four golf courses surrounding Gullane; Nos 1, 2 and 3 and the world-famous **Muirfield**, where you need an introduction to play. Golf may be Gullane's *raison d'être*, but **windsurfing** has recently been gaining in popularity.

Between Gullane and North Berwick is the attractive little village of **Dirleton**, dominated by the ruins of **Dirleton Castle**. The original castle dates from the 12th century and was added to over the following three centuries, until it was destroyed by Cromwell's army. The very lovely **gardens**, which date from the 16th century, are well worth a visit. ■ *Apr-Sep daily 0930-1830; Oct-Mar Mon-Sat 0930-1630, Sun 1400-1630. £2.80, £2 concession. T01620-850330 (HS).* At the eastern end of the village a road runs north for a mile or so to **Yellowcraigs**, where there's a lovely clean beach and views across to **Fidra island**.

Sleeping & eating

In **Aberlady** is the **D-C** *Old Aberlady Inn*, T01875-870503, on the main street. A cosy wee place to stay, with good food and ales in its traditional bar. There's also a **campsite**, T01875-870666, open Mar-Oct, on the Haddington Rd.

There are several hotels and B&Bs in **Gullane**, but pick of the bunch is undoubtedly the **L** *Greywalls Hotel*, T01620-842144, open Apr-Oct, a supremely charming and elegant Edwardian country house designed by Sir Edwin Lutyens. It overlooks Muirfied golf course and has an enviable reputation for superb cuisine (expensive). If you can't afford a meal, call in for tea and shortbread. It's not cheap (£7.50), but it does give you a chance to enjoy the house – and the lovely gardens designed by Gertrude Jekyll. The best place to eat in Gullane, or anywhere else in Southeast Scotland outside Edinburgh, was always *La Pontinière*, T01620-843214, on the main street. Unfortunately this cosy French bistro is is currently closed but may re-open late 2002. Disappointed gastronomes can always head for *The Old Clubhouse*, T01620-842008, a pleasant bar/bistro just off the main street. Open till 2200; mid-range prices.

In **Dirleton** is the enticingly named **A** *Open Arms Hotel*, T01620-850241. A traditional country house hotel opposite the castle, it's a friendly and comfortable place with a highly rated, and expensive, restaurant. Across the Green is the much cheaper **D** *Castle Inn*, T01620-850221.

North Berwick

Phone code: 01620
Colour map 6, grid A2
Population: 4,850

The dignified and slightly faded Victorian seaside resort of North Berwick is 23 miles east of Edinburgh and easily visited as a day trip from the capital. The town's chief attractions are its fine sandy **beaches** and the two excellent **golf courses**, the West Links and the Glen, but there are several other points of interest for visitors.

Ins & outs

The **train station** is a 10-min walk east of the town centre. There's a frequent rail service to and from **Edinburgh** (30 mins). There are also regular **buses** (X5, 124) from Edinburgh, via Aberlady and Gullane. These stop on the High St. There are also regular buses from Edinburgh to Dunbar via Haddington (X6/106). *First Edinburgh* buses, T0131-6639233. The **TIC** is on Quality St, T892197. Apr and May Mon-Sat 0900-1800; Jun and Sep Mon-Sat 0900-1800, Sun 1100-1600; Jul Mon-Sat 0900-1900, Sun 1100-1800; Aug Mon-Sat 0900-2000, Sun 1100-1800; Oct-Mar Mon-Fri 0900-1700.

Sights

The biggest attraction is the **Scottish Seabird Centre** on the harbour. It's a bit like a hi-tech hide, with remote control cameras on the Bass Rock transmitting live pictures to screens placed in the visitor centre. You can control the cameras yourself, rotating, panning and zooming so that you can get the best view possible. Cameras are also trained on Fidra, so that you can watch the puffins too. If you come during the winter, when the gannets and puffins have left, you can watch the grey seals that pup on the nearby Isle of May in December. There's also a very popular café here, with great views across the water. ■ *Summer daily 1000-1800; winter Mon-Fri 1000-1600, Sat, Sun 1000-1730. £4.50. T890202, www.seabird.org*

Next to the harbour are the remains of the **Auld Kirk**, the 12th-century Church of St Andrews, scene of one of the strangest events in Scottish history. In 1590, while King James VI was returning from Europe with his new wife, Anne of Denmark, Francis Stewart, Earl of Bothwell was plotting against him. The Earl summoned the witches of East Lothian to the church to meet the 'Devil' (actually Bothwell in disguise) and attempted by means of witchcraft to cause a storm in the Firth of Forth in order to drown King James and his new wife. The attempt failed and, when James got wind of this satanic treachery, several witches were tried and executed. Bothwell himself was imprisoned but later escaped.

North Berwick is overlooked by **Berwick Law**, a 613-ft volcanic crag, topped by the ruins of a watchtower built during the Napoleonic Wars, and an arch made from a whale's jawbone. It's an easy walk to the top and the views on a clear day are rewarding. Take Law Road out of town and then follow the signs. Three miles east of town, off the A198, are the mid-14th-century ruins of **Tantallon Castle**, perched dramatically on the edge of the cliffs, looking out to the Bass Rock. This formidable fortress was the stronghold of the 'Red Douglases', Earls of Angus, until Cromwell's attack in 1651, which left only the massive 50-ft high curtain wall intact. ■ *Apr-Sep daily 0930-1830; Oct-Mar Mon-Wed and Sat 0930-1630, Thu 0930-1200, Fri and Sun 1400-1630. £2.80, £2 concession. T892727 (HS). To get there, take the Dunbar bus from North Berwick (see below).* There's a great **beach** a few miles south of Tantallon which is well worth the slight detour. Turn left off the A198 at Auldhame farm, follow the road for about a mile to the gate (£1 toll charge) and beyond to the car park, then walk.

Three miles offshore is the 350-ft high **Bass Rock**, a massive, guano-covered lump of basalt, used as a prison in the 17th century but now home to millions of nesting gannets and other seabirds including guillemots, razorbills and fulmars. There are also puffins nesting on the nearby island of **Fidra**.

A-B *The Marine Hotel*, Cromwell Rd, T892406, F894480. 83 rooms. North Berwick's premier hotel, overlooking the seafront and with an open-air pool. There are many excellent **guesthouses** and **B&Bs** to choose from, including: **D** *The Glebe House*, on Law Rd, T/F892608; **E** *The Studio*, T895150, on Grange Rd; **E** *Tantallon House*, T892873, open Apr-Oct, at 2 West Bay Rd; and **D** *Palmerston*, T892884, at 28b St Andrew St. There's a **campsite** at *Tantallan Caravan Park*, T893348, open Mar-Oct, on Dunbar Rd, overlooking the Glen golf course.

There are several very good places to **eat** in North Berwick. *The Grange*, 35 High St, T895894. Good contemporary Scottish cuisine in classy surroundings, mid-range-expensive prices. *Quadrant*, 7-9 Quality St, T895110. Surprising to find such a hip café-bar in this corner of East Lothian, stylish design and the food ain't bad either. Open daily till 2300. *Millars*, Market Pl, T890437, is a good bistro serving dishes like fajitas, wraps and bruschetta; while the *café* at the Scottish Seabird Centre is also worth trying. *Millennium Spice*, High St, T895418, serves good Indian food; and *Poonthai*, at 7 High St, is a good Thai restaurant. If you fancy a good cup of tea and a cake, try the *Westgate Gallery*, Westgate, T894976.

Sleeping & eating

There are lots of places to stay in North Berwick, but it's advisable to book ahead at weekends and in the busy season as it's very popular with golfers

Southern Scotland

Southern Scotland

Tours There are **boat trips** from North Berwick, weather permitting, to the Bass Rock and Fidra, daily between May and Sep with *Fred Marr*, T892838. Trips cost £5.00 per person and last about 1¼ hrs. You can also arrange in advance to be dropped off on Bass Rock and picked up 3 hrs later for £10 per person, but you'll need to be a dedicated bird-watcher to put up with the stench of guano.

Dunbar
Phone code: 01368
Colour map 4, grid C2
Population: 5,800

Twelve miles southeast of North Berwick, just off the main A1 from Edinburgh to the south, is the little fishing port of Dunbar. The town's main claim to fame is as the birthplace of **John Muir**, the explorer naturalist who founded Yellowstone National Park in the US and became known as the father of the Conservation movement. **John Muir House**, 128 High Street, is his childhood home. It has been refurbished in period detail and contains a small museum dedicated to his life and work. ■ *Jun-Sep Mon-Sat 1100-1300 and 1400-1700, Sun 1400-1700. Free. T860187.* Also on the High Street is the 16th-century **Town House Museum**, one of the oldest of Dunbar's houses, formerly a prison and now a small local history and archaeology museum. ■ *Apr-Oct daily 1230-1630. Free. T863734.*

There are regular **buses** from Edinburgh. Dunbar is on the main London-Edinburgh rail line and there are regular **trains** to and from Edinburgh (40 mins) and south to England. The **Tourist Information Centre** is at 143 High St, T863353. May Mon-Sat 0900-1700; Jun and Sep Mon-Sat 0900-1700, Sun 1100-1600; Jul Mon-Sat 0900-1900; Sun 1100-1800; Aug Mon-Sat 0900-2000, Sun 1100-1800.

The scant remains of **Dunbar Castle** stand beside the old **harbour**. A two-mile clifftop trail leads west from the castle to **John Muir Country Park**, a vast area comprising the Tyne estuary and Belhaven Bay, and covering a variety of habitats which are home to numerous bird species. As well as the excellent beachcombing possibilities, there's also fishing and horse riding in the park. For more details contact the TIC in town, or phone, T01620-827318. Dunbar is also well known as the home of **Belhaven beers**, which are still brewed on the original site (signposted off the Edinburgh road). Guided tours can be arranged if you contact them in advance, T864488.

Sleeping and eating There are several **guesthouses** and **B&Bs**. A popular choice is **C-D** *Muirfield House*, 40 Belhaven Rd, T/F862289. Nearby, also on Belhaven Rd is **E** *Springfield Guest House*, T862502. There's also the *Belhaven Bay Caravan & Camping Park* in John Muir Country Park, just off the A1087 to the west of town, T8659568. The best place to eat in town is *The Creel*, near the harbour, T863279, which serves good, moderately priced seafood and other dishes. Open Tue-Sun.

Haddington and around

Phone code: 01620
Colour map 6, grid A2
Population: 8,000

Handsome Haddington is the archetypal prosperous country town. It sits on the River Tyne, only 15 miles east of Edinburgh, making it ideal for a pleasant day out from the rigours of city life. The town dates from the 12th century but most of it was built during the 17th to 19th centuries, when Haddington benefited from its role as the driving force behind the Agricultural Revolution which transformed farming in East Lothian. Haddington was also the birthplace of firebrand preacher **John Knox**, founder of the Presbyterian Church in Scotland, whose famous tract entitled *The First Blast of the Trumpet Against the Monstrous Regiment of Women* did little to endear him to either Mary of

Guise, regent of Scotland, Mary, Queen of England or Elizabeth I (see page 646). Also born here were Alexander II of Scotland, in 1198, and Samuel Smiles (1812-1904), author of *Self-Help*.

There's no tourist office in Haddington, but there are information boards at places of interest, and a booklet, *A Walk Around Haddington* (£1.50), is available from newsagents.

The compact town centre is very attractive and makes for a pleasant stroll. No **Sights** fewer than 129 buildings have been listed as historically interesting, including the graceful **Town House**, in tree-lined Court Street, which was built in 1748 by William Adam, father of Robert. At the east end of the High Street, Church Street leads to **St Mary's Collegiate Church**, the largest parish church in Scotland, dating from the 14th century and restored in the 1970s. It's a particularly beautiful ecclesiastical building, with lots of interesting nooks and crannies, and enjoys a lovely setting on the river. There are public services, brass rubbings on Saturday, concerts on Sunday afternoons in the summer and also a tearoom. ■ *Apr-Sep Mon-Sat 1100-1600, Sun 1400-1630. Free (donations welcome). T823109.* Nearby at Haddington House are the peaceful medicinal gardens of **St Mary's Pleasance**, which are free and open during daylight hours. Buried in the churchyard is Jane Welsh (1801-66), wife of essayist and historian Thomas Carlyle. The **Jane Welsh Carlyle House**, at 2 Lodge Street, was her home until her marriage, and part of it is open to the public. ■ *Apr-Sep Wed-Sat 1400-1700. £1.50, £1 concession. T823738.*

A mile south of Haddington is **Lennoxlove House**, seat of the Duke of Hamilton. The sprawling confection of styles consists of a medieval tower house with gradual extensions and additions over the centuries. Inside the house are some fine paintings and furniture, but the *pièce de résistance* is the death mask of Mary, Queen of Scots, and a silver casket in which she kept her letters, given to her by her first husband, Francis II of France. ■ *Easter-Oct Wed, Thu and some Sats and Sun 1400-1630. £4, £2 concession. T823720.*

About four miles northeast of Haddington, on the B1347 at East Fortune, is the excellent **Museum of Flight**, Scotland's National Museum of Aviation. Housed in a complex of Second World War hangars and nissen huts is a vast and impressive collection of old aircraft – from the Tigermoth to the Vulcan bomber – and wartime memorabilia. ■ *Apr-Jun, Sep and Oct daily 1030-1700; Jul and Aug daily 1030-1800; Nov-Mar Mon-Fri 1100-1500. £3, children free. T880308.*

Six miles east of Haddington, at **East Linton**, is the very photogenic **Preston Mill**, an 18th-century water wheel and grain mill, which includes an exhibition on milling. ■ *Easter and May-Sep Mon-Sat 1100-1300 and 1400-1700, Sun 1330-1700; weekends in Oct 1330-1600. £2.50, £1.75 concession. T860426. First Edinburgh bus No 106 from Edinburgh to East Linton (T0131-6639233).* Just to the south of East Linton is **Traprain Law**, which offers fantastic views of the coast and hinterland of East Lothian as well as being the site of a prehistoric hillfort. Near the foot of Traprain Law are the extensive 13th-15th-century ruins of **Hailes Castle**.

Five miles south of Haddington, on the B6369, is the pretty little village of **Gifford**, birthplace of the Reverend John Witherspoon (in 1723), who was a signatory to the American Declaration of Independence. Gifford makes a good base for hiking in the **Lammermuir Hills** to the south. It's possible to follow trails across the hills and meet up with the Southern Upland Way (see page 138).

Southern Scotland

Sleeping & eating	There are some top-class hotels in and around town, such as the **B** *Maitlandfield House Hotel*, 24 Sidegate, T826513, www.maitlandfieldhotel.fsnet.co.uk, which boasts 2 very fine restaurants; and **B** *Browns Hotel*, 1 West Rd, T/F822254, www.browns-hotel .com, an elegant Regency town house. A couple of miles out of town is **C** *Abbey Mains*, T823286, a large stone farmhouse with its own kitchen garden. Evening meals also available. A cheaper option is the **E** *Plough Tavern*, at 11 Court St, T823326, a traditional inn serving decent food; or **B&B** at **E** *Schiehallion*, 19 Church St, T825663.

There are several very good places to eat, including vegetarian-friendly *The Waterside*, T825674, by the river near Nungate Bridge, where you can enjoy excellent French bistro-style food at mid-range prices. Open 1200-1400, 1730-2200 (1200-2200 at weekends). Also good is *Poldrate's*, T826882, in a converted mill on the road to Gifford (mid-range). Another place in Gifford worth trying is the Tweedale Arms, on the High St, T810240, which serves tasty bar food 1100-2300 (mid-range) and good ales; also rooms, **C**. A great place for a pub lunch is the *Drover's Inn* in **East Linton**, T860298, where you can sit outside on a sunny day, or stay inside in the cosy bistro. Either way, the food is excellent and worth the trip alone. The *Victoria Inn*, T823332, on Court St, also does decent bar meals as well as hosting the Haddington Folk Club on Wed nights.

Transport	First *Edinburgh* run regular **buses** to and from Edinburgh, T0131-6639233. There are also hourly buses to **North Berwick** (Mon-Sat, less frequently on Sun; 45 mins) and hourly buses to **Gifford** (20 mins).

The Borders

The Scottish Borders covers a huge swathe of southern Scotland to the east of the M74. It's an unspoiled wilderness of green hills, rushing rivers and bleak, barren moors, and it has an austere beauty which would surprise those who think that real Scotland starts somewhere north of Perth. The Borders' proximity to England also gives it a romantic edge and makes it even more essentially Scottish. This is a region which is drenched in the blood of countless battles with the English, and its many ruined castles and abbeys bear witness to Scotland's long, turbulent relationship with its belligerent southern neighbour. It should come as no surprise, then, that this southern corner of Scotland has so inspired the country's greatest poets and writers. Robert Burns and John Buchan often spoke of its rare charms, but it is Sir Walter Scott, inspired not only by the stark beauty of the countryside but also by its lore and legends, who is most closely associated with the region.

The wildest and most spectacular scenery is to be found in the southern part of the region, along the Yarrow Water, between Selkirk and Moffat, the upper reaches of the Tweed valley, south of Peebles, and in Liddesdale, southwest of Jedburgh. But it is along the central valley of the River Tweed, between Peebles in the west and Kelso in the east, where you'll find most of the historic attractions, including the fascinating Traquair House, Sir Walter Scott's mansion at Abbotsford. Together with Selkirk, and the textile-producing towns of Galashiels and Hawick, these towns form the heart of the Borders.

Ins and outs

Getting around	There's a good network of **buses** serving the region's main towns. Bus timetables are available from local tourist offices. For all bus information, call the *Borders Council*

The Riding of the Marches

The Border people's passion for rugby is matched only by their enthusiastic celebration of the Riding of the Marches, which takes place throughout the early summer months in each of the major towns. This ancient ritual dates back to the Middle Ages, when the young men – or 'Callants' – would ride out to check the boundaries of common lands owned by the town.

Each town has its own variations of the Riding ceremonies, and have other activities including concerts, balls, pageants and various festivities lasting several days. Others also commemorate local historical events. For instance, the Selkirk Gathering, which is the oldest and largest of the Ridings, ends with the Casting of the Colours, which commemorates Scotland's humiliating defeat at the Battle of Flodden.

Transport Division, T01835-825200. The main operator is *First Edinburgh*, T0131-6639233. There are numerous buses running between the main towns of **Galashiels**, **Melrose**, **Peebles**, **Hawick**, **Selkirk**, **Jedburgh** and **Kelso**. There are also buses connecting the Border towns with **Edinburgh** and **Berwick-upon-Tweed**. There are regular buses from Berwick-upon-Tweed (Traveline T0870-6082608). *National Express*, T08705 808080, runs services from Newcastle to Edinburgh via **Jedburgh**, **Galashiels** and **Melrose**.

The regular bus service is supplemented during the summer months (Jul-Sep) by the *Harrier Scenic Bus Services*. Buses make round-trip tours once a week on the following routes: **Melrose-Moffat**, via Galashiels, Selkirk, Bowhill House, Yarrow, St Mary's Loch (on Thu); **Selkirk-Eyemouth** via Galashiels, Melrose, Kelso, Coldstream, Berwick-upon-Tweed; **Hawick-Eyemouth** via Jedburgh, Town Yetholm, Berwick-upon-Tweed. Current timetables are available at local tourist offices.

The main London-Edinburgh **railway line** follows the east coast from **Berwick-upon-Tweed** north to **Dunbar** in East Lothian. There is no rail link with the Border towns, so you'll have to get off at Berwick and take a bus from there.

There's a good **road network** which allows you to explore the region easily by car. The best way to see the Borders, though, is on foot or by bike. The 90-mile **Tweed Cycleway** runs past the most important sights, while the **Southern Uplands Way** takes you through the region's most beautiful and spectacular scenery (see page 138).

There are plenty of opportunities for **walking** in the Borders, whether it's a gentle stroll or a serious hike across open country. There's a comprehensive network of paths and forest trails plus a programme of Ranger-led walks. For more details see *Walking in the Scottish Borders* and *Ranger-led Walks*, both available free at tourist offices.

There are nine tourist information centres throughout the region. The ones in Jedburgh and Peebles are open all year, and the others (in Coldstream, Eyemouth, Galashiels, Hawick, Kelso, Melrose and Selkirk) are open from Apr to Oct. Details are given under each town. For any of their free publications call T0870-6070250, and for information on Borders festivals, such as the Melrose Rugby Sevens or the Ridings, call the Events Line, T01750-20054.

Information
Visit www. scot-borders.co.uk, or call the information line, T01835-863435

Peebles

Due south of Edinburgh is the pleasant little town of Peebles, on the banks of the river Tweed, surrounded by wooded hills. The river here is wide and fast, whereas the pace of life on the town's broad High Street is altogether more sedate. Things liven up somewhat during the week-long **Beltane Fair**, the

Phone code: 01721
Colour map 6, grid B1
Population: 7,000

Southern Scotland

Southern Scotland

 Cycling around Peebles

There are many graded cycle routes through the Glentress, Cardrona and Elibank and Traquair forests. At Walkerburn, east of Innerleithen, you can link up to the fully signposted 90-mile **Tweed Cycleway***. See the tourist board leaflet* Cycling in the Scottish Borders. *For bike hire try* **Scottish Border Trails***,*

T720336, open Apr-Oct, at Glentress, a mile or so east of town on the A72. Mountain and touring bikes cost from £12 per day during peak season. They also organize bicycle tours. Bikes can also be hired from **Crossburn Caravan Cycle Hire***, T/F720501, on the Edinburgh Road. Mountain bikes cost from £8-14 per day.*

great Celtic festival of the sun which is held in June and marks the beginning of summer. Another good time to visit is during the **Peebles Arts Festival**, which is held over two weeks at the end of August and beginning of September. Peebles is only a 45-minute drive from Edinburgh, and makes a convenient base for a tour of the Tweed valley.

Ins & outs There are hourly **buses** to **Edinburgh** (1 hr), **Galashiels** and **Melrose** and, less frequently, to **Selkirk** and **Biggar**, with **First Edinburgh**, T720181. Buses stop outside the post office, near the TIC, on Eastgate.

The town's **Tourist Information Centre** is on the High St, T720138, peebles@ scot-borders.co.uk Apr and May Mon-Sat 0930-1700, Sun 1000-1400; Jun Mon-Sat 0930-1730, Sun 1000-1600; Jul and Aug Mon-Fri 0900-2000, Sat 0900-1900, Sun 1000-1800; Sep Mon-Sat 0930-1730, Sun 1000-1600; Oct Mon-Sat 0930-1700, Sun 1000-1400; Nov and Dec hours vary. All hours may change.

Sights The **Tweeddale Museum** on the High Street is housed in the Chambers Institute, which was a gift to the town from William Chambers, a native of Peebles and founding publisher of the Chambers Encyclopaedia. It houses two notable friezes: one is a copy of the Elgin marbles taken from the Parthenon in Athens (and yet to be returned to their rightful home); the other is the 19th-century Triumph of Alexander. Temporary exhibitions are also staged throughout the year. ■ *Apr-Oct Mon-Fri 1000-1200 and 1400-1700, Sat 1000-1200, 1400-1600; winter hours vary. Free.*

Just to the west of town, on the A72, is **Neidpath Castle**, perched high on a rocky bluff overlooking the Tweed. The medieval Tower House enjoys an impressive setting, but there's little to see inside which would justify the entrance fee. ■ *Easter-late May holiday daily 1600-1900, late June-early Sep 1100-1800. £3, £2.50 concession.* The castle can be reached by following the trail along the River Tweed from Hay Lodge Park in town. The walk passes a beautiful picnic spot beneath the castle and you can swim in the river (but take care). The trail continues through lovely wooded countryside and you can cross the river and return at Manor Bror (a three-mile round trip) or further on at Lyne footbridge (an eight-mile round trip). Details of this and other local walks can be found in the *Popular Walks around Peebles* leaflet available at the tourist office.

Two other good woodland walks are in **Glentress Forest**, just over a mile east of town on the A72, and **Cardona Forest**, on the south side of the Tweed, four miles out of town on the B7062. Also on the B7062 to Traquair (see below), about two miles from town, is **Kailzie Gardens** with a walled garden, greenhouses, woodland walks, trout fishing pond and excellent courtyard tearoom. ■ *Apr-Oct daily 1100-1730; Nov-Mar 1100-1700 £2. T720007.*

Eight miles southwest of Peebles, a mile beyond the village of Stobo on the B712, is **Dawyck Botanic Gardens**, an outstation of Edinburgh's Royal Botanic Garden, which contains a fine collection of trees and shrubs and landscaped wooded paths. ■ *Daily Mar-mid Nov 0930-1800; closes 1600 in Nov. T760254.*

Sleeping

There's no shortage of accommodation in and around Peebles, from upmarket hotels to modest B&Bs

A *Cringletie House Hotel*, T730233, F730244, www.cringletie.com, 2 miles north of town just off the A703 to Edinburgh. Lovely 19th-century baronial house set in 28 acres of grounds, with an excellent restaurant (see below) and friendly service. A *Peebles Hotel Hydro*, Innerleithen Rd, T720602, www.peebleshotelhydro.co.uk Large resort hotel with excellent sports facilities and a whole host of activities for kids, good restaurant. Also good is **B-C** *Castle Venlaw Hotel*, on the Edinburgh Rd, T720384, enquiries @venlaw.co.uk, www.venlaw.co.uk, a lovely old baronial castle with good views over the town; the **D** *Green Tree Hotel*, 41 Eastgate T720582, and the **C-D** *Kingsmuir Hotel*, T720151, www.kinsmuir.com, which does good bar meals. Amongst the dozens of **guesthouses** and **B&Bs** is the excellent **E** *Rowanbrae*, on Northgate, which runs off the east end of the High St, T721630; and **E** *Grey Gables*, on Springwood Rd, T721252, which uses organic produce and can provide vegetarian breakfasts. About a mile and a half out of town is **E** *The Shieling*, Eshiels T722577, theshieling@skynow.net There's **camping** at Rosetta Caravan & Camping Park, on Rosetta Rd, a 15-min walk north of the High St, T720770. Open Apr-Oct.

Eating

The best place to eat is the Cringlethie House Hotel (see above) which serves delicious Scottish cuisine at mid-range/expensive prices. Open 1230-1400, 1900-2100. Otherwise, there's the *Horse Shoe Inn*, T730225, at Eddleston, about 5 miles north of Peebles on the A703. It serves very good, moderately priced food throughout the day and evening. A great place in the centre of town is *The Sunflower Restaurant*, 4 Bridgegate, T722420, which serves coffee, cakes and Mediterranean style lunches – as well as evening meals on Thu, Fri and Sat. There is lots of choice there for veggies. The *Park Hotel*, on Innerleithen Rd, does decent bar meals. An excellent deli in town is *The Olive Tree*, at 7 High St. It sells a wide selection of continental delicacies and local produce and specializes in cheeses. Another good deli is *Cooks Fine Foods*, next to the TIC.

Biggar and around

Eighteen miles west of Peebles, via the A72, A701 and A702, is the old market town of Biggar, just across the regional border, in South Lanarkshire. Biggar stands on the A702, the main route from the M74 to Edinburgh, and makes a pleasant and convenient stopping-point for those driving to the capital from the south. The town centre has had a recent makeover and there are enough places of interest to warrant a few hours here.

Phone code: 01899
Colour map 5, grid B6

Ins & outs

Getting there There are several daily **buses** to **Edinburgh**.There are also regular daily buses to **Lanark**. Traveline T0870-6082608, have information on all public transport. A *Postbus* service, T01752-494527, runs to **Tweedsmuir**, **Abington** and **Wanlockhead** (see page 169).

The **Tourist Information Centre** is at 155 High St, T221066. Open Easter-Sep Mon-Sat 1000-1700, Sun 1200-1700.

Sights

The **Moat Park Heritage Centre**, T221050, is housed in a renovated church near the foot of Kirkstyle, off the High Street. It includes displays on local history, archaeology and geology as well as some very interesting tapestries. ■ *Easter-Oct Mon-Sat 1030-1700, Sun 1400-1700. £2/£1.50.* Ask here

Southern Scotland

about details of **Hugh McDiarmid's Cottage**, which is three miles north of town. It was the home of the poet until his death and can be viewed by appointment. only.

There are four other museums in Biggar. Close by, on North Back Road, is **Gladstone Court Museum**, which features a Victorian street with shops, a bank and schoolroom preserved just as they were 150 years ago. ■ *Apr-Oct Mon-Sat 1030-1700, Sun 1400-1700. £2/£1.50.* The Gladstone family, ancestors of the 19th-century Liberal Prime Minister, William Ewart Gladstone, are buried in the churchyard of **St Mary's Church**.

The **Greenhill Covenanters' Museum**, on Burnbrae, traces the development of the Covenanting movement. ■ *May-Sep daily 1400-1700. £1, £0.70 concession.* Nearby is the **Gasworks Museum**, the only surviving coal-fired gasworks in Scotland. ■ *Jun-Sep daily 1400-1700. £1, £0.50 concession.*

On Broughton Street is the **Puppet Theatre**, set up by Purves Puppets, a touring theatre company. The museum features puppets from all over the world, including some very strange ones indeed. There are also regular workshops, backstage tours and shows are held all year round in the Victorian theatre. ■ *Museum open Easter-end Aug Mon-Sat 1000-1630, Sun 1400-1630. May also be open outwith these hours – call first to check. All seats £5. T220631.*

Biggar is overlooked by **Tinto Hill** (2,333 ft), near the village of Symington, four miles southwest of town at the junction of the A72 and A73. It's a fairly easy walk from the village to the summit, from where the views are fantastic. There's also a Druidic Circle and Bronze-Age burial cairn. A good track starts from near the Tinto Hill farm shop on the A73. Allow about three hours. Regular Biggar-Lanark buses pass through Symington.

Sleeping & eating

A recommended place to stay is **D** *Skirling House*, at **Skirling**, about 3 miles northeast of Biggar, T860274, www.skirlinghouse.com, open Mar-Dec, a wonderful B&B with superb home cooking. Another excellent B&B is **D-E** *Lindsaylands House*, 1 mile west of Biggar, T220033. The *Elphinstone* and *Cornhill House* hotels both serve good bar meals, and there's the usual selection of cafés and takeaways along the High Street. Don't miss the wonderful ice cream at *The Chocolate Box* on the High St (open daily 0900-1700, Sun from 1300); or try that of its neighbour, and rival, *Taylors of Biggar*.

Around Biggar

Five miles east of Biggar, at the junction of the B7016 and A701, is the village of **Broughton**, childhood home of novelist John Buchan, who wrote the classic best-seller *The Thirty Nine Steps*. Just to the south of the village is the **John Buchan Centre**, a small museum dedicated to the life and work of the man who went on to become Governor General of Canada. ■ *Easter Weekend and May to mid-Oct daily 1400-1700. £1.50. T01899-221050.*

About 10 miles south of Broughton, on the A701 to Moffat, is the historic **D** *Crook Inn*, just to the north of tiny **Tweedsmuir**, T01899-880272. The old country inn has strong literary associations. **Robert Burns** wrote his poem '*Willie Wastle's Wife*' in what is now the bar, and Sir Walter Scott used to pay the occasional visit. From the inn you can climb **Broad Law** (2,756 ft), the second highest hill in southern Scotland. A steep and winding single-track road climbs east from Tweedsmuir, past the Talla Reservoir, to meet the A708 from Moffat to Selkirk by the shores of **St Mary's Loch** (see page 154).

The Tweed Valley: Peebles to Galashiels

Seven miles east of Peebles is the village of Innerleithen, home of **Robert Smail's Printing Works**, on the main street, where you can see how printing was done at the beginning of the 20th century. You can watch the printer at work on the original machinery and even try your hand at typesetting. ■ *Easter and 1 May-30 Sep Mon-Sat 1000-1300 and 1400-1700, Sun 1400-1700; weekends only in Oct Sat 1000-1300 and 1400-1700, Sun 1400-1700. £2.50, £1.70. T830206 (NTS).*

Innerleithen
Phone code: 01896
Colour map 6, grid B1

Sleeping and eating There are some excellent places to stay and eat in Innerleithen, including the **D** *Traquair Arms Hotel & Restaurant*, on the Traquair Rd, T830229, traquair.arms@scotborders.com A local favourite for its fine food and real ales. **E** *Caddon View* , 14 Pirn Rd, T830208, caddonview@aol.com There's a **campsite** at *Tweedside Caravan Park* on Montgomery St, T831271, open Apr-Oct. Note that accommodation is usually fully booked during the Traquair Fair in Aug (see below). For great ice cream, head for *Caldwell's* on the High St.

Transport *First Edinburgh*, T01721-720181, bus No 62 runs regularly to Innerleithen and Peebles from **Edinburgh**.

The big attraction in these parts is the amazing Traquair House, one of Scotland's great country houses. It lies about a mile south of Innerleithen, on the south side of the Tweed. Traquair is the oldest continually inhabited house in the country and is still owned by the Maxwell Stuarts, who have been living here since 1491. Its history goes much further back, however, and parts of the house are believed to date from the 12th century. The original Tower House was added to over the next five centuries, and most of what you see today dates from the mid-17th century. It has been visited by no fewer than 27 monarchs, including Mary, Queen of Scots, who stayed here with her husband, Darnley, in 1566. The place is steeped in Jacobite history, but the family paid for its Catholic principles. The fourth earl was imprisoned in the Tower of London, and sentenced to death, for his part in the Jacobite rising of 1715, but managed to escape with the help of his wife who smuggled him out disguised as a maid. The fifth earl served two years in the Tower of London for his support of Bonnie Prince Charlie in 1745. By the turn of the 18th century the family had lost most of its estates and had neither the money nor the motivation to undertake any major rebuilding.

Traquair House

As a result, visiting Traquair is genuinely like stepping back in time, and there's a uniquely nostalgic and spooky atmosphere missing from so many other historic houses. One of the most interesting rooms is the **priest's room**, where a succession of resident priests lived in hiding until the Catholic Emancipation Act of 1829 allowed them to give mass. Amongst the many fascinating relics is the cradle used by Mary, Queen of Scots for her son, James VI, and some letters written by the Stuart pretenders.

Also worth seeing are the **gardens**, where you'll find a maze, craft shops, a cottage tearoom and an 18th-century working **brewery** producing several ales including *Bear Ale* and *Jacobite Ale*, which can be purchased in the tearoom and gift shop. A **craft and music fair** is held in the grounds of the house every August. ■ *Apr-Jun and Sep-Oct daily 1230-1730; Jun-Aug daily 1030-1730; £5.30 (£2.80 child). T830323. Bus No C1 runs once a day to Traquair from Peebles.*

Southern Scotland

Galashiels
Phone code: 01896
Colour map 6, grid B2
Population: 13,700

At the junction of the A72 and A7 Edinburgh-Carlisle road is the gritty, workmanlike textile town of Galashiels, strung out along the banks of the Gala river for more than two miles. Galashiels is one the largest towns in the Borders region, and a transport hub, but there's precious little to detain passing tourists.

There are frequent **buses** to and from **Edinburgh** (1 hr 25 mins); **Peebles, Melrose** (20 mins), **Hawick** (40 mins), **Selkirk** (15 mins) and **Carlisle** (2 hrs). The main operator is *First Edinburgh*, T0131-663 9233, Galashiels Bus station, T01896-752287. The **Tourist Information Centre** is at 3 St John's St, T755551. Apr-May Mon-Sat 1100-1600, Jun and Sep Mon-Sat 1000-1700; Jul and Aug Mon-Sat 1000-1800, Sun 1100-1300; Oct Mon-Sat 1000-1600.

Galashiels has played a vital role in the Borders economy for over 700 years as a major weaving town, producing tartans, tweeds and woollens, and is the home of the Scottish College of Textiles, though the industry has gone into decline in recent times. The only real attraction is **Lochcarron Cashmere and Wool Centre** in Huddersfield Street, a working mill with a visitor centre, textiles museum and reasonable mill shop. ■ *Open all year round daily for guided tours, phone for times; T751100.*

Melrose and around

Phone code: 01896
Colour map 6, grid B2
Population: 2,300

Nestled at the foot of the mystical Eildon Hills, by the banks of the Tweed, is little Melrose, the loveliest of all the Border towns. It's an engaging mix of cute little shops and cottages and dignified Georgian and Victorian houses, and boasts one of the most famous ruins in Scotland (see below). The normally soporific atmosphere is shattered every April during the week-long **Melrose Sevens**, when the town is taken over by rugby fans from all over the world for the acclaimed seven-a-side rugby tournament which has been going since 1883.

Melrose makes a great base for exploring the beautiful landscapes of the middle stretch of the Tweed which so inspired Sir Walter Scott, the famous son of the Borders. Two of the area's main sights, **Dryburgh Abbey** and **Abbotsford House**, are inextricably linked with the writer's life and work. They can be reached by public transport, but you'll need your own transport if you want to get off the beaten track.

Ins & outs

Getting there There are regular buses to **Galashiels** (15 mins), **Kelso** (several daily; 35 mins), **Jedburgh** (30 mins), **Peebles** (several daily; 1 hr 10 mins), and **Selkirk** (hourly Mon-Sat, less frequently on Sun; 40 mins). To get to **Hawick**, it's easier to catch a bus to Galashiels and then change (see page 656). Buses to Melrose stop in Market Square, close to the abbey and tourist office.

The **Tourist Information Centre** is next to the abbey ruins in Abbey St, T822555. Apr-May Mon-Sat 1100-1600, Sun 1000-1300; Jun Mon-Sat 1000-1730, Sun 1000-1300; Jul and Aug Mon-Sat 0900-1830, Sun 1000-1700; Sep Mon-Sat 1000-1730, Sun 1000-1300; Oct Mon-Sat 1000-1600, Sun 1000-1300. Hours may vary. Those who wish to explore the area by bike can **hire cycles** in Galashiels, at *Gala Cycles*, T757587, at 58 High St.

Sights

The bitter wars that ravaged the Scottish borders for centuries did irrevocable damage to Melrose Abbey, but even in ruins it remains toweringly beautiful and impressive. It was founded in 1136 by the prolific David I (who helped to found

The Legends of the Eildons

The three-peaked Eildon Hills were considered a sacred place by the ancient Celts and have long been shrouded in mystery and associated with a number of legends. For a start, they are believed to have been created by the wizard/alchemist Michael Scott, and it was here that the mystic Thomas the Rhymer was given the gift of prophecy by the Faerie Queen. Most startling of all, though, is the claim that King Arthur and his knights lie asleep beneath the hills, victims of a terrible spell.

all four of the great Border Abbeys) and was the first Cistercian monastery in Scotland. It was attacked in 1322 by Edward II, but soon restored thanks to the financial assistance of Robert the Bruce. In 1385 it was largely destroyed by Richard II of England, then completely rebuilt, only to be ravaged again, this time by Henry VIII, in the mid-16th century. The abbey as it stands today dates from the 14th and 15th centuries, and was preserved by the money of the Duke of Buccleuch and the energy and talent of Sir Walter Scott. His great narrative poem *The Lay of the Last Minstrel* painted an eloquent picture of the abbey and helped him on the road to fame.

The red sandstone ruins show an elaborate Gothic style and some of the finest figure sculpture in Scotland. Of particular note are the humorous gargoyles, which include a pig playing the bagpipes on the roof of the south side of the nave. The abbey's real claim to fame is that the **heart of Robert the Bruce** was buried here, at his request, after it had been taken to the Holy Land to help in the Crusades. The lead casket believed to contain the heart was finally excavated in 1996 and now takes pride of place in the abbey museum, in the **Commendator's House**, next to the church. ■ *Apr-Sep daily 0930-1830; Oct-Mar Mon-Sat 0930-1630, Sun 1400-1630. £3.30, £2.50 concession. T822562 (HS).*

Next to the abbey is **Priorwood Garden**, where plants are grown specifically for dried flower arrangements. There's also a dried flower shop on site. ■ *Apr-Sep Mon-Sat 1000-1730, Sun 1330-1730; Oct-Dec Mon-Sat 1000-1600, Sun 1330-1600. £2, £1 child. T822493 (NTS).*

On Market Square is the **Trimontium Exhibition**, a small but interesting centre which tells the story of the Roman occupation of the area and includes some archaeological finds. ■ *Apr-Oct daily 1030-1630, Sat, Sun closed 1300-1400. £1.50, £1 concession. T822651.* The more adventurous can follow the **Trimontium Walk**, a four-mile guided tour of Roman sites in the area, including the site of the Trimontium (Three Hills) fort at Newstead. ■ *Apr-Oct Thu 1330-1700. £2. T822651.*

Walks around Melrose

The three peaks of the **Eildon Hills** can be seen from all parts of the Central Borders region and can be climbed quite easily from Melrose. Starting from Market Square, head along the B6359 to Lilliesleaf, and after 100-yd the path is signed to the left and leads to the saddle between the North and Mid hills (Mid Hill is the highest, at 1,385 ft). The path leads to the summit of North Hill, then Mid Hill, and finally West Hill, to the south. There are several routes back to town, but heading via the golf course makes a nice circular walk of two miles. Allow about 1½ hours. The route is detailed in the *Eildon Hills Walk* leaflet available from the tourist office.

Melrose is the starting point for the **St Cuthbert's Way**, a 60-mile walk which finishes at **Lindisfarne** (the Holy Isle). The much longer **Southern Upland Way** also passes through the town (for more details see page 138).

Sleeping There's not a huge amount of accommodation in Melrose, considering its appeal, so it's best to book in advance during the summer and especially during the Melrose Sevens in mid-Apr. The best hotel is **C** *Burts Hotel*, on Market Sq, T822285, www.burtshotel .co.uk This refurbished traditional 18th-century inn is very comfortable, and renowned locally for its excellent modern Scottish cuisine (lunch mid-range; dinner expensive). Also on the square is the small, comfortable **C** *Millars Hotel*, T822645. Pick of the **B&Bs** and **guesthouses** is the excellent **E** *Dunfermline House Guest House*, on Buccleuch St, T822148, www.dunmel.freeserve.co.uk Best of the rest are **E** *Braidwood*, also on Buccleuch St, T822488; **E** *Little Fordel*, T822206, on Abbey St; and **E** *Collingwood*, on Waverley Rd, T822670, open Apr-Oct, on the outskirts of town. No smoking.

There's a very good and very popular **F** *Youth Hostel*, in a large mansion on the edge of town, overlooking the abbey from beside the A6091 bypass, T822521, open all year. There's also a **campsite** at *Gibson Park*, T822969, at the end of the High St opposite the Greenyards rugby ground.

Eating
Finding a good place to eat isn't too difficult
Best of all is *Burt's Hotel* (see above), where you can dine in style in the dining room or opt for their excellent pub grub. Another hotel recommended for food is the moderately priced *King's Arms*, on the High St, T822143. On the other side of the river, in the village of Gattonside, is the *Hoebridge Inn Restaurant*, T823082, which offers good quality Scottish fare at mid-range prices and is well worth the walk. A good French-style bistros is *Marmions Brasserie*, T822245, on Buccleuch St near the abbey (daily 0900-1800, 1830-2200). Mid-range prices.

Entertainment The Wynd Theatre is a tiny **theatre** which stages regular drama productions and musical events, T823854. Check at the TIC for the current programme.

Abbotsford House One of the Borders' top tourist attractions is Abbotsford House, home of Sir Walter Scott from 1812 to 1832 and a Mecca for the great novelist's many admirers. For an account of his life, see page 656.

Scott spent a small fortune transforming the original farmhouse into a huge country mansion befitting a man of his status and, though Abbotsford may not be to everyone's taste, the house is an intriguing mix of styles and enjoys a beautiful setting. The house is still lived in by Scott's descendants, and the library and study have been preserved much as they were when he lived here, including the collection of over 9,000 antiquarian books. There's also an amazing assortment of Scottish memorabilia, including Rob Roy's purse, Bonnie Prince Charlie's drinking cup and Flora MacDonald's pocketbook.

The house is well worth visiting and sits in pleasant grounds, about three miles west of Melrose between the Tweed and the B6360. Take the Melrose-Galashiels bus and get off at the Tweedbank traffic island. From there it's a 15-minute walk. ■ *Mid-Mar to May and Oct Mon-Sat 0930-1700, Sun 1400-1700; Jun-Sep daily 0930-1700. £4, £2 child. T750043.*

Dryburgh Abbey Five miles southeast of Melrose on the B6404, near the village of St Boswells, is Dryburgh Abbey. Its setting amongst ancient cedars on the banks of the Tweed, also make it the most beautifully idyllic, romantic and evocative of the Border abbeys. It dates from around 1150, when it was founded by Hugh de Morville for Premonstratensian monks from Alnwick in Northumberland.

The 12th- and 13th-century ruin is remarkably well-preserved and complete, and was chosen as the burial place for Sir Walter Scott. His final resting place is in the north transept of the church. Close by lies Field Marshal Earl Haig, the disastrous First World War commander. ■ *Apr-Sep 0930-1830; Oct-Mar Mon-Sat 0930-1630, Sun 1400-1630. £2.80, £2 concession. T01835-822381.*

If you're travelling by public transport from Melrose, take the **Jedburgh** bus as far as St Boswells (10 minutes), then walk north from the village for about a mile. If you're driving, make sure you pass **Scott's View**, on the B6356, which offers a sweeping view of the Eildon Hills and Tweed valley. Scott came here many times to enjoy the view (hence its name) and to seek inspiration. There's an even better view from the hill on the other side of the road. In the abbey grounds is the **B-C** *Dryburgh Abbey Hotel* (T01835-822261, www.dryburgh.co.uk).

North of Melrose on the main A68 is the stolid market town of **Lauder**, which merits inclusion because of Thirlestane Castle, one of Scotland's oldest and finest castles, which stands on the eastern edge of town. The castellated baronial house is the seat of the Earls of Lauderdale and has been owned by the Maitland family since the 16th century. Inside, the 17th-century plaster ceilings are particularly notable. ■ *End Mar-end Oct daily (except Sat) 1030-1700 – last admission 1615. £5.30, £3 child. T01578-722430.*

Thirlestane
Castle

Selkirk and around

About six miles southwest of Melrose, on the A7 to Hawick, is the little town of Selkirk, standing on the edge of the Ettrick Forest which rises steeply from the Ettrick Water. Selkirk has been a textile centre since the early 19th century when the growing demand for tweed could no longer be met by the mills of Galashiels. Those mills are closed now and Selkirk is a quiet, unassuming place that only comes to life during the **Selkirk Gathering** in June, the largest of the Border Ridings (see page 145). Selkirk is handily placed for visiting the other Border towns and sights, and makes a good base for touring the area.

Phone code: 01750
Colour map 6, grid B2
Population: 6,000

Getting there The A7 runs south to Hawick and north to Galashiels and Melrose, while the A699 heads east to Kelso, via St Boswells. The A708 runs southwest towards Moffat (see below) and the A707 takes you northwest to meet the A72 to Innerleithen and Peebles. *First Edinburgh* bus No 95 runs frequently to and from **Edinburgh** and **Hawick**, via Selkirk and Galashiels. There are also regular daily buses to **Langholm** and **Carlisle**. There's a bus to **Moffat**, on Sat only. All buses leave from Market Sq.

Ins & outs

The **Tourist Information Centre** is next to Halliwell's House (see below) on Market Sq, T20054. Apr-May, Jun, Sep Mon-Sat 1000-1700, Sun 1400-1600; Jul, Aug Mon-Sat 0930-1730, Sun 1400-1700; Oct Mon-Sat 1000-1600, Sun 1400-1600. Hours may vary.

Halliwell's House Museum and Robson Gallery features an 18th-century ironmongers and tells the story of the town and its industry. The gallery has a changing programme of temporary exhibitions. ■ *Same opening hours as the tourist office. Free. (Closed for renovations until Apr 2002.) T20096.* Also on Market Square is **Walter Scott's Courtroom**, where Sir Walter Scott served as Sheriff of Selkirk from 1799 to 1832. It houses an exhibition on his life and writings. ■ *Apr-end Sep Mon-Sat 1000-1600; Jun-Aug also Sun 1400-1600; Oct Mon-Sat 1300-1600. Free.* Outside the courtroom is a statue of the great novelist, and at the other end of the High Street is a statue of **Mungo Park** (1771-1805), the famous explorer and anti-slavery campaigner who was born in Selkirkshire. At the northern end of town, on the A7 to Galashiels, is **Selkirk Glass**, a thriving local industry, where you can see glass-blowing displays. ■ *Mon-Sat 0900-1700, Sun 1100-1700. Free. T20954.*

Sights

Southern Scotland

Sleeping **A-B** *Philipburn Country House Hotel*, Linglie Rd, T720747, info@philipburnhousehotel
.co.uk Upmarket accommodation and good food. There are also cheaper hotels in
town, such as the dependable, family-run **D** *Glen Hotel*, Yarrow Terr, T/F20259,
glenhotel@hotmail.com; and the **D-E** *Heatherlie House Hotel*, at Heatherlie Park,
T21200, www.heatherlie.freeserve.co.uk There are some good value B&Bs, including
E *Hillholm*, 36 Hillside Terr, T21293; and **E** *Sunnybrae House*, 75 Tower St, T21156. The
cheapest place around is the **F** *SYHA Broadmeadows Youth Hostel* at Yarrowford,
T76262; open end-Mar to end Sep, 5 miles west of Selkirk on the A708, beyond Bowhill
(see below). There's a **campsite** at *Victoria Park Caravan & Camping Site*, T20897,
beside the river next to the indoor swimming pool.

Eating Possibilities for eating are limited. The *County Hotel*, T21233, on the High St, serves
decent bar meals; and the *Court House Coffee Shop*, on Market Sq, does snacks and
high teas. There's also a coffee shop at the Selkirk Glass Visitor Centre. Or you can try the
local speciality, Bannock bread, from Jackie Lunns on Market Sq.

Bowhill House
& Country Park Three miles west of Selkirk, where the B7009 turns south off the A708, is the
entrance to Bowhill House and Country Park, home of the Scotts of Buccle-
uch and Queensberry since 1812. They were once the largest landowners in
the Borders and fabulously wealthy, a fact made evident by the fantastic collection of French antiques and European paintings on display. There are
works by Canaletto, Guardi, Reynolds and Gainsborough. The wooded hills
of the Country Park can be explored via a network of footpaths and cycle
trails. There's no public transport to Bowhill, but the weekly *Harrier Scenic
Bus Service* runs near Bowhill from Selkirk and Melrose in the morning,
returning in the afternoon. It runs from July to September (see page 144).
■ *House open Jul daily, 1300-1630. £4.50. £2 child, wheelchair users free.
Country Park Apr-Jun and Aug daily except Fri 1200-1700; Jul daily
1200-1700. £2.*

Yarrow Water
& Ettrick Water
*OS Landranger Nos
73 and 79*

The A707 heads southwest from Selkirk to Moffat, following the beautiful
Yarrow Water to **St Mary's Loch**, where the road is crossed by the **Southern
Upland Way**. A few miles west of Selkirk is the turning south on to the B7009
which follows the course of the Ettrick Water to meet the B709, which continues south, past the village of **Ettrick**, to **Eskdalemuir** and on to **Langholm**
(see page 167).

This is one of the most remote and beautiful parts of Scotland, and an area
inextricably linked with **James Hogg** (1770-1835), 'The Ettrick Shepherd',
who was a great friend of Sir Walter Scott. Hogg was a notable writer himself
and his most famous work, *The Confessions of a Justified Sinner*, is important
in Scottish literature. Hogg was born in Ettrick and spent his entire life in the
Ettrick and Yarrow valleys. He and Scott would often meet in **E-D** *Tibbie
Shiels Inn*, T01750-42231, on the narrow strip of land separating **St Mary's
Loch** from the ethereal **Loch of the Lowes**. It's still a famous watering hole
and popular stop along the Southern Upland Way. It also serves bar meals
(Easter-Nov daily; Nov-Easter closed Mon, Tue, Wed). From *Tibbie Shiels
Inn* you can follow the Southern Upland Way south to Ettrick Water, where
an unclassified road leads east to the village of Ettrick, or continue southwest
all the way down to Moffat (see page 168). Alternatively, head north along the
eastern shore of St Mary's Loch to the A708, then continue north to Traquair
House (see page 149), then east towards Yair Hill Forest, where you can turn
south to the *Broadmeadows Youth Hostel* (see above). These are strenuous
hikes and you should be fit and well equipped (see page 60).

At Cappercleuch, on the west shore of St Mary's Loch, a spectacular single-track road twists and turns its way up to the Megget Reservoir and then down past the Talla Reservoir to the tiny village of **Tweedsmuir**, on the A701 (see page 148). East of St Mary's Loch, the A708 is crossed by the B709 which runs north to Innerleithen and south and then east to Hawick. At the road junction is the **E** *Gordon Arms Hotel* (T01750-82232), said to be the last meeting place of Scott and Hogg. It's a popular stopping point for walkers, and offers bar food and local ales.

Jedburgh

Ten miles from the English border is the attractive little town of Jedburgh, straddling the Jed Water at the edge of the northern slopes of the wild, barren Cheviot Hills. Jeburgh was strategically the most important of the Border towns, due to its proximity to England, and as a result received the full brunt of invading English armies. These days the only invaders are tourists. Jedburgh is the most visited of the Border towns and there are a number of interesting sights.

Phone code: 01835
Colour map 6, grid B2
Population: 4,000

Getting there The bus station is close to the abbey and there are good connections around the Borders. First *Edinburgh*, T0131-6639233, runs frequent daily **buses** to Hawick, Kelso and Galashiels. There are also buses daily to and from **Edinburgh**.

Ins & outs

The town's **Tourist Information Centre** is on Murray's Green. It's a large and well-stocked office with leaflets detailing local walks, T863435. Apr, May and Oct Mon-Sat 1000-1700, Sun 1100-1600; Jun and Sep Mon-Sat 0930-1800, Sun 1100-1700; Jul and Aug Mon-Fri 0900-2000, Sat 1000-1900, Sun 1000-1800; Nov-Mar Mon-Sat 1000-1700. Hours may vary.

The town is dominated by **Jedburgh Abbey**, founded in 1138 by David I for Augustinian canons from northern France. The site had much older religious significance, however, and stonework in the abbey's museum dates from the first millennium AD. Malcolm IV was crowned here and Alexander III married his second wife in the abbey in 1285. Their wedding feast was held at nearby Jedburgh Castle (see below) and, like the castle, the abbey came under attack during the many English invasions, most devastatingly in 1523 when it was bombarded and burned. Despite this, the abbey church is remarkably complete, particularly the tower. Excavations have recently uncovered the remains of the cloister buildings, and among the finds is the priceless 12th-century 'Jedburgh comb', which is on display in the excellent **visitor centre** which brilliantly tells the abbey's long and fascinating history. ■ *May-end Sep daily 0930-1830; Oct-Mar Mon-Sat 0930-1630, Sun 1400-1630. £3.30, £2.50 concession, £1.20 child. T863925.*

Sights

Nearby, at the top of the Castlegate, is **Jedburgh Castle Jail and Museum**, which was formerly the county jail. It was built in 1823 on the site of the 12th-century castle, which changed hands many times until it was destroyed by the Scots because of its value to the English. The displays in the cell blocks depict prison life in the 19th century, and there's an exhibition on the town's history. ■ *Easter-end Oct Mon-Sat 1000-1630, Sun 1300-1600 £1.50, £1 concession. T864750.*

At the other end of the town centre is **Mary, Queen of Scots House**, a beautiful 16th-century building of rough-hewn stone which contains a small bedroom occupied by Mary during her stay at Jedburgh in 1566. She spent

Southern Scotland

several weeks here recovering from illness after her famous 30-mile ride to Hermitage Castle (see page 157) to visit her injured lover, the Earl of Bothwell. The ensuing scandal was only exacerbated by the murder of her husband Darnley the following year at Holyrood Palace in Edinburgh. Many years later, during her long incarceration, Mary regretted the fact that she hadn't died while staying in Jedburgh. This episode in Scottish history is told through a series of displays, and there are various artefacts associated with Mary. ■ *Mar-Nov Mon-Sat 1000-1630, Sun 1200- 1630. £2.60, £1.50 concession. T863331.*

Sleeping There are a few hotels in town, but the most luxurious place to stay is the **B** *Jedforest Hotel*, in the village of Camptown, 6 miles south of Jedburgh, on the A68, and only 5 miles from the border, T840222, www.jedforesthotel.freeserve.co.uk The self-proclaimed 'First Hotel in Scotland' is very comfortable, with a fine restaurant. Also recommended is the **D** *Glenfriars Hotel*, The Friars, T862000, bookings@ edenroad.demon .co.uk A lovely Georgian house near the north end of the High St. There are several **B&Bs** in and around town, but few can match the sheer style and value-for-money of **E-D** *Hunalee House*, T/F863011, sheila. whittaker@btinternet.com Open Mar-Oct. This early 17th-century house is a mile south of town on the A68, set in 15 acres of gardens and woodlands. Also out of town and great value is **E-D** *Ancrum Craig*, T/F830280, ancrumcraig@clara.net Open Jan-Dec. A quiet 19-century country house 2 miles from the A68 near the village of Ancrum. In town is the **E** *Kenmore Bank Guest House*, on Oxnam Rd, T862369, www.hotelsjedburgh.co.uk, overlooking the Jed Water; and the more characterful **E** *Meadhon House*, 48 Castlegate, T/F862504, meadhon@aol.com

There are a few **campsites** close to Jedburgh. 4 miles south of town on the A68 is the *Jedwater Caravan Park*, T840219, open Apr-Oct. 5 miles to the north of Jedburgh is *Lilliardsedge Holiday Park and Golf Club*, T830271, open Easter-end Oct; while the *Elliot Park Camping & Caravanning Club*, T863393, open Apr- Oct, is a mile north of town.

Eating There's not a great deal of choice for eating in Jedburgh. Best of all is *Simply Scottish*, T864696, on the High St, which offers modern, bistro-style Scottish fare all day at cheap-mid-range prices. There's also the *Castlegate Restaurant*, T862552, on the corner of the High St and Abbey Close, which serves traditional meals and snacks. On the High St is *The Sunrise*, T863503, a popular Indian restaurant (open 1200-1430, 1800-2300). Eleven miles south of Jedburgh, is the *Carter Bar*, the first/last pub in Scotland, standing on the border with England in the Cheviot Hills.

Sport & Jedburgh's Common Riding, the **Callant's Festival**, takes place in late Jun/early Jul
festivals (see also 'Borders Festivals', on page 145). In early Feb is the **Jedburgh Hand Ba'** game, a bruising and exhausting contest between the 'uppies' (those born above the Market Place) and the 'downies' (those born below), who endeavour to get a leather ball from one end of the town to the other. Visitors from south of the border may wish to note that the game used to be played with the heads of vanquished Englishmen. **Horse riding** is available for experienced riders at *Ferniehurst Mill Lodge*, T863279, 2 miles south of Jedburgh on the A68. They offer accommodation and tailor-made riding holidays.

Hawick

Phone code: 01450
Colour map 6, grid B2
Population: 15,700

Fourteen miles southwest of Jedburgh and 12 miles south of Selkirk is Hawick (pronounced 'Hoyk'), the largest town in the Borders and centre of the region's knitwear and hosiery industry for over 200 years. Hawick is not a place noted for its great beauty, but it does attract lots of visitors who come to shop at its many factory outlets where you can buy all the classic brand names in knitwear. A list of knitwear suppliers is available at the TIC (see below).

There are hourly **buses** to and from **Jedburgh** (35 mins) and **Galashiels** (40 mins), and regular daily buses to and from **Selkirk** (20 mins), **Edinburgh** (2 hrs) and **Carlisle** (1 hr 15 mins). There's also a service to **Melrose** (40 mins), but it may be quicker to go to Galashiels and change there.

The **Tourist Information Centre** is in Drumlanrig Tower on the High St, T372547. Easter-May and Oct Mon-Sat 1000-1700, Sun 1200-1700; Jun and Sep Mon-Sat 1000-1730, Sun 1200-1730; Jul and Aug Mon-Sat 1000-1800, Sun 1200-1800. Hours may vary.

In the same building as the TIC is a **museum**, which outlines the tower's role in Anglo-Scottish wars from the 16th century. ■ *Same opening hours as the tourist office. £2.50, £1.50 concession.* In Wilton Lodge Park is the **Hawick Museum and Scott Art Gallery**, which has an interesting collection of mostly 19th-century textile exhibits. ■ *Oct-Mar Mon-Fri 1300-1600, Sat closed, Sun 1400-1600; Apr-Sep Mon-Fri 1000-1200 and 1300-1645, Sat, Sun 1400-1645. Free. T373457.*

A mile from town, on the A698 to Kelso, is the **C** *Mansfield House Hotel*, T373988, www.mansfield-house.com A traditional mansion house hotel offering good food (lunch cheap; dinner mid-range). Also good is **D** *Kirklands Hotel*, West Stewart Pl, T372263. There are plenty of cheaper B&B alternatives, including **E** *Oakwood House*, Buccleuch Rd, T372814. Eating options are pretty much confined to the hotel bars and restaurants.

The A7 runs southwest from Hawick through the dramatic scenery of **Teviotdale** to the tiny village of **Teviothead**, where it then exchanges the valley of the River Teviot for the **Ewes Water**. The Ewes then meets the River Esk at **Langholm**, in Dumfries and Galloway. The A7 continues its route south, to meet the A74(M) just north of **Carlisle**.

A much more beautiful route south is to take the A698 northeast out of Hawick, then turn off on to the A6088 which heads southeast. Just beyond the tiny village of **Bonchester Bridge**, take the B6357 which leads you into lovely **Liddesdale**. The B6357 follows the course of the Liddel Water all the way south to the village of **Canonbie** (see page 167), where it meets the A7.

A few miles north of **Newcastleton**, the B6357 meets the B6399 which runs north back to Hawick. Four miles north of the junction is the turning to **Hermitage Castle**, one of the great Border strongholds. The oldest part of the castle dates from the 13th century and it was in the hands of the Earls of Douglas until 1492, when it passed to the Earls of Bothwell. The fourth Earl of Bothwell, James Hepburn, was the third husband of Mary, Queen of Scots, following the murder of her second husband, Darnley, and is thought to have been behind the plot to murder him. It was to Hermitage that Mary made her famous ride to visit her future husband who had been injured in a border raid. Mary's marriage to Bothwell in 1566 was ill-advised and only succeeded in uniting their enemies; and led ultimately to her imprisonment in Lochleven Castle. Bothwell meanwhile fled to Norway, where he was captured and later died a prisoner himself, in 1578. Hermitage became largely irrelevant following the Union of Crowns in 1603 and fell into disrepair. Much of what you see today dates from the 19th century when the Duke of Buccleuch ordered its repair. The vast and eerie ruin is said to be haunted, which is not surprising given its grisly past. One owner, William Douglas, starved his prisoners to death in the ghoulish dungeons, which can still be seen. ■ *Apr-Sep daily 0930-1830. £2, £1.50 concession. There is no public transport service from Hawick. T01387-376222 (HS).*

Sleeping There are a couple of places to stay in the village of **Newcastleton**, 5½ miles south of Hermitage. The **E** *Liddlesdale Hotel*, T/F01387-375255, also serves local specialities such as pheasant and salmon; and there's the very pleasant **E-D** *Borders Honey Farm*, T/F01387-376737, 3 miles north of Newcastleton on the B6357.

Kelso and around

Phone code: 01573
Colour map 6,
grid B3
Population: 6,000

The little market town of Kelso, at the confluence of the Tweed and Teviot rivers, is one of the most picturesque of the Border towns, with its cobbled streets leading into a wide market square bounded by elegant, three-storey 18th- and 19th-century town houses. The main **festivals** are the **Border Union Agricultural Show** and the town's **Riding of the Marches**, both of which take place in July. Kelso also hosts its own Rugby Sevens in early September.

Ins & outs The **bus station** is on Roxburgh St, a short walk from The Square. There are regular **buses** to and from **Galashiels**, **Melrose**, **Jedburgh**, **Coldstream** and **Kirk Yetholm**. Services are less frequent on Sun. For more details, contact the main bus operator *First Edinburgh*, T0131-663 9233, or *Traveline*, T0870-6082608. There are also several buses (Mon-Sat) to and from **Berwick-upon-Tweed** (see below).

Kelso's **Tourist Information Centre** is in the Town House, on The Square, T223464. Apr-May Mon-Sat 1100-1600, Sun 1000-1300; Jun and Sep Mon-Sat 0930-1700, Sun 1000-1300; Jul and Aug Mon-Sat 0900-1830, Sun 1000-1700; Oct Mon-Sat 1000-1600, Sun 1000-1300; winter Mon-Sat 1100-1600. Hours subject to change.

Sights **Kelso Abbey** was once the largest and richest of the Border abbeys, but suffered the same fate as its counterparts, Jedburgh, Dryburgh and Melrose. Kelso was a strategic point in the Border wars between the Scots and the English and the abbey, founded in 1138 by King David, was laid to waste by successive English invasions, most devastatingly in 1545 by the Earl of Hertford. This latter attack was part of Henry VIII's so-called 'Rough Wooing', when the king took exception to the Scots' refusal to ratify a marriage treaty between his son and the infant Mary Stuart. Today, little remains of the abbey, and it is the least complete of those in the Borders. The nearby octagonal **Old Parish Church**, built in 1773, is unusual. ■ *Apr-end Dec daily (Sun afternoon only). Free.*

Aside from the abbey, the town's only other major attraction is the pleasant **Cobby Riverside Walk**, which leads along the banks of the Tweed to Floors Castle (see below). Leave The Square by Roxburgh Street, and follow the signposted alley to the start of the walk. The route passes the junction of the Tweed and Teviot rivers, a spot famous for its salmon fishing.

Floors Castle, the vast ancestral home of the Duke of Roxburghe, stands imperiously overlooking the Tweed, about a mile northwest of the town centre. The original Georgian mansion was designed by Robert Adam and built in 1721-26, though it was later remodelled by William Playfair in the 1840s, with the addition of many flamboyant features. Only 10 rooms are open to the public but they are undeniably elegant and palatial, and amongst the many priceless family items on display are outstanding collections of European furniture, porcelain and paintings by Picasso, Matisse and Augustus John, and a

15th-century Brussels tapestry. Floors is the largest inhabited castle in Scotland and the current occupier, the 10th Duke of Roxburghe, is a close personal friend of the royal family. The house also has a restaurant and a coffee shop. ■ *Mid Apr to end Oct daily 1000-1630 (last admission 1600). £5.50, £4.75 concession. T223333.*

The most luxurious place to stay hereabouts is **L** *The Roxburghe Hotel & Golf Course*, at the village of Heiton, a few miles from town on the A698 to Hawick, T450331,www.roxburghe.net This country mansion, owned by the Duke of Roxburgh, stands in hundreds of acres of park and woodlands on the banks of the Teviot, and offers grand style, superb cuisine and a championship golf course. Less salubrious but nevertheless highly recommended is the slightly more affordable **B** *Ednam House Hotel*, on Bridge St, T224168, F226319. A family-run Georgian mansion overlooking the Tweed and close to the town centre. Excellent food served all day (lunch cheap; dinner mid-range) in a restaurant with great views over the river. There are also some fine guesthouses and B&Bs, including **E** *White Swan Inn*, Abbey Row, T225800; and the non-smoking **E-D** *Bellevue House*, Bowmont St, T/F224588, bellevue.kelso@virgin.net The nearest **youth hostel** is at Kirk Yetholm (see below). There's a **campsite** at *Springwood Caravan Park*, T224596, admin@springwoodcaravanpark.co.uk, open Mar-Oct, overlooking the Tweed on the A699 heading west towards St Boswells.

Sleeping

The best places to eat are the Roxburghe and *Ednam House Hotels* listed above. The other hotels in town also offer food, most notably the *Queens Head* , T224636, at 24 Bridge St, and the *Black Swan Hotel*, T224563, on Horsemarket. Both are just off The Square and offer cheap bar meals. There's also *Cobbles*, a cost dining pub on Belmont Pl, and *Cottage Garden Tea Room*, opposite the abbey, which offers tea, coffee and light lunches (closed Sun & Wed, Nov-Easter, and Mon Jan, Feb).

Eating

Six miles northwest of Kelso on the B6397 is the village of Smailholm, where a turning leads to Smailholm Tower, a classic Scottish tower house and an evocative place full of history and romance. The 15th-century fortified farmhouse, built by the Pringles, squires to the Earls of Douglas, stands on a rocky pinnacle above a small lake. Sir Walter Scott's grandfather owned the nearby farm and the young Scott came here as a sickly child in the 1770s to improve his health. So began the writer's long love affair with the lore and landscapes of the Scottish Borders which inspired so much of his poetry and prose. Scott would write a ballad about this gaunt tower house – *The Eve of St John* – as part of a deal with the owner to save it. Today Smailholm houses a small, unremarkable museum relating to some of Scott's works, but the views from the top of the tower are rewarding. ■ *Apr-Sep daily 0930-1830; Oct-Mar Sat 0930-1630, Sun 1400-1630. £2, £1.50 concession. T460365.*

Smailholm Tower

Northwest of Kelso, on the A6089 to Gordon, is the signpost for Mellerstain House, home of the Earl of Haddington and one of Scotland's great Georgian houses. This 18th-century architectural masterpiece was designed by William Adam and his son Robert and perfectly characterizes the elegant symmetry of the period. The superb exterior is more than matched by the exquisitely ornate interiors. There is also furniture by Chippendale and Hepplewhite, as well as paintings by Constable, Gainsborough, Veronese and Van Dyck. The formal Italian gardens, laid out in the early 20th century, are equally impressive. ■ *Easter weekend and May-Sep Sun-Mon 1230-1700 (last admission) 1630. £5, £4.50 concession; café/shop 1130-1730. T410225.*

Mellerstain House

Southern Scotland

Kirk Yetholm &
Town Yetholm
There are regular
buses to and from
Kelso, 20 mins away

Six miles southeast of Kelso on the B6352 are the twin villages of Kirk Yetholm and Town Yetholm, lying within a stone's throw of the English border on the edge of the Cheviot Hills, at the northern end of the **Pennine Way** which runs up the spine of northern England. The villages are also on **St Cuthbert's Way**, which runs from Melrose to Lindisfarne in Northumberland (see page 138).

Sleeping There's accommodation in Kirk Yetholm, at the excellent **C-D** *Border Hotel*, T420237, overlooking the village green, which marks the end of the Pennine Way. Kirk Yetholm was once the home of the king of the gypsies (you can still see his pretty little cottage by the green) and the bar is full of pictures of the former gypsy inhabitants. It serves a welcome pint of ale and good food, too. There are several B&Bs, including **D-E** *Valleydene*, T420286, valleydene@rdplus.net, on the High Street. There's also a **F** *Youth Hostel* in Kirk Yetholm, T420631, open mid-Mar to end Oct. There's a caravan park (does not take tents) at *Kirkfield Caravan Park*, on Grafton Road in Town Yetholm, T420346, open Apr-Oct. A good pub is *The Border*, on The Green, popular with hikers.

Coldstream
Phone code: 01890
Colour map 6, grid B3

Standing on the north bank of the River Tweed, which marks the border with England, is the little town of Coldstream. The busy A697 linking Newcastle-upon-Tyne with Edinburgh runs through the centre of town, but Coldstream has little to offer visitors other than history.

Ins &outs There are several **buses** daily (Mon-Sat) between Kelso and Berwick-upon-Tweed, T0870-6082608.The well-stocked **Tourist Information Centre**is in the Town Hall on the High St, T882607. Apr, May Jun Mon, Thu, Sat 1300-1700, Tue, Wed, Fri 1000-1400; Jul, Aug Mon-Sat 1000-1700, Sun 1100-1600, Sep Mon-Sat 1000-1700, Sun 1100-1600; Oct Mon 1030-1700, Tue, Wed, Fri 1030-1500, Thu 1200-1630, Sat 1100-1600; winter hours vary.

Sights The town gave its name to the famous regiment of Coldstream Guards, formed by General Monck in 1659 before he marched south to support the restoration of the Stuart monarchy a year later. The regiment had originally been sent to Scotland as part of Cromwell's New Model Army, but Monck was persuaded to change allegiance. No doubt the offer of the title, first Duke of Albermarle, had something to do with his decision. The Guards remain the oldest regiment in continuous existence in the British army and you can find out all about their proud history in the **Coldstream Museum**, on Market Square, off the High Street. ■ *Apr-Sep Mon-Sat 1000-1600, Sun 1400-1600; Oct Mon-Sat 1300-1600. Free. T882630.*

Near the handsome five-arched bridge which spans the river at the east end of town is the 18th-century **Toll House**, where eloping couples from England were once granted 'irregular marriages'. On the western edge of town is the 3,000-acre **Hirsel Country Park**, seat of the Earls of Home. Hirsel House isn't open to the *hoi polloi*, but you can wander around the grounds. ■ *Open all year during daylight hours.*

Four miles southeast of Coldstream, across the border near the village of Branxton, is **Flodden Field**. In 1513 James IV crossed the Tweed at Coldstream to attack the English, while Henry VIII was busy fighting in France. The invasion was a diversion to assist the French, but Henry sent an army north to meet the threat and James IV's army was routed. The king, his son and some 9,000 men were slain in one of Scotland's greatest military disasters.

Southern Scotland

Not such a Dunce

Duns was also the birthplace of John Duns Scotus (1266-1308), a medieval scholar and theologian of some note, who taught at the universities of Oxford and Paris. He opposed the orthodox views of Thomas Aquinas, and his teachings divided the Franciscans and Dominicans. After his death his ideas quickly fell out of favour and those who held them were derided as being stupid, and so we now have the word 'dunce', derived from the heterodox views of John Duns Scotus.

Sleeping and eating   There are a few places outside town including **E** *Fernyrig Farm*, Birgham, T830251, and **E** *Old School House*, Birgham, T830612. In town is **E** *Garth House*, 7 Market St, T882477; and **E** *Attadale*, 1 Leet St, T883047. The *Coldstream Caravan & Camping Park* is at the southern edge of town, T882333. Just over the border in England is *The Old Mill*, Wark Rd, Cornhill on Tweed, T883524.

Duns
Phone code: 01361
Colour map 6,
grid B3

The quiet market town of Duns lies in the middle of Berwickshire, surrounded by the fertile farmland of the Merse. Duns is best known as the birthplace of Jim Clark (1936-68), a former farmer who went on to become world motor racing champion twice in the 1960s and who remains one of Britain's greatest ever racing drivers. His successful career was tragically cut short when he was killed in a crash while practising at Hockenheim in Germany. The **Jim Clark Room**, 44 Newton Street, is a museum dedicated to his life. ■ *Apr-Sep Mon-Sat 1000-1300 and 1400-1630, Sun 1400-1600; Oct Mon-Sat 1300-1600. £1.30, child free. T883960.*

There are some good **local walks**, detailed in the leaflet *Walks Around Duns*. The best walk is to the top of **Duns Law** (714 ft), from where there are terrific views of the Merse and the Lammermuir Hills to the north. Also at the top is the **Covenanter's Stone**, which marks the spot where the Covenanting army camped in 1639, awaiting the arrival of Charles I's troops.

Sleeping and eating   The best place to stay, if you can afford it, is the **B** *Chirnside Hall Hotel*, T818219, F818231, www.chirnsidehallhotel.com, a mile east of Chirnside on the road to Berwick. This Victorian mansion house offers luxurious accommodation and excellent food all day at mid-range prices (booking essential). A cheaper alternative is **D** *Wellfield House*, Preston Rd, T883189, www.wellfieldhouse.com, a traditional Georgian house offering great value (no smoking). Also recommended is the non-smoking **D-E** *St Albans*, T883285, www.scottishbordersbandb.co.uk, on Clouds, a lane behind the police station.

Eating   The best place to eat in the area is the award-winning *Wheatsheaf at Swinton* in the village of Swinton, about 5 miles south of Duns on the A6112, T860257, www.wheatsheaf-swinton.co.uk   The food is 1st-class but expensive. Open Tue-Sun 1200-1400, Tue-Sat 1800-2100. Alternatively, you can get cheap bar meals at the *Whip and Saddle*, on Market Sq, T883215.

Transport   There are several **buses** daily (fewer on Sun) to and from **Kelso** and **Berwick-upon-Tweed**.

Duns lies only a few miles south of the **Lammermuir Hills**, a low-lying range running east to west and acting as a natural boundary between the Borders and East Lothian. The hills are criss-crossed by numerous paths and ancient droving trails, including the easterly section of the **Southern Upland Way** from **Lauder**, on the A68, to **Cockburnspath** by the A1 on the coast. You can

Around Duns

Southern Scotland

walk the final 10 miles of the route, starting from the hamlet of **Abbey St Bathans**, northwest of Duns on the Whiteadder Water.

Two miles east of Duns, on the A6015, is **Manderston House**, described as the finest Edwardian country house in Scotland. No expense has been spared in the design and decoration and the whole effect, from the silver staircase to the inlaid marble floor in the hall, is one of quite staggering opulence. Take a good look at the staircase – it had tarnished badly over the years (one panel is left to show how black it was) and was voluntarily and lovingly cleaned up by a retired couple. The 56 acres of beautiful gardens should not be missed. There are wonderful displays of rhododendrons late in May. ■ *Mid-May to Sep Thu and Sun 1400-1700. £6.50 (£3 concession) house and gardens, £3.30 (£1.50 concession) gardens only. T01361-883450, www.manderston.co.uk*

Twelve miles east of Duns, and five miles west of Berwick-upon-Tweed off the B6461 to Swinton, is **Paxton House**, a grand neoclassical mansion designed by John and James Adam, the less-famous brothers of Robert, for Patrick Home,who had fallen in love with a Prussian aristocrat at the court of Frederick the Great. She was a great favourite of Frederick's and he strongly opposed the marriage, which never went ahead. She and Patrick corresponded for years and vowed never to marry anyone else while the other was alive. Both kept their promise. Inside there's an impressive display of Chippendale and Regency furniture, and the Picture Gallery is an outstation of the National Gallery of Scotland. In the 80 acres of grounds beside the River Tweed is a Victorian boathouse and a salmon-fishing museum. ■ *House open Easter-Oct daily 1115-1700 (1615 last tour). £5, £4.75 concession. Grounds open Apr-Oct 1000 till sunset.*

Eyemouth
Phone code: 018907
Colour map 6, grid B3
Population: 3,500

Five miles north of the border on the Berwickshire coast is the busy fishing port of Eyemouth. Fishing has been the life and soul of Eyemouth since the 13th century and the **Eyemouth Museum**, in the Auld Kirk on Market Place, has displays on the town's fishing heritage. The centrepiece is the Eyemouth Tapestry, made by local people in 1981 to mark the centenary of the Great Disaster of 1881, when 189 local fishermen were drowned during a violent storm. ■ *Same opening hours as tourist office. £1.75, £1.25 concession.* The two main events in Eyemouth's calendar naturally have a fishing theme. The week-long **Herring Queen Festival** takes place in late July.

Ins & outs There are several **buses** daily to and from **Edinburgh** (1 hr 40 mins), and there are a couple of daily buses (Mon-Fri) to and from **Kelso**, via **Duns**. There's also a daily service to and from **Berwick-upon-Tweed**. If you're driving, the best route north is the scenic A1107 which joins the fast A1 near Cockburnspath.

In the same building as the museum is the **Tourist Information Centre**, T50678. Open Apr-Jun and Sep Mon-Sat 1000-1700 and Sun 1230-1430; Jul and Aug Mon-Sat 0930-1730, Sun 1200-1700; Oct Mon-Sat 1000-1600. Hours subject to change.

There are a number of excellent coastal **walks** around Eyemouth, particularly the seven-mile **Burnmouth to St Abbs walk** described below. There are also shorter walks, which are described in the *Walks in and around Eyemouth* leaflet, available at the tourist office. The waters around Eyemouth are excellent for **scuba diving**. They form part of the **St Abbs and Eyemouth Voluntary Marine Reserve**, one of the best dive sites in Scotland, with a wide variety of marine life and the spectacular Cathedral Rock.

Sleeping and eating B-C *Churches* is a small hotel on Albert Rd in Eyemouth, T50401, www.churcheshotel.co.uk Otherwise there are several **B&Bs** in and around town, including **E** *Hillcrest*, Coldingham Rd, T50463, and **C-D** *Gunsgreen Lodge*, Gunsgreen Park, T752085, bookings T07713-101486. There's also a **campsite** at the *Eyemouth Holiday Park*, T751050, overlooking the beach at the north end of town.

Eating options are fairly limited. There's a string of pubs and hotels along the harbour serving fresh fish and standard bar meals, the best being *The Ship*, T50224. Otherwise try the *Old Bakehouse*, opposite the tourist office, which serves cheap snacks and meals all day.

Three miles north of Eyemouth on the A1107 is the village of **Coldingham**, notable only for its medieval **priory**, founded by King Edgar in 1098, then rebuilt in the 13th century before suffering further attacks in 1545 and 1648. The remaining sections have been incorporated into the present parish church.

Here the B6438 turns north and winds its way down to the picturesque little fishing village of **St Abbs**, nestled beneath steep cliffs. There's a little museum and a Visitor Centre for the Marine Reserve in the Old School House – open summer, hours vary with volunteer staff. St Abbs is also a good base for divers wishing to explore the **St Abbs and Eyemouth Voluntary Marine Reserve** (see above). There are a number of boats offering dive charters as well as birdwatching boat trips. Try Peter Gibson, T018907-71681, Alistair Crowe, T018907-71412, Billy Atkinson, T018907-71288, or ask down at the harbour.

Just north of the village is the **St Abb's Head National Nature Reserve** (NTS), which comprises almost 200 acres of wild coastline with sheer cliffs inhabited by large colonies of guillemots, kittiwakes, fulmars and razorbills. To get to the reserve, follow the trail from the car park at Northfield Farm on the road into St Abbs. The path ends at the lighthouse, about a mile from the car park. An excellent coastal walk, from Burnmouth, south of Eyemouth, to St Abbs is described below.

A side road turns off the B6438 at Coldingham and leads a mile down to the coast at **Coldingham Sands**, a tiny resort with a fine sandy beach. It's a popular spot for **surfing** and **diving**. The dive shop at *Scoutscroft Holiday Centre*, T71669 (see below), rents out equipment and runs diving courses.

St Abb's Head
Phone code: 01890
Colour map 6, grid B3

Southern Scotland

Sleeping and eating In St Abbs there's the excellent **E** *Castle Rock Guest House*, Murrayfield, on the cliffs above the harbour, T771715; and nearby is **E** *Wilma Wilson's* B&B, 7 Murrayfield, T771468. There is also bunkhouse accommodation at **F** *The Rock House Dive Centre*, T71288, right on the harbour. **At Coldingham Sands** is **C** *Dunlaverock Country House Hotel*, T771450, a small, comfortable hotel offering excellent food. There's also a **F** *youth hostel* at Coldingham Sands, on the cliffs above the south end of the bay, T771298, open mid-Mar to end Sep. There are a few **campsites**, including *Scoutscroft Holiday Centre*, T771338, open Mar-Nov, which also rents diving equipment and offers courses. A good place to eat if you're going to St Abb's Head is *Northfield Farm Visitor Centre* by the car park, which has a pleasant tea room with tables outside. There is also a good pottery and a gallery/artist's workshop. Hours vary.

Transport Buses between **Edinburgh** and **Berwick-upon-Tweed** pass through **Transport** Coldingham several times daily. There's also an hourly service between St Abbs, Coldingham, Eyemouth and Berwick. Traveline, T0870-6082608

Burnmouth to St Abbs coastal walk
OS Landranger No 67

The Berwickshire coast offers some good walking opportunities along high cliffs with lots of birdlife to see. This walk starts at **Burnmouth**, a few miles south of Eyemouth. To get there, take the hourly bus service from Coldingham, which connects in Berwick with services to other Border towns. The seven-mile route is waymarked and is mostly on good paths, though there is some rough ground. Allow about four hours and take care at some points along the clifftop.

To get to the cliff path, get off the bus at Burnmouth primary school, go through the gate by the houses and walk up the side of the field. Continue along the path towards Eyemouth, past some dramatic scenery at **Fancove Head**, the highest point of the cliffs, at 338 ft. When you reach the golf course, follow the signs around the seaward edge and then left across the golf course, then right towards **Eyemouth harbour**.

Cross the bridge near the lifeboat mooring and walk along the quayside to the end of the promenade, where you cross a short section of beach and then climb the steps to the headland and the remains of Eyemouth Fort. Walk around the seaward side of the Caravan Park and turn right to cross the fields and then return to the cliff path. The path descends to **Linkum Shore** and crosses the beach. Follow it around Yellow Craig to reach **Coldingham Bay**. At the far end of the bay, climb the steps and then follow the tarmac path which leads to the village of **St Abbs**. From here you can follow Creel Path to reach the B6438, and from there it's a short walk into Coldingham.

Berwick-upon-Tweed
Phone code: 01289

Yes, we know, Berwick-upon-Tweed is in England, but the town has strong historical ties with Scotland, and its football team plays in the Scottish league. It also makes a convenient stopping point if you've had a long journey north. The town, which takes its name from a river which has its source in Scotland, wasn't always in England. It changed hands more than a dozen times between 1147 and 1482, when it was finally taken for England by Richard, Duke of Gloucester, later Richard III. Berwick was a strategic base for English attacks on the Borders and large sections of the town wall, built by Edward I to repel the Scots, still survive. It has also retained its medieval street plan, and many of its steep, cobbled streets are worth exploring.

Sleeping There is plentiful accommodation. The highly recommended **B** *Marshall Meadows Country House Hotel*, T331133, is a Georgian mansion set in 15 acres of grounds only a few hundred yards from the border. Rather more central is the **D-E** *Dervaig Guest House*, 1 North Rd, T307378, only a few mins from the train station. Also close to the station is **E** *Whyteside House*, 46 Castlegate, T/F331019.

Transport There are regular **buses** to and from **Edinburgh** (2 hrs). Buses also run to **Kelso**, **Duns**, **Galashiels** and **Eyemouth** with *First Edinburgh*, T01896-752237, and *Swan's Coaches*, T01289-306436. Berwick is on the main London-Aberdeen **rail line** and there are fast and frequent trains to and from **Edinburgh**. For rail information, T08457-484950.

The Tourist Information Centre is at 106 Marygate, T330733. Oct-Mar Mon-Sat 1000-1200 and 1300-1600; open longer hours from Easter to Oct.

Dumfries and Galloway

Dumfries and Galloway is one of Scotland's forgotten corners, forsaken by most visitors for the cities of Edinburgh and Glasgow or the grandeur of the Highlands. But the southwest has much to offer those prepared to leave the more-beaten track. Away from the main routes west from Dumfries to Stranraer and north to Glasgow, traffic and people are notable by their absence, leaving most of the region free from the tourist crush of more popular parts.

Some of the most beautiful scenery is to be found along the Solway coast, west from Dumfries to the Mull of Galloway. Here you'll find the romantic ruins of Caerlaverock Castle, Threave Castle and Sweetheart Abbey, along with Whithorn Priory, known as the 'Cradle of Christianity' in Scotland. Also on this lovely coast is the beguiling town of Kirkcudbright, inspiration for some of Scotland's most famous artists and still a thriving artistic colony. Rising behind the coastline are the Galloway Hills which form part of the 150,000-acre Galloway Forest Park, a vast area of mountains, moors, lochs and rivers, criss-crossed by numerous trails and footpaths suitable for all levels of fitness. Running right through the heart of the Galloway Hills is the 212-mile Southern Upland Way, one of the country's great long-distance walks (see page 138). The southwest also has strong literary associations. The great poet, Robert Burns, lived and died here, in Dumfries, and the town boasts several important Burns sights.

Ins and outs

The region has a good network of **buses**. The main operators are *Stagecoach Western*, **Getting around**
T01387-253496, and *McEwan's*, T01387-256533. *National Express*, T08705-808080, has long-distance coaches from London, Birmingham, Glasgow and Edinburgh to Stranraer, for the **ferry** crossing to Belfast and Larne in Northern Ireland. There are 2 **train** routes from Carlisle to Glasgow, via Dumfries and Moffat. There's also a line from Stranraer to Glasgow. For rail information, T08457-484950. Dumfries & Galloway council has a **travel information line**, T08457-090510, for all public transport services. Open Mon-Fri 0900-1700.

The **Dumfries and Galloway Tourist Board** has its head office in Dumfries, at 64 **Information**
Whitesands, T01387-245550, info@dgtb.ossian.net, www.galloway.co.uk They have a range of free brochures and guide books for the region, including Accommodation, Birdwatching, Cycling, Fishing, Walking and Golfing. There are also tourist offices in Stranraer, Castle Douglas, Gatehouse of Fleet, Gretna Green, Kirkcudbright, Moffat and Newton Stewart.

Cutting through the region is the A74(M), the congested main route from **Annandale**
England to Scotland. Most people whizz straight through this eastern part of Dumfries & Galloway on their way north, but away from the main roads there are a few interesting places to visit.

The first place you encounter across the border is the nondescript little village **Gretna Green**
of Gretna Green. It's not a particularly interesting place to visit, but Gretna *Phone code: 01461*
Green has been synonymous with marriage ceremonies for many years and *Colour map 6,*
thousands of couples still come here to tie the knot. *grid C1*

The **World Famous Old Blacksmith's Shop** houses a visitor centre with a small exhibition on Gretna Green's history as well as gift shops. ■ *Jan-Mar and Nov-Dec daily 0900-1700; Apr-May and Oct daily 0900-1800; Jun and Sep*

Southern Scotland

Wedding bellows

In Scotland, a marriage declaration made before two witnesses used to be legally binding, and anyone could perform the ceremony. This meant that eloping couples from south of the border came to Scotland to have their weddings witnessed by whomever came to hand. As Gretna Green was the first available community on the main route north, it became the most popular destination for runaway lovers. In their desperation, many tied the knot at *the first place to hand after getting off the stagecoach, and in Gretna this happened to be the local blacksmith's shop, situated at the crossroads.*

The marriage business boomed in the village, until 1940 when marriage by declaration was made illegal. However, under Scots law young couples can still marry at 16 without parental consent, and Gretna Green still attracts its fair share of Romeos and Juliets.

---

daily 0900-1900; Jul and Aug daily till 2000. £2, £1.50 concession. T338224, www.gretnagreen.com

Opposite is the **tourist office**. ■ *T337834. Apr-Jun and Sep-Oct daily 1000-1630; Jul and Aug till 1800.* There's also a rival blacksmith's shop, the **Gretna Hall Blacksmith's Shop**, at the **B-C** *Gretna Hall Hotel*, T338257, www.british-trust-hotels.com This was where better-off runaway couples would come to maintain a class distinction. ■ *Apr-Oct daily 0900-2000; Nov-Mar daily 0900-1700. £0.80, children free. T337635.*

Transport Buses runs to and from **Dumfries**. Service operators are *Stagecoach Western*, T01292-613500, and *MacEwans*, T01389-256530. Gretna Green is also on the Dumfries-Carlisle rail line and there are regular **trains** in either direction. For train information, T08457-484950.

**Ecclefechan &
Lockerbie**
Phone code: 01576
Colour map 6, grid C1

Nine miles northwest of Gretna Green on the A74(M) is the neat little village of Ecclefechan, birthplace of the great writer and historian **Thomas Carlyle** (1795-1881), one of the most powerful and influential thinkers in 19th-century Britain. His old home, The Arched House, is now a tiny museum known as **Carlyle's Birthplace** and features a collection of personal memorabilia. ■ *Apr-30 Sep Fri-Mon 1330-1700. £2.50/£1.70. T300666.*

About eight miles north of Ecclefechan is **Lockerbie**, a quiet, unassuming little town which hit the headlines on 21 December 1988 when a Pan-Am jumbo jet, flying from Frankfurt to New York, was blown up by a terrorist bomb, killing all 196 passengers and crew. The plane's fragments fell on the town, killing a further 11 people. After many months of exhausting diplomatic efforts, the two suspects were extradited from Libya, tried in a Scottish court set up in the Netherlands, and sentenced to life imprisonment. But for the people of Lockerbie life has never been the same.

Sleeping There are several places to stay in **Ecclefechan**, including the refurbished 18th-century **B** *Kirkconnel Hall*, T300277, www.kirkconnelhall.com; and **F** *Carlyle House*, opposite Carlyle's Birthplace, T/F300332. There's also a **campsite** at *Cressfield Caravan Park*, T300702, open all year, at the southern end of the village; and at *Hoddom Castle Caravan Park*, T300251, open Apr-Oct, 3 miles west of Ecclefechan in the grounds of Hoddom Castle.

Transport Ecclefechan is served by **buses** that run between Lockerbie and Annan.

Langholm

Langholm sits at the confluence of three rivers – the Esk, Lewes and
Wauchope – on the A7, one of the main routes north to Edinburgh, and a
less stressful alternative to the A74(M). During the 18th century
Langholm became a thriving textile town and is still a major centre of the
Scottish tweed industry.

Phone code: 01387
Colour map 6, grid C2

Langholm was the birthplace of the great **Hugh McDiarmid** (1892-1978),
poet and co-founder of the Scottish National Party. He is also buried here,
against the wishes of the local nobs, who took great exception to his radical
views. On the hill above the town is the **McDiarmid Memorial**, a stunning
modern sculpture which looks like a giant metallic open book. A path leads
for about half a mile to another memorial, from where there are wonderful
views across the Southern uplands and the Solway Firth. A signed single-track
road leads off the A7, about half a mile north of Langholm, to a path which
leads to the memorials.

This is clan Armstrong country and the **Clan Armstrong Trust Museum**
is a must for anyone with that particular surname. Neil was here, but we don't
know if Gary has ever been. ■ *Easter-Oct Tue-Sun 1400-1700. £1.50.
T380610.* Local festivals include the town's **Common Riding**, which takes
place on the last weekend in July, the **Langholm & Eskdale Festival of Music
and Arts** which is held in the last week in August, and the **Eskdale Agricultural Show** held at the end of September.

There are a couple of hotels in town. **D-E** *The Reivers Rest*, 81 High St, T381343,
www.reivers-rest.demon.co.uk Serves bar meals and real ales. There are several **B&Bs**
including **E** *Border House*, 28 High St, T380376, cairns@borderhouse.fsnet
.co.uk There's also a **campsite** at *Ewes Water Caravan & Camping Park*, T380386,
open Apr-Sep, close to town.

**Sleeping
& eating**

Langholm is on the No 95 **bus** route between **Carlisle** and **Galashiels**, and buses pass
through several times daily. Bus No 124 (Yellow Bus) runs between Langholm and
Eskdalemuir, and No 112 (MacEwans) runs betwenn Eskdalemuir and **Lockerbie**.

Transport

The A7 runs north to Hawick and on to Edinburgh. It also runs south to
Carlisle, via **Canonbie**, through an area known as the Debatable Land until
the border was settled in 1552. From Canonbie the B6357 provides a more
scenic alternative route to the Borders, running through lovely **Liddesdale**
towards Hawick and Jedburgh (see page 157). A shorter route to Liddesdale is
to take the single-track road heading east off the A7 just to the north of
Langholm, which joins the B6357 at **Newcastleton**. The best place to eat in
this area is the C *Riverside Inn* in Canonbie, T371512, www.langholm
.com/riverside which serves superb pub food. It's also a good place to stay.

**Around
Langholm**

Another scenic route from Langholm to the Borders region is the B709. It
runs northwest to the tiny village of **Eskdalemuir**, 14 miles from Langholm,
then north through the Eskdalemuir and Craik forests to **Ettrick**, where it follows the valley of the Ettrick Water to Selkirk (see page 154). About 1½ miles
north of Eskdalemuir is the **Kagyu Samye Ling Tibetan Monastery**. This
Tibetan Buddhist centre was founded in 1967 for study, retreat and meditation, and incorporates the Samye Temple, the first Tibetan Buddhist monastery in the west. There are guided tours for visitors, regardless of faith (prices
vary from £2-£5), and a programme of weekend courses and teachings.
There's also a café and shops on site and pleasant walks through the gardens.

■ *Daily 0900-1800 (tea room and shops 1000-1700). Bus No 112 from Lockerbie stops at the centre. T373232.*

Moffat

Just to the east of the A74(M), at the northern end of Annandale, is the attractive market town of Moffat, with its wide High Street and long, eventful history. Moffat was once something of a fashionable spa town and its sulphur springs attracted the great and the good. Now it's a centre for the local woollen industry.

Ins & outs

There are frequent **buses** to Edinburgh, Glasgow (No X74) and Dumfries (Nos 114 and 199). Bus No 199 also runs to Edinburgh, via the A708, on Fri and Sat. Bus No 382 runs to Carlisle, via **Lockerbie** and **Gretna Green**, and bus No 130 runs to **Galashiels**, via **Selkirk**, along the scenic A708. The main operator is *Stagecoach Western Buses*, T01387-253496. There's also the Harrier Scenic Bus Service, which runs once or twice a week between Jul and Sep – useful for walkers (see also page 144). For *Harrier Service* bus times call *First Edinburgh*, T0131-6639233.

The **Tourist Information Centre** is on Ladyknowes, T220620. Apr, May, Sep and Oct daily 1000-1700; Jun-Aug 0930-1830.

Amongst the local festivals is the Moffat Agricultural Show, held on the last Sat in Aug

Near the TIC is the **Moffat Woollen Mill**, where you can see a demonstration of traditional weaving and trace your Scottish ancestry. There's also a shop selling woollens and tartans. ■ *T220134. Mar-Oct daily 0900-1730; Nov-Feb daily till 1700. Free.* Nearby is the **Moffat Museum**, which tells the town's history. ■ *Easter to end Sep Mon, Tue and Thu-Sat 1030-1300 and 1430-1700, Sun 1430-1700. £1. T220868.*

The tourist office has a selection of leaflets detailing the many local walks. For a pleasant short stroll along the River Annan follow the 'Waterside Walk' sign from the High Street. There are more strenuous walks in the Lowther Hills and along the Southern Upland Way (see next page).

Sleeping

There's plenty of accommodation in Moffat and you should have no problems finding a room. Of the several hotels lining the High St, the best is the very fine **C** *Moffat House Hotel*, T220039, www.moffathouse.co.uk Also on the High St is the **D** *Star Hotel*, T220156, www.famousstarhotel.com, the narrowest hotel in the UK. Overlooking the town is the **C** *Wellview Private Hotel*, Ballplay Rd, T220184, www.wellview.co.uk A Victorian house with an excellent restaurant which offers a 6-course dinner using the best of local produce (expensive). Amongst the many **guesthouses** and **B&Bs** is the highly rated **D-E** *Hartfell House*, Hartfell Cres, T220153, robert.white@virgin.net Many of the B&Bs are on Beechgrove, which is a 5-min walk from the town centre. These include **E** *Queensberry House*, T220538. There's also a **campsite** at *Hammerlands Farm*, T220436, open Mar-Nov, about a mile east of town by the A708.

Eating

Try the excellent Greenmantle ale

The *Wellview* and *Moffat House Hotels* are the best places to eat in town. The hotels and pubs along the High St all serve **bar meals**, including the *Buccleuch Arms Hotel*, the historic *Black Bull Hotel* and the *Balmoral*. Traditional food is available at *The Lime Tree*, High St, T221654. Alternatively, try *Claudio's Restaurant*, T220958, in the old police station at Burnside, which serves a wide range of Italian dishes. Open Sun-Thu till 2130, Fri/Sat till 2200, Sep-May closed on Mon. There are also several cafés on the High St.

Moffat makes a convenient base from which to explore the Lowther Hills **Around Moffat**
to the west and the wild and barren southwest Borders to the east, either by
car or on foot. The Southern Upland Way passes only about a mile east of
town, by the A708, which runs northeast for 22 miles to Selkirk in the Borders (see page 153).

Stagecoach Western bus No 130 from Moffat to Galashiels runs along
this very beautiful route which passes through the most stunning parts of
the Southern Uplands. Ten miles northeast of Moffat on the A708 is the
spectacular **Grey Mare's Tail** waterfall, which plunges 200 ft from a hanging valley. The base of the falls can be reached from the road by a steep
footpath, which continues past the head of the falls to the remote **Loch
Skeen**, from where experienced walkers can climb to the summit of **White
Coomb** (2,696 ft). This is also a popular birdwatching area. The A708 carries on into the Borders region and passes the famous **Tibbie Shiels Inn**,
on the shores of **St Mary's Loch** (see page 154).

Another scenic route from Moffat is the A701 which runs north towards
Edinburgh. En route it meets the A72, which heads east to Peebles and
along the Tweed valley. Six miles north of Moffat on the A701 you get a
great view of the **Devil's Beef Tub**, a vast, deep natural bowl once used by
Border Reivers (rustlers) for hiding stolen cattle (hence the name). The
Tub was also used as a hide-out by persecuted Covenanters during Charles
II's 'killing times'.

Further north the road enters **Tweeddale** and passes through tiny
Tweedsmuir, where a spectacular side road climbs up into the hills to
meet the A708 at St Mary's Loch (see page 148). *Stagecoach Western* bus
No 199 runs along this route to Edinburgh, but only on Fridays and Saturdays, T01387-253496.

West of Moffat, between the A74(M) and Nithsdale, are the wild and bare **The Lowther**
Lowther Hills. About 13 miles north of Moffat, at **Elvanfoot**, the B7040 **Hills**
leaves the A74(M) and crosses the hills, passing through the old lead-min-
ing villages of **Leadhills** and **Wanlockhead** to meet the A76 a few miles
south of **Sanquhar** (see page 174).

Leadhills is a rather forlorn-looking place, but a few miles south is
Wanlockhead, the highest village in Scotland at 1,500 ft and home of the
Museum of Lead Mining. The visitor centre gives an introduction to the
mining industry and there's a **guided tour** of an old lead mine, miners'
cottages and the 18th-century library. ■ *1 Apr -31 Oct daily 1000-1630.
£3.95, £2.75 concession (prices subject to change). T01659-74387, www.
leadminingmuseum.co.uk* Wanlockhead was also a gold mining centre
and you can try your hand at gold panning at the museum. The **Scottish
and British Gold Panning Championships** are held there during the second last weekend in May.

Sleeping and transport Wanlockhead is on the Southern Upland Way, and
there's a youth hostel in the village **F** *Lotus Lodge*, T01659-74252, open Apr-Oct.
There's a **bus** (No 223) to Leadhills from Sanquhar which passes through
Wanlockhead. For times call the Travel Information Line, T08457-090510.

Dumfries

Phone code: 01387
Colour map 5, grid C6
Population: 31,000

Dumfries is the largest town in southwest Scotland, straddling the River Nith, a few miles from the Solway Firth. Known as the 'Queen of the South', Dumfries has long been a thriving market town and seaport for a large agricultural hinterland, and its strategic position made it a prime target for English armies. Its long history of successive invasions began in 1306, when Robert the Bruce committed the first act of rebellion against Edward I by capturing Dumfries Castle, which led to the Wars of Independence.

But it was town planners in the 1960s who did more to destroy the town centre than invading armies. Nevertheless, Dumfries is a pleasant and convenient base from which to explore the beautiful Solway coast, and its associations with Robert Burns, who spent the last years of his life here, also make it worth a visit in its own right. There are many interesting sights lying within easy distance of Dumfries, including **Caerlaverock Castle** to the southeast, and **Ellisland Farm** and **Drumlanrig Castle** to the north in Nithsdale.

Ins & outs
For transport details, see next page

The **bus station** is only a short walk west of the High St, at the top of Whitesands beside the river. The **train station** is on the east side of town, a 5-min walk from the centre. The **Tourist Information Centre** is at 64 Whitesands, on the corner of Bank St, T253862. Apr, May and Oct daily 1000-1700; Jun-Sep daily 0930-1800.

Sights

Most of the town's attractions and facilities are on the east side of the river. A tour of the main sights should begin on the pedestrianized High Street, at the **Burns Statue**, at its northern end. It shows the great bard sitting on a tree stump with his faithful dog at his feet. A few minutes' walk along the High Street is the **Midsteeple**, built in 1707 to serve as a courthouse and prison. Nearby, at 56 High Street, is the **Globe Inn**, T252335, one of Burns' regular drinking haunts, where you can sit in the poet's favourite chair and enjoy a drink (see 'Eating' below). Continue down the High Street and follow the signs for **Burns' House**, in Burns Street, where the poet spent the last few years of his life, and died in 1796. It contains some interesting memorabilia, including original letters and manuscripts. ■ *Apr-Sep Mon-Sat 1000-1700, Sun 1400-1700; Oct-Mar Tue-Sat 1000-1300, 1400-1700. Free. T255297.* Just to the south is the red sandstone **St Michael's Church**. In the churchyard is the **mausoleum** where Burns lies buried.

On the other side of the river, on Mill Road, is the award-winning **Robert Burns Centre**, housed in an old water mill. It tells the story of Burns' last years in the town. ■ *Apr-Sep Mon-Sat 1000-2000, Sun 1400-1700; Oct-Mar Tue-Sat 1000-1300 and 1400-1700. T264808.* On the hill above, centred around an 18th-century windmill tower, is **Dumfries Museum**, which has good local history, natural history and anthropology displays. ■ *Apr-Sep Mon-Sat 1000-1700, Sun 1400-1700; Oct-Mar Tue-Sat 1000-1300 and 1400-1700. Free. T253374.* On the top floor of the windmill tower is a **Camera Obscura**. ■ *Apr-Sep (also open Mar weather permitting). Mon-Sat 1000-1700, Sun 1400-1700. £1.50, £0.75 concession.*

Also on the west bank of the river, at the west end of the 15th-century Devorgilla Bridge, is the **Old Bridge House**, built in 1660 and the town's oldest house. It is now a museum of town life over the centuries. ■ *Apr-Sep Mon-Sat 1000-1700, Sun 1400-1700. Free. T256904.*

There's no shortage of accommodation in Dumfries, though some of the nicest places are out of town (see 'Around Dumfries' below). Among the many hotels is the **B** *Cairndale Hotel*, English St, T254111, www.cairndalehotel.co.uk 91 rooms. Popular with business visitors and boasts a full range of leisure facilities as well as hosting a ceilidh on Sun nights (May-Oct). Also good is the newly refurbished **B** *Station Hotel*, 49 Lovers Walk, T254316, www.stationhotel.co.uk 32 rooms. Very handy for the train station and has a good restaurant. A short walk west of the town centre is Laurieknowe, where you'll find several places to stay, including **D** *Edenbank Hotel*, T252759, and **D** *Dalston House Hotel*, T/F254422, www.dalstonhousehotel.co.uk

There are lots of good **guesthouses** and **B&Bs** near the train station on Lovers Walk, such as **E** *Morton Villa*, at No 28, T255825; **E** *Fulwood Hotel*, at No 30, T252262; and **E-F** *Torbay Lodge*, at No 31, T253922. Also near the train station is **E** *Hazeldean House*, 4 Moffat Rd, T266178, www.hazeldeanhouse.com There are also some nice places on the west side of the river, including **E-F** *The Merlin*, 2 Kenmure Terr, T261002, near the Burns Centre.

Sleeping

Apart from the hotels listed above, one of the best places to eat is *Hullabaloo*, on Mill Rd, T259679, above the Burns Centre in a converted old water mill. Open Tue-Sat. For good Italian food try *Bruno's*, at 3 Balmoral Rd, T255757. Next door and run by the same family is the *Balmoral Fish & Chicken Bar*, which is reputed to sell the best chips in southwest Scotland. Open Wed-Mon 1800-2200. Another good Italian-style restaurant is the moderately priced *Benvenuto*, at 42 Eastfield Rd, T259890; or try *Mambo Italiano*, 113 Queensbury St,

Eating

Southern Scotland

Dumfries

To Edinburgh (A701)

River Nith

Lover's Walk

Sleeping
1 Fulwood
2 Merlin
3 Morton Villa
4 Station
5 Torbay Lodge

Eating
1 Globe
2 Mambo
3 Opus
4 Pumpernickel

N

0 metres 100
0 yards 100

T265888. For **vegetarian** food try *Opus*, 95 Queensbury St, T255752. Cheap-mid-range prices. Open Mon-Sat 0900-1700. The pubs in town all serve cheap bar meals, but the most atmospheric place is the *Globe Inn*, 56 High St, once frequented by a certain poet of this parish. A good place for coffees and light lunches is *Pumpernickel*, 60-62 Friars Vennel, T254475.

Festivals Dumfries hosts quite a few festivals throughout the year, including the **Dumfries Book Fair** at the beginning of May, and **Guid Nychburris Festival** in the middle of Jun, which features a week of entertainment and ceremonies. On the **2nd Sat in Aug** is the **Dumfries & Lockerbie Agricultural Show**. For a full list of dates, check with the tourist office.

Transport There are regular **buses** to Kirkcudbright (Nos 76, 501, X74). No 500 and X75 go twice
For all bus times, call daily to **Newton Stewart** (1 hr 20 mins) and **Stranraer** (2 hrs), for the ferry to Belfast.
the Travel Information *National Express*, T08705-808080, runs a daily service between **London** and **Belfast**, via
Line, T08457-090510, Dumfries and **Stranraer** and towns in between. *Stagecoach Western*, T01292-613500,
or Traveline has 2 buses daily to and from **Edinburgh** (No 100; 2 hrs 20 mins). There are also regular
T0870-6082608 buses to **Carlisle** (No 79; 50 mins) and to **Moffat** (No 114 or X74; 1 hr). Bus No 500 runs to
Castle Douglas (45 mins) and No 246 to **Cumnock**, via **Sanquhar** (50 mins). There are also buses to **Thornhill**, **Dalbeattie** via **Rockcliffe**, **Moniaive**, **Glencaple/Caerlaverock Castle** and **Annan** via **Ruthwell**.

There are frequent **trains** Mon-Sat to and from **Carlisle** (35 mins) and several daily (Mon-Sat) to and from **Glasgow** (1 hr 30 mins), via **Kilmarnock**, where you change for trains to Stranraer. There's a reduced service on Sun. For all rail enquiries, T08457-484950.

Directory **Car hire** *Arnold Clark*, New Abbey Rd, T247151. Open Mon-Fri 0800-1800, Sat 0830-1700, Sun 1100-1700. From £18 per day. **Cycle hire** *Nithsdale Cycle Centre*, 46 Brooms Rd, T254870. For bike repairs and parts, *Kirkpatrick Cycles*, 13-15 Queen St, T254011. Also *Riks Bike Shed* in Mabie Forest (see page 174).

Caerlaverock Eight miles from Dumfries, on the east bank of the Nith estuary where it enters
Castle the Solway Firth, is Caerlaverock Castle, everyone's idea of the perfect medieval fortress, and one of the best-preserved ruins in Scotland. The unusual triangular-shaped castle, which dates from around 1277, was the stronghold of the Maxwells, the Wardens of the Western Marches. But though surrounded by a moat and impregnable-looking, it has fallen several times over the course of its long history. It was first besieged in 1300 by Edward I of England during the Wars of Independence and soon captured, then destroyed by Robert the Bruce. It was repaired in the 1330s, then 300 years later refurbished in the trendy Renaissance style by Robert Maxwell, first Earl of Nithsdale. But several years later it was attacked again, this time by the Covenanters, who captured it after a 13-week siege and proceeded to trash the place. Caerlaverock was never occupied again. ■ *Apr-Sep 0930-1830; Oct-Mar Mon-Sat 0930-1630, Sun 1400-1630. £2.80, 2. To get there, take Stagecoach Western bus No 371 from Dumfries. T770244 (HS).*

A few miles further on is the WWT **Caerlaverock Wetlands Centre**, an absolute must-see attraction for birdwatchers, and also recommended for those with only a passing interest in our feathered friends. The 1,350 acres of wild reserve attract many thousands of birds, most notably barnacle geese, migrating here in the winter. A series of hides and observation towers allow you to get very close to the birds, and during the summer months there are nature trails through wildflower meadows, where you may see the rare natterjack toad. There's also a Visitor Centre and a Fair-Trade coffee shop. ■ *Daily 1000-1700. £4.00, children £2.50, WWT members free. T770200, www.wwt.org.uk*

About seven miles east of Caerlaverock along the B724 is the turning to the lit- **The Ruthwell** tle village of **Ruthwell**. Inside the village church is the remarkable **Ruthwell** **Cross** **Cross**, which dates from the late seventh century when the whole of southern Scotland and northern England, from the Humber-Mersey line to the Forth, was controlled by the Angles. The two main faces of the 18-ft high cross are carved with religious and secular figures and bear inscriptions in both Latin and runes. ■ *Free. Key to church from Mrs Coulthard. T870249. Take bus No 79 from Dumfries.*

Sleeping If you want to stay, the very comfortable, family-run **D-E** *Kirkland Country House Hotel*, T870284, is right next to the church. For something a bit more luxurious, try **A-B** *Comlongon Castle*, T870283, www.comlongon.com, a 14th-century, family-owned castle and adjacent mansion house hotel, which is very popular for weddings. To get there, head north from Ruthwell for about a mile to Clarencefield, where a signposted road turns left (west) for another mile to the castle.

The A76 runs northwest from Dumfries all the way to Kilmarnock in Ayrshire. **Nithsdale** Along the way are several places of interest, starting with **Ellisland Farm**, six miles from Dumfries. This was the home of Robert Burns from 1788 to 1791, during which time he built the farmhouse and tried to introduce new farming methods. Ultimately, this venture collapsed and he moved to Dumfries, but not before writing his famous ghost story, *Tam o' Shanter*, and Hogmanay favourite, *Auld Lang Syne*. The farmhouse is now a museum displaying various personal items. ■ *Apr-Sep Mon-Sat 1000-1300 and 1400-1700, Sun 1400-1700; Oct-Mar Tue-Sat 1000-1700. £2.50, £1 concession. T01387-740426.*

Eight miles further north is **Thornhill**, where the A702 heads eight miles west to the peaceful little conservation village of **Moniaive**. There are a couple of **B&Bs** in the village, including **E-F** *Bainoon*, on the High Street, T01848-200266. The *George*, on the High Street, is a lovely old pub for a drink and a meal. Bus No 202 runs to Moniaive from Dumfries.

A short drive from Moniaive by Glenkiln Reservoir (between Dunscore and Shawhead) is an extraordinary collection of **sculptures**, placed on the wild Glenkiln Estate by Sir William Keswick. There are six works in all, the easiest ones to find being *John the Baptist* by Rodin, which stands at the head of the reservoir, and *Standing Figure* by Henry Moore. There are other works by Moore as well as one by Epstein, which is hidden in a copse of Scots Pine. A good place to stay in this area is **C-D** *Speddoch*, a large country house, a short drive from the sculptures, which has been owned by the same family for 300 years. The family is very hospitable, there are cosy log fires and good home cooking – if you choose to eat there you'll dine with the family at night. It's a Wolsey Lodge – private homes offering accommodation where you're treated like a family guest. T01387-820342, www.wolsey-lodges.co.uk

Four miles north of Thornhill is the turning for **Drumlanrig Castle**, more French château than Scottish castle. This sumptuous stately home of the Duke of Buccleuch and Queensberry is renowned for its superb art collection, which reflects the mind-boggling wealth of its owners. Included are works by such luminaries as Rembrandt, Leonardo Da Vinci, Holbein, Breughel and Van Dyck, as well as numerous family portraits by Allan Ramsay and Godfrey Kneller. After all that you may need to clear your head with a stroll round the extensive **country park**. You can also hire mountain bikes and explore a network of cycle trails. There's also a **bicycle museum**, commemorating the fact that the bicycle was invented nearby, at Keir Mill. ■ *Castle 27 Apr to 11 Aug and 24 Aug-8 Sep, gardens 27 Apr-30 Sep Mon-Sat 1100-1600, Sun 1200-1600.*

Southern Scotland

£6/£4. *T01848-330248, www.drumlanrigcastle.org.uk Drumlanrig is 1½ miles from the A76.*

Seven miles north of Drumlanrig, the B797 turns right (east) off the A76 and climbs up to **Wanlockhead**, the highest village in Scotland (see 169). A few miles further, on the A76, is the neat little town of **Sanquhar**, which lies on the Southern Upland Way.

South of Dumfries South of Dumfries are some of the area's loveliest sights. The A710 runs past New Abbey and the ruins of **Sweetheart Abbey**, then follows the Solway Coast past the quiet little coastal villages of **Rockcliffe** and **Kippford**, before looping around to Dalbeattie, where it meets the A711 which runs from Dumfries to Kirkcudbright. Bus No 372 runs from Dumfries to Dalbeattie, stopping in New Abbey, Kirkbean, Rockcliffe and Kippford, T710357.

Four miles south of Dumfries is the turn-off to **Mabie Forest**, a large area criss-crossed by forest paths and cycle trails. You can hire bikes at *Riks Bike Shed*, T270275. They also run tours of the forest; daily in summer 1000-1800; winter Monday and Friday-Sunday 1000-1800. Bikes cost £10 per person per day. Mabie Forest is a good place to take children as there are plenty of walks and cycle trails. At Mabie Farm Park, Burnside Farm there's a tea room and grass toboggan rides (well, it's different). T259666. Apr-Oct Mon-Sun 1000-1700; Nov-Mar Sat, Sun 1000-1700.

New Abbey
Phone code: 01387
Colou rmap 5, grid C6

Seven miles south of Dumfries, in the pretty little village of New Abbey, are the graceful red sandstone ruins of **Sweetheart Abbey**, founded by Cistercian monks in 1273. The abbey gets its name from the extreme marital devotion of its patron, Lady Devorgilla de Balliol, wife of John, who founded Balliol College, Oxford. On his death she had his heart embalmed and carried it around with her, until her own death in 1290. Now both she and the heart are buried in the presbytery. ■ *Apr-Sep daily 0930-1830; Oct-Mar Mon-Wed and Sat 0930-1630, Thu 0930-1200, Fri and Sun 1400-1630. £1.80, concession £1.30. T01387-850397 (HS).*

Just north of the village is **Shambellie House Museum of Costume**, a Victorian country house set in beautiful gardens, which houses a collection of period costumes from the late 18th to the early 20th centuries. ■ *Apr-Oct daily 1100-1700. £2.50, concession £1.50. T01387-850375.* New Abbey is dominated by **Criffel Hill** (1,867 ft). One and a half miles south of the village take the turning for Ardwell Mains Farm, from where a track leads to the summit. The views from the top are magnificent, stretching all the way south to the lakes and across to the Borders.

A few miles south of New Abbey, at **Kirkbean**, is the turning for the **John Paul Jones Cottage**, birthplace of the US naval hero. It's now a small museum and includes an exhibition and audio visual of his amazing life. ■ *Apr-Jun Tue-Sun 1000-1700; Jul and Aug daily 1000-1700. £2 (£1). T01387-880613.* South of Kirkbean, at **Southerness**, there's an excellent championship **golf course**.

Sleeping There are a couple of places to stay on the village square; the **D-E** *Abbey Arms Hotel*, T01387-850489, enquiries@abbeyarms.netlineuk.net; and **D-E** *Criffel Inn*, T01387-850244. Both are also great village pubs and serve bar meals.

Rockcliffe &
Kippford
Phone code: 01556
Colour map 5, grid C6

The A710 turns west south of Kirkbean and parallels the Solway Coast, past the wide **Sandyhills Bay** to Colvend. About a mile beyond, a side road turns off to the little village of Rockcliffe, nestled in a beautiful rocky cove at the mouth of the Urr estuary. From Rockcliffe you can walk about 1½ miles to neighbouring Kippford, a popular sailing centre, along the **Jubilee Path** (NTS). The path passes the **Mote of Mark**, an ancient Celtic hillfort. Another path runs south from Rockcliffe along the cliff tops, to **Castlehill Point**. From Kippford, at low tide, you can walk across the causeway to **Rough Island**, a 20-acre offshore bird sanctuary owned by the NTS. During May and June, when the terns and oystercatchers are nesting, it's out of bounds.

Sleeping and eating There's a decent choice of accommodation along this stretch of coast. In **Rockcliffe** is the very fine **B** *Barons Craig Hotel*, T630225, www. baronscraighotel.co.uk; and the more modest **E** *Millbrae House*, T630217. In **Kippford** is the **D-E** *Anchor Hotel*, T620205, which also serves superb pub food and is the perfect spot for a great pint of real ale after the walk from Rockcliffe. Also in Kippford is **E** *Rosemount Guest House*, T620214. At **Sandyhills**, a couple of miles east on the A710, is the baronial splendour of **D-E** *Craigbittern House*, T01387-780247 and the comfortable **D-E** *Cairngill House Hotel*, T01387-780681. There are also a few **campsites** in the area, including *Kippford Holiday Park*, T/F620636, www .kippfordholidaypark.co.uk; and *Castle Point Caravan Site*, T630248, open Mar-Oct, near Rockcliffe.

Beyond the turnings to Rockcliffe and Kippford is the town of Dalbeattie, where there's a decent range of shops. Three miles north of town is the **Mote of Urr**, a 12th-century motte-and-bailey castle. About four miles south, near **Palnackie**, is the turn-off for the 15th-century **Orchardton Tower**, the only circular tower house in Scotland. On the first Sat in August Palnackie hosts the **World Flounder Tramping Championships**, an unusual event which involves trying to catch the biggest flounder – with your feet!

Dalbeattie & around

From Dalbeattie the A711 runs southwest to Kirkcudbright, and the A745 heads west to Castle Douglas, about five miles away.

Castle Douglas and around

The neat little town of Castle Douglas, standing on the edge of lovely little **Carlingwark Loch**, was laid out in the 18th century by Sir William Douglas, a local lad who made his fortune in the Americas. There's nothing of note in the town itself, but there are a few worthwhile attractions in the surrounding area You can find out all about these, and other local sights, at the TIC (see below).

Phone code: 01556
Colour map 5, grid C5
Population: 3,500

McEwan's bus Nos 501 and 505 run frequently from **Dumfries** to **Kirkcudbright**, stopping in Castle Douglas. Bus No 520 runs north along the east shore of Loch Ken from Castle Douglas to **New Galloway** and **Dalry**.

Ins & outs

   Tourist Information Centre, Market Hill Car Park. Apr-Jun, Sep and Oct daily 1000-1630; Jul and Aug daily 1000-1800. T502611. A good way to explore the area is by bike, and you can **rent bikes** at *Ace Cycles*, 11 Church Street, T504542. Mountain bikes cost £10 per person per day.

A mile southwest of town, off the A75 or reached by the lochside road, is **Threave Garden**, the NTS horticultural school's magnificent floral extravaganza. The best time to visit is early spring when over 200 types of daffodils burst into bloom, but it's a very colourful experience at any time of the year. In Spring 2002 Threave House will open to the public for the first time. It will contain a horticultural implement museum. ■ *Gardens open daily all year from 0930 till sunset. Visitor Centre open Mar-Good Friday Wed-Sun 1000-1600; Easter-31 Oct daily 0930-1730; Nov-Christmas Wed-Sun*

Sights

1000-1600 (hours subject to change). Check times and prices for House. £5, £.4 concession. T502575.

Two miles further west at Bridge of Dee, a country lane branches north (right) and leads for about a mile to the start of a footpath which takes you to the gaunt tower of **Threave Castle**, standing alone on an island in the middle of the River Dee. Threave was built in the 14th century by Archibald 'the grim', third Earl of Douglas, and head of the 'Black' Douglas line. The Douglases were one of Scotland's most powerful baronial families and the main line, the 'Black' Douglases, were descended from 'the Good' Sir James, trusted friend of Robert the Bruce. The outer wall of the castle was added in 1450 in an unsuccessful attempt to defend it against King James II, who was determined to break the power of the maverick Border family. The Covenanters reduced Threave to its present ruinous state in 1640, and little remains of the interior. It's a romantic ruin nevertheless, especially as you have to be ferried across to the island. It's a 10-minute walk from the car park, then ring the bell for the custodian to take you across in a small rowing boat. ■ *1 Apr-30 Sep daily 0930-1830. £2.20, concession £1.60. T0131-6688800 (HS).*

The A713 runs north from Castle Douglas along the shores of long and skinny **Loch Ken** to New Galloway (see page 180). The loch is a popular watersports centre, with sailing, windsurfing, water-skiing, canoeing, rowing and fishing. There's also an RSPB nature reserve on the west bank, and walking trails. *Loch Ken Marina*, T01644-470220, at the village of **Parton**, on the east bank eight miles north of Castle Douglas, hires motor boats for water-skiing. It's open Easter-31 October daily 0900-1700. *Galloway Sailing Centre*, T01644-420626, www.lochken.co.uk, also at Parton, offers watersports tuition and hire, as well as other activities such as quad biking and gorge scrambling, and basic dormitory accommodation (**F**). It's open 1 April-31 October daily 0900-1900; November-March daily till 1700. Fishing permits and boats are available at the marinas and the caravan parks. The village of Parton hosts the **Scottish Alternative Games** on the first Sunday in August. The various traditional Scottish games include the world finals of the Gird'n'Cleek competition, whatever that may be.

Sleeping & eating There's lots of accommodation in Castle Douglas, including **C-D** *Crown Hotel*, T502031, www.TheCrownHotel.co.uk, the pleasant **D** *Douglas Arms Hotel*, T502331; and **D** *Inperial Hotel*, T502086. All are on King St and serve decent food. There are also many good value **B&Bs** and **guesthouses**. Try **E** *Craigvar House*, 60 St Andrew St, T503515, open Mar-Oct; or **E** *Albion House*, 49 Ernespie Rd, T502360, open Feb-Oct. There are several other places to stay along Ernespie Rd. A few miles northeast of town, at Haugh of Urr, is the peaceful and attractive **E** *Corbieton Cottage*, T660413. Thirteen mile south of Castle Douglas, on the A711, is the village of **Auchencairn**, overlooking a lovely bay. There's a range of accommodation here, including the luxurious, award-winning **B** *Balcary Bay Hotel*, T640217, which has an excellent restaurant. There's also a **campsite** at *Lochside Caravan & Camping Site*, beside the loch, T503806, open Easter-late Oct; and at *Loch Ken Holiday Park*, by the village of Parton, T01644-470282, open late Mar-early Nov.

Apart from the hotels listed above, the best place to eat in Castle Douglas is *Carlo's*, 211 King St, T503977, a moderately priced Italian restaurant. Eleven miles out of town, on the A712 near Crockettford, is *Craigadam*, T/F650233, www.craigadam.com, where you can enjoy good home cooking at mid-range prices. They also offer B&B (**D-E**).

Hero and villain

John Paul Jones (1747-92) was a hero to the Americans, but the British saw him as a pirate. Early on in his nautical career, as plain John Paul, he was imprisoned in Kirkcudbright Tolbooth for the manslaughter of his ship's carpenter. His fortunes changed, along with his name, in later life when he joined the US fleet in 1775. Four years later, during the American War of Independence, in command of a few American and French ships, he won a dramatic victory against a powerful British force off the English coast and became an American hero. He is generally regarded as the father of the modern US Navy.

Kirkcudbright

Kirkcudbright (pronounced 'kir-koo-bree') sits at the mouth of the river Dee, 10 miles southwest of Castle Douglas. With its colourful waterfront and streets of elegant Georgian villas and Victorian town houses, it is without doubt the most attractive town in the southwest and makes the ideal base from which to explore the beautiful Solway coast. The Glasgow Boys (see below) started to come here in the late 19th century and established an artists' colony, and ever since then Kirkcudbright has been a favourite haunt of artists. The town's name comes from the now-vanished Kirk of Cuthbert, which relates to St Cuthbert, who converted much of southern Scotland to Christianity.

Phone code: 01557
Colour map 5, grid C5
Population: 3,500

Southern Scotland

Kirkcudbright is 25 miles west of Dumfries and can be reached via the A75 or A711. It is 50 miles east of Stranraer on the A75. **Bus** 500 runs between **Dumfries** and **Stranraer** passing through **Castle Douglas** and **Newton Stewart**. Bus Nos 501, 502 and 505 run between Kirkcudbright and Dumfries.

Ins & outs
A local firm offers cruises of Kirkcudbright Bay; ask at the TIC for details

The town's **Tourist Information Centre** is beside the harbour. They will book accommodation for you during the busy summer season, and sell the leaflet *Walks Around Kirkcudbright*, which details many local walks. T330494. Apr-Jun, Sep and Oct daily 1000-1700; Jul and Aug daily 0930-1800.

Near the harbour is **MacLellan's Castle**, which is a castellated town house rather than a defensive fortress. It was built in the 1570s by the then-provost, Thomas MacLellan of Bombie, using stone from the adjoining ruined monastery. The castle is relatively complete, except for the roof, and inside there's a warren of rooms to explore. ■ *Apr-Sep daily 0930-1830. £1.80, concession £1.30. T331856 (HS).*

Sights

Nearby, at 12 High Street, is the wonderful **Broughton House**, the Georgian town house which was bought in 1901 by E A Hornel, the renowned artist and member of the 'Glasgow Boys', an influential late 19th-century group of painters who established an artists' colony in Kirkcudbright (see also page 214). Many of Hornel's works are on display here, in the excellent Hornel Gallery. The artist also designed the beautiful **Japanese Garden**, which leads from the house down to the river. ■ *House and Garden open Apr-Oct daily 1300-1700, opens at 1100 in Jul (hrs may vary). £3.50, concession 2.50. T330437 (NTS).*

Only a few minutes' walk along the High Street is the early 17th-century **tolbooth**, which now houses the **Tolbooth Art Centre**. As well as featuring a display of works by Hornel and his fellow 'colonists', including local artist Jessie King, the centre also tells the story of the town's artists colony from the late 19th century to the present day, and there are temporary exhibitions of local arts and crafts and photography. ■ *All year Mon-Sat 1100-1600 and Sun 1400-1700. £1.50, concession £0.75. T331556.* Another of the town's art galleries is the **Harbour Cottage Gallery**, which hosts a variety of shows throughout the year. ■ *Mar-Nov daily 1030-1230 and 1400-1700.* Both are among the venues used during the **Kirkcudbright Arts Festival**, which takes place over two weeks in late August and early September.

One of the town's most interesting sights is the **Stewatry Museum**, on St Mary Street, which boasts an extraordinarily diverse collection of exhibits reflecting the social and natural history of this part of the Solway coast, once known as the Kirkcudbright Stewatry because it was administered by the kings' stewards during the 14th and 15th centuries. ■ *Same opening hours and admission charge as Tolbooth Art Centre. T331643.*

About seven miles southeast of Kirkcudbright is the lovely wee village of **Dundrennan**, site of the ruins of **Dundrennan Abbey**, a 12th-century Cistercian establishment standing in a beautifully bucolic setting in a secluded valley. You may not be too surprised to learn that the abbey has associations with Mary, Queen of Scots. She spent her last night on Scottish soil here. Bus No 505 between Kirkcudbright and Dumfries passes through Dundrennan, or if you're feeling energetic it's a lovely five-mile walk along quiet country roads. ■ *Apr-Sep daily 0930-1830; Oct-Mar Sat 0930-1630 and Sun 1400-1630. £1.80, concession £1.30. T500262.*

Sleeping There's a wide range of accommodation available in and around town, but it's best to book in advance during the summer months. The top hotel is the **C** *Selkirk Arms Hotel*, on the High St, T330402, www.SelkirkArmsHotel.co.uk 17 rooms. This beautifully refurbished Georgian hotel in the old part of town has attractive rooms and also has the town's finest restaurant (see below). Another cracking place to stay is **D** *Gladstone House*, at 48 High St, T331734. 3 rooms. This wonderful, superior guesthouse has a secluded garden and also offers afternoon tea. No smoking. Fantastic value. A cheaper alternative is **E** *Gordon House Hotel*, 116 High St, T/F330670.

There are many **B&Bs**, including **D-E** *Mrs Black*, at 1 Gordon Pl, T330472; **E** *Mrs Caygill*, at 'The Marks', T330854, www.marksfarm.co.uk **D-E** *Millburn House*, Millburn St, T339166; **D-E** *Mrs McLaughlin*, 14 High St, T330766, (Apr-Sep); **D-E** *Number 3*, 3 High St, T330881; and **E** *Mrs Durok*, at 109a High St, T331279, open Mar-Oct. A few miles north of town in the village of Twynholm, is the excellent **D-E** *Fresh Fields*, on Arden Rd, T860221, open Jan-Oct.

There are also a couple of **campsites** near the town. *Silvercraigs Caravan & Camping Site*, T503806, open Easter to late-Oct, is on an elevated site overlooking the town, about a 10-min walk from the centre; and *Seaward Caravan Park*, T870267, open Mar-Oct, is part of a new leisure complex at Brighouse Bay, with a wide range of facilities including heated pool, 9-hole golf course and pony trekking.

Eating The best place to eat is the *Selkirk Arms Hotel* (see 'Sleeping' above), whose highly skilled chef is something of local celebrity. Food is served daily 1200-1400 and 1800-2130 (dinner expensive; lunch cheap-mid-range). Another good place to try is the *Auld Alliance Restaurant*, 5 Castle St, T330569. As the name suggests, it's a mixture of Scottish and French culinary styles, and features Solway scallops and local salmon. Open Easter-Oct Mon-Sat 1830-2130, Sun also 1200-1400 (dinner expensive; lunch cheap).

Gatehouse of Fleet

The quiet little town of Gatehouse of Fleet lies 10 miles west of Kirkcudbright, a mile or so north of the A75. It's an attractive place on the banks of the Water of Fleet, surrounded by forested hills. The town's **Tourist Information Centre** is in the car park on the High Street. ■ *Mar, Apr and Oct daily 1000-1630; Jun and Sep till 1700; Jul and Aug till 1800. T814212.* Nearby is the **Mill on the Fleet Museum**, housed in a restored 18th-century cotton mill complete with working water wheel. The museum traces the history of the town's cotton industry which lasted from the mid-18th century until the early 19th century. There's also a bookshop and a pleasant café with riverside terrace. ■ *Easter-Oct daily 1030-1730. £1.50 (price may change). T814099.*

There are several pleasant walks in the surrounding countryside, including to **Cardoness Castle**, about 1½ miles to the south, standing on a hill overlooking the B796 which connects Gatehouse with the main A75. The remarkably well-preserved ruin was the home of the MacCullochs and is a classic example of a 15th-century tower house. There are excellent views across Fleet Bay from the top floor. ■ *Apr-Sep daily 0930-1830; Oct-Mar Sat 0930-1630 and Sun 1400-1630. £2.20, concession £1.60. T0131-6688800 (HS).* Details of other local walks are given in a leaflet which is on sale at the tourist office. In the grounds of Cally Palace Hotel are **Cally Gardens**, a specialist nursery and walled garden centre, with around 3,500 varieties of plant. ■ *Apr-Sep Tue-Fri 1400-1730, Sat, Sun 1000-1730 £1.50.* About 2½ miles south of town off the A75 is **Cream o'Galloway**, Rainton Farm, a family business where award-winning ice cream is made. There's a viewing gallery where you can watch the ice cream being made, and a children's woodland play area. ■ *Easter-Sep daily 1100-1800, Oct 1100-1700. Charge for adventure playground. T01557-814040, www.creamogalloway.co.uk*

Set in 500 acres of its own grounds is **A** *Cally Palace Hotel*, T814341, www.callypalace.co.uk A very exclusive Georgian mansion and former home of local laird James Murray who amassed a massive fortune from the cotton industry, it now offers impeccable luxury and top-class facilities. Rather more down-to-earth are the **B-C** *Murray Arms Hotel*, on Ann St, T814207. Also serves good bar meals; and **E** *The Bobbin Guest House*, at 36 High St, T814229. **B&B** accommodation is on offer at **D-E** *The Bay Horse*, T814073, at 9 Ann St. A little way out of town is the highly recommended **D-E** *High Auchenlarie Farmhouse*, T840231, open Mar-Oct. **Sleeping**

Bus No 500 between **Dumfries** and **Stranraer** stops in Gatehouse of Fleet. No 500 and X75 run between Gatehouse of Fleet and **Newton Stewart**. **Transport**

The A75 runs west from Gatehouse to **Creetown**, standing on the east shore of Wigtown Bay, overlooked by the distinctive bulk of Cairnsmore of Fleet hill (2,330 ft). It's a lovely stretch of road as it hugs the shore, with good views across the bay. In Creetown is the **Gem Rock Museum**, which has a wide range of precious stones on display. ■ *Easter-Sep daily 0930-1800; Oct and Nov daily 1000-1600; Dec-Feb Sat and Sun 1000-1600, £2.90, concession £2.40 T01671-820357,* www.gemrock.net East of Gatehouse, off the A75 at Burnbrae, Twynholm is a museum dedicated to Formula 1 star **David Coulthard** who was born in the area. The collection includes memorabilia from his go-carting days up to the present. There's a popular tearoom too called *The Pit Stop* – presumably you have to eat very **Around Gatehouse**

Phone code: 01557
Colour map 5, grid C5

Southern Scotland

quickly. Also good bar meals at the *Star* pub opposite. ■ *Apr-Oct Mon-Tue, Thu-Sat 1000-1600, open Wed 1000-1600 in Jun. £2.50, £1.50 concessions. T860050.*

New Galloway & Galloway Forest Park
Phone code: 01644
Colour map 5, grid C5

Nestled in the valley of **The Glenkens**, which runs north from Loch Ken, is New Galloway, a pleasant little village of whitewashed houses surrounded by beautiful countryside and close to the Galloway Forest Park. A few miles north of New Galloway is the village of **Dalry**, or St John's town of Dalry, to give it it's full name, sitting beside the Water of Ken and giving access to the Southern Upland Way. About five miles farther north on the A713 is the turning to **Polmaddy Settlement**, a reconstructed Galloway village dating from before the Clearances of the 18th and 19th centuries.

To the west of New Galloway lies Galloway Forest Park, the largest forest park in Britain, covering 300 square miles of forested hills, wild and rugged moorland and numerous lochs. It's a vast and beautiful area criss-crossed by waymarked Forestry Commission trails and longer routes, such as the Southern Upland Way (see page 138). It's also home to a rich variety of fauna, such as feral goats, red deer, falcons and even golden eagles. Those wishing to hike in the park should be properly equipped and buy the relevant Ordnance Survey maps. The OS Outdoor Leisure Map No 32 covers Galloway Forest Park. Also useful is *The Galloway Hills: A Walker's Paradise*, by George Brittain. See also under **Newton Stewart** below.

The A712 runs southwest from New Galloway, cutting through the southern section of the Galloway Forest Park, to Newton Stewart. This 19-mile stretch of scenic road is known as **The Queen's Way**. Seven miles southwest of New Galloway the road skirts **Clatteringshaws Loch**, hidden amongst the pine trees, with a 14-mile footpath running round it. This path joins the Southern Upland Way which winds its way north towards the **Rhinns of Kells**, a range of hills around 2,600 ft that form the park's eastern boundary. On the shores of the loch is the **Clatteringshaws Forest Wildlife Centre**, which gives an introduction to the park's flora and fauna. ■ *Easter-Oct daily 1000-1700. Free. T420285.* From the centre you can follow the lochside trail to **Bruce's Stone**, a huge boulder marking the spot where Robert the Bruce is said to have rested after yet another victory over those troublesome southern neighbours.

About a mile southwest of the Forest Wildlife Centre is the **Raiders' Road**, a 10-mile timber road and erstwhile cattle rustlers' route which runs from the A712 and follows the Water of Dee southeast to Stroan Loch and then turns north to meet the A762 just north of Mossdale. About halfway along the trail is **the otter's pool**, in a clearing in the forest, a great place for paddling or swimming. The Raider's Road is only open between April and October, and there's a toll charge. The A762 heads north along the western shore of Loch Ken back to New Galloway, making a circuit of about 20 miles, starting and ending in New Galloway.

About three miles southwest of Clatteringshaws Loch along The Queen's Way is the **Galloway Red Deer Range**, where you can get close up to the deer, stroke them and take photos. ■ *End of Jun to mid-Sep Tue and Thu 1100 and 1400, Sun 1430. £2.50, £1 child. T07771 748401.*

Sleeping and eating There are several hotels and B&Bs in the village. On the High St, there's the small and comfortable **E** *Leamington Hotel*, T420327, www.leamington-hotel.com, which does evening meals; and the **D-E** *Cross Keys Hotel*, T420494, where you can also get bar food. A few miles to the east, in the village of

Balmaclellan, is **E-F** *High Park*, T420298, a farmhouse B&B. There's also a **F** *youth hostel* at Kendoon, T01644-460680, 5 miles north of Dalry on the B7000, close to the Southern Upland Way and the A713. It's open mid-Mar to early Oct. Take the Castle Douglas-Ayr bus and ask to get off near the hostel. At the bottom of the High St is **E-F** *The Smithy*, T420269, which offers B&B accommodation and is also a café/restaurant/bookshop. It provides essential information on walks in the forest park, **rents bikes** and also serves home-cooked meals and tasty snacks (try their oatcakes). It's open daily Mar, Apr and Sep 1000-2000, May-Aug till 2100 and Oct till 1800.

Transport Yellow Bus S2, **Castle Douglas** to **Dalry**, stops in New Galloway. Some of these buses continue to Ayr. There are also regular buses to Dumfries, nos 503 and 501.

Newton Stewart and around

The town of Newton Stewart is set on the west bank of the River Cree at the junction of the main A75 and the A714, amidst beautiful wooded countryside. It's a popular base for **hiking** in the hills of Galloway Forest Park, especially around **Glen Trool** (see below). Newton Stewart is also a major centre for **salmon and trout fishing**. The season runs from March till mid-October. Permits, guides and the hire of fishing gear can all be arranged at the *Creebridge House Hotel* (see below).

Phone code: 01671
Colour map 5, grid C4
Population: 3,200

The **tourist office** is on Dashwood Square, just off the main street and opposite the bus station. They can book accommodation for you as well as provide lots of information on walking in Galloway Forest Park. ■ *Apr and Oct daily 1000-1630; May, Jun and Sep till 1700; Jul and Aug till 1800. T402431.* The **Forestry Commission**, T402121, also produces a series of leaflets on its various marked trails through the forest park. See also **Galloway Forest Park** above.

As a major walking and fishing centre, Newton Stewart has plenty of accommodation across the range. Top of the list is the fabulous **A** *Kirroughtree House*, T402141, www.kirroughtreehouse.co.uk 17 rooms. This grand 18th-century country mansion is set in its own grounds and offers impeccable standards of comfort and service. It's superb restaurant (expensive) has a well-deserved reputation for its gourmet Scottish cuisine. Another fine choice, and a lot cheaper, is the charming **B** *Creebridge House Hotel*, across the river in the village of Minnigaff, T402121, www.creebridge.co.uk 19 rooms. Arranges fishing permits and offers very good food at mid-range prices.

Sleeping

There are also lots of **B&Bs** to choose from. Many of these are on Corsbie Rd and include **D** *Rowallen House*, T402520, www.rowallan.co.uk **E** *Oakbank*, T402822, open Feb-Nov; and **E** *Stables Guest House*, T402157. Also good is the friendly **E-F** *Kilwarlin*, 4 Corvisel Rd, T403047, open Apr-Oct. There's a **F** *SYHA Youth Hostel*, T402211, open mid-Mar to end-Oct, in the village of **Minnigaff**, which is on the other side of the river, across the bridge.

There are a couple of Forestry Commission **campsites** in **Glen Trool** (see below). There's the *Caldons Caravan & Camping Site*, on the western shore of Loch Trool, T840218, open Apr-Sep (possibility of closure so check with tourist office first), and the *Glen Trool Holiday Park*, T840280, open Mar-Oct, near Glen Trool village, just off the A714.

The best places to eat are *Kirroughtree House* and *Creebridge House Hotel*. The latter also serves fine ales. Alternatively, try *The Brig End Pantry*, a tearoom and restaurant overlooking the Cree bridge, T402003; or *The Riverbank*, a popular lunch stop near the main car park, T403330. About ½ mile out of town on the A714 heading south is the *Black Sheep Inn*, where there is a licensed restaurant and bar, T404326.

Eating

Southern Scotland

Transport Newton Stewart is on the main A75 between **Dumfries** and **Stranraer** and there are regular **buses** to and from each of these destinations, including Nos X75 and 500. There's also a No 430 bus to Stranraer and No 500 to **Gatehouse of Fleet**. Newton Stewart is the departure point for buses south to **Wigtown** and **Whithorn** (No 415). There's a service (No 359) north along the A714 to **Girvan**, via Bargrennan and **Glen Trool** village several times a day Mon-Sat (less frequently on Sun).

Around Newton Stewart

Newton Stewart lies at the heart of the most scenically stunning part of Galloway and makes an ideal base for exploring this most beautiful part of the country. About three miles east, near Palnure, is the **Kirroughtree Visitor Centre**, the southern gateway to Galloway Forest Park. A series of waymarked trails and cycle routes lead from here into the forest. There's also a tea room serving light meals.■ *Apr-Sep daily 1030-1700, Oct closes at 1630. T402165.*

Four miles north of town, reached via the A714, is the **Wood of Cree Nature Reserve**, T402861, the largest ancient woodland in southern Scotland. This RSPB reserve is home to a huge variety of birdlife, including pied flycatchers, redstarts and wood warblers. There are nature trails running for two miles through the forest in the Cree Valley.

The prime attraction around Newton Stewart is **Glen Trool**, one of the most accessible and loveliest parts of Galloway Forest Park. Ten miles north of Newton Stewart at **Bargrennan**, on the A714, a narrow road winds its way for five miles past Glen Trool village to **Loch Trool**, hemmed in by the wooded slopes of the glen. Halfway up the loch is **Bruce's Stone**, which marks the spot where Robert the Bruce's guerrilla band ambushed the pursuing English force in 1307, after they had routed the main army at Solway Moss.

There are a number of excellent **hiking trails** which start out from here, including the one to the summit of **Merrick** (2,766 ft), the highest peak in southern Scotland. It's a tough climb of about four hours, but fairly straightforward and well worth the effort. There are also numerous Forestry Commission trails for the less fit/experienced/adventurous. Part of the **Southern Upland Way** (see page 138) runs through Glen Trool and along the southern shores of Loch Trool, then continues east towards Clatteringshaws Loch. On the road to Loch Trool, about a mile from the village, is the **Glen Trool Visitor Centre**. ■ *Apr-Oct daily 1030-1730. T01671-402420.*

The Machars

South of the A75 is the peninsula of fertile rolling farmland known as the Machars. It's a somewhat neglected corner of the southwest but has strong early-Christian associations, and there are many important sites. The Machars is served by *Stagecoach Western* (T01776-704484) **bus** No 415 which runs regularly between **Newton Stewart** and **Isle of Whithorn**, via Whithorn and Wigtown.

Wigtown

Phone code: 01988
Colour map 5,
grid C4

The disconsolate little town of Wigotwn sits on the northwesterly shore of Wigtown Bay and is notable for its large number of bookshops (18 at the last count). It is now gaining a reputation as Scotland's National Book Town with festivals held throughout the year, www.wigtown-booktown.co.uk If you need to buy a book in the southwest, then this is the place to do it. The town overlooks the salt marshes and sands of Wigtown Bay which attract thousands of birds, including greylag and pinkfoot geese, ducks and waders in the winter. In 1685 two female Covenanters – Scottish Presbyterians persecuted by Charles II – were drowned at the stake by the rising tide on Wigtown Sands. The **Martyr's Stake** marks the site of their death. About three miles northwest is **Torhouse Stone Circle**, a Bronze Age site of 19 standing stones forming a ring 60 ft across.

Sleeping There are a couple of **B&Bs** in town: **E-F** *Glaisnock House*, 20 South Main St, T/F402249, www.glaisnock-house.co.uk; and **E-F** *Craigenlee*, 8 Bank St, T402498.

Eleven miles south from Wigtown is Whithorn, a remote and forlorn village but one which occupies an important place in Scotland's history. It was here in the late fourth century, that **St Ninian** established a mission and built the first Christian church north of Hadrian's Wall. The tiny church, which he called **Candida Casa** (the White House), has not survived but after Ninian's death a priory was built to house his tomb. This became a famous seat of learning and an important place of pilgrimage for penitents from England and Ireland, as well as from Scotland.

Whithorn
Phone code: 01988
Colour map 5, grid C4/5

The ruins of the 12th-century priory are being excavated and can be visited as part of the **Whithorn Visitor Centre and Dig** on George Street. In the visitor centre there are exhibitions and artefacts (including the 12th century Whithorn crozier) and an audio-visual display. You can visit the excavations going on behind the visitor centre, but there's not much to see and you won't be able to make much sense of the ruins without the help of the complimentary guiding service. The adjacent **Priory Museum** contains some important interesting archaeological finds and early-Christian sculpture, including the Latinus Stone which dates from 450 AD and is the earliest Christian memorial in Scotland. ■ *Apr-Oct daily 1030-1700. £2.70, concession £1.50. T500508.*

Four miles away is the misnamed Isle of Whithorn, which isn't an island at all but an atmospheric old fishing village built around a natural harbour. The village is the site of the ruined 13th-century **St Ninian's Chapel**, built for pilgrims who landed here from England and Ireland. Along the coast to the west of the village is **St Ninian's Cave**, said to have been used by the saint as a private place of prayer. It is reached via a footpath off the A747 before entering the Isle of Whithorn.

Isle of Whithorn
Phone code: 01988
Colour map 5, grid C5

Sleeping There are a couple of places to stay in the village. Try the **D-E** *Steam Packet Inn*, T500354, a popular fishermen's pub with rooms on the quayside, which serves good, cheap bar meals. There's also B&B at **F** *Dunbar House*, on Tonderghie Rd, T500336. About 11 miles west of Whithorn, near the village of **Port William**, is the sumptuous **B** *Corsemalzie House Hotel*, T860254, www.corsemalzie-house.ltd.uk, a highly rated hotel and restaurant. Open Mar-Jan.

From Whithorn the A747 heads west to meet the coast and then runs northwest along the east shore of **Luce Bay** for 15 miles till it meets the A75 at the pretty little village of Glenluce. Two miles north of the village, signposted off the A75, is **Glenluce Abbey**, founded in 1192 by Roland, Earl of Galloway for the Cistercian order. The remains, set in a beautiful and peaceful valley, include a handsome early 16th-century Chapter House with a vaulted ceiling noted for its excellent acoustics. The abbey was visited by Robert the Bruce, James IV and, you guessed it, Mary, Queen of Scots. It was also the home of the 13th-century wizard and alchemist, **Michael Scott**, who appears in Dante's *Inferno* and who, according to legend, cast a spell on King Arthur and his knights and sent them to sleep under the Eildon Hills overlooking Melrose (see page 151). ■ *Apr-Oct 0930-1830; Oct-Mar Sat 0930-1630, Sun 1400-1630, £1.80, £1.30 concession.*

Glenluce
Colour map 5, grid C4
Buses 430 and 500 between Newton Stewart and Stranraer stop in Glenluce village and you can walk from there

Stranraer

Phone code: 01776
Colour map 5, grid C3
Population: 10,700

Stranraer wins no prizes for beauty or tourist appeal, but as Scotland's main ferry port for Northern Ireland it's an important town which sees a lot of through traffic. It sits on the shores of sheltered Loch Ryan on the **Rhinns of Galloway**, a windswept peninsula shaped like the head of a pick-axe at the end of the Solway coast.

Ins & outs

Transport links are all conveniently located close to each other. The **train station** is on the ferry pier, close to the Stena Line **ferry terminal** (T08705-707070), from where car and passenger ferries leave for Belfast. A few minutes' walk south is the **bus station**. P&O ferries to Larne (T08705-980666, www.poirishsea.com) leave from **Cairnryan**, 5 miles north of Stranraer on the A77. Bus No 358 and X58 runs to Cairnryan from Stranraer. For details on services to Northern Ireland, see page 36. For information on buses and trains, see 'Transport' below.

The **Tourist Information Centre** is at 28 Harbour St, T702595. Apr-Jun, Oct and Nov Mon-Sat 0930-1730, Sun 1000-1600; Jul-Sep daily 0930-1800; Dec-Mar Mon-Sat 1000-1600.

Sights

The main attraction is the medieval tower which is all that remains of the 16th-century **Castle of St John**, one of the main headquarters of Graham of Claverhouse, the fanatical persecutor of the Protestant Covenanters in the late 17th century. Many of them died in the castle dungeons. It was later used as a prison in the 19th century. Inside, an exhibition traces the castle's history. ■ *Apr-mid Sep Mon-Sat 1000-1300 and 1400-1700. £1.20, concession £0.60. T705544.* Also worth a peek is the **Stranraer Museum** on George Street, which features displays on local history and has a section devoted to the life of Arctic explorer Sir John Ross (1777-1856), whose expeditions to find the Northwest Passage to the Pacific led to the discovery, in 1831, of the North Magnetic Pole. His house, called North West Castle, is now a hotel (see below). ■ *Mon-Fri 1000-1700, Sat 1000-1300, 1400-1700. Free. T705088.*

Three miles east of Stranraer are **Castle Kennedy Gardens**, famous for their riotous rhododendrons and magnificent monkey puzzle trees. The 75 acres of landscaped gardens are set on a peninsula between two lochs and two castles (Castle Kennedy and Lochinch Castle). ■ *Apr-Sep daily 1000-1700. £3, £2 concession. T702024.* **Loch Ryan**, the huge inlet which protects Stranraer from the stormy Irish Sea, is a haven for a variety of birdlife. The mudflats of **Wig Bay**, on the western shore offer good opportunities for birdwatching.

Sleeping

As you'd expect in a major ferry port, there's no shortage of places to stay. The most unusual choice has to be the **L** *Corsewall Lighthouse Hotel*, 11 miles northwest of town at Corsewall Point, T853220, corsewall-lighthouse@msn.com 6 rooms. This cosy hotel is housed in a working lighthouse, set in 20 acres of its own grounds on the wild and windy clifftops, a surreal experience. The owners can arrange transport from Stranraer. The most luxurious choice is the superb **B** *North West Castle Hotel*, T704413, www.northwestcastle.co.uk 73 rooms. The former home of Sir John Ross (see 'Sights' above) also offers full leisure facilities and excellent cuisine.

There are lots of cheaper **B&Bs** and **guesthouses** to choose from, including the centrally located **E** *Windyridge Villa*, 5 Royal Cres, T889900; and **E** *Fernlea*, Lewis St, T703037. Also good is **E** *Glen Otter*, Leswalt Rd, T703199. Close to Castle Kennedy is the lovely **D-E** *Chlenry Farmhouse*, T705316. There's also **hostel** accommodation at **F** *Sally's Hoose*, Balyet Farm, Cairnryan Rd, T703395. It only has 6 beds but is open all year.

There's a **campsite** at *Aird Donald Caravan Park*, T702025, open all year, 1 mile from town; and *Wig Bay Holiday Park*, T853233, 4 miles to the north, open Mar-Oct.

The most expensive place to eat is *North West Castle Hotel* (see above). A bit cheaper is **Eating** *L'Aperitif*, on London Rd, T702991. It serves good Italian food Mon-Sat 1200-1400 and 1730-2100. There's also *Bar Pazzerello*, 57 George St, T706585 and Venezia Ristorante, on Hanover St, T703987. For good Scottish food try *The Bay House*, Ladies Walk. Otherwise, you can try the hotel bar meals or the numerous fast food outlets.

For details on **ferry** services to Northern Ireland, see 'Ins and outs' above. **Transport**
Bus *National Express* (T08705-808080, www.gobycoach.com) No 920 runs between **London** and **Belfast** via Stranraer – it's an overnight service. *Stagecoach Western* has a service from **Glasgow** (3 hrs) to Ayr (X77), change at Ayr for Stranraer. There are regular buses to **Newton Stewart**, **Kirkcudbright**, **Dumfries** and other towns along the A75. There are also regular daily buses to **Ayr** (2 hrs), and daily buses to **Portpatrick** (25 mins), **Port Logan** (35 mins) and **Drummore** (45 mins). **Train** There are several trains daily to **Belfast** via Larne. There's also a daily service to and from **Glasgow** (2 hrs) and **Ayr** (1 hr 20 mins). For all rail enquiries call T08457-484950.

Portpatrick

Nine miles southwest of Stranraer on the beautiful and rugged west coast of the Rhinns is the picturesque old port of Portpatrick. Until the mid-19th century it was the main departure point for Northern Ireland but is now a peaceful little holiday resort and a good base from which to explore the southern part of the peninsula. Portpatrick is also the starting point for the **Southern Upland Way**, the 212-mile coast-to-coast route which ends at Cockburnspath on the Berwickshire coast (see page 138). The whole route may be beyond most mortals, but you can walk the first section to Stranraer (nine miles), or continue for a further four miles to Castle Kennedy Gardens and return to Portpatrick by bus, via Stranraer. You can arrange **sea fishing trips** from Portpatrick. These cost £8 for half a day, T810468.

Population: 600
Phone code: 01776
Colour map 5, grid C3

By far the best place to stay in this area is the very wonderful **L** *Knockinaam Lodge Hotel*, **Sleeping** T810471, which offers great sea views, exquisite and unmatched cuisine (expensive) and impeccable service. It is rated as one of the best hotels in the south of Scotland. Those without the means to enjoy such splendour can try the **B** *Fernhill Hotel*, T810220, www.fernhillhotel.co.uk, which overlooks the village. Its reputation has a fine reputation (lunch cheap to mid-range; dinner mid-range). Also good is **C** *The Waterfront Hotel*, North Cres, T810800, www.waterfronthotel.co.uk

There's also plenty of cheaper accommodation, such as: **E** *Carlton Guest House*, South Cres, T810253; **E** *The Knowe*, North Cres, T810441; **E-F** *Ard Choille Guest House*, 1 Blair Terr, T810313; and nearby **E-F** *Albony Guest House*, 4 Blair Terr, T810568. There are a few **campsites** on the hill above the village: *Galloway Point Holiday Park*, T/F810562, open Easter-Oct; *Castle Bay Caravan Park*, T810462, open Mar-Oct; and *Sunnymede Caravan Park*, T/F810293, open Mar-Oct. All have good facilities and enjoy good views.

The best places to eat are the *Knockinaam Lodge* and *Ferhill Hotels*. Cheaper options **Eating** include the *Mount Stewart Hotel* and the *Harbour House Hotel*, both on the seafront and both of which serve decent bar meals. Also worth trying are *Campbells*, a seafood restaurant on South Crescent, T810314; and the bistro in *The Waterfront Hotel*.

Southern Scotland

Transport **Buses** run regularly between Portpatrick and **Stranraer**. T0870-6082608.

South of From Portpatrick the road runs south to the Mull of Galloway through lush,
Portpatrick green farmland which receives high average rainfall. The Rhinns are also warmed
by the Gulf Stream which gives the peninsula the mildest climate in Scotland and
means it's almost frost-free. This is beautifully demonstrated at **Logan Botanic
Garden**, an outpost of Edinburgh's Royal Botanic Garden, about a mile north of
the tiny village of **Port Logan**. The garden boasts a vast array of exotic, subtropical
flora from the southern hemisphere, including tree ferns and cabbage palms.
■ *Mar-Oct daily 0930-1800. £3, £2.50 concession. T860231.*

Bus No 407 from Stranraer passes through Port Logan on its way to
Drummore, a fishing village on the east coast of the Rhinns. Five miles further
south is the **Mull of Galloway**, a dramatic, storm-lashed headland and Scotland's most southerly point, only 25 miles from Ireland and the Isle of Man.
The narrow isthmus is an **RSPB nature reserve** and the home of thousands of
seabirds such as guillemots, razorbills and puffins. There's a small information centre. ■ *Late May-Aug. T01671-402861.*

Ayrshire

*The region of Ayrshire is best known as the birthplace of **Robert Burns**, Scotland's great poet, loved and revered the world over. The vast majority of visitors
come here to visit the many sights associated with the great bard, but the Ayrshire
coast is also famed for its excellent golf courses, such as Turnberry, Troon and
Prestwick. There are a few other reasons for visiting Ayrshire, most notably
Culzean Castle to the south of Ayr, one of Scotland's top tourist attractions. One
of the region's main attractions is the beautiful Isle of Arran, but it is covered in
the Argyll chapter (see page 278).*

*The most attractive part of Ayrshire is the south, from the main town, Ayr,
south to Girvan. North of Ayr is a series of low-key resorts interspersed with ports
and industrialized towns stretching to the mouth of the Clyde.*

Ins and outs

Getting around South Ayrshire is served by a reasonable **bus** service along the coast and there's also a
train line from Stranraer to Ayr, via Girvan and Maybole. The busy A77 runs north from
Stranraer along the coast to Turnberry, where it turns inland to Maybole and bypasses
Ayr, before heading northeast towards Glasgow. Near Prestwick it meets the A78
which runs north along the Firth of Clyde coast before turning east towards Glasgow.

Information Ayrshire's tourist services are run by the **Ayrshire and Arran Tourist Board**, whose
head office is in Prestwick, T01292-678100, www.ayrshire-arran.com There are also
seasonal offices in Irvine, Largs, Girvan and Millport (open Easter-Oct).

Girvan Between Stranraer and Ayr is the seaside resort of Girvan, where there's a seasonal
Phone code: 01465 **Tourist Information Centre** on Bridge Street, near the harbour, T678100,
Colour map 5, which has a full list of accommodation. Open April-May and October Mon-
grid B4 day-Friday 1100-1600, Saturday 1200-1600; June Monday-Saturday 1030-1630;
July and August Monday-Saturday 1030-1630, Sunday 1100-1600; September
Monday-Friday 1030-1600, Saturday 1200-1600. The **McKechnie Institute** in
Dalrymple Street houses temporary museum exhibitions and has a gallery
upstairs featuring local artists' work. ■ *Tue, Fri 1300-1600 and Sat 1000-1700.*

Sleeping and transport **D-E** *Glendrissaig Guest House*, on Newton Stewart Rd, T714631, open Apr-Oct, which offers vegetarian meals. **E** *St Oswalds*, 5 Golf Course Rd, T713786. Or if you want to play the famous **Turnberry Championship Golf Course**, you can stay at the luxurious **L** *Turnberry Hotel*, T01655-331000, www.turnberry.co.uk, 5 miles north of Girvan. There are several daily **trains** to and from **Ayr** and **Stranraer**. There's a **bus** service (No 923) between **Glasgow** and **Stranraer** which passes through Ayr.

Ten miles west of Girvan is Ailsa Craig, a huge uninhabited lump of granite (once quarried and famed in Curling circles), 1,114 ft high and two miles in circumference, which resembles a giant floating muffin. It's now a **bird sanctuary** and home to thousands of gannets. It earned the nickname '**Paddy's Milestone**' as it's halfway between Belfast and Glasgow.

Tours Boats leave from Girvan harbour for the trip to Ailsa Craig at least once a day between May and Sep. Several companies sail around the rock but only the *MV Glorious* is allowed to land (weather permitting). It's necessary to book at least a week in advance, T713219. A 4-hr trip costs £12 per person, a 6-hr trip costs £14 per person. There are also trips to Ailsa Craig from Troon, on board the paddle steamer *Waverley* in summer (see also under Ayr below).

Culzean Castle & Country Park
Colour map 5, grid B4

Twelve miles south of Ayr is Culzean (pronounced 'cullane'), one of Scotland's great castles and the National Trust for Scotland's most visited property. It is one of Ayrshire's few non-Burnsian attractions and well worth a detour if you're in the vicinity. Culzean enjoys a magnificent setting, perched high on a clifftop above a rocky shore and surrounded by 563 acres of country park. The scale of the house and the country park is overwhelming and you should allow more than a few hours to do it justice.

Culzean was designed by Robert Adam and built in 1772-90 for David Kennedy, 10th Earl of Cassilis, as a replacement for the original 15th-century castle. The grand exterior gives no hint of the almost overweening opulence inside. Adam's customary meticulous attention to detail and love of classical embellishment reaches its zenith here. The magnificent oval staircase is regarded as one of his greatest achievements, and the perfect symmetry of the circular saloon is a deliberate counter-balance to the seascapes on view from the windows. The castle contains a collection of paintings and 18th-century furniture and an armoury, and there's an Eisenhower Room, which celebrates the former US President's military career and his association with Culzean. He stayed several times as a guest of the Kennedys, and the top floor was given to him by the erstwhile owners.

The vast **country park** is also well worth exploring and was Scotland's first, created in 1969. It features a network of woodland paths, clifftop trails and the shoreline below, formal gardens, the ice house, pagoda and the beautiful Swan Pond. There's also a walled garden with a Victorian vinery. The best place to start is the **visitor centre** housed in the Home Farm buildings, with a café, shop and exhibits. Here you can pick up free leaflets and maps to help you find your way around, or you can take a guided tour. ■ *Castle Easter-Oct daily 1100-1700 (last admission 1630); Visitor centre open Easter-Oct daily 1030-1730. Country Park open all year daily 0900-sunset. Castle and park £8, concession £6; park only £4.50, concession £3. Guided tours of castle daily at 1530, also at 1100 in Jul and Aug; tours of grounds Apr-Jun daily at 1430, Jul-Aug daily at 1100 and 1430, Sep 1430. T01655-884455. Accommodation is available (L) in six double bedrooms on the top floor. There's also a top-class, and very expensive, restaurant for residents only.*

Southern Scotland

Kirkoswald &
Crossraguel
Abbey
Phone code: 01655
Colour map 5, grid B4

A few miles inland from Culzean, on the A77, in the tiny village of Kirkoswald, is the refurbished thatched cottage which was the home of John Davidson, village souter (shoemaker), who was the original Souter Johnnie of Robert Burns' *Tam o' Shanter*. Life-sized stone figures of the souter, Tam himself, the innkeeper and his wife are in the restored ale-house in the garden, and there are Burns' relics in the cottage. ■ *Apr-Sep daily 1130-1700; also weekends in Oct 1130-1700. £2.50, concession £1.70. T760603. There's an hourly bus service between Ayr and Girvan which stops in Kirkoswald.*

Two miles south of **Maybole** on the A77 are the ruins of **Crossraguel Abbey**, a Clunaic establishment founded in the 13th century by the Earl of Carrick, and much rebuilt during the next three centuries. The remarkably complete remains include the church, cloister, chapter house and much of the domestic premises. ■ *Apr-Sep daily 0930-1830. £2.00, concession £1.50. T883113.* About five miles northwest of Maybole on the A719 coastal road to Ayr, you'll pass a curious local phenomenon known as the **Electric Brae**. Because of an optical illusion, it appears that you're travelling uphill rather than down.

Sleeping There are a few places to stay in and around Maybole. On the B7023 heading west of town towards Culzean is **E** *Homelea*, 62 Culzean Rd, T882736. There are also a couple of **campsites**. The *Culzean Bay Holiday Park*, T01292-500444, www.newandusedcaravans.co.uk, open Mar-Oct, is 8 miles south of Ayr on the A719 coast road; and the *Walled Garden Camping & Caravan Park*, T740323, www.walledgardencp@clara.co.uk, open Apr-Oct, is at Kilkerran Estate, 7 miles south of Maybole off the B741.

Ayr

Phone code: 01292
Colour map 5, grid B4
Population: 50,000

The largest town in southwest Scotland, looking west out on to the Firth of Clyde and Arran, Ayr has been a popular seaside resort since Victorian times. The town's 2½ miles of sandy beach, together with Scotland's most important racecourse, continue to attract hordes of visitors from nearby Glasgow. Ayr is best known for its many connections with Scotland's national poet, **Robert Burns**, who was born in the neighbouring village of **Alloway** and who famously praised the town for its 'honest men and bonnie lasses'. For information on Burns' life and work, see page 656.

Ins & outs The **bus station** is in the centre of town at the foot of Sandgate, close to the post office. The **train station** is a 10-min walk east, on Station Rd. There are frequent buses and trains to and from Glasgow, Dumfries and Stranraer. There are **trains** every 30 mins to and from Glasgow Central (50 mins), and several daily to **Stranraer** (1¼ hrs). For all rail enquiries, call T08457-484950. For a **taxi**, call *Central Taxis*, T267655.

The **Tourist Information Centre** is at 22 Sandgate near the Town Hall, at the opposite end of the main shopping street from the bus and rail stations, T678100. Apr-June Mon-Sat 0900-1700; Jul-Aug Mon-Sat 0900-1800, Sun 1000-1700; Sep Mon-Sat 0900-1700, Sun 1100-1700; Oct-Mar Mon-Sat 0900-1700.

Sights Most of Ayr's important sights are contained within the **Burns National Heritage Park** in Alloway (see below), but there are a few places of interest dotted around the cramped streets of Ayr's **old town**, to the south of the River Ayr. To the west of Sandgate, off Bruce Terrace, is **St John's Tower**, the only surviving part of the 12th-century Church of St John the Baptist. It was here, in 1315, that Robert the Bruce called a meeting of the Scots parliament to decide his successor to the throne. In 1652 Cromwell's army incorporated the church into a fort which they built. Guided tours are available for groups by arrangement with Sheena Andrew at the Carnegie Library, Main Street (T282109), or you can get the key to the tower from the Council offices on Burns Statue Square (£2 deposit required).

As compensation for taking over the Church of St John, in 1654 Cromwell donated money to build the **Auld Kirk** at the end of Kirk Port, a narrow lane leading off the High Street. The church retains its original canopied pulpit, and in the lych gate you can see iron grave-covers used to protect corpses from the body snatchers who sold them to medical schools. A short distance away is the **Auld Brig**, the 13th-century bridge immortalized by Burns in his poem *Twa Brigs*. At 230 High Street is the **Tam o' Shanter Inn**, an ancient thatched pub where the eponymous hero enjoyed an evening of alcoholic excess before mounting his trusty mare, Meg, and setting off on his near-disastrous journey home to Kirkoswald. The pub is now a shrine to the bard and its walls are covered with many of his greatest quotes. A few yards away on the High Street is the **Wallace Tower**, which commemorates the Scottish patriot, William Wallace, who was imprisoned in the town in 1297, for setting fire to a barn with 500 English soldiers inside.

Southern Scotland

Ayr

■ Sleeping	8 Queens Guest House	2 Hunny Pot
1 Belmont Guest House	9 Richmond Guest	3 Stables & Coffee House
2 Craigallan Guest House	House	4 Tudor
3 Crescent	10 Savoy Park	
4 Dargil Guest House	11 SYHA Hostel	● Bars & pubs
5 Daviot House		5 Tam o'Shanter Inn
6 Fairfield House	● Eating	
7 Glenmore Guest House	1 Fouters	

At the top of the High Street, where it meets Sandgate, is the impressive spire of the **Town Buildings**, and opposite is **Loudoun Hall**, a former merchant's house which dates from 1470 and has been recently refurbished (tours by arrangement with Sheena Andrew, Carnegie Library, see above). Turn left before you reach New Bridge and head along South Harbour Street to reach the **harbour**, where you can arrange a **cruise** on board the *Waverley*, the world's last ocean-going paddle steamer. They leave on Tuesday and Wednesday only from early July to the end of August. For bookings or further information, T0141-243 2224, or check at the tourist office. Also ask at the tourist office for details of other boat trips from Ayr harbour.

The **beach** lies to the southwest of the town centre, overlooked by the long Esplanande and backed by a grid-iron of streets lined with elegant Victorian villas. This is where you'll find most of the guesthouses, particularly around Wellington Square. There are also many guesthouses and B&Bs on Carrick Road at the south end of town, and Prestwick Road at the north end.

Buses run from Alloway to Ayr (No 361) regularly. Change at Ayr and get the X77 or No 4 bus to go to Glasgow

The heart of Burns country is Alloway, formerly a separate village a few miles south of Ayr, but now swallowed by its spreading suburbs. On the road to Alloway from Ayr is the impressive **Rozelle House and Park**. Built originally around 1760, the house now holds the *Tam o' Shanter* series of paintings by Alexander Goudie, a must for those who want an insight into Burns' colourful work. It also houses the Ayrshire Yeomonry Museum, and has various temporary exhibitions. Good coffee shop and craft shop focussing on quality local crafts. ■ *Oct-Mar Mon-Sat 1000-1700, and Apr-Nov Sun 1400-1700. Free. T445447.* A 10-minute walk down the road brings you to the **Burns National Heritage Park**. For details of transport to Alloway, see below under **Transport**.

The best place to start is the **Burns Cottage and Museum**, the low, thatched, whitewashed 'auld clay biggin' where the poet was born on 25 January 1759 and spent the first seven years of his life. The museum contains original manuscripts, books, paintings and other memorabilia, plus a brief history of his life. ■ *Apr-Sep daily 0930-1730, Oct-Mar daily 1000-1700. £3, concession £1.50. T441215.* Nearby is the **Tam o' Shanter Experience**, a modern building housing an audio-visual theatre telling the story of *Tam o' Shanter*, a funny and frightening poem and a cautionary tale of the consequences of alcoholic over-indulgence. There's also a well-stocked gift shop and a restaurant. ■ *Same opening hours as above. £1.50, £0.75 concession. T443700.*

Across the road are the ruins of **Alloway Kirk**, where Robert Burns' father, William, is buried. This was the setting for the famous scene in *Tam o' Shanter* when Tam stumbles across a wild orgy of witches, warlocks and demons. When he gets carried away watching one particularly winsome witch, Nannie, and screams out his encouragement, the ghouls give chase and Tam and his mare, Meg, narrowly escape, minus Meg's tail, across the **Brig o' Doon**, the 13th-century humpbacked bridge which still stands nearby, spanning the River Doon. Overlooking the bridge is the ostentatious **Burns Monument**, a Neoclassical temple which houses a display. There are statues of various Burns characters in the gardens. ■ *Same opening hours as the Burns Cottage and Museum in summer; closed winter. £1, £0.50 concession.*

As a change from Robert Burns you can visit the **Dunaskin Heritage Centre**, Waterside, Dalmellington Road, about 12 miles south of Ayr off the A713. It deals with the iron-working heritage of the area and has two audio-visual presentations, an interactive computer quiz and a restored 1914 iron worker's cottage. As it is in the heart of mining country there is also a simulated mine tour. ■ *Apr-Oct daily 1000-1700. £4.50, £3.75 concession.*

No arguments about the best hotel in town: the **L-A** *Fairfield House Hotel*, 12 Fairfield Rd, T267461, www.fairfieldhotel.co.uk 45 rooms. Near the seafront, luxury facilities and excellent restaurant and conservatory brasserie. In Alloway is the **A** *Ivy House*, T442336, www.theivyhouse.uk.com 5 rooms. This comfortable country house is convenient for the Burns Trail and has a good restaurant. Another high-class hotel is the **B** *Savoy Park Hotel*, 16 Racecourse Rd, T266112, www.savoypark.com There's also the comfortable **B** *Brig O'Doon Hotel*, T442466, www.costley-hotels.co.uk, which has a good restaurant.

There are numerous comfortable **guesthouses** and **B&Bs** in the Victorian new town, in the streets and squares between Alloway Pl and the Esplanade. On Queens Terr are: **E** *Craggallan Guest House* at No 8, T264998, www.craggallan.com **E** *Dargil Guest House* at No 7, T261955; **E** *Daviot House* at No 12, T269678, www. daviothouse.com; and **E** *Queens Guest House* at No 10, T265618. There are also several small guesthouses and B&Bs on the streets between Alloway Pl and Burns Statue Square. On Bellevue Cres are **E** *The Crescent*, at No 26, T287329, www.26 crescent.freeserve.co.uk; and **E** *Glenmore Guest House* at No 35, T269830, www.glenmoreguesthouse.co.uk On Park Circus are **E** *Belmont Guest House* at No 15, T265588, belmontguesthouse@bt.internet.com; and **E** *Richmond Guest House* at No 38, T265153, www.richmond-guest-house.co.uk

Cheaper accommodation is available at the **F** *SYHA Youth Hostel*, at 5 Craigweil Rd, about a 20-min walk south of the town centre, off Alloway Pl, T262322, www.syha.org.uk, open Mar-Dec. There are a couple of good **campsites** in and around Ayr. *Craigie Gardens Caravan Club Site*, is only a 10-min walk from the centre, T264909, www.caravanclub.co.uk, open all year; and *Heads of Ayr Caravan Park*, 5 miles south of town on the A719 to Culzean, T442269, open Mar-Oct.

Sleeping
There's plenty of accommodation, but during the busy high season and important race meetings it's still a good idea to book in advance

There are several eating places which stand out. Best of all is *Fouters*, 2a Academy St, T261391. This bistro/restaurant in a converted bank basement opposite the town hall offers superb French-influenced cuisine using the very best of local fish, seafood, game and beef. Lunch cheap; dinner expensive. Open Mon-Sat. Also recommended is *The Stables Coffee House & Restaurant*, Queens Ct, 41 Sandgate, T283704. A small, friendly place offering traditional Scottish dishes and excellent cakes, scones and ice cream, all at cheap prices. No smoking. Open daily till 1700 (closed Sun during winter). Another fine place to eat is the *Tudor Restaurant*, 8 Beresford Terr, T261404. More of a café really and serves great home-cooked meals and high teas. Open Mon-Sat 0900-2000, Sun 1200-2000 (Jun, Jul and Aug and 1st 2 weeks in Sep till 2100). Another great cafe is the *Hunny Pot*, at 37 Beresford Terr, T263239, Mon-Sat 0900-2200, Sun 1030-2100.

Many of the pubs also serve cheap lunches. There are many bars clustered around Burns Statue Sq, and of course there's the *Tam o' Shanter Inn*, T611684 (see 'Sights' above).

Eating

Cycling *AMG Cycles*, 55 Dalblair Rd, T287580. Rents bikes for £15 per day, or £15 per weekend. **Golf** There's an excellent 18-hole public course at *Belleisle Park*, T441258. **Horse racing** Ayr Racecourse is at 2 Whitletts Rd, T264179, www.ayr-racecourse.co.uk It's the premier racecourse in Scotland and holds 25 days of racing throughout the year, including the Scottish Grand National in mid-Apr. **Horse riding** *Ayrshire Equestrian Centre*, South Mains, Corton Rd, T266267. Cross country course, hacks and lessons from £14 per hr.

Sport

Communications Internet: there's a cybercafé at Carnegie Library, 12 Main St, T286385, jcastle@lib.south.ayrshire.gov.uk

Directory

Southern Scotland

Kilmarnock, Prestwick & Troon

Troon is the Scottish port for Seacat Services to/from Northern Ireland (see page 36)

Immediately north of Ayr, and well served by buses and trains from Ayr, is **Prestwick**, home of another fine Ayrshire golf course and also an **international airport** (for flight details, see page 31). If you need to stay in Prestwick try the **C-D** *Parkstone Hotel*, Esplanade, T01292 477286, which also serves good bar meals. North of Prestwick the A77 turns northeast towards Glasgow, bypassing the distinctly uninspiring industrial town of **Kilmarnock**, best known as the home of Johnnie Walker whisky. It is also home to a little-known attraction **Dean Castle and Country Park** (follow signs from A77). Set in parkland with a Rare Breeds Farm, this 14th-century Keep with 15th-century Palace houses a collection of European arms and armour, early musical instruments and items relating to Burns. ■ *Apr-Oct daily with hourly tours from 1215 to 1615 weekdays and 1215-1515 weekends. Free.* There is also a tearoom, (1000-1700 summer, 1100-1500 winter). In the centre of Kilmarnock is the **Dick Institute**, Elmbank Avenue which has a fine collection of paintings, including works by Turner, and social and natural history collections. ■ *Mon, Tue, Thu, Fri 0900-2000, Wed 0900-1700, Sat 1000-1700. Free. T01563 554343.* From Kilmarnock the A76 heads southeast to Dumfries, passing through **Mauchline**, where Robert Burns married Jean Armour and where their cottage is now another Burns Museum. The A78 meanwhile runs northwards, passing the quiet, staid resort of **Troon**, famous amongst the golfing fraternity for its excellent **golf course**, T01292-311555.

Irvine

Phone code: 01294
Colour map 5, grid B4

The next town heading north is Irvine, once one of Glasgow's main trading ports and now redeveloped as a new town. The **Tourist Information Centre** is on New Street near the **train station** and the huge shopping centre, T678100 (open Easter-October, 1000-1600. Hours liable to change).

Down at the old harbour, by Gottries Road, is the **Scottish Maritime Museum**, a genuinely interesting exhibition of various ships which you can board. Amongst the assorted vessels moored at the museum docks is a Clyde 'puffer', an old tug and the *Carrick*, the world's oldest clipper (still undergoing restoration). There's also a reconstructed shipyard worker's tenement flat, a coffee shop and souvenir shop, and regular guided tours. ■ *Daily 1000-1700. £2.50, concession £1.75. T278283.* Nearby is the **Magnum Leisure Centre**, the largest in Scotland, with a pool, cinemas, ice rinks and much more besides. ■ *Daily 0900-2200.* On the Harbourside at Irvine is **The Big Idea**, the area's newest and brightest attraction. It celebrates a thousand years of inventions, with visitors interacting with the exhibits using an electronic key. Exhibits range from showing how levers and pulleys work, to giving you the chance to programme a robotic arm. ■ *Mon-Fri 1000-1700, Sat, Sun 1000-1800. £7.95, concession £5.95. T08708-404030.*

Between Irvine and Kilmarnock on the A759 is Royal **Dundonald Castle**. This was the first home of the Stuart kings, built in 1371 by Robert II and much restored since. ■ *Apr-Sep daily 1000-1700. £2, concession £1. T01563-851489 (HS).*

Sleeping **E** *Harbourside Hotel*, 86 Montgomery St, T275515, is at the harbourside and handy for transport and pubs and restaurants. A good place for a pub meal is *The Ship Inn*, 122 Harbour St, T279722.

Transport There are regular **trains** to Glasgow and Ayr. *Stagecoach* **buses**, T01292-613500, leave from Irvine Cross on the High Street to Ayr, Glasgow, Kilmarnock and Largs. 7 miles north of Irvine is the dismal town of **Ardrossan**, from where *Caledonian MacBrayne*, T0990-650000, **ferries** depart for Brodick on the Isle of **Arran**. For details of ferry sailings see page 279). **Trains** leave **Glasgow Central** (1 hr; regularly during the high season (Apr-Oct), to connect with the ferries.

The most attractive town on the North Ayrshire coast is the resort of Largs, backed by high wooded hills and facing the island of **Great Cumbrae**, a few miles offshore and reached by ferry from Largs. The town is not only a traditional family holiday centre, but its extensive **marina** is popular with yachties, and the **Sportscotland National Centre** at Inverclyde, T674666, hosts numerous national indoor competitions.

Largs
Phone code: 01475
Colour map 5, grid A4
Population: 10,000

The **bus** and **train stations** are next to each other on Main St, a short walk from the **ferry pier**. There are hourly **trains** to and from **Glasgow Central** (1 hr. There are also hourly **buses** to **Glasgow**, and to **Ayr**, **Ardrossan** and **Irvine** with *Stagecoach*, T01294-607007. The **Tourist Information Centre**, T678100, is at Largs railway station. Apr-Jun Mon-Sat 0900-1700; Jul and Aug Mon-Sat 0900-1800, Sun 1000-1700; Sep-Oct Mon-Sat 0900-1700.

For details of ferry sailings, see under Great Cumbrae below

The award-winning **Vikingar!** at the north end of the promenade is a multi-media exhibition which fully describes the Viking influence in Scotland, which ended with the Battle of Largs in 1263 (see below). Other facilities include a theatre and cinema, swimming pool, café, bar and gift shop. ■ *Apr-Sep Mon-Fri and Sun 1030-1730, Sat 1230-1530; Oct and Mar Mon-Fri and Sun 1030-1530, Sat 1230-1530; Nov and Feb Sat 1230-1530, Sun 1030-1530. £3.80, children £2.90. T689777, www.vikingar.co.uk* The Battle of Largs is commemorated by the **Pencil Monument**, about a mile south of town along the shoreline footpath. The defeat of the Vikings by the Scots effectively marked the end of Norse sovereignty over the mainland and Western Isles.

There are banks with ATMs and shops on Main St. The post office is just off Main St, on Aitken St

Hidden away in Largs' Old Kirk on Bellman's Close, just off the High Street, is **Skelmorlie Aisle**, an absolute gem of Renaissance architecture unique in Scotland. Built in 1636 as a mausoleum for Sir Robert Montgomerie of Skelmorlie and his wife, the burial vault sits within an aisle with a richly painted timber barrel-vaulted roof. The decoration features the family coat of arms, biblical scenes and representations of the four seasons. The tomb was decorated by Scottish masons following Italian patterns and also includes the coat of arms. ■ *Jun-Aug Mon-Fri 1400-1700; keys from museum next door. Free.*

A few miles south of Largs on the A78 is **Kelburn Castle and Country Centre**, the 13th-century home of the Earls of Glasgow, which boasts a vast range of activities designed for kids. As well as the castle itself, there's a walled garden, secret forest, horse riding, adventure playground, Marine assault course and a woodland glen with a network of trails leading past waterfalls. ■ *T568685, www.kelburncountrycentre.com Easter-end-Oct daily 1000-1800. £4.50, concession £3. Guided tours of castle every afternoon from Jul to Aug, an extra £1.50 per person. Take bus 585 from Largs station.*

You can also take a **boat trip** during July and August from Largs to Rothesay and the Kyles of Bute with *Clyde Marine Cruises* of Greenock, T01475-721281. The old paddle steamer *Waverley* departs from Largs on Tuesdays during the summer, T0141-2218152, to Arran and Bute. Details also from the tourist office.

Sleeping Those who wish to splash out can try the **B** *Brisbane House Hotel*, on the seafront promenade, T687200, www.maksu-group.co.uk It is comfortable and offers very fine Scottish cuisine at mid-range prices. A few miles north town on the A78 is

Southern Scotland

B *Manor Park*, an elegant Victorian country mansion offering b&b, set in 15 acres of grounds overlooking the Firth of Clyde, T520832. There are lots of **guesthouses** and **B&Bs** in town, including: **E** *Belmont House*, 2 Broomfield Pl, T676264, www.belmont.i12.com; **E** *St Leonards Guest House*, 9 Irvine Rd, T673318, stleaonards @blackaw98.freeserve.co.uk; and **E-D** *Tigh-Na-Ligh Guest House*, 104 Brisbane Rd, T/F673975, www.s-h-systems.co.uk/a06156 The cheapest place to stay is **F** *Biscayne House*, 110 Irvine Rd, T672851, www.biscayneguesthouse.co.uk, open all year, an independent hostel. There's a **campsite** about 4 miles north on the A78 at *Skelmorlie Mains Caravan Park*, T520794, open Mar-Oct.

Eating The *Brisbane House Hotel* (see above) is the best place in town for a full-blown meal. Also good is *Fins Seafood Restaurant*, T568989, about 5 miles south of Largs on the A78. It serves great fish and seafood daily except Mon (lunch mid-range; dinner expensive). Don't leave town without visiting the legendary *Nardini's*, T674555, on the promenade. This authentic 1950s Italian café is an institution and is reckoned by some to be the best café in Scotland. It's owned by the family of the actress Daniella Nardini. The décor alone is worth the detour, but the ice cream makes this a truly magical experience. Also good Italian food and coffee. Open daily 2230 in summer.

Great Cumbrae Island   Only a few minutes from Largs by ferry is the hilly island of Great Cumbrae. At only four miles long and a couple of miles wide, it's ideally suited for a day or half-day trip from Largs and is best explored on foot or by bike. Great Cumbrae is a major water sports centre and Millport beach is a popular place for **windsurfing**.

Ferries leave **Largs** every 15 mins during the summer and every 30 mins in winter for the 10-min sailing to the slip on the northeast shore. **Buses** meet the ferry for the 4-mile trip to Millport. The return far is £3.15 per person and £13.35 per car, or £3.60 and £15.70 respectively at peak times. Bikes cost £2 return. For more information, contact *CalMac*, T08705-650000, or at Largs pier, T674134.

The **Tourist Information Centre** at 28a Stuart St, Millport, T01292-678100. Easter fortnight daily 1200-1600, Apr-May Sat, Sun 1200-1600, Jun and Sep Mon-Sat 1200-1600; Jul, Aug daily 1000-1700; Oct Sat, Sun 1200-1600. **Bike hire** is available in Millport at *Mapes & Son*, 3-5 Guildford St, T530444, for £4 per day.

The only settlement of any size is **Millport**, which is home to Europe's smallest cathedral, the beautiful **Cathedral of the Isles**, built in the mid-19th century. ■ *Daily 1100-1600 except during services.* About a mile east of town is the **Marine Life Museum**, part of Glasgow University Marine Biology department, which contains an excellent aquarium. ■ *Mon-Fri 0930-1215 and 1400-1645; Jul-Sep also Sat. £1.50, £0.75 children. T530581.* The nicest parts of the island are away from Millport and are best explored by bike. The 14-mile main road runs right round the edge of the island, or there's a narrow Inner Circle Road which passes **The Glaidstone** (417 ft), the highest point on the island. More information on these cycle routes is available from the TIC.

Sleeping and eating Next to the cathedral is **E** *College of the Holy Spirit*, T530353, www.argyll.anglican.org, an Anglican retreat which offers comfortable B&B. There's also **E** *Cir Mhor*, 35 West Bay, T530723. For eating you're limited to *Minstrels Wine Bar & Restaurant*, T531080, on Cardiff St, or the wonderful *Ritz Café* which has been serving great ice cream, chips and cappuccino for almost a century.

Glasgow

5

Glasgow

There's an old saying that Edinburgh is the capital but Glasgow has the capital. This dates back to the late 19th century, when Glasgow was the "Second City of the Empire". It was a thriving, cultivated city grown rich on the profits from its cotton mills, coal mines and shipyards, and a city that knew how to flaunt its wealth.

The heavy industries have long gone, but Glasgow has lost none of its energy and excitement, and its people possess a style and swagger that makes their Edinburgh counterparts look staid and stuffy by comparison. Just take a stroll round the revived Merchant City or along Byres Road in the West End, and sit in one the countless stylish bars and restaurants, and you'll witness a degree of posing that is Continental in its fervency. The licensing laws may not be Continental but they're more liberal than they are in London and the atmosphere is infused with those vital Glasgow ingredients missing from so many large British cities – warmth and humour. Glasgow is without doubt the friendliest of Britain's large cities. Perhaps that's because it doesn't feel British. Glasgow is often described as European in character; for the remarkable diversity of its architecture, for the accessibility of its art, and for the optimism and openness of its people. It is also compared with North America; for its gridiron street system and for the wisecracking of its streetwise citizens.

Ins and outs

Getting there

Phone code: 0141
For flight, bus and
train details, see
pages 237 and 31.

Air **Glasgow International** airport, T8871111, is 8 miles west of the city, at junction 28 on the M8. It handles domestic and international flights. Terminal facilities include car hire, bank ATMs, currency exchange, left luggage, tourist information (T8484440) and shops, restaurants and bars. There's also a Travel Centre in the UK Arrivals concourse, T8484330 (open daily 0800-2200 in summer and till 1800 in winter) and a Thomas Cook Hotel and Travel Reservations desk in the International Arrivals concourse, T8877220. To get into town take a Glasgow Airport Link bus from outside Arrivals. They leave every 10-15 mins to Buchanan bus station, with drop-off points at Central and Queen St train stations; 25-30 mins, £3.30 single, £5 return. Tickets can be bought from the driver. Buses to the airport leave from Buchanan St bus station and stop outside the main TIC (see below). A taxi from the airport to the city centre costs around £12.

Glasgow Prestwick, T01292-511006, www.gpia.co.uk, is 30 miles southwest of the city. It is used by *Ryanair* from London Stansted, also for flights from Paris Beauvais, Dublin, Franfurt Hahn and Brussels. Trains to and from Central Station leave every 30 mins (45 mins; £2.50 single).

Bus All long-distance buses to and from Glasgow arrive and depart from Buchanan Bus station, on Killermont St, T3327133, 3 blocks north of George Sq. A number of companies offer express coach services day and night around the country and to most English cities; these include *Citylink Coaches*, T08705-505050, and *National Express* T08705-808080.

Train Glasgow has two main train stations: Central station is the terminus for all trains to southern Scotland, England and Wales; and Queen St serves the north and east of Scotland. A shuttle bus runs every 10 mins between Central station (Gordon Street entrance) and Queen St, at the corner of George Sq. It takes 10 mins to walk between the two. For information on rail services and fares, call National Rail Enquiries, T08457-484950 (advance credit/debit card bookings T08457-550033).

Getting around

Further details are
available from the
Strathclyde Travel
Centres (see below)

The best way to get around the city centre sights is by walking, although some of the hills are very steep. If you want to explore the West End or South Side, you'll need to use the public transport system, which is efficient and comprehensive. The best way to get from the city centre to the West End is to use the city's **Underground**, or subway as it's also known, whose stations are marked with a huge orange 'U' sign. This is less effective for the South Side but there's a vast range of buses from the city centre. There's also an extensive suburban train network which is a fast and efficient way to reach the suburbs south of the Clyde. It is relatively easy to get around Glasgow by car, especially as the M8 runs right through the heart of the city. Parking is not a problem either. There are sufficient street meters and 24-hr multi-storey car parks dotted around the centre, at the St Enoch Centre, Mitchell St, Oswald St, Waterloo St and Cambridge St. For car hire companies, see page 238. Taxis are plentiful and reasonably priced and can be hailed from anywhere in the city.

The *Roundabout Glasgow* ticket covers all Underground and train transport in the city for one day and costs £3.50. This gives a £1.50 discount on a city bus tour. Valid Mon-Fri after 0900 and weekends. A *Discovery* ticket (£2.50) gives unlimited travel on the Underground for 1 day (valid after 0930 Mon-Fri and weekends). There's also a *Daytripper* ticket which gives unlimited travel on all transport networks throughout Glasgow, the Clyde coast and Clyde valley. It's valid for one day and costs £7.50 for 1 adult and 2 children, or £13 for 2 adults and up to 4 children.

Things to do in Glasgow ★

- See an amazing show at the world-renowned Citizens' Theatre.
- Find out all about the city's fascinating history through the eyes of its people at the People's Palace.
- Take a tour round the School of Art, Charles Rennie Mackintosh's Art Nouveau masterpiece.
- Wander round the Barras market listening to the famous Glasgow East End patter and maybe you'll unearth a hidden treasure.
- See how you fare at the Transport Museum, one of the city's less obvious attractions and a delight to young and old alike.
- Get your freak on at the Arches, home to some of Glasgow's best club nights.

Orientation & information

Glasgow city centre covers the large area from **Charing Cross** train station and the M8 in the west to **Glasgow Green** in the east, near the cathedral. It is built on a grid system across some steep hills on the north side of the River Clyde. The heart of the city is **George Square**. Here you'll find the tourist office, and the two main train stations (Central station and Queen Street) and the Buchanan bus station are all within a couple of blocks. Immediately to the east of George Square is the renovated **Merchant City** which, together with the streets west of George Square, forms the commercial and business centre. The main shopping streets in the city centre are **Sauchiehall Street**, which runs parallel to the river, west as far as Kelvingrove Park, the pedestianized **Buchanan Street**, which runs south from the east end of Sauchiehall Street, and **Argyle Street**, at the south end of Buchanan St.

The **West End** begins on the other side of the M8, which cuts a swathe through the city. This is the home of the University and is the city's main student quarter, with many of its best bars, cafés and restaurants. The West End is well connected with the city centre by the Underground. South of the Clyde are the more sedate suburbs, know as the **South Side**. To the southwest, in Pollock Country Park, are two of Glasgow's main tourist attractions, **Pollock House** and the **Burrell Collection**, which can easily be reached from the city centre by train or bus.

The main **Tourist Information Centre** is at 11 George Sq, T2044400, F2213524, www.seeglasgow.com (open May daily 0900-1800; Jun and Sep daily 0900-1900; Jul and Aug daily 0900-2000; Oct-Apr Mon-Sat 0900-1800). They provide an excellent service, including a wide selection of maps and leaflets and a free accommodation booking service. You can also buy travel passes, theatre tickets, arrange car rental and exchange currency at their *bureau de change*.

South of George Sq, in front of the giant St Enoch Centre, is the **Strathclyde Travel Centre**, T2264826 (open Mon-Sat 0830-1730). They can provide maps, leaflets and timetables. Their free *Visitor's Transport Guide* includes a particularly useful map of the city. There are other **travel information centres** at Buchanan Bus station, T3327133 (open Mon-Sat 0630-2230, Sun 0700-2230), Hillhead Underground Station, on Byres Rd, T3333673 (open Mon 0800-1730, Tue-Sat 0830-1730), and at Glasgow airport (see page 198).

Glasgow

History

Glasgow was founded in 543 AD when St Mungo built a church in what was then called *Glas-ghu* (meaning "dear green place"). The establishment of a cathedral in the 12th century and Scotland's second university in the 15th century brought status to the city and it was made a royal burgh in 1454.

But Glasgow played little part in the political or economic history of medieval Scotland. It was largely ignored during the bitter wars with England and most of the country's trade was with the Low Countries via the east coast ports.

The city's commercial prosperity came in the 17th century, when it began importing tobacco, sugar, cotton and other goods from the Americas. It began to expand westwards from the medieval centre of the High Street (with the exception of the cathedral, nothing of medieval Glasgow remains). Glasgow's location in the Clyde valley, surrounded by developing coalfields and with deep-water docks only 20 miles from the sea, ensured its development during the Industrial Revolution, in the late 18th century. The city grew rapidly with an influx of immigrants, mainly from the West Highlands, to work in the cotton mills. The deepening of the Clyde up to the Broomielaw, near the heart of the city, and the coming of the railway in the 19th century made the city one of the great industrial centres of the world.

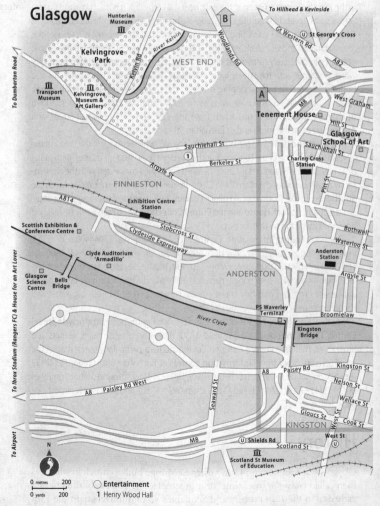

Glasgow

Hunterian Museum 🏛

To Hillhead & Kevinside

B

Gt Western Rd · U · St George's Cross

Kelvingrove Park

River Kelvin

Kelvin Rd

Woodlands Rd

A82

WEST END

To Dumbarton Road

Transport Museum 🏛

Kelvingrove Museum & Art Gallery 🏛

A

M8

West Graham

Tenement House □

Hill St

Glasgow School of Art □

Sauchiehall St

Sauchiehall St

1

Berkeley St

Charing Cross Station ▣

Pitt St

Argyle St

FINNIESTON

A814

Exhibition Centre Station

Stobcross St

Bothwell

Waterloo St

Clydeside Expressway

Scottish Exhibition & Conference Centre □

Anderston Station ▣

Clyde Auditorium 'Armadillo' □

ANDERSTON

Argyle St

To Ibrox Stadium (Rangers FC) & House for an Art Lover

Glasgow Science Centre □

Bells Bridge

PS Waverley Terminal □

River Clyde

Broomielaw

Kingston Bridge

Kingston St

Paisley Rd

A8

Nelson St

A8 Paisley Rd West

Seaward St

Wallace St

KINGSTON

Gloucs St

West St

Cook St

To Airport

N

M8

U Shields Rd

Scotland St

West St U

Scotland St Museum of Education 🏛

0 metres 200
0 yards 200

◯ **Entertainment**
1 Henry Wood Hall

It continued to expand rapidly between the late 18th and early 19th centuries, growing five-fold in only 50 years, and was further swelled by thousands of Irish immigrants fleeing Ireland to escape famine and to seek work. By the mid-19th century Glasgow's population had reached 400,000 and it could justifiably call itself the "second city of the empire". The Victorians built most of the city's most notable buildings, along with the acres of congested tenements that would later become notorious slums.

Since the Second World War and the decline of shipbuilding and heavy industries, Glasgow's population has fallen from over a million to less than 700,000: the result of planning policies designed to decant its population from slum tenements into "new towns" such as East Kilbride and Combernauld outside the city. During the recession of the late 1970s, Glasgow suffered more than most but instead of confronting central government, Glasgow embarked on a bold plan to reinvent itself and shake off the shackles of its industrial past. With its customary energy and wit, the city launched the "Glasgow's Miles Better" promotional campaign in 1983 which led to the 1988 Garden Festival,

Glasgow

Detailed maps
A Glasgow City Cen-
tre, page 204

Related maps
B Glasgow West End,
page 216

Guided Tours

There are various **guided walks** around the city. The **Scottish Tourist Guides Association**, T/F01786-447784/ 0870-607071, offer a variety of entertaining and informative tours. **Mercat Tours**, T7720022, offer the chilling 'Gruesome Glasgow Tour', daily at 1900, and 'Ghosts and Ghouls Tour', daily 2100, which leave from outside the TIC in George Square, from 1 June to 30 September. All these walking tours last one and a half hours. There's also **The Glasgow Literary Tour**, T0131-2266665 (£5/3.50), which is both witty and fascinating. Walkabout Tours are audio-guided tours (£5) of the city centre and Cathedral Precinct which leave from the TIC. For details visit www.walkabout-tours.com

There are sightseeing **guided bus tours** of the city with **Guide Friday**, 2nd floor, St George's building, 5 St Vincent Place, T2487644, and **Scotguide Tourist Services**, 153 Queen St, T2040444, www.scotguide.com These are on board open-top buses and the all-day ticket allows you to hop on and off as you please. Tours run from April to October, and buses leave from George Square every 20 minutes. Fares are £7.50 per person per adult.

There are also a number of **cruises on the Clyde**, see page 222 for details.

1990's year as European City of Culture and, most recently, City of Architecture and Design, in 1999. Glasgow may still suffer the problems of urban deprivation, but it has regained its old confidence and transformed itself into a thriving, post-industrial city with a bright future.

Sights

It's no accident that Glasgow was chosen as both City of Culture and, more recently, UK City of Architecture and Design. Its main attractions are its magnificent Victorian buildings, its museums and art galleries (most of which are free). Sir John Betjeman, Poet Laureate and architectural enthusiast, described Glasgow as the "greatest Victorian city in Europe" and many examples of its rich architectural legacy can be found in the commercial centre (from George Square west to the M8).

To the east of George Square is the **Merchant City**, where the Palladian mansions of the Tobacco Lords have been cleaned up and reclaimed by the professional classes as a fashionable place to eat, drink and play. Further east, in almost surreal contrast, is the **East End**, a traditional working-class stronghold, and to the north is the oldest part of Glasgow, around the medieval **cathedral**.

West of George Square is **Buchanan Street**, one of the city's principal shopping thoroughfares, along with **Sauchiehall Street**, at its northern end, and the more downmarket **Argyle Street**, at the southern end. From here the streets rise towards **Blythswood Square**, a much quieter area of elegant late Georgian buildings filled with office workers. Beyond **Charing Cross**, across the ugly scar of the M8, is the city's **West End**, an area of grand Victorian townhouses and sweeping terraces and home of some of the city's best **museums**.

On the city's **South Side**, across the River Clyde, is **Pollock Country Park**, home of two of Glasgow's finest museums, the **Burrell Collection** and **Pollock House**. The **River Clyde** itself has been added to the list of visitor attractions. The **Clydeside Walkway**, running from Victoria Bridge in the east to the River Kelvin in the west, is an attempt to direct Glasgow's great river towards a post-industrial future of leisure and tourism.

Perhaps not surprisingly, given the origins of its name, Glasgow boasts quite a few green spaces – more per head of population than any other city in Europe. There are more than 70 parks in all, from **Glasgow Green** in the East End to **Kelvingrove Park** in the West End, and **Queen's Park** and **Pollock Country Park**, both in the South Side.

George Square and around

The heart of modern Glasgow is George Square, which makes the obvious starting point for a tour of the city centre, as the **Tourist Information Centre** is located here, on the south side. Amongst the many statues which adorn the square are those of Queen Victoria, Prince Albert, Sir Walter Scott, Robert Burns, Sir Robert Peel and James Watt. The square is surrounded by fine Victorian buildings, most notable of which is the grandiose **City Chambers**, which fills the east side, a wonderful testament to the optimism and aspiration of Victorian Glasgow. It was designed in Italian Renaissance style by William Young and the interior is even more impressive than its façade. The imposing arcaded marble entrance hall is decorated with elaborate mosaics and a marble staircase leads up to a great banqueting hall with a wonderful arched ceiling, leaded glass windows and paintings depicting scenes from the city's history. One wall is covered by a series of murals by the Glasgow Boys (see page 214). ■ *There are free guided tours of the City Chambers, Mon-Fri at 1030 and 1430. T2872000.*

Several of the sights listed below may be closed for restoration work, and some of the churches are only open during services. For details of opening times, ask at the TIC in George Sq

On the northwest corner of George Square, opposite Queen Street station, is another fine building, the **Merchants' House**, now the home of Glasgow Chamber of Commerce. ■ *Free. Entry by appointment only. T2218272.*

Just to the south of George Square, facing the west end of Ingram Street, is **Royal Exchange Square**, which is almost completely filled by the Gallery of Modern Art (GOMA). The building dates from 1778, when it was built as the Cunninghame Mansion, home to one of Glasgow's wealthy Tobacco Lords. It passed to the Royal Bank of Scotland in 1817 and ten years later the magnificent portico was added to the front and the building then became the Royal Exchange, the city's main business centre. It then housed a library, until its reopening in 1996 as one of the city's newest, and its most controversial, art venues, drawing the ire of many a critic for its unashamed eclecticism and populism.

The Gallery of Modern Art

The gallery features contemporary works from artists worldwide over four themed levels: the **Earth Gallery** on the ground floor; the **Fire Gallery** in the basement; the **Water Gallery**; and the **Air Gallery**. It's a bold, innovative art space, making excellent use of the fabulous original interior. It includes interactive computers and art workshops. There's also a superb top-floor **café**, with great views across the city's rooftops (see Cafés). ■ *Mon-Thu and Sat 1000-1700, Fri and Sun 1100-1700. Free. T2291996, www.glasgow.gov.uk*

The Merchant City

The grid-plan of streets to the east of George Square as far as the High Street form the Merchant City, where the Tobacco Lords built their magnificent Palladian mansions. They made Glasgow the most important tobacco trading city in Europe and can also take the credit for it being one of the lung cancer capitals of the world by the mid-20th century.

Glasgow

Glasgow city centre

N

0 metres 100
0 yards 100

Sleeping
1 Adelaide's *B2*
2 Art House *B3*
3 Babbity Bowster *C5*
4 Cathedral House *B6*
5 Euro Hostel *D3*
6 Glasgow Hilton *C2*
7 Groucho Saint Judes *B3*

8 Langs *A4*
9 Malmaison *B2*
10 Merchant Lodge *C4*
11 Millennium *C4*
12 Old School House *A2*
13 Pipers' Tryst *A3*
14 Rennie Mackintosh *A2*
15 Victorian House *A2*
16 Willow *A2*

Eating
1 Amber Regent *B3*
2 Axiom *D1*
3 Bargo *C5*
4 Borders *C4*
5 Buttery *C1*

6 Café Cosmo *A3*
7 Café Cossachock *D5*
8 Café Gandolfi *C5*
9 Cameron's *B2*
10 Canton Express *A2*
11 City Merchant *C5*
12 Costa *C3*
13 Doocot Café & Bar *C3*
14 Fratelli Sarti *B3*
15 Glasgow Noodle Bar *B3*
16 Gordon Yuill & Company *B3*
17 Granary *D4*
18 Green Room *B4*
19 Ho Wong *D3*
20 Ichiban Japanese
Noodle Café *C4*

Glasgow (side tab)

Glasgow

21 Le Bouchon *D5*
22 Miss Cranston's Tearooms *C3*
23 Pattaya *A1*
24 Rogano's & Café Rogano *C4*
25 Schottische *C5*
26 Wee Curry Shop *A3*
27 Where the Monkey Sleeps *B3*
28 Willow Tea Rooms *B3*

⬤ **Bars & pubs**
29 Bar 10 *C3*
30 Bar 91 *C5*
31 Blackfriars *C5*
32 Cask & Still *B3*
33 Gate *A2*
34 Griffin *B2*

35 Havana *C3*
36 Horse Shoe Bar *C3*
37 Mitre Bar *C5*
38 Mojo *B3*
39 Rab Ha's *C4*
40 Scotia Bar *D4*

◯ **Entertainment**
1 Archaos *C4*
2 Arches *D3*
3 Bennet's *C4*
4 CCA *A2*
5 Citizens' Theatre *E4*
6 City Halls & Ticket Office *C5*
7 Garage *A1*
8 Glasgow Film Theatre *B3*

9 King's Theatre *B2*
10 King Tut's Wah Wah Hut *B2*
11 Mitchell Theatre *B1*
12 Nice 'n' Sleazy *A2*
13 Royal Concert Hall *B4*
14 Royal Scottish Academy of
   Music & Drama (RSAMD) *B3*
15 Theatre Royal *A3*
16 Tron Theatre *D5*
17 Tunnel *C3*

Related maps
A Glasgow West End,
page 216

This part of the city was once a bustling trade centre and money has been poured into the restoration of its 18th century warehouses and homes in an attempt to revitalise and regenerate the city's old historic core. Though many of the buildings are little more than façades, the investment has succeeded in attracting expensive designer clothes shops and a plethora of stylish bistros, cafés and bars, which are packed with the city's young professionals and media types. It's a very pleasant and interesting area to explore, and when all that neo-classical architecture gets too much, you can pop into one of the trendy café-bars for some light relief.

A good place to start is **Hutchesons' Hall**, at 158 Ingram Street, a distinguished Georgian building which is now the National Trust for Scotland's regional headquarters. It was built by David Hamilton in 1805 in neo-classical style with a traditional Scottish "townhouse" steeple. It was once home of the Scottish Educational Trust, a charitable institution founded by the 17th century lawyer brothers George and Thomas Hutcheson which provided almshouses and schools for the city. Their statues gaze down towards the site of the original almshouse in Trongate. Inside is a shop and information room with an audio-visual programme about the history of the Merchant City. ■ *Mon-Sat 1000-1700. Free. T5528391.*

In nearby Glassford Street is Glasgow's oldest secular building, the **Trades Hall**, designed by Robert Adam and built in 1794 as the headquarters of the city's trade guilds. It still serves its original purpose. ■ *T5522418. Entry by appointment only.* At the corner of Ingram Street and Glassford Street is the lavish **Trustee Savings Bank** building, designed by that prodigious talent, JJ Burnet in 1900. Nearby, on Ingram Street, is another fine building, **Lanarkshire House**, designed by his father, John Burnet, along with two more of Glasgow's greatest architects, David Hamilton and James Salmon Jnr. It dates from 1879 and has recently been opened as a combination of bars, restaurants and meeting rooms.

Running off Ingram Street is Virginia Street, whose name recalls Glasgow's trading links with America. Here you'll find a rather dilapidated collection of early 19th century buildings, **Virginia Buildings**. Behind the southernmost of these buildings is **Crown Arcade**, formerly the tobacco and sugar exchange and now beautifully converted to a glass-roofed arcade of antique and craft shops. Parallel to Virginia Street is Miller Street, where you'll find the Merchant City's oldest surviving house (No 42), the **Tobacco Laird's House**, dating from 1775.

Trongate to the East End

Glasgow Cross & around
Just south of Trongate, around King St, is a lively area crammed with contemporary art galleries and studios. Many of the works are for sale so it's a good hunting ground for original gifts

The Merchant City is bounded to the east by the High Street and to the south by Trongate. These two streets meet at Glasgow Cross, once the centre of trade and administration and regarded as the city centre, until the coming of the railway in the mid-19th century. In the centre of the intersection stands the 126 ft-high **Tolbooth Steeple**, one of only three crowned steeples in the country. This is the only remnant of the original tolbooth built in 1626, which housed the courthouse and prison (described by Sir Walter Scott in *Rob Roy*). The **Mercat Cross** next to the steeple is a 1929 replica of the medieval original.

The nearby **Tron Steeple** is the only surviving part of St Mary's Church, built in 1637. This church was accidentally burned down by drunken members of the aptly-named Glasgow Hellfire Club in 1793. After a meeting, they went to the church to warm themselves by a fire, which they built up until it got out of control. The steeple has been incorporated into the modern frontage of the **Tron Theatre** (see page 235), and the interior of the replacement church forms the theatre auditorium. Nearby, at 14 King Street, is the **Sharmanka Kinetic Gallery and Theatre**, which puts on performances by mechanical sculptures made from carved wooden figures and old bits of junk. A great place to take the kids. ■ *Performances on Sun at 1500 (short programme for children) and 1800, Tue 1300, Thu 1900. £3 (£2 children). T5527080, www.sharmanka.co.uk* To the south, on Bridgegate, is the **Merchants' Steeple**, built as part of the **Fishmarket** in 1872. The 164 feet-high steeple, with details in Gothic and Renaissance style, is all that's left of the old Merchants' House, built in 1651-59.

East of Glasgow Cross, Gallowgate and London Road lead into the city's **East** **The Barras**
End, only a stone's throw from the Merchant City. It may look shabby and rundown by comparison but this is where you can sample a slice of pure Glasgow, especially in The Barrows ("The Barras"), a huge market spread out around the streets and alleys south of Gallowgate. You could spend days rummaging around through acres of cheap, new and second-hand goods. A lot of it's junk (dodgy computer games, pirate videos etc) but there are plenty of bargains to be found and there's every chance of unearthing some valuable antique. The real attraction, though, is the unique atmosphere of the place and wit and repartee of the market traders. ■ *The market is held every weekend, 1000-1700, and the entrance is marked by the huge red gates on Gallowgate.*

South of The Barras is the wide expanse of Glasgow Green, said to be the oldest **Glasgow Green**
public park in Britain. It has been common land since at least medieval times and Glaswegians still have the right to dry their washing here. Bonnie Prince Charlie reviewed his troops here in 1745 before they were hung out to dry by the English at Culloden. The Green has always been dear to the people of Glasgow and some of the city's major political demonstrators have held meetings here, including the Chartists in the 1830s and Scottish republican campaigners in the 1920s. There are various **monuments** dotted around the park, including a 144 feet-high monument to Lord Nelson, erected in 1806, and one to James Watt. Just to the north of the Green are two of the city's oldest churches, dating from the mid-18th century. In St Andrew's Square is **St Andrew's Church**, and nearby is the episcopal **St Andrew's-by-the-Green**, once known as the Whistlin' Kirk because of the introduction of its organ, a radical move in those days.

On the edge of the green, to the east of the People's Palace (see below), is **Templeton's Carpet Factory**, a bizarre structure designed in 1889 by William Leiper in imitation of the Doge's Palace in Venice. It's Britain's best example of polychromatic decoration (in other words, very colourful). The building is now used as a business centre.

On the northern end of the green, approached from London Road, is the People's **People's Palace**
ple's Palace, opened in 1898 as a folk museum for the East End. The recently refurbished museum gives a real insight into the social and industrial life of this great city from the mid-18th century to the present day. Its galleries display a wealth of artefacts, photographs, cartoons and drawings, and a series of films, music and people's anecdotes. A visit to the People's Palace should be on everyone's itinerary, particularly if you're interested in scratching beneath the city's surface and getting to know it better. Equally recommended is the **Winter Gardens**, a huge conservatory at the rear of the museum, where you can enjoy a cup of tea or coffee in tropical surroundings. ■ *Mon-Thu and Sat 1000-1700, Fri and Sun 1100-1700. Free. T5540223.*

Glasgow

The Cathedral area

Until the 18th century Glasgow consisted only of a narrow ribbon of streets running north from the river past the Glasgow Cross and up the High Street to the cathedral. Then came the city's rapid expansion west and the High Street became a dilapidated backwater. At the top of the High Street stand the two oldest buildings in the city, **Glasgow Cathedral** and **Provand's Lordship**.

Glasgow Cathedral The rather severe-looking early Gothic structure is the only complete medieval cathedral on the Scottish mainland. It was built on the site of St Mungo's original church, established in AD 543, though this has been a place of Christian worship since it was blessed for burial in AD 397 by St Ninian, the earliest missionary recorded in Scottish history. Most of the building was completed in the 13th century though parts were built a century earlier by Bishop Jocelyn. The choir and crypt were added a century later and the building was completed at the end of the 15th century by Robert Blacader, the first Bishop of Glasgow.

During the Reformation, the city's last Roman Catholic Archbishop, James Beaton, took off for France with most of the cathedral treasures, just ahead of the townsfolk who proceeded to rid the building of all traces of "idolatry" by destroying altars, statues, vestments and the valuable library. The present furnishings mostly date from the 19th century and many of the windows have been renewed with modern stained glass. The most outstanding feature in the cathedral is the fan vaulting around St Mungo's tomb in the crypt, one of the very finest examples of medieval architecture in Scotland. There's also fine work in the choir, including a 15th century stone screen, the only one of its kind left in any pre-Reformation secular (non-monastic) church in Scotland.

Behind the cathedral looms the **Western Necropolis**, a vast burial ground overlooking the city from the top of a high ridge. It's the ideal vantage point from which to appreciate the cathedral in all its Gothic splendour and many of the tombs are wonderfully-ornate. Interred here are the great and the good (and not so good) of Victorian Glasgow, overseen by a statue of John Knox, the 16th century firebrand reformer. ■ *Apr-Sep Mon-Sat 0930-1800, Sun 1400-1700, Oct-Mar Mon-Sat 0930-1600, Sun 1400-1600. Free. T5526891.*

Cathedral Precinct In front of the cathedral is the weetabix-coloured **St Mungo Museum of Religious Life and Art**, which features a series of displays of arts and artefacts representing the six major world religions, as well as a Japanese Zen garden in the courtyard outside – great for a few moments of quiet contemplation. Highlights include Salvador Dalí's astounding painting *Christ of St John of the Cross*, purchased by the city from the artist in 1951. Don't miss the extremely interesting comments on the visitors' board. There's also a bookshop and café serving hot meals, snacks and drinks. ■ *Mon-Thu and Sat 1000-1700; Fri and Sun 1100-1700. Free. T5532557.* Across the street the **Provand's Lorship**, the oldest remaining house in Glasgow, built in 1471 as part of a refuge for the city's poor and extended in 1670. It has also served as an inn of rather dubious repute in its time. Now it's a museum devoted mainly to medieval furniture and various domestic items. ■ *Same phone number and opening hours as above.*

Buchanan Street to Charing Cross

Glasgow's commercial heart is the area between Buchanan Square and the M8 to the west. This vast grid-plan – which inspired town planners in the USA – is home to the city's main shopping streets and arcades, as well as its businesses and

24 hours in Glasgow

Twenty-four hours in Glasgow is just not enough, but if you're really pushed for time the following suggested itinerary will give a brief indication of why this is now considered one of the most exciting cities in Europe.

Start the day at the **People's Palace** on Glasgow Green for an introduction to the city's history. Head across to Sauchiehall Street for mid-morning coffee in the **Willow Tea Rooms** and admire the elegant interior design of Charles Rennie Mackintosh. Down to **Princes Square** for a spot of shopping, followed by a walk around the **Merchant City**. Lunch in **Babbity Bowster**.

After lunch take the St Enoch subway to Kelvin Hall, for the **Kelvingrove Museum & Art Gallery**, then take a stroll through Kelvingrove Park to the **Hunterian Art Gallery**. Then walk up to the **Botanic Gardens** and enjoy afternoon tea in the **Kibble Palace**. Subway back to Buchanan Street and head to **Rogano** for a drink. Take a taxi to **Café India** for dinner, then finish up with a nightcap at **Café Insomnia** on Woodlands Road.

Glasgow

financial institutions. It is also where you'll find many of its architectural treasures.

At the bottom (south) end of Buchanan Street is St Enoch Square, dominated by the **St Enoch Centre**, a gigantic glass-covered complex of shops, fast-food outlets and an ice rink. There's also a subway station and transport centre in the square. St Enoch Square looks onto Argyle Street, one of Glasgow's most famous shopping streets. Though its status has been usurped in recent decades by the more fashionable streets to the north, it does boast the **Argyle Arcade**, Scotland's first ever indoor shopping mall, built in 1827 in Parisian style, at the junction with Buchanan Street.

Argyle Street runs west from here under the railway bridge at **Central station**. This bridge has always been known as the 'Heilanman's Umbrella', owing to the local joke that Highlanders would stand under it for shelter rather than buy an umbrella.

A short walk north on Buchanan Street is **Princes Square**, one of the most stylish and imaginative shopping malls in Britain. Even if you're not buying or looking, it's worth going in to admire this beautifully-ornate Art Nouveau creation, or to sit at the top-floor café and watch others spend their hard-earned cash in the trendy designer clothes shops below. A little further north, on the opposite side of the street, is a branch of the famous **Willow Tea Rooms** (see below) with replicas of Mackintosh designs. Almost opposite is **Borders Bookshop**, housed in the huge and impressive former Royal Bank of Scotland (1827), which backs onto Royal Exchange Square.

Lovers of architecture should head west into Gordon Street and then south (left) into Mitchell Street, where you'll find The Lighthouse, another of Glasgow's hidden gems. It was designed by the ubiquitous Charles Rennie Mackintosh in 1893 to house the offices of the Glasgow Herald. The Herald vacated the premises in 1980 and it lay empty, until its recent transformation into **Scotland's Centre for Architecture, Design and the City**, a permanent legacy of the Glasgow's role as UK City of Architecture and Design in 1999. This stunning 21st century building also contains the **Mackintosh Interpretation and Review Gallery**, which features original designs and information on the life and work of the great architect. A 135-step spiral staircase leads to the viewing tower, which affords great views over the city. There's also a shop and café. ■ *Mon, Wed, Fri and Sat 1030-1730, Tue 1100-1700, Thu 1030-1700, Sun 1200-1700. £2.50, £2 concession. T2216362.*

The Lighthouse

A fishy tale

Though it is many years since salmon were caught in the Clyde, two appear in the city's coat of arms. Each fish has a ring in its mouth, recalling an old local legend.

The Queen of Strathclyde was given a ring by her husband but then promptly gave it to her lover. The king found the lover wearing the ring as he slept beside the Clyde. He took the ring and threw it *into the water, and then went to his wife and asked her to show it to him. The Queen prayed to St Mungo for help, and immediately, one of her servants miraculously found the ring in the mouth of a salmon he had caught. The king then had to accept his wife's pleas of innocence, despite knowing something fishy was going on.*

Buchanan Street north & St Vincent Street

Further north on Buchanan Street, close to Buchanan Street Underground, are two more interesting buildings: **St George's Tron Church**, designed in 1808 by William Stark and the oldest church in the city centre, and the **Athenaeum**, designed in 1886 by JJ Burnet and showing early signs of his later modernism. Running west from George Square, between Argyle Street and Sauchiehall Street, is St Vincent Street, where you'll find two of the city's extraordinary buildings. **The Hatrack**, at No 142, was designed in 1902 by James Salmon Jnr. It's a very tall, narrow building, like many in the city centre, with a fantastically-detailed roof which looks like an old hat stand.

Further along St Vincent Street, near the intersection with Pitt Street, is one of the jewels in Glasgow's architectural crown, the **St Vincent Street Church**, designed in 1859 by Alexander 'Greek' Thomson, the city's "unknown genius" of architecture. Much of his work was destroyed in the 1960s and this is his only intact Romantic Classical church, now on the World Monument Fund's list of the 100 most endangered sites. The Presbyterian church is fronted by Ionic columns like those of a Greek temple and the church also shows Egyptian and Assyrian decoration. The main tower is Grecian in style while the dome could have come straight out of India during the Raj.

A series of streets climb northwards from St Vincent Street up to Sauchiehall Street, another of the city's main shopping thoroughfares. If there's one thing Glaswegians like to do it's spend money and Glasgow is second only to London in the UK in terms of retail spending. The newest of the city's shopping centres is the upmarket **Buchanan Galleries**, next door to the **Royal Concert Hall** (see page 234), at the north end of Buchanan Street, where it meets the east end of Sauchiehall Street.

Sauchiehall Street

There are a few notable places of interest on Sauchiehall Street, including Charles Rennie Mackintosh's wonderful **Willow Tea Rooms**, at No 217, above *Henderson's* the Jewellers. This is a faithful reconstruction on the site of the original 1903 tea room, designed by CRM for his patron Miss Kate Cranston, who already ran three of the city's most fashionable tea rooms, in Argyle Street, Buchanan Street and Ingram Street. The tea room was very much peculiar to Glasgow, promoted by the Temperance Movement as a healthy alternative to the gin palaces, popular throughout the country in the late 19th century, and Miss Cranston's were the *crème de la crème* of tea rooms. They offered ladies-only rooms, rooms for gentlemen and rooms where both sexes could dine together. In addition, her tea rooms offered a reading room, a billiards room for the gentlemen and a smoking room, not forgetting the unrivalled splendour of the decoration.

Mackintosh had already worked with Miss Cranston on her other tea rooms, but Sauchiehall Street was their *tour de force*. Sauchiehall means "alley of the willows" and this theme was reflected not only in the name, but throughout the interior. Mackintosh was allowed free rein to design the fixtures and fittings; everything, in fact, right down to the teaspoons. The exclusive Salon de Luxe, on the first floor, was the crowning glory, and the most exotic and ambitious part of the tea rooms, decorated in purple, silver and white, with silk and velvet upholstery. Visitors today can relive the splendour of the original tea rooms as they relax in the distinctive high-backed chairs with a cup of tea, brought to them by the specially selected high-backed waitresses. ■ *The tea rooms are open from 0930 to 1630 (see also 'Cafés' on page 230).*

A few yards west, on the opposite side of the street, are the **McLellan Galleries**, another fine example of classical architecture. The galleries are currently closed but when they re-open will host a wide of touring and temporary exhibitions. ■ *To check re-open date T3311854. Opening times and admission charges change with each exhibition.*

Further down the street, on the same side, is the **Centre for Contemporary Arts (CCA)**, housed in the Grecian Buildings, a former commercial warehouse designed by Alexander 'Greek' Thomson in 1867-68. The centre presents a changing programme of contemporary theatre, dance and other cultural events. It also has two excellent café-bars (see 'Cafés', page 230). ■ *Centre open Mon-Sat 0900-2400; Sun 1200-1900. Galleries open Mon-Sat 1100-1800; Sun 1200-1700. Free. T3327521.*

A very steep walk up from Sauchiehall Street, at 167 Renfrew Street, is the **Glasgow** Glasgow School of Art, one of the city's most important buildings, and one of **School of Art** the most prestigious Art Schools in the country. The building was designed by Charles Rennie Mackintosh, after his proposal won a competition set to find a design for the school, in 1896. It was built in two stages from 1897-1899 and completed in 1907.

Much of the inspiration for his design came from nature and from his drawings of traditional Scottish buildings. He was also influenced by the Art Nouveau style, particularly the illustrations of Aubrey Beardsley. The school is now regarded as Mackintosh's architectural masterpiece and gives full expression to his architectural ideals. It is rooted in tradition, with a thoroughly modern-looking exterior of extreme austerity, and there are medieval, castle-like features such as turrets and curving stair wells.

The interior is both spacious and utilitarian and shows perfectly his desire to create a unified and harmonious working environment for both students and teachers. The studio walls and high ceilings are painted white, with huge windows allowing light to pour into the spaces. The corridors and staircases are decorated with glazed coloured tiles to help guide students and staff around the massive building. In the spectacular two-storey library Mackintosh also designed the light fittings, bookcases and the oak furniture. There are symbols of nature everywhere throughout the building, used to inspire the students to produce their own works of art. And who could fail to be inspired in such a stunning environment.

Entry to the school is by guided tour only which visits the main rooms containing many of the well-known pieces of furniture and includes the famous library. It is still a working art school, so take note of the annual closing. ■ *Tour times Sep-Jun Mon-Fri at 1100 and 1400, Sat 1030 and 1130; Jul-Aug Mon-Fri 1100 and 1400, Sat/Sun 1030, 1130 and 1300. Closed late Jun for graduation and from Christmas through to New Year. £5, £3 students. Booking is advised. T3534526, www.gsa.ac.uk*

Glasgow

Other Mackintosh buildings

Aside from the Mackintosh buildings listed separately, there are a number of his lesser known works scattered around the city centre. These include the **Martyrs' Public School** (1895), at Parson Street, just off the High Street and M8 (open daily 1300-1600, free, T2878955), the **Daily Record Building** (1901), at 20-26 Renfield Lane (external viewing only), the **Royal Fusiliers Museum** (c1903), at 518 Sauchiehall Street (ring for opening times, T3320961), Ruchill Church Hall, Shakespeare Street (open Monday-Friday 1030-1430, closed July/August, free) and the former **Glasgow Society of Lady Artists' Club** (1908), at 5 Blythswood Square (external viewing only). At 870 Garscube Road is **Queen's Cross Church**, CRM's only church and a fascinating piece of architecture. Beautifully simple, with echoes of the symbolism of his other buildings, it now functions as the headquarters of the Charles Rennie Mackintosh Society. There's an information centre, a small display and a gift shop. ■ *Mon-Fri 1000-1700, Sat 1000-1400, Sun 1400-1700. T9466600. £2, £1 concession. Contact the CRM Society at the church, Glasgow G20 7EL, T9466600, F9452321, www.crmsociety.com Buses 21, 61 and 91 from Hope St (west side of Central station), or Underground to St George's Cross and walk 10 mins on Maryhill Rd.*

The Tenement House

A few hundred yards northwest of the School of Art, down the other side of the hill, at 145 Buccleuch Street, is the Tenement House, a typical late Victorian tenement flat. This was the home of Miss Agnes Toward, a shorthand typist, for 50 years until she moved out in 1965. It's a fascinating time-capsule of life in the first half of the 20th century and retains most of the original features such as the bed recesses, kitchen range and coal bunker. The whole experience is a little voyeuristic, as the flat includes many of Agnes' personal possessions, and in the parlour the table is set for afternoon tea, lending a spooky atmosphere redolent of the Marie Celeste. On the ground floor is an exhibition on tenement life. The property is owned by the NTS. ■ *1 Mar-31 Oct, daily 1400-1700. £3.50, £2.50 concession. T3330183.*

On the other side of Cowcaddens Road, behind the huge Royal Scottish Academy for Music and Drama, is the **Piping Centre**, at 30-34 McPhater Street. It's a kind of centre for the promotion of the bagpipes and contains rehearsal rooms, performance spaces and accommodation for aficionados of the instrument which divides opinion so sharply. There's also a very fine **café** and a **museum** which features a collection of antique pipes. ■ *Mon-Sat 1030-1630; Sun in summer. £3, £2concession.*

The West End

The bustling hub of the West End is Byres Rd, running south from the Great Western Road past Hillhead Underground. It's an area populated mostly by students and full of fashionable shops, bars, cafés and restaurants

On the other side of the M8 is the West End, an area which contains many of the city's major museums, as well some of its finest examples of Victorian architecture. During the course of the 19th century the West End grew in importance as wealthy merchants moved here, away from the dirt and grime of the industrial city. By the middle of the 19th century the **Park Conservation Area** had been established and was described as one of the finest pieces of architectural planning of the century. Perhaps the most impressive of all the terraces in the conservation area are **Park Quadrant** and **Park Terrace**, with glorious views across **Kelvingrove Park**. Soon after, in 1870, the **university** also moved west, to its present site overlooking Kelvingrove Park, and in 1896 the Glasgow District Subway was extended west. In 1888 the park was used to stage an international

Charles Rennie Mackintosh

To say that Barcelona has Gaudi and Glasgow has Rennie Mackintosh is not overstating the case. He is not only one of Scotland's most celebrated architects, but one of the creative geniuses of modern architecture.

Charles Rennie Mackintosh was born in Glasgow in 1868 and at 15 began work as a draughtsman with a local firm of architects. At the same time, he continued to pursue his studies at the Glasgow School of Art where his talent as an artist soon earned him recognition, and his experimental, decorative style brought him into contact with kindred spirits Herbert MacNair and two sisters, Frances and Margaret MacDonald. They became known as 'The Four' and together they developed their unique form of art and design, which became known as the 'Glasgow Style'

Mackintosh was as much an artist and interior designer as an architect but he saw no conflict in this. He considered architecture to be "...the synthesis of the fine arts, the commune of all the crafts", and he used his diverse talents to great effect, designing every detail of a building, down to furniture, carpets and decoration. This can be seen to greatest effect in his most important building, the Glasgow School of Art.

In the late 1890s he began his Argyle Street tea room project for Miss Cranston, and developed his distinctive, elegant high-backed chairs, for which he is probably best known today. In 1900 he married Margaret Macdonald (Herbert MacNair and Margaret's sister were married the previous year) and they began to design the interior of their own flat, creating their distinctive colour schemes of white and grey, pink and purple, and the light and dark interiors representing the masculine and feminine.

Throughout his career, Mackintosh's talents were far better understood abroad than at home, where his designs were often criticised as being iconoclastic and too modern. He was forced to leave Glasgow in 1914 due to lack of work and soon became depressed and alcoholic, and though his fortunes improved after moving to London, he died, a tragic but romantic figure, in 1928.

It is only in the past few decades that his genius has been fully recognised and serious efforts made to preserve his artistic legacy. The restoration of the Willow Tea Rooms, Scotland Street School, Queen's Cross Church and the Mackintosh House at the Hunterian Art Gallery, as well as The Hill House in Helensburgh, are all testimony to his prodigious talents.

Glasgow

exhibition and the profits were used to build the **Kelvingrove Museum and Art Gallery**, which housed the second international exhibition, in 1901.

Glasgow's greatest art gallery (with the possible exception of the Burrell Collection) is the Kelvingrove Art Gallery and Museum, which stands below the university, on the other side of the River Kelvin, at the most westerly end of Argyle and Sauchiehall Streets, near Kelvingrove Park. This massive sandstone Victorian building houses one of the finest municipal collections of Scottish and European paintings in the country, and should not be missed. The art gallery and museum, first opened to the public in 1902, can be entered from the "rear", leading to one of the most popular urban myths, that it was mistakenly built back to front and when the architect found out he was so distraught that he jumped from one of the towers. It was actually designed by two architects, Sir JW Simpson and Milner Allen, and is a wonderful structure, especially the breathtaking atrium. At one end of the atrium is a huge set of organ pipes, and recitals are still held here. On the

Kelvingrove Museum & Art Gallery
Check that the museum is open before visiting as a lengthy refurbishment is pending, probably starting in late 2002

The Glasgow Boys

With the coming of the industrial age, Glasgow had grown rapidly from a small, provincial town into the "Second City of the Empire". This sudden growth in size and wealth led to the beginnings of the famous and long-standing rivalry between Glasgow and Edinburgh, and, by the 1880s, to a new departure from the cultural mainstream, when a group of students nicknamed the Glasgow Boys, united in protest against Edinburgh's dominance of the arts.

This group of five painters – Guthrie, Hornel, Lavery, Henry and Crawhall – rejected the traditional concept of art which was confined to historical melodrama, sentimental "poor but happy" cottagers and grandiose visions of the Highlands inspired by Sir Walter Scott. They referred to these paintings as "gluepots" for their use of megilp, a treacly varnish that lent the paintings a brown

patina of age. Instead, they experimented with colour and, inspired by the European Realists, chose earthy, peasant themes. This not only shocked and offended the genteel Edinburgh art establishment, but also scandalized their fellow citizens.

The Glasgow Boys left Scotland to study in Paris, where their work met with great acclaim. Subsequently their art began to fetch high prices from the new rich of Glasgow, eager to buy status through cultural patronage. But once the group had achieved the artistic respect and commercial success its members craved, they sadly lost their freshness.

The influence of the Glasgow Boys cannot be underestimated. They shook the foundations of the art establishment and were the inspiration for the next generation of great Scottish painters, known as the "Colourists".

ground floor is the **Scottish Natural History Museum** and, on the opposite side of the main hall, a rather jumbled collection of pottery, porcelain, silverware, costumes, tapestry and a collection of arms and armour.

But it is the art gallery upstairs which makes this such a fascinating attraction. Displayed in a series of rooms are some superb works, including Botticelli's *Annunciation*, Giorgione's *The Adultress Brought Before Christ* and Rembrandt's *Man in Armour*. There are also outstanding examples of French Impressionism, Post-Impressionism and Dutch schools, including works by Degas, Monet, Turner, Bonnard, Pissaro, Vuillard, Braque and Derain. There are also excellent works by many of Scotland's finest artists, including, Sir Henry Raeburn, Horatio McCulloch and Alexander Naysmith. The Glasgow Boys are also well represented, with works by George Henry, Joseph Crawhall, Sir James Guthrie and Sir John Lavery. There's also a room dedicated to Charles Rennie Mackintosh, featuring a marvellous collection of furniture. ■ *Mon-Thu and Sat 1000-1700; Fri and Sun 1100-1700. Free. There's a cheap self-service café on the ground floor. Also free guided tours most days from the enquiry desk. T2872690. To get there, take any bus heading for the Dumbarton Rd (Nos 9, 16, 42, 62, 64,). Nearest Underground station is Kelvin Hall.*

Transport Museum Opposite the Kelvingrove Museum and Art Gallery and behind the **Kelvin Hall**, just off Argyle Street, is the Transport Museum, whose name may lack appeal but which is one of the country's most fascinating museums. There are collections of trams, trains, motor cars, horsedrawn vehicles, bicycles, motorbikes, as well as a whole room dedicated to models of Clyde-built ships. Everything you ever wanted to know about the history of transport but were too disinterested to ask. Well, this place will change all that. There's also a reconstruction of a 1938 cobbled street, an old Underground station and a cinema showing old films of Glaswegians heading "doon the watter". Something for everyone, as they say in the tourist brochures. ■ *Mon-Thu and Sat 1000-1700, Fri and Sun 1100-1700. Free. T2872720.*

The **Kelvin Walkway** follows the River Kelvin from Kelvingrove Park through the northwest of the city to Dawsholm Park, about three miles away. It goes through the Botanic Gardens and under the Forth and Clyde Canal. With the appropriate maps you could follow one waterway out and return by the other. The path starts just west of the Transport Museum, by the bridge on the Dumbarton Road.

The university's roots go back to 1451 when Pope Nicholas V authorised William Turnbull, Bishop of Glasgow to found a seat of learning in the city. At first there was just an Arts faculty and lectures were held in the cathedral crypt and neighbouring monastery. In the 17th century the university moved to new premises in the High Street, but these became too small and, in 1870, it moved to its present site, on Gilmorehill, overlooking Kelvingrove Park. The Gothic buildings were designed by Sir George Gilbert Scott, though the Lion and Unicorn balustrade on the stone staircase opposite the Principal's Lodging is a relic of the old High Street colleges, as is the stonework of the lodge gateway. Bute Hall, which is now used for graduation and other ceremonies, was added in 1882. The **university chapel** is also worth seeing.

Glasgow University & the Hunterian Museum

Contained within the university buildings is the **Hunterian Museum**, named after William Hunter (1718-83), a student at the university in the 1730s. His bequest to the university of his substantial collections led to the establishment of the Hunterian Museum in 1807, Scotland's oldest public museum. It has displays of social history, archaeology and geology and includes Roman relics from the Antonine Wall and one of the largest coin collections in Britain. Beneath the museum is the **University Visitor Centre**, which features interactive displays on the university and a coffee bar. There's also a **Zoology Museum**, housed in the Graham Kerr Building, a few minutes' walk from the main museum. ■ *Mon-Sat 0930-1700. Free. T3304221, www.hunterian.gla.ac.uk*

Across the road, at 82 Hillhead Street, is the Hunterian Art Gallery, a modern building containing the more interesting part of Hunter's bequest, the fabulous art collection. The gallery holds an important collection of European paintings including works by Rembrandt, Koninck, Rubens, Pissaro and Rodin, as well as 18th century British portraits by Ramsay and Reynolds. There is also a fine collection of Scottish 19th and 20th century paintings including works by McTaggart, Guthrie and Fergusson. The *piece de resistance* is the huge collection of works by the American painter, James McNeill Whistler. There are some 70 paintings and a selection of his personal possessions on show, making it the largest display of his work outside the USA.

Hunterian Art Gallery & Mackintosh House

Attached to the gallery is the **Mackintosh House**, a stunning reconstruction of the main interiors from 78 Southpark Avenue, the Glasgow home of Charles Rennie Mackintosh and his wife, Margaret MacDonald, from 1906 to 1914. A stairway leads to an introductory display containing numerous drawings and designs, including those for his major buildings, furniture and interiors. From there you are led into the cool, soothing rooms, lovingly reconstructed and exquisitely furnished with some 80 original pieces of his furniture. These give the perfect example of just why this innovative designer and architect is so revered. Among the highlights are the Studio Drawing Room, decorated in white and flooded with natural light, and the guest

Glasgow

bedroom from Northampton, a later commission, with its bold and dazzling geometric designs. When George Bernard Shaw, a guest, was asked if the décor would disturb his sleep, he replied, "No, I always sleep with my eyes closed." ■ *Mon-Sat 0930-1700. Mackintosh House closed daily 1230-1330. Free. T3305431, www.hunterian.gla.co.uk To get there take buses 44 and 59 from the city centre (Hope St), or the Underground to Hillhead and walk. Opposite the entrance is the student refectory.*

Botanic Gardens At the top of Byres Road, where it meets the Great Western Road, is the entrance to the Botanic Gardens, a smallish but perfectly formed park where you can lose yourself along the remote paths that follow the wooded banks of the River Kelvin. There are two large hothouses in the park, one of which is the **Kibble Palace**, built as a conservatory for the Clyde Coast home of Glasgow

Glasgow West End

KELVINSIDE

A To Dumbarton — Devonshire Gdns [10] — Great Western Rd — **Botanic Gardens** — Kibble Palace ▣

B — Hydland Rd — Saltoun St — Cresswell St [5] — Ruthven La — Gt George St — [17] [11] [21] ⓤ Hillhead [2] [12] — Ashton La — [10] [1] [6]

Partickhill Rd — Highburgh Rd — [20] — **Hunterian Gallery & Mackintosh House** ▥ — **Western Infirmary** ✚

C [9] — Hyndland St — White St — [22] — Byres Rd

Kelvinhall [26] ⓤ — [4] — Argyle St — ▥ **Transport Museum** — **Kelvin Hall Sports Arena**

West of Scotland Cricket Ground — Dumbarton Rd — River Kelvin — Old Dumbarton Rd

D ⓤ Partick — To Anniesland

1 **2** **3**

N — 0 metres 100 / 0 yards 100

■ Sleeping
1 Berkeley Globetrotters *D6*
2 Glasgow Backpackers Hostel *C5*
3 Heritage & Botanic *B4*
4 Hillhead *B4*
5 Hillview Guest House *B4*
6 Kelvin Park Lorne *D4*
7 Kirkland House
8 Kirklee
9 Number Thirty Six
10 One Devonshire Gardens & Amaryllis Restaurant *A1*
11 Sandyford *D5*
12 SYHA Youth Hostel *C5*
13 Townhouse Hotel *D5*
14 Wickets

● Eating
1 Air Organic *D5*
2 Ashoka Ashton Lane *B3*
3 Ashoka West End *D4*
4 Beetlenut *C2*
5 Brasserie Metro *B3*
6 Brel *B3*
7 Café India
8 Canal
9 Cottier's *C2*

businessman, John Kibble, and then shipped to its present site in 1873. The domed glasshouse, which contains a collection of ferns and palms from around the world, is thought to have been designed by Sir Joseph Paxton who designed the Crystal Palace in London, as well as Kelvingrove Park. The **main glasshouse** is more attractive, with outstanding collections of orchids and begonias. ■ *Gardens open daily 0700 till dusk. Free. Kibble Palace and all glasshouses open daily 1000-1645 in summer, 1000-1615 in winter.*

South Side

South of the River Clyde is a part of Glasgow largely unknown to most visiting tourists, except for two of the city's most notable attractions, the **Burrell Collection** and **Pollock House**, both set in the sylvan surrounds of **Pollock**

Glasgow

10 Cul de Sac & Attic Bar *B3*	**19** Stravaigin *B5*	**27** Uisge Beatha *B5*
11 Deirfiuracha *B3*	**20** Tinderbox *C3*	
12 Grosvener Café *B3*	**21** Ubiquitous Chip *B3*	○ **Entertainment**
13 Insomnia *C6*	**22** University Café *C2*	**1** Grosvenor Cinema *B3*
14 La Parmigiana *B4*		**2** Henry Wood Hall *D5*
15 Mother India *D5*	● **Bars & pubs**	**3** Mitchell Library & Theatre *C6*
16 Nairn's *C6*	**23** Brewery Tap *D4*	
17 Puppet Theatre *B3*	**24** Firebird *D4*	
18 Sal & Pepe *B4*	**25** Halt Bar *C6*	
	26 Living Room *C2*	

Related maps
A Glasgow City Centre,
page 204

Alexander 'Greek' Thomson: the unknown genius

Alexander Thomson was the greatest architect of Victorian Glasgow, who did as much to shape the city as the famous Charles Rennie Mackintosh. In the middle of the 19th century, when the "Second City of the Empire" was a growing, dynamic place, he brought a distinctive flair to all manner of buildings: warehouses and commercial premises, terraces and tenements, suburban villas and some of the finest Romantic Classical churches in the world.

Despite his nickname he never visited Greece and was not a conventional Greek Classicist. In fact, he thought the architects of the Greek revival had failed "because they could not see through the material into the laws upon which that architecture rested. They failed to master their style, and so became its slaves". Instead, Thomson evolved a distinctive manner of building using a Greek style but in an unconventional way and incorporating modern inventions such as iron beams and plate glass. Thomson

was struck by "the mysterious power of the horizontal element in carrying the mind away into space and into speculations on infinity". This dominance of horizontality has led to comparisons with Frank Lloyd Wright, though Thomson predates him by 40 years.

Thomson was a truly original and brilliant architect yet was shamefully neglected after his death in 1875. In the 1960s, in a frenzy of destruction, the city planners did their best to wipe out this man's amazing achievements completely. Finally, though, the city paid tribute to one of their most talented sons with a major exhibition about his work as part of the City of Architecture and Design year.

For more information on Alexander "Greek" Thomson and his surviving buildings, see the tourist office's Glasgow architectural guide 1. The only building open to the public is Holmwood House, in Cathcart (see below).

Country Park. There are other reasons to venture south of the river, however, not least of these being to see Charles Rennie Mackintosh's **House for an Art Lover** in nearby Bellahouston Park. Further east is another stop on the Mackintosh trail, the **Scotland Street School Museum of Education**. To the south, in Cathcart, is **Holmwood House**, Alexander 'Greek' Thomson's great architectural masterpiece.

The Burrell Collection
Three miles southwest of the city centre is Glasgow's top attraction and a must on any visit, the Burrell Collection, standing in the extensive wooded parklands of Pollock Country Park. The magnificent collection contains some 8,500 art treasures, donated to the city in 1944 by the shipping magnate, William Burrell (1861-1958) who sold his shipping interests in order to devote the remainder of his life to collecting art. He began collecting in the 1880s, and in 1917 bought Hutton Castle near Berwick-on-Tweed to house his collection. There it stayed, until the modern, award-winning gallery was built with the £450,000 donated by Burrell for the purpose of displaying his hugely eclectic bequest. The building opened to the public in 1983.

The collection includes ancient Greek, Roman and Egyptian artefacts, a huge number of dazzling oriental art pieces, and numerous works of medieval and post-medieval European art, including tapestries, silverware, textiles, sculpture and exquisitely-lit stained glass. There's also an impressive array of paintings by Rembrandt, Degas, Pissaro and Manet amongst many others.

The gallery is a stunning work of simplicity and thoughtful design, which allows the visitor to enjoy the vast collection to the full. The large, floor-to-ceiling windows afford sweeping views over the surrounding woodland and allow a flood of natural light to enhance the treasures on view. Some sections of the gallery are reconstructions of rooms from Hutton Castle and incorporated into the structure are carved stone Romanesque doors. There's also a café and restaurant on the lower ground floor. ■ *Mon-Thu and Sat 1000-1700, Sun 1100-1700. Free. T6497151, www.glasgow.gov.uk Buses 45, 47 and 57 from the city centre (Union St) pass the park gates on Pollockshaws Rd. From the gates it's a 10-min walk to the gallery, or there's a twice hourly bus service. There are also regular trains from Central station to Pollockshaws West station. A taxi from the city centre costs £6-7.*

Pollock House & Country Park

Also in Pollock Country Park, a 10-minute walk from the Burrell, is **Pollock House**, designed by William Adam and finished in 1752. This was once the home of the Maxwell family, who owned most of southern Glasgow until well into the last century. It contains one of the best collections of Spanish paintings in Britain, including works by Goya, El Greco and Murillo. There are also paintings by William Blake, as well as glass, silverware, porcelain and furniture. The most interesting part of the house are the servants' quarters downstairs, and there's a good tearoom in the old kitchens. ■ *Daily 1000-1700. £4, £3 child/concession. Nov-Mar free. T6166410.* If the weather's fine, the park is worth exploring. There are numerous trails through the woods and meadows and guided walks on Sundays with the park rangers. There are two golf courses within the park grounds, as well as a herd of highland cattle. ■ *Entry to the park is from Pollockshaws Road, or Haggs Road if you're on foot. Car parking is at the Burrell Collection and costs £1.50. T6329299.*

House for an Art Lover

On the ground floor is an excellent café, which is popular with locals (see 'Cafés' on page 230)

A short distance north of Pollock Park is Bellahouston Park, site of the most recent addition to the Charles Rennie Mackintosh trail, the House for an Art Lover. Although the building was designed in 1901 as an entry to a competition run by a German design magazine, it was not completed until 1996, when it became a centre for Glasgow School of Art postgraduate students, though a number of rooms on the lower floor are open to the public. Mackintosh worked closely with his wife on the design of the house and there is distinctive evidence of her influence, especially in the exquisite **Music Room** with its elaborate symbolism, particularly the rose motif, which is used throughout. But though the detail is, as ever, intense, the overall effect is one of space and light. The exterior of the house is equally impressive and totally original. ■ *Apr-Sep Sun-Thu 1000-1600, Sat 1000-1500; Oct-Mar Sat 1000-1500, Sun 1000-1600; call for weekday access times T3534449. £3.50, £2.50 concession. T3534770. To get there take the Underground to Ibrox station and walk (15 minutes), or bus 91 from Hope St.*

Scotland Street School Museum of Education

Directly opposite Shields Road Underground is another of Charles Rennie Mackintosh's great works, the Scotland Street School, which opened in 1906 and closed in 1979. The entire school has been preserved as a museum of education and is a wonderfully evocative experience. There's a fascinating collection of school memorabilia and reconstructed classrooms from Victorian times up to the 1960s, as well as changing rooms, science room and headmaster's office (straighten your tie and comb your hair before entering).

This was the most modern of Mackintosh's buildings and is notable for its semi-cylindrical glass stair towers, the magnificent tiled entrance hall and his customary mastery of the interplay of light and space. There's also a café, but don't worry, they don't serve authentic school food. ■ *Mon-Thu 1000-1700,*

Glasgow

Fri-Sun 1100-1700. Free. T2870500. Underground to Shields Rd, or buses 89, 90, 96 and 97 from the city centre.

East of Pollock Park
To the east of Pollock Country Park, by Pollockshaws Road, is **Queen's Park**, named after Mary, Queen of Scots, whose reign ended after defeat here, at the Battle of Langside, in 1568. A memorial outside the park marks the site of the battle. It's a pleasant place for a stroll and the views north across the city make it even more enjoyable. Close by, in Mount Florida, is **Hampden Park**, home of Scottish football and now also the home of the new **Scottish National Football Museum**, which describes the history of the game in Scotland. This may strike some as a rather masochistic idea given some of the more infamous and embarrassing episodes, but there have been highs (Wembley '67 and Lisbon '69) as well as lows (Wembley '66 and Argentina '78). ■ *Mon-Sat 1000-1700, Sun 1100-1700. £5, £2.50 concession.Tour of the stadium £2.50. T6166100, www.scottishfootballmuseum.org.uk Regular trains to Mount Florida station from Central station (turn left out of station and head straight downhill till you see the stadium; there are no signs.Buses 5, 12, 31, 37 or 44A.*

Holmwood House
South of Queens Park and Hampden, at 61-63 Netherlee Road in Cathcart, is Holmwood House, designed by Alexander "Greek" Thomson, Glasgow's greatest Victorian architect. Holmwood was built for James Couper, a paper manufacturer, between 1857 and 1858 and is the most elaborate and sumptuously decorated of all the villas Thomson designed for well-to-do industrialists on the outskirts of Glasgow. It was rescued from decline by the National Trust for Scotland in 1994 and is well worth a visit.

The building is a work of genuine originality and has become a monument of international importance, as Thomson was the first modern architect to apply a Greek style to a free, asymmetrical composition. The house also includes features reminiscent of Frank Lloyd Wright, which pre-date the great American architect by some forty years. Thomson designed everything in the house and conservation work is revealing very beautiful and elaborate stencilled decoration and friezes with Greek motifs. The best description of Holmwood comes from Thomas Gildard who wrote in 1888: "If architecture be poetry in stone-and-lime – a great temple an epic – this exquisite little gem, at once classic and picturesque, is as complete, self-contained and polished as a sonnet". ■ *Easter-31 Oct, daily 1330-1730, but access may be restricted at certain times; phone in advance. £2.40, £1.60 child/concession. T6372129. Trains every ½ hr to Cathcart from Central station, or take buses 44 and 46 from the city centre to Cathcart bridge, turn left onto Rannon Rd and walk 10mins to gates.*

Along the Clyde

Arriva buses 23 and 24 go to the Science Centre from Jamaica St
After all the years of neglect, it is good to see that Glasgow's newest, most dazzling development is to be found on the Clyde. The £75 million **Glasgow Science Centre**, 50 Pacific Quay, opened late in 2001 on the south side of the Clyde on the former garden festival site. This enormous complex aims to demystify science, bringing it life with imaginative displays and interactive exhibits covering everything from the human body to the internet. Make time to visit the Glasgow Tower too, which is the tallest free standing building in Scotland at 300 ft. Each of its floors has a theme and takes a serious look at aspects of science, from the basic rules of nature to cloning and genetic modification. At the top there's a viewing cabin and great views over Glasgow and the Clyde. The Centre also contains an IMAX theatre. ■ *Science Mall daily*

1000-1800; Glasgow Tower Sun-Wed 1000-1800, Thu-Sat 1000-2100; IMAX Theatre Sun-Wed 1100-1700, Thu-Sat 1000-2030 (hours subject to change). Science Mall £6.50, £4.50 concession, family available; IMAX or Glasgow Tower £5.50, £4 concession, family available; discounts available. If you purchase tickets to more than 1 attraction. T4205010, www.gsc.org.uk

Opposite the Science Centre is the **Scottish Exhibition and Conference Centre (SECC)**, built in 1987 on the site of the former Queen's Dock and now the country's premier rock and pop venue. Next door is the controversial **Clyde Auditorium**, known locally as the 'Armadillo', which was designed by Sir Norman Foster and built in 1997. Further west, also on the north bank of the Clyde, is a romantic looking sailing ship, the *SS Glenlee* – otherwise known as the **Tall Ship at Glasgow Harbour**, 100 Stobcross Road. Launched in 1896, this three masted ship was built on the Clyde and is one of only five Clydebuilt sailing ships that remain afloat in the world. The tour offers a vivid insight into the daily lives of the sailors and the conditions on board ship in 1896. ■ *Daily 1000-1700, £4.50, £3.95 concession. T3390631, www.glenlee.co.uk*

Further west still, at Braehead, is **Clydebuilt,** a museum charting the close relationship between Glasgow and the Clyde. There's an audio-visual presentation on the history of shipbuilding and displays on a whole range of themes related to the river, from the cotton and tobacco trades, to emigration and immigration. There are also plenty of 'hands-on' activities for kids and temporary exhibitions throughout the year. ■ *Clydebuilt is at junction 25a (west-bound) off the M8 or can be reached .on the Clyde waterbus (see below). T8861013 Mon-Sat 1000-1800, Sun 1100-1700, £3.50, £1.75 concession.*

At Anderston Quay, east of the Science Centre, is **The Waverley**, the world's last ocean going paddle steamer and one of a former fleet of pleasure boats that used to take Glaswegians on trips 'doon the watter' to Clyde coast resorts. She has now had a £4 million refit and has been restored to her original glory. You can take still take day trips on the Waverley along the Clyde to destinations like Dunoon, Largs, the Kyles of Bute and Arran. ■ *Sailings take place from Easter-mid May and from Jun to late Aug, Fri-Mon. T2218152, www.waverleyexcusions.co.uk Office open summer Mon-Sat 0900-1700, winter Mon-Fri 0900-1700. Trips range from £10-30.*

Trips along the Clyde

Next to the Tall Ship is **Seaforce**, a company offering high speed powerboat trips along the Clyde. Trips range from a 15 minute 'taster' (£2.50, £1.50 concession) to a four hour trip to the village of Kilcreggan (includes a chance to visit the village) £30, £15 concession. There's also a mystery tour which goes to, well, it's a surprise.■ *Apr-Sep daily 1300-dusk, Oct-Mar trips can be booked. Office hours 0800-2200. T4007737, www.seaforce.co.uk.*

The **Clyde Waterbus**, Pride of the Clyde, is a river taxi that runs along the Clyde between Broomielaw and Braehead (where there is the large Braehead shopping centre and Clydebuilt maritime museum). ■ *Trips go about every 1½ hrs and include a commentary on the history of the river. T7786635 Services run Mon-Fri from 1045-1815, Sat from 0945, Sun from 1145. £3*

The most unusual tour must be that offered by **glasgowDucks**. This company have several brightly coloured amphibious vehicles that take you through the city and along the Clyde. Tours last 90 minutes and start at Pacific Quay, by the Science Centre. The commentary gives you an insight into the shipbuilding industry on the Clyde and takes you past the last private shipyard on the river. ■ *Tours operate at Easter holidays and from Jun-Oct, weekends only Nov, Dec. £11.50, £8.50 children, booking recommended. T5728381 (bookings T0870-0136140), www.glasgowducks.com*

Glasgow

Clyde Walkway   The Clyde Walkway is a 40-mile walking route which is being developed to link the centre of Glasgow to the Falls of Clyde at Lanark, via the Clyde Valley (see page 241). Sections of the waterfront walk are still rather empty and depressing but the central part, between Victoria Bridge and the SECC, is interesting and takes in some of the more distinguished bridges and much of Glasgow's proud maritime heritage.

Start the walk at **Victoria Bridge**, built in 1854 to replace the 14th century Old Glasgow Bridge, and continue past the graceful **Suspension Bridge**, built in 1851 as a grand entrance to the 'new town' on the south bank. You can cross from here to **Carlton Place**, whose impressive Georgian façades have been restored and which were designed to front the never-completed 'new town'. Back on the north bank is **Customs House Quay** and, further west beyond George V Bridge, **Broomielaw Quay**. From here, Henry Bell's *Comet* inaugurated the world's first commercial passenger steamboat service. This was also the departure point for many Scottish emigrants to North America, and, later, for thousands of holidaying locals heading "doon the watter" to the Firth of Clyde seaside resorts. Further west, at Anderston Quay, is the **P.S. Waverley Terminal** (see above). Between here and the SECC is the huge 175ft high **Finnieston Crane**, which was once used for lifting railway locomotives at a time when Glasgow was the largest builder of these in the world outside North America. Close by is the **Rotunda** (1890-96) which was once the northern terminal of the complex of tunnels which took horse-traffic and pedestrians under the river, until the building of a new road tunnel in the 1960s. The Rotunda has been restored as a restaurant complex. Soon you come to the **Scottish Exhibition and Conference Centre (SECC)** and the **Clyde Auditorium** (the "Armadillo"), sitting opposite the new **Glasgow Science Centre**.

Essentials

Sleeping

The Tourist Information Centre can help find somewhere to stay and also publishes a free accommodation guide   Glasgow has a good range of accommodation. Most of the hotels, guest houses, B&Bs and hostels are in the city centre and the West End or south of the river, around Queen's Park. The best area to find good value mid-range accommodation is the West End, around Kelvingrove Park and the university. This is a good area to stay in, as it's convenient for several of the city's major sights as well as many of the best bars and restaurants. Glasgow has undergone something of a revolution on the hotel front in recent years and the market is highly competitive. A large number of big chains have opened up in the city, offering everything from deluxe accommodation to simple low cost lodging – meaning that there are often good deals available to travellers prepared to shop around. The city also has several boutique hotels, offering stylish accommodation with more character than the international chains. Finding a decent room for the night can be difficult during the major festivals (see page 235) and in Jul and Aug and it's best to book ahead at these times.

City Centre   **L** *Glasgow Hilton*, 1 William St, T2045555, F2045044, www.hilton.com 319 rooms. Gigantic, futuristic-looking luxury hotel regarded as one of the city's best. Full facilities include leisure centre and shopping mall. Their restaurant, *Cameron's*, is also widely held to be one of the finest around (see Eating). **L-A** *Glasgow Moat House*, Congress Rd, T3069988, F2212022, www.moathousehotels.com 283 rooms. Massive glass structure next to the SECC and 'Armadillo' on the banks of the Clyde. 2 excellent restaurants, *Mariner's* and *Dockside No 1*. **L** *Malmaison*, 278 West George St, T5721000, F5721002, glasgow@malmaison. com 72 rooms. Sister hotel of the one in Edinburgh and equally chic and stylish. Superior in every way. Their brasserie is also highly recommended. **A** *Millennium Hotel*, George Sq, T3326711, F3324264, www.millennium-hotels.com 117 rooms. Huge 18th century hotel in the heart of the city, next to Queen St station. Conservatory bar on the ground floor is good for people-watching.

B *Groucho Saint Judes*, 190 Bath St T3528800, F3528801, www.grouchosaintjudes .com An intimate boutique hotel with only 6 bedrooms and a fine dining restaurant. Largest of all and more of a style hotel is the far from cheap **B-L** *Langs Hotel*, 2 Port Dundas Pl, T3320330, www.langshotel.co.uk Has 110 contemporary bedrooms, a trendy bar and Californian inspired restaurant.

C *The Art House*, 129 Bath St, T2216789, www.arthousehotel.com. Stylish refurbishment of former education authority building. Well located and good value. Features Scotlands's first Japanese Teppan-yaki grill. **C-D** *Adelaide's*, 209 Bath St, T2484970, F2264247, www.adelaides.co.uk 8 rooms. Beautiful "Greek" Thomson restoration in the heart of the city centre. **C-D** *Babbity Bowster*, 16-18 Blackfriars St, T5525055. 6 rooms. A local institution and one of the first of the Merchant City townhouses to be renovated. Typical Glaswegian hospitality, a near-legendary pub (see 'Bars' below) and an excellent restaurant (see 'Eating').

D *Cathedral House*, 28/32 Cathedral Sq, T5523519, F5522444. 8 rooms. Overlooking the cathedral. Wonderfully-atmospheric old building with comfortable rooms and very good moderately-priced restaurant (open daily 1030-2400). **D** *The Merchant Lodge*, 52 Virginia St, T5522424, F5524747. 33 rooms. Renovated old building in quiet side street close to the Merchant City's stylish bars and restaurants. Great value.

The city centre also has a range of moderately priced hotels and guesthouses like the **E** *Greek Thomson Hotel*, 140 Elderslie St, T3326556. 17 rooms. Named after Glasgow's less famous architectural son. More of a guest house, with the service that goes with it, and great value. **E** *Rennie Mackintosh Hotel*, 218-220 Renfrew St, T3339992, F3339995. 24 rooms. Another homely guest house exploiting a great architect's name, but they also offer friendly service and superb value for money. **E** *Pipers' Tryst Hotel*, 30-34 McPhater St T353 0220, www.thepipingcentre.co.uk Well established, situated in the piping centre it has 8 rooms. **E** *The Victorian House*, 212 Renfrew St, T3320129, F3533155. 60 rooms. Large, friendly guest house very close to the art college. Superb location and just about the best value in the city centre. There are many other guest houses along Renfrew St, including **E** *The Old School House* ,No 194, T3327600 and **E** *Willow Hotel*, No 228, T3322332.

F *Euro Hostel*, 318 Clyde St, T2222828, F2221095, www.euro-hostels.com 364 beds, all rooms with en suite facilities, includes continental breakfast. A huge multi-storey building overlooking the Clyde.

L *One Devonshire Gardens*, 1 Devonshire Gdns, T3392001, F3371663, www. **West End** one-devonshire-gardens.co.uk 27 rooms. Highly- acclaimed hotel which is the very last word in style and comfort. There are few, if any, classier places to stay in the country. Their restaurant is sensational and is run by celebrity chef Gordon Ramsay (see 'Eating').

B *Kelvin Park Lorne Hotel*, 923 Sauchiehall St, T3149955, F3371659, www.regalhotels.co.uk 100 rooms. Dependable old stalwart and well located for galleries, museums etc.

C *Wickets Hotel*, 52 Fortrose St, T/F3349334, www.wicketshotel.co.uk 10 rooms. Overlooking the West of Scotland cricket ground and close to Partick rail station and Underground. Family-run hotel with good restaurant and its own beer garden.

D *Heritage and Botanic Hotel*, 1 Alfred Terr, by 625 Great Western Rd, T3396955, F3371812, www.hotelsglasgow.com 16 rooms. Good value Victorian townhouse

Glasgow

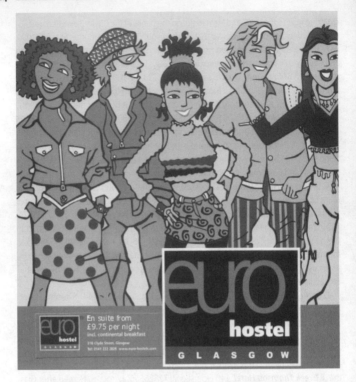

Glasgow

close to the West End action. **D** *Jury's Glasgow Hotel*, Great Western Rd, T3348161, F3343846, www.jurysdoyle.com 137 rooms. Nothing too fancy, but comfortable rooms and good facilities including pool, sauna and gym. Free parking. Very good value. **D** *Kelvin Hotel*, 15 Buckingham Terr, Great Western Rd, T3397143, F3395215, www.scotland2000.com/lomondkelvin 33 rooms. Comfortable guest house in lovely Victorian terrace near Byres Rd and Botanic Gardens. In the same terrace is the smaller **D** *Lomond Hotel*, T3392339. **D** *Kirkland House*, 42 St Vincent Cres, T2483458, kirkland@gisp.net 5 rooms. Small, family-run guest house with that little bit extra. Close to Kelvingrove Park. A few doors down, at No 36, is **D** *Number Thirty Six*, T2482086. **D** *Kirklee Hotel*, 11 Kensington Gate, T3345555, F3393828, www.scotland2000.com/kirklee/9rooms. Lovely Edwardian townhouse with beautiful garden. Close to bars and restaurants on Byres Road and the Botanic Gdns. **D** *The Sandyford Hotel*, 904 Sauchiehall St, T3340000, F3371812, www.sandyfordhotelsglasgow. co.uk 60 rooms. Comfortable and good value hotel convenient for the SECC and art galleries. **D** *The Townhouse*, 4 Hughenden Terr, T3570862, F3399605, www. thetownhouseglasgow.com 10 rooms. Just off the Great Western Rd. Lovely Victorian townhouse offering comfort, hospitality and great value. **D** *The Townhouse Hotel*, 21 Royal Cres, T3329009, F3539604, www.hotels.glasgow.com 20 rooms. Yet another elegantly-restored Victorian townhouse, set back off Sauchiehall St. Good value.

E *Hillhead Hotel*, 32 Cecil St, T3397733, hillhotel@aol.com 11 rooms. Small, friendly hotel ideally placed for the Byres Rd nightlife and close to Hillhead Underground. **E** *Hillview Guest House*, 18 Hillhead St, T3345585, F3533155, kdmcmillan@msn.com 10 rooms. Friendly, good value B&B close to university and Byres Rd.

F *SYHA Youth Hostel*, 7/8 Park Terr, T3323004. 144 beds. This former hotel has been converted into a great hostel with dorms for 4-6, many with en suite facilities. Price includes continental breakfast. It gets very busy in Jul/Aug so you'll need to book ahead. Open 24 hrs. It's a 10-min walk from Kelvinbridge Underground station, or take bus 44 or 59 from Central station and get off at the first stop on Woodlands Rd, then head up the first turning left (Lynedoch St). Close by is **F** *Glasgow Backpackers Hostel*, 17 Park Terr, T3329099, www.scotlands-top-hostels 90 beds. Open 3 Jul-23 Sep. Independent hostel housed in university halls of residence. Also very popular, and cheaper than the *SYHA*. **F** *Berkeley Globetrotters*, 63 Berkeley St, Charing Cross, T2217880/2045470. 30 beds. Open all year, very cheap and popular, so phone ahead to book. It's just past the Mitchell library, on the other side of the M8 heading west from Bath St. Take a 57 bus from the city centre. It incorporates the *BlueSky Backpackers Hostel*, T2211710, next door, which is also open all year. Also in the West End is **F** *Bunkum Backpackers*, 26 Hillhead St, T5814481, www.easyhostel.com It has 32 beds and kitchen facilities.

A-B *Best Western Ewington*, Balmoral Terr, 132 Queen's Dr, T4231152, www.countryhotels.net 43 rooms. Friendly and comfortable hotel in a secluded terrace facing Queen's Park. Their restaurant, *Minstrels*, is superb value and worth a visit in its own right. **A-C** *Sherbrooke Castle Hotel*, 11 Sherbrooke Av T4274227, www.sherbrooke.co.uk is a small hotel (25 rooms) with a bit more character than the chains. It's a good base for exploring the attractions of the south side as it's only about a mile from the Burrell collection.

South Side

   D *Boswell Hotel*, 27 Mansionhouse Rd, T6329812. Just to the south of Queen's Park, off Langside Rd. Lively and informal hotel better known for its excellent pub where you can hear live folk and jazz. **E** *Reidholme Guest House*, 36 Regent Park Sq, T4231855. Small, friendly guest house in a quiet side street near Pollockshaws Rd.

The *University of Glasgow* has a range of **self-catering** accommodation, available Jul-Sep, contact the Conference and Visitor Services, 81 Great George St, T3305385, www.gla.ac.uk/vacationaccommodation *Cairncross House*, 20 Kelvinhaugh Place, off Argyle St near Kelvingrove Park, has rooms to let. It also has **B&B** accommodation at *Dalrymple Hall in the West End*, **E**, available Mar-Apr and Jul-Sep. The *University of Strathclyde*, T5534148, www.strath.ac.uk/department/rescat/sales/index.html A wide range of **B&B** accommodation in its various halls of residence across the city, mostly available Jun-Sep, though a few are open all year round. **E** *Baird Hall*, 460 Sauchiehall St. Open all year. 191 rooms (all shared bathrooms). The pick of the bunch. A beautiful Art Deco high-rise building in a great location. Also cheaper than most of the others. **E** *Chancellors Hall*, Rottenrow East (on campus). 218 en suite rooms. **E** *Garnett Hall*, Cathedral St (on campus). 124 rooms. Also self-catering from £260-330 per week. **E** *Murray Hall*, Collins St (on campus). 70 rooms. Farther out of town, but the cheapest of the lot, is **F** *Jordanhill Campus*, 76 Southbrae Dr. 189 rooms. More salubrious accommodation is available at the **C** *Strathclyde Graduate Business School*, 199 Cathedral St, T5536000, F5536002, www.sgbs.strath.ac.uk/hotel 107 en suite rooms. Open all year.

Campus accommodation & self-catering

There is also plenty of self-catering and serviced accommodation in the city, much of which is quite upmarket. There are *West End Apartments*, 401 North Woodside Rd, T3424060, F3348159, www.glasgowhotelsandapartments.co.uk close to Kelvinbridge Underground, which have 4 apartments to let from £259 per week, and *The Serviced Apartment Company*, SACO House, 53 Cochrane St, T2044610, F2481919, www.sacoapartments.co.uk which has 12 apartments in the Merchant City. Weekly rates from £420.

Glasgow

Camping The only campsite anywhere near the city is *Craigendmuir Park*, Campsie View, Stepps, T7794159/2973. It's four miles northeast of the city centre and a 15-minute walk from Stepps station.

Eating

For those on a tight budget, many city restaurants offer cheap business lunches. Pre-theatre dinner menus also provide an opportunity to sample some of the finest food at affordable prices, if you don't mind eating before 1900. Many of Glasgow's restaurants are open 7 days a week

Glasgow's culinary renaissance continues unabated. Glasgow has always boasted a wide selection of ethnic eateries, particularly **Indian**, **Chinese** and **Italian** restaurants, and these have been joined by a growing number of cuisines from around the globe. **Scottish** cuisine is also well represented, reflecting the growing trend of marrying traditional Scottish ingredients with continental and international flavours and styles. **Vegetarians** are also well catered for. Though there aren't too many exclusively vegetarian or vegan restaurants, most places now offer substantial and imaginative vegetarian menus. Glasgow also reflects the move away from strict culinary national boundaries and towards a more international style. Its many bistros and brasseries feature wide-ranging menus which incorporate everything from Mediterranean cooking to Pacific Rim specialities. They also tend to be more lively and informal places to eat, as well as offering good value for money. And this is one of the city's great strengths. Compared to other cities (ie London), you can eat well and in some style without breaking the bank.

The greatest concentration of eating places is around **Byres Road** in the West End, which is heavily populated by students and therefore the best area for cheap, stylish places to eat. The **Merchant City** contains most of the designer brasseries, which are more expensive, but many of the **bars** serve good food at reasonable prices. Some of the places listed below also appear in the **Bars** section. **Cafés** are often good value places to eat, and these are also listed separately below.

City Centre **Expensive** *The Buttery*, 652 Argyle St, T2218188. Victoriana abounds in this old favourite with its clubby atmosphere. Consistently rated as one of the best in the city, with an emphasis on the finest Scottish fish, seafood and game. Good high-quality wine list. Open Mon-Fri 1200-1430, 1900-2230; Sat 1900-2230. Downstairs is the much cheaper and less formal *The Belfry*, open Mon-Fri 1200-1500, 1700-2300; Sat 1700-2300. *Cameron's*, 1 William St, T2045555. In Glasgow's *Hilton Hotel*. Sublime Scottish cuisine. Pricey but well worth it. No smoking area. Open Mon-Fri 1200-1400, 1900-2200; Sat 1900-2200. *Groucho St Judes*, 190 Bath St, part of the chic small hotel but open to non residents. Very much the in-place for Glasgow's movers and shakers. Modern Scottish food with lots of char-grilled fish and meat and very good puddings. *Ho Wong*, 82 York St, T2213550. Tucked away just off Argyle St, this Chinese restaurant doesn't look much from the outside but inside awaits a memorable Cantonese culinary experience and the city's finest Szechuan food. Not cheap but worth every penny. You can BYOB. Open Mon-Sat 1200-1400, 1800-2330; Sun 1800-2330. *Rogano's*, 11 Exchange Pl, T2484055. A Glasgow culinary institution. Designed in the style of the Cunard liner, *Queen Mary*, and built by the same workers. Looks like the set of a Hollywood blockbuster and you'll need a similar budget to pay the bill, but the seafood is truly sensational. Open daily 1200-1430, 1830-2230. Downstairs is *Café Rogano*, which offers a less stylish alternative, but it's a lot easier on the pocket. Open Sun-Thu 1200-1430, 1830-2230.

Mid-range *Amber Regent*, 50 West Regent St, T3311655. Plush and very upmarket restaurant serving classic Chinese cuisine. Those on a tight budget can also indulge themselves, with half price main courses before 1900 Wed-Sat and all night Mon/Tue. BYOB. Open Mon-Thu 1200-1415, 1730-2300; Fri 1200-1415, 1730-2330; Sat 1200-2400. *Axiom*, Lancefield Quay, 154 Hydepark St, T2212822. Wide-ranging menu featuring contemporary Scottish dishes. Superb value. Open Mon-Sat 1100-2300. *Café Cossachock*, 10 King St, T5530733. Near the Tron Theatre. Cosy, authentic-feeling Russian restaurant with a relaxed, informal atmosphere. Art gallery upstairs. More than just a good meal, it's an entire cultural experience. Open Mon-Sat 1030-late; Sun 1600-late. *Café Gandolfi*, 64 Albion St, T5526813. The first of Glasgow's style bistro/brasseries back in 1979, which almost makes it antique by today's contemporary design standards. Still comfortably continental, relaxed and soothing. Good place for a snack or a leisurely late breakfast. Open Mon-Sat 0900-2330. *City Merchant*, 97-99 Candleriggs, T5531577. The best of Scottish meat and game but it's the fish and seafood which shine. Absolutely superb. It's at the top end of this price range but their two- and three-course set menus are more affordable and excellent value (available 1200-1900). Very popular and a good atmosphere. BYOB. No smoking area. Open Mon-Sat 1200-2300, Sun 1700-2300.

Gordon Yuill and Company, 257 West Campbell St T572 4052, Mon-Sat 0800-2230. New venture from the Rogano's former manager. Smart Pacific Rim food and chic looking interior. *Fratelli Sarti*, 121 Bath St, T2040440. Everything you'd expect from a great Italian restaurant, and a lot more besides. Exceptional value food washed down with the best value bottle of wine in the city. No wonder it's always busy. No smoking area. Open Mon-Sat 0800-2300; Sun 1200-2300. *The Green Room*, Glasgow Royal Concert Hall (see 'Entertainment'), 2 Sauchiehall St, T3323163. Much more than a good place to eat before the show. A superb restaurant in its own right where you can indulge in the finest of Scottish produce at reasonable prices. Good vegetarian selection. No smoking area. Open Mon-Sat 1200-1430, 1730-2130; also Sun (performance days only). *Le Bouchon*, 17 King St, T5527411. A genuine Parisian bistro offering classic French dishes at unbeatable value. Their cheap lunchtime set menu is hugely popular with local professionals. They also do a cheap 2-course pre-theatre supper. Open Mon-Thu 1200-1400, 1730-2400; Fri/Sat 1200-1430, 1700-0100.

Pattaya, 437 Sauchiehall St, T5720071. Top-class, well-presented Thai cuisine in calm, casual surroundings. Good value. Open Mon-Thu 1200-1400, 1730-2330; Fri/Sat 1200-1400, 1730-2400; Sun 1800-2330. *Schottische*, 16-18 Blackfriars St, T5527774. Upstairs from the legendary *Babbity Bowsters* (see below). The best of Scottish food at very affordable prices. Leave room for their diet-busting puddings. Open Mon-Sat 1230-1530, 1830-2100. *Tron Theatre*, Chisholm St, T5528587. Refurbished restaurant offers a dining experience that's worth applauding. The 2-course set lunch is exceptional value. No smoking area. The effortlessly stylish bar is perfect for that pre-prandial tipple. Open Mon-Sat 1200-2200; Sun 1030-1600, 1800-2200.

Cheap *Babbity Bowster*, 16-18 Blackfriars St, T5525055. You can't get away from this place, and why would you want to? Buzzing café-bar housed in a magnificent 18th century building in the heart of the Merchant City. Traditional Scottish and French dishes served with flair. Outrageously good value. The bar is one of the city's perennial favourites (see 'Bars'). Open Mon-Sat 0800-2400; Sun 0900-2400. *Bargo*, 80 Albion St, T5534771. Impressively stylish designer bar serving excellent value bar snacks and meals of superior quality. Definitely a place to be seen in (see 'Bars'). Open Mon-Sat 1100-2400; Sun 1200-2400. *Café Gandolfi @ Habitat*, Buchanan Galleries, 200 Buchanan St, T3311254. From the people who brought you *Café Gandolfi* (see above), a new café-bar made for weary shoppers. Quality Scottish ingredients with flavours from around the world. *Café Clear*, 51 Greendyke St T5526454 Tue-Sun noon-midnight. Part of the Homes for the Future innovative complex of buildings by Glasgow Green, this bar/café serves Mediterranean dishes, sandwiches and soups. *Café Source*, 1 St Andrews Sq (in the church) T5486020, Mon-Fri 1100-2300, Sat 1100-midnight, Sun noon-2300. Great contemporary café offering everything from fishcakes to savoury vegetarian tart. Or just chill out with a latter and read the papers. Live music every Wed from 2000. *Canton Express*, 407 Sauchiehall St, T3320145. No-frills, cheap and filling Chinese fast food at any hour of the day or night. Open daily 1200-0500.

Glasgow Noodle Bar, 482 Sauchiehall St, T3331883. Oriental fast food eaten from disposable containers with plastic chopsticks or forks. Very cheap chow and great after a heavy night on the town. Open daily 1200-0500. *The Granary*, 82 Howard St, T2263770. Behind the St Enoch Centre. Serves good, honest and wholesome vegetarian food. Big portions, big value, fast counter service. Popular with office workers and shoppers at lunchtimes. No smoking area. Open Mon-Sat 0900-1730; Sun 1100-1700. *Ichiban Japanese Noodle Café*, 50 Queen St, T2044200. Excellent value, healthy Japanese specialities in cool, modern surroundings. BYOB. No smoking. Open Mon-Fri 1200-1600, 1730-2300; Sat 1200-2300; Sun 1300-2200. *Tempus at the CCA*, 350 Sauchiehall St, T3327959. Set in the recently refurbished Centre for Contemporary Arts this café/restaurant serves contemporary Scottish dishes. The menu is flexible and you can just drop in for a coffee and a snack if you don't want lunch. Upstairs (also reached via Scott St) is the *CCA Bar* which serves sandwiches and coffees. It is notable for its décor, designed by artist Jorge Pardo, which is a psychedelic creation with lots of bright colours and carved wood. Daily 1100-midnight (last order for food 2130). *Wee Curry Shop*, 7 Buccleuch St, T3530777. Son of *Mother India* (see below). Small in every sense except flavour and value. Quite simply the best cheap curry this side of Bombay, in a cosy, relaxed atmosphere. Good vegetarian options and incredible value 3-course buffet lunch. BYOB. Open Mon-Sat 1200-1430, 1730-2300; Sun 1730-2300.

West End **Expensive** *Amaryllis*, 1 Devonshire Gdns, T3392001. Part of the luxurious *One Devonshire Gardens Hotel* (see 'Sleeping').Award-winning restaurant run by celebrity chef, Gordon Ramsay. Nuff said. No smoking. Open Sun-Fri 1230-1400, 1915-2200; Sat 1915-2200. *La Parmigiana*, 443 Great Western Rd, T3340686. This sophisticated Italian restaurant is one of Glasgow's finest eating establishments. Recommended for a special occasion. Open Mon-Sat 1200-1430, 1800-2300. *Nairn's*, 13 Woodside Cres, T3530707. Much-hyped restaurant run by TV chef Nick Nairn, but deserving of all the praise. Exceptional cuisine and superb value. Open daily 1200-1400, 1800-2200. *Puppet Theatre*, 11 Ruthven La, T3398444. Very stylish, very intimate dining. Menu is Scottish with an international flavour. Good value set lunches. Open Sun and Tue-Fri 1200-1430, 1900-2230; Sat 1900-2300. *Stravaigin*, 28-30 Gibson St, T3342665. Hard to define but difficult to resist. An eclectic mix of exotic Asian flavours and prime Scottish ingredients to produce the most sublime results. Expensive but you won't get better value for money in this category and totally justifies its many awards. Upstairs is a café-bar where you can sample some of that fabulous food at more affordable prices. Open Mon-Thu 1200-1430, 1700-2230; Fri/Sat 1200-1430, 1700-2300; Sun 1700-2230. *The Ubiquitous Chip*, 12 Ashton La, T3345007. A ground-breaking, multi award-winning restaurant and still the city's favourite place for Mctastic Scottish food, especially venison and seafood. All served in a plant-filled, covered courtyard patio. Open Mon-Sat 1200-1430, 1730-2300; Sun 1230-1430, 1830-2300. Upstairs is their bistro, *Upstairs at the Chip*, which doesn't make you feel quite as special but is much easier on the wallet. Open daily 1200-2300.

Mid-range *Air Organic*, 36 Kelvingrove St, T5645200/5201. Ultra-cool bistro. The type that could only really exist in Glasgow. Styled on Miami International Airport and serving organic and orgasmic food. Try their Thai or Japanese offerings. No smoking area. Open Mon-Thu and Sun 1100-2300; Fri/Sat 1100-2400. *Ashoka Ashton Lane*, 19 Ashton La, T3371115. First-class Indian restaurant, part of the famous west coast chain. Very popular with students and Byres Road trendies. Open Mon-Thu 1200-2400; Fri/Sat 1200-0030; Sun 1700-2400. *Ashoka West End*, 1284 Argyle St, T3393371. The oldest in this ever-popular chain of excellent Indians. Great value and a vegetarian-friendly menu. Open Mon-Thu 1200-1400, 1700-0030; Fri 1200-0100; Sat 1700-0100; Sun 1700-0030. *Beetlenut*, 142 Dumbarton Rd, T3371145. Imaginative, international-flavour food served in a relaxed atmosphere. Good at any time of the day and child-friendly. New addition to the West End's already busy cuisine scene but manages to fill a gap. Open Mon-Sat 1100-0100; Sun 1200-0100. *Brel*, 39-43 Ashton La. Another stylish continental eating establishment in Glasgow's hippest culinary quarter. This time it's Belgian. Great food and great value, especially during the half price happy hour (1700-1900). Open Mon-Thu and Sun 1000-2300; Fri/Sat 1000-2400.

Café India, 171 North St, T2484074. Cavernous Indian restaurant that's big on style and has a deserved reputation for fine food. Good value buffet downstairs. No smoking area. Open Mon-Thu 1200-2400; Fri/Sat 1200-0030; Sun 1500-2400. *Cottier's*, 93-95 Hyndland St, T3575825. Very elegant Latin American restaurant housed in a converted church. The food is heavenly and the ambience spiritually rewarding. These dear souls are also great with kids, bless them. Stylish bar and theatre downstairs on the ground floor where you can often hear live music (see 'Live music venues' below). Open Mon-Thu 1700-2230; Fri/Sat 1700-2400; Sun 1200-2230. *Cul de Sac*, 44-46 Ashton La, T3344749. Effortlessly fashionable, laid back and oh, so boho. A great place to sit back, soak up the atmosphere and enjoy good French-style food. Their famous crêpes are half price between 1700 and 1900, as are the tasty burgers and pasta. Good vegetarian choices, too, and it's a great place to work of last night's excesses with a hearty Sun brunch. Open Sun-Thu 1200-2300; Fri/Sat 1200-2400. *Deirfiuracha*, 29 Ashton La T3373636. Unusual Gaelic restaurant run by two sisters and very popular with those in the know. Puddings are particularly good. Tue-Sat 1800-2130. *Mother India*, 28 Westminster Terr, Sauchiehall St, T2211663. Exquisite Indian cooking at affordable prices. Friendly and informal atmosphere. Strong vegetarian selection. Cheap set lunch and pre-theatre menus. BYOB (no drinks licence). Open Mon-Thu 1200-1400, 1730-2300; Fri 1200-1400, 1700-2330; Sat 1200-2330; Sun 1700-2300. *Oblomov*, 372-374 Great Western Rd, T3399177. A deliciously decadent slice of Eastern Europe. The dark, sumptuous decor and classic cuisine are enhanced by an accompanying string quartet. Open Sun-Thu 1100-2300; Fri/Sat 1100-2400.

Cheap *The Canal*, 300 Bearsden Rd, T9545333. Stylish and upmarket American diner beside the Forth and Clyde Canal. Good grub, and beer from its very own microbrewery on the premises. Open Sun-Thu 1200-2200; Fri/Sat 1200-2300. *Grassroots Café*, 97 St Georges Rd, T3330534. Vegetarian and vegan food at this intimate café near St Georges Cross. Lots of soups and salads and filling main courses. Mon-Sun 1000-2200. *Otago*, 61 Otago St T3372282. There's a cool, minimalist look to this Mediterranean bistro that offers lots of veggie choices. Good selection of wines too. Mon-Sat 1100-2200. *Sal e Pepe*, 18 Gibson St, T3410999. This little Italian is one of those places you just can't stop talking about (or writing about). It is, quite simply, perfect in every sense. And as if that weren't enough, there are half price pizza and pasta offers weekdays between 1500 and 1800. What more could you want? Open Mon-Sat 0930-1100; Sun 1200-2300.

Mid-range *Arigo*, 67 Kilmarnock Rd T6366616. Good Italian restaurant offering high quality fresh food. The sort of place that doesn't need to advertise. Mon-Fri noon-1430, 1700-2230, Sat noon-1600, 1700-2230, Sun noon-1630, 1700-2230. *Ashoka Southside*, 268 Clarkston Rd, T6370711. Small and intimate Southside version of this venerable chain of Indian restaurants. Open Mon-Sat 1700-2400; Sun 1700-2300. *Cul de Sac Southside*, 1179 Pollockshaws Rd, T649-1819. Wee sister to the West End original (see above). Same excellent food and atmosphere. Open Mon-Thu 1200-1430,

South Side

Glasgow

1700-0100; Sat/Sun 1200-0100. *Spice Garden*, 11-17 Clyde Pl, T4294422. There's an enormous choice at this popular Indian restaurant that prides itself on its cleanliness. It's conveniently open all night so good for those desperate for a post-club curry. Daily 1800-0430.

Cheap *Buongiorno*, 1021 Pollockshaws Rd, T6491029. The best pizza in Glasgow – at these prices? Impossible, surely. Well, check it for yourself. Impeccable Italian family cooking, with cosy ambience to match. They even have a pre-theatre two-for-one deal! Are they crazy? Simply unbeatable, so book ahead. Open Mon-Sat 0900-2300; Sun 1000-2200.

Cafés

The cafés listed below also serve food and are often the most economical option for a midday snack or meal

Glasgow prides itself on its café society and many of the new, trendy designer cafés make it seem more like Barcelona or Greenwich Village than the west coast of Scotland. Glasgow is also full of authentic Italian cafés where you can enjoy a cheap fry-up washed down with frothy cappuccino. Whatever your preference, you won't have any trouble finding the right place for that essential caffeine shot during a hard day's sightseeing or shopping. Glasgow is also the home of the tearoom and those who insist on their mid-afternoon infusion won't be disappointed.

City Centre *Borders*, 98 Buchanan St, T2227700. Inside *Borders* bookshop. Browse while you enjoy some good coffee (free refills) and delicious cakes and scones, or a fresh fruit smoothie, or a light snack. Also live jazz bands on Fri nights (see 'Entertainment'). No smoking area. Open Mon-Sat 0800-2300; Sun 1100-2130. *Café Cosmo*, 12 Rose St. Part of the Glasgow Film Theatre (see 'Entertainment') and definitely worth knowing about, even if you're not a movie buff. It's a great cheap lunch venue, especially for vegetarians. Open daily 1200-2100. *Costa*, Royal Exchange Square. Part of the reputable chain which has several other outlets in the city. Good quality coffee and a good range of snacks, salads and meals. Open daily 0800 till late. *The Doocot Café and Bar*, The Lighthouse, 11 Mitchell Lane, T2211821. There's a 1950s retro look at this café on the top of the Lighthouse (see sights). Stop for soups, sandwiches and light meals before immersing yourself in the world of architecture. *Miss Cranston's Tearooms*, 33 Gordon St T2041122. You could miss this traditionally run tea-shop as it's hidden above a baker's shop. This is the place to come for a full blown afternoon tea with sandwiches, scones, cakes and gallons of tea. *Willow Tea Rooms*, 217 Sauchiehall St, T3320521. A recreation of the original Miss Cranston's Tearooms, designed by Charles Rennie Mackintosh and filled with many of his original features. Most visitors come here for the interior design, but they also offer a good selection of reasonably-priced teas, sandwiches, cakes and scones, as well as hot meals. There's also a sister branch at 97 Buchanan St (T2045242), which is licensed. No smoking area. Open Mon-Sat 0930-1630; Sun 1200-1615. *Where the Monkey Sleeps*, 182 West Regent St, T2263406 is a relaxed exhibition space/café. Good cappucinos and sandwiches, as well as soups from Eurasia (see above). Exhibits and sells works of new artists, including graduates of Glasgow and London schools of art. Mon-Sat 0700-1900, Sat 1000-1900, Sun 1100-1900.

West End Brasserie Metro, 8 Cresswell La, T3388131. Big and bright West End café/deli just off Byres Rd that's popular with students. Wide-ranging menu makes it a good, cheap choice for lunch. No smoking area. Open Mon-Sat 0800-1800; Sun 0900-1800. *Grosvener Café*, 31 Ashton La, T3391848. Behind Hillhead Underground. A perennial favourite with local students who come for the wide selection of cheap food (filled rolls, soup, burgers, pizzas, etc). Cosy and friendly atmosphere. Good Sun brunch, and Thai food in the evenings. Open Mon 0900-1900; Tue-Sat 0900-2300; Sun 1030-1730.

Insomnia, 38-42 Woodlands Rd, T5641700. 24-hr café/deli where the menu changes with the mood. Still the best place for late-night refuelling, whether it's a caffeine kick, herbal infusion or a cheap bite to eat. BYOB. No smoking area. Open daily. *Tinderbox*, 189 Byres Rd, T3393108. Coffee shop which looks and feels more like a style bar. Great coffee, good magazines to read and a large no smoking, child-friendly area. Open daily 0800-2200. *University Café*, 87 Byres Rd, T3395217. A gloriously authentic Italian Art Deco café, where grannies and students sit shoulder-to-shoulder enjoying real cappuccino, great ice cream and good, honest and cheap mince and tatties, pie and chips, sausage rolls, gammon steak and all the other golden oldies. Open Mon-Fri 0900-2200; Sat 0900-2230; Sun 1000-2200.

Art Lovers' Café, Bellahouston Park, Drumbreck Rd, T3534779. Housed in CRM's exquisite House for an Art Lover. A nice place to chill and a good selection of light snacks and hot and cold meals. Also live jazz on Sat nights in the bar. No smoking. Open Sun-Fri 1000-1700; Sat also 1830-2400. *Chisholm's*, 145 Kenmure St. No-nonsense traditional caff serving very cheap filled rolls and fry-ups to a grateful public. Open Mon-Fri 0900-1730; Sat 0930-1700; Sun 1100-1700.

South Side

Bars and pubs

Forget all the tired old clichés about Glasgow and Glaswegians, a night out in Scotland's largest city is a memorable experience – for all the right reasons. Glasgow is bursting at the seams with bars and pubs to suit all tastes, from ornate Victorian watering holes to the coolest of designer bars, where you can listen to thumping dance beats before heading off to a club. DJs normally start at 2100 till 2400 and entry is usually free, with some places charging after 2300 when they transform into clubs. One of the best areas for the sheer number and variety of pubs and bars is the **West End**, with its large student population.

Most pubs and bars open till 2400, though a few are open later, and many of them close at 2300 on weekdays and Sun

Note that there's bound to be some overlap between bars, cafés, bistros and restaurants. Many of the bars listed below, especially those in the Merchant City and West End, serve very good food at reasonable prices, and the best of these are also included in the 'Eating' section. Similarly, many of the **cafés** and **bistros** listed under their respective sections are among the best places to enjoy a drink. Also note that many bars feature regular **live bands** and **comedy nights**, and the most notable of these are listed separately (see 'Comedy' and 'Live music venues' below).

The Arches Café Bar, 253 Argyle St. Part of the legendary club, this stylish basement bar is the perfect place to linger over a Belgian beer or enjoy their food. Open daily 1200-2000; bar open 1100-2400. *Babbity Bowster*, 16-18 Blackfriars St. Prime Merchant City pub that has everything; lively atmosphere, wide selection of real ales and good food (see also 'Eating'). *Bar 10*, 10 Mitchell St. This converted warehouse is Glasgow's original style bar and still as cool as ever. Good food on offer and a popular pre-club meeting place at weekends with regular DJs. *Bar 91*, 91 Candleriggs. Another cool style bar, but comfortable and relaxed and a good place to eat. Happy hour specials 1700-2000. *Bargo*, 80 Albion St (see also 'Eating'). Stylish and spacious Merchant City bar/bistro with surprisingly good food and a high posing quotient. *Blackfriars*, 36 Bell St. Merchant city favourite which pulls in the punters with its vast range of international beers and lagers. Also a wide range of excellent grub, live music and comedy at weekends and that inimitable Glasgow atmosphere (see also 'Comedy' and 'Live music venues' below). *The Cask and Still*, 154 Hope St. Formerly the *Pot Still* and famous for its massive range of malts (around 500 of them). They also have a selection of cask ales and decent pub grub. Closed Sun. *The Gate*, 408 Sauchiehall St. New addition to the long list of style bars and another popular pre-club place. Cool and intimate at the

City Centre

same time and great value for lunch. Happy hour is 1200-2000 (!) and DJs pump up the volume Thur-Sat. *The Griffin*, 226 Bath St. Opposite the King's Theatre. Turn of the century pub (not the most recent one) recently renovated but losing none of its style. Still the best place in the city for pie and chips and a drink (only £2.75!). Other traditional dishes, plus vegetarian, at amazing value.

Havana, 50 Hope St, T2484466. Is it a bar, is it a restaurant, or is it a club? All three, in fact. Latin grooves, Latin food and Latin spirit, all rolled into one. Coming here is like stepping into a Bacardi advert. Ay, Caramba! (See also 'Nightclubs'). Open Mon-Wed and Sun 1200-2400; Thur-Sat 1200-0100. *The Horse Shoe Bar*, 17 Drury La, between Mitchell St and Renfield St, near the station. Classic Victorian Gin Palace that is still one of the city's favourites. Its much-copied island bar is the longest continuous bar in the UK, so it shouldn't take long to get served, which is fortunate as it gets very busy. Incredibly good-value lunch served till 1430, then all day till 1900 upstairs and perhaps the cheapest pint in town. If you only visit one pub during your stay, then make sure it's this one. *The Lounge*, 142 West Regent St. Stylish, yet comfortable basement bar that's very popular with city suits due to its great value lunch specials. *The Mitre Bar*, 12-16 Brunswick St. A great traditional Glasgow pub in the midst of the Merchant City's cool designer bars. Good *craic*, cheap grub and fine ales. *Mojo*, 158a Bath St. One of Glasgow's funkiest bars with cool sounds for that pre-club drink. Good food served through the back in a more intimate atmosphere (see 'Eating'). *Rab Ha's*, 83 Hutcheson St. This old Merchant City stalwart still packs 'em in. It has an enviable reputation for its food and is above the restaurant of the same name. *The Scotia Bar*, 112 Stockwell St. This old East End pub also claims to be the oldest in town, and its low ceilings and wooden beams support a convincing argument. Its also the best place in town for folk music (see 'Live music venues' below), and much-frequented by writers, poets and drinking thinkers (or thinking drinkers).

West End *The Attic*, 44-46 Ashton Pl. Above the *Cul de Sac* restaurant (see 'Eating'). Stylish designer bar where you can enjoy tasty tapas and a bottle of plonk in cool, calm surroundings. Also good for a sandwich and fresh fruit smoothie at lunchtime. *The Brewery Tap*, 1055 Sauchiehall St. Classic student haunt, within skiving distance of the university. Convivial atmosphere, cheap food and a good selection of ales on tap are all major attractions, as are the weekday happy hour (1700-1900) and regular live music sessions (see 'Live music venues' below). *Firebird*, 1321 Argyle St. Yet another of the city's never-ending stream of new style bars, but this one has the distinct advantage of providing excellent food, especially their pizzas. Happy hour 1700-1900 daily and DJs Thu-Sun. *The Halt Bar*, 160 Woodlands Rd. T5641527. This erstwhile tram stop (hence the name) is one of Glasgow's great unspoiled pubs with many of the original Edwardian fixtures intact. Also a good place to see live music two or three times a week (see 'Live music venues' below).

The Living Room, 5-9 Byres Rd. Near Kelvinhall Underground. Cool, relaxing space with good music and a wide choice of food throughout the day. Plenty of drinks promos, a happy hour, and DJs five nights a week are other reasons to pay a visit. *Uisge Beatha*, 232 Woodlands Rd. The "water of life" is one of those pubs you go into for a wee drink and you're still there many hours later, the day's plans in ruins around your feet. Looks and feels like a real Highland hostelry. Cosy and welcoming and serving ridiculously cheap food. Scottish in every sense, right down to the effigy of Mrs T's head strung up by a tartan scarf (if only it were real!).

South Side *Boswell Hotel*, 27 Mansionhouse Hotel. Lively Queen's Park favourite with a good selection of real ales and regular live music sessions. Noted for its good food; also has rooms (See also 'Sleeping'). *The Church on the Hill*, 16 Algie St. Popular Southside bar housed in an old church. Stained glass windows, beer garden, contemporary menu and DJs preach to the converted at weekends. *Heraghty's Free House*, 708 Pollockshaws Rd. The best pint of Guinness in Glasgow in an old-style Irish pub with old-style hospitality and old-style prices (no need for happy hours here). And they even have a ladies' toilet, proving that everything comes to those who wait! *Samuel Dow's*, 69-71 Nithsdale Rd. Or Sammy Dow's as it's known by its many Shawlands regulars. A friendly Southside local serving good ale and cheap bar food. Also regular live folk music nights. *The Taverna*, 778 Pollockshaws Rd. Popular Southside venue near the Tramway Theatre and Queen's Park. Nice, bright Mediterranean look and feel which extends to their love of kids. Good selection of ales and European beers and good value food, especially their pre-theatre dinner. Next door is a good Greek restaurant.

Entertainment

It's been a few years now since Glasgow was chosen as 'City of Culture' but the legacy lives on and the city continues to enjoy a wide span of art, theatre, film and music. The majority of the larger **theatres, concert halls** and **cinemas** are concentrated in the city centre, though its two most renowned theatres, the Citizens' and the Tramway, are to be found south of the Clyde.

Details of all the city's events are listed in the two local newspapers, *The Herald* and the *Evening Times*. Another excellent source of information is the fortnightly listings magazine *The List*, which also covers Edinburgh and which is on sale in most newsagents. To book **tickets** for concerts or theatre productions, call at the Ticket Centre, City Hall, Candleriggs (open Mon-Sat 0900-1800; Sun 1200-1700). Phone bookings T2874000 (Mon-Sat 0900-2100; Sun 0900-1800). Note that some of the **live music venues** don't have their own box office. For tickets and information go to Tower Records, on Argyle St, T2045788.

When it comes to **nightlife**, Glasgow is a city of energy and passion. Its **club scene** is amongst the most vibrant in the UK. Opening times are pretty much the same all over with doors opening from 2300-0300. Entry costs vary from £2-5 for smaller mainstream clubs and £5-10 for the bigger venues, up to £20 for some of the special club nights with top class DJs.

Art galleries Apart from the large, main galleries listed under 'Sights', there are many small, independent galleries showcasing contemporary local, Scottish and international artists. The *Glasgow Galleries Guide*, free from any of the galleries, lists all current exhibitions. The following galleries are amongst the most interesting. *Art Exposure Gallery*, 19 Parnie St (behind the *Tron Theatre*), T5527779. Open Mon-Sat 1200-1700. *Collins Gallery*, 22 Richmond St, T5482558. Part of Strathclyde University campus. Open Mon-Fri 1000-1700; Sat 1200-1600. *Compass Gallery*, 178 West Regent St, T2216370. Open Mon-Sat 1000-1730. *Cyril Gerber Fine Art*, 148 West Regent St, T2213095/2040276. Open Mon-Sat 0930-1730. *Fireworks*, 35a Dalhousie St, T3324969. Open Tue-Sat 1000-1800. Ceramic gallery and workshop. *Glasgow Print Studio Gallery*, 1st floor, 22 King St, T5520704, www.gpsart.co.uk Open Tue-Sat 1000-1730. Opposite is *The Original Print Shop*. *Street Level Gallery*, 26 King St, T5522151. Open Tue-Sat 1000-1730.

Cinemas There are mainstream multiplexes throughout the city, such as the 9-screen *Odeon Cinema*, at 56 Renfield St, T0870-5050007 . For more discerning film-goers, there's the *Glasgow Film Theatre* (*GFT*), at 12 Rose St, T3326535, with an excellent programme of art-house movies and a good bar for discussion later. In the West End is the *Grosvener*, in Ashton La, off Byres Rd, T3394928. An old 2-screen cinema showing art-house and mainstream films.

Glasgow

Comedy venues	*The Stand Comedy Club*, 333 Woodlands Rd, T0870-6006055. Top notch comedy Thu-Sun. *Blackfriars*, 36 Bell St, T5525924. Regular slots on Sun nights. Also live jazz (see below). *Curlers*, 256 Byres Rd, T3386511. Next to Hillhead Underground. Real student hole which claims to be the oldest pub in the city. Live comedy on Wed nights, also live bands (see below) and DJs at weekends. *The State Bar*, 148 Holland St, T3322159. Good comedy club on Thu nights. Also live blues on Tue and a good selection of real ales. Not a bad pub, actually. *Waxy's*, 20 Candleriggs, T5528717. In the Merchant City. Comedy on Thu nights, and added attractions such as cheap cocktails and mega-cheap lunches.

Concert halls *City Halls*, Candleriggs, T2875024. Smaller-scale classical music events. Home of the Scottish Chamber Orchestra. *Henry Wood Hall*, 73 Claremont St, T2044540/2263868. HQ of the Royal Scottish National Orchestra. *Royal Concert Hall*, 2 Sauchiehall St, T3326633. Prestigious venue for orchestras and big-name rock, pop and soul acts. *The Royal Scottish Academy of Music and Drama*, 100 Renfrew St, T3324101. Varied programme of international performances. *Theatre Royal*, Hope St, T3329000. The home of the generally excellent Scottish Opera and Scottish Ballet, also regularly hosts large-scale touring theatre and dance companies and orchestras.

Gay clubs & bars Glasgow's gay scene has grown around the trendy bars and cafés of the Merchant City, especially Virginia St, Wilson St and Glassford St. *Bennet's*, 90 Glassford St, T5525761. Glasgow's main gay club. Wed-Sun 2300-0330. *Café Delmonica's*, 68 Virginia St, T5524803. Daily 1200-2400. Free. A fun place and a very up-for-it crowd. DJs at weekends. *Revolver*, 6a John St, T5532456. Mon-Sat 1100-2400, Sun 1230-2400. Free. Sexy new bar with interesting theme nights. *Polo Lounge*, 84 Wilson St, T5531221. Mon-Thu 1700-0100, Fri-Sun 1700-0300. £5 or free before 2300 Mon-Thu. Very classy bar popualr with young professionals. Very busy at weekends. *Sadie Frost's*, 8-10 West George St, T3328005. Mon-Sat 1200-2400, Sun 1400-2400. Free. Underneath Queen St station. Very busy and noisy. Sun is women only in the Blue Room. *Waterloo Bar*, 306 Argyle St, T2295891. Mon-Sat 1200-2400, Sun 1230-2300. Glasgow's oldest gay bar, attracts a more mature working-class clientele. Unpretentious and great fun.

Live music venues *Barrowlands*, Gallowgate, T5524601. Famous old East End ballroom and now Glasgow's liveliest and best-loved gig venue. Popular with acts just breaking through and big names trying to rediscover what it's all about. Cathouse, 15 Union St, T2486606. Glasgow's only rock club. Ideal for seeing bands before they make it big. *Clutha Vaults*, 167 Stockwell St, T5527520. Well-known pub which has live music nights from a wide range of local talent. *Cottier's*, 93-95 Hyndland St, T3573868. Good venue for more esoteric music acts, also jazz and blues (see also 'Eating'). *The Garage*, 490 Sauchiehall St, T3321120. Medium-sized venue for bands on the verge of a breakthrough. *The Halt Bar*, 160 Woodlands Rd, T5641527. Popular bar featuring live indie/pub rock bands two or three times a week (see also 'Bars'). *King Tut's Wah Wah Hut*, 272a St Vincent St, T2215279. Glasgow's hallowed live music venue. Many a famous band has made the break in this cramped, sweaty club. Good bar downstairs for a pre-gig drink. *Nice 'n' Sleazy*, 421 Sauchiehall St, T3330900. Great bar and music venue. Everything from indie to rock downstairs while musos hang out in upstairs bar. *The Scotia Bar*, 112 Stockwell St, T5528681. A Glasgow institution and home of Glasgow's folk scene. *Scottish Exhibition and Conference Centre (SECC)*, Finnieston Quay, T2483000. Gigantic multi-purpose venue with all the atmosphere of a disused aircraft hangar. Plays host to the likes of Robbie Williams and Pavarotti. *13th Note Café* , 50-60 King St, T5531638. Another major player on the alternative live music scene. Popular and lively venue for up-and-coming indie/rock bands. Also good veggie food in the bar upstairs (see 'Eating'). Also *13th Note Club*, 260 Clyde St, T2432177, which plays host to unsigned bands.

Alaska, 142 Bath La, T2481777. Home of the city's Soma label, so hosts some of the **Nightclubs**
best club nights. *Archaos*, 25 Queen St, T2043189. A younger more dressy crowd
come here for house, techno and club classics in this massive venue. *The Arches*, 253
Argyle St, T0901-0220300. Cavernous space under Central station. Glasgow's finest
and always at the cutting edge of the UK dance scene. *Babaza*, 24 Royal Exchange
Sq, T2040101. Unusual interior, up-for-it crowd who love their R&B and hip hop.
Cube, 34 Queen St, T2268990. Increasingly popular plays host to a musical mix of
club nights 5 nights a week. Gay nights on Mon and Tue. *Fury Murry's*, 96 Maxwell St,
T2216511. Behind the St Enoch Centre. An eclectic crowd get down to a mix of dance
and student faves. *The Garage*, 490 Sauchiehall St, T3321120. Downbeat, sticky student haunt featuring the usual cheesy retro stuff that they seem to love, and cheap
drinks, which always go down well. Occasional live bands. More of an old-fashioned
getting bevvied up and copping off kind of place. *Havana*, 50 Hope St, T2484466
(see also 'Bars'). More of a bar with dancing, and only open till 0100 at weekends, but
they play the hottest Latin grooves you can find. *MAS*, 29 Royal Exchange Sq,
T2217080. Temporary home of the legendary *Sub Club*, which will open up soon
after suffering fire damage at its real home on Jamaica St. Privilege, Hope St,
T2045233. Crazy club with busy club nights, especially 'Shagtag', an appropri-
ately-named night of house and tance where you're guarantted to score. *The Tunnel*, 84 Mitchell St, T2041000. A new Millenium and still going strong as one of the
city's prime club venues. *The Velvet Rooms*, Sauchiehall St, T3320755. Small and stu-
diously hip bar/club for those who wish to worship at the altar of groove.

The Arches, 30 Midland St, T2219736. In the railway arches under Central station. Pres- **Theatre**
ents more radical and experimental theatre. Also home to one of the city's major clubs
(see 'Nightclubs' above). *Centre for Contemporary Arts* (CCA), 350 Sauchiehall St,
T3327521. Hosts contemporary dance and theatre, as well as staging various art exhibitions. *Citizens' Theatre*, 119 Gorbals St, T4290022. Just across the river. Home to
some of the UK's most exciting and innovative drama. Main auditorium and two
smaller studios. Big discounts for students and the unemployed. *King's Theatre*, 294
Bath St, T2485153. The city's main traditional theatre presenting musicals, panto and
that kind of thing. *Mitchell Theatre*, 3 Granville St, T2874855. At Charing Cross. Stages
various drama productions as well as occasional jazz concerts. *Theatre Royal* (see 'Concert Halls' above). Primarily a concert hall but also stages high-brow theatre, darling.
Tramway Theatre, 25 Albert Drive, T4222023. Just off Pollockshaws Rd. Interna-
tionally-renowned venue with varied programme of innovative and influential theatre,
dance, music and art exhibitions. *Tron Theatre*, 63 Trongate, T5524267. Major contemporary theatre productions. Also musical performances and big-name comedy acts.
Home to a very fine bar and restaurant (see 'Eating').

Festivals

Glasgow doesn't like to be overshadowed by Edinburgh, and has a few notable festivals of its own. Things kick off in the last 2 weeks of **Jan** with the **Celtic Connections**
music festival, featuring artists form around the world. It is held in the *Royal Concert
Hall* (T3538000). The city's biggest festival is the **West End Festival**, 2 weeks of
music, theatre and various free events held over 2 weeks in **Jun** (T3410844). Other
festivals include the **RSNO Proms**, at the Royal Concert Hall in **Jun**, the **Glasgow
International Jazz Festival** (T5523552) in **Jul**, and the **World Pipe Band Championships** (T2215414) which are held on Glasgow Green in **mid-Aug**. **Glasgay** is Britain's largest lesbian and gay arts festival held in various venues from **late Oct** to **early
Nov**. T3347129. For further information, contact Glasgow City Council's events
department (T2872000).

Shopping

Glasgow is a shopaholic's paradise. The best city in the UK after London provides endless opportunities for retail therapy. **Merchant City** is the home of the *Italian Centre*, Glasgow's most upmarket shopping area. This is the home of *Armani* and *Versace*, as well as some other upmarket shops, cafés and restaurants. There's also a branch of *Cruise* on Ingram St. Not far away is *Innhouse* on Wilson St, which has lots of contemporary designer homeware by names like Alessi. *Hutcheson's Hall* on Ingram St (see above) is a good place for original crafts by Scottish designers. The art galleries on *King St* like Glasgow Print Studio (see sights above) are all good places in which to seek out new and original artworks. Also on King St, in Kings Court, is *ESD*, which sells funky ladies clothing and retro designs. And of course there's *The Barras*, The Barras Centre, London Rd (Sat, Sun 0900-1700), Glasgow's famous East End market with over 1000 traders flogging their wares. Worth coming if only to hear their patter.

On **Buchanan St** the possiblities are endless. You can not only find all the usual high street stores, but designer names and some specialist stores. At the top of Buchanan St, just minutes from Queen St station, is the city's newest shopping centre *Buchanan Galleries*. Along Buchanan St itself you'll find plenty of good clothes and shoe shops like *Press and Bastyan*, *Diesel*, *Hobbs* and *Office*. Trendies will also want to check out *Urban Outfitters* which is full of '70s items and retro gear. There's also a *Fraser's* department store and a large branch of *Graham Tiso*, the outdoor shop, which has 5 floors of boots, waterproofs and anything else you'll need for exploring the hills. If you've set your heart on a kilt make for *Hector Russell*, kiltmakers who also do kilts for hire. Booklovers won't find any of these shops however as they'll be blissfully browsing in the large branch of *Borders*. Also on Buchanan St is the extremely stylish Princes *Square*. Clothes and shoe shops include *Karen Millen*, *French Connection*, *Calvin Klein*, *Pied a Terre* and *Phase Eight* for women and *Ted Baker*, *Hugo* and *Lacoste* for men. For unusual gifts there's *Illuminati* and for cosmetics and perfumes there's *Space NK Apothecary* and *Penhaligons*.

Off Buchanan St is the *Argyll Arcade* a specialist shopping centre with over 30 jewellery shops. For more standard high street chains there is the *St Enoch* shopping centre at the very bottom of Buchanan St, and there's also Argyle St which again has high street stores. On Howard St is the famous and enormous menswear store *Slaters* which has become something of a Glasgow institution. If you like designer clothing but don't want to pay full price, go to *Designer Exchange*, off 17 Royal Exchange Sq near Rogano. It has loads of nearly new designer clothes, samples and accessories. Tue-Sat. There are also branches of *T K Maxx* on Sauchiehall St and in the St Enoch Centre, which are great places for seeking out designer goods at very low prices.

The **West End** is a great place for browsing as it's full of quirky, off beat shops. There are several good jewellery shops. *Bethsy Gray* is a jewellery designer with a shop/workshop in Starry Starry Night on Downside Rd. She specializes is working with silver. *Orro* on Bank St is a sleek contemporary jewellers'. You can also find jewellery, as well as antiques, pottery, 'Glasgow Style' artefacts etc in *De Courcey's Arcade* in Cresswell La, which has a brilliant selection of goods from different traders. If you're a booklover there are plenty of good second hand bookshops to explore. *Bookpoint*, on Hyndland Rd has lots of books on Scotland and Glasgow, while *Voltaire and Rousseau* on Otago St is an old established antiquarian bookstore. For academic books there's a branch of *John Smith and Son* on University Av. Also worth trying is the *Oxfam* bookshop on Byres Rd.

There are several great delis around here full of treats to help you put together a delicious picnic if the weather's good. *North Star Provisions* on Queen Margaret Dr has Portuguese specialities, while *Ian Mellis*, on Great Western Rd is a wonderful cheese shop full of unusual varieties of cheese ranging from strong blues, to creamy bries.

Then there's *Peckham's* on Byres Rd, and *Heart Buchanan*, also on Byres Rd. For fresh fruit and veg try *Roots and Fruits* on Byres Rd. For fresh Scottish produce bought straight from the farmer you can also try the *Farmers' Market* held every other weekend (usually Sat) in Mansfield Park on the corner of Hyndland Rd and Dumbarton Rd. 1000-1500.

Transport

Air Glasgow International airport is the main departure point in Scotland for flights to North America. There are also regular flights to several European destinations and many domestic flights. There are also flights to **Glasgow Prestwick**. For airline addresses and phone numbers, see 'Directory' below.

Long distance
See also pages 198 and 31

Bus *Scottish Citylink* has buses to most major towns in Scotland. There are buses to **Edinburgh** every 15 mins (1¼ hrs, £3 single); hourly buses to **Stirling** (45 mins, £3.60) and **Inverness** (4 hrs, £14); 15 buses daily to **Aberdeen** (4 hrs, £15); 4 daily to **Oban** (3 hours, £11.20); 4-5 daily to **Fort William** (3 hrs, £11.80); 3 daily to **Portree** (7 hrs, £20); and hourly to **Perth** (1½ hrs, £7.50) and **Dundee** (2¼ hrs, £8). *Midland Bluebird* (T01324-613777) runs buses to **Milngavie**, at the start of the West Highland Way (30 mins, £1.50).

Train *Scotrail* also operates the West Highland line from Queen Street north to **Oban** (3 daily, 3 hrs), **Fort William** (3 daily, 3¾ hrs) and **Mallaig** (3 daily, 5¼ hrs). *ScotRail* also run services to **Edinburgh** (every 30 mins, 50 minutes, £7.50 cheap day return), **Perth** (hourly, 1 hr), **Dundee** (hourly, 1 hr 20 mins), **Aberdeen** (hourly, 2½ hrs), **Stirling** (hourly, 30 mins) and **Inverness** (3 daily, 3½ hrs).

Bus Routes are shown on the *Visitor's Transport Guide*. For short trips in the city fares are £0.80. On most buses you'll need to have exact change. After midnight, till 0400, there's a limited night bus service (more frequent at weekends). Full details from Travel Centres. A good way to get around town is to buy a ticket for one of the **guided bus tours**.

Local

Taxi There are taxi ranks at Central and Queen Street train stations and Buchanan bus station. To call a cab, try *Glasgow Wide TOA* (T3326666), who also run city tours. Minimum fare around the city centre is £1.50-2. To the Burrell collection from the city centre (about three miles) should cost around £6-7.

Train Trains leave from **Glasgow Central** mainline station to all destinations south of the Clyde, including to Greenock (for ferries to Dunoon), Wemyss Bay (for ferries to Rothesay), Ardrossan (for ferries to Arran) and to Prestwick airport. There's a low-level station below Central station which connects the southeast of the city with the northwest. This cross-city line serves the SECC and a branch runs north to Milngavie, at the start of the West Highland Way. There's also a line from **Queen Street** which runs west all the way to Helensburgh, via Partick and Dumbarton. Branches of this line run to Balloch, at the south end of Loch Lomond, and Milngavie.

Underground Locals affectionately call it the "Clockwork Orange", as there's only one circular route serving 15 stops and the trains are bright orange. It's easy to use and there's a flat fare of £0.90, or you can buy a day ticket for £2.50. Trains run roughly every 5-8 mins from approximately 0630 till 2235 Mon-Sat and from 1100 till 1750 on Sun.

Directory

Airlines *Aer Lingus*, 19 Dixon St, T0645-737747. *British Airways*, 66 Gordon St, T08457-733377 (Glasgow Airport T8891311). *Icelandair*, Glasgow Airport, T0345 -581111. *Lufthanasa*, 78 St Vincent St, T08457-737747.

Glasgow

Banks *Bank of Scotland*, 235 Sauchiehall St, 110 Queen St, 55 Bath St and 63 Waterloo St. *Royal Bank of Scotland*, 98 Buchanan St, 22 St Enoch Square, 140 St Vincent St and 393 Sauchiehall St. *Clydesdale Bank*, 14 Bothwell St, 7 St Enoch Square, 30 St Vincent Place, 344 Argyle St and 120 Bath St. **English banks** include *Barclays*, 90 St Vincent St and *Lloyds TSB*, 12 Bothwell St. **Exchange**: *American Express*, 115 Hope St, T2214366, open Mon-Fri 0830-1730, Sat 0900-1200. *Thomas Cook*, Central station, T2044496, open Mon-Wed and Sat 0800-1900, Thu and Fri 0800-2000, Sun 1000-1800.

Bicycle hire *Dales*, 150 Dobbies Loan, T3322705. Close to Buchanan bus station. *West End Cycles*, 16 Chancellor St, T3571344, at the south end of Byres Rd. £12 per day for mountain bikes, £50 per week. ID and £50 deposit required.

Car hire *Arnold Clark*, 10-24 Vinicombe St, T3349501 (also at the airport, T8480202). *Avis*, 161 North St, T2212877 (also at the airport, T8872261). *Budget*, 101 Waterloo St, T2264141 (also at the airport, T8870501). *Hertz*, 106 Waterloo St, T2487736 (also at the airport, T8877845). *Melvilles Motors*, 555 Sauchiehall St, 192 Battlefield Rd, Langside and at airport, T0345-525354.

Communications Internet *EasyEverything*, 57 St Vincent St, huge facility and the cheapest service in town. *The Internet Café is* at 569 Sauchiehall St, T5641052. It charges £2-2.50 per ½ hr on line. *Internet Exchange*, 136 Sauchiehall St, T3530535. *Café Internet*, 153-157 Sauchiehall St, T3532484. The main **post office** is at 47 St Vincent St, T0345-222344. Services include poste restante, currency exchange and cash withdrawal at the *German Savings Bank*. Open Mon-Fri 0830-1745, Sat 0900-1900. Also branches at 85-89 Bothwell St, 216 Hope St and 533 Sauchiehall St. Post offices in some supermarkets are open on Sun.

Football *Celtic Football Club* are based at Celtic Park, 95 Kerrydale St, T5562611, off the London Rd in the East End. Their bitter opponents, *Rangers*, play at Ibrox Stadium, 150 Edmiston Dr, T4278500, in the South Side. Tickets for league matches start at around £15-20.

Gay & lesbian contacts Lesbian and Gay Switchboard, T3328372, open daily 0700-2200. **Stonewall Scotland**, LGBT Centre, 11 Dixon St, T2040022.

Medical services *Glasgow Royal Infirmary* is at 84 Castle St, T2114000, near the cathedral. The *Southern General Hospital* on Govan Rd, T2011100, is the main South Side hospital. For **dental emergencies** go to the *Glasgow Dental Hospital*, 378 Sauchiehall St, T2119600. **Pharmacies**: *Superdrug*, Central station, T2218197; open Mon-Wed and Sun till 2000, Thu-Sat till 2100. *Munroes'*, 693 Great Western Rd, T3390012; open daily till 2100.

Left luggage There's an office at Buchanan bus station, open daily 0630-2230. Also lockers at Central and Queen Street train stations (£2 per day).

Police 945 Argyle St, T5323200. Free emergency numbers are T999 or T112.

Travel agents *USIT*, Glasgow University Campus, The Hub, Hillhead St, T3570608; and 122 George St, T5531818. *Glasgow Flight Centre*, 143 West Regent St, T2218989.

Around Glasgow

Glasgow is surrounded by a series of drab satellite towns, once major centres of coal and steel, or shipbuilding, which are struggling to recover their identity. It's tempting to pass through this depressed hinterland, especially as the delights of the West Highlands lie just beyond the city's boundary, to the northwest, but there are some interesting sights for those with the time or the inclination. The 18th century model community of **New Lanark** and the spectacular **Falls of Clyde** nearby are well worth the trip from Glasgow, and there are a couple of interesting historical sights near Hamilton, namely **Bothwell Castle** and **Chatelherault**.

Within easy reach of the city, north of the suburb of Milngavie (pronounced 'Mullguy'), is **Mugdock Country Park**, sitting between Glasgow and the **Campsie Fells** (see Stirling section, page 350). It offers some fine walking along marked trails and includes the first section of the **West Highland Way**, which starts in Milngavie (see page 59). There are regular trains from Central station to Milngavie. You can either walk from here for three miles across Drumclog Moor or take the Mugdock bus from the station.

West of Glasgow, close to the airport, is the town that gave its name to the famous fabric design copied from Kashmiri shawls. Paisley grew up around its 12th century roots and by the 19th century was a major producer of printed cotton and woollen cloth, specializing in the production of the eponymous imitation shawls.

Paisley
Phone code: 0141
Population 78,000

Ins and outs There are frequent **trains** to Paisley's Gilmour St station from Glasgow Central. There are also frequent **buses**, which stop at the abbey. Buses depart from Gilmour St station every 10 mins for Glasgow Airport, 2 miles north of town. The **Tourist Information Centre** is at 9A Gilmour St. Open Oct-Mar Mon-Sat 0900-1700 (closed 1330-1430); Apr-Sep Mon-Sat 0930-1730, Sun 1200-1700. They will help you find accommodation, though there's no reason to stay in Paisley as it's so close to Glasgow.

In the town centre, opposite the town hall, is **Paisley Abbey**, founded in 1163 but destroyed during the Wars of Independence in the early 14th century. It was rebuilt soon after, but fell into ruin from the 16th century. Successive renovations took place, ending with a major restoration in the 1920s. The façade doesn't do justice to the wonderfully spacious interior, which includes exceptional stained glass windows and an impressive choir. Also of note is the 10th century Barochan Cross, at the eastern end of the north nave. The best time to visit is during one of their open days, held one Sat a month (phone the tourist office for details), when the 150-feet high tower is open to the public. The views form the top are great. ■ *Mon-Sat 1000-1530. Free. T8897654. To get there, follow Gilmour St from the train station to The Cross, then turn left into Gauze St and cross the river.*

In the High Street is the **Museum and Art Gallery**, with a huge collection of the world famous Paisley shawls and an interesting display of the history of weaving. ■ *Tue-Sat 1000-1700, Sun 1400-1700. Free. T8893151.* Also on the High Street is another imposing ecclesiastical monument, the **Thomas Coats Memorial Church**, built by the great Victorian thread maker and one of the grandest Baptist churches in Europe. ■ *May-Sep Mon, Wed and Fri 1400-1600, T8899980.* Above the High Street, on Oakshaw Street, is the **Coats Observatory**, which has some interesting displays on climate, seismology and astronomy. ■ *Tue-Sat 1000-1700, Sun 1400-1700. Free. Public telescope viewing Thu 1930-2130 Oct-Mar. T8892013.* Another interesting sight is the **Sma' Shot Cottages**, in George Place, off New Street. These are fully restored and furnished 18th century weavers' cottages, with photographs and various artefacts. There's also a tearoom with home baking. ■ *Open Wed and Sat 1300-1700 Apr-Sep. T8891708.* To the south of Paisley is the **Gleniffer Braes Country Park**, which is a great place for a walk in the hills. To get there, take the B775 south of town.

Glasgow

The Firth of Clyde

West of Glasgow, the banks of the Clyde are still lined with the hulking ghosts of this great river's shipbuilding heritage. West of the **Erskine Bridge**, which connects the north and south banks of the Clyde, is **Port Glasgow**, the first of a series of grim towns which sprawl along the southern coast of the Firth of Clyde. It was developed as the city's first harbour in the late 17h century, but there's little to detain visitors today. Just before Port Glasgow, however, at Langbank, just off the M8/A8, is **Finlaystone Estate**, a Victorian mansion house set in sprawling grounds and featuring a walled garden, visitor centre and conservatory tearoom. ■ *Gardens open all year daily 1030-1700. Tearoom open daily Apr-Sep 1100-1630. House open Apr-Aug (Sun tours at 1430 and 1530). £3, £2 concession. T01475-540285.*

Greenock
Phone code: 01475
Population: 50,000

About 30 miles west of Glasgow, Greenock was the first dock on the Clyde, back in the early 18th century and was the birthplace, in 1736, of James Watt, whose development of the steam engine contributed so much to the Industrial Revolution. Greenock today doesn't look particularly appealing, but it has its attractions. On the quay is the **Customs House Museum**, housed in the 19th century neoclassical former Customs House, where Robert Burns and Adam Smith were once employees. The museum charts the history of the Customs and Excise service, which is a lot more interesting than it sounds. ■ *Open Mon-Fri 1000-1600. Free. T726331.* While you're here, you should also visit the **McLean Museum and Art Gallery**, at 15 Kelly Steet, near Greenock West station. The museum contains a collection of items belonging to the town's most famous son, James Watt, and the small gallery on the ground floor has works by the Glasgow Boys as well as Fergusson, Cadell and Peploe. ■ *Mon-Sat 1000-1700. Free. T723741.*

Tourist enquiries are handled by the local council, T712555

Sleeping and eating The best hotel for miles around is the superb **A** *Gleddoch House Hotel*, T540711, at Langbank (see above) near Port Glasgow. This former home of the Lithgow shipping family is extremely comfortable, with marvellous views across the Clyde and a reputation for excellent cuisine. There are a few decent and cheap places to eat in Greenock itself, including *Bennick's Brasserie*, at 49 West Blackhall St, and *Aldo's*, at 121 West Blackhall St.

Transport There are regular **trains** to Greenock from Glasgow Central and **buses** every hour from Buchanan bus station.

Gourock & Wemyss Bay

Three miles west of Greenock is the shabby old seaside resort of Gourock. Gourock is the terminal for the *CalMac* ferry to **Dunoon**, on the Cowal peninsula (see page 251).

Transport Ferries leave frequently every day on the 20-min crossing. For details call *CalMac* T650100. *Western Ferries*, T01369-704452, also runs a ferry service (every ½ hr) between Gourock and Dunoon. They leave from McInroy's point, two miles from the train station, from where *Citylink* buses also depart. *Clyde Marine*, T721281, runs a frequent passenger-only ferry service to **Kilcreggan** (10 mins) and a less frequent service (40 mins) to **Helensburgh** (see page 248), Mon-Sat. *Clyde Marine* also run **cruises** on the Firth of Clyde, to Brodick on Arran, Tighnabruaich, or Tarbert on Loch Fyne. Note that these leave from Princes Pier in Greenock.Gourock train station is next to the *Calmac* ferry terminal. Trains and buses to Glasgow are the same as for Greenock.

Eight miles south of Gourock is Wemyss Bay, departure point for ferries to

Rothesay, on the Isle of Bute. Every summer this place used to be packed full of holidaying Glaswegians heading "doon the watter" to Rothesay, and the magnificent Victorian train station is a proud legacy of those days. *CalMac* ferries run frequently (see page 253), and trains run every hour to Glasgow.

Once the capital of the ancient Britons of Strathclyde, Dumbarton dates back as far as the fifth century, when it was an important trading centre and of strategic importance. Today, though, it's a pretty awful place, and of little importance to tourists. It's best to avoid the town and head straight for the spectacular **Dumbarton Castle**, perched on top of Dumbarton Rock, which is surrounded by water on three sides and commands excellent views over the Clyde estuary. This has been a strategic fortress for 2,000 years, though most of the current buildings date from the 18th century or later. ■ *Apr-Sep daily 0930-1830; Oct-Mar Mon-Sat 0930-1630, Sun 1400-1630. £2, £1.50 comcession. T732167.* If you're interested in shipbuilding then you should visit the **Scottish Maritime Museum**, on Castle Street. It has a working ship model experiment tank; the oldest one in the world, in fact. ■ *Open Mon-Sat 1000-1600. £1.50. T763444.*

Dumbarton
Phone code: 01389

The **Tourist Information Centre**, T742306, is out of town, on the A82, which runs north to Balloch and Loch Lomond. It's open daily mid Oct-Mar 1000-1600; Apr- mid May 1000-1700; mid May-mid Jun 1000-1800; mid Jun-late Aug 1000-1900. **Trains** to Dumbarton Central and Dumbarton East stations run regularly from Helensburgh and Balloch, and from Glasgow Queen St. Get off at Dumbarton East station for the castle.

The Clyde Valley

The River Clyde undergoes a series of changes as it begins the journey from its source, 80 miles southeast of Glasgow, through the orchards and market gardens of pretty Clydesdale and the abandoned coal mines of North Lanarkshire on its way to the former shipyards of Glasgow. The M74 motorway follows the course of the river, straddled by the valley's two largest towns, **Hamilton** and **Motherwell,** the latter still reeling from the recent closure of its steelworks. Sandwiched between them is **Strathclyde Country Park**, a huge recreational area which features a 200-acre man-made loch and is massively popular with water-sports enthusiasts. The M74 then turns south towards the border with England, while the A72 takes up the task of shadowing the river to **Lanark**, the most interesting focus of this area, standing as it does beside the fascinating village of **New Lanark**.

This town, now more of a suburb of Hamilton, is famous as the birthplace of **David Livingstone**, the notable Victorian missionary and explorer, who felt the white man's burden more than most and took off to Africa in 1840 to bring Christianity to the natives. He was born in the humble surroundings of a one-roomed tenement, in 1813, and worked in the local cotton mill before educating himself and taking a medical degree. The entire tenement block, at 165 Station Road, has been transformed into the **David Livingstone Centre**, which tells the story of his life, including his battle against slave traders and that famous meeting with Stanley. There's also an African-themed café, gift shop and garden. The centre is a short walk from the train station. ■ *Open Mon-Sat 1000-1700, Sun 1230-1700. £3, £2 child/concession. T823140.*
A 30-minute walk down the river towards Uddingston brings you to the substantial red sandstone ruin of **Bothwell Castle**. This is commonly

Blantyre
Phone code: 01698
Population: 18,500

regarded as the finest 13th century stronghold in the country and was fought over repeatedly by the Scots and English during the Wars of Independence. It has withstood the ravages of time well and is still hugely impressive. ■ *Open Apr-Sep Mon-Sun 0930-1830. £2, £0.75 child. T816894.* Southwest of Blantyre is the **Museum of Scottish Country Life**, Philipshill Road, Wester Kittochside, East Kilbride, which gives an insight into the lives of people in rural Scotland. ■ *Daily 1000-1700, £3, £1.50 concession, children free. T01355 224181, www.nms.ac.uk. Take First Bus 31 from the St Enoch Centre in Glasgow to Stewartfield Way, or a train to East Kilbride.*

Transport Trains to Blantyre leave from Glasgow Central every ½ hr. It's a 20-min journey. Buses run regularly from Buchanan bus station; take nos 63 or 67 for Blantyre and nos 55 or 56 for Bothwell.

Hamilton

Phone code: 01698
Population: 51,500

Hamilton has the longest history of any town in the area, with associations with Mary, Queen of Scots, Cromwell and the Covenanters, who were defeated by Monmouth at nearby Bothwell Bridge, in 1679. The town today is unremarkable but a mile or so south, at Ferniegair, are the gates to **Chatelherault**, an extensive country park and impressive hunting lodge and summer house, built in 1732 by William Adam for the Dukes of Hamilton. There are ornamental gardens and 10 miles of trails to explore along the deep wooded glen of the Avon, past the 16th century ruins of **Cadzow Castle** and into the surrounding countryside. The Ranger service offers guided walks around the park. ■ *Visitor centre open Mon-Sat 1000-1700, Sun 1200-1700. Free. House open Mon-Thu and Sat 1030-1630, Sun 1230-1630. Free. T426213.* Within the bounds of nearby Strathclyde Park is the **Hamilton Mausoleum**, a huge burial vault of the Hamilton family. It's an eerie place with an amazing 15-second echo: the longest in Europe, Europe, Europe…■ *Mausoleum tours Apr-Sep on Wed, Sat and Sun at 1500; also at 1900 in Jul and Aug. Oct-Mar Sat, Sun and Wed 1400. £1.15, £0.80 child.*

Lanark & New Lanark

Population: 9,000
Phone code: 01555

The little market town of Lanark sits high above the River Clyde. Most people come here to visit the immaculately-restored village of **New Lanark**, one of the region's most fascinating sights, a mile below the town, beside the river. **Ins and outs** Lanark is 25 miles southeast of Glasgow. There are hourly trains from Central station. There's an hourly bus service from Lanark train station to the village, but the 20-min walk is recommended for the wonderful views. The last bus back uphill from the village leaves at 1700. To book a taxi, call *Clydewide*, T663221. Lanark is home to Scotland's largest residential **horse riding centre**, at the *Race Course Stables*, T01470-532439.

There's a **Tourist Information Centre** in Lanark, in the Horsemarket, 100 yds west of the train station, T661661. It's open May-Sep Mon-Sat 1000-1800, Sun 1200-1700, Oct-Apr Mon-Sat 1000-1700. They can book accommodation and there's plenty to choose from, though the most interesting places to stay are in New Lanark.

The community was founded in 1785 by David Dale and Richard Arkwright as a cotton-spinning centre, but it was Dale's son-in-law, Robert Owen, who took over the management in 1798 and who pioneered the revolutionary social experiment. He believed in a more humane form of capitalism and believed the welfare of his workers to be crucial to industrial success. He provided them with decent housing, a co-operative store (the forerunner of the modern co-operative movement), adult educational facilities, the world's first day nursery and the social centre of the community, the modestly-titled **Institute for the Formation of Character**. Here, in the **Visitor centre** you can see an introductory video about New Lanark and its founders, join the Millennium Ride (an atmospheric 'dark ride') and see original textile machinery In Robert Owen's School for Children audio visual technology allows you to see the 'ghost' of Annie McLeod (an imaginary mill girl) on stage, telling you the story of life in 19th century New Lanark. The programme lasts 15 minutes. There is also a reconstruction of an early classroom. You can wander through the village and see the 1920s shop, a restored mill-worker's house and even **Robert Owen's House**. There's also a tearoom and gift shop. ■ *Visitor centre open daily 1100-1700. Passport tickets to all attractions £4.75, £3.25, concession, children. Access to the village at all times. T661345, www.newlarnark.org*

Just beyond the village lies the wooded **Falls of Clyde Nature Reserve**, managed by the Scottish Wildlife Trust (SWT). You can visit the **SWT Wildlife Centre**, housed in the old dyeworks, which provides information about the history and wildlife of the area. ■ *Centre Easter-Oct Mon-Fri 1100-1700, Sat and Sun 1300-1700;Nov-Dec, Feb-Easter Sat and Sun 1300-1700. £1, £0.50 children. T665262.*

Sleeping and eating The **F** *New Lanark Youth Hostel*, T666710, new.lanark@syha.org.uk is beautifully situated in Wee Row by the river. It's open all year and includes continental breakfast. There's also the **B-C** *New Lanark Mill Hotel*, T667200, hotel@newlanark.org which has a restaurant and serves moderately-priced lunches and dinners. There are plenty of place to eat in Lanark, including the usual hotels and pubs, cafés, chip shops and Indian restaurants. The best place is *Ristorante La Vigna*, at 40 Wellgate, T630351, a moderately-priced Italian of some renown. It's open daily for lunch and dinner, but is popular, so book in advance. If you're in town on a Mon, which is market day, it's well worth trying the *Market Bar and Restaurant*, at Lanark Market on Hyndford Rd.

You can walk from the village to the stunning **Corra Linn** waterfalls and beyond. Starting from the village, walk past the SWT centre and up the stone steps into the nature reserve above Dundaff Linn, the smallest of the three waterfalls on the walk. A riverside boardwalk takes you past a 200-year-old weir, and just beyond the end of the boardwalk go right at a junction to pass Bonnington power station. Steps then lead up to a viewing platform above the dramatic Corra Linn, the highest falls on the Clyde, where the river plunges 90 ft in three stages. Continue up the steps and follow the path through woodlands to reach another set of falls at **Bonnington Linn**. You can retrace your steps back to the village, or extend the walk by crossing the weir at Bonnington Linn and turning right down the track on the opposite bank, taking a narrow path on the right after a few hundred yds. Take care here as the path is very close to the lip of the gorge! After about a mile, the path leads you to the crumbling ruin of Corra Castle. To return to Bonnington Linn, retrace your steps for about 100 yds and then follow the vehicle track on the right.

Walk to the Falls of Clyde
The total distance, including the extension, is about 5½ miles. Allow 3-4 hrs there and back and wear boots or strong shoes as some parts can be muddy

Five miles northwest of Lanark is the village of **Crossford**, from where you can visit Craignethan Castle, an ornate tower-house standing over the River Nethan. It was built by Sir James Hamilton for James V, in 1530, and was last major castle to be built in Scotland. Mary, Queen of Scots left from here to do battle at Langside (at Queen's Park in Glasgow), where she was defeated and fled to France before her eventual imprisonment. The castle, like so

Craignethan Castle

Glasgow

many others in Scotland, is said to be haunted by her ghost. ■ *Apr-Sep Mon-Sat 0930-1630, Sun 1400-1630, Mar and Oct Mon-Wed, Sat and Sun 0930-1630, Thu 0930-1230. £1.50. To get there, take a bus from Lanark to Crossford, then it's a 15-min walk.*

Argyll

6

Argyll

Stretching north from the Mull of Kintyre almost to Glencoe and east to the shores of Loch Lomond, the region of Argyll marks the transition from Lowland to Highland. It's a region of great variety, containing all the ingredients of the classic Scottish holiday: peaceful wooded glens, heather-clad mountains full of deer, lovely wee fishing ports, romantic castles and beautiful lochs.

Argyll also has its own particular attractions in the shape of its numerous prehistoric sites. Much of the region was once part of the ancient **Kingdom of Dalriada**, established by the Irish Celts (known as the Scotti, hence Scotland) who settled here in the fifth century. Their capital was at **Dunadd**, near Lochgilphead, from where they gained ascendancy over the native Picts. Argyll has since been ruled by Norse invaders, then by Somerled, whose successors, the powerful MacDonalds, Lords of the Isles, were in turn dislodged by the Campbells, allies of Robert the Bruce. They became the **Dukes of Argyll**, and even today are still one of the largest landowners in the region.

Despite its proximity to the massive Glasgow conurbation, Argyll is sparsely populated. Its largest town, **Oban**, has only 8,000 inhabitants. Oban is also the main ferry port for Argyll's Hebridean islands.

This chapter covers mostly mainland Argyll, plus the smaller coastal islands. Also included are the Firth of Clyde islands of **Bute** and **Arran**, the most accessible of Scotland's more southerly islands, and the most popular. Bute is actually part of Argyll and Bute, created in the recent regional government reorganization, while Arran was tacked on to Ayrshire to form Ayrshire and Arran.

Ins and outs

Getting there　Most visitors' approach to Argyll is west from Glasgow. At Dumbarton there's a choice of route: the more popular one is north on the busy A82 along the west bank of **Loch Lomond** (see page 351); the other route is along the north shore of the Firth of Clyde, through **Helensburgh** and along the shores of **Gare Loch** and **Loch Long**. Both routes converge at **Arrochar**, the gateway to the real Argyll. The latter road is much quieter but is not exactly a scenic alternative, as it passes through an industrial wasteland that includes the submarine base at Faslane and the oil tanks at Finnart.

Getting around

During the peak summer months it's essential to book ferry tickets in advance

Public transport is limited in much of Argyll, though the main towns are served by **buses**. The main bus operators are *Scottish Citylink*, T0990-505050, and *Oban & District Buses*, T01631-562856. The Oban to Glasgow rail line passes through the northern part of the region. For rail enquiries, T0345-484950. For general public transport enquiries contact Argyll & Bute Council, T01546-604695. Times of local buses and trains can also be checked at local tourist offices.

Most **ferries** to the islands and remote peninsulas are run by *CalMac*, T08705-650000, www.calmac.co.uk If you're planning on taking more than 1 or 2 ferries, especially with a car, it may be more economical to buy an **Island Hopscotch** ticket. They can be used on a variety of route combinations and are valid for 1 month. They require advance planning but are better value than buying single tickets. For example, the Bute-Cowal-Kintyre Hopscotch ticket allows you to travel by ferry from Wemyss Bay to Rothesay, from Rhubodach to Colintraive and from Portavadie to Tarbert for £6.30 per passenger plus £29.50 for the car.

Tourist information　Most of this chapter is covered by the *Argyll, the Isles, Loch Lomond, Stirling & Trossachs Tourist Board*, F01369-706085, www.scottish.heartlands.org The main offices, which are open all year round, are in **Oban**, **Inveraray**, **Dunoon**, **Rothesay** and **Campbeltown**. There are smaller seasonal offices in **Lochgilphead**, **Tarbert**, **Ardgarten** and **Helensburgh**. The island of **Arran** is covered by the *Ayrshire & Arran Tourist Board*, T01292-262555, F269555, www.ayrshire-arran.com

Helensburgh

Phone code: 01436
Colour map 2, grid A1
Population: 14,000

On the west coast, the Lowlands and Highlands are separated by the Firth of Clyde, which leads eventually into the heart of the city of Glasgow. Twenty-three miles northwest of Glasgow on the A814, overlooking the Clyde, is the town of Helensburgh, its wide, grid-plan streets lined with elegant Georgian houses. The town boasts a few very notable connections; both **Henry Bell**, originator of the steamship, and **John Logie Baird**, who invented the television, were born here.

Ins & outs　**Getting there**　There is a daily ferry service to and from Gourock. There are also 2 train stations: one for Glasgow trains, and the other for trains to Oban and Fort William. See transport below.

The **tourist information centre** is in the clock tower on the waterfront, T672642. Open Apr to mid-May daily 1000-1700; mid-May to Jun daily 0930-1800; Jul-Sep daily 0930-1900; early Oct Mon-Fri 1000-1630, Sat-Sun 1000-1700.

Sights　Helensburgh is most famously known for its connection with the great Glasgow architect, **Charles Rennie Mackintosh**. In the upper part of the town, on Upper Colquhoun Street, is **Hill House**, one of the best examples of

Things to do in Argyll

- Take a cruise on Loch Etive, inaccessible except by boat, and one of Scotland's great hidden treasures.
- Explore the archaeological treasures of Kilmartin Glen.
- Drive down to Tighnabruaich in Southwest Cowal and enjoy the wonderful views across the Kyles of Bute.
- Take a look round the magnificent Gothic fantasy of Mount Stuart.
- Enjoy the finest of piscine cuisine at the Inverawe Fisheries and Smokery.

Mackintosh's work. The house was designed for Glasgow publisher Walter Blackie in 1902-04, and is now owned by the National Trust for Scotland. The house is a masterpiece of balanced perfection and artistry and there's much to admire. The attention to detail, the use of natural light, the symbolism of the floral patterns and use of light and dark – hallmarks of his personal Art Nouveau style – are all very much in evidence. After exploring the house, you can visit the kitchen, which has been tastefully converted into a tearoom (open 1330-1630). ■ *T673900. Apr-Oct daily 1330-1730. Adult £6, concession/children £4.50. To get there from the Central Train Station, walk about a mile and a half up Sinclair St, then turn left at Kennedy St and follow the signs. From Helensburgh Upper Station (see below) it's a 5-min walk.*

Sleeping The most upmarket place to stay is **C-D** *The Commodore Hotel*, 112-117 West Clyde St, T676924, F677112. 45 rooms. West Clyde Street overlooks the loch and is where you'll find most of the hotels and guest houses, including **E** *Ardmore Guest House*, T673461, www.scoot.co.uk/ardmore_guest_house There are lots of B&Bs, including **E** *Ava Lodge*, 44 Glasgow St, T677751, norma@cantello.prestel.co.uk

Transport There's a daily passenger-only *CalMac* **ferry** service from Helensburgh to **Kilcreggan** (30 mins) and **Gourock (42 mins)**, from where there are regular trains to Glasgow Central and other ferries to Dunoon (see page 251). Helensburgh has 2 **train** stations. The Central Station has a regular service (every 30 mins) to and from **Glasgow** (45 mins), while the Upper Station serves **Oban** (3 times daily; 2 hrs 15 mins) and **Fort William** (4 daily Mon-Sat, 3 on Sun; 3 hrs). For times, contact *Scotrail*, T08457-484950.

Cowal Peninsula

The Cowal Peninsula reaches out into the Firth of Clyde, framed by Loch Fyne and Loch Long. This is the most visited part of Argyll due to its proximity to Glasgow, but, despite the summer hordes, much of it is undisturbed. Most people head straight for **Dunoon**, the main ferry port and one of the major Clyde seaside resorts, leaving more adventurous souls to enjoy the forests and mountains of **Argyll Forest Park** in the north or the peace and tranquillity of the southwest coastline.

Colour map 3, grid C6

The northern part of the peninsula is largely covered by the sprawling **Argyll Forest Park** which extends from Loch Lomond south to Holy Loch. This area contains the most stunning scenery in Cowal, and includes the **Arrochar Alps**, a range of rugged peaks north of Glen Croe which offer some of the best climbing in Argyll. The most famous of these is Ben Arthur (2,891 ft), better known as "**The Cobbler**", but this, and the other "Alps" are only for the more serious hill walker. Rather less imposing are the hills south of Glen Croe,

Argyll

between Loch Goil and Loch Long, in an area known as **Argyll's Bowling Green** (not because it's flat, but an English corruption of the Gaelic *Baile na Greine*, meaning "Sunny Hamlet"). There are also numerous footpaths and cycle tracks threading their way through the park, and details of these can be found in the Forestry Commission leaflets available at the **tourist office** in Ardgarten (see below).

Arrochar
Phone code: 01301
Colour map 3, grid C6

The gateway to Cowal sits at the head of Loch Long on the main A83, only a few miles west of Tarbet and the shores of Loch Lomond. It's a small, unremarkable place but the setting is dramatic, with The Cobbler towering overhead.

Sleeping and eating There are plenty of hotels and B&Bs, including **D** *The Village Inn*, T702279, F702458, www.maclay.com, which also serves decent grub; and the very friendly **E** *Lochside Guest House*, T/F702467, lochsidegh@aol.com, which also serves food and which is very close to the village's main pub.

Transport *Scottish Citylink* **buses** between Glasgow and Oban stop off at Arrochar (1 hr 10 mins to Glasgow; 1 hr 40 mins to Oban), 3 daily in each direction (twice on Sunday). Arrochar shares a **train** station with Tarbet, on the main west coast line. Trains heading north to Oban (1 hr 45 mins) or Fort William (2 hrs 30 mins) or south to Glasgow (1 hr 15 mins) stop 3-4 times daily.

Ardgarten, Glen Croe & Lochgoilhead

A few miles beyond Arrochar, on the shores of Loch Long, is **Ardgarten**, where there's a **tourist office and visitor centre**, T702342, which is open daily April-October 1000-1700, till 1800 in July and August, and provides useful advice and information on hillwalking and wildlife, as well as organizing various activities.

From Ardgarten the A83 climbs steeply up **Glen Croe** to reach one of Scotland's classic viewpoints at the top of the pass, the **Rest and be Thankful**. The hordes of like-minded tourists, eager for that memorable photograph, cannot detract from the majestic views of the surrounding craggy peaks.

Here the road forks. The A83 continues towards **Inveraray** (see page 256) and the single-track B828 heads southwest to meet the B839, which runs down to the village of **Lochgoilhead**, in a beautiful setting on Loch Goil. There are several **hotels** and **B&Bs** as well as an unsightly village of self-catering holiday chalets next door. At the end of the road, several miles down the west side of Loch Goil, are the ruins of 15th-century **Castle Carrick**.

Sleeping In Ardgarten there's an **SYHA youth hostel**, T702363, open Feb-Dec and Forestry Commission **campsite**, T702293, open Easter-Oct.

Ardkinglas Woodland Garden

The A83 meanwhile runs down through **Glen Kinglas** to reach the village of **Cairndow**, at the head of Loch Fyne. Nearby is the Ardkinglas Woodland Garden, which contains an impressive collection of exotic rhododendrons, as well as the largest conifers in Europe, over 120-ft high and 30-ft in girth. ■ *Daily dawn till dusk. Free. T01499-600263.*

A mile or so further on towards Inveraray, at **Clachan**, at the head of Loch Fyne, is the highly acclaimed *Loch Fyne Oyster Bar*.

Younger Botanic Garden

Just before Cairndow, the A815 branches left and runs south down the eastern shore of Loch Fyne. At **Strachur** it turns inland and heads down to **Loch Eck**, a very beautiful and narrow freshwater loch, popular with trout fishermen. At the southern end of Loch Eck, at **Benmore**, is the Younger Botanic Garden, a lovely woodland garden and offshoot of the Royal Botanic Garden in Edinburgh. Its 140 acres are laid out with over 250 species of rhododendrons and feature an avenue of Giant Redwoods. ■ *1 Mar-31 Oct daily 0930-1800. Adult £3, concession £2.50, children £1. T01369-706261.*

Dunoon

The largest town in Cowal, and indeed the largest in Argyll, with 13,000 inhabitants, is Dunoon, one-time favourite holiday destination for Glaswegians, who came in their hordes on board the many paddle steamers that sailed "doon the watter" from Glasgow. Dunoon still attracts visitors, albeit in much smaller numbers, but the town has fallen on desperately hard times with the recent closure of the US nuclear submarine base on nearby Holy Loch, which was the town's life blood.

Phone code: 01369
Colour map 2, grid A1

Nevertheless, the town still comes to life during the **Cowal Highland Gathering**, held on the last weekend of August. This is the world's largest Highland Games and culminates in a spectacular march of massed pipes and drums through the streets.

Getting there There are 2 **ferry** crossings to Dunoon from Gourock, with **train** connections to and from Gourock to Glasgow. There are also buses to Colintraive, Inveraray and Lochgoilhead. Cowal's main **tourist information centre** is on Alexandra Parade, T703785. Open Apr Mon-Fri 0900-1700, Sat 1100-1730, Sun 1100-1500; May Mon-Fri 0900-1730, Sat-Sun 1000-1700; Jun and Sep Mon-Fri 0900-1800; Jul-Aug Mon-Sat 0900-1900; Oct Mon-Fri 0900-1730.

Ins & outs

Argyll

There's not much to keep you in Dunoon but, if the weather's bad and you need to kill time, you could head for the **Castle House Museum**, on Castle Hill, which dominates the town centre, where you can bone up on Cowal's often grisly past. ■ *Easter-Oct Mon-Sat 1030-1630, Sun 1400-1630. Adult £1.50, concession/children free.* A mile northwest, along the A855 to Sandbank, is the **Cowal Bird Garden**, an aviary with exotic birds such as parrots and macaws plus a small rare-breeds farm. ■ *Easter-Oct daily 1030-1800, Nov-Easter Sun only 1100-1600. Adult £3, children £2.*

Sights

There are more than enough hotels and guesthouses to choose from. One of the best is the **A** *Enmore Hotel*, Marine Parade (near Hunter's Quay), T702230, F702148, www.enmorehotel.com A small, family hotel in its own grounds overlooking the sea and with a reputation for good food (restaurant open to non-residents; mid-range-expensive). Also good is **B** *Ardfillayne House*, a mile south of town on the Innellan Rd, T702267, F702501, www.argyll-business.directory.com A Victorian country house offering fine Scottish/French cooking (booking required). 3 miles north of Dunoon, on the A815, is **C** *The Anchorage Hotel & Restaurant*, T/F705108, www.anchorage.com Also has a reputation for fine food (lunch mid-range; dinner expensive).

Sleeping & eating

There's lots of **B&B** accommodation, which can be booked at the tourist office (see below), and there are 2 **campsites** nearby: *Cot House Caravan & Campsite* is at Kilmun, a few miles north of town, on the shores of Holy Loch, T840351; open Apr-Oct; and a few miles further north, at the southern end of Loch Eck, is *Stratheck Caravan Park*, T/F840472; open Mar-Dec.

Aside from the hotels listed above, the best food can be found at *Chatters*, 58 John St, T706402, an informal and outstanding little restaurant offering French-style Scottish cuisine (lunch mid-range; dinner mid-range-expensive). Open Mon-Sat.

Sport **Cycle hire** *Highland Stores*, 156 Argyll St. **Pony trekking** *Velvet Path Riding & Trekking Centre*, Rowan House, Innellan, by Dunoon, T830580.

Transport The most popular ferry crossing is the *CalMac* car and passenger ferry which makes the 20-min trip daily all year round every 30 mins. The first leaves Gourock at 0620 and the last returns from Dunoon at 2105. There's also a *Western Ferries* service every 30 mins which arrives at Hunter's Quay, a mile north of the town centre, T01369-704452. For times and details of **train** connections from **Gourock** to **Glasgow**, T01475-650100. There are **buses** to **Colintraive** 2-3 times daily Mon-Sat (40 mins), to **Inveraray** (on Tue, Fri-Sat; 1 hr 15 mins) and to **Lochgoilhead** (Mon and Fri; 1 hr 15 mins). For times, contact *Western Buses*, T01700-502076.

Tighnabruaich

Phone code: 01700
Colour map 5, grid A3

One of the most beautiful parts of Argyll is the southwest of Cowal, particularly the route down to the little village of **Tighnabruaich**. The A8003 runs down the west side of Loch Riddon and there are few lovelier sights than the view from this road across the **Kyles of Bute**, the narrow straits that separate Cowal from the island of Bute. Tighnabruaich gets busy in the summer with visitors who come here to enjoy some of the best sailing on the west coast. Much of the accommodation is booked up by those enrolled at the **Tighnabruaich Sailing School**, T811717, which offers dinghy sailing and windsurfing courses at all levels. There is a bank in the village and buses leave from here to **Portavadie** (1-3 times daily; 25 minutes), **Colintraive** (see below) and **Rothesay** (1-2 times daily Monday-Thursday; one hour).

Sleeping The **SYHA youth hostel**, T811622, open Apr-Sep, sits high above the village with great views across the Kyles and is often full. There's also **D** *The Royal Hotel*, T811239, F811300, royalhotel@btinternet.com, on the waterfront, with a multi-gym and sauna, and excellent restaurant serving cheap lunches and mid-range-expensive dinners. There are a couple of cheap **B&Bs** in the village, including **E-F** *Ferguslie*, T811414, open Apr-Sep. In neighbouring **Kames**, there's the **C** *Kames Hotel*, T811489, F811283, tcandrew@aol.com, with great views, and live music in the bar.

Transport It's also possible to reach **Bute** from southwest Cowal. The A8003 turns off the main A883, which runs right down the west of the peninsula and the east side of Loch Riddon to **Colintraive**, at the narrowest point in the Kyles, only a few hundred yards wide. A small car and passenger *CalMac* ferry crosses to **Rhubodach** on Bute (for details, see next page). There are buses from **Colintraive** to **Tighnabruaich** (1-2 times daily Mon-Thu; 35 mins), and to **Dunoon** (see previous page).

South of Tighnabruaich

A few miles southwest of Kames, is **Portavadie**, on the west coast of Cowal. A *CalMac* car and passenger **ferry** sails from here to **Tarbert**, on the Kintyre Peninsula, saving a lot of time if you're heading for the islands of **Islay, Jura** or **Colonsay**. The ferry to Tarbert makes the 25-minute crossing every hour daily from 0800 till 1915. The one way trip costs £3.15 per passenger and £13.35 per car.

About 10 miles further up the deserted west coast of Cowal is **Otter ferry**. There used to be a ferry link from here to Lochgilphead, but not for the small, amphibious mammals. It gets its name from the gravel bank that juts out into Loch Fyne (*An Oitir* means gravel bank in Gaelic). It's still worth stopping here, if only for the excellent oyster bar and pub, *The Oystercatcher*, T01700-821229, which overlooks the lovely sandy beach.

Isle of Bute

Barely a stone's throw off the south coast of Cowal is the island of Bute, another favourite holiday destination for people from Glasgow and Ayrshire, who come here in droves during the busy summer months. But though the island is small (15 miles long by five miles wide), it's deceptively easy to escape the hordes, who tend to congregate around the east coast resort of Rothesay, leaving the delights of the sparsely populated west coast free for those who enjoy a bit of peace and quiet.

Phone code: 01700
Colour map 5, grid A3
Population 7,500

Bute has been a popular place since late Victorian times, when a gaggle of Glasgow grannies could be seen being pushed along the promenade in their bath-chairs under tartan blankets, taking the invigorating sea air. Now, the island is successfully reinventing itself as a haven for walkers and cyclists. Some of the island's walks are described below.

Ins and outs

Bute is easily accessible from Glasgow. Take a **train** from Glasgow Central to the **ferry** terminal at Wemyss Bay (1 hr 10 mins), and from there it's a 35-min crossing to Rothesay. There are also **buses** to Rothesay from Tighnabruaich in Southwest Cowal (see above) once or twice a day Mon-Thu (1 hr). For times, contact *Western Buses*, T502076. See also Transport on page 256.

Getting there

The *Western Buses* service around Bute is fairly good, though limited on Sun. The best way to see Bute is by **bicycle**. The island is fairly flat and the roads are quiet and in good condition. See also Transport on page 256.

Getting around

Argyll

Bute

The Tourist Information Centre has recently moved into The Winter Gardens on the Promenade, in Rothesay, T502151. Open Apr and Oct Mon-Fri 0900-1730, Sat 1000-1730, Sun 1100-1500; May Mon-Fri 0900-1730, Sat-Sun 1000-1700; Jun and Sep Mon-Fri till 1800; Jul-Aug Mon-Sat till 1900; Nov-Mar Mon-Thu 0900-1730, Fri 0900-1700.

Tourist information

Rothesay

The sole town on Bute is Rothesay, which, like Dunoon, is a hugely popular holiday destination. There the similarity ends, however, for Rothesay is a genteel and tasteful Victorian seaside resort, with its handsome period mansions lining the broad sweep of bay, its elegant promenade lined with palm trees and the distinctive 1920s **Winter Gardens**, now refurbished and housing a cinema and restaurant.

Rothesay was the hometown of child singing sensation, Lena Zavaroni, who died tragically in 1999 from anorexia

Sights One thing you must do before leaving Rothesay is spend a penny in the palatial **Victorian public toilets**. Rather more than that (£300,000 to be exact) has
already been spent on restoring this architectural gem to its former glory.
Gents get the best deal but the ladies can also take a peek. ■ *Daily Easter-Oct
0800-2100, Nov-Easter 0900-1700. 10p.*

Rothesay Castle is also worth visiting. Built around the 12th century, the
castle was attacked by Vikings, before becoming a favourite with the Stewart
kings. It fell into English hands during the Wars of Independence and was
retaken by Robert the Bruce in 1311. It was also occupied by Cromwell's New
Model Army after the Civil War and partly dismantled, but restoration work
has helped preserve much of this impressive circular, moated ruin. ■ *Apr-Sep
Mon-Sat 0930-1830, Sun 1400-1830; Oct-Mar Mon-Sat 0930-1630, Sun
1400-1630 (closed Thu-Fri afternoon). Adult £1.80, concession £1.30, children
£0.75. To get there, follow the signs from the pier.*

Behind the castle is **Bute Museum**, which features interesting displays covering the island's history, wildlife and archaeology. ■ *Oct-Mar Tue-Sat
1430-1630; Apr-Sep Mon-Sat 1030-1630, Sun 1430-1630. Adult £1.20, children £0.40.*

Around Bute

Mount Stuart One of Bute's main attractions is Mount Stuart, a unique Victorian Gothic
house set in 300 acres of lush woodland gardens, three miles south of
Rothesay. This magnificent architectural fantasy reflects the Third Marquess
of Bute's passion for astrology, astronomy, mysticism and religion, and the
sheer scale and grandeur of the place almost beggars belief. This is truly one of
the great country houses of Scotland and displays breathtaking craftsmanship
in marble and stained glass, as well as a fine collection of family portraits and
Italian antiques. Much of the existing house dates from 1877, and was built
following a terrible fire which destroyed the original, built in 1719 by the Second Earl of Bute.

Equally impressive are the **landscaped gardens** and woodlands, established by the Third Earl of Bute (1713-92), who advised on the foundation
of Kew Gardens in London. It's worth spending a whole day here in order to
take in the amazing splendour of the house and to explore the beautiful gardens. And if the weather's fine, why not bring a picnic and enjoy the wonderful sea views.

■ *Easter weekend and 1 May-17 Oct daily except Tue and Thu. Gardens open
1000-1700; House open 1100-1630. Admission to House/Gardens: adult £6.50,
concession £5, children £2.50. Gardens only: adult £3.50, concession £3, children
£2. T503877, www. Mountstuart.com A regular bus service runs from Rothesay
to the gates of the House (see 'Getting around' above).*

Just before Mount Stuart is the tidy little village of **Kerracroy**, designed by the
wife of the Second Marquess of Bute and featuring an interesting mix of building styles. South of Mount Stuart and the village of Kingarth is **Kilchattan
Bay**, an attractive bay of pink sands and the start of a fine walk down to
Glencallum Bay, in the southeastern corner of the island (see below). There's
accommodation at Kilchattan Bay, at **E** *St Blane's Hotel*, T/F831224.

Southwest of Kilchattan Bay is **St Blane's Chapel**, a 12th-century ruin in a
beautifully peaceful spot near the southern tip of the island. The medieval
church stands on the site of an earlier monastery, established in the sixth century by St Blane, nephew of St Catan, after whom Kilchattan is named. The

Kilchattan Bay to Glencallum Bay walk

*The route is waymarked, but if you want to take a map, it's OS Landranger sheet 63 A longer walk is the circular route from **Kilchattan Bay** south to **Glencallum Bay** and back, via **St Blane's Chapel**. The walk is five miles in total. Allow about three hours. For buses to and from Rothesay, see 'Getting around' above.*

*Follow the signpost for 'Kelspoke Path' beside Kiln Villas and take the track which climbs steadily before turning sharply back on itself. Go through a gate and shortly before the next gate turn right. Follow the rough track, which swings right, then left over open ground to the ruins of **Kelspoke Castle**.*

Continue along the grassy path, past a reservoir on your right, then cross the stile and go down and across a small burn. Turn left and follow the burn, before heading right to join the shore path and follow this past the lighthouse on your left and around the headland to Glencallum Bay. Continue round the shoreline and at the far end of the bay follow the waymarks as the path climbs to cross the headland. The path then levels out and from here

*there are great views across to the mountains of **Arran**.*

*The path then reaches the col above **Loch na Leighe**. Drop down to the loch and follow the waymarks south over open ground. Before reaching a farm called 'The Plan', go right over two footbridges, then left below a low ridge. Keep to the right of the buildings, following the waymarks across open ground to the stile that crosses to the ruins of St Blane's Chapel (see below). Leave the chapel by the gap in the boundary wall and go through a gate, turning left on a clear track which climbs steadily to a stile. Cross the stile and turn right, following the edge of the field down to a gate. Walk uphill on the left side of the field to Suidhe Hill. At the top of the field, cross the fence and keep going, turning right at the corner of the fence. Go through a gate at the next corner and look for a waymark about 100 m downhill. Follow the path steeply downhill, passing through a kissing gate and staying close to the wall. You then reach a drying green at the foot of the hill; turn left and follow a path around the buildings and back on to the road at Kilchattan.*

Argyll

---

ruin can be reached by road from Rothesay, or as part of the walk from Kilchattan Bay (see above).

Four miles north of St Blane's, on the west coast, is **Scalpsie Bay,** the nicest beach on the island and a good place for seal-spotting. A little further north is **St Ninian's Point**, looking across to the island of Inchmarnock. At the end of the beach are the ruins of a sixth-century chapel, dedicated to St Ninian.

The Highland-Lowland dividing line passes through the middle of Bute at **Walks** Loch Fad, which separates the hilly and uninhabited northern half of the **on Bute** island and the rolling farmland of the south. The highest point on the island is **Windy Hill** (913 ft) in the north, from where there are great views across the island.

A less strenuous walk is up **Canada Hill**, a few miles southwest of Rothesay, above Loch Fad. Walk along Craigmore promenade and turn off at the old pier to Ardencraig Gardens. Then continue uphill along the golf course to the top of the hill for great views of the Firth of Clyde.

Essentials

Most of the island's accommodation is in and around Rothesay, and the tourist office will **Sleeping** book your hotel or B&B. Convenient for the ferry is **B** *Cannon House Hotel*, Battery Pl, T502819, F505725. A comfortable Georgian townhouse. Also central is **E** *The Commodore*,

12 Battery Pl, T/F502178, spearcommodore@aol.com One of the nicest guest houses. There are lots of other guest houses and B&Bs on Battery Place. North of town, in **Ardbeg**, is the **D** *Ardmory House Hotel & Restaurant*, T502346, F505596, ardmory.house.hotel@dial.pipex.com, with a restaurant open to non-residents. 3 miles south of town, at **Ascog**, is the excellent-value **E-F** *Ascog Farm*, T503372.

Eating The best place to eat on the island is the *New Farm Restaurant*, T831646, which is 6 miles south of Rothesay, near Mount Stuart House and Gardens (see above). This whitewashed cottage farmhouse is set on a working sheep farm and dairy and uses local produce to great effect. The atmosphere is friendly and informal. Booking is essential for lunch (mid-range) and dinner (expensive). They also offer B&B (**E**, or **D** including dinner). In town, there's *Fowler's*, housed in the Winter Gardens, T500505, offering good-value lunches and dinners. It is an absolute culinary must while you are on Bute to sample the superb fish and chips at the award-winning *West End Café*, 1-3 Gallowgate, T503596. It's open for takeaways all year round, and for sit-down meals Easter-Sep 1200-1400 and 1600-2400 (closed Mon).

Festivals The island holds its own *Highland Games* on the last weekend in **Aug**. There's also the *Isle of Bute International Folk Festival* and *World Ceilidh Band Championships*, a massive festival of music and dance held over the third weekend in **Jul**, and the *Isle of Bute Jazz Festival*, during the **May** Bank Holiday weekend.

Sport **Golf** *Rothesay Golf Course*, T503554, scenic 18 holes with great views at Canada Hill. **Pony trekking** *Rothesay Riding Centre*, at Ardbrannan Farm, Canada Hill, T504791. **Sailing** *Bute Sailing School*, Cannon House, Battery Pl, T502819. Open Mar-Nov. Runs all RYA courses, as well as cruises on their own luxury yacht.

Transport **Buses** connect with the arriving ferries at Rothesay and run to: Mount Stuart (hourly; 15 mins), Kilchattan Bay (4 daily Mon-Sat, 3 on Sun; 30 mins) and Rhubodach (1-2 daily Mon-Sat; 20 mins). For **cycle hire** try *Mountain Bike Centre*, 24 East Princes St, Rothesay, T503554, open daily Apr-Sep 0800-2000, or at *Mount Stuart House*, T502333.

Ferries sail daily every 45 mins from 0715 till 1945 (later on Fri, Sat and Sun). For times, T01700-502707. The one-way trip costs £3.25 per passenger and £13.15 per car. There's also a ferry to Rothesay from Brodick on Arran (2 hrs), once a day on Mon, Wed and Fri in the summer only. Bute can also be reached from the Cowal Peninsula. A small car/passenger ferry makes the 5-min crossing from Colintraive to Rhubodach, at the northern end of Bute, daily every half hour or hour; from 0530-1955 Mon-Sat and 0900-1955 Sun in the summer (21 Apr-27 Aug). The one-way trip costs £1 per passenger and £6.60 per car.

Inveraray

Phone code: 01499
Colour map 3, grid C6
Population: 700

Inveraray is the classic 18th-century planned village, with its straight wide streets and dignified Georgian houses, and enjoys the most stunning of settings, on the shores of Loch Fyne. It was rebuilt by the third Duke of Argyll, head of the Campbell clan, at the same time as he restored the nearby family home, which now attracts hordes of summer visitors. As well as its natural beauty and elegance, and fine castle, Inveraray has several other notable attractions in and around the town and you could quite happily spend a few days here, whatever the weather.

Ins & outs **Getting there** Inveraray is on the main Glasgow-Oban and Glasgow-Campbeltown bus routes, and *Scottish Citylink* **buses** from Glasgow (1 hr 45 mins) stop in Front St, 6 times daily Mon-Sat (4 on Sun). Three of these buses (2 on Sun) continue to Oban (1 hr

5 mins), and 3 continue (2 on Sun) to Lochgilphead and Campbeltown (2 hrs 30 mins). For times, T0990-505050.

Getting around Inveraray is a small village and most of the sights below are within easy walking distance.

Tourist Information Centre On Front St, T302063. Open Apr Mon-Sat 0900-1700, Sun 1200-1700; May-Jun Mon-Sat 0900-1700, Sun 1100-1700; Jul-Aug Mon-Sun 0900-1800; Sep-Oct Mon-Sat 0900-1700, Sun 1200-1700; Nov Mon-Fri 1100-1600, Sat-Sun 1200-1600; Dec-Jan Mon-Fri 1000-1500, Sat-Sun 1100-1500; Feb-Mar Mon-Fri 1100-1600, Sat-Sun 1200-1600.

Inveraray Castle One of Argyll's most famous castles, Inveraray has been   Sights
the clan seat of the Campbells for centuries and is still the family home of the Duke of Argyll. The present neo-Gothic structure dates from 1745, and its main feature is the magnificent armoury hall, whose displays of weaponry were supplied to the Campbells by the British government to quell the Jacobite rebellion. The elaborately furnished rooms are also on display, as is the fascinating and troubled family history in the Clan room. There are extensive grounds with fine walks, particularly up to the hill-top folly. ■ *Apr-Jun, Sep-Oct Mon-Thu and Sat 1000-1300 and 1400-1745, Sun 1300-1745; Jul-Aug Mon-Sat 1000-1745, Sun 1300-1745. Adult £5.50, concession £4.50, children £.50. T302203.*

Inveraray Jail The Georgian prison and courthouse in the centre of the village has been brilliantly restored as a fascinating museum that gives a vivid insight into life behind bars from medieval times up till the 19th century. You can sit in on an 1820 courtroom trial, then visit the cells below and learn all about some of the delightful prison pursuits, such as branding with a hot iron, ear nailing and public whipping. The whole experience is further enhanced by the guides, who are dressed as warders and prisoners. Makes you want to stay on the right side of the law, though, thankfully conditions have improved – as you will see for yourself. ■ *Apr-Oct daily, 0930-1800, Nov-Mar daily 1000-1700. Adult £4.90, concession £3.10, children £2.40. T302381.*

Inveraray Maritime Museum Another worthwhile diversion, especially if you've got kids in tow, is the *Arctic Penguin*, one of the world's last iron sailing ships, which is moored at the loch-side pier. Below decks are lots of interesting displays on Clyde shipbuilding and the Highland Clearances, as well as various 'hands-on' activities. ■ *Apr-Sep daily 1000-1800, Oct-Mar daily 1000-1700. Adult £3, concession £2, children £1.50. T302213.*

All Saints Church One sight which has great appeal is the **Bell Tower** of All Saints Church, which attracts campanologists from near and far to ring the second heaviest set of church bells in the world. It's worth a visit, not just to dangle from the end of a rope, but to climb the tower and admire the panoramic view of the town below. ■ *Mid-May to end-Sep daily 1000-1300 and 1400-1700. Tower: adult £2, children £0.75.*

Argyll Wildlife Park A few miles southwest of town, on the A83 to Lochgilphead, Argyll Wildlife Park is another great place for kids. Amongst the native wildlife wandering around the forest-clad hills are pine martens, badgers, foxes, deer, wildcats, wild goats, a variety of wildfowl and birds of prey, racoons and wallabies, though the more informed of you will have noted that the last two are not native to Scotland. There's also the obligatory tearoom and gift shop. ■ *Daily 1000-1700. Adult £3.75, concession £2.50, children £1.95. T302264.*

Auchindrain Township Three miles beyond Argyll Wildlife Park is Auchindrain, a complete reconstruction of an original West Highland village.

Argyll

The thatched cottages, barn and blacksmith have all been perfectly restored, and are all furnished and equipped to give a real insight into what rural life must have been like in the Highlands before the Clearances. There's also an informative visitor centre, with a bookshop and tearoom. ■ *1 Apr-30 Sep daily 1000-1700. Adult £3.80, concession £3, children £1.80. T500235.*

Note that the gardens may close in 2001 prior to being taken over by the NTS

Crarae Gardens Four miles further down the A83 is one of Scotland's very best public gardens, dramatically set in a deep wooded glen on the shores of Loch Fyne. There are marked woodland walks winding their way through a spectacular array of rhododendrons, azaleas and numerous other exotic plants towards the tumbling waterfalls of the "Himalayan Gorge". May is a good time to see the gardens in full bloom, as is autumn for the vast variety of deciduous trees, but any time of year is worth it. ■ *Mar-Oct 0900-1800, from dawn till dusk in winter. Adult £2.50, children £1.50. T01546-886614.*

Sleeping There are several good **hotels** to choose from, such as the historic **A-B** *Argyll Hotel*, Front St, T302466, F302389, formerly the *Great Inn*; or the **B** *Loch Fyne Hotel*, just of town on the A83, T302148, F302348. Also good is the **C** *Fernpoint Hotel*, T302170, F302366, fernpoint.hotel@virgin.net, a lovely Georgian house overlooking the loch; and the **D** *George Hotel*, T302111.

There's also lots of **B&Bs** in town, including **E** *Newton Hall*, Main St, T302484, a converted church, open Mar-Dec; as well as a **F** *SYHA Youth Hostel*, Dalmally Rd, T302454, open mid-Mar to end-Oct; and a **campsite**, at *Argyll Caravan Park*, T302285, 2½ miles south of town on Loch Fyne, with excellent facilities.

Eating The best place to eat for miles around is the *Loch Fyne Oyster Bar*, T600264, about 9 miles east of town on the A83 near Clachan. This restaurant, shop and smokehouse attracts customers from miles around to enjoy their famous oysters and other "Fyne" foods such as the renowned smoked kippers. Open Nov-Mar daily 0900-1800, from mid-Mar onwards 0900-2100 (booking essential at weekends). The *George Hotel* in town offers good, cheap bar food and good ale in a lively atmosphere. The *Loch Fyne Hotel* also does good food, but is a bit more expensive.

Sport **Pony trekking** *Argyll Riding & Activities*, Dalchenna Farm, T302611.

Loch Awe and Loch Etive

Colour map 3, grid B/C 6

North of Loch Fyne is Loch Awe, the longest freshwater loch in Scotland and, further north, the beautiful Loch Etive. There's enough here to justify a couple of days' exploration, particularly the little-visited west shore of Loch Awe, but if you're pressed for time, there are a few conveniently placed sights along the A85 from Glasgow to Oban.

The A819 north from Inveraray joins the A85 at the northeastern tip of Loch Awe, between the villages of of **Dalmally** and **Lochawe**. Just west of the junction is the romantic ruin of **Kilchurn Castle**, on a promontory jutting out into the loch. The castle ruin can be visited by boat from the pier in Lochawe village.

Sleeping There's a good selection of places to stay in Dalmally and Lochawe. A place with an especially nice view is the **D** *Loch Awe Hotel*, T01838-200379, open Feb-Dec.

Transport Both Dalmally and Lochawe are on the Glasgow-Oban rail and bus routes. **Trains** in either direction stop 3 times daily and there are several *Scottish Citylink*

buses daily. These buses also stop at **Inveraray** (see above) and **Taynuilt** (see below) en route from Glasgow to Oban and vice versa.

A few miles west of Lochawe, and almost a mile inside Ben Cruachan (3,695 ft) is the underground **Cruachan Power Station**, or "Hollow Mountain". From the visitor centre on the shores of Loch Awe, a guided bus trip takes you deep into the heart of the mountain through massive tunnels until you reach the generating room. ■ *Apr-Nov 0930-1700; Jul-Aug 0930-1800. Adult £3, children £1.50. Between Loch Awe and Loch Etive runs the River Awe, which squeezes through the dark and ominous* **Pass of Brander***, so steep and narrow that legend has it that it was once held against an entire army by an old woman brandishing a scythe.*

Ben Cruachan & Pass of Brander
Colour map 3, grid B6

Further west, and 12 miles east of Oban, is the tiny village of Taynuilt, near the shore of Loch Etive. Just before the village, at **Bridge of Awe**, is a sign for **Inverawe Fisheries, Smokery & Country Park**, T822446, www.smokedsalmon.co.uk, where you can take fishing lessons, learn about traditional smoking techniques, or wander along a series of nature trails. If the weather's fine, you can buy some of their delicious smoked products and have a picnic (see box above).

Taynuilt
Phone code: 01866
Colour map 3, grid B5

The main attraction though, is **Bonawe Iron Furnace**, north of the village on the shores of Loch Etive. Founded in 1753 by a group of Cumbrian ironmasters, Bonawe used the abundant woodlands of Argyll to make charcoal to fire its massive furnace. At its height, it produced 600-700 tons of pig-iron a year. This was then shipped out to the forges of England and Wales. Iron production ceased at Bonawe in 1876 and it has now been restored as an industrial heritage site, with displays explaining the whole production process. ■ *Apr-Sep, daily 0930-1830. Adult £2.50, concession £2, children £1.T822432.*

Beyond the Bonawe Heritage Site is the pier from which **Loch Etive Cruises** depart. The loch is inaccessible except by boat, and the three-hour cruise of one of Scotland's great hidden treasures is definitely worth it. You'll see the mountains of Glencoe, seals on the rocks, deer on the hillsides and maybe even a golden eagle flying above, and you won't stop talking about it for weeks, or months. ■ *Cruises depart at 1000, 1200 and 1400 (except Easter-30 Apr, Sat-Sun, 1-14 Oct, at 1400 only). Adult £8, children £4, no booking necessary but arrive in plenty of time. T822430.*

Running south from the village is the very lovely and very quiet **Glen Lonan**. About four miles along the Glen Lonan road is **Barguillean's Angus Garden**, one of Argyll's youngest and smallest gardens, but also one of the most peaceful and evocative, set around the shores of little Loch Angus. It was created in 1957, in memory of Angus MacDonald, a journalist and writer killed in Cyprus in 1956. ■ *Daily 0900-1800. No admission charge but there's an honesty box. T822333.*

Sleeping and eating There's a good selection of accommodation in and around Taynuilt. On the main road is the welcoming **D-E** *Taynuilt Hotel*, T822437, F822721; and there are also several B&Bs. The most luxurious places to stay, and the best places to eat, are in **Kilchrenan**, south of Taynuilt on the shores of Loch Awe. **L** *Ardanaiseig Hotel*, T833333, F833222, www.ardanaiseig-hotel.com 3 miles east of Kilchrenan village on an unclassified road. Open Feb-Dec. Offers opulence and style, beautiful surroundings and views, and exquisite food (lunch mid-range; dinner expensive). **B** *Taychreggan Hotel*, T833211/833366, F833244. Not as grand as the *Ardanaiseig Hotel*, but with equally wonderful views and superb cuisine (lunch mid-range; dinner expensive).

Argyll

Piscine cuisine

The whole philosophy of smoking fish varies from one producer to another. At **Inverawe Fisheries and Smokery** (see below) they buy smaller farmed salmon because they believe the lower fat content makes them tastier than larger ones. Traditional methods prevail here. The fish are dry salted, washed, smoked over oak logs for anything from 16 to 24 hours, depending on conditions, and then hand-sliced. The result is a rich and freshly oaky taste in a huge range of formats from a 112 g sliced pack (£5.95) to a whole side (£20.65), as well as gravadlax, smoked trout, eel and halibut, plus a whole range of pre-packed hampers.

Knipoch Smokehouse, in South Lorn near Oban (T01852-316251, www.knipochsmokehouse.co.uk), on the other hand, believes that large salmon, weighing 6-7 kg, produce the best quality. Its approach involves a dry salt cure strengthened with sugar, whisky, juniper and rowan berries, plus a lengthy 2-3 day smoke. The fish comes out so black it has to be washed and trimmed to look presentable, and the taste is a rather unusual one: strong, sweet, sharp and almondy. A whole side costs £45, but it can be cut to any size: sliced at £17.60 per 500 grams, unsliced at £15.95.

Walking around Loch Awe

These routes are all outlined, with accompanying maps, in the Forestry Commission leaflet, 'A Guide to Forest Walks and Trails in North Argyll', available at tourist offices

A single-track road runs southwest of Kilchrenan along the shores of Loch Awe to the tiny villages of **Dalavich** and **Ford**, through the very beautiful **Inverinan Forest**, a Forestry Commission property which has a series of undemanding marked trails running through the hills overlooking the loch.

The first walk starts out from the little hamlet of **Inverinan**. Red waymarkers lead you from the car park into the woods surrounding the gorge of the River Inan. Part of the route follows the old drove road along which cattle were driven from the Highlands down to the markets in south and central Scotland. The walk is three miles long and should take around an hour and a half.

Further along the road, half a mile north of Dalavich, is a car park at **Barnaline Lodge**, the starting point for a nine-mile bike route, a waymarked walk through the **Caledonian Forest Reserve**, and a couple of other woodland walks. The longest of the walks is the five-mile route that leads along the River Avich, then along the shores of Loch Avich before returning to the lodge.

Two and a half miles south of Dalavich is a car park, which marks the starting point for a blue waymarked walk along the shores of Loch Awe. The route passes through **Mackenzie's Grove**, a sheltered gorge containing some of the largest conifers on the west coast. The route then runs along the shores of the loch, from where you can see the remains of a *crannog*, one of over 40 of these Iron-Age settlements on Loch Awe. The route then heads back to the car park; about three miles in total.

Oban

Phone code: 01631
Colour map 3, grid B5
Population: 8,000

Oban lies at the centre of the northerly part of Argyll, known as Lorn, which stretches north as far as Appin, south to Ardfern and east to the shores of Loch Awe. It also comprises several relatively peaceful islands, including Lismore, Kerrera, Seil and Luing. It's a busy little place: not only is it the largest port in northwest Scotland and the main departure point for ferries to the Hebrides, it is also the main tourist centre in Argyll. Not surprisingly, it gets very crowded in summer, with passing traffic and people using it as a base for exploring the region. It has a wide range of hotels, guest houses, B&Bs, restaurants and shops, and a number of tourist attractions, which is useful to know if

Argyll

you're stuck here in bad weather. The town lies in the beautiful setting of a wide, crescent-shaped bay, backed by steep hills, with the island of Kerrera, just offshore, providing a natural shelter. It has been a favourite with tourists since Victorian times, when Queen Victoria pronounced it as 'one of the finest spots we have ever seen'. More recent royal comments, made by Prince Philip (who else?), in relation to the drinking habits of the local populace, have been less than flattering.

Ins and outs

Oban is reasonably well served by **buses** and **trains** from Glasgow, Fort William and Inverness, and there are a number of west coast local bus services to and from Lochgilphead, Dalmally and Kilmartin.

Getting there
See page 264 for transport details

There are regular local buses around town and around Lorn, including to Clachan Seil, North Cuan, Isle of Luing, North Connel, Dalavich, Bonawe, and Ganavan Sands. These are mostly operated by *Oban & District Buses* or *Royal Mail Postbuses*, T01463 -256200.

Getting around

The **Tourist Information Centre** is on Argyll Sq, T563122, and has internet access. Open 1-29 Apr Mon-Fri 0900-1700, Sat-Sun 1000-1700; 30 Apr-17 Jun Mon-Sat 0900-1730, Sun 1000-1700; 18 Jun-1 Jul Mon-Sat 0900-1830, Sun 1000-1700; 2 Jul-2 Sep Mon-Sat 0900-2000, Sun 0900-1900; 3-23 Sep Mon-Sat 0900-1830, Sun 1000-1700; 24 Sep-28 Oct Mon-Sat 0900-1730, Sun 1000-1600; 29 Oct-31 Mar Mon-Fri 0930-1700, Sat/Sun 1200-1600.

Tourist information

Sights

The town's great landmark is **McCaig's Folly**, an incongruous structure that resembles Rome's Coliseum and which dominates the skyline. The tower was built by local banker John Stuart McCaig in the late 19th century, as a means of providing work for unemployed stonemasons. Unfortunately, McCaig died before the project was complete, and to this day no one is quite sure of his intentions. There's not much to see, apart from the exterior walls, but the views of the town and bay are quite magnificent and well worth the climb up. There are various routes on foot, but the most direct is to go up Argyll Street and on the left beside the church climb the set of steps known as Jacob's Ladder, which lead to Ardonnel Terrace. Turn left here and the tower soon comes into view and is well signposted.

Another good walk is to the ruins of **Dunollie Castle**, north of town on the Corran Esplanade towards Ganavan, from where there are also wonderful views. The castle was built on the site of an ancient stronghold of the King of Scots, and was then taken over in the 13th century by the MacDougalls, Lords of Lorn.

The principal seat of the MacDougalls was **Dunstaffnage Castle**, three miles north of Oban, off the A85. The 13th-century fort is built on an impressive site, and much of the huge curtain wall remains intact. The ruins of the little chapel nearby are worth a look. The castle served as a temporary prison for Flora MacDonald. ■ *Apr-Sep daily 0930-1830; Oct-Mar daily Sat-Wed 0930-1630. Castle grounds open all year round. Adult £2, concession £1.30, children £0.75. T562465.*

Two miles east of Oban along the Glencruitten Road is the **Rare Breeds Farm Park**. It's a fun place, especially for kids, with lots of strange-looking, yet familiar animals native to these shores. The animals are in pens, or roam free, and are very friendly and approachable. ■ *Late Mar to late Oct daily 1000-1730 (mid-Jun to end of Aug till 1930). Adult £5, concession/children £3.50. There are 3 buses daily Mon-Fri to and from Oban train station. T770608.*

If the weather's bad you can take a tour round the **Oban Distillery**, at the end of Stafford Street, which is opposite the North Pier. ■ *Easter to Oct Mon-Fri 0930-1700, and Sat 0930-1700; Jul-Sep Mon-Fri 0930-2030. Adult £3.50. T572004.*

Boat trips   Boat trips can be made from Oban, to **Mull, Iona, Staffa** and **The Treshnish Islands** with *Gordon Grant Tours*, on Railway Pier, T562842. There are other boat operators around the harbour, on the North, South and Railway Piers. You can also rent boats from *Borro Boats*, Dungallan Parks, Gallanach Road, T563292.

Essentials

Sleeping   There's no shortage of hotels, guest houses and B&Bs, most of which are very reason-
■ *on map*   ably priced, and many of which are on or near the seafront. There are also lots of B&Bs
Price codes: in the streets below McCaig's Folly. Though it shouldn't be a problem finding a room
see inside front cover   for the night, Oban is the main ferry port for the islands and gets very busy in the summer with through traffic. It's often a good idea to get the tourist office to find a place,
which costs a little more, but can save a lot of time and effort.

There are dozens of   **A** *Caledonian Hotel*, Station Sq, T563133, F562998, www.miltonhotels.com 70
B&Bs on Ardconnel Rd   rooms. Huge old Victorian Gothic building which is hard to miss. Full of 'character',
which hides a multitude of sins, but it's very handily placed for the ferry and train station. **A** *Manor House Hotel*, Gallanach Rd, T562087, F563053. 11 rooms, open
Feb-Dec. Overlooking the bay on the road south out of town towards the Kerrera
ferry. Offers comfort, style and superb cuisine.

C *Dungallan House Hotel*, Gallanach Rd, T563799, F566711, dungallanhotel-
oban.co.uk 13 rooms, open Jan, Mar-Oct and Dec. A Victorian house set in 5 acres of
woodland, offering great views, hospitality and fine food.

D *Barriemore Hotel*, Corran Esplanade, T/F566356. 13 rooms, open Mar-Nov.
More of a guesthouse, and a superior one at that. Victorian style and elegance coupled with great views and a friendly atmosphere mean that this is much more than
all right. **D** *Glenburnie Hotel*, Corran Esplanade, T/F562089. 15 rooms, open Apr-Oct.
Another very good guesthouse along the seafront, which is lined with more
upmarket guest houses and small hotels.

E *Glenbervie Guest House*, Dalriach Rd, T564770, F566723. 8 rooms. Lovely Victorian house high above the town on a street full of good quality accommodation, very
good value.

The official **F** *SYHA Youth Hostel*, T562025, open all year from Mar, is on Corran
Esplanade, just beyond St Columba's Cathedral. Cheaper and more central is the independent hostel, **F** *Oban Backpackers*, T562107, on Breadalbane St. Open Mar-Oct and
Dec 21-Jan 14. Cheaper still and with breakfast included is the much smaller and
quirkier **F** *Jeremy Inglis Hostel*, T565065, at 21 Airds Cres, opposite the TIC.

Argyll

There are 2 **campsites** nearby: the *Oban Divers Caravan Park*, T/F562755, open Mar-Nov, on the Glenshellach Rd, about 1½ miles south of the ferry terminal; and the *Oban Caravan & Camping Park*, T562425, F566624, open Apr to mid-Oct, on Gallanach Rd, 2 miles south of town near the Kerrera ferry.

Expensive The best food in Oban can be found at the excellent *Manor House Hotel* (see above).

Mid-range *The Reservation*, 108 George St, T563542. Very good bistro-style lunches and dinners and a wide vegetarian selection, open summer daily 1130-2200. *The Studio*, Craigard Rd, T562030. Good-value 3-course set dinner and good à la

Eating

There are numerous cheap options around town, none of which are particularly memorable

Oban

To Connel, Glasgow & Fort William (A85)

To Dunollie Castle & Ganavan Sands

St Columba's Cathedral

Oban Bay

Dunollie Rd
Croft Rd
Croft Av
Longsdale Rd
Swimming Pool
Highland Theatre
McCaig's Folly
Oban Cycles
North Pier
Stafford St
Oban
Jacob's Ladder
Laundrette
Bus Stops
Railway Pier
Train Station
Station Sq
Argyll Sq
CalMac Ferry Terminal
South Pier
Gallanach Rd
Villa Rd
To Oban Divers Caravan Park
To Glasgow
Tesco Supermarket
To Lochgilphead & Campbeltown (A816)
To Oban Rare Breeds Park, Glen Lonan & Taynuilt
To Kerrera Ferry, Oban Caravan & Camping Park & Dungallan House Hotel

Argyll

| | metres | 200 |
| | yards | 200 |

N

■ **Sleeping**		6 Manor House		2 Ee'usk Fish Café
1 Barriemore		7 Oban Backpackers Hostel		3 Gathering & O'Donnell's Bar
2 Caledonian		8 SYHA Youth Hostel		4 McTavish's Kitchens
3 Glenbervie Guest House				5 Oban Inn
4 Glenburnie		● **Eating**		6 The Reservation
5 Jeremy Inglis Hostel		1 Café na Lusan		7 The Studio

carte menu, popular with locals, so you'll need to book, open daily 1700-2200 (cheap 'early bird special' served 1700-1830). *Ee'usk Fish Café*, George St, T565666. Good value for luscious fresh fish. Then name isn't meant to sound like you've just eating something nasty, it's actually the phonetic spelling of the word fish in Gaelic. Open daily 1200-1430 and 1800-2130. *The Gathering*, Breadalbane St, T564849. Good, honest home cooking in one of Oban's oldest restaurants. Downstairs is *O'Donnell's* (see below).

Cheap Bar meals are available at pubs and hotels, and there are the ubiquitous fish and chip shops, the best of which is *Onorio's* on George St. *Café na Lusan*, on Craigard Rd, T567268, is one of the few places offering veggie and organic food, with homebaking and a relaxed, welcoming atmosphere. Also internet access (see next page). Open daily 1100-2100 in summer, 1100-1800 in winter. The much-publicised *McTavish's Kitchens*, 34 George St, T563064. There's a self-service cafeteria downstairs (open from 0900) and the restaurant upstairs (open 1200-1400 and 1800-2230) has a 'Scottish Show' (see below).

Bars & entertainment The town is not exactly the party capital of Scotland, so don't expect much in the way of late-night diversion. Your best bet is *O'Donnell's*, beneath The Gathering (see above) an Irish pub which has live music most nights, including ceilidhs. Serves bar meals till 2300 and stays open till 0100. There's also Scottish music and dancing every night at *McTavish's Kitchens* May-Sep 0830-2230 (£3 admission, £1.50 if dining). Otherwise, there's the *Oban Inn*, by the north pier, which is the nicest pub in town and serves bar food.

The local cinema, confusingly called *The Highland Theatre*, is at the north end of George St, T562444, and shows most of the popular current releases.

Festivals
Precise dates change annually: check the latest details at the TIC

The *Highlands & Islands Music & Dance Festival* is held at the **end of Apr/beginning of May**. At the beginning of **Jun** is the *Oban Mod*, and at the beginning of **Aug** it's the *Lorn Agricultural Show*. The *Argyllshire Gathering* (Oban Games) is held at the end of **Aug** in Mossfield Park.

Sport **Cycling** You can rent bikes from *Oban Cycles*, 9 Craigard Rd, T566966. For details of cycle routes through the forests of Argyll, see the Forest Enterprise leaflet, *Cycling in the Forest*, available free at the tourist office.

Diving *Puffin Dive Centre*, Gallanach Port, Gallanach Rd, T566088. Diver training centre and facilities (open 0800-2000).

Fishing Excellent trout and coarse fishing on Loch Awe and Avich. Permits and boat hire from *The Angler's Corner*, 114 George St, T566374. Open Mon-Sat 0930-1700, Sun 1000-1500.

Golf *Glencruitten Golf Club*, T562868/564115, is an 18-hole course on the edge of town; £16 per round per day.

Pony trekking *Melfort Riding Centre*, Melfort Village, Kilmelford by Oban, T01852-200322. Also at *Achnalarig Farm*, Glencruitten, T562745.

Swimming *Atlantis Leisure*, Dalriach Rd, T566800.

Walking The *Oban Walkers* organize walks throughout Argyll and beyond every fortnight. For more details contact the tourist office, where you can also pick up the Forestry Commission guides to *Forest Walks and Trails in North Argyll and Knapdale, Kintyre & Kilmichael*.

Windsurfing *Linnhe Marine Watersports Centre* at Lettershuna (see page 267).

Transport **Bus** There are regular daily buses to and from **Fort William**, via Benderloch and Appin (1¾ hrs) with *West Coast Motors*, T01586-552319, *Highland Country Buses*, T01463-233371 and *Oban & District Buses*, T562856. There's a regular daily service to and from **Glasgow** (3 hrs) with *Scottish Citylink Coaches*, T08705-505050, and to **Inverness** (1¼ hrs). There are regular daily buses to and from **Dalmally**, via Cruachan Power Station, Lochawe and Taynuilt Hotel, operated by *Oban & District*, *Scottish Citylink*, *Awe Service Station*, T01866-822612 and *LF Stewart*, T01866-833342. There's a service to **Lochgilphead**, via Kilmartin, a couple of times a day (Mon-Sat), operated by *Oban & District*, *Scottish Citylink* and *West Coast Motors*.

 Car hire *Flit Van & Car Hire*, Glencruitten Rd, T/F566553. From £33.50 per day. *Practical Car & Van Rental*, Robertson's Motor Repairs, Lochavullin Industrial Estate, T570900. From £36 per day. *Hazelbank Motors*, Lynn Rd, T566476, F566783. From £35 per day.

 Ferry Oban is the main ferry port for many of the Hebridean islands. The *CalMac* ferry terminal, T566688, is on Railway Pier, to the south of the town centre. Only 100 yds away is the train station, T563083, which is next to the bus terminal. Details of ferries out of Oban are on page 290. For ferries to Lismore, see page 267.

 Train There are 3 trains daily to **Glasgow**, via Crianlarich, where the Oban train connects with the Mallaig/Fort William-Glasgow train. For times, contact *Scotrail* (T08457-484950).

Banks All the major banks have branches with ATMs in the town centre and you can also change foreign currency at the TIC. **Communications** Internet *Café na Lusan* (see Eating on previous page), £1.50 per 20 mins. The TIC and *Oban Backpackers* both charge £1.50 for 15 mins

*(margin)* Directory

*(margin, rotated)* Argyll

A good place to get away from the crowds and enjoy some peace and quiet and some fine walking is the island of Kerrera, which protects Oban Bay. It's only five miles by two, so can be explored easily on foot or by bike.

*(margin)* Isle of Kerrera
Phone code: 01631
Colour map 3, grid C5

Ins and outs The departure point for ferries to Kerrera is 1½ miles along the Gallanach Rd. They leave several times daily between 0845 and 1800 (between 1030 and 1700 on Sun). The trip takes 5-10 mins and costs £2.50 return (£1.50 for children and £0.50 for bikes), T563665.

The highest point on the island is 600 ft, from where there are great views across to Mull, the Slate Islands, Lismore and Jura. Otherwise, there's a good trail down to the ruins of **Gylen Castle**, built by the MacDougall's in 1582, which is perched on a cliff-top on the south coast. Near the castle is the **F** *Kerrera Bunkhouse*, T570223, which has six beds, is open April-September, and can also arrange a lift to and from the ferry. There's also a tearoom here, which serves tea, coffee, juices, cakes and snacks.

 The ferry lands at the spot where King Alexander II was mortally wounded while defeating the Vikings in battle in 1249. A mile northwest of here is **Slatrach Bay**, a nice sandy beach and a great place for a picnic.

North of Oban

Five miles north of Oban an impressive steel cantilever bridge carries the A828 across the mouth of Loch Etive at **Connel**. It's worth stopping here to see the **Falls of Lora**, a wild tide-race created by the narrow mouth of the sea loch and the reef that spans most of it, thus restricting the flow of water. The result is the impressive rapids, which are best seen from the shore in the village or from halfway across the bridge. There are several cheap **B&Bs** in Connel village, should you wish to stay, but the nicest place is the **D** *Ards House*, T710255, which offers good food.

(margin) *Phone code: 01631*
Colour map 3, grid B5

Five miles east of Connel Bridge, on the north shore of Loch Etive, **Archattan Priory Garden** is worth a detour if the weather's fine. You can wander amongst the 13th-century priory ruins and the gardens, which are at their best between July and September, though spring is also a good time. There's also a tearoom. ■ *1 Apr-31 Oct 0900-1800. T750274.*

A few miles north of Connel Bridge at **Benderloch**, a road turns west (signed South Shian) to the *Tralee Dive Centre*, T/F720262, where you can charter boats for fishing. Nearby is *Tralee Rally Karting*, T720297, which is open July-September daily 1000-1800.

Barcaldine Castle
Continue on this road to reach Barcaldine Castle, built by the Campbells in the late 16th century. The tower house is still occupied by Campbells, having been sold in the mid-19th century and then bought back as a ruin 50 years later. It's now open to the public and, though there are no real treasures, there are interesting stories to be told, secret passages to explore, a dungeon (with obligatory ghost) and a tearoom where you can try Mrs Campbell's home baking. ■ *Jul-Aug Tue-Sun 1200-1700. £3.25. T720598.*

Sleeping You can spend the night in the castle; there are 2 rooms (**D-E**) for B&B from Jun-Sep. If the thought of a night in a haunted castle doesn't appeal, there are several B&Bs in the village of Benderloch. If money's no object, then treat yourself to the luxurious **L** *Isle of Eriska Hotel*, T720371, F720531. 17 rooms. Argyll's only 5-star hotel, situated on its own private 300-acre island off the northern point of Benderloch.

Oban Sealife Centre
Near Barcaldine Castle, on the main A828, is the Oban Sealife Centre, on the shore of Loch Creran. It's enormous fun and also environmentally friendly as they rescue seals and other aquatic life and then release them back into the wild at the end of the season. You can see lots of strange underwater creatures at close quarters and even touch some of them. It's the ideal place to come with kids, or if it's raining. There's also a self-service restaurant. ■ *Daily 0900-1800 (1000-1700 in the winter months). Adult £6.50, concession £5.50, children £4.50. Various discount vouchers are in operation. Ask at the TIC or phone directly; T720386. Buses to from Oban to Fort William pass by the Sealife Centre (see page 264).*

Port Appin
Phone code: 01631
Colour map 3, grid B5
The road runs around Loch Creran and enters the district of Appin, made famous in Robert Louis Stevenson's *Kidnapped*, which was based on the 'Appin Murder' of 1752. A road turns southwest off the main Fort William road to Port Appin, on the western tip of the peninsula, the departure point for the passenger ferry to **Lismore** (see next page).

Sleeping and eating There are a couple of hotels in this attractive little fishing village, the best of which is the superb **L** *Airds Hotel*, T730236, F730535. 12 rooms. This classy little roadside hotel boasts one of the very best restaurants in the whole country and is recommended in all the best guide books. There's also the **C** *Pierhouse Hotel*, T730302, F730400. Sitting right by the tiny pier, this cosy little hotel has a deserved reputation for excellent, moderately priced local seafood. If your budget doesn't stretch that far, then there's the **E** *Fasgadh Guest House*, T730374.

Castle Stalker
To the north of Port Appin is the irresistibly photogenic Castle Stalker. Standing on its own tiny island with a background of islands and hills, it's probably second only to the famous Eilean Donan in its portrayal of Scotland's romantic image. It was built in the 16th century by the Stewarts of Appin before

falling into Campbell hands after the ill-fated 1745 rebellion. The current owners open it to the public for a limited period in July and August. Check opening times at the tourist office in Oban.

At **Lettershuna**, just beyond Port Appin, is the **Linnhe Marine Watersports Centre**, where you can hire motor boats, sailing dinghies or windsurfing boards, take sailing or windsurfing lessons, or try water-skiing, pony trekking or even clay pigeon shooting. ■ *May-Sep 0900-1800. T730227, Cell 0421-503981.*

Isle of Lismore

The island of Lismore lies only a few miles off the mainland, in Loch Linnhe, yet feels a world away. It makes an ideal day trip and offers great opportunities for walking and cycling, as well as wonderful views across to the mountains of Morvern and Mull, the Paps of Jura to the south and Ben Nevis to the north. It's a fertile little island (the name *leis mór* is Gaelic for "the big garden") and once supported a population of 1,400, though the present population is about a tenth of that.

Phone code: 01631
Colour map 3, grid B5

Lismore has a long and interesting history. It was the ecclesiastical capital of Argyll for several centuries and the **Cathedral of St Moluag** was founded here in the 12th century, just north of Clachan. All that remains is the choir, which is now used as the parish church. The cathedral occupies the site of a church founded by the Irish saint, who established a religious community on the island about the same time as St Columba was busy at work in Iona. Legend has it that the two saints were racing to the island, in an attempt to be the first to land and found a monastery. Such was Moluag's religious zeal that he cut off his finger and threw it on to the shore, thus claiming possession. This sort of behaviour is, of course, frowned upon in Olympic rowing events.

Not far from the church, is the 2,000-year-old **Broch of Tirefour**, one of the best-preserved prehistoric monuments in Argyll, with surviving circular walls up to 16-ft high. Other interesting sights include **Castle Coeffin**, a 13th-century fortress built by the MacDougalls of Lorn, on the west coast, and in the southwest of the island the 13th-century **Achadun Castle**, built for the Bishops of Argyll. It's a short walk from here to **Bernera Island**, which can be reached at low tide (but don't get stranded).

Sleeping and eating There are a couple of B&Bs on the island, including **F** *The Schoolhouse*, T760262, just beyond Clachan, 1½ miles north of the ferry pier. There's also a shop and post office at Clachan.

Transport The *CalMac* car ferry from Oban lands at **Achnacroish**, about halfway up the east coast (2-4 daily Mon-Sat; 50 mins; £1.80 single, £19.15 per car). A passenger ferry leaves from Port Appin pier to the island's north point (daily every 1-2 hrs; 10 mins). There's a limited postbus service which runs Mon-Sat (see the *Lorn Area Transport Guide* for times), or you can hire bikes from *Mary MacDougall*, T760213.

South Lorn and the Slate Islands

Eight miles south of Oban the B884 turns west off the A816 to the tiny Slate Islands, so called because in the mid-19th century, the island's slate quarries exported millions of roofing slates every year. The quarrying industry has long since gone, leaving behind dilapidated old buildings as well as pretty little villages of whitewashed cottages built for the slate workers.

Phone code: 01852
Colour map 3,
grid C4/5

Argyll

Ins & outs
It can be a rough crossing and times are subject to sailing conditions

Getting there A passenger **ferry** sails from Ellanbeich on Seil to Easdale, making the 5-min trip at regular intervals between 0745 and 1900 Mon-Sat (between 0930 and 1500 on Sun), partly to schedule, partly on request. Check times at Oban tourist office. A car ferry to Luing (South Cuan) sails from South Cuan on Seil (5 mins), Mon-Sat every 15-30 mins from 0745 to 1815 (later in summer) and on Sun every 30 mins from 1100 to 1800. Check times at Oban tourist office.

Getting around A *Postbus* service runs from Oban train station to Clachan Seil, Balvicar, Ellenbeich and North Cuan on Seil. There's also a circular postbus service on Luing, from South Cuan to Cullipool and Toberonochy. Check times at Oban tourist office. Fares for both routes are £1 (£0.50 for children).

Isle of Seil
Phone code: 01852

The most northerly of the Slate Islands is Seil, which is reached from the mainland across the impressive Clachan Bridge, better known as the 'Bridge over the Atlantic', built in 1792, with its elegant, high arch to allow ships to pass beneath. Beside the bridge is an old inn, *Tigh an Truish*, or 'House of the Trousers', where islanders would have to swap kilt for trousers in order to conform to the post-1745 ban on the wearing of Highland dress.

Two miles south, at **Balvicar**, the road turns right and climbs up and over to the main village of **Ellanbeich**, an attractive wee place with rows of white cottages around the harbour. This was once a tiny island itself until the intensive slate quarrying succeeded in silting up the narrow sea channel. The village is also, rather confusingly, known by the same name as the nearby island of **Easdale**, so renowned was the latter for its slate deposits. Another road runs south from Balvicar to **North Cuan**, from where the car ferry sails across the treacherous Cuan Sound to **Luing** (see below).

Sleeping There's B&B accommodation on Seil, at **E** *Mutiara* , T300241, open May-Nov.

Isle of Easdale
Phone code: 01852

Easdale is separated from Seil by a 500-yd-wide channel which has to be dredged to keep it open. The island, only 800 yds by 700 yds, was the centre of the slate industry and the old dilapidated workers' cottages can still be seen, lending an air of melancholy to the place. There was once a population of over 450 here, but the quarries were flooded during a great storm in 1881 and the industry collapsed. The present population numbers around 50. The old quarries can still be seen, filled with water, with the derelict work buildings standing forlorn as the surrounding vegetation takes over. The fascinating history of the island is explained at the **folk museum** near the main square in the village. ■ *Apr-Oct daily 1030-1730. £2. T300370.*

There are no roads on the island, which only takes about half an hour to walk around. There's a tearoom by the pier and some of the old cottages have been modernized and turned into self-catering accommodation (details from the Tourist Information Centre in Oban, see page 261).

Isle of Luing
Phone code: 01852

The long, thin island of Luing (pronounced 'Ling') once had a population of around 600 which was drastically reduced during the Clearances to make way for cattle. The island is still well known for its beef, and is the home of a successful new breed named after it.

The island is small, six miles by two, and mostly flat, making it ideal for exploring by bike. Bikes can be hired in the pretty little village of **Cullipool**, a mile or so southwest of the ferry (contact *Isle of Luing Bike Hire*, T314256). There's also a tearoom, post office and general store. On the road to Cullipool is the island's only B&B, **E-F** *Bardrishaig Farm*, T314364.

The only other village is **Toberonochy**, three miles from Cullipool on the east coast. It's another village of attractive white cottages built for slate workers and nested below a ruined church.

South of the turn-off to the Slate Islands is **Arduaine Gardens**, a beautiful place and an absolute must for all gardening enthusiasts. The 20-acre garden, now owned by the National Trust for Scotland, is best visited in May and June when you can enjoy the spectacular rhododendrons, but there are also beautiful herbaceous borders, ponds filled with water lilies, woodland and sweeping lawns to admire, as well as great views across to Jura and the Slate Islands. ■ *Daily all year 0930 till sunset. Adult £3, concession £2, children £1. T200366.*

South Lorn
Phone code: 01852

Sleeping If you want to stay around here, there's the superb **A-** *Loch Melfort Hotel*, T01852-200233, F200214, www.loch-melfort.co.uk 26 rooms. Open all year. It enjoys great views and a reputation for the finest seafood. If you can't afford such luxury, there's a **campsite** nearby, or **B&B** at **E-F** *Willow Cottage*, T200202.

This is boating country, and just south of Arduaine, on the northern coast of the **Craignish Peninsula**, is surreal **Croabh Haven**, a yachting marina built in the style of a reproduction 18th-century fishing village. You can go for comfort and stay at the **D-E** *Buidhe Lodge*, T01852-500291, www.buidlodge.com or opt for the faded charm of **E-F** *Lunga*, T01852-500237, F500369, coline@lunga.demon.co.uk

South of Croabh Haven is another yachting marina at **Ardfern**, where there's a hotel and B&B accommodation, a popular pub, restaurant and delicatessen. You can arrange boat trips from Ardfern around Loch Craignish and to the offshore islands with *Ruby Cruises*, T/F500616.

Mid-Argyll

The area south of Oban and north of Kintyre is commonly known as Mid-Argyll, a very attractive region of sea lochs, rolling hills and the huge forest of Knapdale, which offers some fine walking. The greatest attraction in Mid-Argyll, though, is Kilmartin Glen, which is littered with Neolithic, Bronze-Age and Iron-Age monuments, and is one of the most interesting and least-known prehistoric sites in Europe.

Lochgilphead

The main town in the area, and administrative centre for the entire Argyll and Bute region, is Lochgilphead, a sleepy little place at the head of Loch Gilp, an arm of Loch Fyne. Lochgilphead started life as a planned town, but the industries came and went, leaving it with the customary grid plan of wide streets but little else. Today it serves as a useful base for exploring the area, with a decent range of accommodation, a bank and supermarket.

Phone code: 01546
Colour map 3, grid C5
Population: 6,000

Public transport is thin on the ground, but with a little time and patience it is possible to explore the area by bus. *Scottish Citylink*, T08705-505050, runs a daily service from Glasgow to Campbeltown which stops in Lochgilphead. The **Tourist Information Centre** is on Lochnell Street, T602344, F606254. You can find out times of buses here, or pick up a free copy of Argyll & Bute Council's Mid-Argyll timetable. Open Apr-Oct.

Ins & outs

Argyll

South of Lochgilphead, and almost a continuation of the town, is the village of **Ardrishaig**, where you'll find the *Castle Riding Centre*, at Brenfield Estate and Farm, T603274. Here you can enjoy cross-country horse riding, beach gallops, pub rides or hire mountain bikes, sail boards, boats, or even try clay pigeon shooting and archery. There's a nice easy walk from the car park at **Kilmory Castle Gardens**, about a mile east of town, up to **Kilmory Loch**. It takes about an hour there and back and is well marked. The gardens also make a pleasant stroll and there are other marked walks, including up to Dun Mór (360 ft).

Sleeping & eating There are several hotels, guesthouses and B&Bs in and around Lochgilphead. Best of the bunch is **B-D** *Cairnbaan Hotel*, T603668, F606045, a lovely 18th-century coaching inn overlooking the Crinan Canal in the village of Cairnbaan, just north of Lochgilphead. In the town itself is **E** *The Argyll Hotel* on Lochnell St, T602221, F603576, argyll.hotel@ btclick.com which has a moderately priced restaurant and lively bar. Just outside of town, at Bank Park, is a **caravan park**, where you can pitch a tent. It has the full range of facilities and also hires out mountain bikes, T602003.

In **Ardrishaig** is the recently refurbished **E** *Grey Gull Inn*, T606017, F606167, www.greygull.co.uk Breakfast not included but still very good value and serves snacks and meals all day. A cheaper alternative for eating out is *The Stables*, or the bar of the *Stag Hotel*, both on Argyll St. If you fancy a picnic, then try the *Alba Smokehouse*, an excellent deli in Kilmory, just east of town.

Sport **Cycle hire** *Crinan Cycles*, The Pier, Ardrishaig, T603511. Also *Lochgilphead Caravan Park* (see above).

Transport There are **buses** from Lochgilphead to Cairnbaan, Crinan, Achnamara and Tayvallich several times daily Mon-Sat. There are buses and shared taxis to Oban via Kilmartin (Mon-Sat) and a postbus to Inveraray (Mon-Sat). There's also a local service to and from Ardrishaig. For details of shared taxis, or to book a taxi, contact *Mid Argyll Taxis*, 4 Slockavullin, Kilmartin, T01546-510318.

Directory **Banks** *Bank of Scotland*, Poltalloch St.

Kilmartin Glen

Phone code: 01546
Colour map 3, grid C5

North of Lochgilphead, on the A816 to Oban, is Kilmartin Glen, an area of Neolithic and Bronze-Age chambered and round cairns, stone circles, rock carvings, Iron-Age forts and duns, Early-christian sculptured stones and medieval castles. Most notable of all is the **linear cemetery**, a line of burial cairns that stretch southward from Kilmartin village for over two miles. The largest and oldest of the group is the Neolithic cairn, **Nether Largie South**, which is over 5,000 years old and big enough to enter. The other cairns, **Nether Largie North**, **Mid Nether Largie** and **Ri Cruin**, are Bronze Age and the huge stone coffins show carvings on the grave slabs. Nearby are the **Temple Wood Stone Circles**, where burials took place from Neolithic times to the Bronze Age.

On the other side of the A816, and visible from the road, is a group of monuments which can all be reached from **Dunchraigaig Cairn**. This is a huge Bronze-Age cairn with some of the covering stones removed to reveal three stone coffins. From here a path is signed to **Ballymeanoch Standing Stones**, the tallest of which is 12-ft high. Two of the stones are decorated with cup marks, prehistoric rock carvings that can be found at numerous locations throughout the Kilmartin area. There's also a henge monument in the same field. These were generally round or oval platforms with an internal ditch, and it's thought they were used for ceremonial purposes.

The best example of rock carvings is at **Achnabreck**, near Cairnbaan village, the largest collection anywhere in Britain. The purpose and significance of these cup- and ring-marked rocks is still a matter of debate.

Before exploring this fascinating area, it's a good idea to stop off at **Kilmartin House**, the multi award-winning interpretive centre, housed in the old manse next to the parish church in the tiny village of Kilmartin. The imaginative and interesting museum helps to explain the bewildering array of prehistoric sites lying all around, and includes artefacts from the various sites and prehistoric music. Upstairs is an audio-visual display which tells the story of this unique corner of Scotland. The café/restaurant does not disappoint either, and serves cheap snacks and meals, using local produce, and excellent coffee from 1230 till 1700. ■ *Daily all year 1000-1730. Adult £3.90, concession £3.10, children £1.20. T510278.*

Kilmartin
Population: 60

Next door in the church graveyard are the **Kilmartin crosses**, dating from as far back as the ninth and 10th centuries. Also within the graveyard is one of the largest collections of medieval grave slabs in the West Highlands.

Two miles north of Kilmartin, sitting high above the A816, is **Carnasserie Castle**, an imposing 16th-century tower house built by John Carswell, Bishop of the Isles, who translated *The Book of the Common Order* in 1567, the first book to be printed in Gaelic. Entry to the castle is free, but it's a little way from the car park.

A few miles south of Kilmartin village is the Iron-Age hill fort of Dunadd, which stands atop a rocky outcrop and dominates the surrounding flat expanse of Moine Mhór (Great Moss), one of the few remaining peat bogs in the country and now a Nature Reserve. Dunadd Fort became the capital of the ancient kingdom of Dalriada around 500 AD and is one of the most important Celtic sites in Scotland. The views from the top are wonderful and worth the visit alone, but you can also see carved out of the exposed rock, a basin and footprint, thought to have been used in the inauguration ceremonies of the ancient kings of Dalriada. There's also an inscription in *ogham* (a form of early writing from Ireland) and the faint outline of a boar, possibly of Pictish origin.

Dunadd

If you want to spend more time exploring Kilmartin Glen, there are a few accommodation options. Opposite the church is **D** *Kilmartin Hotel*, T510250, F606370, which is comfortable and serves meals all day. There are also a couple of cheaper B&Bs to choose from, including **E** *Burndale*, T510235, and **E** *Tibertich*, T/F810281, www.tibertich.com, a working sheep farm just north of the village. A good place for lunch is the café at Kilmartin House (see above), otherwise, there's *The Cairn* restaurant, T510254, which serves very good, moderately priced Scottish and European dishes using local produce (open Mar-Oct from 1700).

Sleeping & eating

Kilmartin Glen is bordered to the south by the Crinan Canal, a nine-mile stretch of waterway linking Loch Fyne at Ardrishaig with the Sound of Jura. It was designed and built by Sir John Rennie in 1801, with the assistance of the ubiquitous Thomas Telford, to allow shipping to avoid the long and often hazardous journey round the Mull of Kintyre and to help stimulate trade in the islands. These days you're more likely to see pleasure yachts and

Crinan Canal
Phone code: 01546
Colour map 3, grid C5

Argyll

cruisers sailing on the canal than the cargo vessels which once transported coal and other goods to the islands and returned with livestock. You don't need to come in a boat to appreciate the canal. You can walk or cycle along the towpath that runs the entire length of the canal, from Ardrishaig to Crinan, and watch boats of all shapes and sizes negotiating a total of 15 locks. The best place to view the canal traffic is at **Crinan**, a pretty little fishing port on Loch Crinan at the western end of the canal. Here you can take a boat trip with *Gemini Cruises*, based at Crinan harbour, T/F830238. They offer two-hour wildlife spotting cruises round Loch Craignish (£9 per person), or longer trips out to the Gulf of Corrievreckan.

Sleeping and eating Crinan boasts one of Scotland's finest hotels, the **A** *Crinan Hotel*, T830261, F830292, www.crinanhotel.com Not only is this one of the most beautifully located hotels in the country, but its celebrated restaurants are amongst the best on the west coast. The bar next to the *Lock 16* restaurant on the top floor offers cheaper lunches, for those who can't afford such indulgence. A cheaper **B&B** alternative is **E** *Tigh-Na-Glaic*, T830245, F830243.

Knapdale
Phone code: 01880
Colour map 5, grid A2

Argyll

Running south from the Crinan Canal down to Kintyre is Knapdale, a forested, hilly area that gets its name from its Gaelic description, *cnap* (hill) and *dall* (field). It's an area worth exploring, for there are many walking trails and superb views from the west coast across to the Paps of Jura.

Immediately south of the canal is **Knapdale Forest**, which stretches from coast to coast over hills dotted with tiny lochs. The Forestry Commission has marked out several lovely trails. Three fairly easy circular trails start from the B8025 which runs south from **Bellanoch**, just east of Crinan. One sets out from the car park at the Barnluasgan Interpretation Centre and runs up to a point beyond Loch Barnluasgan, with great views over the forest and the many lochs. It's a mile in total. A second trail, also a mile long, starts from a car park a little further along the B8025 and heads through the forest to the deserted township of Arichonan. The third trail starts out from the car park between the starting points for the first and second trails. It runs right around Loch Coille-Bharr and is three miles long. A more strenuous walk starts from a car park about 100 yds into the forest, off the B841, about half a mile west of Cairnbaan, and climbs up to the peak of **Dunardy** (702 ft).

At the Barnluasgan Interpretation Centre a little side road turns south down the eastern shore of beautiful **Loch Sween**, past the village of **Achnamara**, to the 12th century **Castle Sween**. First impressions of the castle, situated on the shores of the lovely loch with the forested hills all around, are completely ruined by the criminally distasteful caravan park nearby. Unfortunately, the caravans were not there when Robert the Bruce attacked the castle, otherwise he might have done us all a favour by razing them.

Three miles south is the ruined 13th-century **Kilmory Knap Chapel**. A new glass roof protects the carved stones inside. The most notable of these is the 8-ft high, 15th-century MacMillan's Cross, which shows the Crucifixion on one side and a hunting scene on the other.

Sleeping The best place to stay in Knapdale is the highly recommended **C** *Kilberry Inn*, T01880-770223, www.kilberryinn.com, west of Tarbert on the B8024. 3 rooms, open Easter-Oct, it offers superb food and perfect peace.

Kintyre

The long peninsula of Kintyre is probably best known as the inspiration for Paul McCartney's phenomenally successful 1970s dirge, 'Mull of Kintyre', but don't let that put you off. Kintyre has all the usual Highland ingredients, such as great scenery, wildlife, bags of history, golf and whisky, but also has the added attraction of being one of Scotland's least explored spots.

Colour map 5, grid A/B2

The peninsula would be an island, were it not for the mile-long isthmus between West and East Loch Tarbert, a fact not lost on King Magnus Barefoot of Norway. In the 11th century he signed a treaty with the Scottish king, Malcolm Canmore, giving him all the land he could sail round, and promptly had his men drag his longboat across the narrow isthmus, thus adding Kintyre to his kingdom. Getting around Kintyre without your own transport requires time and patience. There's a bus service running up and down the west coast (see above), and also a limited service from Campbeltown to places around the peninsula (see page 276).

Tarbert

The fishing village of Tarbert sits at the head of East Loch Tarbert, in a sheltered bay backed by forested hills, and is one the most attractive ports on the west coast. Tarbert (the name derives from the Gaelic *An Tairbeart* meaning "isthmus") has a long tradition of fishing, and in the 18th and 19th centuries was a major herring port. Today, prawns and other shellfish are the main catch and though there is still a sizeable fleet, fishing has declined in importance to the local economy. Tourism, meanwhile, is a growing source of income, and Tarbert attracts its fair share of yachties, particularly in May when the village hosts the second largest racing series in the UK after Cowes attracting hundreds of boats and thousands of visitors. The town also hosts an excellent **folk music festival**, over a weekend at the end of September (for details, T820343).

Phone code: 01880
Colour map 5, grid A3
Population: 1,000

Argyll

There are **buses** from Tarbert to **Kennacraig** (for ferries to Islay) several times daily Mon-Sat. Also from Tarbert to **Claonaig** (for ferries to Lochranza on Arran) and **Skipness** (2-3 daily Mon-Sat). Details from Argyll & Bute Council, T01546-604695, or the TIC. The **Tourist Information Centre** is on Harbour St, T820429. Open 6-29 Apr Mon-Fri 1000-1700, Sat-Sun 1200-1700; 30 Apr-1 Jul Mon-Sat 1000-1700, Sun 1100-1700; 2 Jul-2 Sep Mon-Sat 0930-1800, Sun 1000-1700; 3 Sep-28 Oct Mon-Sat 1000-1700, Sun 1200-1700.

Ins & outs
For ferry details, see next page

Overlooking the harbour is the dramatically sited ruin of **Robert the Bruce's** 14th-century castle. There's not much left to see, other than the five-storey 15th-century keep. It's unsafe to investigate the ruins too closely, but the view alone is worth the walk. There are steps leading up to the castle, next to the *Ann Thomas Gallery* on Harbour Street. Behind the castle there are several marked trails leading up into the hills, with great views over Loch Fyne and the islands. Less strenuous is the short walk at the end of Garvel Road, on the north side of the harbour, which leads to the beach. At the end of East Pier road, beyond the Cowal Ferry, is another interesting walk, to the Shell Beaches. You can also explore the lovely gardens at *Stonefield Castle Hotel* (see below).

Sights

Just south of town, on the main A83, is the **An Tairbeart Heritage Centre**, which tells you all you need to know about the area's fascinating history, as well as providing a whole host of activities such as woodturning and sheep shearing. There's also a good, moderately priced restaurant offering local specialities such as venison and oysters. ■ *Easter till early Jan daily 1000-1900. Free. T820190, www.an-t.co.uk*

Sleeping Three miles north on the A82 to Lochgilphead is the sumptuous **L-A** *Stonefield Castle Hotel*, T820836, F820929. Price includes dinner. A magnificent Baronial Victorian mansion set in 60 acres of beautiful woodland garden, with great views across the loch and an acclaimed restaurant to boot. There's a good selection of places to stay in Tarbert itself, including the **B** *Columba Hotel*, T/F820808, www.columbahotel.com, on East Pier Rd. 10 rooms. Price includes dinner (**C** without). This refurbished and comfortable Victorian hotel is on the waterfront and features fine cooking (mid-range) in its restaurant. The popular bar offers cheap, imaginative meals. Just outside the village is the **B** *West Loch Hotel*, T820283, F820930, a traditional 18th-century coaching inn on the main A83 overlooking West Loch Tarbert. Price includes dinner (**D** without) There's also plenty of B&B accommodation, mostly **E**, and a **campsite** at Escart Bay, in a secluded spot overlooking West Loch Tarbert, T820873.

Eating Pick of the bunch is *The Anchorage*, on Harbour St, T820881. Wonderful food, particularly the local seafood and fish, and mid-range prices. Small and cosy so book in advance. Otherwise the best food is available at the hotels. There's the above-mentioned *Columba* and *Stonefield Castle* Hotels but also recommended is the *Victoria Hotel*, T820236, aliatvic@aol.com, which is on the right as you enter the village from Lochgilphead.

As you'd expect with a place popular with yachties, Tarbert boasts some very fine restaurants

Shopping *Earra Gael Craft Shop*, T820428, in the old Weighbridge on Harbour St. Open daily Apr-Oct 1000-1730. *Ann Thomas Gallery*, Harbour St, T820390. Good selection of books, local prints and stationery; open daily (Mon-Sat 0900-1830, Sun 1100-1830 in summer).

Transport **Ferries** There is a car and passenger ferry from **Portavadie** on the Cowal peninsula to Tarbert (25 mins), which leaves daily every hour in summer, less frequently in winter. There are ferries from Tarbert to **Lochranza** on Arran and a summer ferry (Apr to mid-Oct) goes to Lochranza from **Claonaig** on the west coast of Kintyre, south of Kennacraig (see page 279). Ferries leave from **Kennacraig**, 5 miles south of Tarbert, to **Islay** (see page 310) and to **Colonsay** (see page 308).

Directory **Banks** *Bank of Scotland* and *Clydesdale Bank* are both on Harbour St, and both have ATMs.

Isle of Gigha

Population: 120
Phone code: 01583

The small island of Gigha (pronounced "Gee-a" with a hard "g") translates from Norse as "God's Island". A grand claim, perhaps, but there's no question that this most accessible of islands is also one of the loveliest. It's only a 20-minute ferry ride away, and only six miles by one mile, so it can be visited easily in a day, which is just about enough time to appreciate why the Vikings loved it so much. Like so many of the Hebridean islands, Gigha has had a long list of owners, including various branches of the MacNeils and, more recently, in 1944, Sir James Horlick, he of bedtime drink fame. Now, though, the islanders are the new proud owners of their own little piece of paradise, thanks to a successful buy-out in 2001. {check}

It was Horlick who created the island's single greatest attraction, the wonderful **Achamore Gardens**, one mile south of the ferry terminal. Thanks to Gigha's mild climate, the 50-acre woodland garden has an amazing variety of tropical plants, including rhododendrons, azaleas, camellias as well as other, more exotic, species. There are two marked walks through the gardens, which start out from the walled garden. The gardens are best seen in early summer, when the rhodies are in full bloom. ■ *Daily all year 0900 till dusk. £2. Also rooms to let, T505254, F505244.*

The island's other delights include some good **walks**, white sandy **beaches** and fantastic views across to Jura on one side and Kintyre on the other. One of the best walks is to take the path left after the **nine-hole golf course**, signed Ardaily, past Mill Loch to the Mill on the west shore. The views from here are just magnificent. Another good idea is to walk, or cycle (see below for bike hire) to the peninsula of **Eilean Garbh** at the north of the island. About half a mile beyond Kinererach Farm a path leads left to the peninsula where two crescent-shaped beaches are separated by a thin spit of land. And if the weather's good enough for a picnic, make sure you try some of the island's famously distinctive cheese.

Walks on the island

The ferry port and only village is **Ardminish**. Here you'll find the **C** *Gigha Hotel*, T505254, F505244, open Mar-Oct, which offers comfort, great views and good bar food. Another option is the **E** *Post Office House*, T505251, a short walk from the ferry. The McSporrans also run the post office and general store, provide good home cooking and even rent out bikes.

A good alternative to staying on the island, at the ferry port of **Tayinloan**, is the **C** *Tayinloan Inn*, T441233, a small and cosy 18th-century coaching inn offering the best food south of Tarbert.

Sleeping & eating

The small *CalMac* car and passenger ferry leaves from Tayinloan to the ferry pier at Ardminish, daily all year round (hourly 0800-1800 Mon-Sat, 1100-1700 Sun). The return trip costs £4.75 per passenger and £17.90 per car (though a car is totally unnecessary).

Transport

Campbeltown

At the southern end of the Kintyre Peninsula is the "metropolis" of Campbeltown, originally called Kinlochkilkerran (*Ceann Loch Cille Ciaran*) but renamed in the 17th century by the Earl of Argyll, who was, of course, a Campbell. This may be the largest town by far in this part of Argyll, but it has a real end-of-the-line feel, due in part to its geographical isolation, but also because the town has long since lost its raison d'être – whisky.

Phone code: 01586
Colour map 5, grid B2
Population: 6,500

Getting there There are flights from Glasgow to Machrihanish. Buses run to and from the **airport** from Campbeltown (2 daily Mon-Fri; 10 mins). There are several daily **buses** to and from Glasgow; also to Machrihanish, Carradale, Saddell and Southend.

Tourist Information Centre, on the Old Quay, T552056. Open Apr Mon-Fri 0900-1730; May-Sep Mon-Fri 0900-1730, Sat-Sun 1100-1700; Oct Mon-Fri 0930-1730, Sat-Sun 1000-1600; Nov-Mar Mon-Fri 1000-1600.

Ins & outs
For transport details, see next page

Campbeltown's whisky production was such that the town even has its own particular regional subgroup of single malt named after it, but of the 34 distilleries once in production, only one remains, the **Springbank distillery**. This family-run distillery is in Well Close, off Longrow, and guided tours are

Sights

by appointment only, T552085. Whisky aficionados should also pay a visit to **Eaglesome** on Longrow South, where you can choose from over 400 single malts. To find out more on the town's history, you can visit the **Campbeltown Heritage Centre**, on the Southend road, housed in the former Lorne Street church, or "Tartan Kirk" as it is known locally, due to its distinctive façade of alternating stone and red brick. ■ *Apr-Oct Mon-Sat 1100-1700, Sun 1400-1700. Adult £2.* The most interesting sight in town is the wonderfully evocative **"Wee Picture House"** on Hall Street, first opened in May 1913. This rare art deco treasure was closed in 1983, but such was the storm of local protest that it was lovingly refurbished and reopened in 1989. No visit to Campbeltown would be complete without witnessing the glories of a bygone era in the oldest surviving cinema in Scotland. Films are shown six nights a week (Friday night is bingo night).

Sleeping & eating   There's plenty of accommodation in town. Pick of the bunch is **L-B** *Craigard House*, Low Askomil, T554242, F551137, www.craigard-house.co.uk, 8 en souite rooms, with great views over the loch. There's the comfortable **C** *Ardshiel Hotel*, T552133, F551422, on Kilkerran Rd or the **D** *White Hart Hotel*, T552440, F554972, on Main St. There are also several cheap **B&Bs**. Aside from the aforementioned hotels, the culinary scene is not worth mentioning.

Festivals   If you're around at the end of **Aug**, don't miss the *Mull of Kintyre Music Festival*, 3 days of the best in traditional Celtic music, held in various venues throughout the town, with numerous impromptu pub sessions.

Sport   **Horse riding** *Mull of Kintyre Equestrian Centre*, Homeston Farm (2 miles south on the B842 to Southend), T552437. Dinner and B&B also available.

Transport   **Air** There are 2 **flights** daily (35 mins), all year round from Glasgow to Machrihanish airport. For times and reservations, contact *British Airways Express*, T08457-733377.

   Bus There are several daily buses from Glasgow to Campbeltown (4½ hrs), via Inveraray, Lochgilphead, Kennacraig and Tarbert. For details: T01586-552319 or T0141-3329191, or *Scottish Citylink* (T08705-505050). There are buses from Campbeltown to **Machrihanish** (hourly Mon-Sat, 3 on Sun; 15 mins), to **Carradale** (45 mins) and **Saddell** (4 daily Mon-Sat, 2 on Sun; 25 mins), to **Southend** (several daily; 25 mins).

   Car It's about a 3-hr drive from Glasgow to Campbeltown. The most direct route is by the A82 to Tarbert on Loch Lomond, then the A83 via Inveraray and Lochgilphead. If you want to hire a car, there's *Campbeltown Motor Company*, T01586-552030, or *Fona taxis & minibuses*, T01586-554001.

Around Campbeltown   If the weather's good, it's worth taking a walk up to **Beinn Ghulean**, which overlooks the town and loch. Follow the signs for the A83 to Machrihanish until you reach Witchburn Road. After passing the creamery on your left, turn left into Tomaig Road and continue till you come to a wooden gate. Cross over the stile and follow the track through the fields, crossing two more stiles, before you reach the Forest Enterprise sign which marks the start of the walk. It's about four miles there and back from the end of Tomaig Road.

   One of the most popular day trips is to the uninhabited **Davaar Island**, connected to the peninsula by a tidal breakwater. Here you can see the cave painting of the Crucifixion, completed in secret by a local artist in 1877. The island can be visited at low tide from Kildalloig Point, a couple of miles east of town. Check tide times at the tourist office before setting out.

Six miles from Campbeltown, on the west coast of Kintyre, is Machrihanish, site of Campbeltown's airport and a magnificent beach – five miles of glorious unspoiled sand backed by dunes and washed by gigantic Atlantic breakers. Not surprisingly, this is a cracking place for **windsurfing** and **surfing**; one of the very best in the country, in fact. It also boasts a dramatic 18-hole championship golf course, whose first hole was described by Jack Nicklaus as the world's greatest opening hole. The beach can be approached either by walking north from the village, or south from the car park on the main A83 to Tayinloan and Tarbert, where it leaves the coast.

Machrihanish
Phone code: 01586
Colour map 5, grid B2

Sleeping A good option is **D** *Ardell House Hotel*, overlooking the golf course, T/F810235. Open Mar-Oct, 10 rooms. Cheaper and simpler is **E** *Mrs Catherine Raiston*, at East Drumlemble, T810220, open Easter-Sep. There's also a **campsite** at East Trodigal, T810366; open Mar-Sep, with full facilities. It's on the right just before the village heading west from Campbeltown.

It's only a short drive south from Campbeltown to the tip of the peninsula, the Mull of Kintyre, eulogised by one-time resident Paul McCartney in the irritating eponymous hit single. There's nothing much to see in this bleak, storm-battered place, apart from the coast of Ireland, a mere 12 miles away and clearly visible on a good day. The road out to the lighthouse, built in 1788 and remodelled by Robert Stevenson, grandfather of Robert Louis, is pretty hairy, to put it mildly. It's possible to walk from here up to Machrihanish (about 10 miles), past the ruined township of Balmavicar and the Largiebaan Bird Reserve. The views are great and there's a chance of seeing golden eagles.

Southend & the Mull of Kintyre

The southernmost village on Kintyre is **Southend**, a bleak, windswept place with a wide sandy beach. At the east end of the beach, jutting out on a rocky promontory, are the scant remains of **Dunaverty Castle**, once a Mac-Donald stronghold, where 300 Royalists were brutally massacred in 1647 by the Covenanting army of the Earl of Argyll, despite having already surrendered. To the west of Southend, below the cliffs, is the ruined 13th-century **Keil Chapel**, which is said to mark the spot where **St Columba** first set foot on Scottish soil, before heading north to Iona. Close by is a pair of footprints carved into the rock, known as **Columba's footprints**.

Sleeping Should you wish to spend time here, there are a couple of good **B&Bs** in Southend, including **E** *Ormsary Farm*, T830665, open Apr-Sep.

The east coast

The slow and winding single track B842 meanders up the east coast from Campbeltown to Skipness and Claonaig, departure point for the ferry to Arran (see page 279). The scenery en route is gentle and pleasant, with nice views of Arran, and there are some worthwhile places to stop, but public transport is somewhat limited (see page 276).

Ten miles up the coast are the idyllic ruins of **Saddell Abbey**, a Cistercian establishment founded by Somerled in 1160. The abbey fell into ruin in the early 16th century and much of the stone was used in the building of Saddell Castle for the Bishop of Argyll. Though little remains, there are some impressive medieval grave slabs, depicting knights, monks, ships, animals and other images.

Argyll

Carradale
Phone code: 01583
Colour map 5, grid B2

A few miles further north is the village of Carradale, the only place of any size on the east coast, nestling in the sandy sweep of beautiful Carradale Bay. There are several pleasant marked walks through the woods between the B842 and the shore. The shortest of these walks (with green waymarkers) starts from the Network Centre (see below) and is a mile long. There's a three-mile walk with red waymarkers which starts at the Port Na Storm car park and follows the forest road to the left. After 150 yds the route turns left again at the road junction. A mile further on, you turn right off the road and follow the track up to the summit of Cnoc-nan Gabhor, from where there are great views of Kintyre and across to Arran. A third walk (six miles; blue waymarkers) also starts from the Port Na Storm car park. This time the route heads right at the junction 150 yds beyond the car park and then runs north along the shore, with a chance of seeing dolphins and basking shark. The path then swings west towards the road, then turns south with views of Carradale Glen.

If the weather's bad, there's the **Network Carradale Heritage Centre**, which features displays of fishing, farming and forestry. ■ *Easter to mid-Oct Mon-Sat 1030-1700, Sun 1230-1600.* A little further north is the **Grogport Tannery**, which produces organically tanned, naturally coloured sheepskins. ■ *Daily 0900-1800.*

Twelve miles north of Carradale the B842 ends at **Claonaig**, which is actually nothing more than a slipway for the ferry to Arran (see below). From here the B8001 heads west to meet the A83 near the Kennacraig ferry pier. A dead-end road runs north for a few miles to the tiny village of **Skipness**, where you can visit the substantial ruins of the 13th-century **Skipness Castle** and nearby chapel. You might want to stop here and enjoy some fresh seafood or good home baking at the *Seafood Cabin*, T01880-760207, open daily 1100-1800 from end May-end September.

Sleeping and eating There are a couple of hotels in Carradale, including the **D** *Carradale Hotel*, T/F431223, carradaleh@aol.com, which offers excellent food and a lively bar with a good selection of local malts and cask ales. There are also several **B&Bs** and a **campsite** at Carradale Bay, with full facilities, T431665; open Easter-Sep.

Isle of Arran

Phone code: 01770
Colour map 5, grid B3

In the wedge of sea between Ayrshire and Kintyre lies the oval-shaped and very beautiful island of Arran. It manages to combine the classic features of the Northwest Highlands with the more sedate pleasures of the Southern Lowlands, thus earning the sobriquet, "Scotland in Miniature". This obvious appeal, coupled with its easy accessibility, makes Arran a very popular destination, but it remains unspoiled, and at 25 miles long is big enough never to feel crowded.

The island attracts all sorts of visitors: hill-walkers and climbers come to tackle the 10 summits over 2,000 ft and dozens of ridge routes; golfers are driven by their desire to play on no fewer than seven courses; the beaches of the southeast are popular with the bucket and spade brigade; and the island is a big hit with geology students, who come here in droves to marvel at the unique rock formations.

Although tourism has become Arran's main income earner, the island is large enough to sustain a relatively stable population of around 4,500, only slightly more than the number of red deer which roam wild in the beautiful mountain glens. Arran was tacked on to North Ayrshire in the recent local government reorganisation, but its geological, historical and cultural links are with the Highlands and Islands, hence its inclusion here.

Ins and outs

The main **ferry** route to Arran is from the distinctly unappealing Ayrshire town of Ardrossan to the island's main town, Brodick. The *CalMac* car/passenger ferry makes the 55 min journey 6 times daily Mon-Sat, 4 times on Sun. A one-way fare costs £4.55 per passenger and £32.50 per car (£26.50 off peak). A 'Day Saver' return (available Apr-Oct) costs £61 for a car and up to 4 passengers. A 5-day return costs £42.50 per car, £7.70 per passenger (subject to availability). There's a regular train connection between Ardrossan and Glasgow Central. There's also a bus connection to/from Edinburgh. By **car**, from the south the main route to Arran is from the M74 motorway, on to the A71 via Kilmarnock, to Irvine and Ardrossan. For more ferry information, contact Ardrossan ferry office, T01294-463470, or Brodick, T01770-302166.

The other **ferry** routes to Arran are from Claonaig, near Skipness on the east coast of Kintyre, to Lochranza in the north of the island. The non-bookable car/passenger ferry makes the 30-min trip 8-11 times daily during the summer (Apr-Oct), less frequently in winter. A one-way journey costs £4.10 per passenger and £18.50 per car. A 'Day Saver' return costs £37.00 for a car and up to 4 passengers. There is also a limited service from Tarbert to Lochranza (1 hr 35 mins). An Island Hopscotch ticket allows you to journey to Brodick and leave from Lochranza or vice versa, giving you more freedom on the island. Adult £7.80, car £41.00. For ferry times, T08705-650000, www.calmac.co.uk; for reservations on sailings to Lochranza, T01880-730253.

Getting there
For details of bus services to Claonaig, T01546-604695

Argyll

Arran

Getting around Fifty seven miles of main road run right around the coastline and pass through every village, making it easy to see much of the island by **car** in a short space of time. There are also two roads, "The String" and The Ross Road, which bisect the island. Arran is best appreciated on a **bike**, however, and for details of bike hire, see below under Brodick.

It's possible to explore the island using public transport, as there are regular **bus** and postbus services. However you should bear in mind that buses to the north and south of the island leave as soon as passengers have disembarked from the ferry, so you need to be organised: there is no time to go to the tourist office or banks first if you're in a hurry to explore the island. There are regular daily buses from Brodick to Blackwaterfoot (30 mins) via "The String"; to Lamlash (10 mins) and Whiting Bay (25 mins) and on to Blackwaterfoot (1 hr 10 mins); to Corrie (20 mins), Sannox (25 mins), Lochranza (45 mins), Catacol (50 mins), Pirnmill (1 hr), Machrie (1 hr 10 mins) and Blackwaterfoot (1 hr 20 mins). There's also a postbus service from Brodick to Corrie, Sannox, Lochranza, Catacol, Pirnmill, Machrie, Blackwaterfoot and back to Brodick; and from Brodick to Lamlash, "The Ross", Kildonan, Whiting Bay and back to Brodick.

A rural daycard gives you unlimited travel on Arran for £3. For bus times and more information contact the tourist office in Brodick, where you can pick up a free copy of the *Arran Transport Guide*, or contact *Arran Rural Rover*, T302000, or *Postbus*, T01546 604695.

Brodick

The largest and busiest settlement on Arran, and main ferry port, is Brodick, lying in a wide bay (hence its Norse name *breidr vik*, meaning "broad bay") backed by a range of steep crags. It's not the most attractive village on the island, and consists of little more than one long street that sweeps round the bay, but you'll find a wide range of tourist facilities and services here. Brodick also makes a convenient base from which to explore the island, particularly if you intend climbing Goatfell, Arran's highest mountain, or walking in Glen Rosa (see page 284).

Ins & outs **Getting around Cycle hire** *Mini Golf Cycle Hire*, T302272, F302903, *Brodick Cycles*, T/F302460, and *Brodick Boat & Cycle Hire*, T302868, are all on the seafront and all charge around £9 per day for mountain bikes.

Tourist Information Centre Beside the ferry pier and bus terminal. T302140, F302395, www.ayrshire-arran.com Mar-Sep Mon-Sat 0900-1930, Sun 0900-1700, also open daily in winter, all hours can vary greatly so do check beforehand.

Sights A few miles north of town is the impressive **Brodick Castle**, one of the island's top sights and a flagship NTS property. Until recently this was the family seat of the Dukes of Hamilton, erstwhile owners of the island. The oldest part of the castle dates from the 13th century, with extensions added in the 16th, 17th and 19th centuries. The hour-long tour of the sumptuously furnished rooms and huge kitchens is very interesting and can be perfectly rounded off with a visit to the castle restaurant, where you can enjoy cheap and tasty, home-cooked meals or light snacks and excellent home baking. On a good day you can even sit outside on the castle terrace and have lunch whilst admiring the views over Brodick Bay. The walled garden is also worth a look, and the surrounding country park includes 11 miles of way-marked trails. ■ *Castle and restaurant open 1 Apr-30 Jun and 1 Sep-31 Oct, daily 1100-1630; 1 Jul-31 Aug, daily 1100-1700. Garden and country park open all year, daily 0930-1700 (country park – sunset). £6 (£4.50 concession); garden and country park only £2.50 (£1.70). T302202.*

Halfway between the village and the castle is the **Arran Heritage Museum**, which consists of a pile of old tools and furniture in a converted 18th-century farm. Strictly for the enthusiast or the terminally bored. It also has a tearoom.
■ *Apr-Oct daily 1000-1630. £2.25, £1.00 child.*

Brodick boasts some pretty high-class accommodation, the best of which is the **A** *Kilmichael Country House Hotel*, T302219, F302068, www.kilmichael.com 7 rooms. Take the road north towards the castle, turn left at the golf course and follow the signs for about a mile. Refined elegance and gracious living in the heart of the countryside in the island's oldest house. Their award-winning restaurant is quite simply the best on the island, and that's really saying something, and booking is essential for non-residents. No children under 12.

    Just beyond the turning to Kilmichael is the road leading to **B-C** *Auchrannie Country House Hotel*, T302234, F302812, www.auchrannie.co.uk 28 rooms (also self-catering and time-share lodges). May lack the charm of Kilmichael but makes up for it with superb facilities and state-of-the-art leisure complex. It also has a 36-bedroom spa resort.Their *Garden Restaurant* is also highly rated and the popular *Brambles Bistro* offers less expensive bar meals.

    There are several hotels closer to the ferry along the seafront, is the **D** *Dunvegan House Hotel*, T/F302811, which offers good quality cooking for residents only. There is also plentiful **B&B** accommodation, including the secluded **E** *Glen Cloy Farmhouse*, Glen Cloy Rd, T302351, which is a cut above the rest, or the consistently-good **E** *Tigh-na-Mara*, on the seafront, T302538, www.arran.net/brodick/tighnamara The nearest **campsite** is *Glen Rosa*, T302380, open Apr-Oct, two miles from town on the road to Blackwaterfoot.

Aside from the hotels, and the castle restaurant mentioned above, there's the excellent *Creelers Seafood Restaurant*, at the Home Farm, a mile or so north of town on the road to the castle, T302810. Some of the best seafood in the whole country served in an informal atmosphere. Taste their Scandinavian smoked salmon and die. For a cheaper alternative try the *Brodick Bar*, behind Wooley's bakery and opposite the post office. Superior pub grub served in the bar or restaurant next door at cheap-mid-range prices.

Arran has an enviable reputation for producing fine foods, and *Home Farm*, just north of the village, has a couple of places you won't want to miss if you're looking for a tasty souvenir. The *Island Cheese Company*, T302788, produces a range of cheeses for sale, including soft cheeses, flavoured cheddars and the famous Arran Blue Cheese. You can also watch the cheese-making process. On the opposite side of the courtyard is *Creelers Smokehouse*, T302797, where you can find a vast range of delicious smoked fish, shellfish, poultry and game, and an excellent restaurant (see Eating above). Next door is *Arran Aromatics*, T302595, open daily 0930-1730, which produces a wide range of unique and beautifully packaged natural soaps and body care products. A rare treat for the olfactory organ. Chocolate lovers shouldn't miss the *Arran Chocolate Factory*, Invercloy, Shore Road, T302873, where you can drool as you watch chocolates being made. Finally there's the *Arran Brewery Company* at Claddach T302061, which has a viewing gallery where you can watch beer being made.

    On the main street is the excellent *Wooley's of Arran*, a highly-acclaimed bakers producing great rolls and their own oatcakes. For more basic provisions, there's the *Co-op supermarket* near the ferry terminal.Directory

Banks The *Bank of Scotland* and *Royal Bank* are both on the seafront, both with ATMs. **Communications** Post office: Just off the seafront, opposite the petrol station and pharmacy. NB These are the only banks on the island.

Sleeping

Eating

Shopping

Directory

Argyll

Lamlash The south of Arran is a fertile landscape of rolling hills and pretty little seaside villages, where you'll find the bulk of the island's population and tourists. A few miles south of Brodick is Lamlash, a quiet and attractive place set in a wide, sheltered bay but with an unappealing mud beach. Lying just offshore is the humpbacked **Holy Island**, which is owned by a group of Scottish Buddhists who have retired here for peace and meditation. A ferry runs to and from the island several times daily from 1 May to 4 September (limited service 5 September to 30 October), and costs £8 return. The first ferry departs Lamlash at 1000 and the last one returns at 1715, leaving you just enough time to climb up to the highest point, **Mullach Mór** (1,030 ft). Boats can be hired for **fishing trips** from the pier, T600998. For fishing supplies or information on **scuba diving**, contact *Johnson's Marine Stores* at the Old Pier, T600333.

The main reason for visiting Lamlash is the excellent **Arran Fine Foods**, at the Old Mill, at the southern entrance to the village, T600606. Here you'll find a mouth-watering selection of locally produced mustards, preserves and chutneys. Don't leave Arran without them!

Sleeping and eating The **C** *Glen Isle Hotel*, T600559, does a good, moderately priced 3-course dinner. Otherwise there's the **D** *Lilybank Guest House*, T600230, which also serves good food. There are several cheaper **B&B** options and also a **campsite** T600251, open mid-Apr to mid-Oct, a short way south of town. Good pubs in which to get a decent bar meal are: the *Pierhead Tavern*, T600380, and *The Drift Inn*, T600656.

Whiting Bay Down in the southeast of Arran, Whiting Bay enjoys a beautiful setting and makes a pleasant alternative to Brodick as an island base, with some good accommodation and restaurants. Whiting Bay is also the starting point for the lovely walk up to **Glenashdale Falls** (see page 284).

Sleeping and eating C-B *Argentine House Hotel*, T700662, F700693, www. argentinearran.co.uk 5 rooms, on the seafront and easily recognisable by the flags flying outside. Swiss owners are friendly, hospitable and professional. Excellent cooking with a continental touch. Dinner is also available to non-residents but booking is essential. **C-D** *Burlington Hotel*, T700255, F700232, www.milford.co.uk/go/ burlingtonarran.html 9 rooms, open Easter-Oct. Comfortable rooms and a reputation for superb seafood; moderately priced set 3-course dinner in dining room or à la carte in bistro. There are also **B&Bs** and **guesthouses**, such as **E** *Swan's Guest House*, Rowallan, T700729, Feb-Nov; and a *SYHA Youth Hostel* on the seafront by the bridge, T700339; open end-Feb to end-Oct.

A cheaper alternative to the hotels mentioned above is the *Coffee Pot* on Golf Course Rd, T700382, where you can enjoy tasty but cheap snacks and home baking. Open Easter-Oct daily, 1000-1700 (Jul/Aug 1000-1900). There are two good places to eat on Shore Road, *Cameronia*, T700254, or the very popular *The Pantry*, T700489 (booking essential for the latter).

Transport *Whiting Bay Garage*, T/F700345, for car hire, taxis, or island tours. *Whiting Bay Hires*, on the jetty, T700382, for cycle hire.

South of Whiting Bay The main road runs south from Whiting Bay, then swings west along the south coast of Arran, with great views south across to the distinctive mound of Ailsa Craig, lying off the coast of South Ayrshire. There are some good sandy beaches along this stretch, particularly at **Kildonan**, a village set back off the main road and with a ruined castle looking out to the island of **Pladda**. Anyone with a sudden urge to throw themselves off the nearest cliff can try their hand at **paragliding**, at *Flying Fever*, No 2 Coastguard House in Kildonan, T820292, www.flyingfever.net

About four miles west of Kildonan are the tiny villages of **Torrylinn**, **Lagg** and **Kilmory**, where you can stop off at the **Torrylinn Creamery** to buy some excellent local cheese and watch it being made, T/F870240, open Sunday-Friday 1000-1600. You can stay here at the **C** *Lagg Hotel*, T870255, an 18th century coaching inn set in acres of woodland by the river, or at the local **campsites**, at *Breadalbane Lodge*, T820210, and *Kildonan Hotel*, T820207, where there's also a **bunkhouse**. Just beyond these villages the Ross Road branches off northeast up Glen Scorrodale to Lamlash. The A841 meanwhile continues north to Blackwaterfoot, on the southwest coast.

The little fishing village of Blackwaterfoot is set round an attractive bay with a tiny harbour – smaller than some people's jacuzzis. There's plenty to do around these parts. Two miles north along the coast are the **King's Caves**, where, according to legend, Robert the Bruce watched a spider try, try and try again and was thus inspired to secure his own and Scotland's destiny. It's a 45-minute walk from where you leave the car to the cathedral-like main cave, which has an iron gate to keep out wandering sheep. There's also **pony trekking** at *Cairnhouse Riding Centre*, T860466, which caters for beginners and experienced riders, and **fly fishing**, at *Port-Na-Lochan Fishery*, T860276.

Blackwaterfoot
The village maintains its quiet charm, even at the height of the summer, and is the ideal place to escape the crowds and enjoy some peace and quiet

A couple of miles northeast of Blackwaterfoot, at **Shiskine**, on the "String Road" which cuts across the middle of the island to Brodick, is the **Balmichael Visitor Centre**, a good place to bring the kids, with a motor museum, adventure playground and a quad bike track. ■ *Mon-Sat 1000-1700, Sun 1200-1700 (closed Mon and Tue in winter). T860430*.

Four miles north of Blackwaterfoot, off the main coast road, is **Machrie Moor**, site of the most impressive of Arran's Bronze-Age **stone circles**. Park by the *Historic Scotland* sign and then walk for one and a half miles along the farm track to reach an area boasting no fewer than six stone circles. Many of them are barely visible above the ground, but the tallest is over 18 ft high.

A few miles further on, just south of the turn-off to Machrie village, is another Historic Scotland sign, this time for **Moss Farm Road Stone Circle**, which lies about a half mile walk along the farm track. There's another Bronze-Age site nearby, at **Auchagallon**.

Sleeping There are a couple of options should you wish to stay here. **B-C** *Kinloch Hotel*, T860444, F860447, www.kinloch-arran.com The largest hotel on the island with 51 rooms and full leisure facilities including swimming pool, sauna, gym and squash court. The are also plenty of **B&Bs**, which are cheaper and of rather more modest proportions, including **E** *Morvern House*, T860254, **E** *Lochside*, T860276, and **E** *The Greannan*, T860200.

North Arran

The north half of Arran contrasts sharply with the southern part. It looks and feels more like the Scottish Highlands – desolate, unspoiled and much of it accessible only to the serious hill-walker. But though the north is scenically more spectacular, it attracts relatively few visitors.

Six miles north of Brodick is Arran's loveliest village, Corrie; a row of perfect, whitewashed fishermen's cottages lining the seafront. Corrie has a couple of hotels and B&Bs, a good pub, and makes an attractive alternative to Brodick

Corrie

as a starting point for the ascent of Goatfell (see page 285).

The main coastal road continues north from Corrie to **Sannox,** with its sandy beach, then it cuts inland and climbs steeply northwest towards Lochranza. It's worth taking your time on this part of the road to admire the wonderful views of the mountains and on the other side of the pass, in **Glen Chalmadale,** you can see red deer heading down to the shore at dusk.

Sleeping D *Tigh-na-Achaidh*, T810208, offers self-catering accommodation. E *Corrie Hotel*, T810273. Friendly, unassuming and good value with a lively bar. E *Blackrock Guest House*, T810282. Open Mar-Oct.

Shopping *Corrie Stores* on Shore Rd is a good place to stock up on locally produced food and drink, as it sells everything from oatcakes to beer.

Lochranza

The most spectacular introduction to Arran is to arrive at Lochranza, the most northerly village and second ferry port. This charming village is guarded by its ruined 13th-century castle and backed by looming mountains. **Lochranza Castle** can be visited free of charge (the key is available from the *Lochranza Stores*).

Lochranza is also the site of Scotland's newest distillery, **Isle of Arran Distillers,** which opened in 1995 and is the first legal whisky distillery on the island for over 150 years. There are guided tours of the distillery, followed by the obligatory dram, and also an excellent restaurant (see below). ■ *T830264, www.arranwhisky.com Mar-Oct daily 1000-1800. Guided tours held throughout the day. £3.50, £2.50 child.* A couple of miles southwest of Lochranza is the tiny village of **Catacol,** whose whitewashed cottages are know as 'The Twelve Apostles'. Here, the bar of the *Catacol Bay Hotel* serves good, cheap pub food and also puts on live music.

Sleeping and eating Lochranza has a decent selection of places to stay, best of which is **D** *Apple Lodge*, T/F830229. A lovely country house with four double rooms, offering high quality home cooking (for residents only). Around the same price but lacking the charm, is **D** *Lochranza Hotel*, T830223, whose bar is the social hub of the village. A cheaper option is **E** *Castlekirk*, T830202, a converted church opposite the castle, or the slightly austere **E** *Benvaren*, T830647. Cheaper still is **F** Croftbank Cottage, T830201, next to the Post Office; or the *SYHA Youth Hostel*, T830631, open Feb-Dec, overlooking the castle. There's a beautifully situated **campsite** next to the golf course, with full facilities, T820273, office@lochgolf. demon.co.uk, open Apr-Oct.

The best place to eat is *Harold's Restaurant*, T830264, arranvc@aol.com, on the upper floor of the distillery visitor centre. Here you can enjoy innovative Scottish/Caribbean cuisine in bright, modern surroundings. Open till 2100. Mid-range prices. The only alternative is the *Lochranza Hotel* which does cheap bar meals. Further round the coast at Pirnmill is the very popular Lighthouse tea room.

Walks on Arran

OS map No 69 covers these walks. Ask local advice during the deer stalking season (late Aug to late Oct)

Arran is a hill walker's paradise. The north part of the island boasts ten peaks of over 2,000 ft and dozens of ridge walks while the gentler south features a variety of less strenuous forest walks. Note that you should only attempt these routes in good weather and avoid climbing any rockfaces. Some ridge walks (A'Chir, Witches Step, Suidhe Fherghas and Cioch Na Oighe) involve quite a lot of scrambling and can be dangerous. They should only be attempted by fit and experienced climbers. Ropes and good OS maps should also be taken.

Argyll

Arran's most popular peak, Goatfell, is also its highest, at 2,866 ft. There's a
path leading up from Corrie, but most people begin the walk from the car
park at **Cladach sawmill**, near Brodick Castle. The path is well marked, easy
to follow and, apart from the final section, relatively easy. It runs initially
through the **Brodick Country Park**, then follows the **Cnocan burn** as it
rises steadily through woodland before crossing the **Mill burn**. Beyond the
burn is a deer fence which runs across the entire island to keep the deer from
the north away from the farming in the south. Above the deer fence the landscape changes to heather moorland and the path begins to climb the flanks
of the mountain. The final 650 ft up to the top is steep and rocky and the path
is not always clear. The last section requires some scrambling on loose scree
but the views that greet you at the top on a clear day are magnificent, stretching right across from Ireland to Mull.

The walk to the summit and back should take about five hours. Though it's
considered a fairly straightforward ascent, remember that this should be
treated with the same caution and respect as any Scottish mountain. You
should be dressed and equipped appropriately and be prepared for any sudden change in the weather. There are also numerous ridge walks around
Goatfell as well as other high peaks to climb.

Many of the walks start from **Glen Rosa Farm**. One of these takes in the
three Beinns; **Beinn Nuis**, **Beinn Tarsuinn** (2,681 ft) and **Beinn
A'Chliabhain**. Start at Glen Rosa Farm and go up the Wood Road to the
High Deer Gate, then to Torr Breac and the 'Y' junction at the top of the
Garbhalt and on to the path which runs round the Three Beinns. This is a full
day's walk.

Another excellent walk is from Glen Rosa to the head of the Glen; then
take the path up into the **Coire Buidhe** and on to the ridge between **Cir
Mhor** (2,617 ft) and **A'Chir** (known as the **Ceems Ridge**). Then follow the
path around the west side of A'Chir. This is not easy to find, but takes you
around the back of A'Chir to **Bowman's Pass** and the north end of **Beinn
Tarsuinn**. From here take the path to **Beinn A'Chliabhan** and down to the
foot of **Garbhalt Ridge** and back down to Glen Rosa.

Cir Mhor can also be climbed from Glen Rosa. Before going over into
Glen Sannox take the steep path straight up. On the way back down, head
into Coire Buidhe and back down the glen. You can also continue from the
top of Cir Mhor and take the path around the west side of A'Chir to the
north end of the Bowman's Pass up on to Beinn Tarsuinn and along the
ridge to Beinn Nuis, then down the path to the Garbhalt Bridge.

Finally, you can also climb **Caisteal Abhail** (2,818 ft) from Glen Rosa. Go
straight up into Coire Buidge on to the Ceems Ridge. Then take the path
round the west side of the A'Chir through the Bowman's Pass and on to Beinn
A'Chliabhain down the side of the Garbhalt to Glen Rosa.

There are also several walks in and around lovely Glen Sannox. It's a
pleasant walk just to make your way up the head of the Glen and return
the same way. You can walk up the Glen to beyond the old mine then
make your way up towards the **Devil's Punchbowl** until you reach the
main path and follow that down into the Coire. Take the main path back
down into Glen Sannox instead of trying to climb out of the Devil's
Punchbowl. You can also walk from **Glen Sannox** to **Glen Rosa**, which
takes around four hours.

Goatfell

Glen Rosa

Argyll

Glen Sannox

Walk to Glenashdale Falls and Giants' Graves

This is one of the most popular walks on the island. It's a steady, easy climb through woodland with the considerable incentive of a beautiful waterfall at the end of it. Both walks can be done together and should take around two to three hours in total, though you should allow some time to enjoy the falls. If you want to take a picnic, pop into the Village Shop which has a wide range of deli-type foods and local cheeses.

The trail starts by the bridge over **Glenashdale Burn**, *next to the Youth Hostel. There's a map board here showing the route. Walk up the track alongside the burn till you see the sign for the path leading to the left up to the* **Giants' Graves**. *It's about 40-45 minutes up to the graves and back to this point, but it's a stiff climb up a steep staircase of 265 steps. At the top continue left along a path through the trees, which then curves right till you reach a*

clearing and the graves, which are chambered tombs, believed to be around 5,000 years old. Depending on the light, this can be a very eerie, but almost magical place.

Return back down the steps, and head left along the main path as it climbs steadily above the burn, past smaller falls, till you reach the main falls. The setting is stunning and the falls are spectacular as they plummet 140 ft into the pools below. You can rest and have a picnic at the top of the falls, or follow the paths down to the pools below which you can swim. The path back down to **Whiting Bay** *passes the scant remains of an* **Iron-Age fort**, *then turns back uphill to reach a broad track. Turn right, cross a small burn by stepping stones, then follow the track downhill all the way to the main road, a short way along from the car park.*

Inner Hebrides

7

Inner Hebrides

The Inner Hebrides comprise the great swathe of islands lying off the western coast of Scotland – east of the Outer Hebrides, south of Skye and west of the Kintyre peninsula. Each is very different in appearance and atmosphere and each has its own distinct appeal.

The most accessible of the islands is **Mull**, a short ferry ride from Oban. It's also the most popular by far, and with some justification. The variety of scenery on offer is astounding and its capital, Tobermory, is the most attractive port in western Scotland. A stone's throw from Mull is tiny **Iona**, one of the most important religious sites in Europe, with some divine beaches. Boat trips can be made from Mull or Iona to the dramatic island of **Staffa**, looming out of the sea like a great cathedral and the inspiration for Mendelssohn's 'Hebrides Overture'. Further west, windswept **Coll** and **Tiree** offer miles of unspoilt beaches and some great windsurfing and, to the south, **Colonsay** is a stress-free zone that makes Mull seem hectic.

Those who enjoy a good malt whisky should head for **Islay**, famed for its distilleries, while neighbouring **Jura** is a wild and beautiful place, perfect for some off-the-beaten-track hiking. If you're after some peace and quiet on Jura then you're in good company, for this is where George Orwell came to write '1984'. Furthest north are the "small islands" of **Eigg**, **Muck**, **Rùm** and **Canna**, reached from Mallaig, but ignored by most tourists. People come here for the fine bird watching and superb walking.

Inner Hebrides

Ins and outs

Getting there

Car space on ferries is limited during the summer months, so it's advisable to book ahead

There are **flights** from Glasgow to Port Ellen (**Islay**): 2 daily Mon-Fri and 1 on Sat (40 mins), all year round. From Glasgow to Tiree: 1 flight daily Mon-Sat (45 mins), all year round. For flight times, call *British Airways Express*, T08457-733377, the local **Tourist Information Centres**, or Port Ellen airport, T01496-302022, and Tiree airport, T01879-220309.

CalMac car and passenger **ferries** sail to and from Mull, Islay, Coll, Tiree, Colonsay and Gigha, and passenger-only ferries sail to Iona and the Small Isles (Eigg, Muck, Rùm and Canna). The departure point for ferries to Mull, Coll, Tiree and Colonsay is **Oban**. Ferry times change according to the day of the week and time of the year, so they aren't listed in full below. Services listed below under each separate island are for the summer period (2 Apr-16 Oct). For full details see the *CalMac* Ferry Guide or call *CalMac*, T08705-650000, reservations@calmac.co.uk (reservations); T01475-650100, www.calmac.co.uk (general enquiries).

For details of **bus** connections from Oban to Glasgow, contact *Scottish Citylink*, T08705-505050. For **train** services from Mallaig to Fort William and Glasgow, contact *Scotrail*, T08457-484950. See also page 46. There are regular daily train and bus services from Glasgow. For full details, see page 261, or contact the TIC in Oban, T01631-563122. The departure point for ferries to Islay (and on to Jura), and some ferries to Colonsay, is **Kennacraig**. There are daily bus services from Glasgow, via Tarbert (see page 273). **Mallaig** is the ferry port for the Small Isles of Eigg, Muck, Rùm and Canna. There are regular bus and train services from Glasgow, via Fort William (see page 471). For bus, train and ferry times, pick up Argyll & Bute Council's free *Area Transport Guides to Lorn, Mull and Islay & Jura*, available at most tourist offices. For times of buses and trains to Mallaig, for the Small Isles, see the *South Highland Public Transport Travel Guide* (£1), available at main tourist offices. For details on how to get around the Inner Hebrides by public transport, see under the relevant island destination.

Getting around

Island Hopscotch Tickets are a cheaper way to get around the islands with a **car**. There are various route options, and tickets give you 30 days' unlimited travel on each route. For example, a ticket for the Oban-Craignure-Tobermory-Kilchoan-Mallaig-Armadale route, allowing you to visit Mull and Skye, costs £8.55 per passenger and £53 per car. See the *CalMac* guide or call the numbers above for full details of the Island Hopscotch Tickets, and the **Island Rover Ticket**, which gives unlimited travel on most *CalMac* routes for 8 or 15 days.

Tourist information

There are **Tourist Information Centres** in Oban (see page 261), Craignure and Tobermory (Mull), Bowmore (Islay), and Mallaig (see page 486). Oban tourist office has information on all the islands covered in this chapter, with the exception of the Small Isles, information on which can be got from Mallaig tourist office.

Isle of Mull

Colour map 3, grid B3/4

The island of Mull is the third largest of the Hebridean islands and, after Skye, the most popular. Everyone has their own favourite island, but Mull has enough going for it to appeal to most tastes: spectacular mountain scenery; 300 miles of wild coastline; castles; wildlife; a narrow-gauge railway; some of the best fishing in Scotland; and some of the prettiest little villages; all in an area roughly 24 miles from north to south and 26 miles from east to west. It's worth spending time on Mull to fully appreciate its pleasures and to take advantage of the great hospitality of an island where people don't even have to lock their doors at night.

Things to do in the Inner Hebrides

- Take a boat trip to the spectacular island of Staffa and the cathedral-like Fingal's cave, which inspired Mendelssohn.
- Hire a bike and explore the island of Iona, especially the very wonderful Bay at the Back of the Ocean.
- Take a walk on the wild side on the remote and windswept island of Jura.
- If you're a golfer, tee off at Machrie, a memorable golfing experience.
- If you're into windsurfing, head for the island of Tiree for the ultimate challenge.

Ins and outs

Mull is well served by **ferry** services. From Oban to Craignure (40 mins) 6-8 times daily Mon-Sat and 5 times daily on Sun. One-way tickets cost £3.55 per passenger and £24.55 per car. *CalMac* offices: Oban, T01631-566688, and Craignure, T01680-812343. From Kilchoan to Tobermory 7 times daily Mon-Sat and 5 times daily on Sun (Jun-Aug). A one-way tickets cost £3.40 per passenger and £18.05 per car. From Lochaline to Fishnish (15 mins) hourly 0700-1910 Mon-Sat and 0900-1800 Sun. A one-way ticket costs £2.15 per passenger and £9.65 per car. Some ferries from Oban to Coll and Tiree call in at Tobermory.

Getting there
Mull is one of the most accessible of the Hebridean islands

You can get to most parts of the island by **bus**. Services given below are for Apr-Oct. Winter services are less frequent. There's a bus from Tobermory post office to Dervaig and Calgary, 5 times a day Mon-Fri and twice on Sat (operated by *RN Carmichael*, T01688-302220). The Craignure to Tobermory via Salen service runs 5 times a day Mon-Fri, 8 times on Sat and 3 times on Sun (operated by *Bowman's Coaches*, T01680-812313, and *Highlands & Islands Coaches*, T01680-812510). There's a bus from Craignure to Fionnphort (for Iona) 6 times a day Mon-Fri, 4 times on Sat and 1 on Sun (*Bowman's* and *Highlands & Islands*). There's also a postbus service from Salen to Burg (Kilninian) via the Ulva Ferry twice a day Mon-Sat (*Royal Mail*, T01463-256200). For bus times, contact the operators or pick up a free copy of the *Mull Area Transport Guide* at the tourist office in Oban, Tobermory or Craignure. This also includes ferry times.

Getting around

The island's 140 miles of **roads** are almost all single-track and mostly in poor condition, so allow plenty of time to get from place to place. The best sections are from Craignure to Salen and the few miles south from Tobermory towards Salen. Petrol stations are few and far between, so it's best to fill up before leaving Oban, on arrival in Craignure, or in Tobermory. Another point worth noting is that the sheep on Mull are even more fearless and stubborn than in other parts of the Highlands and Islands and regard the roads very much as their own, which can slow you down even more. If you want to try your luck, you can hire a car from *Mackay's Garage* in Tobermory, or at the *Bayview Garage* just outside Craignure, on the road to Toronsay Castle. Expect to pay around £32-35 a day.

Cycling is a good way to get around and there are a number of places to rent bikes. In Tobermory there's *Tom-a' Mhuillin* on the Salen Rd, T01688-302164, *Brown's Hardware* shop on Main St, T01688-302020, or try the youth hostel (see page 296). In **Salen** there's *On Yer Bike*, T01680-300501, which also has a shop by the ferry terminal in **Craignure**, T01680-812487. Expect to pay around £8-10 per day.

The best time to visit is generally May and Jun and late Aug to Sep. At these times midges and clegs (horse flies) are not so much of a problem. But Mull is the wettest of the Hebridean islands and rain can fall at any time, even in the summer months, so you'll need to come prepared.

Climate

Inner Hebrides

Festivals & events A great time to be on Mull is during the annual **Mull Music Festival**, known as the Whisky Olympics, is held on the last weekend of Apr, when you can enjoy a feast of Gaelic folk music and, of course, whisky. The focus of the festival is the bar of the *Mishnish Hotel* in Tobermory (for details T01688-302383). Another great musical event is the **Mendelssohn on Mull Festival**, held over 10 days in early Jul to commemorate the famous composer's visit here in 1829. **The Sound of Mull**, a day long celebration of local rock and pop acts, takes place at the end of Sep. The **Tobermory Highland Games** take place annually on the 3rd Thu in Jul. Rally enthusiasts should not miss the **Tour of Mull Rally** held in early Oct, which is part of the Scottish Championship. Anyone who's complained about the state of Mull's roads (and who hasn't?) should watch the professionals hurtle around the island at over 60 mph!

Like many of the Hebridean islands, the people of Mull, or *Muileachs*, suffered greatly during the Clearances, when they were forced off their land to make way for sheep. The subsequent decline in population was exacerbated by the terrible potato famine of 1846, and the population fell dramatically from a peak of 10,600 in 1820. Numbers have stabilized to around 2,500 in recent years, mainly through the replacement of native islanders by English and Scottish incomers, known as 'White Settlers'. This is something of a sore point and the locals sarcastically refer to their island as 'The Officer's Mess', when the resident population rises to around 8,000 during the summer.

With around 600,000 visitors a year, tourism is an important contributor to the island's economy, supplementing the traditional fishing, crofting and whisky distilling. Despite the numbers, Mull remains unspoiled, though the main roads become congested at the height of the season and accommodation can be hard to find, as there are few large hotels or campsites on the island.

Mull

Craignure and around

The arrival point for most visitors is the tiny village of Craignure, which is little more than a row of houses scattered along the seafront. There are a few places to eat, a tourist office and some basic services, but precious little else in the way of diversions, though Torosay Castle is just down the road. Directly opposite the pier is the **Tourist Information Centre**, in the same building as the *CalMac* office, T812377. ■ *Easter to end of Oct, Mon-Thu and Sat 0900-1900 (Sat till 2015 in Jul and Aug), Fri 0900-1700, Sun 1030-1700 (till 1900 Jun-Aug). Also Nov-Easter Monday-Sat 0900-1700, Sun 1030-1200 and 1530-1700.*

Not far from the pier, on the main road heading south, is **D** *Craignure Inn*, T812305, www.craignure-inn.co.uk 3 rooms, open all year. Its cosy bar serves decent cheap-moderately priced food and is a good place to seek refuge on a wet day. There are also several guesthouses and B&Bs around Craignure, all in the **E** category (details from the tourist office). A little further south of the *Craignure Inn*, on the opposite side, is the turning to *Shielings Holiday Campsite*, T812496, which is beside the terminal for the little steam railway to Torosay Castle (see below). As well as a campsite with full facilities, there's accommodation in self-catering "shielings", which are carpeted cottage tents (**F**). On the north side of the ferry pier is *MacGregor's* restaurant, T812471, a general store and post office.

> **Sleeping & eating**

Three miles south of Craignure, at Lochdon, is the **D** *Old Mill Guest House & Restaurant*, T/F812442. 3 rooms. Their cosy little restaurant has a deserved reputation for fine cuisine, so you'll need to book in advance.

One and a half miles south of Craignure is **Torosay Castle**, more of a baronial family home than a full-blown castle. Inside everything is informal and, refreshingly, there are invitations to sit down, or touch things, or even look through old family scrapbooks. There is some fine Edwardian furniture and paintings by Landseer and Sargent. The real attraction though, is the fabulous garden, designed by Lorimer, especially the Italianate statue walk. In the castle grounds you can watch traditional weaving methods at the **Isle of Mull Weavers**, or visit the gallery and workshops of **Kells Gold and Silversmiths**, T812526, open daily 0900-1800. You can walk to the castle along a forest path starting just to the south of Craignure, but the best way to arrive at the castle is by the **Mull and West Highland Railway**. The little steam and diesel engine pulls the miniature carriages along the narrow-gauge track on the 20-minute journey from Craignure. ■ *The castle is open Easter-mid Oct daily 1030-1730. Gardens open all year daily 0900-1900. Admission to house and gardens £4.50, children £1.50; gardens only £3.50, child £1. Free parking, tearoom and shop. T812421. Isle of Mull Weavers open all year daily 0900-1700. Free. Mull and West Highland Railway open Easter-mid Oct (T812494 for times). Fares: £2.50 adult single, £3.50 return.*

> **Torosay Castle**

A couple of miles east of Torosay is **Duart Castle**. The 13th-century ancestral seat of the Clan Maclean stands imperiously at the end of a promontory, commanding impressive views over Loch Linnhe and the Sound of Mull. The castle's main feature is the tower house, built in the late 14th century when it became the main residence of the Macleans of Duart. Mull belonged to the clan until it was forfeited when the Macleans supported young Prince Charles Edward Stuart, who was defeated at Culloden in 1746. The castle was deserted for the next century and a half, then in 1911 Colonel Sir Fitzroy Donald

> **Duart Castle**

Maclean, chief of the clan, bought the castle from Murray Guthrie of Torosay and restored it as the clan chief's residence. Today it's a fascinating place to visit, with many relics and artifacts on display. There's also an excellent tea-room serving delicious home-baked scones. ■ *May-mid Oct daily 1030-1800. Adult £3.80, concession £3, children £1.90. T812309.*

Salen
Phone code: 01680

Midway between Craignure and Tobermory on the main A849 is the pretty village of Salen. It stands on the east coast at the narrowest point on the island, and is only three miles from the west coast, making it a good base from which to explore the island. **Bicycles** can be hired from *On Yer Bike* (T300501) for around £10 per day.

There are a couple of interesting sights around Salen. Just to the north, over-looking the bay, is the ruin of **Aros Castle**, built in the 14th century and one of the strongholds of the Lords of the Isles. Tradition holds that the treasure of the Spanish galleon sunk in Tobermory Bay in 1588 (see page 294) was recovered by the Macleans and still lies buried beneath the ruins of Aros Castle.

Four miles southwest of Salen, near **Gruline** and **Loch Ba**, is the **MacQuarrie Mausoleum**, which houses the remains of Major-General Lachlan MacQuarrie (1761-1824). He took over as Governer-General of New South Wales from the unpopular William Bligh, formerly of the *Bounty*, and became known as the "Father of Australia". The mausoleum is maintained by the National Trust for Scotland, on behalf of the National Trust of Australia.

Wildlife tours can be made from Aros, just to the north of Salen, with Richard Atkinson at *Island Encounter Wildlife Safaris*, Arla-Beag, Aros, T300441. Full-day wildlife safaris with a local guide cost £25 including lunch. You'll see golden eagles, white-tailed sea eagles, hen harriers, divers, merlins, peregrine falcons, seals and porpoises, to name but a few.

Sleeping and eating In the village is **B-C** *Salen Hotel*, T300324, F300599. 18 rooms, open all year. Near the MacQuarrie Mausoleum, at Gruline, is **D** *Gruline Home Farm*, T300581, F300573. There are also several **B&Bs** in and around Salen, mostly in the **E** category. About 5 miles south, just before the turn-off to the Fishnish to Lochaline Ferry, is *Balmeanach Park Caravan & Campsite*, with full facilities; and *Cynthia's Tearoom*, T300342, which serves snacks, lunches and a cheap to mid-range 3-course dinner.

Tobermory

Phone code: 01688
Population: 800
Tobermory is the only Highland town to have a Womble named after it

There is no prettier port in the west of Scotland than Tobermory, Mull's main village, which is set on the side of a steep hill in a wooded, sheltered bay. The brightly painted houses that line the harbour front date from the late 18th century when the British Fisheries Society built Tobermory as a planned herring port. It never really took off as a fishing port, however, and nowadays you're more likely to see pleasure yachts anchored in the protected waters of the natural harbour. Lying at the bottom of the harbour is a galleon of the Spanish Armada, which sank in mysterious circumstances, along with its treasure of gold doubloons which has eluded salvage crews ever since (see box on page 297).

Ins & outs

Getting there Tobermory is a 30-40 min drive north from the ferry pier at Craignure. There are regular daily buses from Craignure which coincide with ferry arrivals. For more details see page 291.

The **Tourist Information Centre** is in the same building as the *CalMac* ticket office, at the far end of Main St, T302182. It's open 6-29 Apr Mon-Fri 1000-1700,

Things to do on Mull when it's wet

It rains a lot on Mull, but luckily there's a fairly large number of indoor options to keep you nice and dry until the weather changes. If you've just arrived off the ferry from Oban and it's chucking it down, then head straight for **Torosay Castle**, *just to the south of Craignure. And if the weather changes whilst exploring the interior, don't miss the gardens. Just beyond the castle is* **Wings Over Mull**, *a bird of prey cpnservation centre which offers indoor hawk-handling and a chance to learn about the island's incredible bird life. Nearby is Mull's greatest fortification,* **Duart Castle**, *which is also worth a peek. If all that*

history gets too much then you could do worse than hole up in the bar of the **Craignure Inn** *and relax in front of their roaring log fire.*

In the north of the island, the most appealing option by far is the **Old Byre Heritage Centre**, *not far from the picturesque village of Dervaig. When in Tobermory do as the locals do, and get yourself down to the bar of the Mish, though you shouldn't really need the excuse of inclement weather. Meanwhile, over in Fionnphort, the departure point for the pilgrimage to Iona, you can seek spiritual assistance with a wee dram in the cosy* **Keel Row Bar**.

Sat-Sun 1200-1700; 30 Apr-1 Jul Mon-Fri 1000-1700, Sat-Sun 1100-1700; 2 Jul-2 Sep Mon-Sat 0930-1800, Sun 1000-1700; 3 Sep-28 Oct Mon-Sat 1000-1700, Sun 1200-1700.

Sights

The harbour front – known as **Main Street** – is where you'll find most of what you want: hotels, guesthouses, restaurants, pubs and shops and the tourist office. Mercifully, though, it's free from the tartan tat that blights so many other tourist hot-spots. Here you'll find the **Mull Museum**, housed in an old bakery. It's worth visiting on a rainy day and you'll learn all about the island's history. ■ *Easter-end Oct Mon-Fri 1030-1630, Sat 1030-1330. £1. T302493.*

At the foot of the main road down to the harbour is the tiny **Tobermory Distillery** which offers a guided tour rounded off with a sampling of the island's single malt. ■ *Easter to end-Oct Mon-Fri 1000-1700. Adult £2.50, concession £1, under 18 free. T302645.* At the top of Back Brae, on Argyll Terrace, is **An Tobar**, an excellent new arts centre housed in an old schoolhouse and featuring a varied programme of exhibitions, music and workshops. Or you can just have a coffee and admire the view. ■ *Mon-Sat all year 1000-1800. T302211, www.antobar.co.uk*

Sleeping

L *Western Isles Hotel*, T302012, F302297. 23 rooms. Open all year, the biggest and grandest hotel on the island, set high above the harbour with great views from the comfortable rooms, has 3 excellent restaurants, including the lovely conservatory bar. **B-C** *Tobermory Hotel*, 53 Main St, T302091, F302254. Good value and great location. Also on the harbour front, close to the ferry port is the famous **D** *Mishnish Hotel*, Main St, T302009, www.mishnish.co.uk Open all year, 10 rooms. Its bar is the live music focus of the town and social hub (see below). Best of the guesthouses on the harbour front is the excellent **E** *Failte Guest House*, T/F302495. Open Mar-Oct, 7 rooms. Also on Main St is the **F** *SYHA Youth Hostel*, T302481. Open end-Feb to end-Oct and rents out bikes.

There are many guesthouses and B&Bs uphill from the harbour, which are often better value. These include: **E** *Copeland House*, Jubilee Terr, T302049/302422. 3 en suite rooms with seaviews. **F-E** *Ivybank*, Argyll Terrace, T302250. Friendly and comfortable. A short walk from town is **E** *Baliscate Guest House*, T302048, F302666. 4 en

Inner Hebrides

suite rooms. They also organize fishing and wildlife trips (see 'Trips from Tobermory' below). Six miles from Tobermory on the Dervaig road is **C *Glencorm Castle***, T302321, a private house offering B&B year round.

Eating The best eating in town is to be had in the ***Western Isles Hotel*** (see above), where you can choose between 3 restaurants. A 3-course à la carte in the dining room or the oriental ***Spices Bistro*** is expensive to mid-range, while cheap bar meals are served in the excellent ***Conservatory Bar***. Not so stylish or tasty, but cheaper is the ***Highland Cottage Hotel*** on Breadalbane St, which does a moderately priced 4-course dinner.

The harbour front is filled with places where you can eat your fill, including the bar

Tobermory

To Golf Course

To Lighthouse

Mrs MacKinnon's B&B ■

Raeric Rd

Erray Rd

Western Rd

Copeland House B&B ■

Ruarigan Terr

Jubilee Terr

Isle of Mull Landrover
Wildlife Expeditions ○

Back Brae

Western Rd

Western Isles ■

An Tobar
Arts Centre ○

Tobermory Chocolate
Company ○

Mishnish ○

Victoria St

Church Brae

Back Brae

Seafare Chandlery
& Diving Services ○

CalMac
Ferry Terminal

Hebridean Whale & Dolphin Trust ○
SYHA Youth Hostel ■

Mull Museum 🏛

Dervaig Rd

Post Office
Brae

Island Bakery
Failte Guest House ■

Albert Street

Argyll Terr

Main St

Highland
Cottage Hotel ●

Ivybank B&B ■

West St

Tobermory ■

Harbour

Breadalbane St

Prison Brae

To Isle of Mull Cheese & Dervaig

To Isle of Mull Cheese & Dervaig

Tobermory River

Eas Brae

MacGochan's
Bar/Bistro ●

To Aros Park

Baliscate
Guest House ■

Mull
Pottery ○

Mull Silver Company ○

To Salen & Craignure

N

0 metres   100
0 yards   100

Inner Hebrides

Shiver me timbers!

The history of 16th-century Europe is littered with the remains of carefully forged and hastily broken political alliances between the various superpowers. One such deal between England and Spain was broken in 1588, prompting Philip II of Spain to send the Spanish Armada, a massive force of 130 ships, to take on the English navy. Originating in Cadiz, the Spanish force moved north and left Lisbon on 20 May. They met Queen Elizabeth's ships in the English Channel, where they were duly routed.

A number of Spanish ships fled up the east coast, chased by the British fleet as far as the Firth of Forth. Denied entry into the estuary by further British naval forces, the tattered remnants of these great Spanish galleons were no longer considered to pose a threat and were left to their own fate.

Many continued up the east coast of Scotland, only to be wrecked in the perilous North Sea. Not all the crews drowned, however, and several integrated into local communites, where their descendants still live to this day. Most of their offspring were distinctively black haired and there is strong facial resemblance even today between some on the northeast coast of Scotland and the residents of Cadiz, from where the Armada originally sailed.

Some Spanish ships headed for the west coast, but were lost in a violent storm in the Hebrides. One galleon, the Florida, was lost in Tobermory harbour, reputedly carrying £300,000 worth of gold bullion. However, during recent dives all that was found on the seabed were rotted timbers, a sailor's bangle and a silver spoon.

---

of the **Mishnish Hotel**, where you can attempt to munch your way through their monumental portions and, if you're not sleeping on the same street, also attempt the walk uphill on an over-filled stomach. Also on the harbour front is the excellent **Island Bakery**. A worthwhile detour is to walk to the edge of town to the excellent **Green Barn** which is run by *Isle of Mull Cheese* (see below). Here you can enjoy good old home baking in the unusual surroundings of a plant-filled glass barn.

An absolute must when in Tobermory is a night in the **Mish**. After one of their pub **Entertainment** meals and several pints of ale, bending over the pool table is an effort, not to mention getting down to some good live folk music. For the sake of choice, other pubs and live music venues are available, namely **MacGochan's**, at the other end of the harbour, near the distillery. There are also music events at **An Tobar** (see 'Sights' above).

Despite its popularity, Tobermory hasn't succumbed to the dreaded tartan disease that **Shopping** afflicts so many other tourist hot-spots. You're more likely to find shops selling fishing tackle or diving gear than tacky souvenirs, and the ones that do cater for the tourist market, such as **Mull Pottery**, T302057, and the **Mull Silver Company**, T302345, open 0900-1730, are tastefully done and enjoyable places to browse in on a wet afternoon. At the foot of Back Brae, which leads steeply up from the harbour to the upper part of the village, is the **Tobermory Chocolate Company**, T302526, open May-Oct Mon-Sat 0930-1730, where you can try out their speciality – chocolate made with the local whisky . On the edge of town, 500 yds off the Dervaig Rd, at Sgriob-Ruadh Farm, is **Isle of Mull Cheese**, T302235, where you can savour their award-winning traditionally made cheese and their wonderful glass barn (see above). Open Apr to end-Sep Mon-Fri 1000-1600.

Whale and dolphin watching trips can be made from Tobermory with **Sea Life Surveys**, **Tours** T302787. A full-day tour costs £45 (£48 in Jul/Aug), and there's a maximum of 12 people per trip. You can find out more at the **Hebridean Whale and Dolphin Trust**, a charity which aims to protect the marine environment through education, at 28 Main St, Tobermory, T302620, F302728, www.gn.apc.org/whales open daily 1000-1700 all year round.

Inner Hebrides

Fishing trips can be made with *Amidas Sea Fishing & Wildlife Trips*, based at Baliscate House (see 'Sleeping' above), or book at *Tackle & Books*, T302336. Trips cost around £15 for 3 hrs, or £30 for a full day. Permits for trout fishing are available from *A Brown & Son*, 21 Main St, Tobermory, T302020, F302454. For more details pick up the *Tobermory Angling Association* leaflet from the tourist office.

Diving trips and courses are available with *Seamore Diving*. Book through *Seafare Chandlery & Diving Service*, Main St, Tobermory, T/F302277.

Wildlife expeditions with *Isle of Mull Landrover Wildlife Expeditions*, at *Ulva House Hotel*, T302044 (David Woodhouse). Full-day tour costs £27.50/£19.50 per person.

Directory **Banks** Mull's only permanent bank is the *Clydesdale Bank* on Main St. There's also a mobile bank which tours the island; for details T08457-826818. **Communications** Internet access at the *SYHA* on Main St (£1.50 per 15mins), *An Tobar* (£1 per 15 mins), *Posh Nosh* above the *CalMac* terminal (£1.50 per 15 mins) and *The Corner Store* (£3 per hr).

The West Coast

Mull's west coast is where you'll find some of the island's most stunning scenery. The B8073 winds its way anti-clockwise from Tobermory in a series of tortuous twists and turns as it follows the contours of the deeply indented coastline. It starts off in terrible condition and soon deteriorates into something resembling a poorly maintained farm track.

Dervaig
Phone code: 01688

The road climbs west from Tobermory then makes a dramatic descent, with innumerable hairpin bends, to Dervaig. This section of road is closed to the public for the annual car rally in October. Dervaig is a lovely village of whitewashed cottages, beautifully situated at the head of Loch Cuin, where the old folk still converse in Gaelic.

It has two very notable features (quite a lot for such a tiny place). One is **Kilmore Church**, which has a very unusual pencil-shaped spire (the only other one in Scotland is at Dunfermline in Fife). Dervaig's real claim to fame, though, is the **Mull Little Theatre**, the smallest professional theatre in Britain, with only 43 seats. It puts on an impressive programme of plays throughout the summer (May-September), and common sense dictates that advance booking is essential (T400245).

One mile beyond Dervaig take the turn-off to Torloisk to reach the **Old Byre Heritage Centre**, which stands out as one of the few genuinely interesting examples of these places. It also features a video of Mull's history and an excellent tearoom (see below). ■ *Easter to end-Oct daily 1030-1830. Adult £3, concession £2, children £1.50. T400229.*

Sleeping and eating Dervaig has a wide choice of places to stay. The nicest is **A** *Druimard Country House Hotel*, T400291, F400345, www.druimard.co.uk 6 rooms, open end Mar-Oct. This Victorian country house offers peace and comfort in beautiful surroundings and is right beside the *Mull Little Theatre*; the room rate includes dinner in the excellent restaurant. They offer a pre-theatre 4-course dinner for non-residents (expensive). There are several B&Bs and guesthouses in and around the village, including the wonderful **D** *Balmacara*, T/F400363, open all year, 3 double rooms, one with a 4-poster bed, and the excellent **D** *Cuin Lodge*, overlooking Loch Cuin, T400346, cuin-lodge@mull.com, open Mar-Oct. If you're on a tight budget there's **F** *The Dervaig Bunkroom*, T400492, at the community hall, which has 10 beds and is open all year.

Aside from the *Druimard Country House*, probably the best food around is at the *Old Byre Heritage Centre* (see above), whose tearoom serves delicious but cheap snacks and home baking. There's also the 16th-century *Bellachroy Hotel*, where you can get decent bar meals. Opposite is *Coffee and Books*, for good coffee and, funnily enough, books.

Five miles west of Dervaig is Calgary Bay, Mull's most beautiful beach ringed by steep wooded slopes with views across to Coll and Tiree. Any Canadians reading this, may be interested to note that the large city in Alberta was named after the former township. Many emigrants were forcibly shipped to Canada from here during the Clearances. There are some wonderful paths through Calgary Wood, just past Calgary Farmhouse Hotel, including a half hour circular walk past the millpond and some unusual modern sculptures.

Calgary Bay
There can be no better end to a day than dinner at the Dovecote followed by a stroll along the beach at sunset

The road down the west coast passes through a series of tiny settlements before reaching the turn-off to Ulva Ferry. A couple of miles before the turning, it's worth stopping at **Eas Fors**, a spectacular waterfall that tumbles straight into the sea from under the road bridge. There's a path down to the bottom and you can swim in the sea, below the falls.

Sleeping and eating Near Calgary Bay is the wonderfully peaceful and relaxing **D** *Calgary Farmhouse Hotel*, T01688-400256. 9 rooms, open Apr-Oct. This restored farmhouse is one of Mull's gems, and the adjoining *Dovecote Restaurant* serves excellent, moderately priced food using the best of local seasonal produce. There's also a tea-room, *The Carthouse*, which offers cheap and delicious light lunches and home baking.

If you have the time and need to escape the hectic bustle of Mull, then take a day out on idyllic Ulva (meaning 'wolf island' in Norse), just off the west coast. You won't see any wolves around, but you're almost guaranteed to spot deer, golden eagles, buzzards and seals offshore. There are several well-marked woodland and coastal trails across the island, including one to the southwest where there are basalt columns similar to those on Staffa, or you can follow the trail to the top of the hill for spectacular views across to the Cuillins on Skye (on a clear day), or cross to Ulva's even smaller neighbour **Gometra** by a causeway. There's also a track to Livingstone's Cave where archaeologists have found signs of human life dating back as far 5,650 BC.

Isle of Ulva
Colour map 3, grid B3 No accommodation but ask the ferry operators about camping

It's hard to believe, but the island once sustained a population of over 850, until they were completely cleared between 1846 and 1851. The derelict crofts can still be seen around the island, along with the lovely little church, which still holds services for the remaining population of around 20. For more information on the island walks and on its history, visit the *Boathouse Heritage Centre* close to the ferry slip on Ulva. There's also a licensed tearoom where you can try the local oysters with Guinness. ■ *Easter-Oct Mon-Fri 0900-1700 and Sun Jun-Aug only. The entry price is included in the ferry fare (see below). T01688-500241, ulva@mull.com*

Transport A small bicycle/passenger-only ferry makes the 2-min crossing on demand from Ulva Ferry, Apr-Oct Mon-Fri 0900-1700, and on Sun Jun-Aug; £4.50 adult return, £2 children (£0.50 for bikes). This includes entry to the Boathouse Heritage Centre, Sheila's Cottage (a musuem of island life) and access to all walks. At other times, phone to make arrangements, T500226.

Inner Hebrides

Staffa
& the
Treshnish Isles
Colour map 3,
grid B3

The tiny uninhabited island of Staffa, five miles off the west coast of Mull, is one of the most spectacular sights not just in Scotland but anywhere in the world. It consists of immense, hexagonal, basalt pillars which loom up out of the sea, like a giant pipe organ.

Staffa was formed 60 million years ago by the slow cooling of Tertiary basalt lavas. These have been carved by the pounding sea into huge cathedral-like caverns such as the mightily impressive **Fingal's Cave**. The sound of the sea crashing against the black crystalline columns made such an impression on Felix Mendelssohnn in 1829 that he immortalized the island in his *Hebrides Overture*. The composer was obviously aware of its original name in Gaelic, which means 'The Melodious Cave'.

You can land on the island – if the weather is good enough – and walk into the cave via the causeway; an experience not be missed. But even if the seas are too rough, it's worth making the 90-minute boat trip just to witness the huge columns and gaping black hole of the cave.

Most boat trips to Staffa include a memorable tour of the uninhabited Treshnish Isles to the northwest. The two most northerly islands, **Cairn na Burgh** and **Cairn na Burgh Beg** have ruined castles, while another, **Bac Mór**, is better known as **Dutchman's cap** because of its curious shape. The largest island, **Lunga**, is the main bird sanctuary and a haven for thousands of seabirds, including razorbills, guillemots, kittiwakes, shags, fulmars, skuas and puffins so tame you'll need to tread carefully to avoid them. In the surrounding seas there are seals, dolphins, minke whales, porpoises, and maybe even basking sharks and killer whales! Most boat trips include time ashore on Lunga and all are dependent on sea conditions.

Boat trips to Staffa and the Treshnish Isles leave from Oban, Dervaig, Ulva Ferry, Iona or Fionnphort, weather permitting. A full-day cruise including Staffa and the Treshnish Isles costs £33 per person (£17 for children); a cruise to Staffa only costs around £14.50. *Turus Mara*, T08000-858786 (freephone), www.turusmara.com, leave from Ulva Ferry, daily May-Sep and Sep-Oct subject to weather and demand . They also run this trip from Oban; £33.50 including ferry and courtesy bus form Craignure to Ulva Ferry. *Inter-island Cruises* leave from Croig near Dervaig, T/F01688-400264. They're a little bit more expensive than the others, but also have trips to Coll and Muck. *Alternative Boat Hire*, T01681-700537, offer trips around the coastline and handline fishing on a traditional wooden boat. You can hire by the hour or for an afternoon, May-Oct, from Fionnphort and Iona.

Ben More & the
Ardmeanach
Peninsula

From Ulva Ferry the B8073 heads east along the north shore of **Loch na Keal** then enters a wide flat valley, where the road forks east to Salen (see page 294) and west along the south shore of Loch na Keal. This part of Mull is dominated by **Ben More** (3,170 ft), the island's highest mountain. All around is a spectacular region of high jutting mountains and deep glens, extending west to the **Ardmeanach Peninsula**. The road passes Dishig, the best point from which to begin the steep walk to the summit (see page 302), then cuts through the towering Gribun cliffs, with the tiny island of **Inch Kenneth** lying offshore. There are also great views of Ulva, Staffa and the Treshnish Isles. The road then turns south across the peninsula as it climbs over the pass and down to Loch Scridain, where it joins the A849 which runs through the beautiful and dramatic **Glen More** to Craignure.

The peninsula may look impenetrable, but with the proper walking gear can be explored on foot. On the north coast, about a mile from the road, is the massive entrance to **MacKinnon's Cave**, which runs for about 100 yards back under the cliffs. Make sure to visit only at low tide and also watch out for the evil spirits who live inside and who are said to have caused the deaths of an entire party of adventurous – or foolish – men. The area around the headland, now owned by the National Trust for Scotland, is known as '**The Wilderness**'. Near the headland is **MacCulloch's Tree**, a remarkable fossilized tree 40 ft high and thought to be 50 million years old, which was discovered in 1819. The tree is only accessible by a seven-mile footpath which begins at Burg Farm. You should call in at the farm to let them know of your intentions and also to get directions. You should have a good map of the area and also time your arrival with low tide.

The Ross of Mull

Mull's southernmost peninsula stretches west for 20 miles from the head of Loch Scridain as far as Iona. Most visitors use it merely as a route to Iona but, if you've got the time and the weather's good, there are a couple of interesting little detours along the way.

Phone code: 01681

The first village is **Pennyghael**, which has two hotels overlooking the loch, **D** *Pennyghael Hotel*, T704288, F704205, which is open from Easter to October and has an excellent restaurant and **D** *Kinloch Hotel*, T704204, which serves cheap bar meals. A tortuous, twisting side road leads south from Pennyghael over the hills and down to **Carsaig Bay**, from where you can head east or west along the shore for some dramatic coastal scenery. For a description of these walks, see page 302.

The next village is **Bunessan**, a fairly unappealing place but convenient for an early ferry to Iona. You can also find out everything about local history and culture at the **Ross of Mull Historical Centre**, on Pier Road. ■ *Easter-Oct daily 1000-1630. £1.* There's a wide range of accommodation, including **E** *Bremenvoir House*, Ardtun, T/F700527, acey@bremenvoir.u-net.com, a modern farmhouse run by Mrs Acey. Open all year.

Two roads lead south from Bunessan. One leads to **Scour**, near where is a great beach at Kilveockan. The other road splits near the coast: the left branch leads to **Uisken Bay**, where there's a nice beach; the righthand branch leads to **Ardlanish Bay**, which also has a good beach. You can spend the night at Uisken Bay at **C-D** *Ardachy House Hotel*, Uisken, by Bunessan, T/F700505, open Mar-Sep, 7 en suite rooms, or the idyllic **E** *Uisken Croft*, T700307, open from April to October.

The road ends at Fionnphort, the departure point for the small passenger-only ferry to Iona, just a mile across the Sound of Iona. The village is little more than a car park, a row of houses, a pub and a shop, but there are several inexpensive B&Bs for those arriving too late to make the crossing. Even if you're not staying, it's worth stopping off in the village to visit the **Columba Centre**, a museum which relates the saint's life story. ■ *Mid-May to end-Sep Mon-Sat 1000-1800, Sun 1100-1800. Adult £2, children £1.*

Fionnphort

A road runs south from Fionnphort a mile to a **campsite** at *Fidden Farm*, T700427. Further south is **Knockvologan**, opposite **Erraid island**, which is accessible at low tide. The island has literary connections, for it was here that Robert Louis Stevenson is believed to have written *Kidnapped*. **Balfour Bay** on the south of the island is named after the novel's hero who was shipwrecked here.

Inner Hebrides

Sleeping and eating Just before Fionnphort is **E** *Achaban House*, T700205, F700649, www.achabanhouse.co.uk 7 rooms. This former manse is comfortable and well-furnished, and also offers dinner. **E-F** *Burnside*, T700208. 1 room. 2 mins from ferry pier, friendly with great views of Iona. Eating options are limited to the *Keel Row Bar & Restaurant*, where you can get moderately priced meals and enjoy a drink by the fire in the cosy bar.

Walks on Mull

OS Landranger Nos 47, 48 & 49

Mull presents numerous walking opportunities, ranging from gentle forest trails to wild and dramatic coastal routes, or even a spot of Munro-bagging for the more intrepid.

Ben More

With the exception of the Cuillins on Skye, Mull's highest peak (3,169 ft) is the only Munro not on the mainland. The trail starts at a lay-by on the B8035, at Dishig, and is fairly clear, though it can be tricky near the top. Return the same way, or more experienced climbers could continue down the narrow ridge to the eastern summit, **A'Chioch**, then descend the eastern face to the road that skirts **Loch Ba**. The views from the top are magnificent, across the other Hebridean islands and even as far as Ireland. If it's a cloudy day, it's worth postponing the ascent until there's clear weather. Allow around six hours for the round trip.

Coastal walks

There are a couple of excellent coastal walks which start out from Carsaig Bay. A good path heads west along the shore to **Carsaig Arches** at Malcom's Point. The path runs below the cliffs out to the headland and then around it, and after about a mile reaches **Nun's Cave**, a wide and shallow cave where the nuns of Iona took refuge after being expelled during the Reformation. The path continues for another mile or so, but becomes a bit exposed in places and traverses a steep slope above a sheer drop into the sea. The famous arches are columnar basalts worn into fantastic shapes. One is a free-standing rock stack and another is a huge cave with two entrances. You'll need to allow about four hours in total plus some time at the arches.

Heading east from Carsaig Bay is a spectacular 4½-mile walk to **Lochbuie**, past Adnunan stack. It starts out through woodland, then follows the shore below the steep cliffs, with waterfalls plunging straight into the sea. It's easy at first but then gets very muddy in places and there's quite a bit of wading through boggy marsh, so make sure you've got good walking boots. Allow about five to six hours in total.

A shorter walk takes you to the bronze age **Lochbuie Stone Circle** at the foot of Ben Buie. Leave your car at the stone bridge before you reach the village. Look for the green sign on the gate to your left and follow the white marker stones across the field. The stone circle is hidden behind a wall of rhododendrons, so follow the marker stones across the plank bridge until you see it. It takes about 30 minutes.

Forest walks

For detailed maps and more information pick up the free Guide to Forest Walks and Trails in North Argyll leaflet at any tourist office

There are a few marked trails through Forestry Commission land on Mull. The first walk is to **Aros Park**, on the south side of Tobermory Bay. Start out from the car park near the distillery in Tobermory and follow the shoreline for about a mile to Lochan a'Ghurrabain, which is good for trout fishing (see page 297). From here there is also a marked path around the loch (1 mile).

A longer walk is to **Ardmore Bay**, three miles north of Tobermory. The trail/cycle path starts at the car park by the road that runs northwest from

Tobermory. From here, it runs out almost to Ardmore point and back again, passing a couple of ruined villages on the way. There's a good chance of seeing seals and lots of sea birds in Ardmore Bay. The trail is four miles in total.

Four miles north of Craignure is the car park and picnic site at **Garmony Point**, where a two-mile trail leads to the Ferry terminal at **Fishnish**, hugging the shore all the way. Another trail (four miles) runs out to Fishnish Point and back through the forest to the car park by the old harbour.

Isle of Iona

*Iona is a small island – barely three miles long and a little over a mile wide – but its importance to Christianity is out of all proportion to its size. Iona's place in religious history was guaranteed when **St Columba** arrived with his 12 disciples and founded a monastery there in 563 AD. The Irish monk then set about converting practically all of pagan Scotland and much of northern England. Iona went on to become the most sacred religious site in Europe and has been a place of pilgrimage for several centuries. Today that pilgrimage has turned into more of an invasion, with hordes of daytrippers making the five-minute ferry trip from Mull to visit the abbey. Few, however, venture beyond the main village, **Baile Mór**, and it's easy to find a quiet spot, particularly on the west coast with its sparkling silver beaches washed by turquoise sea. It's worth spending a day or two here to soak up the island's unique spiritual peace, so well conveyed in the words of Dr Johnson: "that man is little to be envied whose…piety would not grow warmer among the ruins of Iona".*

Phone code: 01681
Colour map 3, grid C3
Population: 130

Ins and outs

A passenger-only **ferry** leaves from **Fionnphort**, Mull (5 mins) frequently 0845-1815 Mon-Sat and hourly 0900-1800 Sun; return trip £3.30.

Getting there

Iona is small enough to get around easily on foot, or you can **hire mountain bikes** at *Finlay Ross (Iona) Ltd*, in Baile Mór village, T700357, F700562, for around £10 per day.

Getting around

History

Iona is known as the 'Cradle of Christianity in Scotland', and was a centre of the arts. The monks produced elaborate carvings, manuscripts, ornate gravestones and Celtic crosses. Their greatest work was the beautiful *Book of Kells*, which dates from AD 800, and which is now on display in Dublin's Trinity College. This proved to be the high point of the church's history. Shortly after came the first of the Viking raids, in AD 806, when many monks were slaughtered at Martyrs' Bay, followed by another in AD 986 which destroyed the work of many years. The relentless pressure from the established church ended with the suppression of the Celtic Church by King David in 1144.

In 1203 Iona became part of the mainstream church with the establishment of a nunnery for the Order of the Black Nuns, as well as a Benedictine Abbey by Reginald of the MacDonalds of the Isles. Iona became overshadowed by the royal city of Dunfermline, and its final demise came with the Reformation when buildings were demolished and all but three of the 360 carved crosses destroyed.

The abbey lay in ruins until in 1899 the island's owner, the eighth Duke of Argyll, donated the buildings to the Church of Scotland on condition that the

The Story of St Columba

St Columba (Colum Cille in Gaelic), a prince of Ireland and grandson of the Irish King, Niall of the Nine Hostages, came to Scotland not as a missionary, but as an act of self-imposed penance for his actions. He stubbornly refused to hand over his copy of the Gospels, illegally copied from St Finian's original, which led to a bitter dispute with the king. This ended in a pitched battle in which Columba's supporters prevailed, but he was so overcome with remorse at the bloodshed he had caused that he fled Ireland, finally settling on Iona as it was the first place he found from where he couldn't see his homeland. Columba, however, was not retiring into obscurity. His missionary zeal drove him to begin work on building the abbey. He also banished women and cows from the island, declaring that "where there is a cow there is a woman, and where there is a woman there is mischief". Workers at the abbey had to leave their womenfolk on nearby Eilean nam Ban (Women's Island). Not content with that, he also banished frogs and snakes from Iona, though there are plenty on Mull. He is even said to have pacified the Loch Ness Monster during a visit to Inverness. He went on to found the Celtic Church, or the Church of the Culdees, with centres throughout Scotland, which differed in many ways from the Church of Rome.

abbey church was restored for worship. Then in 1938 the Reverand George Macleod founded the Iona Community as an evangelical Church of Scotland brotherhood, with the abbey buildings as its headquarters, and by 1965 had succeeded in rebuilding the remainder of the monastic buildings. Now the abbey complex has been completely restored and the island of Iona, apart from the abbey buildings, is owned by the National Trust for Scotland.

The Abbey

The present abbey dates from around 1200, though it has been rebuilt over the centuries and completely restored in the 20th century. The oldest part is the restored **St Oran's Chapel**, to the south of the abbey on the right, which is plain and unadorned save for its splendid 11th-century Norman doorway. It is said that Columba was prevented from completing the building of the original chapel until a living person had been buried in the foundations. His friend Oran volunteered and was duly buried. Columba later asked for the face to be uncovered so that he could bid a final farewell to his friend, but Oran was found to be alive and claimed he had seen Heaven and Hell, describing them in such blasphemous terms that Columba ordered he be covered up immediately!

Surrounding the chapel is the **Reilig Odhrain**, the sacred burial ground, which is said to contain the graves of 48 Scottish kings, including Macbeth's victim, Duncan, as well as four Irish and eight Norwegian kings. The stones you see today are not the graves of kings but of various important people from around the West Highlands and Islands. The most recent is that of **John Smith**, leader of the British Labour Party from 1992 until his untimely death in 1994.

Beside the **Road of the Dead**, which leads from the abbey church to St Oran's Chapel, stands the eighth-century **St Martin's Cross**. This is the finest of Iona's Celtic high crosses and is remarkably complete, with the Pictish serpent-and-boss decoration on one side and holy figures on the other. Standing in front of the abbey entrance is a replica of **St John's Cross**, the other great eighth-century monument. The restored original is in the **Infirmary Museum**, at the rear of the abbey, along with a fine collection of medieval gravestones.

No part of St Columba's original buildings survives, but to the left of the main entrance is **St Columba's Shrine**, the small, steep-roofed chamber which almost certainly marks the site of the saint's tomb. You get a good view of the whole complex from the top of the small grassy knoll opposite the abbey entrance. This is **Torr an Aba**, where Columba's cell is said to have been. The **Abbey** itself has been carefully restored to its original beautiful simplicity and inside, in a side chapel, are marble effigies of the eighth Duke of Argyll and his third wife, Duchess Ina. ■ *The abbey is open all year and at all times. Admission is free but you're asked to give a £2.80 donation at the entrance, where you can pick up a plan of the abbey.*

Baile Mór

The passenger ferry from Fionnphort on Mull lands at Baile Mór, Iona's main village, which is little more than a row of cottages facing the sea. There are over a dozen places to stay but, as demand far exceeds supply during the busy summer season, it's best to book in advance at one of the tourist offices on Mull, or in Oban. There's also a post office, a very good craft shop and general store in the village.

Just outside the village, on the way to the abbey, are the ruins of the **Augustinian nunnery**. Just to the north, housed in the parish church manse, built by Thomas Telford, is the **Iona Heritage Centre**, which features displays on the island's social history. ■ *Apr-Oct Mon-Sat 1030-1630. Adult £1.50.* Nearby stands the intricately carved 15th-century **Maclean's Cross**.

B-C *Argyll Hotel*, T700334, F700510, www.argyllhoteliona.co.uk 17 rooms, open Apr-Oct. This is the better of the island's 2 upmarket hotels, and its very good restaurant serves cheap lunches and mid-range-expensive 4-course dinners. Among the island's B&Bs is **E** *Iona Cottage*, T700579, open year round. It's worth the walk down to **F** *The Iona Hostel*, T700642, an exceptional hostel with views to the Treshnish Islands about a mile from the ferry along the path past the abbey. It's best to book ahead in summer. Apart from the *Argyll Hotel*, there's the *Martyrs' Bay Restaurant*, which serves soup and snacks.

Sleeping & eating
There are 15 B&Bs on the island; ask at the post office for a full list

Around the island

On the west coast are some lovely beaches of white sand and colourful pebbles. The best of the lot is the **Bay at the Back of the Ocean**, beside the golf course, and only a mile and a half walk from the ferry. This was one of John Smith's favourite places and it's easy to see why. At the southern tip of the island is another sandy beach at **St Columba's Bay**, believed to be the spot where the saint first landed. The small cairns here are said to have been built by the monks as penance for their sins (they obviously had a lot on their conscience). You can also seek answers to difficult questions by walking round the labyrinth, whose twisting route makes use of your left and right brain and makes you think. Around the corner, at Rubha na Carraig-géire on the southeastern tip, is the **marble quarry**, disused since 1915. The rusting remains of the cutting equipment are still lying around.

Do yourself a real favour by taking the time to explore the island and enjoy its natural beauty as well as its spiritual peace

Another good walk is to the top of **Dun I**, the only real hill, which rises to a height of 300 ft. To get there, continue on the road north from the abbey, past MacDougal's Cross, then go through a gate to the right of Bishop's Walk Farm and follow the fence up to where you join a footpath up to the top. It's only about half an hour up and down and there are great views from the top of the entire island and the coastline of Mull.

Inner Hebrides

Isles of Coll, Tiree and Colonsay

Coll

Phone code: 01879
Colour map 3,
grid B3
Population: 170

The low-lying, treeless and windswept island of Coll offers the simple pleasures in life, and is so peaceful and quiet that it makes some of the more popular islands appear crowded by comparison. There's little to do here other than stroll along the magnificent, deserted beaches and enjoy the relatively long hours of sunshine. Tourism, though, remains low on the list of priorities, and those who do come prefer it that way. Even by Hebridean standards there are few facilities, and accommodation is scarce.

Ins & outs　**Getting there**　There's a **ferry** from Oban to Coll (2 hrs 40 mins) and Tiree (55 mins) once daily on Mon, Tue, Wed, Fri and Sat. One way ticket to Coll or Tiree costs £11.40 per passenger and £65 per car. From Coll to Tiree costs £2.90 and £16.65.

　　Getting around　The *CalMac* ferry from Oban calls in at Coll's only village, Arinagour, where half of the island's population live and where you'll find the post office and a few shops. There's no petrol station, but you should leave the car behind anyway. The island is only 13 miles long by 4 miles wide and the best way to get around is on foot or by bike.

The best of Coll's beaches are on the west coast, at **Killunaig**, **Hogh Bay** and **Feall Bay**. The latter is separated from the nearby **Crossapool Bay** by giant sand dunes up to 100 ft high. These are now owned by the RSPB to protect the resident corncrake population. Nearby, at the head of Loch Breachacha, is the restored medieval **Breachacha Castle**, built by the Macleans of Coll and once owned by them but now used as an adventure-training school for young overseas aid volunteers. The castle is sometimes open to the public; check with the tourist office in Oban for details. The dilapidated 18th-century mansion nearby is where Boswell and Dr Johnson stayed when they were stranded here for 10 days during their grand Highland tour in 1773.

　　It's worth taking a walk up **Ben Hogh** (341 ft), the island's highest point, overlooking Hogh Bay on the west coast, to get a good overview. The east coast, north from Arinagour to **Sorisdale**, is an uninhabited wilderness which is ideal for some gentle hillwalking.

Sleeping　In Arinagour is the **C** *Coll Hotel*, T230334, F230317. A family hotel with a good restaurant,
& eating　and is the social hub of the island. Also in the village is **E** *Taigh Solas*, T/F230333. A few miles to the west is **E** *Achamore*, T230430. A lovely old farmhouse. Down in the southwest, at Breachacha Bay, is **E** *Garden House*, T/F230374. Nearby, in the walled garden of the castle, is the island's **campsite** (open Apr-Oct; phone as for *Garden House*). The only alternative to hotel or guesthouse food is the trendy bistro in Arinagour.

Tiree

Phone code: 01879
Colour map 3,
grid B2
Population: 800

Tiree claims to be the sunniest place in Scotland, and has a comparatively low average rainfall, but it's also one of the windiest places in the country. So windy, in fact, that Tiree has become the windsurfing capital of Scotland and is known as the 'Hawaii of the North'. International windsurfers are attracted by the huge Atlantic rollers that break on the island's countless, long, clean and silver beaches.

Getting there Tiree has an **airport** and there are regular daily flights (except Sun) all year round from Glasgow. The airport is at The Reef, Crossapol (T220309). For full details, see page 290. There are *CalMac* car and passenger **ferries** to the island from Oban, via Coll and, occasionally, Tobermory. The ferry port is at Scarinish (T220337). From Oban to Tiree (55 mins) once daily on Mon, Tue, Wed, Fri and Sat. One-way ticket to Tiree costs £11.40 per passenger and £65 per car. From Coll to Tiree costs £2.90 and £19.90.

Ins & outs

Getting around There's a **shared taxi** service which operates on request Mon-Fri 0930-1500 (limited service on Sat), also Mon-Wed and Fri 1600-1730. There's also a Tue evening service for arriving ferries, but only in the summer. For private taxi hire call *Island Cabs*, T220344 (evenings and weekends only). There's a **postbus** service around the island, including to and from the airport. The timetable is available at Scarinish Post Office. **Bicycle hire** is available at the *Tiree Lodge Hotel* (see below), or contact Mr N Maclean, T220428.

Tiree is much greener and more fertile than its neighbour. It was once known as the breadbasket of the Hebrides and its Gaelic name, *tir-iodh*, means 'Land of Corn'. The island supported a population of 4,450 in 1831, but was ruthlessly cleared by its owner, the Duke of Argyll, so that by 1881 the population had been halved. Not content to stop there, he even drafted in the marines in 1885 to evict those crofters who dared to protest. Today Tiree enjoys relative prosperity, and crofting is the mainstay of the economy, with cattle and sheep grazing the miles of rich machair. Tourism is also a major contributor and during the height of the season the island's population approaches the levels of the early 19th century.

Tiree is a low, flat island, only about 11 miles long and six miles across at its widest, and is also known by the nickname *Tir fo Thuinn*, or "Land below the waves". When seen from a distance most of it disappears below the horizon, save its two highest hills, **Ben Hynish** (462 ft) and **Beinn Hough** (390 ft), on the west coast. Being flat and small, it obviously makes good sense to explore it by bicycle, but remember that the constant wind varies from strong to gale force.

Around the island

The ferry port is at **Gott Bay**, half a mile from **Scarinish**, the island's main village and home to a *Co-op* supermarket, post office and bank (there's a garage at the pier head). About four miles from Scarinish, is Vaul Bay, where the well-preserved remains of **Dun Mor**, a Pictish Broch built around the first century AD, stand on a rocky outcrop to the west of the bay. A few miles west of here is the **Clach a'Choire**, or 'ringing stone', a huge glacial granite boulder covered in Bronze-Age cup marks which makes a metallic sound when struck. Legend has it that should it ever shatter, or fall off its pedestal, then Tiree will sink beneath the waves.

The island's main road runs northwest from Scarinish, past the beautiful beach at **Balephetrish Bay** to **Balevullin**, where you can see some good examples of restored traditional thatched houses. Just to the south, at **Sandaig**, is the **Thatched House Museum** which tells of the island's social history. ■ *Jun-Sep Mon-Fri 1400-1600.*

In the southwestern corner of the island is the most spectacular scenery of all, at the headland of **Ceann a'Mara**, or Kenavara. The massive sea cliffs are the home of thousands of sea birds and you can see seals on the rocky shore. East from here, across the golden sands of Balephuil Bay, is the island's highest hill, **Ben Hynish**, topped by a radar-tracking station resembling a giant golf

Inner Hebrides

ball. Despite this, it's worth the climb to the top for the magnificent views over the island and, on clear days, across to the Outer Hebrides. Below Ben Hynish, to the east, is the village of **Hynish**, where you'll find the **Signal Tower Museum**, which tells the fascinating story of the building of the **Skerryvore Lighthouse** (1840-44) by Alan Stevenson, an uncle of Robert Louis Stevenson. This incredible feat of engineering was carried out from Hynish, where a dry dock/reservoir was built for shipping materials by boat to the Skerryvore reef, 10 miles to the southwest.

Sleeping & eating

There are several guesthouses and B&Bs, the best of which is the wonderful **C** *Kirkapol House*, T/F220729, in a converted Victorian church overlooking Gott Bay. Price includes dinner. **D** *The Glassary Guest House & Restaurant*, is at Sandaig, T/F220684. 4 en suite rooms, open all year, very good food (mid-range). There are 2 hotels: the **C** *Scarinish Hotel*, T220308, F220410, is in the village; and **D** *Tiree Lodge*, T220368, F220994, at Gott Bay. It's possible to **camp** free on the island, but ask for permission first.

The best food on offer is at the *The Glassary* (see above). There's also the option of bar lunches and suppers at the *Tiree Lodge* and *Scarinish Hotel*. For afternoon tea or coffee you're limited to the *Alan Stevenson Centre* in Hynish, open 1430-1630, or *Glebecraft* in Scarinish.

Sports

Windsurfing tuition is available at Loch Bhasapol, T220559 (summer only). The major windsurfing event is the *Wave Classic*, held annually in Oct.

Colonsay

Phone code: 01951
Colour map 3, grid C3
Population: 100

Colonsay is the epitome of the island haven: remote, tranquil and undemanding. It has abundant wildlife (150 species of resident or migrant birds), beautiful plants and flowers (over 500 species) and glorious beaches. All this has become accessible to daytrippers, with a ferry round trip (see below), leaving you six hours ashore. This does scant justice to the island's peculiar charms, however, and judging by the ever-growing number of holiday homes and self-catering accommodation on Colonsay, it's a view shared by many.

Ins & outs

Getting there There are **ferry** sailings from Oban (2 hrs) once daily Wed, Fri and Sun, arriving at Scalasaig on the east coast. From Kennacraig there is 1 sailing (3 hrs 35 mins) on Wed. From Port Askaig there is 1 sailing (1 hr 10 mins) also on Wed. One-way Oban/Kennacraig-Colonsay costs £10.10 per passenger and £48.50 per car; Port Askaig-Colonsay £3.55 and £18.75. Ferries need to be booked well in advance during the summer months.

Getting around There's a limited **bus** and postbus service around the island Mon-Sat, for those without their own transport. On Wed in the summer, a tour bus meets the ferry and takes visitors round the island. As the island is only 8 miles long by 3 miles wide, you might want to consider hiring a bicycle. **Bike hire** from *A McConnel*, T200355.

Around the island

The island is rich in archaeological & historical remains

Colonsay's population lives in the three small villages, the largest of which is **Scalasaig**, the ferry port. The island's only hotel is here and there's also a restaurant, a post office/shop, a petrol pump and a heritage centre by the pier. A few miles north of the ferry, in the middle of the island, is **Colonsay House**, dating from 1772. The house was sold, along with the rest of the island, in 1904 to Lord Strathcona, who had made his fortune in Canada with the Hudson Bay Company and went on to found the Canadian Pacific Railway. The house is not open to the public but the lovely gardens and woods, full of rhododendrons, giant palms and exotic shrubs, are worth a stroll. The estate cottages are now self-catering holiday homes.

There are several standing stones, the best of which are **Fingal's Limpet Hammers**, at Kilchattan, southwest of Colonsay House. There are also Iron Age forts, such as **Dun Eibhinn**, next to the hotel in Scalasaig (see below). Colonsay is also home to a wide variety of **wildlife**. You can see choughs, one of Britain's rarest birds, as well as corncrakes, buzzards, falcons, merlins and perhaps even the odd golden eagle or sea eagle. There are also otters, seals and wild goats (said to be descended from the survivors of the Spanish Armada ships wrecked in 1588).

The jewel in the island's crown, though, lies six miles north of Scalasaig, past Colonsay House, at **Kiloran Bay**. The beach here is described as the finest in the Hebrides, and who could argue. The magnificent half mile of golden sands, backed by tiers of grassy dunes, with massive breakers rolling in off the Atlantic, is worth the two-hour ferry crossing alone.

Accommodation on Colonsay is limited and must be booked up well in advance. **B** *Isle of Colonsay Hotel*, T300316, F200353, www.colonsay.org.uk A few hundreds yards from the ferry, 11 rooms, a cosy 18th-century inn with a friendly bar and excellent food; they also arrange various trips around the island. Attached to the hotel is *Viragos*, a coffee house and well-stocked bookshop. A cheaper option is the excellent **E** *Seaview*, T200315, at Kilchattan, near the standing stones. Open Apr-Oct. **F** *Colonsay Bakcpacker's Lodge*, T200312, www.colonsay.org.uk, is an old keeper's cottage 2km from the ferry, sleeps 16 and is open all year, phone ahead for lift from ferry. Aside from the hotel bar, you can eat at *The Pantry*, T200325, near the ferry pier. It is open Mon-Sat and offers simple home cooking as well as teas and cakes.

Sleeping & eating

Apart from 1 hotel and a couple of B&Bs, all accommodation is self-catering. Caravans and camping are not allowed on the island

Just off the southern tip of Colonsay is the island of Oronsay, two miles square with a population of six and one of the highlights of a visit to Colonsay. The name derives from the Norse for 'ebb-tide island', which is a fitting description as Oronsay can be reached on foot at low tide, across the mud flats known as 'The Strand'. It takes about an hour to walk from the south end of Colonsay to the ruins of a 14th-century **Augustinian Priory**. This was the home of some of the most highly skilled medieval craftsmen in the Western Highlands. A surviving example of their work is the impressive Oronsay Cross and the beautifully carved tombstones, on display in the **Prior's House**.

Isle of Oronsay

Legend has it that St Columba first landed here after leaving his native Ireland, but he could still see his homeland from the top of Ben Oronsay and so decided to continue north to Iona, where he founded the community that was to become the centre of Christianity in northern Britain (see page 303).

Make sure you take wellies for the walk across The Strand and check on the **tides**. Tide tables are available at the hotel or shop. Spring tides (new and full moon) allow about three to four hours to walk across and back, which is just enough time to see the priory but little else. Fast walkers may also have time to pop into *The Barn*, T200344, for home cooking and crafts.

Isle of Islay

Islay (pronounced eye-la), the most southerly of the Hebridean islands and one of the most populous, with around 4,000 inhabitants, has one very important claim to fame – single malt whisky. Islay produces a very distinctive, peaty malt and

Phone code: 01496
Colour map 5, grid A1

Inner Hebrides

connoisseurs are in for a treat, as the island has no fewer than seven working distilleries. Aside from whisky, people also come here to watch birds. The island is something of an ornithologists' wonderland, and from October to April plays host to migrating barnacle and white-fronted geese flying down from Greenland in their thousands for the winter.

If that leaves you cold, then there's always the spectacular coastal scenery, from the wild Mull of Oa to the glorious beach at Laggan Bay. Compared to other islands like Skye, Mull or Arran, Islay receives few visitors, mainly due to its distance from the mainland, giving it a really isolated feel.

Ins and outs

Getting there Islay can be reached by **air** from Glasgow (for flight details, see page 290). The airport is at Glenegedale, a few miles north of Port Ellen on the road to Bowmore.

The **ferry** to Islay (and Jura) from Kennacraig to Port Ellen (2 hrs 10 mins) sails 1 daily on Mon and Sun and 2 daily on Tue, Thu, Fri and Sat; and to Port Askaig (2 hrs) 1 daily on Tue, Wed, Thu, Fri and Sat and 2 daily Mon. One-way to Port Ellen/Port Askaig costs £7.25 per passenger and £38.50 per car. The ferry from Oban to Port Askaig sails on Wed (4 hrs 15 mins); one-way £10.35 per passenger and £50 per car. From Colonsay to Port Askaig (1 hr 10 mins) there is a sailing on Wed; one-way £3.65 and £19.25. *CalMac* offices: Kennacraig, T01880-730253; Port Ellen, T01496-302209.

It takes about 2½ hrs to **drive** to Kennacraig from Glasgow, and there's a daily **bus** from Glasgow to Kennacraig (with *West Coast Motors*) which connects with the ferry to Islay (for bus times, contact Buchanan Street bus station, T0141-3333708, or Traveline T0870-6082608).

Getting around For those without their own transport, there's a regular bus service around the island,
Because the with Islay *Coaches*, T840273, and *Royal Mail Postbuses*, T01246 546329. There are
island is partially buses from Portnahaven to Port Ellen, via Port Charlotte, Bridgend, Bowmore and the
Gaelic-speaking airport; from Port Askaig to Port Ellen via Ballygrant, Bridgend, Bowmore and the air-
the road signs port; from Port Ellen to Ardbeg, Bowmore, Port Askaig and Portnahaven, and also a
are bilingual **postbus** to Bunnabhain. Buses run regularly at least from Mon-Sat, but only once on Sun. For bus times, pick up a copy of the timetable from the tourist office in Bowmore, Tarbert, Lochgilphead or Oban, or contact the Public Transport Helpline, T015456-604695

For **car hire** there's D&N *Mackenzie* at Glenegedale, T302300. **Taxi hire** at *Carol's Cabs*, Frederick Cres, Port Ellen, T302155. **Bicycle hire** at *Port Ellen Playing Fields Association*, T07831-246911; the Post Office, Bowmore, T810366; and *Mick Stuart*, Lennox St, Port Ellen, T302391, who is also a wildlife guide.

Information Islay's only official **Tourist Information Centre** is in Bowmore, T810254. Apr-Jun Mon-Sat 0930-1700 (and Sun 1400-1700); Jul-Sep Mon-Sat 0930-1730, Sun 1400-1700; Sep and Oct Mon-Sat 1000-1700, Oct-Mar Mon-Fri 1200-1600. They'll find accommodation for you.

Port Ellen and around

Port Ellen is the largest place on Islay and the main ferry port, yet it still has the feel of a sleepy, wee village. It was founded in 1821 by the laird, Walter Frederick Campbell, and named after his first wife. There are shops, hotels, B&Bs, restaurants, a bank, a couple of filling stations, a post office and an information centre of sorts, based in a caravan beside the *White Hart Hotel*, making Port Ellen a good base from which to explore the delights of the southern half of Islay.

The places listed below are in and around Port Ellen. Four miles to the north, overlooking Laggan Bay, is **A** *Machrie Hotel*, T302310, F302404, www.machrie.com 18 rooms. Golfing hotel right by a great beach and a great golf course, does golfing packages. The bar and restaurant make the perfect end to 18 perfect holes. Also by the golf course is the excellent **B-C** *Glenmachrie*, T/F302560. 5 rooms. A genuine farmhouse offering genuine hospitality and superb food. The price includes dinner, and you'd be crazy to book B&B only and deny yourself the pleasure. Nearby is **D** *Glenegedale House Hotel & Restaurant*, T302147, F302210, which is very handy for the airport. At Kintra beach (take the Oa road and follow the signs for Kintra) is **E-F** *Kintra Farmhouse*, T302051. Open Apr-Sep, 3 rooms. Also an independent hostel, the **F** *Kintra Bunk Barns Hostel*, T302051, open Apr-Sep, and a very good restaurant (see below). This is a great place for camping, and there's a **campsite** with full facilities (open Apr-Sep).

There are several places to stay in the village itself. **E** *The Trout-Fly Guest House*, T/F302204, is right beside the ferry terminal and has a decent restaurant (for residents only). **E** *The Bothy*, 91 Lennox St, T302391, mickstuart@thebothyislay.freeserve .co.uk Run by the versatile Mick Stuart who also hires out bikes and acts as a wildlife guide. Keen divers might want to try the *Islay Dive Centre*, 10 Charlotte St, T302441, which has apartments to rent (**E**).

Apart from the places mentioned above, there's very good, cheap food available at the *Old Granary* at Kintra Farm, T302051, open 1730-2300, Jul/Aug 1200-2300.

There are a number of excellent day trips from Port Ellen. A road runs east out to **Ardtalla**, where it ends. Along the way, it passes three distilleries, first **Laphroaig**, then **Lagavulin** and lastly, **Ardbeg**, all of which offer guided tours (see page 314). Between the Lagavulin and Ardbeg distilleries is the dramatically sited 16th-century ruin of **Dunyvaig Castle**, once the main naval base and fortress of the Lords of the Isles (see also page 313). A mile further on is the impressive **Kildalton Cross**, standing in the graveyard of the ruined 13th-century chapel. The eighth-century cross is remarkably well preserved and one of Scotland's most important Early Christian monuments, and the carvings depict biblical scenes. At the end of the road is Ardtalla, from where you can begin the ascent of **Beinn Bheigeir** (1,609 ft), the island's highest hill, with spectacular views from the summit.

Southwest of Port Ellen a road runs out to a little, rounded peninsula known as **The Oa**, an area of varied beauty, both wild and pastoral, and with a wonderful coastline. The road runs as far as **Upper Killeyan**, from where it's about a mile uphill to the spectacular headland at the **Mull of Oa**. Here you'll see the strange-looking **American monument**. The obelisk commemorates the shipwrecks offshore of two US ships, the *Tuscania* and the *Ontranto*, both of which sank in 1918 at the end of the war. There's a great walk north from the Mull of Oa up to Kintra, but it's best to start out from Kintra (see below).

A turn-off from the road to The Oa leads north to **Kintra**, at the south end of **The Big Strand** at Laggan Bay, with five miles of glorious sands and dunes. There's a restaurant and accommodation here, and it's a great place for camping (see below). The restaurant is at the end of the road, with the beach on one side and on the other a wild and spectacular coastal walk to the **Mull of Oa**. There's a detailed map of the route in the restaurant. Just to the north of Kintra is the **Machrie golf course**, a memorable golfing experience.

The A846 runs north from Port Ellen, straight as a pool cue, to Bowmore, the island's administrative capital and second largest village. Founded in 1768 by the Campbells, it's an appealing place, laid out in a grid plan with the main street running straight up the hill from the pier to the unusual **round church**, designed to ward off evil spirits, who can hide only in corners. Thankfully, the nice spirit stayed behind and can be found at the **Bowmore Distillery**, just to the west of Main Street. This is the oldest of the island's distilleries, founded in 1779, and the most tourist-friendly.

Sleeping and eating D *Harbour Inn*, Main St, T810330, F810990. 4 rooms. Completely refurbished to a high standard, great views across the bay and superb food in their acclaimed restaurant (mid-range/expensive). D *Lochside Hotel*, Shore St, T810244, F810390. 8 rooms. Friendly and good-value hotel with a mind-boggling selection of single malts. On the road between Bowmore and Port Charlotte, at Bridgend, is C *Bridgend Hotel*, T810212, F810960. 10 rooms, nice and peaceful and good bar meals. There are also several B&Bs in Bowmore.

The Rinns of Islay

North of Bowmore, at **Bridgend**, the A846 joins the A847 which runs west to the hammerhead peninsula known as the Rinns of Islay ("rinns" is derived from the Gaelic for promontory). A few miles west of Bridgend the B8017 turns north to the **RSPB Reserve** at **Loch Gruinart**. The mudflats and fields at the head of the loch provide winter grazing for huge flocks of barnacle and white-fronted geese from Greenland, arriving in late October. There's an

Islay

RSPB visitor centre at **Aoradh** (pronounced "oorig") which houses an observation point with telescopes and CCTV, and there's a hide across the road. In total there are about 110 species of bird breeding on Islay, including the rare chough and corncrake.

The coastal scenery around the Rinns is very impressive, particularly at **Killinallan Point**, a beautiful and lonely headland at the far northeast of Loch Gruinart. Also impressive is **Ardnave Point**, west of Loch Gruinart, and further west along the north coast, **Sanaigmore.** The best beaches are at **Saligo** and **Machir Bay** on the west coast, past Loch Gorm. Both are lovely, wide, golden beaches backed by high dunes, but swimming is forbidden due to dangerous undercurrents. You can stay at **Kilchoman**, near Machir Bay, at **E-D** *Kilchoman House*, T850382, F850277, a former Georgian Manse that offers self catering accommodation. Open April-October, book in advance.

Port Charlotte
There are a few good beaches around

Port Charlotte is without doubt the most charming of Islay's villages, with rows of well-kept, whitewashed cottages stretched along the wide bay. It, too, was founded by the prolific Walter Frederick Campbell, in 1828, and named after the other important woman in his life, his mother.

But Port Charlotte is not just a pretty face. The **Islay Wildlife Information and Field Centre** is a must for anyone interested in flora and fauna. It's very hands-on, with good displays on geology and natural history, a video room and reference library. It's also a great place for kids, and has activity days when staff take tours of the surrounding area. ■ *T850288. Easter-Oct Mon, Tue, Thu, Fri and Sun 1000-1500. £2.*

Also worth visiting is the compact **Museum of Islay Life**, to the east of the village, where you can find out all about illegal whisky distilling on the island. It also has interesting archival material. ■ *Easter-Oct Mon-Sat 1000-1700, Sun 1400-1700. £2.*

Sleeping and eating Accommodation is somewhat limited in Port Charlotte. The best place to stay is the **C** *Port Charlotte Hotel*, T850361, F850361. 10 rooms. Restored Victorian inn with gardens and conservatory on seafront; their restaurant features local seafood and is the best around. There's also a B&B **E** *Mrs Wood*, T850225, open Apr-Oct; and a *SYHA hostel*, T850385, open Mar to end-Oct, next to the Wildlife Information Centre. Aside from the hotel, the best place to eat is the *Croft Kitchen* (T850230). It's a coffee and gift shop by day and moderately priced restaurant by night, open Mar-Oct daily 1000-2030, best to book in season.

Portnahaven

At the southern end of the Rinns is the picturesque little fishing and crofting village of Portnahaven, its Hebridean cottages rising steeply above the deeply indented harbour. A mile south is Portnahaven's twin settlement, **Port Wemyss**, also named after the laird's wife, would you believe (she was a daughter of the 8th Earl of Wemyss).

Sleeping Amenities are few and far between in this remote corner. If you want to stay, you can find a bed at **E** *The Old School House*, in Portnahaven, T860242.

Around Port Askaig

Ballygrant

The A846 runs east from Bridgend out to Port Askaig passing a couple of interesting sights on the way. A mile and a half beyond Bridgend is the **Islay Woollen Mill**, which was established in 1883 on the site of a 17th-century mill. The road then passes through **Ballygrant**, just to the south of **Loch**

The Whisky Trail

Though the whisky distilling process is basically the same everywhere, some distilleries have more beautiful locations and more interesting tours. Islay's seven distilleries enjoy the most scenically stunning settings and are full of character and history. Islay also offers the unique opportunity to visit several of Scotland's most impressive distilleries in one day, and their distinctive peaty malts are considered to be among the finest.

Laphroaig (pronounced 'la-froyg') is the closest to Port Ellen, and its wonderful setting is summed up by its name, meaning "The beautiful hollow by the broad bay" in Gaelic. According to many this is the ultimate in malt whisky and is at its best after dinner. The free distillery tours are by appointment only, T302418.

Lagavulin (pronounced 'laga-voolin') is a mile along the shore by the romantic ruin of Dunyveg Castle. Their 16-year-old single malt is one of the classics and also makes the ideal after-dinner tipple. They also offer a very interesting tour (£3), Monday-Friday by appointment only, T302400.

Ardbeg distillery is a mile further east and produces a robust and powerful single malt. Established in 1815, it was closed for a while, but was recently acquired by Glenmorangie and runs tours (£2) Monday-Friday from

1030 till 1530, and also on Saturday and Sunday June-August, T302244.

Bowmore is the oldest distillery on Islay and still uses all the old traditional methods to produce its fine single malt, also at its best after dinner. Their hour-long tours are the most professionally done and even include a video. Tours (£2) all year round from Monday-Friday at 1030 and 1400, in the summer months at 1030, 1130, 1400 and 1500, T810441.

Caol Ila (pronounced 'coal-eela') was founded in 1846 and lies close to Port Askaig, with great views across the Sound of Islay to Jura. Unlike most of its island peers, this single malt is best before dinner. Tours of the distillery (£3) all year round by appointment only, T840207.

Bunnahabhain (pronounced 'bun a havan') is the most northerly of the distilleries, set in a secluded bay with great views across to Jura. Free tours are also by appointment only, T840646.

Bruichladdich (pronounced 'brook-laddie') is in the village of the same name on the road south to Port Charlotte. Recently voted distillery of the year by the readers of America's Malt Advocate. They offer tours (£3) all year round Mon-Sat at 1030, 1130 and 1430, www.bruichladdich.com

Finlaggan. Here, on two crannogs (artificial islands), were the headquarters of the Lords of the Isles, the ancestors of Clan Donald. The MacDonalds ruled from Islay for nearly 350 years, over a vast area covering all of the island off the west coast and almost the whole of the western seaboard from Cape Wrath to the Mull of Kintyre. There's a new **visitor centre** to the northeast of the loch, where you can learn more about the history of the site and see some of the archaeological remains. ■ *Easter-Oct Tue, Thu and Sun 1400-1630. £1.50.* You can walk across the fen to **Eilean Mor**, where there's a collection of carved gravestones near the ruins of a medieval chapel. A smaller island, **Eilean na Comhairle** ('The Council of the Isle'), is where the Lords of the Isles met to decide policy.

Sleeping There's accommodation at the superb **D** *Kilmeny Farmhouse*, T/F840668. Comfort, style, excellent food and a warm, friendly atmosphere. The only drawback is that there are only 3 rooms, so book well in advance. Otherwise, there's the **D** *Ballygrant Inn*, T/F840277, which is comfortable and serves great pub grub.

Port Askaig is Islay's other ferry port, with connections to the mainland and to the islands of Jura and Colonsay. It's little more than a dock, a car park and a few buildings huddled at the foot of a steep, wooded hillside. If you're arriving by the late ferry, there's accommodation at **C-D** *Port Askaig Hotel*, T840245.

Port Askaig

A short walk north along the coast is the **Caol Ila distillery**, and a couple of miles further north, at the end of the road which branches left before you enter Port Askaig, is the beautifully situated **Bunnahabhain Distillery**.

Isle of Jura

The words 'wild' and 'remote' tend to get overused in describing the many Hebridean islands, but in the case of Jura they are, if anything, an understatement. The short ferry crossing from neighbouring Islay takes you into another world, pervaded by an almost haunting silence. Jura has one road, one hotel, six sporting estates and 5,000 red deer, which outnumber the 200 people by 25:1, the human population having been cleared to turn the island into a huge deer forest. Rather appropriately, the name Jura derives from the Norse 'dyr-ey', meaning deer island.

Phone code: 01496
Colour map 5,
grid A1/2

Ins and outs

A small car and passenger **ferry** makes the regular 5-min crossing daily from Port Askaig on Islay to Feolin Ferry. For times, contact Cerco Denholm, T01496 840681. A one-way ticket costs £10 per car and £1.80 per passenger.

Getting there

Amazingly enough, there is a **bus** service on Jura, which runs from Feolin Ferry to Craighouse several times a day, Mon-Sat. A few buses continue to Lagg and Inverlussa and return to Craighouse. Note that some journeys are by request only and must be booked the day before, T820314.

Getting around
For bus times, see the timetable, available free at TICs

Around the island

Jura is one of the last, great wildernesses in the British Isles and perfect for some real off-the-beaten-track walking. Its main attractions are the beautiful **Paps of Jura**, three breast-shaped peaks that dominate not only the island itself but also the view for miles around. From Kintyre, Mull, Coll and Tiree, and from the mountains of mainland Scotland from Skye to Arran, they can be seen on the horizon. The Paps provide some tough hill-walking and require good navigational skills, or a guide. It takes a good eight hours to cover all three peaks, though during the Paps of Jura fell race they are covered in just three hours. A good place to start is by the three-arch bridge over the Corran river, north of **Leargybreack**. The first pap you reach is **Beinn a'Chaolais** (2,408 ft), next is the highest, **Beinn an Oír** (2,571 ft) and the third is **Beinn Shiantaidh** (2,476 ft). To find out about guides, ask at the hotel in Craighouse (see below). The island's west coast is completely uninhabited and inaccessible to all but the hardiest and most dedicated of walkers.

The Paps

One of the island's main draws is the Corryvreckan whirlpool at the very northern tip, between Jura and the uninhabited island of **Scarba**. The notorious whirlpool, the most dangerous tide race in Scotland, is best appreciated one hour after low tide, and its awesome roar can be heard long before you reach it. It is named after a Viking, Bhreacan, who anchored his boat here for

Corryvreckan whirlpool & the north

Inner Hebrides

three days and nights by a rope woven from the hair of virgins. Unsurprisingly, the rope parted under the strain, casting doubt on the status of one of the contributors, and Bhreacan drowned. To get there, follow the rough track from **Ardlussa** to **Kinuachdrach**, or get someone to drive you, then it's a two-mile walk. Before setting out, ask at the hotel for information and directions.

Also in the north of the island is **Barnhill**, the completely isolated and forlorn-looking cottage where **George Orwell** wrote *1984* between 1946 and 1948 (hence the book's title). Though the house attracts literary pilgrims, it remains closed, although it can be rented from £400 per week from April to December; T01786-850274.

Craighouse The only village on Jura is Craighouse, eight miles from Feolin Ferry on the southeast coast. Here you'll find the **Jura distillery**, which welcomes visitors. Tours are by appointment, T820240. Beside the distillery is the island's one and only hotel, the **C** *Jura Hotel*, T820243, F820249, overlooking the lovely small isles bay. They'll provide information on island walks, and the pub is the social hub. There's cheaper accommodation with **E** *Mrs Boardman*, T820379, open April-September; or **E** *Zoe Newton*, Ivy Cottage, T820322 (dinner available for £12).

Three miles south of the village, at **Ardfin**, is **Jura House**, with its beautiful walled garden, filled with wild flowers and Australasian plants and trees. ■ *Daily during daylight hours. £2.*

The Small Isles

Phone code: 01687
Colour map 3

The Small Isles is the collective name given to the four islands of Eigg, Muck, Rùm and Canna, lying south of Skye. Seen from the mainland, they look a very tempting prospect, especially the jagged outline of Rùm and the curiously shaped Eigg. But visiting the islands is not easy, as ferry transport is purely designed for the inhabitants and not geared towards the convenience of island-hopping tourists. Furthermore, the island populations are small, and accommodation and facilities are limited. But the determined traveller with time on their hands will be well rewarded, particularly on mountainous Rùm, with its superb walking and abundant wildlife.

Ins and outs

Getting there A *CalMac* passenger-only **ferry** sails from Mallaig to all four islands. From Mallaig to **Eigg** (1½ hrs) on Mon, Tue, Thu and Sat; Mallaig to **Muck** (2 ½ hrs) on Tue, Thu and Sat; Mallaig to **Rùm** (1¾ -3½ hrs) on Mon, Wed and Sat; Mallaig to **Canna** (3 hrs) on Mon, Wed, Fri and Sat. One-way Mallaig to: Eigg £4.75; Muck £7.25; Rùm £7.10; Canna £8.10. From May-Sep the *CalMac* ferries from Mallaig are supplemented by cruises from Arisaig with *Arisaig Marine*, T01687-450224. For details, see page 485.

Getting around There are ferries between Eigg, Muck, Rùm and Canna; for details contact the *CalMac* office in Mallaig, T01687-462403. On Sat in the summer a ferry leaves at 0500 and sails Mallaig-Canna-Rùm-Muck-Eigg, allowing those with limited time to at least see the islands from close up. A second ferry leaves on summer Sat, making it possible to spend either 9½ hrs on Canna, or 7½ hrs on Rùm, or 5 hrs on Muck, or 3½ hrs on Eigg. At Eigg, Muck and Rùm passengers are transferred to small boats as there are no suitable piers.

Eigg

Little Eigg (pronounced 'egg') has had something of a chequered past. In 1577 it was the scene of one of the bloodiest episodes in the history of Clan warfare, when 395 MacDonalds, almost the entire population, were trapped in a cave and suffocated by a raiding party of Macleods from Skye, who lit a fire at the entrance. More recently it has been at the heart of a bitter land ownership debate. Having endured a succession of absentee landlords, ranging from the merely eccentric to the criminally negligent, the 65 remaining islanders seized the moment and bought the island themselves, in conjunction with the Scottish Wildlife Trust. Now everyone can enjoy the island's wildlife, which includes otters, seals, eagles and many other birds, such as the Manx shearwater, guillemots and black-throated divers.

Colour map 3, grid A/B 4

The island is dominated by **An Sgurr**, a 1,289 ft flat-topped basalt peak with three vertical sides. It can be climbed easily by its western ridge, and there's a superb view from the summit. Sitting in the shadow of the Sgurr, at the southeastern corner, is the main settlement, **Galmisdale**. This is where the ferries drop anchor (passengers are transferred to a smaller boat), and there's a post office, shop and tearoom, all by the pier. At the northern end is the small township of **Cleadale**, on the Bay of Laig. Just to the north are the "**Singing Sands**", a beach that makes a strange sound as you walk across it.

Two croft houses at Cleadale offer B&B: **D** *Lageorna*, T482405, www.isleofeigg.org, also offers full board with packed lunch, and caters for vegetarians; and **D** *Laig Farm*, T482437. There's also an independent **hostel** with 24 beds, **F** *The Glebe Barn*, T482417, open Apr-Oct.

Sleeping

Muck

Tiny Muck is the smallest of the four islands and is flat and fertile, with a beautiful shell beach. It has been owned by the MacEwan family since 1879. The island gets its unfortunate name (*muc* is Gaelic for pig) from the porpoises, or "sea pigs", that swim round its shores. The ferry drops anchor near **Port Mór**, and you can stay at **D** *Port Mór House*, T462365. The price includes dinner which is also available to non-residents. Alternatively, you can ask permission to camp at the tearoom, which does snacks and sells fresh bread.

Colour map 3, grid B3

Inner Hebrides

Rùm

Rùm, or Rhum (the extra 'h' was added to avoid alcoholic associations) is the largest of the islands and the most wild, beautiful and mountainous. The island is owned and run by Scottish Natural Heritage as an enormous outdoor laboratory and research station, and most of the 30 or so inhabitants are employed by them. Studies of the red deer population are among the most important areas of their work, and access to parts of the island is restricted. This is not prohibitive, though, and there are many marked nature trails, walks and bird-watching spots. The island is a haven for wildlife, and perhaps its most notable resident is the magnificent white-tailed sea eagle, successfully re-introduced on to Rùm in the 1980s and now spreading beyond the island. Rùm is also home to golden eagles, Manx shearwaters and, less appealingly, millions of midges. The island is the wettest of the Small Isles and a haven for the little pests.

Colour map 3, grid A3

Rùm's other great attraction is its mountain range, which rivals that of the Cuillins of Skye. The highest point is **Askival** (2,664 ft), which can be reached by the main ridge from **Hallival**, though the route involves some rock scrambling and is only advised for fit and experienced walkers. Before setting out, you'll need to ask permission from the manager of the reserve office at the *White House* (T462026).

Though it looks like a wilderness, Rùm once supported a population of 300. Most of them were shipped off to Canada in the mid-19th century, leaving behind an uninhabited deer forest for sporting millionaires. One of these, John Bullough, bought it in 1888 and passed it on to his son, Sir George Bullough, who built the extravagant and extraordinary **Kinloch Castle**. No expense was spared on this massive late-Victorian mansion, constructed of red sandstone from Arran in a bizarre combination of styles; to describe it as over-the-top would be a gross understatement. It is currently undergoing a £14 mn refurbishment.

The castle stands at the head of narrow Loch Scresort by the little hamlet of **Kinloch**, where you'll find a well-stocked shop, a post office and a coffee shop in the community hall. Ferries are anchored in the loch and passengers are transferred to a smaller craft and dropped a few minutes' walk along the shore from Kinloch.

The Bullough family mausoleum, built in the style of a Greek Doric temple, stands incongruously on the west coast at **Harris Bay**. It's an interesting 7½ mile walk across to the mausoleum from Kinloch.

Sleeping If you plan to stay longer than a day, book well in advance. Rooms in *Kinloch Castle* are no longer available but there is cheap hostel accommodation in the old servants' quarters, including double rooms; open Mar-Oct. For bookings and more information, T462037, castlemanager@rumcastle.free_/online.co.uk There are also a couple of cheap and basic **bothies** (F); and **camping** is allowed at Kinloch. Contact the reserve manager, T462026.

Accommodation on the island is limited: most people visit on a day trip

Canna

Canna is the most westerly of the Small Isles and is owned by the National Trust for Scotland. It's a small island, five miles long by one mile wide, bounded by cliffs and with a rugged interior, fringed by fertile patches. It's attached to its smaller neighbour, **Sanday**, by a narrow isthmus which is covered, except at low tide. The main attraction for visitors is some fine walking. It's about a mile from the ferry jetty up to the top of **Compass Hill** (458 ft), so called because its high metallic content distorts compasses. The highest point on the island is **Carn a' Ghaill** (690 ft). During the summer, a day trip from Mallaig allows you over nine hours in which to explore Canna and enjoy the fantastic views across to Rùm and Skye.

Colour map 3, grid A3 There are no shops on Canna, so you'll need to bring your own supplies

The population of 20 mostly work on the island's farm. Canna was gifted to the National Trust by its benevolent owner, Dr John Lorne, a notable Gaelic scholar who still lives there. The island continues to be run as a single working farm and, since it was sold in 1938, has been an unofficial bird sanctuary with 157 recorded bird species, including Manx shearwater and puffins.

Sleeping Those wishing to stay put, can **camp** rough, with permission from the National Trust for Scotland, or rent out their self-catering cottage, T0131-226 5922.

Central Scotland

8

*Central Scotland is not a distinct region but rather the sum of disparate parts of other regions, including **Perthshire**, **Stirling**, the **Trossachs**, **Loch Lomond** and **Fife**. The historically important regions of Perthshire and Stirling straddle the Highland Boundary Fault, the diving line between the heavily populated Central Lowlands and the wild, remote Highlands. Just across this 'border' are the Trossachs, a beautiful area of mountains and forests eulogized by Sir Walter Scott that stretches west from Callander, and the glens of Perthshire, steeped in the rich broth of Scottish history and seasoned with lochs and mountains.*

To the east, bounded by the Firth of Tay to the north and the Firth of Forth to the south, is the Kingdom of Fife, once isolated from the rest of the country. Even since the building of the Forth and Tay bridges, the region has managed to retain its own peculiar flavour. The small peninsula juts out into the North Sea like the head of a little terrier dog. Rather apt, given the proud Fifers' fight to preserve the identity of their own 'Kingdom' when it was threatened by local government reorganization in 1975 and 1995.

Perthshire and Stirling

*As the main access route between the wild, remote Highlands and heavily popu-
lated Central Lowlands, Perthshire and Stirling have been at the very heart of
the main events which have shaped the Scotland's destiny. Many of the most
important battles have been fought here and the region is littered with remnants
of the past.*

*Standing between Edinburgh and Glasgow, yet only a short distance from
some of the country's most beautiful scenery, the ancient town of **Stirling** is synonymous with the country's two greatest historical heroes, Robert the Bruce and
William Wallace. Stirling is the gateway to the **Trossachs**, a beautiful area of
mountains, forests, lochs and steep-sided glens. Northeast of Stirling is the town
of **Perth**, whose surrounding glens are dotted with numerous castles. Nearby is
Scone Palace, where every Scottish king was crowned – all 42 of them. Numerous castles are scattered around the glens of Perthshire, including **Blair Castle**,
one of the country's top attractions and home to the only legitimate private
army in Britain.*

*The region has other attractions, not least of which is the spectacular and var-
ied landscape, ranging from the rolling hills of Strathearn to the rugged peaks of
the Grampian Mountains. There are Munros aplenty for the climbing, and in the
far west of the region, on the eastern shores of **Loch Lomond**, is the **West Highland Way**, Scotland's most popular long-distance hike. There are numerous
cycle trails through the forests and glens, and a long-distance cycleway runs from
Glasgow, through the Trossachs and along the shores of Loch Tay to Pitlochry.
There's also **skiing** at Glenshee, **salmon fishing** on the river Tay, **watersports** on
loch Earn and **golfing** at glorious Gleneagles, all within easy reach of Edinburgh
and Glasgow.*

Ins and outs

**Getting
around** Though the more remote northerly parts of Perthshire and Stirling are difficult to reach
by public transport, much of the region is easily accessible. The towns of Perth and
Stirling are transport hubs and one of the country's main train lines, from Glasgow to
Inverness, passes through the region. A good network of intercity and local buses connects all the main towns and villages. The main road north to Inverness, the A9, runs
through the eastern part of the region, and the main route north from Glasgow, the
A82, forms its western boundary.

**Tourist
information** Stirling, Falkirk, parts of the Ochils, the Campsies, the Trossachs and Loch Lomond are all
covered by the *Argyll, the Isles, Loch Lomond, Stirling & the Trossachs Tourist Board*,
info@scottish.heartlands.org, www.scottish.heartlands.org, with tourist offices in Aberfoyle, Alva, Balloch, Callander, Drymen, Dunblane, Falkirk, Killin, Stirling, Tarbet and
Tyndrum. The rest of the region, from Kinross in the south to Blair Atholl in the north and
from Glenshee in the east to Rannoch Moor in the west, is covered by the *Perthshire
Tourist Board*, www.perthshire.co.uk, info@perthshire.co.uk, with tourist offices in Aberfeldy, Auchterarder, Blairgowrie, Crieff, Dunkeld, Kinross, Perth and Pitlochry. Both tourist
boards can provide information and literature on accommodation and various outdoor
activities such as walking, cycling, golf and fishing. Two good walking guides are
Hallewell Publications' pocket guides, and *Walk Loch Lomond and the Trossachs*.

Things to do in Central Scotland

- Find the Roman in the gloamin' at the lovely Perthshire village of Fortingall, said to be the birthplace of Pontius Pilate.
- Travel the road from Aberfoyle to Callander, through the spectacular Duke's Pass, one of the most beautiful routes in the country.
- Play hunt the royal in St Andrews, medieval university town and ancient home of golf.
- Explore historic Stirling, home of Braveheart and scene of Scotland's greatest military triumph.
- Meander through the string of pretty fishing villages in the East Neuk of Fife.

Perth

'The Fair City' of Perth is aptly named. Situated on the banks of Scotland's longest river, the Tay, Perth and its surrounding area boasts some of the most beautiful scenery in the country. Perth was once the capital of Scotland, and there are many interesting sights to visit (most of which are free). The jewel in Perth's crown, though, is undoubtedly Scone (pronounced 'scoon') Palace, on the outskirts of town. Scone was the home of the Stone of Destiny for nearly 500 years, and the site where every Scottish king was crowned.

The town makes a convenient and very pleasant base for exploring this beautiful Highland region. There are many colourful parks and historic buildings, excellent shopping opportunities and plenty of places to eat, drink and relax. Perth also has a proliferation of leisure and sporting facilities – and not many towns can boast a golf course on an island in the middle of a river.

Phone code: 01738
Colour map 4, grid C3
Population: 48000

Ins and outs

Perth is easily accessible from almost anywhere in the country. It's only 1½ hrs from Edinburgh or Glasgow, and half an hour from Dundee, by road, and on the main train lines to these cities, as well as on the main lines north to Aberdeen and Inverness. The **train** and **bus stations** are almost opposite each other at the west end of town, where Leonard St meets Kings Pl.

Getting there

The town centre is very compact and lies on the western bank of the Tay, between 2 large parks; North Inch and South Inch. It's easy to get around on foot, but Scone Palace and many of the B&Bs are on the eastern bank of the river, so you may wish to take a bus. **Local buses** are run by *Stagecoach*, T629339. For a **taxi**, call *Ace Taxis*, T633033. An enjoyable way to see the sights is to use the *Guide Friday* bus tour of Perth. Tour tickets are valid all day, so you can get on and off as often as you please and you can join the tour at various locations throughout the city. T0131-5562244 for more details, or contact the tourist office.

Getting around

The **Tourist Information Centre** is housed in the Lower City Mills, West Mill St, T450600. It is open Apr-Jun, Sep and Oct Mon-Sat 0900-1730, Sun 1100-1600; Jul and Aug Mon-Sat 0900-1830, Sun 1100-1700; Nov-Mar Mon-Sat 0900-1600.

Tourist information

Central Scotland

Sights

Town centre The heritage of Perth is easy to trace owing to the number of interesting historical sites within walking distance of each other. Its position on the River Tay ensured that Perth became a busy trading port which still has a bustling harbour, the only inland harbour in Britain. In years gone by, salmon and wool were major exports from Perth, while claret was imported from Bordeaux in France.

Between the High Street and South Street is **St John's Kirk**, still standing on its original site. It was founded in 1126, though most of the present church dates from the 15th century. In 1559 firebrand preacher John Knox gave one of his trademark sermons, inspiring the good folk of Perth to destroy the local monasteries. The church gave the town its original name of 'St John's town', a name upheld in the local football team, St Johnstone.

Central Scotland

Perth

■ Sleeping	● Eating	
1 Kinnaird Guest House & Marshall House	1 Auld Hoose	6 No 63
2 Pitcullen Crescent Guest Houses	2 Caffé Cantaro	7 Time Out
3 Quality Station	3 Exceed	8 Seafood
	4 Let's Eat Again	9 Paco's
	5 Let's Eat Bistro	10 Scaramouche

N

0 metres   200
0 yards   200

A few minutes' walk north, on North Port, is the **Fair Maid's House**, the fictional home of Sir Walter Scott's virginal heroine in his novel, *The Fair Maid of Perth*. The novel was set in the 14th century, at the time of the Battle of the Clans which took place on the North Inch, just to the north, across Charlotte Street. Close by, at the corner of Charlotte Street and George Street, is the **Museum and Art Gallery**, with displays on local history, art, archaeology, natural history and whisky. ■ *Mon-Sat 1000-1700. Free. T632488.*

In the 18th century the world-famous Black Watch regiment was raised in Perth, and the **Black Watch Museum**, housed in the 15th-century Balhousie Castle, is well worth a visit even to the most un-military minded. The museum is on Hay Street, on the edge of the North Inch, to the north of the town centre. ■ *May-Sep Mon-Sat 1000-1630, closed last Sat in Jun; Oct-Apr Mon-Fri 1000-1530. Free. T0131-310 8530.* Back in the town centre, in West Mill Street is **Lower City Mills** (also home to the tourist office), a restored and working 19th-century oatmeal mill powered by a huge water wheel (closed to visitors at the time of writing).

Perth's other museum contains the excellent **Fergusson Gallery**, a display of works by the renowned Scottish colourist, John Duncan Fergusson. The gallery is found at the south end of Tay Street, near South Inch, in a splendid neo-classical building which was once Perth's waterworks. ■ *Mon-Sat 1000-1700. Free. T441944.*

Those with souvenirs to buy may be interested in a visit to the **Caithness Glass** factory, on Inveralmond Industrial Estate, two miles north of the town centre on the A9, where you can also watch the glass-blowing process. ■ *Easter-Oct Mon-Sat 0900-1700, Sun 1000-1700; Nov-Mar Mon-Sat 0900-1700, Sun 1200-1700. Free. T492320.*

For those with more horticultural leanings, **Branklyn Garden**, at 116 Dundee Road, has been described as 'the finest two acres of private garden in the country'. With an impressive collection of rare and unusual plants, it includes superb examples of Himalayan poppies. Well worth a visit at any time of year, many of the plants grown there are on sale in the shop. ■ *Mar-Oct daily 0930-sunset. £3, £2 child/concession, T625535 (NTS).*

Kinnoull Hill Woodland Park is a beautiful wooded area on the outskirts of the city. The trip to the top of Kinnoull Hill (783 ft) itself affords an astounding view across Perth, down to the Tay estuary and through Fife to the Lomond hills. To the north, the views stretch from Ben More in the west to Lochnagar in the northeast.

There are four walks through the Woodland Park – Nature Walk, Tower Walk, Jubilee Walk and Squirrel Walk – and each of these is graded according to how difficult it is and what type of conditions the walker can expect. However, none of the walks are extremely strenuous, though the Squirrel Walk is most suitable for the less able. If you're feeling particularly energetic, cycling and horse riding take place in specific zones in the park, principally in the Deuchny Wood area. There is a Countryside Ranger Service in the park and they will be happy to answer any questions you may have about their work or the park itself. Also ask at the tourist office in town for details.

Situated a few miles outside Perth on the A93 Braemar Road, is the unmissable **Scone Palace**, one of the most historically important places in the country. The home of the Earls of Mansfield, Scone has a long and fascinating history. It was the capital of the Pictish Kingdom in the sixth century and home of the Celtic church. Here, Kenneth MacAlpin united Scotland, and in

838 AD, placed the stone of Scone (or 'Stone of Destiny') on Moot Hill, opposite the palace entrance. This became the ancient crowning place of Scottish kings, including Macbeth and Robert the Bruce. The Royal City of Scone became the seat of government, and the kings of Scotland resided at the Palace of Scone before their coronations. The coronation stone was removed to Westminster by that most hated foe, Edward I, in 1296, and only recently returned to Scotland in a desperate, but failed, Conservative attempt to win back support north of the border. The famed stone currently resides in Edinburgh Castle (see page 80). In 1651, the last coronation in Scotland took place when King Charles II was crowned by the Scots on the Moot Hill. The ceremony was attended by Lord Stormont, forefather of the present occupier, Lord Mansfield. Part of the church where this took place still remains.

Aside from its hugely impressive history, the palace also houses beautiful collections of porcelain, needlework, royal furniture, clocks, ivories and many other absorbing artefacts. You could also spend a few hours walking in the magnificent 100-acre gardens, filled with bluebells, rhododendrons, roses and rare trees, with strutting peacocks and Highland cattle roaming around. There's also a maze, picnic park and children's adventure playground, plus a gift shop and coffee shop with delicious home baking. ■ *Early Apr to late Oct daily 0930-1730 (last admission 1645). Palace and grounds £6.20, £5.30 concession; grounds only £3.10, £2.50 concession. T552300.*

Huntingtower Castle Though not as impressive as Scone, Huntingtower Castle, three miles west of Perth on the A85 to Crieff, is well worth a visit. It consists of two complete towers dating from the 15th and 16th centuries, linked by a 17th-century range, and features some fine 16th-century painted ceilings. The castle, once owned by the Ruthven family, has some interesting history of its own. Prior to the building of the range, a daughter of the house once leapt between the two towers to avoid being caught in her lover's bedroom. ■ *Apr-Sep daily 0930-1830; Oct-Mar Mon-Wed and Sat 0930-1630, Thu 0930-1200, Sun 1400-1630, closed Fri. £2.00, £1.50 concession. T627231 (HS).*

Essentials

Sleeping
There are numerous places to stay in and around Perth

Pick of the bunch is the **A** *Ballathie House Hotel*, at Kinclaven, near Stanley, 2 miles north of Perth, just off the A9, T01250-883268, www.ballathiehousehotel.com 43 rooms. This elegant, award-winning 19th-century former hunting lodge has a reputation for superb Scottish cuisine (expensive). Another excellent option is the **B** *Huntingtower Hotel*, T583771, F583777, www.huntingtowerhotel.co.uk, 1 mile west of Perth off the A85 to Crieff, 34 rooms. Elegant country house hotel in its own landscaped gardens, good food in the dining room (mid-range) and bar meals in the conservatory (cheap). Next to the train station, on Leonard St, is the **B-C** *Quality Station Hotel*, T624141, admin@gb628-u-net.com 70 rooms. A grand old Victorian edifice close to the town centre. **D-C** *Sunbank House Hotel*, 50 Dundee Rd, T624882, F442515. 9 rooms. A lovely little hotel overlooking the River Tay and close to Branklyn Garden and Kinnoull Hill, great value.

There are plenty of **B&Bs** and **guesthouses** in town. You'll find lots of them along Dunkeld Rd, heading north out of town towards the A9, including: **E** *Almond Villa Guest House*, No 51, T629356, almondvilla@compuserve.com; **E** *Clark Kimberley*, No 57-59, T637406; **E** *The Gables Guest House*, No 24, T/F624717, www.thegablesgh.co.uk; and **E** *Strathcona*, No 45, T626185. There are also several places on Marshall Pl, which overlooks the South Inch, including the highly recommended **E** *Kinnaird Guest House*, No 5, T6280121, www.Kinnaird-guesthouse.co.uk Next door at No 6 is **E** *Marshall House*, T442886.

Perhaps the best place to look is Pitcullen Cres, on the A94 Coupar Angus road, where almost every house on the street offers B&B. The most recommended include **E** *Achnacarry Guest House*, No 3, T621421; **E** *Adam Guest House*, No 6, T/F627179; **E** *Clunie Guest House*, No 12, T/F623625, ann@clunieperth.freeserve.co.uk; and **E** *Pitcullen Guest House*, No 17, T626506, www.pitcullen.guesthouse@virgin.net

The excellent **F** *SYHA Youth hostel* is at 107 Glasgow Rd, T623658, open Mar-Oct, about half a mile west of the town centre (take bus No 7). There's a **campsite** at *Cleeve Caravan Park*, on Glasgow Rd, near the ring road, about 2 miles from town, T639521, open Apr-Oct. There's also the *Scone Palace Camping & Caravan Club Site*, T552308, open Apr-Oct.

Perth is packed with pubs and restaurants to suit all tastes. Restaurant-wise, quite a few come with glowing references from diners. *Let's Eat Bistro*, T643377, on Kinnoull St, is a very classy establishment which provides a modern Scottish menu with Mediterranean influences, all meals cooked fresh to order. Open Tue-Sat 1200-1400, 1830-2130. Its sister bistro, *Let's Eat Again*, T633771, is at 33 George St. Open the same hours but until 2145. Both are in the mid-range category. *No. 63*, T441451, is a swish restaurant down by the river at 63 Tay Street which serves contemporary Scottish food. Open Tue-Sat 1200-1400, 1830-2100. *Exceed*, T621189, at 65 South Methven St, has a more general menu but it's just as appetizing; as is the menu at *Time Out*, T567056, at 80 George St, close to the museum. For something a little more expensive, try *The Seafood Restaurant*, T449777, at 168 South St, which specializes in delicious fish and game. *Paco's*, T622290, 3-5 Mill St, has a more 'Tex-Mex' feel to it, serving fajitas, enchiladas, steaks and a fine line in chicken dishes, while also serving up a children's menu of burgers and pizzas. For a good cappucino or a panini try *Caffe Canto*, T451938, a popular chic café at 62 George St.

Of the **pubs** in town, *The Auld Hoose*, T624136, on the corner of South St and King Edward St, does a nice bar lunch; as does *Mucky Mulligan's*, T636705, at 97 Canal St. *Scaramouche*, T637479, 103 South St, is a very popular bar; as is the *Cherrybank*, T624349, at 210 Glasgow Rd, where the bar lunches and suppers come very highly recommended.

Eating & drinking

Perth Theatre, 185 High St, T621031, is a beautiful Victorian-era theatre with an excellent reputation for high-class productions. The *Playhouse* **cinema** at 6 Murray St, T623126, offers a dose of escapism on the big screen. For the younger (and young at heart) traveller, there are 2 **nightclubs** in Perth: *Curly Lloyd's* at 40-48 Canal St, T630503; and the *Ice Factory* at 6 Shore Rd, T630011.

Entertainment

The **Perth Highland Games** are held on the second Sun in Aug, T627782, on the same weekend as the **Perth Show**, which takes place on South Inch. There are also regular **jump racing** events during the summer at **Perth Racecourse**, near Scone Palace, T551597.

Festivals & events

Outdoor equipment *Mountain Man Supplies*, 133 South St, T632368.

Shopping

For sports and leisure, Perth takes a bit of beating. Four sports centres in the city ensure there's no excuse for 'couch-potato' inactivity. *Perth Leisure Pool*, T492410, open daily 1000-2200, west of the town centre on the Glasgow Rd, claims to have the best leisure swimming pool in Scotland. Next door is *Dewar's Rinks*, T624188, where the visitor can curl, ice skate or bowl. *Bell's Sports Centre*, on Hay Street, T622301, open daily 0900-2200, covers virtually every sport and leisure activity imaginable.

Scotland is famed for its superb fishing and Perth has more than its fair share of **game and course fishing** facilities. Too many, in fact, to detail here, so we'll mention just one, which is recommended: the *Sandyknowes fly-fishery* at Bridge of Earn,

Sports

Central Scotland

T813033, a few miles southeast of Perth. Located between the rivers Earn and Tay, there are facilities for the novice, right up to the most experienced angler with great fishing in a beautiful landscape. The season runs from Mar-Dec and currently costs £10 per day. Details of all the Perthshire fisheries are available from the Tourist Information Centre at West Mill Street.

Another sport Scotland is renowned for is **golf**, and Perth is particularly worthy of mention in this respect as it has a golf course in the middle of the River Tay! Moncrieff Island is worth playing a round on, if only to be able to tell your friends that the golfers don't shout 'fore' on this course, they shout 'ahoy there!' Details from the Tourist Information Centre, or contact *King James VI Golf Club*, T625170.

Perth is also well-placed for other outdoor activities such as **walking**, **cycling** and **skiing**. *Glenshee ski centre* is on the A93 north of Blairgowrie and is easily reached from Perth (see page 336). The tourist office can provide suggested cycle routes, and stocks the *Cycle Routes in Highland Perthshire* booklet. For walkers, a recommended guidebook is *Perthshire, Angus and Fife Walks*, which details 28 routes.

Transport Scottish *Citylink* **buses** (T08705-505050) run frequently to **Glasgow** (1 hr 25 mins), **Edinburgh** (1½ hrs), **Dundee** (35 mins), **Aberdeen** (2½ hrs) and **Inverness** (2½ hrs). *Stagecoach* (T629339) run local buses to Dunkeld, Pitlochry, Aberfeldy and Crieff; and *Strathtay Scottish* (T01382-228054) buses serve Blairgowrie, Alyth and Dundee.

There's an hourly **train** service (Mon-Sat; 2-hourly on Sun) to **Glasgow Queen St** (1 hr); and frequent trains to **Edinburgh** (1 hr 20 mins). There are also hourly trains to **Stirling** (30 mins), **Dundee** (25 mins) and **Aberdeen** (1 hr 40 mins), and several daily to **Inverness** via **Pitlochry** (30 mins) and **Aviemore**.

Car hire *Arnold Clark*, St Leonard's Bank, T442202.

Directory **Medical services** *Perth Royal Infirmary*, Taymount Terr, T623311.

North of Perth

Perth is the main gateway to the eastern side of the Highlands and the A9, the road north, is a gentle introduction to the wild northern reaches of Scotland. The Perthshire Highlands may lack the sheer magisterial grandeur of the northwest but have their own serene beauty. The route north from Perth is served by regular trains and buses.

Dunkeld and Birnam

Phone code: 01350
Colour map 4, grid B3

Twelve miles north of Perth is the attractive village of Dunkeld, standing right on the Highland line. Dunkeld is surrounded by beautiful scenery offering excellent **walking** opportunities, details of which are available from the **Tourist Information Centre** at The Cross, T727688, in the heart of the village. ■ *All year round: Apr-Jun, Sep and Oct Mon-Sat 0930-1730, Sun 1100-1600; Jul and Aug Mon-Sat 0900-1830, Sun 1100-1700; Nov and Dec Fri-Mon 1000-1600.*

Sights It's definitely worth making a stop here, if only to admire the **cathedral**, in the most idyllic situation on the banks of the fast-flowing, silvery Tay. Half of it is still in use as a church and the other half is in ruins. The oldest part of the cathedral is the 14th-century choir, which now forms the parish church, while the 15th-century nave and tower are also still standing. Much of the original was damaged during the orgy of ecclesiastical destruction that accompanied the Reformation. It was damaged again in the Battle of Dunkeld in 1689, fought between supporters of the protestant William of Orange and the Stuart monarch James VII. ■ *Apr-Sep 0930-1830 (HS). Free.* On your way to the cathedral you'll pass a collection of lovely little whitewashed cottages, beautifully restored by the National Trust of Scotland (NTS). More details are available at the Ell Shop nearby.

Across the bridge from Dunkeld is **Birnam**, made famous in Shakespeare's *Macbeth*, though the play's protagonist was in reality a very different character from the evil villain portrayed by the Bard. Birnam was the inspiration for another famous literary figure, **Beatrix Potter**, who spent her childhood summers here. Visitors can explore the origins of the *Peter Rabbit* stories at the **Beatrix Potter Exhibition.** ■ *Daily 1000-1700. Free. T727674.*

A short distance north of Dunkeld on the A9 is the turning to **The Hermitage**. A marked woodland walk starts from the car park and follows the river Braan to the Black Linn Falls, overlooked by Ossian's Hall, an 18th-century folly built by the Duke of Atholl. It's a lovely spot, which has inspired the likes of Wordsworth and Mendelssohn. Further on is Ossian's Cave. Buses to Pitlochry (see below) stop at the turning for The Hermitage.

A few miles northeast of Dunkeld, off the A923 to Blairgowrie, is the **Loch of the Lowes Visitor Centre**, managed by the Scottish Wildlife Trust. There's a hide with binoculars for viewing a pair of ospreys which breed here and which can be seen on the loch from early April to early September. ■ *Apr-Sep daily 1000-1700. Free (donation advised). T727337.*

The top hotel in the area is **L** *Kinnaird House*, at Dalguise, about 8 miles north via the A9 and the B898, T01796-482440. The setting, the style, the service and the restaurant are all excellent. In the village is the luxurious **L** *Hilton Dunkeld*, T727771, www.dunkeld.hilton.com, former home of the Duke of Atholl, now with full leisure and outdoor activity facilities. More modest options include **D** *The Bridge B&B*, 10 Bridge Street, T727068, www.visitscotland.com/thebridge; or **B&B** at **E-D** *The Pend*, 5 Brae St, T727586, www.thepend.com; and **E** *Birnam Guest House*, 4 Murthly Terr, Birnam, T727201. There's also a **hostel**, the *Western Caputh Independent Hostel*, at Caputh, 5 miles east of Dunkeld, on the A984 to Coupar Angus, T01738-710617. It has 18 beds and is open all year.

Sleeping & eating

Eating options are mostly limited to the hotels. *Kinnaird House* is particularly good (see baove). Bar meals are offered by the *Atholl Arms* (see above) and the *Birnam House Hotel*, T727462, on the main road through Birnam. There is a café at the Beatrix Potter Exhibition (see above).

Citylink **buses** between Perth and Inverness stop at the train station by Birnam several times daily in either direction. *Stagecoach* buses from Perth to Pitlochry and Aberfeldy stop in Dunkeld, and *Strathtay Scottish* buses between Blairgowrie and Aberfeldy also stop in the village (twice daily Mon-Sat). There are several **trains** daily, T08457-484950, to and from Perth and Inverness.

Transport

Pitlochry

Despite being one of the busiest Highland tourist towns in the summer, Pitlochry's lovely setting on the shores of the River Tummel, overlooked by Ben y Vrackie, makes it a pleasant base for exploring this beautiful area. The town also has a few worthwhile attractions of its own.

Phone code: 01796
Colour map 4, grid B3
Population: 2,500

Getting there The bus and **train stations** are on Atholl Road. *Scottish Citylink* **buses** run almost every hour between **Glasgow** (2 hrs 15 mins), **Edinburgh** (2 hrs 45 mins) and

Ins & outs

Central Scotland

Inverness (2 hrs) via Pitlochry. Stagecoach buses run daily except Sun to **Aberfeldy**, **Dunkeld** and **Perth**. Pitlochry is on the Perth-Inverness rail line and there are several daily **trains** (Mon-Sat; fewer on Sun) to Perth (30 mins).

Getting around   Cycle hire *Escape Route*, 8 West Moulin Rd, T/F473859. Touring and off-road bikes for £14 per day. **Taxi** *Elizabeth Yule Transport*, T472290.

The **Tourist information Centre** is at 22 Atholl Rd, T472215. Apr to mid-May, mid-Sep and Oct Mon-Sat 0900-1800, Sun 1100-1700; mid-May to mid-Sep Mon-Sat 0900-1900, Sun 0900-1800; Nov-Mar Mon-Fri 0900-1700, Sat 1000-1400.

Sights   There are two whisky distilleries to visit. The larger of the two is Bell's **Blair Atholl Distillery**, at the southern end of town, heading towards the A9 to Perth. ■ *Easter-Sep Mon-Sat 0900-1700, Sun 1200-1700; Oct Mon-Fri 1000-1700, Nov-Easter Mon-Fri 1000-1600 tours every 10 mins. £3. T482003.* A couple of miles east of town, on the A924, is the **Edradour Distillery**, the smallest in Scotland. ■ *Mar-Oct Mon-Sat 0930-1700, Sun 1200-1700; Nov and Dec Mon-Sat 1000-1600. Free. T472095.*

Pitlochry's main attraction is the **fish ladder**, part of the **power station and dam** which formed man-made **Loch Faskally** when it was constructed on the River Tummel. The ladder allows salmon to swim up to their spawning grounds and you can watch them leaping spectacularly in the spring and summer. The best months are May and June. The fish ladder is across the river, a short distance from the *Pitlochry Festival Theatre* (see below). In summer 2002 the Scottish Plant Collectors Garden will open in the grounds of the theatre. Contact the theatre for further information.

Walks around Pitlochry
OS Landranger maps Nos 43 and 52 cover all the walks, and the OS Explorer map No 21 (Pitlochry and Loch Tummel) covers them in greater detail

The tourist office sells a useful leaflet *Pitlochry Walks* which describes four long local walks, and there are many other fine walks in the surrounding area. The greatest walking attraction is **Ben y Vrackie** (2,758 ft), a steep six-mile walk (there and back) from the tiny hamlet of Moulin, a mile north of Pitlochry on the A924 (turn left at the *Moulin Inn*). The path is well trodden and the going is relatively easy, across bleak moorland, until the steep final ascent on scree. On a clear day the views from the summit of the Trossachs are wonderful, so it's best not to attempt this on a cloudy day. In spite of its proximity to Pitlochry, you need to be properly equipped and take the usual safety precautions (see page 60).

Another excellent walk from Pitlochry, described in the tourist office leaflet, leaves town on the north road and turns left past the boat station. It then crosses the Cluanie footbridge and follows the road to Loch Faskally and up the River Garry to Garry Bridge over the **Pass of Killiecrankie** (see page 331). The path returns to Pitlochry along the west bank of the River Garry, before turning west up the River Tummel, passing close by the **Linn of Tummel**, then crossing the Tummel and following the west shore of Loch Faskally to the dam and fish ladder.

Sleeping   There's plenty of accommodation to choose from. The best hotel in town is the superb **B** *Pine Trees Hotel*, Strathview Terr, T472121, www.pinetreeshotel.co.uk This Victorian country house is set in 10 acres of gardens away from the tourist bustle. Its *Garden Restaurant* has a fine reputation. A few miles north of Pitlochry, in the village of Killiecrankie, is the **B-C** *Killiecrankie Hotel*, T473220, www.killiecrankiehotel.co.uk Open Mar-Dec. 10 rooms. It's a quiet, cosy country house hotel which offers quite possibly the very finest food in the area. Another top-class hotel is the **C-D** *Dunfallandy Country House Hotel & Restaurant*, T472648, dunfalhse@aol.com, a mile out of town on the road to Logierait. 8 rooms. This Georgian mansion offers great views, peace and quiet and superb cuisine, no smoking, excellent value.

Falls of Bruar walk

A well-maintained path leads from the lower falls along the gorge of the Bruar River to the upper falls and back down the other side. It's a 1½ mile round trip. From the House of Bruar, turn right by the adventure playground, then left up the river bank. The path passes under a railway arch and through a kissing gate. It then heads through open forest to a rocky outcrop, from where you can see the lower falls. A series of wooden steps leads down from the outcrop, then a ricky path climbs up till it forks. Go right, then cross the bridge, from

where there's a good view of the lower falls. From here a clear path leads up the far side till it reaches a deer fence. Climb up to the gate, go through it and continue uphill through trees till the path levels out high above the gorge. Further on there's a picnic area, then the path curves left down to the upper bridge, which is a great vantage point from which to admire the stunning view. The path heads left through more trees. It then crosses a stream before descending to thelower bridge and then back to the car park.

There are numerous guesthouses and B&Bs, far too many to list here. The tourist office will provide a full list. Among the most recommended are **D-E** *Craigroyston House*, 2 Lower Oakfield, T472053; **E** *Arrandale House*, Knockfarrie Rd, T472987; and **E** *Craigatin House & Courtyard*, 165 Atholl Rd, T472478. There's an **F** *SYHA Youth Hostel*, T472308, on Knockard Rd overlooking the town centre is open all year.

Eating The *Killiecrankie Hotel* (see above) is expensive but the best place to eat. The bar is less formal and cheaper than the restaurant. In town try *Port-na-Craig Inn & Restaurant*, T472777, which is just below the Festival Theatre on the banks of the River Tummel. It offers great Scottish cooking at mid-range prices in a bistro ambience. Another good choice is the *Old Smithy*, at 154 Atholl Rd, T472356, which is moderately priced and open daily till 2100; or *The Old Armoury*, Armoury Rd, T474281. A couple of miles south of Pitlochry on the old A9 road is the *East Haugh Country House Hotel & Restaurant*, T473121, www.easthaugh.com, a 17th-century country house with excellent and elegant dining and great bar lunches (lunch mid-range; dinner expensive). A few miles north of Pitlochry, at Moulin on the A924 is the wonderful *Moulin Inn*, T472196, www.moulin.u-net.com, which serves good, hearty, cheap pub food and fine real ales (try their 'Braveheart') in a great atmosphere. Food daily till 2130.

Entertainment The *Pitlochry Festival Theatre*, T484626, is across the river from the town centre. It stages a different play every night for 6 nights a week during its season from May to Oct.

Shopping *MacNaughton's*, Station Rd. A vast range of everything tartan and lots more besides. Come here first.

Around Pitlochry

Four miles north of Pitlochry the A9 cuts through the **Pass of Killiecrankie**, a spectacular wooded gorge which was the dramatic setting for the Battle of Killiecrankie in 1689, when a Jacobite army led by Graham of Claverhouse, Viscount 'Bonnie Dundee', defeated the government forces under General Hugh Mackay. One government soldier evaded capture by making a jump of Olympic gold medal-winning proportions across the River Garry at **Soldier's Leap**. An NTS **visitor centre** has displays on the battle and the local natural history. ■ *Apr-Oct daily 1000-1730. Free (honesty box; £1 donation advised). T473233.*

Central Scotland

Blair Atholl &
Blair Castle
Phone code: 01796
Colour map 4, grid B3

Seven miles from Pitlochry, and a mile from the village of Blair Atholl, is Blair Castle, traditional seat of the Earls and Dukes of Atholl. This whitewashed, turreted castle dates from 1269 and presents an impressive picture on first sight. This is the headquarters of Britain's only private army, the Atholl Highlanders, and one of them usually pipes in new arrivals. Thirty-two rooms in the castle are open for public viewing and are packed full of paintings, furniture, armour, porcelain and much else besides, presenting a startling picture of aristocratic Highland life in previous centuries. The most outrageously sumptuous of the rooms are the Tapestry Room and the ballroom. The surrounding landscaped grounds are home to peacocks and Highland cattle, and there are woodland walks and a walled Japanese water garden to enjoy. ■ *Apr-Oct 1000-1800 (last admission 1700). Open 0930 Jul, Aug. House and grounds £6.25, grounds only £2.00, various concessions. T481207.*

There's a **caravan park** within the castle grounds, T481263, open April-October, with good facilities. A very good **walk** starts from the caravan park and heads up into **Glen Tilt**. It's about 10½ miles there and back along estate roads, though this can be shortened by four miles or lengthened by six miles. A leaflet describing the routes is available from the castle or caravan park.

Sleeping and eating There's a selection of accommodation in Blair Atholl village. The **C-D** *Atholl Arms Hotel*, T481205, near the train station, does B&B and serves bar meals. The best food hereabouts is to be found at the *Loft*, Golf Course Rd, T481377, www.theloftrestaurant.co.uk, which offers superior Modern Scottish/Mediterranean food at mid-range/expensive prices.

Transport Not all **trains** stop at Blair Atholl. *Elizabeth Yule Transport* (see Pitlochry Transport above) runs a service between Pitlochry and Blair Atholl, via Killiecrankie, a few times daily, except Sun. You can **hire bikes** from *Atholl Mountain Bikes*, T473553, for £12 per day. They have a leaflet listing various cycle routes, including the Glen Tilt route above.

Falls of Bruar

Eight miles from Blair Atholl, just off the A9, are the Falls of Bruar. There's a short walk from the car park to the lower falls, but it's worth continuing to the more dramatic upper falls, which are less visited (see above). By the car park is the excellent **House of Bruar**, a huge shopping emporium designed like a Victorian hunting lodge where you can buy just about any kind of souvenir and enjoy some very fine Scottish cooking.

Loch Tummel
& Loch
Rannoch
Phone code: 01796
Colour map 4, grid B2

The B8019 turns off the B8079 road from Pitlochry to Blair Atholl and runs west along the shores of beautiful lochs Tummel and Rannoch, best seen in the autumn when the trees change their colours. At the eastern end of Loch Tummel is **Queen's View**, a spectacular viewpoint which looks down the loch and across to Schiehallion. There's a **visitor centre** here, with displays and audio-visual programmes about the area. ■ *Apr-Oct daily 1000-1730. Free, but £1 parking charge. T473123..*

OS sheet No 51

Schiehallion (3,552 ft) is one of Scotland's best-loved mountains, whose distinctive conical peak made it ideal for use in early experiments in 1774 to judge the weight of the earth. These were not an unqualified success, but led to the invention of contour lines as an aid to surveying the mountain. The walk to the summit is fairly straightforward, except for the very rocky final stretch. You'll need to be properly clothed and equipped (see page 60) and take a map and compass. The route to the summit starts at the car park on the B846 Kinloch Rannoch to Aberfeldy road, near Braes of Foss.

Beyond Loch Tummel is the little village of Kinloch Rannoch, where back-packers can stock up on supplies before heading into the hills. There are a few **places to stay** in the village, including the characterful **C** *Dunalastair Hotel*, T01882-632323, www.dunalastair.co.uk; and **E** *Bunrannoch House*, T01882-632407, www.bunrannoch.co.uk, a former Victorian shooting lodge which offers good cooking.

Kinloch Rannoch
Colour map 4, grid B2

Sixteen miles west of the village the road ends at Rannoch station, where you can catch trains north to Fort William or south to Glasgow. You can grab something to eat here at the little tearoom. Beyond the west end of Loch Rannoch is bleak Rannoch Moor which extends all the way to Glen Coe. By the station is the **E-D** *Moor of Rannoch Hotel*, T01882-633238, which does good, moderately priced meals. There's a daily (except Sunday) **postbus** service, T472386, from Pitlochry to Rannoch station, via Kinloch Rannoch, or check with *Elizabeth Yule Transport* (see Pitlochry **Transport**).

Aberfeldy

The little town of Aberfeldy stands on the banks of the River Tay, on the A827 which runs between the A9 and Loch Tay. It's well placed geographically for exploring the northern part of Perthshire, though Pitlochry has better tourist facilities.

Phone code: 01887
Colour map 4, grid B2
Population: 2,000

Getting there *Stagecoach* **buses** run regularly (Mon-Sat) to **Pitlochry** (45 mins), **Dunkeld** (1¼ hrs) and **Perth** (1¾ hrs). *Strathtay Scottish* has twice daily (except Sun) buses to **Blairgowrie**, via Dunkeld. There's also a **postbus** service to **Killin** and another to **Glen Lyon** once a day, except Sun, T820400.

Ins & outs

Tourist Information Centre is housed in an old church on The Square, in the centre of town. T820276. Apr-Jun, Sep and Oct Mon-Sat 0930-1730, Sun 1100-1600; Jul and Aug Mon-Sat 0930-1830, Sun 1100-1700; Nov-Mar Mon-Fri 0930-1730, Sat 1000-1400.

The River Tay is spanned by **Wade's Bridge**, built by General Wade in 1773 during his campaign to pacify the Highlands. Overlooking the bridge is the **Black Watch Monument** which commemorates the famous regiment becoming part of the British Army's peacekeeping force here, in 1739. In Mill Street is the **Aberfeldy Water Mill**, built in 1825 and restored in 1983 to produce stone-ground oatmeal in the traditional Scottish way. ■ *Easter-Oct Mon-Sat 1000-1700, Sun 1200-1630. £2.50.* Just outside Aberfeldy is **Dewar's World of Whisky**, one of a new breed of distillery visitor centres. You start your visit in the heritage centre where there's an audio guide and interactive exhibits informing you all about whisky and the Dewar family. Then you go on a guided tour of the distillery which ends, of course, with a chance to taste the product. ■ *Apr-end Oct Mon-Sat 1000-1800, Sun 1200-1600, Nov-Mar Mon-Fri 1000-1600. £3.95, £3.00 concession. T822010, www.dewars.com/worldofwhisky.*

Sights

A mile west of Aberfeldy, across the Tay at Weem, is **Castle Menzies**, an impressive, restored 16th-century 'Z-plan' fortified tower-house, the former seat of the chief of Clan Menzies. ■ *Apr-mid Oct Mon-Sat 1030-1700, Sun 1400-1700. £3.50, £3.00 concession. T820982.* Not far away at Castle Menzies Farm, is **House of Menzies**, a tourist store with a coffee shop. It's got an excellent selection of New World wines and is a good place to buy gifts such as Scottish jewellery. ■ *Apr-end Oct Mon-Sat 1000-1700, Sun 1100-1700; Oct-Dec closed Mon; Jan-Apr, Thu, Fri 1000-1700, Sat, Sun 1100-1700. T829666.*

Central Scotland

A popular local walk is to the **Falls of Moness**, through the famous **Birks of Aberfeldy**, forever associated with the poet Robert Burns who was inspired by the birks (birch trees) to write his eponymous song. It's a fairly easy walk along a marked trail (see map) up to the impressive falls, and the views of Strathtay and the surrounding hills on the descent also make it worthwhile. It's about four miles there and back.

Sleeping & eating There are several hotels in and around town, the best of which is the magnificent 15th-century **L-A** *Farleyer House Hotel* in Weem, T820332, 100127.222@compuserve.com Also recommended are: **B** *Guinach House*, T820251, a family run country house hotel in a lovely setting by the Birks and with a superb restaurant (expensive); and the very friendly **C** *Weem Hotel* T820381, in Weem, about a mile west of Aberfeldy on the B846 to Strathtummel. Also in Weem is the excellent **C** *Ailean Chraggan*, T820346, which serves very good food in the bar (mid-range). There are many **guesthouses** and **B&Bs**, including **D-E** *Fernbank House*, Kenmore St, T820345; **E** *South Lodge*, T820115, by Castle Menzies and **E** *Tigh'N'Eilean Guest House*, T820109, on Taybridge Dr, all of which are recommended and offer good value.

There's not a great deal of choice for **eating**, other than the hotels in town or a bar lunch in one of the pubs. The *Breadalbane Bakery*, at 37 Dunkeld St on the way out of town, is recommended for home baking and their Aberfeldy Whisky Cake. There's also the coffee shop at House of Menzies which sells snacks such as panini and baguettes, as well as home-made cakes.

Around Loch Tay

Kenmore
Colour map 4, grid B2

The 14-mile-long Loch Tay is surrounded by some of the loveliest scenery in Perthshire and is well worth exploring, though public transport around its shores is limited to one postbus service a day. At the northeast end of Loch Tay is Kenmore, a neat little village of whitewashed cottages dominated by a huge archway which stands at the gateway to Taymouth Castle, built by the Campbells of Glenorchy in the early 19th century and now a very fine **golf course**, T830228. Near the village, on the southern bank of the loch, is **The Scottish Crannog Centre**, an authentic reconstruction of a *crannog*, an artificial Bronze-Age island-house built for the purpose of defence. ■ *Mar and Nov daily 1000-1600; Apr to mid-Oct 1000-1730. £4.25, various concession £3.85. T830583.* Loch Tay is a major **watersports** centre, and close by the Crannog Centre is *Croft-Na-Caber*, T830588, Scotland's best watersports and activities centre, where you can try water-skiing, windsurfing, sailing, rafting, jet biking, river sledging, fishing, parascending, clay-pigeon shooting, hill walking and Nordic skiing. You can **hire bikes** from *Perthshire Mountain Bikes*, T830291.

Sleeping and eating There's accommodation at the **D** *Croft-Na-Caber Hotel*, T830236. Also in Kenmore is the *Loch Tay Boating Centre*, T830291, open Apr-Oct, where you can hire speedboats, fishing boats and canoes. The best place to stay in Kenmore is the **C** *Kenmore Hotel*, T830205, which claims to be Scotland's oldest coaching inn, dating from 1572. Whether or not this is true, there's no denying that it's full of character and very comfortable. There's also a **campsite** at the *Kenmore Caravan and Camping Park*, T830226, complete with its very own golf course. The best food is to be had in the lovely bar of the *Kenmore Hotel* (mid-range).

Kenmore to Amulree
Colour map 4, grid B2

For those with their own transport, one of the most scenic routes in this part of the country is the spectacular road which winds its way south from Kenmore high up into the mountains, across a bleak and barren plateau and down the

Climbing Ben Lawers

The north side of Loch Tay is dominated by Ben Lawers (3,987 ft), the highest mountain in Perthshire. Its massif of seven summits includes six Munros which are linked by an eight-mile ridge which can be walked in one day by fit and experienced hill walkers. The best access to the ridge is from Glen Lyon. You'll need OS sheet No 51. The trek to the main summit starts from the **NTS Visitor Centre**, two miles along a track which turns off the main A827 about halfway between Kenmore and Killin (see page 358). This track continues over a wild pass to Bridge of Balgie in Glen Lyon. Leaflets describing the climb are available from the visitor centre. It's a seven-mile walk there and back, and though the route is straightforward and easy to follow, it's a very steep, tough climb of 2,700 ft from the centre to the summit. Allow 5-6 hours. You should be fit, properly clothed (see page 60) and have some previous hill-walking experience, but the views from the top on a clear day are amazing, across to the North Sea in the east and the Atlantic Ocean in the west. There's also a much easier one-mile nature trail, and an accompanying booklet describing the rare Alpine flora is available at the centre. Near the turn-off to the NTS Visitor Centre is the **E** Ben Lawers Hotel, T01567-820436.

---

other side to the tiny hamlet of **Amulree**. This road is often closed in the winter and there are gates at either end. From Amulree you can continue south to Crieff (see page 337), through the gentler, but equally stunning scenery of the **Sma' Glen**. Alternatively, you could head north to Aberfeldy and then complete the circuit back to Kenmore.

A few miles west of Kenmore a minor road turns off the A827, which runs along the north bank of the loch, and heads to Fortingall, a tiny village of classic beauty which features on many a calendar. It's little more than a row of thatched cottages which wouldn't even get a mention were it not for two amazing claims. The 3,000-year-old yew tree in the churchyard is claimed to be the oldest living thing in Europe. More astonishing is the claim that this is the birthplace of **Pontius Pilate**, said to be the son of a Roman officer who was stationed here. Furthermore, it is believed that Pilate returned here to be buried, and a gravestone in the churchyard bears the initials 'PP'. There's **accommodation** in the village at the wonderful, and very popular, **D** *Fortingall Hotel*, T01887-830367, hotel@fortingall.com, next to the churchyard.

Fortingall & Glen Lyon
Colour map 4, grid B2

If you have your own transport, make a detour up Glen Lyon, one of the most beautiful of all Scottish glens. On a summer's day there can be few lovelier places on earth, as the River Lyon tumbles through corries and gorges and through flowering meadows, with high mountain peaks on either side and eagles soaring overhead. It's no surprise that Wordsworth and Tennyson waxed lyrical over its qualities. The road from Fortingall runs all the way to the head of the glen, at Loch Lyon. This is walking and fishing paradise. There are several Munros to 'bag' and fishing permits are available at the *Fortingall Hotel* (see above).

Blairgowrie and Glenshee

The other major road running north from Perth is the A93, which passes the Glenshee ski resort on its way to Braemar and then heads east through Deeside to Aberdeen (see page 419). The respectable town of Blairgowrie, or Blairgowrie and Rattray to give it its full title, lies amidst the raspberry fields of

Phone code: 01250
Colour map 4, grid B4

Central Scotland

Glenshee ski centre

Glenshee ski centre is at the crest of the Cairnwell Pass (2,199 ft), the highest main road pass in Britain, on the border of Perthshire and Aberdeenshire. It is the most extensive skiing area in Scotland, with 38 pistes, as well as Nordic skiing. **Ski rental** is around £13 per day (£12 for snowboards) and lessons are £18 for four hours. A one-day **lift pass** costs £18, or £72 for five days, including tuition and hire. For more information, call Ski Glenshee (T01339-741320, www.ski.scotland.net). For the latest snow and weather conditions, call the Ski Hotline (T0900-1-654656).

The only public transport is a daily **postbus** service (Monday-Saturday only) from Blairgowrie to Spittal of Glenshee, or to the ski resort from Braemar and Ballater.

Strathmore and is conveniently placed to serve as an accommodation centre for Glenshee Ski Centre (see below).

Ins & outs **Getting there** *Strathtay Scottish*, T01382-228054, **buses** run hourly (Mon-Sat; less frequently on Sun) to and from **Perth** (45 mins) and **Dundee** (1 hr).

The **Tourist Information Centre** is at 26 Wellmeadow in the centre of town. T872960. Apr-Jun, Sep and Oct Mon-Sat 0930-1730, Sun 1100-1600; Jul and Aug Mon-Sat 0900-1830, Sun 1100-1700; Nov-Easter Mon-Fri 0930-1730, Sat 1000-1400.

There's little of real interest to detain passing tourists, but **Keathbank Mill**, off the A93 to Braemar, is worth a look. This huge 19th-century jute mill has a steam turbine dating from 1862 driven by the largest water wheel in Scotland. There's also a heraldry museum, model railway and woodcarving workshops. ■ *Apr to early Oct daily 1030-1700. £4.25.* T872025. Three miles south of Blairgowrie, just off the A93 by **Meikleour**, is a 100-ft-high **beech hedge**, the highest hedge in the world.

Sleeping There's a good selection of accommodation. Top of the range is the **L** *Kinloch House* **& eating** *Hotel*, T884237, www.kinlochhouse.com, a luxurious country house 3 miles west of town on the A923 to Dunkeld. It offers excellent cuisine (expensive) and sporting facilities. More affordable is the **C** *Altamount House Hotel*, T873512, on the Coupar Angus Road, which also offers top-class cooking (mid-range to expensive). There are plenty of cheaper options, including **D-E** *Rosebank House*, T872912, on Balmoral Road. **Camping** is available at the *Blairgowrie Holiday Park*, T876666, in Rattray, across the River Ericht. Some 20 miles north of Blairgowrie, at **Spittal of Glenshee**, is *Gulabin Lodge*, T885255, a **hostel/bunkhouse** run by Cairnwell Mountain sports which rents out skis, boards and mountain bikes and also gives skiing tuition. Nearby is one of the area's top hotels, **B-C** *Dalmunzie House Hotel*, T885224, a grand old Highland sporting lodge set in a 6,000-acre estate and boasting the highest 9-hole golf course in Britain.

There are several decent eating places, best of which is *Cargills*, T876735, a nice-looking bistro housed in a converted mill store by the river. (mid-range). Closed Mon. The *Angus Hotel* and *The Driftwood* pub, both on Wellmeadow, serve decent bar meals, as does the lovely **D-E** *Bridge of Cally Hotel*, T886231, 6 miles north of town on the A93.

Strathearn

Strathearn is the wide valley (or strath) of the river Earn, which stretches west from Perth to Loch Earn, on the border of the Perthshire and Stirling regions. The Highlands officially begin in the western part of Strathearn and the Highland Boundary Fault runs through the village of Comrie, near Crieff.

Crieff and around

The well-groomed town of Crieff sits on the slopes of the Grampian foothills overlooking the wide Strathearn valley. It's a popular tourist centre and a good base for exploring the western part of Perthshire and the Trossachs. People have been coming here since Victorian times, when Crieff was a popular spa town, and its position between the Highlands and Lowlands made it an important livestock market in the 18th century, with traders coming from as far afield as the Isle of Skye to buy and sell cattle. The **Crieff Highland Gathering** takes place on the penultimate Sunday in August.

Population: 6,350
Phone code: 01764
Colour map 4, grid C2

Getting there *Stagecoach* **buses**, T01738-629339, run every hour (Mon-Sat) to Perth (45 mins) and Comrie. Some buses continue to St Fillans. There are regular buses to Stirling, via Muthill, and also to Auchterarder via Muthill. *Stagecoach* also runs a special 'Tourist Trail' bus around Perthshire and Stirling, stopping at Pitlochry, Aberfeldy, Dunkeld, Comrie, St Fillans and various other places.

Ins & outs

    Getting around Cycle hire *Crieff Ski Shop*, 66 Commissioner St, T654667, and *Finnie's Cycle Hire*, T652599.

    The **Tourist Information Centre** is in the town hall on the High Street. T652578. Apr-Jun, Sep and Oct Mon-Sat 0930-1730, Sun 1100-1600; Jul and Aug Mon-Sat 0930-1830, Sun 1100-1700; Nov-Mar Mon-Fri 0930-1730, Sat 1000-1400. In the basement of the town hall is a free exhibition on the town's history, where you can see the 1000-year-old Burgh Cross. Open same hours as the tourist office.

A mile from town, just off the A85 to Comrie, is **Glenturret Distillery**, Scotland's oldest distillery, established in 1775. It has a good restaurant which serves food all day (lunch cheap/mid-range; dinner expensive). In 2002 a new visitor centre will open dedicated to the Famous Grouse brand of whisky. There'll be tours and tastings, as well as a shop. ■ *Feb-Dec Mon-Sat 0930-1800 (last tour 1630), Sun from 1200 to 1630. Guided tours around £5; tasting tour around £10. T656565.*

Sights

    Five miles southeast of Crieff, off the B8062, is **Innerpeffray Library**, Scotland's first ever public library (founded in 1680), with a huge collection of rare and ancient books (but don't make too much noise about it). ■ *Apr-Sep daily (except Thu) 1000-1245 and 1400-1645, Sun 1400-1600, Feb, Mar, Oct, Nov closes at 1600; Dec, Jan by appt only. £2.50 with guided tour. T625819.* The chapel next door dates from 1508 and is also interesting.

    Two miles south of Crieff, on the A822 to **Muthill**, is the turning to the very wonderful **Drummond Castle Gardens**, one of the finest formal gardens in Europe. Even the most horticulturally ignorant of people could not fail to be amazed by the graceful harmony and symmetry, in particular the magnificently laid-out flower beds celebrating family and Scottish heraldry. If you have the feeling you've seen them before, that's because they were featured in the film *Rob Roy*. ■ *Easter weekend and May-Oct daily 1400-1800 (last entry 1700). £3.50, £2.50 concession. T681257. To get there, take bus No 47 towards*

Central Scotland

Muthill and get off at the gates, then walk 1 mile up the castle drive. In the village of Muthill itself is an ancient **church bell tower**, which dates from around 1250, and a small Village Museum, open during the summer.

Sleeping & eating

There's a good selection of accommodation in Crieff. Most of the hotels are to be found on Perth Rd and Comrie Rd, but the best place to stay is the enormous **L** *Crieff Hydro*, T655555, www.crieffhydro.com which first opened in 1868 as the *Strathearn Hydropathic*. Turn off the High Street at the *Drummond Arms Hotel* then continue uphill and follow the signs. It offers a huge range of leisure activities and a fine restaurant.

Best of the cheaper accommodation is **E** *Merlindale*, Perth Rd, T655205. Also good is **E** *Comely Bank Guest House*, 32 Burrell St, T653409, bookings@comelybank.demon.co.uk

Other than the hotels in town and the Glenturret Distillery (see above), there isn't a huge choice of decent places to eat. Pick of the lot is *The Bank*, 32 High St, T656575, which offers modern Scottish food. Also worth trying are *Blue Med*, 24 West High St, T656161, which serves Mediterranean dishes and also does morning coffees; and *The Gallery*, 15 Hill St, T653249.

Shopping

The Strathearn Gallery & Pottery, 32 West High St, T656100, www.strathearn-gallery.com, open Mon-Sat 1000-1700, Sun 1300-1700.

Comrie
Colour map 4, grid C2

Seven miles west of Crieff is the pleasant village of Comrie, which has the distinction of being the most earthquake-prone place in Britain due to its position on the Highland Boundary Fault. The world's first seismometer was set up here, in 1874, at the **Earthquake House**, which is at The Ross, about one mile west of the village, just off the A85. ■ *Apr-Oct daily.*

A great place for kids is the **Auchingarrich Wildlife Centre**, a few miles south of Comrie on the B827 on a windy hillside. It has a large collection of wild and exotic animals which you can feed and pet. ■ *All year daily 1000 till dusk. £4, £3 child. T679469.*

A recommended **walk** from Comrie is to the **Devil's Cauldron**, a spectacular waterfall in **Glen Lednock** which extends six miles into the hills northwest of Comrie. It's a pleasant mile-long woodland walk to the waterfall, and from there you can climb up to **Melville Monument**, at the top of Dunmore Hill (840 ft), from where there are excellent views across Strathearn and the Ochil Hills. Five miles further west is the village of **St Fillans**, at the east end of **Loch Earn**. The A85 runs along the northern shore of the loch to **Lochearnhead**, where it continues northwest towards **Crianlarich** (see page 357).

Sleeping   There are a few places to stay in Comrie, including the very comfortable **B** *Royal Hotel* on Melville Sq, T679200, www.royalhotel.co.uk, which has a good restaurant and great pub round the back serving real ales. At the other end of the price scale is **F** *Braincroft Bunkhouse*, T670140, an independent hostel 2 miles east of Comrie on the road to Crieff.

Auchterarder & Dunning
Phone code: 01764
Colour map 4, grid C3

South of Strathearn is the trim little town of Auchterarder, overlooked by the **Ochil Hills** to the south and surrounded by rich farmland. There's a Tourist Information Centre on the High Street. T663450. Apr-Jun, Sep and Oct Mon-Sat 0930-1730; Jul and Aug Mon-Sat 0900-1800, Sun 1100-1600; Nov-Mar Mon-Fri 1000-1400 (do check opening hours). The adjacent **heritage centre** tells of centuries of local history – from agriculture to education – including information on the local textile industry which has been going here since the 16th century. Most people come here to play **golf** at the world-renowned *Gleneagles Hotel* (see below).

Five miles east of Auchterarder, and eight miles southwest of Perth, is the historically interesting little village of Dunning, once the capital of the Picts and the place where Kenneth I, king of the Picts and Scots, died in 860. The village was burned to the ground by the Jacobites in 1716 and the only surviving building is the 12th-century Norman tower of **St Serf's church**. A mile west of the village, by the B8062, is **Maggie Walls Monument**, which commemorates the burning of a local witch in 1657.

Sleeping and eating L *Gleneagles Hotel*, T662231, www.gleneagles.com, a luxury 5-star hotel and leisure resort with 3 top-class golf courses. If you can afford it, there is no better way to pamper yourself. The restaurant, *Andrew Fairlie at Gleneagles* (T694267), is equally impressive and expensive. Slightly cheaper is the 19th-century baronial splendour of *Auchterader House*, T663646.

Transport There are daily **buses** with *Docherty's Midland Coaches*, T662218, to and from **Dunning, Crieff, Stirling** and **Perth**.

Stirling

As you'd expect with such a strategically important town, Stirling has a long and fascinating history and is packed with major historical sights. The town is best known for its castle, perched high on a rocky crag above the town and every bit as impressive as Edinburgh's. Also the Wallace Monument, a huge monolith high on Abbey Craig to the northeast of town which commemorates William Wallace, portrayed by Mel Gibson in the movie Braveheart.

Being so close to both Edinburgh and Glasgow, the sights of Stirling can be visited in a day from either city, but it's also a very pleasant place to stay. It may lack the cosmopolitan feel of Edinburgh but has a lively buzz of its own during the busy summer months and there is a wide range of accommodation and other tourist facilities.

Phone code: 01786
Colour map 2, grid C2
Population: 37,000

Ins and outs

Stirling is easily reached from Edinburgh, Glasgow, Perth and most other main towns and cities by regular **bus** and **train** services. The **train station** is on Station Rd, near the town centre, and the **bus station** is close by, on Goosecroft Rd, behind the Thistle Shopping Centre.

Getting there

Most of the important sights, except Bannockburn and the Wallace Monument, are within easy walking distance of each other. There's an open-topped 'hop on, hop off' Heritage Bus Tour which runs from Jun to Sep and includes the castle and Wallace Monument. There are tours every 30 mins from 1000 till 1700. A day ticket costs £6.50. Check details at the TIC.

Getting around

The TIC is at 41 Dumbarton Rd in the centre of town. It is the main office for Loch Lomond, Stirling and the Trossachs and stocks a wide range of books, guides, maps and leaflets. It also has information on the various **guided walks** of the town, including the popular **ghost walks** which take place Tue-Sat at 1930 and 2130. Alternatively, there are personal stereo guides available from *Stags Audio Walks*, at 24 Broad St. T475019. All year Jun and Sep Mon-Sat 0900-1800, Sun 1000-1600; Jul and Aug Mon-Sat 0900-1930, Sun 0930-1830; Oct-May Mon-Sat 1000-1700.

Tourist information

Central Scotland

Stirling

To Callander & The Trossachs

Sleeping
1 Ashgrove House *G3*
2 Castlecroft *B1*
3 Forth Guest House *C5*
4 Garfield House *E2*
5 Golden Lion Milton *E4*
6 No 10 *G3*
7 Park Lodge *G2*
8 Portcullis *C2*
9 Stirling Highland & Scholars Restaurant *E4*
10 SYHA Youth Hostel *D3*
11 Terraces *G4*
12 XI Victoria Square *F2*

Eating
1 Barnton Bar & Bistro *D4*
2 Berties *E3*
3 Darnley Coffee House *D3*
4 East India Company *D4*

Central Scotland

Central Scotland

**Map labels:**

To University, Bridge Of Allan, Wallace Monument & Ravenswood Guest House

Stirling Old Bridge

Causewayhead Rd

Lovers Walk

River Forth

Dean Cres

James St

Forrest Rd

Alexandra Pl

Edward Av

Millar Pl

Edward Rd

Argyll Av

Forth Street

Rosebery Pl

Ronald Pl

Forth Cres

Shore Rd

Riverbank View

3

Forth Pl

Seaforth Pl

River Forth

Train Station

Murray Pl

Rd

Thistle Centre

Bus Station

Upper Craigs

Wellgreen Rd

Wellgreen

Nelson Pl

Colquhoun St

5

6

To Bannockburn & Edinburgh

History

It was once said that whoever controlled Stirling held the key to Scotland. Consequently the town and its surrounds have witnessed many crucial struggles between the Scots and the English. In fact, its name is a derivation of 'The Striveling', meaning place of strife. It was here that the Scots under William Wallace defeated the English at the **Battle of Stirling Bridge** in 1297. A more famous battle was fought just a few miles away, at **Bannockburn** in 1314, when Robert the Bruce's small army routed Edward II's much larger English force. For the next three centuries, until the Union of Crowns in 1603 and James VI's move to England, Stirling Castle was the favourite residence of the Stuart monarchy and the setting for the coronation, in 1543, of the young Mary, the future Queen of Scots.

Sights

The obvious place to begin a tour is the immensely impressive castle which stands 250 ft above the flat plain atop the plug of an extinct volcano. From the west there's a sheer drop down the side of the rocky crag, making the castle seem a daunting prospect to would-be attackers, and now presenting visitors with fantastic views of the surrounding area. There's been a fortress here since the Iron Age, though the current building dates mostly from the 15th and 16th centuries, when it was the favourite residence of the Stuart kings.

On the esplanade is a **visitor centre** which shows an introductory film giving a potted history of the castle. From here you proceed to the **Upper Square**, where you can see the magnificent **Great Hall**, built by James IV and which was recently restored to its original condition. He also built the royal residence known as the **King's Old Building**, which now houses the

Stirling Castle

Central Scotland

museum of the Argyll and Sutherland Highlanders, which traces the history of this famous regiment from its inception in 1794 to the present day. James V, whose wives were both French, brought masons from France to create the spectacular **Palace** (1540-42), the finest Renaissance building in Scotland. This was where the young Mary, Queen of Scots spent much of her life until her departure for France, in 1548.

The interior of the royal apartments is largely bare but you can still see the **Stirling Heads**, 56 elegantly carved oak plaques which once decorated the ceiling of one of the rooms. Also impressive is the interior of the **Chapel Royal**, built by James VI in 1594 for the baptism of his son. The 16th- century **kitchens** are also interesting and have been restored to recreate the preparations for a royal banquet. ■ *Apr-Oct daily 0930-1800 (last entry 1715); Nov-Mar till 1700 (last entry 1615). £6.50, £5 concession (includes admission to Argyll's Ludging). T450000 (HS).*

The Old Town
The Old Town grew from around the 12th century, when Stirling became a royal burgh, and spread from the castle down the hill towards the flood-plain of the River Forth. Most of the historic sights are clustered around these medieval cobbled streets.

The Old Town was fortified with massive **town walls**, built in the mid-16th century as protection against Henry VIII's constant attacks in order to force Mary, Queen of Scots to marry his son and unite the two kingdoms – the so-called 'Rough Wooing'. These walls are the best surviving in Scotland and can be followed along a path known as the **Back Walk**, which starts near the tourist office in Dumbarton Road and runs around the base of the Castle Rock and back up to the Old Town. On the way the path passes Gowan Hill, site of the **Beheading Stone**, used in numerous executions, most notably that of Murdoch, Duke of Albany, in 1425.

Five minutes' walk downhill from the castle is **Argyll's Ludging** (lodging), the finest and most complete surviving example of a 17th-century town house in Scotland. It was built by William Alexander, founder of Nova Scotia, and then, on his death, was bought by the ninth Earl of Argyll. In the 18th century the house became a military hospital, and in the 1960s was used as a youth hostel. It has recently been restored to its former glory and rooms are furnished as they would have been in the late 17th century. ■ *Same opening hours as the Castle. £2.80, or joint ticket with the Castle. T450000.*

Further down Castle Wynd, at the top of Broad Street, is **Mar's Wark**, the ornate façade of a dilapidated town house, started by the first Earl of Mar, Regent of Scotland, in 1569 but left to fall into ruin following his death two years later. It was further damaged during the 1745 Jacobite Rebellion. A little further down Castle Wynd is the medieval **Church of the Holy Rude**, where the infant James VI was crowned in 1567. The oldest parts, the nave and tower, date from 1456 and the church also features one of the few surviving 15th-century timber roofs. Behind the church is **Cowane's Hospital**, built in 1637 by the wealthy merchant John Cowane as an almshouse for 'Decayed members of the Guild of Merchants'. It now houses a tartan display and computer database for those wishing to trace their roots. ■ *Apr-Sep Mon-Sat 0900-1700, Sun 1300-1700. Free. T472247.*

A short way down St John Street is the impressively refurbished **Old Town Jail**, where the rigours of life behind bars in times gone by is brilliantly brought to life by enthusiastic actors. A glass lift then takes you up to the roof for spectacular views across the town and Forth Valley. ■ *Apr-Sep daily 0930-1800; Oct daily till 1700; Nov-Feb daily till 1600; Mar till 1700. £3.95, £2.75 concession. T450050.*

Opposite the jail is Broad Street, centre of the medieval town and site of the **Mercat Cross**, which is topped by a Unicorn known locally as the 'Puggy'.

Nearby is the **Tolbooth**, built in 1705 as the town's administrative headquarters by Sir William Bruce (who designed the Palace of Holyroodhouse in Edinburgh) and used as a courthouse and jail in the 19th century. Early in 2002 it will open as a performance venue with a 200-seater theatre and a studio/rehearsal space. Comedy clubs and events will take place throughout the year and there will be a bar/restaurant. At the bottom of Broad Street is **Darnley's House**, where Mary, Queen of Scots' second husband, Lord Darnley, is said to have stayed. It now houses a coffee shop (see Eating below). In the Thistle Shopping Centre you can visit The Bastion Jail (opposite Marks and Spencer), which is all that remains of a defensive tower that formed part of the old town wall. You can look down into the Thieves Pit where prisoners were kept. ■ *Mon-Sat 0900-1800, Sun 1200-1500. Free.*

At the bottom of Spittal Street, where it joins King Street, turn into Corn Exchange Road and then head west up Dumbarton Road to reach the **Smith Art Gallery and Museum**, which houses some interesting displays about the town's history and culture, as well as a fine collection of paintings. ■ *All year Tue-Sat 1030-1700, Sun 1400-1700. Free. T471917.*

The Lower Town

At the north end of the town, a 20-minute walk from the town centre, is the 15th-century **Old Bridge**, which was the lowest crossing point on the River Forth, and one of the most important bridges in Scotland until Kincardine Bridge was built in 1936. The bridge was built to replace earlier structures, including the famous wooden bridge, scene of the battle in 1297 in which William Wallace defeated the English.

Two miles northeast of the town, near the University and Bridge of Allan, is the Wallace Monument, an impressive Victorian Gothic tribute to Sir William Wallace, hero of the successful but hugely inaccurate film, *Braveheart*. Wallace was knighted by Robert the Bruce for his famous victory at Stirling Bridge, but following defeat later at Falkirk he went off to Europe in search of support for the Scottish cause. During his absence he was betrayed by the Scots nobles and on his return found guilty of treason and cruelly hanged, drawn and quartered in London.

Wallace Monument
A new statue to Wallace located in the car park was decapitated by locals because it bore too strong a resemblance to Mel Gibson

Inside the monument are various exhibits including a Hall of Scottish Heroes and Wallace's mighty two-handed sword (5 ft 4 in long – about the same height as the actor who played him in the film). There are fantastic views from the top of the 220-ft tower – if you can manage the climb up its 246-step staircase. There's a shuttle bus which runs from the foot of the hill up to the tower every 15 minutes. An open-topped **tour bus** runs to the monument from Stirling Castle every half hour (see Ins and outs above). ■ *Jan, Feb, Nov and Dec daily 1030-1600; Mar-May and Oct 1000-1700; Jun 1000-1800; Jul, Aug and Sep 0930-1830. £3.95, £2.75 children. T472140.*

A mile east of Stirling are the ruins of Cambuskenneth Abbey, founded in 1147 by David I for Augustinian canons, and once one of the richest abbeys in the country. Robert the Bruce held his parliament here in 1326, and King James III (1451-88) and his wife, Queen Margaret of Denmark, are buried in the grounds. The only substantial surviving feature is the 14th-century belfry. The abbey can be reached from Stirling on foot, via a footbridge over the River Forth, and from the Wallace Monument which is just a mile to the north. ■ *Open all year. Free.*

Cambuskenneth Abbey

Central Scotland

Bannockburn A few miles south of Stirling is the site of Scotland's greatest victory over the English (no, not Wembley 1967), when Robert the Bruce defeated Edward II's army, on 24 June 1314. It was the **Battle of Bannockburn** which united the Scots and led to the declaration of independence at Arbroath in 1320 (the 'Declaration of Arbroath'). There's not an awful lot to see, but the **Bannockburn Heritage Centre** puts flesh on the bones and brings to life the full scale of the battle. Outside is an equestrian statue of Bruce, on the spot where he is said to have commended his forces, and the site of the bore stone, where Bruce planted his standard after victory. What's left of the original bore stone is on display in the visitor centre, safe from souvenir hunters. ■ *Site open all year, Heritage Centre open Apr-Oct daily 1000-1730; Oct-Mar 1030-1600; closed Jan, Feb. £2.50, £1.70 child/concession. To get there, take buses Nos 51 and 52 from Stirling (every 30 mins). T812664 (NTS).*

Essentials

Sleeping
■ *on map*
Price codes:
see inside front cover

B *Stirling Highland Hotel*, Spittal St, T272727, F272829. 78 rooms. Converted former school refurbished to high standards with full facilities, including a pool and saunas. Their *Scholars Restaurant* is highly recommended (see Eating below). **B** *Golden Lion Milton Hotel*, 8 King St, T475351, F472755. 71 rooms. Large Victorian hotel which is convenient for sights, shops and restaurants. **C** *Park Lodge Hotel*, 32 Park Terr, T474862, F449748. 10 rooms. Luxurious Georgian/Victorian town house beautifully situated close to town centre, overlooking the park and castle, with a very fine restaurant. **C-D** *The Portcullis*, Castle Wynd, T472290, F446103. 6 rooms. 200-year-old hotel next to castle, some rooms have great views over the town. **C-D** *Terraces Hotel*, 4 Melville Terr, T472268, is a Georgian house set off the main road.

There are lots of **B&Bs** and **guesthouses** in the King's Park area, to the south of the tourist office. Try the extremely comfortable **D** *X1 Victoria Square*, T475545, which has great views of the castle; or, also on Victoria Sq, **E** *Garfield House*, T473730. **E** *Firgrove*, 13 Clifford Rd, T475805, is a large, comfortable, Victorian house. Also worth trying are **E** *Number Ten*, Gladstone Pl, T472681; and **E** *Castlecroft*, Ballengeich Rd, T474933. A short distance south of the tourist office is **D-E** *Ashgrove House*, 2 Park Av, T/F472640. A short walk north of the train station is the recommended **E** *Forth Guest House*, 23 Forth Pl, T471020. A few miles out of town is **D-E** *West Plean House*, Denny Rd, T812208, a large house which is set in its own grounds. There are also lots of B&Bs and guesthouses on Causewayhead Rd, which leads to the University. These include **E** *Ravenswood Guest House*, at No 94, T475291.

There's **campus accommodation** at Stirling University, a couple of miles north of the town centre near **Bridge of Allan** (**E**, T467141, open Jan, Feb and Jun-Sep). Also on campus is the **C-D** *Stirling Management Centre*, T451712, open all year, which offers more luxurious B&B accommodation and full board (**A-B**). There are regular buses (Nos 53 and 58) to the campus which leave from Murray Pl.

A cheaper option is the **F** *SYHA youth hostel*, in a converted church on St John St at the top of the town, T473442, open all year. There's an excellent **campsite** at *Witches Craig Caravan Park*, at Blairlogie, 3 miles east of Stirling on the A91, T474947, open Apr-Oct.

Eating
Mid-range *Scholars Restaurant* at the *Stirling Highland Hotel* (see above) has an excellent reputation for modern Scottish cuisine. *Hermann's*, 32 St John St, T450632, at the Tolbooth on the road up to the castle, is an upmarket choice. It offers excellent Scottish/Austrian cuisine at moderate prices (and a cheap set lunch). Also on the road up to the castle is *Stirling Merchant Bar Bistro*, 39 Broad St, T473929, which serves modern Scottish dishes, while *Leonardo's at the Riverhouse*, Castle Business Park, T465577, offers good quality Scottish/Mediterranean dishes.

Cheap The best curry in town can be had at the *East India Company*, 7 Viewfield Pl, T471330, with a cheaper pakora snack bar upstairs. A good Italian restaurant is the busy *Italia Nostra*, 25 Baker St, T473208, which serves cheap-moderate food daily till 2300; or try *La Ciociara*, 41 Friars St, T451552, which also serves coffees and pastries during the day. On the same street, at No 5, is *Olivia's Restaurant*, T446277, which offers good Scottish food in an informal atmosphere (cheap to mid-range prices, open Mon-Sat 1200-1430 and 1830-2200). *Berties* is a café-bistro in the Albert Hall on Dumbarton Rd, T446930, and a cheap and relaxing place for lunch (open daily 1000-1700). A firm favourite with students is the *Barnton Bar & Bistro*, opposite the post office on Barnton St, T461698. It's cheap, open daily till 2400 (0100 at weekends) and serves great all-day breakfasts. A good place for coffee and a snack is the elegant *Darnley Coffee House*, 18 Bow St, T474468.

Bars & pubs Two of the best **pubs** in Stirling are the *Portcullis*, T472268, on Castle Wynd, below the castle; and the *Settle Inn*, further down on St Mary's Wynd, which is the oldest hostelry in town (1773) and very popular with Stirling's large student population. *Pivo*, on Corn Exchange, T451904, is a trendy Czech bar which also serves light meals. The lively *Barnton Bar & Bistro* (see above) is also a good place for a drink, as is Whistlebinkies, on St Mary's Wynd.

Entertainment **Ceilidhs** are held during Jul/Aug on Wed evenings in the Golden Lion Hotel. Check details at the tourist office. The *MacRobert Arts Centre*, T461081, on the campus of **Stirling University** shows a good selection of mainstream and arthouse **films** and **drama** productions. Buses run from the town centre (see 'Sleeping').

Transport Scottish *Citylink* **buses** run at least every hour to and from **Dundee** (1½ hrs) and at least every 30 mins to **Perth** (50 mins) and **Glasgow** (1 hr). There are also regular buses to Inverness (3½ hrs) and **Aberdeen** (3½ hrs), but you'll probably need to change at Perth and Dundee respectively. Buses also run to Edinburgh, but as the journey takes 1½ hrs you might prefer to take the train. Local buses are run by *First Edinburgh*, T01324-613777. There are frequent services to **Dunblane**, **Doune** via **Blair Drummond** (30 mins), **Callander** (45 mins), Dollar (35 mins), Falkirk (30 mins) and Linlithgow (1 hr), and several daily to Aberfoyle (45 mins).

There are ScotRail **trains,** T08457-484950, every 30 mins (Mon-Sat; hourly on Sun) to **Edinburgh** (45 mins) and **Glasgow** (45 mins; £3.70), and regular services to **Perth** (35 mins), **Dundee** (1 hr) and **Aberdeen** (2¼ hrs).

Car hire *Arnold Clark*, Kerse Rd, T478686. From £16 per day. **Cycle hire and tours** *Wildcat Bike Tours*, Stirling Enterprise Park, Unit 102, John Player Building, T/F464333; or Stewart Wilson Cycles, Barnton St, T465292 (£12 per day). **Taxis** *Woodside Taxis*, T450005.

Around Stirling

Dunblane
Phone code: 01786
Colour map 4, grid C2

Four miles north of Stirling is the attractive little town of Dunblane, which was suddenly and horrifyingly catapulted into the media spotlight in 1996 when Thomas Hamilton walked into the local primary school and gunned down 15 children and their teacher. The town has been an ecclesiastical centre since it was founded in the seventh century by St Blane who lived at the nearby dun (fort), hence the name.

There's a seasonal **Tourist Information Centre** on Stirling Road, T824428, open May-September. The main attraction is the beautiful **cathedral**, dating mainly from the 13th century, though the lower part of the tower is Norman. The cathedral was restored to its former glory in the late 19th century. ■ *Apr-Sep Mon-Sat 0930-1830, Sun 0930-1800; Oct-Mar Mon-Sat 0930-1630, Sun 1400-1630 (HS). Free.* Close by on the square, housed in the 17th-century Dean's house, is the tiny cathedral **museum**, with a display on local history. ■ *May-Oct Mon-Sat 1000-1230 and 1400-1630. Free.* Nearby is **Leighton Library**, the oldest private library in Scotland, now open to the public. ■ *May-Oct Mon-Fri 1000-1230 and 1400-1630.*

Outside Dunblane at Bridge of Allan is **Bridge of Allan Brewery** on Queens Lane, a micro brewery that offers free tours and tastings. T834555, www.bridgeofallan.co.uk, open daily 1000-1700.

Sleeping There are a couple of very exclusive hotels in and around Dunblane. Overlooking the town is the luxurious Victorian **A** *Hilton Dunblane Hydro*, T825403, set in 44 acres of woodland. 4 miles north of town, near Kinbuck on the B8033, is **L** *Cromlix House*, T822125, one of Scotland's best country-house hotels, with its own loch and chapel. Excellent service and cuisine (expensive). It's worth coming here for dinner or Sun lunch. Rather less expensive is *Boozy Rouge at the Sheriffmuir Inn*, T823285, on the wild moors of **Sheriffmuir** south of Dunblane, where the Jacobite Earl of Mar took on the government forces in 1715. The inn dates from the same period and serves fine food and ales, and is a wonderful place in the summer.

Transport There are regular **buses** to Dunblane from Stirling (see Stirling Transport), and also frequent **trains** to and from Stirling, Edinburgh and Glasgow.

Doune
Phone code: 01786
Colour map 4, grid C2

Seven miles northwest of Stirling is the quiet village of Doune, which is worth visiting for its well-preserved late-14th-century courtyard **castle**, overlooking the River Teith. Built for the Regent Albany, it passed into the hands of the Earls of Moray (who still live there) following the execution of the Albany family by James I. Its most striking feature is the combination of tower, gatehouse and domestic quarters, which includes the Lord's Hall with its carved oak screen and musicians' gallery. ■ *Apr-Sep daily 0930-1830; Oct-Mar Mon, Wed and Sat 0930-1630, Thu 0930-1230, Fri and Sun 1400-1630, £2.50, £1.90 concession. T841742.*

A few miles south of Doune, off the A84 to Stirling, is the **Blair Drummond Safari Park**, Scotland's only wildlife park, with lions, tigers, elephants, monkeys, rhinos, giraffes, zebras and various other exotic animals. There's a safari bus for those without their own transport. There are also sea lion shows and numerous other kids' activities. ■ *Mar to early Oct daily 1000-1730, last admission 1630. £8.50, £4.50 children. T841203.*

Transport There are regular **buses** to Doune from Stirling, via Blair Drummond (see Stirling Transport above).

Falkirk and Linlithgow

Colour map 5, grid A6

Stretching southeast from Stirling along the Firth of Forth is an area noted more for its industry than its scenic beauty, though there are one or two interesting historical sights, most notably **Linlithgow Palace**.

Falkirk
Phone code: 01324

Falkirk is the main town between Stirling and Edinburgh, and a busy shopping centre. There's accommodation in Falkirk, details of which can be obtained from the **Tourist Information Centre**, 2-4 Glebe Street, T620244. It's open April to May daily 0930-1700, June to October daily 0930-1800, and August daily 0930-1900 (hours subject to change).

Falkirk is at the confluence of the Forth and Clyde Canal and the Union Canal, and southwest of the town centre is Scotland's newest engineering achievement, The Falkirk Wheel. Due to open in spring 2002 this huge steel structure will be the world's first rotating boat lift – it basically transfers boats from one canal to another. Falkirk's main attraction is **Callendar House**, a huge turreted mansion extensively altered over the years but thought to date originally from the 14th century. It has several interpretative rooms bringing to love trades of the early 19th century, and is well worth a visit if only for its excellent working Georgian kitchens. ■ *Mon-Sat 1000-1700 all year, Apr-Sep also Sun 1400-1700. £3.00, £1.50 concession. T503770.*

North of Falkirk, near Airth, on the B9124, is **The Pineapple**, one of the most bizarre buildings in Scotland. This 45 ft-high pineapple was built in 1761 as a garden folly for the fourth Earl of Dunmore. It is now owned by the NTS. ■ *All year daily from 0930 till sunset.*

Sleeping There are regular **trains** from **Stirling**, **Perth**, **Glasgow Queen Street** and **Edinburgh** to Falkirk Grahamston station, which is a 5-min walk from the TIC.

Linlithgow
Phone code: 01506

Halfway between Falkirk and Edinburgh is the pleasant little West Lothian town of Linlithgow, home of the magnificent Renaissance **Linlithgow Palace**, one of the most romantic and impressive historic buildings in Scotland. It's off the beaten track and relatively little-visited but well worth the detour, for this is a real gem. The 15th-century ruin is set on the edge of Linlithgow Loch and is associated with many of Scotland's main historical players, including James V (1512) and Mary, Queen of Scots (1542), who were both born here. James V was also married here, to Mary of Guise, and Bonnie Prince Charlie popped in for a visit during the 1745 rebellion. One year later the palace was badly damaged by fire during its occupation by General Hawley's troops, prior to their defeat by Jacobite forces under Prince Charles at the Battle of Falkirk. The ruin still conveys a real sense of the sheer scale of the lavish lifestyle of the court, from the ornate fountain in the inner courtyard to the magnificent Great Hall with its massive kitchens. ■ *Apr-Sep daily 0930-1830; Oct-Mar Mon-Sat 0930-1630, Sun 1400-1630. £2.80, £2.00 concession. T842896.*

Next to the palace is **St Michael's Church**, the largest pre-Reformation church in the country, with its controversial crown and spire, added in 1964. ■ *Oct-Apr Mon-Fri 1030-1500, May-Sep 1000-1630.* On the High Street is the **Linlithgow Story**, which relates the history of the royal burgh. ■ *Easter-Oct daily 1000-1700. £1.*

West of town, at **Cairnapple Hill**, are ancient stone circles dating from around 2500BC to 500BC. Details of how to get there from the **Tourist Information Centre**, in the Burgh Halls at The Cross. They will also provide details of accommodation, though Linlithgow is easily reached from Edinburgh and Stirling. The best place in town for a bar lunch (and a good pint of ale) is *The Four Mary's*, on the High Street. ■ *T844600. The tourist office is open Easter-Sep daily 1000-1700.*

North of Linlithgow, at Bo'ness, is the **Bo'ness and Kinneil Railway**, a privately run steam railway. Steam trips are arranged throughout the year, and there are also restored locomotives and carriages to see at Bo'ness station. (T0150-6 822298, www.srps.org.uk).

Eating 2 miles northeast of town, at the junction of the A904 and A803 is the seriously good and seriously expensive *Champany Inn*, T834532, which specialises in beef.

Rather more modest is the busy and welcoming *Four Marys*, 65 High St, T842171, which serves cheap bar meals and real ales; 1200-1430, 1730-2030, 1230-2030 Sun.

Transport Regular **buses** from Stirling and Edinburgh stop at The Cross. The **train station** is at the southern end of town. There are hourly **trains** to and from **Edinburgh** (20 mins), **Glasgow Queen Street** (30 mins) and **Stirling** (35 mins).

The Ochils

Colour map 4, grid C3 The Ochil Hills rise sharply from the flat flood-plain of the River Forth and stretch northeast, through **Clackmannanshire**, into Perth and Kinross. This unfashionable and little-known range of hills is characterized by the shapely, rounded tops divided by steep-sided glens. There are good walking opportunities and some surprisingly dramatic scenery. At their feet, the pretty little towns and villages known collectively as 'the Hillfoots' were once Scotland's second-largest wool-producing region, after the Borders. Today visitors can explore the region's tweedy heritage on the **Mill Trail**, starting in **Alva** and linking the main mill centres along the A91, which runs east all the way to St Andrews in Fife.

A few miles northeast of Stirling, in the village of **Blairlogie**, is the crumbling 16th-century **Logie Old Kirk** and its ancient graveyard full of fascinating old stones, beautifully located by Logie Burn.

A few miles further east is the little town of **Alva**, home to the **Mill Trail Visitor Centre**, in Glentana Mill on Stirling Street. Here you'll see what life was like for mill workers in the mid-19th century (pretty grim apparently), and learn about the history of textile production from the Industrial Revolution onwards. ■ *Jan-Jul and Sep-Dec 1000-1700; Aug 0900-1700. Free. T01259-769696.*

Alloa
Phone code: 01259
Colour map 4, grid C3

A few miles south of Alva is the unappealing brewery town of Alloa, notable only for the beautifully restored **Alloa Tower**, which stands in a park a short walk from the town centre. The 15th-century tower house, one of the largest surviving medieval tower houses in Scotland, is the ancestral home of the Erskine family, Earls of Mar and Kellie, who were custodians of the young Mary, Queen of Scots. Of particular note is the Italianate staircase, the original oak rood beams and the pit dungeon. There are also excellent views from the parapet walk. ■ *Apr-Sep daily 1330-1730; Oct weekends only 1330-1730. £3, £2 concession. T211701 (NTS).*

Sleeping Try **L** *Dunmar House Hotel*, T214339, www.dunmarhouse.co.uk on Tullibody Rd, a luxurious Edwardian mansion house hotel in 4 acres of grounds.

Dollar
Phone code: 01259
Colour map 4, grid C3

Top of the bill in these parts is the well-heeled little town of Dollar, 11 miles east of Stirling and well worthy of a day trip. Looming above the town at the head of magical **Dollar Glen**, is the spectacularly sited **Castle Campbell**, standing between two deep ravines and formerly known as Castle Gloom, until it passed into the hands of the Campbells in the 15th century. The castle was sacked by Cromwell's troops in 1654, but the tower is well preserved and there are fantastic views down Dollar Glen from the parapet. There's an excellent marked walk from the town up to the castle through the narrow, steep-sided glen, said to be the home of fairies and other woodland spirits. ■ *Apr-Sep daily 0930-1830; Oct-Mar Mon-Wed and Sat 0930-1630, Thu 0930-1230, Sun 1400-1630. £2.80, £2 concession. T742408 (HS).*

Alva Glen walk

*A fine walk from Alva heads up Alva Glen to the summit of **Ben Cleuch** and then down Mill Glen to **Tillicoultry**. It's a total distance of eight miles and should take around four to five hours. It's mostly on good paths and tracks, but walking boots are recommended, as well as waterproofs, warm clothing, food and drink.*

Starting from the car park head up the glen, cross the bridge, climb a series of steps and then go under a large pipe and past the water works to reach a gate giving access to the open hill. Follow a clear path across the hill until it reaches a track. Follow this track up to the head of the glen and, just before it turns left, leave it and take a path on the right which climbs towards the summit of Ben Buck. First, you'll reach a false summit, from where there are great views north to the mountains of Breadalbane, near Callander and Loch Earn.

*Follow the fence line to the right and, after a fence junction, take a clear path up to the rocks at the summit of Ben Cleuch. Having taken in the views, leave the summit along the same fence line. Near a fence junction, keep to the right and take the path which climbs up to **The Law** (2,093 ft), from where there is a wonderful view across the Forth. Follow the path which descends steeply and is eroded, taking care especially near the foot of the hill. Cross the burn by the footbridge and, at the path junction beyond, take the right-hand lower path, which winds down*

*the steep-sided **Mill Glen**, re-crossing the burn several times.*

Once you reach the road, go down Upper Mill Street as far as the main road. You can head left into Tillicoultry to catch a bus back to Alva, or enjoy a pint at The Woolpack. To continue the walk, head right and take the next right along a rough road heading up to the quarry. Continue straight ahead on a clear track leading up beside the golf course and through woodland until you reach The Farriers hotel, restaurant and craft shop complex. At the entrance to the Woodland Park car park, go right and follow a broad path uphill through the trees. The path levels out then crosses the Silver Burn, where silver was mined in the 18th century. Go through a kissing gate and then head back to the start of the walk. OS Landranger No 58.

Sleeping and eating There's not a huge choice of accommodation, but the **D** *Castle Campbell Hotel*, T/F742519, is comfortable and does good meals. If you're after a sandwich or something for a picnic, then look no further than *Nesbits*, a popular local deli on the main street.

Transport There are regular **buses** to Dollar from **Stirling**. There are also buses to and from **Alloa**.

The A91 passes through the gloriously named hamlet of **Yetts o' Muckhart**,   **East of Dollar** at the junction with the scenic A823 which runs north through Glen Devon to meet the A9 Stirling-Perth road, near the famous **Gleneagles Hotel** (see page 338). A few miles north of Yetts o' Muckhart, at the village of **Glendevon** is a basic **F** *SYHA Youth Hostel*, T781206, open mid-March to early October, which provides information on walks in the Ochil Hills. South of Yetts o'

Central Scotland

Muckhart is **Rumbling Bridge**, at the junction of the A823 and A977, from where there are breathtaking views down into a deep gorge.

Kinross &
Loch Leven
Phone code: 01577
Colour map 4, grid C3

The A91 meets the M90 Edinburgh-Perth motorway by the town of Kinross, which is mostly bypassed by tourists speeding north to the Highlands or south to the capital. Kinross comes under the remit of the **Perthshire Tourist Board** and you don't even have to venture too far from the motorway to visit the helpful local **Tourist Information Centre**, which is next to the service area at Junction 6, T863680 April-June, September-October Monday-Saturday 0930-1730, Sunday 1100-1600; July, August Monday-Saturday 0930-1800, Sunday 1100-1700.

On an island in the middle of Loch Leven, and visible from the M90, is the lonely tower of **Loch Leven Castle**, where Mary, Queen of Scots was imprisoned for almost a year at the behest of Queen Elizabeth. She made a dramatic escape in May, 1568, with the help of her young, impressionable jailer. There's not much left of the 14th-century ruin, but it's an evocative place full of romance and history. During the summer a **ferry** leaves from Kinross to the island. ■ *(HS) Apr-Oct Mon-Sat 0930-1730 (ends 1630 Oct). £3.*

Not far from Loch Leven – Junction 5 off the M90 – is the RSPB reserve at **Vane Farm**, T862355. There are several nature trails to follow and three hides from which to observe the rich bird life of the loch. In autumn and winter you can see thousands of geese, as well as birds such as tufted duck, teal and peregrine. In September you may also see ospreys hunting for fish on the loch. ■ *Daily 1000-1700. £3, £2 concession.*

Sleeping and eating If you're passing by around lunchtime there's a good restaurant only a few hundred yards away, *The Grouse and Claret*, at Heatheryford Country Centre, T864212. They serve game and seafood and also cater for vegetarians (mid-range, open daily except Mon). They also have three rooms for **B&B** (**D**). Another good place to eat, and cheaper, is in the café of *Dobies* garden centre T863308, next to the tourist office, or *The Butterchurn*, T01383-830169, just off Junction 4 on the M90. In Kinross itself is *Carlin Maggies*, 193 High Street, T863652, a restaurant serving contemporary Scottish food.

The Campsies

Colour map 4, grid C2

Running southwest from Stirling to Loch Lomond, and bordered by the broad farmlands of the **Carse of Stirling** to the north and the northern suburbs of **Glasgow** to the south, are the **Campsies**. This is an area of gently rolling hills and fertile farmland, comprising the **Fintry, Gargunnock, Strathblane** and **Kilsyth Hills** and the **Campsie Fells**. Other than weekend hikers from Glasgow, the Campsies attract few visitors and this unspoiled peace and beauty is their main attraction. There's a string of picturesque villages nestled in the hills, amongst them **Killearn**, **Kippen**, **Gargunnock** and **Balfron**, birthplace of Alexander 'Greek' Thomson, Glasgow's great Victorian architect (see page 218). There's plenty of good walking to be done here. For details of the **Campsie Fells Trail**, contact the **Stirling TIC**, T01786-475019.

Fintry
Phone code: 01360

Lying at the heart of the Campsies is the attractive little village of Fintry, at the head of the Strathendrick valley, and regular winner of the 'Scotland in Bloom' competition. Two miles east of the village is the 90-ft-high **Loup of Fintry** waterfall. There are a few places to stay in Fintry, including the wonderful

B *Culcreuch Castle Hotel*, T860228, www.culcreuch.com, a 14th-century castle set in the 1,600-acre Culcreuch Country Park. A cheaper option is the **E** *Fintry Inn*, T860224, which also offers pub food.

At the western end of the Campsie Fells is the village of Drymen, the busiest of the Campsie villages due to its proximity to the eastern shores of Loch Lomond. Drymen also lies on the **West Highland Way** (see page 59). There's a seasonal **tourist office** in the library on The Square. ■ *T660068. May-Sep.* There's a decent selection of **accommodation** in Drymen. Best hotel is the **B-C** *Buchanan Arms Hotel*, T660588. There are lots of **B&Bs**, including **E** *Easter Drumquhassle Farm*, T660893, http://members.aol.com/juliamacx, on Gartness Road. A highly recommended place to eat is the moderately priced *Clachan Inn*, T660824, on The Square, or you can try the Winnock Hotel nearby, T660245. You can rent **bikes** at *Lomond Activities*, 64 Main Street, T660066.

Drymen
Phone code: 01360

South of **Killearn** on the A81 is the **Glengoyne Distillery**, ■ *T550254. Mon-Sat 1000-1600, Sun 1200-1600; £3.75, £2.75 concession, £10 nosing session,* which is the starting point for two excellent walks in the Strathblane Hills, to the top of **Dumgoyne Hill** (1,400 ft) and **Earl's Seat** (1,896 ft), the highest point in the Campsies.

Further west, on the other side of Strathblane, is **Queen's View** on **Auchineden Hill**, from where there are wonderful views up Loch Lomond as far as Ben Ledi. Queen Victoria was particularly impressed with the view – hence its name. The path to the top starts from the busy car park on the A809 Bearsden to Drymen road. It takes about 45-50 minutes each way. From the car park a path also leads up to **The Whangie**, a deep cleft in the rock face with sheer walls rising over 30 ft on either side. A path runs for 100 yd through the narrow gap.

Walks

There are several **buses** daily to Drymen from **Glasgow**, via Queen's View. There are also buses through the region from **Stirling**. A **postbus** service, T01752-494527, www.royalmail.com/postbus, leaves from **Denny**, five miles south of Stirling, to Fintry (Mon-Sat at 0955), from where two buses (Mon-Sat) run to Balfron. There are regular buses to Denny from **Stirling** bus station.

Transport

Loch Lomond

Britain's largest inland waterway, measuring 22 miles long and at certain points up to five miles wide, is Scotland's most famous (uninhabited!) loch, thanks to the Jacobite ballad about its "bonnie banks". These same banks are now one of the busiest parts of the Highlands, due to their proximity to Glasgow (only 20 miles south along the congested A82). During the summer the loch becomes a playground for day-trippers who tear up and down the loch in speedboats and on jet skis, obliterating any notion visitors may have of a little peace and quiet. In spring 2002 this area will become Scotland's first National Park.

Colour map 4, grid C1

The **west bank** of the loch, from Balloch north to Tarbet, is one long, almost uninterrupted development of marinas, holiday homes, caravan parks and exclusive golf clubs. The most picturesque village on the west bank, **Luss**, is the setting for the Scottish TV soap *Take the High Road*, and is full of visitors buying souvenir tea towels and hoping to catch a glimpse of one of the 'stars'.

Central Scotland

The **Loch Lomond Authority Visitor Centre**, T01301-702785, next to the large car park in the village, has information on the loch's natural history, flora and fauna. ■ *Easter-Oct daily 1000-1800.*

Balloch to Tarbet
Phone code: 01389

At the southern end of the loch is the resort town of **Balloch**, packed full of hotels, B&Bs, caravan parks and any number of operators offering **boat trips** around the loch's overcrowded waters. Try *Sweeney's Cruises*, T752376, or *Mullen's Cruises*, T751481, which both offer a wide range of trips, starting at around £4-5 for an hour. A daily 2½-hour cruise from Balloch to Luss leaves at 1430 (£7). **Loch Lomond Shores**, T01389-721500, is a large visitor centre and orientation centre as you come into town, which operates as the gateway to the National Park. At the 100-acre site you can see a film celebrating the area in addition to shops, restaurants and the restored steamer 'Maid of the Loch'. There are plans to move the tourist office here too. During the early stages of the park's development the old **Tourist Information Centre** near the station, T753533, is also likely to remain open; April-June, September and October daily 1000-1700; July and August daily 0930-1830.

North of **Tarbet**, at the narrow northern end of the loch, things quieten down a great deal and the road to **Ardlui**, at its northern tip, is very beautiful and peaceful. The A82 continues north of Ardlui, past **Inverarnan**, to meet the A85 at **Crianlarich** (see page 358). There's a **Tourist Information Centre** in Tarbet, T01301-702260; April-October; and a **Visitor Centre** at Inveruglus, T01301-704392.

East bank & Ben Lomond
OS Landranger map 58

The tranquil **east bank** of Loch Lomond is a great place for walking. The **West Highland Way** (see page 59) follows the east bank all the way from **Drymen**, through **Balmaha**, **Rowardennan** and **Inversnaid**. Beyond Rowardennan this is the only access to the loch's east bank, except for the road to Inversnaid from the Trossachs. From Rowardennan you can climb **Ben Lomond** (3,192 ft), the most southerly of the Munros. It's not too difficult and the views from the top (in good weather) are astounding. There are two routes: the easier one starts from the car park at the end of the road just beyond the *Rowardennan Hotel*; the other route, known as the 'Ptarmigan Route', starts from beyond the youth hostel. You can also go up by one route and return by the other. Allow about five to six hours there and back.

An easier climb is **Conic Hill**, on the Highland fault line and very close to Glasgow. The route starts from the Balmaha car park. It takes about 1½ hours to reach the top, from where the views of the loch are stunning.

Sleeping & eating
There are numerous hotels and B&Bs in Balloch, Luss, Inverbeg and Tarbet

In **Balloch**, the **D** *Balloch House*, T752579, near the A82, has a good restaurant. Best of the B&Bs is the **E** *Gowanlea Guest House*, T752456, on Drymen Rd. There's a good **campsite** at *Lomond Woods Holiday Park at Tullichewan*, T755000, on the Old Luss Rd, where you can hire **mountain bikes**. A few miles further on up the west bank, in **Arden**, is **F** *Loch Lomond SYHA Youth Hostel*, T850226, www.syha.org.uk a grand 19th-century turreted mansion complete with the obligatory ghost. A few miles north of Luss, at **Inverbeg**, is the **C-B** *Inverbeg Inn*, T01436-860678, which does good food.

On the **eastern shore** there's an **F** *SYHA Youth Hostel* at **Rowardennan**, T01360-870259, open Feb-Oct. There's also the **C** *Rowardennan Hotel*, T01360-870273, which offers a bit more comfort and serves bar meals. There are a couple of **campsites** on the east bank, at *Milarrochy Bay*, T01360-870236, open end-Mar to Oct, near Balmaha, and the Forestry Commission campsite at *Cashel*, T01360-870234, www.forestholidays.co.uk, a few miles further north. On the northeast shore, and only accessible by road via the B829 from Aberfoyle, is the splendidly isolated **D** *Inversnaid Hotel*, T01877-386223.

In **Ardlui**, at the northern tip of the loch, is the comfortable **C** *Ardlui Hotel*, T01301-704243, www.ardlui.co.uk. A few miles north, at **Inverarnan**, is the *Drover's Inn*, T01301-704234, the famous Highland watering hole, with smoke-blackened walls, low ceilings, bare floors, open fires, a hall filled with stuffed animals, barman in kilt and a great selection of single malts. The perfect place for a wild night of drinking in the wilderness. It simply doesn't get any better than this.

Scottish *Citylink*, **buses** run regularly from Glasgow to **Balloch** (45 mins), and on to **Transport** Luss and **Tarbet** (1 hr 10 mins). Some buses go to **Ardlui** (1 hr 20 mins) and on to **Crianlarich**. There are 2 **rail** lines from Glasgow to Loch Lomond. One runs to **Balloch** every 30 mins (35 mins;) the other is the West Highland line to Fort William and Mallaig, with a branch line to Oban. It reaches Loch Lomond at **Tarbet** and there's another station further north at **Ardlui**.

There's a passenger **ferry service** across the loch between **Inverbeg** and **Rowardennan**, T01360-870273, 3 times daily (Apr-Sep). There are also ferries between **Inveruglas** and **Inversnaid**, T01877-386223. Ardleish to Ardlui ferry (Apr-Oct) summon from shore by raising ball up signal mast (0900-1900). Out of season by arrangement with Ardlui Hotel (T01301-704243).

The Trossachs

Strictly speaking, the Trossachs is the narrow wooded glen between **Loch Katrine** *and* **Loch Achray**, *but the name is now used to describe a much larger area between Argyll and Perthshire, stretching north from the* **Campsies** *and west from* **Callander** *to the eastern shore of Loch Lomond. It's a very beautiful and diverse area of sparkling lochs, craggy mountains and deep, forested glens, and for this reason is often called the 'Highlands in miniature'. Visit in the autumn when the hills are purple and the trees are a thousand luminous hues, from lustrous gold to flaming scarlet and blazing orange.*

The Trossachs was one of the country's first holiday regions, and remains a major tourist destination. Its enduring appeal is due in no small measure to Sir Walter Scott, who eulogized its great natural beauty in his epic poem, Lady of the Lake, and whose historical novel, Rob Roy, brought to public attention the region's other great attraction, Rob Roy MacGregor, one of the great romantic Highland figures.

Ins and outs

The *Trossachs Trundler* is a **bus** which makes a circuit of the Trossachs, linking **Getting around** Stirling, Callander, Aberfoyle and Port of Menteith, and stopping off at various scenic places en route. It also connects with departures of the *SS Sir Walter Scott* on Loch Katrine. It runs from Jun-Sep (not Wed) and costs £8 for a day ticket. Contact the local TIC for details.

The Trossachs is superb walking country. The two most challenging peaks are **Walking in** **Ben Venue** and **Ben A'an** around Loch Katrine and Loch Achray, about 10 **the Trossachs** miles west of Callander. **Ben Venue** (2,385 ft) is the more difficult climb. It *OS Landranger maps* starts from behind the *Loch Achray Hotel* and is waymarked, but it's a strenu- *56 and 57* ous climb which requires hill walking experience, proper clothing and all the usual safety precautions (see page 60). Allow about five hours for the return trip. **Ben A'an** (1,520 ft) isn't a giant of a hill, but it's a steep climb from the start, from the car park of the former *Trossachs Hotel* (now a timeshare development) on the north bank of Loch Achray, and there's a bit of scrambling

Central Scotland

involved near the summit. It takes about 1½ hours to the top. The views from both hills are stupendous on clear days, but remember that the weather is as unpredictable in the Trossach mountains as anywhere else in the Highlands. A useful guide is Collins' *Walk Loch Lomond and the Trossachs*.

Both these mountains lie within the **Queen Elizabeth Forest Park**. This vast and spectacular wilderness of 75,000 acres borders Loch Lomond to the west and incorporates Loch Ard, Loch Achray and Loch Lubnaig, as well as Ben Venue, Ben A'An and **Ben Ledi**, which overlooks Callander. The park is run by the Forestry Commission and is criss-crossed by a network of less difficult waymarked trails and paths which start from the Queen Elizabeth Park **Visitor Centre**, about half a mile north of Aberfoyle on the A821. Available at the centre are audio-visual displays on the park's flora and fauna and information on the numerous walks and cycle routes around the park. ■ *Mar-Oct daily 1000-1800; Oct-Dec 1100-1600 (parking £1). Full details of the park are available from the Forest Enterprise in Aberfoyle, (same tel no). T01877-382258.*

Aberfoyle

Phone code: 01877
Colour map 4, grid C1

The sleepy village of Aberfoyle suddenly bursts into life in the summer with the arrival of hordes of tourists. It lies on the edge of the Queen Elizabeth Forest Park and, along with Callander to the east, is one of the main tourist centres for the Trossachs. It makes an ideal base for walking and cycling in the surrounding hills. There's plentiful accommodation, though you'll have to book during the busy summer season.

Ins & outs   **Getting there** There are regular **buses** to and from **Stirling**,T0870-6082608. There are also daily services from **Glasgow**, via Balfron. There's a **postbus service**, T01752-494527, www.royalmail.com/postbus, from Aberfoyle to **Inversnaid** on Loch Lomond (see page 352).

The **Tourist Information Centre** is on the main street. Apr-Jun, Sep and Oct daily 1000-1700; Jul and Aug 0930-1900, weekends only Nov-Mar (hours subject to change). T382352.

Sights   Three miles east of Aberfoyle is the **Lake of Menteith**, the only lake in Scotland (as opposed to loch). On Inchmahome island in the middle of the lake are the beautiful and substantial ruins of **Inchmahome Priory**, the 13th-century Augustinian priory where the four-year-old Mary, Queen of Scots was sent in 1547, safe from the clutches of Henry VIII. A **ferry** takes visitors over to the island from **Port of Menteith**. ■ *Apr-Sep Mon-Sun 0930-1830. £3.30, £2.50 concession. T385294 (HS).* The lake is also a popular spot for **fly-fishing** and you can rent boats from *Lake of Menteith Fisheries*, T385664, April-October.

To the north of Aberfoyle is Doon Hill, better known as the **Fairy Knowe**. The tree at the top is said to be the home of the 'People of Quietness', and in 1692 a local minister was less than discreet in telling the world of their secrets. As punishment he was taken away to fairyland, and his spirit has languished there ever since. If you go round the tree seven times, your wish will be granted, but go round it backwards and… well, we won't be held responsible. It's about an hour up and back. Cross the bridge over the Forth and head past the cemetery, then follow the signs.

Sleeping   The best place to stay in the area is the **A-B** *Lake Hotel*, in Port of Menteith, situated on the lakeshore overlooking Inchmahome, T385258, www.lake-of-menteith-hotel.com.

Central Scotland

Rob Roy

As the tourist board never tires of reminding us, the Trossachs is Rob Roy country. Rob Roy ('Red Robert' in Gaelic) was one of Scotland's most notorious outlaws or one of the bravest Highland heroes, depending on your point of view. It is true that he was a freebooter, but he was also defending Highland clan culture and more specifically fighting for the very survival of his own clan against proscription and persecution by the government and its supporters.

Rob Roy MacGregor (1671-1734) was born in Glengyle, to the northwest of Loch Katrine. The MacGregors' lands included those previously owned by the rival Campbells but bestowed on the MacGregors for services rendered to Alexander II in his conquest of Argyll. For a long time the clan kept possession of their lands by right of the sword, but the

constant attempts by neighbouring clans to displace them led to retaliation by the MacGregors and earned them a reputation for being aggressive. Rob Roy did little to change this image, and his bitter feud with the powerful Duke of Montrose led to his being outlawed and eventually captured and sentenced to transportation. He was pardoned and returned to **Balquhidder***, where he stayed for the rest of his life. He now lies buried in the churchyard.*

The Rob Roy story was first popularized by Sir Walter Scott's eponymous 19th-century novel, and his life continues to be romanticized, most recently in the 1995 film starring Liam Neeson and Tim Roth. Like Robin Hood before him, his courage in refusing to bow to the forces of authority seems to strike a chord with people.

It's stylish, comfortable, very romantic and boasts a fine restaurant (lunch mid-range; dinner expensive). There are dozens of **B&Bs** in and around Aberfoyle, including **E** *The Barns of Shannochill*, by Aberfoyle, T382878, a barn annexe in the country; and the lovely **D-E** *Creag-Ard House* in Milton, 2 miles west of Aberfoyle overlooking Loch Ard, T382297, with fishing and boat hire available.

Camping is available at *Cobeland Campsite*, T382392, open Apr-Oct, 2 miles south of Aberfoyle on the edge of the Queen Elizabeth Forest Park; and the excellent *Trossachs Holiday Park*, T382614, open Mar-Oct, set in 40 acres with **mountain bike hire**.

There are several decent **eating** places in the village. The *Forth Inn Hotel*, T382372, and *The Coach House*, T382822, both on Main St, serve good pub food. The best place to eat is the excellent and very popular *Braeval Old Mill*, T382711, a few miles east on the A873 to Port of Menteith. **Eating**

The A821 route north from Aberfoyle, through the spectacular **Duke's Pass**, and then east past Loch Achray and Loch Vennachar, is one of the most beautiful routes in the country and not to be missed. There are a couple of worthwhile diversions along the way. About five miles north of Aberfoyle, a track branches to the right and runs through Achray Forest and along the shores of Loch Drunkie, before rejoining the A821 further north. A few miles further on, a road turns left to **Trossachs Pier** on the eastern shore of **Loch Katrine**. This is the departure point for **cruises** on the *SS Sir Walter Scott*, T376316. In the mornings (daily except Wed) it sails to the remote settlement of **Stronachlachar** on the far western shores of the loch and back. In the afternoons (daily) it only sails around the loch for an hour. ■ *Cruises depart Apr to end of Oct: at 1100 to Stronachlachar, returning at 1200, and around the loch at 1345 and 1515. Cruises cost from £6 (£4 morning cruise one way).* There's a road and cycle path around the loch as far as Stronachlachar, and you could **Aberfoyle to Callander** take the morning cruise there and then cycle back to the pier. **Cycle hire** from *Trossachs Cycle Hire*, T382614, for £6.50-10 per half day and £10-16 for a whole day.

The road then swings east along the northern shores of luscious Loch Achray and Loch Venachar, past **Brig o' Turk**. Just past the village, on the A821, is the wonderful *Byre*, T01877-376292, a cosy bar serving good ales and hearty food (mid-range), ideally placed for walkers and cylists.

Callander

Phone code: 01877
Colour map 4, grid C2
Population: 2,500

Callander sits at the eastern end of the Trossachs, 14 miles northwest of Stirling, its wide streets totally and unashamedly devoted to tourism and lined with tearooms, restaurants and craft shops. The town's overworked **Tourist Information Centre** is on the main street, in Ancaster Square, T330342. Same opening times as visitor centre below. It shares the same building as the **Rob Roy and Trossachs Visitor Centre** which gives an entertaining account of the life of Rob Roy MacGregor. ■ *Mar-May and Oct-Dec daily 1000-1700; Jun 0930-1800; Jul and Aug 0900-2000; Sep 1000-1800; Jan and Feb weekends only 1000-1600. £3.25.*

Ins & outs There are regular **buses** to and from **Stirling** (45 mins). There's a *Scottish Citylink* service once daily in summer between Edinburgh and Fort William which stops in Callander. A **postbus** leaves daily, except Sun, at 0915 to **Trossachs Pier** and connects with **cruises** on Loch Katrine (see 'Aberfoyle to Callander' above). There's also a postbus between Callander and **Aberfoyle**, via **Port of Menteith** (Mon-Fri in the afternoon).

Walks & cycle routes
OS Landranger No 57

Callander is also a good base for exploring the Trossachs. A recommended local walk is to **Bracklinn Falls**, reached by a woodland trail which leads from Bracklinn Road. It's about 30 minutes each way. Another trail from Bracklinn Road leads up to **Callander Crags**, from where there are great views of the surrounding area. Allow 1½ hours there and back. The most challenging walk in the area is to the summit of **Ben Ledi** (2,857 ft), but it's a tough climb and you'll need to be fit, experienced and prepared (see page 60).

Two miles north of Callander, on the A84 route to the Highlands, are the

Callander

Sleeping
1 Arden House
2 Dunmor Guest House
3 Priory

Eating
1 Dun Whinny's
2 Pip's Coffee House

Falls of Leny, in the narrow and dramatic Pass of Leny. The falls are accessible from the car park by the roadside or via the **Callander to Strathyre Cycleway,** which follows the old train line to Oban, from Callander north along the west bank of **Loch Lubnaig.** This forms part of the **Glasgow to Killin Cycleway,** which runs from the centre of Glasgow, via Balloch, Aberfoyle, Callander, Balquhidder and Lochearnhead, to Killin. This is the best way to see the Trossachs. You can **hire bikes** in Callander from *Wheels,* Invertrossachs Road, T331100, for £6-10 per day.

If you want something a wee bit special, then head for the **A** *Roman Camp Country House Hotel,* T330003, www.roman-camp-hotel.co.uk An exquisite 16th-century hunting lodge set in extensive grounds by the river, away from the hoi polloi. Queen Victoria was quite taken with the place. Also serves superb Scottish cuisine (expensive). For something a bit more down-to-earth, there's a huge selection of **B&B** accommodation, including **D-E** *Brook Linn Country House,* T330103, open Easter-Oct, a fine Victorian house overlooking the town; **D-E** *Arden House,* T/F330235, open Mar-Nov, on Bracklinn Rd; **D-E** *The Priory,* T/F330001, open Apr-Sep, also on Bracklinn Rd; and **D-E** *Dunmor Guest House,* T330756, open Apr-Oct, on Leny Rd. You can also try **B** *Leny House,* a 5-star B&B in the parkland of the Leny Estate, T331078, www.lenyestate.com, open Apr-Oct. A couple of miles out of town, along the Invertrossachs Rd which turns off the A81, is the **F** *Trossachs Backpackers,* T331200, trosstel@aol.com, an independent hostel which also **rents bikes.** There's also **camping** at *Gart Caravan Park,* Stirling Rd, T330002, open Easter to mid-Oct.

> **Sleeping & eating**

The best place to eat is the *Roman Camp Hotel* (see above). Otherwise the hotels and pubs offer bar meals. Most of the places along the main street are overpriced, but the *Ben Ledi Café* offers good-value basic grub (well it was good enough for Prince William when he visited the town). If you want a cake or a sandwich try *Dun Whinny's,* 9 Bridge St, T331257, or *Pip's Coffee House* on Ancaster Sq. There's also an internet café, *The Cooler* on the Main St. A few miles north of town, at Kilmahog, is the highly rated *Lade Inn,* T330152.

North of Callander

The A84 heads north from Callander along the east bank of Loch Lubnaig, and beyond towards **Loch Earn.** At the northern end of Loch Lubnaig, in **Strathyre,** is *C-D Creagan House,* T384638, a family-run 17th-century farmhouse offering excellent food (mid-range to expensive) and comfortable accommodation, open Mar-Jan.

> *Colour map 4, grid C2*

A few miles further north, a side road branches left to the tiny village of **Balquhidder,** famous as the burial place of Rob Roy. His grave in the churchyard, where his wife and two of his sons are also buried, is thankfully understated. The road continues west along the north shore of Loch Voil to **Inverlochlarig,** from where there are numerous excellent opportunities for experienced hill walkers.

Eating The best place by far to stay in these parts is the small, family-run **C** *Monachyle Mhor Hotel,* T01877-384622, on the road to Inverlochlarig. It offers great views of the loch, peace and quiet and fabulous Scottish/French cuisine (lunch mid-range; dinner expensive).

A few miles north of the turning to Balquhidder, where the A84 meets the A85 from Crieff to Crianlarich, is Lochearnhead, at the western tip of Loch Earn. The loch is a highly popular **watersports centre** and at *Lochearnhead*

> **Lochearnhead**
> *Phone code: 01567*

Watersports, T830330, you can try water-skiing, canoeing and kayaking. Lochearnhead is also a good base for **walking** in the surrounding hills.

Sleeping and eating D-E *Clachan Cottage Hotel*, T830300 or E *Mansewood Country House*, T830213. Most other options are **self-catering** cabins and caravans and include *Earnknowe*, T/F830238, cottages for rent, from £135-£330 per week for up to six people. The best place to eat is the *Four Seasons Hotel*, T685333, at St Fillans, at the east end of the loch.

Killin
Phone code: 01567

In the far northwestern corner of Stirling region, just to the west of Loch Tay, is Killin, a pleasant little village which makes a good base for walkers wishing to explore the wild mountains and glens of the ancient district of **Breadalbane** (pronounced Bread-*al*binn). Killin's picture-postcard setting, with the beautiful **Falls of Dochart** tumbling through the centre of the village, makes it a popular destination for tourists.

The **Tourist Information Centre** overlooks the falls. In the same building is the **Breadalbane Folklore Centre**, which has displays on local clan history and contains the sacred healing stones of the seventh-century missionary, St Fillan. ■ *Tourist office and Folklore Centre both open Mar-May and Oct daily 1000-1700; Jun and Sep till 1800; Jul and Aug 0930-1830. £2.00, £1.25 concession. T820254.*

Sleeping and eating The best place to stay is the **D** *Dall Lodge Country House Hotel*, T820217, www.dallodgehotel.co.uk, open Mar-Oct, which offers idiosyncratic style and very good food. Next best choice is the **D-E** *Killin Hotel*, T820296, www.killinhotel.com Amongst the dozens of **B&Bs** is **E** *Invertay House*, T820492, invertay@btinternet.com, open Mar-Nov; and *Mansewood Country House*, T830213. There's also a **F** *Youth Hostel*, T820546, open Mar to end-Oct, at the northern end of the village. The **outdoor centre**, T820652, on the main road, hires out mountain bikes, as well as climbing equipment.

Transport There are **buses** to Killin from **Stirling** via **Callander** (1 hr 45 mins). There's a **postbus** from **Callander** once daily Mon-Fri (1 hr), which continues to **Crianlarich** and **Tyndrum**. There's also a postbus service from **Aberfeldy** (see page 333).

Crianlarich & Tyndrum
Phone code: 01838
Colour map 4, grid C1

Twelve miles west of Killin is Crianlarich, at the crossroads of the A82 Glasgow-Fort William road and the A85 to Perth, and at the junction of the Glasgow to Fort William and Oban **rail lines**. It is a staging post on the **West Highland Way**. There are many places to stay, including an **F** *SYHA Youth Hostel*, T300260, open all year except 3-27 January. Try also **D** *Ewich House*, T300300, a refurbished farmhouse in stunning scenery; or **D***Ben More Lodge*, T300210. Six miles further north is tiny **Tyndrum**, which shot to prominence a few years ago after the discovery of gold in the surrounding hills. There's a seasonal **Tourist Information Centre**, T400246, on the Main Road, April-June and September-November daily 1000-1700; July, August 0930-1800.

Transport There are 2 **train stations** at Tyndrum. One serves the Glasgow to Oban line and the other the Glasgow to Fort William line. There are **trains** from both villages to Fort William, Oban and Glasgow (T03457-484950). *Scottish Citylink* **buses**, between Glasgow and Oban and Fort William stop in both villages. There's also a **postbus** service between Crianlarich and Tyndrum and Killin (Mon-Sat).

Fife

*For such a small region, Fife is a very diverse place. The difference between the blighted industrial landscape of the southwest and the prosperous-looking rural northeast couldn't be more marked. Northeast Fife consists of **St Andrews** and the **East Neuk** and if you only have a few days in which to visit, then this is the area to see. **St Andrews**, in particular, is important and attractive enough to visit on its own. The ruins of its cathedral and castle bear witness to its former importance, while the Royal and Ancient Golf Club is the sport's spiritual home and stands on the world's most famous links course. It also has the oldest university in Scotland **The East Neuk of Fife** is a string of picture-postcard old fishing villages, Those with more time on their hands could also venture inland to explore **Falkland**, **Cupar** and the **Howe of Fife**. Here, you'll find **Falkland Palace**, one of Scotland's most remarkable historic buildings.*

Ins and outs

Getting around The main transport route through the region is the M90 which runs from Edinburgh north to Perth and skirts Fife's western boundary. A more scenic alternative is the beautiful coastal route, which branches east off the M90 just north of the Forth Road Bridge as the A921 to Kirkaldy, the A955 from there to Leven and the A917 from Leven through the East Neuk villages and on to St Andrews. The coastal route also affords easy access into the centre of Fife. The Tay Road Bridge leads south from Dundee into Fife, via the A914 and A919 southeast to St Andrews and the A92 southwest to Glenrothes and Kirkaldy. It meets the A91, which runs east from the M90 and gives access to Falkland Palace, the Scottish Deer Centre, Cupar and also St Andrews.

The **train** line north from Edinburgh follows the coast as far as Kirkaldy and then cuts inland towards Dundee, stopping at Cupar and Leuchars. From Leuchars a **bus** can be taken to St Andrews. It is possible to explore the peninsula using public transport, but it can be a slow and time-consuming business as buses to the more remote parts are few and far between.

Tourist information The various Tourist Information Centres provide free and comprehensive information on all that Fife has to offer, including where to stay. They also sell tickets for events, attractions, trips and tours, provide exchange facilities and stock maps and guide books. Details of the TICs are given under the relevant town. You'll find them in St Andrews, Kirkaldy, Anstruther, Crail, Dunfermline and North Queensferry.

Visit the Fife Tourist Board website, www.standrews.com

Southwest Fife

Travelling north from Edinburgh across the Firth of Forth, you pass through this industrial corner of the Kingdom. The area was once a major producer of coal, but a succession of pit closures has left a scarred and depressed wasteland. However, the area is not without its attractions. Dunfermline boasts an impressive history and the coastal route takes you through some attractive villages.

Dunfermline

Phone code: 01383
Colour map 4, grid C3
Population: 52,000

A mere 5 km inland, just off the M90, the town of Dunfermline is steeped in history. It was once the capital of Scotland, from the 11th century to the Union of Crowns in 1603, and its great abbey and royal palace still dominate the skyline. Until the late 19th century, Dunfermline was one of Scotland's most important linen producers and a major coal-mining centre. Those traditional industries have long since gone but the town still thrives economically and has grown considerably in size.

Ins & outs

See page 362 for transport details

Trains from Edinburgh connect with Dunfermline. The train station is a 15-min walk southeast of the centre, halfway down St Margaret's Drive. There's an hourly bus service from Edinburgh, and services every 2 hrs from Glasgow, Perth and Dundee. The bus station is in the Kingsgate Centre, on the north side of town, T621249. **Tourist Information Centre** is at 13/15 Maygate (next to the Abbot House). T720999. Mon-Sat 0930-1730, Sun 1100-1600; closed on Sun, Oct-Mar.

History

In the 11th century, Malcolm Canmore, King of Scotland, offered hospitality in his tower in Dunfermline to the English heir to the throne, Edgar Atheling and his family, on their flight from William the Conqueror and the Norman Conquest. Edgar's sister, Princess Margaret, a devout Catholic and later 'Saint Margaret', married the King in 1067, and was largely responsible for introducing the religious ideas of the Catholic Church into Scotland. Horrified by the lax ways of the Celtic Church, she began to build a new church which was founded in 1072 (see below).

Sights

Dunfermline **Abbey** stands on the site of the Benedictine Priory, built by Queen Margaret in the late 11th century. When she endowed the priory, she set up a shrine, with a relic of the 'True Cross' and encouraged pilgrims to come from miles away to venerate it. Her son, David I, raised the priory to the rank of abbey and began building the new abbey church in 1128, on the foundations of Margaret's church. These foundations were rediscovered in modern times and can now be seen through a grating in the floor. Frequently sacked and burned over the centuries, today's building is a combination of different tastes and styles. Much of the present abbey was built long after King David's death but the superb Norman nave, with its massive pillars, is still there to be admired. The Norman decorations above the west doorway are rare examples of such work in Scotland. The north porch, northwest tower, west front and massive buttresses are all the work of William Shaw, Master of works to Anne of Denmark in the 16th century. The other part of the abbey church was added in the 19th century and today serves as the parish church.

Close to the east gable of the parish church are the foundations of the shrine of St Margaret where she and her husband are buried. But they were not the only royal persons to be buried in the abbey. Six Scottish kings also lie there, with the grave of Robert the Bruce beneath the pulpit. He was buried in the abbey in 1329 but over the years the exact position of his grave became uncertain. Then, in 1818, when the foundation of the new church was being prepared, Bruce's tomb was rediscovered, the skeleton covered in a shroud of gold and the breast bone severed where his heart had been removed in order to take it to the Holy Land, in accordance with his wishes. Unfortunately, it never made it and now lies in Melrose Abbey. In 1889, Robert the Bruce's descendent, the Earl of Elgin, gifted a memorial brass to mark the tomb. To celebrate the historic find, an over-enthusiastic architect designed the vast inscription round the top of the square tower, which no-one can fail to notice.

The Abbey church stands adjacent to the ruined **monastery** building and the **Royal Palace**, which are linked by a pend or alleyway.

The palace, built when Malcolm and Margaret married, has fallen into ruins, but what little remains still hints at its undoubted magnificence. For centuries, it was a favourite residence of the Kings of Scotland. David II, James I and Charles I were all born here, the latter being the last monarch to be born in Scotland. ■ *Apr-Sep daily 0930-1830; Oct-Mar Mon-Wed & Sat 0930-1630, Thu 0930-1230, Sun 1400-1630. £2, £1.50 concession, £0.75 children. Disabled access. T739026.*

Dunfermline may have been the home to many Scottish monarchs, but its most famous son was born in more modest surroundings. Andrew Carnegie (1835-1919), the son of a humble linen weaver, emigrated to the USA and made a fortune in steel. One of the great philanthropists, he gave away £350 mn for the benefit of mankind and was particularly generous to his home town, giving it Pittencrief park, public baths, a library and an annual Festival of Music and Arts. The **Andrew Carnegie Birthplace Museum** is the small cottage in Moodie Street where Carnegie was born. The rooms are furnished as they were in his lifetime and the millionaire himself sits at the his desk in his study. ■ *Apr-Oct Mon-Sat 1100-1700, Sun 1400-1700. Groups in winter by appointment only. £2, £1 concession, children free. T724302.*

The beautiful and lavishly endowed **Pittencrief Park**, known locally as 'the Glen', is opposite the west door of the Abbey. Inside the park is **Pittencrief House Museum**, built in 1610 and also bought by Carnegie for the people of Dunfermline. It features displays of local history, costumes and an art gallery. The glasshouses (free entry) are filled with tropical plants and flowers, and the art deco pavilion has a restaurant. Here also stands the ruin of **Malcolm's Tower**, where King Malcolm and his bride lived before the building of the palace. Dunfermline – which means 'fort by the crooked pool' – takes its name from the tower's location. ■ *Museum open Apr-Sep daily 1100-1700; Oct-Mar daily 1100-1600. Free. T722935.*

In the Maygate is the **Abbot House**, which was the home of Robert Pitcairn, the post-Reformation Abbot of the Abbey. The house is one of the oldest in Scotland, possibly 14th century, and was restored in 1963. There's a café serving snacks and light lunches. ■ *All year daily 1000-1700. £3, £2 concession, children free (if accompanied by an adult. T733266.*

The 19th-century **Town House** in Bridge Street was designed in the French and Scottish Gothic style, said to be very fashionable at the time. Among its interesting features are the gargoyles and grotesques, depicting the heads of King Robert the Bruce, King Malcolm, Queen Margaret and Queen Elizabeth.

Incongruously housed in the stone building in Chalmers street car park is the entrance to **Saint Margaret's Cave**. The saintly queen often retired here for moments of secret devotion. Her husband, suspicious of her frequent visits to the cave, followed and discovered her kneeling in prayer. Overjoyed that his suspicions were groundless, he had the cave fitted up for her as a place of devotion. ■ *Easter to end-Sep daily 1100-1600. Free.*

Dunfermline Museum is at Viewfield Terrace, south of the East Port. The Victorian villa has displays concentrating on local history, including the weaving and damask linen industries, for which the town was famous and which greatly contributed to Fife's economic well-being. ■ *All year, Mon-Fri. Free. Phone 24 hrs in advance for admission; T313838.*

Central Scotland

Four miles north of the town centre, just off the A823, is **Knockhill Racing Circuit**, T723337, www.knockhill.co.uk, Scotland's national motorsport centre, which stages major car and motorbike racing events (as well as rally, race and 4x4 driving courses) between April and October, usually on Sunday. ■ *£5-20 depending on the event, children under 16 free, OAP/concession half price.*

Sleeping
■ *on map*
Price codes:
see inside front cover

A-B *Pitbauchlie House Hotel*, Aberdour Rd, T722282, F620738. 50 rooms with bathroom, set in landscaped gardens, only a few mins from the M90, with recommended restaurant. Very good. **B** *Garvock House Hotel*, St John's Dr, Transy, T621067, F621168, www.garvock.co.uk 12 rooms with bathroom, elegant country house in woodland setting, short break deals available. Excellent. **B-C** *Davaar House Hotel*, 126 Grieve St, T721886, F623633. 10 en suite rooms, within walking distance of the town centre and bus and rail stations, good restaurant. Very good. A few miles west of Dunfermline, at Crossford, is **B** *Keavil House Hotel*, T736258, F621600, www.keavilhouse.co.uk 40 en suite rooms, excellent accommodation and restaurant, leisure club. **E** *Pitreavie Guest House*, 3 Aberdour Rd, T/F724244. 6 rooms with 2 shared bathrooms, B&B.

Eating

Aside from the hotel restaurants listed above and the usual array of ethnic restaurants and fish and chip shops, there's the *Town House*, 48 East Port, T432382, open 1200-2130 Sun-Thu, till 2230 Fri/Sat. Mid-range à la carte, cheap 2-course business lunch. Near the abbey in Guildhall St is *Somewhere Else*, a pub serving good value home-made soup, sandwiches and Belhaven beer.

Transport

Buses run frequently to **Stirling**, **Edinburgh** (30 mins), **Dundee** (1½ hrs) and **Kirkcaldy** (30 mins). *Scottish Citylink*, runs buses hourly to **Edinburgh** and **Perth**. **Train** to **Edinburgh** every hour (30 mins).

Directory

Banks There are several banks with ATMs in the High St. **Communications** The *Post Office* is in Pilmuir St, near the bus station.

Culross
Phone code: 01383
Colour map 4, grid C3

Pronounced 'kooros', this beautifully restored village contains the finest surviving examples of Scottish vernacular architecture from the 16th and 17th centuries. Culross was then one of the largest ports in Scotland, and enjoyed a flourishing trade in coal and salt with other Forth ports and the Low Countries. Following the industrial revolution, however, the little town went into near-terminal decline until the National Trust rescued it from decay in 1932.

Getting there Culross lies off the A985, 12 km west of the Forth Road Bridge. Take a Fife *Scottish* No 14/14a bus on the Dunfermline-Glasgow route, T621249. There are also services from Falkirk, and from Glasgow, via Stirling and Alloa.

To appreciate the town's unique sense of history fully, explore its narrow cobbled streets on foot. A good starting point is the **National Trust Visitor Centre**, in the **Town House**, or Tolbooth, on the main road beside the palace, which dates from 1626. Here you can watch an excellent video charting the history of the town.

The **Palace** was built between 1597 and 1611 by local merchant, Sir George Bruce, who made his fortune from coal and salt panning. It's not so much a palace as a grand house, but its crow-stepped gables and pan-tiled roofs give a delightful example of Scottish architecture from this period. Inside, the many small rooms and connecting passageways make it feel much larger than it is.

The main features are the wonderful original painted ceilings and wood panelling. The National Trust has filled the house with 17th and 18th century furniture and restored the garden which now features a variety of vegetables, herbs and perennials from the period.

A steep, cobbled street known as **Back Causeway** leads up behind the Town House to a tiny market place, where you'll find another distinctive building, the late-16th-century **Study**, a restored house that takes its name from the small room at the top of the corbelled tower, reached by a turnpike stair.

Further up the steep hill, past the many wonderfully restored little houses, is **Culross Abbey**, founded in 1215 by Cistercian Monks on land given to the church by the Earl of Fife. The original choir and tower are now the site of the parish church, which contains the beautiful family tomb of Sir George Bruce. There is little remaining of the rest of the abbey, but it's worth the climb for the peaceful surroundings and views over the Forth.

■ *Palace, Study and Town House open daily Apr, May, Sep and weekends in Oct 1230-1630; Easter weekend and Jun-Aug 1000-1700. Combined ticket for the Palace, Town House and Study is £5, £4 child/concession, £14 Family. Most of the exhibition and the ground floor of the Palace have wheelchair access, also parking and toilet facilities. T880359, www.nts.org.uk*

Sleeping and eating E *St Mungo's Cottage*, Low Causeway, T882102. 3 rooms, 1 with bathroom, very good. The café in the *Bessie Bar Hall* in the *Palace* (see above) serves home-made food and is open 1030-1630.

Along the shore, is the ruin of **St Mungo's Chapel**, built in 1503 by Archbishop Blackadder. It was here, in the sixth century, that St Kentigern was born. Affectionately nicknamed 'Mungo', he went on to build Glasgow Cathedral, around which the city later grew. About 10 km east of Culross is **Charlestown**, an 18th-century village with a picturesque harbour, built by the 5th Earl of Elgin for sailing vessels trading with Europe. It was the 7th Earl of Elgin who took the ancient Greek marble sculptures from the Parthenon in Athens and sold them to the British Museum in 1816 for £35,000. These became known as the 'Elgin Marbles' and continue to be a bone of contention between Britain and Greece. For a **guided tour** round the village, contact the *Charlestown Lime Heritage Trust*, T01383-872006 (walks from May till end-September, Sundays at 1430 and Wednesdays at 1900, £2.50, £1 child/concession.

East from Culross

One-and-a-half kilometres further east lies the charming village of **Limekilns**, which takes its name from the lime kilns that used to be one of its main industries. If you fancy a drink, try the *Ship Inn*, which featured in Robert Louis Stevenson's 'Kidnapped', and while for a restaurant serving good Italian cooking try *Il Pescatore*.

Situated at the foot of the Forth Rail Bridge, North Queensferry was originally the northern terminal of the ferry established by Queen Margaret to carry pilgrims to Dunfermline. It remained a ferry terminal until the road bridge was opened in 1964. Now it is home to a yacht marina and provides the ideal vantage point from which to wonder at the fantastic engineering feat of the Forth Rail Bridge. Also here is the popular **Deep Sea World**, Scotland's award-winning national aquarium, which boasts the world's largest underwater viewing tunnel, through which you pass on a moving walkway, coming face-to-face with sharks, conger eels and all manner of strange sea creatures. There is also a display of species from the Amazon rainforest. ■ *Apr-Oct daily 1000-1800;*

North Queensferry, Inverkeithing & Aberdour
Phone code: 01383
Colour map 4,
grid C3/4

Central Scotland

July/Aug 1000-1830; Nov-Mar daily 1100-1700. £6.25, £4.55 concession, £3.95 child, under 3 free. T411880, www.deepseaworld.com

The desolate shipbreakers yards at **Inverkeithing**, a stone's throw from North Queensferry, give no hint that this is one of the oldest Royal Burghs in Scotland. Granted a charter by King William the Lion around 1165, Inverkeithing was for centuries a place of trade and commerce with a small harbour and local coal workings. Born in the town in 1735 was Samuel Greig, often described as the founder of the Russian Navy. The son of a local shipmaster, he initially had a career in the British Navy, but following secondment to Russia he organized the Russian fleet for Catherine the Great, for which he received a knighthood.

Five miles east of the Forth bridges, on the A921, is **Aberdour**. The castle at the southern end of the main street, was built by the Douglas family on lands originally granted to Thomas Randolph, Earl of Moray, by King Robert the Bruce in 1325. The 14th-century tower is the oldest part of the castle, the other buildings having been added in the 16th and 17th centuries, including the unusual Dovecote (pronounced doocot) and the attractive walled garden. Nearby is St Fillan's Church, which is part Norman, part 16th century. The church has a peaceful, timeless quality which entices the visitor to linger in quiet contemplation. Note the leper-squint in the west wall, formerly used by sufferers who were not allowed to worship within the church. ■ *Castle open Apr-Sep daily 0930-1800; Oct-Mar Mon-Wed & Sat 0930-1600, Thu 0930-1200, Sun 1400-1600. £2, £1.50 concession, £0.75 children.*

Sleeping On the north side of the Forth Road Bridge is the **B-C** *Queensferry Lodge Hotel*, T410000, F419708, home of the **Forth Bridges Exhibition** which tells the story of the bridges through models, artefacts and a 40-min video (daily 0900-2100, free). The hotel is also home to the **Forth Valley Tourist Information Centre**, T417759, and offers comfortable accommodation in 77 en suite rooms with great views of the Forth and a restaurant. In Aberdour are **C-D** *Aberdour Hotel*, High St, T860325, F860808, www.aberdourhotel.co.uk 16 en suite rooms, restaurant, and **D** *Hawkcraig House*, Hawkcraig Point, T860335. Excellent B&B run by Mrs Barrie, 2 en suite rooms, price includes dinner.

Transport Trains run hourly from North Queensferry, Inverkeithing and Aberdour stations to **Kirkcaldy** and **Edinburgh**. There are 2 buses every hour to **Dunfermline**, and a bus runs about every 2 hrs to **Edinburgh**.

Burntisland & Kinghorn
Phone code: 01592
Colour map 4, grid C4

Three miles east of Aberdour is Burntisland, once famous for shipbuilding but now more popular as a holiday resort. The **Highland Games** held in mid-July are reputed to be the second oldest in the world and take place, like most of the town's summer activities, on the busy seafront Links. The church of **St Columba** was the first to be built in Scotland after the Reformation. The General Assembly of the Kirk of Scotland was held here in 1601, when in the presence of James VI, it was proposed that there should be a new translation of the Bible, the Authorised version, published in 1611. **Rossend Castle** is a 15th-century tower house that was recently restored and is now occupied by a firm of architects. It was here that the impetuous French poet, Chastelard, propositioned Mary, Queen of Scots in 1563, and was promptly beheaded for his impertinence.

Sleeping B-C *Inchview Hotel*, 69 Kinghorn Rd, T872239, F874866, inchview@msn.com 12 en suite rooms, restaurant. **B-C** *Kingswood Hotel*, Kinghorn

Rd, T872329, F873123, www.kingswoodhotel.co.uk 9 en suite rooms, very comfortable, set in 2 acres of gardens and woodland, views across the Forth, offers good bar meals, high teas and dinners. There are many **B&Bs** along the Links. Particularly good is **E** *Gruinard*, 148 Kinghorn Rd, T873877.

Transport Trains as for Aberdour. Buses run 3 times every hour to Kirkcaldy.

A few miles along the coast from Burntisland, at Kinghorn, you'll pass a monument beside the road in the shape of a Celtic cross. This is where Alexander III was thrown from his horse and killed, an event that completely changed the course of Scottish history. The king had been heading home from Edinburgh to his new wife, whom he had married only six months earlier in an attempt to provide himself with an heir. There was a violent storm that night, but he insisted on being ferried across the Forth before galloping east towards Pettycur, where his still-barren queen was waiting. His horse stumbled on the cliff edge and the king was thrown to his death, thus plunging the country into many years of bitter conflict and power struggles. Today, Kinghorn is a busy summer resort with a sandy beach, a golf course and a wide range of guesthouses. Transport details are as for Burntisland above.

Kinghorn

Kirkcaldy

Fifteen miles east of the Forth bridges is Kirkcaldy (pronounced kirkoddy), called the 'Lang Toon' because of its main street which, running along the seafront, is all of four miles long. It's perhaps unkind to say that Kirkcaldy was once famous (or infamous) for its terrible stench, but at the height of its thriving linoleum industry you could smell the place for miles around. Nowadays, the town's economy has diversified and the smell has thankfully gone. Also gone is much of its shipping trade, and the area around the harbour bears witness to a once thriving sea port. Some of the little streets and wynds (steep alleyways) opposite the harbour are worth exploring, such as Kirk Wynd or Sailor's Walk, which have been lovingly restored by the NTS. Today, the town is best known as Fife's main shopping centre, but if you're passing through there are a few other attractions aside from the many high street chain stores.

Population: 49,570
Phone code: 01592
Colour map 4, grid C4

Getting there The **train** station is in the upper part of town. The **bus** station is 1 block uphill from the High St. Kirkcaldy is on the main **Edinburgh** to **Dundee** and **Aberdeen** rail line, with regular services each way. Numerous buses run to **St Andrews**, **Dunfermline**, **Edinburgh** and the **East Neuk**.

The **Tourist Information Centre** is at 19 Whytescauseway. T267775. Mon-Fri 1000-1700, Sat 1000-1300 and 1400-1700. They will book accommodation and explain how to get there, which is invaluable as hotels and guesthouses are limited and scattered around the outskirts of town.

Ins & outs

The **Museum and Art Gallery** is in the War Memorial Gardens next to the railway station. There is a good archaeological collection and you can learn about the area's social, industrial and natural history. The small art gallery has an excellent collection of Scottish colourists, including work by William McTaggart, Peploe, Lowry, Sickert and Raeburn. There are also displays of the local Wemyss Ware pottery. ■ *All year daily Mon-Sat 1030-1700, Sun 1400-1700. Free. T412860.*

Across from the War Memorial Gardens is the **Adam Smith Centre**, named after one of the town's most famous sons, the pioneer economist and author of *The Wealth of Nations* in 1776. The centre stages live theatre and

Sights

Central Scotland

concerts and also has a cinema and restaurant/bar, T412929. In the High Street among the many shops, you'll find the birthplace of Adam Smith. At the old burgh school there's a plaque recording that both he and Robert Adam, the famous architect, were pupils there in the 1730s, and that Thomas Carlyle, the historian and essayist, taught there nearly 100 years later.

Ravenscraig Castle towers dramatically above the park of the same name, at the east end of the town, on a rocky promontory guarding the wide bay. The ruin dates from 1460, when James II intended it as a dower house for his wife. The castle was the first in Britain to be designed specifically for defence by and against cannon fire and you can see the wide gun loops in the massive thick walls. Near the castle, the steps that lead from the high-rise flats in Nether Road down to the beach should number 39 and are said to have inspired John Buchan to write his famous novel.

Dysart, the eastern suburb of Kirkcaldy, is a little burgh dating back to the 16th century and is full of character, with its delightful little wynds and court-yards and old houses with crow-stepped gables and pan-tiled roofs. Dysart was once a busy trading port with the Netherlands. Now all that remains is the little harbour, perfectly set below the ancient battlements of St Serf's church. The **Pan Ha'**, an area of 17th-century houses, was restored by the NTS, as was the **McDougall Stuart Museum**. This house, dated 1575, was the birthplace of John McDougall Stuart, the first man to cross Australia from north to south, in 1866. The award-winning museum charts the story of Stuart and his fascinating and often dangerous expedition. ■ *Jun-Aug daily 1400-1700. Free. T412860.*

Sleeping

Kirkcaldy's guesthouses and B&Bs are spread throughout the town's residential districts

C *Dunnikier House Hotel*, Dunnikier Way, T268393, F642340, www.dunnikier-house-hotel.co.uk 15 en suite rooms set in pleasant grounds, good food. **B-D** *Parkway Hotel*, 6 Abbotshall Rd, T262143, F200433. 35 en suite rooms, comfortable, near the rail station. Among the recommended guesthouses and B&Bs are **E** *North Hall Guest House*, at 143 Victoria Rd, T268864. Run by Norie and Agnes Cairns, 2 mins from the train station, **E** *Bennochy Bank Guest House*, 26 Carlyle Rd, T200733.

Eating

There are lots of unremarkable places to eat in the High St, including the usual array of bakers, pubs, chip shops and Indian and Chinese restaurants. The best restaurant by far is the *Old Rectory*, in Dysart, a few miles east, T657211. It is moderately priced and open Tue-Sat for dinner; Tue-Sun for lunch. The best fish and chips here, or anywhere else, can be found at *Valente's*, 73 Oventon Rd, east of town centre. Open till 2300, closed Wed.

Entertainment

Every Apr for 5 days, Kirkcaldy's esplanade is closed to traffic for 5 days during the **Links Market**, one of the largest and oldest street fairs in Britain.

Around Kirkcaldy

Balgonie Castle has been described as one of the scariest places on Earth in an American TV show

A few miles east along the coast from Dysart are the villages of **East and West Wemyss**, so called from the many 'weems', or caves, found on this particular stretch of Fife coast. The famous caves lie along the foreshore of East Wemyss, below the ruins of **MacDuff's Castle**, reputed to be the home of Macduff of Shakespeare's *Macbeth*. Within the caves you'll find Britain's earliest picture of a boat, as well as hunting scenes, portrayed by craftsmen of Pictish times. King James IV was so impressed by one of the caves that he held court there and it is now known, unsurprisingly, as Court Cave.

The A92 runs from the northeastern outskirts of Kirkcaldy to **Glenrothes**, a sprawling new town, developed since 1950, which was originally designed to meet the housing needs of new colliery workers. Coal mining, however, declined in Fife, and Glenrothes instead attracted the trailblazers of Scotland's new light electronics industries. Two miles east of Glenrothes on the B921 off the A911, is the splendid 14th-century **Balgonie Castle**. This was the 17th-century home of Field Marshall Sir Alexander Leslie, Lord General of the Scottish Covenanting Army and First Earl of Leven, and was garrisoned by Rob Roy MacGregor with 200 clansmen in 1716. Restoration continues in this family home and living museum. ■ *Daily 1000-1700, for a personal guided tour.*

Sleeping L *Balbirnie House Hotel*, Balbirnie Park, Markinch, T610066, F610529, www.www.balbirnie.co.uk This magnificent Georgian mansion is set in 400 acres of country park with its own 18-hole golf course and is the height of luxury, 30 en suite rooms and restaurant.

North Fife and the Howe

In stark contrast to the industrial landscape of Kirkcaldy and Glenrothes, the ***Howe of Fife*** *(Howe means valley) is a low-lying area of patchwork fields, woodlands and farming communities which runs from the attractive market town of* ***Cupar*** *in the east to* ***Falkland****, at the foot of the* ***Lomond Hills****. The area makes a worthwhile stopping off point on the way to or from St Andrews. It is reached from the M90 and is well served by regular buses to and from Dundee and Kirkcaldy. The main Edinburgh to Dundee and Aberdeen train also stops here, at Cupar.*

Tucked away at the foot of the Lomond Hills, off the A912, the ancient and beautiful village of Falkland is the most royal of Fife's Royal Burghs and holds a unique place in Scottish history, as it is the site of **Falkland Palace**, the favourite residence of the Stuart monarchs. More than three centuries have passed since the last of the kings left Falkland, but it still retains a delightful charm, thanks to the NTS Little Houses Improvement scheme.

Falkland
Phone code: 01337
Colour map 4, grid C4

The great **Royal Palace** stands in the heart of the village, which is a surprise in itself as it shows a remarkable lack of class distinction; rare in medieval Scotland. But it is not only the location of the palace that is exceptional. It is one of the grandest buildings in the country and its variety of styles is part of its charm. Facing the street, the south front is a splendid example of Scottish Gothic with its buttresses, niches and statues of Christ and the saints. The magnificent courtyard frontage in the classical style, with pillars and medallions, strikes an altogether different mood and an air of gracious living. Scotland has few surviving buildings that were in the mainstream of Renaissance architecture, but this one is by far the best.

Though the building shows a strong French influence, there is a flavour about it that is unmistakably Scottish. Most of the existing palace was built in the early 16th century by James IV and his son James V. It was designed as a hunting lodge and was much loved by the Stuart kings and queens who came here to hunt deer and wild boar in the surrounding forests. There was also royal (or real) tennis to ease the strains of government. The royal tennis court, built in 1539 and the oldest in Britain, is still in use.

But though the monarchy, from James II to Charles II, spent some of their happiest days at Falkland, the best known event to happen there was the tragic death of King James V. He had come to the palace after his defeat at Solway Moss in 1542 and died of a broken heart on hearing of the birth of a daughter, the future Mary, Queen of Scots. When the news was broken to him he exclaimed "Farewell, it cam with ane lass and it will pass with ane lass". He then turned his face to the wall and died. The king's bedchamber is one of the many attractions inside the palace, morbid though it may be. A guided tour lasts 40 minutes and includes the Chapel Royal (still used for Mass), the superb Flemish Tapestry Gallery, the King's Bedchamber and Queen's Room, as well as the gardens and Tennis Court. ■ *Apr-Oct Mon-Sat 1000-1730, Sun 1330-1730. £5 (£2.50 garden only), £4 child/concession (£1.70 garden only), £14 family.T857397.*

Falkland is a good base for **walks** in the **Lomond Hills**. A narrow road leads from the village to a pass between East and West Lomond. It's about one hour to the pass and a further 45 minutes to the summit of West Lomond (1,712 ft). The views from the top on a clear day are wonderful.

Sleeping and eating C-D *Covenanter Hotel*, is near the palace, T857224, F857163, www. covenanterhotel.com. 6 comfortable en suite rooms, excellent food served in the restaurant (mid-range) and bistro (cheap) downstairs. **E** *Oakbank House*, The Pleasance, T857287. 2 en suite rooms, excellent value. **F** *Falkland Backpackers*, Back Wynd, T857710, falkland@backpackers.connectfree.co.uk Open Apr-Dec.

Aside from the *Covenanter*, there's cheap food in the *Hunting Lodge Hotel*, opposite the palace, and good home baking at *Kind Kyttock's Kitchen*, Cross Wynd. Open daily except Mon. A nice cosy place for lunch or a drink is the *Stag*, a low, whitewashed 17th century pub in Mill Wynd

Transport **Buses** run daily to Kinross and from Perth, Kirkcaldy and Cupar. The nearest train station is 5 miles away at Markinch, on the Edinburgh to Dundee line.

Cupar and around

Phone code: 01334
Colour map 4,
grid C4
Population: 7,610

The main centre in the Howe of Fife is Cupar, a thriving market town that was once the administrative centre of Fife. There's an air of relative well-being about the place, verified by an array of shops catering to the retail connoisseur. In the heart of the burgh is the Castlehill which played a notable part in Cupar's history. There, the Thanes of Fife had their principle residence in ancient times and later it became the home of Sir David Lindsay. Sir David was a dramatist with a devastating wit and his play *Ane Pleasant Satyre of the Three Estaits* earned him considerable fame. It was by far the most popular play of its day and is still popular at the Edinburgh Festival.

Ins & outs Cupar is on the **Edinburgh** to **Dundee** rail line and **trains** depart in each direction roughly every hour, or every 2 hrs on Sun. **Buses** from **Dundee** to **Kirkcaldy** pass through the town, and there are direct buses to **St Andrews** every 20 mins.

Sights
The cottage at the foot of the tower can be rented from the NTS for around £250 per week, T0131-2439331

One of the main reasons for stopping off at Cupar is to visit **Hill of Tarvit,** two miles south of the town and one mile from Ceres (see below). This Edwardian mansion house was beautifully remodelled by Robert Lorimer in 1906. Among the fine collection of treasures inside are Flemish tapestries, Chinese porcelain, Dutch paintings and 18th-century French, Chippendale and vernacular furniture. The gardens are laid out in the French style, with box hedges and yew trees, and there is a woodland walk to a hilltop toposcope with a lovely view of the house. The estate includes the fine **Scotstarvit Tower**, three quarters of a mile west of the mansion house, dating from 1579. ■ *House and garden open Easter & May-Sep, weekends in Oct. £5, £4 child/concession; garden and gounds only £2/£1. Admission to tower free; key held at house.*

The **Scottish Deer Centre**, three miles west of Cupar on the A91, is both enjoyable and educational. Here you can see many species of deer at close hand,

and even feed, stroke or photograph them during a ranger-led tour. There are indoor and outdoor adventure parks for the kids as well as a restaurant and winery. ■ *Easter-31 Oct daily 1000-1800; Nov-Easter daily 1000-1700. £4, £3 child, £3.50 concession, £13 family. T01337-810391.* Those who prefer more exotic animals can head a few miles further west on the A91 to the **Fife Animal Park** at Collesie, where you can see ostriches, wallabies, emus, bison and llamas as well as more familiar breeds. ■ *Apr-May daily 1000-1800; Jun-Aug till 1900; Sep-Mar till 1600. £3.50, £3 child/concession. T01337-831830.*

B *Fernie Castle Hotel*, near Letham, 5 miles north of Cupar, T01337-810381, F810422, www.ferniecastle.demon.co.uk A beautifully restored 14th-century castle set in 17 acres of grounds with its own loch, 15 comfortable en suite rooms, lovely dining room and bar. **B-C** *Eden House Hotel*, 2 Pitscottie Rd, T652510, F652277, www.eden-group.com. Elegant Victorian town house with 11 en suite rooms and excellent restaurant, also arranges golfing packages. **D** *Lordscairnie*, Moonzie near Cupar, T/F01337-870252. Superior B&B with 4 en suite rooms, dinner available on request. **D** *Rathcluan Country House & Restaurant*, Carslogie Rd, T/F650000, www.rathcluan.co.uk. 2 en suite rooms and 3 with shared bathroom, parking and wheelchair access.

Sleeping & eating

 In the town centre there are bakeries, fish and chip shops and the obligatory Indian and Chinese restaurants and takeaways. The best place to eat in town is undoubtedly *Ostler's Close*, 25 Bonnygate, T655574, which does a 3-course lunch for under £20. The best place in the area is the renowned *Peat Inn*, 3 miles southeast of Ceres on the B940, T840206, and well worth a detour, for here, in the 18th-century building, you can sample some of the finest food in the entire country. The proprietors have a Michelin star to verify this and the French-influenced décor and ambience match the culinary excellence.

Once described as the most attractive village in Scotland, **Ceres** lies three miles south of Cupar. Whether or not you agree with that assertion, the village does present an appealing picture with its pan-tiled cottages surrounding a historic village green. Tradition says that the village and ancient cobbled bridge have been there for more than 650 years, that the men of Ceres marched across the bridge on their way to the battle of Bannockburn and on their return celebrated their victory with games on the village green. The **Highland Games** are still an annual event, on the last Saturday in June, with the Ceres Derby the highlight of the day.

Ceres

 Another special feature of Ceres is the **Fife Folk Museum**, housed in part of the 17th-century Tolbooth Weigh House and two adjoining cottages. The award-winning museum displays crafts and trades, costumes, tools and utensils of a bygone age in rural Fife. ■ *Easter and mid-May to Oct daily 1400-1700. £2.50, £2 concession, children free. T828250.* Also worth visiting is the **Griselda Hill Pottery**, at Kirkbrae. Here you can see a revival of the production of Wemyss Ware, the best-known Scottish pottery. ■ *T828273. Summer and Christmas Mon-Fri 0900-1630, Sat and Sun 1400-1700, Mon-Fri 0900-1630 in winter. Free.* A good place for a bar lunch is *Meldrums Hotel*, on Main Street, T828286.

North Fife

Four miles northwest of St Andrews is **Leuchars**, best known as an RAF base, but in the centre of the village is one of the oldest churches in Scotland. The 12th-century chancel and apse, incorporated into the parish church, are exceptional examples of Norman architecture. One mile east of Leuchars is

Colour map 4, grid C4

the privately owned **Earlshall Castle** built in 1546 by Sir William Bruce, ancestor of the present owners. This is a fine example of a 16th-century Scottish castle, very strongly built with 5-ft thick walls, battlements and gun loops. The castle is set among beautiful gardens with unusual topiary chessmen, but is not open to the general public.

Just beyond Leuchars is the B945 turning for **Tentsmuir Forest**, on the northeastern tip of Fife. There is an excellent broad sandy beach, the perfect spot for a picnic, as well as a Nature Reserve where you can see wildfowl waders and a large colony of seals sunning themselves on the sands. In 1957, on a site near Morton Farm on the Tentsmuir peninsula, evidence was found of a settlement visited seasonally by hunter-gatherers about 8,000 years ago. This remarkable site is one of the earliest human habitations in Scotland. Finds from the site are in the Dundee Museum and the Museum of Scotland in Edinburgh.

Nearby, on the shores of the Tay, is the unremarkable village of **Tayport**, from where a ferry used to cross the river to Dundee. Tayport's church tower dates from the 17th century and a plaque commemorates General Ullysses Grant's visit on his way to see the first Tay Rail Bridge, which was blown down in 1879 while a train was passing over it. A new bridge has been built since, along with the **Tay Road Bridge** (£0.80 toll), which carries you from Fife into the city of Dundee.

Five miles west of the Tay Rail Bridge, off the A914, is **Balmerino Abbey**, on a hill overlooking the river. It was founded in the 13th century by Alexander II, whose mother Ermengarde, widow of William the Lion lies buried there. Little of the abbey remains today. In 1547 it was set on fire by the English Army during the 'Rough Wooing' (see page 641) and in 1559 Knox's Reformers completed the destruction on their way back to St Andrews after 'reforming' Lindores (see below). Some of the pillars and part of the cloisters are still visible and in the orchard is a great Spanish chestnut tree, planted by the monks some 700 years ago. Unfortunately, the buildings are unsafe and inaccessible. ■ *All year. £1 (honesty box).*

Newburgh
Phone code: 01337

Lying on the south shore of the River Tay, close to Fife's western boundary, Newburgh is a Royal Burgh with a pretty little harbour and a long history. On the hill to the south of the town are the remains of MacDuff's Cross, the legendary place of sanctuary for any MacDuff who had committed a murder in hot blood. To achieve pardon, the murderer had to touch the cross, wash himself nine times at Ninewells nearby and forfeit nine cows, each of which had to be tied to the cross. If you're passing through, it's worth stopping to visit the **Laing Museum**, which shows excellent exhibitions including fossilised fish discovered in the area, a feature on Scottish emigration and Victorian displays. ■ *Apr-Sep, Mon-Fri 1000-1700, Sat-Sun 1400-1700; Oct-Mar, Wed and Fri 1200-1600, Sun 1400-1700. Free. T840223.*

Standing above the town are the ruins of **Lindores Abbey**, founded in the 12th century by David, Earl of Huntingdon. Not much of the great abbey now remains – only the gateway, part of the tower and fragments of the great walls. The abbey never recovered form the devastation visited upon it in 1559 by John Knox and his 'Congregation of the Godly'. Its ruins became a quarry whenever any building stone was needed. The views from the ruins across the Tay are lovely, especially on a summer evening.

The story of Newburgh, however, dates back much further than its abbey. A thousand years earlier, history was already being made on the eastern outskirts of the town, at Carpow. Here, in 208 AD, the Romans built a great fortress which was to be the base for their campaign against the tribes of Angus and Mearns. Unlike England, Scotland never became Romanized, and the fortress at Carpow was eventually demolished by the Romans when they withdrew to the south. Evidence of human settlement around Newburgh extends even further back in time. People built and lived in the hillfort on top of Norman's Law during the last four centuries BC. Today, its remains are accessible by public footpath from the roads north and south of the Law. Three circles of fortification can easily be traced.

St Andrews and the East Neuk

This well-groomed seaside resort on the northeastern coast of Fife is the 'Home of Golf' and a mecca for aficionados of the sport the world over. Here is the headquarters of the game's governing body, the Royal and Ancient Golf Club, and the world's most famous golf course, the Old Course. But it's not all Pringle sweaters and five irons. St Andrews has an air of calm dignity tinged with an inherent sense of history, as you'd expect from a place that was once the ecclesiastical capital of Scotland and the country's oldest seat of learning. St Andrews has avoided becoming stuffy and remains one of Scotland's smartest towns – especially now that royal pin-up Prince William is an undergraduate at its ancient university.

Phone code: 01334
Colour map 4, grid C5
Population: 13,000

Ins and outs

St Andrews, 13 miles south of Dundee and 55 miles north of Edinburgh, is not on the **train** line. The nearest station is 5 miles away at Leuchars, on the Edinurgh- Dundee-Aberdeen line. Regular **buses** make the 15-min journey from there to St Andrews. A **taxi** costs around £7. The bus station is on City Road, at the west end of town. There are frequent buses to Dundee (30 mins), the East Neuk villages and Cupar (20 mins). There is also a service to Stirling. Buses run from Edinburgh to St Andrews via Kirkcaldy.

Getting there

St Andrews is a compact town and best explored on foot. A hop- on-hop-off tour bus takes in all the main sights (see page 377). If you're driving, parking in the town centre is difficult. You need to buy vouchers (£0.80 for up to 2 hrs) from the TIC or from local shops. Taxis are available from *Golf City Taxis*, 13 Argyle St, T477788, or *St Andrews Taxis*, T477272.

Getting around

The **Tourist Information Centre**, 70 Market St, T472021, has comprehensive information about St Andrews and Northeast Fife. Open Apr-May Mon-Sat 0930-1800, Sun 1100-1600; Jun Mon-Sat 0930-1900, Sun 1100-1800; Jul-Aug Mon-Sat 0930-2000, Sun 1100-1800; Sep to mid-Oct Mon-Sat 0930-1900, Sun 1100-1800; mid-Oct to Mar Mon-Sat 0930-1700.

Information

History

St Andrews is, of course, synonymous with Scotland's patron saint. Andrew was the first of the disciples and among his many converts was the wife of the Roman Governor of Patras in Western Greece. The governor was so furious and jealous of his wife's conversion that he had Andrew crucified. Andrew asked to be tied to an X-shaped cross so that he would not appear to be emulating Christ – thus giving the Scottish flag its distinctive Saltire Cross.

According to legend, a saintly monk called Rule, or Regulus, who lived in Patras, was divinely inspired to take some of the Apostle's bones and make a

Central Scotland

journey far to the west. St Rule set off and was shipwrecked on the rocks just to the west of St Andrews harbour. After converting the Pictish king to Christianity, St Rule enshrined the sacred relics on the headland where the ruins of the 12th-century cathedral now stand. The shrine became a place of worship for Christian pilgrims from far and wide and a special ferry was kept on the river Forth to transport them. St Andrew became Scotland's patron saint and his city the ecclesiastical capital of the country.

Sights

Cathedral St Andrews' street plan has not changed since the Middle Ages. It basically consists of three main streets – North Street, Market Street and South Street – which still converge on the Cathedral standing proudly, overlooking the harbour at the eastern end of the town. Founded in 1160, it was consecrated 160 years later, in 1318, by Robert the Bruce. Medieval pilgrims came in their thousands to pray at its many altars. This explains the exceptional width of North Street, which enabled the vast numbers to proceed to the cathedral. Perched on the cliffs above the harbour are the foundations of the Church of **St Mary of the Rock**, all that remains of the ancient Celtic settlement. It fell into disuse as the church of St Rule and the Cathedral prospered.

Though devastated over the years by fire and by zealous religious reformers, the Cathedral ruins are still impressive, giving adequate proof that this was by far the largest ecclesiastical building ever to be erected in Scotland. The

St Andrews

Sleeping		
	6 Doune House	13 St Andrews
1 Amberside Guest	7 Glenderran	Tourist Hostel
House	8 Hamilton Wall	14 West Park House
2 Aslar Guest House	9 Hazelbank	
3 Cameron House	10 Old Course	● Eating
4 Craigmore Guest	11 Rusacks	1 Brambles
House	12 St Andrews Golf	2 Broons
5 Deveron House	& Ma Belles	3 Doll's House

imposing Romanesque **St Rule's Tower** is where the holy relics of the Apostle were kept until the Cathedral was completed. It's a long hard climb to the top of the tower, but the view on a clear day is well worth the effort.

The Cathedral visitor centre has a fine collection of early Christian sculptured stones from the church of St Mary of the Rock. Of particular interest is the unique eighth century Pictish sarcophagus. ■ *Cathedral and Tower open Apr-Sep daily 0930-1830; Oct-Mar Mon-Sat 0930-1630, Sun 1400-1630. £2, £0.75 child, £1.50 concession. Joint ticket with Castle £4, £1.25 child, £3 concession. T472563.*

Poised on a rocky headland overhanging the sea stands the ruin of **St Andrews Castle**. It was built at the end of the 12th century as the place and stronghold of the Bishops of St Andrews and has witnessed many violent incidents in the blood-stained history of the Scottish Church. Many reformers suffered imprisonment here, including George Wishart, whom the infamous Cardinal Beaton had burnt at the stake in front of the castle in 1546. His initials can be seen picked out in cobble-stones on the roadway near the entrance.

Castle

Following the martyrdom of Wishart, a group of avenging Protestants gained entry to the castle disguised as stone masons and brutally murdered Beaton. His body was then hung over the battlements for all to see. After the murder the reformers held the castle against siege for a year until they capitulated to the French fleet. The castle fell into ruin in the 17th century, but two very notable features remain. In the northwest tower is the grim bottle dungeon, hollowed out of solid rock and from which death was the only release. Also of note is the mine and countermine, tunnelled through the rock during the siege that followed Cardinal Beaton's murder. The besiegers started their tunnel, but were thwarted by the defenders who tried to intercept them. Uncertainty about who was there led to its abandonment. A fascinating exhibition in the visitor centre brings the history of the castle to life. ■ *Opening times as for the Cathedral. £2.80, £1 child, £2 concession. Joint ticket with Cathedral available (see above). T477196.*

North Sea

St Andrews Castle

E Scores

Museum of St Andrews Preservation Trust

Cathedral

Kirk Hill

Queen Mary's House

St Rule's Tower

The Pends

Shorehead

Pier Harbour

East Sands

St Leonard's School

Abbey St

Abbey Walk

Castle St

N Castle St

6

To Crail, Anstruther & Grange Inn (A917)

4 Get Juiced
5 Jahangir
6 Janetta's
7 La Posada
8 New Balaka Bangladeshi
9 Peter Michael's
10 The Vine Leaf

11 Victoria Café

● Bars & pubs
12 Drothy Neeboars
13 Dunvegan
14 Ogston's
15 West Port

The University of St Andrews, founded in 1410 by Henry Wardlaw, Bishop of St Andrews, is the third-oldest in Britain after Oxford and Cambridge. Among its many fine buildings is the **Church of St Salvator** in North Street. The first of its colleges, St Salvator's was founded by Bishop Kennedy in 1450. The Bishop's niece, Kate, was said to be so beautiful that all the students were in love with her. Today's students still pay homage to her pulchritude in the

University
The university was thrust into the media spotlight recently due to the arrival of a certain William Windsor as an undergraduate

Central Scotland

The Home of golf

The Royal and Ancient Golf Club of St Andrews is the ruling house of golf worldwide and a mecca for all who play or follow the game. On any one day during the summer, you'll see many addicts staring reverentially across the most famous stretch of golf course in the world. The imposing 1854 clubhouse overlooks the first and 18th holes and you can enter by invitation only. Anyone, however, can play on the six courses at St Andrews, including the historic Old Course itself.

The citizens of St Andrews have been playing golf on these Links for a very long time, even before 1457 when the Scottish Parliament tried to ban the game. No one in the town took the ban seriously and by 1553 they had an inalienable right to play golf on the Links. The game developed and acquired popularity in the highest circles – even Mary, Queen of Scots was known to indulge in the odd round or two. The new craze was getting out of hand, however, and towards the end of the 16th century there was a spate of church absenteeism caused by people slipping off for a quick 18 holes. Two men were brought before the Kirk session in 1598 for "prophaning of the Saboth day in playing at the gouf eftir nune". As it was a first offence they got off with an admonition.

By the 17th and 18th centuries St Andrews was very much in decline, but exciting things were happening in the world of golf. In 1754 some 22 noblemen, mostly landowners in Fife, decided to move their golfing activities from Edinburgh to St Andrews. And so the exclusive Society of St Andrews Golfers, the forerunner of the Royal and Ancient Golf Club, came into existence. It was that fortunate decision that saved St Andrews turning into a ghost town and it has never looked back since.

Kate Kennedy Pageant (see below). The bishop's tomb is in the church, along with a magnificent mace from his time, which is still carried on special occasions. The pulpit is the very one from which John Knox delivered his firebrand sermons in the Parish Church. The initials PH laid in the pavement outside the entrance mark the spot where Patrick Hamilton, one of the early reformers, was burned in 1528.

Other parts of the University include **St Mary's College**, in South Street, founded in 1537 by Archbishop James Beaton, uncle of the notorious cardinal. **Queen Mary's House**, in South Street by the Cathedral, is where the ill-fated queen stayed in 1563. Charles II also stayed here, in 1650. The house was restored in 1927 and is now used as St Leonard's school library. During her stay Queen Mary planted a thorn tree that still flourishes in the quadrangle of St Mary's college. **St Leonard's College**, on Pends Road which leads from the end of South Street down to the harbour, was founded in 1512 but then amalgamated with St Salvator's in 1747. The present buildings now house a private girls' school.

Other sights St Andrews has many other notable historic buildings and monuments. The **West Port** (c.1580) at the west end of South Street, was the main entrance to the old town and is one of the few surviving city gates in Scotland. All that remains of **Blackfriars Chapel**, a small Dominican church, is a single apse. Rebuilt around 1515, its remains are in South Street, beside Madras College. Opposite the Tourist Information Centre in South Street is the **Holy Trinity Church**, rebuilt in 1410, which was modified in the late 18th century and restored in the 20th century. Inside, Archbishop Sharp's monument graphically records his brutal murder in 1679 on Magus Muir.

History envelops St Andrews; every street and building has its own story. So it's a real pleasure just to wander aimlessly through its narrow alleyways (or

Central Scotland

'closes') that connect the medieval streets and discover its many hidden delights. A good example is **Louden's Close**, between Blackfriars and the West Port. Alternatively, stroll down **The Pends** by the Cathedral to the quaint old harbour; here, during term time, you might see the Sunday Parade of University students processing from the chapel in their scarlet medieval gowns that were introduced so that they could be spotted easily when entering the local brothels.

As well as an impressive history, St Andrews has other attractions. There are two fine sandy **beaches**, the **East and West Sands**, that enclose the town like golden bookends. The latter provided the setting for the opening sequence in the film *Chariots of Fire*. If you've got children, then the huge **St Andrews Aquarium** is a must. Situated on The Scores, at the west end of town near the Golf Museum (see above), this is where you can legally indulge in any number of piscean pleasures with an array of weird and wonderful sea creatures. ■ *Daily in summer 1000-1800; phone for winter opening hours. £4.50, £3.50 child, £3.85 concession, £17 family. T474786, www.standrewsaquarium*

The history of golf, and the town's intimate association with it, are all to be discovered in the **British Golf Museum**, standing directly behind the Royal and Ancient Clubhouse on Bruce Embankment. It is the most exciting of its kind, and audio-visual displays and touch activated screens bring the game to life and trace its development through the centuries. ■ *Easter to mid-Oct daily 0930-1730; mid-Oct to Easter Thu-Mon 1100-1500. £3.75, £1.50 children, £2.75 concession, £9.50 family. T460046, www.britishgolfmuseum.co.uk*

The **St Andrews Preservation Trust Museum**, at 12 North Street, has a number of fascinating displays including 19th-century shop interiors. ■ *Easter weekend 1100-1700 and May-Oct daily 1400-1700. Free. T477629.* Also worth a visit is the **St Andrews Museum**, in Kinburn Park near the bus station, which charts the history of the town from earliest times. ■ *Apr-Sep daily 1000-1700; Oct-Mar Mon-Fri 1030-1600, Sat/Sun 1230-1700. Free. T412690.* The **Botanic Gardens** on Canongate offer a peaceful retreat, only 10 minutes walk south of South Street. ■ *Daily all year 1000-1600. £2, £1 child/concession. T476452.*

Two miles west of the town centre on the B939 is **Craigtoun Country Park**. The park has an **Italian Garden**, a **Dutch Village** surrounded by an ornamental lake, a miniature railway, putting green, boating, trampolines a licensed restaurant and picnic area. ■ *End-Apr to end-Aug daily 1030-1730; Apr and Sep weekends only 1030-1730. £3, £2.50 child, £2 concession, £10 family. T473666.*

Essentials

St Andrews has plentiful accommodation, from humble B&Bs to international-class hotels, but advance booking is still advisable during the summer months.

L *Old Course Hotel*, T474371, F477668, www.oldcoursehotel.co.uk Internationally renowned golf resort and spa overlooking the 17th hole, 125 en suite rooms, bar and restaurants. **L** *Rufflets Country House Hotel*, Strathkinnes Low Rd, T472594, F478703, www.rufflets.co.uk Small country house set in 10 acres of grounds on the outskirts of town by the B939, with 25 en suite rooms and good restaurant. **L** *Rusacks Hotel*, Pilmour Links, T474321, F477896, www.heritage-hotels.com Recently refurbished, bar and restaurant overlooking the 1st and 18th holes, 48 en suite rooms. **L** *The Parkland Hotel*, Kinburn Castle, Double Dykes Rd, T473620, F460850, www.parklandstandrews.com A 19th-century castle in the town centre, its restaurant is highly-praised.

Sleeping
■ *on map*
Price codes:
see inside front cover

There are several hotels lining The Scores, overlooking the bay. At No 40 is **L-A** *St Andrews Golf Hotel*, T472611, F472188, www.standrews-golf.co.uk 22 comfortable en suite rooms, good restaurant with extensive wine list, specialize in golfing breaks. Cheaper but still comfortable is **B-C** *Hazelbank Hotel*, at No 28, T/F472466, www.hazelbank.com 10 en suite rooms.

Most of the **guesthouses** are around Murray Pk and Murray Pl between The Scores and North Street. Among those recommended are: **D-E** *Amberside Guest House*, 4 Murray Pk, T/F474644, amberside@talk21.com; **D-E** *Cameron House*, 11 Murray Pk, T472306, F479529, www.cameronhouse-sta.co.uk; **C-D** *Craigmore Guest House*, 3 Murray Park, T472142, F477963; **D-E** *Doune House*, 5 Murray Pl, T/F475195, dounehouse@aolc.om; **C-D** *Glenderran*, 9 Murray Pk, T477951, F477908, glenderran@telinco.com Also in the centre of town are **D** *Aslar Guest House*, 120 North St, T473460, F477540, www.aslar.com, and **D-E** *West Park House*, 5 St Mary's Pl, T475933, F476634, rosemary@westparksta.freeserve.com

Between Jun and Sep, the **university** rents out rooms on a B&B basis, with dinner optional, in **D** *Hamilton Hall* and **C-D** *New Hall*, at 79 North St, T462000, F462500, www.st-and.ac.uk/services/resbus/Homepage.html; or book through the TIC. The cheapest option is the new **F** *St Andrews Tourist Hostel*, Inchcape House, St Mary's Pl, T479911, F479988, www.hostelsaccommodation.com

Eating

There is no shortage of restaurants, cafés and bars,

Expensive The best restaurant in the area, and one of the best in Britain, is the *Peat Inn*, about 7 miles south of St Andrews, on the B940 (see page 369). Another excellent restaurant out of town is *The Grange Inn*, on the Crail Rd, near Kinkell Braes overlooking the East Sands, T472670, F462604. Many of the hotels have good restuarants, such as the *Parkland*, *St Andrews Golf* and the *Rusacks*. *The Vine Leaf*, 131 South St, T477497, has a deservedly high reputation which is matched by the prices.

Mid-range The *New Balaka Bangladeshi Restaurant*, T474825, at the corner of St Mary's Pl and Alexandra Pl, is *the* place to go for a curry. It was recently voted "Best Curry in Scotland". Another good Indian restaurant is *Jahangir*, 116a, South St, T470300. There's also *Café India*, at 64 Market St, T477778, which offers a 'Student Special' 3-course meal plus 2 drinks for under a tenner. One of the nicest places for lunch, a light snack or coffee and cakes is *Brambles*, 5 College St beside the Market Sq. *The Dolls' House*, 3 Church Sq, T477422, is run by Carol Smillie's husband and offers a good value set lunch and early dinner. *Broons*, 117 North St, is a stylish new bistro next dooro to the *New Picture House*. For Mexican food try *La Posada*, on St Mary's Pl, T470500, open daily 1100-2300.

The best places for cheap food are the pubs and bars (see below)

Cheap The *Victorian Café*, 1 St Mary's Pl, is a popular student hang-out, serving snacks and drinks. The best chip shop is *Peter Michael's* on the coner of Market St and Union St. The best place for ice cream is the wonderful *Janetta's*, at 31 South St, near the Byre Theatre (don't confuse with the smaller branch at the other end of South St). You can choose from 52 flavours, including Irn Bru sorbet. *Get Juiced*, 149 South St, T472927, is a juice bar, also with panini and wraps and internet access.

Pubs & bars

There are a lot of good pubs to satisfy the large student population

Ogston's, 116 South St, T473473, is a good café-bar/bistro serving a wide range of moderate-cheap dishes. The *Central Bar*, on Market St, is a favourite with locals and students. In the basement of the *St Andrews Golf Hotel* is *Ma Belle's*, T472611, open daily till 2400, which attracts students and locals alike (it is Prince William's local) and serves cheap bar meals. *West Port*, South St by the West Port, is a stylish bar offering a good selection of sandwiches and vegetarian dishes, nice beer garden. Restaurant upstairs serves Pacific Rim cuisine. There's always a warm welcome at the *Dunvegan*, in Pilmour Pl, the most convivial of drinking dens. A good pub for real ales is *Droothy Neebors*, in South St near West Port. They serve food all day.

The **Byre Theatre**, on Abbey St, T475000, www.byretheatre.com, stages an excellent range of productions throughout the year and began its life in a cowshed of the old Abbey St Dairy Farm, hence its name. The **Crawford Arts Centre**, in North St, T474610, has a changing programme of art exhibitions, professional theatre and music performances in its drama studio and galleries. The only cinema in town is the **New Picture House**, in North St.

Lammas Fair is Scotland's oldest surviving medieval market, with showmen from all over Britain setting up stalls and booths in the three main streets. This bright, lively carnival is held in early **Aug**. The other main event in the town's calendar is the **Kate Kennedy Pageant**, usually held on the 3rd Sat in **Apr**.

St Andrews has a good range of independent shops, most of which are in South St, Market St, Bell St and Church St. Two of particular interest are in Burghers Close, a little cobbled courtyard at 141 South St: *Di Gilpin Designer Knitwear*, T476193, open daily 1000-1800; and *Wind & Water*, T460600, which sells a wide range of kites. A good out- door equipment shop is *Aktive 8*, at 109A South St, T473999, www.active8.co.uk And of course there's the **St Andrews Woollen Mill**, overlooking the 18th holf of the Old Course, the palace of Pringle and capital of cashmere, where you can purchase those essential tactile souvenirs.

Golf As well as the legendary Old Course, there are no fewer than 5 other 18-hole courses in and around the town: Duke's Course (T474371); Eden Course; Jubilee ; New ; and Strathtyrum. For information and reserving tee-times on all except the Duke's, T466666. Green fees range from £17 up to £80 for the Old Course (day ticket). **Sports Centres** *University of St Andrews*, St Leonard's Rd, T462190, www.st-and.ac.uk Open Mon-Fri 0900-2200, Sat 0900-2100, Sun 1100-2100. Gym, squash courts, sunbed, fitness suite, etc.

The open-top tour bus is a hop-on-hop-off service which leaves from the bus station every hour from 0930 till 1630, Fri-Mon May-Oct; also Tue, Wed and Thu Jul/Aug. Stops include TIC, Golf Museum, Cathedral and Botanic Gardens. £5.50, £2.75 child, £4.50 concession. T474238. *The Original St Andrews Witches Tour* run Apr-Sep on Fri at 2000 (also Sun in Jun and Thu and Sun in Jul/Aug), Oct-Mar Fri at 1930. £6, £4 child. T655057. *St Andrews Guided Walks* leave from Church Sq at 1100 on Wed till end-Oct. £4, £3.50 concession, child under 12 free. T850638.

Banks There are banks with ATMs in Market St and South St. Also bureau de change at the TIC. **Medical services** Accident and Emergency (A&E) 24 hrs at Memorial Hospital, Abbey Walk, T472327. Health Centre, Pipeland Rd, T476840, 24 hrs. **Communications** Internet access at *Get Juiced* (see above). **Police** North St, T418900. **Toilets** Church Sq (disabled and baby changing facilities); on City Rd; at the Harbour; West Sands car park.

The East Neuk

Fife was described by King James VI as "a beggar's mantle fringed with gold". The golden fringe to which he referred was the East Neuk (or nook, meaning corner). Here, on Fife's easternmost stretch of coastline are some of the kingdom's greatest attractions. From Largo Bay to Fife Ness lies a string of picturesque villages, each with its own distinctive character and charm. These were once thriving seaports trading with the Low Countries. The Dutch influence lives on in their architectural styles. The red pan-tiled roofs and crow-stepped gables lend a particular continental feel to one of the most attractive corners of Scotland.

Robinson Crusoe

In a humble cottage down by the shore at Lower Largo, Alexander Selkirk spent his boyhood. By the age of 15 he was a strapping lad with a fierce temper, and in one particular incident the Minister and Kirk session were appalled to hear that he had threatened to blow out both his brother's and father's brains.

Young Alex went to sea after that and, in 1704, he set off for the South Seas as a sailing master in the vessel Cinque Ports. Eight months had elapsed when Selkirk had a violent quarrel with the captain and, at his own request, went ashore on the uninhabited island of Juan Fernández, off the coast of Chile.

Four years and four months later, Selkirk saw two ships approaching the island and, lighting a fire to attract their attention, ran along the shore to meet them. He was dressed completely in goat skins. However, by the time he returned home to Lower Largo, he had amassed a small fortune in pirate booty and his clothes were somewhat more elegant. So much so that his mother didn't even recognize him.

This was the story that was related to Daniel Defoe when the two met in a London coffee house in 1715 – the fiery-tempered Fifer was later immortalized in Defoe's tale of Robinson Crusoe.

Ins & outs   **Getting there**   The No 95 **bus** runs every hour between **Dundee** and **Leven**, via St Andrews, Crail, Anstruther, Pittenweem, St Monans and Elie.

Lundin Links & Largo
Phone code: 01333
Colour map 4, grid C4

Lundin Links is the most westerly of the East Neuk villages. It is popular with the golfing fraternity and boasts some fine courses. On the ladies course you can see three large standing stones, reminders of the Bronze Age peoples who once populated this area. Next door to Lundin Links is **Lower Largo**, best known as the birthplace of Alexander Selkirk, the real-life Robinson Crusoe. His statue can be seen in the main street running behind the *Crusoe Hotel*. This was once an important fishing centre. Now it is a popular holiday resort with its golden crescent of sand and picturesque little harbour, framed by an impressive railway viaduct.

Sleeping and eating L-C *Old Manor Hotel*, Leven Rd, Lundin Links, T320368, F320911, www.oldmanorhotel.co.uk Overlooking Largo Bay, 24 en suite rooms, good seafood menu in bistro and bar. For good bar meals try the *Crusoe Hotel*, by the harbour in Lower Largo. *Scotland's Larder*, T360414, on the road east out of Upper Largo, provides a real insight into Scottish food with its restaurant, shop and cooking demonstrations. Booking for dinner is essential. Open Apr-Nov daily 1000-late, Nov-Mar Sun-Thu 1100-1500, Fri and Sat from 1100.

Elie & Earlsferry
Phone code: 01333
Colour map 4, grid C5

Heading east from Largo, the next coastal villages are Elie and Earlsferry, which are really two halves of the same place. This is one of Fife's most popular resorts, with a mile of lovely sandy beaches, and is very popular with sailors and windsurfers. There are also two golf courses – a nine-hole and an 18-hole.

There is an exclusive air about Elie, which is only enhanced by the tale that, at one time, fish and chips were banned from the town! Like its neighbours, though, it shares the distinctive Dutch-influenced architecture. The **Lady's Tower**, a short walk from the harbour, recalls a more aristocratic past. The tower was built as a bathing box for Lady Janet Anstruther, a noted beauty of the 18th century. The whole town knew when Lady Janet was bathing, for she sent a bellman round the streets to warn the inhabitants to stay away.

Elie's westerly neighbour is the much older burgh of Earlsferry. There are three caves in the rock face at **Kincraig Point**, the headland at the far end of a broad sandy beach: the Deil's (Devil's) Cave; Doo's (dove's) Cave; and the spectacular MacDuff's Cave, where the Thane (Earl) of Fife is said to have hidden from Shakespeare's Macbeth, until fishermen rowed him across the Forth to safety. Hence the town's name.

Sleeping and eating B-C *The Golf Hotel*, Bank St, Elie, T330209, F330381, www.golfhotel.co.uk Very comfortable accommodation, 22 en suite rooms, restaurant, will arrange teeing off times for St Andrew and local courses. For tasty bar meals and a good pint try the *Ship Inn*, down by Elie harbour. The best place to eat is the highly acclaimed *Bouquet Garni*, on the High St, T330374. It's open for lunch and 1900-2100; closed Sun. No smoking. Mid-range.

Sports *Elie Waterpsorts* by the harbour, T330962, offer windsurfing, sailing, water-skiing and canoe hire and instruction and also hire out mountain bikes (£9 per day).

Further along the coast, St Monans was once one of Scotland's busiest fishing ports, a fact that is emphasized by the presence of Miller's boatyard by the harbour. This is one of the oldest surviving boat-builders, established in 1747 and still producing traditional fishing boats. Other reminders of the town's sea-faring past remain. The tiny fishermen's church stands so close to the sea that during winter storms the spray rises over the churchyard wall to wash the gravestones in the cemetery. The present foundations of the church date from 1362, but the original church dates from a century earlier.

St Monans
Phone code: 01333
Colour map 4, grid C5

Eating It's worth stopping at the *Seafood Restaurant & Bar*, 16 West End, just off the A917, T730327 for some excellent seafood. Mid-range. Open 1200-1500 (1230 on Sun) and 1800-2300 Sat. Closed Mon.

This is the home of the East Neuk fishing fleet with a thriving fish market and harbour crammed with fishing boats. It is well worth rising early to come here and witness the landing of the catch. At the east end of the harbour is **The Gyles**, an attractive group of 16th- and 17th-century houses beautifully restored by the NTS and boasting some fine examples of Dutch-style gables.

The oldest house by far in Pittenweem is in **Cove Wynd**, which climbs steeply up to the High Street from the East Shore overlooking the harbour. In the seventh century the early Christian missionary, **St Fillan** lived here in a **cave**, dug deep into the rock. All through the middle ages pilgrims came to visit the cave. This primitive dwelling gave the town its name, for in the Pictish tongue, the word means 'place of the cave'. ■ *To visit the cave, collect the key from the Gingerbread Horse in the High St. T311495.*

The pilgrims who visited the shrine received hospitality at the 12th-century **Priory**, established by Augustinian monks from the Isle of May. The remains can be seen in the Marygate, behind the Episcopal church. Nearby, in the High Street is the impressive 16th-century Parish church and **Kellie Lodge**, also 16th-century, town house of the Earls of Kellie and an excellent example of vernacular style architecture.

Three miles inland from Pittenweem, on the B9171, stands **Kellie Castle**, one of the oldest and most magnificent of Scottish castles. This is 16th- and 17th-century domestic architecture at its best, though the oldest part of the castle dates from 1360. Owned by the Oliphants for over 250 years, then by the Earls of Mar and Kellie, the castle was saved from ruin over a century ago by Professor James Lorimer. The interior is notable for its superb plasterwork ceilings, which were then the height of fashion. The castle's 16 acres of

Pittenweem
Phone code: 01333
Colour map 4, grid C5

Central Scotland

beautifully landscaped gardens were designed by Lorimer's son, Robert, who became a well-known architect specializing in restoration. Among his works is the Hill of Tarvit, near Cupar (see page 368). His grandson, the sculptor Huw Lorimer, also lived here. ■ *Castle open Easter to end-Sep, and weekends in Oct, 1330-1730. Garden and grounds open Apr-Sep daily 0930-2100; Oct-Mar till 1630. £5, £4 concession/child, £14 family. Bus Nos 61A/B runs from St Andrews to Arncroach and passes the castle entrance four times daily, except Sun (1 hr).*

Anstruther

Phone code: 01333
Colour map 4, grid C5
Population: 3,270

Known locally as Anster (pronounced enster), this is the largest of the East Neuk villages. Today, it is best known as the home of the Scottish Fisheries Museum, but it was Scotland's main fishing port at the end of the 19th century, with almost 1,000 boats in its fleet. Next to the Fisheries museum is the helpful **Tourist Information Centre**; open Easter to mid-September Monday, Friday-Saturday 1000-1700, Tuesday-Thursday 1000-1300 and 1400-1700, Sunday 1200-1700. T311073.

Like its neighbours, Anster traded with the Low Countries and Scandinavia, before becoming an important centre for herring fishing. This proud heritage has been well preserved in **The Scottish Fisheries Museum**, which faces the harbour on the site of the pre-Reformation St Ayles chapel. The museum, established in 1969, gives a fascinating insight into the life and work of a fishing community and is well worth a visit. There's also a fine collection of actual and model fishing boats, equipment, maps and compasses, as well as an aquarium. ■ *Apr-Sep Mon-Sat 1000-1730, Sun 1100-1700; Oct-Mar Mon-Sat 1000-1630, Sun 1200-1630. £3.50, £2.50 concession/child. T310628.*

Moored in the harbour opposite the museum is the **North Carr Lightship**. For more than 40 years she did service off Fife Ness and is now a museum where you can picture what life must have been like for the seven-man crew in those cramped conditions for weeks on end.

Three miles north of Anstruther, just off the B9131 to St Andrews at Troy Wood, is **Scotland's Secret Bunker**, one of Fife's most fascinating attractions. This was to have been the government HQ for Scotland in the event of nuclear war and was only opened to the public in 1994. In fact, part of the complex is still operational and remains secret, as do the equivalent centres in England and Wales. The approach is through an innocuous-looking farmhouse, then visitors descend via a huge ramp to the bunker, 30 m underground and encased in 5 m of reinforced concrete. The bunker could house 300 people and was to be fitted with air filters, an electricity generator and its own water supply. It even had a couple of cinemas, which are now used to show a rather frightening 1950s newsreel giving instructions to civilians on what to do in the event of nuclear attack. Aside from the café and gift shop, the bunker has been left exactly as it was in the 1950s. ■ *Apr to end-Oct daily 1000-1700. £6.95, £3.75 child, £5.45 concession. T310301, www.secretbunker.co.uk The direct St Andrews to Anstruther bus takes you to the turn-off for Troy Wood, then it's a 1-mile walk.*

During the summer months boats from Anstruther visit the **Isle of May**, five miles offshore, guarding the mouth of the Firth of Forth. The approach to the island's impressive cliffs is spectacular. The island became a national Nature Reserve in 1956 and is home to a large population of puffins, shags, guillemots, razorbills and kittiwakes as well as seals. The island has an intriguing history. It was home to the Benedictine Priors who came in remembrance of St Adrian, the Christian missionary who was murdered there in AD 870 and the remains of whose chapel can still be seen. The first lighthouse in

Scotland, built here in 1636, can also be seen. The present lighthouse was built by Robert Louis Stevenson's grandfather in 1816. ■ *There is one sailing daily from May to end-Sep (not on Fri from May-mid Jul). £13, £6 child, £11 concession. T310103 (24 hours).*

Sleeping and eating B-C *Craw's Nest Hotel*, Bankwell Rd, T310691, F312216, www.smoothhoud.co.uk/hotels/crawsnes.html Very good hotel with restaurant and full range of facilties, 50 en suite rooms. There are plenty of good **guesthouses** and **B&Bs**. **D-E** *Beaumont Lodge*, 43 Pittenweem Rd, T/F310315, reservations@beau-lodge.demon.co.uk. Superior guesthouse with 4 en suite rooms which also serves good evening meals. **D-E** *The Grange*, 45 Pittenweem Rd, T/F310842, www.thegrangeanstruther.fsnet.co.uk 7 en suite rooms. **E** *The Sheiling*, 32 Glenogil Gardens, T310697.

Several hotels and pubs serve bar meals, including the *Craw's Nest* and the cosy *Dreel Tavern*, on High St West, while the *Anstruther Fish Bar*, on Shore St, does a mean takeaway fish supper. A restaurant of particular note is *The Cellar*, 24 East Green, just behind the Fisheries Museum, T310378. The seafood here is among the finest in the country and will set you back around £30 for a 3-course dinner.

Crail

Phone code: 01333
Colour map 4, grid C5

Three miles northeast of Anstruther and 10 miles from St Andrews is the most ancient and picturesque of all Fife's Royal Burghs. Crail was once the largest fishmarket in Europe and for centuries its ships returned from the Low Countries and Scandinavia laden with cargo. Today you're more likely to see tourists than fishermen, but you can still buy fresh lobster and shellfish here.

Centuries ago, the town's rich merchants built their handsome houses round the market place. At the far end of the Marketgate, is the **Collegiate Church of St Mary**, whose origin goes back to the 12th century. During the building of the church the Devil is said to have hurled a great boulder at it from the Isle of May. The boulder split as it flew through the air and one part landed only 30 m from the churchyard gate. It still sits there, bearing the Devil's thumbprint.

At the other end of the Marketgate is the **Tolbooth**, dating from the early 16th century, now serving as the town hall. In the striking Dutch tower is a bell dated 1520, cast in Holland. Also in the Marketgate is the **Museum and Heritage Centre** which shows much of the history of the town. ■ *Apr-May weekends and public holidays 1400-1700; Jun-Sep Mon-Sat 1000-1300 and 1400-1700, Sun 1400-1700. Free.* There's a **Tourist Information Centre** at the Museum and Heritage Centre, T450869, open Easter-September. Crail's real attraction, however, is its beautiful **harbour**, surrounded by whitewashed cottages with pan-tiled roofs and crow-stepped gables. It is one of the most photographed locations in all of Scotland and a favourite with artists. To reach the old harbour you go down the steep, winding Shoregate. At the foot of the Shoregate is the 19th-century customs house.

Sleeping and eating D-E *Marine Hotel*, 54 Nethergate, T450207, F451145. 9 en suite rooms, restaurant, good cheap bar meals. **E** *Caiplie Guest House*, 53 High St, T/F450564. 3 en suite rooms and 2 with shared bathroom. Excellent 3-course dinner available. Also good for cheap bar food is the *Golf Hotel*.

Central Scotland

Northeast Scotland

9

Northeast Scotland

The northeast of Scotland is the huge triangle of land
that thrusts defiantly into the harsh North Sea and
comprises the regions of Aberdeenshire, Moray and
Angus, and the cities of **Aberdeen** and **Dundee**,
Scotland's third and fourth largest cities respectively. This
is a hard-working region based on agriculture, fishing
and, more recently, the oil industry, and its people typify
the stereotype of the dour, determined and thrifty Scot.

The region may lack the sheer drama and majesty of
the northwest, but the coast and countryside between the
Firth of Tay and the Moray Firth have their own, more
subtle charms – and better weather. The **Moray Firth**,
from the hardy fishing port of Fraserburgh west to the
Findhorn community, has some of the country's most
dramatic coastal scenery, with perfect little fishing
villages clinging for dear life to storm-battered cliffs.
There are also long stretches of apricot-coloured beaches,
long hours of sunshine, and even dolphins frolicking in
the waters offshore. Flowing into the Moray Firth is the
River Spey, whose gentle, wooded valley is the centre of
Scotland's malt whisky industry.

Another of the region's assets is its rich history. This is
castle country and there are over 70 in Aberdeenshire
and Moray alone. One of the most famous is Balmoral
Castle, forever linked to the royal family since Queen
Victoria came, saw and purchased in 1852. So strong is
the connection that this area is better known as 'Royal
Deeside' and visitors can indulge in a bit of royal
spotting at the annual Braemar Gathering, the local
Highland Games.

Northeast Scotland

Ins and outs

Getting around Dundee and Aberdeen are connected by the fast A90 which runs inland through Angus before linking up with the coastal A92 near Stonehaven. Regular **buses** ply between the two cities, and there's a good **rail** link, connecting Aberdeen and Dundee to Edinburgh. Trains also run northwest from Aberdeen to Inverness, passing through Elgin and other inland towns. There's a fairly good bus service throughout the north-east, as well as a limited network of **postbuses** serving the Angus glens. Only the most remote and mountainous parts of the region cannot be reached by public transport. For more details of transport in Aberdeenshire and Moray, see page 411, and for Dundee and Angus see page 393.

Dundee

Phone code: 01382
Colour map 4, grid B4
Population: 177,500

Scotland's fourth largest city sits on two prominent hills, Balgay and the Law, overlooking the River Tay. Few cities in Britain can match Dundee's impressive setting, seen at its breathtaking best from across the Tay, in Fife. But, despite the common consensus that the views of the city are indeed spectacular, certain guide books have suggested that visitors keep their distance. Which just goes to show how out of touch they are, for Dundee has transformed itself into a vibrant, thriving city and an increasingly popular destination for tourists.

One of Dundee's big attractions is Captain Scott's ship, the Discovery, *and such is the civic pride engendered by its return home that Dundee has become widely known through its slogan – City of Discovery. There are other, less publicized, attractions, such as the Law Hill, which commands fantastic views over the city and the Tay estuary, and the attractive seaside suburb of Broughty Ferry. Dundee also has a thriving arts scene and plenty of good shops, bars and restaurants. But the city's best kept secret is its people. The accent may at first be somewhat impenetrable, but Dundonians have an endearing earthy humour and are the friendliest bunch of people you'll find anywhere on the east coast of Scotland.*

Ins and outs

Getting there Dundee's **airport**, T643224, is on Riverside Drive, about a 5-min drive west of the city centre. There are no buses to the centre. A taxi will cost around £2. For flight information, see page 393. The **bus station**, T228345, is on Seagate, a few hundred yards east of the City Square. All regional and national buses arrive here (for details, see page 393). **Trains** into Dundee arrive at Taybridge Station, T228046, a few hundred yards south of the High St, across the dual carriageway at the foot of Union St. For details of train services, see page 393. By **car** the best approach is from the south, across the Tay Road Bridge (80p toll; payable heading south only), which gives a spectacular introduction to the city. Alternatively, the city is reached via the A90, from Aberdeen to the north or Perth to the west. Coming from Perth, turn on to Riverside Drive at the Invergowrie roundabout for the city centre.

Getting around Dundee city centre is fairly compact and most of the sights are within walking distance of each other. For outlying sights, the city is served by an efficient bus service. **Buses** heading west along the Perth Rd pass along the High St, stopping at the city square. Heading northwards, buses leave from Albert Square, behind the McManus Galleries, and buses heading east towards Broughty Ferry leave from outside Littlewoods on the High St.

Northeast Scotland

Things to do in Northeast Scotland

- Head down to the attractive little fishing village of Auchmithie and enjoy some superb seafood at the But'n'Ben restaurant.
- Visit Dufftown, self-proclaimed 'Malt Whisky Capital of the World' and begin the tour of the region's many distilleries.
- If you're not all castled-out, then crack on down to Crathes, the perfect fairytale castle, which, unbelievably, is almost overhshadowed by its gorgeous gardens.
- If all that royal-spotting leaves you cold, then head for the Lonach Highland Gathering, held in August, and frequented by the likes of Billy Connolly and Judi Dench.

For information on city buses, phone Dundee District Council Transport Division, T433125. Local services are run by *Travel Dundee*, T201121, and *Strathtay Scottish*, T228054. Day passes (£3) can be bought on board buses or at the Travel Dundee shop at the top of Commercial St. There are **taxi** ranks on Nethergate and High St, or call *City Cabs*, T566666, or *Tele Taxis*, T889333.

The very helpful **Tourist Information Centre** is at 21 Castle St, T527527, F527551, www.angusanddundee.co.uk, a short walk from the train station. They provide extensive details and free leaflets for all Dundee's attractions. They also sell bus tickets, book accommodation and have a good souvenir shop. You can pick up a free copy of the monthly *What's On* listings magazine here. Open Jun-Sep Mon-Sat 0900-1800, Sun 1200-1600; Oct-May Mon-Sat 0900-1700.

Information
The two local newspapers the Courier & the Evening Telegraph are good sources of information

History

The name Dundee is derived from the Gaelic words 'dun' meaning hill or fort and 'daig', who was thought to be an early local chieftain. Dundee has been settled since prehistoric times, and Pictish earthworks and chambers can still be seen at Tealing, Ardestie and Carlungie, just beyond the city's boundaries. The city was an important trading port as long ago as the 12th century, and it was here that Robert the Bruce was proclaimed King of Scots in 1309. Its importance, however, made it a prime target for a succession of English invaders. It was captured by Edward I, besieged by Henry VIII, destroyed by Royalists and Cromwell's army during the Civil War, and then again by Viscount Dundee prior to the Battle of Killiecrankie. The young William Wallace, the fiery Scottish patriot, was educated in Dundee, and during its occupation by Edward's forces Wallace stabbed the son of an English overlord for daring to insult him, and had to flee south. A plaque on the High Street marks the spot where the incident took place.

Dundee is famous within Scotland as the city of the three J's; **Jute**, **Jam** and **Journalism**. These three industries were part of the city's commercial success, and the jute mills in particular, from the early 19th century, were the foundation of the city's wealth. Along with Edinburgh, Dundee became a centre for investment trusts which sunk cash into ventures all over the world, particularly the USA. In 1873 Dundee jute man Robert Fleming set up the Scottish Investment Trust to channel money into US cattle ranches, mining companies and railways. The biggest cattle ranch in the USA was run from Dundee until 1951 and the Texas oil industry was largely financed by Dundee jute wealth. The jam-making came about almost by accident, when a ship carrying a cargo of oranges was forced to put into Dundee harbour during a storm. A

Northeast Scotland

local grocer bought the oranges, which his wife then made into marmalade, and an industry was born.

Journalism is the only 'J' still in operation in the city. DC Thomson are now the city's largest employers outside the health and leisure industries, and continue to produce many newspapers and magazines. Perhaps their most famous creations are the children's comics *The Dandy* and *The Beano*, begun in 1937 and 1938 respectively and still going strong. Generations of British children have been brought up on the antics of *Dennis the Menace*, *Desperate Dan*, *The Bash Street Kids* et al, and the popularity of these cartoon characters is reflected in the choice of the comic-inspired lettering for Dundee's promotional logo.

While the three 'J's' were undoubtedly important to Dundee, other industries also played a substantial role in the city's history. Dundee was a major centre for shipbuilding and ships were built for both the whaling industry and for the import and export of jute and other cargoes. Dundee has a proud maritime heritage and for many years was the capital of the British whaling industry. In these more enlightened times we may shudder at the decimation of the whale stocks that led to the demise of the industry, but whale oil was a very valuable commodity, and the men who sailed the freezing Arctic seas to catch whales suffered terrible privations and hardships. On one famous occasion the whalers did not have to travel very far in search of their quarry. In December 1883 a humpback whale swam into the Tay estuary and foundered on the sandbanks. Large crowds gathered to watch the doomed animal's attempts to return to the sea, and it was harpooned on 7 December before finally being landed, completely exhausted, on 8 January the following year. It was put on public display before being sold, and the skeleton of the 'Tay whale' now resides in the city's McManus Galleries (see below).

Sights

Discovery Point
The obvious place to begin your tour of the city is Discovery Point, the impressive riverside location of Dundee's main attraction, the **Royal Research Ship** *Discovery*. This excellent facility, which attracts tens of thousands of visitors each year, is across the road from the train station, next to the Leisure Centre and *Hilton Hotel*. When Dundee was an important shipbuilding centre its speciality was wooden ships, and it was the Royal Geographical Society who commissioned the *Discovery*, which was launched on the Tay on 21 March 1901. She was the first specially designed scientific research ship and spent two winters in the Antarctic, where her wooden hull was able to withstand the enormous pressures of the pack ice. Famous as Captain Scott's ship, the *Discovery* and Scott parted company after his expedition in 1904. Another Dundee-built vessel, the *Terra Nova*, carried Scott to the South Pole in 1911 – the fateful expedition from which he never returned. After being purchased by the Maritime Trust, the *Discovery* was returned to Dundee in 1986 and moored at its present specially built quay with an excellent **visitor centre** at her side. The state-of-the-art centre presents an entertaining introduction, with audio-visual displays and an exhibition. On board the vessel you can see the cabins used by Scott and his crew, and hear some interesting anecdotes from the enthusiastic guides. ■ *Daily Apr-Oct 1000-1700 (Sun 1100-1700), Nov-Mar till 1600. £5.95, £3.85 child, £4.45 concession. £10.15/£7.75 for joint ticket with Verdant Works. T201245, www.rsdiscovery.com*

A short distance west of *Discovery*, in Victoria Dock on the other side of the road bridge, is Dundee's other major floating attraction, the **HM Frigate** *Unicorn*. Built in 1824, this is the oldest British warship still afloat, probably because it never fired a shot in anger. It was used variously as a gunpowder store and a training vessel, until it was rescued from the scrapyard in 1968 by a preservation society. A tour of the ship gives some idea of the cramped conditions in which the 300 men had to live and work, and the unused cannons are still on display. ■ *Mar-Oct daily 1000-1700; Nov-Feb Mon-Fri 1000-1600. £3.50, £2.50 child/concession. T200900.*

The focal point of the city centre is City Square, which is surrounded by shops and cafés, the imposing **Caird Hall**, the city's main concert hall, and the **City Chambers**, scene of much shady dealing in the 1960s and 70s, which led to the demolition of the city's medieval core. The resulting shopping mall, the infamous Overgate, has itself been replaced by a brand new retail complex. In front is the **Old Steeple**, the highest surviving medieval tower in the country. ■ *Apr-Sep Mon-Sat 1000-1700, Sun 1200-1600; Oct-Mar 1100-1600.*

Around the centre

The pedestrianized Reform Street leads north from City Square to **Albert Square**, site of the **McManus Galleries**, housed in Gilbert Scott's impressive Victorian Gothic edifice. Inside are some very fine exhibits detailing the city's history from the Iron Age to the Tay Bridge Disaster. The latter event was chronicled by the inimitable William McGonagall, the 'World's Worst Poet', and here you can read his excruciatingly awful verse, along with an equally painful account of the famous 'Tay Whale', the skeleton of which is also on display. Upstairs is the superb **Albert Hall**, which contains various antique collections, and the **Victoria Gallery**, whose 19th- and 20th-century collections include some notable Scottish painters such as McTaggart. ■ *Mon 1100-1700, Tue-Sat 1000-1700. T432020. Free.* Also in Albert Square are the huge red sandstone offices of local publishing giant, DC Thomson, who have entertained generations of British kids with their *Beano* and *Dandy* comics. A five-minute walk west, along Meadowside and Ward Road, across the dual carriageway and up Guthrie Street, is the excellent **Verdant Works** heritage centre, in West Henderson's Wynd. This former jute mill gives a rare insight into what life was like for mill workers, and details the history of the jute industry. ■ *Same opening hours and prices as Discovery (see above). T225282, www.verdantworks.com* Behind the DCA, on Greenmarket, is **Sensation**, one of those hands-on, interactive kind of places, so loved by kids.   *Open from 1000. £5.50, £ 3.99 child. T228800.*

The most prominent feature of the city is the Law Hill, a 571ft-high ancient volcanic plug. The views from the summit, over the entire city and south to Fife across the River Tay and its two bridges, are fantastic. It's a steep climb to the foot of the Law from the city centre, up the Hilltown, so it's best to take a bus (Nos 3 or 4) from Albert Square. The 1½-mile-long **Tay Road Bridge** was opened in 1966, while the **Tay Rail Bridge** is over two miles long and the longest railway bridge in Europe. It was built in 1878 but the following year the final section collapsed during a terrible storm. No one could alert the driver of the approaching train and it plunged into the cold, dark waters of the Tay, killing the crew and 75 passengers. A replacement section was built in 1887 and still stands today.

Law Hill & Balgay Hill

About a mile west of the Law, is Balgay Hill, site of the **Mills Observatory**, a free public facility which houses a planetarium as well as displays on astronomy and space exploration. ■ *Apr-Sep Mon-Fri 1100-1700, Sat 1400-1700; Oct-Mar Mon-Fri 1600-2200, Sat 1400-1700. Free. Take bus Nos 2, 36 or 37 to Balgay Road, at the entrance to Balgay Park. T435846.*

Northeast Scotland

Broughty Ferry

There are frequent buses to Broughty Ferry leaving from outside Littlewoods on the High St

Four miles east of Dundee, is the attractive seaside resort of **Broughty Ferry**. 'The Ferry' was once a separate settlement, with fishermen's cottages lining the shore and the large villas of wealthy jute barons climbing the hills behind, but it has since been swallowed up by the city's eastern suburbs. There's a long sandy beach, which is sadly polluted, and several good pubs and places to eat. The 15th-century **Broughty Castle** stands on the seafront, guarding the mouth of the Tay, and now houses an interesting **museum** of local history which includes a detailed description of the whaling industry. ■ *Apr-Sep Mon-Sat 1000-1600, Sun 1230-1600; Oct-Mar closed Mon. Free. T436916.*

Essentials

Sleeping

There's not a huge amount of top-class accommodation in Dundee, and many of the best hotels are outside the city. There are plenty of good-value guesthouses, though, particularly in the West End, on and around the Perth Rd, and in the eastern suburb of Broughty Ferry.

A *Queen's Hotel*, 160 Nethergate, T322515, F202668. 47 rooms. Perennial old favourite, conveniently located for all the main sights and with car parking round the back, also handy for West End pubs and restaurants, the Rep Theatre and almost next door to the DCA. A *Swallow Hotel*, Kingsway West, T641122, F568340. 107 rooms. Conveniently situated by the large roundabout where Riverside Dr meets the city ringroad (Kingsway) and A90 to Perth, tastefully refurbished and extended Victorian mansion with full leisure facilities and extensive grounds. In Brought Ferry is the B *Woodlands Hotel*, 13 Panmure Terr, T480033, F480126. 38 rooms. Set in extensive grounds and with pool and gym. C *Shaftesbury Hotel*, 1 Hyndford St, T669216, F641598. 12 rooms. In a converted jute baron's mansion just off the Perth Rd about a mile from the city centre. Comfy, relaxed, with a decent restaurant.

Most of the **guesthouses** and **B&Bs** are to be found to the east and west of the city centre, but if you want to be smack in the centre of town, then try the E *Auld Steeple Guest House*, 94 Nethergate, T/F200302. 11 rooms. Nothing fancy but clean and tidy and only a few mins' walk from the train station. A short walk north of the city centre is D *Hillside Guest House*, 43 Constitution St (off Constitution Rd), T/F223443, TildaB@aol.com. Comfortable, friendly and non-smoking. E *Nelson Guest House*, 8 Nelson Terr (off Victoria Rd), T225354. A 10-min walk from the bus station. In the east, heading towards Broughty Ferry, is D *Aberlaw*, 230 Broughty Ferry Rd, T/F456929. There are lots of places along the Arbroath Rd, including D *Anlast*, No 379, T456710; and E *Ash Villa*, No 216, T450381. There's also a good selection of guesthouses/B&Bs in the West End, including D *Bracklinn*, 5 Fort St (off Richmond Terr), T/F566563. The *University of Dundee* offers B&B accommodation (E, shared bathrooms) from Jun-Sep in its halls of residence at *West Park*, 319 Perth Rd, T647181, g.anderson@dundee.ac.uk. It also has self-catering flats for weekly rental, T344039.

There's a wide range of places to stay in **Broughty Ferry**. One of the best is D *Hollies Orchard*, 12 Castelroy Rd, T776403, mediamack@sol.co.uk. Also recommended is the E *Beach House Hotel*, 22 Esplanade, T776614. Further east towards **Monifieth** is E *Auchinean*, 177 Hamilton St, T774782. There are lots of places on Monifieth Rd, including E *Invermark House*, No 23, T739430. There's a **campsite** at Carnoustie, 10 miles east of Dundee city centre: *Woodlands Caravan Park*, T01241-854430, which is open Apr-Oct.

Eating

There's no shortage of places to eat in Dundee, from the ubiquitous burger bars, pizza parlours, fish and chip shops and takeaways to upmarket continental cuisine. Many of the city's pubs provide excellent value meals. Most of the better restaurants, bars and

Northeast Scotland

pubs are to be found in the West End, around the University and Perth Rd, and there's also a wide selection of places to eat in Broughty Ferry.

Expensive *Raffles*, 18 Perth Rd, T226344. There was a time when this was *the* place to eat but some say its new trendy image is the victory of style over content. Good (and reasonably priced) for Sun brunch, though. Open Tue-Sun. Best of the lot is *South Kingennie House*, T350562, near Kellas, off the B978 which runs north from Broughty Ferry. It's a bit of a schlep from town but well worth it for the superb traditional Scottish cooking. Open daily except Sun evening and Mon, lunch cheap to mid-range; dinner expensive.

Mid-range Another excellent out-of-town place is *11 Park Avenue* in Carnoustie T/F01241-853336. Open Tue-Sat. *Agacan Kebab House*, 113 Perth Rd, T644227. Brightly decorated and cosy Turkish restaurant, nice ambience and tasty grills, open Tue-Sun. *Café Buongiorno*, 11 Bank St, T221179. Small, intimate Italian, popular as a café by day and restaurant by night. *Cul de Sac*, 10 South Tay St, next to the Rep, T202070. Café-bar/restaurant with a cool, laid back atmosphere. Open daily 1200-2230. They also run *The Het*, the Rep Theatre's foyer café-bar. *Jute Café-bar*, 152 Nethergate, in Dundee Contemporary Arts. So stylish you could be in Glasgow, and a great vibe. Small but interesting menu. Open daily 1030-2400 (Sun till 2300). *Mandarin Garden*, 40-44 South Tay St, T227733. Excellent Chinese cuisine, served by friendly, efficient staff. Try the house banquet. Open daily except Sun for lunch and 1700-2300. *Pizza Express*, 31a Albert Square, T226677. Part of the acclaimed pizza chain. Great pizza, elegant surroundings. *Royal Oak*, 167 Brook St, T229440. In an unlikely setting, near Verdant Works and the Hawkhill, great pub food with an Indian emphasis, large portions. There are lots of restaurants in **Broughty Ferry**, but don't miss a trip to

Dundee

To Law Hill

To Arbroath, Montrose, Forfar & Aberdeen

Dudhope Park

A923

West Henderson's Wynd

North Marketgait

Victoria Rd

Bell St

Verdant Works

McManus Galleries

Meadowside

Waterstone's Bookshop

Broak St

Ward Rd

Bank St

Commercial St

Seagate

HM Frigate Unicorn

Marketgait

Dock St

Marketgait

A92

City Square

Overgate Ln

Old Steeple

High St

Trades House

Overgate Centre

Hogshead

South

Olympia Leisure Centre

Tay Road Bridge

West Port

Sun Tay St

Nethergate

Rep Theatre

Taybridge Train Station

University of Dundee

Sensation

Discovery Point

Art College

Perth Rd

Dundee Contemporary Arts & Jute Café-Bar

River Tay

Hawkhill

Roseangle

Riverside Dr

To Couper Angus & Blairgowrie

To St Andrews & Edinburgh

To Broughty Ferry, Arbroath & Montrose

Northeast Scotland

N

0 metres 200
0 yards 200

■ Sleeping	**4** Pizza Express	**10** Phoenix
1 Auld Steeple Guest House	**5** Raffles	**11** Royal Oak
2 Queen's Hotel		**12** Tally Ho's
	● **Bars & pubs**	
● **Eating**	**6** Globe	○ **Entertainment**
1 Cafe Buongiorno	**7** Laing's	**1** Circus
2 Cul de Sac	**8** O'Neill's	**2** Fat Sam's & Mardi Gras
3 Mandarin Garden	**9** Parliamentary	

Visocchi's, 40 Gray St, T779297. A genuine Italian café serving the best capuccino in town and the best ice cream for miles. Nearby, at 43a, is *Nawab*, T731800, an excellent Indian Balti house that's a cut above the rest.

Bars & clubs

Dundee's nightlife is concentrated in a relatively small area of the city centre, based around the West Port and Nethergate

Bars *Cul de Sac* and the *Jute Café-bar* (see above) are both civilized places to chill, but for something a bit livelier, try any of the busy bars along the Nethergate, especially the *Phoenix* and *Parliamentary Bar*, on opposite sides of the street by the junction with West Marketgait. At the top of South Tay Street is the West Port, where you'll find a clutch of student bars, including *Tally Ho's* and *The Globe*. On the other side of the Hawkhill are the *West Port Bar* and, nearby in Brown St, the *Freelance & Firkin*, which has live music at weekends. Further up the Perth Rd, opposite Duncan of Jordanstone Art College, Roseangle branches left, and here you'll find *Laing's*, which is hugely popular with the 20-30s and boasts a beer garden with views across the Tay. It also serves pretty decent grub. In the city centre is *O'Neill's Irish Bar*, 80 North Lindsay St, a cheap and cheerful pub with a wide range of good-value pub food and live folk music. On Union St is *Hogshead*, which serves 6 ales and decent bar grub. At the top of Union St is the sumptuous *Trades House*, a converted bank which has received some favourable accounts. Broughty Ferry is a good place for a drink on a summer's evening, especially the *Ship Inn*, a cosy old pub right on the seafront with a reputation for fine food. Also recommended is the *Fisherman's Tavern*, 12 Fort St. It's popular with nautical types and is rightly famed for its superb real ales and good pub food.

Clubs There's no shortage of post-pub venues, though the best places are to be found around the West Port area. *Fat Sam's*, at 31 South Ward Rd, attracts a slightly older crowd (ie out of short trousers), and has a large chill-out area. Next door is *Mardi Gras*, a vast club open every night except Tue. It's popular with teenagers. Just around the corner, in Ward Rd, is *The Circus*, Dundee's newest and biggest club.

Entertainment

Cinema and theatre The *UGC* multiplex, at Kingsway West near the entrance to Camperdown Park, T0870-9020407 shows mainstream movies. *Dundee Contemporary Arts*, 152 Nethergate, T432000, is Dundee's cultural hub, housed in a superb modern building, with two cinema screens showing current arthouse releases, also exhibition spaces, print studio, visual research centre and the *Jute Café-bar*. Dundee's excellent *Rep Theatre* is on Tay Square, off South Tay St, T223530. It stages locally produced contemporary theatre and hosts various national touring companies. It is also a jazz venue and has a good café-restaurant in the foyer.

Shopping

The new Overgate Centre is on Nethergate and has all the usual High Street shops, including *Debenhams* and *H&M*. The main bookshops are *James Thin*, 7 High St, and *Waterstone's*, 34 Commercial St.

Sport

Football Dundee has two Premier League football clubs, the cosmopolitan *Dundee FC*, who strut their stuff at Dens Park, T826104, and their bitter rivals *Dundee United* (aka the 'Arabs'), who reside at Tannadice, T833166, which is just across the street. **Golf** There are two public courses, at *Caird Park*, Mains Loan, T434706, and Camperdown, in *Camperdown Park*, T432688. *Downfield Golf Club*, on Turnberry Av, T825595, is a fine private course which allows visitors. Dundee is also within 30 mins' drive of *Carnoustie* and *St Andrews*, both of which have famous championship courses. **Leisure centres** *Olympia Leisure Centre*, Earl Grey Place (next to the RRS Discovery), T434888. Pool with water slides and wave machines, also gym, sauna and climbing wall. Open Mon-Fri 0900-2100, Sat-Sun 0900-1700. *Stack Leisure Park*, Harefield Rd. Multiplex cinema and 10-pin bowling.

Air   There are direct flights to Dundee from **London City Airport**, 4 times daily, with
Scot Airways, T0870-6060707.

Bus   *National Express*, runs 4 services daily to and from **London** (10 hrs direct).
Scottish Citylink, operates an hourly service to and from **Edinburgh** (2 hrs) and **Glasgow** (2¼ hrs). Most Edinburgh and Glasgow buses stop en route in **Perth** (35 mins).
There are also hourly buses to **Aberdeen** (2 hrs). Some Aberdeen buses go via **Forfar**
(25 mins) and others go via **Arbroath** (30 mins). *Strathtay Scottish*, T01382-228054,
runs buses at least every 30 mins to **Blairgowrie** (1 hr), **Forfar** (30 mins), **Brechin** (via
Forfar, 1¼ hrs) and **Arbroath** (1 hr); and hourly to **Perth** (1 hr), **Kirriemuir** (1 hr 10 mins)
and **Montrose** (1¼ hrs). Their Rover ticket (£5) gives unlimted travel 1 day.

Train   There are trains at least every hour, Mon-Sat, to and from **Glasgow** (1½ hrs)
and **Edinburgh** (1½ hrs). Trains run less frequently on Sun. Trains run every 30 mins to
and from **Aberdeen** (1¼ hrs), via **Arbroath, Montrose and Stonehaven**.

Car hire   *National*, 45-53 Gellatly St, T0870-4004508. *Arnold Clark*, 14-22 Trades
Lane, T225382. *Hertz* 18 Marketgait, T223711. **Cycle hire**   *Just Bikes*, 57 Gray St,
T732100. *Nicholson's*, 2-4 Forfar Rd, T461212.

Banks   *Bank of Scotland*, 2 West Marketgait, T317500. *Lloyds TSB*, 96 Albert St,
T453535. *Royal Bank of Scotland*, 133 Albert St, T462256. **Currency exchange**:
Thomas Cook, City Sq, T200204. Open Mon-Fri 0900-1730, Sat 0900-1700. Also at the
TIC. **Communications**   Internet: *Megabyte Internet Bistro*, 31 Hilltown (behind
Wellgate Centre), T200134. **Post office**: 4 Meadowside, T203532. Open Mon-Fri
0900-1730, Sat 0900-1900. **Medical services**   Hospital: *Dundee Royal Infirmary*, Barrack Rd, T660111. 24-hr accident and emergency. **Pharmacy**: *Boots*, High St. Open
Mon-Wed, Fri-Sat 0830-1745, Thu till 1900. Sun opening on rota basis; check local
press. **Travel agents**   *Campus Travel*, Airlie Pl, T200412. *Ramsay Travel*, Crichton St,
T200394. **Useful addresses**   Police: *Tayside Police HQ*, Bell St, T223200.

Angus

The fishing and farming county of Angus was formerly part of the giant Tayside
region but is now a separate authority with its own distinct identity. Angus isn't a
name that rolls off many tourists' tongues, but it has much to recommend it to
those who prefer to escape the summer hordes. The east coast, from Arbroath
north to Montrose, is particularly attractive with its sheer red cliffs punctuated by
sweeping bays of golden sand. In the north are the Angus Glens, stretching deep
into the heart of the Grampian peaks and offering excellent walking opportuni-
ties. The heart of the county is the wide valley of Strathmore, with its string of neat
market towns. This was part of the ancient Pictish Kingdom and there are still
many interesting carved stones scattered around the area.

Ins and outs

The towns along the main Dundee-Aberdeen routes are easy to get to by bus or train,
but public transport to the more remote parts is limited. For more information pick up
a copy of Angus Council's *Public Transport Map & Guide*, available from tourist offices, or
call the *Transport Team*, T01307-461775, or *Strathtay Scottish*, T01382-228054. For rail
enquiries, T0345-484950.

Angus is covered by the *Angus & Dundee Tourist Board*, which has offices in Arbroath,
Brechin, Carnoustie, Forfar, Kirriemuir and Montrose. They have a website: www.
angusanddundee.co.uk

Arbroath

Phone code: 01241
Colour map 4, grid B5
Population: 23,500

The A92 coast road to Aberdeen bypasses the little coastal town of **Carnoustie**, whose **championship golf course** is revered worldwide, and heads to Arbroath, 17 miles northeast of Dundee. This is the home of that great Scottish delicacy, the **Arbroath smokie** – haddock smoked over oak chips – which you can buy in the tiny smokehouses around the harbour. But though Arbroath was once a thriving fishing and trading port, today it has the look of a place that's down on its luck, with high unemployment and a town centre blighted by insensitive planning.

Ins & outs   The **train** station is on Keptie St, about 5 mins' walk from the tourist office. The **bus** station is nearby, on Catherine St, T870646. Arbroath is on the Dundee-Aberdeen rail line and there are trains every 30 mins to and from **Dundee** (20 mins). For rail enquiries call T01382-228046. There are *Scottish Citylink* **buses** every 2 hrs to **Aberdeen** (1½ hrs) via **Montrose** and **Stonehaven**, and to **Dundee** (25 mins). *Strathtay Scottish*, T01382-228054, runs regular buses to **Brechin** via **Montrose**, and less frequently to **Auchmithie**.

The **Tourist Information Centre** is on Market Pl, right in the centre of town, T872609. Apr-May Mon-Fri 0900-1700, Sat 1000-1700; Jun-Aug Mon-Sat 0930-1730; Sun 1000-1500; Sep Mon-Sat 0930-1730; Oct-Mar Mon-Fri 0900-1700, Sat 1000-1500.

Sights   The chief attraction is undoubtedly **Arbroath Abbey**, on Abbey Street, near the top of the High Street not far from the tourist office. Founded by William the Lion in 1178 (who's buried here), it went on to become one of the wealthiest monasteries in the country. It is also one of the most important sites in Scottish history. It was here, on 6 April 1320, that the Declaration of Arbroath was issued, asking Rome to reverse its excommunication of Robert the Bruce and recognize him as King, thus asserting Scotland's independence from England. Pope John XXII finally agreed to the claim four years later. You can buy copies of the declaration (the original is in Edinburgh) which contains the stirring words: "For so long as a hundred of us remain alive, we will yield in no least way to English dominion. For we fight, not for glory, not for riches, nor for honour, but only for freedom, which no good man surrenders but with his life".

After the Reformation the abbey suffered badly and, like so many other important ecclesiastical buildings in Scotland, was used as a quarry for the building of the town. However, enough of the abbey survives to give you a good idea of just how magnificent it must have been; in particular the massive west front and the south transept (containing a circular window which was once lit up as a beacon to guide ships). In 1951 the **Stone of Destiny** found a temporary home here following its theft from Westminster Abbey by Scottish Nationalists. It was duly returned, where it stayed until its recent move to Edinburgh Castle (see page 80). ■ *Apr-Sep Mon-Sat 0930-1830, Sun 1200-1830; Oct-Mar Mon-Sat till 1630, Sun 1400-1630. £1.80, £1.30 concession. T878756.*

Beside the harbour is the **Signal Tower Museum**, housed in the elegant Regency building that was once the shore base and family living quarters for the keepers of the Bell Rock Lighthouse, 12 miles offshore. The museum has some interesting local history displays, including re-creations of a fisherman's cottage and a schoolroom. ■ *Mon-Sat 1000-1700, also Sun 1400-1700 in Jul-Aug. Free. T875598.*

A mile northwest of the town centre is **St Vigeans**, where the red sandstone church is perched right on top of a hill in the centre of the village. Beside the hill is tiny **St Vigeans Museum**, which contains an excellent collection of Pictish and medieval carved stones. ■ *Apr-Sep Mon-Sat 0930-1830, Sun 1400-1830. Free (collect the key from No 7).*

There are several **B&Bs** around the centre, including the **E** *Harbour Guesthouse*, 4 The Shore, by the harbour, T878047; and **E** *Scurdy Guesthouse*, 33 Marketgate, T872417, near the High St. A mile south of town on the A92 to Dundee and overlooking the golf course, is **D-E** *Five Gables*, T871632.

    The best place to eat is the cosy *But'n'Ben* restaurant, T877223, by the harbour in Auchmithie (see below). Their seafood is superb and great value (mid-range). Open daily except Tue 1200-1500 for lunch, 1600-1730 for high tea and 1900-2200 for dinner. Four miles northwest of town, signposted off the A933 Brechin Rd, is the *Letham Grange Resort*, T890373, www.lethamgrange.co.uk, a beautifully restored baronial mansion now functioning as a top-class golf resort hotel. It has a more formal restaurant (mid-range) and a conservatory for lunches and light meals (cheap). It will come as no surprise that Arbroath boasts an excellent fish and chip shop, *Peppo's*, at 51 Ladybridge St, by the harbour (closed Sat).

Sleeping & eating

Five miles north of Arbroath by road is the attractive little fishing village of Auchmithie, perched precariously on the cliff-top with a steep descent to the harbour and quay. Auchmithie is the true home of the smokie and, though Arbroath later took the credit, the village can at least lay claim to the region's best seafood restaurant, the *But'n'Ben* (see above). You can walk to the foot of Auchmithie along a marvellous cliff path which starts at the far end of **Victoria Park**. There are numerous caves to explore and lots of seabirds to see along the three-mile route. You should pick up a free copy of *The Arbroath Cliffs Nature Trail Guide* from the tourist office.

Auchmithie

Montrose

Fourteen miles north of Arbroath is the elegant town of Montrose, the most pleasant and interesting of the Angus towns, rich in history and with great beaches to the north and south. It stands at the mouth of a vast tidal basin, covering 2,000 acres and bordered by 17 miles of roads. The basin is home to a multitude of wild birds such as ducks, geese, swans and waders who come here to search for food on the wide expanse of mud flats. The **Montrose Basin Wildlife Centre** is at Rossie Braes, a mile out of town on the A92. They have superb viewing facilities, with binoculars and high-powered telescopes as well as remote-control video cameras. There are also guided walks around the reserve. ■ *Apr-Oct daily 1030-1730; Nov-Mar daily 1030-1600. £2.50. T676336.*

Phone code 01674
Colour map 4, grid B5

The **train** station is on Western Rd, 1 block from the High St. There are trains every 30 mins to Aberdeen and Dundee. **Buses** stop in the High St. There are frequent buses to and from **Aberdeen** (1¾ hrs), though you have to change at **Stonehaven**. *Strathtay Scottish*, T01382-228054, runs regular buses to **Brechin** and **Forfar**. The tiny **Tourist Information Centre** is next to the library, T672000. Apr-Jun and Sep Mon-Sat 1000-1700; Jul-Aug 0930-1730.

Ins & outs

Montrose was once a thriving port, trading with various European countries, and the wealthy 18th- and 19th-century merchants built their houses gable-end to the street, in imitation of the Continental style. This earned the townsfolk the nickname of 'gable-endies', which has stuck to this day. The

Sights

sole remaining gable-ended houses can be seen on the High Street, which is the widest in Scotland. The south end of the High Street is overlooked by a statue of **Sir Robert Peel**, a local man who was British Prime Minister and founder of the present-day Police Force. From his name came the old slang term for police, 'The Peelers'.

A few blocks from the High Street, on Panmure Place, is **Montrose Museum and Art Gallery**, housed in a fine neoclassical Victorian building and one of the first purpose-built museums in Scotland. Among the displays are Bronze-Age axe-heads, Montrose pottery and silver (the town had its own assay mark, a rose, and pieces are much sought after). The Maritime Gallery has a fleet of model ships, relics of the once-thriving whaling industry, and Napoleonic items, including a cast of his death mask. ■ *Mon-Sat 1000-1700. Free. T673232.* Outside the museum is a lifesize bronze sculpture of a boy by local sculptor, William Lamb (1893-1951). More of his work can be seen at the **William Lamb Sculpture Studio** on Market Street, where his famous subjects include the Queen, Queen Mother and the great Scots poet Hugh McDiarmid. The studio was left by the artist as his memorial gift to the town. ■ *Jul-Sep Tue-Sun 1400-1700. Free.* Near the museum, on the same side of the street, up an alley (or close), are **Taylor's Auction Rooms**, T672775. Every second Saturday, people come from far and wide to bid for paintings, jewellery, furniture and many other items. It's well worth a visit, and you might even come away with a piece of locally hall-marked silver.

On the A92 heading north out of town is the **Aerodrome Museum**. Montrose was Scotland's first airport, used in both world wars for the training of pilots. The museum documents the lives of many of the men who lost their lives, including the chilling tale of Lieutenant Desmond Arthur whose ghost is said to haunt the former air base. There are also assorted aircraft on display outside. ■ *Sun 1200-1700, or at other times by appointment. T675401.*

Traill Drive leads to the town's impressive **beach**, which stretches all the way north to St Cyrus (see page 411). About four miles south of Montrose, reached by turning off the A92, is the great sweep of **Lunan Bay**, a stunningly beautiful, and usually deserted, sandy beach, once popular with smugglers. Like many beaches on the northeast coast, there are strong currents, so do not swim beyond your capabilities. There's a variety of **wildlife** around, including nesting puffins on the red sandstone cliffs. Overlooking the beach is the 12th-century ruin of **Red Castle**, which was originally a royal hunting lodge.

Three miles west of Montrose on the A935 is the **House of Dun**, built in 1730 for David Erskine, Lord Dun. It is a very attractive Georgian building in the Palladian style, designed by William Adam, who was at the forefront of Scottish architecture between the Jacobite risings of 1715 and 1745, but otherwise somewhat eclipsed by his sons Robert and James. Lady Augusta Kennedy-Erskine, daughter of William IV and the actress Mrs Jordan, also lived there, and the house contains many royal mementos. Alas, the huge sword which was driven into a tree in the grounds by one of the Erskines was removed by the present owners, the National Trust, for safety reasons. The courtyard has recently been restored, and *Angus Handloom Weavers*, Scotland's last handloom linen weavers, are based there. Fine linen is for sale by the yard, as well as linen goods. There's an attractive café and shop. ■ *Easter and 1 May-30 Jun daily 1330-1730; 1 Jul-31 Aug 1100-1730; weekends in Oct 1330-1730. Garden and grounds all year daily 0930 to sunset. £6, £4.50 concession, £1 child. Garden and grounds only £1. T810264. Strathtay bus No 30 to Brechin passes the entrance, ask to get off.*

C *The Links Hotel*, Mid Links, T671000. A short walk from the beach, comfortable town **Sleeping &**
house hotel offering good Scottish/French cooking at mid-range prices. For **B&B** **eating**
accommodation try the **E** *Limes Guesthouse*, T677236, thelimes@easynet.co.uk, at 15
King St. For something a bit more scenic, there's **E** *Lunan Lodge*, T01241-830267,
b&b@lunanlodge.sol.co.uk. An 18th-century country house in the village of Lunan
overlooking Lunan Bay. On the coast road north to St Cyrus there's B&B in the old fishing station at **B** *Woodston*, T01674-850226, info@woodstonfishingstation.co.uk, evening meal available, great bird watching down on the sands.

Apart from the hotels, eating options are limited. *Murray Lodge Hotel* at the end of
Murray St does a tasty lunch. *Steeple Computers Systems* is a **cyber café** opposite the
Old Kirk, T662160. Open Tue-Sat.

Brechin

Nine miles west of Montrose is Brechin, a quiet little town on the banks of the   *Phone code: 01356*
River South Esk, whose main attraction is its 14th-century **cathedral**, in   *Colour map 4, grid B5*
Bishop's Close off the High Street. There's been a church here since the ninth   *Population: 7,500*
century though most of what you see dates from the beginning of the 20th
century when major restoration work was carried out. The adjacent 106-ft
high **round tower** dates from the 11th century and is one of only two such
structures in the country.

Scottish *Citylink* **buses** run every 2 hrs to **Aberdeen** (1 hr), **Dundee** (50 mins) and   **Ins & outs**
Forfar (20 mins). Buses leave from Panmure St. *Strathtay Scottish*, T01382-228054,
has services to **Edzell** several times daily (20 mins) and daily every hr to **Montrose** (20
mins), from South Esk St. The **Tourist Information Centre** is at 10 St Ninian's Pl, opposite the library. They have information on hiking in Glen Esk. T623050. Apr-Jun and Sep
Mon-Sat 1000-1700; Jul-Aug Mon-Sat 0930-1730.

The small **Brechin Museum** is housed in the library on St Ninian's Square   **Sights**
and is the usual collection of local curiosities and memorabilia. ■ *Mon, Tue,*
Thu-Fri 0930-1800, Wed 0930-1900, Sat 0930-1700. Free. Also on St Ninian's
Square is the terminus of the **Caledonian Railway**, which runs steam trains
on a four-mile section of line between Brechin station and Bridge of Dun, a
mile from the House of Dun (see under Montrose above). ■ *Trains run six*
times daily on Sun only, from Jun to early Sep. £4.50 return, £2.50 child/conces-
sion. T810318.

Just off the A90, is the **Brechin Castle Centre**, which is a Country Park with
garden centre, pets corner, miniature railway (open April-September), picnic
areas and waterside walks. There's also a coffee shop. Part of the centre is
Pictavia, which gives a fascinating glimpse into Scotland's Celtic past. You'll
help to solve the riddles of the stones, see the mysterious Pictish standing
stones and hear the sounds of battle in the Tower of Sound. ■ *Open all year.*
T626813.

Five miles north of Brechin on the B966 is **Edzell**, an impossibly neat and pic-   **Excursions**
turesque planned village lying at the foot of Glen Esk. At the entrance to the   *Phone code: 01356*
village is the impressive **Dalhousie Arch** which leads on to the wide main   *Colour map 4, grid B5*
street, lined with quaint little tearooms and shops selling Victoriana. A mile
west of the village is the red sandstone ruin of **Edzell Castle**, a 16th-century
tower house which, over the course of its life, has been visited by Mary, Queen
of Scots, James VI and, less happily, Cromwell's troops. But it is the magnificent **garden**, or 'Pleasance', which is the real attraction. Created by Sir David

Northeast Scotland

Lindsay in 1604, the superb heraldic and symbolic sculpted wall panels are rare examples of European Renaissance Art in Scotland. ■ *Apr-Sep 0930-1830; Oct-Mar Mon-Wed and Sat 0930-1630, Thu 0930-1200, Fri and Sun 1400-1630. £2.50, £1.90 concession. T648631.*

Three miles southwest of Edzell, on either side of the road, are the **Brown Caterthun** and **White Caterthun**, two remarkable Iron-Age forts, defended by ditches and ramparts over 900-ft high. These were occupied by the Picts around the first few centuries AD and the views from the top are amazing. To get there, follow the road west of the castle and turn left at Bridgend, then take the left fork. Or take the road southwest from Edzell and take the first right after Dunlappie. There's no public transport. It's an easy walk from the road to either fort.

Sleeping Accommodation is limited. In **Brechin** there's the **D** Northern Hotel, 2 Clerk St, T625505, which also serves moderately priced meals; and **B&B** at **E-D** *Doniford*, 26 Airlie St, T62236 In **Edzell** the pleasant **C** *Glenesk Hotel*, T648319, does bar and restaurant meals. There's also **B&B** at **E-F** *Inchcape*, T647266, on the High St; and **E-F** *The Gorse*, T648207, on Dunlappie Rd.

Forfar and Glamis

Phone code: 01307
Colour map 4, grid B4
Population: 12,650

Fourteen miles north of Dundee, just off the main A90, is Forfar, the county capital of Angus. Forfar was the ancient capital of the Picts and, though it wouldn't be picked as a top tourist destination today, it is only a few miles from the county's star attraction, **Glamis Castle**. The town is best known for its contribution to Scottish cuisine, the famous **Forfar Bridie**, a gigantic shortcrust pastie filled with mince and onions (see next page).

Ins & outs Scottish *Citylink* **buses** run to and from **Dundee** every 2 hrs (25 mins) and **Aberdeen** (1 hr 20 mins), via **Brechin** (20 mins). Buses stop opposite the church in East High St. *Strathtay Scottish*, T01382-228054, runs buses every hr to **Kirriemuir** (25 mins) and to **Brechin** via **Aberlemno**. Forfar's **Tourist Information Centre** is at 45 East High St, T467876. Apr-Jun and Sep Mon-Sat 1000-1700; Jul-Aug Mon-Sat 0930-1730.

Sights **The Meffan Gallery and Museum**, at 20 West High Street, illustrates the colourful history of town and county, and includes Pictish remains and a grisly account of the witch-hunts of the 17th century. ■ *Mon-Sat 1000-1700. T464123. Free.* Two miles east of town, off the B9113, are the ruins of **Restenneth Priory**. The 12th-century Augustinian priory was chosen by King Robert the Bruce as the last resting place of his son, Prince John. ■ *Open at all times. Free.* About four miles southeast, on the road to Letham, is **Dunnichen Hill**, once known as Nechtansmere, scene of a Pictish victory in 685 AD over Ecgfrith, King of the Angles, thus assuring Scotland's independence.

Five miles northeast of Forfar, along the B9134, is the tiny village of **Aberlemno**, home to some of the country's best **Pictish stones**. In the churchyard, just off the main road, is an eighth-century cross-slab with a Celtic cross, entwined beasts on one side and an elaborate depiction of the Battle of Nechtansmere on the other. There are three other stones with Pictish and early-Christian symbols by the roadside. There are plans to move the stones to a protected site, so check with the TIC before visiting. ■ *Open access except Nov-Mar. Free. Buses from Forfar to Brechin stop in Aberlemno.*

The best place to eat is *O'Hara's*, 41-43 West High St, T464350. Bar-bistro offering **Eating** great food with an inventive twist and real ales. Food served Mon-Sat lunch and evening. Also good is the *Chapelbank House Hotel*, at 69 East High St, T463151. They serve a good, cheap lunch daily except Mon, and moderately priced dinner daily except Sun and Mon. Several bakeries in town sell bridies, but the locals will tell you that the best place to sample this delight is *McLaren's*, next to the *Queen's Hotel* on West High St

Five miles southwest of Forfar is the county's star attraction, Glamis Castle **Glamis Castle** (pronounced Glamz), the fabulous family home of the Earls of Strathmore **& village** and Kinghorne. Glamis is every inch the archetypal Scottish castle, and one of *There are several* the most famous. This was the setting for Shakespeare's *Macbeth*, but its royal *places to stay in* connection doesn't end there. It was the childhood home of Her Majesty *Forfar, but Kirriemuir* Queen Elizabeth the Queen Mother, and the birthplace of Her Royal High- *is nicer and equally* ness the Princess Margaret. The setting matches the impeccable pedigree. As *convenient for Glamis* you approach down the long, tree-lined drive, the castle suddenly appears in *Castle* all its glory, the jumble of turrets, towers and conical roofs rising up against the backdrop of the Grampian Mountains like one of Walt Disney's fairy-tale fantasies. Most of the building you see dates from the 15th century, though the glamorous touches were added in the 17th century.

The five-storey, L-shaped castle grew from its humble beginnings as a mere hunting lodge, used by the Kings of Scotland in the 11th century. In 1372 King Robert II gave it to his son-in-law, Sir John Lyon, whose descendants, the Earls of Strathmore and Kinghorne, have lived here ever since. The 14th Earl was the Queen Mother's father.

Highlights of the tour include the 17th-century drawing room, with its impressive plasterwork ceilings, and the ghostly crypt, haunted by Lord Glamis and Crawford who was entombed within its walls as punishment for playing a few hands of gin rummy with the Devil on the Sabbath. The 17th-century chapel, with its biblical frescoes, is also haunted, this time by the 'grey lady', the ghost of the sixth Lady Glamis, who was burnt as a witch by James V. Duncan's Hall is reputedly where King Duncan was murdered by Macbeth, though, like much else in the play, this is very doubtful. You can also see the Royal Apartments, including the Queen Mother's bedroom, and the extensive grounds are also well worth exploring. There's a restaurant on site. ■ *Late Mar to end Oct daily 1030-1730 (Jul-Aug from 1000), last admission 1645. Guided tours last one hour and leave every 15 mins. £6.50, £4.80 concession, £3.20 child. T840393. There's a limited bus service from Dundee, Forfar and Kirriemuir. Contact Strathtay Buses, T01382-228054.*

In the village of **Glamis**, just off the square, is the **Angus Folk Museum**. It's housed in a picturesque row of 18th-century cottages which are divided into domestic and agricultural sections. The changes in living and farming in Angus over the last 200 years are vividly illustrated with the help of a vast collection of local artefacts. ■ *Easter and 1 May-Sep daily 1100-1700; weekends only in Oct 1100-1700. £2.40, £1.60 child/concession. T840233.*

Kirriemuir

Kirriemuir, or Kirrie as it's known locally, is the ideal spot for those wishing to *Phone code 01575* explore the beautiful Angus Glens, or visit Glamis Castle, only five miles *Colour map 4, grid B4* south, or simply for those who wish to get off the tartan trail and stay in a *Population: 5,300* lovely, unspoiled wee town.

Northeast Scotland

Ins & outs *Strathtay Scottish*, T01382-228054, runs hourly **buses** (Mon-Sat, less frequently on Sun) to and from **Dundee** (1 hr 10 mins). There are also buses every hr to **Forfar** (25 mins) and twice a day (except Sun) to **Glamis**. There's a **postbus service**, T01463-256200, from Kirriemuir to **Glen Prosen** (once daily except Sun) and **Glen Clova** (twice on weekdays, once on Sat).The **Tourist Information Centre** is on Cumberland Cl, T574097. Apr-Jun and Sep Mon-Sat 1000-1700; Jul-Aug Mon-Sat 0930-1730.

Sights Kirrie's claim to fame is as the birthplace of JM Barrie (1860-1937), creator of Peter Pan, the little boy who never grew up. Barrie was the son of a hand-loom weaver and ninth of 10 children. His classic tale of *Peter Pan and the Lost Boys*, written in 1904, is said to have been inspired by the memory of his older brother, who died while still young. Kirrie is the fictional Thrums of Barrie's autobiographical novel, *A Window in Thrums*. **Barrie's birthplace** can be visited at 9 Brechin Road. The humble little weaver's cottage is now managed by the NTS, and the upper floor is furnished as it would have been when he lived there. The adjacent house features an exhibition of his literary and theatrical works. The outside wash-house is said to have been his first theatre and the model for the house built for Wendy by the Lost Boys in Never-Never Land. Barrie is also buried in Kirrie, at the nearby St Mary's Episcopal Church. ■ *1 Apr-30 Sep Mon-Sat 1100-1730, Sun 1330-1730. Weekends only in Oct Sat 1100-1730, Sun 1330-1730. £3, concession £2, child £1. T572646. .*

At the top of Kirriemuir Hill is a **camera obscura**, which offers a panorama of the surrounding Strathmore countryside and the glens to the north. At the southern end of town, at Bellies Brae, is the **Aviation Museum**, which houses a large, eclectic collection of Second World War memorabilia. ■ *Apr-Sep Mon-Sat 1000-1700, Sun 1100-1700. Free (donations welcome).* Birdwatchers should head a few miles west of town, just off the B951, to the **Loch of Kinnordy** and **RSPB Reserve**, where there are two hides overlooking the loch and wetlands.

Sleeping There's not a huge choice of accommodation in Kirrie. Best of all is the **D** *Airlie Arms Hotel*, St Malcom's Wynd, T572847. A converted medieval monastery now a small, comfortable hotel, offers cheap bar meals and decent, moderately priced evening meals. Among the few **B&Bs** are **E** *Woodlands*, at Lisden Gdns, T572582; and **E** *Crepto*, at 1 Kinnordy Pl, T572746. Those wishing to stay longer can rent a self-catering cottage next door to Barrie's birthplace, for £250-320 per week for up to 4 people. Contact the National Trust for Scotland head office (see page 39).

Eating & The best restaurant in the area is the *Lochside Lodge*, by the Loch of Lintrathen, **entertainment** T560340, 6 miles along the B951, then take the turning left for Bridge of Lintrathen. This converted farmstead serves moderately priced modern Scottish cooking and also rents rooms (**D**). In town, the *Airlie Arms* (see above) and the *Thrums Hotel*, Bank St, T572758, both serve decent food. A great café is *Visocchi's* on the main street, which has been serving delicious ice cream since 1953.

Kirriemuir is well known for its **Folk Festival**, held on the first weekend in **Sep** each year. The best venues for live music are the *Airlie Arms* (see above), the *Roods Bar* nearby, and *Three, Bellies Brae*, which may be an unusual name for a pub, but is a very welcoming watering hole.

The Angus Glens

East of Perthshire, south of the Grampians and north of Dundee are the Angus Glens, a series of five glens running parallel to each other and all of them beautiful, peaceful and offering plenty of relatively painless hillwalking opportunities.

Colour map 4, grid B4

Getting there and around Kirriemuir is the gateway to **Glens Isla, Prosen** and **Clova**, while the other two, **Glens Lethnot** and **Esk**, are reached via Brechin. There are regular **buses** to Brechin and Kirriemuir from Dundee, but getting around the glens is not easy without your own transport as there is only a limited postbus service.

Ins & outs

Running parallel to Glen Shee (see page 336), lovely Glen Isla is the furthest west of the Angus Glens and can also be reached from the little town of Alyth, east of Blairgowrie. At the southern end of the glen, five miles north of Alyth by Bridge of Glenisla, is **Reekie Linn**, a series of waterfalls that plunge through a deep, wooded gorge. A path leads for 200 yds from the car park and picnic site on the road between Bridge of Glenisla and Bridge of Lintrathen. Nearby is the excellent *Lochside Lodge* restaurant and *Peel Farm Coffee and Craft Shop*.

Glen Isla
Phone code:01575

Six miles north, at **Kirkton of Glenisla**, on the B951, is the **C** *Glenisla Hotel*, T582223, glenislahotel@sol.co.uk, an impossibly cosy 17th-century inn with log fires, real ales, good grub and plenty of local characters. It's worth the trip just to spend a night here. Further north a side road turns off the B951 and runs to **Auchavan**, at the head of the glen. There are paths from here into the wild and mountainous **Caenlochan Forest**. A **postbus** runs Mon-Sat from Blairgowrie to Auchavan. At the mouth of the glen is the tiny village of **Meigle**, home to Scotland's most important collection of early-Christian and Pictish carved stones. They are housed in the superb **Meigle Museum**. ■ *Apr-Sep daily 0930-1830. £1.80.*

Five miles north of Kirriemuir is the tiny village of **Dykehead**, at the foot of Glen Clova, where a side road branches northwest and runs into Glen Prosen. Both glens penetrate deep into the Grampian Mountains and are blessed with a rugged beauty, but Glen Prosen carries little of the cachet of its neighbour and is consequently a much more peaceful option for hillwalkers. The little road runs deep, into the glen but it's best explored on foot.

Glen Prosen
Phone code: 01575

A good walk is the relatively straightforward four-mile **Minister's Path**, which connects the two glens. It starts from behind the kirk in Glenprosen village and heads over the hilly moorland and down to the B955 just before Clova village. You can catch the **postbus** back to Kirriemuir from the *Clova Hotel* (see below). The Kirriemuir to Glen Prosen postbus runs once daily except Sun.

Glen Clova is only 30 miles north of Dundee yet you could be in the heart of the Highlands, with craggy mountains towering overhead and heather-clad slopes populated by deer and grouse. Glen Clova leads north into Glen Doll, from where you can follow the old **drove roads** which lead to Ballater and Braemar in Deeside. These ancient routes were used by whisky smugglers, government troops and rebels, as well as cattle drovers, and though they may look straightforward on the map, they can be as treacherous as any of the Scottish mountains. Only fit and experienced walkers should attempt these walks.

**Glen Clova
& Glen Doll**
Phone code: 01575
*OS Landranger
Nos 43 & 44*

One of the best walks is the famous **Jock's Road** to Braemar. The 14-mile route starts from the Glen Doll youth hostel and it's a tough seven-hour hike

Northeast Scotland

up to the summit at Crow Craigies (3,108 ft) and down to the head of Loch Callater. The descent is very steep and may require crampons in winter. From the loch, the path follows the Callater Burn till it reaches the main A93, two miles from Braemar (see page 419). Another excellent walk is the **Loops of Brandy**, which starts from behind the *Clova Hotel* and climbs up into the mountains, around Loch Brandy and back again. It's a four-hour walk there and back.

Drivers should note that the B955 from Dykehead divides just before the bridge of the River South Esk. The west branch is traditionally used by vehicles heading up the glen, while the east branch should be for traffic returning down the glen. The two roads meet up again six miles further on, at the tiny hamlet of **Clova**, which consists of little more than the **D** *Clova Hotel*, T550222, which is a very friendly and popular climbers' retreat. As well as bar meals, the hotel lays on regular barbecues, ceilidhs and a multitude of various activities. There's also an eight-bed bunkhouse outside (**F**) which is open all year. It has a kitchen, but no shower.

Four miles further north, near the end of the road, in Glen Doll, is a campsite, T550233, by the bridge. It's open during the summer and has only basic facilities. A few hundered yards north is **F** *Glendoll Youth Hostel*, T550236, open 10 March-31 October. It has 45 beds and boasts a squash court as well as the standard facilities. Note that access is limited between 1030 and 1700. There's a **postbus** service to Glen Clova from Kirriemuir twice a day Monday-Friday and once on Saturday. The 0830 departure runs as far as the hostel and the 1500 departure (Monday-Friday only) stops at the *Clova Hotel*. The afternoon service leaves from the hotel at 1530.

Glen Esk
Phone code: 01356

North from Edzell, the road runs 13 miles to the head of beautiful **Glen Esk**, the most easterly of the Angus Glens and, like the others, quiet and empty. Nine miles north of Edzell along the Glen road is the **Glenesk Folk Museum**, housed in an old shooting lodge known as 'The Retreat'. The museum's extensive local folk history collection gives a fascinating insight into the lives of the Glen's inhabitants. It also has a good tearoom (try their rhubarb jam and home baking). ■ *Easter-May Sat-Mon 1200-1800; Jun to mid-Oct 1200-1800. Adult £2. T670254.*

OS Landranger No 44

Four miles further on, beyond Tarfside village, the public road ends at **Invermark Castle**. This is the start of one of the Mounth Roads, ancient rights of way leading from the Angus Glens across the mountains to Deeside. This route leads eventually to Ballater or **Glen Tanar**, near Aboyne. For a description of the latter route in reverse, see under **Deeside** (page 421). You can also hike from here to the summit of **Mount Keen** (3,081ft), Scotland's most easterly Munro, but – like the Mounth Road – this is a tough walk and you'll need full hill-walking equipment and a map. An easier walk is to the **Queen's Well**, three miles from the car park across the river from Invermark Castle. It's about three hours there and back. Altenatively, you can head west from the castle, past the lovely old church and along the north shore of **Loch Lee.**

Aberdeen

Scotland's third largest city, and Britain's most isolated, is a hard place. Hard because of the grey granite of its buildings, and hard because of the nature of its people, who are industrious, thrifty, proud and uncompromising. First impressions are often determined by the weather: when it rains it's about as appealing as cold porridge. Sometimes leaden skies hang low over a uniform greyness, and a howling gale blows in from the North Sea, but when the clouds do part and the sun shines down, the tiny mica chips, which form a natural part of granite, sparkle and glisten like a display in a jeweller's window. Whatever the impression, it is a place that elicits a strong response. Lewis Grassic Gibbon, the northeast's most famous writer, wrote: "One detests Aberdeen with the detestation of a thwarted lover. It is the one haunting and exasperatingly lovable city in Scotland."

Phone code: 01224
Colour map 4, grid A6
Population: 217,260

Ins and outs

Aberdeen **airport** is 7 miles northwest of the city centre, at Dyce, off the A96 to Inverness. There are regular domestic flights to Scottish and UK destinations, including Orkney and Shetland, as well as international flights to several European destinations. For airport information, T722331. There's car hire and currency exchange at the airport. Buses 27 and 27A run at peak times to and from the city centre (35 mins, £1.35 single). For more information, T650065. Alternatively, take a train to Dyce station and a bus (Mon-Fri only) or taxi from there. A taxi from the airport to Dyce railway station costs around £5, and £10 to the city centre.

Getting there
For more details see pages 31 & 411

Aberdeen is linked to Lerwick in Shetland and Stromness in Orkney by P&O **ferries**, T572615. There are regular sailings from the passenger terminal in the harbour, a short walk east of the train and bus stations.

The **bus** terminal is next to the train station, on Guild St. *National Express* has daily buses from London and *Scottish Citylink* runs buses to all major Scottish towns. *Bluebird*, T212266, are the main regional operator. The **train** station is on Guild St. There are regular services from London, and major Scottish towns and cities. For all rail enquiries, T08457-484950.

Aberdeen city centre is compact and the best way to get around is on foot, though you may need to use local buses to reach some of the outlying sights, such as Old Aberdeen and the University. Almost all **buses** pass along Union St, the city's main thoroughfare. The most useful services are: Nos 18, 19, 24 and 24A from Union St to Great Western Rd; Nos 6, 20 and 26 to Old Aberdeen; No 14 to the Beach and Footdee; and Nos 17 and 26 to Duthie Park from Union St. A good idea, if you're using public transport frequently, is to buy a prepaid **Farecard** (for £3, £5 or £10), which works like a phonecard. These are available at the tourist office (see below), where you can also pick up the free *Public Transport Guide* which includes a map of bus routes. For a **taxi**, call *Mair's*, T724040.

Getting around

The main sights can be visited in a couple of leisurely days, and many of them are free. Most of the **museums and art galleries** are clustered around the compact city centre and can be covered on foot. From the centre it's only a short walk down to the **harbour**, with its bustling fish market and interesting **Maritime Museum**. The outlying sights, such as the suburb of **Old Aberdeen**, **Duthie Park** and the city's **beach** can all easily be reached by bus. The best way to get around is to take one of *Grampian Coaches'* open-topped **bus tours** of the city, which leave from the tourist office. These run from Jun-Sep and cost £4 per person for a 90-min tour, or £6 per person for a full day *Explorer ticket*, which allows you to hop on and off official tour buses as well as use any other buses around the city. Tickets can be bought from the driver, at the sales kiosk in St Nicholas St, or at the head office at 395 King St, T650024.

Northeast Scotland

Information The very helpful **Tourist information Centre** is now in Provost Ross' House, in Shiprow by the harbour, T288828. As well as the usual accommodation booking service, they also will also book tickets for theatres and events, trips and tours. They have a wide selection of leaflets on walks in Aberdeen, and run bus tours (see below). The tourist office also gives out free monthly listings magazines, *Listings Aberdeen* and *What's On*, and has a 24-hr *What's On Line*, T636363. Another good source of information on current events are the local newspapers, the *Press and Journal* and *Evening News*. Open Jun and Sep Mon-Sat 0900-1700, Sun 1000-1400; Jul-Aug Mon-Fri 0900-1900, Sat 0900-1700, Sun 1000-1600; Oct-May Mon-Fri 0900-1700, Sat 1000-1400, T632727, www.castlesandwhisky.com

History

Aberdeen lies between two rivers, the Don to the north and the Dee to the south, backed by a fertile hinterland and facing the wild North Sea, which has brought the city great wealth since the discovery of oil in the early 1970s. Its maritime history, however, dates back to its foundation as a Royal Burgh in 1124. In the past Aberdeen had strong trading links with Scandinavia and the Low Countries. Fast clipper ships, built in the city, brought tea from India and other goods from all over the world. Until some years after the Second World War, Aberdeen's lifeblood was fishing and shipping. It was the biggest fish market in the country and still lands considerable catches. Then came the discovery of North Sea oil and gas and Aberdeen became Boom City, flaunting its new-found wealth with an almost unseemly fervour. The glory years of the early 1980s may have gone, but Aberdeen still exudes an air of self-confidence and prosperity rare in other regional UK cities.y

Aberdonians also have an inordinate amount of civic pride, which can verge on the overweening. This may have been enhanced in recent years by its new-found status and wealth, but has its roots in the 14th century, when the townsfolk offered protection to Robert the Bruce during the Wars of Independence. In return, Bruce rewarded the town with 'Freedom Lands' for which he had previously received rent. The money saved was diverted into a Common Good Fund, to be spent on amenities. Today this money is still used to pay for the upkeep of its many fine parks and to keep the city looking its best. This sense of pride in its parks and public buildings makes Aberdeen an extremely pleasant place to visit. It's also a very lively place, and its many bars, restaurants, nightclubs, theatres and shops are as vibrant and thriving as you'd expect in any city with money in its pockets.

Sights

City centre Aberdeen's main artery is **Union Street**, one mile long and built on pillars (an amazing and expensive engineering feat). The street is a fascinating mix of Victorian Gothic and modern glass and concrete and is perpetually packed with buses, cars and pedestrians. The oldest part of the city is the 13th-century **Castlegate**, at the eastern end of Union Street, now dominated by the 17th-century **Mercat Cross**, which was the focus of Aberdeen's long history as a major market town and trading centre. Opposite, at the corner of Union Street and King Street, in the Town House, is the **Tolbooth** which dates from the 14th century. Not only did it serve as a collection point for tolls and taxes but it was also used as the Wardhouse, housing prisoners held on remand.

A little further west down Union Street is Broad Street, where you'll find the tourist office. 50 yds beyond it, at 45 Guestrow, is Aberdeen's oldest surviving private house, the 16th-century **Provost Skene's House**. Its distinctive style, with boldly pointed stone and little turrets, stands out from the adjacent modern buildings. It was only the intervention of the Queen Mother which saved this little historical gem from the same fate as its neighbours. The interior features a series of ornate tempera-painted ceilings dating from 1622, which somehow survived the orgy of vandalism in the wake of the Reformation. There are also furnished period rooms and an interesting display of memorabilia, including mementos of John Brown, ghillie and companion of Queen Victoria. There is a pocket watch given to him by the widowed queen, also a silver pipe and case from the same donor. ■ *Mon-Sat 1000-1700, Sun 1300-1600. Free. T641086.*

Across the road from the tourist office is the imposing **Marischal College** (pronounced 'Marshall'), the second largest granite building in the world, after the Escorial in Madrid. This massive neo-Gothic sculpture is loved and loathed in equal measure, but cannot be ignored. Aberdeen was the seat of two universities, the Catholic King's College (see 'Old Aberdeen' below) and the Protestant Marischal College, founded in 1593 by the 5th Earl of Marischal. The two colleges combined in 1860 to form Aberdeen University. The **museum**, entered through the main quadrangle and up the stairs, is open to visitors and worth visiting. It is divided into two exhibitions, the 'Encylopaedia of the Northeast', which depicts the region's distinctive culture, and 'Collecting the World', which features many wonderfully diverse items collected from around the globe. ■ *Mon-Fri 1000-1700, Sun 1400-1700. Free. T274301.*

From Marischal College, head down Upperkirkgate, past the Bon Accord and St Nicholas Shopping Centres, and up Schoolhill to the city's magnificent

Aberdeen

Sleeping	2 Gerard's	6 Wild Boar
1 Brentwood	3 Lemon Tree	
2 Caledonian Thistle	4 Owlie's	**Bars & pubs**
	5 Poldon's,	7 Ministry of Sin
Eating	Ma Cameron's Inn	8 Oh'Henry's
1 Carmine's Pizza	& Old Town School	

Northeast Scotland

A rose by any other name

*Aberdeen is known as the 'Granite City',
and Rubislaw Quarry still bears
testament to the vast quantities of
granite hewn there and used to build its
striking Victorian Gothic buildings. But it
has a softer side, and is also known as the
'City of Roses'.*

There is a profusion of blooming

*flowers that fill the parks, gardens, traffic
islands and roadways, creating a stark
contrast to the grey streets and buildings.
In fact, flower power is so prevalent here
that Aberdeen has been debarred from
entering the 'Britain in Bloom'
competition, in order to give other places
a chance!*

Art Gallery, a most elegant building of marble steps with a pillared gallery overlooking a central well. At the top of the stairs stands a showcase of lovely Meissen china. There are changing displays of costumes and applied arts. All the big names are here; there's a Degas bronze, and paintings by **Dante Gabriel Rossetti**, **Monet**, **Pissarro**, **Millais**, **Legros**, **Sargent**, **Sisley**, **Russell Flint**, **Holman Hunt**, **Landseer**, **Augustus John**, **Raeburn**, **McTaggart** and **Sir George Reid**, amongst many others. **William Roelofs**' large oil of *Waterlilies* is a fitting rival to Monet. There are also several works by **Joan Eardley**, who lived near Stonehaven. A large number of the paintings were bequeathed by local granite merchant, Alex MacDonald, in 1900. Downstairs is a white-walled circular room which commemorates the 167 people who lost their lives in the Piper Alpha oil rig disaster in 1988. There's also a well-stocked shop, café and craft gallery. ■ *Mon-Sat 1000-1700, Sun 1400-1700. Free. T646333.*

West of the Art Gallery are the sunken **Union Terrace Gardens**, which make a pleasant escape from the traffic on Union Street. Here, at the end of Union Terrace, stand three buildings at right angles: the Central Library, His Majesty's Theatre and St Mark's Church, always known locally as 'Education, Damnation and Salvation'. They are obligingly pointed out by a huge statue of William Wallace, brandishing his sword. At the West End of Union Street, Bon Accord Terrace leads south into Justice Mill Lane, home to many of the city's best bars and nightclubs, and also to the **Sartrosphere**, a fun-focused hands-on science and technology discovery centre. ■ *Apr-Oct Mon-Sat 1000-1700, Sun 1330-1700, Mar-Nov Mon-Fri (closed Tue) 1000-1600, Sat 1000-1700; Sun 1330-1700. £5, £3 children/concession. T640340.*

Anyone interested in military history should not miss the **Gordon Highlanders Museum** at St Luke's in Viewfield Road, which is off Queen's Road (buses 14 or 15 from Union Street). ■ *Apr-Oct Tue-Sat 1030-1630, Sun 1330-1630. £2, £1.50 concession. T311200.*

The harbour From the Castlegate, Shiprow, a steep cobbled street, leads down to the harbour and the gleaming glass and steel of the excellent new **Maritime Museum**, which traces Aberdeen's long seafaring history from earliest times up to the present day. In the entrance is a list, up-dated daily, of ships in harbour. The Lloyd's register is there if you ask. As you go up the stairs (there's a lift, if needed), the first things that you will see are the lenses from Rattray Head lighthouse. The sounds are authentic: the cry of seagulls and the crash of the sea on shale. A huge board lists all the ships built in Aberdeen from 1811 until 1991, including the famous fast clippers. Most dramatically, down the stairwell hangs a model of an oil rig. The methods in use in oil and gas exploration and production are explained. The auditorium (which has an induction

Northeast Scotland

City slickers

When oil was discovered in the North Sea in 1970, it was assumed that 'black gold' would bring nationwide prosperity. But while many in the country would argue that the huge oil revenues flowed south with little benefit accruing to the Scottish people, the people of Aberdeen have a different tale to tell.

Oil transformed Aberdeen from a relatively impoverished northern backwater to a flourishing and prosperous city, where every oil company, exploration firm, tool manufacturer and diving supplier now base themselves. Aberdeen quickly became the oil capital of Europe. Millions were invested in infrastructure, such as the harbour and airport, the population increased rapidly, average earnings soared and unemployment plummeted. Aberdeen was suddenly a city brimming with confidence. New, upmarket restaurants,

bars and shops opened to cater for a population with money to burn. Ironic, really, in a city whose people have a reputation for being less than extravagant with their cash.

But it couldn't last. In the mid-1980s the price of oil slumped from US$80 a barrel to US$10 and recession struck the northeast. Jobs vanished, house prices dropped and Aberdonians woke up to the realization that they were completely dependent on oil for their economic well-being. But predictions of the city's demise were greatly exaggerated. In recent years oil prices and production have risen to the levels of the early 1980s and house prices are once more on the up. Oil looks set to continue flowing in from the North Sea for a very long time to come. And this time around everyone will surely heed the dangers of the past and learn to be a bit more Aberdonian.

---

loop system) features good explanatory videos. There is a hands-on children's area and a layout of bunks. The museum spills over into the adjoining **Provost Ross' House** dating from 1593, the oldest building in the city, which now houses the **Tourist Information Centre**. There's also a shop and a good licensed café. ■ *Mon-Sat 1000-1700, Sun 1200-1500. Free. T337700.*

At the foot of Shiprow is Market Street, which runs the length of the harbour. It's still a busy place and on any one day you'll see a huge variety of vessels from all over the world. Follow your nose and the screech of seagulls down to the **fish market**, where fish has been landed and traded since the 13th century. The best time to see it is early in the morning, before 0800. At the northeast corner of the harbour is the old fishing village of **Footdee** (pronounced 'Fittie'), which is interesting to explore and an easy walk from Market Street, via Regent and Waterloo Quays and York Street, or south from the Beach Esplanade. Ask at the tourist office about guided walks, or pick up one of their leaflets.

At the southern end of Market Street, North Esplanade leads to **Duthie Park**, a 10-minute bus ride from town, on the banks of the Dee. The park features a beautiful rose garden, known as 'Rose Mountain', which is best seen in summer. Also in the park are the Winter Gardens, a gigantic hothouse full of tropical plants and birds. It covers an amazing two acres and is possibly the largest of its kind in Europe.

A 20-minute bus ride northwest of the city centre, on the banks of the Don, is the beautifully preserved suburb of Old Aberdeen, with its cobbled streets and peaceful atmosphere. An independent burgh until 1891, Old Aberdeen is clustered around **St Machar's Cathedral**, with its soaring twin spires. The cathedral was founded in the sixth century and is one of the oldest granite

Old Aberdeen

Northeast Scotland

buildings in the city, dating from the 15th century. It is also one of the few examples in the country of a fortified cathedral. Legend has it that Machar, a follower of Columba, was sent to establish a church at a place near the sea where the river was shaped like the crook on a Bishop's crozier, hence its site. Inside, the heraldic ceiling is particularly impressive. ■ *Daily 0900-1700, free, services on Sun at 1100 and 1800. T485988.* Next to the cathedral is the **Cruickshank Botanic Garden**, with beautiful floral displays. ■ *May-Sep Mon-Fri 0900-1630, Sat-Sun 1400-1700; Oct-Apr Mon-Fri 0900-1630. Free.*

A short walk south of St Machar's is **King's College**, founded in 1495 by Bishop Elphinstone. The most notable of the college buildings is the 16th-century **King's College Chapel**, with its distinctive crowned spire. The interior is remarkably well preserved and features some rare and beautiful medieval woodcarving in the ceiling and choir stalls. ■ *Mon-Fri 0900-1700. Free. T272137.* The **King's College Visitor Centre** houses a multimedia display on the university's often turbulent history. ■ *Mon-Sat 1000-1700, Sun 1200-1700. Free. T273702.* There are **guided walks** around the cathedral and University from June-August, leaving from King's College on Wednesday at 1900 and Sunday at 1430. The guides are extremely helpful and well informed.

Just to the north of St Machar's Cathedral, on the banks of the Don, is **Seaton Park**, another of the city's fine open spaces. North of the park, the Don is spanned by the **Brig o' Balgownie**, completed in the 14th century with money from the Common Good Fund. It is the oldest Gothic bridge in Scotland, and over the years has charmed the likes of Byron. On the north bank of the Don is **Bridge of Don**, home to the city's two finest golf courses, the Royal Aberdeen and Murcar.

The beach Between the mouths of the rivers Don and Dee, and less than a mile east of Union Street, is Aberdeen's beach, a two-mile stretch of glorious golden sand. But though the northeast gets a large share of Scotland's sunshine, don't expect to sunbathe comfortably as the beach is exposed to the bitter North Sea winds. And as you watch parents coaxing their reluctant children into the water, note that a few miles offshore, oil rig workers are being warned of the dangers of perishing in these freezing seas. At the southern end of the esplanade is **Aberdeen Fun Beach**, a huge leisure complex with multi sports facilities, swimming pool, bar and cafés, ice arena, multiplex cinema, nightclub and Scotland's largest permanent fun fair. Nearby is Pittodrie Park, home of Aberdeen FC. The northern end of the long, long beach is backed by a succession of golf links.

Essentials

Sleeping
Though full of transient oil workers and business people during the week, many hotels offer discounts at the weekend, when prices fall by up to 50%. Note that single rooms are at premium and very poor value

Aberdeen has plenty of accommodation but its hotels are relatively expensive. The best value are the B&Bs and guesthouses, many of which can be found on Bon Accord St and Crown St, both running south off Union St, and along Great Western Rd. The cheapest options are the youth hostel and university residences left vacant during summer vacation. There's also a campsite in the suburbs. The tourist office has a free guide and will book accommodation.

L *Caledonian Thistle Hotel*, Union Terr, T640233, F641627. 78 rooms. Superior city-centre hotel in a grand old Victorian building. Full facilities, friendly service and good restaurants. **L** *The Marcliffe at Pitfodils*, North Deeside Rd, T861000, reservations@marcliff.com. 42 rooms. This outstanding, luxurious country house hotel on the outskirts of town offers an unbeatable mix of baronial elegance and modern comforts, as well as exceptional hospitality and service, and superb cuisine.

A *Simpson's Hotel Bar/Brasserie*, 59 Queen's Rd, T327777, address@simpsonshotel .com 37 rooms. Very stylish, modern hotel with a Mediterranean look and feel. The attached restaurant has won many plaudits for its excellent Scottish/international cuisine (see 'Eating').

C *Atholl Hotel*, 54 King's Gate, T323505, info@atholl-aberdeen.co.uk 35 rooms. 1 of many elegant granite mansions in the West End, this one has an excellent reputation for its reliability, service and good food. **C** *Brentwood Hotel*, 101 Crown St, T595440, reservations@brentwood-hotel.demon.co.uk 65 rooms. Good-value business hotel and therefore often full on weekdays, on a street full of similar hotels, but better than most, close to the action on Union St; its cellar bar does very good bar meals (see 'Bars'). **C** *Craiglynn Hotel*, 36 Fonthill Rd, T584050, www.craiglynn.co.uk 8 rooms. Intimate and comfortable Victorian house close to the town centre, also has a good reputation for its food. **C** *Mannofield Hotel*, 447 Great Western Rd, T315888, mannofield _hotel@tartan-collection.co.uk 9 rooms. Small, friendly and elegant hotel about a mile west of Union St.

D *Cults Hotel*, 328 North Deeside Rd, T/F867632. 6 rooms. 4 miles from the town centre on the A93 to Deeside, good value. **D-E** *Speedbird Inns*, Argyll Rd, Dyce, T772884. 99 rooms. Large, purpose-built hotel chain at the airport; good value.

There are many **guesthouses** on Bon Accord St, including: **E** *Applewood Guesthouse*, No 154, T580617; **E** *Crynoch Guesthouse*, No 164, T582743; and **E-F** *Denmore Guesthouse*, No 166, T587751. There are also numerous small, family-run guesthouses along Great Western Rd: **E** *Aberdeen Springdale Guesthouse*, No 404, T316561; **D-E** *Fourways Guesthouse*, No 435, T310218; **E** *Kildonan Guesthouse*, No 410, T316115; and **D-E** *The Noble Guesthouse*, No 376, T313678. Another good place to look is along King St, where you'll find **D-E** *Campbell's Guesthouse*, No 444, T625444, cam44@zetnet.co.uk; and the very highly rated **D-E** *The Jays Guesthouse*, No 422, T638295, jaysguesthouse@clara.net

F *Aberdeen Youth Hostel* is at 8 Queen's Rd, T646988, a mile west of the bus and train stations (take buses 14 or 15 from the bus station). It's open all year till 0200 and has 116 beds. The nearest **campsite** is *Hazelhead Caravan Park & Campsite*n on the A944, with a swimming pool nearby. Take buses 14 or 15 from town. Open Apr-Sep.

Campus accommodation is available at the *University of Aberdeen* **C** *Kings Hall* (open all year) and **C** *Crombie Johnston Hall* (open Mar-Apr and Jun-Sep), both well situated in Old Aberdeen. Contact: Conference Office, Regent Walk, Old Aberdeen, T272664, j.m.pirie@admin.abdn.ac.uk *Robert Gordon's University*, T262134, also has self-catering flats throughout the city. For more details check with the TIC.

Expensive *Courtyard on the Lane*, Alford La, T213795, just off the west end of Union St. Highly rated bistro serving imaginative Scottish/European menu, with a more formal restaurant upstairs. Open Tue-Sat. *Gerard's*, 50 Chapel St, T639500. This *très cher* traditional French restaurant has been around for as long as anyone can remember and remains one of the best; the set meal is less of a strain on the bank balance. Open daily. *Silver Darlings Restaurant*, Pocra Quay, North Pier, Footdee, at the southern end of the Beach Esplanade, T576229. Highly recommended as serving the best seafood in town, also a great location overlooking the harbour entrance, best to book in advance. Open Mon-Fri 1200-1400, Mon-Sat 1900-2130. *Simpson's*, 59 Queen's Rd, T327777 (see also 'Sleeping'). Designer brasserie serving superb Scottish cuisine with an international flavour. Open daily.

Mid-range *Little Italy*, 79 Holborn St, T515227, near the west end of Union St. Usual pasta and pizza fare. Open late (till 2400 Mon-Wed and till 0200 Thu-Sat). *Owlie's*, Littlejohn St, T649267. French brasserie food with some interesting variations and good vegetarian/vegan options, very popular, so good atmosphere and good value. Open Mon-Sat. *Poldino's*, 7 Little Belmont St, T647777, one of the city's favourite Italian restaurants, so it's always busy. *The Royal Thai*, Crown Terr (off Crown St), T212922.

Eating
There's no shortage of good places to eat in Aberdeen, though prices tend to be higher than elsewhere in the region. Many of the city's pubs and bars serve good-value meals, though many of them don't serve food in the evening

Northeast Scotland

Long-established Thai restaurant with wide-ranging menu. Open daily for lunch and 1900-2300. *The Wild Boar*, 19 Belmont St, T625357. Popular bar-bistro serving good-value food, plenty of vegetarian choices, and just look at those cakes! Open daily.

Cheap *Ashvale*, 46 Great Western Rd, T596981. The northeast's most famous, and best, fish and chips, quite simply unmissable. This is the original branch and it's huge, with seating for 300; also takeaway. Open daily till late. Another superb chippie, some say better, is *The New Dolphin* on Chapel St. Mostly takeaway and open till 0100 (0300 at weekends). *Carmine's Pizza*, 32 Union Terr, T624145. Best pizza in town and excellent-value 3-course lunches. Open Mon-Sat 1200-1730. *The Lemon Tree*, 5 West North St, T642230. Café inside the excellent arts centre (see also 'Entertainment'). Relaxed and laid-back place for a light vegetarian lunch, or coffee and cakes. Open Wed-Sun 1200-1500.

Bars & nightlcubs

Like most busy ports, Aberdeen has a large transient population with lots of cash to spend. Consequently, its numerous loud, flashy bars and traditional pubs are usually packed with people out for a good time. *The Prince of Wales*, 7 St Nicholas La, just off Union St, T640597. The best pub in the city, with a great selection of real ales and a real flagstone floor. Also does very cheap bar food and gets very crowded. Traditional fiddel music on Sun evenings. There are lots of trendy bars in Justice Mill Lane, off the West End of Union St, which fall in and out of fashion, but *Bex* is a perennial fave. *Café Society*, 9 Queen's Rd, opposite the youth hostel. A bit of an oil workers' pick-up joint, but has a good beer garden and serves food till 2200. *Cocky Hunters*, 504 Union St. Very popular with students and young professionals, and features regular live music. *The Globe*, 13 North Silver St. Down-to-earth café-bar which serves decent food at lunch-time. *Ma Cameron's Inn*, Little Belmont St. The city's oldest pub, though the old bit now constitutes only a small section, serves food at lunch and early evening. In the same street is *The Old Town School*, which is more of a modern theme bar but has a good selection of ales and does food. *O'Neill's*, 9 Back Wynd. An Irish theme pub which serves decent grub, a good selection of Irish beers, stout and whiskeys, and has live folk music at weekends. Wild club upstairs (see below). *Under the Hammer*, North Silver Street, along from *The Globe*, a basement wine bar which attracts a more mature crowd. Open evenings only.

Aberdeen also has numerous nightclubs to choose from, most of which close at 0200. Pick of the bunch is *Ministry of Sin*, 16 Dee St, T211661, off Union St. The faithful congregate in this converted church for a heavenly mix of cool sounds and atmosphere. Popular with students and oldies. Often has big-name guest DJs and open 7 days. *The Works*, 9 Belmont St. Subterranean and sub-twenties, sweaty and lively kind of a place. Open Thu-Sat till 0200. *Oh'Henry's*, 20 Adelphi Close, just off Union St. Very studenty and therefore very retro (70s and 80s). *The Pelican* at the *Metro Hotel*, Market St. Basement club featuring live indie bands and guest DJs. Open Thu-Sat. *O'Neill's*, 9 Back Wynd. Upstairs in Irish theme pub. Nominal cover charge gets you a wild, raucous night of Irish music till 0200. Lots of stamina needed, hence the younger crowd.

Entertainment

Tickets for most plays and concerts can be booked at the box office, next to the Music Hall on Union St, T641122. Open Mon-Sat 1000-1800

Cinema Among the city's mainstream cinemas is *Virgin*, T572228, a huge 9-screen complex on Beach Esplanade; and the *Odeon*, T916422, on Justice Mill Lane. **Theatre** *His Majesty's*, Rosemount Viaduct, T637788. Aberdeen's main theatre, with a programme featuring opera, ballet, musicals and panto. *Music Hall*, Union St, T632508. The main venue for classical music concerts, as well as big-name comedy acts. *Capitol Theatre*, 431 Union St, T583141. Venue for smaller touring rock and pop bands. *Aberdeen Arts Centre*, 33 King St, T635208. Stages a variety of theatrical productions and exhibitions, and also shows arthouse movies. *The Lemon Tree*, 5 West North St, T642230. The hub of the city's arts scene, with a wide and varied programme of events, including live jazz and folk, comedy and contemporary drama. Also has a good café/bar-restaurant (see 'Eating').

Air There are domestic flights to and from London and several provincial airports, and to a few European destinations.

Transport
*See also pages
30 & 403*

Boat *P&O* ferries, T572615, have daily evening departures (Mon-Fri) to **Lerwick** on Shetland. The trip takes 14-20 hrs. From Jun-Aug there are departures on Tue and Sat to **Stromness** on Orkney; Sat only the rest of the year. See also under **Orkney & Shetland** (page 596).

Bus *Scottish Citylink* runs direct buses to **Dundee** (2 hrs), **Perth** (2½ hrs), **Edinburgh** (4 hrs), **Stirling** (3½ hrs) and **Glasgow** (4½ hrs). *Bluebird Buses*, T212266, is the major local bus operator. Service No 10 goes every hour to **Inverness** via **Huntly** and **Elgin**. Service No 201 goes every 30 mins (hourly on Sun) to **Banchory**, every hour (Mon-Sat; less frequently on Sun) to **Ballatar** and several times daily to **Braemar**. There are also buses to **Stonehaven** (Service No 103), **Alford** (Service No 220), **Peterhead** (No 263), **Fraserburgh** (Nos 267/268) and **Ellon** (Nos 290/291). For more details pick up a free copy of the *Aberdeenshire & Moray Public Transport Guide* at the bus station or tourist office, or call the Public Transport Unit, T664581.

Car hire *Budget*, Powis Terr, Great Northern Rd, T488770; also at the airport, T771777. *Arnold Clark*, Girdleness Rd, T249159. *Thrifty*, 76 Huntly St, T621033. **Cycle hire** *Aberdeen Cycle Centre*, 188 King St, T644542. *Alpine Bikes*, 64 Holburn St, T211455. From £12 per day. Open daily.

Train There are services to **Edinburgh** (2½ hrs), **Glasgow** (2¾ hrs), **Dundee** (1¼ hrs), **Perth** (1¾ hrs), **Stirling** (2¼ hrs) and **Inverness** (2¼ hrs).

Banks All the major banks have branches with ATMs on and around Union St. **Currency exchange**: *Thomas Cook*, 335-337 Union St, T212271. Open Mon-Sat 0930-1730; or the tourist office on Broad St. *American Express* office at *Lunn Poly*, 3-5 St Nicholas St, T633119. Open Mon-Fri 0900-1730, Sat 0900-1700. **Communications** Internet facilities at the Central Library, also at *RSC Internet*, 15 Marischal St, T585113. The main **post office** is in the St Nicholas Centre, T633065. **Medical services** *Aberdeen Royal Infirmary*, T681818, is on Foresthill, northeast of the town centre. It has a 24-hr A&E. **Pharmacy**: *Boots*, 161 Union St, T211592. Open Mon-Sat 0800-1800. **Tour operators** *Grampian Heritage Tours*, T01358-789513, run various day tours around the region, leaving from the tourist office. Tickets also from tourist office. *STA Travel*, 30 Kirkgate, T658222. **Useful addresses** Left luggage: 24-hr lockers at the train station. **Police**: Queen St, T639111.

Directory

South Aberdeenshire

The main A90 runs north from Dundee to Aberdeen and passes through the Howe of the Mearns, an agricultural district so evocatively described by local author, Lewis Grassic Gibbon, in his brilliant trilogy A Scots Quair. *His home can be visited at Arbuthnott. The coastal route (A92) from Dundee runs north from Montrose and meets the A90 by the little fishing port of Stonehaven, which is close to the dramatic ruins of Dunnotar Castle, one of the area's main attractions. Other places of interest include Fasque House, family home of Victorian prime minister Gladstone.*

Montrose to Stonehaven

North of Montrose on the A92, is the little coastal village of St Cyrus, whose church steeple is seen to great effect for miles around. Thanks to a bequest in the will of one John Orr in 1844, four local brides benefit each year in the most

St Cyrus
*Phone code: 01674
Colour map 4, grid B5*

unusual way. The eldest, the youngest, the tallest and the shortest (all of them carefully measured by the local minister) receive a dowry from the interest on the money which he left for that purpose. Thus they are known as The Dowry Brides. The annual interest is in fact divided in five. The final fifth is used to buy comforts for the poor. The town is also known for its strict enforcement of the 30 mile per hour speed limit (this applies to Kincardine O'Neil on Deeside too). There's a wonderful sandy **beach** here, and the **National Nature Reserve**, complete with marine-life tank and visitor centre, is interesting, T830736, May-Sep.

Sleeping and transport E *Kirkside Bothy*, near the beach, T830780, Apr-Oct. There's also a **campsite** at *East Bowstrips Caravan Park*, T850328. At Lauriston, turn right at the *Bush Hotel* for Milton Haven. *Bluebird Buses*, service No 101 between Stonehaven and Montrose, pass through St Cyrus and Johnshaven hourly Mon-Fri (less frequently Sat-Sun).

Johnshaven
Phone code: 01561
Colour map 4, grid B5

A few miles further on is the old fishing village of Johnshaven, a thriving fishing port until quite recently, and in the early 18th century probably the largest in Scotland. The village is unusual because of the great number of people who are called McBay. They are all mostly descended from two cousins, Long Ned and Little Ned, one of whom had seven sons, and the other 10. Johnshaven is a good spot for buying lobster and crab, and its annual **Fish Festival** is getting more and more popular. It takes place on either the first or second Saturday in August. The date depends upon the tides, which have to be suitable for visiting craft. There's accommodation in the village at E *Ellington B&B*, Station Place, T362756.

The three-mile walk north along the shore to **Gourdon**, is one of the most pleasant and one of the easiest in the area. Very often, cormorants bask in the sun out on the rocks, spreading their wings to dry. Rather less often dolphins tumble past, their fins cutting a path through the water. In Gourdon you can buy fish from several fish houses on the harbour.

Inverbervie
Colour map 4, grid B6

A few miles further on from Johnshaven lies Inverbervie, birthplace of Hercules Linton, designer of the *Cutty Sark*. The village is probably better known for the *Bervie Chipper* which was recently voted the best fish and chip shop in the UK. You can either eat in or takeaway (either way it's excellent value); just don't leave town without finding out what all the fuss is about.

By decree of King David, son of Robert the Bruce, Inverbervie is a Royal Burgh and residents enjoy several privileges, such as free fishing in the local river. Many anglers know this, but the fish seem to know as well as they are not very plentiful. For full-blooded **fishing** make for either the North Esk River at Edzell (see page 397) or somewhere along its length before it flows out to the sea by the two bridges just north of Montrose. The old bridge in Inverbervie, built in 1799, is the oldest single span bridge in the British Isles. To see it, turn left to the north of the village, just before the memorial to Linton. In the village square is *Mingei,* which has a good selection of Japanese and European antiques.

Just to the south of the village, on the left heading north, is the **Mill of Benholm** (pronounced 'Ben-um'). This is a water mill powered by the water from the miller's dam. There's also a little tearoom and an easy signed walk nearby.

Transport *Bluebird Buses,* service No 101 between Stonehaven and Montrose, pass through Inverbervie and Kinneff (see below) hourly Mon-Fri (less frequently Sat-Sun).

Five miles inland from Inverbervie, between the A92 and A90, is Arbuthnott, birthplace of the amazingly prolific author Lewis Grassic Gibbon (1901-35), and where he spent his formative years. From 1928 till his untimely death at the age of 34, he wrote an astonishing 17 books. *Sunset Song*, the first part of the *Scots Quair* trilogy, is his best-known work. It remains one of the true classics of Scottish literature and is an absolute must for anyone exploring this area. The **Grassic Gibbon Centre**, at the east end of the village, traces his life and points out the places he wrote about. There is also a café and bookshop. ■ *Apr-Oct daily 1000-1630. £2, £1.25 child/concession. T361668.* Grassic Gibbon is also buried here, under his real name of James Leslie Mitchell, in a corner of the churchyard, about half a mile away at the other end of the village. The parish church itself is one of the few intact pre-Reformation churches in Scotland and is notable for its 13th-century chancel. Near the centre is **Arbuthnott House**, a fortified manorhouse dating from the 15th century. ■ *The gardens are open all year daily 0900-1700, the house on certain days in the summer. Details from Bervie Information and Activity Centre in the main street.*

Arbuthnott
Phone code: 01561
Colour map 4, grid B6

A few miles north of Inverbervie, on the road to Stonehaven, you'll see a sign on the right to the **Old Church**, Kinneff, where the Scottish Crown Jewels – the Royal Regalia – were hidden in 1651 to protect them from Cromwell's greedy paws. Here they lay buried under the church floor for nearly 10 years. It's a mile and a half down to the church, where there's a memorial to the Reverend James Grainger, who hid the treasures and thus saved the 'Honours of Scotland': the crown, sceptre and sword. There are various stories of how they were smuggled out of nearby Dunnottar Castle (see below). In *Tales of a Grandfather*, Sir Walter Scott relates how Christian Grainger, the minister's wife, accompanied by her serving maid, carried them out of Dunnottar in collaboration with the Governor and his wife. Another version tells how they were lowered on ropes down the castle wall. There, on the beach, a fishwife gathering seaweed hid the sword in a bundle of flax and the crown in her creel (used for catching lobsters). So, the 'Honours' were saved and are now displayed in Edinburgh castle.

Kinneff
Colour map 4, grid B6

Just to the north of Kinneff, at **Crawton**, is the **Fowlsheugh RSPB Reserve**. The spectacular 250-ft high cliffs are home to tens of thousands of seabirds, including shags, guillemots, kittiwakes, fulmars, razorbills and puffins. They're best seen in early summer (May-July). You can see them from the top of the cliffs, but take great care. Better still, take a boat trip from Stonehaven (May-July on Tuesday and Friday at 1830).

Stonehaven

The solid and tidy old fishing port of Stonehaven lies 15 miles south of Aberdeen, where the coastal A92 joins the main A90 from Dundee. Nowadays Stonehaven is better known as a seaside resort, attracting a fair few visitors in the summer months.

Phone code: 01569
Colour map 4, grid B6
Population: 9,000

Stonehaven is on the Aberdeen-Dundee rail line and there are regular **trains** in either direction. The train station is a 15-min walk from the square. It is also served by **buses** 101, 107 and 707 from **Aberdeen**. There are also buses to and from **Montrose**, passing through the coastal villages described above. It's possible to head straight from Stonehaven to **Deeside** by taking the A957 (known as 'The Slug') to **Crathes** (see page 416).

Ins & outs

Northeast Scotland

The **Tourist Information Centre** is at 66 Allardyce St, the main street past the square, T762806. Apr, May and Oct Mon-Sat 1000-1300 and 1400-1700; Jun and Sep Mon-Sat 1000-1300 and 1400-1800, Sun 1300-1800; Jul-Aug Mon-Sat 1000-1900, Sun 1300-1900.

Stonehaven is famous for its strange fireball-swinging festival on Old Year's Night, an ancient pagan ritual

Not least of the town's attractions is its wonderful art deco outdoor, heated salt-water **swimming pool**, one of only two in Scotland (the other is at Gourock). It is kept at a constant 82°F. The pool is only open from the first Saturday in June till the the end of August, 1100-1930 (there's also a midnight swim; ask for details at the TIC). By the harbour is the **Tolbooth**, built around 1600, and the town's oldest building. It now houses a seafood restaurant (see below) and local history **museum**. ■ *Jun-Sep Mon and Thu-Sat 1000-1200 and 1400-1700, Wed and Sun 1400-1700. Free.* Another attraction is the town's highly respected **folk festival**, held over three days in mid-July. Away from the harbour and old town is the market square, where you'll find banks with ATMs and most of the shops. Just off the square is *Just Scottish*, an excellent arts and crafts shop (open Mon-Sat 1000-1730).

Sleeping & eating

A couple of recommended places are **C** *Heugh Hotel*, Westfield Rd, T762379; and **D** *Arduthie House*, Ann St, T762381. The best place to eat in town is the excellent *Tolbooth Restaurant*, T762287, upstairs from the museum on the harbour. It's expensive but worth it for the excellent seafood. Open Tue-Sat 1830-2130 (1730-2200 Sat). The restored *Carron Tearooms* serve traditional high tea Wed-Mon 1330-1600 and boats a wonderful art deco interior. Six miles north of town at Netherley, on the B979, is the friendly and welcoming *Lairhillock Inn & Restaurant*, T01569-730001, a charming old coaching inn which offers excellent local produce in beautifully rustic surroundings at mid-range prices. Also has rooms. A few miles south of Dunnotar Castle is the turn-off to Catterline, where you'll find the wonderfully cosy *Creel*, renowned for its seafood.

Dunnottar Castle

The main reason for coming to Stonehaven is to visit the impressive and impregnable Dunnottar Castle, two miles south of town just off the A92. Dating from the 12th century, this ancient ruin was a stronghold for the Earls Marischal of Scotland. Standing 160 ft high, with the sea on three sides and a huge drop and 'curtain wall' on the fourth, it is not far short of an island. It is worth devoting considerable time to exploring one of the country's most outstanding castles, which is approached by a steep 400-yd walk from the car park. So dramatic is its setting, that it was used as the backdrop for Zeffirelli's film version of *Hamlet*, starring Mel Gibson. But the fortress has a dramatic and bloody history all of its own. In 1297 William Wallace (another of Mel Gibson's characters, strangely enough) burnt alive an entire English garrison here; later, in 1685, a large group of Covenanters was imprisoned, tortured and then left to rot in the castle dungeons. The castle was reduced to its present state in 1716, during reprisals for the Earl Marischal's Jacobite activities. ■ *Easter-Oct Mon-Sat 0900-1800, Sun 1400-1700; Nov-Mar Fri-Mon 0930-1600. £3.50, £1 child. The castle can also be reached by a footpath from Stonehaven; contact the tourist office for the relevant leaflet. T762173.*

The Howe of the Mearns to Deeside

Colour map 4, grid B5

Fourteen miles south of Stonehaven, just off the main A90 is **Laurencekirk**. A few miles east, off the tiny B9120, is the **Hill of Garvock** (908ft), which gives great views over the Howe of the Mearns. It is topped by the Tower of Johnston (which lies up a footpath), built to commemorate Britain's victory over Napoleon in the Peninsula Wars. On the other side of the hill is a depression called the **Sheriff's Kettle**. Here, at Baileys Farm in 1420, disgruntled local lairds boiled the Sheriff and 'supped the brew'.

Four miles west of Laurencekirk on the B9120 is the village of **Fettercairn**, famous for its handsome arch, built in 1861 following a visit from Queen Victoria. A mile west of the village is the **distillery**, one of the oldest in Scotland, with free guided tours and a 'dram' at the end. ■ *May-Sep Mon-Sat 1000-1630. T01561-340205.* The village holds its annual **Highland Games** on the first Saturday in July. They're authentic and the setting is lovely.

A few miles north on the B974 is the 18th-century **Fasque House**, erstwhile home of four-times British prime minister, William Gladstone. The family still lives in the west wing. Closed at the outbreak of the Second World War and only reopened in the 1970s, the faded grandeur of the place is wonderfully tangible. Though the house is interesting because of its historic connections with the former prime minister, it is also an excellent example of an 'Upstairs-Downstairs' country house and gives a fascinating insight into the lifestyle of a wealthy Victorian landowner. The estate also includes extensive grounds filled with deer. ■ *T01561-340569. May-Sep daily 1100-1730. £3.50, £2.50 concession.*

Beyond Fasque the B974 wends its way through rich farming country, with its distinctive red soil, up to the **Cairn O' Mount** (1,492 ft) and on to **Banchory**. Before you start the actual steep ascent, the road to the right, over a water splash, leads to the **Glen of Drumtochty**. This is a delightful detour, ending up in the little town of **Auchinblae**. Nearby is *Drumtochty Castle Stables*, T01561-320082, which sleeps up to four, from £250/350 per week. If you decide not to divert and feel like some refreshment, park on the left and climb the steps to the *Clatterin' Brig restaurant*, T01561-340297. Opened originally by a Bowes-Lyon, kinswoman of Queen Elizabeth the Queen Mother, it is open all year round. When you eventually reach the summit of the Cairn O' Mount, stop for a moment to admire the view. The cairn dates from 2000 BC.

Take your mountain bike in May and enter the Great Drumtochty Challenge, www.drumtochtychallenge.fsnet.co.uk

Deeside

The River Dee rises in the Cairngorms and flows down through the surrounding hills, eastwards to the sea at Aberdeen. The valley of the Dee is known as Deeside, or rather Royal Deeside, for its connections with the royal family, who have holidayed here, at Balmoral, since Queen Victoria first arrived in 1848. Originally, Queen Victoria and Prince Albert were looking for an estate further west, but were advised that the Deeside climate would be better for Albert's delicate constitution. The queen fell in love with this area and its people, and following Albert's death she sought out the company of straight-talking northerners, preferring their down-to-earth honesty to the two-faced toadies she endured at court.

Colour map 4, grid A4-6

Today, Deeside's royal associations have made it the tourist honeypot of the northeast, but the royal presence has also saved it from mass development. There's an air of understated affluence and refinement in the villages strung out along the A93 that runs along the north bank of the Dee and, as well as the obvious attraction of Balmoral, there are many other fine examples of baronial castles. Deeside is also a great area for various outdoor activities, such as hiking in the surrounding mountains, mountain biking, canoeing and skiing.

Ins and outs

Getting there & getting around All the main tourist attractions on Deeside can be reached by **bus** from Aberdeen. *Bluebird Northern* service No 201, T01224-212266, runs every 30 mins (Mon-Sat) to Banchory, via Cults and Crathes, and every hour to Braemar, via Aboyne, Dinnet, Ballater and Crathie (for Balmoral). On Sun, the bus runs every hour and 2 hrs respectively. If you wish to explore Deeside along a less popular route (though even in the summer, crowds are never great) take the B976 along the south bank of the River Dee.

Information For details of the **Castle Trail**, **Victorian Heritage Trail** and **Deeside Tourist Route**, contact the TIC in Aberdeen, or in any of the towns along the way.

Aberdeen to Banchory

Colour map 4, grid A5/6 The first sight of interest heading west from Aberdeen is **Drum Castle**, three miles west of **Peterculter** (pronounced 'Petercooter'). It's a combination of a 13th-century square tower, Jacobean mansion house and later Victorian additions. It was given to one William de Irvine by Robert the Bruce for service rendered at Bannockburn and was in the family's hands for over 650 years, until it was taken over by the National Trust for Scotland in 1976. There's a beautiful walled garden and a trail through the 100-acre ancient Wood of Drum which forms part of the castle grounds. ■ *Mid-Apr-31 May and 1-30 Sep daily 1330-1730; 1 Jun-31 Aug daily 1100-1730; weekends in Oct 1330-1730. Gardens same dates daily 1000-1800. Grounds all year daily 0930 till dusk. Castle, gardens and grounds £6, £4.50 concession, £1 child; garden and grounds only £1 (honesty box). T01330-811204.*

A few miles southeast of Peterculter is its sister village, **Maryculter** (pronounced 'Marycooter'), where you'll find **Storybook Glen**, the northeast's answer to Disneyland. This very attractive and tasteful 'theme park' is a great place to take the kids and features giant tableaux and lifesize characters from many childhood fairy tales and nursery rhymes. ■ *Daily Mar-Oct 1000-1800; Nov-Feb weekends only 1100-1600. £3.50, children £1.75. T01224-732491.*

Crathes Castle & gardens
Opposite the castle gates is The Milton Restaurant T01330-844566, serving excellent, moderately priced food daily till 2200 (lunch only on Sun) Fifteen miles west of Aberdeen, where the A93 meets the A957 from Stonehaven, is Crathes Castle, a perfect 'fairytale' castle built over 40 years in the mid-16th century. The turreted tower-house is still furnished with many period pieces and wall hangings, and is notable for its superb painted ceilings. There are narrow spiral staircases leading to tiny rooms, one of which is said to be inhabited by the obligatory ghost. The castle is well worth exploring but is almost overshadowed by the exceptional gardens, which shouldn't be missed. There are no fewer than eight of them, so take your time. There's also a visitor centre, restaurant and shop. ■ *Castle, visitor centre and shop open 1 Apr-30 Sep daily 1030-1730; 1-31 Oct daily 1030-1630 (last admission to castle 45 mins before closing). Licensed restaurant open 10 Jan-31 Mar and 1 Nov-23 Dec Wed-Sun 1030-1600; 1 Apr-31 Oct daily 1030-1730. Grounds and garden open all year daily 0900-dusk. Castle only £3.50, concession £3; castle and grounds combined £7, concession £5. T01330-844525.*

Banchory

Phone code: 01330 Colour map 4, grid A5 Banchory makes a very pleasant base for exploring the area, with the River Dee burbling through, but there's not a great deal to do here, apart from salmon fishing, which is popular in these parts. You can watch salmon leaping spectacularly at the **Bridge of Feugh**, to the south of town. There is a sad tale, though, of a lady-in-waiting who was staying at Balmoral when the royal family were in residence some years ago. She was standing fishing in the river, in quite deep water, and wearing chest-height waders, when the sovereign rode by. Seeing the king, she curtsied, whereupon the water flowed quickly into her waders and she sank beneath the water and drowned.

The **Tourist Information Centre** is in the local museum, on Bridge St, behind the High St. It can provide information on walking and fishing in the area. It's open Apr-Jun Mon-Sat 1000-1300, 1400-1700; Jul-19 Aug Mon-Sat 0930-1800, Sun 1300-1800; 20 Aug-27 Oct Mon-Sat 1000-1300, 1400-1700. *Adventure Scotland*, T850332, dlatham@netcomuk.co.uk, is a Banchory-based company offering a wide range of adventure activities, including white-water rafting, mountain biking, skiing and hiking.

Sleeping & eating

There are some very fine places to stay in and around Banchory. Three miles north of town on the A980 is the very wonderful **B** *Raemoir House Hotel*, T824884. A country mansion set in 3,500 acres of woods and parkland, 20 rooms. Another excellent choice is the **B** *Banchory Lodge Hotel*, T822625, a sporting lodge-type hotel superbly situated on the banks of the river near the town centre. It's also a great place to stop and have a bite to eat for lunch. The river runs past the lawn and you can watch the salmon leap as you perhaps enjoy the fruits of their labour. Also recommended is the **B** *Tor-na-Coille Hotel*, T822242, tornacoille@ btinternet.com, outside town on the Inchmarlo Rd. This tastefully furnished Victorian country house hotel is set in lovely grounds and boasts a considerable reputation for its modern Scottish cooking (lunch mid-range; dinner expensive). There are also plenty of good guesthouses and B&Bs, including **E** *Towerbank House*, at 93 High St, T824798, diane@dawps.fsnet.co.uk; and the excellent **E** *June Little*, 73 High St, T824666. There's also a **campsite**, *Silver Ladies Caravan Park*, T822800, at Strachan, just outside Banchory.

Aside from the hotels listed above, the best place to **eat** is probably the *Burnett Arms Hotel* on the High St, T824944. There's also *Le Bistroquet*, which has a varied menu, and *The Shieling*, a good café and gift shop..

Lumphanan
Colour map 4, grid A5

From Banchory you can head northwest on the A980 to Alford, in the Don Valley (see page 423). Roughly halfway is the village of Lumphanan, which was thought to be the burial place of Macbeth, the Scottish king so misrepresented by Shakespeare (he is actually buried on Iona). **Macbeth's Cairn** is instead a prehistoric cairn. Just to the south of the village is the **Peel Ring**, a 12th-century Motte, or castle mound, and one of Scotland's earliest medieval sites.

Aboyne
Phone code: 01339
Colour map 4, grid A5

The attractive little village of Aboyne is 30 miles west of Banchory on the A93. There are a couple of very good places to eat in and around Aboyne. In the village itself is *The Black-faced Sheep*, T887311, a coffee shop with excellent home baking. A good pub for food is *The Boat*, on Charleston Road, off the A930. South of Aboyne, in **Glen Tanar** (see 'Walks in Deeside' below), is *Glen Tanar Equestrian Centre*, T886448, which offers riding in the forests and hills.

Dinnet
Colour map 4, grid A4

A few miles further on is Dinnet. In the **Muir of Dinnet National Nature Reserve** you can explore the Burn o' Vat, a sheltered valley which attracts many butterflies and dragonflies. During the walk, you'll come to a huge circular stone chamber and, in nearby Loch Kinord, there are crannogs, which are ancient man-made islands.

Ballater and Balmoral

Phone code: 01339
Colour map 4, grid A4

The neat little town of Ballater is proud of its royal connections. You can buy meat from the butcher with his 'By Royal Appointment' sign, or clothes from royal outfitters. This is where Lizzie and Phil pop down to the shops for a pint of milk or perhaps to choose a video. Ever since Queen Victoria first arrived by train from Aberdeen in 1848, the royal family have been spending their holidays here in their summer residence, Balmoral. She was not amused at the prospect of having an unsightly rail station on her doorstep, so the line ended eight miles east, at Ballater. The line has been closed for some time, but you can still visit the old train station, which now houses an elegant tearoom.

The **Tourist Information Centre** is housed in the old Royal Station, T755306. It's open Easter-May and Oct Mon-Sat 1000-1300, 1400-1700, Sun 1300-1700; Jun and Sep Mon-Sat 1000-1300, 1400-1800, Sun 1300-1800; Jul-Aug Mon-Sat 1000-1300, 1400-1900, Sun 1300-1900.

The royals are not the only famous summer visitors. The poet Byron (who attended Aberdeen Grammar School) spent many childhood summer holidays at Ballaterach, a few miles east of Ballater. He had a narrow escape when he slipped and nearly fell into the fast flowing stream at the Linn of Dee, beyond Braemar. He was rescued just in time and went on to wax poetic about the beautiful hills which are Ballater's other great attraction. The town makes the ideal base for **hiking** (see below) as well as a number of other outdoor activities. Many of the walks set off from **Loch Muick** (pronounced 'Mick'), nine miles southwest of Ballater, at the head of Glen Muick. (For details, see 'Walks in Deeside' below). There's a visitor centre and car park at Spittal of Glenmuick. From here a track leads along the west shore of the loch to the lodge where Queen Victoria met John Brown. For guides and equipment for canoeing, climbing, mountain biking and skiing, contact *Adventure Scotland* in Banchory (see above).

Sleeping There's plenty of accommodation in Ballater, from expensive hotels to reasonably priced B&Bs. Pick of the bunch is the **A-B** *Darroch Learg Hotel*, T755443, darroch.learg @exoams.wk.com, half a mile from town, off the A93 heading west to Braemar. 18 rooms, open Feb-Dec. Friendly country house hotel with fine views and a reputation for superb food (expensive), good value. **A-B** *Hilton Craigendarroch*, on the Braemar Rd, T755858, www.hilton.com 44 rooms. Victorian country house converted into a modern resort hotel with full leisure and sports facilities, 2 good restaurants. **B** *Balgonie Country House Hotel*, T/F755482, on the western outskirts of town, off the A93. 9 rooms, open Feb-Dec. Friendly and comfortable country house hotel, excellent food (expensive). **C** *Glen Lui Hotel*, Invercauld Rd, T755402, www.glen-lui-hotel. co.uk 19 rooms. Another comfortable hotel offering fine food (lunch cheap; dinner mid-range). **E** *Deeside Hotel*, set back from the A93 heading out of town towards Braemar. T755420, www.royal-deeside.org.uk Friendly, good value and good food (mid-range). Among the many B&Bs is the recommended **E** *Inverdeen House*, 11 Bridge Sq, T755759, www.inverdeen.com French, German and Polish spoken, great breakfasts, no smoking. Also good is **E** *Moorside House*, T/F755492, on the Braemar Rd. There's a **campsite** at *Anderson Road Caravan Park*, T755727, open Apr-Oct.

Eating Apart from the hotels listed above, there are lots of places to eat. Best of all is *The Green Inn*, T/F755701, on the green in the town centre. It boasts a well-deserved reputation as one of the very best restaurants in the region, classic Scottish cooking with

Northeast Scotland

an imaginative and health-conscious twist, expensive. Open daily 1900-2100 (closed Sun Oct-Mar); also has 3 rooms upstairs (**B-C** full board). Also good is the family-friendly *La Mangiatoia*, T/F755999, on Bridge Sq (lunch cheap-mid-range; dinner mid-range to expensive).

Eight miles west of Ballater is the area's main attraction, Balmoral Castle. The 16th-century tower house, formerly owned by the local Gordon family, was bought for Queen Victoria by Prince Albert in 1852 and converted into today's baronial mansion. It has been the royal family's summer retreat ever since. Only the ballroom and the grounds are open to the likes of you and me, and only for three months of the year. **Pony trekking** and **pony cart rides** are available around the estate grounds and are favourite ways of enjoying the wonderful scenery. Opposite the castle gates is **Crathie Church**, which is used by the family when they're in residence. There's a small souvenir shop next to the main gates and a visitor centre which gives a lot of information on the castle and its owners. Also at Crathie is the *Inver*, an 18th-century inn which serves good, honest food (best to book, T01339-742345). ■ *Mid-Apr to end Jul, daily 1000-1700 (closed on Sun in Apr-May). £4.50, concession £3.50, children £1. T742334. Buses to Braemar from Aberdeen stop by the gates.*

Balmoral Castle
Colour map 4, grid A4

Braemar

Nine miles west of Balmoral, is Braemar, the final town on Deeside, lying at the foot of the awesome, brooding **Cairngorm** massif, which dominates the Eastern Highlands. Even at the height of summer you can see a dab of snow still lying in a hollow in the surrounding mountains, and Braemar is an excellent base for **hiking** (see below), and winter **skiing** at Glenshee (see page 336). It's an attractive little place, much loved by Queen Victoria and much visited during its annual **Braemar Gathering** (or games), which attracts tens of thousands of visitors each year, amongst them members of the royal family.

Phone code: 01339
Colour map 4, grid A3

The **Tourist Information Centre** in Braemar is in Balmoral Mews, on Mar Rd. It's open daily Jan-May and Sep-Dec 1000-1700, Jun 0930-1800, Jul-Aug 0930-1900. T741600. The **Braemar Highland Heritage Centre**, in Balmoral Mews by the tourist office, includes informative talks (in several languages) on the area, an exhibition and shops. Daily Apr-Sep 0900-1800 (Jul-Aug till 2000), Oct-Mar 1000-1700. Free. T741944. For rental of ski equipment, try the The Braemar Ski School Hire, in Victoria Hall on Glenshee Rd.

The games are held on the first Sat in Sep. Booking is essential and tickets can be bought in advance from the Booking Secretary, BRHS, Coilacreich, Ballater, AB35 5UH, T755377

Just north of the village, and well signposted, is **Braemar Castle**, dating from 1628. This impressive fortress was used by Hanoverian troops after the Jacobite Rising of 1745. It is L-shaped, with a star-shaped defensive wall and a central round tower with a spiral stair. There are barrel-vaulted ceilings and an underground prison. The world's largest cairngorm (a semi-precious stone, a variety of quartz, which is yellow, grey or brown in colour) weighing 52 lbs is on display in the morning room. There's also a piece of tartan worn by Prince Charles Edward, Bonnie Prince Charlie. ■ *Mid-Apr to end Oct Sat-Thu 1000-1800. £3, concession £2.50, children £1. T741219.*

A very scenic side trip from Braemar is to the **Linn of Dee**, six miles west of the village, at the end of the road. Here, the river thunders through a narrow gorge to spectacular effect. There are numerous walks from here along the river, or for the more adventurous, the famous **Lairig Ghru**, which runs

Braemar Gathering

There has been a gathering (or games) of some sort at Braemar for 900 years, ever since Malcolm Canmore set contests for the local clans so that he could pick the strongest and bravest of men for his army. These events take place up and down the country throughout the summer, but none are as famous, or well attended, as Braemar's. Queen Victoria attended in 1848 and the Gathering is still patronized by the royal family. Crowds come from all over the world to proclaim the monarch as Chieftain of the Braemar Gathering.

At the gathering the visitor will see contests in traditional Scottish events, such as tossing the caber, Highland dancing and bagpipe competitions and displays. There is an inter-services tug o' war championship, a medley relay race and a hill race up Morrone. The sounds of the massed pipes echoing around the encircling heather-clad hills and a plethora of tartan also help to make this a real tourist highlight. The royal connection (and the crowds) apart, many other local communities hold similar games.

through the Cairngroms to Aviemore (see below). Between the Linn of Dee and the tiny settlement of **Inverey**, a mile to the east, there's a very basic **youth hostel** (open mid-May to early October), which has no phone, so book through Braemar hostel (see below). A postbus runs in the afternoon (Monday-Saturday) from Braemar to the Linn of Dee, via the hostel.

Sleeping & eating
Accommodation is hard to find before and during the Braemar Gathering, but at other times of the year there's plenty to choose from

Best of all is the **C** *Braemar Lodge Hotel*, T741627, on the outskirts of the village on the road south to Glenshee and Blairgowrie. There's also the **B** *Invercauld Arms Hotel*, T741605, and the **D-E** *Callater Lodge Hotel*, Glenshee Rd, T741275, www. hotel-braemar.co.uk Small and comfortable. There are plenty of guesthouses and B&Bs, including **E** *Schiehallion House*, T741679, open Jan-Oct on Glenshee Rd; and **E** *Clunie Lodge*, T741330, on Cluniebank Rd. There's a **F** *SYHA Youth Hostel*, T741659, open all year, at Corrie Feragie on Glenshee Rd; and also **F** *Rucksacks*, 15 Mar Rd, T741517, a cheap and friendly bunkhouse that's popular with hikers and also rents out mountain bikes. There's **camping** at *Invercauld Caravan Site*, T741373, open Dec-Oct, on Glenshee Rd.

The only decent places to eat are the bars of the larger hotels, which are a bit on the expensive side. *Braemar Lodge* serves meals 1200-1400 and 1800-2100.

Walks in Deeside

Ballater and Braemar are ideal bases for walking in the surrounding Grampian Mountains, and if you feel like 'bagging a Munro' (ie climbing a mountain over 3,000 ft), there are some close at hand. All of this area is to be included in the new **Cairngorms National Park**, due to open in early 2003. This will be the largest national park in Britain, covering a vast 4,500 sq km, from Aboyne in the east to Dalwhinnie in the west, and from Blair Atholl north to Grantown-on-Spey.

Lochnagar
OS Landranger No 44

The best walk in the area is to the summit of Lochnagar (3,786 ft), made famous by Prince Charles in the book he wrote for his brothers when young, *The Old Man of Lochnagar*. The noble and mysterious mountain dominates the Royal Forest of Balmoral and takes its name from a small loch at its foot (it's also known as the White Mounth). This fine granite mass is approached from the car park by the Rangers' **visitor centre** at Spittal of Glen Muick. For information on their free guided walks, T755377. The path to the top is well trodden and well marked, though steep as you near the summit. It's 10 miles there and back, so allow a full day for the climb. You'll need to be properly equipped and take a map.

An easier walk is to Cambus o' May, on the river, about four miles east of Ballater. It's a great spot for a picnic, or to swim in the river, or to enjoy a stroll along the riverbank. A good walk from Braemar is to the summit of Morrone (2,818 ft), the mountain to the southwest. The walk takes about four hours in total.

Cambus o' May & Morrone
OS Landranger No 43

Another good climb is the route up **Mount Keen** (3,077 ft), the most easterly Munro, which lies between Deeside and Glen Esk, the loveliest of the Angus glens (see page 402). Again, you should allow a whole day for this expedition.

Glen Tanar to Glen Esk
OS Landranger No 44

It can be approached from the Visitor Centre in **Glen Tanar**, at the end of the little road that runs southwest off the B976, across the river from Aboyne. You can climb to the summit and return by the same route but, if your party has two cars, it is well worth walking over to Glen Esk, 14 miles away. Drive around to the Invermark car park at the head of Glen Esk and park one car there. From Glen Tanar follow the old drove road which at times runs with the Mounth road. Skirting the Home Farm with its Arboretum and its dammed lake, the fairly flat track winds along Glen Tanar through the forest for about four miles. Then comes the Halfway Hut, used for rest and repast by former shooting parties. You will pass shooting butts *en route*. The next stretch is through open country with the **Clachan Yell** (626 ft) on the left.

The walk proper then begins to take shape. Cross the stone bridge of Etnach, and then the path begins to lead up to the Shiel of Glentanar. The second bridge forks left and the track heads for the summit. The rough path continues along a ridge, the shoulder of Mount Keen. From the summit with its stone marker, Dinnet and its two lakes is visible to the north, and the River Esk glints its way down the valley to the south. Watch out for adders around here. On the descent, you'll pass the **Queen's Well**, used by Queen Victoria when she and her party went down to Fettercairn posing as a wedding party. The well is decorated with a graceful granite crown which was erected in 1861. The royal party covered much of the climb on hill ponies. The stone arch at Fettercairn commemorates this visit.

The Don Valley

North of Royal Deeside is the lesser-known valley of the Don, Aberdeen's second river. This relatively little-visited corner of the northeast is an historian's and archaeologist's dream, as it's littered with medieval castles, Pictish stone circles and Iron-Age hillforts. A quarter of all Britain's stone circles can be found here (if you look hard enough). Local tourist offices have free leaflets on the region's archaeological sites, with background information and details of how to find them. The main sites are included in the tourist board's 'Stone Circle Trail'. There's also a well-signposted 'Castle Trail', which includes the area's main castles. One of these castles, Corgarff, stands at the southern end of the notorious Lecht Road, which runs from Cock Bridge to Tomintoul. This area, known as The Lecht, is one of Scotland's main ski centres.

Colour map 4, grid A4/5

Ins and outs

There are regular **trains** and **buses** to Inverurie, from Aberdeen and Inverness. *Bluebird Northern*, T01224-212266, No 220 runs regularly every day from Aberdeen to Alford (1¼ hrs).

Getting there

Getting around Travelling around the Don Valley without your own transport is not easy. Bus No 219 runs from Alford to Strathdon (Mon-Sat), but services beyond Strathdon are virtually non-existent.

Inverurie and around

Phone code: 01467
Colour map 4, grid A5

The solid farming town of Inverurie is 17 miles northwest of Aberdeen on the A96 to Inverness. It makes a useful base for visiting the numerous castles and ancient relics dotted around the area. The **Tourist Information Centre** is in the Town Hall on Market Place. T625800. Open April-June and September Monday-Saturday 0930-1700; July-August 0930-1800. The **Thainstone Mart**, south of town just off the A96, is one of the largest livestock markets in the country, and interesting if you like that sort of thing. It's held Monday, Wednesday and Friday around 1000.

Sleeping The best place to stay around Inverurie is the magnificent **B** *Pittodrie House Hotel*,
& eating near Chapel of Garioch, T681444, www.macdonald.hotels.co.uk 27 rooms. This fine baronial mansion originally belonged to the Earls of Mar, and the 2,000-acre estate was granted to them by Robert the Bruce for their loyalty at the Battle of Bannockburn. The opulent surroundings are matched by the superb cuisine. **B** *Thainstone House Hotel*, to the south of Inverurie off the A96, T621643, is a luxurious country mansion offering excellent cuisine and leisure facilities. There's also a decent selection of cheaper guesthouses and B&Bs, including **E** *Breaslann Guest House*, Old Chapel Rd, T621608.

Around About six miles southwest of Inverurie, off the B993 (turn first left after the
Inverurie village of Kemnay), is the magnificent **Castle Fraser**, built in 1575 by the 6th Earl of Mar and similar in style to Crathes and Craigievar. The interior was remodelled in 1838 and many of the furnishings date from that period. There's a walled garden, tearoom and trails through the estate. ■ *Castle open Mid-Apr-31 May and 1-30 Sep daily 1330-1730; 1 Jun-31 Aug daily 1100-1730; weekends in Oct 1330-1730. Garden open all year daily 0930-1800. Grounds all year daily 0930 till dusk. Castle, garden and grounds £6, concession £4.50. Garden and grounds only adult £2, concession £1.30. T01330-833463 (NTS).*

Close by, and signed off the B993, is the 4,000 year-old **Easter Aquhorthies Stone Circle**. This archaeological site is overshadowed by **Bennachie** (1,732 ft), by far the best hill in the area and thought to be the site of Mons Graupius, in 83 AD, when the Romans defeated the Picts. It's a straightforward two-hour walk to the summit and the views from the top are great. There are various trails, though the most commonly used route starts from the **Bennachie Centre**, at Esson's car park, a mile beyond **Chapel of Garioch** (pronounced 'Geery'), signposted off the A96 at Pitcaple, and about five miles northwest of Inverurie. ■ *Apr-Oct Tue-Sun 1000-1700; Nov-Mar Wed-Sun 1000-1700. For more details of the various Bennachie Hill walks and the 'West Gordon Way', T794161. Bennachie Centre, T681470.* Near here is the **Maiden Stone**, a 10-ft high Pictish gravestone with relief carvings showing what looks like an elephant, along with other creatures not normally found around these parts.

A few miles west of the turn-off to Chapel of Garioch, the B9002 heads west off the A96 to the village of **Oyne**, site of the **Archaeolink Prehistory Park**. This state-of-the-art interpretative centre takes you on a journey back in time. It's a great introduction to the numerous ancient sites in the area and explains why the stone circles were built and what the various carved symbols mean.

The 40-acre park includes various interesting features such as a reconstructed Iron Age farm, Stone-Age settlement and Roman camp, as well as a hilltop Iron-Age fort. The Archeodrome features audio-visual presentations which bring to life the ancient history of the area. ■ *Apr-Oct daily 1000-1700. £3.90, children £2.35. T01464-851544, www.archaeolink.co.uk*

Near the village of **Daviot**, north of the A96 off the B9001 from Inverurie, or reached via the A920 west of **Oldmeldrum**, is the **Loanhead of Daviot Stone Circle**. This impressive 6,000 year-old site is 500 yds from the village and consists of two stone circles, the smaller of which encloses a cremation cemetery dating from 1500 BC.

Thirteen miles north of Inverurie is **Fyvie Castle**, off the A947 between Oldmeldrum and Turriff. This grandest of Scottish baronial piles is a major feature on the 'Castle Trail' and shouldn't be missed if you're in the vicinity. The castle's five towers are each named after one of the five families who have had the pleasure of living here over the centuries. The last lot only moved out in 1980 so it has a rare lived-in feel to it. The oldest part of the castle dates from the 13th century and, apart from the great wheel-stair and the 17th-century morning room, the extravagantly opulent interior is largely from the Edwardian era. There's a superb collection of portraits including works by the likes of Raeburn, Batoni, Gainsborough and Hoppner, as well as 17th-century tapestries and collections of arms and armour. The landscaped grounds and Fyvie Loch are also worth exploring, and even the tearoom is great. ■ *Easter to 31 May and 1-30 Sep daily 1330-1730; 1 Jun-31 Aug 1100-1730; weekends only in Oct 1330-1730. Grounds open all year daily 0930-dusk. £6, £4.50 concession, £1 child. T01651-891266 (NTS).*

Alford and around

The main tourist centre on Donside is the little country town of Alford (pronounced 'Ah-ford'), 25 miles west of Aberdeen. The principal point of interest in town is the **Grampian Transport Museum**, which features a comprehensive and fascinating display of transport history, with collections of cars, buses, trams, steam engines and some more unusual exhibits. ■ *End Mar to end Oct daily, 1000-1700. £3.80, £3.10 concession, £1.60 child. T562292.* Almost next door is the terminus for the **Alford Valley Railway**, a narrow-gauge passenger steam railway that runs for about a mile to Murray Park and back again (total journey time one hour). ■ *Steam engine runs 1st Sun of month. Diesel engine runs Apr-May and Sep Sat-Sun 1300-1700; Jun-Aug daily 1300-1700. £2, £1 child. T562811.*

Phone code: 01975
Colour map 4, grid A5

Northeast Scotland

The railway station is also where you'll find the **Tourist Information Centre**. T562052. Open April-May and September Monday-Saturday 1000-1300, Sunday 1300-1700; June-August Monday-Saturday 1000-1200, 1230-1700, Sunday 1300-1700. Also in town is the **Alford Heritage Centre**, on Mart Road, which has a large display of agricultural and domestic items. ■ *Apr-Oct Mon-Sat 1000-1700, Sun 1300-1700. T562906.* Alford is close to The Lecht ski centre (see page 426) but you can also ski here all year round on the local dry ski slope at the **Alford Ski Centre**, on Greystone Road, T563024. There's also snowboarding, instruction and equipment hire.

About a mile west, at Bridge of Alford, is the **D** *Forbes Arms Hotel*, T562108, where you can get decent bar food (prices cheap to mid-range). There's also **B&B** accommodation in Alford at **E** *Dunvegan*, 26 Gordon Rd, T563077; and **E** *Bydand*, 18 Balfour Rd, T563613.

Sleeping & eating

Craigievar Castle Six miles south of Alford is one of the northeast's most gorgeous castles, the classic tower house of Craigievar, with its impressive turrets, balustrades and cupolas. The castle remains much as it was when it was built in 1626 by wealthy local merchant, William Forbes. Unfortunately, though, its popularity led to its deterioration and the NTS now restricts entry to only a small number of visitors at a time to prevent further damage. The castle stands in well-tended grounds. ■ *Castle open mid-Apr-30 Sep daily 1330-1730 (last admission 1645). Grounds open all year daily 0930-dusk. Adult £7, £5 concession. Grounds only £1 (honesty box). T01339-883280.*

Kildrummy Castle
Phone code: 01975

Six miles west of Alford, the A944 meets the A97 which heads north towards the town of Huntly, on Speyside (see page 428). A few miles south of the junction stand the extensive and impressive ruins of Kildrummy Castle, Scotland's most complete 13th-century castle. Amongst the most infamous events in the castle's long and bloody history was the treacherous betrayal of Robert the Bruce's family to the English during the Wars of Independence. It was the seat of the Earls of Mar and used as an HQ for the Jacobite rebellion of 1715, after which the sixth Earl of Mar ('Bobbing John') fled to exile in France and the castle fell into ruin. ■ *Apr-Nov daily 0930-1830. £2, £1.50 concession, £0.75 child. T571331.*

Across the other side of the river from the castle ruins is one of the very best hotels in the northeast, the spectacularly sited **L-A** *Kildrummy Castle Hotel*, T571288, www.kildrummycastelhotel.co.uk, a baronial country mansion set in beautiful grounds (see above). It also has an excellent restaurant.

Strathdon
Phone code: 01975
Colour map 4, grid A4

The tiny village of Strathdon, 10 miles southwest of Kildrummy, is famous for its **Highland Games**, known as the *Lonach Highland Gathering*, held on the third Saturday in August, and a healthy blast of authenticity in comparison to the rather more glitzy affair at Braemar on Deeside (see page 420).

As you head west through Strathdon, you'll see a sign which appears to tell you that you're lost, but in fact is pointing the way to the wonderfully named village of **Lost**, four miles north of Strathdon, in the middle of nowhere. Take the turning off the A944 at Bellabeg. This road also leads to the excellent **Lost Gallery**, which shows work by contemporary artists and is well worth visiting. ■ *Wed-Sun 1100-1700. T651287.*

Corgarff Castle Five miles west of Strathdon the A944 meets the A939 Ballater-Tomintoul road. A few miles beyond the junction is the austere Corgarff Castle, a 16th-century tower house, later turned into a garrison post, with an eventful and gruesome history. Here Margaret Forbes and her family were burned alive by the Gordons in 1571 during the bitter feud between the two families. In the wake of the ill-fated 1745 rebellion the government remodelled the castle, building a star-shaped defensive wall, and garrisoned 60 men to maintain order and communications in this part of the Highlands. Corgarff continued in use into the 19th century when English Redcoats were stationed here in order to prevent whisky smuggling. Today it's managed by Historic Scotland. ■ *Apr-Sep daily 0930-1830; Oct-Mar weekends only. £2.80, £2 concession, £1 child. T651460.* Just before the castle an old military road leads for about a mile to **F** *Jenny's Bothy*, T651449. Open all year, a basic but wonderfully remote bunkhouse.

Beside Corgarff is the hamlet of **Cock Bridge**, standing at the end of one the most beautiful and notorious stretches of road in the country. In winter, the Tomintoul to Cock Bridge road is almost always the first road in Scotland to be blocked by snow (you have been warned!). From Cock Bridge the A939 rises steeply to the Lecht Pass (2,089 ft) before dropping dramatically to **Tomintoul**, the highest village in the Highlands. Tomintoul is a bit of a one-horse town and, like so many others in this area, is an 18th-century planned village, built by the local laird to keep an eye on his tenants. It lies roughly midway between the Don Valley and Speyside, and is therefore well-placed for both the Whisky and Castle Trails. It is also the nearest settlement of any size to **The Lecht**, one of Scotland's top five ski resorts (see next page), and it marks the end of the long-distance **Speyside Way** (see page 428), so is popular with walkers and skiers.

Tomintoul
Phone code: 01807
Colour map 4, grid A4
Altitude: 1,600 ft

Getting there There are **buses** to Tomintoul from **Keith** via **Dufftown** (Tue and Sat only), from **Elgin** (Thu only) and from **Aberlour** (on schooldays, with connection to Elgin). For details call *Roberts of Rothiemay*, T01466-711213. The **Tourist Information Centre** is in the village square, T580285, tomintoul@agtb.ossian.net It's open 2 Apr-2 Jun Mon-Sat 0945-1300, 1400-1700; 4 Jun-8 Jul Mon-Sat 0930-1300, 1400-1700; 9 Jul-19 Aug Mon-Sat 0930-1800, Sun 1300-1800; 20 Aug-1 Sep Mon-Sat 0930-1300, 1400-1700; 3 Sep-27 Oct Mon-Sat 0945-1300, 1400-1700.

On the village square is the **Museum and Visitor Centre**, which has a display of local history, wildlife, landscape and outdoor activities. ■ *Jun-Sep Mon-Sat 1000-1600; Oct-May Mon-Fri 1000-1600. Free. T673701.* Ten miles north of Tomintoul on the B9008 is the **Glenlivet Crown Estate** (see also page 427), with an extensive network of hiking paths and cycle trails, as well as lots of wildlife, including reindeer. Information and free maps are available from the **ranger's office** in Tomintoul, T580283.

Sleeping and eating There are a few hotels around the main square, the nicest of which is the **D-E** *Glenavon Hotel*, T580218. It is also the best place for a drink, and popular with après-skiers, tired walkers and locals. There's also a B&B **B** *Livet House*, Main St, T580205. The **F** *SYHA Youth Hostel*, on Main St, T580282, is hoping to reopen in 2002. Other than the hotels, the best place to eat is the *Clockhouse* on the Square.

Northeast Scotland

Speyside

*The River Spey is Scotland's second longest river, rising in the hills above Loch Laggan and making its way northeast to where it debouches at Spey Bay, on the Moray coast. Speyside is one of Scotland's loveliest valleys and is synonymous with two of Scotland's greatest products, salmon and whisky. The upper part, Strathspey, is equally famous for its hiking, skiing and watersports. It is covered in the Highlands chapter (see page 530). This section covers the lower part of the valley and comprises the famous **Malt Whisky Trail**. There are more malt whisky distilleries in this small area than in any other part of the country, including some famous brands such as Glenlivet and Glenfiddich. However, it's not all whisky in these parts: there's also some fine walking along the 45-mile Speyside Way, which runs from Spey Bay south to Tomintoul.*

Colour maps 2, grid C3/4

The Lecht

The Lecht is a ski resort for all seasons. It offers dry-slope skiing throughout the year and its snowmaking facilities mean that the winter season can be extended beyond January and February. The Lecht's gentler slopes make it ideal for beginners and intermediates and the emphasis is on family skiing. There's a snowboard fun park with half pipe, log slide, gap jump and table top. However, there are also more difficult runs for the more experienced skier, and extensive off piste skiing.

*A **day ticket** costs £15 for adults, and £8 for children; a half-day ticket costs £12. There's a ski school and equipment hire at the base station, T01975-651440, thelecht@sol.co.uk. For latest snow and weather conditions call the base station, or the Ski Hotline, T09001-654657.*

There's also a summer acitvity area with quad bikes, a tubing slope and funkarts.

Dufftown

Phone code: 01340
Colour map 2, grid C4

A good place to start your whisky tour is Dufftown, founded in 1817 by James Duff, the fourth Earl of Fife, and the self-proclaimed 'Malt Whisky Capital of the World'. There's more than a grain of truth in that assertion, for there are no fewer than seven working distilleries here. This is indeed the town that was built on seven stills.

Ins & outs *Bluebird Buses*, T01224-212266, run a daily service from **Elgin** (No 336). There's also a service (Nos 360 & 361) which connects Dufftown with **Keith** and **Aberlour** (Mon-Fri). For details call *W W Smith*, T01542-882113.

Dufftown's **Tourist Information Centre** is inside the Clock Tower in the centre of the main square, T820501. They have maps and information on the whisky trail. Open Apr-8 Jul Mon-Sat 1000-1300, 1400-1700; 9 Jul-19 Aug Mon-Sat 1000-1800, Sun 1300-1800; 20 Aug-27 Oct Mon-Sat 1000-1300, 1400-1700.

Sights Just outside of town, on the A941 to Craigellachie, is the **Glenfiddich Distillery**, the town's most famous distillery and one of the best known of all malt whiskies (see box, page 427). Behind the distillery are the 13th-century ruins of **Balvenie Castle**, built by Alexander 'Black' Comyn, then added to in the 15th and 16th centuries, and visited by Mary, Queen of Scots in 1562. ■ *Apr-Sep daily 0930-1830. £1.50, £1.10 concession , £0.50 child. T820121 (HS).* Four miles north of Dufftown, at the junction of the A941 and A95, is the little village of **Craigellachie**, site of the **Speyside Cooperage** (see below) and where you can see Thomas Telford's beautiful bridge over the River Spey. At nearby Aberlour is the home of *Walkers Shortbread*, T01340-871555.

About eight miles southwest of Craigiellachie, on the A95 to Grantown-on- Spey, is beautiful **Ballindalloch Castle**, a mile west of the village of Marypark. The castle is one of the loveliest in the northeast and has been lived in continuously by its original family, the Macpherson-Grants, since 1546. It houses a fine collection of Spanish paintings and the extensive grounds are home to the famous Aberdeen-Angus herd of cattle, bred here since 1860. ■ *Easter-Sep daily 1000-1700. £4 entry plus £1 parking. T01807-500206.* Also in Ballindalloch is the **Glenfarclas Distillery**. ■ *Tours Apr-Sep Mon-Fri 0930-1700; Jun-Sep also Sat 0930-1630; Oct-Mar Mon-Fri 1000-1600. £3.50, under 18s free. T01807-500245, www.glenfarclas.co.uk*

Northeast Scotland

The Malt Whisky Trail

*Speyside is Scotland's most prolific whisky-producing region and the **Malt Whisky Trail** is a well-signposted 70-mile tour around seven of the most famous distilleries, plus the Speyside Cooperage. Most of the distilleries offer guided tours, and most (with the exception of Glenfiddich) charge an entry fee, which can then be discounted, in full or in part, from the cost of a bottle of whisky in the distillery shop. Tours also include a free dram. Those listed below are the most interesting. For more information, visit www.maltwhiskytrail.com*

*The **Spirit of Speyside Whisky Festival** is a celebration of "the water of life" with various whisky-related events taking place throughout the region (3-6 May 2002). For details www.spiritofspeyside.com*

***Strathisla**, in Keith, is the oldest working distillery in the Highlands (1786) and perhaps the most atmospheric, in a beautiful setting on the River Isla. This is a relatively rare malt, which is also used in the better-known Chivas Regal blend. T01542-783044. Open Feb to end Nov Mon-Sat 0930-1600, Sun 1230-1600. £4 (includes £2 discount voucher).*

***Speyside Cooperage** is near iellachie Craig, four miles north of Dufftown. Here you can watch the oak casks for whisky being made. T01340-871108. Open Jun-Sep Mon-Sat 0930-1630; Oct-May Mon-Fri 0930-1630. £2.25.*

***Dallas Dhu** is a bit off the beaten track, a mile south of Forres off the A940. It no longer produces whisky but it's a beautifully preserved Victorian distillery which you can explore on your own. T01309-676548. Open daily Apr-Sep 0930-1830; Oct-Mar Mon-Wed and Sat 0930-1630, Thu 0930-1200, Fri and Sun 1400-1630. £3, £1.90 concession.*

***Cardhu** is seven miles west of Craigellachie, at Knockando on the B9102. This lovely little distillery is now owned by United Distillers, and their fine malt is one of many used in the famous Johnny Walker blend. T01340-872555. Open Mar-Nov Mon-Fri 0930-1630, Sun 1100-1600; Jul-Sep also Sat 0930-1630 and Sun 1100-1600; Dec-Feb Mon-Fri 1000-1600. £3 (includes £2 discount voucher).*

***Glen Grant** is in Rothes, on the A941 to Elgin. This distillery tour has the added attraction of a Victorian garden and orchard, woodland walks by the burn and the rebuilt 'Dram Pavilion'. T01542-783318. Open mid-Mar to end Oct Mon-Sat 1000-1600, Sun 1130-1600; Jun-Sep Mon-Sat 1000-1700, Sun 1130-1700. £3 (includes £2 discount voucher).*

***Glenfiddich** is just north of Dufftown, on the A941. Probably the best known of all the malts and the most professionally run operation. It's the only distillery where you can see the whisky being bottled on the premises, and the only major distillery that's free (including the obligatory dram). T01340-820373. Open all Apr to mid-Oct Mon-Sat 0930-1630 and Sun 1200-1630; mid-Oct to Mar Mon-Fri only. Free.*

***Glenlivet** is 10 miles north of Tomintoul on the B9008. This was an illicit whisky until it was licensed in 1824. The distillery was later founded in 1858 and this malt has gone on to become one of the world's favourites. It was then taken over in 1978 by Seagram's. T01542-783220. Open mid-Mar to end Oct Mon-Sat 1000-1600, Sun 1230-1600; Jul-Aug till 1800. £3 (includes £2 discount voucher).*

A restored old train powered by a diesel engine runs from Dufftown to Drummuir (5 miles) and on to Keith (10 miles) on Saturday and Sunday, T821181, at 1330 and 1500. Adult ticket £6.

The best place to stay is the superb **A** *Craigiellachie Hotel*, T881204. Also recommended is the **B** *Minmore House Hotel*, T01807-590378, minimorehouse@ukonline.co.uk, open May-Oct, 10 miles southwest of Dufftown, in the village of Glenlivet. Right beside the distillery and is the former home of the owner. Also in Craig iellachie is the **E** *Highlander Inn*, on

Sleeping & eating

The Speyside Way

The Speyside Way follows the River Spey from its mouth at Spey Bay inland as far as Ballindalloch, then crosses high moorland to Tomintoul. The 45-mile route takes three to five days to complete. Much of it is on an old railway line and passes close to several small villages, meaning that it can easily be broken down into shorter walks. It also passes several distilleries along the way. There are plans to extend the route in the next few years, from Buckie, on the Moray coast, to Aviemore.

There is no guidebook to the Speyside Way, but OS Landranger maps Nos 28 & 36 cover the entire route. Further information and route leaflets are available from the **Moray Council Ranger Service**, *at Boat of Fiddich, Craigellachie. The office is open Easter-Oct daily 0900-1700 (T01340-881266, www.moray.org/area.speyway/webpages/swhome.htm).*

Victoria St, T/F881446. Popular and serves decent bar meals. There's a fairly wide selection of accommodation in Dufftown itself. Two good **B&Bs** are **E** *Tannoch Brae*, T820541, and **E** *Tullich House*, T821008, whoch also provides dinner.

The new *La Faisandarie*, T821273, has a good reputation, book first. Also good is the moderately priced *A Taste of Speyside*, on Balvenie St, T820860. *The Fife Arms Hotel*, T820220, on the square does cheap bar meals. As far as entertainment goes, the *Commercial Hotel*, T820313, on Church St has ceilidhs every 2nd Thu during the summer.

Huntly

Phone code: 01466
Colour map 2, grid C5

Ten miles east of Dufftown is the pleasant and prosperous-looking little town of Huntly. Close to the Whisky Trail and on the main Aberdeen to Inverness train route, it makes a convenient base from which to explore this area. The **Tourist Information Centre** is on the main square, T792255. It's open April-October daily 1000-1700; July-August till 1900.

The town also boasts a lovely little castle all of its own. The 16th-century **Huntly Castle** stands in a beautiful setting on the banks of the River Deveron, on the northern edge of town. It was built by the powerful Gordon family and is notable for its fine heraldic sculpture and inscribed stone friezes, particularly over the main door. ■ *Apr-Sep daily 0930-1830; Oct-Mar Mon-Wed and Sat 0930-1630, Thu 0930-1200, Fri and Sun 1400-1630. £2.80, £2 concession, children £1. T793191 (HS).* Near the castle is the **Nordic Ski Centre**, T794428, the only year-round cross-country ski centre in the UK. The centre also hires out ski equipment and mountain bikes.

Seven miles south of town, near the village of Kennethmont, is **Leith Hall**, an unprepossessing mid-17th-century mansion house. The house contains the personal possessions of successive Leith lairds, most of whom saw military service overseas, but more interesting are the extensive grounds which include a six-acre garden, 18th-century stables and ice house, two ponds, a bird observation hide and countryside walks. ■ *Easter and 1 May-30 Sep daily 1330-1730; weekends in Oct 1330-1730. Garden and grounds open all year daily 0930-dusk. £6, £4.50 concession, £1 child. T01464-831594 (NTS).*

Sleeping & eating

There's a decent selection of accommodation in and around Huntly. The most impressive place to stay is **C** *The Castle Hotel*, T792696, castlehot@enterprise.net The former home of the Duke of Gordon, it's approached through the castle entrance and then over the river. There are several good **B&Bs** in town, including **E** *Greenmount Guesthouse*, 43 Gordon St, T792482; **E** *Mrs Alden*, 10 Church St, T792324; and **E-F** *Strathlene*, on

The Tap o' Noth walk

OS Landranger No 37 covers the route. The total distance is three miles. Allow at least two hours there and back.

Eight miles south of Huntly on the A97 is the village of **Rhynie**, *where you turn off for one of the best walks in the northeast. The Tap o' Noth (1,851 ft) dominates this part of rural Aberdeenshire and the panoramic views from the top make it a worthwhile climb. It's also a fairly easy walk to the conical summit, where there's a vitrified fort.*

It's believed that the name derives from the Gaelic taip a'nochd, *which translates as look-out top. But there's also a local legend that the hill's giant, Jack o'Noth, stole the sweetheart of his neighbour, Jack o'Bennachie. In retaliation, the cuckolded neighbour hurled a huge boulder and flattened Jack on his own hilltop.*

Start the walk from the car park at **Scurdargue**, *a few miles west of Rhynie, off the A941. Leave the car park and head straight up the track to a gate. Go through the gate and cross some rough pasture into woodland. At the northwest corner of the wood, go through another*

gate and turn left onto a track. Follow this grassy track uphill beside a fence until you see another area of forestry ahead, with rough pastureland on the right. Follow the faint track across the pasture to the broad track which then climbs up the Tap's western slopes. Follow this all the way to the top, up the tight zig-zag on the southern flank and through the eastern entry to the hillfort, into a large enclosure. On the way back down look out for a subsidiary path under the fort's western ramparts. This path desc- ends steeply to the left, south of the main track. It then joins the main track and you can retrace your steps back to the car park.

MacDonald St, T792664. The hotels in town serve bar food, as does the *Auld Pit*, which is a good pub. Another good pub, especially for real ale, is the *Borve Brew House*, in Ruthven, a few miles off the A96 to Keith.

The Northeast Coast

The northeast coast holds some of Scotland's best coastal scenery, particularly the Moray Coast from Spey Bay to Fraserburgh. Here you'll find some picturesque little villages clinging to the cliffs like limpets, and miles of windswept, deserted sandy beaches. Portsoy, Pennan, Gardenstown and Crovie are all well worth visiting, and there are great beaches at Cullen, Lossiemouth, Rosehearty and Sunnyside. Other highlights in the region include the beautiful Duff House, the working abbey at Pluscarden, and Findhorn, famous worldwide for its alternative, spiritual community.

Colour map 2, grid C3-6

Ins and outs

The two largest towns along the coast are the hard-working, no-nonsense fishing ports of Peterhead and Fraserburgh, both linked by a regular bus service from Aberdeen. Fochabers, Elgin and Forres are all on the main Aberdeen-Inverness **bus**

Getting around

Northeast Scotland

route and served regularly, and **trains** between Aberdeen and Inverness stop at Elgin and Forres. Otherwise, public transport is somewhat limited and it can be difficult getting to the more out-of-the-way places without your own transport.

North of Aberdeen

The A90 runs north to Peterhead. Fifteen miles north of Aberdeen is the turn-off to **Ellon**, and five miles west of Ellon, on the A920 to **Oldmeldrum**, are **Pitmedden Gardens**. The centrepiece of the property, the Great Garden, was originally laid out in 1675 by Sir Alexander Seton, and the elaborate, orderly floral patterns have been lovingly recreated. Also on the 100-acre site is the **Museum of Farming Life**, where you can see how the estate workers lived. There's also a visitor centre, tearoom and a woodland walk. ■ *1 May-30 Sep daily 1000-1730. £5, £4 concession, £1 child. T01651-842352 (NTS).*

A mile north of Pitmedden, a side road turns left off the B999 to **Tolquhon Castle** (pronounced 'tee-hon'). This early 15th-century tower was built for the Forbes family and later extended with a large mansion around a courtyard. The most impressive feature is the ornamental gatehouse, but there are also other interesting original features to discover. ■ *T01651-851286. Apr-Sep daily 0930-1830, Oct-Mar weekends only. £1.80, £1.30 concession.*

Haddo House Four miles north of Pitmedden, reached via the B9005 from Ellon, is the elegant Palladian mansion of Haddo House, one of the most impressive of Scotland's country houses. Designed by William Adam for the 2nd Earl of Aberdeen in 1732, and later refurbished in the 1880s, the house beautifully marries graceful Georgian architecture with sumptuous late-Victorian interiors. Home of the Gordon family for over 400 years, Haddo is a wonderfully tasteful legacy of how the other half lived. The house sits in 177 acres of country park, where you can stroll around the woodland and lakes, home to abundant wildlife such as deer, red squirrels and pheasants. Haddo also hosts a varied programme of music, drama and arts events. For details of forthcoming productions, contact the *Haddo Arts Trust*, T01651-851770, or the National Trust. ■ *Easter and 1 May-30 Sep daily 1330-1730, weekends in Oct (last admission 1645), guided tours Mon-Sat; garden and country park open all year 0930-dusk. £6, £4.50 concession, £1 child. T01651-851440 (NTS).*

Fyvie Castle Seven miles west of Haddo House is Fyvie Castle, off the A947 between Oldmeldrum and Turriff. This grandest of Scottish baronial piles is a major feature on the 'Castle Trail' and shouldn't be missed if you're in the vicinity. The castle's five towers are each named after one of the five families who have had the pleasure of living here over the centuries. The last lot only moved out in 1980 so it has a rare lived-in feel to it. The oldest part of the castle dates from the 13th century and, apart from the great wheel-stair and the 17th-century morning room, the extravagantly opulent interior largely dates from the Edwardian era. There's a superb collection of portraits including works by the likes of Raeburn, Batoni, Gainsborough and Hoppner, as well as 17th-century tapestries and collections of arms and armour. The landscaped grounds and Fyvie Loch are also worth exploring and even the tearoom is great. ■ *Easter to 30 Jun and Sept daily 1330-1730, Jul-Aug 1100-1730, weekends only in Oct, grounds open all year daily 0930-dusk. £6, £4.50 concession, £1 child. T01651-891266 (NTS).*

Eleven miles north of Aberdeen, the A975 turns off the A90 and makes an interesting little detour along the coast before rejoining the A90 a few miles south of Peterhead. The road crosses the mouth of the River Ythan at **Newburgh** and passes the dramatic **Sands of Forvie**, which are now part of the **Forvie National Nature Reserve**, one of Britain's largest dune systems and home to a vast array of birdlife.

Newburgh to Cruden Bay

Eight miles north is the little town of **Cruden Bay**, at the northern end of a wide sweep of sandy beach. Close by, perched on the clifftop, are the gaunt, storm-lashed ruins of **Slains Castle**, built in 1597 by the Earls of Errol. So eerily evocative is the ruin that it fired the imagination of Bram Stoker and inspired him to write *Dracula* during one of his holiday visits. The castle ruin is a 15-minute walk from Cruden Bay. From the car park at the end of the main street, head along the cliffs.

Three miles north of Slains Castle is the **Bullers of Buchan**, an amazing 245-ft deep circular basin of rocky cliff where the sea boils in through an eroded archway. In spring and summer the cliffs are home to countless thousands of seabirds. You can also reach this point from the A975, via the footpath from the car park. Take great care near the edge of the chasm and watch out for kamikaze seabirds.

Cruden Bay also has a terrific **golf course**, rated as one of the best links courses in the UK, T01779-812285. You can stay in town at the **B** *Red House Hotel*, T01779-812215.

Thirty miles north of Aberdeen is the harsh, uncompromising town of Peterhead, Europe's busiest white-fish port. Fish is Peterhead's *raison d'être* and everything revolves around its huge harbour. Local fishermen have not been having it so good in recent years, however, as North Sea fish stocks have become dangerously depleted and EU quotas have threatened livelihoods. The town's alternative sources of income are the power station and the high-security prison.

Peterhead
Phone code: 01779
Colour map 2, grid C6
Population: 18,500

Peterhead may not be the most appealing prospect, but the town is rightly proud of its seafaring heritage. The **Peterhead Maritime Heritage Museum** is housed in an attractive new building on South Road. It tells the story of the whaling and fishing industries and depicts the life and times of the townsfolk through a series of interactive displays and a video presentation. ■ *T473000. Apr-Oct Mon-Sat 1000-1700, Sun 1200-1700; Nov-Mar Sat 1000-1600, Sun 1200-1600. £2.50, £1.50 child.* At the north end of town on Golf Road, at the mouth of the River Ugie, is the **Ugie Fish House**, Scotland's oldest working fish house. Salmon and trout have been smoked here since 1585 and you can still see traditional methods being employed, and then purchase the finished product. ■ *T476209. All year Mon-Fri 0900-1700, Sat 0900-1200. Free.*

Nine miles west of town at Mintlaw, is the **Aden Country Park** (pronounced 'Ah-den'). It's a great place for kids, with numerous walks around the estate, various organized activities and events, and the **Aberdeenshire Farming Museum**, which features a semi-circular farmstead built in the early 19th century and a working farm dating from the 1950s. ■ *T01771-622906. May-Sep daily 1100-1700; Apr and Oct weekends only 1200-1630. Free. Bus No 286 daily to and from Peterhead.*

Sleeping and eating There's no tourist office in town, but the best place to stay is the modern **A** *Waterside Inn*, T471121, on the road heading out of town to Fraserburgh, by the River Ugie. A cheaper option is **E** *Carrick Guesthouse*, T470610, at 16 Merchant St. A good fish and chip shop is the *Dolphin*, on Alexandra Par by the harbour.

Northeast Scotland

Transport *Bluebird Buses*, T01224-212266, run every 30 mins (Mon-Sat; every hour on Sun) from **Aberdeen**, via **Ellon** (No 260) and **Cruden Bay** (No 263).

Fraserburgh

Phone code: 01346
Colour map 4, grid C6
Population: 13,000

Eighteen miles north of Peterhead, at the very northeastern tip of the northeast coast, is the hardy, windswept fishing town of Fraserburgh. At the northern tip of the town is **Kinnaird Head Castle and Lighthouse**, which now houses Scotland's **Lighthouse Museum**. This bizarre structure started out as a 16th-century castle which was then converted by the Northern Lighthouse Company in 1787 into one of mainland Scotland's first lighthouses. The museum offers a truly fascinating illumination of the engineering skill and innovation involved in the design and workings of the lighthouse, with displays of the huge lenses and prisms, as well as a history of the Stevenson family (Robert Louis' father and grandfather) who designed many of Scotland's lighthouses. The highlight is the guided tour to the top of Kinnaird Head Lighthouse itself. ■ *Apr-Oct Mon-Sat 1000-1800, Sun 1200-1800; Nov-Mar till 1600. T511022.* The **Tourist Information Centre** is at 3 Saltoun Square. T518315. Apr-Jun and Sep Mon-Sat 1000-1300 and 1400-1700; Jul-Aug Mon-Sat 1000-1300 and 1400-1800, Sun 1300-1700.

Sleeping and eating Accommodation is fairly thin on the ground. There's the **A** *Saltoun Arms Hotel*, T518282; or **B&B** at **E-F** *Clifton House*, 131 Charlotte St, T518365. There's also a **campsite** 5 miles west of town at **Rosehearty**, which has a good beach. The best place to **eat** is *Findlays*, at Smiddyhill Rd and Boothby Rd, for good fish and Aberdeen Angus steaks. Eat in the *Lighthouse Museum* restaurant for the wonderful surroundings.

Transport *Bluebird Buses*, T01224-212266, run regular buses to and from **Aberdeen**, via **Mintlaw**, and **Peterhead**. There are also buses to **Banff** via **Pennan** and **Gardenstown** (No 273; Mon-Sat).

Pennan, Crovie & Gardenstown

Colour map 2, grid C5/6

Between Fraserburgh and Macduff/Banff lies a trio of charming little coastal villages, clinging hungrily to the sea cliffs like babies to their mothers' breasts. The most easterly is **Pennan**, which shot to fame in 1982 when the hit British movie *Local Hero* was filmed here. The tiny hamlet lies just off the road, at the foot of a very steep hill, and consists of little more than a row of neat, whitewashed cottages, bravely challenging the North Sea. The only place to **eat and sleep** is the cheap and cosy **E** *Pennan Inn*, T01346-561201.

A few miles west, on the other side of Troup Head, is the equally lovely little fishing village of **Gardenstown** (or Gamrie, pronounced 'Game-ree'), whose streets are so precipitous you almost need to be roped up to get around on foot, never mind trying to drive a car. You can also sleep here, at **E** *The Palace Farm*, T01261-851261, March-Nov; or **E** *Bankhead Croft*, T01261-851584, both of which provide dinner. A stone's throw away is the even tinier village of **Crovie** (pronounced 'Crivvie'), which is so narrow its residents have to walk sideways.

Banff & Macduff

Phone code: 01261
Colour map 2, grid C5

The road west from Pennan leads on to the busy fishing port of Macduff, separated only by a bridge from neighbouring Banff, whose town centre still retains its faded Georgian elegance. The great attraction in the area is **Duff House**, on the Banff side of the River Deveron, a short walk upstream from the bridge. This magnificent Georgian mansion was designed by William Adam in 1735 for local entrepreneur William Duff, who later became Earl of Fife. The house was supposed to act as the capital of Duff's huge estate, but the whole project collapsed after a major disagreement between architect and patron and ended with a lawsuit in 1747. The wings were never built but Duff House remains one of the finest Georgian baroque houses in Britain. After a variety of uses and a period of dereliction, the house has been meticulously restored and reopened as an important outpost of the **National Gallery of Scotland**. The extensive collection on display includes works by Scottish artists Ramsay and Raeburn, as well as an El Greco. ■ *Apr-Oct daily 1100-1700, Nov-Mar Thu-Sun 1100-1600. £4, £3 child/concession. T818181.*

The house is surrounded by extensive grounds with some lovely walks through sylvan settings. The best, though, is along the banks of the river Deveron to the beautiful **Bridge of Alvah**, spanning the river across a deep gorge. It's about four miles there and back from Duff House. Leaflets showing the route are available free from the tourist office in Banff (see below).

A mile southwest from Banff, on the A97 to Huntly, is the **Colleonard Sculpture Garden**, a peaceful space populated by wooden sculptures carved out of tree trunks, the work of Frank Bruce, who lives in the house and can often be seen around the site. ■ *Daily 0930-1700. Free.*

In Macduff is the **Macduff Marine Aquarium**, at 11 High Shore. Various weird and wonderful specimens from the Moray Firth are displayed in Britain's deepest aquarium tank. ■ *T833369. Daily 1000-1700. £2.75, £1.50 child.* The local **Tourist Information Centre** is in Banff, at Collie Lodge, opposite the gates of Duff House. ■ *Apr-Sep daily 1000-1300 and 1400-1700; Jul-Aug Mon-Sat till 1800, Sun 1300-1800. T812419.* They offer a free hour-long walkman tour (£1 deposit) which takes you around the elegant Georgian upper town.

Sleeping and eating In Banff C *Banff Springs Hotel*, T812881, is on the western outskirts of town on the A98 to Elgin. It's a friendly, modern hotel with a good restaurant (mid-range). There are several very good **guesthouses** and **B&Bs**, including **E** *Links Cottage*, T812223, Mar-Nov, overlooking Boyndie Bay; **E** *Bryvard Guesthouse*, Seafield St, T818090, bryvard@aol.com; and **E** *The Orchard*, Duff House, T812146, jma6914291@aol.com. There's a **campsite** at *Banff Links Caravan Park*, T812228; open Mar-Oct, on Boyndie Bay. **In Macduff** **D** *The Highland Haven*, T832408, on Shore St; and the **D-E** *Knowes Hotel*, T832229, on Market St.

For **places to eat** try the highly-rated *Fagin's*, a few miles west of Banff, in the little village of Whitehills, T861321. Mid-range prices; open Fri-Sun for lunch and Wed-Sat 1900-2200.

Transport *Bluebird Buses*, T01224-212266, run services from Banff to **Fraserburgh** (Mon-Sat) via **Gardenstown** and **Pennan**, and from Macduff to **Huntly/Keith** (Mon-Sat). Bus No 305 leaves hourly (Mon-Sat; less frequent on Sun) to **Aberdeen**, and to **Elgin** via **Portsoy**, **Cullen** and **Buckie**.

West of Banff are two of the most attractive towns on the Moray coast, Portsoy and Cullen. Portsoy is particularly lovely, with its 17th-century harbour, restored merchants' houses and narrow streets. The famous Portsoy marble, used in the building of Versailles, was quarried nearby. The best time to visit is in late June, when you can enjoy the town's excellent *Scottish Traditional Boat Festival* which features local food, street theatre and music. Six miles west is the town of Cullen, dramatically sited beneath a series of striking 19th-century railway viaducts and fronting an impressive sweep of sand. Walk east from Cullen harbour along the coast for a few miles to the lovely, deserted beach at **Sunnyside**, overlooked by the lemming-like ruin of **Findlater Castle**. There's another great beach at **Sandend**, between Portsoy and Cullen.

Portsoy & Cullen
Phone code: 01542
Colour map 2, grid C4/5

Northeast Scotland

Sleeping and eating The best places to stay in **Cullen** are **B-C** *The Seafield Arms Hotel*, T840791, www.theseafieldarms.co.uk; and **D** *The Bayview Hotel*, T841031, both on 57 Seafield St. There are also several **B&Bs**. The local delicacy (and delicious it is, too) is Cullen Skink, a soup made with smoked haddock and cream. For food try the hotels listed above. Two good pubs for food are the *Royal Oak* and *Cullen Bay*, both on the A98 east towards Banff.

Fochabers & around

Phone code: 01343
Colour map 2, grid C4

The A98 runs inland, bypassing the coastal town of **Buckie**, to reach the pleasant little town of Fochabers, 12 miles west of Cullen. The town is best known as the home of the famous Baxter family, whose name has become synonymous with food, especially soup. The Baxters factory now stands west of the bridge over the Spey by the A98, and the **Baxter's visitor centre** tells the story of the famous food-producing family from 1868, when George and Margaret Baxter opened their grocery shop in Spey Street. There are also factory tours on weekdays, and cooking demonstrations. The Baxter's *Spey Restaurant* serves good cheap meals and snacks. ■ *Factory tours Mon-Fri 1000-1130 and 1230-1600. Free. T820666, www.baxters.com*

Five miles north of Fochabers, at the mouth of the River Spey, is **Spey Bay**, site of the **Tugnet Ice House**, which was built in 1830 to store ice for packing salmon, and now houses an exhibition on the salmon industry and the wildlife of the Spey Estuary. ■ *May-Sep daily 1100-1600. Free. T01309-673701.* Next door is the **Moray Firth Wildlife Centre**, which has an exhibition on the Moray Firth dolphins, as well as other local wildlife, including grey and common seals, otters and ospreys. The centre also houses a research unit studying the resident bottlenose dolphins (for more on the dolphins, see page 450). ■ *Mar-Dec daily 1100-1630; Jul-Aug 1030-1900. £1.50, £0.75 concession. T820339. Mfwc@dial.pipex.com*

Sleeping There's accommodation in town at the **C-D** *Gordon Arms Hotel*, 80 High St, T820508. Also **E** *Mrs Shand*, at Castlehill Cottage, Blackdam, T820761.

Transport Fochabers is on the main A96 Aberdeen-Inverness route and there are regular buses to and from various towns en route, such as **Elgin**, **Forres** and **Nairn**. There are also *Bluebird Buses*, T01224-212266, to **Banff**, via **Cullen** and **Portsoy**.

Elgin

Phone code: 01343
Colour map 2, grid C3
Population: 20,000

Nine miles west of Fochabers and 38 miles east of Inverness, is the busy market town of Elgin, which dates back to the 13th century. Elgin has retained much of its medieval streetplan, making it one of the loveliest towns in the country. There's also a good range of shops, and banks with ATMs, in the town centre.

Ins & outs Elgin is well-served by public transport. **Trains** run hourly every day to **Aberdeen** and **Inverness**, stopping at **Forres** and **Nairn**. *Bluebird Buses*, T01224-212266, run hourly to **Aberdeen** (3 hrs) and **Inverness** (1¼ hrs) via **Nairn** (40 mins) and **Forres** (25 mins). There are buses every 30 mins to **Lossiemouth** (20 mins) and hourly to **Burghead** (Mon-Sat, 30 mins). There are buses along the coast to **Banff** and **Macduff**, hourly to **Dufftown** (1 hr) and to **Findhorn** (Mon-Sat, 20 mins). There's also a bus once a day (schooldays only) to **Pluscarden**, T01542-882482. The **bus station** is central, on Alexandra Rd, 1 block north of the High Street. The **train station** is about 750 yds south of town, on Station Rd, off Moss St, which runs south from the High St.

The **tourist office** is at 17 High St, T542666. Apr, May and Oct Mon-Sat 1000-1300 and 1400-1700, Sun 1300-1700; Jun and Sep daily till 1800; Jul and Aug daily till 1900.

Fochabers to Spey Bay walk

There's an excellent walk from Fochabers to Spey Bay, along the first section of the Speyside Way. Start by the old Spey Bridge and follow the B9104 for about 800 yds until you reach the 'Speyside Way' sign which takes you away from the road on to the riverside footpath. Follow this path for two miles, then, as the river swings left, look for the sign on the right showing where you leave the riverside track. Continue along this path for 500 yds, then turn left on to a minor track and, after a further 400 yds, you join a wider track and follow this all the way to Spey Bay.

You can take an alternative route back to Fochabers by turning right at the old railway track (Scottish Wildlife Trust sign) on to a track leading down to the river and then up on to the old railway viaduct and across the river. At the road bridge, take the steps on the left and go up to the road, then turn left and follow this minor road all the way back to the A98, about half a mile west of Baxters. Instead of turning left at the end of the

viaduct, you can make a short diversion into the little village of Garmouth. Here, a plaque marks the spot where King Charles II signed the Solemn League and Covenant in June 1650, thus accepting the proposed Reformation of the Church. The total distance covered is nine miles, and you should allow between four and five hours. There's no public transport to Spey Bay.

The main tourist attraction is **Elgin Cathedral**, on North College Street, round the corner from the tourist office. Though partially ruined, the scattered remains still bear testament to what was once a majestic and beautiful cathedral. Founded in 1224, the cathedral was considered the finest in Scotland until 1390 when it was burned to the ground by the big, bad 'Wolf of Badenoch', the name given to Alexander Stewart, the illegitimate son of Robert II, following his excommunication by the bishop. And if that weren't bad enough, it was rebuilt, only to suffer further damage during the orgy of vandalism that followed the Reformation. There are still some 13th-century features remaining amongst the ruins, particularly the Pictish cross-slab and the octagonal chapterhouse.

■ *Apr-Sep Mon-Sat 0930-1830, Sun 1400-1830; Oct-Mar Mon-Wed and Sat 0930-1630, Thu 0930-1200, Sun 1400-1630. £2, £1.50 concession, joint ticket with Spynie Palace (see below) £2.80, £2.10 concession. T547171.*

Also in town is the **Elgin Museum**, at 1 High Street. It has excellent displays of fossils and Pictish relics, as well as some interesting anthropological collections. ■ *T543675. End Mar-Oct Mon-Fri 1000-1700, Sat 1100-1600, Sun 1400-1700. £1.50, £0.75 concession.* A new distillery not yet on the Malt Whisky Trail is **Glen Moray Distillery**, on Bruceland Road on the western outskirts of town. ■ *Tours all year every hour 0930-1530 Mon-Fri (Sat Jun-Sep). £2 .*

Two miles north of Elgin is **Spynie Palace**, the residence of the Bishops of Moray from the 14th century till 1686, when they were abolished in the Scottish Church. The palace is now a ruin, though the massive tower built by

Sights

Northeast Scotland

The Northern Lights

A feature of visiting the far north of Scotland in winter is the chance of seeing the Aurora Borealis, or Northern Lights, which decorate the night skies like a gigantic laser show. The best time to see them is between October and March – especially during December and January. Try to get as far north as you can, though there are no guarantees of a sighting as cloud cover can obscure visibility. Any of the north-facing coastal villages are a good bet.

Bishop David Stewart remains, affording spectacular views over Spynie Loch and the Moray Firth. ■ *Apr-Sep Mon-Sat 0930-1830, Sun 1400-1830; Oct-Mar weekends only till 1630. £1.80, £1.35 concession, joint ticket with Elgin Cathedral available (see above).*

Six miles southwest of Elgin, set in a sheltered valley, is the giant hulk of **Pluscarden Abbey**. The abbey was founded in 1230, but in 1390 became another victim of the incredibly vengeful Wolf of Badenoch (see above). It recovered, but then fell into disrepair after the Reformation, until 1948 when it was rebuilt by an order of Benedictine monks, who still inhabit the abbey, making it the only medieval monastery in Britain that still houses a monastic community. Today it is a residential retreat for men and women and is open all year round. It has 26 single rooms and two doubles. Maximum stay stay is two weeks and charges are by donation. There are also guided tours. ■ *Daily 0445-2045. Free. T890257, www.pluscardenabbey.org*

Sleeping There's a wide range of accommodation in Elgin. Best of the hotels is the **A** *Mansion House Hotel*, The Haugh (north of the High St, overlooking the river), T548811. 23 rooms. Full leisure facilities and a good restaurant in an elegant and comfortable town house. Also recommended is the **C** *Mansfield House Hotel*, on Mayne Rd (1 block south of the High St), T540883. 21 rooms. Centrally located, elegant town house. Its restaurant is very popular with locals and reputed to be the best in town (expensive).

There are many fine **guesthouses** and **B&Bs**, including the highly rated **D-E** *The Pines Guesthouse*, T542766, kath-pos@hotmail.com, on East Rd, a short walk from the town centre. Also good are **E** *The Lodge*, 20 Duff Av, T549981; **D-E** *The Croft*, 10 Institution Rd, T546004; and **E** *Ardgye House*, T850618, which is 5 mins' drive from town on the A96 west to Inverness. For something a bit different, there's **D-E** *The Old Church of Urquhart*, T843063, a converted church in the tiny village of Urquhart, 5 miles east of Elgin, off the A96 to Aberdeen.

Eating The best place to eat in town is the *Mansfield House Hotel* (see above). There are plenty of cheaper places in town, including *Littlejohn's*, 193 High St, a Tex-Mex/Cajun restaurant chain that's child-friendly. Nearby, at 181 High St, is *Ca'Dora*, a fish and chip shop. *Gordon and McPhail*, 50-60 South St, is an excellent deli, with a lip-smacking variety of fine foods and a huge range of malt whiskies. A good pub is the 17th-century *Thunderton House*, in Thunderton Pl, off the High St.

Lossiemouth to Burghead
Colour map 2, grid C4
There are regular buses to Lossiemouth and Burghead from Elgin (see above)

Six miles north of Elgin is **Lossiemouth**, funnily enough at the mouth of the River Lossie. The old fishing port is blessed with two fine beaches, to the east and west of town, and an excellent golf course, making it a popular seaside resort in summer. The town's real claim to fame, though, is as the birthplace of James Ramsay MacDonald (1866-1937), Britain's first Labour prime minister. Between 'Lossie' and Burghead, south of the coast road, is the scattered village of **Duffus**. The old part is home to a ruined

14th-century motte and bailey castle and an interesting 13th-century church, while the newer part is better known for its close neighbour, **Gordonstoun School**, the public school favoured (but not necessarily loved) by the royal family.

Six miles west of Lossie is the fishing village of **Burghead**, ancient Pictish capital of Moray and site of an important Iron-Age fort. The only real surviving feature is the well in King Street (key from No 69 King Street). The village gave its name to the **Burghead Bulls**, a series of remarkable Pictish stone carvings, some of which can be seen in the Elgin Museum (the others are in the Royal Museum in Edinburgh and the British Museum in London). The old Pictish New Year is still celebrated in the village on 11 January, when a burning tar barrel – the Clavie – is carried around. To the west of the village a wide sweep of sandy beach stretches all the way west to Findhorn (see below). There's a good chance of seeing the Moray Firth's resident population of bottlenose **dolphins** from here.

Sleeping and eating There are a few **campsites** between Lossiemouth and Burghead. A couple of miles east of Burghead is *Hopeman Sands Caravan Park*, T830880, open Apr-Nov; and overlooking the beach to the west of Lossiemouth there's the *Silver Sands Leisure Park*, T813262, open Apr-Oct. A good pub for food is *Skerry Brae*, on Stotfield Rd.

Forres and Findhorn

Twelve miles west of Elgin is the solid little town of Forres. On Invererne Road is **Benromach Distillery**, which is on the Malt Whisky Trail. ■ Oct-Mar Mon-Fri 1000-1600; Apr-Sep Mon-Sat 0930-1700; also Sun Jun-Aug 1200-1600. £2.50. T675968, www.benromach.com On the eastern edge of town is the 20-ft high **Sueno's Stone**, one of the most remarkable and important Pictish carved stones in Scotland.

Phone code: 01309
Colour map 2, grid C3

Forres is on the main Aberdeen to Inverness bus route and rail line, and there are regular **buses** and **trains** in either direction. *Bluebird Buses* Nos 310 and 311 run from **Elgin** to **Forres**, via **Kinloss** and **Findhorn** several times daily (Mon-Sat).There's a **Tourist Information Centre** at 116 High St, T672938. Easter-Jun, Sep and Oct Mon-Sat 1000-1300 and 1400-1700; Jul-Aug Mon-Sat till 1800, Sun 1300-1800.

About six miles south of Forres is one of the northeast's best-kept secrets, the very beautiful **Randolph's Leap**, a spectacular gorge on the River Findhorn which is the perfect place for a picnic, or a swim in the river. To get there, head south on the A940 and just beyond **Logie Steading** take the right fork (the B9007) for a half a mile. It's on the right side of the road as you head south. It's also worth stopping at Logie Steading, where you can buy good-value arts and crafts. ■ *May-Oct daily 1100-1700, weekends from 1200*. A few miles west of Forres is **Brodie Castle** (see 'Highlands' chapter, page 454).

There's a surprisingly wide range of accommodation in Forres. Best of the hotels are the excellent **A** *Knockomie Hotel*, T673146, overlooking the town on the A940 south to Grantown; and the **B** *Ramnee Hotel*, T672410, on Victoria Rd. Both have highly acclaimed restaurants. Among the many fine **guesthouses** and **B&Bs** are **D-E** *Springfield*, T676965, hbain@globalnet.co.uk, on Croft Rd; **D-E** *Sherston House*, T671087, at Hillhead; and **E** *Tormhor*, T673837, at 11 High St.

Sleeping

Northeast Scotland

The Findhorn Foundation

A combination of hard work and serendipity led three hard-pressed caravan dwellers in the early sixties – Peter and Eileen Caddy and Dorothy Maclean – to establish a garden in the Kinloss dunes which quickly became renowned far and wide for its miraculous abundance, owing, they claim, not only to organic methods but directions from the kingdom of nature spirits. Attracting the like-minded and curious, it grew into a pioneering community where, with an emphasis on the spiritual, the philosophy of the ecological movement was put into practice, following angelic guidance regularly channelled by two of the founding fathers.

Caravans are slowly being replaced by energy efficient houses using environmentally safe building materials, including upturned whisky barrels salvaged from a nearby distillery, with reed bed sewage systems and turf roofs. A strong educational bias brings 4,000 people annually from all over the world to participate in residential courses in personal development, community living and ecological building, or to complete a year-long 'foundation course'. In a vibrant, hot-house atmosphere overshadowed by pine trees in a warren of densely packed houses, is a community centre and a stone and timber arts centre/café architecturally inspired by the tenets of Rudolph Steiner, all giving shelter against the sea winds in order to promote plant life and greenery. Extending worldwide by reputation, the influence of the Foundation has also spread locally, attracting kindred spirits to settle in the area and establish initiatives such as native reforestation of the Highlands, a Steiner School and complementary health practices.

All but the most world-weary of cynics will find the Foundation a fascinating, and possibly enlightening, experience. There are guided tours around the site daily at 1400 throughout the summer.

Findhorn A few miles northeast of Forres is **Kinloss**, site of a major RAF base. The B9011 heads north from Kinloss and past the RAF base; on the right is a sign to the 'Findhorn Bay Caravan Park'. In the shadow of the RAF base in a landscape of gorse and pine-clad dunes, the caravan park is the original site and nucleus of the **Findhorn Foundation**, a world-renowned spiritual community.

A mile north of the Caravan Park is the traditional fishing village of Findhorn, sparkling white under a huge sky, on the eastern shore of Findhorn Bay. The bay provides sheltered waters for boating and watersports, which can all be arranged from the village. On the other side of the bay you can walk on the dunes of Culbin Sands, explore the forest and look for dolphins in the Moray Firth. You may even see osprey fishing for trout or salmon. In the village itself is the **Findhorn Heritage Centre**. ■ *Easter, Jun, Jul-Aug daily (except Tue) 1400-1700; May and Sep also weekends 1400-1700.*

Sleeping and eating You can join the community as a short-term guest, eating and working on-site and staying at local recommended **B&Bs**, and there's a full programme of courses and residential workshops on spiritual growth and healing etc. For more information, T690311. The excellent on-site **shop/deli** by the car park sells books, new-age paraphernalia and a huge variety of organic food (open Monday-Friday till 1800; weekends till 1700). There's also a very good vegetarian **café**. The caravan park is open to the public and you can **camp** beside the Foundation, T690203, caravan@findhorn.org

A good place to eat in the village is the *Kimberley Inn*, T690492, which serves seafood and real ales in a colourful pub atmosphere. Off the A96 is the Crown & Anchor, a very child-friendly pub offering good value food and.

The Highlands and Skye

10

The Highlands and Skye

The Highlands is the part of the country which reflects perfectly most people's romantic image of Scotland. The main town is Fort William, which lies in the shadow of **Ben Nevis**, Britain's highest mountain. North from here stretches a dramatic shoreline of deep sea lochs and sheltered coves of pure white sand backed by towering mountains and looking across to numerous Hebridean islands. West of Fort William, via the lyrical 'Road to the Isles', is Mallaig, now the main departure point for ferries to Skye. Further north is Ullapool, one of the main ferry ports for the Outer Hebrides and the ideal base from which to explore the wild and near-deserted far northwest.

Inverness is the largest town in the region and 'capital of the Highlands'. It lies at the northeastern end of the Great Glen, which cuts diagonally across the southern Highlands to Fort William, linking deep and mysterious **Loch Ness** with the west coast and giving access to **Glencoe**, one of the most beautifully evocative Highland glens and a major climbing and skiing centre. Inverness is also ideally situated for exploring the northeast coast, with its charming old fishing ports, and the storm-lashed north coast, running west from John O'Groats to **Cape Wrath**, as wild and remote a place as you could ever wish for. Then, of course, there's the **Isle of Skye** – the misty isle – mecca for climbers and the most scenically diverse and spectacular of all the islands.

Ins and outs

Getting there
For more transport details, see page 31

Inverness is linked to the south by the fast A9 from Edinburgh and Perth, to Aberdeen by the A96 and to Fort William by the A82, and is well served by buses. Wick, Thurso, Ullapool and Kyle of Lochalsh can all be reached by bus from Inverness. The rail line from Edinburgh closely follows the A9 to Inverness, and there are connections north to Wick and Thurso, west to Kyle of Lochalsh and east to Aberdeen. **Fort William** is easily reached from Glasgow by buses and trains, which continue to Mallaig for the ferry to Skye.

Getting around
By far the most scenic route to the Highlands is the spectacular West Highland Railway, one of the world's great rail journeys, particularly the section from Fort William to Mallaig

Getting around in the Highlands is a lot easier with your own transport, especially in the more remote parts, but it's not difficult to reach the main tourist centres by bus or train. Getting off the beaten track can be a little more complicated, but with forward planning is easily achievable. Much of the time you'll need to rely on the local postbus service, which runs between the various remote post offices throughout the region. Timetables are available at most post offices or Tourist Information Centres. A good idea is to purchase the Public Transport Travel Guides for South Highland and/or North Highland and Orkney. These are available at main tourist offices for £1. Details of ferries from the mainland ports to Skye, are on page 536. Ferries to the Outer Hebrides and Orkney are given in the respective island chapters.

Information

Roughly speaking, this chapter covers the northern half of mainland Scotland plus the Isle of Skye, and is covered by the **Highlands of Scotland Tourist Board**, T01997-421160, www.highlandfreedom.com, which publishes free accommodation guides for the region. They will also book accommodation for a nominal fee. Note that many of the smaller offices are closed during the low season. There's also a local website which has lots of information, including maps, at www.cali.co.uk/highexp/

Climate

The beauty of the northwest Highlands is only enhanced by the notoriously unpredictable weather and that ever-present travelling companion, the midge. That's a lie. The midge is the scourge of many a Highland holiday: a ferocious, persistent and unbelievably irritating little beast who will drive you to the edge of insanity. For details on how best to combat this little terror, see page 65.

The only predictable thing about the weather is its unpredictability. You can have blazing sunshine in Apr, pouring rain in Jul and a blizzard in May. So, you'll need to be prepared for everything. Climbers and walkers especially must take heed of all weather warnings. It can be hot enough for bikinis in the car park at the foot of a 2,000-ft mountain, and 2 hrs later near the summit you're faced with driving, horizontal hail, rain or snow and unable to see further than the end of your nose. People die every year on the Scottish mountains simply because they are ill-prepared, and it is essential to take proper precautions (see page 60). Even those who are not intent on bagging the odd Munro should remember the old adage, that there's no such thing as bad weather, only inadequate clothing.

The Highlands and Skye

Things to do in the Highlands and Skye

· Go for a drive up glorious Glen Affric, one of the very loveliest of Highland glens.
· Choose the West Highland choo-choo, one of the world's great train journeys.
· Take a trip from Shiel Bridge to the splendidly isolated village of Glenelg.
· Travel the stunning route to Applecross and enjoy some wonderful seafood in the cosy Applecross Inn.
· Go for a walk along the beach at Sandwood Bay and watch the sun set with a loved one.
· Take a boat trip into the gaping mouth of Loch Coruisk

Inverness

Inverness is the largest town in the Highlands and the busy and prosperous hub of the region. All main routes through the Highlands pass through here at some point, so it's a hard place to avoid. The town's position at the head of the Great Glen and on the shores of the Moray Firth have made it a firm favourite with tourists, who flock here in their legions during the summer months to look for the evasive Loch Ness Monster. Though Inverness has little in the way of major sights, it's a pleasant place to base yourself as you explore the other, more visible attractions on offer in the surrounding area, including the resident population of dolphins in the Moray Firth. The town, though, is not without its own appeal, particularly the leafy banks of the River Ness, which runs through its heart, linking Loch Ness with the Moray Firth.

Phone code: 01463
Colour map 2, grid C2
Population: 42,000

Ins and outs

There are daily **flights** to and from London Gatwick, Glasgow and Edinburgh with *British Airways* (continuing to Kirkwall and Sumburgh), and daily flights to and from London Luton with *easyJet*. There are also flights to and from Stornoway Mon-Sat with *British Airways Express*. The airport is 7 miles east of the town, at Dalcross (T232471). A twice-daily airport bus to and from the town centre connects with London and Stornoway flights. It takes 20 mins and costs £2.50. A taxi to/from the airport costs £10.

The **bus station** is nearby, just off Academy St (T233371). Left luggage costs £1 per item, open Mon-Sat 0830-1800, Sun 1000-1800.

The **train station** is at the east end of Academy St (T238924). There are regular services to Aviemore, Perth, Glasgow, Edinburgh and Kyle of Lochalsh (for Skye). Left luggage lockers at the train station cost £2-4 per 24 hrs.

Getting there
For further details see page 449.
Inverness is 109 miles from Aberdeen,
161 miles from Edinburgh and
117 miles from Perth

Inverness town centre is compact and easy to explore on foot, and most of the hotels and guesthouses are within a 15-min walk of the TIC. Loch Ness is not within walkable distance, so you'll need your own transport, or alternatively book a tour (see page 457). **Cycle hire** *Barney's Bicycle Hire & Shop*, 35 Castle St, T232249. Open 0900-2100. Mountain bike hire from £7 per day. Also bikes for hire from *Bazpacker's Hostel* (see 'Sleeping').

Getting around

The **TIC**, T234353, is on Castle Wynd, near Ness Bridge, 5-mins walk from the train station. It stocks a wide range of literature on the area, can book accommodation and transport and gives out free maps of the town and environs. Tickets for all the tours listed on the next few pages are available from the TIC. Open 2 Apr-27 May Mon-Sat 0900-1700, Sun (Easter and from 6 May) 1000-1600; 28 May-24 Jun Mon-Sat 0900-1800,

Tourist Information

The Highlands and Skye

Sun 0930-1700; 25 Jun-22 Jul Mon-Sat 0900-1900, Sun 0930-1700; 23 Jul-19 Aug Mon-Sat 0900-2030, Sun 0930-1800; 20 Aug-2 Sep Mon-Sat 0900-1900, Sun 0930-1700; 3 Sep-30 Sep Mon-Sat 0900-1800, Sun 1000-1600; 1 Oct-21 Oct Mon-Sat 0900-1700, Sun 1000-1600; 22 Oct-Apr Mon-Fri 0900-1700, Sat 1000-1600.

History

One of the town's first visitors was that much-travelled cleric, St Columba, who came in AD 565 to confront the Pictish King Brude, whose fortress was reputedly at **Craig Phadraig**, a few miles west of Inverness. Around the mid-12th century King David I built the original castle and made Inverness a royal burgh on the strength of its growing importance as a trading port. Furs, hides, wool and timber were all exported as far afield as the Mediterranean. The town's economic prosperity and status as the most important northern outpost, however, made it a prime target for marauding Highland clansmen, and during the Wars of Independence in the 13th century Inverness was also a regular target for both English and Scots armies.

The town's renaissance came with the completion of the Caledonian Canal and rail links with the south in the 19th century. These improved communications heralded something of a tourist boom amongst the wealthy and fashionable who came north to the Highlands to shoot anything that moved in the name of sport. In the mid-19th century Queen Victoria decided to embrace all things Scottish, which only boosted the town's popularity. Over recent decades Inverness has grown rapidly, not only as a prime base for visiting tourists, but also as the main administrative and commercial centre for the Highlands.

Sights

The castle   The town is dominated by its red sandstone castle. Built in 1834, this Victorian edifice is very much the new kid on the block in terms of Scottish castles. The original castle dates from the 12th century and was built on a ridge to the east of the present structure. Nothing remains of the old castle, which is unsurprising given its bloody and eventful history. It was here that King Duncan of Scotland was slain by Macbeth, an event dramatically (and erroneously) portrayed in Shakespeare's eponymous work. The castle was occupied three times during the Wars of Independence in the 13th century, and when Robert the Bruce recaptured it in 1307 he destroyed it. In the mid-17th century Cromwell ordered his men to build a stone version on the same site. In 1715 James Francis Edward was proclaimed king there, but not long after it was destroyed by the Jacobites to prevent it from falling into enemy hands following the defeat of Bonnie Prince Charlie at Culloden (see page 464).

The present castle houses the Sheriff Court and also stages the **Castle Garrison Encounter**, where you can sign up as a mid-18th-century soldier. New recruits (that's you) pass through the Quartermaster's Store and are introduced to the Sergeant of the Guard, before being accosted by a female camp follower and finally led out through the garrison shop. ■ *Mar-Nov Mon-Sat (Sun only in Jul/Aug) 1030-1730. Adult £3, concession £2.70, children £2. T243363.*

Around   On the castle terrace is a statue of **Flora MacDonald**, to honour her part in
the castle   helping the prince to escape (see page 544). Below the castle is **Inverness Museum and Art Gallery**, on Castle Wynd beside the Tourist Information

Tours of Inverness

*An open-top double-decker **Bus Tour** around Inverness and Culloden is run by **Guide Friday.** Tours leave from Bridge Street near the tourist office at 1000 and then every 45 minutes till 1645, from May to October. Tickets can be bought at their booth in the train station, T224000; open Mon-Fri 0900-1730, Sat 0830-1745, or on*

board the bus. A full day ticket: adult £7.50, concession £6 , children £2.50. The city only tour costs £5.50/£4/£2.50.

*The **Inverness Terror Tour** leaves from outside the tourist office at 1900 nightly and tells the tale of the town's horrific past, complete with witches, ghosts, torture and murders.*

Centre . The museum gives a decent overview of the history of the town and the region, while the gallery is eminently missable. ■ *Mon-Sat 0900-1700. Free.*

Just around the corner, on High Street, is the Gothic-style **Town House**, where Prime Minister Lloyd George held an emergency cabinet meeting in 1921, the first ever to be held outside London.

Opposite, on the corner of Bridge Street and Church Street, is the **Tolbooth Steeple** which dates from 1791 and which had to be repaired after an earth tremor in 1816. Church Street also boasts the town's oldest building, **Abertarff House** (built around 1592), which is now owned by the National Trust but not open to the public. Almost opposite is the much-restored **Dunbar's Hospital**, built in 1688 as an almshouse for the town's poor. At the end of Church Street, where it meets Friar's Lane, is the **Old High Church**, founded in the 12th century and rebuilt in 1772, though the 14th-century vaulted tower remains intact. In the adjoining graveyard prisoners taken at Culloden were executed, and you can still see the bullet marks left by the firing squads on some of the gravestones. ■ *The church is open Fri 1200-1400 and during services; guided tour at 1230.*

Church Street

At the corner of Huntly Street and Ness Bridge, is the **Kiltmaker Centre**, where you can learn everything you ever wanted to know about tartan (including what Scotsmen wear under their kilts). You can also see kilts being made in the factory and, in the shop downstairs, be measured up for one of your own. ■ *Mid-May-end Sep Mon-Sat 0900-2100, Sun 1000-1700; Oct-mid-May Mon-Sat 0900-1700. Adult £2. T222781, www.hector-russell.com*

West Bank

Nearby, directly opposite the castle, is the neo-Gothic **St Andrews Cathedral** which dates from 1869, and is worth a peek if you're passing by. Continuing south along Ness Bank, past the **Eden Court Theatre** (see 'Entertainment' below), you reach **Bught Park** (see 'Sleeping'), which overlooks the **Ness Islands**, joined by footbridge to both banks. The islands are attractively laid out as a park and are a favourite with local anglers. This also happens to be a lovely place for a peaceful evening stroll.

Essentials

You shouldn't have much trouble finding somewhere to stay in Inverness, though in Jul and Aug it's advisable to book ahead. This can be done through the tourist information centre, or in the train station at the Thomas Cook booth, but you'll be charged a booking fee (see page 40). There are several good quality hotels in and around town and plenty of B&Bs. The best places to look are along both banks of the river south of

Sleeping
■ *on map*
Price codes:
see inside front cover

The Highlands and Skye

the Ness Bridge, Old Edinburgh Rd, Southside Rd, Culduthel Rd and Ardconnel St, all to the east of the castle, and on the west bank, behind Balnain House, around Kenneth St and Fairfield Rd. There are also several budget hostels in and around the centre, and a couple of large campsites.

L *Culloden House Hotel*, Milton of Culloden, about 3 miles east of town near the A9. T790461, F792181. 28 rooms. Superb Georgian mansion with 1st-class facilities, service and restaurant. **L** *Dunain Park Hotel*, about 3 miles southwest of the town

Inverness

To Moray Firth Cruises, Black Isle, Wick & Edinburgh (A9)

Sleeping
1 Bazpackers Hostel
2 Brae Ness
3 Eastgate Backpackers Hostel & La Deja Vú
4 Felstead House
5 Glenmorriston Town House
6 Ho Ho Hostel
7 Inverness Student
8 Ivybank Guest House
9 Kinkell House

● **Eating**
1 Café No 1
2 Castle Restaurant
3 Dickens
4 Glen Mhor Hotel
5 Lemon Tree
6 Raja
7 Shapla
8 Steakhouse No 10

● **Bars & pubs**
9 Blackfriars
10 Chili Palmers
11 Johny Foxes
12 Lafferty's
13 Phonix Bar

The Highlands and Skye

centre, just off the A82 Fort William Rd. T230512, F224532, dunainparkhotel@
btinternet.com 12 rooms. An elegant Georgian mansion house with its own grounds,
lovely and peaceful with an excellent restaurant (see below) and its own indoor pool.
L *Glenmoriston Town House Hotel*, 20 Ness Bank. T223777, F712378. 15 rooms.
Recently refurbished and now one of the classiest places in town, with a superb Italian restaurant (see below). **L** *Inverness Marriot*, Culcabock Rd, 1 mile south of the
town centre near A9, T237166, F225208. 81 rooms. Large, modern hotel with excellent rooms, service and facilities.

B *Glenruidh House Hotel*, Old Edinburgh Rd South, 2 miles from the town centre
(phone for directions). T226499, F710745, glenruidhhousehotel@btinternet.com 6
rooms. No smoking. Comfortable and peaceful hotel in secluded setting, with friendly
service and excellent food.

D *Moyness House Hotel*, 6 Bruce Gardens, T/F233836, kayjonesmoyness@msn.com
Fine Victorian villa in a quiet area near the theatre, with comfortable rooms and very
good food. **D** *Brae Ness Hotel*, 17 Ness Bank. T712266, F231732. 10 rooms. No smoking. Family-run Georgian hotel overlooking the river and Eden Court, with a licensed
restaurant for residents. **D** *Felstead House*, 18 Ness Bank. T/F231634,
felstead@jafsoft.com 8 rooms, 5 with bathroom en suite. Family-run Georgian guesthouse, large and comfortable rooms, good breakfast and overall good value.
D *Ivybank Guesthouse*, 28 Old Edinburgh Rd. T/F232796. 5 rooms, 3 with en suite
bathroom. Georgian house with lots of character, nice garden and friendly welcome.
D *Kinkell House*, 11 Old Edinburgh Rd. T235243, F225255, clare@kinkell.
freeserve.co.uk 7 rooms, 3 with en suite bathroom. Comfortable Victorian family
home with spacious rooms, decent value (£2 charge for credit card payment).

F *Bazpackers Hostel*, 4 Culduthel Rd (at the top of Castle St), T717663. 48 beds in
dorms of 4-8, twin and double rooms available, cooking facilities and garden for barbecues, also has laundrette, good atmosphere. **F** *Eastgate Backpackers Hostel*, 38
Eastgate (above *La Déjà Vu* restaurant), T/F718756, www.hostelsaccommodation
.com 47 beds in 5 dorms, 2 twins rooms and 1 family room, free tea and coffee, and
continental breakfast for £1.50. Discount for ISIC holders. **F** *Inverness Student Hotel*, 8
Culduthel Rd, next door to *Bazpackers*, T236556. 9 dorms with 57 beds, some dorms
have good views. Friendly and laid-back atmosphere with all the usual facilities.
F *SYHA Youth Hostel*, Victoria Drive, off Millburn Rd, T231771, F710349. 166 beds.
Huge hostel in former school hall of residence. Another cheap option is the **F** *Ho Ho
Hostel*, T221225, at 23a High St. **Bught Caravan and Camping Site**, Bught Park, on the
west bank of the river near the sports centre, T236920. The largest and most centrally
located campsite, with good facilities; £4.30-11.40 per pitch.

As you'd expect in a major tourist centre, there's the usual plethora of pubs, cafés and **Eating**
restaurants serving cheap and basic food for the non-discerning palate, but those *No shortage of*
looking for a higher standard of cuisine won't be disappointed either. There are also *places to eat in*
loads of takeaways, particularly on Academy St and Eastgate around the train station, *Inverness*
and on Young St, just across the Ness Bridge. A good bakery is *Asher's* in Church St.

Expensive *Dunain Park Hotel* (address as above). Award-winning Scots-French
cuisine in elegant surroundings, and a superb list of malts. Take a stroll in the lovely gardens afterwards. *Glen Mhor Hotel*, 9-12 Ness Bank, T234308. *Riverview* restaurant at
the front is good, especially for seafood. *La Riviera*, at the *Glenmoriston Town House
Hotel* (see above). Excellent Italian food.

Mid-range *Café No 1*, 75 Castle St, T226200. Stands head and shoulders above
everything else in the town centre in terms of quality and imagination, has nice contemporary décor, good selection of vegetarian options, open for lunch and
1800-2200. *Dickens*, 77 Church St, T713111. Offers a mix of oriental and international
dishes with an emphasis on fish; business lunch for £6.50; open 1200-1400 and

The Highlands and Skye

1730-2300. *La Déjà Vu*, 38 Eastgate, T231075. Very good French provincial cooking in an informal atmosphere; their 3-course business lunch is great value at £7; open daily 1200-1400 and 1700 till late. *Nico's Bistro* at the back is also good for traditional Scottish dishes. *Raja*, behind the post office on Post Office Av, T237190. Highly rated Indian restaurant. *Shapla*, 2 Castle Rd, T241919. Good Indian restaurant with Tandoori and Balti menu and good views of the river in the upstairs lounge, open till 2330. *Steakhouse No 10*, 10 Bank St, T714884. Specializes in crêpes and steaks, offers reasonably priced snacks 1100-1500, and à la carte lunch and dinner.

Cheap *Castle Restaurant*, 41 Castle St. Glorified greasy spoon serving huge portions of stodgy, filling grub, convenient for backpacker's hostels, open till 2100. *The Lemon Tree*, 18 Inglis St. Located in the pedestrianized town centre, family-run café offering good home baking and basic but filling meals. The best bet for a cheap lunch or evening meal is one of the city's many pubs and bars, where you can get a main course for £5-6. The most favoured options are *Johnny Foxes*, *Chilli Palmers* and *No 27* (see below).

Entertainment

Bars At 108 Academy St is the *Phoenix*, one of the best pubs in town and always lively. Next door is an Irish theme pub, *Lafferty's*, which features Scottish/Celtic live music on Fri and Sat. Across the street is *Blackfriars*, which is another good pub. *Gellions*, on Bridge St, has varied live music throughout the week; and *Johnny Foxes*, at 26 Bank St, features Irish folk music every night in summer as well as boasting one of the most unusual pub menus around. *Chilli Palmers*, on the corner of Queensgate and Church St, is a trendy new bar offering decent food and a DJ at weekends, and you can enjoy a Jazz Lunch on Sun at *No 27*, on Castle St.

Theatre and cinema *Eden Court Theatre* is on Bishops Rd, overlooking the River Ness. It offers a varied programme of theatre, dance and all kinds of music. There's also a bar and self-service restaurant with good food and views over the river. The attached cinema shows a programme of art-house and newly released movies, for information: T234234. Prices vary depending on the performance. The 7-screen *Warner Village* is on the A96 Nairn Rd, about 2 miles from the town centre. Cinema tickets cost from £4.

Festivals There are numerous events held in and around Inverness throughout the year. These range from a humble pub ceilidh to a full-blown Highland Games. For details contact the Tourist Information Centre or visit their website. The best of the local folk festivals are held over the Easter weekend (T01738-623274), and the excellent *Highland Festival* takes place over 3 days at the end of **Jun** (T711112, www.highlandfestival.demon.co.uk). There's also a festival of *folk music* in **Jul** and **Aug** at Balnain House (see 'Sights' above).

Shopping

Inverness is a good place to buy a **kilt**, or practically anything else in tartan. To find your own clan tartan, head for the *Scottish Kiltmaker Visitor Centre* (see 'Sights' above). Other places which sell highland dress and traditional gifts are *Chisholm's Highland Dress*, 47-51 Castle St, T234599, open 0900-1730 and 1900-2130 in Jul and Aug; and *Hector Russell*, 4-9 Huntly St, T222781. At *James Pringle Weavers* (Holm Mills, Dores Rd, T223311), you can see tartan rugs being made in the weaving mill, then spend your cash in their extensive mill shop, and eat in the restaurant. The Eastgate Shopping Centre houses all the usual high street branches, and the Victorian Market on Church St has a wide range of shops. The largest **bookshop** in town is *James Thin*, 29 Union St, T233500, which has an excellent range of Scottish books and maps. There's also a branch of *Waterstone's*, at 50-52 High St, T717474.

Sports

10-pin bowling at *Roller Bowl*, 167 Culduthel Rd, T235100. Open Mon-Fri 1200 till late, Sat-Sun 1100 till late. The best golf course in the area is at Nairn (see page 453). There's an 18-hole municipal course at Torvean, 2 miles from town on the A82 to Fort William, T711434. The *Highland Riding Centre* is at Borlum Farm, Drumnadrochit, T/F01456-450358. The *Aquadome Leisure Centre* is at Bught Park, T667500. Open Mon-Fri 0730-2200, Sat-Sun 0730-2100. Competition-sized pool, flumes, wave machine and kiddies' pool, also health suites, gym and other indoor sports facilities. The *Inverness Tennis and Squash Club* is at Bishop's Rd, T230751.

Bus There are regular daily buses to **Glasgow** and **Edinburgh** via **Aviemore,** **Transport** **Pitlochry** and **Perth** with *Scottish Citylink* (T0990-505050). Change at Perth for **Dundee**. There are regular daily *Citylink* buses to **Ullapool**, connecting with the ferry to **Stornoway**; also to **Fort William** and **Oban**. There are daily *Citylink* buses to **Kyle of Lochalsh**, **Portree** and **Uig** (connecting with ferries to **Tarbert** and **Lochmaddy**). There are regular *Citylink* buses to **Fort Augustus** via **Drumnadrochit** and **Urquhart Castle** (also with *Highland Bus & Coach*, T233371), and to **Scrabster**, for the ferry to **Stromness**, via **Wick** and **Thurso**; also with *Morrison's Coaches*, T01847-821241.

To **Ullapool** via **Gairloch** and **Aultbea**, there are daily buses with *Spa Coaches* (T01997-421311), *Bluebird Northern* (T239292) and *Westerbus* (01445-712255). To **Tain** and **Lairg** there are daily services with *Bluebird* and *Rapson's* (T710555). To **Tain** and **Helmsdale**, via **Dornoch** there are regular daily buses with *Citylink*, *Morrison's* and *Bluebird*. To **Lochinver** via **Ullapool** there's a daily service with *Spa* coaches and *Rapson's of Brora* (01408-621245). To **Durness** via **Lairg** and **Tongue**, or via **Ullapool** (not in winter) there's a daily service with *Royal Mail Postbuses* (T0131-228 7407). To **Grantown-on-Spey**, daily service with *Highland Country Buses* (T233371) and *Highland Bus & Coach*. *Inverness Traction* and *Highland Country Buses* have services to places around Inverness, including **Nairn**, **Forres**, **Culloden**, **Beauly** and **Dingwall**. *Bluebird* have regular buses to **Aberdeen**, via **Nairn**.

Car hire *Avis* is at the airport (T01667-462787); *Budget* is on Railway Terr behind the train station (T713333); *Europcar* has an office at the Highlander service station on Millburn Rd (T235337), and at the airport; *Thrifty* is at 33 Harbour Rd (T224466). Expect to pay from around £30 per day.

Ferry For details of connections to Stornoway (Lewis) see page 560, or contact the *CalMac* office in Inverness, T717681. For Scrabster to Stromness, see page 596.

Taxi *Rank Radio Taxis*, T221111/220222; *Tartan Taxis*, T233033.

Train There are direct trains to/from **Aberdeen**, **Edinburgh** via Aviemore, and **Glasgow**. There are several daily services to/from **London King's Cross**, via Perth and Edinburgh, including a sleeping car service (see page 36). There is also a regular service to **Wick** and **Thurso**, via Tain, Lairg and Helmsdale. The journey from Inverness to **Kyle of Lochalsh** (for Skye) is one of the most scenic in Britain. There are 3 trains daily (none on Sun). Phone T0845-7484950 for all rail enquiries.

Banks All the major banks can be found in the town centre. The *Royal Bank* is oppo- **Directory** site the post office on Queensgate; the *Bank of Scotland* is opposite the Town House on the High St; the *Clydesdale* is opposite the train station; and *Lloyds TSB* is on Church St. Foreign currency can also be exchanged at the tourist office's bureau de change at 2.5% commission (see below for address and opening hours). Also *Thomas Cook*, 9-13 Inglis St, T711921, Mon-Fri 0900-1700; and *Alba Travel* (American Express agents), 43 Church St, T239188, Mon-Sat 0900-1700.

Communications Internet: *MTC Internet*, 2 Grant St, T715450. *Invernet* is in the process of moving premises, agrainger@yahoo.com *The Gate* café bar, opposite the

The Highlands and Skye

Tours from Inverness

Orkney Islands Day Tours leave from Inverness every day throughout the summer. The tour departs daily 1 Jun-2 Sep from Inverness bus station at 0730; returns 2100. Booking essential; £44 per person, under 16 *half price. Details from the tourist office, or contact John O'Groats Ferries, Ferry Office, John O'Groats, Caithness. T01955-611353, F611301, www.jogferry.co.uk (for tours from John O'Groats, see page 516).*

post office, has internet facilities and serves drinks and snacks from 1000-2100. **Post office:** the main branch is at 14-16 Queensgate, T234111. Open Mon-Thu 0900-1730, Fri 0930-1730, Sat 0900-1320.

Cultural centres Inverness library is just around the corner from the bus station. It has an excellent genealogical research unit. Consultations with the resident genealogist cost £12 per hr; T236463, for an appointment. The library also houses the Highland archives, where you can research the history and culture of the region. Open Mon-Fri 1100-1300 and 1400-1700; Oct-May 1400-1700 only.

Medical services *Raigmore Hospital* is on the southeastern outskirts of town near the A9 (T704000) for accidents and emergencies. **Pharmacies:** *Boots* is in the Eastgate Shopping Centre; open daily 0900-1730, Thu till 1900.

The Moray Firth

Colour map 2, grid C2 *East of Inverness along the Moray Firth stretches a long coastline of cliff-top walks, fine beaches, attractive old towns and many historic sites and castles. The Moray Firth is perhaps best known for its large resident population of **bottlenose dolphins**, the largest dolphins in the world. Over 100 of these beautiful and intelligent mammals live in the estuary, the most northerly breeding ground in Europe, and there's a very good chance of seeing them, particularly between June and August. The Moray Firth dolphins have become a major tourist attraction and several companies run dolphin-spotting boat trips. You can also see them from the shore. Two of the best places are **Chanonry Point**, on the southern shore of the Black Isle (see page 518), and **Fort George**, on the opposite shore (see below). The **Kessock Bridge**, which crosses the Moray Firth to the Black Isle, is another good dolphin-spotting location and also has a **visitor centre**, where you can can listen in to their underwater conversations.*

The busy A96 runs parallel to the coast and the region is well served by public transport. The attractions listed below can be visited as day-trips from Inverness.

Culloden The eerie and windswept Culloden Moor, five miles to the east of Inver-
Colour map 2, ness on the B9006, was the site of the last major battle fought on the British
grid C2 mainland. The Jacobite cause was finally lost here, on 16 April 1746, when the army of Prince Charles Edward Stuart was crushed by the superior Government forces, led by the Duke of Cumberland, whose savagery earned him the nickname 'Butcher'. Now owned by the National Trust for Scotland, Culloden is a melancholy place and by far the most painfully evocative of Scotland's battlefields, particularly on a bleak and windy winter's day.

The battlefield has been restored to its original state (minus the dead bodies). The Visitor Centre is the obvious starting point and gives a graphic

Battle of Culloden

The second Jacobite rebellion of 1745 was ill-fated from the start. Bonnie Prince Charlie's expedition south lacked sufficient support and was turned back at Derby. After their long and dispiriting retreat north, the half-starved, under-strength army – exhausted after an abortive night attack on Hanoverian forces at Nairn – faced overwhelmingly superior forces under the command of the ambitious Duke of Cumberland at Culloden.

The open, flat ground of Culloden Moor was hopelessly unsuitable for the Highlanders' style of fighting, which relied on steep hills and plenty of cover to provide the element of surprise for their brave but undisciplined attacks. In only 40 minutes the Prince's army was blown away by the English artillery, and the Jacobite charge, when it finally came, was ragged and ineffective. Cumberland's troops then went on to commit the worst series of atrocities ever carried out by a British Army. 1,200 men were slain, many as they lay wounded on the battlefield. Prince Charlie, meanwhile, fled west where loyal Highlanders protected him until he made his final escape to France.

But the real savagery was to come. Cumberland resolved to make an example of the Highlands. Not only were the clans disarmed and the wearing of Highland dress forbidden, but the Government troops began an orgy of brutal reprisals across the region. Within a century the clan system had ended and the Highland way of life changed forever.

audio-visual description of the gruesome episode. From the Visitor Centre paths lead across the field to the clan graves, marked by simple headstones which bear the names of the clans who fought. Next to the Visitor Centre, the restored cottage of Old Leanach – which was used by the Jacobites as a head-quarters, and where 30 Highlanders were burnt alive – is now a museum. A memorial cairn, erected in 1881, is the scene each April of a commemorative service organized by the Gaelic Society of Inverness.

To get there by public transport, Highland Country Bus No 12 leaves from Inverness Post Office Monday-Saturday (last bus back at 1830). The *Guide Friday* tour bus leaves from Bridge Street, May to September from 1030, last bus returns at 1745.

■ *Site open daily all year. Visitor Centre and shop open 15 Jan-31 Mar and 1 Nov to 31 Dec daily 1000-1600; 1 Apr-31 Oct daily 0900-1800. Visitor centre, including audio-visual presentation, and Old Leanach cottage. £4, concession £3, children £1. Wheelchair access, bookshop, restaurant.*

Clava Cairns This impressive and important Bronze-Age site lies only a mile southeast of Culloden and is well worth a short detour. The 5,000 year-old site consists of three large burial cairns encircled by standing stones, set in a grove of trees. The less imaginative visitor may see it as merely a pile of stones but no one can fail to be affected by the spooky atmosphere of the place. This is even more perceptible when no one else is around!

To get there, continue on the B9006 past Culloden Moor, then turn right at the Culloden Moor Inn and follow the signs for Clava Lodge. Look for the sign on the right of the road.

The big blue

There are various **dolphin-spotting cruises** around the Moray Firth, but there is a code of conduct for boat operators. Before you choose a cruise, make sure the company is part of the Accreditation Scheme. One such company, based in Inverness, is **Moray Firth Dolphin Cruises**, T717900, morayfirth.cruises@virgin.net Trips are £10 (£8 concession), last 1½ hours and leave from Shore Street Quay (beyond the roundabout at the far end of Chapel

St). Buses run from the tourist information centre 15 minutes before sailings. Also in Inverness are **McAuley Charters**, Harbour offices, Longman Drive, T717337. Dolphin-spotting cruises also leave from Cromarty (see page 519) and Buckie. Buckie is also the home of the **Moray Firth Wildlife Centre**, which houses a **dolphin exhibition**, where you can find out evrything you ever wanted to know about them.

Fort George

Colour map 2, grid C2
Fort George is 11 miles NE of Inverness and 6 miles W of Nairn Highland Bus and Coach No 11 from the Post Office in Inverness, several daily except Sun; also buses from Nairn.

Standing proudly on a sandy spit that juts out into the Moray Firth is Fort George, Europe's finest surviving example of 18th-century military architecture. Begun in 1748, it was the last in a chain of three such fortifications built in the Highlands – the other two being Fort Augustus and Fort William – as a base for George II's army to prevent any potential threats to Hanoverian rule. It was completed in 1769, by which time the Highlands were more or less peaceful, but was kept in use as a military barracks. Today it remains virtually unchanged, and there are even armed sentries at the main gate. You can walk along the ramparts to get an idea of the sheer scale of the place and also enjoy the sweeping views across the Moray Firth. You may even be lucky enough to see a school of dolphins. Within the fort are the barracks, a chapel, workshops and the Regimental Museum of the Queen's Own Highlanders, which features the fascinating Seafield Collection of arms and military equipment, most of which dates from the Napoleonic Wars. ■ *Apr-Oct daily 0930-1830; Oct-Mar Mon-Sat 0930-1630, Sun 1400-1630. £4.50, concession £3.50, children £1.50. Wheelchair access, café.*

Cawdor Castle

Highlights include the impressive paintings and tapestries, fascinating kitchen and the genuinely witty captions that have visitors laughing all over the castle

Though best known for its legendary association with Shakespeare's *Macbeth*, Cawdor Castle post-dates the grisly historical events on which the great Bard based his famous tragedy. The oldest part of the castle, the central tower, dates from 1372, and the rest of it is mostly 16th or 17th century. But despite the literary disappointment, the castle is still one of the most appealing in Scotland. It has been in the hands of the Cawdor family for over six centuries and each summer they clear off, leaving their romantic home and its glorious gardens open for the enjoyment of ordinary folks like us. There's also a nine-hole golf course.

According to family legend, an early Thane of Cawdor, wanting a new castle, had a dream in which he was told to load a donkey with gold, let it wander around for a day and watch where it lay down, for this would be the best spot for his new castle. He duly followed these instructions and the donkey lay down under a thorn tree, the remains of which can still be seen in the middle of a vaulted chamber in the 14th-century tower. ■ *May to mid-Oct daily 1000-1730. £5.40.* To get to Cawdor by public transport, take the *Highland Country Buses* No 12 from Inverness Post Office. It runs several times daily (except Sunday), the last bus returns around 1800. There are also regular buses from Nairn. In the village of Cawdor, close by the castle, is the *Cawdor Tavern*, T/F01667-404777, a traditional country pub serving excellent food in a friendly atmosphere. Perfect for lunch or dinner after visiting the castle. Prices are cheap to mid-range.

The Highlands and Skye

Just to the west of Cawdor is **Kilravock Castle**, a lovely 15th-century stately home which is closed to the public, but can be visited by prior appointment. The castle (pronounced 'Kilrawk') is still the seat of the Rose family, who now run it as a guesthouse on strictly Christian principles. ■ *T01667-493258. The castle gardens are open to the public Mon-Sat 1000-1600, and worth visiting. Free.*

Nairn

The genteel seaside resort of Nairn claims the driest and sunniest climate in the whole of Scotland. This alone should be reason enough to pay a visit, but there are other attractions besides the sunshine. There are miles of sandy beach stretching east to the Culbin Forest, a **championship golf course** (which hosted the 1999 Walker Cup), and two of the best castles in the country are within easy reach – **Cawdor Castle** (see above) and **Brodie Castle** (see below).

Phone code: 01667
Colour map 2, grid C2
Population: 11,190

Getting there There are regular daily **buses** from Inverness (30 mins) with *Highland Country Buses* and *Bluebird* (see Inverness Transport above). Nairn is on the Inverness-Aberdeen rail line, and there are several **trains** daily from Inverness (20 mins). The **Tourist Information Centre** is at 62 King St, T452753. Open Easter-May and September-October Monday-Saturday 1000-1700; June-August daily 0900-1800.

Ins & outs

Nairn began life as an important commercial centre in the 12th century, and by the early 17th century had grown to such an extent that King James VI was able to boast of a town in his northern kingdom so large that people at one end of the High Street didn't understand the language spoken by those at the other end (the different languages being English and Gaelic). The town was a major fishing port in the 19th century and the tiny houses of the **Old Fishertown**, huddled together around the harbour, are very different from the town centre, which is known as **New Fishertown**. Both lie apart from the substantial villas and hotels of the seaside resort that developed with the arrival of the Highland Railway in the mid-19th century.

Background

Today Nairn is still a tourist favourite, with its seafront full of people munching chips and ice cream. There are banks with ATMs in the High Street, a post office on Cawdor Street, a swimming pool on Marine Road, and cinema on King Street. The town hosts its annual **Highland Games** in August.

The **Fishertown Museum** in Old Fishertown is interesting and tells of the building of the harbour by Thomas Telford in 1820 and the subsequent decline of the herring industry. The harbour is now mainly used by pleasure craft. ■ *The museum is open from Jun to Aug Mon-Sat 1000-1700. Free.*

Sights

About two miles east of Nairn, in the little village of **Auldearn**, is a 17th-century doocot (dovecote) from where the royal standard was flown, in 1645, by the victorious troops of Charles I led by the Marquis of Montrose against the Covenanters. Displays in the doocot tell of the battle (entry £1.50).

The most luxurious here is **L** *The Golf View Hotel*, on Seabank Rd next to the golf course, T452301, scotland@morton-hotels.demon.co.uk 47 rooms, pool, sauna, spa, gym, tennis courts and fine restaurant. **B** *Clifton House*, Viewfield St, T453119. This unique hotel offers superb hospitality and a touch of class, every room is different and the place is full of antiques. They host musical and theatrical evenings and dinner is also quite an event.

Sleeping
There's lots of accommodation to choose from right across the range

The Highlands and Skye

There are lots of guesthouses and B&Bs, including the very fine **E** *Bracadale House*, Albert St, T452547, neil.macleod@ lineone.net There's a good **campsite** 1½ miles from town: *Spindrift Caravan & Camping Park*, at Little Kildrummie, T453992, open Apr-Oct.

Eating Aside from the hotels in town, one of the best places to eat is the *Boat House*, T455469, 2 miles east of Nairn in the little village of Auldearn (prices mid-range). If you fancy a fish supper, try *Friar Tuck's*, at 30 Harbour St. For a hot snack there's *Asher's Bakery*, 2 Bridge St, which is recommended, and run by the same folk as the one in Inverness.

Sport **Cycling** Bike hire from *The Bike Shop*, 178 Harbour St. **Pony trekking** *Heatherfield Riding Centre*, Lochloy Rd, T456682.

Around Nairn

Ten miles south of Nairn on the A939 to Grantown is **Dulsie Bridge**, a very popular local beauty spot which is a great place for a summer picnic or to swim in the River Findhorn. On the southern shores of the Moray Firth, just east of Nairn, is Culbin **Sands**, a stretch of sand home to a host of birdlife. The best time to visit is from autumn to spring when bar-tailed godwits, oystercatchers, knots, dunlins, ringed plovers, redshanks, curlews, shellducks, red breasted mergansers, greylag geese and snow buntings, to name but a few, come here in their droves.

Brodie Castle

The castle is 8 miles E of Nairn, just off the main A96 to Forres Bluebird buses run to Brodie from Inverness, via Culloden and Nairn; 45 mins

Here is one of Scotland's finest castles, still lived in by the Brodie family. The oldest part of the castle, the Z-plan tower house, is 16th-century, with additions dating from the 17th and 19th centuries, giving it the look of a Victorian country house. The interior of the house is the epitome of good taste, with some fabulous ceilings, and you can look round several rooms, including the huge Victorian kitchen. The collections of furniture and porcelain are wonderful but most notable are the outstanding paintings, which include Edwin Landseer and Scottish Colourists. The grounds, too, are a delight, especially in spring when the daffodils are in bloom. There's also a tearoom. ■ *Castle open 1 Apr-30 Sep Mon-Sat 1100-1730, Sun 1330-1730; Oct weekends only Sat 1100-1730, Sun 1330-1730. Grounds open all year daily 0930-sunset. Castle: £6, concession £4.50, children £1; grounds only £1 (honesty box). T01309-641371.*

West of Inverness

*West of Inverness, the Moray Firth becomes the **Beauly Firth**, a relatively quiet little corner despite its proximity to Inverness, as most traffic heading north crosses the Kessock Bridge on the main A9. The A862 west to Beauly offers a more scenic alternative, and the chance to visit a **13th-century priory**, and a **distillery**. South of Beauly, the A831 leads to two of Scotland's most beautiful glens, **Glen Strathfarrar** and **Glen Affric**.*

Beauly

Phone code: 01463 Colour map 2, grid C1

The sleepy little market town of Beauly is 10 miles west of Inverness, where the Beauly river flows into the Firth. It's a lovely wee place – hence its name. According to local legend, when Mary, Queen of Scots stayed here, at the priory, in 1564, she was so taken with the place that she cried (in French, of course) "Ah, quel beau lieu!" (What a beautiful place!).

At the north end of the marketplace is the ruin of **Beauly Priory**, founded in 1230 for the Valliscaulian order, but like so much else of Scotland's ecclesiastical heritage, destroyed during the Reformation. ■ *11 June-30 Sep daily 0930-1830. £1.20, concession £0.90, children £0.50.*

Sleeping and eating The most expensive place to stay is **L** *The Priory Hotel*, on the main street, T782309. At the opposite end of the main street is the **C** *Lovat Arms Hotel*, T782313, lovat.arms@cali.co.uk, which is the best place to stay. A relaxed and comfortable place with an excellent restaurant and great bar food, lots of tartan and the occasional ceilidh. A cheaper **B&B** option is **F** *Ellengowan*, Croyard Rd, T782273 (open Apr-Oct). The best food is at the *Lovat Arms Hotel*, which offers cheap meals in the bar or an expensive 4-course dinner in the restaurant. Otherwise, you could try the *Beauly Tandoori* on The Square, T782221, for a cheap curry; or the *Friary* for an even cheaper fish supper.

Transport There are *Inverness Traction* **buses**, T239292, every hour to Beauly, and on to Muir of Ord, from Inverness and from Dingwall. There's also a *Ross's Minibus* service from Beauly 3 days a week, T761250.

Four miles east of Beauly, at Balchraggan just off the main Inverness road, is **Moniack Castle Winery**, where you can try a whole range of wines, including elderflower and birch. ■ *Mon-Sat 1000-1700.* Four miles to the north is the **Glen Ord Distillery**, on the outskirts of **Muir of Ord**, just off the A832. ■ *Mar-Oct Mon-Fri 0930-1700; Jul-Sep also Sat 0930-1700 and Sun 1230-1700. T01463-872004. Take a bus from Inverness or the train.* The River Beauly is one of Scotland's best salmon-fishing rivers, and five miles south of Beauly at **Aigas** is a fish lift, where you can watch salmon bypass the dam with the aid of technology. ■ *Mon-Fri 1000-1500.*

Southwest of Beauly are glens Affric and Strathfarrar. **Glen Strathfarrar**, the lesser known of the two, is unspoiled and considered by some to be the more beautiful. To get there, take the A831 nine miles south from Beauly to **Struy** and follow the signs. Access to the glen is restricted by the owners, Scottish Natural Heritage, to 12 cars at a time and you have to leave by 1900. The glen is also closed from mid-August to October. But once you're in there is a tremendous feeling of peace, and there's good climbing, fishing and walking. The little ungraded road runs for 14 miles all the way to the impressive Monar Dam at the head of the glen. Glen Strathfarrar can also be reached from Drumnadrochit, via Cannich (see below).

Glen Strathfarrar & Glen Affric
Colour map 1, grid C6
Most of the walks and cycle routes here are covered by OS Landranger Nos 25 and 26

The A831 continues south from Struy through **Strathglass** to the village of **Cannich**, gateway to glorious **Glen Affric**, a dramatic and beautiful gorge, with the River Affric rushing through it, and surrounded by Caledonian pine and birch forest (this is one of the few places where you can still see the native Scots pine). There are few, if any, more stunning sights in the Scottish Highlands and it's perfect for walking, or even just to drive through and stop for a picnic on a nice, sunny day.

Colour map 3, grid A6

Glen Affric reaches west into the very heart of the Highlands and is great for a spot of Munro-bagging. Beyond Loch Affric the serious walking starts. From Affric Lodge, nine miles west of Cannich, begins a 20-mile trail west to Morvich, near **Shiel Bridge**, on the west coast near Kyle of Lochalsh (see page 487). This strenuous walk is for experienced hikers only, and takes around 10 hours. You can stop off halfway at one of the most remote **youth hostels** in

The Highlands and Skye

Scotland, *Glen Affric Youth Hostel*, at Allt Beithe (no phone; open mid-March till end October).

There are also many shorter, easier walks around Glen Affric. There are some short, circular marked trails at the end of the road which runs west from Cannich almost to Loch Affric, and also from the car park at the impressive **Dog Falls**, 4½ miles from Cannich and a great place to stop for a picnic and swim. Cycling in the forests around Cannich is good too – you can hire bikes at *Cannich Caravan and Camping Park*.

Glen Affric can also be reached from **Drumnadrochit** (see page 457) by heading west on the A831 through **Glen Urquhart** to Cannich. Just before Cannich, on the road from Drumnadrochit, a single track road leads left (south), past the Caravan and Camping Park, to the tiny village of **Tomich**. From here, it's a three-mile hike up a woodland trail to a car park. A few hundred yards down through the trees takes you to the lovely **Plodda Falls**. An old iron bridge affords a spectacular view of the waterfall as it plunges 150 yards into the foaming waters below.

Sleeping There are several options in and around **Cannich**. One of the best hotels in the area is the **B** *Mullardoch House Hotel*, in Glencannich, on the road to Beauly, T/F01456-415460. An excellent B&B is **C-D** *Kerrow House*, in Cannich village, T415243, F415425, stephen@kerrow-house.demon.co.uk There are also a couple of **hostels**: the **F** *SYHA Cannich Youth Hostel*, T415244, open mid-Mar to end Oct; and the slightly cheaper independent **F** *Glen Affric Backpackers*, T/F415263, which is open all year.

In the village of **Tomich** is **B** *The Tomich Hotel*, T01456-415399, F415469. The price includes dinner, and it's a comfortable place with good food and free use of the nearby indoor heated pool; also great for fishing holidays. Near Tomich is the independent hostel **F** *Cougie Lodge*, T01456-415459, which is open Apr-Sep and will pick you up from Tomich or Cannich if you phone ahead.

Transport *Highland Bus & Coach*, T01463-233371, runs buses 3 days a week Mon-Fri from Inverness to Cannich and Tomich, via Drumnadrochit. There are also buses from Inverness to Cannich and Tomich, via Beauly (2 on Tue and Fri, and 1 on Sat).

Loch Ness to Fort Augustus

Colour map 4,
grid A1/2

One of Scotland's biggest attractions is the narrow gash of Loch Ness, Britain's deepest body of fresh water, stretching 23 miles from Fort Augustus in the south almost to Inverness in the north. The loch is scenic in its own right, with rugged hills rising steeply from its wooded shores, but visitors don't come here for the views. They come every year, in their hundreds of thousands, to stare across the dark, cold waters in search of its legendary inhabitant, the **Loch Ness Monster***. A huge tourist trade has grown up around 'Nessie', as the monster is affectionately known, and every summer the main A82 which runs along its western shore is jam packed with bus-loads of eager monster-hunters, binoculars trained on the loch surface, desperate for one glimpse of the elusive beast.*

The best way to see the loch is on a cruise from Inverness (see the Monster Tours box on page 457). There are also boat trips from Drumnadrochit and Fort Augustus (see below). Most of the tourist traffic uses the congested A82, which offers few decent views of the loch. By far the best views

Monster tours

There are various monster-spotting tours of **Loch Ness** which leave from the tourist office. **Guide Friday** are based at the train station, T224000. They run half-day coach trips right round the loch, at 1030 and 1430, lasting 3 hours. Tickets: adult £14.50, concession £11.50, children £6.50, available from booking office at the train station or the tourist office.

Coach tours, boat cruises and combined coach and cruise trips round the loch are offered by **Jacobite Cruises** (T233999, jacobite@cali.co.uk) Half day cruises cost £10, half day coach and cruise trips cost £14.50 (including entry to the Loch Ness Monster Exhibition and Urquhart Castle). Trips run from April-October and leave from Tomnahurich Bridge on Glenurquhart Road, 1½ miles south of the town centre. Free buses leave from the TIC 20 minutes before sailing, if tickets are bought here. Otherwise, to get there take **Inverness Traction** buses Nos 3, 3A, 4 and 4A every 15 minutes from Church Street.

---

of the loch are from the quiet and picturesque B862/852 which runs along its eastern shore, from Fort Augustus up to Inverness. It's possible to make a complete circuit of the loch, which is best done in an anti-clockwise direction heading south from Inverness on the A82, but you'll need your own transport (or take a tour), as there are no buses between Fort Augustus and Foyers.

Drumnadrochit

The Nessie tourist trade is centred on the village of Drumnadrochit, 15 miles south of Inverness, where the canny locals have cashed in on the enduring popularity of the monster myth. The monster hype is almost overpowering, with two rival Monster Exhibitions and the inevitable souvenir shops selling all manner of awful tartan tack, including those scary-looking tartan dolls with flickering eyelids, the "See-You-Jimmy" tartan bonnet, complete with ginger 'hair', and not forgetting the Loch Ness Monster novelty hat.

Phone code: 01456
Colour map 2, grid C1

Of the two aforementioned Monster Exhibitions, the **Original Loch Ness Visitor Centre** is the least worthwhile. It's a glorified gift shop with a rather amateurish audiovisual show attached. ■ *T450342. Apr to end of Oct daily 1000-1800 (Jul-Aug till 2100). £3.50, students £3, children and OAPs £2.75.*

Those genuinely interested in the fascinating history of the search for 'Nessie' should visit the recently refurbished **Official Loch Ness Monster Exhibition**. Though it's considerably more expensive, it gives a detailed description of the many eye-witness accounts over the years and also explains the recent research projects carried out in the loch. ■ *T450573. Easter-end May 0930-1730; Jun and Sep 0930-1830; Jul-Aug 0930-2030; Oct 0930-1800; Nov-Mar 1000-1600. £5.95, students £4.50, children £3.50.*

Loch Ness Cruises operate from the Original Loch Ness Visitor Centre from April to October and run daily from 0930-1800. They last one hour and cost £8 per adult and £5 per child.

If it all gets too much, then fear not, for Drumnadrochit gives easy access to one of the most beautiful corners of Scotland. The A831 heads west from the village through **Glen Urquhart** to **Cannich**, about 12 miles away, at the head of **Glen Affric**, a great place for walking or enjoying a picnic (see page 455). If the weather's good, hiring bikes in Drumnadrochit (see below) and cycling into Glen Affric makes for a great day out. There's also **pony trekking** at the Highland Riding Centre, T450358, at Borlum Farm.

The Highlands and Skye

The Great Glen

The Great Glen, which splits the Scottish mainland from Fort William in the south to Inverness in the north, is one of the world's major geological fault lines. The Glen was formed millions of years ago when the northern part of the Caledonian mountains 'slid' more than 60 miles south, leaving behind a massive glen with four freshwater lochs – **Loch Linnhe, Loch Lochy, Loch Oich** *and* **Loch Ness**.
The most famous of these is Loch Ness, which attracts hordes of visitors eager to catch a glimpse of its elusive monster. The renowned engineer, Thomas Telford, succeeded in connecting all these lochs when he built the impressive **Caledonian Canal**. *The canal took 22 years to complete, and when it was opened in 1822 was the first in Britain to take ships from one coast to the other. It remains the only canal in the country capable of carrying ships of up to 500 tons. The best way to appreciate the glen is by boat, through the 38 miles of natural lochs and rivers and the 22 miles of canal, and every summer pleasure craft of all shapes and sizes ply its length. The main A82 runs from Inverness south to Fort William. The southern section, from Fort Augustus, follows the original line of the road constructed in 1727 by General Wade to link the military garrisons at Fort William and Fort Augustus (hence their names). There are regular daily* **bus services** *between Inverness and Fort William, with additional buses between Invergarry and Fort Augustus. Another way to travel through the Great Glen is along the excellent* **cycle route**, *which follows the canal towpaths, forest trails and quiet minor roads to avoid the busy main road. The route is outlined in the Forestry Commission leaflet, available from most Tourist Information Centres.*

Sleeping & eating There's a wide range of accommodation on offer in and around the village of Drumnadrochit. If you can afford it, your best bet is to head for **B** *Polmaily House Hotel*, 3 miles from Drumnadrochit on the A831 to Cannich, in Glen Urquhart, T450343, F450813, polmailyhousehotel@btinternet.com 10 rooms. A comfortable, child-friendly country house far enough away from the madding crowd to offer peace and quiet, many walks nearby, also tennis courts, horse riding and covered pool, and a good restaurant. In the village itself is **D** *The Benleva Hotel*, T450288, F450781. Small, family-run hotel with bar and dining room. There are numerous **B&Bs**, including the excellent **E** *Drumbuie Farm*, T450634, F450595, a modern farmhouse on the right as you enter the village from Inverness, with its own herd of Highland cattle. **D** *Gillyflowers*, T/F450641, gillyflowers@cali.co.uk, is good value. Cheaper still is the **F** *Loch Ness Backpackers Lodge*, at Coiltie Farmhouse in East Lewiston, T450807, immediately south of Drumnadrochit, on the left. It's open all year, has excellent facilities, and arranges boat trips and local walks.

Other than the hotels, which all serve decent bar food, there's the *Glen Restaurant*, T450282, which offers simple fare; and, next door, the more upmarket *Fiddler's Bistro*, T450678, where you can also hire **mountain bikes**.

Transport *Citylink* **buses** between Inverness and Fort William stop at Drumnadrochit several times daily in either direction. Additional services run between Inverness and Urquhart Castle during the summer months. There are also buses from Inverness to Cannich and Tomich, via Drumnadrochit (see page 456).

Castle Urquhart A few miles south of Drumnadrochit are the ruins of Castle Urquhart. The castle bears the scars of centuries of fighting but its setting, perched on a rocky cliff on the loch's edge, is magnificent and, not surprisingly, one of the most photographed scenes in Scotland. Dating from the 14th century, the castle

The Highlands and Skye

The Great Monster Hunt

In a country full of myths and legends, the Loch Ness Monster is the greatest of them all. As elusive as a straight answer from a politician, Nessie has single-handedly sold more tins of tartan-wrapped shortbread to foreign visitors than Edinburgh Castle.

Tales of Nessie go way back to the sixth century, when St Columba is said to have calmed the beast after she had attacked one of his monks. But the monster craze only really took off with the completion of the A82 road along the loch's western shore in 1933. Since then there have been numerous sightings, some backed up with photographic evidence, though the most impressive of these – the famous black-and-white movie footage of Nessie's

humps moving through the water, and the classic photograph of her head and neck – have been exposed as fakes.

In recent decades determined monster hunters have enlisted the help of new technology, such as sonar surveys, but have failed to come up with conclusive evidence. Enter Cyber Nessie, the latest attempt to end the years of rumours, hoaxes and speculation. Nessie's very own website – www.lochness.scotland.net/camera.htm – is a 24-hour real-time video watch of Loch Ness, and has already produced a couple of claimed sightings. But nothing could compare with the excitement of seeing the monster in the flesh.

was a strategic base, guarding the Great Glen during the long Wars of Independence. It was taken by Edward I, held by Robert the Bruce against Edward II, and was then almost constantly under siege before being destroyed in 1692 to prevent it from falling into Jacobite hands. Most of the existing buildings date from the 16th century, including the five-storey tower, the best-preserved part of the complex, from where you get great views of the loch and surrounding hills. At the time of writing, there are plans to build a new visitor centre. ■ *Apr-Sep daily 0930-1830; Oct-Mar daily 0930-1630. £3.80, concession £2.80, children £1.20. T450551.*

Between Drumnadrochit and Fort Augustus is the tiny village of Invermoriston, probably the nicest spot on the entire Inverness to Fort Augustus stretch of the A82. It's a beautiful little piece of Highland scenery, with a photogenic old stone bridge over foaming river rapids. There are marked woodland trails leading off into the hills past some lovely waterfalls.

At Invermoriston the A887 heads west through **Glen Moriston** to meet the A87, which runs from **Invergarry** (see below) all the way through the rugged and dramatic **Glen Shiel** to the awesome mountains of **Kintail** on the west coast near **Kyle of Lochalsh**. *Citylink* buses between Inverness and Kyle of Lochalsh stop at Invermoriston.

Invermoriston
Phone code: 01320
Colour map 4, grid A1

Sleeping There are several B&Bs in the village and, a few miles to the north on the main A82 overlooking Loch Ness, is the **F** *SYHA Loch Ness Youth Hostel*, T351274, open mid-Mar to end Oct. 1½ miles south of Invermoriston, and 6 miles north of Fort Augustus, is the *Loch Ness Caravan & Camping Park*, T351207, right on the shores of the loch with great views and excellent facilities (open Easter-Oct).

Fort Augustus

At the more scenic southern end of Loch Ness stands the village of Fort Augustus, originally set up as a garrison after the Jacobite rebellion of 1715, and headquarters of General Wade's campaign to pacify the Highlands.

Fort Augustus
Phone code: 01320
Colour map 4, grid A1

Today Fort Augustus is a busy little place, full of monster-hunting tourists and boats using the flight of five locks to enter or leave Loch Ness on their journey along the **Caledonian Canal**.

The village hosts **Highland Gatherings** in late June and July, mid-August and early September, featuring traditional dancing and piping competitions, tossing the caber and sheep dog trials.

The **Tourist Information Centre**, T366367, is in the car park next to the petrol station and *Bank of Scotland*. It's open April-June Monday-Saturday 1000-1700; July-August 0900-2000; September-October 0900-1800.

Sights   On the shores of Loch Ness is **Fort Augustus Abbey**, a Benedictine Monastery founded in 1876 on the site of the original fort. The abbey closed in 1998, but there are tours of the grounds and cloisters. ■ *Easter-Oct daily 0900-1700; Nov-Mar 1000- 1600. Adult £3, concession £2. T366233.*

By the canal locks is **The Clansman Centre**, where young guides in traditional dress provide a lively and entertaining presentation of 17th-century Highland family life in an old turf house. There follows a display of weaponry and a mock sword fight in the garden. You can even have your picture taken wearing traditional Highland costume. There's also a craftshop selling the more tasteful kind of souvenirs. ■ *Apr, May, Jun and Sep daily 1100-1700; Jul-Aug 1000-1800. £3, concession £2.50. T366444.*

Loch Ness Cruises with *Loch Ness Ferry Co Ltd*, on board the *Royal Scot*, set off from the jetty in the abbey grounds. ■ *Apr-Oct hourly from 1000. The trip lasts 50 mins and costs £6 per adult. Also boat and bike hire. T01223-208939.*

Sleeping   There's a good selection of places to stay in Fort Augustus, but perhaps the best, and
& eating   certainly the most unique, is the **D** *Lovat Arms Hotel*, T366206, F366677. 23 rooms. A beautiful old mansion house standing above the village. There are lots of **B&Bs** to choose from, including the wonderfully named **D-E** *Mrs Service*, at *Sonas* on the Inverness Rd, T366291; and the friendly **E** *Kettle House* on Golf Course Rd, T366408; open Feb-Nov. The newly converted **F** *Morag's Lodge*, T366289, offers baclpacker accommodation between Mar and Oct. Other than the hotels in the village, there's the cosy *Bothy Bite*, T366710, by the canal bridge, which serves cheap meals from 1200-2100. The *Loch Inn*, by the canal, is the best place for a drink, and also serves decent pub grub.

Sport   **Cycle hire** *Loch Ness Ferry Co Ltd* (see above). **Pony trekking** *Fort Augustus Riding Centre*, Pier House, T366418.

Transport   Fort Augustus is a convenient stopover between Fort William and Inverness, and there are several **buses** daily in either direction. It takes 1 hr to both towns. There is an additional service between Fort Augustus and Invergarry (see below) once a day Mon-Sat.

Fort Augustus   A worthwhile detour from Fort Augustus is to take the B862/852 up the **east
to Dores   shore of Loch Ness** on a mostly single-track road that skirts the loch for much
Colour map 4,   of its length to the village of Dores. It's a much quieter and more scenic route
grid A1/2   than the busy A82 and follows General Wade's original (and very straight) military road which linked Fort Augustus with Fort George. Though it makes a more interesting alternative to the more popular A82 route from Inverness to Fort Augustus, it's best done from south to north, if you have the time.

The road winds its way up into rugged hills before returning to the lochside at **Foyers**, where there's accommodation at **E-F** *Intake-House*, T01456-482258, open April-October; and the small independent youth hostel

F *Foyers House*, T01456-486623. It's worth stopping here to see the impressive **waterfall** where the River Foyers plunges into Loch Ness. To get there, follow the steep (and slippery) track down from opposite the shops.

Three miles further north, at **Inverfarigaig**, is the spooky and sinister **Boleskine House**, once home of Alastair Crowley, who is said to have practised devil worship here. In the 1970s the house was bought by Jimmy Page of Led Zeppelin, but sold some years later after the tragic death of his daughter. Those of a nervous disposition may wish to pass on quickly and continue to the little village of **Dores**, at the northeastern end of the loch, where you can enjoy a good pint of ale and some decent grub at the *Dores Inn*. You can then continue to Inverness, or return via the beautiful hill road that leads up to **Loch Mhor** and back to Fort Augustus via the **Stratherrick** valley. From **Errogie**, at the northern end of Loch Mhor, there's a dramatic section of road that winds down to the loch through a series of tight, twisting bends, reminiscent of an Alpine pass, and great for cyclists. There are also some interesting marked woodland trails around Errogie.

Transport This route is only possible if you have your own transport. There are buses south from Inverness, but they only run as far as Foyers (3 times Mon-Fri, twice on Sat). Alternatively, it can be done by **bike**, as a full-day circular trip from Fort Augustus or from Inverness.

Fort Augustus to Fort William

*South of Fort Augustus, the A82 leaves behind Loch Ness and runs along the west shore of **Loch Oich** and then the east shore of **Loch Lochy**, till it reaches **Spean Bridge**. Here the A82 continues south to **Fort William**, while the A86 branches east through **Glen Spean** to join the A9 Perth to Inverness road finally at **Kingussie**. All along this route are many opportunities to get off the beaten track and explore huge chunks of real wilderness, deserted since the Clearances and soaked in the blood of history.*

The old village of Invergarry stands where the A82 turns west to meet the A87. There's not much to see or do in the village, but the surrounding area merits some exploring, particularly the route west through Glen Garry (see next page), and there are several places to stay.

Inside the entrance to the *Glengarry Castle Hotel* (see 'Sleeping' below) stand the ruins of **Invergarry Castle**, once the stronghold of the MacDonnells of Glengarry and later destroyed by the Duke of Cumberland as he wreaked revenge on the Highlands in the aftermath of Culloden (see page 40). The hotel was later built as the main house of the Ellice family, who made their fortune from the *Hudson Bay Company* in Canada and who were the main driving force behind the creation of the Victorian planned village.

A mile or so south of the village, at **North Laggan**, is a monument by the side of the road standing over **The Well of the Seven Heads**. This tells the grisly story of the Keppoch Murders, one of the most infamous clan murders which took place at **Roy Bridge** (see below) in the 17th century. It all began when the chief of the clan MacDonnell died, leaving two young sons, who were sent away to complete their education before returning to Roy Bridge to celebrate the elder brother's accession to the chiefship. Another branch of the clan present at the celebrations started a fight in which both brothers were

**Invergarry &
around**
Phone code: 01809
Colour map 4, grid A1

The Highlands and Skye

killed. Believing they had been murdered, one of their cousins persuaded a fellow clan member to raise 50 men and march on the murderers' house at nearby Inverlair. The accused murderers – a father and his six sons – were duly slaughtered and their heads cut off, to be displayed before the local laird at Glengarry. On the way to his lodge, the heads were washed here in this well.

A few miles further south, at **Laggan**, where the A82 crosses to the east bank of Loch Lochy, is the site of the Battle of the Shirts. On the east shore of Loch Oich, near North Laggan, is the **Great Glen Water Park**, T501381, an outdoor activities centre offering numerous adventure sports, including white-water rafting, canoeing, mountain biking, rock climbing, sailing, windsurfing, hill walking and water skiing. There are also self-catering lodges for rent.

Sleeping There are various options for sleeping in and around Invergarry, but none can match the splendour of **A** *Glengarry Castle Hotel*, T501254, F501207, castle@glengarry.net, set in 60 acres of woodland running down to Loch Oich. 26 rooms, open Mar-Nov. The hotel has been in the MacCallum family for over 40 years and continues to be one of the best in the Highlands. Rather less luxurious but still comfortable and good value is **D** *Invergarry Hotel*, T501206, F501400, hotel@invergarry.net

South of Invergarry, at South Laggan, is the **F** *SYHA Loch Lochy Youth Hostel*, T501239, open mid-Mar to end-Oct. There are a couple of **campsites** near the village: *Faichem Park*, T501226, open Easter-Oct; and *Faichemard Farm Camping Site*, T501314, open Apr-Oct, which is off the A87.

Tour companies *Glengarry Mini Tours*, T501297, run various minibus day tours in the Great Glen, Glen Coe and Glen Nevis.

Transport Invergarry is on the Fort William to **Inverness** bus route (see Fort Augustus above). It is also on the main **Fort William** to **Kyle of Lochalsh** (and **Skye**) *Citylink* route, and a couple of buses pass through daily in both directions. For times: T0990-505050.

The A87 leads west from Invergarry through Glen Shiel to **Shiel Bridge**, on the way to Kyle of Lochalsh on the west coast (see page 487). About seven miles along the A87, past the turning for Kinloch Hourn (see below), is the Glen Garry viewpoint, from where you get one of the most stunning, and famous, of all Highland views. From this angle Loch Garry looks uncannily like a map of Scotland, so get out the camera for that classic holiday snap.

Glen Garry to Kinloch Hourn
Colour map 3, grid A5/6

A mile or so before the Glen Garry viewpoint, where the A87 begins to leave the shores of Loch Garry, is the turning left for the road through Glen Garry, described as the longest and most beautiful cul-de-sac in Britain. The little single-track road turns and twists for 22 glorious miles along the shores of **Loch Garry** and **Loch Quoich** all the way to **Kinloch Hourn**, at the head of Loch Hourn, a sea loch on the west coast.

Glen Garry is now virtually deserted but was once home to some 5,000 people who were driven out during the infamous Highland Clearances in the 19th century. The road passes the tiny hamlet of **Tomdoun**, once the junction of the main road to Skye, until the massive post-war hydroelectric schemes changed the landscape. Experienced hillwalkers can still follow the old route to Skye, through Glen Kingie, along Loch Hourn and then across the wild **Knoydart peninsula** till they reach the tiny settlement of **Inverie**. From here a little ferry runs twice a day on Mon-Wed and Fri to **Mallaig**.

Getting shirty

One the bloodiest battles in Scottish clan history was the Battle of the Shirts, fought in 1544. It was so named because it was fought on a hot day and the combatants took off their shirts before proceeding to butcher each other. One side – the Frasers – were almost wiped out and their opponents – a combined force of MacDonalds, MacDonnells and Camerons – suffered less heavy losses and claimed victory. In total over 1,000 were killed and a plaque beside the canal locks describes the terrible events.

Beyond Tomdoun the road passes a huge dam, built in the 1950s, which raised the waters of Loch Quoich by over 100 ft, flooding many of the old settlements. Also flooded was Glen Quoich Lodge, which can count Edward VII and Sir Edward Landseer among its notable guests. It was reputedly Glen Garry that gave Landseer the inspiration for his famous painting *The Monarch of the Glen*. The road then reaches its highest point, at 1,200 ft, before descending to **Kinloch Hourn**, once a thriving fishing village but now remote and isolated. Incredible as it may seem, you can actually stay here.

Sleeping B *Skiary*, T01809-511214, open May-Sep, phone ahead to arrange for a boat to meet you. This is perhaps the most remote guesthouse in the Highlands. It is accessible only by boat or foot and has no mains electricity. There are 3 rooms and prices are for full board, and include the boat trip both ways. The food is wonderful and the setting is simply magnificent.

Transport There's a **postbus** from Invergarry post office on Mon, Wed and Fri, which runs to Kingie, which is halfway to Kinloch Hourn. A 4-seater post car runs all the way to Kinloch Hourn from Invergarry on Tue, Wed, Thu and Sat. A more scenic return would be to take the **ferry** from Kinloch Hourn to **Arnisdale** (summer only; daily by arrangement) and then head to **Glenelg**, from where you can take a ferry across to **Kylerhea** on Skye (see page 550).

The main A82 runs down the east shore of Loch Lochy to the village of Spean Bridge, at the head of Glen Spean, beneath the towering Lochaber mountains. The village gets its name from Thomas Telford's bridge across the River Spean. Two miles west are the remains of the old 'Highbridge', built in 1736 by General Wade, and the site of the first clash between Government troops and the Jacobites, three days before Prince Charles raised his standard at Glenfinnan.

Spean Bridge
Phone code: 01397
Colour map 3,
grid B6

Spean Bridge is only eight miles north of Fort William so gets busy in the summer, but it still makes a more peaceful and attractive alternative base for exploring this astoundingly beautiful part of the Highlands. There's a **Tourist Information Centre** just off the main road behind the post office. ■ *Easter-Oct. T712576, F712675*. Spean Bridge is also the starting point for the excellent **Grey Corries ridge walk** (OS Landranger Map No 41).

Sleeping There's no shortage of accommodation in Spean Bridge. Pick of the bunch has to be **A** *Old Pines Restaurant with Rooms*, T712324, F712433, www.lochaber. com/oldpines 8 rooms, just past the Commando Memorial on the B8004; price includes dinner. This Scandinavian-style chalet is a great place to stay, especially if you have kids in tow, and is renowned for its exceptional, award-winning Scottish cuisine. Food is available to non-residents (the 5-course dinner is expensive but lunch is much cheaper). **A** *Corriegour Lodge Hotel*, 9 miles north of Spean Bridge on the A82,

The Highlands and Skye

T712685, F712696. 9 rooms, open Feb-Dec. Lovely Victorian hunting lodge on the shores of Loch Lochy, with fine views and an excellent restaurant (non-residents dinner only; expensive). Further south, on the shores of Loch Lochy, is a very good **B&B**, **D** *Invergloy House*, T712681. In the village itself is **E** *Smiddy House*, T712335, F712043. A comfortable guesthouse with a bistro attached, serving good, cheap meals. Also good is the **D** *Corriechoille Lodge*, T/F712002, www.corrie1.demon. co.uk Open Mar-Nov.

There are lots more guesthouses and B&Bs and a couple of **campsites**, north of the village at *Stronaba Caravan & Camping*, T712259, open Apr-Oct; and west towards Gairlochy at *Gairlochy Holiday Park*, T712711, F712712, open Apr-Oct.

Eating There's also a wide choice of places to eat. As well as those listed above, there's the *Old Station Restaurant*, T712535, in a converted railway station. Has a very good reputation, dinner is expensive; lunch by prior arrangement only, open Apr-Oct, Tue-Sun 1800-2100. Also recommended is *The Coach House Restaurant*, T712680, crann_tara@bigfoot.com, which is about 3 miles north of town on the right-hand side, at Glenfintaig. It's a popular place and small, so you'll have to book ahead for lunch (cheap) or dinner (mid-range to expensive), open late Apr to late Oct, daily 1200-1500 and 1800-2100.

Transport There are regular **buses** to and from Fort William and Inverness (£6 single). Spean Bridge is also on the Fort William-Glasgow **rail** line (see Fort William Transport below).

Loch Arkaig
Phone code: 01397
Colour map 3,
grid A6

A mile north of Spean Bridge on the A82 is the **Commando Memorial**, which commemorates the commandos who trained here during the Second World War. It's worth lingering for a few moments to appreciate the fantastic views all around. From here the B8004 branches west to **Gairlochy**, crossing the Caledonian Canal, then the B8005 heads north to Loch Arkaig, a long, deep and mysterious loch stretching west through the mountains. Bonnie Prince Charlie passed this way, before and after Culloden, through an area which has, for centuries, been the seat of the Camerons of Lochiel. The Camerons were fervent supporters of the Jacobite cause and when Prince Charles landed at Loch nan Uamh, on the road from Fort William to Mallaig, he called on Cameron of Lochiel to join him at Glenfinnan.

You can find out all about the Camerons and their involvement in the Jacobite rebellion of 1745 in the **Clan Cameron Museum**, in the tiny township of **Achnacarry**, nestled between the shores of Loch Lochy and **Loch Arkaig**. The museum is housed in an old cottage rebuilt after being burned by government troops in 1746. ■ *Easter to mid-Oct daily 1330-1700; Jul-Aug 1100-1700. Adult £3, concession £1.50, children free.* T712480.

Beyond the turn-off to Achnacarry, the single-track road runs through the Clunes Forest and **The Dark Mile**, a long line of beech trees which completely cuts out daylight. At the east end of Loch Arkaig, a stone bridge crosses the Caig Burn. Beside the bridge is a car park, from where a path leads up to the spectacular **Cia-Aig Falls** which tumble into a deep, dark pool known as **The Witch's Cauldron**. It was here that an old hag was accused of casting her evil eye over Lochiel's cattle, causing them to fall ill and die. But when she fell into the pool and drowned, the cattle miraculously began to recover from their illness.

Beyond the falls is *Highland Icelandic Horse Trekking*, T/F712427, hihot@compuserve.com, which offers one-hour, two-hour and day rides in the surrounding hills. The road runs along the north shore of Loch Arkaig all the way to the head of the loch, from where experienced and well-equipped hill walkers can hike through the glens to Loch Nevis and Knoydart.

Transport There's no public transport beyond Achnacarry, and there's only 1 **bus** a day to Achnacarry from Lochaber High School in Fort William.

From Spean Bridge the A86 runs east through Glen Spean to meet the A9 Perth to Inverness road which leads to **Aviemore**, Scotland's main ski centre (see page 531). The road passes through **Roy Bridge**, which is the turn-off for **Glen Roy**, noted for its amazing 'parallel roads'. These are not in fact roads, but three gravel ledges etched on to the mountains at different heights. The 'roads' marked the shorelines of a glacial lake formed during the last ice age. Roy Bridge was also the site of the infamous Keppoch Murders (see page 461).

**Glen Roy &
Loch Laggan**
*Phone code: 01397
Colour map 4,
grid A/B1*

The road continues east towards Loch Laggan. After a couple of miles it passes **Cille Choirille**, an ancient church built by a 15th-century Cameron chief as penance for a life of violence. The church fell into disrepair but was restored and reopened in 1932 and now attracts people of all creeds as it's said to inspire peace and spiritual healing. Further east, at the eastern end of Loch Laggan, is the massive **Laggan Dam**, built in 1933 to provide water for the aluminium smelter at Fort William. The water is piped through tunnels up to 15 ft in diameter carved through the core of Ben Nevis. The road runs along the north shore of the loch, past the **Creag Meagaidh National Nature Reserve**, where you can see herds of red deer right by the reserve car park. A track leads from here up to **Lochan a' Choire** (about four hours).

Sleeping and eating There are several hotels in **Roy Bridge**, including the **C** *Stronlossit Hotel*, T712253, F712641, which serves good meals all day from 1100 (cheap lunch; mid-range dinner). There are also 3 independent **hostels**: the **F** *Grey Corrie Lodge*, T712236, F712241, is handy for shops and transport, serves cheap bar meals and also has laundry facilities. A mile and a half from the village is the cheaper **F** *Aite Cruinnichidh* hostel, at Achluachrach, T712315. Five miles east, at Tulloch train station, is **F** *Station Lodge*, T/F732333, which also serves meals (including vegetarian).

Aside from the places listed above, a good place to eat is the *Glenspean Lodge Hotel*, T712223. Lunch served 1230-1430 (cheap) and dinner 1830-2100 (expensive).

Sport Fishing *Fishing Scotland*, T/F712812, www.fishing-scotland.co.uk, runs fishing courses and trips on the surrounding lochs. Loch Arkaig in particular is renowned for its trout fishing. **Hiking and climbing** *Nevis Guides*, Bohuntin, Roy Bridge, T712356.

Transport There are **buses** from Fort William to Roy Bridge (3 times daily Mon-Fri; 1 on Sat). Roy Bridge is also on the Fort William-Glasgow **rail** line.

Fort William and around

Fort William is the gateway to the Western Highlands and one of the country's main tourist centres. It stands at the head of Loch Linnhe, with the snow-topped mass of Ben Nevis towering behind. You could be forgiven for assuming that it's quite an attractive place, but you'd be wrong. Despite its magnificent setting, Fort William has all the charm of a motorway service station. A dual carriageway runs along the lochside, over a litter-strewn pedestrian underpass and past dismal 1960s concrete boxes masquerading as hotels.

*Phone code: 01397
Colour map 3, grid B6
Population: 10,774*

The Highlands and Skye

Most of the good things about Fort William are outside the town. The surrounding mountains and glens are amongst the most stunning in the Highlands and attract hikers and climbers in their droves: **Ben Nevis** – Britain's highest peak at 4,406 ft – and also the very beautiful **Glen Nevis**, which many of you may recognize from movies such as *Braveheart* and *Rob Roy*, see page 471. There's also skiing and snowboarding at nearby **Aonach Mor**, one of Scotland's top ski areas, see page 471, and some good mountain biking around the **Leanachan Forest**, see page 469.

Though it's not a pretty sight, Fort William is the largest town hereabouts and has all the services and facilities you'd expect. There are banks with ATMs on the pedestrianized High Street, as well as a couple of good supermarkets and two well-stocked outdoor-equipment shops.

Ins and outs

Getting there
For more details see 'Transport', on page 470

Fort William is easily reached by **bus**, from Inverness, Glasgow and Oban, and by **train**, direct from Glasgow via the amazing and beautiful West Highland Railway. The train and bus stations are next to each other at the north end of the High St, on the other side of the dual carriageway. If you're driving, parking can be a problem. There's a big **car park** beside the loch at the south end of town, and another behind the tourist office. You can also walk to Fort William, if you have a week to spare, from just north of Glasgow, along the 95 mile-long **West Highland Way** (see page 59).

Getting around

The town is strung out for several miles along the banks of Loch Linnhe. The centre is compact and easy to get around on foot. Many of the **guesthouses** and **B&Bs**, and a few youth hostels, are in **Corpach**, 1½ miles to the north, but there are frequent buses from the town centre. There are also buses to the youth hostel in **Glen Nevis**. For information on these and on **taxis** and **car hire** see under Transport, page 470.

Tourist information

The busy **TIC** is on Cameron Sq, just off the High St, T703781, F705184. They stock a good range of books, maps and leaflets covering local walks. They will also help arrange transport to more remote Highland parts. Open Apr-late May Mon-Sat 0900-1700, Sun 1000-1600; Jun-early Jul Mon-Sat 0900-1800, Sun 1000-1700; Jul-Aug Mon-Sat 0900-2030, Sun 0900-1800; Sep-late Oct Mon-Sat 0900-1800, Sun 1000-1700; Nov-Mar Mon-Sat 1000-1700.

Sights

There's little of real interest in the town, though the **West Highland Museum**, on Cameron Square by the tourist office, is a worthwhile exception. It contains excellent exhibits of Jacobite memorabilia, including a bed in which Prince Charles slept, and a 'secret' portrait of the prince which is revealed only when reflected in a cylindrical mirror. There are also fine displays of Highland clans and tartans, wildlife and local history. ■ *Jun-Sep Mon-Sat 1000-1700; Oct-May 1000-1600; Jul-Aug also Sun 1400-1700. £2, £1.50 concession , £0.50 child. T702169.* The **fort** from which the town gets its name was built in 1690 by order of William III to keep the rebellious Scottish clans in order. The garrison fought off attacks by Jacobites during the rebellions of 1715 and 1745 but was then demolished to make way for the railway line. The scant remains of the fort can be seen on the lochside, near the train station.

The **Ben Nevis Distillery** is at Lochy Bridge, at the junction of the A82 to Inverness and the A830 to Mallaig, about a mile north of the town centre. To get there take a Caol or Corpach bus (see below under Transport). ■ *Visitor Centre open Mon-Fri 0900-1700 (Jul-Aug also Sat 1000-1600). Tours £2 per person. T700200.* Just before the distillery, on the left, are the 13th-century ruins of **Inverlochy Castle**.

Three miles from the town centre along the A830 to Mallaig, in the suburb of Banavie, is **Neptune's Staircase**, a series of eight linked locks on the Caledonian Canal. The locks lower the canal by 90 ft in less than two miles between Loch Lochy and Loch Eil and comprise the last section of the canal which links the North Sea with the Irish Sea. It's a pretty dramatic sight, with equally dramatic views of Ben Nevis and its neighbours behind Fort William. From here you can walk or cycle along the canal towpath. Further along the A830 to Mallaig, in the village of Corpach, is **Treasures of the Earth**, an exhibition of crystals, gemstones and fossils displayed in a huge simulated cave. ■ *May-Sep daily 0930-1900; Oct-Apr 1000-1700. £3, £2.75 concession, £1.50 child. T772283.*

Essentials

Fort William has plentiful accommodation, ranging from large luxury hotels to modest guesthouses and B&Bs. Many of the B&Bs are in **Corpach** and **Banavie** to the north of town. As a main tourist centre, Fort William gets very busy in the high season and you'll need to book ahead at this time. The tourist office will book a room for you, for a small fee, or you can ask for their free *Fort William & Lochaber Visitor Guide* and phone around yourself.

Sleeping
■ *on map*
Price codes:
see inside front cover

L *Inverlochy Castle Hotel*, 3 miles north of town on the A82 to Inverness, T702177, F702953, www.inverlochy.co.uk 16 rooms. One of the best hotels in the country, and everything you'd expect to find in a real castle: unsurpassed elegance, impeccable service and superb food (see Eating below), all set in 500 acres of beautiful grounds.

B *The Moorings Hotel*, 3 miles out of town in Banavie, on the road to Corpach and Mallaig, T772797, F772441. 21 rooms. Overlooks 'Neptune's Staircase'; well situated and comfortable with an excellent restaurant.

C *Alexandra Hotel*, The Parade, T702241, F705554, sales@miltonhotels.com 97 rooms. Large established hotel right in the centre of town, with restaurant. **C** *Glenloy Lodge Hotel*, about 6 miles from town on the B8004 north from Banavie, T/F712700. 9 rooms. Open mid-Dec to late Oct. Friendly and comfortable little hotel tucked away in a quiet, secluded location, and with a good restaurant. **C-D** *Glenlochy Guesthouse*, Nevis Bridge, North Rd, T702909, is recommended. **C** *Highland Hotel*, Union Rd, T702291, F700133. Traditional Highland hotel overlooking the town, with great views across Loch Linnhe. Good restaurant, comfortable; cheaper off-season.

D *Distillery House*, across the road from the *Glenlochy Guesthouse* (opposite the road into Glen Nevis), T700103, F702980. 6 rooms. Comfortable, upmarket guesthouse. **Achintore Rd**, which runs south along the loch, is packed with B&Bs and hotels, many of which are large and characterless. More appealing than most is **D** *Lawriestone Guesthouse*, T/F700777. Running parallel is **Grange Rd**, which is lined with B&B accommodation. Two of the best are **B** *Crolinnhe*, T702709, open Mar-Nov; and **B** *The Grange*, T705516, open Mar-Nov.

There are also plenty of B&Bs which are closer to the **bus and train stations**, mostly on and around Fassifern Rd and Alma Rd. These include **D-E** *Guisachan House*, T/F703797; and **E** *Mrs Heger*, 'Finnisaig', T702453, both on Alma Rd; and **D** 6 *Caberfeidh*, Fassifern Rd, T703756.

There are several more places to stay in **Glen Nevis**, including **E** *Achintee Farm Guesthouse*, T702240, mcy@btinternet.com, by the start of the path to Ben Nevis. For details of how to get there, see Transport below.

There are also cheaper options, in the shape of several hostels and a couple of campsites. The popular **F Fort William Backpackers** is on Alma Rd, 500 yds from the train station, T700711. 3 miles out of town in Glen Nevis, near the start of the path up Ben Nevis, is the large **F SYHA Youth Hostel**, T702336, which gets very busy in summer. A better bet is the independent **F Ben Nevis Bunkhouse**, at Achintee Farm, across the river from the visitor centre (see above). **F Calluna**, T700451, F700489, www.guide.u.net.com, is at Heathercroft, about a 15-min walk from the tourist office (see map). It's run by experienced mountain guide, Alan Kimber. There are 2 hostels in Corpach (see Transport below). **F The Smiddy Bunkhouse**, T772467, bunks@ bunksville.com, is next to Corpach train station, with the Snowgoose Mountain Centre attached. **F Scottish International Backpackers** is at Farr Cottage Activity Centre, T772315, F772247, www.fort-william.co.uk\ farrcottage, which also organizes hill walking trips and rents out mountain bikes. Two miles up the Glen Nevis Rd is **Glen Nevis Caravan & Camping Park**, T702191, open mid-Mar to late Oct, which has excellent facilities. Five miles from town on the road to Mallaig, is **Linnhe Caravan & Chalet Park**, T772376, open Christmas to late Oct, also with full facilities.

Eating

Fort William isn't exactly the culinary capital of the Highlands, but there are some top quality restaurants and a decent choice across the range

Most of the hotels offer lunch and dinner, and the best of these is the *Inverlochy Castle* (see above). It's expensive but the food is superb and the surroundings are the last word in grandeur. Open daily 1230-1345, 1900-2115. Otherwise, by far the best option is the excellent *Crannog Seafood Restaurant*, on the Town Pier, T705589, crannogallan@msn.com Housed in an old smokehouse, the seafood is as fresh as you can get and the surroundings are unpretentious. It gets very busy and service can be slow, so book ahead and take your time (lunch cheap to mid-range; dinner mid-range). Four miles from town is *An Crann*, T772077. Take the A830 to Mallaig, then turn right to Banavie on the B8004. This converted barn is a local favourite and offers good Scottish cooking in a friendly

The Highlands and Skye (side margin)

Fort William

To Ben Nevis Distillery, Banavie, Carpach, Mallaig (A830) & Inverness (A82)

River Lochy
River Nevis
To Glen Nevis

Lochaber Leisure Centre

Safeway Supermarket
Bus Station
Old Fort Ruins
Nevisport

To Camusnagul
To Glencoe & South to Glasgow (A82)

West Highland Museum
Cameron Square
Off Beat Bikes
Loch Linnhe

0 metres 50
0 yards 50

6 Fort William Backpackers Hostel
7 Glenlochy Guesthouse
8 Grange
9 Mrs Heger B & B

■ **Sleeping**
1 6 Caberfeidh
2 Alexandra
3 Calluna
4 Crolinnhe
5 Distillery House

● **Eating**
1 Café Chardón
2 Crannog Seafood
3 Grog & Gruel
4 Indian Garden
5 McTavish's Kitchens

Tours from Fort William

*Top of the Pops as far as tours are concerned has to be the **Jacobite Steam Train** which runs from Fort William to Mallaig during the summer months. Further details from West Coast Railway Company, T01524 732100, www.westcoastrailway.co.uk*

*There are several **cruises** which leave from the Town Pier, giving you the chance to spot local marine wildlife, including seals, otters and seabirds. One of the operators is **Seal Island Cruises** (T705589), who run trips of 1½ hours from April to September.*

---

atmosphere. (Mid-range prices.) Lunch 1230-1500, dinner 1700-2100, closed Sun. Open late Mar to mid-Oct.

A great place for baguettes, filled rolls and pastries to eat in or takeaway is *Café Chardón*, upstairs at Peter Maclennan's store, in a side lane off the High St, T772077. Fort William boasts a very fine curry house, the *Indian Garden Restaurant*, at 88 High St, T705011. It does a cheap lunch, takeaways and is open late. *The Grog & Gruel*, 66 High St, T705078, is a pub-cum-restaurant offering good-value pizza, pasta and Tex Mex, and a wide range of superb cask ales. Open till 2400/0100. Also on the High St is *McTavish's Kitchens*, T702406, serving steaks and seafood at mid-range prices. In summer it hosts nightly Scottish music shows, with dancing and bagpipes, from 2030.

In Glen Nevis, near the SYHA hostel, the *Glen Nevis Restaurant*, T705459, serves a cheap-mid-range 2-course lunch and mid-range 3-course dinner. Open 1200-2200, Apr-Oct. Nearby is *Café Beag*, T703601, a cosy place with log fire. Good vegetarian food.

Canoeing There are several good rivers around Fort William, ranging in difficulty from Grade 1 to 6. Canoe courses are run by *Snowgoose Mountain Centre*, which is attached to *The Smiddy Bunkhouse* (see 'Sleeping' above). A useful contact is the *Nevis Canoe Club*, T705388.

Sports

Fishing *Torlundy Trout Fishery*, at Torlundy Farm in Tomacharich, 3 miles north off the A82, T703015, has 3 lakes filled with rainbow trout and hires out rods. Pony trekking from £15/hr, book in advance.

Hiking and climbing Fort William is a mecca for hikers and climbers. For information on the climb up Ben Nevis and walks around Glen Nevis, see page 471. If you want to hire a guide, try *Lochaber Walks*, 22 Zetland Av, T703828; *Fort William Mountain Guides*, T700451; *Alba Walking Holidays*, T704964; and *Snowgoose Mountain Centre* (see 'Sleeping' above). Fort William has 2 excellent outdoor activity equipment shops: *Nevisport*, T704921, is on the High St, and has a huge selection of books, maps and guides, a bureau de change and bar-restaurant. At the other end of the High St is *West Coast Outdoor Sports*, T705777. There's an indoor climbing wall at the *Lochaber Leisure Centre* (see below).

Mountain biking The Leanachan Forest, below Aonach Mhor, is 4 miles north of Fort William. Access is via the road to the Aonach Mhor ski development. The forest covers a huge area with 25 miles of mountain bike trails, ranging from easy to demanding. There is also the Great Glen Cycle Route, which is mainly off-road and runs all the way from Fort William to Inverness. For the hire, sale or repair of bikes, and good advice on local cycle routes, visit *Off Beat Bikes*, 117 High St, and at the Nevis Range Ski Centre, T704008, www.offbeatbikes.co.uk, open only Jul-Aug.

Skiing The Nevis Range ski centre is at nearby Aonach Mhor. For details, see above, and for ski equipment, try *Nevisport* (see above).

The Highlands and Skye

Riding the rails

Running from Glasgow to Mallaig via Fort William, the West Highland Railway is only 164 miles long but is widely acknowledged as one of the most scenic railway journeys in the world. The great thing about this journey is its variety, taking you from the distinctive red tenements of Glasgow and the former shipbuilding areas of the River Clyde, to the windy wilderness of Rannoch Moor and the chilly splendour of the hills. It's about an hour after leaving Glasgow that you get your first taste of highland scenery when the train hugs the eastern bank of sinewy Loch Long. Then it's on past the 'bonnie banks' of Loch Lomond, Britain's largest body of inland water. It's impossible not to pass this serene loch without thinking of the famous ballad about two Jacobite soldiers captured after the '45 rebellion. The soldier taking 'the low road' is due to be executed, his companion taking the 'high road' is due to be released.

After Ardlui, at the top of Loch Lomond, the countryside gets more rugged. Wherever you look you see something of interest: a waterfall gushing down a hillside, a buzzard surfing on the breeze – perhaps a herd of Highland Cattle wallowing in a river. The West Highland Way, the long distance footpath from Glasgow to Fort William, is close to the line now and at stations such as Crianlarich, Upper Tyndrum and Bridge of Orchy you can often spot footsore walkers with muddy boots - who get on the train looking slightly guilty and collapse on their seats with sighs of relief.

The landscape gets wilder and bleaker as the railway crosses the lonely, peaty wastes of Rannoch Moor and on to Corrour, which featured in the film version of Irvine Welsh's cult book Trainspotting. Then you descend to the lusher country around Tulloch, before pulling in to Fort William. This is a popular visitor centre as it's close to Ben Nevis, Britain's highest mountain, and beautiful Glen Nevis, which has featured in films such as Braveheart and Rob Roy. Now comes the most spectacular part of the journey, for the West Highland Line leaves the best 'till last. Leaving Fort William, the train crosses Thomas Telford's Caledonian Canal - where you can see an impressive series of eight locks known as 'Neptune's Staircase' - hugs the shore of Loch Eil, then crosses the magnificent Glenfinnan Viaduct, a masterpiece in concrete. You soon get superb views of the evocative Glenfinnan Monument that commemorates the start of the 1745 rebellion, before pulling in to Glenfinnan Station. The train now takes you through a landscape of craggy hills and glacial lochs etched with birch and pine trees. You pass Loch nan Uamh, from where Bonnie Prince Charlie fled for France after his defeat at Culloden, then draw in to Arisaig, the birthplace of the man who inspired RL Stevenson's Long John Silver. Next is beautiful Loch Morar, Britain's deepest inland loch and home – so legend has it – to a mysterious monster. Soon you get great views across the water to the craggy islands of Eigg and Rhum, before finally pulling in to the port of Mallaig.

Swimming There's an indoor pool at the *Lochaber Leisure Centre*, off Belford Rd (see map), T704359.

Transport Bus Local: There are buses every 10-20 mins to and from **Caol** and **Corpach**, and every hour on Sun and in the evening. There is an hourly service to **Glen Nevis**, Mon-Sat from 0800-2300, Jun to Sep only (less frequent on Sun). There are 4 buses daily to **Aonach Mhor** during the ski season.

Bus Long distance: There are several daily *Citylink* buses to **Inverness** (1 hr, £7.40); to **Oban** (1¾ hrs, £6.90) via **Glencoe** (30 mins); and to **Uig** (3½ hrs, £17), via

Nevis Range Ski Centre

*The Nevis Range Ski Centre, four miles northeast of Fort William at Torlundy, is situated on the mountain of **Aonach Mhor** (4,006 ft). It's Scotland's highest skiing and snowboarding area and has the longest ski season, running from Christmas to May. It also boasts the country's only cable-car system, built in 1989. The 1½ mile gondola ride is a popular attraction not only with skiers and snowboarders in the winter but also during the summer off-season period, when it's used by hill walkers to gain easy access to the mountains. For most tourists, though, it's an easy way to climb to over 2,000 ft and enjoy the wonderful views from the terrace of the self-service restaurant at the top. There are ski and snowboarding schools and also a dry slope for summer skiing in July and August (open Sunday-Thursday 1100-1230, £18 including gondola).*

The gondola is open all year, except early November to the week before Christmas, 1000-1700 (July-August 0930-1800, Thu-Fri till 2100) and costs £6.75 return (children £4.15). T01397-705825, www.ski.scotland.net

---

Portree and **Kyle of Lochalsh** (1 hr 50 mins). *Citylink* buses also go several times daily to **Glasgow** (3¼ hrs, £11.80), via Glencoe and Tyndrum, and to **Edinburgh** (4 hrs, £16.50), via **Stirling** (3 hrs, £12.90). There is a bus to **Mallaig** (1½ hrs, £4) daily except Sun with *Shiel Buses*, T01967-431272. *Highland Country Buses*, T702373, run several times a day to **Kinlochleven** (50 mins) via Glencoe. There is also a *Postbus* service (Mon-Sat) to **Glen Etive**.

Car hire *Easydrive*, at Lochy Bridge, T701616; *Volkswagen Rental*, at Nevis Garage, Argour Rd, Caol, T702432; *Budget*, at North Rd, T702500, or *Practical Car & Van Hire*, at Slipway Autos, Corpach, T772404. Prices start from around £35 per day. **Taxi**: You can call a taxi on T706070, or T704000.

Ferry There is a passenger-only ferry service to **Camusnagaul**, on the opposite bank of Loch Linnhe, from the Town Pier. It sails several times daily (Mon-Sat) and takes 10 mins. For times etc contact Highland Council, T01463-702695, or ask at the tourist office.

Train There are 2-3 trains daily from **Glasgow** to Fort William (3¾ hrs) via **Crianlarich**. These trains continue to **Mallaig** (a further 1 hr 20 mins) where they connect with ferries to Armadale on Skye (see page 537). There are no direct trains to Oban; you need to change at Crianlarich. There is a sleeper service from **London Euston** (see page 36), but you'll miss the views. For all rail enquiries, T0345- 484950.

Communications The library on the High St offers free **internet** access. Otherwise there;'s *Thing King*, on High St, £1.50/15 mins

Directory

Glen Nevis

Colour map 3, grid B6

Only 10 minutes' drive from Fort William is one of Scotland's great glens, the classic Glen Nevis. The sparkling Water of Nevis tumbles through a wooded gorge, closed in by steep, bracken-covered slopes, with the massive hulk of Ben Nevis watching over. The whole scene is both rugged and sylvan, and the nearest you'll get to a Himalayan valley in the Scottish Highlands. It's not surprising, then, that this is a favourite with movie directors and has featured in films such as *Rob Roy* and *Braveheart*.

There are many walks in and around the glen, not least of which is the trek up to the summit of Britain's highest mountain. Aside from the walks described below, there are several easy, marked forest walks which start from the car park at Achriabhach. There are buses into Glen Nevis, as far as the youth hostel, from Fort William bus station (see 'Transport' above).

Every year many thousands of people make the relatively straightforward ascent of Ben Nevis, and every year a frighteningly high percentage end up injured, or lost, or dead. More people die annually on the 'Ben' than Everest, so this is a mountain that needs to be taken seriously. Though it may be in the 70s in the car park when you set off, the weather changes with alarming speed and you can find yourself in a blizzard at the summit, or, as is usually the case, in a blanket of cloud or hill fog. It goes without saying that you need to be well prepared. You will need a good, strong pair of boots, warm clothing, waterproofs, food and drink. You should also take a map and a compass. Allow six to eight hours for the return trip. In the winter the top part of the mountain is covered in snow and you should not attempt the walk unless you are an experienced hill climber.

The route The main tourist path, built as a pony track to service the now-dilapidated observatory on the summit, starts from the car park at Achintee Farm, on the north side of the river, reached by the road through Claggan. It climbs gradually at first across the flank of Meal an t-Suidhe, before joining the alternative path from the youth hostel. This latter route is shorter but much steeper.

The trail continues to climb steadily as it begins to follow the **Red Burn**, until it reaches a junction, with Lochan Meal an t-Suidhe down to the left. Here, an alternative route down from the summit heads left under the north face of the mountain (see below). This is the halfway point of the main route. The path crosses the Red Burn and then climbs by a series of long and

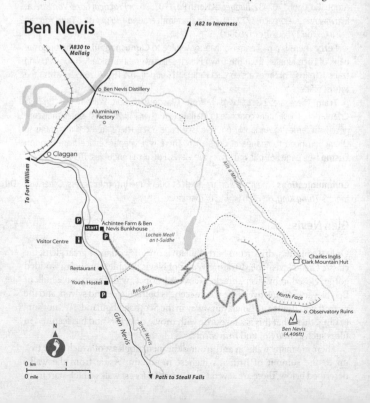

Ben Nevis

A82 to Inverness

A830 to Mallaig

Ben Nevis Distillery

Aluminium Factory

Claggan

To Fort William

Allt a'Mhuilinn

P
start Achintee Farm & Ben Nevis Bunkhouse
P
Visitor Centre
i
Lochan Meal an t-Suidhe

Charles Inglis Clark Mountain Hut

Restaurant
Youth Hostel
P
Red Burn
North Face
Observatory Ruins

Glen Nevis
River Nevis
Ben Nevis (4,406ft)

N

0 km   1
0 mile   1

Path to Steall Falls

Steall Falls

A fairly easy low-level walk is to the spectacular 300 ft-high Steall Falls at the head of the glen. It's a popular walk, especially in the summer when the trail can resemble the queue for the Ladies at a Tom Jones concert, but this doesn't detract from its stunning natural beauty.

The path starts at the end of the road, at the second car park. Before setting off you might like to note the sign by the steep waterfall that cascades down to the edge of the car park. It reads 'Warning! This is not the path to Ben Nevis'. Now, if you need to be warned against attempting to climb up Ben Nevis through a waterfall, you probably shouldn't be left alone in possession of this book, never mind let loose on the Scottish mountains. Once you've shaken your head in disbelief at the apparent mind-numbing stupidity of some of your fellow travellers, follow the track alongside the Water of Nevis. The path climbs steadily through the woods

and becomes rocky, with the river thundering below through the steep gorge. It runs close to the river before emerging from the gorge and opening up into a wide, flower-filled meadow, with a high waterfall at the far end. It's a beautiful, tranquil place and ideal for a picnic. Follow the path across the valley floor till it crosses the river via a precarious bridge that consists of three ropes of thick wire in a V-shape. The path then leads to the bottom of the falls. You can also head left at the bridge and continue up the valley to some ruins. From here the path leads to **Corrour station**, 14 miles away, but it's for fit and experienced hillwalkers only. You can then catch a train back to Fort William. It's a very popular route, and there's even accommodation at the end of it, near the train station, at the **SYHA Loch Lochy Youth Hostel** (T01809-501239; open mid-March to late October).

OS Landranger No 41 covers the route.

The Highlands and Skye

seemingly never-ending zig-zags up to a plateau. The path splits in two, but both paths take you up to the summit, marked by a cairn and emergency shelter, on the ruins of the old observatory. Note that on the upper sloping plateau the path can 'disappear' in mist and snow, and some cairns and beacons have been removed by vandals masquerading as purists. If conditions deteriorate, a compass is a life-saver. There is a shelter on the summit and at least two others on the mountain.

To return simply retrace your steps all the way. If the weather is settled enough and you have time, you can follow the alternative route below the north face. This leads right round the mountain to the Charles Inglis Clark mountain hut, then heads down into the **Allt a' Mhuilinn** glen which leads all the way down to the distillery on the A82, a mile north of the town centre. Note that this route adds an extra three or four miles to the descent and should only be attempted by fit and experienced hillwalkers.

Fort William to Glen Coe

Phone code: 01855
Colour map 3, grid B6

The main A82 south to Glasgow runs down the side of Loch Linnhe towards Glen Coe. About eight miles south of Fort William it passes the **Corran Ferry** to **Ardgour** (see page 481). The ferry makes the five-minute crossing every 30 minutes. Foot passengers are free and cars cost £4.70. By the ferry is the **D** *Nether Lochaber Hotel*, T821235, which serves decent, cheap pub meals.

Less than half a mile south of the ferry is the turning to **Inchree**, where you'll find cheap lodging at the *Inchree Bunkhouse Hostel*, T821287. There's also a good restaurant nearby, the *Four Seasons Bistro and Bar*, T821393, a friendly and informal place that looks like a log cabin. It's open daily except Tuesdays, 1800-2130. Prices are mid-range.

There's an easy 40-minute circular walk up to **Inchree Waterfall**. It starts from the car park at the end of the road beyond the tiny hamlet and is clearly marked. The waterfall is impressive and divided into three sections. The views from the top, down the length of Loch Linnhe, are worth the walk alone. The path continues up past the waterfall to the forest road which leads back downhill to the car park.

Sleeping
A mile south of the ferry are the villages of **Onich** and **North Ballachulish**. There's a wide selection of places to stay here, mostly with good views of the loch, which make an attractive alternative to Fort William. Overlooking the loch are **L** *Allt-nan-Ros Hotel*, T821210, allt-nan-ros@zetnet.co.uk; and **L** *The Lodge on the Loch Hotel*, T821237, laurence@mysteryworld.co.uk, open Feb-Dec. Both are high-quality hotels with great views and good restaurants (lunch mid-range; dinner expensive). A cheaper option is **B** *Onich Hotel*, T821214, which also has loch views and serves good meals (cheap-mid-range) in its busy bar. A good place to dine, but for residents only, is **B** *Cuilcheanna House*, T821226; open Easter-Oct, a comfortable guesthouse just off the main road.

Sport
Alfresco Adventure, T821248, just to the east of North Ballachulish on the B863 to Kinlochleven, offers boat hire and various outdoor activities such as mountain biking and canoeing.

Kinlochleven
Phone code: 01855
Colour map 3, grid B6

The B863 turns east off the A82 at North Ballachulish and heads to Kinlochleven, at the head of Loch Leven. It can also be reached on the same road from Glencoe village, seven miles west. It's an unlikely place to find a huge aluminium factory, but it kept the village alive for many years. Now, though, it's threatened with closure and there's talk of Kinlochleven being developed as a major mountaineering centre.

You can find out all about the long and often tragic history of aluminium-working in Lochaber at **The Aluminium Story**, in the Kinlochleven Visitor Centre and Library on Linnhe Road. ■ *Apr-Oct Tue-Fri 1030-1800, Sat-Sun 1100-1500. Free. T831663.*

The West Highland Way passes through the village and many walkers spend the night here before setting out on the last stretch before Fort William. There are also several good walks in the surrounding hills and glens, a few of which are described below.

Sleeping and eating There's not a huge amount to choose from in the way of accommodation or eating out. The **D** *MacDonald Hotel*, on the Fort William Rd, T831539, open Mar-Dec, serves cheap bar lunches and moderately priced dinners; and the **E** *Tailrace Inn*, on Riverside Rd, T831777, does cheap bar meals all day. There are also several **B&Bs**, as well as an independent hostel, the *West Highland Lodge*, Hostel Brae, T831471.

Transport *Highland Country Buses*, T01397-702373, runs 6 times a day (Mon-Sat) between Fort William and Kinlochleven (50 mins).

There are some fairly easy short walks from Kinlochleven up the glen of the River Leven, including the one to the impressive **Grey Mare's Tail** waterfall. A fairly easy but rewarding half-day walk is to follow the **West Highland Way** south from the village to the top of the **Devil's Staircase**, where it meets the A82 at the eastern end of Glen Coe.

Walks around Kinlochleven
OS Landranger No 41

The route starts from the British Aluminium Visitor Centre, runs around the side of the aluminium factory, then crosses a wooden bridge and climbs gradually on a dirt jeep-track up to Penstock House, at 1,000 ft. At the top, near the house, the track forks to the right and continues on a rough footpath to the **Devil's Staircase**. The path is marked with the West Highland Way thistle sign, so it's easy to follow uphill to the top of the pass (1,804 ft), from where you get great views of Loch Eilde Mór and the Mamores to the north. The path then descends down the staircase to Glen Coe, with breathtaking Buachaille Etive Mór in front of you all the way.

You'll have to return to Kinlochleven by the same route, or you could carry on to the *Kingshouse Hotel* (see below). The return trip from Kinlochleven should take four to five hours, or you can start out from Glencoe (see below). This section of the West Highland Way was once part of the old military road which ran from Fort William to Stirling. The Devil's Staircase was named by the 400 soldiers who had to endure severe hardship while building it in the 17th century.

Another good hike, though more strenuous, is to **Beinn na Callich** (2,507 ft). You'll need to be fairly fit for this steep climb, and allow around six to seven hours for the return trip. The route is well marked and starts from the West Highland Way footpath opposite the school, which is on the road heading out of the village towards Fort William.

The path climbs steeply at first, crosses the tarmac road to Mamore Lodge, then continues till it joins General Wade's old military road, which takes the West Highland Way on its final 11 miles to Fort William. From here, you'll see the path zig-zagging up the mountain. Continue along the old military road for about 400 yd until you cross a wooden bridge. Then follow a path down to another wooden bridge, where the ground is quite boggy. Cross the bridge and the path begins to zig-zag uphill till it levels out on to a plateau, before continuing relentlessly upwards through a long series of zig-zags to the summit, marked by a couple of cairns and a commemorative plaque. The views from the top make the tiring climb worthwhile. You can see down on to Loch Leven, across to Glen Coe and the magnificent Mamores looming close by.

Fit and experienced hill walkers can access the Mamores from the Mamore Lodge road. Once you're up there you have the opportunity to bag several

The Highlands and Skye

Munros, via a series of excellent ridge walks connecting **Am Bodach** (3,386 ft) with **Stob Coire a' Chairn** (3,219 ft), **Na Gruagaichean** (3,461 ft), **An Gearanach** (3,222 ft), **Sgor An Iubhair** (3,285 ft), **Sgurr a'Mhaim** (3,606 ft) and **Stob Ban** (3,278 ft). These peaks and ridges can also be reached from Glen Nevis (see page 471). As well as a good pair of lungs and the proper equipment, take a map and a compass.

Ballachulish
Phone code: 01855
Colour map 3, grid B6

On the southern shore of Loch Leven, a mile or so west of Glencoe village on the A82, is the old slate quarrying village of Ballachulish. There's a good range of accommodation here and many use the place as a base to visit Glencoe.

In the car park just off the main road is the **Tourist Information Centre**, T811296. As well as the usual accommodation booking service they have displays about the quarries. It's open April-May Monday-Saturday 0900-1700, Sunday 1200-1600; June-September Monday-Saturday 0900-1800, Sunday 1000-1700; September-October Monday-Saturday 1000-1700, Sunday 1000-1600.

Sleeping L *The Isles of Glencoe Hotel*, T811602, F811770, reservations@mysteryworld.co.uk 39 rooms. A modern hotel and leisure complex next to Highland Mysteryworld. Excellent location on the shores of the loch, and facilities

Glen Coe & Loch Leven

A82 to Fort William
A82 to North Ballachulish
A82 to Fort William
A828 to Oban
Abhainn Righ
Lochan Lunn Da Bhra
Mullach nan Coirean
Stob Bàn (3,278ft)
West Highland Way
Sgurr a' Mhàim (3,606ft)
Grey Mare's Tail Waterfall
Kinlochleven
Mam na Gualainn
Beinn na Caillich (2,507ft)
North Ballachulish
Caliart
Loch Leven
Garbh Bheinn (2,845ft)
Pap of Glencoe (2,435ft)
Eilean Munde
South Ballachulish
Glencoe
River Coe
Sgurr nam Fiannaidh (3,173ft)
Meall Dearg (3,120ft)
Aonach Eagach Ridge
Am Bodach (3,684ft)
Ballachulish
MacDonald Monument
Signal Rock
Glen Coe
Start of Lost Valley Walk
Gleann a' Chaolais
NTS Visitor Centre
Loch Achtriochtan
Aonach Dubh
Gearr Aonach
The Three Sisters
Meeting of Three Waters
Gleann na Fhiodh
Meall Mór
Stob Coire nan Lochan (3,658ft)
Lost Valley
(2,661ft)
Buchaille Etive Beag
Bidean nam Bian (3,744ft)
Beinn Fhada
Beinn Maol Chalum
(3,143ft)
Sgor na h-Ulaidh

N
0 km 1
0 miles 1

■ Sleeping
1 Ballachulish
2 Ballachulish House
3 Clachaig Inn
4 Isles of Glencoe
5 Kingshouse
6 Leacantium Farm Bunkhouse
7 Red Squirrel Campsite
8 SYHA Hostel

The Highlands and Skye

include heated pool, sauna and gym. The restaurant serves a mid-range to cheap 3-course lunch and expensive to mid-range 3-course dinner. **L** *Ballachulish Hotel*, in South Ballachulish by the bridge, T821582, F821463, reservations @mysteryworld.co.uk 54 rooms. Grand old hotel, handily placed for Glen Coe, Fort William or Oban; restaurant serves meals all day (3-course lunch mid-range to cheap; 3-course dinner expensive). **L** *Ballachulish House*, T811266, F811498, open Mar-Oct. 7 rooms. 200 yd beyond the *Ballachulish Hotel* on the A828 to Oban. This comfortable and elegant hotel/guesthouse is steeped in history and said to be the most haunted house in Scotland. The seat of the Stewarts of Ballachulish since the 16th century, this was where the final order for the Glencoe Massacre was signed (see below). Hospitality is second-to-none and the food is superb; even if you're not staying you can enjoy the experience of dining here (expensive), but book ahead. There's also a wide selection of cheaper B&Bs and guesthouses in the village, including the very good **E** *Fern Villa*, T811393.

Glen Coe

There are many spectacular places in the Scottish Highlands, but few, if any, can compare to the truly awesome scenery of Glen Coe. No one could fail to be moved by its haunting beauty, with imposing mountains, their tops often wreathed in cloud, rising steeply on either side from the valley floor. The brooding atmosphere of the landscape is only enhanced by the glen's tragic history. Once you've heard of the Glen Coe Massacre it sends a shiver down the spine every time you pass this way. Scotland's most famous glen is also one of the most accessible, with the A82 Glasgow to Fort William road running through it. Much of the area is owned by the National Trust for Scotland and virtually uninhabited, leaving huge tracts of glen and mountain which provide outstanding climbing and walking. There's also skiing at the Glencoe Ski Centre (see below), and canoeing on the River Coe and River Etive.

There's a small **National Trust for Scotland Visitor Centre** at the western end of the glen, about three miles south of Glencoe village. It shows a short video on the Glencoe Massacre and has a gift shop selling the usual stuff. ■ *Early Apr to mid-May and early Sep to end Oct daily 1000-1700; mid-May to end Aug 0930-1730. 50p. T811307.*

Binnein Mór

Na Gruagaichean (3,461ft)

Loch Eilde Mór

River Leven

Blackwater Reservoir

Dam

West Highland Way

Devil's Staircase

Altnafeadh

Rannoch Moor

A82 To Crianlarich & Glasgow

(3,032ft)

Buchaille Etive Mór (Great Shepherd of Etive)

(2,963ft)

Glen Etive

River Etive

Museum of Scottish Skiing & Cimbing

To Glencoe Ski Centre ▶

Glencoe Village

Phone code: 01855
Colour map 3, grid B6

At the western entrance to the glen, on the shores of Loch Leven, is Glencoe village, 16 miles south of Fort William just off the A82. There are several places to stay in and around the village, as well as a general store, post office and the thatched **Glencoe Folk Museum**, which has collections of costumes, military memorabilia, and domestic and farm tools and equipment. ■ *Late May to Sep 1000-1730. £1.50.*

Sleeping and eating About 3 miles south of the village, on the old road which leads from the village to the NTS visitor centre is **D** *Clachaig Inn*, T811252, inn@glencoe-scotland.co.uk 19 rooms. Good-value accommodation and one of the great Highland pubs. It's a favourite haunt of climbers and there's a lively atmosphere as well as some fine real ales and decent cheap food. There are also 3 chalets which can be rented on a weekly basis (phone for details), and mountain bike hire (see below).

On the same road, about 2 miles from the village, is the excellent **F** *SYHA Youth Hostel*, T811219. It's open all year and is very popular with climbers, so you should book ahead. Nearby are the **F** *Leacantium Farm Bunkhouses*, T811256, which offer cheap, basic accommodation in 2 bunkhouses and an alpine barn. The same people also run the *Red Squirrel Campsite* further along the road, which charges £3.50 per person per night.

There are several B&Bs and guesthouses in the village itself, including **E** *Scorrybreac Guesthouse*, T/F811354, john@tajones.demon.co.uk, open Dec-Oct; and on the outskirts of the village, at Upper Carnoch, is **E** *The Glencoe Guesthouse*, T811244. To the east of the village, on the shores of Loch Leven, you can camp at *Invercoe Caravans*, T/F811210.

At the east end of the glen, almost opposite the turn-off to the Glencoe Ski Centre, is **D** *Kingshouse Hotel*, T851259. 22 rooms. This is Scotland's oldest established inn and such a landmark that it even appears on maps, marked as 'hotel'. It's on the West Highland Way and is popular with hikers, climbers and skiers who frequently drop in for a refreshing drink in the bar and some good-value food. Apart from the places listed above, you can eat in the village at **C** *The Glencoe Hotel*, T811245, which serves cheap bar lunches and moderately priced 3-course dinner.

Sports **Cycle hire** *Glencoe Mountain Bike Centre* at the *Clachaig Inn* (see above); £12 for a full day, £8 for a half day.

Transport Highland *Country Buses* run several times daily from **Fort William** to Glencoe village (30 mins, £3.40). There are *Citylink* buses to **Glasgow** (2 ½ hrs) and **Fort William**. The daily *Postbus* service from **Fort William** to the *Kingshouse Hotel* and **Glen Etive** stops at the Glencoe crossroads.

Climbing & hiking in Glen Coe

OS Landranger No 41

Glen Coe offers some of Britain's most challenging climbing and hiking, with some notoriously treacherous routes and unpredictable weather conditions that claim lives every year. The routes described below are some of the least strenuous, but you'll still need a map, good boots, warm clothing, food and water, and you should take the usual precautions (see page 60).

One of the most popular walks is the relatively straightforward hike up to the **Lost Valley**, a secret glen where the ill-fated MacDonalds hid the cattle they'd stolen. Allow around three hours for the return trip. Start from the car park by the large boulder (see map, page 477), opposite the distinctive **Three Sisters**. Head down to the valley floor and follow the gravel path which leads down to a wooden bridge across the River Coe. Cross the bridge and follow the path up and over the stile. From here there's a choice of two routes. The less obvious route heads right and offers an easier climb into the valley. This eventually meets the lower, well-worn track, which involves a bit of scrambling but is more

The Glen Coe Massacre

Glen Coe is probably best known as the scene of one of the most shameful and notorious incidents in Scottish history.

Following his succession to the throne, William III wanted all the clans to swear an oath of allegiance by 1 January 1692. After much hesitation, the Jacobite clans of the West Highlands agreed to do so. However, MacIain of Glencoe, chief of a small branch of the MacDonalds, was not only late in setting off on the journey, but mistakenly went to Fort William to sign, instead of Inveraray. By the time he reached Inveraray it was 6 January and the deadline had passed.

The government decided that the rebellious clan be punished, in order to set an example to other clans, some of whom had not taken the oath. A company of 120 soldiers, under the command of Cambell of Glenlyon, were sent to Glen Coe and, since their leader was related by marriage to MacIain, the troops were billeted in

MacDonald homes, in keeping with the long-standing Highland tradition of hospitality.

There they stayed for almost two weeks, until the cold-blooded order came through to '. . . put all to the sword under seventy'. And so, on a cold winter's night, in the early hours of 13 February 1692, the Campbells ruthlessly slaughtered their hosts. MacIain and 37 men, women and children were slain in their beds, while many others fled into the hills, only to die of hunger and exposure. It was a bloody incident which had deep repercussions and proved to be the beginning of the end of the Highland way of life.

There's a monument to the fallen MacDonalds in the village of Glencoe, where members of the clan still gather on 13 February each year. For a powerful and evocative account of the Massacre, you should read Glencoe *by John Prebble (Penguin).*

---

exciting as it follows the rushing waters of the **Allt Coire Gabhail**. The upper and lower paths meet a few miles further up and here you cross the river by some stepping stones. Proceed up the steep scree slope till you reach the rim of the Lost Valley, where many of the MacDonalds fled on the night of the infamous massacre. Once in the valley there are great views of **Bidean nam Bian**, **Gearr Aonach** and **Beinn Fhada** and you can continue for a further 20-30 minutes to the head of the valley. From here it's possible to climb Bidean, but you'll need to be fit, experienced and well equipped.

Glen Coe also offers one of the world's classic ridge walks, the **Aonach Eagach**. It's not for the inexperienced or faint-hearted as there are some fairly exposed pinnacles. The ridge runs almost the entire length of the glen, starting at **Am Bodach** and ending at **Sgor nam Fiannaidh**. Don't make the mistake of descending from the last summit straight down to the Clachaig Inn. This is not the correct route.

Another difficult route is to the summit of **Buachaille Etive Mór**, one of the most photographed mountains in Scotland and one you'll probably recognize immediately the first time you see it from the A82 on the way to or from Glencoe. The mountain is best viewed from the *Kingshouse Hotel* and the route starts from Altnafeadh, a couple of miles west of the hotel. This is also the start or finish point for the fairly easy half-day walk over the **Devil's Staircase**, which is part of the **West Highland Way** (for a description of the route, see page 475).

Glen Etive runs southwest from the hotel. It's a very beautiful and little-visited place, and great for wild camping. There's a postbus service once a day from Fort William.

Finally, there are some short, pleasant walks around **Glencoe Lochan**, an artificial loch created in the mid-19th century by Lord Strathcona for his

The Highlands and Skye

Glencoe Ski Centre

The Glencoe Ski Centre is just over a mile from the Kingshouse Hotel, on the other side of the A82, on **Meall A'Bhuiridh** *(3,636 ft). This is Scotland's oldest ski centre, established in 1956, and remains one of the best, with the longest single descent. At the base station is the* **Museum of Scottish Skiing and Climbing** *where you can see the ice axe used by Chris Bonnington, among other things. It's open May-September daily 0900-1700. There's also a restaurant and café. The chair lift operates daily 0930-1700. A full day pass, including lifts, costs £17 (children £9.50). There's also a combined five-day pass for Glencoe and Nevis Range. T851226, glencoe@sol.co.uk, www.ski.scotland.net*

homesick Canadian wife. Take the left turning off the minor road to the youth hostel just beyond the bridge over the River Coe. There's a choice of three walks of between 40 minutes and an hour, all detailed at the car park.

Mountain guides *Hadrian Mountaineering*, 19b Carnoch, T/F811472, www.glencoe-mountain-sport.co.uk *Glencoe Guides*, T811402. *Dave Hanna*, Ardarroch, Ballachulish, T811620.

Ardgour, Ardnamurchan and Morvern

Colour map 3, grid B4/5

West of Fort William is one of the most remote parts of the Highland region, stretching south from **Loch Ailort** *to the* **Morvern Peninsula***, and west to the wild and beautiful* **Ardnamurchan Peninsula***. This lonely, southwestern corner features a dramatic landscape of rugged mountains, desolate moorland and near-deserted glens, fringed by a coastline of sparkling white beaches and clear turquoise seas with wonderful views across to the isles of Mull and Skye. This is one of the least-populated areas in Britain, mainly due to the legacy of the Highland Clearances in the mid-19th century, when whole communities were evicted by landlords in favour of more profitable sheep.*

With so few people around, this is an area noted for its wildlife, with a huge variety of birds and animals, such as deer, pine martens, wildcats and eagles. If you have both the time and the energy, it's worth exploring on foot. There's a series of footpaths throughout the area, particularly around Ardnamurchan.

Ins and outs

Getting there & getting around
30 walks in the area are listed in a local guide book available at tourist offices. You should also have OS Map numbers 40, 47 and 49, which cover the area

It's an area of few roads. Once you leave the A830 Fort William to Mallaig road, **buses** are few and far between, so it's not easy to get around quickly without your own transport. *Shiel Buses*, T01967-431272, run most of the bus services. There's a bus once a day on Tue, Thu and Sat from Fort William to Lochaline (2 hrs), via the **Corran Ferry**. There's a bus once a day (Mon-Sat) from Fort William to Acharacle (1 hr 30 mins, £4.25), via Lochailort. There's also a bus (Mon-Fri) to Acharacle from Mallaig (1 hr 30 mins). There's a bus once a day (Mon-Sat) from Fort William to Kilchoan (2 hrs 25 mins, £5), via Strontian (1 hr, £2.70), Salen and Glenborrodale.

For details of the **ferry** from Lochaline to Fishnish on Mull and from Kilchoan to Tobermory, see page 291. If you're travelling by **car**, access is via the A861, leaving the A830 before Glenfinnan or at Lochailort. You can also make the 5-min ferry crossing to Ardgour from the Corran Ferry, about 8 miles south of Fort William on the A82, see page 474.

Ardgour

The name Ardgour means 'height of the goats', and you can still see feral goats in this huge, sparsely populated wilderness bordered by Loch Shiel, Loch Eil, Loch Linnhe and Loch Sunart. Access is via the A861 south from Kinlocheil, or on the Corran Ferry to the tiny lochside villages of **Corran** and **Clovulin**. There's accommodation here at **D-E** *The Inn at Ardgour*, T01855-841225.

The attractive little village of Strontian on the shores of Loch Sunart gave its name to the element strontium, which was first discovered in the nearby lead mines in 1790. These now-abandoned mines also produced most of the lead shot used in the Napoleonic wars. Strontian is the largest settlement in these parts and has a couple of shops, a post office and a **Tourist Information Centre**; open April to October Monday-Friday 0900-1700, Saturday 1000-1600 and Sunday 1000-1400. T402131.

Strontian
Phone code: 01967
Colour map 3, grid B5

About two miles north of the village is the **Ariundle Nature Reserve**, which offers a pleasant two-hour nature trail through the glen and a 40-minute forest walk.

Sleeping Strontian has a couple of good hotels. The luxurious **L-A** *Kilcamb Lodge Hotel*, T402257, F402041, open Mar-Nov, stands in its own grounds on the lochside and serves superb food. There are several B&Bs, including the very comfortable **E** *Kinloch House*, T402138, open Jan-Nov.

Morvern

Just east of Strontian the A884 leads south through the bleak, desolate landscape of Morvern to the tiny remote community of **Lochaline** on the Sound of Mull, departure point for the *CalMac* ferry to **Fishnish**.

Phone code: 01967

About three miles before Lochaline is the turning left for the track which leads down the side of Loch Aline to the 14th-century ruins of **Ardtornish Castle**. First you'll come to **Kinlochaline Castle** (keys available at the cottage) and **Ardtornish House**. This house stands on the site of the original house, which was visited on several occasions by Florence Nightingale, who was a family member of the original owners. The author John Buchan spent many summers here in the 1930s. There's a path which leads from the estate office uphill across open moorland for an hour till it reaches **Loch Tearnait**. In the centre of the loch is a 1,500 year-old crannog, an artificial island built for defensive purposes. This walk is detailed in the tourist board's *Great Walks* leaflet, along with the Ariundle Nature Trail, available from local tourist offices. During the stalking season (1 July-20 October) check at the estate office before setting out.

If you want to stay in Lochaline, there are a couple of **B&Bs** and the **L** *Lochaline Hotel*, T421657, which serves decent bar meals. There's also a **scuba diving school** at the ferry pier, T421627.

Sleeping

Ardnamurchan Peninsula

The main places of interest in this area are to be found on the rugged Ardnamurchan peninsula, the end of which is the most westerly point on the British mainland.

The Highlands and Skye

The winding A861 runs west from Strontian along the north shore of Loch Sunart to **Salen**, where the single-track B8007 branches west and runs all the way out to the tip of the peninsula. The A861 meanwhile turns north to **Acharacle**. There's accommodation at Salen in the E *Salen Hotel,* T431661, salenhotel@aol.com, where you can also get food (cheap to mid-range) and information on local walks. A mile or so east of Salen, at **Resipole**, you can pitch a tent at the *Resipole Farm Caravan Park*, T431235. There's also a restaurant and bar on site.

Glenborrodale & Glenmore
Phone code: 01972
Colour map 3, grid B4

The first settlement you reach heading west out to Ardnamurchan Point is Glenborrodale. Before you reach the tiny hamlet look out on the left for the castellated late-Victorian towers of Glenborrodale Castle, once the property of a certain Jesse Boot, who founded a chain of chemist shops which you may have heard of.

Just west of Glenborrodale is the excellent **Glenmore Natural History Centre**, local photographer Michael McGregor's interactive exhibition which features some of his most stunning photographs of local wildlife. The centre is designed to interact with the environment and there's live video action of the surrounding wildlife, including pine martens, birds and even fish in the nearby river. It's a great place for kids, and adults too. There's also a café serving snacks, and a bookshop. ■ *Apr-Oct 1030-1730 (Sun 1200-1730). Adult £2.50, concession £2, children £1.50. T500254.*

A mile to the east is the **RSPB Reserve** where you can see golden eagles, otters and seals. You can take a two-hour wildlife trip to the **seal colonies** – or further afield to Tobermory on Mull or Staffa and the Treshnish Islands – with *Ardnamurchan Charters*, T500208, or T01967-431263.

A few miles west of the centre, the B8007 turns away from the coast. Here you'll see the beautiful bay of **Camas nan Geall**. It's worth stopping at the car park to admire the fantastic views, or take the path down to the beach. A great place to stay in Glenborrodale is C *Feorag House*, T500248, F500285. Between Glenborrodale and Kilchoan, a road runs to the north coast of the peninsula and the beautiful beaches at **Fascadale**, **Kilmory** and **Ockle**.

Kilchoan
Phone code: 01972
Colour map 3, grid B4

The straggling crofting village of Kilchoan is the main settlement on Ardnamurchan. Shortly after passing the sign for the village, you can turn left to the scenic ruin of **Mingary Castle**, built around the 13th century. There's a **Tourist Information Centre** here which provides information on local scenic walks and will help with accommodation. It's open Easter-October Monday-Saturday 0900-1845, Sunday 1030-1715. T510222. A car and passenger **ferry** leaves Kilchoan for Tobermory on Mull. It sails mid-April to mid-October and the crossing takes 35 minutes (see page 291).

Sleeping There's a decent selection of accommodation. B *Far View Cottage*, T510357, www.ardamurchan.com/farview Open Mar-Nov. Superior and friendly B&B with great views and excellent food (mid-range; also for non-residents, but booking essential). B *Meall Mo Chridhe*, T/F510328. Open Apr-Oct. A beautiful 18th-century converted manse with great sea views and fine cooking. Full board also available (**A**). Dinner available for non-residents (expensive), but booking essential. A cheaper option is **E** *Doirlinn House*, T/F510209. A few miles beyond the village, on the road to Ardnamurchan Point, is **D** *Sonachan Hotel*, T/F510211, darie@sonachan.u-net.com You can get lunch (1200-1430; cheap) and dinner (1800-2000; mid-range) at the **C** *Kilchoan House Hotel*, T510200.

Beyond Kilchoan the road leads to the **lighthouse** at mainland Britain's most westerly point, with stunning views (on a clear day) across to the small isles of Rùm, Eigg, Muck and Canna, with the Cuillins of Skye rising behind Rùm. The former lighthouse was designed by Alan Stevenson, father of Robert Louis, and built in 1849. The buildings have been converted into the **Ardnamurchan Visitor Centre**, where you can learn about the history and workings of lighthouses. There's also self-catering accommodation, a café and gift shop. ■ *1 Apr-31 Oct daily from 1000-1800 (1700 in Oct). Adult £2.50, concession/children £1.50. T510210.*

A mile northwest of Kilchoan a road branches to the right to the beautiful long, white beach at **Sanna Bay**. It's worth making the trip here just to walk on the beach, but this is also a good place to spot whales and dolphins. On the road to Sanna Bay is the tiny settlement of **Achnaha**, which is famed for its rare 'ring-dyke' system, a huge, natural rock formation which is the crater of an extinct volcano. You can stay in Achnaha, at **E-F** *Hillview*, T510322.

You'll need your own transport to reach Ardnamurchan Point and Sanna Bay as there are no buses beyond Kilchoan (see 'Getting around' above).

North of Salen on the A861 is the scattered crofting township of Acharacle, at the western end of Loch Shiel surrounded by rolling hills. A couple of miles to the west a road leads to beautiful **Kentra Bay**. Cross the wooden bridge, follow the footpath round the side of Kentra Bay and then follow the signs for Gortenfearn, where you'll find the famous '**singing sands**'. Not only is the beach music to the ears as you walk its length, but the view across to Skye and the small isles is a feast for the eyes.

Three miles north of Acharacle is **Loch Moidart**. Here, perched on a rocky promontory in the middle of the loch, is the 13th-century ruin of **Castle Tioram** (pronounced 'Cheerum'), one of Scotland's most romantic and atmospheric castles. This was the seat of the MacDonalds of Clanranald, until it was destroyed by their chief in 1715 to prevent it from falling into Hanoverian hands while he was away fighting for the Jacobites. There are plans to restore the castle, but you can visit it (free) via the sandy causeway that connects it to the mainland at low tide.

Sleeping The village has several shops, a post office, garage and plenty of places to stay. **C** *Loch Shiel House Hotel*, T431224, F431200. 10 rooms. Comfortable and decent bar meals (cheap lunch; mid-range to cheap dinner). Contact them for details of cruises on Loch Shiel. A couple of good B&Bs are **C** *Belmont House*, T431266; and **D-E** *Ardshealach House*, T431301; open Apr-Sep. Food is also available at the *Clanranald Hotel*, at Mingarry, T431202. About 5 miles east of the village, on a side road off the A861 north to Lochailort and Mallaig, is the very beautiful **D** *Dalilea House*, T431253; open Apr-Oct.

Sports From Dalilea Pier you can cross to The *Achnanellan Centre*, T431265, an outdoor activities centre on the south shore of Loch Shiel at the foot of **Beinn Resipol** (2,772 ft). They hire out mountain bikes, canoes, sail boats and camping equipment, as well as providing cheap, basic bunkhouse accommodation (**F**). It was from Dalilea Pier that Bonnie Prince Charlie left to sail up Loch Shiel to raise his standard at Glenfinnan (see over page).

Ardnamurchan Point & Sanna Bay
Phone code: 01972
Colour map 3, grid B3

Acharacle & Castle Tioram
Phone code: 01967
Colour map 3, grid B4

The Highlands and Skye

The Road to the Isles

*The 46-mile stretch of the A830 from **Fort William** to **Mallaig** is known as 'The Road to the Isles'. It's a very beautiful journey, particularly by train (see page 470), through a landscape that resonates with historical significance. This is Bonnie Prince Charlie country, where the ill-fated Jacobite Rising not only began, but also ended, with the Prince's flight to France.*

Glenfinnan
Phone code: 01397
Colour map 3,
grid B4

It all started on 19 August 1745 at Glenfinnan, 19 miles west of Fort William at the head of Loch Shiel. Less than a month earlier, Prince Charles Edward Stuart had landed on the Scottish mainland for the first time, on the shores of Loch nan Uamh, between Lochailort and Arisaig (see below). He had come to claim the British throne for his father, James, son of the exiled King James VII of Scotland and II of England.

The clan chiefs had expected French support, but when the Prince arrived with only a handful of men they were reluctant to join the cause. Undeterred, the prince raised his standard and his faith was soon rewarded when he heard the sound of the pipes and Cameron of Lochiel, along with 800 men, came marching down the valley to join them. It must have been an incredible moment.

There's a powerful sense of history here. You don't have to be Scottish to feel a shiver run down the spine and a tear well in the eye as you gaze across stunning Loch Shiel stretching into the distance, veiled by steep mountains. You can almost hear the wail of the bagpipes in the distance. A commemorative **tower** stands proudly at the head of the loch, erected in 1815 by Alexander MacDonald of Glenaladale in memory of the clansmen who fought and died for the Prince. You can climb to the top of the tower (mind your head, though) for even better views down the loch. The Glenfinnan Games are held here in mid-August.

On the other side of the road is the National Trust for Scotland **visitor centre**, which has displays and an audio programme of the Prince's campaign, from Glenfinnan to its grim conclusion at Culloden. There's also a café. ■ *1 Apr-18 May and 1 Sep-31 Oct daily 1000-1700; 19 May-31 Aug 0930-1800. Adult £1.50, concession £1. T722250.*

A mile away, in Glenfinnan village, is the **Station Museum**, which is housed in the railway station on the magnificent Fort-William to Mallaig railway line. It has displays of memorabilia from the line's 100-year history. ■ *Apr-Oct daily 0930-1630. £0.50. T722295.* You can also sleep and eat here (see below). The 1,000-ft span of the **Glenfinnan viaduct**, between the visitor centre and the village, is one of the most spectacular sections of the famous **West Highland Railway** (see page 470).

You can take a cruise down Loch Shiel, from Glenfinnan to Acharacle (see above) at its southern end. Contact *Loch Shiel Cruises* at the *Glenfinnan House Hotel* (see below). There are sailings most days from April to October.

Sleeping and eating On the main road, half a mile past the monument on the right, heading west, is **A** *The Prince's House*, T722246, F722307, princeshouse@ glenfinnan.co.uk 9 rooms, open Mar-Nov. Comfortable old coaching inn which offers good food (mid-range). Just off the main road is **B-C** *Glenfinnan House Hotel*, T/F722235. 17 rooms, open Apr-Oct. Historic house with lots of charm, which is more than can be said for the staff. Overpirced. Dinner served from 1930 (expensive to mid-range for 4 courses). You can also walk in the vast grounds or fish on the loch. A much cheaper option is the **F** *Glenfinnan Sleeping Car*, at the train station, T722400. Bunkhouse accommodation for 10 people, also mountain bike hire. You can eat here, too, in the *Glenfinnan Dining Car* (cheap 2-course lunch; mid-range 3-course dinner).

About 10 miles west of Glenfinnan the road passes through the village of Lochailort, where the A861 branches south to the remote Ardnamurchan Peninsula (see above). There's accommodation and food here at the **D** *Lochailort Inn*, T470208, open March-October.

Lochailort
Phone code: 01687
Colour map 3,
grid B5

A couple of miles further on, is **Loch nan Uamh**, where Prince Charles first landed on the Scottish mainland and from where, a year later, he fled for France following the disastrous defeat at Culloden (see page 451). A path leads down from the car park to the **Prince's Cairn**, which marks the beginning and the end of the Jacobite cause.

At the western end of the Morar Peninsula is the little village of Arisaig, scattered round a sandy bay. This was the birthplace of Long John Silver, who worked on the construction of the nearby lighthouse at Barrahead, which happened to be one of many such lighthouses designed by the father of Robert Louis Stevenson. Silver met Robert Louis on a few occasions, and so impressed the young writer that he immortalized him in his classic novel *Treasure Island*.

Arisaig & Morar
Phone code: 01687
Colour map 3, grid A4

There are some nice beaches around, and the road west from the village out to the **Rhue Peninsula** is great for seal spotting. You can also take a **cruise** from Arisaig to the islands of **Rùm, Eigg** and **Muck**. ■ *There are sailings daily Mon-Fri, and also Sat-Sun during the summer months. For details contact Murdo Grant, T450224. See also page 316.*

Between Arisaig and Morar is a string of glorious beaches of white sand backed by beautiful machair, washed by turquoise seas and enjoying magnificent views across to Rùm and the Cuillins of Skye. This is one of the most stunning stretches of coastline in Britain, despite the presence of too many ugly holiday bungalows and caravan sites. Eight miles north of Arisaig is **Morar**, where the famous beach scenes from the movie *Local Hero* were filmed – with not a caravan in sight.

This coastline gets very busy in summer but, like so much of the Highlands, it's easy to get away from it all. A single-track road leads up behind the village of Morar to dark, mysterious **Loch Morar**, the deepest inland loch in the country and home of Morag, Scotland's other, lesser-known monster. Two locals reported seeing her in August 1969 and a scientific investigation two years later uncovered a remarkable number of eye-witness accounts. You could always try to elicit further information from the locals over a wee dram in the bar of the *Morar Hotel*. The road runs along the north shore of the loch for three miles till it reaches the pretty little hamlets of **Bracora** and **Bracorina**. Here the road stops, but a footpath continues all the way to **Tarbet** on the shores of Loch Nevis, from where it's possible to catch a boat back to Mallaig (see below). It takes about three hours to walk to Tarbet (where there's now a bothy), and you'll need to get there by 1530 for the boat.

Sleeping and eating Arisaig has plenty of accommodation and a decent range of services. There are several hotels, including **B** *Arisaig Hotel*, T450210, arisaighotel @dial.pipex.com They serve moderately priced food 1200-1400 and 1800-2100. A good restaurant is *The Old Library Lodge*, T450651, open Apr-Oct, which also has rooms (**B**).

The Highlands and Skye

Mallaig

Phone code: 01687
Colour map 3,
grid A4

The end of the road is Mallaig, a busy fishing port and main departure point for the ferry to Skye. It's not a particularly appealing place, but it's always busy with people waiting for the ferry or the train to Fort William. Mallaig is a small place, huddled round its harbour, and the train and bus stations and *CalMac* ferry office are all within a few yards of each other. Also close by are banks with ATMs and the post office.

Ins & outs

Bus *Shiel Buses*, T01967-431272, run 2 buses daily Mon-Sat from Mallaig to **Fort William** (1½ hrs, £4.50) from Jul-Sep, and on Mon, Thu and Fri the rest of the year.

Ferry *CalMac*, T462403, ferries run throughout the year to **Armadale** on Skye (see page 537), to **Lochboisdale** and **Castlebay** (see page 560), and to the **Small Isles** (see page 486). *Bruce Watt Sea Cruises*, T462320, have trips to the remote village of **Inverie**, on the Knoydart Peninsula (see below), and **Tarbet** on Loch Nevis (see above). They sail on Mon, Wed and Fri throughout the year, departing at 1015 (to Inverie only) and 1415, and returning at 1155 and 1745. They also sail on Sat during Jun-Aug to Inverie, departing at 1030 and returning at 1215.

Train The best way to arrive in Mallaig is by train. There are several services daily (1 on Sun) to and from **Fort William**, with connections to **Glasgow** (see page 470). There's also a steam train which runs in the summer months (see page 470).

The **Tourist Information Centre** is by the harbour, T462170. Apr-Oct Mon-Sat 0900-2000, Sun 1000-1700; Nov-Mar Mon, Tue, Fri 1100-1500.

Sights

Great views over the Sound of Sleat from the indoor swimming pool at the top of Frank Brae (open daily)

If you have some time to kill you could visit **Mallaig Marine World**, an aquarium with indigenous marine creatures as well as displays on the history of the local fishing industry. ■ *Jun-Sep Mon-Sat 0900-2100, Sun 1000-1800; Oct-May Mon-Sat 1200-1730. £2.75, children £1.35. T462292.* Beside the train station is the **Mallaig Heritage Centre**, with interesting descriptions of the local Clearances, the railway line and the fishing industry. ■ *May-Sep Mon-Sat 0930-1700, Sun 1300-1700. £1.80, children £1.*

For something a bit more energetic, there are a couple of good walks around the village. An easy one, which should take around 45 minutes, goes to the little village of **Mallaig Bheag** (Mallaigviag), further east along the coast. Just before the car park at the eastern end of the harbour you'll see a sign, on the right as you head east, which points you towards the old road to Mallaig Bheag. Follow the path up behind the houses and continue into a small glen behind the hill that overlooks the port. The path then rises gradually till you're rewarded with great views of Loch Nevis. It continues through Mallaig Bheag then joins up with the main road back to Mallaig. Follow this till the end of the row of houses on your right, turn right and then left and back down to Mallaig bay and the start of the walk.

Sleeping & eating

C *Marine Hotel*, T462217, Marinehotel@btinternet Next to the train station and much nicer inside than it appears. Their restaurant also serves the best food in town (mid-range). Follow the road round the harbour to East Bay, where you'll find the excellent-value **E-F** *Western Isles Guesthouse*, T/F462320, open Jan-Nov, which serves dinner to guests. Nearby is **E** *Glencairn*, T462412, open Apr-Sep. There are lots of other **B&Bs** to choose from. The cheapest place to stay is **F** *Sheena's Backapackers Lodge*, T462764, a friendly, easy-going independent hostel, with dorm beds, double rooms and kitchen facilities.

The *Cabin Seafood Restaurant* serves cheap to mid-range main courses and a great value 'teatime special'. The *Cornerstone Café* also does cheap meals and snacks, but cheapest of the lot is the cafetería in the *Fisherman's Mission* at the pier.

Knoydart Peninsula

The Knoydart Peninsula, the most remote and unspoilt region in Britain and one of Europe's last great wildernesses, literally lies between Heaven and Hell, for it is bordered to the north by **Loch Hourn** ('Loch of Hell') and to the south by **Loch Nevis** ('Loch of Heaven'). It can only be reached on foot or by boat and consequently attracts walkers, who can wander for days around a network of trails without seeing another soul.

Colour map 3, grid A5

A 2-day **hiking** route starts from Kinloch Hourn, reached by bus from Invergarry (see page 461). The trail winds its way around the coast to Barrisdale and on to Inverie. Another route into Knoydart starts from the west end of Loch Arkaig (see page 464) and runs through Glen Dessarry. Both are tough hikes and only for fit, experienced and well-equipped hill walkers.

An easier way in is by **boat**. *Bruce Watt Sea Cruises* sail from Mallaig to Inverie (see above). There's also a ferry service from **Arnisdale**, on the north shore of Loch Hourn, to Barrisdale. To arrange a crossing, contact Len Morrison, Croftfoot, Arnisdale, T01599-522352. It's a small open boat which takes 5 passengers, and all sailings are subject to weather.

Ins & outs
As mentioned above, the only way in is by boat or on foot

The peninsula's only settlement of any size is tiny Inverie, with just 60 inhabitants. It's the only village in Scotland which can't be reached by road, but still has a post office, a shop, a few places to stay and Britain's most remote pub.

Inverie
Phone code: 01867

The only **guesthouse** is **C** *Pier House*, T462347, which offers good, old-fashioned hospitality and wonderful local seafood (mid-range prices). A cheaper option is **F** *Torrie Shieling*, T462669. It's a bit more expensive than most other hostels, but is very comfortable, and popular with hikers. They also have their own transport for trips around the peninsula and will collect guests from Mallaig by arrangement. The only alternative is the much cheaper, but less appealing **F** *Knoydart Hostel*, T462242, near Inverie House. Another place to eat is *The Old Forge*, T462267, the most remote pub on mainland Britain. You can enjoy some tasty local seafood and a pint of real ale in front of an open fire. There's even the occasional impromptu ceilidh.

Three or four miles up the peninsula's only road is the highly recommended **B** *Doune Stone Lodge*, T462667, standing in splendid isolation. The minimum stay is 3 nights as guests are picked up from Mallaig by boat.

The Great Glen to Kyle of Lochalsh

The A87 is one of the main Highland tourist routes, connecting the Great Glen with the west coast and the Isle of Skye. It runs west from Invergarry between Fort Augustus and Fort William, through Glen Moriston and Glen Shiel to Shiel Bridge, at the head of Loch Duich, and on to Kyle. At Shiel Bridge a road branches off to Glenelg, from where you can sail across to Skye. It's a beautiful journey and by far the best way to reach the island.

The journey from Invergarry to **Shiel Bridge** is worth it for the views alone. Glen Shiel is a spectacular sight, with 3,000 ft-high peaks soaring up on either side. This is one of the most popular hiking areas in Scotland, with the

Glen Shiel
Colour map 3, grid A5

The Highlands and Skye

e magnificent and much-photographed **Five Sisters of Kintail** on the north side of the glen, and the equally beautiful **South Glen Shiel Ridge** on the other.

There are several excellent hiking routes in Glen Shiel, but these mountains are to be treated with great respect. They require fitness, experience and proper equipment and planning. None of the routes should be attempted without a map, compass and detailed route instructions. You should be aware of the notoriously unpredictable weather conditions and also check locally about deer stalking. The season runs from August to October, but for more details contact the local stalkers (T01599-511282, or T01320-340262). A good trekking guide is the SMC's *Hill Walks in Northwest Scotland*.

The **Five Sisters Traverse** is a classic ridge route. It starts at the first fire break on the left as you head southeast down the glen from Shiel Bridge and finishes at Morvich, on the other side of the ridge. Allow a full day (eight to 10 hours). You can also hike from Morvich to *Glen Affric Youth Hostel* at Cannich. It's a strenuous 20-mile walk, but you can stop off midway at the remote *Allt Beithe Youth Hostel* (see page 455).

The magnificent **South Glen Shiel Ridge** is one of the world's great hikes. It starts from above the *Cluanie Inn* (see below). From here, follow the old public road to Tomdoun which meets up with a good stalking path which climbs to the summit of the first Munro, **Creag a' Mhaim** (3,108 ft). The ridge then runs west for almost nine miles and gives you the chance to pick off no fewer than seven Munros. Allow a full day for the walk (nine to 10 hours), and you'll need to set off early.

Sleeping About 9 miles east of Shiel Bridge is one of the Highlands' classic hotels, the **C** *Cluanie Inn*, T0320-340238. It's a firm favourite with hikers and climbers and it's easy to see why. After a hard day's ridge walking, what could be better than jumping into the jacuzzi, then having a hot dinner and a good pint beside a log fire. You can also camp nearby, but why deny yourself the pleasure if you can afford it?

A less salubrious option is the **F** *Ratagan Youth Hostel*, T01599-511243, just outside Shiel Bridge. It's also popular with hikers, and is open all year except Jan. You can **camp** at *Morvich Caravan Club Site*, T01599-511354, open late Mar to late Oct; or at Shiel Bridge, T01599-511211.

Transport *Citylink* buses between Fort William, Inverness and Skye pass through Glen Shiel several times daily in each direction. There's a *Postbus* service between Kyle and Glenelg (see below) and **Highland Country Buses** run from *Ratagan Youth Hostel* to Kyle (30 mins) and on to Plockton (50 mins), on schooldays only, departing at 0755 and returning at 1640.

Glenelg

One of the most beautiful journeys in Scotland is the road from Shiel Bridge to the picturesque little village of Glenelg on the Sound of Sleat, only a short distance opposite Kylerhea on Skye.

The unclassified single-track road turns off the A87 and climbs steeply and dramatically through a series of sharp switchbacks to the top of the **Mam Ratagan Pass** (1,115 ft). From here the view back across Loch Duich to the Five Sisters of Kintail is simply amazing, and the all-time classic calendar shot.

The road then drops down through Glen More to Glenelg, the main settlement on the peninsula, which lies on the old drovers' route which ran from Skye to the cattle markets in the south. This little-known corner of the Western Highlands is Gavin Maxwell country and was featured in *Ring of Bright Water*, his novel about otters. He disguised the identity of this beautiful, unspoiled stretch of coastline, calling it Camusfearna, and today it remains a quiet backwater.

You can see the famous otters at **Sandaig**, on the road running from Glenelg, where Gavin Maxwell lived. The site of his cottage is now marked with a cairn. As well as otters, you can see numerous seabirds, seals and porpoises in the Sound of Sleat, and around the peninsula you may be lucky enough to catch a glimpse of wildcats, pine martens, golden eagles and the recently reintroduced sea eagles.

The village itself consists of a row of whitewashed cottages surrounded by trees and overlooked by the ruins of the 18th-century Bernera Barracks. It's worth stopping in Glenelg, if you've got the time, to experience a night in the wonderfully cosy **E** *Glenelg Inn*, T522273. Even if you can't spend the night, at least spend an hour or two enjoying the atmosphere, good ale and fine seafood. It's one of those places that almost makes you glad it's raining.

Just before the village the road forks. The right turning leads to the **Glenelg-Kylerhea ferry**, which makes the five-minute crossing to Skye. The tiny six-car ferry runs from April to October and is the most scenic and romantic route to the misty isle. For more details, see the Skye chapter (page 537).

A road runs south from Glenelg to Arnisdale. About a mile and a half along this road, a branch left leads to the **Glenelg Brochs** – Dun Telve and Dun Dun Troddan – two of the best-preserved Iron-Age buildings in the country. Dun Telve stands to a height of over 30 ft and the internal passages are almost intact.

The road south from Glenelg continues past Sandaig Bay and runs along the north shore of unearthly Loch Hourn, with great views across the mountains of Knoydart. The road ends at the impossibly cute little fishing hamlet of **Arnsidale**, from where you can take a boat across the loch to Barrisdale on the Knoydart peninsula. For details, see page 487. A bit further along the coast, the road ends at the even tinier hamlet of **Corran**, where there's B&B accommodation at **E-F** *Mrs Nash*.

Transport There's a *Postbus* service from **Kyle of Lochalsh** to **Arnisdale** and **Corran** via Glenelg at 0945 Mon-Sat. It takes 3 ¾ hrs. The return bus from Corran departs at 0725.

One of Scotland's most photographed sights is the stunningly located Eilean Donan, 10 miles west of Shiel Bridge on the A87. It stands on a tiny islet at the confluence of Loch Duich and Loch Alsh, joined to the shore by a narrow stone bridge and backed by high mountains. This great calendar favourite has also featured in several movies, including *Highlander*, which starred Sean Connery.

Eilean Donan Castle
Phone code: 01599
Colour map 3, grid A5

The original castle dates from 1230 when Alexander III had it built to protect the area from marauding Vikings. It was destroyed by King George in 1719 during its occupation by Spanish Jacobite forces sent to help the 'Old Pretender', James Stuart. It then lay in ruins, until one of the Macraes had it rebuilt between 1912 and 1932. Inside, the Banqueting Hall with its Pipers' Gallery is most impressive, and there's an exhibition of military regalia and interesting displays of the castle's history. The views from the battlements are also worthwhile. ■ *Apr-Oct daily 0900-1700. Adult £3.95, concession £3.20, group rates £2.95. T555202.*

The Highlands and Skye

Sleeping and eating There are several places to stay in the nearby village of **Dornie**. **D** *Dornie Hotel*, T555205, is a good option and serves very good food (mid-range). Just across the bridge is **D** *Loch Duich Hotel*, T555213. It offers comfortable accommodation, meals and live music in the bar on a Sun evening. There are several good **B&Bs**, including **E** *Tigh Tasgaidh*, T555242; and **F** *Fasgadale*, T588238. A cheaper place to stay is the 6-bed **F** *Silver Fir Bunkhouse*, Carndubh, T555264.

Aside from the hotels listed above, there are a couple of places in Dornie serving decent food. Across the bridge is *Jenny Js*, T555362, which is moderately priced but can be variable. There's also the *Clachan Pub* where you can enjoy a good-value 3-course evening meal.

Across the bridge is the turning right for Killilan, a tiny hamlet at the head of Loch Long. About ¾ of a mile up this road is the **B** *Conchra House Hotel*, T555233, conchra@aol.com 6 rooms. This historic 18th-century hunting lodge is peaceful, has lovely views and boasts a reputation for good food. At the end of this road, at Camas-luinie, is **F** *Tigh Iseabeal*, T588205, a 10-bed independent hostel.

Transport *Citylink* buses between **Fort William** and **Inverness** and **Skye** stop by the castle.

Kyle of Lochalsh

Phone code: 01599
Colour map 3, grid A5

Before the coming of the controversial Skye Bridge a mile to the north (see page 537), the little town of Kyle, as it is known, was the main ferry crossing to Skye and consequently a place which attracted a busy tourist trade. Now, though, the tourist traffic bypasses Kyle, which is probably the most sensible thing to do as it's not the most attractive of places. There are a couple of banks with ATMs, two small supermarkets and a post office in the village.

Ins & outs **Bus** *Scottish Citylink* buses, T0990-505050, run to Kyle from **Inverness** (3 daily, 2 hrs); **Glasgow** via **Fort William** (4 daily, 5 hrs); and **Edinburgh** via **Fort William** (1 daily, 6 ½ hrs). These buses continue to **Portree** (a further hour) and **Uig** (1½ hrs), for ferries to Tarbert on Harris and Lochmaddy on North Uist. There's also a regular shuttle service across the bridge to **Kyleakin** (every 30 mins).

Train The train journey from Inverness to Kyle, though not as spectacular as the West Highland line, is very scenic. It runs 3-4 times Mon-Sat (2 ½ hrs) and once or twice on Sun from May to Sep. There's also an observation car and dining car in the summer.

The **Tourist Information Centre**, which is at the main seafront car park, T534276. Apr, May and mid-Sep to late Oct Mon-Sat 0930-1730; Jun to mid-Jul and late Aug to mid-Sep Mon-Sat 0930-1900; mid-Jul to late Aug Mon-Sat 0930-2100, Sun 1230-1630.

There are a couple of interesting boat trips which you can take from here. One is on board the *Seaprobe Atlantis*, which is fitted with underwater windows allowing you to watch 'the world beneath the waves'. Check sailing times at the pier, or at If you prefer, you could take a **seafood cruise** – a 2½-hour wild-life-spotting and seafood-eating boat trip. Contact Neil MacRae, T577230.

Sleeping & eating It's a good idea to get the tourist office to book a room for you, as there's not a lot to choose from. There are a couple of hotels, most luxurious of which is the **B** *Lochalsh Hotel*, T534202, with great views across to Skye and good food. Three miles north, at Erbusaig, is the very comfortable **D** *Old Schoolhouse*, T534369, a B&B with a highly rated restaurant. A mile and a half north of Kyle is **E** *Crowlin View*, T534286. There's also cheap hostel accommodation at **F** *Cuchulainn's*, T534492, on Station Rd. 4 miles east of Kyle, at **Balmacara**, you can camp at *Reraig Caravan Site*, T566215.

Just outside the village, on the road to Plockton, is the *Seagreen Restaurant & Bookshop*, T534388, a bistro-cum-bookshop and gallery serving wholefood and local seafood throughout the day (mid-range to expensive). At the railway station is *The Seafood Restaurant*, T534813, which has a good reputation for seafood (mid-range to expensive); open Easter-Oct 1000-1500 and 1830-2100. Another option is the *Lochalsh Hotel*, which does very good bar lunches.

Plockton

If there were a poll taken of visitors' favourite Highland villages then you can bet your bottom dollar that Plockton would come top with most folk. If you look for a definition of picturesque in your dictionary, it'll say "see Plockton". Well, maybe not – but it should.

Phone code: 01599
Colour map 3, grid A4

Plockton's neat little painted cottages are ranged around the curve of a wooded bay, with flowering gardens and palm trees. Yachts bob up and down in the harbour and there are views across the island-studded waters of Loch Carron to the hills beyond. Even on the telly Plockton's charms proved irresistible, and millions of viewers tuned in each week to watch the TV series *Hamish Macbeth*, which featured Robert Carlyle as the local bobby.

There are lots of good walks around the village. One of the best ways to appreciate it is to head up to Frithard Hill, from where there are great views of the bay. Another good walk is along the beach, starting from the High School playing fields at the top of the village.

Plockton's a popular place with artists who are drawn by the village's setting and the wonderful light. A good place to find some of their work, as well as other souvenirs, is *The Studio Craft Shop*, on the corner of the seafront and the road leading out of town.

The best place to stay, and eat, is **C** *The Haven Hotel*, T544223, on Innes St. 15 rooms, open Feb-Dec. Good value and the food in the restaurant is quite superb (5-course dinner; expensive). Nearby is the cosy and comfortable **D** *Plockton Inn*, T544222. There are quite a few places on Harbour St along the waterfront, including the wonderful and busy **D** *Plockton Hotel*, T544274, which serves good food (mid-range) and has a great little beer garden at the front where you can sit and enjoy a drink on a balmy summer evening. There are lots of **B&Bs** to choose from and one of the nicest is the **E** *Shieling*, T544282, at the far end of the harbour. Also on the seafront is **E** *An Caladh*, T544356. There's cheaper accommodation at the **F** *Plockton Station Bunkhouse*, Nessun Dorma, Burnside, T544235.

A few miles out of Plockton, on the road to Achmore, is the **E** *Craig Highland Farm*, T544205, which offers B&B accommodation and self-catering cottages from £235 per week. The farm is also a conservation centre, where you can see and feed rare and ancient breeds of domestic animals. Apart from the hotels listed above, a good place to eat in Plockton is *Off the Rails*, T544423, at the railway station. It's open from 0830 for breakfast, snacks, lunch and evening meals (cheap to mid-range).

Sleeping & eating

A good way to see the local wildlife is to take a boat trip. *Leisure Marine*, T544306, runs one-hour seal- and otter-watching cruises in the summer for £3.50 per person. They also hire out boats. Similar trips are run by *Sea Trek Marine*, T544346.

Tours

The Highlands and Skye

Wester Ross

*From Loch Carron north to Ullapool, is the region of Wester Ross, an area of dramatic mountain massifs, fjord-like sea lochs and remote coastal villages. Here lies some of Europe's most spectacular scenery, from the isolated peninsula of **Applecross** to the mighty peaks of **Torridon**, which offer some of Scotland's best climbing and hillwalking. There are also gentler attractions such as the magnificent gardens at **Inverewe** and the beautiful pink sands of **Gruinard Bay**.*

East from Plockton

East of Plockton, just before the road meets the A890 at Achmore is the **West Highland Dairy**, where you can pick up some good local cheese for a picnic (if the weather's fine). The road passes the turn-off for **Stromeferry** and continues along the east shore of Loch Carron to **Strathcarron** at its northeastern end, on the Inverness to Kyle of Lochalsh rail line.

Sleeping There's **B&B** accommodation at **E** *The Shieling*, T01520-722364, open April-October, by the rail station; and at **F** *Achnashellach Hostel*, T01520-766232.

Transport There's a **postbus** service from Strathcarron to **Shieldaig** and **Torridon** twice a day Mon-Sat.

About a mile further on you come to a road junction. The A890 heads right (east) through Glen Carron to **Achnasheen**, where it meets the A832 nine miles east of **Kinlochewe**. The A832 then continues east till it meets the main A835 which connects **Ullapool** with the A9 north of **Inverness**. The A896 meanwhile heads left (west) to Lochcarron.

Lochcarron
Phone code: 01520
Colour map 1, grid C4
Population: 870

Lochcarron village consists of little more than a main street along the shore of the loch, but it has more facilities and services than most other places in these parts. Here you should take the opportunity to withdraw cash at the *Bank of Scotland* ATM, fill up with petrol and buy some supplies at the small self-service store. There's also a **Tourist Information Centre**, T722357, which will provide details of the many excellent walks in the surrounding hills; it's open April-October. For guided walks around Lochcarron, contact *Island Horizons*, Kirkton Road, T722238. Two miles south of the village on the road to the 15th-century ruins of **Strome Castle** is *Lochcarron Weavers*, where you can see tartan being made and also buy from a vast range of woven goods.

Sleeping and eating There's a wide range of accommodation and several places to eat. Best of the bunch is the **D** *Rockvilla Hotel & Restaurant*, T722379, rockvilla@btinternet.com This small, family-run hotel offers very good food at cheap-mid-range prices. There are lots of B&Bs, including **E** *Bank House*, T722332, in the same building as the Bank of Scotland. About 5 mins' drive from the village, across the loch on the A890, is the excellent *Carron Restaurant*, T722488, mid-range prices.

Applecross
Phone code: 01520
Colour map 1, grid C4

West of Lochcarron at Loch Kishorn, a side road leaves the A896 and heads to Applecross. There are many scenic routes in the Highlands but this one beats them all. The **Bealach na Ba** ('Pass of the Cattle') is the highest road in Scotland and is often closed during the winter snows. It climbs relentlessly and dramatically through a series of tortuous switchbacks – both spectacular and terrifying in equal measure. The high plateau, at 2,053 ft, is cold and desolate, but from here you have the most stunning views: from Ardnamurchan

Peninsula to Loch Torridon, taking in Eigg, Rùm, the Cuillins of Skye, the Old Man of Storr and the Quirang.

The narrow, single-track road then begins its gradual descent to the isolated little village of Applecross, site of one Scotland's first Christian monasteries, founded in 673 AD. The village consists of a row of whitewashed fishermen's cottages looking across to the island of Raasay and backed by wooded slopes. It's a beautifully tranquil place where you can explore beaches and rock pools or enjoy a stroll along sylvan lanes.

Sleeping and eating The reason many people make the long detour is to savour the delights of the venerable **E** *Applecross Inn*, T744262. There are, sadly, too few authentic Highland hostelries where you could quite happily while away a few hours, or even an entire afternoon, but if you have to be holed up somewhere to escape the rotten weather, then this place is as good as any and better than most. The welcome is warm, the crack is good and the seafood is so fresh you can almost see it swimming past as you order (try a half pint of prawns for a fiver or scallops for £7.50). Bar food served 1200-2100, children welcome till 2030, ceilidhs on Fri evening. The rooms upstairs are nothing fancy, but comfortable, with sea views.

If there's no room at the *Inn* there are a few B&Bs a mile to the south in the village of **Camusteel**: **E** *Mrs Cross*, 'Seawinds', T744373; **F** *Mrs Thompson*, 'Raon-Mor', T744260, open Apr-Oct. Just before Applecross is a bakery with a poly-tunnel sheltered restaurant which serves good cheap light meals.

Transport It's possible to reach Applecross by public transport, but only just. A *Postbus* service leaves Strathcarron train station daily (except Sun) at 0955, arriving in **Shieldaig** at 1040. Another *Postbus* then leaves Shieldaig at 1130 and arrives in Applecross at 1300, via the beautiful and winding coast road. No buses run over the Bealach na Ba. A *Postbus* leaves Applecross at 0915 and arrives in Shieldaig at 1010. It continues to **Torridon** (see below) and arrives at 1030. Another *Postbus* leaves Shieldaig at 1045 and arrives at Strathcarron train station at 1130. There are train connections from Strathcarron to Inverness and Kyle (for times T08457-484950).

Torridon

Torridon is perhaps the most striking skyline in the Scottish Highlands. The multi-peaked mountains of **Beinn Alligin**, **Liathach** (pronounced '*Lee*-ahakh') and **Beinn Eighe** ('Ben-*eay*') form a massive fortress of turrets, spires and pinnacles that provides an awesome backdrop to Loch Torridon, as well as the most exhilarating walking and climbing on the Scottish mainland (see below).

Phone code: 01445
Colour map 1,
grid C4/5

The coast road from Applecross meets the A896 from Lochcarron at the lovely little village of **Shieldaig** on the southern shore of **Loch Torridon**. There's a shop, a post office, a campsite, a couple of B&Bs and the **B** *Tigh-an-Eilean Hotel*, T01520-755251, where you can get reasonable meals.

Several miles east, a side road turns off the A896 by **Torridon** village and winds its way along the northern shore of the loch, then climbs through dramatic scenery before dropping to the beautiful little village of **Diabaig** (pronounced 'Jee-a-beg'), 10 miles from Torridon village. It's a worthwhile side trip, as the views across to the Applecross peninsula and Raasay are fantastic. There's also a great seven-mile coastal walk from Diabaig to Redpoint (see 'Walks around Torridon' below).

Much of the Torridon massif is in the care of the National Trust for Scotland, and just before Torridon village is the **NTS countryside centre**,

T791221, where you can get information and advice on walks in the area, as well as books and maps. About 400 yards past the centre is the **Deer Museum**, which has a small display describing the management of red deer in the Highlands as well as some live specimens outside.

Sleeping About a mile south of the turn-off to Torridon village is the magnificent **L** *Loch Torridon Hotel*, T791242, F791296, www.lochtorridonhotel.com 22 rooms. This elegant former hunting lodge sits on the lochside surrounded by majestic mountains and offers the ultimate in style and comfort. It also boasts one of the finest restaurants in the area (expensive). There are several B&Bs, including the excellent **E** *Upper Diabaig Farm*, T790227, open Apr-Sep, in Upper Diabaig. There are also a couple of **F** *SYHA hostels*. One is in Torridon village, T791284, open 29 Jan-31 Oct, with an adjacent campsite. The other is much smaller and more basic, 4 miles north of Diabaig on the trail to Redpoint, at the disused crofting township of Craig (no phone; open 14 May-3 Oct).

Transport The *Postbus* from Applecross to Shieldaig continues to Torridon village (see above). There's a postbus from Strathcarron station at 0955 which arrives in Shieldaig at 1040. *Duncan Maclennan* buses (T01520-755239) have a service which leaves Strathcarron at 1230 and arrives in Torridon at 1330 (daily except Sun). There's also a daily (Mon-Sat) *Postbus* service from Diabaig to Kinlochewe and Achnasheen, via Torridon, at 0955. There are also *Duncan Maclennan* buses between Torridon and Shieldaig and Strathcarron.

Walking around Torridon

OS Outdoor Leisure series No 8 Torridon offers some of the most spectacular walking on the Scottish mainland but also presents some of the most serious challenges. You need to be fit, experienced and well prepared and also be aware of the notoriously unpredictable weather (see page 60). You should have a compass and the relevant map. **Beinn Eighe** (3,309 ft) has nine peaks and is the largest of the Torridon mountains. To traverse its ridge is a mighty undertaking and can take two days. A much shorter and easier walk around the base of the mountain is described below, under **Beinn Eighe National Nature Reserve**.n

For those who are not experienced hill walkers, there's a Ranger Service for visitors. During July and August the ranger, Seamus McNally, takes guided walks up into the mountains three times a week. For more details call, T791221. A recommended local mountain guide is Steve Chadwick, T712455.

Beinn Alligin Beinn Alligin (3,232 ft) is the most westerly of the Torridon peaks and probably the least demanding. The **Allt a'Bhealaich Walk** is a steep but short walk of about two hours. It starts from the car park just beyond the stone bridge that crosses the Abhainn Coire Mhic Nobuil. Follow the path that runs beside the river gorge until you reach the first bridge, cross it and follow the east bank of the Allt a' Bhealaich burn. Higher up, cross the second bridge and continue to follow the track up to the 380-m contour line, then turn back retracing your steps. This walk doesn't include the ascent of the peak but the views are magnificent. Those who wish to climb the three Horns of Beinn Alligin can continue from the 380-m contour line above the second bridge. The track that follows their ridge is exposed and requires rock scrambling experience.

Liathach Seven-peaked Liathach (3,460 ft) stretches over five miles, and the magnificent **ridge walk** is considered by many to be the most impressive in Britain.

This walk requires a high level of stamina and will take at least seven to eight hours. It also helps if you have a car waiting at the end.

A good place to start this long and strenuous challenge is about half a mile or so east of Glen Cottage, which is just over two miles east of the Countryside Centre. A steep climb takes you to a point just west of Stuc a'Choire Dhuibh Bhig (3,000 ft). Then retrace your route to climb the twin tops of Bidein Toll a'Mhuic (3,200 ft), linked by a narrow ridge. The path from here descends to the head of a deep ravine and keeps to the crest of the ridge around the rim of Coireag Dubh Beag which plunges steeply to the north. The ridge then rises across a field of huge and unstable boulders to the highest peak – Spidean a'Choire Leith. The view from this point is stunning, with Coire na Caime before you, surrounded by 2,000 ft sheer cliffs. From here, the path follows a narrow exposed ridge for over a mile towards Mullach an Rathain (3,358 ft). Unless you are an experienced scrambler with a good head for heights, the best way from here is to take the path to the south, below the sharp pinnacles. Beyond the pinnacles the climb to Mullach an Rathain is straightforward. The track from here to Sgorr a'Chadail is a long but fairly easy walk and ends on the path in Coire Mhic Nobuil (see Beinn Alligin above).

Coire Walk

A less difficult walk, but still requiring a fair degree of fitness and taking most of the day, is the Coire Walk. It follows the River Coire Mhic Nobuil to its watershed and down again by the Allt a'Choire Dhuibh Mhoir to the main road in Glen Torridon. Again, two cars will shorten the distance considerably.

The walk starts at the same point as the Beinn Alligin walk above. It follows the path up to the first bridge then branches east and continues on the path that runs north of the river, all the way to its source in the pass between Liathach and Beinn Dearg. Here the ground is boggy between the string of pools and lochans and the path is less distinct, but it becomes clear again in the upper reaches of the Coire Dubh Mor, a huge gully that separates Liathach from Beinn Eighe. A little further on, the track joins a stalkers' path which curves round Sail Mhor to the famous Coire Mhic Fhearchair, considered to be the most spectacular corrie in Scotland (see Beinn Eighe below). The Coire path leads to a ford, which is crossed by stepping stones, then descends following the west side of the burn down to the car park on the Torridon road, from where it's about 4½ miles to Torridon village.

Diabaig to Red Point Walk
OS Landranger No 19

An excellent low-level coastal walk is from Diabaig to Redpoint. It is far less strenuous or daunting than the others described above and there is a clear path. It starts at the wooden gate to the right of the post office in Diabaig and ends at Red Point Farm, seven miles away.

After four miles the coastal path reaches the derelict croft houses in the Craig valley. One of these has been converted into a *SYHA* Hostel (see 'Sleeping' above). There are two possible routes from here. You can follow the footpath above the coastline, or leave the footpath after crossing the wooden bridge over the Craig river and climb through an area of woodland. Take a reference from your OS map and you'll reach the highest point, Meall na h-Uamha, from where there are superb views. You can then descend to rejoin the coastal path and continue till you reach the glorious golden sands of Red Point, with wonderful views across to Skye and Raasay. Keep to the path through the farm till you reach the car park. Unless you've arranged your own transport here, you'll have to walk back the way you came, or catch the schoolbus to Gairloch (see page 498).

Loch Maree

On the north side of the Torridon mountains is beautiful Loch Maree, dotted with islands and bordered by the mass of **Slioch** (3,215 ft) to the north and ancient Caledonian pine forest to the south. Running along its northern shore, from Slioch almost as far as Poolewe, is the remote Letterewe Estate, one of Scotland's great deer forests. The A832 skirts the south shore of the loch, running northwest from **Kinlochewe**, and passes the **Victoria Falls**, a mile or so beyond **Talladale**. The falls commemorate Queen Victoria's visit in 1877. To find them, look for the 'Hydro Power' signs.

Sleeping The village of **Kinlochewe** is a good base for walking in this area. It has a post office, shop, garage and accommodation. The **E** *Kinlochewe Hotel*, T760253, offers B&B as well as cheaper bunkhouse beds and cheap bar meals. There's also **B&B** at **D** *Cromasaig*, on the Torridon road, T760234, cromasaig@msn.com; and a basic campsite a few miles northwest, at *Taangan Farm*, at the head of Loch Maree.

The best accommodation, though, is at **Talladale**, halfway between Kinlochewe and Gairloch. **B** *The Old Mill Highland Lodge*, T760271, open mid-Dec to mid-Oct, is a converted mill set in its own gardens. It's friendly and comfortable, offers great food (price includes dinner), seclusion and great views. **B-C** *Loch Maree Hotel*, T760288, lochmaree@easynet.co.uk This beautifully located hotel is being returned to its former glory. Queen Victoria was here! It also offers superb cuisine (**A** including dinner).

Transport Kinlochewe is 9 miles west of **Achnasheen** rail station which is on the Inverness-Kyle line. There's a daily (except Sun) *Postbus* service. There's also a *Postbus* (Mon-Sat) from Kinlochewe to **Torridon** and **Diabaig**, and a bus to Torridon and **Shieldaig**, T01520-755239. Buses between Gairloch and Inverness (see below) stop in Kinlochewe.

Beinn Eighe National Nature Reserve

While most of the Torridon massif is managed by the NTS, Beinn Eighe (which means 'File Peak' in Gaelic) is under the control of Scottish Natural Heritage. It is Britain's oldest National Nature Reserve, set up in 1951 to protect the ancient Caledonian pine forest west of Kinlochewe. It has since been designated an International Biosphere Reserve and extended to cover 30 square miles. The reserve is the home of a great variety of rare Highland wildlife, including pine martens, wildcats, buzzards, Scottish crossbills and golden eagles. There's also a wide range of flora which can best be appreciated on the excellent mountain trail described below which climbs from the ancient pine woods through alpine vegetation to the tundra-like upper slopes.

About half a mile northwest of Kinlochewe on the A832, is the **Beinn Eighe Visitor Centre**, which has information on the flora and fauna in the reserve and sells pamphlets on the trails described below. Note that camping is restricted to the official campsite at Taangan Farm (see 'Sleeping' above).

The mountain and woodland trails both start and end in the car park at the side of Loch Maree, about two miles beyond the visitor centre. The **woodland trail** heads west along the lochside then crosses the road and climbs for about a mile up to the Conservation cabin before descending back to the starting point. It should take about an hour and is easy to follow, though quite steep in parts, and you'll need a good pair of walking boots.

The **mountain trail** is four miles long and rough and steep in parts. You should be well equipped with good walking boots, waterproofs, food and warm clothing. It should take around three to four hours. The route is well marked with cairns and you should not stray from the path.

The trail heads south from the car park and begins a gentle ascent through woodland to a boggy area and then begins to zigzag up a very steep and rugged section, climbing to over 1,000 ft in less than half a mile. This is the steepest section of the trail, but the views back across Loch Maree to Slioch are fabulous. The summit of the mountain trail is **Conservation cairn** (1,800 ft) from where you can see the tops of 31 Munros on a clear day and enjoy a close-up view of the impressive Beinn Eighe ridge a few miles to the south.

The trail now begins to descend as it heads northwest towards An t-Allt (1,000 ft), turns northwards down to a small enclosure, then heads east to the deep Allt na h-Airidhe gorge. From here the trail continues down to the treeline and runs through woodland to join up with the top of the Woodland Trail. Follow the path to the right and this takes you back to the car park.

Gairloch

Gairloch consists of a string of tiny crofting townships scattered around the northeastern shore of the loch of the same name. It's a great place which attracts a large number of visitors who come for the many beautiful beaches, excellent walks, golf and fishing, and the chance of seeing seals, porpoises, dolphins and whales in the surrounding waters.

Phone code: 01445
Colour map 1, grid C4

There are **buses** to and from Inverness 3 times a week, also buses to Kinlochewe and a local **postbus** service (see Transport on next page).

The **Tourist Information Centre**, T712130, is at the car park in Auchtercairn, where the road branches off to Strath. They will book accommodation for you and sell a wide range of books and maps. Jan-Mar, Nov and Dec Mon-Thu 0900-1230 and 1300-1700, Fri 0900-1230 and 1300-1630; Apr and May, Sep and Oct Mon-Sat 0900-1730, Sun 1300-1800; Jun-Aug Mon-Fri 0900-1800, Sat 1000-1800, Sun 1300-1800

Ins & outs

If the weather's bad (as it sometimes can be) or if you're interested in local history, then visit the **Gairloch Heritage Museum**, which is beside the tourist office on the A832 to Poolewe, a few yards beyond the turn-off to Strath. Included are archaeological finds, a mock-up of a crofthouse room, schoolroom and shop, the interior of the local lighthouse and an archive of old photographs. ■ *Apr-mid-Oct Mon-Sat 1000-1700. £2.50, concession £2, children £0.50. T712287.*

Sights

The waters around Gairloch are home to a wide variety of marine mammals such as seals, otters, porpoises, dolphins, minke whales and even killer whales. You can take a wildlife-spotting cruise with *Sail Gairloch*, T712636. The cruise lasts two hours and leaves daily from Gairloch Pier (subject to weather conditions). It can be booked at the Gairloch Marine Life Centre by the pier. For information on **sea angling trips**, contact the chandlery shop at the harbour, T712458. For those who prefer dry land, try a **quad bike tour** of the Flowerdale Deer Forest with *Highland Trails*. Book at *The Anchorage* post office/craft shop at the harbour or at Flowerdale estate office, T712378.

B-C *Myrtle Bank Hotel*, T712004, F712214, MyrtleBank@email.msn.com 12 rooms. Modern hotel in the centre of Gairloch overlooking the loch, very good food and service in the restaurant (expensive dinner and cheap bar meals). There are numerous cheaper B&Bs scattered throughout the area. Most of the owners will provide maps and information on local walks. On the main street in **Strath**, near the shops, is **F** *Bains House*, T712472, which is friendly and great value. On the road that turns off to the

Sleeping
Gairloch has a wide range of accommodation. The TIC will help you find a room

The Highlands and Skye

right by the *Millcroft Hotel*, beyond the fire station, is **E-F** *Duisary*, T712252, open Apr-Oct. In **Charleston**, by the harbour, is **E** *Mrs A MacIver*, T712388, open Feb-Nov.

Further afield, at **Badachro**, south of Gairloch on the road to Red Point, is **E** *Lochside*, T741295. Also at Badachro is **F** *Badachro Bunkhouse*, T07760-344008. 13 miles north of Gairloch, at the end of the road, is the **F** *Rubha Reidh Lighthouse*, T/F771263, ruareidh@netcomuk.co.uk, which offers comfortable B&B (**D** including dinner) and hostel accommodation. It's best to book ahead in the high season. They also have a tearoom serving home baking, snacks and light lunches; open Easter-Oct Sun, Tue and Thu 1100-1700. Self-catering is also available for private rooms or the hostel. There are buses from Gairloch as far as Melvaig (see below), then it's a 3-mile hike along the road to the lighthouse.

There are a couple of hostels in Gairloch: **F** *Auchtercairn Hostel*, T712131, open Mar-Nov, is at Gairloch Sands Apartments, just before the turn-off to Strath; 3 miles beyond Gairloch, on the road to Melvaig, is **F** *Carn Dearg Youth Hostel*, T712219, open 15 May-3 Oct. There are a couple of **campsites**: *Gairloch Caravan & Camping Park*, T712373, is at Strath, with full facilities and close to all amenities; *Sands Holiday Centre*, T712152, open Easter-Oct, is at Big Sand, about a mile beyond Strath.

Eating The *Myrtle Bank Hotel* (see above) serves very good, expensive, meals, and its bar lunches are good value. The *Scottish Seafood Restaurant*, T712137, next to Gairloch filling station, is good for seafood at mid-range prices (unlicensed). The *Mountain Restaurant*, Strath Sq, T712316, has a terrace overlooking Gair Loch. It is run by mountaineers and offers an interesting menu, as well as accommodation in several themed rooms. There's also *The Steading Restaurant*, T712449, next to the Heritage Museum, which is open daily 0930-2100. For a lite bite, or tea and scones, try the *Conservatory Coffee Shop*, on the square in Strath. For cheap pasta, there's *Gino's Italian Restaurant* at the friendly *Millcroft Hotel* in Strath, T712376. The best place for a good pint of real ale and some hearty pub grub is *The Old Inn*, T712006, near the harbour.

Transport There's a **bus** from **Inverness** to Gairloch 3 times a week (Mon, Wed and Sat) at 1705 with *Westerbus*, T712255. The return bus is at 0805. *Westerbus* also have services to **Kinlochewe** (Mon-Sat at 0730) and to **Mellon Charles/Laide**, via **Poolewe** (Mon-Sat). There's a **Melvaig-Gairloch-Red Point postbus** service Mon-Sat which leaves Gairloch at 0820 heading north to Melvaig and leaves Gairloch heading south to **Red Point** at 1035. On Fri only there's a subsidized taxi service between Gairloch and Melvaig 1030-1230 (to book T712559/712497).

Directory There are shops and takeaways in Strath and Auchtercairn, a petrol station in Auchtercairn, and a bank with ATM near the harbour at Charleston.

Around Gairloch The beach by the golf course at Gairloch is nice, but the beach at **Big Sand**, a few miles northwest of Strath, is better, and quieter. Further north is Melvaig, from where you can walk to **Rubha Reidh Lighthouse** (see 'Sleeping' above). Around the headland from the lighthouse is the beautiful, secluded beach at **Camas Mor**. This is a good place for spotting sea birds, and there's a great walk from here on a marked footpath to **Midtown**, four miles northwest of Poolewe. You'll have to walk or hitch from here as there's no public transport to Poolewe.

Many of the roads in the area were built during the Potato Famine of 1840 in order to give men work, with funds supplied by Dowager Lady Mackenzie of Gairloch. These became know as the 'Destitution Roads', and one of these is the narrow B8056 which runs west for nine miles to **Red Point** from the junction three miles south of Gairloch, at Kerrysdale. This is a lovely little side trip and well worth it, especially on a clear evening to enjoy the magnificent sunsets at Red Point beach. The beach itself is extremely beautiful, backed by steep dunes and looking across to the Trotternish peninsula on Skye. So romantic is this spot that some people (naming no names) have been known to plight their troth here. Red Point is also the start or finish point for the excellent coastal walk to or from **Diabaig** (see page 495). On the road to Red Point is the picturesque little hamlet of **Badachro**, tucked away in a wooded, sheltered bay with fishing boats moored in its natural harbour. It's worth stopping off here on the way back from Red Point for a wee dram at the *Badachro Inn*.

There are lots of other good walks in the area, including to **Flowerdale Falls** and the **Fairy Lochs** and the **USAAF Liberator**. The TIC (see previous page) has a selection of walking guides and OS maps.

Five miles east of Gairloch on the other side of the peninsula is the neat little village of Poolewe, beautifully set at the mouth of the River Ewe, where it cascades into sheltered Loch Ewe. There are some good walks around Poolewe, including the one around **Loch Kernsary** described above. There's also a nice little drive up the side road running along the west shore of Loch Ewe to **Cove**. You can walk from **Midtown**, midway along the road, to **Rubha Reidh**, north of Gairloch (see above).

Poolewe
Phone code: 01445
Colour map 1,
grid B4

Sleeping and eating There are several places to stay in and around **Poolewe** and the TIC in Gairloch will help you find accommodation. On the Cove road by the lochside is the former home of Osgood Mackenzie, the **L** *Pool House Hotel*, T781272, poolhouse@inverewe.co.uk, open Mar- Dec. It enjoys great views and serves good food (expensive). At **Inverasdale**, a few miles up the Cove road, is **E** *Bruach Ard*, T781214, open Apr-Oct. Further up this road, near Cove, is **E** *Mrs MacDonald*, T781354, open Apr-Oct. Above Poolewe, reached by a path that leads from the road beside the campsite, is **E** *Mrs MacIver*, T781389, open Apr-Oct. The excellent *Camping and Caravan Club Site*, T781249, is between Poolewe village and Inverewe Garden.

The best place to eat in Poolewe is probably the licensed restaurant at Inverewe Garden which is open daily 1000-1700 (see below). If you need to grab a quick snack, or fancy a coffee, try the *Bridge Cottage Café*, which is on the left at the turn-off to Cove.

The reason most people come here is to visit Inverewe Garden where you'll find an astonishing collection of exotic subtropical plants growing on the same latitude as Siberia, thanks to the mild climate created by the North Atlantic Drift. This wonderful 50-acre oasis of colour is a mecca for garden lovers, but even those who flinch at the mere sight of a lawn-mower will be bowled over by the sheer scale and diversity of plants and flowers on view.

Inverewe Garden

The garden was created from a treeless wilderness by Osgood Mackenzie, starting in 1862. By the time of his death in 1922 he had produced an internationally renowned walled and woodland garden. His work was continued by his daughter, who then gave the garden to the National Trust for Scotland in 1952. Since then, the plant collection has diversified even more and an intricate maze of paths leads you through ever-changing displays of Himalayan rhododendrons, Tasmanian eucalyptus, many Chilean and South African species, together with a large collection of New Zealand plants.

The garden is well worth visiting in any weather and at any time of the year, but especially from the end of April through the summer when the rhododendrons are in bloom. You should allow at least a couple of hours to do it justice. The garden is about a mile north of Poolewe on the main A832.

There's a visitor centre and gift shop and a good restaurant, which serves snacks and hot meals. ■ *Garden open 15 Mar-31 Oct daily 0930-2100; 1 Nov-14 Mar daily 0930-1700. Visitor Centre open 15 Mar to 31 Oct 0930-1730. Guided garden walks 15 Apr to 15 Sep Mon-Thu at 1330. £5, concession £4, children £1. T781200.*

Around Laide
Phone code: 01445
Colour map 1,
grid B5

North of Poolewe the A832 passes **Aultbea** on its way to **Laide**, where it then skirts the shores of Gruinard Bay, with its lovely coves of pink sand. From Laide Post Office a side road branches north to **Mellon Udrigle** and **Opinan**, both with great beaches. Between Laide and Mellon Udrigle, at **Achgarve**, a road branches left for about half a mile. From the end of this road you can walk all the way to **Slaggan**, a ruined village on the other side of the peninsula. It's a nice spot for a picnic but don't be tempted to swim in the sea as the tidal race makes it dangerous.

Gruinard Bay is a very beautiful part of the northwest coast but will always be synonymous with **Gruinard Island**, standing ominously in the middle of the bay. The island was used as a testing ground for biological warfare during the Second World War and was contaminated with anthrax spores. The Ministry of Defence finally agreed to decontaminate it in 1990 and it has now been declared 'safe'.

Sleeping There are a couple of really good places to stay around here. In the village of **Laide** is the **D** *Old Smiddy Guest House*, T731425, oldsmiddy@aol.com, open Apr-Oct. Its excellent restaurant is also open to non-residents, but it's best to book well in advance (expensive). There's also a **campsite** in Laide, the *Gruinard Bay Caravan Park*, T731225, open Apr-Oct.

Transport There are daily **buses** to Laide from **Gairloch** with *Westerbus*, T712255. Some of them continue to Mellon Udrigle. There are buses between Laide and **Inverness** 3 times a week (Tue, Thu and Fri), leaving at 0805 and returning at 1705. There are also buses on other days between **Gairloch** and **Inverness** which stop at Laide (see above under Gairloch).

Dundonnell
Phone code: 01854
Colour map 1, grid B5

The road heads inland then runs along the southern shore of **Little Loch Broom** to **Dundonnell**, from where there are spectacular views of awesome **An Teallach** (3,483 ft), a mountain of almost mythical status amongst Scottish climbers and spoken of in hushed, reverential tones. The path to the highest of its summits is clear and begins southeast of the *Dundonell Hotel*. It will take a full day and you'll need to be well prepared (OS map No 19) and heed the usual advice. You can stay at the **B** *Dundonnell Hotel*, T633204, selbie@dundonnellhotel.co.uk, open February-December, which does good meals (cheap to mid-range bar meals; expensive three-course dinner). Alternatively there's B&B at **E** *Mrs Ross*, T633237, in Camusnagaul, a few miles back up the loch. Also in Camusnagaul is the *Sail Mhor Croft Independent Hostel*, T633224, sailmhor@btinternet.com, but you should call before arriving.

A few miles beyond Dundonnell, a side road branches left and runs for seven miles to the tiny, remote hamlet of **Badrallach**, where you can stay at the *Badrallach Bothy & Camp Site*, T633281.

Falls of Measach
The A832 coastal road from Gairloch and Poolewe meets the A835 Ullapool-Inverness main road at **Braemore junction**, 12 miles south of Ullapool. Before heading on to Ullapool it's worth stopping at the very

Walk around Loch Kernsary

This straightforward but rewarding walk covers six miles and should take around 2½ to three hours. The track is very boggy underfoot in places, especially after rain, so you'll need good boots.

Start in Poolewe, from the car park by the school near the bridge over the Ewe. Head up the single-track road with the river on your right. Go through the gate, then the track heads away from the river and up into woodland. At the Letterewe Estate gate cross the stile and continue to the next fork. Turn left here to Kernsary Estate, with views of Loch Maree and Beinn Eighe to the south. Follow the track to the next gate, go through and cross the wooden bridge. Continue along the track and you'll see Loch Kernsary on your left. At the next fork, turn left over the bridge and pass Kernsary Cottage on the right. Beyond the cottage, go through the gate and immediately head left down towards the burn, where the ground may be boggy. There's no path here, but cross the

wooden footbridge and continue straight on, past the piles of stones on your left. Cross the stile, and the path follows the length of Loch Kernsary. At the head of the loch, the path climbs to give you views down to Poolewe. Follow the path down till it eventually takes you to the main road. Turn left and follow the road back to the car park. OS Landranger Map No 19 covers the route.

impressive Falls of Measach, just by the junction. The falls plunge 150 ft into the spectacular **Corrieshalloch Gorge** (or 'ugly/fearsome gorge' in Gaelic) and can be crossed by a distinctly wobbly suspension bridge (not for vertigo sufferers). The falls can be reached from the A835, but the most dramatic approach is from the A832 Gairloch road.

Ullapool

The attractive little fishing port of Ullapool, on the shores of Loch Broom, is the largest settlement in Wester Ross. The grid-pattern village, created in 1788 at the height of the herring boom by the British Fisheries Society, is still an important fishing centre as well as being the major tourist centre in the northwest of Scotland and one of the main ferry terminals for the Outer Hebrides. At the height of the busy summer season the town is swamped by visitors passing through on their way to or from Stornoway on Lewis, heading north into the wilds, or south to Inverness. It has excellent tourist amenities and services and relatively good transport links, making it the ideal base for those exploring the northwest coast and a good place to be if the weather is bad.

Phone code: 01854
Colour map 1,
grid B5
Population: 1,800

The Highlands and Skye

Getting there Ullapool is the mainland terminal for **ferries** to Stornoway (Lewis). *Scottish Citylink* buses, T08705-505050, to and from Inverness (twice daily Mon-Sat, 1 hr 20 mins; £12.50) connect with the ferry to and from Stornoway. For further details of ferries, see the Outer Hebrides chapter (page 560), or contact the local *CalMac* office on Shore St, opposite the pier, T612358. There are also buses to places further north, and south along the coast. Buses stop at the pier near the ferry dock.

Ins & outs
See also page 504

The **Tourist Information Centre** is at 6 Argyle St, T612135. It is well run and provides an accommodation booking service as well as information on local walks and trips, and has a good stock of books and maps. Easter-Jun and Sep-Nov Mon-Sat 0900-1800, Sun 1300-1800; Jul and Aug Mon-Sat 0900-1900, Sun 1300-1800; Nov-Easter Mon-Fri 1300-1630.

Sights Ullapool's attractions are very much of the outdoor variety and include the **Falls of Measach**, **Achiltibuie** and **Stac Pollaidh**. There are also many good local walks and cruises to the **Summer Isles** (see 'Tours' below). It's worth taking a stroll around the **harbour** to watch the comings and goings of the fishing fleet and you might even see the occasional seal or otter swimming close to the shore. The only real 'sight' as such is the **Ullapool Museum and Visitor Centre** in a converted church in West Argyle Street. It has some interesting displays on local history, including the story of those who set sail from here in 1773 on board *The Hector*, the first ship to carry emigrants from the Highlands to Nova Scotia in Canada. ■ *Apr-Oct Mon-Sat 0930-1730; Jul and Aug also 1930-2130; Nov-Mar 1200-1600. £2, concession £1.50, children free. T612987.*

Sleeping
■ *on map*
Price codes:
see inside
front cover

There is no shortage of places to stay in Ullapool, ranging from one of the very finest hotels in the UK to numerous guesthouses and B&Bs, a couple of good youth hostels and a campsite.

L *Altnaharrie Inn*, T633230. 8 rooms, open Apr-Oct. This world-renowned hotel is on the other side of Loch Broom and you'll be picked up from town in their own launch. The ultimate Highland retreat, if you can afford it, and unique in every sense, their restaurant is one of most highly acclaimed in the UK. The hotel was closed for the 2001 season; unlikely to re-open in 2002, check.

B *The Ceilidh Place*, 14 West Argyle Pl, T612103, F612886, reservations@ ceilidh.demon.co.uk 23 rooms. This former boat-shed has grown over the years to become one of the most refreshingly different hotels in the country, with comfortable bedrooms, cosy lounge, bookshop, restaurant, bar and coffee shop. They also host a varied programme of arts events such as live music, plays, poetry readings, exhibitions and ceilidhs (see below); a great place to relax and soak up some local culture. Across the road is their clubhouse, with basic but comfortable dorms (**E-F**).

D-C *Harbour Lights Hotel*, Garve Rd (on the left, heading into Ullapool on the A835), T612222, harbour@vacations-scotland.co.uk 22 rooms, open 1 Mar-31 Oct. Modern hotel offering good service and very good food available all day (mid-range). **D** *Ferry Boat Inn*, Shore St, T612366, www.ferryboat-inn.com On the lochside, decent accommodation and food and the best pub in town. **C-D** *Morefield Hotel*, North Rd, T612161. Open May-Oct. On the edge of town heading north, in the middle of a housing estate, motel-style accommodation and a superb seafood restaurant. **D** *Point Cottage Guest House*, 22 West Shore St, T612494, www.pointcottage.co.uk Lovely old fishing cottage at the quieter end of the loch-front.

There are more
guesthouses on Garve
Rd, heading south out
of town, and lots of
B&Bs along Seaforth
Rd and Pulteney St

E *Brae Guest House*, Shore St, T612421. 8 rooms, open May-Oct. Comfortable guesthouse on the loch-front. **E** *Eilean Donan Hotel*, 14 Market St, T612524. Friendly and central. **E** *Strathmore House*, Strathmore, Morefield (1 mile north of town), T612423, murdo@strathmore.fsnet.co.uk Open Apr-Oct. Friendly, comfortable and good value. Ullapool has a very good **F** *SYHA youth hostel* on Shore St, T612254, open Feb-Dec, where you can pick up some good information on local walks, alsobike hire, internet and laundry facilities. There's an independent hostel, **F** *West House*, on West Argyle St, T613126, open all year. It has the full range of facilities, including free internet for guests, hires out mountain bikes and runs local bus tours. The only **campsite** is at *Broomfield Holiday Park*, T6120020, on Shore St at the west end of the village, with great views across to the Summer Isles and a laundrette on site. It's open Easter-Sep.

The *Altnaharrie Inn* (see above) is considered perhaps the finest in the country, and Gunn Erkison's cooking is of world renown. Expensive, and non-residents will need to book well in advance. *Mariner's Restaurant* is part of the *Morefield Hotel* (see above). The setting may be a little incongruous but there's nothing wrong with the food. The seafood is sensational, which is why people travel from miles around and it's always busy. Mid-range prices and excellent value.

Eating
There's plenty of choice across the range, from one of the UK's top hotel/restaurants to the humble seafront chippie

 The Ceilidh Place (see above) is one of those places that tourists seem to hang around for hours or even days. It exudes a laid-back, cultured ambience. The self-service coffee shop does cheap wholefood all day during the summer, while the restaurant serves more expensive full meals, with an emphasis on vegetarian and seafood at night. There's even outdoor seating. Open 1100-2300. Also live music and various other events (see below). *The Tea Store*, opposite the TIC on Argyle St, has good value snacks. *Ullapool Catering* (T612969) make up great picnics from local organic produce at goodo value prices. You can also get decent, cheap pub food at lunchtime and early evening in the *Ferry Boat Inn*, the *Seaforth Inn* and the *Arch Inn* (see below).

Ullapool

To Strathmore Guest House

The Highlands and Skye

N

0 metres 100
0 yards 100

■ Sleeping		Mariner's Restaurant	● Eating
1 Brae Guest House	4 Eilean Donan	8 Point Cottage Guest House	1 Arch Inn
2 Broomfield Holiday Park	5 Ferry Boat Inn	9 SYHA Youth Hostel	2 Seaforth Inn
3 Ceilidh Place	6 Harbour Lights	10 West House Hostel	
	7 Morefield Hotel &		

Entertainment Ullapool's favourite pub has to be the *Ferry Boat Inn* (or 'FBI' as it's known locally), on Shore St. It has a Thu night live music session year round and during the summer you can sit outside on the sea wall and watch the sun go down as you drain your glass. Another good place for a drink is the *Arch Inn*, at the other end of Shore St. The bar of the *Seaforth Inn* has live music on a Fri night, which has been described by one local as 'raucous'. For something a wee bit more sedate and civilized, head for *The Ceilidh Place*, where you can enjoy a quiet drink in the cosy *Parlour Bar* or take advantage of their varied programme of events. There's live music nightly (except Sun) throughout the summer and on a Mon in winter, also ceilidhs and poetry readings. The clubhouse opposite stages plays.

Shopping The town is well supplied with shops. *Boots* the chemist is on Shore St by the pier, and there's a *Safeway* supermarket next to the car park north of Seafield Rd. A good outdoor equipment shop is *Mountain Man Supplies*, opposite the museum on West Argyle St. The best **bookshop** in the northwest is the one at *The Ceilidh Place* (see above). The *Captain's Cabin*, on the corner of Quay St and Shore St, also sells books, as well as crafts and souvenirs. An excellent **jewellers** is the *Knockan Studio*, opposite the TIC on Argyle St, T613365, open Mar-Oct, Mon-Sat 0900-1800. For **pottery**, look no further than *Highland Stoneware*, T612980, on Mill St heading north towards Morefield. You can wander round the studios before browsing in their gift shop, which is pricey but you may have luck in their bargain baskets. They also have a factory in Lochinver (see page 507). Open Mon-Fri 0900-1800 (Easter-Oct also Sat 0900-1700).

Tours During the summer the *MV Summer Queen* runs 4-hr cruises to the **Summer Isles**, with a 45-min landing on Tanera Mór. These leave Mon-Sat at 1000 from the pier and cost £14 per person. There are also 2-hr wildlife cruises around **Loch Broom**, **Annat Bay** and **Isle Martin**, which leave daily at 1415 and also on Sun at 1100, and cost £8 per person. Cruises can be booked at the booth by the pier or by calling, T612472. Walking tours can be arranged daily with *Northwest Frontiers*, T612628, with the very experienced Andy Cunningham, and *Celtic Horizons*, T612429.

Transport Scottish *Citylink* **buses** run 2-3 times daily (except Sun) between Ullapool and **Inverness**, connecting with the ferry to Stornoway. There are also buses daily (except Sun) to and from Inverness with *Rapson's Coaches*, T01463-710555, and *Spa Coaches*, T01997-421311. There's a service to **Lochinver** (1-2 times daily except Sun, 1 hr) with *Spa Coaches* and *Rapson's of Brora*, T01408-621245, and to **Achilitibuie** (twice daily Mon-Thu, once on Sat, 1 hr) with *Spa Coaches*. There's also a daily bus to and from **Gairloch**, which continues to Inverness, during the summer only. **Cycle hire** At *West House* independent hostel (see 'Sleeping' above); £10 per day.

Directory **Banks** The only bank is the *Royal Bank of Scotland* in Ladysmith St.

North of Ullapool

Colour map 1,
grid B5/6

North of Ullapool you enter a different world. The landscape becomes ever more dramatic and unreal – a huge emptiness of bleak moorland punctuated by isolated peaks and shimmering lochs. A narrow and tortuously twisting road winds its way up the coast, past deserted beaches of sparkling white sand washed by turquoise sea. There's not much tourist traffic this far north and once you get off the main road and on to the backroads, you can enjoy the wonderful sensation of having all this astonishingly beautiful scenery to yourself.

The Highlands and Skye

*The region immediately north of Ullapool is called **Assynt**, and is heaven for serious hill walkers and climbers. Though most are not Munros, and not particularly difficult by Scottish standards, they can attract some of the worst weather imaginable, even in the height of summer. Also remember to check locally regarding access during the deer-stalking season which runs from mid-August to mid-October. (See also 'Safety in the Scottish Mountains', page 60.) Amongst the most spectacular of Assynt's distinctive 'island peaks' are **Suilven** (2,398 ft), **Ben More Assynt** (3,275 ft), **Quinag** (2,650 ft) and **Canisp** (2,775 ft). Much of this region is protected in the **Inverpolly and Inchnadamph National Nature Reserves**, home to an extremely rich and diverse wildlife.*

About 12 miles north of Ullapool on the main A835 is the exceptional SNH visitor centre at **Knockan Crag**. It's an interactive display of the geology, flora and fauna of the area and is open all year round 24 hours a day, T666234. From the visitor centre there's a marked trail which leads up to the Crag, and the views from the clifftop are excellent, across to Inverpolly's 'island' peaks of **Cul Mór**, **Cul Beag** and **Stac Pollaidh**.

Inverpolly National Nature Reserve
Phone code: 01854
Colour map 1, grid B5

A few miles north of here is the village of **Knockan**, with accommodation at E *Assynt Guided Holidays*, T666215, open mid-May to mid-Oct. Nearby, at **Elphin**, is the **Highland and Rare Breeds Farm** (open mid-May to end of September, daily 1000-1700). Beyond Elphin is **Ledmore**, where the A837 branches east towards **Lairg** and **Bonar Bridge**. There's a good craft shop at Ledmore where you can buy hand-knitted sweaters.

Between Ullapool and Knockan Crag is the turn-off west (left) to the distinctive craggy peak of **Stac Pollaidh**. A new path has been recently established by the John Muir Trust, which takes you on a circular walk around the peak from the car park. Take the right-hand path and go round at the same level, or climb up the rear to the top, go around the summit and descend by the same path. You'll need a head for heights to reach the summit as much of the route is exposed, but the stunning views are worth it. Be careful not to stray from the path; it's been put there because of the damage inflicted by tens of thousands of pairs of boots each year, resulting in serious erosion on the south face. It's a fairly easy 2½ hour walk.

OS Landrayer No 15

The unclassified single-track road winds its way west past Stac Pollaidh to the turn-off for Achiltibuie. This old crofting village, with whitewashed cottages set back from the sea views across to the beautiful **Summer Isles**, is home to one of the northwest's main tourist attractions. The **Hydroponicum**, or 'Garden of the Future', is a gigantic greenhouse which is pioneering the system of hydroponics to grow plants from all over the world. Hydroponics uses water instead of soil to carry nutrients to the plants and can be carried out anywhere. Here you can see an incredible variety of subtropical trees, orchids, flowers, vegetables, herbs and fruits. A guided tour takes you through the different climatic zones, and you can taste their produce, including the famous strawberries, in the *Lilypond Café*, which serves meals and snacks. ■ *Easter to end of Sep daily 1000-1800. Guided tours every hour on the hour. £4.75, concession £3.50, children £2.75. T622202, www.race.co.uk/hydroponicum*

Achiltibuie
Phone code: 01854
Colour map 1, grid B5

Another worthwhile attraction is the **Achiltibuie Smokehouse**, five miles to the north, at Altandhu. Here you can watch the salmon, herring, trout and other fish being cured before buying some afterwards. ■ *May-Sep Mon-Sat 0930-1700. Free. T622353.*

The Highlands and Skye

Walks around Ullapool

There are several good walking trails which start in Ullapool. One of these is to the top of **Ullapool Hill**, or Meall Mhor (886 ft). Starting from the tourist office, head to the end of Argyle Street, turn left on to North Road and then cross the road at the Far Isles Restaurant. Walk down the lane between Broom Court and the Hydro sub-station and then follow the path which zig-zags up the hillside. There's a good cairned path up to the top of the hill. The views from the top over Glen Achall, and on a clear day, the mountains of Sutherland, are superb. You can return by traversing the hillside to the top of the Braes, or take a track leading to **Loch Achall** and follow the Ullapool river through the quarry road back to the village. The return trip takes one to two hours. A relatively easy, but much longer walk, of five to six hours, is to **Rhidorroch Estate**. Take the A835 north out of Ullapool. Opposite the petrol station and before the bridge, take the road on the right signed 'Quarry'. Go through the quarry keeping to the left, and follow the Ullapool river till you see Loch Achall. Continue along the north bank of the loch for another six miles. **East Rhidorroch Lodge** is on the right; cross the bridge to get there, then skirt the lodge fences and cross to the track which leads up the southwestern hill. This brings you out to **Leckmelm**, about four miles south of Ullapool on the A835. This last section offers wonderful views across Loch Broom to An Teallach. From Leckmelm you can also climb **Beinn Eilideach** (1,837 ft). A good coastal walk is to **Rhue Lighthouse** and back. From the north end of Quay Street go down the steps to the river. Cross the bridges and head left by the football field. Follow the path to the left by the duck pond and cross in front of the bungalow. Then follow the shoreline north for about two miles, climbing up the hillside when the tide is high. Follow the path till you reach the little white lighthouse at Rhue Point. To return, take the single-track road out of Rhue back to the main road and up over the hill to Ullapool. It's about six miles in total. There are many more strenuous hiking routes around Ullapool. The A835 south of town gives access to **Beinn Dearg** (3,556 ft) and the **Fannichs**, a range of hills on the southern side of Dirrie More. There's also **An Teallach**, a favourite with Scottish climbers (see page 500). North of Ullapool are the mountains within the **Inverpolly National Nature Reserve** (see below). These include **Ben Mór Coigach** (2,438 ft), **Stac Pollaidh** (2,011 ft), **Cul Beag** (2,523 ft) and **Cul Mór** (2,786 ft). All routes are covered by OS Maps Nos 15, 19 and 20. They all require hillwalking experience and you should be well prepared for the unpredictable weather conditions. A good climbing guidebook is The Northern Highlands, SMC District Guide, by Tom Strang. North West Frontiers is an Ullapool-based tour company offering guided walking tours around Ullapool and throughout the Northwest Highlands. Contact them at: 18A Braes, Ullapool, IV26 2SZ, T/F612628, NWF@compuserve.com, ourworld.compuserve.com/homepages/NWF

Sleeping and eating   Near the Hydroponicum is the **L** *Summer Isles Hotel*, T622282, F622251, summerislesyhotel@aol.com Open Easter-Oct, which enjoys magnificent views across to the Summer Isles. It also boasts an excellent restaurant (expensive). Even if you're not staying or eating here, it's worth stopping to have a drink on the terrace and watch the sun set over the islands. The basic but very cheap **F** *SYHA Youth Hostel* is a few miles south at Achininver, T622254; open mid-May to early Oct. There are also several B&Bs in Achiltibuie.

Tours Those inviting **Summer Isles** lying offshore can be visited from Achiltibuie pier on board the *Hectoria*. **Cruises** leave Mon-Sat at 1030 and 1415 and last 3½ hrs, with 1 hr ashore on the islands. To book, contact *I Macleod* at Achiltibuie Post Office, T622200, or at home, T622315. Cruises cost £12 per person (half price for children). There are also deep-sea angling trips (1800-2100) which cost £6 per person and £15 per rod.

Transport There are 2 **buses** daily (Mon-Thu) to **Ullapool** with *Spa Coaches*, T01997-421311, leaving Achiltibuie Post Office at 0800 and 1300. The early bus starts in Reiff (at 0740) and the other one leaves from Badenscallie. The journey takes an hour. There's also a bus on Sat, leaving at 0750.

Lochinver

The road from Achiltibuie north to Lochinver is known locally as the 'wee mad road', and you'd be mad to miss this thrilling route which twists and winds its way through some the northwest's most stunning scenery. The village of Lochinver is a working fishing port and the last sizeable village before Thurso. It has a good tourist office (see below), lots of accommodation, a bank with ATM, post office and petrol station.

Phone code: 01571
Colour map 1, grid B5

There's a *Postbus* service from Lochinver to and from **Drumbeg**, via the coast road, which continues to **Lairg**. It runs once a day, Mon-Sat. There are also buses to and from Drumbeg and on to **Ullapool**, once or twice daily except Sun, with *Rapsons of Brora*, T01408-621245, and *Spa Coaches*, T01997-421311.

Ins & outs

The best place to start is the **Assynt Visitor Centre**, which houses the **Tourist Information Centre**. It has displays on the local geology, history and wildlife and there's also a ranger service with guided walks throughout the summer. ■ *The centre is open Apr-Oct Mon-Fri 1000-1700 and Sun 1000-1600. T844330.* Those looking for local souvenirs should head for *Highland Stoneware*, T844376, www.highlandtrail.co.uk/stoneware.html, a local pottery factory just outside the village on the road north. A few miles south of Lochinver, beyond **Inverkirkaig**, is the trail along the river to the **Kirkaig Falls**. The path starts near the *Achins Bookshop*, T844262, which has a good stock of Scottish titles and a café. Follow the path for about two miles till it branches right to the falls in the gorge below. Continue along the main path for about another ¾ mile till you reach Fionn Loch, with superb views of mighty **Suilven**. The walk up to the falls and back should take around 1½ hours. This is one of the main approaches to the foot of the mountain.

Sights

L *Inver Lodge Hotel*, Iolaire Rd, T844496, F844395, inverlodge@compuserve.com 20 rooms, open Apr-Oct. A modern luxury hotel standing above the village with great views and excellent restaurant (lunch mid-range; dinner expensive). **L** *The Albannach Hotel*, at Baddidaroch, T844407, F844285. This wonderful 18th-century house overlooking Loch Inver is one of the very best places to stay in the northwest, and the food offered in the award-winning restaurant is sublime. The price includes dinner. Non-residents are also welcome but booking is essential. There are many comfortable guesthouses and B&Bs, including **E** *Ardglas Guest House*, T844257, ardglass@btinternet.com; and **E** *Polcraig*, T844429, cathelmac@aol.com; **E** *Davar*, T844501, open Mar-Oct; and **E** *Tigh-Na-Sith*, T844740; open Apr-Sep.

Apart from the hotels listed above, the best food can be found at *Lochinver's Larder Riverside Bistro*, T844356, on the way into town on the A837. You can eat in or takeaway and prices are mid-range. Nearby is the cheap and cheerful *Caberfeidh*, T844321.

Sleeping & eating

The Highlands and Skye

Loch Assynt & Inchnadamph
Phone code: 01571
Colour map 1, grid B5/6

The area east of Lochinver is a remote wilderness of mountains and moorland dotted with lochs and lochans. As well as being a favourite haunt of hardy climbers and walkers, Assynt is a paradise for anglers. Most of the lochs are teeming with brown trout, and fishing permits are readily available throughout the area from the TIC in Lochinver or at local hotels, guesthouses and B&Bs. There's also salmon fishing on the River Kirkaig, available through the *Inver Lodge Hotel* (see above), and on Loch Assynt through the *Inchnadamph Hotel* (see below).

The A837 Lochinver-Lairg road meets the A894 to Durness 10 miles east of Lochinver at **Skiag Bridge** by Loch Assynt. Half a mile south of here, by the loch, are the ruins of **Ardvreck Castle**. The castle dates from 1597 and was the stronghold of the Macleods of Assynt until a siege of the castle in 1691, when it was taken by the Seaforth Mackenzies. Before that, the Marquis of Montrose had been imprisoned here following his defeat at Carbisdale in 1650. Access to the castle is free, but the ruins are in a dangerous state and should be approached with care.

To the east of the road lies the **Inchnadamph National Nature Reserve**, dominated by the massive peaks of **Ben More Assynt** and **Conival**, which should only be attempted by experienced hill walkers. A few miles south of the village of **Inchnadamph**, at the fish farm, is a steep, but well-marked footpath up to the **Bone Caves**. This is one of Scotland's oldest historical sites, where the bones of humans and animals such as lynx and bear were found together with sawn-off deer antlers dating from over 8,000 years ago.

Sleeping C *Inchnadamph Hotel*, T822202, inchnadamphhotel@assynt99.freeserve. co.uk An old-fashioned Highland hotel on the shores of Loch Assynt, catering for the hunting and fishing fraternity (see above). Nearby is the **F** *Inchnadamph Lodge*, T822218, assynt@presence.co.uk, or *Assynt Field Centre*, which offers basic hostel accommodation in bunk rooms, as well as twin, double and family rooms. Continental breakfast is included. It's open all year, but phone ahead between Nov and Mar. It's ideally situated for climbing Ben More Assynt and guides are available.

Lochinver to Kylesku: the coast road
Phone code: 01571
Colour map 1, grid B5

The quickest way north from Lochinver is the A837 east to the junction with the A894 which heads to Kylesku. But by far the most scenic route is the B869 coast road that passes moorland, lochs and beautiful sandy bays. It's best travelled from north to south, giving you the most fantastic views of Suilven. Untypically, most of the land in this part of Assynt is owned by local crofters who, under the aegis of the *Assynt Crofters' Trust*, bought 21,000 acres of the North Assynt Estate, thus setting a precedent for change in the history of land ownership in the Highlands.

The trust now owns the fishing rights to the area and sells permits through local post offices and the tourist office in Lochinver. It has also undertaken a number of conservation projects, including one at **Achmelvich**, a few miles north of Lochinver, at the end of a side road which branches off the coast road. It's worth a detour to see one of the loveliest beaches on the west coast, with sparkling white sand and clear turquoise sea straight out of a Caribbean tourist brochure. You can stay here, at the **F** *SYHA Hostel*, T844480, open mid-May to early October; or camp at the *Shore Caravan Site*, T844393, open April-September.

From the beach car park below the hostel a path leads northwest along the coast. Bear left off the sandy path shortly after the white cottage on the hill ahead comes into view, and follow the footpath until the road is reached at **Alltan na Bradhan** , where there are the remains of an old meal mill.

The Highlands and Skye

Continue north from here along the coast for about a mile till you reach a small bay just before **Clachtoll**, the Split Rock. Close by are the remains of an Iron-Age Broch, but don't cause further damage by clambering over the ruins. Return to the beach by the same path. The walk there and back should take about 1½ hours.

The road runs east from Drumbeg, under the shadow of towering **Quinag** (2,654 ft), to meet the A894 heading north to **Kylesku**, site of the sweeping modern road bridge over Loch a'Cháirn Bháin. From Kylesku you can visit Britain's highest waterfall, the 650-ft high **Eas a'Chùal Aluinn**, near the head of Loch Glencoul. **Cruises** leave from the old ferry jetty below the *Kylesku Hotel* to the falls on board the *MV Statesman*, T01571-844446. You can also see porpoises, seals and minke whales en route. You may be able to get closer to the falls by getting off the boat and walking to the bottom, then getting on the next boat. ■ *The 2-hr round trip runs Apr-Sep daily at 1100 and 1400 (Jul and Aug also at 1600), and costs £9, children £3.*

There's also a trail to the top of the falls. It starts at the south end of Loch na Gainmhich, about three miles north of Skiag Bridge. Skirting the loch, follow the track in a southeasterly direction up to the head of the **Bealach a Bhuirich** (the Roaring Pass). Continue until you meet a stream, with several small lochans on your right. Follow this stream until it plunges over the **Cliffs of Dubh** (the Dark Cliffs). You can get a better view of the falls by walking to the right about 100 yards and descending a heather slope for a short distance. Allow about three to four hours for the round trip.

Sleeping and eating Before you leave on the boat trip, pop into the **B** *Kylesku Hotel*, T502231, kylesku.hotel@excite.co.uk, for some delicious and great-value pub seafood, or for B&B, open Mar-Oct. There's also a more formal and expensive restaurant next door. If you want to spend the night here, a cheaper option is the **D** *Newton Lodge*, T/F502070, newtonlge@aol.com, open mid-Mar to mid-Oct. There's also a small hostel at **F** *Kylesku Lodges*, T502003, open Easter-Oct.

Ten miles north of Kylesku is the little crofting community of Scourie, sitting above a sandy bay. Anyone remotely interested in wildlife is strongly advised to make a stop here to visit Handa Island, a sea bird reserve run by the Scottish Wildlife Trust, and one of the best places in the country for bird life. The island is now deserted, except for the warden, but once supported a thriving community of crofters, until the potato famine of 1846 forced them to leave, most emigrating to Canada's Cape Breton. Now it's home to huge colonies of shags, fulmars, razorbills, guillemots and puffins. The best time to visit is during the summer breeding season, from late May to August. There's a footpath right round the island, which is detailed in the free SWT leaflet available at the warden's office when you arrive. You should allow three to four hours.

There's a **ferry service** to the island from **Tarbet Beach**, three miles northwest off the A894, about three miles north of Scourie. It sails continuously, depending on demand. ■ *Apr-Sep Mon-Sat 0930-1700. The 15-min crossing costs £7.50 return. T502077.*

Another excellent wildlife boat trip leaves from **Fanagmore**, a mile from Tarbet on the other side of the peninsula, with *Laxford Cruises*, T502251. They sail around beautiful Loch Laxford, where you can see lots of birds from nearby Handa Island, as well as seals, porpoises and otters. ■ *Trips leave Easter till the end of Sep daily except Sun at 1000, 1200 and 1400 (also at 1600 in Jul and Aug). The trips last 1 hr 45 mins and cost £10 for adults, £5 for children.*

Kylesku
Phone code: 01971
Colour map 1, grid B5

Scourie & Handa Island
Phone code: 01971
Colour map 1, grid A5

The Highlands and Skye

For bookings contact Julian Pearce, who also runs the wonderful *Seafood Restaurant* (mid-range) just above the jetty at Tarbet. If you're up this way, don't miss a visit to this restaurant which serves seafood caught by Julian during his boat trips! It's a great place and you can even stay here, in the self-catering caravan next door, which sleeps up to six.

Sleeping and eating There is lots of accommodation in and around Scourie. Best of all is the **C** *Eddrachilles Hotel*, a few miles south in Badcall Bay, T502080, F502477, eddrachilles@compuserve.com 11 rooms, open Mar-Oct, this is one of the most magnificently situated hotels in the country. The 200 year-old building stands in 300 acres of grounds overlooking the bay, the food on offer is superb, though the atmosphere is a little stuffy (their Eddrachilles heel, you might say). Another excellent place to eat is the **B** *Scourie Hotel*, T502396, www.scourie-hotel.co.uk, open 1 Apr-mid-Oct, a 17th-century former coaching inn popular with anglers (lunch mid-range; dinner expensive). There are several **B&Bs** in the village, but none better than the welcoming **C** *Scourie Lodge*, T502248, open Mar-Oct, which also does good evening meals. There's a **campsite**, T502060, on Harbour Rd.

Transport There's a **Postbus** service to Scourie from Durness and Lairg once a day, Mon-Sat. It leaves Durness at 0820 and arrives at 0935 and continues to Lairg. It returns at 1245 and arrives at 1420. There's also a **Postbus** service between Scourie and **Elphin**, with connections to **Lochinver**.

Kinlochbervie & around
Phone code: 01971
Colour map 1,
grid A5

The road north from Scourie passes **Laxford Bridge**, where it meets the A838 running southeast to **Lairg** (see page 524). The A838 also runs north to Durness, on the north coast (see below). At **Rhiconich**, the B801 branches northwest to Kinlochbervie, a small village with a very big fish market. This is one of the west coast's major fishing ports, and huge container lorries thunder along the narrow single-track roads carrying frozen fish and seafood to all corners of Europe. It's worth heading down to the fish market in the evenings to see the day's catch being landed and sold.

A few miles beyond Kinlochbervie is **Oldshoremore**, a tiny crofters' village scattered around a stunning white beach, and a great place to swim. The less hardy can instead explore the hidden rocky coves nearby.

At the end of the road is **Blairmore**, from where a footpath leads to **Sandwood Bay**, the most stunning and beautiful beach on the west coast. It's a long walk, but because of its isolation you'll probably have this glorious mile-long stretch of white sand all to yourself. The beach is flanked at one end by a spectacular rock pinnacle and is said to be haunted by the ghost of an ancient shipwrecked mariner. Allow three hours for the walk there and back, plus time at the beach. You could take a tent and watch the sunset. Sandwood Bay can also be reached from **Cape Wrath**, a day's hike to the north (see page 512).

Sleeping In Kinlochbervie village is **B** *The Kinlochbervie Hotel*, T521275, F521438, klbhotel@aol.com A nicer place to stay is the **D** *Old School Hotel*, T/F521383, www.host.co.uk, halfway between Kinlochbervie and the A838 at Rhiconich. It used to be a school, as the name implies, and this only adds to the charm. They also serve great food at mid-range prices, daily 1200-1400 and 1800-2000. In Rhiconich is the **A** *Rhiconich Hotel*, T521224, rhiconichhotel@compuserve.com; and also **B&B** at **E** *Benview*, T521242, open Apr-Sep. There's a good **campsite** at Oldshoremore, T521281.

Transport A **Postbus** leaves Kinlochbervie harbour at 0900 and goes to **Scourie** (35 mins) and on to **Lairg** (1 hr 50 mins) from where there are connections to **Inverness**. The same postbus returns from Lairg at 1245, arrives in Kinlochbervie at 1448, then continues to **Durness** (35 mins).

The North Coast

*Scotland's rugged north coast attracts few visitors, but those who do venture this far find that's there's plenty to write home about. This is some of Britain's most spectacular and undisturbed coastline, from the wild and remote **Cape Wrath** in the far northwest, to **John O'Groats**, that perennial favourite of sponsored walkers, in the far northeast. In between lie over 100 miles of storm-lashed cliffs, sheer rocky headlands and deserted sandy coves, all waiting to be explored. It's also a great place for birdwatching, with vast colonies of seabirds, and there's a good chance of seeing seals, porpoises and minke whales in the more sheltered estuaries.*

Getting around the far north without your own transport can be a slow process. Getting to **Thurso**, the main town, by bus or train is easy, but beyond that things get more difficult. Details of what little public transport there is are given under the relevant destination.

Ins & outs

Durness

Durness is not only the most northwesterly village on the British mainland, but also one of the most attractively located, surrounded by sheltered coves of sparkling white sand and machair-covered limestone cliffs. It's worth stopping here for a few days to explore the area. The **Tourist Information Centre**, T511259, arranges guided walks and has a small visitor centre with displays on local history, flora and fauna and geology. Open April-October Monday-Saturday 0900-1800; July and August also Sunday 1100-1900.

Phone code: 01971 Colour map 1, grid A6

A mile east of the village is the vast 200 ft-long **Smoo Cave**. A path from near the youth hostel leads down to the cave entrance which is hidden away at the end of a steep, narrow inlet. Plunging through the roof of the cathedral-like cavern is an 80-ft waterfall which can be seen from the entrance, but the more adventurous can take a boat trip into the floodlit interior.

Around Durness

A few miles east of the Smoo Cave are a couple of excellent beaches, at **Sangobeg** and **Rispond**, where the road leaves the coast and heads south along the west shore of stunning **Loch Eriboll**, Britain's deepest sea loch, which was used by the Royal Navy during the Second World War as a base for protecting Russian convoys.

About a mile northwest of Durness is the tiny hamlet of **Balnakeil**, overlooked by a ruined 17th-century church. In the south wall is a graveslab with carved skull-and-crossbones marking the grave of the notorious highwayman Donald MacMurchow. If you're looking for souvenirs, or an escape from the rat race, then head for the **Balnakeil Craft Village**, an alternative artists' community set up in the 1960s in a former RAF radar station. Here you can buy weavings, pottery, paintings, leatherwork and woodwork in the little prefab huts. There's also a café. ■ *Apr-Oct daily 1000-1800*. Balnakeil has also become well-known in golfing circles. The nine-hole course, T511364, is the most northerly in mainland Britain, and its famous ninth hole involves a drive over the Atlantic Ocean. The beach here is glorious, especially in fine weather

The Highlands and Skye

Old Man of Stoer

A side road turns left off the B869 north of **Stoer** *and runs out to* **Stoer lighthouse***. From here you can walk across the Stoer Peninsula to the* **Old Man of Stoer***, a dramatic rock pillar standing offshore, surrounded by sheer cliffs. Allow about three hours for the circular walk which starts and ends in the lighthouse car park. There is no public transport to the lighthouse, but the Lochinver-Drumbeg postbus runs to Raffin, one mile away. A clear path runs from the car park to the cliffs then follows the line of the cliffs northwards. The path heads inland for a short distance as it bypasses a deep gully then meets the clifftop again, and after a mile or so you can see the Old Man tucked away in a shallow bay, battered by huge waves.*

Beyond the Old Man the path continues to the headland, the **Point of Stoer***, from where it turns back on itself and climbs* **Sidhean Mór** *(532 ft). The views from here are fantastic, across to Harris and Lewis and south to the mountains of Assynt. From here, follow the faint path south, back towards the lighthouse, passing a small loch below Sidhean Beag on your left and an obvious cairn on your right. Then you pass a radio mast and follow the*

clear track back to the lighthouse car park. Nine miles further on, in beautiful **Eddrachillis Bay***, is* **Drumbeg***, a popular place for anglers who come to fish in the many lochs of North Assynt. There's not much accommodation around here other than self-catering cottages, but you can spend the night at* **D** Taigh Druimbeag, *T833209; open Easter to the end of October. OS Landranger Map No 15 covers the route.*

---

when the sea turns a brilliant shade of turquoise. Even better, walk north along the bay to **Faraid Head**, where you can see puffin colonies in early summer. The views from here, across to Cape Wrath in the west and Loch Eriboll in the east, are stupendous.

Cape Wrath There are several excellent trips around Durness, but the most spectacular is to Cape Wrath, Britain's most northwesterly point. It's a wild place and the name seems entirely appropriate, though it actually derives from the Norse word *hwarf*, meaning 'turning place'. Viking ships used it as a navigation point during their raids on the Scottish west coast. Now a lighthouse stands on the cape, above the 1,000 ft-high **Clo Mor Cliffs**, the highest on the mainland, and breeding ground for huge colonies of seabirds.

You can walk south from here to Sandwood Bay (see page 510). It's an exhilarating but long coastal walk, and will take around eight hours. It's safer doing this walk from north to south as the area around the headland is a military firing range and access may be restricted, which could leave you stranded.

Sleeping A good place to stay is the **C** *Cape Wrath Hotel*, T511212, jack@capewrathhotel.co.uk,
& eating which is just off the A838 on the road to the ferry at Keoldale. It overlooks the loch and

is popular with fishermen and passing tourists who stop here to enjoy the great food and superb views. The best value around Durness has to be the **B-C** *Port-Na-Con Guest House*, T511367, portnacon70@hotmail.com, on the west shore of Loch Eriboll, 7 miles from Durness. It's popular with anglers and divers so you'll need to book ahead to take advantage of such comfort amidst all this great scenery. The food in the adjoining restaurant is superb and also great value, especially the seafood. Non-residents are welcome but should book. There are also several B&Bs in Durness, best of which is **E** *Puffin Cottage*, T511208, puffincottage@aol.com, open Apr-Sep. There's a basic **F** *SYHA Youth Hostel*, at Smoo, to the east of the village, T511244; open mid-Mar to early Oct. There's also **camping** at *Salgo Sands Caravan Park*, T511222.

A daily **bus** runs to and from **Thurso**, via Tongue and Bettyhill (Jun-Aug, Mon-Sat) with *Highland Country Buses*, T01847-893123, leaving Thurso at 1130 and Durness at 1500. There's also a daily bus service (May to early Oct) to and from **Inverness** via Ullapool and Lochinver, with *Bluebird/Inverness Traction*, T01463-239292. There's a *Postbus* service to **Lairg** via **Tongue** and **Altnaharra**, Mon-Sat at 1115; also via **Kinlochbervie** and **Scourie** Mon-Sat at 0820. To get to **Cape Wrath**, first take the passenger **ferry** across the Kyle of Durness from Keoldale, 3 miles south of Durness, T511376. It runs May-Sep hourly 0930-1630. The ferry connects with a minibus, T511287, for the 11 miles to the cape (40 mins).

Transport

Durness to Thurso

The road east from Durness runs around Loch Eriboll on its way to the lovely little village of Tongue. A causeway runs across the beautiful **Kyle of Tongue**, but a much more scenic route is the single-track road around its southern side, with great views of **Ben Hope** (3,041 ft) looming to the southwest. The village of Tongue is overlooked by the 14th-century ruins of **Varick Castle**, and there's a great beach at **Coldbackie**, two miles northeast.

Tongue
Phone code: 01847
Colour map 2,
grid A1

Sleeping and eating There are several places to stay in Tongue. The **B-C** *Tongue Hotel*, T611206, is a former hunting lodge of the Duke of Sutherland. It overlooks the Kyle of Tongue and does good food. Also recommended for its food is the excellent **C** *Ben Loyal Hotel*, T611216, Thebenloyalhotel@byinternet.com There are cheaper options, such as the excellent-value **E** *Rhian Cottage*, T611257, jenny.anderson@tesco.net There's also a good **F** *SYHA Youth Hostel*, T611301, open mid-Mar to late Oct, beautifully situated at the east end of the causeway; and a couple of **campsites**: one is at Talmine, T601225, 5 miles north of Tongue by the beach; and the *Kincraig Camping and Caravan Site*, T611218, just to the south of the village. Also at Talmine is the lovely 19th-century **E** *Cloisters*, T601286, reception@cloisteral.demon.co.uk

The A836 runs south from Tongue, through **Altnaharra**, to **Lairg** (see page 524). It also continues east to the crofting community of **Bettyhill**, named after the Countess of Sutherland who ruthlessly evicted her tenants from their homes in Strathnaver to make way for more profitable sheep. The whole sorry saga is told in the interesting **Strathnaver Museum**, housed in an old church in the village. There are also Pictish stones in the churchyard behind the museum. ■ *Apr-Oct Mon-Sat 1000-1300 and 1400-1700. Adult £1.90, concession £1.20, children £0.50. T521418.*

The museum sells a leaflet detailing the many prehistoric sites in the Strathnaver valley which runs due south from Bettyhill. The B871 then branches southeast to meet the A897 to Helmsdale. There are a couple of great beaches around Bettyhill, at **Farr Bay** and at **Torrisdale Bay**, which is the more

Bettyhill
Phone code: 01641
Colour map 2,
grid A2

The Highlands and Skye

impressive of the two and forms part of the **Invernaver Nature Reserve**.

There's a small **Tourist Information Centre** in Bettyhill, T521342, open Easter-September Monday-Saturday.

Sleeping and eating The **E** *Farr Bay Inn*, T521230, www.bettyhill.com, does decent bar food. A good value B&B is **F** *Bruachmor*, T521265, open Apr-Oct.

Melvich & East from Bettyhill the hills of Sutherland begin to give way to the fields of
Dounreay Caithness. The road passes the turn-off to **Strathy Point** before reaching
Colour map 2, grid 2/3 **Melvich**, another wee crofting settlement overlooking a lovely sandy bay.

South from Melvich the A897 heads to Helmsdale (see page 527) through the **Flow Country**, a vast expanse of bleak bog of major ecological importance. About 15 miles south of Melvich, at **Forsinard**, is an **RSPB Visitor Centre**. The peatlands here are a breeding ground for black- and red-throated divers, golden plovers and merlins as well as other species. Otters and roe deer can also be spotted. ■ *Easter-Oct daily 0900-1800. Guided walks through the nature reserve leave from the visitor centre. T01641-571225.*

The north coast of Scotland is ideally suited to the more active type of tourist, and 10 miles west of Thurso you might say that the radioactive tourist is catered for at the **Dounreay Nuclear Power Station**. Though its fast breeder reactors were decommissioned in 1994, the plant is still a major local employer and now reprocesses spent nuclear fuel. There's a permanent exhibition at the **visitor centre**, where you learn all about the 'benefits' of nuclear power. ■ *Easter-Sep daily 1000-1700. Free. T01847-802572.*

Sleeping and eating There's some excellent accommodation in **Melvich**, including **D** *Bighouse Lodge*, T01641-531207, open May-Oct, an 18th-century mansion sitting at the mouth of the Halladale river in 4 acres of its own grounds. Also recommended is **E** *Shieling Guest House*, T/F01641-531256, theshieling@btinternet.com, open Apr-Oct.

Thurso

Phone code: 01847
Colour map 2, grid A3
Population: 9,000

Thurso is the most northerly town on the British mainland and by far the largest settlement on the north coast. In medieval times it was Scotland's chief port for trade with Scandinavia, though most of the town dates from the late 18th century when Sir John Sinclair built the 'new' extension to the old fishing port. The town increased in size to accommodate the workforce of the new nuclear power plant at nearby **Dounreay**, but the plant's demise has threatened the local economy. Today Thurso is a fairly nondescript place, mostly visited by people catching the ferry to Stromness in Orkney.

Ins & outs **Getting there** There are daily buses to and from **Inverness** which connect with buses to **Edinburgh**. There are regular daily buses to and from **Wick airport** (see page 529). **Ferries** to **Stromness** in Orkney leave from Scrabster, 2 miles north of Thurso (see page 596), and a bus service runs between **Thurso train station** and **Scrabster ferry pier**. The **train station** is at the south end of Princes St, 500 yd from the TIC (see below). There are daily trains from **Inverness**.

The **Tourist Information Centre** is on Riverside Rd, T892371. Open Apr-Oct Mon-Sat 0900-1800, Jul and Aug also Sun 1000-1800. They have a leaflet on local surfing beaches.

There's little of real interest in the town centre. Near the harbour are the **Sights**
17th-century ruins of **Old St Peter's Church**, which stand on the site of the
original 13th-century church founded by the Bishop of Caithness. In the town
hall on the High Street is the **Heritage Museum**, which features some Pictish
carved stones. ■ *Jun-Sep Mon-Sat 1000-1300 and 1400-1700. £0.50.*
T892459. Thurso is also known to keen surfers who come here for the unbeatable surf. To the east of town, at **Dunnet Bay**, is a three-mile-long beach with
an excellent reef break and there's another good reef break, at **Brims Ness** to
the west. Further west, at **Strathy Bay** (see above) you'll find rollers that can
match anything in Hawaii (though the water's a lot colder).

A reasonable bet is the huge **B** *Royal Hotel*, Traill St, T893191. 102 rooms. Central, and   **Sleeping**
upgraded to include indoor pool and leisure facilities. The nicest place to stay, though,   *Thurso boasts a*
is the **A** *Forss Country House Hotel*, T861201, jamie@forsshouse.freeserve.co.uk, 4   *wide variety of*
miles out of town at Bridge of Forss. This small family-run hotel is set in 20 acres of   *accommodation,*
lovely woodland and has an excellent restaurant, open to non-residents (mid-range to   *most of it fairly*
expensive). There are lots of cheap B&Bs, including: **E** *Murray House*, 1 Campbell St,   *average*
T895759, murrayhouse.thurso@bigfoot.com; **E** *Annandale*, 2 Rendel Govan Rd,
T893942, thomson@annandale2.freeserve.co.ul; and **E** *Mrs C Murray*, 1 Granville
Cresent, T892993. Thurso also has 3 independent hostels: **F** *Sandra's Backpackers*,
24-26 Princes St, T894575; **F** *Thurso Hostel*, Ormlie Lodge, Ormlie Rd, T/F896888; and

Thurso

Sleeping
1 Murray House
2 Royal
3 Thurso Hostel

Eating
1 Johnston's

The Highlands and Skye

F *Thurso Youth Club*, Old Mill, Millbank, T892964, open 1 Jul-30 Aug. The nearest **campsite** is *Thurso Camping Site*, T607771, north of town on the road to Scrabster.

Eating   The best place to eat in town is *The Upper Deck* in Scrabster, T892814, by the harbour. It has a mid-range surf'n'turf menu. Other than that, your best bet is a bar meal at the *Pentland Hotel*, T893202. A decent café is *Johnston's* on Traill St. There are also the ubiquitous Indian and Chinese restaurants and fish and chip shops. Out of town is the *Forss Country House Hotel* (see above) and *The Bower Inn*, T01955-661292, between Thurso and Wick. To get there, turn off the coast road at Castletown and follow the B876 till you see the sign for Gillock.

Entertainment   **Cinema** At *Viking Bowl*. **Bowling** *Viking Bowl*, Ormlie Rd, T895050. **Swimming** Millbank Rd, T893260.

Transport   **Bus** *Citylink* buses run to and from **Inverness** (3 ½ hrs) 4 times daily, T0870-5505050,
Buses arrive at Sir George's St Port Office and depart from Sir George's St Church   continuing to Scrabster to connect with the ferries to and from Stromness in Orkney. *Citylink* buses to Inverness connect with buses to **Edinburgh**. *Highland Country Buses*, T01847-893123, run local services to **Bettyhill** (3 times daily Mon-Thu, twice on Sat; 1 hr 10 mins) and to **Reay** (4 times daily Mon-Thu, 3 times on Sat). There are regular daily buses to and from **Wick** via **Halkirk** or Castletown. *Highland Country Buses* also run the service between **Thurso train station** and **Scrabster ferry pier** (5-10 mins). *Harrold Coaches*, T01955-631295, run a service to and from **John O'Groats** (4 times daily Mon-Thu, twice on Sat; 1 hr). There's also a *Postbus* service to **Wick airport**, leaving Riverside Rd at 0920 and arriving at 1000.

Car hire *William Dunnett & Co*, T893101. **Cycle hire** *The Bike & Camping Shop*, the Arcade, 34 High St, T896124, rents mountain bikes for £8 per day.

Ferry Ferries to **Stromness** in Orkney leave from Scrabster, 2 miles north of Thurso. For details, see page 596.

Train Three trains leave daily from **Inverness** (3 ½ hrs), 2 of them connecting with the ferries from Scrabster to **Stromness** in Orkney. Trains continue to **Wick** (30 mins) and return trains to Inverness leave from Wick.

Dunnett Head   About 10 miles northeast of Thurso is the most northerly point on the British
Phone code: 01847 Colour map 2, grid A3/4   mainland. No, not John O'Groats, but Dunnet Head. It's reached by turning off the Thurso-John O'Groats road at Dunnett, at the east end of **Dunnett Bay**, a three-mile-long sandy beach that's popular with surfers who come to tackle the gigantic waves of the **Pentland Firth**, the wild and treacherous strait between the mainland and Orkney.

It's a much nicer place than John O'Groats, with marvellous views across to Orkney and along the entire north coast (on a clear day). There's a Victorian lighthouse out at the point, and the dramatic seacliffs are teeming with seabirds. There's also a great little café, the *Dunnett Head Tearoom*, T851774, a few miles from the lighthouse, which serves cheap snacks and meals (open April-October daily 1500-2000).

John O'Groats   If you still feel inclined to visit this dreary tourist trap, then that's your preroga-
Phone code: 01955 Colour map 2, grid A4   tive, but don't say we didn't warn you. It's boring at best and pretty miserable most of the time. It gets its name from the Dutchman Jan de Groot, who was commissioned by King James IV to run a ferry service to Orkney in 1496. Ferries still operate from here to Burwick in Orkney (see Transport below). There's a **Tourist Information Centre** here (T611373, open April-October Monday-Saturday 0900-1700), as well as a post office, craft shops and a chippie.

Two miles east of John O'Groats is **Duncansby Head**, which is far more rewarding. South of the headland a path leads to the spectacular **Duncansby**

Stacks, a series of dramatic rock formations. The 200-ft cliffs are home to countless seabirds and you can see the narrow, sheer-sided inlets known locally as *geos*.

Sleeping and eating C *John O'Groats House Hotel*, T611203, which has a restaurant. There are also several B&Bs, including the very decent **E** *Bencorragh House*, at Upper Gills in Canisbay, a few miles west, T611449, bartonsandy@hotmail.com, open Mar-Oct. Also in Canisbay is the **F** *SYHA Youth Hostel*, T611424, open 19 Mar-31 Oct. There are a couple of **campsites**, at John O'Groats and further west by the beach at Huna. The tourist office will help you find accommodation.

Tours There are **Orkney Islands Day Tours**, which leave daily 1 May-30 Sep at 0900, and return at 1945 (£33 per person, under 16 half price). A shorter day tour departs daily from 1 Jun-2 Sep 1030, and returns at 1800 (£30 per person, under 16 £8). There's also a wildlife cruise 20 Jun-31 Aug, which departs at 1430; £12 per person. Contact: *John O'Groats Ferries*, Ferry Office, John O'Groats, T611353, F611301, www.jogferry.co.uk Tours also leave from Inverness.

Transport There are **buses** to John O'Groats from Thurso (see above under Thurso), and from **Wick** (5 daily Mon-Fri, 4 on Sat) with *Highland Country Buses*.
 Ferries to Burwick (Orkney) sail twice daily from May to September (45 mins, £16 one way). A connecting bus takes passengers on to Kirkwall (40 mins; £25 off-peak return).

The East Coast

*The east coast of the Highlands, from Inverness north to Wick, doesn't have the same draw as the west coast and attracts far fewer visitors, but it has its own, gentler appeal, and there are many lovely little seaside towns to explore. The sea lochs and estuaries of the inner **Moray Firth** are fringed with fields and woods, a fertile lowland landscape dotted with farms and crofts. Fast-flowing rivers drop from the hills through deep, wooded straths. The bulk of **Ben Wyvis** dominates the horizon northwest of Dingwall.*

*Across the **Dornoch Firth** is Sutherland – the south land of the Norsemen – where the coastal strip of fertile land narrows towards Helmsdale, backed by heather-clad hills deep blue in the reflective sea light. Prehistoric sites are abundant throughout East Sutherland, as are Pictish sculptured stones in Easter Ross. The seagoing Norsemen of Orkney used the firths to extend Viking influence into the Pictish lands, lured by good land and timber for shipbuilding. Dingwall was their Thingvallr – or place of assembly. Many existing villages grew up around Celtic Christian missions of the seventh or eighth centuries. From the 11th century **Tain** was an important place of pilgrimage, and the cathedrals at **Dornoch** and **Fortrose**, and **Fearn Abbey**, date from the 13th century.*

The Black Isle

Across the Kessock Bridge from Inverness is the Black Isle, which is neither an island nor black. It shares with the Moray coast long hours of sunshine and low rainfall, rolling acres of barley and stately woods of oak and beech dropping down to the shores. It also has a compelling atmosphere – a combination perhaps of its soft microclimate, lush vegetation and attractive architecture. Its main attractions are the picturesque town of **Cromarty** and **Chanonry**

Phone code: 01381
Colour map 2,
grid C2

The Highlands and Skye

Strathmore to Braemore walk

This walk gives a flavour of the bleak but beautiful landscape of the Caithness hinterland. The 16-mile linear route starts from Strathmore Lodge. To get there, head south from Thurso on the B874. After a short distance turn on to the B870 and follow it for 10 miles to the little hamlet of Westerdale, which stands on the River Thurso. Turn right here on to an unnumbered road and follow this road for about five miles. Just past the white Strathmore Lodge the road splits. Follow the right-hand track which runs through commercial forestry, before emerging on to open moor with Loch More on the left. Where the forestry begins again on the right, the track swings left across an arm of the loch and heads southwards. At the southern end of the loch a track runs left to Dalnaha, but keep going straight ahead, along the valley of the River Thurso. You then reach a cluster of buildings at Dalnawillan Lodge. Ignore the track which heads off to the right and carry straight on, past the house at Dalganachan, over Rumsdale Water and on to the junction before The Glutt, which is a series of

buildings. Turn left here and follow the track for a further four miles till you reach the junction beside Lochan nan Bò Riabach. Continue down the valley of Berriedale Water to Braemore.

There is no public transport from here, so you'll have to arrange your own transport if you don't want to retrace your steps. OS sheet No 11 covers the route.

Point, on the southern side near Rosemarkie, which is one of the best **dolphin-spotting** sites in Europe.

On the north side of the Kessock Bridge is the **North Kessock Tourist Information Centre**, T01463-731505; open daily from Easter to October. Next door is the **Dolphin and Seal Visitor Centre**, which gives details of accredited dolphin cruises. You can see dolphins from the village of **North Kessock** just to the south.

One of the many sacred wells (and caves) in the area is the unmissable **Clootie Well**, on the verge of the main road between Tore and Munlochy Bay Nature Reserve. It was once blessed by St Curitan (see below under Rosemarkie) and is thought to cure sick children. Thousands of rags still flutter from the surrounding trees, though well-worshippers are in danger of being mown down by traffic. Despite the presence of traffic, it's an eerie place. Go at night, if you dare.

Fortrose & Chanonry Point Further east on this road, beyond **Munlochy** and **Avoch** (pronounced 'Och') is the village of **Fortrose**, on the east shore. The magnificent **cathedral** at Fortrose is now largely a ruin where rainwashed carved faces of rose-coloured sandstone peer down from roof bosses, and snapped-off stumps of window tracery are redolent of Reformation vandalism. On the golf course at **Chanonry Point**, overlooking the Moray Firth, a plaque marks the spot where the **Brahan Seer** was boiled in a barrel of tar (see box). Chanonry Point is also a great place for seeing **dolphins**. They come close to shore at high tide and there's a good chance of seeing them leaping above the waves.

A few miles from Fortrose on the north side of Chanonry Point is the tiny vil- **Rosemarkie**
lage of **Rosemarkie**. Celtic saints Curitan and Boniface selected this sheltered spot on the southern shore for their Christian mission in the seventh century. St Boniface is remembered at nearby St Bennet's Well. **Groam Museum** houses a superb collection of Pictish sculptured stones found locally, imaginatively displayed alongside contemporary artwork inspired by them. A year-round programme of events and lectures is devoted to the study of Pictish culture. ■ *Easter-Sep Mon-Sat 1000-1700, Sun 1400-1630; Oct-Apr Sat and Sun 1400-1600. £1.50, concession £1, children £0.50. T620961.*

Beware of fairies, last sighted in the 1970's in **Fairy Glen**, now a nature reserve. A lovely marked trail leads into the glen from the top end of the High Street, through a wooded gorge where you may spot woodpeckers and treecreepers. A couple of places to eat in Rosemarkie are *Crofters*, T620844, on the seafront, which does cheap bar meals; and the *Plough Inn*, near the museum.

Cromarty

On the northeastern tip of the Black Isle Peninsula, at the mouth of the *Phone code: 01381*
Cromarty Firth, is the gorgeous village of Cromarty, one of the east coast's *Cromarty has its*
major attractions. Its neat white-harled houses interspersed with gracious *own website:*
merchants' residences are almost unchanged since the 18th century when it *www.cali.co.uk/*
was a sea port thriving on trade as far afield as Russia and the Baltic. Many emi- *highexp/Cromarty*
grants bound for the New World embarked here. A prosperity based on textiles and fishing led to decline and dereliction.

There are regular daily **buses** from **Inverness** and a bus service twice a week to and **Ins & outs**
from **Dingwall**.

Although restored and much inhabited, Cromarty now has the atmosphere of **Sights**
a backwater, but a very attractive one at that, where you feel as if you're stepping back in time, in stark contrast to the numerous oil rigs moored on the opposite shore in **Nigg Bay** (see below). For a fascinating insight into the history of the area, visit the 18th-century **Cromarty Courthouse**, in Church Street, which houses the town's museum. ■ *Apr-Oct daily 1000-1700; Nov, Dec and Mar daily 1200-1600. £3, concession/children £2; includes loan of headset for recorded tour of the town's other historic buildings. T600418.* Next to the courthouse is the thatch-roofed **Hugh Miller's Cottage**, birthplace of the eminent local geologist and author. ■ *1 May-30 Sep daily 1100-1300 and 1400-1700 (Sun afternoon only). £2.50, concession £1.70, family ticket £7. T600245.* Also worth seeing is the elegant 17th-century **East Church**.

There's a good walk along a coastal path from the east end of the village through woodland to the top of the South Sutor headland, one of the two steep headlands guarding the narrow entrance to the Cromarty Firth. There are excellent views from here across the Moray Firth. Leaflets describing this and other local walks are available at the Cromarty Courthouse.

One of Cromarty's main attractions is its **dolphins**. They can be seen from the shore, or with a **boat trip**, but make sure you go with an accredited operator, such as *Dolphin Ecosse*, T600323. Full-day or half-day trips leave from the harbour and you can see porpoises and seals as well as dolphins, and perhaps even killer whales further out. To the west, the mudflats of **Udale Bay** are an

The Highlands and Skye

RSPB reserve and a haven for wading birds and wintering duck and geese, which can be viewed from a hide. In the winter other birds such as pinkfooted geese and whooper swans use the bay as a roost. **Poyntzfield Herb Garden** is an organic plant nursery specializing in rare and native medicinal herbs. Worth visiting if only for a glimpse of the house, and the view from the car park over the Cromarty Firth through massive beech trees.

Sleeping & eating
It's advisable to book ahead during the summer

For such an appealing place, there's precious little accommodation. The best place to stay is the **C** *Royal Hotel*, on Marine Terr, T600217, royalcrom@cali.co.uk It has a good restaurant, and cheaper meals are available in the bar. There are a couple of B&Bs, including the very good **E** *Beechfield House* at 4 Urquhart Court, T600308, beechfield@cali.co.uk Another good place to eat is *Thistle's Restaurant* on Church St, T600471, which has a moderately priced and imaginative menu, including interesting vegetarian dishes. A great place for tea and scones is *Binnie's Tearoom* on Church St. For cheap bar food try the *Cromarty Arms*, opposite the Cromarty Courthouse, which also has live music some nights.

Transport

A 2-car **ferry** crosses to **Nigg** every half hour from Apr to Oct, 0900-1800. *Highland Bus & Coach*, T01463-233371, runs a **bus** service from **Inverness** to Fortrose and Cromarty (4-7 times daily Mon-Sat). There is also a bus service to and from **Dingwall** on Wed and Thu.

Strathpeffer

Phone code: 01997
Colour map 2, grid C1
Population: 1,384

Strathpeffer gets busy in the summer with coach parties, but it's a pleasant place and there are some excellent walks in the surrounding hills. The little village gained recognition in 1819 when Dr Morrison, a physician from Aberdeen, bathed in its sulphur springs and cured himself of rheumatoid arthritis. He quickly spread the word and Strathpeffer became a fashionable spa resort attracting thousands of visitors. Two world wars intervened and the town's popularity declined. Today the only reminder of its past is the **Water Sampling Pavilion** in the square where you can test the waters.

Ins & outs

There are regular **buses** between Strathpeffer and **Dingwall** (see below). There's a seasonal Tourist Information Centre, on the main square, T421415; open Easter-Nov Mon-Sat 1000-1700.

Just outside Strathpeffer on the road to Dingwall is the **Highland Museum of Childhood** which has many historical displays on childhood in the highlands, as well as collections of dolls, toys and games. ■ *Mar-Oct Mon-Sat 1000-1700, Sun 1400-1700; Jul and Aug Mon-Thu 1000-1700 and 1900-2100, Sat 1000-1700, Sun 1400-1700. £1.50, concession £1. T421031.*

Walks around Strathpeffer
OS Landranger No 26

A fine walk is to **Knock Farrel and the Touchstone Maze**, site of an Iron-Age vitrified fort which lies at the north end of a ridge known locally as the **Cat's Back**. A marked trail starts from Blackmuir Wood car park. Head up the hill from town, turn left up a road immediately before the youth hostel, and the car park is on the left. The walk is six miles in total and takes about three hours. Aside from OS Landranger sheet 26, the route is also described in a Forestry Commission leaflet *Forests of Easter Ross*, available from tourist offices.

Another excellent side trip is to **Rogie Falls**, near Contin, which is three miles southwest of Strathpeffer on the main A835 Inverness-Ullapool road.

The short walk up to the falls starts from the car park three miles north of Contin on the A835. There are also some pleasant woodland walks around here. Experienced hikers can tackle magnificent **Ben Wyvis** (3,432 ft). The route to the summit starts four miles north of **Garve**, seven miles northwest of Contin.

The best accommodation is in **Contin**, 3 miles southwest of Strathpeffer. Top of the list is the excellent **B** *Coull House Hotel*, T421487, www.milford.co.uk/go/coulhouse.html, an elegant 19th-century country house offering fine food. There are several **B&Bs** in Contin, including the very grand-looking **E** *Taigh an Eilein*, T421009, lorna.mac@talk21.com, open Apr-Sep. In Strathpeffer itself is the **C** *Brunstane Lodge Hotel*, on Golf Course Rd, T421261, open Mar-Dec, which serves decent cheap bar meals. There are many good value B&Bs in Strathpeffer, including: **D** *Inver Lodge*, T421392, open Mar-Dec; **E** *White Lodge*, T421730, walter_fleming@lineone.net, open Apr-Oct; and the elegant **D-E** *Craigvar*, on the Square, T421622, www.craigvar.com **Sleeping**

Dingwall and the Cromarty Firth

Dingwall, at the head of the Cromarty Firth, has two major claims to fame. Not only is it believed to be the birthplace of Macbeth, it was also the home for many years of **Neil Gunn** (1891-1973), perhaps the Highlands' greatest literary figure (see also page). It's a fairly dull, though functional town, with good shops and banks (with ATMs) lining its long main street. The **Dingwall Museum** tells the history of this Royal Burgh. ■ *May-Sep Mon-Sat 1000-1700. £1.50, concession £1, children £0.50. T865366.* *Phone code: 01349 Colour map 2, grid C1*

East of Dingwall, before **Evanton**, is **Clanland and Sealpoint**, which has history and wildlife exhibitions and offers the chance to see the local seal population. ■ *All year daily 0930-1730. T830033.* Standing on a hill above Evanton is the **Fyrish Monument**, a replica of the Gate of Negapatam in India, built by local men and funded by local military hero, Sir Hector Munro, to commemorate his capture of the Indian town, in 1781. To get there, turn off the B9176 towards Boath. It's a stiff two-hour climb up to the top.

The Cromarty Firth is a centre for repairing North Sea oil rigs, and many of the villages along its north shore have benefited from the oil industry. One of these is **Invergordon**, just west of Nigg Bay, which has suffered in recent years due to the closure of the local aluminium factory.

Beyond Invergordon, a road branches south to **Nigg Ferry**. The ferry from Cromarty to Nigg was once a major thoroughfare, and now a tiny two-car ferry makes the 20-minute crossing in the summer months (see **Cromarty** above). From the ferry you get a good view of **Nigg Bay**, a vast natural harbour used in both world wars by the Royal Navy. Its entry is guarded by the dramatic headlands of the Sutors, identified in folklore as friendly giants. Also gigantic are the oil rigs ranged along the firth and the oil terminal at Nigg, a dramatic and not unpleasant contrast with Lilliputian Cromarty. Away from the shore, in **Nigg Old Church** (1626) is an old Pictish cross slab. ■ *Easter-Oct daily 1000-1630.*

If you need to stay in **Dingwall**, the smartest place around is **B** *Tulloch Castle Hotel*, T861325, a castle dating from the 12th century. There's hostel accommodation in **Evanton** at the *Blackrock Bunkhouse*, T830917, open 1 Apr-31 Oct. **Sleeping**

Dingwall is on the rail line between **Inverness** and **Kyle of Lochalsh** and Thurso. There are several **trains** daily in each direction (30 mins to Inverness). There are hourly **buses** **Transport**

The Highlands and Skye

A seerious crime

The Brahan Seer was boiled in a barrel of tar in 1660 but not before he had foretold the building of the Caledonian Canal and Kessock Bridge, the Highland Clearances and the Second World War. He also predicted the demise of the local lairds and the Seaforths. It was Lady Seaforth who ordered his execution, after the seer had a vision of her husband in the arms of another woman. Apparently the precise spot where he met his end is now the 13th hole of the golf course at Chanonry Point, which just goes to prove that it is indeed unlucky for some.

---

between **Inverness** and **Invergordon**, via Dingwall. There are also hourly buses between Inverness and Dingwall via **Muir of Ord**. There are buses between Dingwall and **Rosemarkie** (twice a day Mon-Thu), and between Dingwall and **Cromarty** (Wed and Thu).

Tain

Phone code: 01862
Colour map 2, grid B2
Population: 4,110

Squeezed between the Cromarty Firth to the south and the Dornoch Firth to the north is the **Tain Peninsula**, whose largest town is Tain. It has an impressive historical portfolio. Its backstreets are an intriguing jigsaw of imposing merchants' houses, steep vennels, secret gardens and dormer windows.

Ins & outs Tain is on the **Inverness-Thurso** rail line and there are **trains** daily in each direction. There are also daily **buses** to and from Inverness and Thurso.

Sights
Tain is a place with a 1950's time-warp feel

Tain was the birthplace of the 11th-century missionary **St Duthac**. Pilgrims flocked here in the Middle Ages to his shrine, and a ruin near the links is thought to be the original **chapel**. His head and heart, encapsulated in gold and silver reliquaries, were later kept in the still extant medieval **Collegiate church** until their disappearance during the Reformation. The shrine was much favoured by the Stewart kings, notably James IV who on one of his frequent pilgrimages reputedly approached walking penitentially barefoot along the King's Causeway. Tain's status as a place of sanctuary probably explains why Bruce's family fled here during the Wars of Independence.

The Collegiate church is on Castle Brae, just off the High Street, and inside is a 17th-century panel painted with the badges of the trade guilds, a reminder of the town's busy international trade. Another reminder is the imposing 16th-century **Tolbooth** in the High Street. Next to the church is a **museum** housed in the Pilgrimage which charts the town's medieval history in the **Tain through Time** exhibition. ■ *Apr-Oct daily 1000-1800; Nov, Dec and Mar 1200-1600. £3.50, concession £2.50. T894089.*

One of Tain's main attractions is the **Glenmorangie whisky distillery**, just off the A9 to the north of town, where you can see how the world-famous whisky is made and try a sample. ■ *All year Mon-Thu 0900-1700; Jun-Aug also Sat 1000-1600 and Sun 1200-1600. Tours from 1030-1530. £2. T892477.* Also out of town, just to the south off the A9, is the **Aldie Water Mill**, a restored 16th-century mill in working order, with various high-quality craft shops attached. Nearby is **The Tain Pottery**, which you can also visit. ■ *Daily 1000-1700. T893786.*

There are several grand hotels in and around Tain. **L** *Mansfield House Hotel*, Scotsburn Rd, T892052, www.mansfield-house.co.uk 19th-century baronial splendour and superb cuisine. Restaurant also open to non-residents (mid-range to expensive). There's the excellent value **C** *Morangie House Hotel*, on Morangie Rd, T892281. It's popular locally for its food (mid-range) and is open for lunch and dinner. There are also more modest B&B options, such as **E** *Golf View House*, at 13 Knockbreck Rd, T892856, www.golfview.co.uk

Sleeping & eating

Brown's Gallery, Castle Brae. Showcases work by Highland artists. Local mussels can be bought from *Bannerman's*, a fish and seafood wholesalers.

Shopping

Tain is on the **Inverness-Thurso** rail line and there are 3 **trains** daily in each direction. *Citylink* **buses** between Inverness and Thurso pass through Tain 4 times a day. There are also buses to **Portmahomack** (4 times daily Mon-Thu), **Balintore** (5-6 times daily Mon-Sat), **Lairg** via **Bonar Bridge** (3 times daily Mon-Sat) and **Dornoch** via **Bonar Bridge** (once a day Mon-Thu) with *Inverness Traction*, T01463-239292, and *Rapson's of Brora*, T01408-621245.

Transport

The town of Tain serves a vast hinterland. Inland the hills are little-visited backwoods and farm towns, narrow valleys lined with crofts where cattle graze in boggy haughs and, to the west, glens and moorland. Along the seaboard are the windswept fields of the **Tarbat Peninsula**. Good sea angling is to be had from the harbours of the otherwise dull coastal villages such as **Balintore**, and at **Shandwick** is a massive Pictish stone. It is said that unbaptized children were buried near the stone which is now in the Museum of Scotland in Edinburgh.

Around Tain

The seaside village of Portnahomack, or 'port of Colman', is named after the missionary who was keen as mustard to found a religious settlement here. Archaeological work is revealing the importance of this area in Pictish times. The **Tarbat Discovery Centre**, T871790, in Tarbat Old Church, displays recently discovered Pictish stonecarving. From the harbour, with its 18th-century girnals (grain warehouses) and sheltered sandy beach, you can see a huge stretch of the Sutherland coast, and the great sandbanks – the 'gizzen brigs' – at the mouth of the Dornoch Firth. Boat trips are available from the harbour for sea angling. A worthwhile trip is out to **Tarbat Ness lighthouse**, about three miles north.

Portnahomack
Colour map 2, grid B2

Eating A great place to eat out here is *The Oyster Catcher*, T871560, a small café-restaurant serving snacks and lunches, and dinner from 1930 (if booked). Crêpes are a speciality, but it also does pasta, seafood and fish.

South from Portnahomack, just west of the junction of the B9165 and the B9166, is Hill of Fearn. **Fearn Abbey** was moved here around 1250 from its original site near Edderton, where it was too vulnerable to sea raiders. It later became the parish church, but in 1742 lightning struck the roof which fell in, killing 38 Sunday worshippers. A tragedy was preceded by a fairy harbinger sighted at nearby Loch Eye. In Hill of Fearn is the excellent **Anta Factory Shop**, one of the very best places in the country for classy tartan furnishing fabrics, as well as tartan rugs and throws, and pottery. ■ *Mon-Sat 1000-1700 (Jun-Sep also Sun 1000-1600).*

Hill of Fearn
Colour map 2, grid C2

The Highlands and Skye

The Dornoch Firth

Colour map 2, grid B2

Fairies were said to cross the Dornoch Firth on cockle shells and were once seen building a bridge of fairy gold, perhaps a forerunner of the Dornoch Bridge which carries the A9 across the Firth just north of Tain. A more pleasant and interesting route is to follow the A836 along the south shore. From **The Struie**, reached by the B9176 which branches south at Easter Fearn, there's a panoramic view over the Dornoch Firth and the Sutherland hills. In the churches of **Edderton** and **Kincardine** are Pictish stones. Another stands in a field northwest of Edderton, but don't disturb the crops or livestock. A quartz boulder at **Ardgay**, the 'Clach Eiteag', commemorates the cattle tryst and fair which once took place locally.

Ten miles from Ardgay, at the end of lovely **Strathcarron**, is the isolated **Croick church**, one of the most poignant reminders of the infamous Clearances. Here in 1845, 90 local folk took refuge in the churchyard after they had been evicted from their homes in Glencalvie by the Duke of Sutherland to make way for flocks of sheep. A reporter from *The Times* described the 'wretched spectacle' as men, women and children were carted off, many never to return. The report is there to read. Far more evocative and harrowing, though, are the names and messages the people scratched in spidery copperplate in the window panes.

Culrain

North of Ardgay is the **Kyle of Sutherland**, where several rivers converge to flood into the sea through lush water meadows. Montrose was defeated here, at **Carbisdale**, in 1651. Overlooking the Kyle, at **Culrain**, is the 19th-century **Carbisdale Castle**, once home of the exiled King of Norway, which now houses the largest and most sumptuous **F** *Youth Hostel* in Scotland, and possibly anywhere else, T01549-421232. It's open 26 February-31 October (except the first two weeks in May). Trains between Inverness and Thurso stop at Ardgay and Culrain. The youth hostel is half a mile up a steep hill from the station. Buses between Inverness and Lairg (see below) stop in Ardgay and Bonar Bridge.

Bonar Bridge & Invershin

After the Dornoch Ferry disaster of 1809, a bridge was built over the Kyle at **Bonar Bridge**, from where the A949 runs eastwards to join the main A9 just before Dornoch, while the A836 continues north to Lairg (see below). A few miles north of **Invershin** are the **Falls of Shin**, an excellent place to watch salmon battling upstream on their way to their spawning grounds (best seen June to September). A visitor centre and café/restaurant/shop has information about six easy walks in the immediate area; all are under an hour long. The café/restaurant serves good, cheap food daily till 1730.

Lairg

Phone code: 01549
Colour map 2, grid B1

Eleven miles north of Bonar Bridge is the uninspiring village of Lairg, the region's main transport hub. Lairg is best known for its annual lamb sale, when young sheep from all over the north of Scotland are bought and sold.

Ins and outs It is said that all roads meet at Lairg, and it's certainly a hard place to avoid. From here the A839 heads east to meet the A9 between Dornoch and Golspie, and west to meet the A837 which runs out to Lochinver. The A836 heads north to Tongue, and south to Bonar Bridge. The A838 meanwhile heads northwest to Laxford Bridge and on to Durness, near Cape Wrath. **Trains** between **Inverness** and **Thurso** stop at Lairg, and **buses** run from here to **Ullapool**.

There's a **Tourist Information Centre**, T402160, which is open Mon-Sat 0900-1700 and Sun 1300-1700.

There are several interesting walks around the village, some of which lead to prehistoric sites such as the Neolithic hut circles at nearby **Ord Hill**. These walks, and many others in the region, are described with maps in the Forestry Commission's leaflet *Forests of the Far North*, which is available at the Ferrycroft Countryside Centre and the TIC.

There's a bank with ATM in the village and several places to stay, including **D-E** *The Nip Inn*, on the main street, T402243, info@nipinn.co.uk, which also does bar meals. There are several **B&Bs** and a **campsite** too, but the most interesting place to stay is 9 miles east at **Rogart** train station, where you can get cheap hostel accommodation at the **F** *Rogart Railway Carriages*, T01408-641343, rogmail@globalnet.co.uk Two old rail carriages have been converted to sleep 16 people and there's a 10% discount for bike or train users. **Sleeping & eating**

Trains between **Inverness** and **Thurso** stop at Lairg and Rogart stations 3 times daily. *Inverness Traction* **buses**, T01463-239292, run from here to **Ullapool**, with connections to **Lochinver** and **Durness**, from May to early Oct (Mon-Sat). Lairg is also the central point for several **postbus** routes, T01463-256228. **Transport**

Dornoch

Dornoch is another architectural gem with its deep, golden sandstone houses and leafy cathedral square. Bishop Gilbert of Moravia (Moray) built the cathedral circa 1245. His family's success in gaining a foothold in Northeast Scotland against the Norsemen was rewarded with the Earldom of Sutherland. It was trouble with the Jarls which prompted Gilbert to move his power base here from Caithness, mindful that his predecessor had been boiled in butter by the locals. *Phone code: 01862 Colour map 2, grid B2*

Getting there There are **buses** to and from **Inverness** (hourly Mon-Sat, 5 times on Sun). *Citylink* buses between Inverness and **Thurso** also stop in Dornoch 4 daily. The **Tourist Information Centre**, T810400, is on the main square. Open Mon-Sat 0900-1300 and 1400-1700. **Ins & outs**

The 13th-century **cathedral** was badly damaged in 1570, then subjected to an ill-conceived 'restoration' by the Countess of Sutherland in 1835. Among the few surviving features is a series of gargoyles, including a green man, and the effigy of an unknown knight. ■ *Mon-Fri 0730-2000. You can climb the cathedral tower during Jul and Aug.* Opposite the cathedral is the 16th-century **Bishop's Palace**, now a hotel (see below). **Sights**

Nowadays Dornoch is famous for its links **golf course**, rated as one of the world's finests and relatively easy to get on. It overlooks miles of dunes and pristine sandy beach. A stone near the links marks the spot where the last **witch** in Scotland was burned in 1722. Folklore recounts a bloody battle against raiding Vikings in 1259 on the beach at **Embo**, just to the north, in which Sir Richard Murray was killed. The battle is commemorated at the **Earl's Cross**. Trout fishing is available on Dornoch Lochans; enquire locally.

Straggling crofting townships such as **Rogart** (see above) are scattered through the glens and around the coast, all occupied and worked vigorously.

The Highlands and Skye

The coastal population was swollen in the 19th century by tenants evicted from the inland glens, resettled here and encouraged to try fishing at such villages as **Embo**. Others joined the eager flood of emigrants to the New World already under way. Crofting tenancies still exist, but crofters now enjoy more protection (see page 570).

North of Dornoch is **Loch Fleet**, a river estuary with a ferocious tide race at its mouth and an SNH reserve protecting rare birds and plants. The rotting skeletons of the fishing fleet abandoned in the First World War lie in the sand on the south shore west of the car park. Nearby **Skibo Castle** is where Madge and Mr Ritchie tied the knot, in relative secrecy. It is an exclusive club, but details of accommodation are available from the Dornoch tourist office. There are several walks in the forestry plantations in the area.

Sleeping & eating There's plenty of accommodation in Dornoch, which can be booked at the tourist office. **B-D** *Dornoch Castle Hotel*, T810216, www.dornochcastle.com, open Apr-Oct. Formerly the Bishop's Palace, this 16th-century building is full of character and boasts excellent food (expensive). Another fine hotel is **L** *The Royal Golf Hotel*, T/F810283, scotland@morton-hotels.demon.co.uk, next to the first tee. There are also lots of good B&Bs and a **campsite**.

Apart from the hotels listed above, a good place to dine is *The Two Quails*, on Castle St, where you can enjoy an expensive but top-class dinner cooked by a chef trained at the *Ritz*. Next door is *Luigi's*, for excellent coffee and a range of exotic ice creams.

Shopping **Bookshops** *The Dornoch Bookshop* on the High St, T810165, is the only bookshop in the area and stocks local books.

Golspie
Phone code: 01408
Colour map 2, grid B2
Population: 1,650

There is little to recommend the dull little town of Golspie, though it does have a couple of banks and supermarkets. There's an 18-hole golf course, and the *Orcadian Stone Company* has a large display of fossils and geological specimens from the Highlands and beyond. The town lives in the dark shadow of the Sutherlands. On **Beinn a'Bhraggaidh** (1,293 ft), to the southwest, is a huge, 100 ft-high **monument** to the Duke of Sutherland. Those who make it up to the monument and who know something of the Duke's many despicable acts may find the inscription risible, as it describes him as "a judicious, kind and liberal landlord". There's no reference to the fact that he forcibly evicted 15,000 tenants from his estate. Not surprisingly, locals would like to see this eyesore removed from the landscape, broken into tiny pieces and then scattered far and wide. Unfortunately, they have thus far been unsuccessful.

The aptly named **Dunrobin Castle**, one mile north of the village, is the ancient seat of the Dukes of Sutherland, who once owned more land than anyone else in the British Empire. Much enlarged and aggrandized in the 19th century with fairy-tale turrets, the enormous 189-room castle, the largest house in the Highlands, is stuffed full of fine furniture, paintings, tapestries and *objets d'art* and bears witness to their obscene wealth. The castle overlooks beautiful gardens laid out with box hedges, ornamental trees and fountains. In stormy weather you should listen to the sea crashing on the beach beyond the walls. The **museum** is an animal-lover's nightmare and almost a caricature of the aristocracy, with a spectacular Victorian taxidermy collection. There are also local antiquities, some from ancient brochs, and Pictish stonecarvings. ■ *1 Apr-31 May and 1-15 Oct Mon-Sat 1030-1630, Sun 1200-1630; 1 Jun-30 Sep Mon-Sat 1030-1730, Sun 1200-1730. £6, students £5, OAPs & children £4.50. T633177.*

Brora sits at the mouth of the River Brora which, as everywhere on this coast, is the site of a once-lucrative salmon netting industry. At the harbour, the ice house is a relic of the herring boom. Coal mines, opened in the 16th century, salt pans and a brickworks are all defunct. Still very much alive, however, is *Hunter's*, the local weavers of heavyweight traditional tweeds, and a good place to invest in some natty headwear. A mile or so north of town is the **Clynelish distillery**. ■ *Tours all year Mon-Thu 0930-1630. £3. T623000.* **Castle Cole** in lovely **Strath Brora**, eight miles northwest, is one of several ruined brochs. Another, **Carn Liath** (signposted), is by the main road, three miles south of Brora.

Brora
Phone code: 01408
Colour map 2, grid B2
Population: 1,860

Sleeping and eating Next to each other, overlooking Brora's golf course are **L-A** *The Links & Royal Marine Hotels*, T621252, highlandescape@btinternet.com Among the many B&Bs is **D** *Glenaveron*, on Golf Rd, T/F621601, glenaveron@hotmail.com If you're staying or just passing through don't miss *Capaldi's*, on the High St, for exquisite home-made Italian ice cream.

North of Brora is the former herring port of Helmsdale, which gets busy in the summer. The village is most notable for its excellent **Timespan Heritage Centre**, which brings the history of the Highlands to life through a series of high-tech displays, sound effects and an audiovisual programme. ■ *Easter-Oct Mon-Sat 0930-1700, Sun 1400-1700. £3.50, concession £2.80, children £1.75. T821327.*

Helmsdale
Phone code: 01431
Colour map 2,
  grid B2

Ins and outs Helmsdale is on the Inverness-Wick/Thurso **rail** line. Buses and trains are the same as for Wick (see below). The Tourist Information Centre, T821640, is on the south side of the village, by the A9. Apr-Sep Mon-Sat 1000-1700.

The centre also includes a model of Barbara Cartland, which may seem incongruous, until you venture across the road to the *La Mirage* tearoom and see the lady herself in the flesh (pink, of course) – or so it seems. The proprietrix is the inimitable Nancy Sinclair, who has modelled herself, and her tearoom, on the queen of romantic novels. The whole effect is pure kitsch and you never know who might pop in for a plate of fish and chips. Barbara Cartland has been holidaying in Helmsdale for over 60 years. ■ *Daily 1200-2045 (Dec-Apr till 1900).*

Sleeping and eating Another good place to eat is the **B-C** *Navidale House Hotel*, T821258, open Feb-Nov. There are also several **B&Bs**, including **D** *Broomhill House*, T821259, with its distinctive turret; and **E** *Torbuie*, T821424, in Navidale, about a mile south. There's also an *SYHA Youth Hostel*, T821577, open mid-May to early Oct.

North from Helmsdale the A9 climbs spectacularly up the **Ord of Caithness** and over the pass enters a desolate, treeless landscape; an area devastated during the Clearances. To get some idea of the hardships people had to endure, stop at the ruined crofting village of **Badbea**, just beyond **Ousdale**. At **Berriedale** a farm track leads west to the **Wag**, from where you can climb **Morven** (2,313 ft), the highest hill in Caithness, with amazing views across the whole county.

The A9 coast road then drops down into **Dunbeath**, a pleasant little village at the mouth of a small strath (or glen). This was the birthplace of one of Scotland's foremost writers, **Neil Gunn** (1891-1973). His finest works, such as

Dunbeath
Phone code: 01593

The Highlands and Skye

After the Gold Rush

*A short drive from Helmsdale, up the **Strath of Kildonan** (or Strath Ullie), is **Baile an Or** (Gaelic for 'goldfield'), site of the great Sutherland Gold Rush of 1869. It all started after local man Robert Gilchrist returned home from the Australian gold fields only to discover gold here, on his doorstep. His success brought others rushing to Kildonan, and soon a shanty town had sprung up to accommodate them.*

Within a year the gold rush was over, but small amounts are still found today. Anyone who fancies their luck can try a bit of gold panning in the Kildonan Burn at Baile an Or, about a mile from Kildonan train station. You can rent out gold panning kits at Strath Ullie Crafts & Fishing Tackle, T821343, opposite the Timespan Heritage Centre in Helmsdale, for £2.50 per day, and licences are free.

The Silver Darlings and *Highland River*, reflect his experiences of growing up in the northeast and are fascinating accounts of life here during the days of the herring boom, though the sleepy harbour of today is barely recognizable as the erstwhile bustling fishing port. The villages of Dunbeath, and **Latherton** to the north, are included on the *Neil Gunn Trail*, as is the beautiful walk up the glen, described in the leaflet available at the **Dunbeath Heritage Centre**. Here, you can learn all about the life and works of the famous novelist as well as the history of Caithness. ■ *Apr-Sep daily 1100-1700. £1.50, concession £0.50, children free. T731233.* If you fancy something to eat, the **D** *Dunbeath Hotel*, T731208, does good, cheap bar meals.

Just outside the village is the **Laidhay Croft Museum**, a restored traditional longhouse with stable, house and byre all under the same roof. ■ *Apr-Oct daily 1000-1800. £1, children £0.50. T 731370.*

Wick

Phone code: 01955
Colour map 2,
grid A4
Population: 8,000

A century ago Wick was Europe's busiest herring port, its harbour jam-packed with fishing boats and larger ships exporting tons of salted fish to Russia, Scandinavia and the West Indian slave plantations. The fishing industry has long since gone, and the demise of the nearby nuclear power station at Douneray has only added to the sense of a place that's past its best. However, there are some interesting archaeological sites in Caithness, as well as the dramatic landscapes, and Wick makes a useful base for exploring the area.

Ins & outs
See also Transport on next page

Wick has an **airport**, a few miles north of town, with daily direct flights to and from Kirkwall (Orkney), **Sumburgh** (Shetland), **Aberdeen** and **Newcastle**. The train and bus stations are next to each other behind the hospital. There are buses to and from **Inverness** and **Thurso**, and trains to **Inverness**.

The **Tourist Information Centre** is on Whitechapel Rd (just off the High St), T602596. Open all year Mon-Fri 0900-1700, Sun 0900-1300.

Sights

Wick is actually two towns. On one side of the river is Wick proper and on the other is **Pulteneytown**, the model town planned by Thomas Telford for the British Fisheries Society in 1806 to house evicted crofters who came to work here. Now it's one great living museum of fishermen's cottages and derelict sheds and stores around the near-deserted quays. It gives a good idea of the scale of the herring trade during its heyday in the mid-19th century, when over 1,000 boats set sail to catch the 'silver darlings'. Here, on Bank Row, is the superb **Wick Heritage Centre**. The highlight of the centre is its massive

The Highlands and Skye

photographic collection dating from the late 19th century. ■ *May-Sep Mon-Sat 1000-1700. £2, children £0.50. T605393.*

Three miles north of Wick are the impressive 15th-century clifftop ruins of **Sinclair and Girnigoe Castle**. On the A99 heading north out of town is the **Caithness Glass Visitors Centre**, where you can watch the famous glass being blown. ■ *Mon-Thu 0900-1630. The shop is open till 1700. T602286.* There is a good **walk** along the rocky shore east of town to **The Trinkie**, and about a mile further on to the **Brig o' Trams**. Ask for details at the TIC. Before Wick, at Ulbster, is another archaeological site, the **Cairn o' Get**. Opposite the sign are the precipitous **Whaligoe Steps**, which lead down to a tiny, picturesque harbour.

One of the most fascinating archaeological sites in the north are the well-preserved **Grey Cairns of Camster**. These chambered cairns, dating from the third and fourth millenia BC, are burial mounds of stone raised around carefully structured circular chambers with narrow entrance passages.To get there, head a mile east of **Lybster** on the A9, then turn left on to the minor road leading north to Watten. The cairns are five miles along this road, on the left-hand side. They comprise two enormous prehistoric burial chambers dating from 2500 BC. They are amazingly complete, with corbelled ceilings, and can be entered on hands and knees through narrow passageways.

If you wish to stay in Wick, there's a reasonable selection of hotels such as **C** *Mackay's* **Sleeping** *Hotel*, Union St, T602323, www.mackayshotel.co.uk, by the roundabout just across the bridge from the town centre. But you're better off going for the excellent **A-B** *Portland Arms Hotel*, about 15 miles south, in Lybster, T01593-721208, www.portlandarms. co.uk A 19th-century coaching inn, full of character and offering great food (mid-range to expensive). The best of the guesthouses and B&Bs are **E** *Wellington Guest House*, 41-43 High St, T603287, open Mar-Oct; and **E** *The Clachan*, on South Rd, T605384. Also good value is **E** *Greenvoe*, George St, near the town centre, T603942.

The best places to eat are also out of town. These include *The Bower Inn* (see page **Eating** 516), and the *Old Smiddy Inn*, in Thrumster, 5 miles south of Wick, T651256, open daily 1200-2100. Probably the best place in town is the *Queen's Hotel*, on Francis St, T602992, which has a varied menu (mid-range). Alternatively, try *Cabrelli's*, 134 High St, a great caff serving pizza and fish and chips. A few yards away is *Carter's Bar*, which does pub food and is an okay place for a drink at night.

Air Wick has an **airport** (T602215), a few miles north of town, with daily direct flights **Transport** to and from **Kirkwall** (Orkney), **Sumburgh** (Shetland), **Aberdeen** and **Edinburgh** with and *British Airways Express*, T08457-733377. Also direct flights to/from Newcastle with *Eastern Airways*, T01955-603914. There's a **Postbus** service to **Wick airport** Mon-Sat at 1015.

Bus *Scottish Citylink*, T08705-505050, buses between **Inverness** and **Thurso** stop en route in Wick (3 daily). There are also regular local buses to Thurso, via Halkirk or Castletown, and buses to **Helmsdale** (2-6 times daily Mon-Sat, 1-4 on Sun) and **John O'Groats** (5 daily Mon-Sat, 4 on Sun).

Car/bike hire *Richard's Garage*, Francis St, T604123.

Train The train and bus stations are next to each other behind the hospital. Trains leave for **Inverness** (3 daily Mon-Sat, 2 on Sun; 3¾ hrs) via **Thurso**, **Helmsdale**, **Golspie**, **Lairg** and **Dingwall**.

The Highlands and Skye

Strathspey and the Cairngorms

One of Scotland's busiest tourist areas is Strathspey, the broad valley of the River Spey, Scotland's second longest river, which rises high in the hills above Loch Laggan and flows northeast to its mouth on the Moray Firth. The lower reaches are famous for salmon fishing and whisky and are covered in the Speyside section of this guide (see page 425), while the upper reaches attract outdoor sports enthusiasts in droves. Hemmed in between the mighty Monadhliath Mountains to the north and the magnificent Cairngorms, Britain's second highest range, to the south, this is an area which offers excellent hiking, watersports, mountain biking and above all, winter skiing.

The main focus of the area is the tourist resort of Aviemore, a name synonymous with winter sports. It's a fairly tawdry place, but people don't come here for the architecture. Aviemore is surrounded by towering peaks, lochs, rivers and forests of native Caledonian pine which are home to rare wildlife such as pine martens, wildcats, red squirrels, ospreys and capercaillie, and Britian's only herd of wild reindeer. Most of upper Strathspey is privately owned by the Glen More Forest Park and Rothiemurchus Estate which has been in the possession of the Grant family since the 16th century, but both owners allow free access to their lands and provide generous outdoor facilities.

Outdoor sports

Skiing
Phone code: 01479
For latest snow conditions call the Ski Hotline T0900-1654655

Cairngorm is Scotland's longest-established ski resort and, though it cannot compare to anything in the Alps or North America, it remains Scotland's largest ski area, with 28 runs and over 20 miles of pistes. When the sun shines, the snowfall is good and the crowds are thin, it can be a very satisfying experience. The season normally runs from January until the snow disappears, which can be as late as April.

The **Cairngorm Ski Area** is about nine miles southeast of Aviemore, above Loch Morlich in Glen More Forest Park, and reached by a frequent bus service. You can rent skis and other equipment from the Day Lodge at the foot of the ski area (T861261), where you can also buy a lift pass (£21 per day). Ski hire (skis, poles and boots) costs £13 per day, and snowboard hire is £16. There are plans to replace the chair-lift with a funicular railway, much to the anger of environmentalists, but this may be a few years away.

If there's enough snow, the area around **Loch Morlich** and **Rothiemurchus Estate** provides good **cross-country** skiing, though in recent years snowfall has been below average. For more information, see page 61. The tourist office provides a free *Cairngorm Piste Map & Ride Guide* leaflet and a *Ski Scotland* brochure which lists ski schools and rental facilities.

Walking
The walks around Strathspey are covered by OS Landranger map No 36 (1:50,000 scale) or OS Outdoor Leisure Map No 3 (1:25,000 scale)

The Cairngorms provide some of Scotland's most challenging walking, with no fewer than 49 Munros and half of Britain's eight mountains over 4,000 ft (**Ben MacDrui**, **Braeriach**, **Cairn Toul** and **Cairn Gorm**). These mountains come into their own in winter, providing experienced climbers with a wide range of classic ice climbs. They should not be taken lightly. They require a high degree of fitness, experience and preparation (see page 60 for safety precautions).

The summit of Cairn Gorm (4,084 ft) is readily accessible as you take the chair-lift up to the Day Lodge (see above) and from there it's a relatively short climb to the top, though you should be prepared for a sudden change in weather conditions.

There are 50 miles of footpaths through this area, including some lovely walks through the forests. There are also ranger-led guided walks. You can find out more at the **Rothiemurchus Estate Visitor Centre**, T810858, which is a mile from Aviemore along the Ski Road. It's open daily 0900-1700 and can provide a free *Visitor Guide and Footpath Map*. Another good area for walking is around **Glen More Forest Park**. The **visitor centre**, T861220, near Loch Morlich has a *Glen More Forest Guide Map* which details local walks.

The best known of the long-distance trails is the **Lairig Ghru**, a 25-mile hike from Aviemore over the Lairig Ghru Pass to Braemar. The trail is well marked but can take at least eight hours and is very tough in parts, so you'll need to be properly equipped and prepared.

In summer, the main activities are watersports, and there are two centres **Watersports** which offer sailing, canoeing and windsurfing tuition and equipment hire. The **Loch Morlich Watersports Centre** (T861221, lochmorlichw-s@ sol.co.uk; open Apr-Oct) is five miles east of Aviemore. The **Loch Insh Watersports Centre**, T651272, user@lochinsh.dial.netmedia.co.uk, open Apr-Oct, offers the same facilities, plus fishing, mountain bike hire and ski instruction on a dry ski slope.

Fishing is a major pursuit in the area. You can fish for trout and salmon on the **Fishing** **River Spey**, and the Rothiemurchus Estate has trout fishing on its stocked loch at **Inverdruie**, where you can hire rods. Fishing permits cost around £10-15 per day for the stocked lochs and £20-30 per day for the River Spey. They are sold at local shops such as *Speyside Sports* in Aviemore, and at *Loch Morlich Watersports Centre* which also hires out rods and tackle. **Alvie Estate**, T01540-651255, near Kingussie also hires rods.

Rothiemurchus and Glen More estates are great areas for mountain biking, **Mountain** with lots of excellent forest trails. The **Rothiemurchus Visitor Centre** (see **biking** above) at Inverdruie has route maps and you can also hire bikes. Bike hire and good advice on routes is also available at *Bothy Bikes*, Unit 7, Grampian Rd, Aviemore, T810111, open daily 0900-1800. *Aviemore Mountain Bikes*, T811007, at 45a Grampian Rd, organises guided bike tours.

Horse riding and pony trekking are on offer at various places throughout **Horse riding** Strathspey. There's *Alvie Stables*, at Alvie near Kincraig, T01540-651409, mobile T0831-495397; *Carrbridge Trekking Centre*, Station Rd, Carrbridge, T841602; and *Strathspey Highland Pony Centre*, Rowanlea, Faebuie, Grantown-on-Spey, T873073.

Aviemore and around

In the 1960s Aviemore was transformed from a sleepy Highland village into the *jumble of concrete buildings, tacky gift shops and sprawling coach parks that it is* *today. The extent of the tourist tat here is so awful it makes Fort William seem* *charmingly understated by comparison, and there can be few more depressing* *and hideous sights than Santa Claus Land children's theme park on a drizzly* *afternoon in November. In saying that, however, the town is the most important* *tourist centre in the area and has a wide range of facilities.*

Phone code: 01479
Colour map 4, grid A3
Population: 2,500

The town lies just off
the A9, 33 miles
south of Inverness

    The train station, banks, restaurants and pretty much everything else are all *found along Grampian Road. Buses stop here too (see 'Transport' below).*

Getting there There are **buses** to and from Inverness Perth and Edinburgh and direct **trains** to and from Glasgow, Edinburgh and Inverness.

Tourist Information Centre The TIC is on Grampian Rd, about 400 yd south of the train station, T810363. They will book accommodation as well as provide free maps and leaflets on local attractions and change foreign currency. Apr-Oct Mon-Fri 0900-1800, Sat 1000-1700, Sun 1000-1600; Nov-Mar Mon-Fri 0900-1700, Sat 1000-1700.

Sights There's nothing of real interest in Aviemore. The real enjoyment lies in the surrounding mountains and forests, though there are a few interesting places close at hand. A great place for kids is the **Cairngorm Reindeer Centre** in Glen More Forest Park, on the road from Coylumbridge, seven miles from Aviemore. ■ *Guided walks to see the herd and feed them leave daily at 1100 and also at 1430 during the summer. £5, children £3. T861228.*

Sleeping
There's no shortage of accommodation around Aviemore

The best choice in the area is the **A** *Corrour House Hotel*, at Inverdruie, 2 miles southeast of Aviemore, T810220, www.corrourhouse.co.uk, open Dec-Oct. This Victorian country house oozes charm, enjoys wonderful views and offers superb cuisine. Also recommended is the **D** *Rowan Tree Restaurant & Guest House*, at Loch Alvie, 1½ miles south of Aviemore on the B9152, T810207, enquiries@rowantreehotel.com, open Dec-Oct. This is one of the oldest hotels in the area and offers excellent food (lunch cheap; dinner moderate). One mile south of Aviemore, at Lynwilg, is the beautiful **D** *Lynwilg House*, T811685, marge@lynwilg.co.uk, a charming, friendly guesthouse with a reputation for good food. There are lots of **B&Bs** in Aviemore itself, including **C** *Vermont Guest House*, T810470; and **E** *Ravenscraig Guest House*, T810278, ravenscrg@aol.com, both on Grampian Rd.

There are a couple of good hostels in Aviemore. The large **F** *SYHA hostel*, T810345, is on Grampian Rd near the tourist office and open all year. There's also the **F** *Aviemore Independent Bunkhouse and Backpackers Hostel*, T811137, on Dalfaber Rd. There are several good **campsites**, including the *Rothiemurchus Camping & Caravan Park*, T812800, at Coylumbridge; and a *Forest Enterprise* site at Glenmore, T861271.

Eating Apart from the hotels and guesthouses listed above, the best place to eat in Aviemore is the *Old Bridge Inn*, T811137, on Dalfaber Rd. This lovely old pub serves excellent-value food and hosts ceilidhs and Highland dinner dances in the summer months. There's a good lochside restaurant at the *Loch Insh Watersports Centre* at Kincraig, between Aviemore and Kingussie, which doubles as a café during the day.

Transport There are *Scottish Citylink* **buses**, T0990-505050, between Aviemore and **Inverness** (45 mins), **Kingussie** (20 mins), **Pitlochry** (1¼ hrs), **Perth** (2 hrs), **Glasgow** (3½ hrs) and **Edinburgh** (3½ hrs). For **Aberdeen**, change at Inverness. **Car hire** from *MacDonald's Self Drive*, 13 Muirton, T811444.

There are direct **trains** to and from **Glasgow** and **Edinburgh** (3 hrs) and **Inverness** (40 mins). For details T0345-484950. The *Strathspey Steam Railway*, T810725, runs between Aviemore, Boat of Garten and Nethy Bridge. The station is just to the east of the main train station. The *Cairngorm Chairlift Company*, T861261, runs daily **buses** between Aviemore and Cairngorm Ski Centre from late Oct to Apr.

Walk An easy circular walk of about four hours around Loch an Eilean in Rothiemurchus Estate starts from the end of the side road which turns east off the B970 two miles south of Aviemore. From the car park at the end of the road head for the lochside. The route around the loch is clearly marked and it's difficult to lose your way as it follows the loch shore. It's a very pleasant walk through woodland with views of a 14th-century castle ruin on an island in the middle of the loch. You can extend the walk by around a mile by including the circuit around Loch Gamhna. The paths around Loch an Eilein are also connected with the massive network of trails around Rothiemurchus. OS Sheet 36.

Eight miles northeast of Aviemore is the tiny village of Boat of Garten which suddenly shot to fame when a pair of **ospreys**, which had disappeared from these shores, reappeared on nearby **Loch Garten**, two miles east of the village. Now these beautiful birds of prey have established themselves here and elsewhere and there are thought be well over 100 pairs throughout the Highlands. The **Abernethy Forest RSPB Reserve** on the shore of Loch Garten is best visited during the nesting season, between late April and August, when the RSPB opens an **observation centre**. This is the only place in the world to see Scottish crossbills. ■ *Daily in season 1000-1800. £2.50 for non-members.* You can also see ospreys at the Rothiemurchus trout loch at Inverdruie, and maybe even on Loch Morlich and Loch Insh. The reserve is also home to several other rare species such as capercaillie, whooper swans and red squirrels. Guided walks leave from the observation centre at 0930 on Wednesdays.

Boat of Garten
Phone code: 01479
Colour map 4, grid A3

Sleeping and eating There's a good selection of accommodation in the village. **C-D** *Heathbank – The Victorian House*, T831234, is a must for Art Nouveau lovers and offers good French cuisine; while the **C-D** *Boat Hotel*, T831258, offers cheap and tasty meals. **D-E** *Glenavon House*, T831213, open Apr-Oct, is a lovely guesthouse on Kinchurdy Rd; and **D-E** *Moorfield House*, on Deshar Rd, T831646, moorfieldhouse@msn.com, is also a good choice. You can also **camp** at *Campgrounds of Scotland*, T831652.

Transport The best way to get to Boat of Garten is on the *Strathspey Steam Railway* which runs at least 5 times daily from Aviemore, T810725. Loch Garten is not easy to reach without your own transport, but check with one of the local TICs about tours.

At Carrbridge, a pleasant little village seven miles north of Aviemore, is the **Landmark Forest Heritage Park**, a woodland theme park which combines entertainment, education and shopping. There's a raised Treetop Trail for viewing wildlife, a fire tower, maze and various nature trails and fun rides. It manages to avoid being tacky and is good fun for kids. ■ *Apr to mid-Jul daily 0930-1800; mid-Jul to Aug 0930-2000; Sep and Oct 0930-1730; Nov-Mar 1000-1700. Adult £6.85, Adult with children £6.50, children £4.55. T841614.* In the village itself is the decidedly fragile-looking 18th-century **Bridge of Carr**, which is not for vertigo sufferers.

Carrbridge

Sleeping and eating There are several places to stay in Carrbridge. Top of the range is the stylish **B** *Dalrachney Lodge Hotel*, T841252, www.dalrachney.co.uk, a former Victorian hunting lodge with a good restaurant. More down to earth, but nonetheless comfortable, is the **E** *Cairn Hotel*, T841212, cairn.carrbridge@talk21.com, which serves good-value bar meals. There's also the much cheaper option of the *Carrbridge Bunkhouse Hostel*, T841250, at Dalrachney House, half a mile north of the village on the road to Inverness.

Transport There are several **buses** daily (except Sun) to Carrbridge from **Inverness** and **Grantown-on-Spey** with *Highland Country Buses*, T01463-233371.

The Highlands and Skye

Kingussie

Phone code: 01540
Colour map 4, grid A2
Population: 1,500

The quiet village of Kingussie (pronounced King-yoosie) lies 12 miles south-west of Aviemore and makes a pleasant alternative as a place to stay. The **Tourist Information Centre** (T661297) is housed in the Folk Museum (see below) and has the same opening hours.

Sights The main attraction here is the excellent **Highland Folk Museum** which contains a fascinating collection of traditional highland artefacts, as well as a farming museum, an old smokehouse, a water mill and traditional Hebridean 'blackhouse'. During the summer there are also demonstrations of spinning, woodcarving and peat-fire baking. ■ *T661307. May-Aug Mon-Fri 0930-1730, Sat and Sun 1300-1700; Apr, Sep and Oct guided tours only Mon-Fri 1030-1630. Adult £4, concession and children £2.40.*

Another worthwhile attraction is **Ruthven Barracks**, standing on a hillock across the river. This former barracks was built by the English Redcoats as part of their campaign to tame the Highlands after the first Jacobite rising in 1715. It was destroyed by the Jacobites in the wake of defeat at Culloden to prevent it from falling into enemy hands, and it was from here that Bonnie Prince Charlie sent his final order which signalled the end of his doomed cause. Access is free and the ruins are particularly attractive at night when floodlit.

At nearby **Kincraig** village, between Kingussie and Aviemore, is the **Highland Wildlife Park**, which has a captive collection of rare native animals. ■ *Apr, May, Sep and Oct daily 1000-1800; Jun-Aug till 1900; Nov-Mar 1000-1600. Park tours: adult £6.50, concession £5.40, children £4.35. T651270.* Those who mourn the loss of the hit TV show, *One Man and His Dog*, will be excited at the prospect of visiting the **Working Sheepdogs Show** at the nearby Leault Farm, where you can see demonstrations of dogs rounding up a flock of sheep. ■ *Daily. Adult £3.50. T651310.*

Sleeping **B** *The Osprey Hotel*, Ruthven Rd, T661510, www.ospreyhotel.co.uk, is a comfortable little hotel with a very good restaurant (expensive). The **D** *Scot House Hotel*, Newtonmore Rd, T661351, www.scothouse.com, is another good choice and also offers great food (lunch cheap; dinner midrange to expensive). There are several good guesthouses, all on Newtonmore Rd, including: **E** *Arden House*, T661369; **E** *Avondale House*, T661731, walsh.lorraine@talk21.com; and **E** *Homewood Lodge*, T661507, homewood@kingussie.ndirect.co.uk There's also **B&B** at **E** *Glengarry*, T661386, www.scots98.freeserve.co.uk, on East Terrace; and **E** *Greystones*, on Acres Rd, T661052, greystones@ lineone.net

There are several decent **hostels** in the area (all **F**): *The Laird's Bothy*, T661334, is on the High St next to the *Tipsy Laird* pub; *Bothan Airigh Bunkhouse*, T661051, is at Insh, a few miles east of Ruthven Barracks on the B970; *Kirkbeag Hostel*, T651298, is in Kincraig, between Kingussie and Aviemore; and at Balachroick House in Glen Feshie, near Kincraig, is *Glen Feshie Hostel*, T651323. In Newtonmore, a few miles west of Kingussie on the A86, is the *Newtonmore Independent Hostel*, T673360, hostel.newtonmore@dial.pipex.com; and at Laggan Bridge, 8 miles further west on the A86, is the *Pottery Bunkhouse*, T01528-544231, attached to the *Caoldair Pottery*.

Eating The *Osprey Hotel* and *Scot House Hotel* both have very good restaurants, but the outstanding place to eat in this area is the award-winning *The Cross*, T661166, on Tweed Mill Brae, a private drive leading off Ardbroilach Rd. This restaurant with rooms (**L** for dinner, B&B) is expensive but well worth it. Open Mar-Nov & Christmas; closed Tue. The *Tipsy Laird* pub serves good meals and real ales; and *La Cafetière* is a nice café.

Loch Morlich to Lairig Ghru walk

The famous Lairig Ghru is an ancient route through the Cairngorms which passes between Ben Macdui and Braeriach. It is a very strenuous walk and only for fit and experienced hikers. An easier propostion is a 12-mile loop which leads to the start of the Lairig Ghru pass, starting from Loch Morlich. To reach Loch Morlich take the B970 east from the southern end of Aviemore, beyond Coylumbridge. The route starts at the western end of Loch Morlich where a forestry track runs south from the road. It leads to a bridge over the River Luineag. Cross the bridge and continue along the track, keeping straight on where another track heads off left. About a mile further on, another track heads off to the right, but keep to the left fork, signposted for Rothiemurchus Lodge.

The track climbs up towards the lodge. Just before it, turn right on to a clear track which leads up to a reservoir. Soon another track heads off to the right signposted for the Lairig Ghru. Follow this path through heather moorland. The path then heads left, climbing up through open moorland to the lip of the glen. The entrance to the Lairig Ghru is straight ahead.

After about a mile, as the hills begin to encroach on either side, a rough path almost

doubles back to the left. Follow this path up the slope to the gap between Creag a' Chalamain and Creag an Leith-choin. The deep gully, the Chalamain Gap, is filled with huge boulders and requires great care when clambering through it. Beyond the gully a path leads through heather and pine saplings, dropping down to the side of a burn, then climbing up on the other side of the burn. Continue on this path, which then drops steeply down to the side of the burn. Cross the footbridge and climb the slope beyond to reach the main road. Turn left along the road to return to the start of the route.

The Highlands and Skye

Transport Kingussie is on the main Inverness to Perth/Glasgow/Edinburgh routes. All Perth-Inverness **trains** stop here and most *Citylink* **buses**. For rail enquiries, T0345-484950. There's also an infrequent school bus service run by *Highland Country Buses* between Kingussie, **Aviemore**, **Newtonmore** and **Dalwhinnie**.

Grantown-on -Spey
Phone code: 01479
Colour map 4,
grid A3
Population: 3,250

This genteel Georgian holiday town is 15 miles northeast of Aviemore and attracts the more mature tourist by the coach-load. Everything here is geared towards fishing, and anyone wishing to get kitted out in proper style should get themselves down to either *Mortimers* or *Ritchies* on the High Street. The **Tourist Information Centre**, T872773, is also here, open April to October daily 0900-1800.

Sleeping and eating As you'd expect in such a respectable place, there's a wide range of upmarket accommodation and a number of very good places to eat. The best places in town are all on Woodlands Terr: **L** *Culdearn House*, T872106, www.culdearn.com; and **D** *Ardconnell House*, T872104, enquiry@ardconnel.com, both of which offer excellent food.

At **Dulnain Bridge**, a few miles southwest of town, are the elegant **C** *Auchendean Lodge Hotel*, T851347, www.auchendean.com; and the handsome **B-C** *Muckrach Lodge Hotel & Restaurant*, T851257, muckrachlodge@sol.co.uk, both of which have superb restaurants. There are lots of other very good guesthouses and B&Bs to choose from, as well as the *Speyside Backpackers*, T873514, an independent hostel, also known as *The Stop-Over*, at 16 The Square.

Transport There are several **buses** daily (Mon-Sat) between Grantown and **Aviemore** (35 mins), and 2 or 3 buses daily, except Sun, to and from **Inverness** (1¼ hrs)

Isle of Skye

*The Isle of Skye (An t-Eilean Sgitheanach), the most scenically spectacular of all the Scottish islands, gets its name from the Norse word for cloud (skuy) and is commonly known as Eilean a Cheo (the Misty Isle), so it obviously rains a lot here. But when the rain and mist clear, the views make the heart soar. Despite the unpredictable weather, tourism is an important part of the island's economy, and has been since Victorian times when climbers returned home extolling its beauty. In the busy summer months the main roads become choked with coach tours and caravans, but the island is large enough to escape the worst of the crowds if you take the time to explore it. The most popular destination is the **Cuillins**, the greatest concentration of peaks in Britain. They provide Scotland's best climbing and have become a mecca for all serious and experienced walkers. Equally spectacular are the bizarre rock formations of the **Trotternish** Peninsula in the north.*

Skye

The Highlands and Skye

Trotternish is also inextricably linked with one of the most significant characters from the island's colourful past, Flora MacDonald, who is buried at *Kilmuir*. *More of the island's fascinating history can be discovered at Dunvegan Castle, ancient seat of the Macleods and a major tourist landmark. The island's main*

Ins and outs

The most popular, and quickest, route to Skye is across the new **bridge** (£5 toll), from Kyle of Lochalsh to Kyleakin. **Coach** services run to Skye from Glasgow and Inverness, with connections to all main cities in the UK (*Citylink*, T08705-5505050; *National Express*, T08705-808080). There is also a **train** service from Kyle of Lochalsh to Inverness (see page 490).

Getting there

A more scenic approach is by **ferry** from Mallaig to **Armadale**, on the southern Sleat Peninsula. The car and passenger ferry makes the 30-min crossing 7 times daily each way (first one leaves Mallaig at 0840, Armadale at 0925; the last one at 1845 and 1920) Mon-Sat from Mar to Oct, and Sun end of May to mid-Sep. The ferry is passenger - only during the winter; for details contact Mallaig, T01687-462403, or Armadale, T01471-844248. Booking is recommended during the summer months, T08705-650000. The one-way trip costs £2.80 per passenger and £15.65 per car. Trains to and from Fort William and Glasgow Queen St connect with some of the ferries (see page 486). The best way to Skye is from Glenelg to **Kylerhea**, south of Kyleakin. The tiny private car ferry makes the 10-min crossing when required, from Easter to Oct Mon-Sat 0900-1800 till mid-May; Mon-Sat 0900-2000, Sun 1000-1800 from mid-May to end-Aug; Mon-Sat 0900-1800, Sun 1000-1800 end-Aug to end-Oct. Cost per car with up to 4 passengers, £6; day return £10. T01599-511302.

Ferries leave from **Uig**, in the north of Skye, to Lochmaddy on North Uist (1¾ hrs) and to Tarbert on Harris (1¾ hrs). To Lochmaddy on Mon, Wed and Fri at 0945 and 1855, Tue, Thu and Sat at 1400 and Sun at 0940 and 1400; for return times, see page 560. The return trip costs £14.55 per passenger and £69 per car. To Tarbert on Mon, Wed and Fri at 0515 and 1400, Tue, Thu and Sat at 0940 and 1800 (no service on Sun); for return times, see page 560. The return trip costs the same as for Lochmaddy. For more details, contact Uig, T01470-542219.

Skye is the largest of the Hebridean islands, at almost 50 miles long and between 7 and 25 miles wide. It is possible to run up a hefty mileage as the extensive road system penetrates to all but the most remote corners of its many peninsulas. It is possible to get around by public transport midweek, with **postbuses** supplementing the normal services, but, as everywhere in the Highlands and Islands, buses are few and far between at weekends, especially Sun, and during the winter months. **Buses** run between Portree, Broadford, Uig (for ferries to the Western Isles), Kyleakin, Armadale (for ferries to Mallaig), Dunvegan and Carbost, and a more limited service runs from Broadford to Elgol and Portree to Glen Brittle.

Getting around *Getting around by public transport is virtually impossible in winter (Oct-Mar) as bus and postbus services are severely limited*

Skye is well served by all types of accommodation: B&Bs, guesthouses, hostels, bunkhouses, campsites and some very fine hotels. During the peak summer months advance bookings are recommended. These can be made directly or through the island's **Tourist Information Centres**; in Portree (open all year), Broadford, Uig and Dunvegan (see relevant section).

Information

Portree

Portree is the island's capital and main settlement. It's a fairly attractive little fishing port, built around a natural harbour, with a row of brightly painted

Phone code: 01478 Colour map 1, grid C3

The Highlands and Skye

Things to do on Skye when it's raining

Just in case you didn't know, it can rain quite often on Skye and unless you're one of those hardy souls who's prepared to brave the elements, you'll need to know about the island's main indoor attractions. There are numerous opportunities to shelter from the rain, but most of them cost money, and many will leave you regretting it, so here's our list of the top ten things to do. Details of opening times and admission prices are given under each relevant destination.

*Beginning in **Portree**, there's the Aros Experience, which gives a good introduction to the island's history. North of Uig, at Kilmuir on the Trotternish Peninsula, is the **Skye Museum of Island Life**, which pretty much does what it says on the sign. Northwest from Portree is **Dunvegan Castle**, home of the Clan Macleod and top of most visitors' itineraries. On the road to Dunvegan is **Edinbane Pottery**, where you can buy pots of every shape and size and watch them being made.*

*Travelling south from Dunvegan, you'll reach the turn-off to the **Talisker Distillery**, the island's only whisky distillery, where you can sample the distinctive peaty taste. While you're there you can visit nearby **Carbostcraft Pottery**, in the village of Carbost, and indulge in some more gift buying. If you're in need of some refreshment after all that culture and shopping, you could do a lot worse than the bar at the **Sligachan Hotel**, which boasts an impressive array of whiskies and climbers' beards. In the southern peninsula of Sleat, near the Armadale ferry terminal, is **Armadale Castle**, with a visitor centre that is actually worth visiting. Nearby is one of the branches of **Skye Batiks**, with a huge selection of these 'new age' style fabrics in a range of original Celtic designs (the other branch is in Portree). And for that final drink before boarding the ferry to Mallaig, why not pop into the cosy bar of the **Hotel Eilean Iarmain**, which also happens to serve wonderful food.*

houses along the shorefront and the rest of the town rising steeply up to the central Somerled Square.

Ins & outs   **Getting there and around**   Portree is ideally placed for trips to all parts of the island. **Buses** leave from the bus station in Somerled Sq to Dunvegan, Uig, Broadford, Kyleakin, Armadale, the Talisker Distillery and Glenbrittle. There are also services to the mainland. The *Calmac* **ferry** office is on Park Rd, just off Somerled Sq, T612075, F613090. The town is compact enough to get around easily on foot, though there is a regular town bus service for those needing to get into the centre from the outskirts.

The **Tourist Information Centre** is just off Bridge St, T612137. They have bus timetables and a good selection of books and maps. It's open Apr to mid-May Mon-Sat 0900-1730; mid-May to Jul Mon-Sat 0900-1800, Sun 1000-1600; mid-Jul to mid-Aug Mon-Sat 0900-2000, Sun 1000-1600; mid-Aug to Sep Mon-Sat 0900-1800; Oct-Mar Mon-Fri 0900-1700, Sat 1000-1600.

History   The town was so named (*Port Righ* means 'King's Harbour' in Gaelic) to commemorate a visit by King James V in 1540. He came with his fleet to quell a long-standing and bitter feud between the island's main clans, the Macleods and the MacDonalds. The town's other notable royal occasion, in 1746 – one of the most poignant moments in Scottish history – was when Prince Charlie bade farewell to Flora MacDonald in MacNab's hostelry, now the *Royal Hotel*.

Almost a quarter of a century later the town was visited by Dr Johnson and Boswell, who dined in MacNab's, believing it to be 'the only inn on the island'.

Gaelic culture

Outside the Outer Hebrides, Skye is the most important centre of Gaelic culture, with a large proportion of the island's population speaking the Gaelic language in everyday life. This in itself is remarkable given the significant drop in population during the Clearances and the continued undermining of the Gaelic culture ever since, especially through the State education system.

Today, as in other parts of the Hebrides, the native culture is again under threat, this time from the huge influx of 'white settlers' from the south, but there is also a new-found pride and interest in the Gaelic language. This has been helped by the existence of the Gaelic college on Sleat, through Gaelic writers such as the late Sorley Maclean, a radical local newspaper (The West Highland Free Press), economic support from Highlands and Islands Enterprise, and spiritual underpinning from the Sabbatarian Free Church. Gaelic is being taught again in schools and can be heard on television. The ancient heritage of the Highlands and Islands is fighting back and reasserting itself as a major European culture.

That may or may not have been the case in those days, but today Portree offers a wide range of places to eat, hotels, B&Bs, pubs, shops and banks to cater for the huge numbers of tourists that come here in the summer.

Sights

The Aros Experience, on Viewfield Road, half a mile from the town centre on the road to Broadford, is an exhibition and audio-visual display of the island's history and cultural heritage. The island's only theatre is housed here and features a varied programme of events, including drama, traditional music and movies (see 'Entertainment' below). There's also a restaurant serving good value snacks and main meals, a gift shop and a network of forest trails to explore. ■ *Daily 0900-2100 (off season 0900-1800). £3, concession £2, children £1, under 12 free, T613649, aros@demon.co.uk*

The **An Tuireann Arts Centre**, on Struan Road, hosts exhibitions of contemporary visual arts and crafts. It has a fine café (see 'Eating' below). ■ *Mar-Oct Mon-Sat 1000-1700; Nov-Feb Tue-Sat 1000-1700. Free, T613306. norahcampbell@antuireann.demon.co.uk*

If the weather's good, Portree offers many opportunities for a wide variety of outdoor activities. **Boat trips** can be made to the island of Rona, north of Raasay, with the *MV Brigadoon*. Trips leave from the pier (April-September) and cost from £10 per person. Full-day charters are also available for £75-150 (12 passengers). T613718, or ask for Peter Urquhart at the pier. For **horse riding**, *Portree Riding and Trekking Stables* are a couple of miles from the town centre, T582419. Follow the Struan Road (B885) for two miles, then bear right at the fork towards Peiness. Four miles north of Portree, at Borve on the road to Uig, is the *Skye Riding Centre*, T01470-532439. **Mountain bikes** can be hired at *Island Cycles*, on The Green; Monday-Saturday 1000-1700, T613121.

Sleeping
■ *on map page 540*
Price codes:
see inside front cover

There are numerous hotels, guesthouses and B&Bs in Portree, but accommodation can be hard to find in the busy summer season. For a small fee the tourist office will book accommodation for you. Prices tend to be slightly higher in Portree than the rest of the island, though B&Bs on the outskirts of town are usually cheaper.

B *Rosedale Hotel*, Beaumont Cres, T613131. 23 rooms. Open May-Sep. Cosy little hotel by the harbour, converted from fishermen's houses. **C** *Bosville Hotel*, Bosville Terr, T612846, F613434, www.macleodhotels.co.uk/bosville 18 rooms. Comfortable and stylish accommodation with friendly service. Boasts 2 award-winning restaurants (see 'Eating' below). There are also several guesthouses on Bosville Terr and

The Highlands and Skye

many B&Bs on Stormyhill Rd and the streets running off it. **C** *Viewfield House Hotel*, on the road into Portree from the south, T612217, F613517, www.skye.co.uk/viewfield 9 rooms. Open mid-Apr to mid-Oct. Grand old country house full of antiques, set in 20 acres of woodland garden. Log fire adds to the welcoming atmosphere; great value. **E** *Mr & Mrs Mathieson*, 'Grenitote', 9 Martin Cres, T612808, on Viewfield Rd heading south out of town. Good value. **E** *Portree House*, Home Farm Rd, T613713, nigel@potreehouse.demon.co.uk 5 rooms, B&B with reduction on meals in the restaurant.

There are a couple of options for budget travellers. **F** *Portree Independent Hostel*, Old Post Office, The Green, T613737. 60 beds. Right in the centre of town, with laundrette (£3 per wash) and email facilities (£3 per hr). **F** *Portree Backpackers Hostel*, 6 Woodpark, Dunvegan Rd, T613641, F613643. 26 beds. There's a **campsite** at Torvaig, just outside the town, T612209, open Apr-Oct.

Eating **Expensive** *Chandlery Seafood Restaurant*, next door to the *Bosville Hotel* (see under 'Sleeping' for details). Superb French/Scottish cuisine using local produce.

Portree

■ Sleeping			● Eating
1 Bosville	4	Portree Independent	1 Ben Tianavaig
2 Mr & Mrs Mathieson's		Hostel	2 Chandlery Seafood
B&B	5	Rosedale	3 Lower Deck Seafood
3 Portree Backpackers	6	Viewfield House	4 Portree House
Hostel			5 Spicehut

The Highlands and Skye

Lower Deck Seafood Restaurant, on the harbour front at the foot of Quay Brae, T613611. Freshest of seafood and a contender with the *Chandlery* for the best food in town. Open Apr-Oct daily 1100-2200. For a budget treat try the excellent fish and chips from their takeaway next door. *Skeabost House Hotel*, 4 miles north of Portree on the Dunvegan road, T01470-532202, F532454, skeabost@sol.co.uk This peaceful country house in lovely grounds on the shores of Loch Snizort has a reputation for fine food using the best local produce.

Mid-range *Ben Tianavaig*, 5 Bosville Terr, T612 152. Excellent vegetarian bistro. Seating is limited so you'll need to book. Open lunchtimes at weekends, and Tue-Sun 1800-2130. *Bosville Restaurant*, in the *Bosville Hotel* (see 'Sleeping' above). Also recommended. They offer a lunchtime special (soup, sandwich and coffee for £5) which is great value.

Cheap *Tuireann Café*, part of the arts centre (see 'Sights' above). Natural whole-foods and organic produce, home-made bread, cakes and pastries. Excellent quality and value. Open Mar-Oct Mon-Sat 1000-1800, Nov-Feb Tue-Sat 1000-1630. *Spicehut*, Bayfield Rd, T612681. Indian restaurant and takeaway. Open daily 1200-1430 and 1700-2400. For cheap Chinese takeaway food, there's *Steve's Kitchen Takeaway*, on Bayfield Rd, opposite the library. *Portree House*, Home Farm Rd (see above), serves good value food, 1200-1545, 1730-2000.

Entertainment The town's nightlife is mainly confined to eating and drinking. The bar of the *Pier Hotel*, Quay Street, T612094 by the harbour is a real fishermen's drinking den. Also popular is the *Royal Hotel*, Bank Street, T612525. If you fancy a wild Fri night ceilidh, try the *Portree Community Centre*, Camanahd Square, Park Road, T613736. The *Aros Experience* (see 'Sights' above) has a theatre which shows drama, movies and live music. Call the box office for details of their monthly progr -amme; T613750. The **swimming pool** is at Camanahd Square, T612655. The island's annual **Highland Games** are a 1-day event held in Portree in early *Aug*.

Shopping
Most of the shops are within a few streets of Somerled Square

There's a *Safeway* supermarket diagonally opposite the *Bosville Hotel* and a wholefood store, *Jackson's Wholefoods*, at Park Pl, opposite the council offices. *Skye Batiks*, The Green (near the tourist office), T613331. Sells handmade 'batiks' (colourful cotton fabrics), which are pricey but unique souvenirs of Skye (see also under Armadale, page 554). A good pottery is *Carbostcraft Pottery*, on Bayfield Rd, which sells a huge variety of designs (they also have a shop near the Talisker Distillery, see page 549). A good

To Torvaig Campsite & Staffin

To Start of Walk Around Portree

Bars & pubs

6 Steve's Kitchen Takeaway
7 Pier Hotel
8 Royal Hotel

The Highlands and Skye

place to buy woollens is *Over the Rainbow*, at the top of Quay Brae, T612555. Open 0900-2200 in the high season. Knitwear and tartan souvenirs can be found at the *Skye Woollen Mill*, Dunvegan Rd, T612889.

Transport
Ace Taxis, T613600;
A2B Taxis, T613456

There are 4 **buses** daily (Mar-Oct) Mon-Fri (2 on Sat) around the **Trotternish Penin-sula**, in each direction, via **Uig**. There are daily buses (4 Mon-Sat, 3 on Sun) to **Kyleakin**, and 3 buses daily Mon-Sat to **Armadale** via **Broadford**. There are 2 daily buses to **Carbost** (for the Talisker Distillery) and **Fiskavaig** Mon-Fri (1 on Sat), and 2 daily buses to **Glenbrittle** (in the summer only). There are 3 buses daily Mon-Fri to **Glendale** via **Dunvegan** (1 on Sat), and 3 buses to **Waternish** via **Dunvegan** (Mon-Sat). There's a Scottish *Citylink* service from **Inverness** (3 Mon-Sat, 2 on Sun, 3 hrs) and also from **Glasgow** via **Fort William** to **Kyleakin**, **Portree** and **Uig** 3-4 times daily (3 hrs from Fort William to Portree). Winter services are severely limited with only a few buses in each direction each day.

Directory

Banks *Bank of Scotland* and *Clydesdale Bank*, both on Somerled Sq. The *Royal Bank* of Scotland is on Bank St. All have ATMs. **Communications** Internet: At the *Portree Independent Hostel* (see 'Sleeping' above), at the post office and at *Portree Backpacker's Hostel* on Dunvegan Rd. **Post office**: At the top of Quay Brae. **Laundry** At the *Portree Independent Hostel*.

Trotternish Peninsula

Colour map 1, grid C3
Trotternish is best
explored with your
own transport, but
there a few daily buses
covering the circular
route from Portree
(see above)

North from Portree is the 30-mile long Trotternish Peninsula, sticking out like a giant thumb. The interior of the peninsula is a basaltic lava wilderness full of bizarre rock formations. A 20-mile long escarpment of sheer cliffs and towering pinnacles dominates the landscape. The best known of these strange formations, the **Quiraing** and **Old Man of Storr**, can be explored on foot. The A855 and A87 roads follow the coast around the peninsula, and a spectacular minor road bisects the ridge from Staffin Bay to Uig.

Uig
Phone code: 01470
Colour map 1, grid C3

The A87 runs northwest from Portree to the tiny ferry port of Uig, dramatically set in a horseshoe bay and the departure point for ferries to **Tarbert** (Harris) and **Lochmaddy** (North Uist). Everything in the village revolves around the ferry timetables, and the regular bus service to and from Portree coincides with the arrival and departure of the ferries.

Ins and outs For ferry times, see page 537. *Scottish Citylink* runs a service to/from Inverness, Fort William and Glasgow. The **Tourist Information Centre** is inside the *CalMac* office at the ferry pier, T542404, and will book accommodation anywhere on the island; open 1 Apr-31 Oct, Mon-Sat 0845-1830, also Sun 0845-1400 Jul-Sep.

Just outside the village is the magical **Fairy Glen**. Turn right just before the *Uig Hotel* coming down the hill from the Portree direction. About a mile up the single track road you enter an eerie, mysterious world of perfect conical hills, some up to 60-ft high. It's almost inconceivable that these are natural formations and the inevitable mist only adds to the spooky strangeness of the place.

Sleeping and eating B *Uig Hotel*, on the right of the road into the village from Portree, beside a white church and opposite Frazer's Folly, T542205, F542308 17 rooms, open year round. Classy accommodation with great views across the bay, good food and a friendly island welcome. Offers clay pigeon shooting and fly fishing. A cheaper option is **D** *The Ferry Inn*, T542242, F542377, joycemary@supanet .com Amongst the good value **B&Bs** is **E** *Idrigill House*, T542398, F542447, s.watkins@lineone.net The **F** *SYHA Youth Hostel*, T542211, is high above the port on the south side of the village and is open mid-Mar to Oct.

The *Pub on the Pier* (open till 2300) serves cheap bar meals, and the famous Cuillin ales are brewed at the nearby Skye Brewery (tours by appointment, T542477). You can also change foreign currency here. *The Ferry Inn* serves bar meals and you can also eat at the *Uig Hotel* and the café by the filling station.

A few miles north of Uig, on the A855 at **Linicro**, is *Whitewave Activities*, where you can try windsurfing and sea kayaking. There's also a café specializing in vegetarian, seafood and celtic music, and a B&B, T542414, info@white-wave.co.uk Further north, at **Kilmuir**, is **The Skye Museum of Island Life**. The group of thatched houses give a fascinating insight into the way of life of a crofting community at the end of the last century, and is the most authentic of several such museums on Skye. ■ *Easter to Oct Mon-Sat 0930-1700. £2, children £1.*

Uig to Duntulm
Phone code: 01470

Behind the museum, at the end of the road, is **Flora MacDonald's Monument**, which marks the grave of Skye's most famous daughter, with her husband buried alongside. The rather austere memorial is inscribed with Dr Johnson's poignant tribute.

At the northwest tip of the peninsula, 15 minutes' drive from Uig, is **Duntulm Castle**, a fairy-tale ruin dramatically perched on a steep cliff. This 15th-century structure, built on the site of an ancient Norse stronghold, became the chief Skye residence of the powerful MacDonalds and was the most imposing castle in the Hebrides. According to local legend, the castle was abandoned around 1732 when a nursemaid accidentally let the baby heir fall from a window on to the cliffs below.

Sleeping and eating Near the castle is **C** *Duntulm Castle Hotel*, T552213, F552292, www.duntulmcastle.co.uk Open Mar-Nov. Friendly and homely with great views across the Minch to the Outer Hebrides. Idyllic and good value. Restaurant is open to non-residents.

Beyond Duntulm the A855 heads across the tip of the peninsula to the east coast, where the famous bizarre rock scenery is found. At the north end of **Staffin Bay**, a minor road cuts across the peninsula to Uig. This road is the access point for the **Quiraing**, the famous jumble of strangely shaped hills and rocks that is one of the island's classic walks. Even if you don't attempt the walk, the road over the back of the Trotternish ridge from Uig makes a worthwhile detour. A few miles south of Staffin Bay is **Kilt Rock**, an impressive sea cliff which gets its name from the vertical columnar basalt strata overlying horizontal ones beneath. A rather tenuous comparison perhaps, but the cliffs south of Staffin are particularly spectacular, as are the **Lealt Falls**, a torrent of mountain water at the head of a gorge, a few miles south of Kilt Rock. The falls are signposted by the road, so all you have to do is park the car and peer over. Just before the turn for Kilt Rock is a wee museum sporting such finds as a dinosaur bone and bronze age artefacts (open May-October).

Duntulm to Portree
For full details of the routes for the Quiraing and Old Man of Storr walks, see page 555

A few miles further south, and 7 miles north of Portree, is a car park which is the starting point for another of Skye's famous walks: up to the **Old Man of Storr**, the distinctive pinnacle of rock which has detached itself from the cliffs of the Storr behind. For a description of the route, see page 555.

The Highlands and Skye

Flora MacDonald

In Kilmuir graveyard is the memorial which marks the grave of Flora MacDonald, one of the most famous characters in Skye's long history. The memorial bears Dr Johnson's fitting epitaph: "A name that will be mentioned in history, and if courage and fidelity be virtues, mentioned with honour".

It was Flora Macdonald who helped Bonnie Prince Charlie to escape capture following the Jacobite defeat at Culloden in 1746. Pursued by government troops, the prince fled from South Uist 'over the sea to Skye' aboard Flora's boat, disguised as an Irish servant girl by the name of Betty Burke. He then

made his way to Portree, where he bade his farewell to the young woman who had risked her own life to protect his.

When Flora's part in the prince's escape became known, she was immediately arrested and sent to the Tower of London. She was released a year later, married a Skye man and then emigrated to North Carolina where she spent the next 12 years of her life. They returned to her husband's house in Kingsburgh in 1786. Flora died in Skye in 1790, and it is said that her funeral was the largest ever witnessed in the Highlands.

Sleeping and eating   A few miles north of Staffin and 20 miles north of Portree, is **A** *Flodigarry Country House Hotel*, T01470-552203, F552301. Beautifully located at the foot of the mighty Quiraing and with stunning views across Staffin Bay, this is one of the great country house hotels, with a relaxing old-world atmosphere and excellent restaurant. Flora MacDonald's actual cottage is in the grounds and has been tastefully refurbished, giving the chance to stay in a place steeped in the island's history. The lively bar is a good place to enjoy a laugh and a jig. Those that can't afford such luxury can always opt for the more modest **F** *Dun Flodigarry Backpackers Hostel*, T/F552212. 66 beds. Open Mar-Oct. Laundry facilities, breakfast available and only 100 yds from the bar of the *Flodigarry Country House Hotel*. There's a **campsite** south of Staffin Bay, T562213, open mid Apr-end Sep. A good place for food is the *Oystercatcher Restaurant* in the village of Staffin, T562384, closed Sunday. At **Culnacnoc**, just north of the Lealt Falls, is **D** *Glenview Inn and Restaurant*, T562248, F562211. 5 rooms. Cosy and relaxed accommodation with a very fine restaurant. In Staffin is *Columba 1400*, an internet café with cheap food and great views. Open daily in summer, Tue-Sat in winter.

Dunvegan, Waternish and Duirinish

Phone code: 01470   In the northwest of Skye the peninsulas of Waternish (or Vaternish) and Duirinish point out into the Minch towards the Western Isles. The larger Duirinish peninsula holds more interest for the visitor, featuring the beautiful green valley of **Glendale**, an area brimming with history, the dramatic walk to **Neist Point** and **Dunvegan Castle**, Skye's most famous landmark.

The turn-off to this much-visited part of the island is four miles northwest of Portree. The A850 swings west towards Dunvegan, by-passing the tiny village of **Edinbane**. There's a campsite, two hotels, several B&Bs, petrol station, Land Rover tours with *Skyetrak Safari* , T582224, and the renowned *Edinbane Pottery* workshop and showroom, which is a must for souvenir hunters. ■ *Easter-Oct daily 0900-1800. T582234.*

The A850 continues west, and those with their own transport and time on their hands might wish to make an interesting little detour at the **Fairy Bridge**, where the B886 runs north to **Trumpan**, near the tip of the Waternish Peninsula. If the weather's good (and it is, occasionally) this is the best place to watch the sun set, in a blaze of red over the Outer Hebrides. If there's no sunset, then you could always visit *Skyeskins*, the country's only traditional exhibition tannery, at Loch Bay, T592237 or pop into the island's oldest pub, at **Stein**. Either way, you should finish off the day with a meal at the wonderful *Lochbay Seafood*, T592235 for reservations, where you can almost see your dinner being landed. Mid-range prices, open April-October for lunch and till 2030 (closed Saturday).

The ruined church at Trumpan, at the end of the road, has some grisly skeletons in its cupboard (see box above). In the graveyard is the 'trial stone'. A hole in the stone was used to test whether or not an accused person was telling the truth. If they could quickly find the hole and stick their arm through it while blindfolded, they were found innocent, but if not, they were guilty. The church is also the starting point for the strenuous eight-mile **walk** out to **Waternish point** and back.

Waternish Peninsula
Colour map 1, grid C2/3

A few miles further on from the turn-off to Waternish is the little village of Dunvegan. Just to the north of the village is proud Dunvegan Castle, the island's most important tourist attraction. This is the home of the chiefs of the Clan Macleod who have lived here for over seven centuries, making it the oldest inhabited castle in Britain. The present structure dates from the 15th and 16th centuries and, though the Victorian restoration has left it looking more like a baronial house, a look inside reveals its true age. Among the many relics on display is Rory Mor's horn, a huge drinking vessel which the chief's heir must drain 'without setting down or falling down', when filled with claret (about 1½ bottles). There's also a lock of Bonnie Prince Charlie's hair, clipped from his head by Flora MacDonald as a keepsake, but pride of place goes to the **Fairy Flag**. The flag has been dated to between the fourth and seventh centuries and is made of Middle Eastern silk. It is said to have been given to the clan chief by a fairy, and has the power to ensure victory in battle for the clan on three occasions. It has been used twice so far. The lovely castle gardens lead down to the lochside jetty, from where you can take a seal-spotting cruise or a boat trip around the loch. There's also a busy restaurant and gift shop by the castle gates. A bus leaves Portree at 1000, arrives at the castle at 1048 and returns at 1252 (March-October only). ■ *Mid-Mar-Oct daily 1000-1730. Castle: £6, £5.50 concession, £3 children . Seal-spotting cruise: £4, children £2.50. Boat trip: £4, children £2.50 T521206.*

Dunvegan Castle
Colour map 1, grid C2

In the village of Dunvegan is the **Giant Angus MacAskill Museum**, housed in a thatched, whitewashed cottage, which relates the life story of the tallest ever Scotsman, Angus MacAskill, who grew to 7 ft and 9 ins tall. He emigrated to Novia Scotia and toured the United States with the midget General Tom Thumb, who is said to have danced on his outstretched hand. More interesting than the museum, though, are the stories of its owner, Peter MacAskill, in particular the one about the replica coffin, which is worth the admission fee alone. Peter is a descendent of Angus and also runs the museum at Colbost (see below). ■ *Mar-Oct daily 0930-1830. £1. T521296.*

Clan warfare

Violent conflict between neighbouring clan chiefs was so commonplace on Skye and in the rest of the Western Highlands that it was almost accepted as part of the very fabric of society. One particularly gruesome example took place on Eigg in 1577. The Macleod's had taken refuge in a cave but their presence was discovered by the MacDonalds, who piled brushwood at the entrance and set fire to it, burning alive the 395 people sheltering inside, almost the entire population of the island. Revenge came the following year, at Trumpan church in Ardmore Bay. The Macleods landed under cover of the early morning fog and set light to the church, burning the congregation inside.

Sleeping and eating There are several hotels including the very comfortable **B** *Atholl House Hotel*, T521219, F521481, reservations@athollhotel.demon.co.uk A recommended guesthouse is **D** *Roskhill House*, 3 miles south of Dunvegan Castle on the A863, T521317, F521761, stay@roskhill. demon.co.uk 5 cosy rooms, peaceful setting, great food. Just beyond Roskhill is a turning south off the A863 to **B** *Harlosh House Hotel*, T/F521367, harlosh.house@virgin.net 6 rooms. Open Easter to mid-Oct. Cosy, comfortable, great views and a reputation for superb food (evenings only). There are also over a dozen **B&Bs**, mostly in the **E** price range.

There are numerous places to stay in and around Dunvegan, and the Tourist Information Centre in the village will arrange accommodation for you, T521581

Duirinish Peninsula
Colour map 1, grid C2

West of Dunvegan is the Duirinish Peninsula. The northern half is populated along the western shores of **Loch Dunvegan** and in the beautiful and green **Glendale**, an area brimming with history but with hardly an island family left. Glendale is now dubbed 'Little England', owing to the large number of incoming settlers from the south. The area is famed throughout the Highlands and Islands, for it was here in 1882 that local crofters, spurred on by the 'Battle of the Braes' (see page 551), resisted the cruel and petty tyranny of their estate manager. The authorities sent a gunboat to deal with the uprising and arrested the ringleaders, some of whom were imprisoned in Edinburgh and became known as 'the Glendale Martyrs'. This episode sparked a radical movement throughout the Highlands and led to the Crofter's Holdings Act of 1886 which gave the crofters a more secure tenure and fair rent (see page 649). The uninhabited southern half of the peninsula is dominated by the flat-topped hills, Healabhal Bheag (1,601 ft) and Healabhal Mhor (1,538 ft), known as **Macleod's Tables**.

The **Glendale Visitor Route** is signposted from just before Dunvegan village and leads westwards along the shores of the loch and across the peninsula. There are several interesting little sights along the way. Those interested in finding out more about crofting on the island should head for the **Colbost Croft Museum**, housed in a restored 'black house' and with a peat fire burning and an illicit still out the back. The museum is 4 miles from Dunvegan on the B884 to Glendale. ■ *Daily 1000-1830. £1, children free.* T521296. A little further on is *Skye Silver*, where you can buy silver jewellery in traditional Celtic designs. ■ *Daily 1000-1800. T511263, www.skyesilver.com* Further north is the **Borreraig Park Exhibition Croft**, which features a huge display of farm equipment from days gone by. ■ *Daily 0900-1800. £1.50.*

At **Borreraig** is the **MacCrimmon Piping Heritage Centre**, a fascinating place which is more of a shrine to the famous MacCrimmons, who were hereditary pipers to the Macleod Chiefs and the first composers, players and teachers of *piobaireachd* (pibroch), which can be heard in the museum (there's an annual recital at Dunvegan Castle in early August). Opposite are the ruins of the ancient piping college. ■ *Daily all year 1000-1700. £1.50. T511369.*

Moving from the sublime to the ridiculous, in the village of **Glendale** is a **Toy Museum**, which should appeal to kids of all ages. ■ *Mon-Sat 1000-1800. £2.50, children £1. T511240.*

The B884 continues west, then a road turns off left for Waterstein. At the end of this road (just over 2 miles) is a car park which is the starting point for the walk out to the lighthouse at **Neist Point**, the most westerly point on Skye and one of the most pleasant walks on the island. It's about 1½ miles there and back and well worth the effort. The path is easy to follow and the views of the sea cliffs are wonderful. There are lots of nesting seabirds around and you might even spot whales offshore. The **lighthouse**, built in 1909, is now unmanned, and you can stay in one of the self-catering cottages, T/F511200. The graveyard at the lighthouse looks real enough but take a closer look and you'll see the names of the film crew who worked on the superb 1997 film, *Breaking the Waves.*

Sleeping and eating Next to the Colbost Croft Museum is *The Three Chimneys*, T01470-511258, www.threechimneys.co.uk, considered by many to be the best restaurant in the north of Scotland and, judging by the numerous awards they've won, that judgement can't be far wrong. Local seafood, meat, veg and dairy produce and a great wine list. Open daily 1230-1400 (except Sun) and 1830-2130; expensive. They also now have accommodation a few yards away at *A The House Over-By* (6 rooms).

Transport There are 3 **buses** daily (Mar-Oct, Mon-Fri) from Glendale to and from Portree via Dunvegan (see above), and 1 bus on Sat and a daily bus from Dunvegan to Glendale (not Sun).

The Cuillins and Minginish

The district of Minginish is the wildest and least-populated part of the island, but for many it is the greatest attraction, for this is where the Cuillins are to be found. This hugely impressive mountain range, often shrouded in rain or cloud, is the spiritual heartland of the island, and when it's clear their heart-aching grandeur can be appreciated from every other peninsula on Skye. Though officially called the Cuillin 'Hills', these are the most untamed mountains in Britain. The magnificent scenery and vast range of walks and scrambles have attracted climbers and walkers for centuries, but have also claimed many lives. It cannot be stressed too strongly that the Cuillins are the most dangerous mountains in Britain and only for experienced climbers (for more on safety, see page 60).

Colour map 3, grid A3/4 OS Landranger No 32 OS Outdoor Leisure No 8

The Highlands and Skye

Guides and equipment The following guides have all been recommended. *Skye Highs*, Mike Lates, 3 Luib, Broadford, T01471-822116. *Cuillin Guides*, Gerry Achroyd, Stac Lee, Glen Brittle, T01478-640289. *Hugh Evans*, 4d Wentworth St, Portree, T01478-612682. *Richard MacGuire*, 4 Matheson Place, Portree, T01478-613180. *Colin Threlfall*, at *Outdoor Sports* (see below). Two good shops for mountain gear are *Cioch Direct*, 4 Ullinish, Struan, T01470-572307, and *Outdoor Sports;* on Bridge Road (next to *Skye Batiks*), Portree

There are three routes into the Cuillins: from the *Sligachan Hotel* (see below); from Glen Brittle (see below); and from Elgol (see below). The eastern part of the range is known as the **Red Cuillins**. Their smoother, conical granite peaks contrast sharply with the older, darker gabbro of the jagged-edged **Black Cuillins** to the west. The latter are particularly suitable for rock climbing and best approached from Glen Brittle, while the former are accessed from the *Sligachan Hotel*. There are 20 'Munros' (mountains over 3,000 ft in height) in the Cuillins, with the highest being Sgurr Alasdair, at 3,251 ft. Though the sheer majesty of the mountains can only be appreciated at close quarters by the climber, there are impressive views from Elgol, from the road into Glen Brittle and, more distantly, from the west coast of Sleat.

Glen Sligachan is one of the most popular routes into the Cuillin range and the main access point for the more forgiving Red Cuillins, the walk to **Loch Coruisk**, or the ascent of **Marsco**. Every year there's a hill race up nearby **Glamaig**, which was climbed in 55 minutes (up and down) in 1899 by a Gurkha soldier – in bare feet!

Sleeping and eating The legendary rallying point for climbers who come to Skye for the Cuillins is the **C** *Sligachan* Hotel, 7 miles south of Portree, where the A87 Kyleakin-Portree road meets the A863 to Dunvegan, T01471-8650204, F650207. The hotel's *Seamus* bar stocks an impressive selection of malts and also serves the island's real ales as well as meals. The **campsite** opposite is the most popular place to stay in the area.

Elgol
Phone code: 01471
Colour map 3, grid A4

One of the most rewarding drives on Skye is the 14-mile single-track road from Broadford to Elgol (Ealaghol), a tiny settlement near the tip of the Strathaird Peninsula, from where you can enjoy the classic view of the Cuillins from across Loch Scavaig and of the islands of Soay, Rùm and Canna. It was from here, on 4 July 1746, that the Young Pretender finally left the Hebrides. Before leaving, he was given a farewell banquet by the MacKinnons in what is now called **Prince Charlie's Cave**. There's also the added attraction of a dramatic boat trip (see below) to the mouth of **Loch Coruisk**, in the heart of the Black Cuillin. The glacial sea loch, romanticized by Walter Scott and painted by Turner, is over two miles long but only a few hundred yards wide, closed in by the sheer cliffs on either side and overshadowed by the towering mountains of black basalt and gabbro. Elgol is also the starting point for the walk to Camasunary (see page 556). The road to Elgol also gives great views of Bla Bheinn (pronounced *Blaven*), best seen from Torrin, at the head of Loch Slapin.

Sleeping There are several B&Bs in Elgol, but a more attractive option is **E** *Rowan Cottage*, T/F866287, www.rowncott.demon.co.uk Open Apr-Nov, a mile east at Glasnakille.

Transport The only public transport is the *Postbus* from Broadford, which runs twice Mon-Sat and once on Sun, and takes 2 hrs. For details of **boat trips** on the *Bella Jane*, T866244; to book T0800- 7313089 (freephone). Return boat trips take 3 hrs, including about 1½ hrs ashore, and cost £13.50, £6.50 child. You should be able to see seals and porpoises en route. There's also a one-way trip for experienced walkers/climbers who wish to make the return journey on foot or to explore the Cuillins (costs £10). There are also trips on the *Nicola*, T866236. Trips to Rùm or Canna cost £20-35.

Glen Brittle
Phone code: 01478
Colour map 3, grid A3

Six miles along the A863 to Dunvegan from Sligachan is a turning left to Portnalong, Carbost and the Talisker Distillery (B8009), which soon leads to the entrance to Glen Brittle. The road down Glen Brittle affords great views of the western side of the imposing Black Cuillins, until it ends at the campsite and shore at the foot of the glen. From Glen Brittle there are numerous paths leading up to the corries of the Black Cuillins. There are many alternative options for those wishing to continue up to the upper corries or to the Main Ridge. One of the finest of the Cuillin corries is **Coire Lagan**. This walk starts from the beach at Glen Brittle village and takes you up to the lochan in the upper coire, with Sgurr Alasdair, the most difficult of the Munros, towering overhead. A fine Cuillin sampler is the short walk to the spectacular **Eas Mor** waterfall.

Sleeping Apart from the campsite by the shore, T640404, the only accommodation is at the **F** *SYHA Hostel*, T640278, in the village. It's open mid-Mar to end of Oct and has 39 beds.

Transport There are 2 daily **buses** from Portree to Glen Brittle Mon-Sat during the summer only. Otherwise, take the Portree-Carbost-Fiscavaig bus, which leaves twice Mon-Fri and once on Sat, and get off at the turn-off, then walk the remaining 7 miles, or hitch, though it can be slow.

A recommended trip for whisky drinkers, or if it's raining, is to the **Talisker Distillery**, at **Carbost** on the shores of Loch Harport, on the B8009 (not in the village of Talisker itself, which is on the west coast). This is Skye's only whisky distillery and produces a very smoky, peaty single malt. The informative tours last around 20-30 minutes and begin with a complimentary dram. ■ *Apr-Jun Mon-Fri 0900-1630; Jul-Sep Mon-Sat 0900-1630; Oct Mon-Fri 0900-1630; Nov-Mar Mon-Fri 1400-1630. Tours £3.50 (includes discount voucher). T614308, F640401, large groups need to book in advance.*

> **Talisker**
> *Phone code: 01478*
> *Colour map 3, grid A3*

Near the distillery is *Carbostcraft Pottery*, which produces a wide range of traditional and original pottery, including the famous 'torn pots'. It's open Monday-Saturday 0900-1700 from February-December (also Sunday in summer). T640259. They also have a shop in Portree.

Sleeping There are a few places to stay in and around **Carbost**. Further west, in the village of **Talisker**, is **C** *Talisker House*, T640245, F640214, jon_and_ros.wathen@ virgin.net 4 rooms. This excellent guesthouse makes an ideal retreat from the summer hordes, and serves fine food. North of Carbost, near **Portnalong**, are 2 hostels. **F** *Croft Bunkhouse & Bothies*, T/F640254, pete@skyehostel.free-online.co.uk Sleeps 26. Also room for camping, transport from Sligachan or Portree, rents mountain bikes, pub and shop nearby. *Skyewalker Independent Hostel*, T640250, F640420, skyewalker@easynet.co.uk In a converted school beyond Portnalong on the road to Fiscavaig. 32 beds.

Transport There's a regular bus service (weekdays only) from Portree and Sligachan to Portnalong, T01470-532240.

Broadford and around

Eight miles west of Kyleakin is Broadford (An t-Ath Leathann), Skye's second largest village, which basically consists of a mile-long main street strung out along a wide bay. Broadford may be low on charm but it's high on tourist facilities, with plenty of accommodation and places to eat, a tourist office, garage, supermarket and bank (with ATM). There are also a few interesting, and unusual, things to do when it rains, which is always a bonus.

> *Phone code: 01471*
> *Colour map 3, grid A4*

The Highlands and Skye

Ins & outs **Getting there** Buses between **Portree**, **Inverness** and **Fort William** pass through daily. There are also daily buses to and from Kyleakin, Portree and Armadale/Ardvasar. See Transport on next page.

The **Tourist Information Centre** is by the Esso petrol station, which also has internet access, T822361. Open Apr-Oct Mon-Sat 0930-1730; Jul-Aug Mon-Sat 0900-1900, Sun 1000-1700.

Sights One of the most incongruous attractions on the island, or elsewhere in the Highlands, is the **Skye Serpentarium**, where you can see, and touch, all kinds of snakes, lizards and other reptiles. ■ *Easter-Oct Mon-Sat 1000-1700 (also Sun in Jul/Aug). £2.50, children £1.50. T822209.* More familiar but also interesting is the **International Otter Survival Fund** visitor centre. ■ Mar-Oct daily 0930-1700. £1.50. At the north end of the village, near the post office, is **World of Wood**, where you can find out everything you ever wanted to know about wood, and buy all sorts of souvenirs. When the weather's clear you can take a boat trip to the island of **Pabay** with *Family's Pride II*. Trips last 1½ hours, cost £10 and leave daily from the main pier, April-October. T822037.

Sleeping Two notable places are **D** *Lime Stone Cottage*, 4 Lime Park (behind the Serpentarium), *Finding a room shouldn't be a problem, except maybe in the peak months* T822142, kathielimepark@btinternet.com, which is full of rustic charm; and **D** *Ptarmigan*, overlooking the bay, T822744, F822745, www.ptarmigan-cottage.com The **F** *SYHA Hostel* is by the new pier, T822422. Open all year. A mile or so south of the village, at Lower Breakish off the A87 to Kyleakin, is the **F** *Fossil Bothy*, T822297, which has 8 beds and is open Easter-Oct, book in advance.

Eating The best place to eat is the *Seagull Restaurant*, at Breakish, south of Broadford on the main road to Kyleakin, T822001. It serves excellent local food with a European twist. Mid-range. For cheap to mid-range bar meals, try the *Claymore Bar-Restaurant*, at the south end of the village, T822333.

Transport Daily Citylink **buses** run to and from Portree, Inverness and Fort William. *Waterloo* buses run daily to and from Kyleakin, Portree (£6 return) and Armadale/Ardvasar. For **car hire** try *Sutherlands* at the Esso Garage, T822225, F822759, who charge from £30 per day. You can rent **mountain bikes** from *Fairwinds Bicycle Hire*, just past the *Broadford Hotel*, T822270, for £7 per day.

Directory *Bank of Scotland* with ATM by the shops opposite the road to the new pier. Next to the Esso station is a Co-op **supermarket**, and there's a **laundrette** in the petrol station shop (open 24 hrs).

Kyleakin & The opening of the Skye Bridge, linking the island with the Kyle of Lochalsh **Kylerhea** (see page 490), has turned the former ferry terminal of Kyleakin (Caol Acain) *Phone code: 01599* into something of a backwater, as well as infuriating the locals with its £5 per *Colour map 3, grid A5* car toll. The absence of road traffic, though, makes it a quiet place to stay, and it's now a favourite with backpackers, judging by the number of hostels. There's precious little to do here, other than look at the small ruin of **Castle Moil**, but you could take one of the seal cruises organized by *Castle Moil Seal Cruises*, which leave from the ferry pier, taking you to see the seal colony on **Eilean Mahl**. Cruises last 1¼ hours and cost £5.50. T544235.

The Highlands and Skye

The Battle of the Braes

One of the most significant incidents in the island's history took place in April, 1882, when a group of around 100 local crofters and their families fought a pitched battle against a force of 60 police sent by the government from Glasgow. The 'Battle of the Braes', as it became known, was caused, like many other such uprisings throughout the Highlands and Islands (see page 546), by threatened evictions. The local crofters were so incensed by the injustice of the eviction notices served on them that they destroyed the offending documents, leading the government to dispatch its police force. The defeat of the government forces of law and order by a bunch of men, women and children with sticks and stones is often described as the last battle fought on British soil, and led eventually to the setting up of a Royal Commission to look into the crofters' grievances.

Sleeping and eating The large, modern **F** *SYHA Hostel*, T534585 a few hundred yards from the pier, is open all year. Nearby is the **F** *Skye Backpackers Hostel*, T/F534510, open all year, and breakfast £1.40. There's also the **F** *Dun Caan Hostel*, T534087, T/F534795, near the old ferry quay, which is open all year and also hires bikes for £5 per day. There are also several **B&Bs**. The backpacker's pub, *Saucy Mary's*, serves cheap meals, but the best place to eat is *The Crofter's Kitchen*, outside the village on the road to Broadford, T534134. It serves 3-course meals and snacks (mid-range). Open Mon-Sat 1000-2100, Sun 1230-2100.

Transport There are **buses** from Kyleakin to **Portree** via Broadford (4 daily), to **Armadale** and **Ardvasar** via Broadford (3 daily Mon-Sat) and half hourly to **Kyle** via the Skye Bridge. *Kyleakin Private Hire* (T534452) run a **taxi** service and guided tours of the island.

Kylerhea

About four miles out of Kyleakin a road turns left off the A87 and heads southeast to Kylerhea (pronounced Kile-ray). The bridge may be the most convenient route to Skye, but the best way to cross is on the small car and passenger ferry that makes the 10-minute crossing to Kylerhea from Glenelg (see page 488). For full details of times and prices, see page 537. Near Kylerhea is the Forestry Commission **Otter Haven**. An hour-long nature trail takes you to an observation hide where you can look out for these elusive creatures. ■ *Daily 0900 till 1 hr before dusk. Free. T01320-366322.*

Broadford to Portree
Colour map 3, grid A4

The road north to Portree runs between the fringes of the Red Cuillins and the coast, giving good views across to the **Isle of Scalpay**. The road then turns west along the shores of Loch Ainort to the turn-off for the **Luib Folk Museum**, another of Peter MacAskill's island museums. The restored croft house has a smoky atmosphere and has old newspaper cuttings telling of the 'Battle of the Braes' and the 'Glendale Martyrs'. ■ *Daily 0900-1800. £1.*

The road runs north to **Sconser**, departure point for the ferry to Raasay (see below), then runs around Loch Sligachan and heads north to Portree. On the opposite side of the loch from Sconser are the crofting communities known as **The Braes**, who successfully opposed their landlords' eviction notices and brought the crofters' cause to the public's attention.

The Highlands and Skye

Isle of Raasay

Phone code: 01478
Colour map 1,
grid C3/4
OS Landranger No 24
The island is a nature
conservancy, and
you may see seals,
eagles and otters

The lush and beautiful island of Raasay lies only a few miles off the east coast of Skye yet remains well and truly off the tourist trail. Its hilly terrain and superb cliff scenery offer numerous walking opportunities and the views from the highest point, **Dun Caan** (1,456 ft), with the Cuillins on one side and Torridon on the other, are, quite simply, beyond compare. The walk to the distinctive flat-topped summit of this extinct volcano, via an old iron mine, is relatively straightforward and one of the most rewarding anywhere in the islands. So much so, in fact, that Boswell was inspired to dance a Highland jig on reaching the top, in 1773, during his grand tour with Dr Johnson. Another excellent walk starts from North Fearns, at the end of a road running east from **Inverarish**, to the deserted township of **Hallaig**, down the side of Beinn na Leac and back to North Fearns. The circular route is five miles long.

Raasay was for much of its history the property of the Macleods of Lewis, whose chief residence was the ruined **Brochel Castle**, before moving to **Clachan**, where **Raasay House** is now located (see below). The original Raasay House was torched by government troops after Culloden, along with all the island's houses and its boats, as punishment for the Macleods giving refuge to Bonnie Prince Charlie. After the Macleods sold the island in 1843, the Clearances began in earnest and Raasay suffered a long period of emigration, depopulation and poverty. It is not surprising, then, that the island's most famous son, the great poet **Sorley Maclean**, writes so passionately about this lost society. Born in Oskaig in 1911, he writes in his native Gaelic as well as in English, and is highly regarded internationally. Raasay's population now numbers around 150 and the island is a bastion of the Free Church, whose strict Sabbatarian beliefs should be respected by visitors.

Those who make it to the north of the island may wish to note that the two miles of road linking **Brochel** to **Arnish** were the work of one man, Calum Macleod. He decided to build the road himself after the council turned down his requests for proper access to his home. He spent between 10 and 15 years building it with the aid of a pick, a shovel, a wheelbarrow and a road-making manual which cost him three shillings. He died in 1988, soon after its completion, and to this day it is known as 'Calum's Road'.

Sleeping The main settlement on the island is **Inverarish**, a 15-min walk from the ferry dock. Half a mile further on is the *Raasay Outdoor Centre*, housed in the huge Georgian mansion that was Raasay House, which runs many and various adventure courses, from climbing to windsurfing, as well as offering basic accommodation from Mar to mid-Oct, and a **campsite**, T660266. Nearby are the **E** *Isle of Raasay Hotel*, T/F660222, and **E** *Churchton House*, T660260, both of which are open all year. Further north along the coast, at **Oskaig**, B&B is available at **E** *Mrs Mackay*, T660207, including dinner. A rough track leads up a steep hill from the tiny village to the island's **F** *SYHA Hostel*, T660240, open mid-Mar to end-Oct.

Transport The *CalMac* car and passenger ferry runs from Sconser daily Mon-Sat every hour from 0830 till 1800 (2130 in Jul/Aug). Last return is at 1700 (2100 in Jul/Aug). It takes 15 mins and costs £3.65 per person return, plus £15.70 per car and £1 per bicycle (so leave the car behind!).

Sleat Peninsula

East of Broadford is the turn-off to the peninsula of Sleat (pronounced 'slate'), a part of the island so uncharacteristically green and fertile that it's known as 'The Garden of Skye'. Sleat is another entry point to the island. Ferries cross from Mallaig on the mainland to Armadale on the southeastern shore of the peninsula. While the rest of the island is the preserve of the Macleods, Sleat is MacDonald country. The MacDonalds of Sleat are one of the major surviving branches of Clan Donald, and have the right to use the title Lord MacDonald (but not Lord of the Isles, which is now used by the heir to the throne).

Phone code: 01471
Colour map 3, grid A4

Sleeping and eating The clan seat is Armadale Castle (see below), but the home of the present Lord MacDonald is **L** *Kinloch Lodge*, T833214, F833277, www.kinloch-lodge.com, at the head of **Loch na Dal**. Lord and Lady MacDonald's family home is also an award-winning restaurant, offering the rare chance to enjoy superb food in the grandest of settings. The track that leads to the 19th-century Sporting Lodge turns off the A851 about 8 miles south of Broadford. Lady Claire Mac-Donald is one of the best known cooks in Scotland and author of several cookbooks, and if you do decide to treat yourself make sure you leave enough room for their exquisite puddings. The 5-course fixed menu is in our expensive range, but well worth it. Accommodation (in our **L** range) is also available in 10 en suite rooms. Open Mar-Nov. A little further on is **B** *Duisdale Hotel*, T833202, F833404, www.duisdale.com 19 rooms (2 with 4-poster beds). Country house hotel set in lovely grounds with great views across the Sound of Sleat. The restaurant serves good traditional Scottish cooking, and a 5-course meal is in the expensive range.

South of Duisdale is the signed turning for Isle Ornsay, or **Eilean Iarmain** (pronounced eelan yarman) in Gaelic, a very beautiful place in a small rocky bay overlooking the tidal Isle of Ornsay with the mountains of Knoydart in the background. This was once Skye's main fishing port, and the neat white-washed cottages and tiny harbour are still there. It is also largely Gaelic-speaking, thanks mainly to the efforts of its landlord, Sir Iain Noble, who owns the hotel and his own local Gaelic whisky company as well as the northern half of the peninsula, which is known as *Fearan Eilean Iarmain*.

Isle Ornsay

Sleeping and eating **L** *Hotel Eilean Iarmain*, T833332, F833275, www.eileanarmain.co.uk 12 rooms. Award-winning Victorian hotel full of charm and old-world character, with wonderful views. It is utterly lovely and romantic and an absolute must if you're in the area and can afford it. Award-winning restaurant features local shellfish landed only yards away (open to non-residents). A cheaper option is to eat in the cosy **bar** next door, which serves pub grub of an impossibly high standard in a more informal atmosphere. The hotel also offers winter shooting on the local estate, and you can enjoy a tasting of the local whisky, T833266.

A few miles further on is a turn-off to the left to the villages of **Ord**, **Tokavaig** and **Tarskavaig**, on the west coast of the peninsula, from where, on a clear day, there are views across to the Cuillins. Near Tokavaig is the ruin of **Dunsgaith Castle**, home of the MacDonalds of Sleat until the 17th century. Tarskavaig is a typical crofting township. In the early 19th century the MacDonalds wanted the more fertile glens inland for their sheep farms and so evicted the people to coastal townships like Tarskavaig. Just beyond the turn-off to Ord are the remains of **Knock Castle**, yet another MacDonald stronghold.

The Highlands and Skye

Sleeping Nearby, in Toravaig House, is the **F** *Hairy Coo Backpacker Hotel*, T833231, F833393, stotty@hairycooskye.freeserve.co.uk 30 beds, open all year, breakfast on request, also serves bar meals. A few miles further on, at Kilmore, is the **F** *Sleat Independent Hostel*, T844440, F844272. Newly refurbished with all facilities, 24 beds, open all year, and free transport to and from Armadale Pier.

Ostaig At Ostaig is the Gaelic College, *Sabhal Mor Ostaig*, where all subjects are taught in Gaelic, including full-time courses in business studies and media, as well as short courses in Gaelic music and culture during the summer months, T844373. The bookshop has a good selection of books and tapes for those wishing to learn the language. The college was founded by Sir Iain Noble (see above). Ostaig is also the beginning or end (depending on which direction you're heading) of the detour to Tarskavaig, Tokavaig and Ord.

Armadale & Ardvasar Just before the ferry pier at Armadale is **Armadale Castle** which was built in 1815 as the main residence of the MacDonalds of Sleat. Most of the castle is now a roofless ruin but the servants' quarters contain an excellent exhibition and accompanying video explaining the history of the Lordship of the Isles. The Clan Donald Lords of the Isles took over from their Norse predecessors in ruling the Hebrides until their power was broken in 1493. The former stables at the entrance comprise offices, a restaurant and bookshop, while the estate manager's house has been converted to accommodate an extensive library and archives. The castle is surrounded by 40 acres of handsome gardens and woodland, and there are ranger-led walks along nature trails with fine views across to the mainland. ■ *Apr to end-Oct daily 0930-1730. £3.95, concession/children £2.85. T844305, 844275, office@cland.demon.co.uk*

Just beyond Armadale Castle is the tiny village of **Armadale** which is strung out along the wooded shoreline and merges into the neighbouring village of **Ardvasar** (pronounced Ard-*vaa*-sar), which has a post office, general store. Armadale's *raison d'être* is the ferry pier and there's not a huge amount to keep you occupied, but there are a couple of good handicraft shops. At the turn-off to the pier is *Skye Batiks* , which also has a shop in Portree (see page 541). Here you'll find the colourful cotton garments which make a unique souvenir of the island, T844396. They also now have B&B accommodation. On the ferry pier is *Ragamuffin*, T844217, which sells a wide range of knitwear and is open daily 0900-1800. About four or five miles past the ferry port, at the end of the road, is **Aird of Sleat**, a crofting township, from where you walk out to the lighthouse at the **Point of Sleat**. It's a five-mile walk on a clear path across moorland with fine coastal scenery.

Sleeping and eating Just before the turn-off to the ferry pier is **F** *SYHA Hostel*, T844260. 42 beds. Open mid-Mar to end Oct, rents bikes. There's also **B&B** accommodation in Ardvasar, at the lovely **C** *Ardvasar Hotel*, T844223, F844495, www.ardvasar.com, a traditional whitewashed coaching in with 9 rooms, an excellent restaurant and the liveliest pub in the vicinity. Alternative eating options are *Pasta Shed*, on the ferry pier, which does good eat-in or takeaway pizzas; a few hundred yards away, the *Gallery* café/restaurant which serves cheap fish and seafood dishes.

Transport For full details of **ferry crossings to Mallaig**, see page 537. There are 3 **buses** daily, except Sun, from Armadale Pier to **Portree** (1 hr 20 mins) and **Kyleakin** (1 hr) via **Broadford** (40 mins). The first bus leaves at 0935.

Walks on Skye

Skye is one of the best places in Scotland for walking. The walks described below range from easy low-level routes to harder walks requiring a reasonably good level of fitness and a detailed map. As in the rest of the Highlands, you should be prepared for the worst and be properly equipped to cope with the wind and rain, even in the height of summer. Good hiking boots are also essential as the ground underfoot is likely to be boggy once off roads and tracks. See also the safety precautions outlined on page 60.

OS Landranger Nos 23 and 32

A nice, gentle introduction to walking in the area, and an opportunity to stretch your legs before tackling more strenuous routes such as the Old Man of Storr or the Quiraing, starts out from Bosville Terrace. Follow the street as it curves round then take the right fork at the first junction, down towards the shore. Just after the car park to the right the road splits: follow the path to the right along the northern shore of the bay. The path follows the shore and passes a viewpoint and flagpole. It then becomes rougher as it swings round the headland and reaches a gate in a dyke. Go through the gate and cross the muddy field, then follow the fence up to the left till you reach another gate. Go over the gate and continue along the edge of the next field, then cross a stile at the top of the field. Climb up the slope to the clear track and follow this left as it heads uphill. You'll then see some houses; take the track beyond the house on the left and follow it down between two large farm buildings. The path heads down across rough moorland towards Portree. Cross the stile and continue downhill through some woods, then you'll see a hotel on your left before rejoining the original road near the car park. It's about 2½ miles in total and takes about an hour and a half at an easy pace. The path can get very muddy in places.

Around Portree

This dramatic basalt finger of rock, 165 ft high, stands beneath the steep cliffs of The Storr (2,360 ft) and is visible from the A855. The starting point for the 3½-mile walk up and back (1½ hours) is the car park on the left, just over six miles north of Portree, near the northern end of Loch Leathan, which can be reached by bus from Portree.

The Old Man of Storr
For transport details, see page 542

Cross the stile over the wall by the Forestry Commission sign and follow the clear track up through the conifer plantation. The track is a gradual uphill climb until you come out into open grassland. Go through the gate in the fence and then it's a steep climb up the grassy slope with the massive pinnacle towering overhead. Once at the top you enter an area of weird and impressive rock formations. You can follow any of the dozens of paths that lead between the rocks, or just enjoy the fantastic views across to Raasay and the mainland beyond. You can follow the same path back down to the car park.

This four-mile walk is quite demanding, but the dramatic scenery more than compensates. To get to the starting point, drive 19 miles north from Portree on the A855. At Brogaig, just north of Staffin, take the single-track road to Uig. Follow this for about 2½ miles and, just after the road has zig-zagged its way up the face of the ridge, park in the car park to the left.

The Quiraing

Cross the road and follow the well-defined path along the base of the cliffs, with a steep grassy slope down to the right. After about one mile you'll start to see some of the well-known rocky features on the far side of a rough valley. The most imposing of these is **The Prison**, a huge, tilted square block. On the left, among the towering cliffs, is **The Needle**, a shaft of rock about 120-ft

The Highlands and Skye

high. Scramble up the narrow gully to the left of The Needle to reach **The Table**, an area of flat grassland surrounded by high cliffs (local shinty teams used to play here!). From The Table continue along the path at the foot of the cliffs, past a small lochan on the right and through a stone dyke, until you reach the lowest point of the ridge on your left. Scramble up on to the ridge and make your way back along the tops of the cliffs (take care at this point). There's a hard climb up the slopes of Meall na Suirmamach, but the views from the top are spectacular. Continue along the top of the cliffs for just over a mile and you'll see the car park.

Elgol to Camasunary Bay
For transport to and from Elgol, see page 548

This nine-mile coastal walk is quite demanding, but on a clear day the views of the Cuillins make it well worth the effort. It starts from the car park in Elgol. From the car park, walk back up the road for a short distance, then turn left along a track behind some houses, signposted for 'Garsbheinn'. Beside the last of these houses is a sign for the path to Coruisk. Follow this path along a steep grassy slope. The views across Loch Scavaig to the island of Soay and the Cuillins behind are marvellous. The slope gets even steeper beneath Ben Cleat, then comes the point where vertigo sufferers may wish they hadn't started. This is the notorious 'bad step', an overhanging rock with a 30- ft drop to the sea below. Once you negotiate this, you then continue along the foot of Glen Scaladal and cross a burn, which can be tricky if it's in spate. Then it's on along the path beyond Beinn Leacach to Camasunary Bay. The shortest way back to Elgol is to retrace your steps (including bad ones), but as an alternative, follow the clear track from Camasunary up the right side of Abhainn nan Lean over the hills to the east until it joins the B8083 from Broadford. From here it's about 3½ miles back along the road to Elgol.

Outer Hebrides

11

Outer Hebrides

The Outer Hebrides – or Long Island as they are also known – consist of a narrow 130-mile long chain of islands, lying 40 miles off the northwest coast of the Scottish mainland. Relentlessly battered by fierce Atlantic winds, the islands can seem a hostile environment and an unappealing proposition, particularly if you happen to be stuck there on a wet Sunday without your own means of transport. Much of the interior is bleak peat bog, rocks and endless tiny lochs, and the long, straggling crofting communities only add to the feeling of desolation. But there are also miles of superb beaches, wild mountain scenery, numerous archaeological treasures and long hours of summer daylight in which to appreciate it all.

Despite the frequency of transport connections with the mainland, the Outer Hebrides remain remote in every sense. Unlike Skye and the Inner Hebrides, tourism is of far less importance to the local economy. In many ways, the islands are the last bastion of the old Highland life. Though newer industries such as fish farming have been introduced, the traditional occupations of crofting, fishing and weaving still dominate, and outside Stornoway on Lewis (the only decent-sized town in the islands) life is very much a traditional one, revolving around the seasons and the tides. Almost every islander has more than one occupation, so don't be surprised if the landlady of your guesthouse also weaves Harris Tweed, or if her husband drives the Postbus as well as doing a bit of fishing on the side. This creates a network of relationships where everyone knows everyone else.

Ins and outs

Getting there **By air** *British Airways*, T08457-733377, flies daily except Sun from Glasgow to Stornoway on Lewis (1 hr), Barra (1 hr 5 mins) and Benbecula on North Uist (1 hr). There are also flights from Edinburgh to Stornoway (1hr 10 mins), Inverness to Stornoway (40 mins) daily except Sun, and to Benbecula (2 hrs 40 mins) Mon-Fri. Note that weather conditions are so changeable that flights are prone to delay and can be very bumpy. Flights to Barra have an added complication in that they land on the beach, meaning that the runway disappears twice a day under the incoming tide.

By boat *CalMac* car and passenger ferries sail to and from Stornoway (Lewis), Tarbert (Harris), Lochmaddy (North Uist), Lochboisdale (South Uist) and Castlebay (Barra). Ferry times change according to the day of the week and time of the year, so they aren't listed in full below. For full details see the *CalMac Ferry Guide* or call *CalMac*, T0990-650000, reservations@calmac.co.uk, for reservations, and T01475-650100, www.calmac.co.uk, for general enquiries. See also 'Essentials', page 46. Car space is limited during the summer months, so it's advisable to book ahead. For details of bus connections on Skye and on the mainland, contact *Scottish Citylink*, T0990-505050.

To Lewis: *CalMac* ferry from Ullapool to Stornoway (2 hrs 40 minutes) 2-3 times daily Mon-Sat in the summer (Jun-Sep) and twice daily Mon-Sat in the winter. One-way ticket costs £13 per passenger and £62 per car. *CalMac* offices: Ullapool (T01854-612358) and Stornoway (T01851-702361).

To Harris: from Uig (Skye) to Tarbert (1 hr 35 mins) twice daily Mon-Sat. One-way ticket £8.50 per passenger, £40 per car. Contact Uig (T01470-542219) or Tarbert (T01859-502444).

To North Uist: from Uig to Lochmaddy (1 hr 40 mins) 1-2 times daily. One-way ticket £8.50 per passenger, £40 per car. Contact Lochmaddy (T5000337).

To Barra and South Uist: from Oban to Castlebay (5 hrs) and Lochboisdale (6 hrs 40 mins) once daily except Tue and Sun. One-way ticket £18.75 per passenger, £67 per car. From Mallaig to Castlebay (3 hrs 45 mins) on Sun only, and to Lochboisdale (3 hrs 30 mins) on Tue only. One-way ticket £13.85 per passenger, £49.50 per car. From Castlebay to Lochboisdale (1 hr 50 mins) on Mon, Wed, Thu and Sat, and from Lochboisdale to Castlebay on Tue, Thu, Fri and Sun. One-way ticket £5.30 per passenger, £30.50 per car.

To North Uist and Harris: a ferry sails to Otternish (North Uist) from Leverburgh (Harris) 3 or 4 times daily. The trip takes 1 hr 10 mins and a one-way ticket costs £4.75 per passenger, £21.90 per car.

Island Hopscotch Tickets: a much cheaper way to get around the islands with a car is with one of *CalMac's* Island Hopscotch tickets. There are various route options, and tickets give you 30 days unlimited travel on each route. For example, a ticket for the Oban- Castlebay- Lochboisdale- Otternish- Leverburgh- Stornoway- Ullapool route allows you to visit all the main islands and costs £38 per passenger and £164 per car. See the *CalMac* guide or call the numbers above for full details of the Island Hopscotch Tickets, and the **Island Rover Ticket**, which gives unlimited travel on most *CalMac* routes for 8 or 15 days.

Getting around You should allow plenty of time to explore the islands fully. With your own transport and travelling from top to bottom, a week would be enough time for a whistle-stop tour but not enough to explore in any depth or scratch beneath the surface. You will need to allow for the lack of public transport on Sun on most islands, and for the fact that weather conditions frequently affect ferry and flight timetables.

Things to do in the Outer Hebrides

- Visit the standing stones at Callanais, preferably at night when there's a spooky atmosphere.
- Take a stroll along the wonderful Uig sands, the loveliest beach on Lewis.
- Hire a car and drive along the amazing Golden Road, on the east coast of Harris.
- Fly to the island of Barra, where the planes land on the beach.
- Take a trip to St Kilda, home to some of the largest seabird colonies in Europe.

By air *Loganair* (operating as *British Airways*) fly between Barra, Benbecula and Stornoway Mon-Fri. For full details, T08457-733377.

By boat Passenger ferries run regularly between Ludag in South Uist to both Eoligarry in Barra and to the island of Eriskay, T01878-720238/265. **Car ferries** There are *CalMac* ferries between Harris and North Uist, and South Uasdfist and Barra (see above for details).

The car ferry to Eriskay from South Uist no longer operates following the opening of the new causeway in Aug 2001

By bus Bus services have improved and now run regularly to most main towns and villages on the islands. Details of local services are given under each destination. You should also invest in a copy of the *Highlands & Islands Travel Guide* (£1) which is available from the local Tourist Information Centres.

By car Most of the islands' roads are single track but in good condition and, unlike other parts of the Highlands and Islands, not too busy. On Sun you'll barely meet another soul, save for the occasional perplexed tourist looking in vain for somewhere to go. Drivers should note that petrol stations are few and far between, expensive and closed on Sun. The normal rules for single track roads apply and, as elsewhere in the Highlands, you need to look out for wandering sheep. Also note that distances are greater than most people imagine. For example, the distance from Nis (Ness) at the northern tip of Lewis to Leverburgh in the south of Harris is 85 miles. From Stornoway to Tarbert is 37 miles. And the distance from Otternish in the north of North Uist to Lochboisdale, the main ferry port on South Uist, is 50 miles. Several local **car hire** agencies offer reasonable rental deals. Expect to pay around £15-25 per day, depending on the size of engine and age of the car.

Note that you cannot take a rented car off the islands

By bicycle Cycling is a great way to explore the islands. You can fully appreciate the amazing scenery around you without the risk of driving over the edge of a cliff, and it only costs a few pounds to transport a bike by ferry. There is, of course, the major problem of strong winds, which can leave you frustrated and exhausted, especially when cycling into the prevailing easterly wind. **Bike hire** agencies are given under the relevant town.

Orientation & information

The Outer Hebrides is made up of more than 200 islands, only 10 of which are populated: Lewis and Harris; Scalpay; Berneray; North Uist; Benbecula; South Uist; Eriskay; Barra; and Vatersay; giving a total population of just under 30,000. The main population centre is Stornoway on Lewis, the only major town in the islands. The rest of the population is scattered throughout the islands in much smaller villages, mostly strung out along the coast.

Lewis and Harris are actually one island, divided by history and a line of high hills that runs between them. The northern part of Lewis is mostly bleak, flat peat moor, while the south and Harris are more rugged, with rocky peaks and superb beaches. The more southerly islands of North Uist, Benbecula and South Uist, joined together by

Outer Hebrides

Festivals in the Outer Hebrides

As the heartland of Gaelic culture, the Outer Hebrides are host to many music events throughout the year, ranging from a spontaneous ceilidh to one of the three local mods. Mods usually consist of three days of competition in piping, singing, instrumental music, drama and poetry, and are an opportunity to see the best of the local talent. More information can be obtained from An Comunn Gaidhealach, T01851-703487. Also listed below are the various Highland Games and agricultural shows, where you can also see piping competitions and Highland dancing.

Late March: Feis nan Coisir, *Stornoway, Lewis.*
1st Friday in April: Donald Macleod Memorial Piping Competition, *Stornoway, Lewis.*
May-June: Highland Festival, *held in various locations.*
Early June: Harris Mod, *Tarbert, Harris.*
2nd week in June: Lewis Mod, *Stornoway, Lewis.*
Mid June: Uist Mod, *Iochdar, South Uist.*
May-June: Lochmaddy Boat Festival, *Lochmaddy, North Uist.*
Mid July: Berneray Week, *Bearnaraigh (Berneray), North Uist.*
July: Ceolas Music School, *South Uist.*

Early July (2 weeks): Barra Festival.
Early/mid July (1 week): Feis Tir an Eorna, *Paibeil, North Uist;* Barra Highland Games, *Borgh (Borve), Barra.*
11-14 July: Hebridean Celtic Music Festival, *Stornoway, Lewis.*
Mid July: North Uist Highland Games, *Hosta, North Uist.*
Mid/late July: Harris Gala; South Uist Highland Games, *Aisgeirnis (Askernish), South Uist;* Lewis Highland Games, *Tong, Lewis.*
Mid July: Barra Highland Games.
3rd week July: Harris Festival
Late July: Barra Live, *Barra;* West Side Agricultural Show, *Barabhas (Barvas), Lewis;* South Uist Agricultural Show, *Iochdar, South Uist;* South Harris Agricultural Show, *Leverburgh, Harris.*
July: Feis Eilean an Fhraoich, *Stornoway, Lewis.*
Late July/early August: North Uist Agricultural Show, *Hosta, North Uist.*
Early August: Carloway Agricultural Show, *Càrlabhagh (Carloway), Lewis;* Fies Tir a Mhurain, *Lionacleit, Benbecula;* Lewis Carnival, *Stornoway;* Fish Festival, *Stornoway;* Twin Peaks Hill Race, *North Uist.*
2nd week August: Harris Arts Festival, *Tarbert.*

bridges and causeways, are mostly low and flat and peppered with so many lochs they resemble a giant sieve. Toll-free road bridges connect the island of Scalpay with Harris and Great Bernera with Lewis, and a causeway connects Berneray with North Uist. A new causeway connecting Eriskay to South Uist opened in August 2001.

There are **tourist information centres** in Stornoway and Tarbert which are open all year round, and also in Lochmaddy, Lochboisdale and Castlebay which are open early Apr to mid Oct. Full details are given under each destination.

The **Western Isles Tourist Board** produces an accommodation brochure as well as the essential *Western Isles Official Tourist Map* (Estate Publications; £3.95), which gives place names in English and Gaelic. They also have their own website (www.witb.co.uk) which provides lots of information on the islands, including up and coming events. Information about the islands can also be obtained at www.hebrides.com and www. gatliff.ic24.net The *Outer Hebrides Handbook and Guide* (£7.95) is written by local experts and is useful on history, culture, and flora and fauna.

Sleeping Accommodation on the islands is generally not difficult to find, except perhaps at the height of the summer when you should book in advance, either directly or through the

Outer Hebrides

Keeping with tradition

The islands are the 'Gaidhealtachd', the land of the Gael. Gaelic culture has remained more prominent here than in any other part of Scotland, and the way of life and philosophy of the islanders will seem totally alien and fascinating to many visitors. Gaelic is the first language for the majority of the islanders – and the only one for the older generation – but the all-pervading influence of the English media has taken its toll and the language is under threat. Though Gaelic is still taught in schools, the younger generation tends to speak to each other in English. Visitors will not have any language problems, as the Gaelic-speaking inhabitants are so polite they will always change to English when visitors are present, though place names and signposts are in Gaelic.

The church is also an important factor in preserving the language, and services are usually held in Gaelic. In fact, religion is one of the most pervasive influences of Hebridean life, and the islanders' faith is as strong as the winds that pound their shores. The islands are split between the Presbyterian Lewis, Harris and North Uist, and the predominantly Roman Catholic South Uist and Barra. Benbecula, meanwhile, has a foot in either camp. On Lewis and Harris the Free Church is immensely powerful and the Sabbath is strictly observed. Don't expect to travel anywhere by public transport, shops and petrol stations will be closed and you'll be hard pressed to find a place to eat. Even the swings in the playgrounds are padlocked! On the Roman Catholic islands, however, things are a bit more relaxed.

---

local tourist office. There are plenty of **B&Bs** and **guesthouses** scattered throughout the islands, many of which offer better value than the hotels. Most don't have private bathrooms, but they're comfortable, very welcoming and will offer evening meals. It's a good idea to book ahead if you're staying on a Sun. If you're staying in the countryside, you should check if there's a convenient pub or hotel to eat in, and if not, make arrangements to eat at your B&B.

There are numerous self-catering style cottages across the islands, many of which are advertised in the Western Isles brochure published annually by the Western Isles Tourist Board. There are also several official **youth hostels** in converted crofts scattered around the islands in isolated locations. Some are difficult to get to without your own transport, but you can always hitchhike. They are run by the **SYHA** or the **Gatliff Hebridean Hostels Trust** (see page 566). They are basic and adequate, but take a sleeping bag and food. Most of them don't have phones, so you can't book in advance, and try not to arrive or leave on a Sun. The Gatliff Trust has 4 hostels on the islands. Contact them at 71-77 Cromwell Street, Stornoway, or visit their website: www.gatliff. ic24.net There are also several new independent private hostels, which are clean and modern, and more expensive.

Leodhas (Lewis)

Lewis constitutes the northern two thirds of the most northerly island in the Outer Hebrides (which includes Harris to the south). It is by far the most populous of the Outer Hebridean islands and, with over 20,000 inhabitants, makes up two thirds of the total population. Just over 8,000 people live in Stornoway, the largest town in the Hebrides and the administrative capital of the Western Isles.

The majority of the rest of the population live in the long line of crofting townships strung out along the west coast between Port Nis (Ness) and Càrlabhagh (Carloway). The west coast is also where you'll find the island's most interesting

*Phone code: 01851
Colour map 1,
grid A3*

sites, the prehistoric remains of Dùn Chàrlabhaigh (Carloway) Broch and the impressive Calanais (Callanish) Standing Stones, the restored blackhouse village of Garenin and the Arnol Blackhouse. These can all be visited as a day trip from Stornoway, either as an organized tour or on the 'West Side Circular' bus service.

The interior of the northern half is flat peat bog, hence the island's name which means 'marshy' in Gaelic. Further south, where Lewis becomes Harris, the scenery is more dramatic as the relentlessly flat landscape gives way to rocky hills, providing the backdrop to the sea-lochs that cut deep into the coast and the beautiful beaches around Uig.

History

Lewis was dominated by the Vikings, and the Norse influence can be seen in many of the place names, such as Uig (which is Norse for 'a bay'). After the end of Norwegian sovereignty in 1266, the island was ruled by the Macleods, said to be descendants of early settlers from Iceland. Control of the island was wrested from them by the Mackenzies, who then proceeded to sell it, in 1844, to Sir James Matheson. The new owner built Lews Castle in Stornoway and began to develop the infrastructure of the island as well as investing in new industries. Though many crofts were cleared and families sent to Canada, the people of Lewis fared well and certainly much better than their counterparts in the Southern Isles.

The next proprietor was Lord Leverhulme, founder of Lever Brothers, who bought the island (along with Harris) in 1918. He planned to turn Lewis into a major fishing centre and ploughed money into developing the infrastructure. He was forced to abandon his plans, however, partly because of the decline of the fishing industry, and partly owing to the growing conflict between him and the islanders returning from the war who wanted land of their own to farm. As a final benevolent gesture, Lord Leverhulme offered Lewis to the islanders, but only Stornoway Council accepted. The island was then divided into estates and sold, and hundreds emigrated.

Today the economy of Lewis is still based on the traditional industries of crofting, fishing and weaving, though there are other economic activities such as fish farming, which is now a major employer, service industries, tourism, construction and the onshore oil yard at Stornoway.

Steòrnabhagh (Stornoway)

Phone code: 01851
Colour map B1,
grid B3
Population: 8,132

The fishing port of Stornoway, the only town in the Outer Hebrides, is the islands' commercial capital and as such boasts more services and facilities than you might expect in any town of comparable size. It has the full range of banks, shops, hotels, guesthouses, pubs and restaurants, garages, car hire firms, sports facilities, an airport and ferry terminal, and for the visiting tourist it presents a rare opportunity to stock up on supplies.

Stornoway is also the administrative capital and home to the *Comhairle nan Eilean* (The Western Isles Council), which has done much to broaden the local economy and to promote and protect Gaelic language and culture, but is probably best known for its disastrous financial dealings with the Bank of Credit and Commerce International (BCCI), which collapsed in 1991, losing the islands a cool £23 million.

The **tourist information centre** is at 26 Cromwell St. They stock maps, bus timetables and various books and brochures, and sell tickets for minibus tours to Calanais and for wildlife trips around Lewis and Harris. ■ *T703088.*

Apr-May and Sep-Oct Mon-Fri 0900-1800, Sat 0900-1700; Jun-Aug Mon-Fri 0900-2000; Oct-Mar Mon-Fri 0900-1700.

Stornoway is the island's transport hub. The **airport** is 4 miles east of the town centre, a £5 taxi ride away. For details of flights to the other islands and the mainland, see Ins and outs (page 560). The *CalMac* **ferry terminal** is just beyond the **bus station**, which is on South Beach, a short walk from the town centre. Full ferry details are also given in Ins and outs. Buses leave from Stornoway to all parts of the island and also to Tarbert and Leverburgh on Harris. Bus timetables are available from the **tourist office**. See also Transport on page 567.

Getting there & around

The town is compact and most of what you need is within easy walking distance of the tourist office. Some of the B&Bs in the residential areas are quite a distance from the centre, but there's an hourly town bus service, or hire a **taxi** from *Central Cabs* (T706900).

Stornoway

Outer Hebrides

N

0 metres 100
0 yards 100

■ **Sleeping**
1 Mrs Anne Macleod's B & B
2 Mrs MacMillan's B & B
3 Park Guest House
4 Royal
5 Stornoway Backpackers Hostel

● **Eating**
1 Golden Ocean
2 Stornoway Balti House
3 Thai Café

The Gatliff Trust

The Gatliff Hebridean Hostels Trust (GHHT) is a non-profit making charitable organisation run entirely by volunteers, working with the island community to establish, maintain and develop a chain of 'value-for-money' hostels offering clean, cheap, simple, safe, welcoming and traditional croft-style accommodation in dramatic and beautiful locations for visitors to the Outer Hebrides.

The GHHT is independent of the SYHA but has adopted status. Visitors do not have to be members of either organisation to use and stay in the hostels. First established as the Gatliff Trust in 1961 by Herbert Gatliff, the Trust was originally intended to provide young persons of limited means with the opportunity to meet local people and enjoy the unique natural environment and cultural heritage of the islands. However, in recent years visitors of all incomes, ages, nationalities and interests have been encouraged to use the facilities.

The Trust is currently involved in the operation of four hostels situated at Garenin (Isle of Lewis), Rhenigidale (Isle of Harris), Berneray (Isle of North Uist) and Howmore (South Uist). Further hostels may be opened on other islands in the future.

The hostels are open all year and looked after by non-resident wardens who live and practise crofting nearby. No advance bookings are accepted but it is very unlikely that visitors will find themselves turned away and without a bed for the night. There is also limited space for camping at the hostels. Hostels provide bunk/camp beds, cooking facilities and cutlery, piped water, toilets and coal/wood fires, but visitors should bring their own food and a sleeping bag is recommended.

Charges for 2002: (18 and over £6.50, 17 and under £5.00, Camping £3.25, Day Visitors £0.90). Annual Membership: £5.00.

Further information, including membership and contact details, hostel locations and photographs, a reading list and places of interest to visit in the surrounding area can be found at the GHHT website: www.gatliff.ic24.net

Sights Stornoway is short on conventional tourist sights and once you've been to the tourist office and bought the necessities from the local supermarkets, there's not much else to do. The focal point of the town has always been its sheltered deep-water **harbour** and, though the fishing industry has declined since its peak at the end of the last century, there's still a fair amount of activity, especially at the fish market on North Beach on Tuesday and Thursday evenings. The harbour is usually full of seals, giving the town its nickname of Portrona (port of seals). There's a good view across the harbour to **Lews Castle**, a 19th-century edifice built by Sir James Matheson with money earned from opium and tea. The castle now houses a college and its real attraction is the wooded grounds, the only place you'll see trees on the islands.

The **Museum nan Eilean**, on Francis Street, features a range of temporary exhibitions on island life and history. ■ *Apr to Sep Mon-Sat 1000-1730; Oct-Mar Tue 1000-1700 and Sat 1000-1300 . Free. T703773.*

Anyone remotely interested in Harris Tweed should visit the **Lewis Loom Centre**, housed in the Old Grainstore at the northern end of Cromwell Street, just off Bayhead. The 40-minute guided tour includes demonstrations of traditional methods of warping, dyeing and spinning, and a detailed lecture on the history of Harris Tweed. There's also a craft shop. ■ *Mon-Sat 1000-1700. Adult £2. T703117.*

The impressive baronial Town Hall on South Beach currently houses the **An Lanntair Art Gallery**, though plans are afoot to move the gallery into a new arts centre. The gallery features the work of local, national and international artists and also stages various musical events. The coffee shop serves home baking and tasty snacks. ■ *Mon-Sat 1000-1730. Free. T703307, lanntair@sol.co.uk*

As the largest settlement on the islands, Stornoway has a good selection of accommodation from which to choose, though you should book in advance in the peak summer season. The tourist information centre will do this for you, for a small fee.

Sleeping

There are several centrally located hotels, the best of which is the **B** *Royal Hotel*, Cromwell St, T702109, F702142. 24 rooms. Good value, and good food in its restaurant and bistro (see 'Eating' below). On the outskirts of town is **B** *Cabarfeidh Hotel*, Manor Park, T702604, F705572. 46 rooms. Not as convenient as the *Royal* but with the full range of facilities and a decent restaurant. **B** *Park Guest House*, 30 James St, T702485, F703482. 10 rooms. This Victorian townhouse is comfortable, only 500yd from the ferry terminal, and the best of the guesthouses. It also has an excellent restaurant which is recommended even if you're not staying.

There are many **B&Bs** in and around the town centre, most of which offer a 'room only' rate for those requiring an early start to catch the first ferry. There are several along Matheson Rd, which is close to the town centre and the ferry terminal, including, **E** *Mrs Anne Maclead*, at No 12, T702673; and **E** (**F** room only) *Mrs M MacMillan*, 'Fernlea' No 9, T702125. Another option is **F** *Fairhaven*, 17 Keith St, T705862, which can also do meals.

The basic **F** *Stornoway Backpackers Hostel* is at 47 Keith St, T703628. Includes breakfast, open all year. There's also a Bunkhouse Hostel at **F** *Laxdale Holiday Park*, on Laxdale Lane, about a mile out of town on the road to Barabhas, T703234. It has 16 beds, basic facilities and is open all year.

The pubs and hotels serve the usual range of bar meals. Probably the best restaurant in town is at the *Park Guest House* (see 'Sleeping' above), which offers top-class modern Scottish cooking using local fish, lamb and venison. It also caters for vegetarians and is open Tue-Sat. Mid-range to expensive. Also recommended is *The Boatshed*, in the *Royal Hotel* (see 'Sleeping' above), which specializes in seafood. Expensive. Less upmarket and cheaper is their *Barnacle Bistro*.

Eating
Note that pubs are closed on Sun and hotels cater only for residents

A good place for cheap snacks and light lunches is the café at the *Ann Lanntair Gallery* (see 'Sights' above). For a touch of non-Scottish fare, try the *Stornoway Balti House*, near the bus station on South Beach; the *Golden Ocean Restaurant*, on Cromwell St; or the *Thai Café* on Church St. There are several other takeaways offering the standard fare of pizza, kebabs, fish and chips etc. The cheapest option is the all-day breakfast served in the *Co-op* supermarket (see map). For a cheap lunch try the *cafeteria* in the *Deep Sea Fishermen's Mission* on North Beach.

There are 2 large supermarkets in town. *Safeway* is beside the ferry terminal and the *Co-op* is by the first roundabout on the road out to Barabhas. There's also a smaller supermarket opposite the tourist information centre.

Buses leave from Stornoway to all parts of the island. Note that buses do not run on Sun. To **Port Niss (Ness)** via **Barabhas (Barvas)** 4-6 times per day; to **Arnol, Siabost (Shawbost), Càrlabhagh (Carloway), Calanais (Callanish)**, and back to Stornoway ('West Side Circular') 4-6 times per day; to **Bearnaraigh (Great Bernera)** via **Gearraidh na h-Aibhne (Garynahine)** 4 per day; to **Uig District** 3-4 per day; to **Ranais (Ranish)** 6-8 times per day. For full details, T840269. There are also buses from Stornoway to **Tarbert** and on to **Leverburgh** (for the ferry to North Uist) 4-5 times per day (T01859-502441).

Transport

Car and bike rental is available at good rates from *Lewis Car Rentals,* 52 Bayhead St, T703760, F705860. Also *Arnol Motors,* in Arnol (see page 568), T01851-710548 (T0831-823318 mobile), F710248. You can **rent bikes** at *Alex Dan's Cycle Centre,* 67 Kenneth St, T704025, F701712.

Directory **Banks** The *Bank of Scotland* is directly opposite the tourist office and has an ATM. The other major banks are also in the centre of town and also have ATMs. **Internet** *Captions,* 27 Church St, T702238, F706782, bayble@captions.co.uk, www.captions. co.uk Open Mon-Sat till late in the summer months. Internet facilities also available at the public library on Cromwell St. **Post office** On Francis St. **Tour companies** *MacDonald's Coaches,* at the Ferry Terminal, T706267. Coach tours. *Hebridean Exploration,* 19 Westview Tce, T705655 (T0374-292746 mobile). Sea kayak tours. *Elena C,* 5a Knock, Point, T870537, F706384. Wildlife trips from Stornoway harbour.

The West Coast

Phone code: 01851
Colour map 1, grid A3

The west coast of Lewis contains most of what you'll want to see and can be covered in a day trip from Stornoway, either with your own transport, by public bus or as part of a minibus tour.

At **Barabhas (Barvas)** the road forks. The A857 bears right (north) and continues all the way to **Nis (Ness)** and the Butt of Lewis (see page 572), but the road you want to take is the A858, which bears left (west). A few miles along this road is the turn-off for **Arnol**. At the end of the village is the **Blackhouse Museum**, one of the best surviving examples of an original blackhouse in Scotland and well worth visiting. These traditional thatched houses were once common throughout the Highlands and Islands, and inhabited until the 1960s. They were built in the tradition of 'longhouses' which can be traced back 1,000 years to the time of the Viking invaders. The name 'blackhouses' dates back to the 1850s when modern buildings were introduced. These were known as 'white houses' and the older style houses were called 'blackhouses'. The blackhouses were well adapted to the harsh local climate. They had no windows or chimney and were built with local materials – stone, turf and thatch of oat, barley or marram grass, and with a peat fire burning continually in the central hearth – and attached to the living quarters was the cattle byre. This particular blackhouse was built in 1885 and lived in until 1964. ■ *T710395. Apr-Sep Mon-Sat 0930-1830; Oct-Mar Mon-Sat 0930-1630, Sun 1400-1630. Adult £2.80, concession £2, children £1.*

Hebridean Replicas (T710562) in the village offers quality handmade Lewis chess sets from local stone, and provides a welcome alternative to much of the tacky tourist paraphernalia to be found in Stornnoway.

Two miles south of the Arnol turn-off, at **Bragar**, look out for an archway, formed from the jawbone of a blue whale which was washed up on the coast nearby in 1920. A few miles further on is the township of **Siabost (Shawbost)**, where the charmingly ramshackle **folk museum**, which was started originally as a project by local schoolchildren, now contains an interesting collection of Hebridean artefacts. ■ *Mon-Sat 0900-1800, free.* Behind the museum is a **campsite**, T710504, March-October.

Just south of Siabost, beside a small loch, is the sign for the recently restored **Norse Mill and Kiln**, which are a half-mile walk over the hill from the car park. There's not much to see as yet, but it's worth getting out of the car if you want to stretch your legs. A little further on is the turning for **Dail Beag (Dalbeg)**, a lovely secluded beach.

Eating Overlooking a small lochan surrounded by hills beside the car park is the *Copper Kettle*, T710592, an unassuming little house which is actually a superb restaurant. Meals must be booked at least 24 hrs in advance and are moderately priced (last booking 2000). Open 1030 till 1730 for tea, coffee, snacks and home baking (all year Mon-Sat). Next door is a self-catering bungalow for rent (same phone number).

The landscape gradually becomes more undulating and scenically interesting as the road then passes through the village of **Càrlabhagh (Carloway)**, Lord Leverhume's proposed fishing port. Here, a branch road leads to the ruined and deserted 'blackhouse' village of **Gearrannan (Garenin)**. The old village has been undergoing extensive renovation in recent years with the aid of EU funding, and several derelict crofts have now been painstakingly restored to their original style of stone walls and thatched roofs. An old cart track leads down to the bay and wonderful sunsets out at sea. The village now boasts a Gatliff Trust hostel, heritage centre, café and holiday dwellings. Above the village a footpath can be followed through the lazybeds and above the sea cliffs to reveal a stunning view of beautiful **Dal More Bay**. The Atlantic waves seem to break relentlessly on golden sands and the beach is, not surprisingly, the favourite haunt of the surfing jet-set from Stornoway. Swimmers and bathers should be careful, however, because as with many of the west coast beaches there can be a fierce rip-current carrying the unwary into deeper water out at sea.

A little further on, standing a few hundred yards from the main road, is the **Dùn Chàrlabhaigh (Doune Carloway) Broch**, the best-preserved building of its type in the Outer Hebrides. The impressive 2,000 year-old drystone habitation is beautifully situated on a rocky outcrop, commanding great views across Loch Carloway to the sea beyond. The remaining outer wall is 30-ft high and slopes inwards, with an inner wall which rises vertically, leaving chambers between the walls. Parts of the inner wall have collapsed, revealing the interior stairs and galleries. There's also the **Doune Broch Visitor Centre** by the car park, which tastefully complements the architectural style of the site, and which gives a good audio-visual description of how life must have been in one of these structures around 50 BC. ■ *T643338. Doune Broch Centre Apr-Oct Mon-Sat 1000-1800. Free.*

Calanais (Callanish)

Five miles south of Dun Chàrlabhaigh is the jewel in the islands' prehistoric crown, the **Calanais Standing Stones**, which are unique in Scotland and the equal of Stonehenge in historical value. The stones are in a beautiful setting overlooking Loch Roag and are very atmospheric, especially at sunset or at night, when no one's around. They are in the form of a Celtic cross, and in the centre is a circle of 13 stones with a central monolith over 12-ft tall, and a chambered burial cairn. The oldest part of this great ceremonial site – probably the stone circle – dates from around 3,000 BC (older than Stonehenge) and continued in use until about 800 BC. The full significance of the site is not yet known, though it is probably connected to the seasonal cycle, as many of the stones are aligned with the rising and setting moon. There are also a number of smaller and more isolated stone circles a few miles south of Calanais on the road to Gearraidh na h-Aibhne (Garynahine).

Phone code: 01851
Colour map 1, grid B2

Outer Hebrides

Crofting

The word 'croft' is derived from the Gaelic croit, meaning a small area of land, and crofting has been the traditional way of life in the Scottish Highlands for many centuries. Its emotive hold on the psyche of the Highlander comes from the long, hard struggle for security of tenure (see page 649).

A croft is aptly described as a parcel of land entirely surrounded by regulations. Most crofts consist of a few acres of arable land with a proportion of grazing land shared with other crofts. Each crofter is, in effect, a kind of small tenant-farmer, the distinction being that he has almost absolute security of tenure and has the right to assign the croft to a member of his family whether the landlord agrees or not. In fact, over the years the crofter has managed to acquire most of the rights of ownership with few of the disadvantages.

The croft is the area of land involved and not the house which is called the 'croft house'. Crofts can vary in size, from a quarter of an acre upwards. Those on Lewis are small and relatively unproductive, with an average size of only

about five acres, while on the Uists, where the land is more fertile, crofts are up to 50 acres or more.

As well as having the sole tenancy of the croft, the crofter usually also has a share in a huge area of 'common grazing' along with the other members of the crofting community – commonly called a township. They also work together in such activities as fencing, sheep dipping or cutting peat.

In reality, crofting does not provide a viable means of living. Very few crofters rely solely on their smallholding for an income and most need to have several occupations (including running a Bed & Breakfast establishment) to make ends meet. But without the family croft whole communities would just pack up and leave, so crofting functions as a means of preventing the depopulation of remote rural areas.

The crofter's lot may change for the better, however, thanks to the Scottish Parliament's new Land Reform Bill which includes a special right to buy for crofting communities.

Next to the stones is the Calanais Visitor Centre, which features 'The Story of the Stones' exhibition, a restaurant and gift shop. On the other side of the stones is the *Blackhouse tearoom and craft shop*, run by the MacBears and better value if you fancy a bite to eat. ■ *Site open daily all year. Apr-Sep 1000-1900; Oct-Mar 1000-1600. Free. Visitor Centre closed Sun. Exhibition: adult £1.75, concession £1.25, children £0.75. Visitor Centre, T621422, calanais.centre@btinternet.com*

Sleeping & eating If you want to stay near the stones and visit them after dark, there are several inexpensive B&Bs in the village of Calanais, including the friendly **E-F** *Mrs Morrison*, 27 Callanish (200 yd from the site), T621392 (open Mar-Sep). A few miles north, in Tolastadh a' Chaolais (Tolsta Chalois) is the recommended vegetarian B&B **E**, run by *Debbie Nash*, 19 Tolsta Chaolais, T621321. There's also **E** *Aros*, T621266, kateblue@yahoo.com, owned by Kate Kirby.

Aside from the Calanais Visitor Centre or Blackhouse tearoom, places to eat are few and far between, but try *Tigh Mealros*, a few miles south, at Gearraidh na h-Aibhne, T621333. They serve good local grub in a cosy, relaxed atmosphere, with scallops a speciality (closes at 2100).

Transport Local **buses** travel from Stornoway. Contact the tourist office, T703088, in Stornoway, or the bus station, T704327, for details. There are also day trips to Calanais with *Galson Motors*, T840269, leaving from Stornoway bus station and *W. MacDonald*, T706267, leaving from the pier.

The Uig Peninsula

From Gearraidh na h-Aibhne the main A858 runs back to Stornoway, while
the B8011 forks west to the remote Uig peninsula in the southwest of the
island. Four miles down this road is a turning to the right onto the B8059,
which leads to the island of **Bearnaraigh (Great Bernera)**, now connected to
the mainland of Lewis by a single-track road bridge. The main settlement on
the island is **Breacleit (Breaclete)**, where you can find out about the island's
history in the Bernera Museum. ■ *Apr-Sep Mon-Sat 1100-1800*. The rest of
the island is fairly interesting with tiny fishing villages, and one or two brochs
and some standing stones. The nicest part, though, is on the north coast, near
the tiny hamlet of **Bostadh (Bosta)**, where a lovely little sandy bay looks out to
the nearby island of **Bearnaraigh Beag (Little Bernera)**. There are a couple of
good B&Bs on the island which both offer evening meals, one in **Tobson**, on
the west coast (**E**, *Mrs MacDonald*, T612347), and the other in **Circebost
(Kirkibost)**, on the east coast (**E**, *Mrs Macauley*, T612341).

The B8011 continues across bleak moorland, then cuts north to **West
Loch Roag**, which is fringed by some fine sandy beaches and backed by a
much hillier landscape. Just beyond **Miabhag (Miavaig)** is the turn-off
right to **Cliobh (Cliff)**, with its picturesque beach which is unsafe for swimming. A mile further on is the little village of **Cnip (Kneep)**, to the east of
which is the beautiful **Traigh na Berie**, a long sandy beach backed by flat
machair which is ideal for camping.

Phone code: 01851
Colour map 1, grid B2

Gallan Head

Beyond Miabhag, the eerie peninsula of Gallan Head provides a setting befitting of a science fiction drama or Cold War Orwellian novel, with empty,
decaying Ministry of Defence buildings battered by the Atlantic storms.
Wandering around the abandoned site it is easy to form ideas of bizarre,
top-secret government experiments and early-warning missile tracking in
this seemingly edge-of-the-world place far removed from the unwanted pry-
ing eyes of everyday society.

Mangersta

Beyond Ardroil the road continues to **Mangersta** where at Aird Fenish is
some of the most spectacular and photogenic coastal scenery in the Outer
Hebrides. The cliffs plunge dramatically beyond the road to the inaccessible
beach below with a series of crumbling sea stacks battered by the fearsome
waves and seabirds riding the updraughts adding to the sense of natural
beauty, energy and power. Further south at **Brenish**, about a 10-minute walk
from the road, is a menacing blowhole connected to the sea by an underground passage.

Far out into the Atlantic are the haunting **Flannan Islands**, scene of an
unsolved mystery in 1900 following the disappearance of three lighthouse
keepers. Various explanations have been put forward over the years, ranging
from a freak-wave in stormy weather, to a monster sea serpent or even a dispute and fight between the men, but whatever the real reason the legend continues. For possible boat trips to the Flannan Islands contact Island Cruising
in Uig, T01851 672381.

**Timsgearraidh
(Timsgarry)**

At **Timsgearraidh (Timsgarry)** are the **Traigh Chapadail (Uig sands)** at the
village of **Eadar Dha Fhadhail (Adroil)**. This is the loveliest of all the beaches
on Lewis, with miles of sand dunes and machair, but it is famous for an
entirely different reason. It was here in 1831 that a crofter dug up the 'Lewis
Chessmen', 78 pieces carved from walrus ivory and belonging to at least eight

Outer Hebrides

incomplete chess sets from 12th-century Scandinavia. Some are now in the Museum of Scotland in Edinburgh, but most can be found in the British Museum in London.

Sleeping & eating
For details of public transport from Stornoway, see page 567

There are a few places to stay around the Uig bay, the best of which is the beautifully located **D** *Baile Na Cille Guest House*, in Timsgarry, T672242, F672241, RandJGollin @compuserve.com It's open Apr-Sep, offers dinner for residents and non-residents alike, and one of the warmest welcomes in the islands. North of Timsgarry, at Aird Uig, is the *Bonaventure* restaurant and B&B, T672474, which serves lunches and dinners of a French/Scottish style.

North to Nis (Ness)

Colour map 1, grid A3

The A857 leaves Stornoway and runs northwest through barren, treeless and relentlessly bleak moorland to **Barabhas (Barvas)**. The landscape is scarred by deep gashes caused by peat digging, and the unfamiliar smell you detect in your nostrils is peat burning – a strange mixture of burning grass, whisky and coffee. Peat is the main source of domestic fuel used on the islands, and outside most houses you'll see large stacks of peat, or '*cruachs*'.

The road from Barabhas northeast to Nis runs through a series of forlorn-looking, scrawny settlements that all look identical and merge into one. They consist of modern, characterless grey pebble-dash cottages with the ubiquitous piles of peat in the gardens, and the abandoned cars and vans scattered around everywhere only adds to the ugly and depressing scene.

Just beyond Barabhas a sign points left to the **Morvern Art Gallery**, which has a café, making it a welcome refuge in bad weather. A few miles further on is a turning right to **Baile an Trùiseil (Ballantrushel)**, site of the huge **Clach an Trùiseil**, a 20-ft monolith (the largest in Europe), which was the scene of the last major battle on the island, fought between the Morrisons of Nis and the MacAuleys of Uig. This is the first of a number of prehistoric sights between here and **Siadar (Shader)** which may be of interest to the keen archaeologist, but otherwise there's little of note on the road north to Nis as it passes through the typical crofting townships of **Coig Peighinnean Buirgh (Five Penny Borve)**, **Gàbhsann bho Dheas (South Galson)**, **Dail (Dell)**, **Suaineabost (Swainbost)**, **Tàbost (Habost)** and **Lìonal (Lionel)**. In saying that, those interested in buying souvenirs should look in at the *Borgh Pottery*, by the bridge at Coig Peighinnean. Here you'll find a wide range of beautiful and original domestic and decorative ware. ■ *T850345. Mon-Sat 0930-1800.*

The road continues north, passing through a number of straggling villages that collectively make up **Nis (Ness)**, until it ends at the fishing village of **Port Nis (Port of Ness)**. It's a lovely spot, with a picturesque little harbour and golden sweep of beach enclosed by steep cliffs. Each September the locals head out to the island of **Sula Sgeir**, 30 miles to the north, for the annual cull of young gannets (or *gugas*), which are considered something of a delicacy by the people of Lewis. A few minutes to the northwest, the Butt of Lewis lighthouse forms the most northerly tip of the Outer Hebrides.

Just before Port Nis, is **Lìonal**, where the B8015 turns off right and leads to the start of the 10-mile **coastal trail** that works it way round to **Tòlstadh (Tolsta North)** and the beautiful beaches of Traigh Mhor and Garry. Numerous shielings pepper the landscape from an earlier era when local crofters drove their cattle to the summer pastures in the island's interior. The beaches can be reached much more easily by road north from Stornoway. For details of the coastal walk, see the tourist information centre in Stornoway.

Another minor road heads northwest to the tiny hamlet of **Eòropaidh (Eoropie)** (pronounced 'Yor-erpee'). By the road junction that leads to Rubha Robhanais is the ancient **Teampull Mholuaidh (St Moluag's Church)**, thought to date from the 12th century and restored to its present state in 1912. It is now used on certain Sundays by Stornoway's Episcopal Church. From Eòropaidh a narrow road runs to the lighthouse at **Rubha Robhanais (Butt of Lewis)**, which marks the nothernmost tip of the Outer Hebrides. It's a great place for spotting seabirds or whales and dolphins, but also very wild and windy. Half a mile back down the road a path leads down to the tiny beach of **Port Sto**, which is more sheltered.

Sleeping

There are several options should you wish to stay in this part of the island. There's the *Harbour View Gallery & Café*, T810735, which also offers B&B accommodation. At Gàbhsann bho Deas (South Galson), halfway between Barabhas and Port Nis, is the friendly and beautifully restored 18th-century **D** *Galson Farm Guest House*, T850492. Cheaper, more basic accommodation is available in the *Galson Farm Bunkhouse* (same phone number). At Coig Peighinnean Buirgh (Five Penny Borve) there's B&B with **D** *Ms Catriona Macleod*, T810240.

Na Hearadh (Harris)

Harris is not an island, but together with Lewis forms the largest of the Outer Hebrides, with Harris taking up the southern third. The two parts are divided by the long sea lochs of Loch Seaforth in the east and Loch Resort in the west, though this division is rarely shown on maps. Though joined, the two are very different in terms of geography. Harris is largely mountain and rock whereas Lewis is flat moorland.

Harris itself is almost split in two by the sea at An Tairbeart (Tarbert), the largest town and ferry terminal. To the north are the highest peaks in the Outer Hebrides, surrounded by some of the finest unspoilt wilderness in the whole country, while to the south are miles of wonderful sandy beaches and, on the east coast, an almost indescribably strange lunar landscape straight out of a science fiction film.

With your own transport you could 'do' Harris in a day quite comfortably, but if the weather's good enough you'll want to spend more time and appreciate its precious natural beauty. There's a regular bus service between Tarbert and Stornoway, and a less frequent one that travels right around South Harris (see Tarbert transport, on page 575).

Phone code: 01859
Colour map 1, grid B2

History

The separation of Harris and Lewis dates back to Norse times, when the island was divided between the two sons of Leod, progenitor of the Macleods. Harris remained in Macleod hands until 1834. The recent history of Harris is closely bound up with that of Lewis. Both were bought by the soap magnate, Lord Leverhulme (see page 564), whose grandiose schemes for Lewis came to nothing. Leverhulme then turned his attentions to Harris, where the peaceful little village of An t-Ob (Obbe) was renamed Leverburgh and transformed into a bustling port with all manner of public works programmes under development. His death in 1925 brought an end to all his plans for Harris, and instead of becoming a town with a projected population of 10,000, Leverburgh reverted to being a sleepy village, with only the harbour, the roads and the change of name to show for it all.

Since the Leverhulme era there has been no main source of employment for the population of 2,400 on Harris, though a successful fishing industry continues on Scalpaigh (Scalpay). There is still some crofting supplemented by the Harris Tweed industry, though most production is now in Lewis, and whatever employment can be found: road-works, crafts and tourism. The most recent project proposed for Harris, to create one of Europe's largest superquarries, is highly controversial and would involve destroying an area of outstanding natural beauty for the sake of perhaps only a few dozen jobs (see page 579), with potentially disastrous consequences for the island's fragile tourist economy.

An Tairbeart (Tarbert)

Phone code: 01859
Colour map 1, grid B2
Population: 500

Tarbert, the largest settlement on Harris, lies in a sheltered bay on the narrow isthmus that joins North and South Harris. It's a tiny place and there's not much to do, but as it's the main ferry port for Harris it has more facilities than anywhere else, such as shops, a bank, post office and tourist information centre. Tarbert's relatively wide range of accommodation and location makes it the ideal base from which to explore the delights on offer.

The **tourist information centre** is close to the ferry terminal. It can arrange accommodation and is a good source of information on local walks. ■ *T502011. Apr-Oct Mon-Sat 0900-1700. It also opens in the winter (check times) and when the ferry arrives.*

Sleeping **C** *Harris Hotel*, on the main road from Stornoway on the left before the turning for the ferry, T502154, F502281. An old established favourite, but more importantly the only place serving food on a Sun (see below). The bar next door also serves meals and is the social hub of the village. During the BBC television series *Castaway*, the hotel became a popular retreat for homesick 'castaways' craving the creature comforts of civilization. **C** *Leachin House*, 1 mile out of Tarbert on the Stornoway road, T/F502157. **B** including dinner. Luxurious Victorian home with great views and superb home cooking (for residents only). Only 2 rooms so book ahead. **D** *Allan Cottage Guest House*, on the left after the turning into the village, T502146. Open Apr-Sep. Close to the ferry, very comfortable rooms and exceptional food. **B** including dinner. Book ahead. **E** *Macleod Motel*, right beside the ferry pier, T502364. Very handy for the early-morning ferry, also has room-only rate.

There are also several B&Bs within 5 mins' walk of the ferry pier, including the very friendly and welcoming **E-F** *Mrs Flora Morrison*, Tigh na Mara, T502270. Others to try are: **E**, *Mrs Morrison*, T502334; **E** *Mrs Mackinnon*, T502095; and **E**, *Mrs Miller*, T502140. A cheaper option is the new **F** *Rockview Bunkhouse*, on the main street, T/F5022211/502626. Open all year.

Eating Options on places to eat are limited. Most guesthouses and B&Bs will provide dinner on request, but check in advance if they do so on a Sun. Aside from those guesthouses mentioned above, probably the best food in the village is the *Firstfruits Tearoom*, T502349, a cosy joint down by the ferry pier. Open Apr, May and Sep Mon-Sat 1030-1630 and till 1830 in Jun, Jul and Aug. Otherwise it's the *Harris Hotel* (see above) which serves food every day till around 2030. They do a 3-course fixed menu (mid-range) or basic and cheap bar meals, as does the bar next door Mon-Sat. The only other option is the chippy next door to the *Rockview Bunkhouse*, where you can get a decent carry out for £2-3. It's open for lunch and in the evening.

Ferry details are given in the Ins and outs section on page 560. There's a **bus** service 4-5 times per day from **Stornoway** to Tarbert (1 hr 15 mins), which continues to **Leverburgh** (for the ferry to North Uist) via the west coast of South Harris. There's also a service 3-4 times per day from Tarbert to Leverburgh via the east coast (45 mins), along the so-called 'Golden Road'. There are also services to **Huisinis** (2-4 per day on school-days, 45 mins), to **Reinigeadal** (2 per day on schooldays) and to **Scalpaigh** (2-5 per day, 10 mins). Bus timetables are available at the tourist office (see above). **Transport**

Ceann a Tuath na Hearadh (North Harris)

North Harris is the most mountainous part of the Outer Hebrides and its wild, rugged peaks are ideal for hill walking. The A859 south from Lewis gets progressively more scenic as it skirts **Loch Siophort (Seaforth)** and the mountains rise before you like a giant barrier. The road then climbs past **Bogha Glas (Bowglass)** and **Aird a Mhulaidh (Ardvourlie)** with **Clisham** (2,619 ft), the highest peak in the Outer Hebrides, and **Sgaoth Aird** (1,829 ft) towering overhead on either side. Just off the A859 near Ardvourlie is **B** *Ardvourlie Castle Guest House*, T502307, F502348. 4 rooms. Open April-October. This lovingly restored Victorian hunting lodge on the shores of Loch Seaforth just oozes charm and elegance and can't be recommended highly enough. As if that weren't enough, they also happen to serve excellent food. There can be no better end to a day spent walking in the surrounding mountains. *Phone code: 01859 Colour map 1, grid B2*

If you can't afford such luxury but still crave the isolation, then carry on south until you reach the turn-off to **Reinigeadal (Rhenigidale)**, which was the most remote community on Harris and accessible only by sea or by a rough hill track until the access road was built. Here you'll find a Gatliff Trust **youth hostel**, a converted croft house (no phone) which sleeps 11 and is open all year (for details on how to get there on foot, see below). From Reinigeadal an ascent of shapely **Toddun** (528m) provides exhilarating exercise rewarded with fine views east across the Minch to the mainland and in the other direction to the mountain wilderness of North Harris. **Reinigeadal (Rhenigidale)**

The A859 continues west across the crest of the craggy hills then drops down to the turn-off for the single-track B887 which winds its way all the way out to Huisinis (Hushinish) between the impressive mountains of the Forest of Harris on one side and the northern shore of West Loch Tarbert on the other, with views across to the Sound of Taransay and the beaches of South Harris. **Bun Abhainn Eadarra (Bunavoneader) to Huisinis (Hushinish)**

Immediately beyond the turn-off you pass through **Bun Abhainn Eadarra (Bunavoneadar)**, which was a thriving whaling station until 1930 and one of Lord Leverhulme's many schemes for the island. The old whaling station is worth a visit even though the site has not been developed as a tourist attraction.

Just before the village of **Miabhag (Meavaig)** a defined footpath heads north into the hills up Glen Meavaig to Loch Voshimid. Further on, though, is a better opportunity for walking. Just before the gates of **Amhuinnsuidhe Castle** (pronounced 'Avan-soo-ee') is a signpost for Chliostair Power Station. From here you can walk two miles up to the dam, then follow the right-hand track round the reservoir and the left-hand track round the upper loch, before you arrive in a wild and remote glen.

Just beyond the castle gates you'll see a beautiful waterfall spilling straight into the sea. The road then runs right past the front door of the castle, built in 1868 by the Earl of Dunmore, and still a private residence, before passing

Outer Hebrides

through an archway and continuing to the tiny crofting township of **Huisinis** (**Hushinish**), beautifully situated in a sandy bay. This is where the road ends; next stop the USA! Follow the track to the right across the machair where a footpath above the jetty and rocky beach can be followed to the old fishing lodge at **Cravadale** and Loch Cravadale beyond. Make a detour to the golden sands and turquoise waters of **Traigh Mheilein** overlooking Scarp. From the coast strong walkers can follow Glen Cravadale inland eventually rejoining the main road near Amhuinnsuidhe Castle.

The rocky island of **Scarp** supported a population of more than 100 as late as the 1940s but was abandoned in 1971, and now the crofters' cottages are used as holiday homes. The island was the scene of a bizarre experiment in 1934, when a German rocket scientist, Gerhard Zucher, tried to prove that rockets could be used to transport mail and medical supplies to remote communities. His theory went up in smoke, however, when the rocket exploded before it even got off the ground, with 30,000 letters on board.

Tarbert to Carnach An interesting little excursion from Tarbert is the 10-mile return route that runs east through the tiny villages of **Urgha** and **Caolas Scalpaigh** to **Carnach** at the end of the road. Just beyond Urgha, on the north side of the road, is a path which leads across the hills to the **Reinigeadal**. It was originally used by the community in Reinigeadal, and the children would make the daily journey across the hills to Tarbert before the village was connected to the A859 by the new road. The wonderfully engineered zigzag path passes through enchanting scenery above **Loch Trollamarig** in a setting more reminiscent of Scandinavia's Fjordland. A visit can easily be made to the deserted village of **Molinginish** nestled snugly in a small valley above the loch.

Scalpaigh (Scalpay) The island of **Scalpaigh** (**Scalpay**), now connected to Harris by a road bridge opened by Prime Minister Tony Blair in 1998, is a thriving fishing community with a population of over 400. It's a pleasant three-mile walk across the island to Eilean Glas Lighthouse, built by the Stevensons and the first ever on the Outer Hebrides. Those who wish to stay on Scalpay can do so at **E** *Hirta House*, T540394, **F** *New Haven*, T540325, or **F** *Seafield*, T540250. If you'd like to do some diving, contact *Scalpay Diving Services*, T540328.

Ceann a Deas na Hearadh (South Harris)

An absolute must while you're in the Outer Hebrides is the 45-mile circular route around South Harris. If you only do one thing while you're here, then make sure this is it, for the change in scenery from the west coast to the east is utterly fascinating. One thing you're sure to puzzle over as you travel round is the fact that most people live on the harsh and inhospitable east coast, known as **Na Baigh** (**Bays**), while the beautiful west coast with its miles of glorious golden sands is scarcely populated. This is not through choice. The fertile west coast housed most of the population until the end of the 18th century when they were cleared to make way for sheep farms. Some emigrated to Cape Breton, while others chose instead to stay in Harris and moved to the east side.

The west coast The main road from Tarbert runs south, skirting East Loch Tarbert, then cuts inland and heads west through a dramatic lunar landscape of rocks dotted

Harris Tweed

Few visitors to Harris will not have heard of its most famous export, Harris Tweed. But how did it emerge from its humble origins to become a product synonymous with high-quality craftsmanship and a de rigeur item of clothing for any self-respecting aristocrat?

Traditionally the tweed was made by fishermen's wives to clothe their own families using wool from their own sheep. They carried out the whole process themselves by hand. First the wool was washed, then dyed using native plants and bushes, tree bark and lichen, then carded, spun, warped, woven and finally waulked, or made soft, by beating it on a table. Many women could produce more than they needed and the surplus was available for sale or barter. The cloth was made throughout the Outer Hebrides and originally was not known as Harris Tweed, but simply as clo mòr (or big cloth).

All that changed in 1842 when the Countess of Dunmore, who owned a large part of Harris, took great interest and introduced many of her aristocratic friends to Harris Tweed. Very soon, much of the surplus tweed was being sold and becoming quite a fashion statement in high places. By the beginning of the 20th century demand was exceeding supply, stimulated by Royal patronage, and faster and more efficient ways of carrying out the ancillary processes were being developed by some of the larger producers. This led, in 1909, to the setting up of the Harris Tweed Association Ltd, to ensure quality control and to protect the interests of the independent crofter/weavers. So Harris Tweed came officially into being, with its famous Orb trademark, originating from the Coat of Arms of the Countess of Dunmore.

To earn this official stamp of authenticity Harris Tweed must be made from pure Scottish wool, dyed, spun and finished in the Outer Hebrides, and hand woven by the islanders in their own homes. There are now about 750 independent weavers and about 400 millworkers employed in the islands, and each weaver can produce three webs of tweed a week (a web measures 80-90 yds in length). In total the industry produces around 5,000,000 yds of tweed annually, depending on demand. The main production centre is now Lewis, but all over the island you can see the woven tweed lying at the gates of crofts waiting to be collected and sent all over the world.

---

with tiny lochans. It then begins to descend towards the sea and you can see the vast expanse of **Losgaintir (Luskentyre)** beach directly ahead. A single-track road turns off to the right and runs out to the tiny settlement of Losgaintir. The road cuts through the rich machair as it follows the magnificent stretch of bleached white sand that fills the entire bay, washed by turquoise sea and backed by steep dunes. All this set against the backdrop of the mountains to the north. Paradise!

A short distance offshore is the island of **Tarasaigh (Taransay)**, which was well populated at the beginning of the 1900s but was recently abandoned. The island has now gained national prominence as the setting for the popular BBC television series *Castaway* where an assortment of supposedly normal people from a variety of backgrounds were challenged to pit their wits against the elements and themselves for a period of a full year in 2000. Some participants were more committed than others, and rumour has it that the bar in the *Harris Hotel* in Tarbert had never seen such good business.

Sleeping You can **camp** on the machair, but ask for permission at the first house. There are a couple of B&Bs: **E-F** *Moravia*, T550262, open Mar-Oct; and **E-F** *Seaview*, T550263, open Apr-Oct.

The road follows the coast, passing through the tiny settlements of **Seilebost**, **Horgabost** and **Burgh (Borve)**. There's B&B accommodation at Seilebost and Horgabost, but a few miles further on is another beautiful stretch of white sands at **Sgarasta Bheag (Scaristabeg)**.

Sleeping Overlooking the beach in a wonderful setting is **B** *Scarista House*, T550238, F550277, tnpmartin@ukgateway.net 5 rooms, open May-Sep. To add to the peace and quiet, there's no TV, only an extensive library and drawing room with open fires. The food on offer is amongst the best on the islands, particularly the seafood. Even if you're not staying, you should treat yourself to dinner here. Expensive but well worth it. There are also self-catering cottages in the grounds. The golf course over the road is so scenic the views may put you off your swing.

Toe Head Beyond Sgarasta Bheag, the village of **Taobh Tuath** (Northton) provides access to the scenic promontory of **Toe Head**, almost cut off from the rest of Harris by the huge expanse of the golden sands of Sgarasta. At the MacGillivary Machair Centre you can learn about the ecology of the local machair which forms such a distinctive and attractive element of the landscape of the west coast of the Hebrides. A ruined chapel of 16th-century origin is situated on the machair below **Chaipaval** (365m), whose heathery slopes can be climbed for one of the best views out to sea towards St Kilda some 40 miles distant.

Ant-Ob
(Leverburgh)
For buses to Leverburgh see under Tarbert
The road then runs along the south shore till it reaches the sprawling village of **An t-Ob (Leverburgh)**, site of Lord Leverhulme's ambitious plan to turn a sleepy crofting township into a major fishing port (see page 573). A few of the original buildings can be seen near the pier, which is the departure point for *CalMac's* **car ferry** to Otternish on North Uist (for details, see Ins and outs, page 560).

Sleeping and eating The present village consists of little more than a row of incongruous Scandinavian-style wooden houses, but there are several B&Bs within a couple of miles of the ferry port. One of the best is **E-F** *Caberfeidh House*, T520276, which is close to the ferry and also offers room only (**F**). More secluded is **E** *Shieldaig House*, T520378, kwhettall@aol.com, with free cycle hire. Also **E** *Mrs Paula Williams*, T520319, F520146, who caters for vegetarians; and **E** *Mrs Catherine Mackenzie*, T520246, situated on Ferry Rd, a few mins from the ferry terminal. A cheaper option is **F** *Am Bothan Bunkhouse*, T520251, which is close to the ferry, has full facilities, space for tents and is open all year. The *An Clachan* café/restaurant, T520370, and shop is not far from the bunkhouse.

Ròghadal
(Rodel)
Three miles east of Leverburgh, at the southeastern tip of Harris, is Ròghadal (Rodel), dominated by the beautiful 12th-century **St Clement's Church**, something of an unusual sight in such a remote spot and one of the most impressive religious building in the Hebrides (only the Benedictine abbey on Iona is larger). The church stands on a site which goes back 1,500 years and was built by Alastair Crotach (Hunchback) Macleod of Harris in the 1520s. Though impressive from the outside, particularly the huge tower, the real interest lies inside, with a collection of remarkable carved wall tombs. There are three tombs, the most notable of which is that of the founder, Alastair Crotach. The one in the south wall of the choir is also worth a close look.

The Forest Of Harris

The Forest of Harris is a vast tract of mountain wilderness extending north from West Loch Tarbert to Loch Resort that forms the de facto boundary with Lewis. Known as the North Harris Estate, and owned and managed by the family of the Bulmer cider empire, it is one of the most isolated and unspoilt upland landscapes in Scotland and, because of its remoteness, receives very few visitors. For experienced hillwalkers, however, it is a paradise offering rugged mountains, dramatic escarpments, airy ridges and desolate glens. There are endless walking possibilities including a horseshoe walk around Clisham and a long walk through Glen Ulladale to Kinlochresort, a former crofting community now abandoned, but once described as the remotest habitation in Britain. Apart from hillwalking the only other human activities now occurring in this wilderness are fishing and sheep and deer farming. As much of the area is in private ownership it is advisable to seek permission for access from Amhuinnsuidhe Castle (T01859-560262), or get further advice from the TIC in Tarbert (T01859-502011).

Running north from Ròghadal up the east coast of South Harris is the **Golden Road**, so named by the locals because the of the huge expense of building it. This twisting, tortuous single-track road runs through a bizarre and striking moonscape, and driving through it is a unique experience (but keep your eyes on the road or you'll end up in one of the many narrow sea lochs). It seems inconceivable that anyone could survive in such an environment, but the road passes through a string of townships created in the 19th century by the people evicted from the west coast (see page 576). People here have spent years eking a meagre living from the thin soil by building 'lazy beds' (thin strips of piled-up earth between the rocks) for planting potatoes. Weaving and fishing also provide much-needed income.

Na Baigh (Bays)

At **Lingreabhagh (Lingarabay)** the road skirts the foot of **Roinebhal**, the proposed site of one of the largest superquarries in Europe, which would demolish virtually the entire mountain over many decades. Local people and environmentalists are up in arms at the prospect of losing precious fishing grounds, not to mention a unique and precious natural asset.

The road passes through a succession of tiny settlements before joining the A859 just south of Tarbert.

Sleeping Accommodation on this coast is limited. There's also the independent *Drinishader Bunkhouse*, at Drinisiader (Drinishader), 3 miles south of Tarbert, T511255, open all year. Or there's **B&B** at **E-F** *Hillhead*, T511226, at Scadabhagh (Scadabay), between Stocinis and Drinisiadar.

Uibhist a Tuath (North Uist)

North Uist is the largest of the southern chain of the Outer Hebrides, about 13 miles from north to south and 18 miles east to west at its widest point. At first sight it comes as something of a disappointment after the dramatic landscapes of Harris. In fact, it's barely a landscape at all, as over a third of the island's surface is covered by water. The east coast around Lochmaddy, the main settlement, is so peppered with lochs it resembles a giant sieve. But heading west from Lochmaddy the island's attractions become apparent, particularly the magnificent beaches on the north and west coast. Also on the west coast, the Balranald Nature Reserve is

Phone code: 01876
Colour map 1, grid C1
Population: 1,815

Outer Hebrides

the ideal place for bird watching. You're also likely to see otters. There are numerous prehistoric sites scattered across the island, and with all that water around there's obviously plenty of good fishing to be had.

Ins and outs

Getting there There are 3 **car ferry** services to North Uist. One is to Otternish from Leverburgh on South Harris, the others are to Lochmaddy, from Uig on Skye, and from Tarbert on Harris. For more details, see page 560. North Uist is joined to the islands of Benbecula and South Uist to the south by causeway and bridge. There are several **buses** daily (Mon-Sat) from Otternish to Lochmaddy and on to Lochboisdale on South Uist.

Getting around There are 4-6 **buses** per day (not Sun) from Otternish to Lochmaddy. These buses continue to Baile a Mhanaich (Balivanich) on Benbecula, where there is an airport (see page 583), and Lochboisdale and Ludag on South Uist (see page 584). There are 4-7 buses per day from Lochmaddy to Otternish. These continue via the new causeway to the island of Bearnaraigh (Berneray) just off the north coast in the sound of Harris. There are 3 buses per day from Lochmaddy to Clachan na Luib (Clachan-a-Luib) which run in an anti-clockwise direction around the north and west coasts. Two buses per day connect Clachan-a-Luib with Baile Sear (Baleshare) and also with Saighdinis (Sidinish). There are also Royal Mail post buses linking the main settlements. Local bus timetables are available at the tourist office in Lochmaddy (see below).

Loch nam Madadh (Lochmaddy)

Colour map 1, grid C1 Lochmaddy, the island's main village and ferry port, is a tiny place, so small you're almost through it before you realize. Though it's on the east coast and not close to the beaches, it is the best base for exploring the island as it boasts most facilities. It has a bank (next to the tourist office), a hotel and pub, a tourist office, a few shops, post office, hospital (T500325) and petrol station. If you have time the **Taigh Chearsabhagh Museum and Arts Centre** (T/F500293, www.taigh- chearsabhagh.com) is worth visiting and has a café.

The **tourist information centre** is near the ferry pier. *T500321. Mid-Apr to mid-Oct Mon-Sat 0900-1700, and for the arrival of the evening ferry. They'll provide transport timetables.*

Sleeping & eating **C** *Lochmaddy Hotel*, T500332, F500210. Right by the ferry terminal. Open all year. Their restaurant serves great seafood, and the lively bar serves snacks. This is also the place to ask about fishing, as they rent out boats and sells permits for trout and salmon fishing. There are a couple of good B&Bs: **D-E** *The Old Courthouse*, T500358; and **E** *The Old Bank House*, T500275/324, both of which are open all year. Half a mile from the ferry pier is an independent hostel, the *Lochmaddy Uist Outdoor Centre*, T500480. It is open all year and offers a wide range of outdoor activities including kayaking, windsurfing and rock climbing. *The Stag Lodge* restaurant, T500364, F500417, also does B&B (**D-E**).

Around the island There are a number of interesting archaeological sites of different periods dotted around the island. The most notable is **Barpa Langass**, seven miles southwest of Lochmaddy on the slope of Ben Langass, just off the A867 which cuts across the bleak peaty hinterland of North Uist. This is a huge chambered burial cairn dating from around 3,000 BC. Unfortunately, it is now too dangerous to enter. About a mile away, on the southern side of Ben Langass, is the small stone circle known as **Pobull Fhinn**, standing on the edge of Loch Langass. Nearby is **B** *Langass Lodge* (T580285, F580385, langars@ btinternet.com), whose restaurant specializes in local seafood and game. Three miles northwest of Lochmaddy on the A865 are three Bronze Age standing stones called **Na Fir Bhreige** (The False Men), said to be the graves of three spies who were buried alive.

Bearnaraigh (Berneray)

The low-lying island of Bearnaraigh, now connected by a new causeway, is famous as the place where Prince Charles spent a holiday helping out on a croft. It's also the birthplace of the giant Angus MacAskill (see page 545). Its real attraction, though, apart from the splendid isolation, is the three-mile-long sandy beach along its north and west coast.

Phone code: 01876
Colour map 1, grid B1

A *Western Isles Walks* booklet for Bearnaraigh, available from Lochmaddy TIC, describes an enjoyable eight-mile walk around the island visiting all the main places of interest including the 16th-century gunnery at **Baile**, the beaches and machair of the north and west coast, and archaeological sites dating from the Viking period near **Borgh**.

There are a couple of options for those wishing to stay. You can share the prince's crofting experience with Donald (Splash) MacKillop at **E** *Burnside Croft*, T540235, splashmackilloop@burnsidecroft.fsnet.co.uk who also offers cycle hire and stories round the fire for evening entertainment. There's also a *Gatliff Trust Hostel* (12 beds, no phone, open all year) in two restored blackhouses overlooking a lovely sandy beach and old Viking pier about a mile up the east coast from the old ferry pier.

Sleeping

Around the island

The real charms of North Uist are its fabulous beaches on the north and west coasts. Heading anti-clockwise from Lochmaddy, the A865 runs northwest, passing the turning for Otternish and **Bearnaraigh** (see above), which is now connected to North Uist by a causeway. It continues west through the township of **Sollas (Solas)**, where there are a couple of B&Bs, and then past the beautiful sands of **Bhalaigh (Vallay) Strand**. Near the northwestern tip of the island is **Scolpaig Tower**, standing on an islet in Loch Scolpaig, a 'folly' built for famine relief in the 19th century.

Three miles south of here is the turning to Balranald RSPB Reserve, an area of rocky coast, sandy beaches and dunes, machair and lochs. The reserve is ideal for bird watching, especially waders. A two-hour guided walk along the headland allows you to see Manx shearwaters, gannets, skuas and storm petrels, and during the summer you can listen out for the distinctive rasping call of the corncrake, one of the rarest birds in Britain. There's a basic visitor centre, which is open April-September.

Balranald
RSPB Reserve

Sleeping There are a couple of places to stay near Balranald: in **Hogha Gearraidh (Houghgarry)**, overlooking the beautiful beach, is **E** *Mrs Kathy Simpson*, T510312; and in **Ceann a Bhaigh (Bayhead)**, a few miles to the south, is **E-F** *Mrs Morag Nicholson*, T510395.

Also in Ceann a Bhaigh is the **Uist Animal Visitors Centre**, where you can see Highland cattle and other rare native breeds, as well as more exotic species such as llamas. ■ *Mon-Sat 1000-2200. Adult £2.*

Outer Hebrides

Rock 'n' roll suicide

Like Newbury Bypass in England, the proposed Lingarabay superquarry represents a cause célèbre in the classic debate between the clashing interests of environment and development. Redland Aggregates originally proposed to develop the east face of Roineabhal (460 m) as a huge quarry providing a vast source of aggregate material for the construction industry in an economically impoverished part of Scotland perceived to be far removed from the mass tourism market. However, the proposal provoked a local, national and international outcry as environmental groups objected to the likely visual, landscape and ecological impacts in a unique and essentially unspoilt mountain environment designated a National Scenic Area and representative of some of the oldest rock in the world. A Public Enquiry followed in 1994-95 at which Redland presented the case for long-term local employment and the preference of one large quarry in a remote area rather than many smaller

projects on the highly populated mainland. Objectors set out the concerns for the damage to a resource of national importance and the precedent it would set for environmental protection both within and outwith the industry in the future if planning legislation were to be overcome. Following a lengthy follow up the Secretary of State rejected the proposal in 2000. Redland Aggregates who have now been taken over by French company, Lafarge, are now appealing against the decision. In the latest twist in the saga Scottish Natural Heritage and other action groups are now believed to be lobbying the UK government and European Parliament to reinforce the environmental value of the site by designation as a Special Area for Conservation under the EC Habitats Directive, thereby making it illegal to develop the site for industrial purposes. In a case where each side attempts to out-manoeuvre the other the outcome is still far from clear and the saga continues.

Clachan na Luib The road continues south to Clachan na Luib, at the crossroads of the A865 and A867 which heads east back to Lochmaddy. There's a post office and general store, and a few miles south, at **Cladach a Bhaile Shear (Claddach-baleshare)** is **F** *Taigh Mo Sheannair*, T580246, a renovated crofthouse on a working farm which offers good hostel accommodation all year round, rents out bicycles and has space for camping

Offshore is the tidal island of **Baile Sear (Baleshare)**, now connected by a causeway to North Uist, with its three-mile long beach on the west coast. A further five miles west are the **Monach Isles** (also known by their old Norse name of Heisker), which were once connected to North Uist at low tide, until the 16th century when a huge tidal wave swept away the sand bridge, thus isolating them. Even so, the islands were still populated until as recently as the 1930s. Now they are populated by the largest breeding colony of grey seals in Europe.

South of Clachan na Luib South of Clachan, the road runs past **Cairinis (Carinish)** over a series of causeways to the little-visited lobster-fishing island of **Griomasaigh (Grimsay)**, before heading across another causeway to Benbecula. There's accommodation at **C** *Temple View Hotel*, T580676; and B&B at **E** *Bonnieview*, T580211,

Near Cairinis is *Feith na Fala*, or Field of Blood, site of the last battle fought in Scotland solely with swords and bows and arrows, in 1601, between the MacDonalds of Sleat and Macleods of Harris. The bloodshed was provoked by one of the MacDonalds divorcing his Macleod wife. When 60 Skye

Macleods set off to North Uist to wreak revenge, they were met by 16 MacDonalds who literally chopped them to pieces, proving that divorce was a messy affair even then.

Beinn na Faoghla (Benbecula)

Tiny Benbecula may be suffering from delusions of stature. Its Gaelic name means 'mountain of the fords', but the highest point is a mere 407 ft, with the rest of the island as flat as a pancake. It lies between Protestant North Uist and Catholic South Uist, and most visitors use it solely as a means of getting from one to the other via the A865 which cuts straight through the middle.

Phone code: 01870
Colour map 1, grid C1
Population: 1,803

Benbecula's **airport** is at Balivanich (see below) and there are direct flights to Glasgow, Barra and Stornoway (see page 560). The island is connected by causeways to both North and South Uist, and **buses** travelling to and from Lochmaddy and Lochboisdale pass through the villages of Balivanich, Lionacleit (Liniclate) and Creag Ghoraidh (Creagorry). There are also regular island buses which run between these settlements.

Getting there & around

Like North Uist, the east of the island is so pitted with lochs that most people live on the west coast. A large percentage of the population are Royal Artillery personnel and their families stationed at **Baile a Mhanaich (Balivanich)**, a sprawling army base of utilitarian buildings in the northwest of the island. The influx of so many English-speakers has had a less than positive impact on Gaelic culture, and the military facilities have blighted much of the island's natural beauty, but Benbecula has benefited economically from the army's presence. Not only is there an airport here, but also a relatively large number of shops and amenities, including the only NAAFI supermarket in the UK that's open to the public, a Bank of Scotland (with ATM) and post office. There are worries, however, that the base may be run down or closed, which would have a devastating effect on the local economy.

Baile a Mhanaich (Balivanich)

South of Balivanich the B892 runs around the west coast before joining the main A865 at the southern end of the island. It runs past **Culla Bay**, overlooked by **Baille nan Cailleach (Nunton)**. It was from here in 1746 that Bonnie Prince Charlie set off with Flora MacDonald over the sea to Skye, disguised as her maid (see also page 543). To the south is **Poll-na-Crann**, better known as 'stinky bay' because of the piles of seaweed deposited there by fierce Atlantic storms. From the mid-18th century this kelp was used extensively in making glass, and provided a source of income for many communities. By 1820 the so-called kelp boom was over, though it is still gathered today and used for fertilizer.

The B892 ends at **Lionacleit (Liniclate)**, where the new community school serves the Uists and Benbecula. It has extensive facilities, including internet, a swimming pool, library, theatre and even a small local history **museum**. ■ *Mon, Tue and Thu 0900-1600, Wed 0900-1230 and 1330-1600, Fri 0900-2000, Sat 1100-1300 and 1400-1600. Free.*

South to Lionacleit (Liniclate)

Most accommodation is in **Lionacleit**, including the functional **A** *Dark Island Hotel*, T603030, F602347, which is a lot nicer inside than its name may suggest, and has a good restaurant. There's also **D** *Inchyra Guest House*, T602176 as well as a couple of **B&Bs** (both **E**) and the *Shellbay Caravan and Camping Park*, T602447; open Apr-Oct. In **Balivanich** is a new hostel, **F** *Tigh-na-Cille Bunkhouse*, T602522, which is open all year and sleeps 10 in 2 dorms and 2 twin rooms.

Sleeping & eating

Outer Hebrides

Out to lunch

Travelling in the Outer Hebrides can be a very different experience from visiting other parts of Scotland. The pace of life is very different here and the needs of tourists have to come second to the ways of local *people. Take the example of a passenger flight from Glasgow to Benbecula, which was delayed for 30 minutes when the plane had to circle because the air traffic controller was out to lunch!*

By far the best place to eat on the island is the **Stepping Stone Restaurant** in Balivanich, T603377, F603121, which offers good wholesome Scottish food every day from 1000 till 2100. Snacks, sandwiches, takeaways and home baking are all available, as well as 3- or 5-course meals (mid-range to expensive).

Directory **Car hire** *Maclennan Self Drive*, Balivanich (T602191, F603191); *Ask Car Hire*, Lionacleit (T602818, F602933).

Uibhist a Deas (South Uist)

Phone code: 01870
Colour map 3,
grid A1
Population: 2,285

South Uist is the largest of the southern chain of Outer Hebridean islands and the most scenically attractive. Like its southern neighbour, Barra, South Uist is Roman Catholic and generally more relaxed about Sunday openings.

Its 20 miles of west coast is one long sandy beach, backed by dunes with a mile or two of beautiful, flowering machair behind. To the east of the main A865 that runs the length of the island rises a central mountainous spine of rock and peat dotted with numerous lochs. Its two highest peaks, Beinn Mhor (2,034 ft) and Hecla (1,988 ft), tower over the rocky cliffs of an inaccessible eastern coastline indented by sea lochs.

Ins and outs

Getting there
The ferry to Eriskay was replaced by a causeway in Aug 2001

The island's main **ferry port** is Loch Baghasdail (Lochboisdale), which is reached from Oban and Mallaig via Castlebay on Barra (it arrives late at night). There are also inter-island ferries from Ludag, at the southern tip of South Uist: a private **passenger-only** ferry sails to Barra. There are passenger ferry sailings on Sun to and from Barra and a car ferry to Castlebay and Oban, but no ferry arrival from Oban, Mallaig or Castlebay and no bus services. For more details, see page 560.

Getting around

A causeway connects South Uist to Benbecula by road and regular **buses** (4-6 per day Mon-Sat) run between Lochboisdale and Lochmaddy on North Uist, stopping en route at Dalabrog (Daliburgh), Tobha Mòr (Howmore) and Lionacleit and Balinavich on Benbecula. There is also a regular bus service between Lochboisdale and Ludag (for ferries to Barra). For **car hire**, there's *Laing Motors* in Lochboisdale (T700267), and you can **rent bikes** at *Rothan Cycles* (T01870-620283).

History

The dominant family in South Uist was Clanranald, who also owned Benbecula. They were descendants of the first Lord of the Isles, who was a MacDonald. The island's connections with Clanranald came to a sorry end, however, in 1837 when it was sold, along with Benbecula, to pay off bad debts, and became the property of the infamous Lieutenant-Colonel John Gordon

Machair

Machair is the name given to the strips of land that lie behind the many wonderful beaches of northwest Scotland and the islands. Machair is notable for its fertility, in sharp contrast to the poor, acid peat of the interior. In summer these strips are transformed into a blaze of colour when a *multitude of wild flowers bloom – primroses, buttercups, orchids, gentian and wild iris – and this provides good grazing for sheep. The fertility of the machair comes from the calcium-rich shell sand which is blown inshore from the beaches and neutralises the acidity of the peaty soil.*

Cluny. Though all the southern isles suffered during the brutal clearances of the 19th century, the experiences of people on South Uist were particularly cruel and inhumane. Between 1849 and 1851 over 2,000 were forcibly shipped to Quebec in Canada. Those who refused to board the transport ships were hunted down by dogs and bound, before being thrown on board and shipped to Canada, where they were left to starve.

Around the island

At the north of the island a causeway leads across **Loch Bi** (pronounced 'Bee') to the distinctive modern statue of Our Lady of the Isles, standing by the main road on the lower slopes of **Rueval** hill. Further up the hill is the Royal Artillery control centre, known by the locals as 'Space City', due to its forest of aerials and 'golf balls', which tracks the missiles fired from a range on the northwestern corner of the island out into the Atlantic. Near here, at **Loch a' Chairnain (Lochcarnan)**, is the small, modern **D** *Orosay Inn* (T01870-610298, F610390, orosayinn@btinternet.com), which is open all year and offers fine Scottish cooking (cheap to mid-range).

Just to the south of here is **Loch Druidibeag Nature Reserve**, on the site of the large freshwater loch, one of the largest breeding grounds in the British Isles for greylag geese and also a favourite haunt for mute swans (there's a warden nearby at Groigearraidh (Grogarry) Lodge). From here the main road runs down the spine of the island, and all along the way little tracks branch off to the west, leading down to lovely beaches. Not far south of Loch Druidibeag is the turning to the tiny village of **Tobha Mòr (Howmore)**, where you can see a collection of old traditional thatched 'blackhouses' beside the seemingly endless stretch of golden sand. One of the houses has been converted into a *Gatliff Trust Youth Hostel* (13 beds, open all year, no phone) which overlooks the ruins of an ancient church and graveyard. The warden lives at Ben More House, at the junction with the main road. From the hostel it's a five-minute walk across the machair to the sandy beach which stretches almost the entire length of South Uist.

From Tobha Mòr, there are superb walks through the lonely hills of **Beinn Mhor** (620 m), **Beinn Corodale** (527 m) and **Hecla** (606 m) to the picturesque and dramatic valleys of Glen Hellisdale, Glen Corodale and Glen Usinish on the east coast. In 1746 Bonnie Prince Charlie is reputed to have taken refuge in a cave above **Corodale Bay** for three weeks following his defeat and escape from Culloden.

Near **Bornais (Bornish)** another minor road can be followed east of the A865 to **Loch Eynort** that penetrates far inland from the Minch. An old stalkers path can be followed along the north shore of the loch towards the sea, with views of numerous seals and the occasional otter and the steep upper slopes of Beinn Mhor towering above to the north.

Outer Hebrides

A few miles south, at **Gearraidh Bhailteas (Milton)**, a cairn marks the birthplace of that famous Heridean lass, **Flora MacDonald** (see page 543). Nearby is the **Kildonan Museum** (T01878-710343), which has a tearoom.

The A865 continues south for a few miles to the village of **Dalabrog (Daliburgh)**, then heads east to the island's main ferry port, **Lochboisdale**.

Loch Baghasdail (Lochboisdale)

Phone code: 01878
Colour map 3, grid A1
Population: 300

South Uists's largest settlement is set on a rocky promontory in a beautiful island-dotted sea loch. The imposing entrance is guarded by Calvay island with its 13th-century castle ruin. Lochboisdale is a tiny place, with little in the way of tourist sights, though it does have a hotel, bank, post office and **tourist information**, at Pier Road. ■ *T700286. Open early Apr to mid-Oct.*

Sleeping

You should book accommodation in advance, as the ferry arrives in Lochboisdale late in the evening. **C** *Lochboisdale Hotel*, T700332, F700367. This fishing hotel is right by the ferry terminal, and the best place to stay and the only place to have a drink or a meal. There's also **B&B** accommodation by the terminal at **E** *Bayview*, T700329; and **F-E** *Lochside Cottage*, T700472. About a mile from the terminal is **D** *Brae Lea Guest House*, T/F700497, who will collect you from the ferry; and **E** *Kilchoan Bay*, T700517.

About 10 miles south of Lochboisdale, on the southern coast of the island, is **Ludag jetty**, the departure point for the small private passenger ferry to **Eòlaigearraidh (Eoligarry)** on Barra. A few miles to the west of Ludag, at **Pol a' Charra (Pollachar)** is the charming **C** *Polachar Inn*, T700215, F700768, which has great views across the Sound of Barra and its own beach close by. At **Cille Bhrìghde (West Kilbride)** nearby is *Hebridean Croft Originals*, which has a wide range of local crafts on show, as well as a photographic display of local history. It's open daily and has a tearoom.

Eirisgeidh (Eriskay)

Phone code: 01878
Colour map 3, grid A1

The tiny island of Eriskay, with a population of less than 200, gives its name to the native breed of pony, said to have been ridden by King Robert the Bruce at the Battle of Bannockburn in 1314. In the late 1970s it nearly became extinct, but one surviving stallion saved the breed and numbers are growing. A series of paths take you around the island in about three hours. For more details, see the *Cuairt Eirisgeidh* leaflet published by the Western Isles Tourist Board and available at the Lochboisdale Tourist Information Centre.

Most people come to Eriskay to pay a visit to **Coilleag a' Phrionnsa (Prince's beach)**, the sandy beach on the west coast. This is where Bonnie Prince Charlie first stepped on to Scottish soil on July 23, 1745, at the start of the ill-fated Jacobite Rebellion. The rare pink convolvulus which grows there today is said to have been planted by the Prince himself from seeds brought from France. A small memorial cairn situated in the dunes behind the beach was erected by the local school to commemorate the occasion.

As well as the wreck of the *SS Politician* (see box on page 590), another sight worth seeing is **St Michael's**, the Roman Catholic church built in 1903 and funded by the local fishing fleet.

Getting there

Eriskay is reached by a frequent car ferry from Ludag (Mon-Sat only; for times, T01878-720261), which lands at the ferry jetty at **Haun**. Construction of a new causeway was completed in August 2001 linking Eriskay to South Uist.

There is a B&B on the island (T720232), and a self-catering flat (T720274), or you can **Sleeping**
wild camp – though there are few amenities, other than a shop, pub and post office.

Bharraigh (Barra)

It may be tempting to overlook the little island of Barra, only about eight miles Phone code: 01871
long by five miles wide, but this would be a great mistake, as it's one of the most Colour map 3, grid A1
beautiful of all the islands in the Outer Hebrides. Here you'll find the best of the Population: 1,316
*islands in miniature – beaches, machair, peat-covered hills, tiny crofting com-
munities and Neolithic remains – and a couple of days spent on Barra gives a real
taster of Hebridean life. Gaelic culture is also strong here but, with its Catholic
tradition, Barra is a bit more laid-back than many of the other islands in the
Outer Hebrides and doesn't follow the others' strict Sabbatarianism.*

Ins and outs

The best way to arrive is by **air** at Tràigh Mhòr ('Cockle Strand'), the famous airstrip on **Getting**
the beach at the north end of the island. This is the only airport in the UK where flight **there**
schedules are shown as 'subject to tides'. For flight details see page 560. Barra is
reached by **car ferry** from Oban and Mallaig on the mainland (for more details, see
page 560), and also by car ferry from Lochboisdale on South Uist, and by passenger-only ferry from Ludag on South Uist (see page 561).

There is a regular bus/postbus service (5-8 times per day Mon-Sat) that runs from **Getting**
Castlebay to the ferry port of Eòlaigearraidh, via the **aiport**. There are also buses (3-4 **around**
per day Mon-Sat) from Castlebay to Bhatarsaigh (Vatersay). You can also hire a car or a
bicycle to tour the island at your leisure (see below).

Bàgh a' Chaisteil (Castlebay)

The main settlement is Castlebay, on the southern side of the island, situated Colour map 3, grid A1
in a wide sheltered bay and overlooked by **Sheabhal** (383 m), on top of which
is a marble statue of the Blessed Virgin and Child. It's a short but steep walk up
to the top from the town, and the views are well worth it. The once-thriving
herring port is also overlooked by the large Roman Catholic church, Our
Lady, Star of the Sea.

As the main ferry port, Castlebay provides the full range of services: hotels,
B&Bs, shops, a bank (but no ATM) and post office. The **tourist information
centre** is on the main street near the ferry terminal. It has information on local
walks and will book accommodation. ■ *T810223. Apr to mid-Oct Mon-Sat
0900-1700; also open for the arrival of the evening ferry.*

Castlebay's most notable feature is the impressive 15th-century **Kisimul Cas-** **Sights**
tle, built on an island in the middle of the harbour. This was the ancient home
of the Chief of the MacNeils, one of the oldest Scottish clans, who owned the
island from 1427 till 1838. It was then sold to the notorious Colonel Gordon
of Cluny, along with neighbouring South Uist and Benbecula (see page 584),
and the poor people of Barra suffered the same cruel fate, 600 of them being
shipped to Canada to starve. One hundred years later the castle and much of
the island was bought back for the MacNeils by an American architect, Robert
Lister MacNeil, who became the 45th Clan Chief and restored the castle to its
present state before his death in 1970. His son, the new Clan Chief, uses it as

Outer Hebrides

A Fishy Tale

In the 1820s a dead body was washed up in Culla Bay, near Griminish on Benbecula. It was said to have had the upper body of a well-developed four-year-old child, with long, dark glossy hair, and the lower half was like a salmon, but without scales. Many people came from all around to look at the bizarre creature, before the landlord of the estate ordered a coffin and shroud and it was given a decent burial on the shore of Culla Bay. What exactly this creature was has remained a mystery to this day.

his residence when visiting, though it is now in the care of Historic Scotland. ■ *The castle can be visited by boat from the pier, weather permitting, Apr-Sep daily 0930-1830; Oct Mon-Wed 0930-1630, Thu 0930-1230, Sat 0930-1630, Sun 1400-1630. Adult £3, concession £2.30, children £1. T810313.*

If you're interested in finding out about the island's history, you should visit the **Barra Heritage Centre**. ■ *Apr-Sep Mon-Fri 1100-1700. Adult £1. T810403.*

Sleeping & eating
It's a good idea to book in advance if arriving on the evening ferry from Oban or Mallaig. The best place to stay is the **D** *Castlebay Hotel*, by the ferry terminal, T810223, F810445. 14 rooms. Friendly, good food, good value and a great bar. A few miles west of Castlebay is the modern, purpose-built **B-C** *Isle of Barra Hotel* T810383, F810385, BarraHotel@aol.com 30 rooms, open Apr-Oct. Overlooking a lovely beach with fantastic sea views. **D** *Craigard Hotel*, T810200, is a family-run hotel with hearty home cooking.

There are also several guesthouses and B&Bs in and around Castlebay, including **E** *Grianamul*, T810416, F810319,ronnie.macneil@virgin.net **E** *Ceol Mara*, T810294; and **E** *Terra Nova*, T810458, which is situated a 10 min walk from the ferry in Nask. At the moment there are no independent hostels or a Gatliff Trust Hostel on Barra. Although there are also no official campsites on Barra, there are endless opportunities for **wild camping** across the island, with the most popular spots to be found on the machair at Traigh Mhor (north Barra), Borve Point (west Barra) and Ledaig (Castlebay). Generally no permission is required from the landowner, but ensure all waste and litter is removed when you leave the site. For campers, there are 2 or 3 well-stocked mini-supermarkets in Castlebay.

The best food is available at the *Castelbay Hotel* and *Isle of Barra Hotel*, both of which offer excellent local fish and seafood at mid-range prices. For something a lot cheaper, try the *Kismul Galley* on the main street, T810645, which offers all-day breakfasts, snacks and home baking, and is open Mon-Sat 0900-2100 and Sun 1000-1800. There's also a tearoom at the airport.

Transport
Car hire is available from £20 per day at *Barra Car Hire*, T810243, and *MacMillan Self Drive*, T890366. **Bicycles** can be hired at *Barra Cycle Hire*, T810284. **Taxi services** and **island tours** with *Hatcher's Taxis*, T810486; and *Nellie's Taxi*, T810302.

Around Bharraigh

The A888 follows a circular route of 14 miles around the island, making an ideal day's bike tour from Castlebay. Heading west, it passes the turning for the causeway to **Vatersay** (see below), then runs northwest between two hills (**Sheabhal** to the east and **Beinn Tangabhal** to the west) to the west coast, where you'll find the nicest beaches. One of these is at **Halaman Bay**, near the village of **Tangasdal (Tangasdale)**, overlooked by the *Isle of Barra Hotel* (see above). At the turning for **Borgh (Borve)** there are standing stones. Next is the turning for the small settlement of **Baile Na Creige (Craigston)**, where you'll find the **Thatched Cottage Museum**, an original 'blackhouse' and the chambered burial cairn of **Dun Bharpa**. ■ *Museum open Easter-Oct Mon-Fri 1100-1700. £1.* From Dun Bharpa there are pleasant walks into the surrounding hills, with the summit of **Sheabhal** offering tremendous views from the highest point on the island.

North of the turning, near **Allathsdal (Allasdale)**, is another lovely beach, and just beyond are the remains of **Dun Cuier**, an Iron-Age fort. Make a short detour at Greian, and follow the headland to the rugged cliffs at Greian Head.

The A888 then heads east to **Bagh a Tuath (Northbay)**, where a branch left leads to the village of Eòlaigearraidh (Eoligarry), near the northern tip, surrounded by sandy bays washed by Atlantic rollers. A private passenger ferry leaves from here to Ludag on South Uist. **Tràigh Mhòr & Eòlaigearraidh (Eoligarry)**

The road to Eoligarry passes the island's airport at Tràigh Mhòr, the 'cockle strand', which once provided 100 to 200 cartloads of delicious cockles each day. Now the cockleshells are gathered and used for harling, the roughcast wall covering used on many Scottish houses. By the beach is the house that was once the home of Compton MacKenzie, author of *Whisky Galore!* (see page 586). He lies buried at **Cille Bhara**, to the west of the village of Eòlaigearraidh, along with members of the MacNeil clan. This was one of the most important religious complexes in the Outer Hebrides, built in the 12th century, and consists of a church and two chapels. One of these, St Mary's, has been re-roofed and houses several carved medieval tombstones and a copy of a runic stone. The original is in the Museum of Scotland in Edinburgh.

Bhatarsaigh (Vatersay) and Mingulay

A worthwhile trip from Castlebay is to the island of Vatersay, now linked to Barra by a causeway built in an effort to stabilise the island community (the present population is around 70). The island boasts two lovely shell-sand beaches backed by beautiful machair, only a few hundred yards apart on either side of the narrow isthmus that leads to the main settlement of Vatersay. On the west beach, Bagh Siar, is the **Annie Jane Monument**, which commemorates the terrible tragedy in 1853, when the emigrant ship *Annie Jane* was wrecked off the coast of Vatersay, with the loss of 333 lives, many of them islanders.

On a clear day from Vatersay you can enjoy the view of the smaller islands to the south – Sandray, Pabbay and **Mingulay**. The latter was inhabited until 1912, and can still be visited from Barra. It has recently been acquired by the National Trust for Scotland.

Day trips to Mingulay can be arranged with Mr John Allan MacNeil in Castlebay, T810449 (approximately £15 per person), who sails to the island in settled weather when sufficient people can be found to fill the boat. It is one of the most rewarding excursions in the Outer Hebrides, particularly during the puffin season from June to early August. The trip normally includes a two-hour sail from Barra past the neighbouring islands of Sandray and Pabbay, a circumnavigation of Mingulay to view the spectacularly high western sea cliffs, and a landing on the east coast for a three-hour exploration of the beautiful beach of Mingulay Bay, the deserted village and surrounding hills and coast. There are also fine views to the lighthouse on Barra Head, the most southerly outpost of the Outer Hebrides island chain. Similar boat trips can

Outer Hebrides

Tight little island

Between Eriskay and South Uist is the wreck of the famous SS Politician, the island's other claim to fame. In 1941 the 12,000 ton ship went aground just off the island of Calvey and sank with its cargo, which included 20,000 cases of whisky. This not only provided many islanders with a supply of whisky for many years, but also provided the plot for Compton Mackenzie's book Whisky Galore!, *which was later made into the famous Ealing comedy of the same name (it was called* Tight Little Island *in the US) and filmed on Barra. Part of the wreck can be seen at low tide, and there's more information on the famous incident on display in the appropriately named Am Politician pub (open 1230-1430), in the main settlement of Baile (Balla).*

also be organised by Mr George McLeod at the Castlebay Hotel, T810223 or ask at the tourist office in Castlebay.

St Kilda

Over 40 miles west of the Outer Hebrides lie the spectacular and isolated islands of St Kilda, Scotland's first UNESCO World Heritage Site. St Kilda captures the imagination of most visitors to the Outer Hebrides, whether they actually get there or just dream about romantic voyages to mysterious lands across perilous seas.

The largest of the islands, **Hirta**, was the remotest community in Britain, if not Europe, until 1930, when the remaining 36 Gaelic-speaking inhabitants were evacuated at their own request, in one of the most poignant episodes of Scottish history.

In 1957 the islands become the property of the National Trust for Scotland, who in turn leased them to the Nature Conservancy (the forerunner of Scottish Natural Heritage) as a National Nature Reserve. St Kilda is the most important seabird breeding station in northwest Europe. The islands are home to the largest colony of gannets in the world, the largest colony of fulmars in Britain, and one the largest colonies of puffins in Scotland. These huge numbers of seabirds were vital to the islanders' survival. Their eggs provided food in the summer, and gannets and fulmers were caught each season to be plucked, dried and stored for the winter. Their feathers and oil were kept for export to generate income, whilst their bones were shaped into useful tools and their skins into shoes.

Today Hirta is partly occupied by the army as a radar-tracking station for the rocket range on South Uist and managed by **Scottish Natural Heritage**. For more information, contact Scottish Natural Heritage, 135 Stilligarry, South Uist, HS8 5RS, T01870-620238. For details of tours, ask at one of the main tourist information centres in the Outer Hebrides.

Getting there The biggest problem apart from accessibility is cost, although it is definitely possible if you're prepared to break the bank. *Island Cruising* in Uig, on Lewis (T01851-672381, F672212) arranges boat trips to St Kilda from April to October starting from about £300 (4-day all-inclusive). The tour comprises the journey to and from St Kilda and a landing on Hirta with a visit to the museum, the old village and a wider exploration of the island including a climb up to the highest sea cliffs in the British Isles at Conachair (430 m).

The *National Trust for Scotland* also organises two-week long voluntary Work Parties throughout the summer every year to undertake restoration, maintenance

How St Kilda was killed off

Friday 29th August 1930 was the end of the life of St Kilda as it had been for centuries. For a least 1,000 years the inhabitants of this remote group of islands had been tenants of the Macleods of Dunvegan on Skye. In earlier days the trip from Skye, undertaken in longboats, would require 16 hours of rigorous rowing and sailing. Even now, the trip to St Kilda is no easy matter.

St Kilda consists of several islands. Hirta, the main habitable island, is now a permanent home only to the largest colony of fulmars in Britain. Across a narrow channel lies Dun. Nearby Boreray is home to the world's largest colony of gannets. Soay virtually completes the group. There are several dramatic 'stacs' rising sheer from the Atlantic Ocean. At 430 m, the sea cliffs at Conachair are the highest in the British Isles.

Until 1930 the islanders had been supported by the mainland by the provision of a nurse and a post office. But the Scottish Office decided that their subsidy of the islands was no longer economic. This meant that life for the residents without those facilities would be untenable. Now owned by the National trust for Scotland, St Kilda is a National Nature reserve. Each year, during the brief summer months when travel to the islands is possible, teams of volunteers work on Hirta, maintaining what remains of the abandoned houses, studying the wildlife and glorying in the peace and isolation of the place.

But in 1930, to the younger of the 36 residents, including a man with nine children, evacuation was an attractive prospect. There would be better schooling for the children, and better health care. Although many had never seen a tree, a new life in forestry appealed. The more elderly residents,

most of whom had never left the island and who could not speak English, must have viewed the drastic change with alarm. But the younger majority view prevailed and evacuation was planned.

There were five hundred Soay sheep to be moved first. Their coats of fine wool were not sheared but plucked by the inhabitants with just the help of a penknife. The resultant locally woven tweed, either shipped ashore or sold to rare visitors, had provided the inhabitants' only contact with actual money. No taxes on income or on anything else were paid. Their internal economy took the form of barter. The plentiful supply of gannets, when dried, provided winter food. No inhabitant had ever fought in any war. Their distance and isolation earned them no consideration by the rest of Scotland.

Despite protestations by The Canine Defence League, all dogs were destroyed. Just two were put down by injections of hydrocyanic acid. The rest, at the islanders' insistence, had stones tied around their necks and were hurled from the jetty. Small boats, holding only a dozen or so sheep, were used to ferry them out to the SS Dunara Castle. Ten cows with four calves were also evacuated. Then HMS Harebell, of the Fishery Protection Service, came on the final day to take the islanders to the mainland. The Under Secretary of State for Scotland imposed a ban on photography, thus ensuring the people of St Kilda privacy during the evacuation. It was not possible to house all of the inhabitants in Argyll, as had been hoped, so the community was split, their communal lives coming to an end.

The history of the island has been documented in a number of scholarly works, including The Life and Death of St Kilda *by Tom Steel, and* Island on the Edge of the World, *by Charles Maclean.*

Outer Hebrides

and archaeology projects around the old village on Hirta. The groups are very popular, and each volunteer must complete an application form, so apply early. The fortnight costs between £450 and £500 and this covers transport from Oban to St Kilda and all food and lodging costs while on the island. For details contact National Trust for Scotland in Oban, T01631-570000, F570011, stkilda@nts.org.uk

Orkney and Shetland

12

Orkney and Shetland

To some these two archipelagos will never be anything more than distant and overlooked specks of land peppering the wild north Atlantic, above an already remote north coast of mainland Scotland. It is true – they are remote and they have maintained a social and political, as well as geographical, distance from the rest of Scotland which goes a long way to explaining the relatively few visitors each year.

Orkney was under Norse rule until the mid-13th century, and Shetland was only 'given' (as part of a princess' dowry) to Scotland in 1469. Somehow, seeing them as a part of Scotland can be very misleading and each must be seen within the context of its own unique cultural background and unusual geography.

It is these two qualities that make the islands worth visiting and the ones that the tourist boards are keen to plug. Both Orkney and Shetland are littered with outstanding archaeological evidence, not just of Norse occupation, such as at **Jarlshof** at the very southern tip of Shetland, but also of life back in 3000 BC at **Skara Brae** and the **Knap of Howar** in the Orkneys. They are also the best places in Britain to see wildlife as yet untamed by the 21st century. Here you can sail alongside porpoises and seals, and watch a million migratory seabirds nest and bring up their young during the summer months. And, thanks to fast and frequent transport links, it doesn't take an Arctic expedition to get here.

Orkney

Orkney may only be a short step away from John O' Groats, but to the fiercely independent Orcadians, 'Mainland' means the largest of the Orkney islands and not the Scottish mainland.

*Mainland is also the site of the two main towns and ferry terminals: the capital Kirkwall and the beautiful old fishing port of Stromness. Here, you'll also find many of Orkney's most precious archaeological treasures: the **Stones of Stenness**; **Maes Howe**; the **Broch of Gurness**; and the remarkable Neolithic village of **Skara Brae**. Aside from Mainland, there are a dozen smaller islands to explore, including **Hoy**, with its wild, spectacular coastal scenery. The even more remote northerly islands offer miles of deserted beaches, and nothing but the calls of myriad birds to shatter the all-pervading peace and quiet.*

Ins and outs

Getting there   **Air**   There are direct flights to **Kirkwall** airport daily except Sun from Aberdeen, Edinburgh, Glasgow, Inverness and Shetland, with connections to London Heathrow, Birmingham, Manchester and Belfast. All these flights are operated by *Loganair/British Regional Airlines* and can be booked through *British Airways*, T0845-7222111.

Boat   There are several ferry routes to Orkney from the mainland. *P&O Scottish Ferries*, T01856-850655, sail from **Aberdeen** to **Stromness** (8 hrs) twice weekly (Tue and Sat) in 'standard season' (Jun-Aug), and once a week (Sat) the rest of the year. From Aberdeen a standard season passenger fare costs £43.50 single and a car costs £113. There's a 20% discount on passenger fares, and 50% on vehicle fares, for midweek sailings. Cars should be booked in advance.

P&O also sail from **Scrabster** to **Stromness** (2 hrs) twice a day (Mon-Sat; once on Sun) from Apr-Oct, and twice a day (Mon-Fri; once on Sat) from Nov-Mar. A standard season passenger fare costs £16.50 single and a car costs £51. A shuttle bus links Scrabster with the nearby town of Thurso, on the north coast. There are regular bus and train services to Thurso from Inverness (see page 516).

P&O sail from **Lerwick** (Shetland) to **Stromness** (8 hrs) on Fri (all year) and Wed (Jun-Aug), returning on Sun (all year) and Tue (Jun-Aug). A passenger fare costs £40.50 single and a car costs £95. There is a 10% student/senior citizen discount on all *P&O* ferries to Orkney.

John o'Groats Ferries, T01955-611353, www.jogferry.co.uk, operate a passenger-only (and bicycles) ferry service from **John o' Groats** to **Burwick** (2-4 times per day; 45 mins) on South Ronaldsay, from May to Sep. A single fare costs £16 (bicycles an extra £3). An **off-peak return** from John o' Groats to Kirkwall, departing at 1600 or 1800 costs £25. No bookings required. A free bus meets the afternoon train from Thurso at 1430 and connects with the 1600 or 1800 ferry to Orkney. There are bus connections between Burwick and Kirkwall (45 mins) for all ferry sailings. They also operate the **Orkney Bus**, a daily direct bus/ferry/bus service between **Inverness** and Kirkwall, via John o' Groats. It leaves Inverness at 0730 and 1420 from Jun-Sep (at 1420 only in May). It costs £40 return. Journey time 5 hrs. Advance booking is essential.

Getting around   **Air**   There are **inter-island flights** which are operated by *Loganair*, T01856-872494. Eight-seater aircraft fly from Kirkwall daily except Sun to **Stronsay**, **Sanday**, **North Ronaldsay**, **Westray** and **Papa Westray**, and on Wed to **Eday**. To Papa Westray and North Ronaldsay costs only £15 single, and to the other islands listed costs £31 single. Inter-island flights not leaving from Kirkwall cost £14. There are **sightseeing flights** in

Things to do on Orkney and Shetland

- Visit the amazing archaeological wonders of Maes Howe and Skara Brae.
- Explore the winding streets of Stromness, one of the most fascinating fishing villages in Scotland.
- Take time to reflect in the incredible little Italian Chapel, on the island of Lamb Holm.
- Take the spectacular clifftop walk to meet the Old Man of Hoy.
- Fly from Westray to Papa Westray, which takes all of two minutes!
- Visit the tiny island of Mousa to see the best-preserved broch in Scotland.
- Brave the white-knuckle boat trip to Fair Isle, one of the best places on earth for birdwatching.
- Explore the dramatic coastal scenery of Hermaness National Nature Reserve, from where you can look out to Muckle Flugga, site of the most northerly lighthouse in the British Isles.

Jul and Aug which fly over all these islands and cost £30. There's also an *Orkney Adventure ticket* which allows you to fly to 3 islands for £66. Flight schedules are given under each relevant destination in this chapter.

Bus Buses on the Orkney islands are very limited. Apart from the daily service between **Burwick** and **Kirkwall**, which connects with the ferry, there are buses from Kirkwall to **Stromness, Evie/Tingwall, Dounby, St Margaret's Hope, Deerness** and **East Holm**. There's also a bus to **Houton** (Hoy) which connects with the ferry. Bus details are given under each relevant destination and on page 603.

Boat *Orkney Ferries*, T01856-872044, operates daily car and passenger ferries to **Rousay, Egilsay** and **Wyre** from Tingwall; to **Shapinsay, Eday, Stronsay, Sanday, Westray** and **Papa Westray** from Kirkwall; to **Graemsay** and **Hoy** from Stromness; and to **Hoy** and **Flotta** from Houton. There's a ferry on Fri to **North Ronaldsay** from Kirkwall.

Fares: to **Rousay, Egilsay, Wyre, Shapinsay, Hoy, Graemsay** and **Flotta** costs £2.40 per passenger one-way and £7.20 per car. Inter-island fares are £1.20 per passenger. A round-trip costs £4.80. To **Eday, Stronsay, Sanday, Westray, Papa Westray** and **North Ronaldsay** costs £4.80 per passenger one-way and £10.80 per car. An inter-island fare is £2.40, and round-trip costs £9.60. There are also additional Sun sailings in summer (May-Sep); contact *Orkney Ferries* or the tourist board for the latest schedules. Those travelling by car should book all ferry journeys in advance. Ferry details are given under the relevant destination.

Car Only the main population centres on Mainland are served by public transport, and having a car is essential to visit many of the most interesting sights. Bringing a car to Orkney is expensive, but there are several **car hire** firms on the Mainland and on the other islands. Car hire firms are listed under each particular town.

Bicycle Orkney is relatively flat and most of its roads are quiet, which makes it ideal for touring by bike, though the wind can make it difficult if it's blowing in the wrong direction. Bicycles can be hired in Kirkwall, Stromness and on many of the other islands. Details are given in the relevant section.

Organized tours Those with limited time may prefer to book a tour of the islands. Both general sightseeing tours and special interest tours are available. *Go-Orkney*, South Cannigall, St Ola, T01856-871871, www. orknet.co.uk/orkney-tours, runs a series of tours of Mainland, and also to Hoy and Rousay. *Wildabout Orkney*, 5 Clouston Corner, Stenness, T01856- 85 1011, www. wildabout.orknet.co.uk, offers highly rated wildlife, historical, folklore and environmental tours of Mainland for around £16 per person for a full day. *Discover Orkney Tours*, T/F01856- 872865, offer tours of Mainland as well as trips to Westray and Papa Westray.

Orkney and Shetland

Orkney

The **Orkney Tourist Board** (www. visitorkney.com) has tourist offices in Kirkwall and Stromness. They will book accommodation for you, or provide a list of what's available, though many B&Bs are not included in the tourist board scheme. They can also provide information on various sights, walks and the islands' wildlife. Those wishing to leave Mainland and visit the smaller islands should pick up a free copy of the tourist board's excellent information and travel guide, *The Islands of Orkney*. For more background reading, see the *Orkney Guide Book* by Dr C Tait (£14.95).

Many of Orkney's monuments are managed by Historic Scotland. They include the Bishop and Earl's Palaces, Broch of Gurness, Maes Howe, Skara Brae and Skaill House, Brough of Birsay and Noltland Castle. You can buy a joint ticket for all these monuments: summer adult £11, concession £8, children £3.50; winter (Skaill closed) adult £10, concession £7, children £3.

Tourist information

Kirkwall

Orkney's capital is built around a wide sheltered bay and is the main departure point for ferries to the northern islands. First impressions are a little misleading, as the harbour area has been blighted by modern development. More appealing, however, are the narrow winding streets and lanes of the old town, which has not changed much over the centuries. There are many houses dating from the 16th, 17th and 18th centuries, as well as Kirkwall's greatest attraction, its magnificent **cathedral**, the finest medieval building in northern Scotland.

Phone code: 01856
Population: 7,000

Getting around The town is compact and it's easy to get around on foot. The **bus station** is 5 mins' walk west of the town centre. The **airport**, T872421, is 3 miles southeast of Kirkwall on the A960. There are no buses to and from town. A taxi will cost around £6.

Ins & outs
For full details see Transport on page 603

Orkney and Shetland

Viking heritage

The history of Orkney and Shetland is bound up with the history of the Vikings, who first came to the islands in the latter half of the ninth century and stayed for about 650 years. This was part of a great Viking expansion westwards, and in less than a century emigrants from Norway and Denmark settled in Orkney, Shetland, Iceland, Greenland, Caithness, the Western Isles, Isle of Man and parts of Ireland and the northern half of England.

In 872 the King of Norway set up a Norse earldom in Orkney, from which the Vikings ruled Orkney, Shetland and the Western Isles and took part in raids around Britain and Europe, creating the popular image of Vikings as aggressive, bloodthirsty invaders. At home, however, they lived a peaceful life, adhering to the laws of their parliament, the ting, and many converted to Christianity.

In the late 14th century Norway, Denmark and Sweden were united under a Danish king. In 1469 the Royal estates and prerogatives in Orkney and Shetland were pledged to Scotland as part of the marriage dowry of Margaret, daughter of the King of Denmark, on her marriage to Prince James of Scotland, later to become King James III. Orkney and Shetland were to revert to rule by the kings of Norway when the debt was paid, but the pledge was never redeemed and the islands remained under Scottish control.

Soon after assuming control, the Scots began to change the old Norse laws which they had agreed to maintain, and Scottish influence grew. In 1564 Mary, Queen of Scots granted the control and revenues from Orkney and Shetland to her half-brother, Robert Stewart. His prime motivation, however, was to extract as much money as possible through taxes. He was succeeded by his son, the infamous Patrick Stewart, who demanded even more rents, dues and fines. Earl Patrick eventually got his come-uppance when he was executed in Edinburgh for treason, but the changes he had made continued and Scots and English gradually began to usurp Old Norse as the native language of the islands.

The **main street** changes its name from Bridge St, to Albert St, to Broad St and Victoria St as it twists its way south from the busy harbour. The cathedral is on Broad St, and most of the shops and banks are on Broad St and Albert St.

On Broad St, near the cathedral, is the very helpful **Tourist Information Centre**, T872856, info@ otb.ossian.net They will book accommodation and change money, and also provide various useful free leaflets including *The Islands of Orkney* and the *Kirkwall Heritage Guide*. They also stock a wide range of guide books and maps, and have details of forthcoming events. Another good source is the weekly newspaper *The Orcadian*. Open Apr-Sep daily 0830-2000; Oct- Mar Mon-Sat 0930-1700.

Sights The town's outstanding sight is the huge and impressive red sandstone **St Magnus Cathedral**, built by masons who had worked on Durham Cathedral in the north of England. It was founded in 1137 by Rognvald Kolson, Earl of Orkney, in memory of his uncle, Magnus Erlendson, who was slain by his cousin, Haakon Paulson, on Egilsay in 1115. Magnus was buried at Birsay and it is said that heavenly light was seen over his grave. It soon became a shrine, attracting pilgrims from as far afield as Norway. Magnus was canonized in 1133, and four years later his nephew commissioned construction of the cathedral. The building wasn't completed until the 14th century, and major additions were made during the intervening centuries. The most recent addition was a new west window for the nave, to celebrate the cathedral's 850th anniversary in 1987.

The bones of St Magnus now lie in the north choir pillar, while those of St Rognvald lie in the south one. There's also a memorial to John Rae, the

Viking place names

Despite the disappearance of the Norse language, many of the Viking place names have survived. Here are some of the most common Old Norse elements which will help explain the meaning of many place names:

		geo	creek
		grind	gate
		ham(n)	anchorage
		holm	small island
		houb	lagoon
		howe	mound
		kirk	church
a(y)	island	lax	salmon
a, o	stream	ler	mud, clay
aith	isthmus	lyng	heather
ayre	beach	minn	mouth
bard	headland	mool, noup	headland
bister	farm	setter	farm
brae, brei	broad	ting	parliament
fell, field	hill	toft	house site
fors	waterfall	voe	sea inlet
garth	farm	wick	bay

19th-century Arctic explorer who is buried in the graveyard, as well as a monument to the 833 men of the HMS *Royal Oak* who died when it was torpedoed in Scapa Flow in 1939. ■ *Apr-Sep Mon-Sat 0900-1800, Sun 1400-1800; Oct-Mar Mon-Sat 0900-1300 and 1400-1700, Sun service at 1115.*

Looming impressively nearby are the ruins of the **Bishop's Palace**, built in the 12th century as the first Kirkwall residence of the Bishop of Orkney. Here King Haakon of Norway died in 1263 after his defeat at the Battle of Largs. The palace was repaired and extended in the mid-16th century by Bishop Reid, and most of what you see dates from that period. There's a good view of the town from the top of the '*Moosie Too'r*'.

The adjacent **Earl's Palace** was built around 1600 by the notorious Patrick Stewart, Earl of Orkney, using forced labour. Still very much intact, it is one of Scotland's most elegant Renaissance buildings and was occupied by the tyrannical Stewart only for a very short time, until he was imprisoned and later executed. Wandering around both these spectacularly impressive, and solid, buildings is a very good way to get a feel for a period of Orkney's history that is very often ignored, with the likes of Skara Brae just up the road.
■ *Apr-Sep daily 0930-1830. £2, concession £1.50, children £0.75. Joint ticket for all Orkney monuments also available. T871918.*

Opposite St Magnus Cathedral is **Tankerness House and Gardens**, a 16th-century former manse which has been restored and now houses the **Orkney Museum**, which features various archaeological artefacts from Neolithic times to the Vikings. If you are spending any time in Kirkwall at the beginning of your stay, then this is an exceedingly worthwhile exhibition. It is a great way to whet your appetite for the archaeological gems that are lying in wait for you all over the islands, and it also puts them into a useful chronological context. ■ *Oct-Mar Mon-Sat 1030-1230, 1330-1700; Apr-Sep 1030-1700; May-Sep also Sun 1400-1700. Free. T873191.*

Old radio buffs should not miss the **Orkney Wireless Museum**, at Kiln Corner, at the harbour end of Junction Road, which houses a jumble of domestic and wartime communications equipment from the 1930s onwards.
■ *Apr-Sep Mon-Sat 1000-1630, Sun 1400-1630. £2, children £1.*

A mile south of the town centre on the road to South Ronaldsay is the 200-year-old **Highland Park Distillery**, the most northerly of Scotland's whisky distilleries. There are guided tours of the distillery, one of the few that still has its own floor maltings, and a wee dram of this particularly fine single malt at the end. ■ *Tours every half hour Apr-Oct Mon-Fri 1000-1700 (last tour at 1600); Jul and Aug also Sat and Sun 1200-1700; Nov, Dec and Mar Mon-Fri at 1400 and 1530 only. Adult £3, concession £2, children £1.50. T874619.*

Sleeping The top hotel in Kirkwall is the very comfortable **B-C** *Ayre Hotel*, T873001, www.ayrehotel.co.uk, on the harbour front. Another good option is the **B-D** *Albert Hotel*, T876000, enquiries@alberthotel.co.uk, on Mounthoolie Lane in the centre of town. It also has a restaurant and a couple of lively bars (see below).

Kirkwall

■ Sleeping
1 Albert
2 Ayre
3 SYHA Hostel
4 West End

0 metres 200
0 yards 200

N

To Orphir & Faveran Hotel

To Highland Park Distillery & Visitor Centre

Two miles from town on the A964 Orphir road at St Ola is the **D** *Foveran Hotel*, T872389, www.foveranhotel.com, overlooking Scapa Flow. It is friendly and comfortable, and also offers very good food, including vegetarian. The **D** *West End Hotel*, Main St, T872368, www.orkneyisles.co.uk/westendhotel, is central and serves good bar meals.

There are also plenty of cheap **B&Bs**, though most rooms are small and don't have en suite facilities. **E** *Whiteclett*, St Catherine's Pl, T874193. A 200-year-old listed house near the harbour; and **E-F** *Arundel*, Inganess Rd, T873148. A modern bungalow on a quiet road about a mile from the town centre.

F *SYHA Youth Hostel*, T872243, open Apr-Sep. This large, well-equipped youth hostel is on Old Scapa Rd, about 15 mins' walk from the town centre. There's also **camping** at *Pickaquoy Caravan & Camping Site*, T873535. Open May-Sep, on the western outskirts of Kirkwall, off the A965.

Eating

Kirkwall is no gastronome's paradise and you'll be hard-pushed to find somewhere decent to eat in town. The best place to eat is probably the *Foveran Hotel* (see above). Otherwise, the *Albert Hotel* (see above) serves bar meals (made with home-grown produce, cheap to mid-range), as does the *West End Hotel*. The islands' only Indian restaurant is the *Mumtaz*, on Bridge St. The best place for a snack is the *St Magnus Café*, opposite the cathedral. This is a true cafeteria-style café, serving substantial soups and rolls in a bustling and very friendly atmosphere.

Bars & nighlife
Nightlife in Kirkwall revolves around its lively pubs

The *Bothy Bar* at the *Albert Hotel* is a good place for a drink, and sometimes has live folk music. The hotel's *Matchmakers Bar* has a disco at weekends. The *Ayre Hotel* also stages folk music nights. Check details in *The Orcadian*. The town's *New Phoenix* **cinema** is housed in the *Pickaquoy Leisure Centre*, T879900, on Pickaquoy Rd. It also has **sports** and fitness facilities, and a café and bar.

Transport

For details of flights and ferries to Orkney, see page 596. Details of inter-island flights and ferries are given in the relevant island sections.

There's a limited **bus** service around the Mainland. *Peace Coaches*, T872866, runs regular buses Mon-Sat from Kirkwall bus station to **Stromness** 30 mins. They also run 3-5 buses a day, Mon-Sat, to **Houton**, 30 mins, which connect with ferries to Hoy; and a daily bus, Mon-Sat, to **East Holm**, 25 mins, and **Stromness via Dounby**, 55 mins. *Causeway Coaches*, T831444, runs 2-4 buses a day, Mon-Sat, to **St Margaret's Hope**, 30 mins. *Rosie Coaches*, T751227, runs buses to **Tingwall** and **Evie**. The bus service between Kirkwall and **Burwick** is run by *Shalders Coaches*, T850809. Note that there is no Sun bus service on Orkney.

Car hire *Scarth Car Hire*, Great Western Rd, T872125. *WR Tullock*, Castle St, T876262, and Kirkwall airport, T875500. **Cycle hire** *Bobby's Cycle Centre*, Tankerness Lane, T/F875777. Mountain bikes from £8 per day.

Directory

Banks Branches of the 3 main Scottish banks with cash machines are on Broad St and Albert St. Exchange also at the tourist office. **Communications** Post office: Junction Rd. Open Mon-Fri 0900-1700, Sat 0930-1230. **Laundry** *The Launderama*, Albert St, T872982. Open Mon-Fri 0830-1730, Sat 0900-1700. **Medical facilities** Balfour Hospital, Health Centre and Dental Clinic, New Scapa Rd, T885400.

West Mainland

Phone code: 01856

Everything west of Kirkwall is known as West Mainland, an area of rich farmland, rolling hills and moorland, fringed by spectacular cliffs along the Atlantic coastline and with the greatest concentration of pre-historic monuments in Britain. Here you'll find, amongst many others, the well-preserved Neolithic village of **Skara Brae**, silent monuments to human endeavour in the form of the

Never a dull moment

There are numerous events which take place throughout the year.

Amongst the best-known annual events is **The Ba' (ball)**, *held on Christmas Day and New Year's Day in Kirkwall. It is a bit like rugby, basketball and a full-scale riot all rolled into one, and is contested between two sides – the Uppies and the Doonies – representing different districts of the town. As many as 200 'players' may be involved, and a game can last up to seven hours as both sides attempt to jostle the ball along the streets until one reaches their 'goal' to win the prized ba'. One of the most entertaining events on Orkney is the excellent* **Orkney Folk Festival**, *which takes place at various locations throughout the islands over three days at the end of May.*

The most prestigious and popular event is the acclaimed **St Magnus Festival**, *held in June in Kirkwall. It consists of six days of music, drama, literature and the visual arts, and features many internationally renowned performers.*

During July there are several **regattas** *held on most of the islands, while August is marked by numerous* **agricultural shows**, *culminating in the* **Festival of the Horse and Boys' Ploughing Match** *on South Ronaldsay (see page 611).*

The **Orkney Science Festival** *is held in the first week in September, T01856-876214. For details of what's going on and when, buy a copy of* The Orcadian, *which comes out on Thursdays, or pick up a free copy of the Tourist Board's guide.*

---

standing **Stones of Stenness** and the **Ring of Brodgar**, and the chambered tomb of **Maes Howe**, with its many still unresolved mysteries. The sights below are listed in an anti-clockwise direction starting from Kirkwall.

Evie & the Broch of Gurness   Nine miles northwest of Kirkwall is the tiny village of Evie. A track leads from the village towards the coast, past a sandy beach, to the **Broch of Gurness**. Standing on a lonely, exposed headland on the north coast, with warm, gentle views across towards the island of Rousay, this is the best-preserved broch on Orkney, thought to date from around 100 BC. It is surrounded by an Iron-Age village whose houses are also remarkably well-preserved, with the original hearths, beds, cupboards and even a toilet still in evidence. The broch and village were occupied by the Picts right up till Viking times, around 900 AD. Many Pictish artefacts have been found on the site, and the grave of a ninth-century Norse woman was also discovered. ■ *Apr-Sep daily 0930-1830. Adult £2.80, concession £2, children £1. T751414 (HS).*

To the southwest of Evie is the **Birsay Moors RSPB Reserve,** and at **Lowrie's Water** on Burgar Hill there's a bird-hide from where you can watch breeding red-throated divers. Also on Burgar Hill you'll see several huge aerogenerators built to take advantage of Orkney's fierce winds.

Sleeping D *Woodwick House*, T751330. A very comfortable country house hotel offering good food and occasional cultural events. Good value. The *Eviedale Centre* beside the junction of the road to Dounby, T751270, open April-October, has a small **bothy** and **campsite**. *The Mistra* is the local village shop, post office and pub.

Birsay   At the far northwestern corner of the Mainland is the parish of Birsay, which was a favourite residence of the Earls of Orkney in Viking times as well as the first seat of the Bishop, before the building of St Magnus Cathedral in Kirkwall. Earl Thorfinn the Mighty lived here (1014-64) and built Orkney's first cathedral, **Christchurch**, for the new Bishop.

In the centre of the village are the ruins of the **Earl's Palace**, built by the infamous Earl Robert Stewart in the late 16th century, and once described as "a sumptuous and stately dwelling". Not much remains today, but enough to give some idea of the sheer scale of the place. ■ *Open at all times. Free.* T01856-721205.

Close by is **St Magnus church**, built in 1760 on the site of an earlier church, which in turn was built on the foundations of what is believed to be the original Christchurch. Also in Birsay, just south of the A966 and A967 junction, is **Barony Mills**, the last working water-powered mill in Orkney. ■ *Apr-Sep daily 1000-1300 and 1400-1700. Adult £1.50.*

Lying half a mile off the coast near the village is the **Brough of Birsay**, a tidal island jutting out into the north Atlantic and visible from several other points all the way down the west cost of the mainland. It is only accessible for a couple of hours at low tide (times available from Kirkwall and Stromness tourist offices) but, if possible, it is best seen at the end of the day, as the sun sets – and you'll probably have the whole island to yourself. Pick your way over the shell- and bladderack-strewn causeway and wander at your leisure (but don't forget the tide!) amongst the remnants of a Pictish, and then Viking, community. The island was an important Pictish settlement from around the sixth century, and many artefacts have been found here. Some of these can be seen at the small ticket office at the entrance to the island. The Brough was also the site of an important Viking settlement, and there are extensive remains, including the 12th-century **St Peter's church** where St Magnus was buried after his murder on Egilsay. You can also walk out to the island's **lighthouse** along the top of the cliffs and see puffins (amongst other migrating seabirds) and possibly Minke whales, Pilot whales and Killer whales. ■ *The tidal island is now managed by Historic Scotland. Open (when tides permit) 11 Jun-30 Sep daily 0930-1830. Adult £1.50, concession £1.10, children £0.50. Phone the Earl's Palace (see above).*

At the southern end of Birsay Bay are the wild and spectacular 300 ft-high cliffs of Marwick Head, topped by the distinctive **Kitchener Memorial**, erected after the First World War to commemorate Lord Kitchener and the crew of the *HMS Hampshire*, which was sunk by a German mine off the coast in 1916 with the loss of all but 12 of her crew. Marwick Head is also an **RSPB Reserve**, and during the nesting season in early summer is home to many thousands of guillemots, razorbills, kittiwakes and fulmars, as well as a few puffins.

Markwick Head

A mile inland, by the Loch of Isibister, is another RSPB reserve, **The Loons**, an area of marshland where you can see breeding and migrating wildfowl and waders. Further east, between Boarhouse Loch and Hundland Loch, is the **Kirbuster Farm Museum**, the last surviving Orkney 'black house' which was inhabited till the 1960s and gives an insight into 19th-century rural life on the islands. ■ *Mar-Oct Mon-Sat 1030-1300 and 1400-1700, Sun 1400-1900. Free.*

Sleeping Accommodation is limited to the **D-E** *Barony Hotel*, T721327, baronyhotel@btinternet.com Open May-Sep, on the north shore of Boardhouse Loch. It specializes in fishing holidays and is about the only place offering **food** in these parts. There's also **E-F** *Primrose Cottage*, T/F721384, i.clouston@talk21.com, a comfortable **B&B** overlooking Marwick Bay.

Transport On Mon there's a **bus** between Kirkwall and Birsay with *Shalder Coaches*, T850809.

Orkney and Shetland

Skara Brae & Skaill House

South of Birsay, eight miles north of Stromness, in the magnificent setting of the dazzling white sands of the Bay of Skaill, is Skara Brae, the best-preserved Stone-Age village in northern Europe. First revealed in 1850 after a violent storm blew away the dunes, the site dates from around 5,000 years ago and was occupied for about 600 years.

The houses contain stone furniture, fireplaces, drains, beds, dressers and even have damp-proof coursing in the foundations. The whole complex presents a unique picture of the lifestyle of its inhabitants, and there's also a replica 'house' that you can enter, and wander around in through the gloom, empathizing with that 3000 BC lifestyle.

The swish, modern visitor centre has a useful introductory video and exhibition which is definitely worth seeing before you look round the site (and it's also worth buying their guidebook). After leaving the visitor centre, you walk down a 'path of time', which takes you back through landmark achievements of the last seven millennia, gradually building up the suspense and putting the achievements of Skara Brae in perspective - they may only be rudimentary buildings that once had turf for their rooves, but they were built 2000 years before the pyramids of Egypt, and in one of the world's most northerly outposts.

During the summer a ticket to Skara Brae includes admission to nearby **Skaill House**, an early 17th-century mansion which contains a few old artefacts, including Captain Cook's dinner service from the *Resolution*, but is a bit of a let-down after what you will have just witnessed, not 300 yards away at Skara Brae.

■ *Apr-Sep daily 0930-1830. £4.50, concession £3.30, children £1.30. Oct-Mar (Skara Brae only) Mon-Sat 0930-1630 and Sun 1400-1630. Adult £3.50, concession £2.60, children £1.20. Joint ticket for all Orkney Historic Scotland monuments also available. T841815.*

Sleeping There are a few **B&Bs** close to Skara Brae, including **E** *Kierfiold House*, T/F841583, near Loch Harray; and **E-F** *Netherstove*, T/F841625, ann.poke@virgin.net, overlooking the Bay of Skaill. To get to Skara Brae you'll need your own transport, or you can visit as part of a guided tour (see page 596), or walk north along the coast from Stromness, via Yesnaby.

A short distance inland from here, at **Sandwick**, is Orkney's only brewery, housed in the old Quoyloo School. It brews the island's *Raven Ale* and various bottled beers, including *Skull-splitter*, named after the Viking Earl, Thorfinn Skull-splitter. South of the Bay of Skaill is **Yesnaby**, one of the most spectacular places on the islands, where the cliffs have been eroded into a series of stacks and *geos* by the fierce Atlantic seas. An exhilarating, and precarious, half-mile walk south from the car park and old Second World War lookout post brings you to **Yesnaby Castle**, a huge sea stack similar to the Old Man of Hoy. It's a dramatic sight, especially in a full force gale.

Standing Stones of Stenness & Ring of Brodgar

Northeast of Stromness on the road to Kirkwall is the tiny village of **Stenness**, near some of Orkney's most interesting prehistoric sites. The Standing Stones of Stenness comprise the four remaining stones from an original circle of 12 stones, dating from 3000 BC. The largest of the stones stands over 15 ft high. ■ *Free*. A path leads from the stones to the nearby **Barnhouse Settlement**, a recently excavated Neolithic village.

About a mile northwest of Stenness is another stone circle, the Ring of Brodgar. This is a particularly impressive henge monument. It is over 100yds in diameter and 27 of the original 60 stones are still standing, some of them up to 15 ft high. Given the importance of these sites, it is particularly refreshing to realize when you get there that you can walk about amongst the stones in the still calm of a summer evening, with only a few oyster catchers for company, but both do get busy with coach parties during the day. ■ *Free.*

Less than a mile northeast of the Stones of Stenness is Maes Howe, the finest Neolithic burial chamber in Europe. It was built around 2750 BC, making it contemporary with the Standing Stones and Skara Brae, and is amazingly well preserved. A huge mound covers a stone-built entrance passage which leads into a central chamber – over 12 ft square and the same in height – with three smaller cells built into the walls of the tomb. A fascinating feature of the site is that the winter solstice sun sets directly over the Barnhouse Stone, half a mile away, and shines down the entrance passage of Maes Howe and on to the back wall of one of the cells.

Maes Howe

When it was opened in 1861, no human remains or artefacts were found, giving no clues as to its usage. However, in the 12th century Vikings returning from the Crusades broke into the tomb searching for treasure. They found nothing but left behind one of the largest collections of runic graffiti anywhere in the world, as well as carvings of a dragon, serpent and walrus. Many of the inscriptions are pretty basic, along the lines of "Thorfinn wrote these runes", but some are more intriguing, such as "Many a woman has come stooping in here no matter how pompous a person she was".

A guide gives you an excellent overview of the chamber's mysterious architectural attributes, but the fact remains that the history of this extraordinary place is still largely unsolved – something that obviously adds to the site's attraction. Unfortunately, you do not get the chance to spend very much time in the chamber, so you are unlikely to uncover any great secrets.

■ *Tickets to Maes Howe from Tormiston Mill, on the other side of the road, where there's a an exhibition, introductory video and café. Apr-Sep daily 0930-1830; Oct-Mar Mon-Sat 0930-1630 and Sun 1400-1630. £2.80, concession £2, children £1. Joint ticket for all Orkney Historic Scotland monuments also available. T761606.*

Sleeping There are a few places to stay around **Stenness**. On the shores of Loch Harray is the **B** *Merkister Hotel*, T771366, merkisterhotel@ecos.co, which is a favourite with anglers. It has a very good restaurant and a popular bar. On the shores of Loch Stenness is the **D-C** *Standing Stones Hotel*, T850449, standingstones@sol.co.uk There's also the lovely **D-E** *Mill of Eyreland*, T850136, www.orknet.co.uk/mill, a converted mill 3 miles from Stromness.

On the southern shores of West Mainland, overlooking Scapa Flow, is the scattered community of Orphir, which has a few sights worth visiting, especially if you're heading across to Hoy from the ferry terminal at **Houton**, a little further west. The main point of interest in Orphir is the **Orkneyinga Saga Centre**, where a small exhibition and video introduces the saga, written circa 1200, possibly by an Icelander, which tells the history of the Viking Earls of Orkney from around 900 AD to 1200 AD, when the islands became a part of Scotland rather than Norway. As you would expect, there's plenty of gore and Machiavellian goings-on, including an assassination attempt that went disastrously wrong, when a poisoned shirt meant for Earl Harold was unwittingly and fatally worn by his brother Paul instead. ■ *All year daily 0900-1700. Free.*

Orphir

For details of ferries to Hoy and Flotta, see page 613. For details of buses to Houton, see page 603

Orkney and Shetland

Behind the centre is **The Earl's Bu**, looking out across Orphir Bay south to Cava Island. These are the 12th-century foundations of the home of the Norse Earls of Orkney written about in the saga. Inside the cemetery gates is a section of the circular church built by Haakon and modelled on the rotunda of the Church of the Holy Sepulchre in Jerusalem.

Stromness

Phone code: 01856
Population: 2,500

Ferries from Scrabster arrive in Stromness, and the newcomer is greeted by rows of stone-built houses hugging the shore, each with their own jetty. Stromness is a much more attractive town than Kirkwall, and its narrow, winding main street, its wynds and closes, its fascinating shops, and its unique atmosphere make it the ideal base for exploring the West Mainland.

Ins & outs   **Getting there**   For details of **ferries** to Scrabster, Aberdeen and Lerwick, see page 596. For ferries to **Hoy**, see page 613.

The **Tourist Information Centre** is at the new ferry terminal, T850716. Its exhibition, *This Place Called Orkney*, is a useful introduction to the islands, and its free *Stromness Heritage Guide* takes you round all the buildings of interest in the town. Apr-Oct Mon-Sat 0800-1800, Sun 0900-1600; Nov-Mar Mon-Fri 0900-1700.

Though referred to in the Viking Saga as Hamnavoe, the town in fact dates from the 17th century. Its importance as a trading port grew in the 18th century when wars and privateers made the English Channel too dangerous and ships used the northern route across the Atlantic, calling in at Stromness to take on food and water and to hire local men as crew. Until the late 19th century ships of the Hudson Bay Company made Stromness their main base for supplies, and used **Login's Well** as a source of fresh water. Whaling ships bound for Greenland also hired local labour. By the late 19th century the herring boom had reached Stromness and there were 400 boats using its harbour, but within two decades the boom was over due to over-fishing. Today Stromness remains a fishing port, as well as Orkney's main ferry terminal and the headquarters of the Northern Lighthouse Board.

Sights   Stromness consists largely of one narrow, winding main street, paved with
Stromness is one of flagstones, which hugs the shoreline. Running off the street are numerous little
the classic Scottish lanes and alleyways, many with fascinating names such as **Khyber Pass**, and
fishing villages and full of interesting buildings which reflect the town's proud maritime heritage.
a perfect introduction The houses on the seaward side of the street are gable end to the waterfront
to Orkney and each has its own jetty. The town is not designed for the motor car, so you'll have to park by the harbour and explore its delights on foot. The main street changes its name from Victoria Street to Graham Place, Dundas Street, Alfred Street and South End as it runs south from the harbour.

The **Stromness Museum,** at 52 Albert Street, has exhibitions on natural and maritime history, and contains artefacts from Scapa Flow and the days of the Hudson Bay company. ■ *May-Sep daily 1000-1700; Oct-Apr Mon-Sat 1030-1230 and 1330-1700. Adult £2.50, children £0.50. T850025. Opposite the museum is the house where* **George Mackay Brown** (1921-96), Orkney's most famous poet and story-writer, spent the last two decades of his life (see also page 658). On a jetty to the south of the new harbour is the excellent **Pier Arts Centre**, housing a permanent collection of works of the St Ives school, including Barbara Hepworth, Ben Nicholson and Patrick Heron, amongst others, in a lovely gallery. ■ *Tue-Sat 1030-1230 and 1330-1700; Jul and Aug also Sun 1400-1700. Free.*

The best hotel in town is the **C-D** *Stromness Hotel*, T850298, www. **Sleeping**
Stromnesshotel.com, an imposing old building overlooking the harbour, recently
refurbished and offering good-value meals.

Also near the ferry terminal, on John St, is the **E** *Ferry Inn*, T850280,
www.ferryinn.com/ which serves food and has a lively bar. There are several B&B
options, including **E-D** *Stenigar*, T850438. Open Apr-Oct, a converted boatyard on
Ness Rd, just before the campsite, with views of Hoy and **E** *Mrs Worthington*, T850215.
Open Apr-Oct, a traditional gable-ended house at 2 South End. On Victoria St near the
harbour is **E** *Orca Hotel*, T850447, www.theoakleigh.com Also has a bistro (*Bistro 76*)
serving good food. A few miles behind Stromness, at Innertown, is **E** *Thira*, T851181, a
comfortable, friendly and non-smoking modern bungalow with spectacular views of
Hoy. Also serves an excellent cooked breakfast, and will provide a fantastic dinner
made from the finest local ingredients on request.

F *Brown's Hostel*, 45 Victoria St, T850661. This popular independent hostel has no
curfew and is open all year round; unlike the **F** *SYHA Hostel*, on Hellihole Rd, a 10-min
walk south from the ferry terminal, T850589. Open Mar-Oct. There's a **campsite**,
T873535, open May to mid-Sep, at Ness Point, a mile south of the ferry terminal. It's
well equipped and has incomparable views, but is very exposed.

The best place to eat is the *Hamnavoe Restaurant*, at 35 Graham Pl, T850606. It spe- **Eating &**
cializes in local seafood but also offers good vegetarian dishes. Mid-range. Open   **drinking**
Mar-Oct Tue-Sun from 1900. The *Stromness Hotel* bar serves good, cheap meals. The
Ferry Inn also serves cheap bar food. The *Orca Hotel* has a good cellar bistro. Near the
ferry terminal, on John St, is the popular Coffee Shop which serves good, cheap grub.
Open Mon-Sat 0900-1830, Sun 0900-1700 (Mon-Sat till 1700 in winter). The best
places for a drink are the downstairs bar of the *Stromness Hotel*, the *Ferry Inn*and the
bar of the *Royal Hotel.*

Diving *The Diving Cellar*, 4 Victoria St, T850055. Offers diving packages, equipment **Sports**
rental and boat charters. Open Mon-Fri 1100-1400 and 1700-1900, Sat 1300-1700.
Scapa Scuba, 13 Ness Rd, T/F851218. Diving course, guided dives, night dives and
boat charters.

There are several **buses** daily (Mon-Sat) between Stromness and **Kirkwall**, 30 mins. **Transport**
There's also a bus from Stromness to **Birsay** on Mon only, with *Shalder Coaches*,
T850809. **Car hire** *Brass's Car Hire*, Blue Star Garage, North End Rd, T850850. **Cycle
hire** *Orkney Cycle Hire*, 54 Dundas St, T850255. £4.50-8.50 per day.

Banks There are branches of *Bank of Scotland* and *Royal Bank of Scotland*, both **Directory**
with ATMs, on Victoria St. **Laundry** Next to the *Coffee Shop*, T850904. Self-service or
service washes.

East Mainland

The East Mainland is mainly agricultural land though, and it contains little of *Phone code: 01856*
the amazing archaeological wealth of its western counterpart, there are some
attractive fishing villages, fine coastal walks and many poignant reminders of
Orkney's important wartime role.

There is not much to see inland on the road running southeast from Kirkwall **Deerness**
past the airport, but head on towards the Deerness Peninsula and you will be
richly rewarded by a truly serene, gentle beauty. There are sandy bays, which
make for very pleasant short walks and picnics (if you can find a sheltered

spot), jutting cliffs and a great variety of birdlife. The peninsula makes the West Mainland seem like a mad, hectic whirl by comparison, and is one of the best places on the Mainland to 'get away from it all'.

When the weather's good, the view southwest from Sandside Bay to the Isle of **Copinsay** (an RSPB reserve) is glorious, and, as it emerges slowly and gracefully from the wild North Sea, is a perfect example of the whale-like properties that have been attributed to the Orkneys by the islands' most famous poet George Mackay Brown. There is a **footpath** following the coast from Sandside Bay to Mull Head (a Nature Reserve) and round the tip of the peninsula to the Covenanters Memorial (1679), a five-mile circular walk.

If you continue along the B9050, the road ends at The Gloup car park at Skaill Bay, from where it's a 200-yard walk to **The Gloup**, a dramatic collapsed sea cave, separated from the sea by a land bridge about 80 yards wide. The word comes from the Old Norse '*gluppa*', meaning chasm, the local name for a blow-hole. A network of signposted footpaths covers the northeastern part of the peninsula and there are circular walks of between two and five miles which start from The Gloup car park. At the northeastern tip is **Mull Head**, a clifftop nature reserve which is home to guillemots, shags, fulmars, razorbills, terns and skuas.

On the south coast of East Mainland, near the northern end of the Churchill Barriers, is the old fishing village of **St Mary's**, once a busy little place but largely forgotten since the building of the causeways. To the east of the village is the **Norwood Museum**, which features the large and eclectic antique collection of local stonemason Norris Wood. ■ *May-Sep Tue-Thu and Sun 1400-1700 and 1800-2000. Adult £3, children £1. T781217.*

Sleeping and eating The only place to stay or eat around here is the **E** *Commodore Motel*, T781319.

The Churchill Barriers East Mainland is linked to a string of islands to the south by four causeways, known as the Churchill Barriers, built on the orders of Prime Minister Winston Churchill during the Second World War as anti-submarine barriers to protect the British Navy which was based in Scapa Flow at the time. His decision was prompted by the sinking of the battleship *HMS Royal Oak* in October 1939 by a German U-boat which had slipped between the old blockships, deliberately sunk during the First World War to protect Scapa Flow, and the shore. After the war, a road was built on top of the causeways, linking the islands of Lamb Holm, Glimps Holm, Burray and South Ronaldsay to Mainland.

On the island of Lamb Holm camps were built to accommodate the men working on the construction of the barriers, many of whom were Italian Prisoners of War. The camps have long since gone, but the Italians left behind the remarkable **Italian Chapel**, fittingly known as 'The Miracle of Camp 60'. It is difficult to believe that such a beautiful building could have been made using two Nissen huts, concrete and bits of scrap metal, and the chapel's enduring popularity with visitors is a tribute to the considerable artistic skill of the men involved. One of them, Domenico Chiochetti, returned in 1960 to restore the interior paintwork. ■ *Open all year during daylight hours. Free.*

Burray On the island of Burray the road passes the **Orkney Fossil and Vintage Centre**, which houses a bizarre collection of old furniture, various relics and 350 million-year-old fish fossils found locally. There's also an archive room

The graveyard of Scapa Flow

The huge natural harbour of Scapa Flow has been used since Viking times, and in the years leading up to the First World War the Royal Navy held exercises there, sometimes involving up to 100 ships. But Scapa was vulnerable to attack, and over the course of the war defences were improved with 21 blockships sunk at the eastern approaches. Scapa Flow continued to be used as the main naval base in the Second World War, but the blockships were not enough to prevent a German U-boat from torpedoing HMS Royal Oak, and the huge task of building the Churchill Barriers began (see page 610).

Scapa Flow's most famous incident happened at the end of the First World War, when, under the terms of the Armistice, Germany agreed to surrender most of her navy. Seventy-four German ships were interred in Scapa Flow, awaiting the final decision, but as the deadline approached the German commander, Admiral Von Reuter, gave the order for all the ships to be scuttled, and every ship was beached or sank.

*The scuttled German fleet, however, proved a hazard for fishing and a massive salvage operation began. Today seven German ships remain at the bottom of Scapa Flow – three battleships and four light cruisers – along with four destroyers and a U-boat and the Royal Navy battleships HMS Royal Oak and HMS Vanguard, which blew up in 1917. This makes Scapa Flow one of the world's great **scuba diving** sites. Two companies in Stromness (see below) offer diving courses for beginners, and wreck diving for experienced divers.*

where you can browse through old books and photographs, and a coffee shop. Not really something to go out of your way for, but worth a look if it's raining. ■ *Apr-Sep daily 1000-1800; Oct Wed-Sun 1030-1800. Adult £2.*

Sleeping and eating In Burray village, on the south coast of the island, there's **B&B** accommodation at **E** *Vestlaybanks*, T731305, vestlaybanks@btinternet.com, which also provides evening meals. Alternatively, you can eat at the *Sands Motel*, T731298.

South Ronaldsay

South Ronaldsay is the southernmost of the Orkney islands, only six miles from the Scottish mainland across the stormy Pentland Firth, the most dangerous stretch of water in the British Isles. A small passenger ferry crosses to **Burwick** on the southern tip of the island from John O' Groats (for details see page 596).

Phone code: 01856

The main settlement is the picturesque little village of St Margaret's Hope on the north coast. It is said to be named after Margaret, Maid of Norway, who died near here in 1290 at the age of seven while on her way to marry Prince Edward, later Edward II of England. She had already been proclaimed Queen of Scotland, and her premature death was a major factor in the long Wars of Independence with England. The word 'hope' comes from the Old Norse word '*hjop*' meaning bay.

St Margaret's Hope

The village smithy has been turned into the **Smiddy Museum**, with lots of old blacksmith's tools to try out. ■ *Open May and Sep daily 1400-1600; Jun-Aug 1200-1600; Oct Sun 1400-1600. Free.* The museum also features a small exhibition on the annual **Boys' Ploughing Match**, a hugely popular event first held circa 1860. Each year in August, boys from the village (and now girls as well) dress up as horses and parade in the village square (prizes are

Orkney and Shetland

given for the best costume). Afterwards the boys and their fathers, or grandfathers, head for the **Sand of Wright,** a few miles west, and have a ploughing match with miniature ploughs, which are usually family heirlooms. The categories are: best ploughed ring, best *feering* or guiding furrow, neatest ends and best kept plough. This sheltered beach is well worth a visit anyway, ploughing or no ploughing. The views stretch in a spectacular 180 degree panorama, south across the Pentland Firth to Caithness on mainland Scotland, west to South Walls and Cantick Head on Hoy, and northwest to Flotta and the west Mainland. It is also yet another good place to spot snipe, lapwing, curlew and redshank. Arctic terns also nest nearby and you can spot them diving dramatically as they fish in the bay.

To the north of the beach is the **Howe of Hoxa**, a ruined broch where Earl Thorfinn Skull-Splitter was buried in AD 963, according to the Orkneyinga saga. South Ronaldsay is a good place to buy local arts and crafts, and there are several workshops dotted around the island. One of these is the **Hoxa Tapestry Gallery**, three miles west of the village on the way to Hoxa Head. Local artist Leila Thompson's huge tapestries are well worth a visit; you may not like the style, but you cannot help but marvel at the extraordinary amount of work and dedication involved in their creation; many of them take years to finish. ■ *Apr-Sep Mon-Fri 1000-1730, Sat and Sun 1400-1800. Adult £2, concession £1.50, children under 12 free . T/F831395.*

Sleeping and eating There's a good selection of accommodation in St Margaret's Hope. Best of the lot is the award-winning **D** *Creel Restaurant & Rooms*, T831311, www.thecreel.co.uk, on Front Rd. It offers comfortable rooms and superb, though expensive, food using deliciously fresh, locally grown ingredients. Dinner only. For cheaper meals, try the bar of the **E** *Murray Arms Hotel*, T831205, on Back Rd. For a good **B&B** try **E** *Bellevue Guest House*, T831294, or **E** *The Fisher's Gill*, T831711, which also offers seafood dishes. For cheap and basic **hostel** accommodation, head for the *Wheems Bothy*, T831537, open Apr-Oct, which is now an organic farm at Wheems, Eastside, a few miles southeast of St Margaret's Hope.

Transport Details of **buses** between Kirkwall and St Margaret's Hope on page 411.

Tomb of the Eagles At the southeastern corner of South Ronaldsay is the recently-excavated Tomb of the Eagles, one of the most interesting archaeological sights on Orkney. The 5,000-year-old chambered cairn was discovered by local farmer and amateur archaeologist, Ronald Simison, whose family now runs the privately owned site and museum. The interior contents of the tomb were practically intact and there were up to 340 people buried here, along with carcasses and talons of sea eagles, hence the name. Various objects were also found outside the tomb, including stone tools and polished stone axes.

Before visiting the tomb you can handle the skulls and various other artefacts at the small 'museum' in the family home, which actually means their front porch! Then you walk for about five to 10 minutes through a field to visit a **burnt mound**, a kind of Bronze-Age kitchen, where Ronald Simison will regail you with all manner of fascinating insider information about the excavation process, before walking out along the cliff edge to the spectacularly sited tomb which you must enter by lying on a trolley and pulling yourself in using an overhead rope. It is particularly eerie being here because there is generally no-one else around, and as you haul yourself into the tomb, with the sound of the North Sea crashing into the cliffs nearby, you wonder to yourself how those buried here met their fate. There is also a lovely, but generally wild

and windy, walk back along the cliffs, via a different route, to the car park.
■ *Apr-Oct daily 1000-2000; Nov-Mar 1000-1200. £2.50.*

Hoy

To the southwest of the Mainland is Hoy, the second largest of the Orkney
islands. The name is derived from the Norse Ha-ey, meaning High Island,
which is appropriate as much of the island is more reminiscent of the Scottish Highlands than Orkney, with only the southern end being typically low
and fertile.

Phone code: 01856

There are 2 **ferry** services to Hoy, both run by *Orkney Ferries*, T850624. Transport on
Hoy is limited to a minibus between Moaness Pier and Rackwick. **Car and bike hire** is
available from *Halyel Car Hire* in Lyness, T791240.

Ins & outs
*See Transport on
next page*

Orkney's highest point, **Ward Hill** (1,571 ft) is in the north of the island,
and the north and west coasts are bounded by spectacular cliffs. At **St John's
Head** the sheer cliffs rise out of the sea to a height of 1,150 ft, the highest vertical cliffs in Britain. The island is most famous for its **Old Man of Hoy**, a
great rock stack rising to 450 ft. This northern part of Hoy forms the **North
Hoy RSPB Reserve** which has a variety of habitats ranging from woodland
to tundra-like hill-tops and sea cliffs. The reserve is home to a huge variety of
birds including great skuas and Arctic skuas, Manx shearwaters and puffins.
On the hills there are red grouse, curlews, golden plovers and dunlins, as
well as peregrine falcons, merlins, kestrels and even golden eagles. Mountain hares are quite common and, if you are very lucky, you can also see
otters along the Scapa Flow coastline.

Hoy's great attraction is its many excellent **walking** opportunities. A minibus
runs between **Moaness Pier**, where the ferry from Stromness docks (see
Transport below), and **Rackwick**, on the opposite side of the island, but it's a
lovely two-hour walk by road through beautiful **Rackwick Glen**, once populated by crofters and fishermen, but now quiet and isolated. On the way you'll
pass the **Dwarfie Stone**, a huge, lonely block of sandstone which is the only
rock-cut tomb in Britain, dating from around 3000 BC. Be careful, though,
because according to Sir Walter Scott this is the residence of the *Trolld*, a dwarf
from Norse legend. On your return you can take a different route through a
narrow valley between the **Cuilags** (1,421 ft) and **Ward Hill** and **Berriedale
Wood**, the most northerly woodland in Britain. The most popular walk on Hoy
is the spectacular three-hour hike from Rackwick to the cliffs facing the **Old
Man of Hoy**. The path climbs steeply westwards from the old crofting township, then turns northwards before gradually descending to the cliff edge.

Walks on Hoy

On the southeast coast of the island is Lyness, site of a large naval base during
both world wars when the British fleet was based in Scapa Flow. Many of the
old dilapidated buildings have gone, but the harbour area is still scarred with
the scattered remains of concrete structures, and there's also the unattractive
sight of the huge oil terminal on **Flotta**. Lyness has a large **Naval Cemetery**,
last resting place of those who died at Jutland, of Germans killed during the
scuttle and of the crew of *HMS Royal Oak*. The old pump house opposite the
new ferry terminal is now the **Scapa Flow Visitor Centre**, a fascinating naval
museum with old photographs, various wartime artefacts, a section devoted
to the scuttling of the German Fleet, and an audio-visual feature on the history

**Lyness &
South Walls**

of Scapa Flow. Well worth a visit. ■ *Mid-May to mid-Sep Mon-Sat 0900-1630, Sun 1030-1545; Jul and Aug Mon-Sat 0900-1630, Sun 0945-1800; mid-Sep to mid-May Mon-Fri 0900-1630. Adult £2. T791300.*

At South Walls, overlooking Longhope Bay, is **Hackness Martello Tower and Battery** which, along with another tower on the north side at Crockness, was built in 1815 to protect British ships in Longhope Bay against attack by American and French privateers while they waited for a Royal Navy escort on their journey to Baltic ports. ■ *The tower is open to the public. If locked, a sign on the door will tell you where to get the key from.*

Sleeping & eating

There's not much accommodation in the north of the island, except for the two SYHA hostels. The larger of the two, **F** *Hoy Youth Hostel*, is about a mile from Moaness Pier. It's open from May-Sep. The smaller hostel is **F** *Rackwick Youth Hostel* in Rackwick Glen (open mid-Mar to mid-Sep). To book ahead for both hostels, contact Orkney Council, T873535, ext 2404. Near the pier and post office is the *Hoy Inn*, T791313, a bar and restaurant which serves good seafood (closed Mon). There's also an RSPB information centre here.

There are a few very good **B&Bs** in the south of the island. South of **Lyness** is **E** *Stoneyquoy*, T/F791234, www.visithoy.com The owner, Louise Budge, also runs guided tours of the island for £40 for up to 4 people, including lunch. On the other side of the bay in Longhope is **E-F** *Burnhouse*, T701263. Also in Longhope is the **E-F** *Old Custom House*, T701358. Near the ferry terminal in Lyness is **E** *The Hoy Hotel*, T791377. Open Apr-Oct, which serves meals. The *Anchor Bar*, T791356, in Lyness serves lunches. There are shops/petrol stations in Lyness and Longhope.

Transport

A passenger ferry sails between **Stromness** and Moaness Pier in the north (30 mins) 3 times a day Mon-Fri and twice on Fri evenings, twice daily Sat and Sun. There's a reduced winter service (mid-Sep to mid-May). There's also a car and passenger service between **Houton** and Lyness and Longhope (45 mins) up to 6 times daily (Mon-Sat). There's a limited Sun service from mid-May to mid-Sep.

Transport on Hoy is very limited. *North Hoy Transport*, T791315, runs a **minibus** service between Moaness Pier and Rackwick, which meets the 1000 ferry from Stromness. Call the same number for a taxi around the island.

Rousay, Egilsay and Wyre

Phone code: 01856 These three islands lie a short distance off the northeast coast of Mainland and, together with Shapinsay to the southeast, are the closest of Orkney's North Isles to Kirkwall.

Rousay

Rousay is a hilly island about five miles in diameter and known as the 'Egypt of the North' due to the large number of archaeological sites. It also has the important **Trumland RSPB Reserve**, home to merlins, hen harriers, peregrine falcons, short-eared owls and red-throated divers, and its three lochs offer good trout fishing.

Getting around You can take one of the very informative **minibus tours** run by *Rousay Traveller*, T821234. These run from Jun-early Sep Tue-Fri, meeting the 1040 ferry from Tingwall and lasting 6 hrs. Tours: adult £15, students/OAPs £12, children £6. **Bike hire** is available from *Arts, Crafts & Bike Hire* at the pier, T821398.

A road runs right around the island, and makes a pleasant 13-mile bike run, but most of the sights are within walking distance of the ferry pier on the southeast side of the island, where most of the 200 inhabitants live. A short distance west of the pier by the road is **Tavershoe Tuick**, an unusual two-storey burial cairn, which was discovered in the late 19th century by Mrs Burroughs, wife of General Traill Burroughs who lived at nearby Trumland House. A mile further west, to the north of the road, is **Blackhammer**, a stalled Neolithic burial cairn. Further west, and a steep climb up from the road, is **Knowe of Yarso**, another stalled cairn, which contained the remains of at least 21 people. The tomb dates from around 2900 BC.

Most of the island's archaeological sights are to be found along the **Westness Walk**, a mile-long walk which starts from Westness Farm, about four miles west of the ferry pier, and ends at the remarkable Midhowe Cairn. The walk is described in detail in a leaflet available from the tourist offices on Mainland. **Midhowe Cairn** is the largest and longest thus far excavated on Orkney – over 100 ft long and 40 ft wide – and, like the others, dates from around 3000 BC. Housed in a large building to protect it, the 'Great Ship of Death', as it is known, contained the remains of 25 people in crouched position on or under the eastern shelves of the chamber, which is divided into 12 sections. Standing nearby, with fine views across to Eynehallow island, is **Midhowe Broch**, one of the best-preserved brochs on Orkney, occupied from around 200 BC to 200AD. The outer walls are about 60 ft in diameter and up to 14 ft high in places.

Another fine walk on the island is around the **RSPB Reserve**. A footpath leads from beside Trumland House and heads up towards the island's highest point, **Blotchnie Field** (821 ft). A leaflet describing the walk is available from the tourist offices on Mainland or the **Trumland Orientation Centre** by the pier.

Sleeping and eating Accommodation on Rousay is very limited. Near Knowe of Yarso, about 2 miles west of the pier, is the **E-D** *Taversoe Hotel*, T821325, which offers excellent-value meals. The seafood is particularly recommended (closed Mon to non-residents). The only other option is the **F** *Rousay Hostel* at Trumland Organic Farm, T821252, open all year and half a mile from the ferry. It has laundry facilities and you can also camp. The *Pier Restaurant,* beside the pier, serves food at lunchtime (cheap to mid-range).

Transport A small car **ferry** sails from **Tingwall** (20 mins) to **Rousay** 6 times a day (Mon-Sat; 5 times on Sun). Most of the ferries call in at **Egilsay** and **Wyre**, but some are on demand only and should be booked in advance, T751360. A bus connects Tingwall and Kirkwall (see page 603).

These two small islands lie to the east of Rousay and have a couple of interesting sights of their own. Egilsay's claim to fame is the murder here of St Magnus in 1115, and a **cenotaph** marks the spot where he was slain. The island is dominated by the 12th-century **St Magnus church**, built on the site of an earlier church, possibly as a shrine to St Magnus. It is the only surviving example on Orkney of a round-towered Viking church. Much of Egilsay has been bought by the RSPB as a reserve to preserve the habitat of the very rare **corncrake**, whose distinctive rasping call may be heard.

Tiny Wyre features strongly in the Viking saga as the domain of Kolbein Hruga, and the remains of his 12th-century stronghold, **Cubbie Roo's Castle**, and nearby **St Mary's chapel** can be still be seen. Kolbein's home, or *Bu*, was on the site of the nearby **Bu Farm**, where the poet **Edwin Muir** (1887-1959) spent part of his childhood. The far westerly point of the island, known as **the Taing**, is a favourite haunt of seals, and a great place to enjoy a summer sunset.

Egilsay & Wyre

Orkney and Shetland

Shapinsay

Phone code: 01856 Less than 30 minutes by ferry from Kirkwall is the fertile, low-lying island of Shapinsay. The main attraction is **Balfour Castle**, an imposing baronial pile which is in fact a Victorian extension to a much older house called 'Cliffdale'. The house, and the rest of the island, was bought by successive generations of the Balfour family who had made their fortune in India. Today the castle is the home of the Zawadski family and can only be visited as part of an inclusive half-day tour. ■ *Tour leaves from Kirkwall on Wed and Sun May-Sep, on the 1415 ferry. Tours must be arranged in advance at the tourist office in Kirkwall. They cost around £15 per person which includes ferry ticket, guided tour of the castle and gardens (at 1500) and complimentary tea and cakes in the servants' quarters. You can take an earlier ferry if you wish to explore the island. T872856.*

In the village, built by the Balfours to house their estate workers, is the **Shapinsay Heritage Centre**, in the old Smithy. It has displays on the island's history and a tearoom upstairs. ■ *Mon, Tue and Thu-Sat 1200-1630, Wed and Sun till 1730. Free. T711258.*

A mile north of the village is the **Mill Dam RSPB Reserve**, where there's a hide overlooking a loch from which you can see many species of wildfowl and waders. Four miles from the pier, at the far northeast corner of the island, is the well-preserved **Burroughston Broch**, with good views of seals sunning themselves on the nearby rocks. West of here, at **Quholme**, is the original birthplace of the father of **Washington Irving**, author of *Rip Van Winkle*.

Sleeping & eating You can stay at **C** *Balfour Castle*, T711282, www.balfourcastle.co.uk, and enjoy all that Victorian splendour. The price includes dinner. The castle has a private chapel and a boat is available for bird watching and fishing trips for residents. Alternatively, there's comfortable B&B in the humbler surroundings of **E** *Girnigoe*, T711256, near the northern end of Veantro Bay. It also offers evening meals. There's a **pub** in the village, in the old gatehouse. Also 2 shops and a post office.

Transport The small car **ferry** makes 6 sailings daily (including Sun in summer) from **Kirkwall** (25 mins).

Eday

Phone code: 01857 The long, thin and sparsely populated island of Eday lies at the centre of the North Isles group. It is less fertile than the other islands, but its heather-covered hills in the centre have provided peat for the other peatless Orkney islands. Eday's sandstone has also been quarried, and was used in the building of St Magnus Cathedral in Kirkwall.

Ins & outs **Getting there** There are **flights** from Kirkwall to Eday airport (called London Air-
See Transport on next page port). There are also **ferries** from Kirkwall. The ferry pier is at Backaland, on the southeast of the island, a long way from the main sights. **Getting around** *Orkney Ferries*, T872044, also run the **Eday Heritage Tour**.

The island has numerous chambered cairns and these, along with the other attractions, are concentrated in the northern part. They are all covered in the signposted five-mile **Eday Heritage Walk**, which starts from the *Community Enterprises Shop* and leads up to the Cliffs of Red Head at the northern tip. The walk takes about three hours to complete, and it's worth picking up the *Eday Heritage Walk* leaflet.

The walk starts at Mill Bay and heads past **Mill Loch**, where an RSPB hide allows you to watch rare red-throated divers breeding in spring and summer. Further north is the huge, 15-ft tall **Stone of Setter**, the largest standing stone in Orkney and visible from most of the chambered cairns. Close by are the **Fold of Setter**, a circular enclosure dating back to 2000 BC, and the **Braeside** and **Huntersquoy** chambered cairns. Further north along the path is **Vinquoy Chambered Cairn**, one of the finest in Orkney and similar to the better-known tomb at Maes Howe, dating from around the same time. An acrylic dome provides light to the main chamber, which can be entered by a narrow underground passage.

The path continues to the summit of **Vinquoy Hill**, which commands excellent views of the surrounding islands of Westray and Sanday. From here you can continue north to the spectacular red sandstone cliffs at **Red Head**, home to nesting guillemots, razorbills and puffins in summer, or head southeast along the coast to **Carrick House**. Built for Lord Kinclaven, Earl of Carrick, in 1633, the house is best known for its associations with the pirate, John Gow, whose ship ran aground during a failed attack on the house. He was captured and taken to London for trial and hanged. Sir Walter Scott's novel, *The Pirate*, is based on this story. ■ *Mid-Jun to mid-Sep guided tour at 1400. £2. T622260.*

Sleeping & eating

There's B&B at **E** *Mrs Poppelwell's*, T622248, at Blett, Carrick Bay, opposite the Calf of Eday. She also provides evening meal and packed lunch, and has a self-catering cottage nearby for up to 3. Also **D** *Mrs Cockram*, T622271. Open Jun-Mar, at Skaill Farm, just south of the airport. Price includes dinner. There's a basic *Youth Hostel*, T622206, open Apr-Sep, run by Eday Community Enterprises, just north of the airport.

Transport

There are **flights** from **Kirkwall** to Eday with *Loganair*, T872494, on Wed only. There are **ferries** from **Kirkwall** (1 hr 15 mins to 2 hrs) twice daily via **Sanday** or Stronsay.

Orkney Ferries, T872044, also run the **Eday Heritage Tour** every Sun from mid-Jun to mid-Sep. It leaves Kirkwall at 0920 and return at 1955 and costs around £30 per person, which includes ferries, guided walks or minibus tour, entry to Carrick House and lunch. Book with *Orkney Ferries* or at the tourist office in Kirkwall. You can hire a **taxi** from Mr A Stewart by the pier, T622206; or **hire bikes** from Mr Burkett at Hamarr, near the post office south of Mill Loch.

Sanday

Sanday is the largest of the North Isles, 12 miles long and flat as a pancake except for the cliffs at Spurness. It is well-named, as its most notable feature is its sweeping bays of sparkling white sand backed by machair, and turquoise seas.

Phone code: 01857

Ins & outs

There are **flights** to Sanday from Kirkwall and also a **ferry** service. The ferry arrives at **Loth**, at the southern tip of the island, and is met by a **minibus** which will take you to most places.

There are numerous burial mounds all over the island, the most impressive being **Quoyness Chambered Cairn**, a 5,000 year-old tomb similar to Maes Howe. The 13 ft-high structure contains a large main chamber with six smaller cells opening through low entrances. Most of the burial tombs remain unexcavated, such as those at **Tofts Ness** at the far northeastern tip, where there are over 500 cairns, making it potentially one of the most important prehistoric sites in Britain. At **Scar**, in Burness, a spectacular Viking find was made recently, and at **Pool** a major excavation has uncovered the remains of at least 14 Stone-Age houses.

Sanday is known for its **knitwear**, though the factory unfortunately closed down recently. You can still visit the *Orkney Angora craft shop*, in Upper Breckan, near the northern tip of the island, T600421.

Sleeping & eating

There are a couple of hotels, the **E** *Belsair Hotel*, T600206, joy:@sanday.quista.net, which serves meals; and the **E** *Kettletoft Hotel*, T/F600217, which also serves meals and has a lively bar. Both are in Kettletoft, where the ferry used to dock. There's also a handful of **B&Bs** including **E-F** *Quivals*, T600467, run by Tina and Bernie Flett. Tina also runs the ferry bus service and Bernie runs a **car and bike hire** service, T600418. Bernie also runs full-day **tours** of the island, on Wed and Fri, from mid-May to early Sep, departing from **Kirkwall** pier at 1010 and returning at 1940 (around £30 per person, minimum of 4 people).

Transport

There are *Loganair* **flights** to Sanday from **Kirkwall** twice daily Mon-Fri and once on Sat. There's a **ferry** service twice daily from **Kirkwall** (1 hr 30 mins).

Stronsay

Phone code: 01857

The peaceful, low-lying island of Stronsay has some fine sandy beaches and cliffs which attract large colonies of grey seals and nesting seabirds. There are few real sights on this largely agricultural island, but the coastline has some pleasant walks. One of the best is to the **Vat of Kirbister** in the southeast, a spectacular '*gloup*' or blow-hole spanned by the finest natural arch in Orkney. To the south of here, at **Burgh Head**, you'll find nesting puffins and the remains of a ruined broch, and at the southeastern tip, at **Lamb Head**, is a large colony of grey seals, lots of seabirds and several archaeological sites.

Ins & outs

There are **flights** to Stronsay from Kirkwall, as well as a **ferry** service. See also Transport below.

The main settlement is the quiet village of **Whitehall**, on the northeast coast where the ferry arrives. It's hard to believe it now, but this was one of the largest herring ports in Europe. During the boom years of the early 20th century 300 steam drifters were working out of Whitehall and nearly 4,000 fishing crew and shore workers were employed. In the peak year of 1924 over 12,000 tons of herring were landed here, to be cured (salted) and exported to Russia and Eastern Europe. Whitehall developed considerably and the *Stronsay Hotel* was said to have the longest bar in Scotland. On Sundays during July and August there were so many boats tied up that it was possible to walk across them to the little island of **Papa Stronsay**. By the 1930s, however, herring stocks were severely depleted and the industry was in decline. The old **Fish Mart** by the pier houses a **heritage centre** with photos and artefacts from the herring boom days. It also has a café and hostel (see below). ■ *May-Sep 1100-1700. Free. T616360.*

Prior to the herring boom, Stronsay's economic mainstay was the **kelp industry**. By the end of the 18th century 3,000 people were employed in the collection of seaweed and production of kelp for export, to be used in making iodine, soap and glass.

The **F** *Stronsay Fish Mart Hostel*, T616360. Open all year, is well-equipped and comfortable (see above). The **E** *Stronsay Hotel*, T616213, www.stronsayhotel.com, is being refurbished and offers cheap bar food. There's **B&B** at **F** *Stronsay Bird Reserve*, T616363, on Mill Bay to the south of Whitehall; where you can also **camp** overlooking the wide sandy bay. At the southern end of the island is the very basic and very cheap *Torness Camping Barn*, T616314, on the shore of Holland Bay near Lea-shun Loch. They also organize nature walks to the nearby seal-hide. Phone for pick-up from the ferry. Other eating options are the café at the *Fish Mart*, which does cheap meals, and the *Woodlea Takeaway* along the shore (open Wed 2130-2300, Fri-Sun 1630-1830 and 2100-2300).

Sleeping & eating

There are *Loganair* **flights** to Stronsay from Kirkwall, twice daily Mon-Fri. A **ferry** service runs from **Kirkwall** (1 hr 30 mins) twice daily Mon-Sat (once on Sun), and once daily Mon-Sat from Eday (35 mins).

Car hire and **taxis** are available from *DS Peace*, T616335. Taxis and **island minibus tours** are available from M Williamson, T616255.

Transport

Westray

Westray is the second largest of the North Isles, with a varied landscape of farmland, hilly moorland, sandy beaches and dramatic cliffs. It is also the most prosperous of the North Isles, producing beef, fish and seafood, and supports a population of 700. The main settlement is **Pierowall**, in the north of the island, but, though it has one of the best harbours in Orkney, the main ferry terminal is at **Rapness**, on the south coast.

Phone code: 01857

Getting there There are **flights** to Westray from Kirkwall. The airport is in the far northeastern corner of the island. There's a **car ferry** service from **Kirkwall** to Rapness, on the south coast of the island.

Getting around There are **guided minibus tours** of Westray which connect with the ferry at Rapness. For more information and details of cycle hire and other tours, see next page.

Ins & outs

Pierowall is a relatively large village for the North Isles and there are several shops, a post office, a hotel and the **Westray Heritage Centre**, with displays on local and natural history, and a tearoom. ■ *Early May to late Sep Tue-Sat 0930-1230 and 1400-1700. £2.* Also in the village is the ruined 17th-century **St Mary's church**. About a mile west of the village is Westray's most notable ruin, the impressive **Notland Castle**, a fine example of a 16th-century fortified Z-plan tower-house. ■ *The castle is managed by Historic Scotland. 11 Jun-30 Sep daily 0930-1830. Adult £1.50, concession £1.10, children £0.50. Phone Skara Brae T01856-841815.*

Pierowall

There are some great coastal **walks** on the island, particularly to the spectacular sea cliffs at **Noup Head**, at the far northwestern tip, which are an **RSPB Reserve** and second only to St Kilda in terms of breeding seabirds, with huge colonies of guillemots, razorbills, kittiwakes and fulmars, as well as puffins. The cliffs on the west coast of Westray are five miles long and there's an excellent walk down the coast from Noup Head, past **Gentleman's Cave**, used as a hiding place by four Jacobite lairds in 1746. Near the southern end of the walk is **Fitty Hill** (554 ft), the highest point on the island, which you can climb for great views, and the walk ends at **Inga Ness**, where you can also see puffins. The best place to see puffins is at **Castle o' Burrian**, a sea stack on **Stanger Head**, on the southeastern coast near the Rapness ferry terminal.

Walks on the island

Orkney and Shetland

Sleeping The best place to stay is **C-D** *Cleaton House Hotel*, T677508, www.orknet.co.uk/cleaton A converted Victorian manse about 2 miles southeast of Pierowall. It serves excellent meals in the restaurant (1900-2100) and in the bar (1200-1400, 1800-2100). In the village is the **E** *Pierowall Hotel*, T677208, www.orknet.co.uk/pierwall, which is less stylish, but comfortable and friendly. It also serves good-value bar meals. There are also several B&Bs, including **E-F** *Sand o' Gill*, T677374, where you can also camp or hire their self-catering caravan.

Transport **Flights** to Westray with *Loganair* depart Kirkwall twice daily Mon-Fri and once on Sat. There's a **car ferry** service from **Kirkwall** to Rapness, on the south coast of the island (1 hr 30 mins). It sails twice daily in summer (mid-May to mid-Sep) and once daily in winter. There's also a **passenger ferry** from Pierowall to **Papa Westray** (see below).

There are **guided minibus tours** of Westray with Alex Costie of *Island Explorer*, T677355, which connect with the ferry at Rapness and cost £20 for a full day. *J & M Marcus* at Pierowall also run bus tours and offer **car hire**. For **cycle hire** contact Mrs Groat at *Sand o' Gill* (see above); or Mrs Bain at *Twiness*, T677319. For **boat trips** to Papa Westray contact Tom Rendall, T677216. *Discover Orkney*, T/F01856-872865, run **day tours** on a Sun to Westray from Kirkwall, leaving at 0940 and returning at 2015, and costing around £30 per person including ferry. They also run a day tour on a Mon to Papa Westray.

Papa Westray

Phone code: 01857 Tiny Papa Westray, known locally as 'Papay', can be reached on the world's shortest scheduled flight – all of two minutes – from Westray, but there are other reasons to visit this little island, one of the most remote of the Orkney group.

Ins & outs As well as the above-mentioned 2-minute **flight** from Westray, there is also a direct
See Transport below flight from Kirkwall. There's a **passenger ferry** from **Pierowall** on Westray, and **car ferry** from **Kirkwall**.

Papay is home to Europe's oldest house, the **Knap of Howar**, which was built around 5,500 years ago and is still standing (they knew how to build 'em in those days). It's on the west coast, just south of the airport. Half a mile north is **St Boniface Kirk**, one of the oldest Christian sites in the north of Scotland, founded in the 8th century, though most of the recently restored building dates from the 12th century. Inland from the Knap of Howar is **Holland Farm**, former home of the lairds of the island, where you can rummage around the farm buildings and the small **museum**. ■ *Open at all times. Free.*

Papay is famous for its birds, and **North Hill**, on the north of the island, is an important **RSPB Reserve**. The cliffs are home to many thousands of breeding seabirds, and at Fowl Craig on the east coast you can see nesting puffins. The interior is home to the largest arctic tern colony in Europe, as well as many arctic skuas. If you wish to explore you have to contact the warden at Rose Cottage, T644240, who runs regular guided walks.

It's worth taking a boat trip to the even tinier, deserted **Holm of Papay**, off the east coast. This is the site of several Neolithic burial cairns, including one of the largest **chambered cairns** on Orkney. You enter the tomb down a ladder into the main chamber which is nearly 70 ft long, with a dozen side-cells. ■ *Contact Jim Davidson, T644259, for boat trips between May and Sep.*

Sleeping There are few options for sleeping. One is the **D-E** *Beltane House Guest House*,
& eating T644267, a row of converted farm workers' cottages to the east of Holland House. It

offers dinner (mid-range). It's run by the island community co-operative, as is the 16-bed **F** *Papa Westray Hostel*, T644267. Open all year, housed in the same complex at Beltane. The co-operative also runs a shop and restaurant serving lunch and evening meals. They have a **minibus** which takes ferry passengers from the pier to anywhere on the island.

The famous **flight** from Westray leaves twice daily Mon-Sat (£14 one-way). There is also a direct flight to Papay from **Kirkwall** daily Mon-Sat, except Fri (£15 one-way). There's a **passenger ferry** from **Pierowall** on Westray 3-6 times daily (25 mins). The **car ferry** from **Kirkwall** to Westray continues to Papa Westray on Tue and Fri (2 ¼ hrs).

Transport

North Ronaldsay

Remote and storm-battered, North Ronaldsay is the most northerly of the Orkney islands and a place where old Orcadian traditions remain. It seems remarkable that anyone should live here at all in these extreme conditions, but 'North Ron'–as it is known locally–has been inhabited for many centuries and continues to be heavily farmed. The island's sheep are a hardy lot and live exclusively off the seaweed on a narrow strip of beach, outside a 13-mile stone dyke which surrounds the island. This gives their meat a unique, 'gamey' flavour.

This small, flat island, only three miles long, has few real attractions, except to keen ornithologists who flock here to catch a glimpse of its rare migrants. From late March to early June and mid-August to early November there are huge numbers of migratory birds. The **Bird Observatory**, in the southwest corner of the island by the ferry pier, gives information on which species have been sighted, as well as providing accommodation. There are also colonies of grey seals and cormorants at **Seal Skerry**, on the northeast tip of the island.

You can stay at the **E** *North Ronaldsay Bird Observatory*, T633200, alison@nrbo.prestel.co.uk It offers wind-and solar-powered full-board accommodation in private rooms or dorms. Full-board accommodation is also available at **D-E** *Garso House*, T633244, christine.muir@virgin.net, about 3 miles from the ferry pier. They also have a self-catering cottage (up to 5 people) and can arrange **car hire, taxis** or **minibus tours**. The *Burrian Inn and Restaurant* is the island's pub, and also serves **food**. **Camping** is possible on the island, contact, T633222.

Sleeping & eating

There are *Loganair* **flights** from **Kirkwall** twice daily Mon-Sat, T01856-872494. There's a car and passenger **ferry** which sails from **Kirkwall** (2 hrs 40 mins) once a week (usually Fri) and also on some Sun between May and Sep. Contact *Orkney Ferries* for details, T01856-872044.

Transport

Shetland

Shetland is so far removed from the rest of Scotland it can only be shown as an inset on maps. In fact, it is easier and quicker to get there from Norway than it is from London. This seems entirely appropriate, for Shetland is historically and culturally closer to Scandinavia than Britain. Many of its place-names are of Norse origin, and people here still celebrate ancient Viking festivals, such as Up Helly-Aa.

Modern-day visitors tend to come by plane rather than longboat, and usually bring binoculars, for Shetland is a birdwatchers' paradise. It is home to countless bird species, many of them seeking refuge from the madding crowds. And, let's face it, there's no better place than here to get away from it all.

Ins and outs

Getting there

Air Shetland has good air connections with the rest of the UK. There are regular flights to and from several mainland airports which are operated by *British Airways'* franchise partners *Loganair* and *British Regional Airlines*, T08457-733377. Shetland's main airport is at **Sumburgh**, 25 miles south of Lerwick, T01950-460654.

There are direct daily flights from **Aberdeen** (4 Mon-Fri; 2 on Sat and Sun), which has frequent services to all other major British airports. There are also direct flights from **Glasgow** (daily), **Edinburgh** (daily except Sun), **London Heathrow** (daily), **Inverness** (Mon-Fri), **Orkney** (daily except Sun), **Wick** (Mon-Sat) and **Belfast** (daily except Sat). There are also international flights to and from **Bergen** and **Oslo** (Norway) on Thu and Sun.

Flying to Shetland is expensive. From Aberdeen a special return fare costs £110-180, and a standard one-way ticket is around £125. A special tourist fare of £80-90 return is available between Orkney and Shetland. For details of the excellent value **Highland Rover Pass**, see page 44.

There's a 50% discount on vehicle fares on some midweek sailings

Boat *P&O Scottish Ferries*, T01224-572615, www.poscottishferries.co.uk, operate car ferries to **Lerwick** from **Aberdeen** and **Stromness** (Orkney). There are sailings from Aberdeen once a day Mon-Fri; the journey takes 14 hrs. Passenger fares for a seat with no accommodation cost from £58 one-way (return costs double), depending on the times of year. Cars cost from £179-188 return. For details of ferries from Stromness, see page 596. Children aged 4-14 travel for half price and under 4s go free. There are also ferries from **Norway**, **Iceland** and the **Faroe Isles**, see page 36.

Getting around

Air There is a regular scheduled inter-island service from **Tingwall Airport** near Lerwick, with *Loganair*, T01595-840246, to the islands of **Foula** (£42 return), **Fair Isle** (£74 return), **Papa Stour** (£32 return) and **Out Skerries** (£36 return).

A frequent ferry service links the larger islands with the Shetland Mainland

Boat There are regular daily car ferries between **Lerwick** and **Bressay** (5 mins), **East Mainland** and **Whalsay** (30 mins), **North Mainland** and **Yell** (20 mins), **Yell** and **Unst** (10 mins), and **Yell** and **Fetlar** (25 mins). Fares on all these routes are £1.20 per passenger and £2.90 per car. There's a less frequent car ferry service between **East Mainland** and **Skerries** (Mon, Fri, Sat and Sun; 1 hr 30 mins), and **Lerwick** and **Skerries** (Tue and Thu; 2 hrs 30 mins). Fares on these routes are £2.10 per passenger and £2.90 per car. Bookings are essential. There's also a passenger/cargo ferry service between **West Mainland** and **Papa Stour** (Mon, Wed, Fri, Sat and Sun; 40 mins), **West Mainland** and **Foula** (Tue, Sat and alternate Thu; 2 hrs), **Scalloway** and **Foula** (alternate Thu; 3 hrs), **South Mainland** and **Fair Isle** (Tue, Sat and alternate Thu; 2 hrs 30 mins), and **Lerwick** and **Fair Isle** (alternate Thu; 4 ½ hrs). Fares on these routes are £2.20 for an adult single and bookings are also essential.

Hitching is also a feasible way to get around and is relatively safe

Road Shetland has around 500 miles of good roads, and an extensive public **bus service** links Lerwick with all towns, villages and tourist sights. There are several bus operators. For detailed information on all bus services, call T:01595-694100 (Mon-Sat 0900-1715). A Shetland Transport Timetable, published by Shetland Islands Council, contains details of all air, sea and bus services throughout the islands. It is available from the tourist office in Lerwick.

The best way to explore the islands is with your own **private car**. It is cheaper to **hire** a car in Lerwick rather than at the airport. For a list of car hire firms see page 626. **Cycling** is a good way to experience the islands, though most places are very exposed and the winds can be strong.

Lerwick

Lerwick is the capital and administrative centre of Shetland and the only size-able town. Though the islands have been inhabited for many centuries, Lerwick only dates from the 17th century, when it began to grow as a trading port for Dutch herring fishermen, thanks to its superb natural sheltered harbour, the Bressay Sound. The town spread along the waterfront, where merchants built their *lodberries*, which were houses and warehouses with their own piers so that they could trade directly with visiting ships. By the late 19th century Lerwick had become the main herring port in northern Europe.

Phone code: 01595
Colour map 6, grid B2
Population: 7,600

Lerwick has continued to grow and is now home to a third of Shetland's population. The discovery of **oil** in the North Sea in the early 1970s led to the building of the **Sullom Voe Oil Terminal**, and the effect on Lerwick has been dramatic. It is now the main transit point to the North Sea oil rigs and there have been major extensions to the harbour area, bringing increased shipping and prosperity to the town.

Ferries from Aberdeen arrive at the main Holmsgarth terminal, which is about a mile north of the old harbour. There's a regular **bus** service between Lerwick and Sumburgh airport (50 mins) run by *John Leask & Son*, T693162. **Taxis** (around £25) and **car hire** are also available. All island bus services start and end at the Viking bus station, which is on Commercial Road, a short distance north of the town centre. The town is small and everything is within easy walking distance.

Ins & outs

The main **Tourist Information Centre** is at Market Cross, on Commercial St, T693434,

Lerwick

	Sleeping		4 Grand	● Eating
■	1 Alder Lodge Guest House		5 Kveldsro House	1 Monty's Bistro
	2 Carradel Guest House		6 Old Manse	
	3 Fort Charlotte Guest House		7 Queens	
			8 Solheim Guest House	
			9 SYHA Hostel	

N
0 metres 200
0 yards 200

www.shetland-tourism.co.uk As well as booking accommodation, they are an excellent source of information, books, maps and leaflets, and will change foreign currency. Open May-Sep Mon-Fri 0800-1800, Sat 0800-1600, Sun 1000-1300; Oct-Apr Mon-Fri 0900-1700.

Sights The town's heart is the attractive **Commercial Street**, which runs parallel to the Esplanade. At the southern end are many old houses and *lodberries*, and you can continue south along the cliffs to the **Knab** or to lovely **Bain's beach**. *Lerwick Walks* is a leaflet detailing many interesting walks in and around town.

Overlooking the north end of Commercial Street is **Fort Charlotte**, built in 1665 and later rebuilt in 1780 and named after Queen Charlotte, George III's consort. It has since been used as a prison and Royal Naval Reserve base and, though there's little to see in the fort, there are fine views of the harbour from the battlements. ■ *Jun-Sep daily 0900-2200; Oct-May 0900-1600. Free.* One of Lerwick's most impressive buildings is the Victorian **town hall**, on Hillhead. The stained-glass windows of the main hall depict episodes from Shetland's history. ■ *Mon-Fri 1000-1200 and 1400-1530. Free.*

Opposite the town hall, above the library, is the **Shetland Museum**, which gives a useful introduction to the islands' history. Amongst the artefacts on display is a replica of the St Ninian's Isle treasure. ■ *Mon, Wed and Fri 1000-1900; Tue, Thu and Sat till 1700. Free. T695057.*

Also in town is the **Up Helly-Aa Exhibition**, in the Galley Shed off St Sunniva Street. This gives a taste of the famous Viking fire festival held annually in Lerwick on the last Tuesday in January, when a torch-lit procession through the town by hundreds of people dressed in Viking costumes (*guizers*) is followed by a replica Viking longship built especially for the event. At the end of the procession the ship is set ablaze when the *guizers* throw their flaming torches on to it. ■ *Mid-May to mid-Sep Tue 1400-1600 and 1700-1900, Fri 1700-1900, Sat 1400-1600. Adult £2.50, concession £1.*

A mile west of town are the substantial remains of **Clickimin Broch**, a fortified site occupied from 700 BC to around the fifth or sixth century AD. A path leads to the site from opposite the *Safeway* supermarket on the A970. ■ *Always open. Free.*

About a mile north of the ferry terminal is the **Böd of Gremista**, a restored 18th-century fishing *böd* (booth) which was the birthplace of Arthur Anderson (1791-1868), co-founder of the Peninsular and Oriental Steam Navigation Company, now *P&O*. One of the rooms features an exhibition on Anderson's life and involvement with *P&O*. ■ *Jun to mid-Sep Wed and Sun 1000-1300 and 1400-1700. Free.*

Sleeping Shetland's best accommodation is outside Lerwick, whose hotels are mostly geared towards the oil industry. During the peak months of Jul and Aug and the Folk Festival in Apr, it's a good idea to book in advance.

The most luxurious hotel in town is the **B** *Kveldsro House Hotel*, Greenfield Pl, T692195, www.kghotels.co.uk Pronounced 'kel-ro', it overlooks the harbour and has an upmarket (and expensive) restaurant as well as cheaper bar food. Directly opposite the ferry terminal is the modern **B** *Shetland Hotel*, T695515; and 10 mins from the centre is the **B** *Lerwick Hotel*, 15 South Rd, T692166, reception@lerwickhotel.co.uk, which has a reputation for fine cuisine. In the centre is the **B** *Grand Hotel*, Commercial St, T692826, which features Shetland's only nightclub; and by the harbour is the rather faded **B-C** *Queen's Hotel*, Commercial St, T692826.

There are several pleasant guest houses and B&Bs, including **D-E** *Fort Charlotte Guest House*, 1 Charlotte St, T695956; **D** *The Old Manse*, 9 Commercial St, T696301; **D** *Alder Lodge Guest House*, 6 Clairmont Pl, T695705, **D-E** *Carradel Guest House*, 36 King Harald

Island tours

Shetland Wildlife Tours,T01950-422483, www.shetland-wildlife-tours.zetnet.co.uk Offer a number of guided tours to see the islands' outstandingly rich selection of wildlife; ranging from the excellent-value £20 trip around Noss and Bressay, where , if you go at the right time of year, you are almost guaranteed to see seals, porpoises and the astounding gannetry on the spectacular cliffs of Noss' east coast, to the more upmarket week-long 'Ultimate Shetland' tour, at around £700.

*There are also Noss & Bressay Wildlife Cruises with **Bressaboats**,T01595-693434, and **Shetland Sea Charters** (same phone number), which cost around £20. Bressaboats and Shetland Wildlife Tours both run a full-day Hermaness and Muckle Flugga Cruise which costs around £70 per person. A variety of **bus tours** are available with **John Leask & Son**, The Esplanade, Lerwick, T01595-693162. These cost from around £10 up to £20 depending on the destination.*

St, T692251; and next door, **D-E** *Solheim Guest House*, T695275. Lerwick's clean, well-run **F** *SYHA* hostel is at Islesburgh House, King Harald St, T692114, open Apr-Sep.

There's **camping** at *Clickimin Caravan & Camp Site*, T741000, near Clickimin Leisure Centre and loch on the western edge of town.

The best place to eat in Lerwick is *Monty's Bistro & Deli*, 5 Mounthooly St, T696655. It offers good modern Scottish cooking in a cosy, informal setting. Lunch cheap; dinner mid-range. Closed Sun. The next best choice is dinner or bar lunch at the *Kveldsro Hotel* and *Lerwick Hotel* (see above). Best place for a curry is the moderately-priced *Raba* Indian Restaurant, 26 Commercial Rd, T695585. *Osla's Café*, T696005, on Mounthooly St, is a cosy café serving a wide range of coffees, pancakes and other snacks and boasting the islands' only beer garden. Open Mon-Sat till at least 1900, Sun 1200-1600.

Eating
Despite a ready supply of fresh local produce, Shetland is a gastronomic desert

The best place for a drink is the upstairs bar in the *Lounge*, on Mounthooly St near the tourist office, where local musicians usually play on Sat lunchtimes and some evenings. The town's only **nightclub** is *Posers*, at the *Grand Hotel*. **Folk music** has a strong following in Shetland and the islands play host to 2 of Scotland's top folk events. In **mid-Apr** the islands are alive with the sound of music as musicians from around the globe come to play at the *Shetland Folk Festival*. Later, in **mid-Oct**, is the *Shetland Accordion and Fiddle Festival*. For details of both events, contact the Folk Festival office, 5 Burns Lane, Lerwick, T694757. To find out what's going on, buy a copy of the *Shetland Times* on Fri, or check out their website, www.shetland-times.co.uk Also check the tourist board's Events phoneline, T694200.

Bars & entertainment

Clickimin Centre, Lochside, T741000. Sports and fitness centre open daily 0800-2300.

Sport

There are regular daily **buses** (Nos 3 and 4) to and from **Sumburgh airport** which connect with flights. These buses also stop at several main sights, including **Jarlshof**, **Sandwick** (for Mousa Broch) and **St Ninian's Isle**. Bus No 2 runs to **Scalloway** (Mon-Sat). There are also buses (daily except Sun) to **Walls**, **Sandness**, **Aith**, **Skeld**, **North Roe**, **Hillswick**, **Vidlin**, **Toft** and **Mossbank**. Buses depart from the Viking bus station. Full details are given in the **Shetland Transport Timetable**.

Car hire *Bolts Car Hire*, Toll Clock Shopping Centre, 26 North Rd, T693636. *John Leask & Son*, Esplanade, T693162. *Star Rent-a-Car*, 22 Commercial Rd, T692075. Both also have offices at Sumburgh Airport. **Cycle hire** *Grantfield Garage*, North Rd, T692709, Mon-Sat 0800-1300 and 1400-1700. There are several **taxi** companies in Lerwick: *6050 Cabs*, T696050; *Sheilds Taxis*, T695276; *Abbys Taxis*, T696666.

Transport
See page 622 for details of ferries and flights to and from Lerwick

See page 622 for details of ferries and flights to and from Lerwick

Orkney and Shetland

Close encounters of the bird kind

Shetland is famous for its birds. As well its huge seabird colonies, the islands attract Arctic species and are an important crossroads for migrating birds. Over 340 species have been recorded on Fair Isle, including rare and exotic birds from Asia and America. Twenty-one out of the 24 seabirds common to Britain breed in Shetland. These can be found around the coastline, but the largest colonies are at the **Hermaness** and **Noss** reserves.

Amongst the many species which can be seen are the puffin. About one fifth of Scotland's puffins breed in Shetland. Its cousins in the auk family, guillemots, and razorbills, are also here in abundance during the summer months, along with kittiwakes, shags and that most common of seabirds, the fulmar. Britain's largest seabird, the gannet, can be seen diving spectacularly for fish at Hermaness, Noss, Fair Isle and Foula, while its smallest seabird, the storm petrel, is best seen around dusk on the tiny island of Mousa.

Summer heralds the return of the Arctic tern which breeds along low coastlines, as do the eider, oystercatcher, ringed plover and black guillemot, or tystie, which stays here all year round. The best place to see waders and shelduck are the nutrient-rich tidal mudflats at the Pool of Virkie in the South Mainland.

Many birds breed on agricultural land, and these include the lapwing, skylark, meadow pipit and wheater. The hills and moorland provide breeding grounds for many summer visitors such as that pirate of the skies, the great skua, or bonxie, and the Arctic skua. Another Arctic species, the whimbrel, also nests here, mainly in Unst, Yell and Fetlar. Moorland habitats are also favoured by the curlew, golden plover and merlin, Shetland's only bird of prey, while the lochs are home to large numbers of red-throated divers. Fetlar is home to 90% of the population of one of Britain's rarest birds, the red-necked phalarope.

Many of Shetland's bird habitats are protected as **RSPB Reserves** and **National Nature Reserves,** and it is an offence to disturb the birds and their young at or near their nests. You also risk being dive-bombed by some of the more aggressively protective species. For a full list of all species recorded on the islands and more practical birdwatching information, be sure to get a copy of the **Shetland Bird Chart** by Joyce Gammack, available from the tourist office in Lerwick.

Directory **Banks** *Bank of Scotland*, **Clydesdale** and *Royal* are on Commercial St. *Lloyds TSB* is on the Esplanade. **Communications** **Post office** Commercial St (open Mon-Fri 0900-1700, Sat 0900-1200), also in Toll Clock Shopping Centre, 26 North Rd. **Embassies and consulates** Denmark, Iceland, Netherlands and Sweden at *Hay & Company*, 66 Commercial Rd, T692533; Finland, France, Germany and Norway at *Shearer Shipping Services*, Garthspool, T692556. **Laundry** *Lerwick Laundry*, 36 Market St, T693043, closed Sun. Service washes only. **Medical facilities** *Gilbert Bain Hospital*, Scalloway Rd, T743000. Opposite is the *Lerwick Health Centre*, T693201. **Travel agents** *John Leask & Son*, Esplanade, T693162.

Around Lerwick

Bressay & Noss
Colour map 6, grid B2/3

Lying to the east of Lerwick across the Bressay Sound is the island of Bressay (pronounced 'bressah'), which creates a sheltered harbour for the capital and led to its establishment as a major trading port. Bressay is only seven miles long by three miles wide, and makes an ideal day trip for **cyclists**. Another good way to get around is on foot, and there's a fine walk to the top of **Ward Hill** (742 ft), the highest point, from where you get great views of the island and as far afield as Foula and Out Skerries. There are also some good coastal

Shetland

walks, particularly along the cliffs from Noss Sound south to **Bard Head, The Ord** and **Bressay Lighthouse**, where you can see large colonies of seabirds.

Serious birdwatchers should head for **Noss**, a tiny, uninhabited island off the east coast of Bressay, which is a **National Nature Reserve** with over 100,000 pairs of breeding seabirds. A walk around the perimeter of the island takes at least three hours but is highly recommended. At the east side is the **Noup of Noss**, where the 600-ft cliffs are packed full of nesting gannets. The reserve is managed by Scottish Natural Heritage who have a small **visitor centre** at Gungstie.

Sleeping D-E *Maryfield House Hotel*, T820207, near the ferry terminal.

Transport Noss can only be visited from late May to late Aug daily, except Mon and Thu, from 1000-1700. There are regular car **ferries** from the old harbour in Lerwick to Bressay (see page 622). From the 'Wait here' sign overlooking Noss sound on the east side of Bressay an inflatable dinghy shuttles back and forth to Noss during the island's opening hours (see above). The trip costs £3 return. In bad weather, call the tourist office, T693434, to check if it's sailing. A **post car** service runs once a day (except Sunday) from Maryfield ferry terminal to Noss Sound, T820200.

Central Mainland

Scalloway
Phone code: 01595
Colour map 6, grid B2

The Central Mainland is Shetland's slim waist, and only a few miles of land separates the east and west coast. Six miles from Lerwick on the west coast is Scalloway, once the capital of Shetland and now a fishing port and fish-processing centre. In 1942, during The Second World War, Scalloway became the headquarters of the **Shetland Bus** operations. This was the name given to the Norwegian fishing boats which sailed to Shetland during the night from German-occupied Norway, bringing refugees to safety and returning with ammunition and resistance fighters. An interesting exhibition on the 'Shetland Bus' can be seen at **Scalloway Museum** on Main Street. ■ *May to Sep Tue-Thu 1400-1630, Sat 1000-1230 and 1400-1630. Donation requested.*

The harbour is dominated by the ruins of **Scalloway Castle**, built in 1600 by the notorious Earl Patrick Stewart using local slave labour (see page 600). After his execution the castle fell into disrepair, though the four-storey main block and one wing remain. Inside, an interpretative display explains its history. Next to the castle is the **Shetland Woollen Company**, T880243, where you can buy the famous Shetland wool and Fair Isle sweaters.

South of Scalloway lie the islands of **Trondra** and **Burra**, now connected to the Mainland by bridges. At Burland on Trondra is the **Spirit of Shetland**, T880437, where you can buy Shetland knitwear, while on West Burra is the attractive little fishing village of **Hamnavoe**.

Sleeping and eating There are a few places to stay in Scalloway. In the upper part of the village is **E** *Hildasay Guest House*, T880822, which has disabled facilities and arranges fishing trips. Eating options are limited to a bar meal at the *Scalloway Hotel* or *Kiln Bar*, or *Da Haaf Restaurant*, T880328, which is a canteen-style restaurant in the North Atlantic Fisheries college and specializes in (yes, you guessed it) seafood. Does a good fish supper, as well as having a more up-market menu for the evenings. Open Mon-Fri 0900-2000.

Transport There are several daily **buses** (except Sun) between Lerwick and Scalloway, operated by *Shalder Coaches*, T880217.

North of Scalloway, the B9074 runs through the fertile Tingwall Valley, past a nine-hole **golf course** at Asta, and the **Loch of Tingwall**, which is good for brown trout fishing and also home to swans and otters. At the northern end of the loch is a promontory called **Law Ting Holm**, which was the site of the *Althing*, or parliament, during the period of Norse rule. Overlooking the loch is **Tingwall Kirk**, built in the late 18th century on the site of the earlier church of St Magnus which dated back to the early period of Norse Christianity. In the graveyard is the old burial vault with several interesting old grave slabs. Nearby is **Tingwall Agricultural Museum**, which houses a collection of old crofting implements. ■ *Jun-Aug Mon-Sat 1000-1300 and 1400-1700. Adult £1.50.*

Tingwall
Phone code: 01595
Colour map 6, grid B2

Sleeping Near the airport, by the crossroads, is the **C** *Herrislea House Hotel*, T840208, www.herrislea-house.shetland.co.uk, which offers good home cooking daily till 2100, and live music in its *Starboard Tack* bar. In nearby Wormadale is the modern **C-D** *Westings Hotel*, T840242, www.westings.shetland.co.uk, which is a good place to stop for lunch.

Transport North of the museum is **Tingwall Airport**, T840246, which has flights to most of the smaller islands (see page 622). Getting to and from the airport is straightforward, as regular buses between Lerwick and Westside (see below) stop in Tingwall.

The A971 continues northwest towards Weisdale. At the head of **Weisdale Voe** the B9075 branches north to **Weisdale Mill**, which now houses the **Bonhoga Gallery**, a purpose-built art gallery featuring varied exhibitions of local, national and international works. There's also a nice café serving snacks. ■ *Wed-Sat 1030-1630, Sun 1200-1630. T830400.*

Weisdale
Phone code: 01595
Colour map 6, grid B2

Weisdale Mill was part of the Kergord estate, known until 1945 as Flemington, and was built from the stones of evacuated crofthouses. Over 300 crofters were forcibly evicted in the mid-19th century during the 'Clearances', when lairds expanded their more profitable sheep-farming activities. In 1940 the mill was requisitioned as the intelligence and administrative HQ for the 'Shetland Bus' operations (see Scalloway above). The Kergord estate today is the largest area of woodland in Shetland, and attracts a variety of migratory birds.

On the west shore of Weisdale Voe, south of the mill, are the ruins of the house where **John Clunies Ross** (1786-1854) was born. He settled in the Cocos Islands in the Indian Ocean in 1827 and proclaimed himself 'King'. After his death, the islands were ruled by his offspring until they became Australian territory, no doubt to the relief of the islanders.

The Westside

The western Mainland of Shetland, stretching west from Weisdale to Sandness, is known as The Westside. This part of Shetland is notable for its varied landscape of spectacular sea cliffs, rolling green hills, bleak moorland, peaty freshwater lochs and numerous long sea lochs, or *voes*. This is excellent **walking** country, with many fine coastal routes, especially around **Culswick** and **Dale of Walls**. It is also great for **birdwatching** and **trout fishing**, and there are many opportunities for spotting **whales, dolphins** and **otters**.

OS Landranger maps Nos 3 & 4

There are a few interesting archaeological sites here, too. At **Stanydale**, signposted from the road between the villages of **Bixter** and **Walls**, is the site of a Neolithic settlement with the remains of houses, field boundaries and clearance cairns. Near the **Brig o' Waas**, just north of Walls, is the **Scord of Brouster**, a prehistoric farm site which has been excavated.

A böd for the night

There is only one youth hostel in Shetland, but budget travellers shouldn't panic. The Shetland Camping Böd project has developed a network of camping böds (pronounced 'burd') which provide basic and cheap accommodation throughout the islands.

A Böd was a building used to house fishermen and their gear during the fishing season and the name has been used to describe these types of accommodation which are similar to English 'camping barns'. They are all located in scenically attractive places and

each has its own fascinating history.

They are very basic and the more remote ones have no electricity or lighting. You'll need to bring a stove, cooking and eating utensils, sleeping bag and torch (flashlight). All böds must be booked in advance through the tourist office in Lerwick. They cost £5 per person per night, though they can also be booked for exclusive use by large groups. They are open from the beginning of April till the end of September. There are at present six camping böds on Shetland and these are listed in the relevant places.

Walls
Phone code: 01595
Colour map 6, grid B1

The pretty little village of **Walls** (pronounced 'waas') is set around a sheltered natural harbour and is a popular spot with visiting yachts. It also attracts many visitors during its Agricultural Show in August, the biggest such event on Shetland.

Sleeping Walls also boasts the best accommodation on the Westside. Two miles southwest of the village is **B** *Burrastow House*, T809307, burr.hs.hotel@zetnet.co.uk, a restored 18th-century house overlooking Vaila Sound. It's full of character and has a reputation for serving superb cuisine (some say the best on the islands, so you'll need to book ahead). There's a **camping böd** in Walls, at *Voe House*, a restored 18th-century house overlooking the village. Open Apr-Sep. Book through Lerwick tourist office. A mile or so north of the village is **E** *Skeoverick*, T803349, a friendly B&B. At Gruting, east of Brig o' Waas is **E-F** *Pomona*, T810438.

Transport There are daily **buses** to Walls from Lerwick, Mon-Sat, with *Shalder Coaches*, T01595-880217. A **minibus** runs to Sandness from Walls once a day (except Sun). Contact Mr P Isbister, T809268.

Sandness
Northwest of Walls, the A971 crosses bleak moorland before descending to the crofting township of Sandness (pronounced 'saa-ness'), surrounded by fertile land and facing little Papa Stour, about a mile offshore. There's a good **beach** here and also a **woollen spinning mill**, where you can watch how they spin the famously fine wool into yarn. ■ *Mon-Fri 0800-1700, free.*

Foula
Walls is the departure point for **ferries** to the remote island of Foula, whose name derives from the Norse *fugl ey*, meaning 'bird island'. Lying 15 miles west of the Shetland Mainland, tiny Foula is the second most remote inhabited island after Fair Isle. It supports a population of around 40 people, who are greatly out-numbered by the many thousands of seabirds, including a small colony of gannets and the rare Leach's petrel. There are also about 2,500 pairs of great skuas, the largest colony in the UK. The island is dominated by its sheer cliffs, which reach their most awe-inspiring peak at **The Kame** (1,220 ft), the second highest sea cliffs in Britain after St Kilda.

An interesting feature of the island's people is that they still observe the old **Julian calendar**, replaced in 1752 in Britain by the present Gregorian system which deleted 11 days from the year. Remote areas of the country kept to the old calendar, adding an extra day in 1800, which was a leap year, and some parts of Shetland continued to observe festivals 12 days after the dates in the new calendar. The most remote areas kept to the old calendar longest, and the people of Foula still celebrate Christmas on 6 January and New Year's Day on 13 January.

Sleeping Those wishing to celebrate 2 Christmases or New Year's Days, or to stay and admire the bird life, can stay on the island at **E** *Leraback*, T753226, which includes dinner in the price. There is also self-catering accommodation available on the island, £90-150 per week for a cottage sleeping 4-6 people. Contact Mr R Holbourn, T753232.

For details of ferries and flights to Foula, see page 622.

A ferry sails from **West Burrafirth** on the Westside, near Sandness, to the little island of Papa Stour, only a mile offshore. The island, which has a population of around 30, is mostly made up of volcanic rock which has been eroded to form an amazing coastline of stacks, arches and caves, most spectacular of which is **Kirstan's Hole**. The island is home to large colonies of auks, terns and skuas, and also has a fascinating history of its own. Pick up the island trails leaflet from the tourist office in Lerwick.

Papa Stour
Colour map 6, grid B1

Essentials You can stay on the island at **D** *North House*, T873238, which offers full board. There's no shop on the island. For details of **ferries** and **flights** to Papa Stour, see page 622. Ferries should be booked with *W Clark*, T810460.

South Mainland

From Lerwick a long, narrow finger of land points south. The main road runs down the east coast for 25 miles till it ends at **Sumburgh Head**, near Shetland's main airport. This southern part of the Shetland Mainland holds the islands' two most important archaeological sights and main tourist attractions.

Phone code: 01950

About 10 miles south of Lerwick, just to the south of **Cunningsburgh**, is the **Catpund Quarries**, where soft soapstone was quarried from Neolithic to medieval times, and made into a variety of stone implements and utensils.

Fifteen miles south of Lerwick, the scattered crofting communities of **Sandwick** look across to the **Isle of Mousa**, site of the best-preserved broch in Scotland. This fortified tower was built around 2,000 years ago and still stands close to its original height of 45 ft. It's a very impressive structure when you see it from the inside and has chambers, galleries, an internal staircase and a parapet. The broch features in a Viking saga of the 12th century when the mother of Harald, Earl of Orkney, took refuge there with her lover. The Earl, who did not approve of the liaison, laid siege to the broch, but it proved impregnable and he gave up.

Mousa
Colour map 6, grid C2
Entry to the broch is free

Mousa island is also home to many seabirds and waders, most notably the Storm Petrel, which is best seen at dusk as they return to their nests amongst the beach rocks. You can also see seals on the white-sand beach at West Voe. If you have time, it's a good idea to walk right around the coast, starting from the landing stage at West Ham and first heading south to the broch. A **passenger ferry** sails to the island from **Leebitton harbour** in Sandwick daily from mid-April to mid-September, weather permitting, at 0930, 1230 and 1400, allowing visitors 2½ hours to see the island. The trip takes 15 minutes and costs £6.50 per adult. For bookings, call Tom Jamieson.

Allow about 2 hrs, and watch out for dive-bombing terns

Orkney and Shetland

Sleeping There's accommodation in Sandwick at the **E** *Barclay Arms Hotel*, T431226, which offers evening meals; and **F-E** *Solbrekke*, T431410.

Transport There are several daily **buses** (Mon-Sat; 2-3 on Sun) between Lerwick, Sandwick and Sumburgh Airport.

South of Sandwick At Hoswick, between Sandwick and Levenwick, is **Da Warp and Weft Visitor Centre**, which houses an exhibition on weaving, crofting, fishing and island life. ■ *May-Sep Mon-Sat 1000-1700, Sun 1200-1700. Free*. Next door is the **Shetland Woollen Company**, where you can buy knitwear.

Further south on the east coast, at Boddam, is the **Shetland Crofthouse Museum**, a restored thatched crofthouse with 19th-century furniture and utensils. ■ *May-Sep daily 1000-1300 and 1400-1700. £2*.

St Ninian's Isle to Quendale
Colour map 6, grid C2

On the west coast, near Bigton village, a signposted track leads to the spectacular sandy causeway (known as a tombolo) which leads to St Ninian's Isle. The tombolo is the best example of its kind in Britain, and you can walk across to the island which is best known for the hoard of Pictish treasure which was discovered in 1958 in the ruins of the 12th-century church. The 28 silver objects included bowls, a spoon and brooches, probably dating from around 800 AD, and are now on display in the Royal Scottish Museum in Edinburgh, though you can see replicas in the Shetland Museum in Lerwick. Two daily **buses** (not Sunday) run to Bigton from Lerwick, though you have to change at Channerwick junction.

The west coast south of Bigton is beautiful with long, sandy beaches interspersed with dramatic cliff scenery. On the other side of the road from the long, sheltered beach at **Scousburgh Sands** is the **Loch of Spiggie RSPB Reserve**. The loch is an important winter wildfowl refuge, particularly for Whooper Swans, and during the summer you can see various ducks, waders, gulls, terns and skuas. There's a hide on the northern shore with an information board. Nearby is the *Spiggie Hotel*, T01950-460409, which offers bar meals, afternoon tea or dinner.

A few miles south of the loch is the village of **Quendale,** overlooking a wide, sandy bay. Here you'll find the beautifully restored and fully working 19th-century **Quendale Mill**, the last of Shetland's watermills. ■ *May-Sep daily 1000-1700. Adult £1.50*.

Not far from here, between Garth's Ness and Fitful Head, lies the wreck of the *Braer* oil tanker which ran on to the rocks in 1993. A disaster of epic proportions was averted by the hurricane-force gales which dispersed the huge oil spillage.

Transport Two **buses** daily (Mon-Sat) run to Quendale from Lerwick, with a change at Channerwick junction.

Sumburgh & Jarlshof
Colour map 6, grid C2

At the southern tip of Mainland is the village of Sumburgh, site of Shetland's main **airport** for external passenger flights and for helicopters and planes servicing the North Sea oil industry. South of the airport is Shetland's prime archaeological site, **Jarlshof**, a hugely impressive place which spans 4,000 years of occupation, from Neolithic times through Norse settlement to the 16th century. The original Stone-Age dwellings are topped by a medieval broch, Pictish wheelhouses, Viking longhouses and, towering over the whole complex, the ruins of a 16th-century mansion. This remarkable site was only discovered at the end of the 19th century when a violent storm ripped off the top layer of turf. Jarlshof is, in fact, not a genuine name, but the exotic invention of Sir Walter Scott in his novel *The Pirate*. A helpful guidebook available from the visitor centre helps to bring the place to life. ■ *Apr-Sep daily 0930-1830. Adult £2.80, concession £2, children £1. T460112 (HS).*

South of Jarlshof the Mainland ends abruptly at **Sumburgh Head**, an RSPB Reserve. The **lighthouse** on top of the cliff was built by Robert Stevenson in 1821, and the keepers' cottages are now rented out as self-catering accommodation. The lighthouse isn't open to the public, but from its grounds you can see many nesting seabirds such as puffins, kittiwakes, fulmars, guillemots and razorbills. Just to the east of the airport is **Pool of Virkie**, another good birdwatching area.

Sleeping Accommodation is limited. There's the **C** *Sumburgh Hotel*, T460201, next to Jarlshof in a converted laird's house. It has a bar and restaurant. There's also a **camping böd** in *Betty Mouat's Cottage*, next to a recently excavated site at Scatness next to the airport. It sleeps up to 8 and is open Apr-Sep. Book through Lerwick tourist office.

Transport There are regular daily **buses** from **Lerwick**, which stop at the hotel, **Scatness** and **Grutness Pier** (for Fair Isle) en route to the airport.

Fair Isle

Fair Isle is the most isolated of Britain's inhabited islands. Only three miles long by 1½ miles wide, the island has a population of around 70 and is best known for its intricately patterned knitwear, which is still produced by a co-operative, Fair Isle Crafts. Co-operative could be said to sum up the friendly islanders, whose lifestyle is based on mutual help and community effort.

Phone code: 01595
24 miles SW of
Sumburgh and
27 miles NE of North
Ronaldsay in Orkney

Getting to Fair Isle requires patience, persistence and a strong stomach to survive the white-knuckle 4 ½-hr **ferry** sailing. There are also **flights** from **Tingwall Airport**. See Transport below.

Ins & outs

For more information on Fair Isle visit www.fairisle.org.uk, or call the National Trust for Scotland (T0141-616 2266, www.thenationaltrustforscotland.org.uk).

Fair Isle is a paradise for **birdwatchers**, and keen ornithologists form the majority of the island's visitors. Celebrity birdwatcher and former Goodie, Bill Oddie, has dubbed it the "the Hilton of the bird world". It stands in the flight path of many thousands of migrating birds, and over 340 species have been recorded here at the **Fair Isle Bird Observatory**, which also offers accommodation and where visitors are welcome to take part. As well as the almost obscenely rich birdlife there are around 240 species of flowering plants, making the island an especially beautiful haven for naturalists. Fair Isle's coastline, especially in the north and west, also boasts some outstanding cliff scenery.

The bird observatory was the brainchild of George Waterston, an ornithologist who first visited in 1935 and then bought the island in 1948 to begin his task of building the observatory. The island was given to the National Trust for Scotland in 1954 and declared a National Scenic Area. It was recently designated a place of outstanding natural beauty and cultural heritage by the Council of Europe. The **George Waterston Memorial Centre** has exhibits and photographs detailing the island's natural history, as well as the history of crofting, fishing, archaeology and knitwear. ■ *May to mid-Sep Mon and Fri 1400-1600, Wed 1030-1200. Donations welcome.*

Sleeping There are a few places to stay on the island, but accommodation must be booked in advance and includes meals. The **C** *Fair Isle Lodge and Bird Observatory*, T760258, www.fairislebirdobs.co.uk, offers full-board accommodation in private rooms or in a dormitory (**E**). Alternatively, there's full board at **D** *Schoolton*, T760250; and **D** *Upper Leogh*, T760248, kathleen.coull@lineone.net There's also a **self-catering cottage** for 4 from £210 weekly (T760248). There are no hotels, pubs or restaurants.

Transport For details of **ferries** to Fair Isle from **Grutness** (near Sumburgh) or **Lerwick**, and **flights** from **Tingwall Airport**, see page 622. A day-return flight allows about 6 hrs on the island. You can also fly from **Kirkwall** on Orkney, which allows 2 ½ hrs on the island, T01856-872420. Ferries should be booked with *J W Stout*, T760222.

North Mainland

Phone code: 01806
Colour map 6, grid B2

The main road north from Lerwick branches at **Voe**, a peaceful and colourful little village nestling in a bay at the head of the Olna Firth. One branch leads to the Yell car and passenger ferry terminal at **Toft**, past the turn-off to the massive **Sullom Voe Oil Terminal**, the largest oil and liquefied gas terminal in Europe. The other road heads northwest to Brae (see below).

Sleeping and eating You can stay in Voe at the *Sail Loft* by the pier. This former fishing store is now Shetland's largest **camping böd**, open Apr-Sep. Food is available at the *Pierhead Restaurant and Bar*, T588332.

Transport Regular **buses** from **Lerwick** to Brae and Hillswick to the northwest, and Toft and Mossbank to the north, pass through Voe daily except Sun.

Brae
Colour map 6, grid B2

Brae is not a very pretty place and was built to accommodate workers at the nearby Sullom Voe oil terminal. It does boast a good selection of accommodation and decent facilities, though, and makes a good base from which to explore the wild and wonderful coastal scenery around the Northmavine peninsula to the north. There's also good walking and spectacularly good westerly views around the island of **Muckle Roe** to the southwest, and up the island's small hill, South Ward (554 ft). But be careful of the overly protective bonxies, or great skuas, which will attack if you get too close. The island is attached to the mainland by a bridge.

Sleeping The best place to stay around Brae, or anywhere else on Shetland, is the **B** *Busta House Hotel*, T522506, www.mes.co.uk/busta A luxurious and wonderfully atmospheric 16th-century country house overlooking Busta Voe about 1½ miles from Brae village. The superb restaurant (mid-range to expensive) is the finest on Shetland, with a selection of malts to match, and there are also meals in the bar. There are also several B&Bs to choose from, including **D** *Valleyfield Guest House*, T522563; and **E** *Drumquin Guest House*, T522621, both with dinner available. On Muckle Roe is **E** *Westayre*, T522368, which is a working croft. A good place to **eat**, other than *Busta House*, is the *Mid Brae Inn* which serves great food daily till 2100.

Transport **Buses** from **Lerwick** to Hillswick (see below) and to **Toft/Mossbank** (see under Yell below) stop in Brae.

Mavis Grind, the narrow isthmus where it's claimed you can throw a stone from the Atlantic to the North Sea, leads into Northmavine, the northwest peninsula of North Mainland. This is excellent **walking** country, and it's a good idea to abandon the car and explore it on foot. **Hillswick Ness**, to the south of **Hillswick** village, is a nice walk, but further west, around the coastline of **Eshaness**, is the most spectacular cliff scenery and amazing natural features, all with unusual and evocative names.

North of the lighthouse are the **Holes of Scraada**, **Grind o' da Navir** and the **Villians of Hamnavoe**, which are not the local gangs but eroded lava cliffs with blowholes, arches and caves. East of Eshaness are the **Heads of Grocken** and **The Drongs**, a series of exposed sea stacks, which offer superb diving. Further north, overlooking the deep sea inlet of **Ronies Voe**, is the dramatic red granite bulk of **Ronies Hill** (1,477 ft), with a well-preserved burial cairn at the summit. The coastal scenery to the north and west of here is even more breathtaking, but very remote and exposed. You should be well equipped before setting out. A useful guide is *Walking the Coastline of Northmavine* by Peter Guy.

Between Eshaness and Hillswick, a side road leads south to the **Tangwick Haa Museum**, which features displays and photographs on the history of fishing and whaling and the hardships of life in these parts. ■ *May-Sep Mon-Fri 1300-1700, Sat and Sun 1100-1900. Free.*

Sleeping and eating Accommodation is available at **E** *Almara*, T503261, at Upper Urafirth. In Hillswick is *The Booth*, Shetland's oldest pub, which serves food daily in summer.

In **Hamnavoe**, reached by a side road which branches north from the road between Hillswick and Eshaness, you can stay at *Johnny Notion's Camping Böd*, birthplace of John Williamson, known as 'Johnny Notion', an 18th-century craftsman who developed an effective innoculation against smallpox. It's open Apr-Sep and has no electricity. Book through Lerwick tourist office.

Transport There is a daily **bus** service from **Lerwick** to Hillswick (Mon-Sat; £1.90), departing at 1710 and arriving at 1825. From there, a feeder service continues to Eshaness (20 minutes). Contact *Whites Coaches*, T809443.

Whalsay and Out Skerries

South of Voe, the B9071 branches east to **Laxo**, the ferry terminal for the island of **Whalsay**, one of Shetland's most prosperous small islands owing to its thriving fishing industry, which helps support a population of around 1,000. The fleet is based at **Symbister**, the island's main settlement. Beside the harbour at Symbister is the **Pier House**, a restored böd which was used by the Hanseatic League, a commercial association of German merchants who traded in Shetland from the Middle Ages to the early 18th century. Inside is an exhibition explaining the history of the Hanseatic trade, and general information on the island. ■ *Mon-Sat 0900-1300 and 1400-1700, Sun 1400-1700. 50p.*

One of Scotland's great poets, **Hugh McDiarmid** (Christopher Grieve), spent most of the 1930s in Whalsay, where he wrote much of his finest poetry, until he was called for war work in 1942, never to return. His former home, at Sodom near Symbister, is now a **camping böd**. It's open April-September and has no electricity.

Northmavine
This is one of Shetland's most dramatic and beautiful areas, with rugged scenery, spectacular coastline and wide empty spaces

Phone code: 01806
Colour map 6, grid B3
In the seas around Whalsay you can see porpoises, dolphins, minke whales and orcas, hence its Viking name which means 'island of whales'

Orkney and Shetland

Battling Betty

Betty Mouat was quite a woman. In 1886, at the age of 60, she was on a boat heading for Lerwick when the captain was swept overboard and the two crewmen went to rescue him, leaving Betty alone. They were unable to get back to the boat which drifted for nine days before ending up in Norway. Betty survived the ordeal.

Transport There are regular daily car and passenger **ferries** between **Laxo** and **Symbister** (see page 622). To book, call T566259. There are daily **buses** to **Laxo** and and **Vidlin** (see below) from Lerwick, run by *Whites Coaches*, T01595-809443.

Out Skerries The Out Skerries is a small group of rocky islands about five miles from Whalsay and 10 miles east of Shetland Mainland. It's made up of three main islands: the larger islands of **Housay** and **Bruray**, which are connected by a road bridge; and the uninhabited island of **Grunay**. The Skerries boast some spectacular and rugged sea cliffs which are home to many rare migrant seabirds in spring and autumn.

Transport There are **ferries** to the Skerries from **Lerwick**, and also from **Vidlin**, about 3 miles northeast of Laxo (see page 622). For bookings, call *G W Henderson*, T515226. There are also **flights** from **Tingwall Airport** (see page 622).

Yell, Fetlar and Unst

Yell
Phone code: 01957
Colour map 6, grid A/B 2

Yell, the second largest of the Shetland islands, was described rather damningly by Shetland-born writer Eric Linklater as 'dull and dark'. And it's true that the interior is consistently desolate peat moorland. But the coastline is greener and more pleasant and provides an ideal habitat for the island's large **otter** population. Yell is also home to a rich variety of birds, and offers some good coastal and hill walks, especially around the rugged coastline of **The Herra**, a peninsula about half way up the west coast.

At **Burravoe**, about five miles east of the ferry terminal at **Ulsta**, is the **Old Haa Museum**, housed in Yell's oldest building which dates from 1672. It contains an interesting display on local flora and fauna and history. ■ *Late Apr-Sep Tue-Thu and Sat 1000-1600, Sun 1400-1700. Free. T722339.*

The island's largest village, **Mid Yell**, has a couple of shops, a pub and a leisure centre with a good swimming pool. About a mile northwest, on the hillside above the main road, are the reputedly haunted ruins of **Windhouse**, dating from 1707. To the north is the **RSPB Lumbister Reserve**, where red-throated divers, merlins, great and Arctic skuas and many other bird species come to breed. The reserve is also home to a large number of otters. A pleasant walk leads along the nearby steep and narrow gorge, known as the **Daal of Lumbister**, filled with many colourful flowers. The area to the north of the reserve provides good walking over remote moorland and coastline.

The road continues north past the reserve and around **Basta Voe,** where you can see otters. North of **Gutcher**, the ferry port for Unst, is the village of **Cullivoe**, with some good walks along the attractive coastline.

Sleeping and eating There's accommodation on Yell at **E** *Hillhead*, T722274, in Burravoe; at **E** *Pinewood Guest House*, T702427, in South Aywick, between Burravoe and Mid Yell; and at the friendly **E-F** *Post Office*, T744201, in Gutcher. You can also stay at *Windhouse Lodge*, which is a **camping böd** below the ruins of haunted Windhouse. It's well-equipped and open Apr-Sep. Eating options are limited to the **café** in the *Old Haa Museum*, the *Seaview Café* in Gutcher, or the *Hilltop Restaurant and Bar* in Mid Yell.

Transport   There are frequent car and passenger **ferries** from **Toft** on North Mainland to **Ulsta** on the south coast of Yell (see page 622). It's not essential, but a good idea to book in advance, T722259. Three **buses** daily (Mon-Fri; 2 on Sat, 1 on Sun) run between Lerwick and Toft (1 hr; £1.90). There's a bus service on Yell which runs between Ulsta and Cullivoe and stops at villages in between, T744214.

Fetlar is the smallest of the North Isles but the most fertile, and known as 'the garden of Shetland'. Indeed, the name derives from Norse meaning 'fat land', as there is good grazing and croftland and a rich variety of plant and bird life. The whole island is good for birdwatching, but the prime place is the 1,700 acres of **North Fetlar RSPB Reserve** around Vord Hill (522 ft) in the north of the island. This area has restricted access during the summer months, and visitors should contact the warden at Bealance, T733246. The warden will also let you know if and when you can see the one or two female Snowy Owls which sometime visit.

> **Fetlar**
> *Phone code: 01957*
> *Colour map 6,*
> *grid A3*

The north cliffs of the reserve are home to large colonies of breeding seabirds, including auks, gulls and shags, and you can also see common and grey seals on the beaches in late autumn. Fetlar is home to one of Britain's rarest birds, the **red-necked phalarope**, which breeds in the loch near **Funzie** (pronounced 'finnie') in the east of the island. You can watch them from the RSPB hide in the nearby marshes. Red-throated divers and whimbrel also breed here. The island is also good for **walking,** and a leaflet describing some of the walks is available from the tourist office in Lerwick.

The main settlement on the island is **Houbie**; on the south coast. Here you'll see a house called Leagarth, which was built by the island's most famous son, Sir William Watson Cheyne, who with Lord Lister pioneered antiseptic surgery. Nearby is the excellent **Fetlar Interpretive Centre** which presents the island's history and gives information on its bounteous birdlife. ■ *May-Sep Tue-Sun 1200-1700. Free.*

Sleeping and eating   There's **B&B** at **E** *The Gord*, T733227, in Houbie, and at **E** *The Glebe*, T733242, a lovely old house overlooking Papil Water. You can also **camp** at *Gerth's Campsite*, T733227, which overlooks the beach at Tresta and has good facilities.

Transport   There are regular car and passenger **ferries** between **Oddsta** in the northwest of the island and **Gutcher** on Yell and **Belmont** on Unst (see page 622). There's a **post car** service which runs around the island from the ferry once a day on Mon, Wed and Fri, T733227.

Unst is the most northerly inhabited island in Britain, but there is more to the island than its many 'most northerly' attractions. It is scenically one of the most varied of the Shetland islands, with spectacular cliffs, sea stacks, sheltered inlets, sandy beaches, heather-clad hills, fertile farmland, freshwater lochs and even a sub-arctic desert. Such a variety of habitats supports over 400 plant species and a rich variety of wildlife. Unst is a major breeding site for gannets, puffins, guillemots, razorbills, kittiwakes, shags, Arctic and great skuas and whimbrels, amongst others, and in the surrounding waters you can see seals, porpoises, otters and even killer whales.

> **Unst**
> *Phone code: 01957*
> *Colour map 6,*
> *grid A3*

In the east of the island, north of **Baltasound**, is the **Keen of Hamar National Nature Reserve**, 74 acres of serpentine rock which breaks into tiny fragments known as 'debris', giving the landscape a strange, lunar-like

Orkney and Shetland

appearance. This bleak 'desert' is actually home to some of the rarest plants in Britain. Baltasound is the island's main settlement, with an airport, hotel, pub, post office, leisure centre with pool and Britain's most northerly brewery, the **Valhalla Brewery** which can be visited by appointment, T711348.

To the north of here is the village of **Haroldswick**, home of Britain's most northerly post office, where your postcards are sent with a special stamp to inform everyone of this fact. Here also is **Unst Boat Haven**, where you can see a beautifully presented collection of traditional boats and fishing artefacts. ■ *May-Sep daily 1400-1700. Free.* A little way further north is the **Unst Heritage Centre**, which has a museum of local history and island life. ■ *Same opening hours as Boat Haven and also free.* Nearby is an RAF radar-tracking station at Saxa Vord. The road ends at Skaw, where there's a lovely beach and Britain's most northerly house. The road northwest from Haroldswick leads to the head of **Burra Firth**, a sea inlet flanked by high cliffs, and site of Britain's most northerly golf course.

To the west of Burra Firth is the remote **Hermaness National Nature Reserve**, 2,422 acres of dramatic coastal scenery and wild moorland which is home to over 100,000 nesting seabirds including gannets, and the largest number of puffins and great skuas (or 'bonxies') in Shetland. There's an excellent **visitor centre** in the former lighthouse keeper's shore station, where you can pick up a leaflet which shows the marked route into the reserve, and see the artistic efforts of many of Unst's children. Whilst in the reserve, make sure you keep to the marked paths to avoid being attacked by bonxies: they are highly protective and rest assured that they will attack if they think that their territory is being threatened. ■ *0830-1800. T711278 daily late Apr to mid-Sep.*

The views from Hermaness are wonderful, out to the offshore stacks and skerries including **Muckle Flugga**, and then to the wide open north Atlantic ocean. Muckle Flugga is the site of the most northerly lighthouse in Britain, built in 1857-58 by Thomas Stevenson, father of Robert Louis Stevenson. The writer visited the island in 1869, and the illustrated map in his novel *Treasure Island* bears a striking similarity to the outline of Unst. Beyond the lighthouse is **Out Stack**, which marks the most northerly point on the British Isles. With nothing between you and the North Pole but water, this is the place to sit and contemplate what it feels like to be at the end of the world.

Sleeping and eating There's a decent selection of accommodation on Unst. Top choice has to be **D** *Buness House*, T711315, buness@zetnet.co.uk, a lovely old 17th-century Haa in Baltasound. Staying here is a bizarre and rather surreal experience, given that you are on the most northerly island in Britain. The house is crammed full of Indian Raj relics, and the stuffed eagle, tiger and leopard skins hanging in the hallway are a wildlife close-up almost as impressive, though considerably more unsettling and un-'PC', as the Hermaness Nature Reserve in the north of the island that the family own. The food is excellent and the accommodation comfortable. Another good place is **E** *Prestegaard*, T755234, a Victorian house at Uyeasound on the south coast near the ferry. Also in Baltasound are the **E** *Cligera Guest House*, T711579; and the independent *Gardiesfauld Hostel*, T755259; open Apr-Sep, which also **hires bikes**.

There's also **B&B** in Haroldswick at **E** *Gerratoun*, T711323. Eating options are limited, though all the B&Bs serve evening meals on request. The **D** *Baltasound Hotel*, T711334, serves meals and drinks to non-residents.

Transport There are regular car and passenger **ferries** to Belmont from **Gutcher** on Yell. Booking is advised, T722259. There's an island **bus** service which runs a few times daily (except Sun) between **Baltasound**, **Belmont** and **Haroldswick**, T711666.

Background

13

640

Background

History

Scotland's earliest known inhabitants are the hunter-gatherers of around 6000-5000 BC .By 2000-1500 BC these Mesolithic people had been joined by **Beaker folk**, so named from their distinctive pottery, and grain-cultivating Megalithic people, arriving by sea via Spain and Portugal, who were tempted to settle by a then prevailing near-Mediterranean climate. Several climate changes for the worse triggered much population movement and also, along with extensive deforestation, caused the formation of peaty soil, now characteristic of much of Scotland, by around 1000 BC.

The pottery and other artefacts of the Beaker people have been found in burial mounds or cairns, such as **Maeshowe** on Orkney Mainland (see page 607), from around this time and suggest a complex social structure and perhaps, more importantly, a belief in the afterlife, as do the prehistoric settlements and monuments in Caithness, Orkney, Shetland and the Outer Hebrides, notably at **Skara Brae** (page 606), **Stenness**, and the **Ring of Brodgar** on Orkney Mainland, and **Callanish** on Lewis (see page 569). But throughout Scotland there are hundreds of standing stones and circles, a legacy of the megalithic peoples. In Aberdeenshire surveys reveal precise orientations indicating their use as observatories charting lunar cycles and eclipses. The layout of **Clava Cairns**, near Inverness (see page 270), bears similarities to the great temple at Newgrange in Ireland. And at **Kilmartin** in Argyll (see page 451), cup and ring marks, stone alignments and burial cairns, formed in a complete 'landscape temple', suggest a geomantic sophistication that has now been forgotten.

At the beginning of the first millennium BC, **Bronze-Age** traders from far afield were busy around the coasts. Celts arrived from Germany, bringing with them new agricultural technology and weaponry such as swords and shields, which in turn necessitated impressive earthwork defences in the form of hillforts and crannogs (see page 653) as competition for land increased. In about 200-100 BC more Celts arrived with superior iron working skills, and consequently, more fortifications were also built. The **brochs**, or towers, the remains of many of which can still be seen dotted along the west coast and in the islands, date from this time (see also page 653).

Indigenous Iron-Age tribes inhabited most of the country and were identified by the Romans as 'Picts' – possibly meaning 'painted, or tattooed, people'. They thwarted Roman imperial ambition in Alba, the land north of the Forth and Clyde, in around AD 80, and a string of Roman military outposts along the Highland line remain from this abandoned campaign. At **Fortingall** near Aberfeldy, the ancient yew tree is said to mark the birthplace of Pontius Pilate, possibly the son of a Roman soldier who later found preferment in Rome. To add credence to this theory, a gravestone marked 'PP' was found.

Defensive **walls** built by Emperors **Hadrian** (built circa AD 123 from the Solway Firth to the Tyne) and **Antoninus** (from the Clyde to the Forth circa AD 143) against the Picts inadvertently set a precedent for the eventual polarization of Scotland and England, beginning around the ninth century, out of the mass of tribal kingdoms. An endlessly disputed border led to centuries of retaliatory raids and devastation on either side.

Picts south of the Antonine wall became semi-Romanized and were known as **Britons**, kin to the Welsh. Their kingdom of Strathclyde, with a stronghold on **Dumbarton Rock** near Glasgow, once extended into Lancashire and retained a separate identity into the 11th century. The Lothians, territory of the British Gododdin, was overrun by Anglians from Northumbria. In the seventh century the Anglians challenged the Picts in Alba and were finally defeated at Dunnichen.

Meanwhile an Irish tribe, **the Scots**, who claimed descent from an Egyptian Pharaoh's daughter, had been settling in Pictish territory in Argyll from around the fourth century. Once in Argyll, the sons of the Scots' leader, Erc, established a kingdom called **Dalriada**, sharing it between themselves under a high king at **Dunadd** (see page 271). When their fellow countryman, **Columba**, arrived in the sixth century on **Iona**, they were aided in their cause by his diplomatic skills at the hostile Pictish court of King Brude, in Inverness. In the ninth century the Scots under **Kenneth MacAlpin** took over the Picts. Although their written records were destroyed, or falsified by the conquering Scots, they left a rich legacy of unique sculptured stones denoting a civilized and artistic culture. When Kenneth set up at **Scone**, and Alba became Scotland, the seven kingdoms of Pictland in the north and east survived as great earldoms.

The early Church   Some claim Joseph of Arimathea brought Christianity to **Whithorn** in Galloway, which had been a religious centre since the first century. Around AD 397 **Ninian** founded a Christian Mission in Whithorn, along eastern Mediterranean monastic lines vastly different from the Roman model. From here he and countless missionaries such as Kentigern, Moluag and Comgan went north to convert the Picts, as far as St Ninian's Isle in Shetland. Their communities, oak churches and cells are remembered in innumerable place names, wells and simple cross-marked stones, often established on pre-Christian sacred sites.

In AD 563 Columba arrived on **Iona** (see page 303), where he went on to found the Celtic Church, or the Church of the Culdees, with centres throughout Scotland, which differed in many ways from the Church of Rome. Iona became known as the 'Cradle of Christianity in Scotland', but the arrival of the Vikings inhibited sea travel and the monks were driven from Iona. About this time, the Scots took over the Pictish nation and the Columban church moved to **Dunkeld**, with Columba's relics transported in the *breacbannoch*, or Monymusk reliquary. This was carried at Bannockburn and is now in the Museum of Scotland in Edinburgh.

St Andrews later became the principal seat of the church, although Iona retained special status. Communities of Culdees (one of which was at St Andrews) survived into the 13th century, outwith the Columban and later Roman church. These were thought to be adherents of Ninian's church, preserving elements of pre-Christian druid religion.

A common origin for the cross symbol found on both the **Pictish cross slabs** and the free standing crosses of **Iona and Islay** is the chi-ro, or wheeled cross, as found at Whithorn. However, the enigmatic symbols, vivid hunting scenes and mythical beasts of the Pictish stones found throughout Pictland are unique, and their function remains a mystery. Another mystery is the brief flourishing in the early 13th century of an accomplished school of sculptors around Loch Awe, in Argyll. In ancient burial grounds throughout **Knapdale** are found grave slabs depicting swords, warriors, and foreign ships, thought to mark the graves of the **Knights Templar** who fled here from France.

The Vikings   Pagan Norsemen in dragonships are first heard of in Argyll in AD 795, the first of many such coastal raids of unimaginable savagery, which included ritual killings. Colonies of monks were not spared; 68 suffered the 'red martyrdom' on Iona in 807, and its library, 'a shop window crammed with the loot of centuries' was a magnet for raiders. By the late ninth century Norsemen had colonized **Orkney** (see page 600), and from Birsay Palace Earl Sigurd wielded power as far south as Moray. A renegade bunch of mixed Norse and Gaelic ancestry, the **Gall-Gaels**, appeared in the Hebrides and Galloway. Some of these, like chieftain Ketil Flatnose's family, became early settlers of Iceland.

Once surrounded by aggressive Norse colonies, now also in Dublin and York, the newly formed 'Scotland' survived through a combination of fighting spirit and a network of shifting alliances with the various Norse powers. Some of these alliances were enduring. In the ninth century 'Torf' Einar, credited with introducing peat cutting, founded a dynasty from which sprang the Earls of Angus.

After the Dublin colony collapsed in 1014, a Viking kingdom of 'Man and the Sudreys' (Hebrides) filled the vacuum, and the isles continued to be ravaged by warring Norsemen. By around 1100 Norwegian king Magnus Barelegs' empire included the entire northern and western seaboard. Against this backdrop, pursuing his own interests, appears **Somerled**, Hebridean hero of Norse-Gaelic blood, progenitor of Clan Donald and the powerful Lordship of the Isles. In 1153 he supported a rebellion against the Scottish crown. Later, in the early 13th century, he built a series of castles around the coast, such as Sween, Tioram, Mingary and Dunstaffnage, which foiled the intermittent attempts made by the Scottish crown to assert control.

The last of the great Norse kings, Hakon, was defeated by the Scots in 1263 at Largs, with the aid of bad winter weather. Orkney and Shetland were only returned to Scotland in the 15th century. A Norse dialect was spoken there into the 18th century, and vestiges of Norwegian law still survive, as does the Viking St Magnus Cathedral in Kirkwall.

Macbeth, the earl-king of the vast land of Moray, rose to high kingship with popular support, reigning for a relatively long (1040-57) and peaceful time with his queen Gruoch, grand-daughter of Kenneth III of Scots. The popular image of Macbeth as portrayed by Shakespeare is, in fact, a false one. The great bard vilified Macbeth in order to please his James VI, who claimed descent from Duncan, Macbeth's rival. But it was Duncan who was the nasty piece of work, and he was slain not at Glamis, as in the famous play, but on the battlefield, while invading Macbeth's territory. Indeed Duncan is remembered in the *Orkneyinga saga*, the 'bible' of Viking history, as Karl Hundason, 'low-born son of the hound'.

**Macbeth &
the battle for
kingship**

Competition for the throne was a part of Pictish custom. A suitable 'tanist' or candidate was elected from anyone whose great-grandfather had been king, and the candidates would then fight it out: in practice survival of the fittest. This competition for the right to be king was complicated by the ancient dynastic rivalry among the Dalriadic Scots and perpetuated when they merged with the Picts under Kenneth MacAlpin. This later precipitated the Wars of Independence.

One part of Shakespeare's *Macbeth* which is historical fact is the Birnam Wood incident, when Malcolm, Duncan's son, and his Northumbrian allies used tree branches as camouflage to advance on Macbeth in his Dunsinnan stronghold near Perth. He was later hunted down and slain at Lumphanan by Malcolm's ally, MacDuff, Earl of Fife, and is buried on Iona.

Macbeth, the last truly Celtic king, was also one of the most able early kings. He was the first to establish and implement a fair legal system and, a firm supporter of the Celtic church, he went on pilgrimage to Rome where an Irish monk observed him liberally scattering money to the poor. Further evidence of the great disservice done to his memory by Shakespeare.

Macbeth's usurper, the uncouth **Malcolm III**, Canmore (meaning 'big head'), was an illegitimate son of Duncan and a miller's daughter. In 1067 Malcolm married Margaret, a Saxon princess born in Hungary and sister of Edgar Atheling, the English heir to the throne, who had fled north with his family to escape William the Conqueror and the Norman conquest. Margaret was a devout Catholic and was largely responsible for introducing the religious ideas of the Roman Catholic Church into Scotland, for which she was canonized in 1251. In 1072 she founded **Dunfermline Abbey** and

**The Canmores
& the Norman
conquest**

Background

introduced southern manners to the Scottish court. Her private chapel survives in Edinburgh Castle, and is one of the oldest surviving buildings in Scotland.

Malcolm's belligerent instincts were not curbed by the influence of the saintly Margaret, however, and one of his many raids into Northumberland provoked a visit from William the Conqueror. The result was that Malcolm was forced to swear allegiance to William, an oath he didn't take too seriously, as he continued to raid England at whim, but one which would lead to a greater degree of southern interference in Scottish constitutional matters.

The Normans began to exert their influence over Scotland in many other ways. They were granted land as far as the Highland fringes, establishing a feudal system based on loyalty to the crown. The traditional patriarchal tribal culture was eroded, causing constant rebellions in the North and Galloway. The Norman successor to the Scottish throne, **David I**, like many of his Norman friends, had English estates, acquired through his wife. This wealth built the great Border abbeys and established the Roman church more fully. New parishes and dioceses revolutionized administration, and burghs were founded to develop international trade, attracting **Flemish** settlers. Society in medieval Scotland became more typically European than England or even France.

One of the depressingly familiar themes running through Scottish history has been the unwillingness of the Scots nobility to resist English ambitions towards Scotland. This has always been their Achilles heel and, in 1290, it provoked a crisis of succession, when the new child queen, Margaret, Maid of Norway, died en route from Norway. Margaret had been recognised as heiress of Scotland, the Hebrides and the Isle of Man, but was taken ill on her way to England and a child marriage to the prince who would become Edward II, son of Edward I. Following her death, no fewer than 13 rival contestants materialized. Two main factions emerged: the Balliols and Comyns against the Bruces. But instead of reverting to the traditional method of tanistry, or 'natural selection', the pusillanimous Scots nobles appealed to Edward I of England to adjudicate.

Wallace &
Bruce: the
Wars of
Succession

Edward eventually chose John Balliol, and he was crowned king at Scone in June 1292. Balliol was anxious to prove to his fellow Scots that he was not as weak as they claimed him to be. He negotiated a defensive agreement with the French, the beginning of the Auld Alliance. He then invaded Cumberland in 1296, but in retaliation Edward attacked Berwick and slaughtered its inhabitants. The Scottish army was then defeated at Dunbar, and thereafter the castles of Edinburgh, Roxburgh, Perth and Stirling were captured.

In the same year, Balliol abdicated at Stracathro and went into exile. Edward then destroyed the great Seal of Scotland and, worse still, moved the Stone of Destiny, the traditional crowning throne for all Scottish kings, to Westminster Abbey, where it lay under the Coronation Chair for 700 years. Scotland, as a result, was left in disarray.

However, resistance found a leader in **William Wallace**, son of a Renfrew laird. He began a revolt against the English in 1297 and built up a substantial army. By September of that year he he had secured a small but strategic victory against English forces at **Stirling Bridge**. This galvanized support, and he was quickly declared 'Guardian of the Realm'. Following his defeat at Falkirk he was betrayed to Edward by one of the Scots noblemen, captured and taken south to be executed (disembowelled, then hung, drawn and quartered) in Smithfield, London, in 1305.

This stirred **Robert the Bruce** to take up the cause of independence. Encountering his treacherous rival, 'Red' Comyn, in a Dumfries church, he seized the initiative, stabbing him at the altar. With Comyn dead, and the support of patriotic church leaders, as well as Sir James, 'The Black Douglas', Bruce was able to consolidate his gains, and he was crowned king with full ceremony at Scone before the inevitable blow of Papal excommunication fell. But it was not only that Rome refused to recognize Bruce as king. Edward I, the self-proclaimed 'Hammer of the Scots', was not best pleased, and for the next seven years Bruce was a virtual outlaw fighting a guerrilla campaign against Edward from hiding in the west.

During this time the indomitable Edward died, and Bruce felt bold and confident enough to raid the northern counties of England as far south as Appleby and Richmond. Of his castles captured by the English, only Stirling remained to be wrested from Edward's successor, Edward II. So the scene was set for the most significant battle in Scottish history, at **Bannockburn**, near Stirling, in 1314, where Bruce confronted Edward II's vastly superior army. His incredible victory, aided by Angus Og of the Isles, and a number of Knights Templar recently arrived seeking sanctuary from persecution in France, has ensured him a place in the heart of every patriotic Scot.

Bannockburn brought the Scots a rare victory over their southern enemy, and led to the signing of the **Declaration of Arbroath**, manifesto of Scotland's independence, in 1320. There followed a temporary peace with England, and Bruce was finally recognized as king by the Pope, before he died in 1329. His friend Douglas, as requested, took Bruce's heart on pilgrimage to the Holy Land, but when Douglas died en route it was returned to **Melrose Abbey**.

From Robert the Bruce's title of 'High Steward' sprang the dynasty of Stewart kings. The early Jameses (of whom there were seven in all) all followed a tragic pattern: succeeding as infant kings, imprisoned throughout childhood, and suffering untimely deaths. James I and III were both murdered, and James II blew himself up accidentally with a cannon. Unscrupulous regents frequently took charge, and hugely powerful nobles like the house of Douglas competed both amongst themselves and against the king. James II hot-bloodedly murdered the Earl of Douglas over dinner at Stirling Castle by throwing him out of the window. The Lords of the Isles were put down by the Earl of Mar and his followers in one of the bloodiest battles of all, 'Red Harlaw' near Inverurie. Like the Douglases, they too were finally forfeited, in 1543.

The Stewart Dynasty

However, the early Stewarts made progress towards rescuing the country from anarchy by laying the foundations for a modern state through a series of constitutional reforms. They embodied the democratic 'Kings of Scots', answerable first to the common people. Mostly cultured and progressive, they found time to write poetry (James I wrote the *King's Quair*), to build Renaissance palaces, and to father sufficient illegitimate 'James Stewarts' to fill numerous ecclesiastical sinecures (James IV and V). James IV was a true Renaissance prince with a glittering court, but a self-destructive streak led to his early death – along with most of the nobility – at Flodden, in 1513, sacrificed for the long-standing 'Auld Alliance' with France.

There is no more tragic and romantic figure in Scottish history than Mary, Queen of Scots. Raised in France for safekeeping as a Catholic, her brief reign was dogged by bad luck, bad judgement and bad timing. She arrived back in Scotland in 1561, a young widow, at the height of Reformation turmoil in which both France and Catholicism were inimical. Something of a loose cannon, she was embroiled in a power struggle not helped by her disastrous choice of husbands. Implicated in the celebrated murder of the first one, her cousin, Henry Lord Darnley, she then swiftly married one of the chief suspects, the Earl of Bothwell, incurring the fury of everyone else. Imprisoned after the Battle of Carberry on the island fortress of Loch Leven, she escaped only to throw herself on the mercy of her cousin Queen Elizabeth I, who, mindful that in Catholic eyes Mary had the better claim to the English throne, locked her up at Fotheringhay for 19 years before deciding to do away with her altogether.

Mary, Queen of Scots

Background

Reformation & the roots of Scottish education The Reformation, converting the Catholic church to Protestant, came relatively late to Scotland and the motives were as much political as religious, though, of course, in 16th-century terms the two were inextricably linked. A pro-English Protestant faction had grown over decades, opposing the French Catholic Regent, Mary of Guise, and in 1560 a rebel parliament banned Catholic Mass, thus shattering for good the Auld Alliance with France, first formalized in 1295.

The casualties of the Reformation were countless, and included religious buildings, works of art and even whole libraries. It amounted to a complete obliteration of the past over which even today amnesia prevails, though, unlike in England, there were very few martyrs. So began 100 years of bitter struggle to establish the reformed church. Cue the Protestant exile, **John Knox**, a Calvinist rabble-rouser of dubious character and little diplomacy who was prone to blasting his trumpet off against the 'monstrous regiment of women,' namely Mary, Queen of Scots. Knox's skills as a colourful orator, and his self-appointed role as official historian of the Reformation, have allowed him to eclipse the real hero, **Andrew Melville**, who sacrificed his career of reforming university education to devote himself to the nuts and bolts of church reform.

Schooling for all as a passport to intellectual freedom and moral probity was a dream of the reformers. While grammar and song schools already existed, by the end of the 17th century most parishes had schools using the bible as textbook. The 'Dominie' (schoolmaster) was until recently a hugely influential community figure. Prior to the Reformation the **Universities** of St Andrews (1412), Glasgow (1451) and Aberdeen (1495) had been established, and Edinburgh University was added to the list in the 1580's.

James VI & the Union of Crowns After Elizabeth's death, Mary's son became James VI of Scotland. **Jacobean Scotland** was vibrant and vigorously European. Religious extremists were checked by James VI, the 'Wisest fool in Christendom,' and unprecedented peace allowed Renaissance culture to blossom. But trouble was brewing. In 1603 James VI ascended to the English throne as James I, with the Union of Crowns. At this time the Scottish Parliament had so little power that James VI/I was able to write from his palace in London: "Here I sit and govern Scotland with my pen. I write and it is done." In contrast, the English parliament had begun to assume some genuine power.

Charles I & the Covenanters James believed in the Divine Right of Kings – the God-given right of monarchs to rule their subjects. It was a belief that he passed on to his son Charles I, who succeeded in 1625 and quickly proved that he had little desire to consult parliament in either Scotland or England. Although he was born in Dunfermline, he showed little interest in Scotland and was essentially an absentee monarch. He did not even bother to come to Scotland to be crowned until 1633, calling a parliament at the same time – and then overseeing proceedings, making sure that the voting went his way.

Charles also showed little tact and diplomacy in matters ecclesiastical, and by reasserting the powers of the bishops he rode roughshod over the authority of the General Assembly of the Church of Scotland. Not surprisingly, the rumblings of revolution could soon be heard.

The struggle of the kirk (church) against the king erupted into full scale civil war, with hostility towards bishops the recurrent theme. A riot in St Giles in Edinburgh expressed public feeling and resulted in **The National Covenant**, signed in Edinburgh in 1638, pledging faith to 'the true religion' and affirming the authority of the powerful General Assembly of the Church of Scotland in all matters spiritual. Covenanters and king came to blows, followed by an extremist group of Presbyterians allying with the English parliament against the king, in the **Solemn League and Covenant**. Battle-hardened Scots flooded back from European campaigns to take up arms.

A supporter of the original Covenant, **Montrose**, led a spirited but doomed campaign for the king against the extremists. At Ardvreck in Assynt he was betrayed to his arch-enemy 'King Campbell', Duke of Argyll, who gave him a traitor's death in Edinburgh. After the Restoration Argyll found himself on the wrong side and met the same end on the same spot.

Civil War

Throughout the 17th century the dark side of religious idealism – fanaticism and paranoia – were epitomized by the 'kirk sessions': courts in which the church conducted an orgy of scapegoating and witch-hunts. Fundamental differences of ideology, constitution and culture between two countries only recently 'twinned', opened cracks in the alliance with the Parliamentarians. The following year Civil War broke out in England, with parliamentarians led by **Oliver Cromwell** fighting to wrest power from the king. In 1649 Charles was executed and England became a republic. The Scots, however, wanted to keep the monarchy and proclaimed his son, Charles II as their king, despite falling under Cromwell's military 'Protectorate'. Cromwell acted swiftly to bring the country under his control. In 1651 he forbade the Scots from holding their own parliament – forcing them to send representatives to Westminster instead.

Charles II & Restoration

The Commonwealth under Cromwell lasted until 1660, when Charles II was restored to the English throne. The Scottish Parliament was revived and met again in 1661. This time the Presbyterian Covenanters, who had gained such control of Parliament prior to the Commonwealth, were tamed. The Scottish Parliament was again largely run by nobles loyal to the king.

Although Charles II's was greeted with wild rejoicing, the reinstatement of the bishops once again proved problematic. Some unconsenting ministers of the church were outlawed and, finding a loyal following, especially in the southwest, they held illegal services, 'Conventicles', in the open air. Crippling fines and brutal persecution from officers of the crown, including Graham of Claverhouse, merely increased their resistance, and many died in the 'Killing Times' as martyrs to high principle.

Religion & the Monarchy

Scotland and England continued to disagree, both about the succession and about religion. Charles II's brother and successor, James VII/II, was a Roman Catholic, and in 1687 he tried to introduce more tolerant policies towards Catholics. His actions were seen as a threat to the privileged position held by the Church of England, which since the time of Henry VIII had been the official church in England, and also displeased Presbyterians in Scotland. At first the feeling was that this state of affairs wouldn't last: James was ageing, and as both his daughters were Protestants, the Protestant succession seemed safe. However, when his heir James Francis Edward was born and brought up as a Catholic, a crisis was precipitated, James was ousted from the throne, and fled ignominiously in 1689. His Protestant daughter, Mary, and her husband William of Orange, were invited to take the throne of England, and were later reluctantly accepted by the Scots under the terms of the **Revolution Settlement**.

The Darién Scheme

Although both countries shared a monarch, England was growing significantly wealthier than Scotland. Like other European countries, it was thriving economically through trade generated by its colonies. Scotland, however, had no colonies of its own. To remedy this, a monopoly company was founded with the approval of the King, modelled on the English East India Company. Wealthy Scots helped to fund it, but much of the capital was raised in England. However, the English East India Company exercised its considerable power to protect its monopoly. Strings were pulled and the House of Commons soon threatened to prosecute the Scottish company's

English directors. The King, who had agreed to its establishment, now came under pressure to oppose it. Not surprisingly, most of the English backers withdrew and Scotland saw it as a matter of national pride to raise the starting capital itself – a sum of £400,000, roughly half the nation's capital.

The intention of the scheme was to establish a permanent colony at Darién, on the Panama Isthmus in Central America. Darién was a strategically important site, and the plan was that goods sent to and from Europe would sail to Panama, be carried overland across the isthmus, then reshipped – the new Scottish company carrying out this lucrative work.

However, the project had not been thoroughly researched. For one thing, the land was owned by Spain, a major world power who King William could not afford to offend. Consequently, he ordered English colonists in the area not to help the Scottish settlers defend their new home against the Spanish. In addition the terrain was hostile (which was why the Spanish had not set up a similar scheme already), and diseases like malaria and yellow fever were rife. Within months large numbers of colonists had died. Another attempt was made and was also unsuccessful, and by 1700 the colony had been abandoned.

The consequences were far reaching. Scotland lost a vast proportion of her wealth; national pride and confidence were dented; and the country lost faith in the dual monarchy. The King had sided with his wealthiest subjects – and Scotland felt betrayed.

Union of Parliaments While Darién produced much anti-English feeling, a number of Scots began to feel that greater co-operation with England could be economically advantageous. At around the same time a further constitutional crisis was brewing. William of Orange had no children and was to be succeeded by James VII/II's daughter, Anne, who was Protestant. However, Anne had no surviving children and English politicians began to search for an heir – who had to be both Protestant and have Stuart blood. They decided on the Hanoverians, who were descended from the daughter of James VI/I. In 1701 the English parliament passed the **Act of Settlement**, ruling that on Anne's death the throne should pass to the House of Hanover. In 1702 William died and the throne passed to Anne.

The assumption was that the Scots would follow England's lead and accept the Hanoverian succession. But the nation was still smarting over Darién and, as Anne turned out to have little interest in Scotland, relations were strained. The difficulties over having two separate governments under one monarch would not go away. In 1703 the Scottish parliament passed the **Act of Security** which declared that on Anne's death Scotland would take a different successor to England, unless some settlement could be agreed upon that restored 'the honour and sovereignty of this Crown and Kingdom'. They wanted to guarantee the power of the Scottish parliament; the freedom of Scottish religion; and freedom of trade. In addition Parliament ordered people to arm themselves and prepare to fight. It was sabre rattling that the English could hardly ignore.

Although Anne signed the Act of Security, Scotland's triumph was shortlived. England passed the **Alien Act**, which declared that all Scots except those resident in England should be treated as aliens, and Scottish trade with England was to be blocked. The Act was to remain in force until Scotland agreed to make moves towards parliamentary union, or accepted Hanoverian succession.

There were obvious economic advantages to closer ties with England, and Scotland was in a vulnerable position. Not only had the Darién venture weakened the economy, the country was also suffering from several years of harvest failure which had led to famine. Although public opinion was against union with England, it counted for little. It certainly appealed to many in parliament. Financial inducements were offered – and accepted, causing Robert Burns to comment later that Scotland had been "bought and sold for English gold". The Church of Scotland, initially suspicious of Union, withdrew its objections when it was assured that Presbyterianism would be safeguarded. A propaganda campaign was carried out on both sides of the border, many of the pamphlets being written by the author Daniel Defoe. The English were assured that union would end the threat of invasion from Scotland; the Scots assured of great economic benefits.

The people were not swayed. There were violent demonstrations in the streets, and riots in Glasgow, Dumfries and Edinburgh. Opponents even went as far as claiming that union would be sinful. The riots in Edinburgh were particularly violent, causing Defoe, who was acting as a spy for the English government, to say: "A Scots rabble is the worst of its kind. 'The Scots', he said, 'were a hardened and terrible people'. Pro union MPs were attacked, and plans were made in Lanarkshire to raise an army to march on Edinburgh. But public opinion was not of consequence. The Duke of Argyll, for instance, made paper kites out of anti-union petitions and flew them around Parliament. Although some members, notably Andrew Fletcher of Saltoun, were opposed to union, the treaty was comfortably passed by the Scottish Parliament on 16th January 1707. It had to be signed in secret in Edinburgh to protect politicians from the mob.

In April the act was passed in the English Parliament, and on 1st May 1707 the Union came into effect. The Kingdoms of Scotland and England were united into Great Britain, though Scotland preserved its separate legal system, educational system and church. Despite the vigorous opposition, threats and bribery assured that a bankrupt and exhausted Scotland was, in popular mythology, sold to England for £398,085 – part compensation for Darién, part wages for the Commissioners who closed the deal.

Rebellion against the imposition of William of Orange began in 1689, when William's government redcoats clashed with supporters of James II (the Jacobites) at **Killiecrankie** (see page 330). They were led by Graham of Claverhouse, 'Bonnie Dundee', who was killed in the battle. In 1692 an expedition to weed out the Jacobites in the Highlands resulted in the **Glencoe massacre**, which provoked unprecedented public outcry (see page 479).

Jacobite rebellion & the Clearances

The Act of Settlement was not forgotten, and dwindling trade and increased taxation fuelled dissatisfaction with the Union. A lively underground resistance, aided by long-standing French connections, revolved around the Jacobite court in exile at St Germain. Sympathy also came from English quarters.

Four attempts ensued to reinstate a Stewart monarchy, supported erratically by France, and culminating at **Culloden** in 1746 (see page 451). Much support came from north of the Tay, which was Catholic and Episcopalian country. The term 'Jacobite' popularly denoted anti-establishment and Episcopalian. Also, pejoratively, Highlander, and was evocative of a linguistic, social and cultural divide between Lowlander and Highlander whihch had grown since the 15th century.

Highland culture and independence was not diminished after the demise of the Lords of the Isles, hence the rise of the Campbells to enormous power as government agents, dealing for instance with the troublesome MacGregors. Claiming descent from Kenneth MacAlpin, the MacGregors were almost annihilated in 1603, and outlawed until 1774. They played a significant part in the Jacobite rebellions (see also page 355).

Although traditionally indifferent to the monarchy, many clans came out in support of Prince Charles (of 'Bonnie Prince Charlie' fame) in 1745. After defeat at Culloden, savage reprisals were led by the 'Butcher' Cumberland. Rebels were beheaded or hanged, estates confiscated, and the pipes and Highland dress proscribed until 1782. Clansmen were enlisted into Highland regiments and 1,150 were exiled,

Background

swelling the ranks of emigrants to the colonies. Gaelic culture was effectively expunged and Scotland as a whole suffered disgrace.

Rise and fall of Bonnie Prince Charlie

Charles Edward Stuart, the 'Young Pretender', grandson of James II, was born in Italy. First setting foot on Scottish soil aged 23 with seven companions (the Seven Men of Moidart), his forceful personality persuaded reluctant clan chiefs to join him in raising the Standard for his father at Glenfinnan in 1745. Inadequately prepared government troops under 'Johnny Cope' (of ballad fame) enabled his swift progress to Edinburgh, where he held court at Holyrood, dazzling the populace with a grand ball. Edinburgh was charmed but embarrassed.

With sights set on the English throne, he reached Derby. Encouraging reports about panic in London were offset by news of advancing government troops which prompted retreat. The pursuing redcoats were outwitted as far as Inverness, and the ensuing bloodbath at **Culloden**, though Charles' only defeat, was decisive. Fleeing to the Hebrides, he was given shelter by **Flora MacDonald** (see page 544) and then spent a summer as a lone fugitive. Despite a £30,000 reward for his capture, he managed to escape on a French frigate in 1746. Too late by a fortnight, 40,000 *louis d'ors* then arrived from France, enough to revive the whole campaign.

This failure has been ascribed to a fatal weakness of character and a collapse of resolve at Derby. He ended his days a degenerate and broken man, ensuring the complete collapse of the Jacobite cause. But Bonnie Prince Charlie is remembered in numerous nostalgic songs, a toast to 'the King over the Water', and a host of memorabilia.

The Enlightenment

Intellectual life flourished in late 18th-century Scotland. Embracing all the arts, its roots lay in the philosophical nature, shaped by European thought, underlying Scots law, education and the church. The sceptic **David Hume** (1711-76) was the foremost of a school of philosophers, best known for his *Treatise on Human Nature* and *Essays, Moral and Political*. Kirkcaldy-born **Adam Smith** pioneered political economy in his *Wealth of Nations* (1776), a powerful impetus to later political reform.

An emphasis on research and practicality in the sciences fostered inventiveness in applied science, contributing much to industry and agriculture. **James Watt** (1736-1819) developed the steam engine which powered the machinery of the Industrial Revolution, medicine flourished at Edinburgh University, and further generations spawned engineers and inventors like **Alexander Graham Bell** and **John Logie Baird**, inventors of the telephone and television respectively.

Classicism was espoused in architecture and by painters like **Allan Ramsay, Raeburn** and **Naysmth**, and gave way in literature to the Romanticism of **Robert Burns** whose work profoundly influenced popular culture and notions of democracy.

Sir Walter Scott's best selling historical novels worked miracles for Scotland's public image. It was he who stage-managed the visit of George IV, who sportingly donned a kilt and, for modesty's sake, pink tights for the occasion. Later on, Queen Victoria was inspired to adopt a Highland home and, with the craze for 'Balmorality', the Highlands assumed a romantic glamour, becoming a fashionable resort for southern sportsmen.

Industrial revolution

Until around 1750 half of Scotland's population lived north of the Clyde and Tay. **Emigration** to the Lowlands or North America was already a problem, as a money economy threatened traditional ways of life. The decision of landlords to resettle their tenants on the coasts, replacing black cattle with sheep, was a disastrous economic and social experiment, with brutal evictions in some areas – although popular myth forgets that famine, disease and overpopulation were rife and many went willingly. Eventually, in 1886, crofters' rights were to some extent recognized (see also page 551).

The gap between Highland and Lowland life continued to widen as overgrazing, deforestation for industry, and deer 'forests', led to desolation in the Highlands, while improvements and drainage transformed Lowland agriculture.

At the same time **industrialization** was soon to bring a massive population shift. Wool, cloth and linen, long established as cottage industries, were undergoing mechanization. By 1820 mills were established in the coalfields of Lanark, Renfrew and Ayr. Linen declined in favour of cotton, spun and woven in Paisley and New Lanark, while tweed was first woven in Galashiels in 1830. Dundee substituted jute for linen and Kirkcaldy developed linoleum. Thriving on trade with America, Glasgow's population mushroomed, absorbing many from the Highlands, as well as thousands of Irish refugees from the potato famine of the 1840's. Poor housing, overcrowding and disease became chronic.

By 1900 iron and later steel, mainly in the west, had become manufacturing mainstays, serviced by new canals, railways and roads. As well as emigrants, Scotland supplied goods to North America: locomotives, girders, bridges, textile machinery and tools. Shipyards flourished on the **Clyde**. The first iron steam ships were launched around 1800, although fast wooden clippers like the *Cutty Sark* were still competitive in the mid-19th century, when major shipping companies such as Cunard came to the fore. From 1880 skilled labour built steel ships for world markets as well as for the Royal Navy. Business boomed during the First World War, when political activity among skilled workers inspired by the Bolshevik revolution, led by Marxist and Scottish Nationalist **John Maclean**, gave rise to the myth of 'Red Clydeside'.

20th-century Scotland

Post-war slump hit all industries in the 1920s, from which they never really recovered. A dangerous dependency on mining, metalworking and heavy engineering was a crucial factor in industrial decline, and the innovative spirit of the 19th century is only now re-emerging among pioneering computer software development companies in the central belt.

In a long Liberal tradition dedicated to political reform, the issue of Home Rule reared its head repeatedly after the 1880s. The first stirrings of nationalism were heard after the First World War and voiced by writers in the 1920's, such as Lewis Spence, Hugh MacDiarmid, Grassic Gibbon and Neil Gunn. These sentiments took political shape as the **Scottish National Party** (SNP) in 1934. Support grew through the 1950s and 1960s, and in 1967 the SNP was revealed as a potent political force when Winifred Ewing won the Hamilton by-election.

Nationalist fervour reached its height in the 1970s, roused by expectations that revenue from the **oil and gas** recently discovered in the North Sea would reverse economic decline. These hopes were dashed by oil revenues disappearing into the British Treasury at Westminster. In 1974, 11 SNP MPs were elected to Westminster – and, although many felt that this was a protest vote, Labour felt concerned. In 1979 it held a referendum on the establishment of a Scottish Assembly. Turnout was low and support was lukewarm, so no assembly was established.

Labour were soon ousted from office and the Thatcher government swept to power in 1979, bringing with them a disdain for Scotland that was to have far reaching consequences. The new Conservative government also introduced policies that did not sit easily with most Scots. When the unpopular Poll Tax, which notoriously taxed 'dukes the same as dustmen', was introduced in Scotland a year earlier than in the rest of Britain, the country felt that it was increasingly being governed by politicians who cared little for its people. Years of Tory rule served only to widen the gap between Scotland and Westminster, and it was almost inevitable that some form of devolution would follow.

Great Scots

*For such a small country, Scotland has produced a remarkable number of intellectual geniuses who have been peculiarly influential. Many of them were great scientists, like **James Clerk Maxwell**, described by Einstein as the most important physicist after Newton, and who paved the way for Einstein's theory of relativity. There was also **John Napier**, the inventor of logarithms, **Lord Kelvin**, who devised the second law of thermodynamics, and **James Hutton**, **Roderick Murchison** and **Charles Lyell**, who together created modern geology.*

*In medicine, Scotland led the world. **Robert Liston** and **James Young Simpson** discovered the benefits of chloroform, and **Alexander Fleming** discovered penicillin, the most effective*

*antibiotic ever devised. The number of technologists is incredible, and includes **James Watt**, who developed the steam engine, **R W Thomson**, who invented the fountain pen and pneumatic tyre, **John Macadam**, who gave the world the metalled road, **Charles Mackintosh**, who invented waterproof fabric, **Alexander Graham Bell**, who invented the telephone, and not forgetting **John Logie Baird**, the father of television.*

Scotland has also given the world the Bank of England, the decimal point, colour photographs, the fax machine, the photocopier, the bicycle, the bus, the thermos flask, the thermometer, the gas mask, the gravitating compass, the fridge, the grand piano, fingerprinting, Bovril, interferon, insulin, the gel-filled bra and Dolly, the cloned sheep.

The new parliament Twenty years on, the Scots voted emphatically in favour of devolution, and the **Scottish Parliament** reconvened after 292 years on 12 May, 1999. The new Parliament has 129 MSPs (Members of the Scottish Parliament) who were elected by proportional representation. It has the power to pass legislation and to alter the rate of taxation. However, defence and foreign affairs are still handled by Westminster. The early years of the Parliament have not been without controversy, and its relationship with Westminster has at times proved frosty. The most pressing issue is the so-called 'West Lothian Question', the anomaly that allows Scottish MPs at Westminster to vote on issues solely affecting England, while English MPs cannot vote on solely Scottish issues. MSPs, for example, recently voted to fund all care for all elderly people in Scotland. Yet this went against the policy of the Labour government, leading to the possible scenario of Scottish Labour MPs at Westminster voting against such funding for the elderly in England. As one commentator said: "The English have been the silent and uninvited guests at the devolutionary feast". In addition, Scotland still benefits from higher spending per head than any other part of Britain – a situation which is almost certain to change.

The new parliamentary building has attracted controversy as its estimated £50 mn construction costs have spiralled to around £300 mn. And, although it was due to be completed in summer 2001, it is now unlikely to be finished until December 2003. Further controversy followed the tragic and sudden death of Donald Dewar, the first First Minister, when his successor Henry McLeish resigned in the face of allegations of financial shenanigans. His own successor, Jack McConnel, immediately had to contend with the tidal wave of tabloid sex scandal. Despite these teething troubles, Scotland's Parliament is finding its feet – and there's no chance that an arrogant monarch (or arrogant Prime Minister) will succeed in controlling it again. Whether devolution is a step on the road to full independence remains to be seen.

Culture

Architecture

A thousand years before Stonehenge, a Neolithic architect was supervising the construction of **Maes Howe** (see page 607) in Orkney. Dramatically accompanied by two stone circles, its massive precision-cut stonework houses a tomb. Religious architecture evolved into the Bronze Age, and over 22 centuries of chambered tombs survive, notably at **Camster** and **Kilmartin**. Henges and stone circles, as at Cairnpapple, also abound. At **Skara Brae** (see page 606) is a 5,000 year-old village, a Neolithic Pompeii where stone furniture and utensils survive in rooms straight out of the 'Flintstones'.

    Brochs, fortresses not dissimilar to diminutive industrial cooling towers such as at **Mousa** on Shetland (see page 632), appeared around 75 BC. A staircase ascended within double walls and a well often provided water for the besieged within. On duns and hilltops, timber laced forts, built from 700 BC into the Middle Ages, are sometimes found to have been fired to such an extent that stonework fused solid or vitrified. Whether this was intentional, or the result of attack, remains a mystery.

    Ninth-century wheelhouses, with stone piers radiating from a central hearth, are visible at **Jarlshof** on Shetland, and appeared later in the Hebrides. Timber began to be used for Pictish hall houses, **crannogs** – lake dwellings on wooden rafts – and early churches (such as at Whithorn).

    In the 11th century **round towers**, such as those at Brechin and Abernethy, were used for defence and as belfries by Culdee communities. Around this time the first cathedrals were built. The one at Birsay on Orkney, founded in 1050 by Earl Thorfinn, was soon replaced by another in Kirkwall commemorating the Norse **St Magnus** (see page 600). This was built by masons from Durham Cathedral after working at Dunfermline Abbey, also Romanesque, built for St Margaret. She also commissioned St Rule's in St Andrews, whose tall square tower suggests Northumbrian influence, echoed in those at Muthill, Dunning (in Strathearn) and Dunblane.

Early structures: from brochs to towers

David I (1124-53) granted land to Roman monastic orders and two centuries of abbey and cathedral building ensued, though mostly in the Lowlands. Years of neglect and depredations by English troops and iconoclastic reformers leave many as picturesque ruins, stripped of magnificent wood and stone carving, stained glass and wallpainting. The wallpaintings at Fowlis Easter, 15th-century collegiate churches, are a rare survivor. The ruins of Oronsay Priory and the Valerian clad cloisters of **Iona's** nunnery (see page 304) are the legacy of the Augustinians.

Abbeys & cathedrals

Symbols of feudalism built by Norman settlers appear in the form of timber motte and bailey fortresses – timber towers with defensive earthworks – though they are found mostly south of the Forth and Clyde.

    Square or oblong tower houses, with a defensive entry at first floor level, barrel vaulting and great hall, were to be an enduring form of dwelling, evolving from the 14th century into the 17th. More elaborate are L-plan and Z-plan versions, with one or two towers added at the corners to defend the entry.

Medieval castles

While ordinary folk lived in thatched turf and stone hovels (some into the 20th century), the cosmopolitan and cultured Stewart kings set about building new palaces and improving existing residences.

    The old castle at **Linlithgow** had emerged by 1540, a wholly residential Renaissance palace ranged around a quadrangle, which even impressed the French Mary of Guise. While the Great Hall at **Stirling** is a triumph of late Gothic, the later Palace

Renaissance palaces

block (1540-42) reveals many Renaissance features, such as the recessed bays along the exterior with sculpted figures, and the famous carved wooden ceiling medallions, the 'Stirling Heads'.

The Tower house A minor building boom in the late 16th century was a result of church land being transferred over a long period into private hands. The old tower house formula found favour, preferred over earlier royal examples of Renaissance innovation. Everyone from nobility to minor gentry was afforded both defence against troublesome neighbours as well as gracious living. **Claypotts** in Dundee is a good example of 'the castle with a country house built on top', while at **Craigievar** (see page 424), finished as late as 1626, idiosyncratic inventiveness reaches its apogée where the roofline explodes in a flurry of fairytale turrets. Families of masons developed individual styles detectable in Aberdeenshire where many tower houses, great and small, are still inhabited or have been recently revived. Defensive features like gun loops (apertures for guns) survived less out of necessity than as status symbols, and interiors, especially timber ceilings, were vividly painted, with exuberant imagery, as at **Crathes** (see page 416).

16th-century townhouses 'New towns' to promote trade were established by David I and settled with English and Flemish merchants, with a strict hierarchy of trading rights and privileges. Stone houses first replaced wood in the east coast burghs in the 16th century, setting a precedent for future urban design. Every burgh had its symbols of commerce and government at its centre: the Mercat (market) cross and the Tolbooth (town hall).

Two centuries later, the spirit of vernacular architecture had not changed dramatically. Nor had urban layout, many houses still being built gable end on to the street. The multi-storey tenement became a distinctive feature of urban living, pioneered in Edinburgh's Canongate, where buildings such as **Gladstone's Land** are still intact.

William Bruce & the 17th-century mansion Less defensive and more comfortable was the country mansion, a concept pioneered by Alexander Seton, paragon of a new kind of architectural patron, at **Pinkie House** in Musselburgh, a daring essay in elegance and erudition. In an urban setting, **Culross Palace** and **Argyll's Ludgings** in Stirling are outstanding examples of grand town houses.

Post Restoration, William Bruce exemplifies a new concept: the architect. Introducing classical symmetry to existing buildings such as Holyrood and Thirlestane, he also designed **Hopetoun** in 1699-1703. The innovative oblong shape and hipped roof of Kinross are characteristic of his many other country house designs with their Anglo-Dutch interiors and plasterwork. He also revolutionized garden and landscape design.

Bruce's protégé, James Smith, was a pioneer of British Palladianism. Rising from master mason to King's Master of Works and private architect, his own house, Newhailes (c1690), was the inspiration for countless lairds' houses, both grand and humble, built throughout Scotland in the 18th century.

Victorian Baronial Not content with Classicism, architects raided the Gothic, Tudor, Jacobean and Scottish past, even Asia and Europe, for ideas. Late 18th-century country houses by Gillespie Graham were asymmetrical and castellated. Inspired by the picturesque movement, they are the harbingers of the High Victorian revival of Scottish baronial which reached its peak in the 1860s. New and unprecedented wealth found industrial tycoons and landowners beating a path to the doors of fashionable architects like Burn and Bryce, to build colossal and fantastic country seats with room for entertaining on a huge scale, and the latest in comforts – like plumbing. Some followed Queen Victoria's example at Balmoral, building extravagant Highland shooting lodges. Most eclectic of all is **Mount Stuart** on Bute (1870s) a neo-Gothic/Renaissance palace whose sumptuous interior even includes details from Charlemagne's tomb (see page 254).

Flamboyant design extended to monumental industrial buildings like textile mills and foundries, also railway stations, viaducts and bridges.

Glasgow grew phenomenally through the 19th century to become the 'Second City of the Empire'. While acres of tenements housed artisans and middle class families, earlier Georgian suburbs were abandoned for commodious villas for the prosperous, designed by leading architects in areas like Kelvingrove. Many, especially on the south side, were designed by Alexander 'Greek' Thomson using Classical Greece and Egypt as inspiration. The best known of his public works is the Greek Revival church in St Vincent St (1858). The originality of his work is itself currently enjoying a long-overdue revival.

Glasgow's heyday: Thomson & Mackintosh

While **Glasgow University** (1870) by Gilbert Scott was inspired by medieval Flemish cloth halls, banks were modelled on Renaissance palazzos. Thomson designed Egyptian-style warehouses, and Burnet in the 1890s returned from New York to design tall, narrow-fronted buildings with steel frames. By 1896 and Charles Rennie Mackintosh's debut, Glasgow had the most exciting architecture in Europe.

The forward-looking Beaux-Arts rationalism of Burnet and company was challenged by Traditionalists reacting against aggressive modernity and advocating traditional building materials and craftsmanship, and referring back to 16th- and 17th-century vernacular architecture. **Rennie Mackintosh** was a leading, if independent exponent, as exemplified at **Hill House** in Helensburgh (see page 248), while a more mainstream Arts and Crafts aesthetic was adopted by **Robert Lorimer** who 're-stored' many early houses, as well as designing anew.

20th century: Traditionalism & modernism

In contrast, Art Déco was favoured by architects such as Glasgow's **Jack Coia** and, by the mid-century, **Basil Spence** was a champion of Modernism. Traditionalism versus Modernism was to become an enduring theme.

Economic depression and dramatic social change brought an urgent need for solutions to both rural depopulation, and urban overpopulation and decay. Already by the 1930s two contrasting visions of social progress were being proposed: restoration of organic unity versus modernist utopia.

A desperate need for housing resulted in massive building projects into the 1970's transforming cities. Many historic buildings were demolished and city centres gutted in an effort to remedy post-war dereliction. Edinburgh had the worst slums in Europe, where overpopulated tenements were literally collapsing. The first residential tower-blocks, the epitome of the Modern Functionalist brave new world, appeared, most notoriously in Glasgow's Gorbals. Urban over-spill was re-housed in New Towns such as Cumbernauld which, although internationally acclaimed in the 1960s, was unpopular with its inhabitants.

Post-war to present day

Traditionalists meanwhile continued to advocate experiments in vernacular style, and a move was made to protect historic buildings. Most prominent of recent public buildings is the new wing of the **Museum of Scotland in Edinburgh**. Completed at a time of renewed national confidence and cultural awareness, historical references are foremost. The sandstone-clad exterior is reminiscent of a medieval fortress, and from within the view over the adjacent Greyfriar's church, scene of the signing of the National Covenant in 1638, has been emphasized.

With the building of the **Scottish Parliament** at Holyrood by Eric Miralles still under way, it is not inappropriate that its temporary home is in the Assembly Rooms of the Church of Scotland, that most democratic of institutions.

Background

Scottish literature

Burns, Scott
& Stevenson
Any overview, no matter how brief, of Scotland's literary tradition must begin with a poet who has become inextricably linked with the image of Scotland and all things Scottish across the globe. **Robert Burns** was born on 25 January 1759 in a small cottage in Alloway, Ayrshire, where he lived until the age of eight. His father was a market gardener and Burns later referred to himself as 'a very poor man's son'.

Following the death of their father in 1784, Robert and his brother rented another farm, but luck wasn't on their side, as they fought against failing crops and an increasing struggle to provide for the family. To combat the anxiety of this situation, Burns found a refuge in his writing. Within the next two years he had composed poetry which encompassed many subjects but mainly concerned itself with life as he was living it. He was also keen to point out what he saw as a kinship between all living things, such as in his famous 'To A Mouse'. The most frequently quoted lines of this poem; 'The best laid schemes o' mice an' men – Gang aft a-gley,' has entered the language, as have many sayings originated by Burns, and is a perfect summing up of his point of view.

Burns wrote in the dialect of plain country people and about the lives they led, but the emotions he described were so genuine that they appealed to all classes. The first three-shilling volume of his poetry was released in July, 1786, by a publisher in Kilmarnock and his wife, Jean Armour, but only got as far as Greenock. However, by this time he had made a reputation for himself in Edinburgh and changed course for the capital to seek his fortune. The 'ploughman-poet' was fêted by the cultured Edinburgh society but, despite these attentions and his growing popularity, he remained a son of the soil at heart, unimpressed by the fuss his presence caused.

In 1788 Burns and his wife set up a home at Ellisland but, given his previous lack of success as a farmer, he accepted a job as an Exciseman in Dumfriesshire. It was during this period, possibly inspired by coming into contact with so many people through his job, that he wrote of the joys of human companionship in what is perhaps his most celebrated work, *Auld Lang Syne*. Sung or spoken, this poem stands to this day as a symbol of friendship, and is practically an anthem when friends gather to celebrate New Year around the world. His love of the companionship of friends is also a focus of *Tam O'Shanter*, which also serves as a cautionary warning against overindulgence and is a ghost story in the tradition of the mythic, while his irritation against the assumed superiority of some was put into words in *A Man's A Man For A' That*, which also returns to his theme of kinship:

"It's coming yet, for a' that,
That man to man, the world o'er,
Shall brothers be for a' that".

In 1791 Burns quit farming and moved to Dumfries. His poems of this period were a return to the form of traditional ballads, such as *Bannockburn* (often mistakenly referred to as *Scots, Wha Hae*) which celebrates the resolute spirit of his ancestors during the battle.

After a period of ill health, Burns died on 21 July 1796, and was buried in St Michael's Churchyard, Dumfries. A statue was erected in his honour by the citizens of Dumfries in 1822 and, to this day, visitors may still be shown around Burns' Cottage in Alloway and view the poet's birthplace, while his memory is celebrated every year on 25 January, his date of birth, now referred to as Burns Night.

Another man regarded as one of the nation's greatest literary figures is **Sir Walter Scott**, who was profoundly influenced by Burns. Born in 1771, the son of a wealthy Edinburgh lawyer, Scott contracted polio as a child, leaving him lame in the right leg. His parents moved to the New Town, while young Scott was sent to his uncle's farm at Sandyknowe in the Borders for a period of recuperation. This period was to last five years, during which time he immersed himself in tales and ballads of Jacobites and Border heroes, giving him a passion for history which would infuse his later work.

Following spells at Edinburgh High School and University, Scott became a solicitor in his father's firm before becoming an advocate in 1792, while devoting his spare time to the love of poetry and literature which had seen him writing verse at the age of 11 and translating poems from their original German. In 1797 he married Charlotte Carpenter, and the marriage was to last for the rest of her life. At the time he had been collecting local material which would eventually become poems in his three volumes of *Minstrelsy Of The Scottish Border* which established his name as a literary figure. Other romantic poetic works followed, such as *The Lady Of The Lake*, as with Burns, employing the Scottish dialect.

In 1811 Scott purchased Abbotsford, a farmhouse near Melrose, and his alterations and rebuilding were to drain his finances over the next 14 years. It was during this period that he would find the style which would remain his best-remembered contribution to literature, the historical novel. Collectively known as the *Waverley* novels, these included *Old Mortality*, *Rob Roy* and *The Heart Of Midlothian*.

The original *Waverley* was a romantic tale of the Jacobite Rebellion of 1745 and the Highland society of the time. By 1819 Scott had moved beyond purely Scottish history and wrote *Ivanhoe*, set in 12th-century England. It remains his most enduring work, and he followed it with *Kenilworth*, *Redgauntlet* and *The Talisman*. Scott's fascination with history went beyond his fictional work and, in 1817, he and some friends discovered the ancient Honours of Scotland, the royal sword, crown and sceptre – which had remained hidden behind a sealed door at Edinburgh Castle since the days of Charles II.

In 1825 Scott was the victim of multiple tragedies. His publishers and a printing company in which he was a partner collapsed with disastrous financial consequences. Added to that, his beloved Charlotte died, and he threw himself into his work so ferociously that he suffered four strokes. Trips to Malta and Italy didn't succeed in improving his health and he died at Abbotsford on 21 September 1832. His huge popularity was believed to have kept the spirit of Scotland alive and he is commemorated by the Scott Monument in Princes Street, Edinburgh.

This tradition for romantic historical adventures continued in the work of another of the triumvirate of the nation's most famous authors. **Robert Louis Stevenson** was born at 8 Howard Place, Edinburgh, on November 13th, 1850. Like Scott, he was trained in law. He was also fond of travel. It was these travels which led to his employment as a writer of travel articles and essays. While staying in Braemar in 1881, Stevenson drew pirate maps of an island, and these became the basis of his tale, which had the working title of *The Sea Cook*. When he offered it to *Young Folks* magazine the editor suggested a new title and so, in the autumn of 1881, *Treasure Island* appeared in serial form, written by one 'Captain George North', a suitably seafaring pseudonym for Stevenson.

Two years after the serial appeared, it was released as a novel, this time under Stevenson's own name, and sold out almost immediately. For Stevenson it was just the first of the many adventure tales, including *Kidnapped*, its sequel, *Catriona* and *The Master of Ballantrae*, he wrote before his death in Samoa on 3 December 1894.

Apart from adventure stories, he was also fond of the macabre, as shown in stories like *The Bottle Imp* and *The Bodysnatcher*, and he was responsible for one of the classics of horror literature, *The Strange Case of Doctor Jekyll and Mister Hyde*, at once an update of the werewolf myth of man-turning-beast, as well as exploration of the dual nature of man. The tale was inspired by Edinburgh's notorious Deacon Brodie, a respectable pillar of the community by day and a robber and highway man by night. Stevenson wrote the first draft in a few days, but it shocked his wife to such an extent that he burned it and rewrote it, injecting some moral points to appease his spouse.

Sherlock Holmes is regarded by many as the quintessential English detective, even though his creator, **Sir Arthur Conan Doyle**, was very much a Scot. Born at Picardy Place, Edinburgh, on 22 May 1859, Conan Doyle was schooled in Lancashire before returning to study medicine at Edinburgh University in 1876. It was while serving as an out-patient clerk at Edinburgh Royal Infirmary that Doyle met Doctor Joseph Bell, the man who was to influence most the creation of his famous character. "His strong point", Doyle later noted, "was diagnosis, not only of disease, but of occupation and character".

Doyle was living in London and had published several short stories and essays when memories of his former mentor, combined with a love of the detective fiction of Edgar Allan Poe, inspired him to write *A Study In Scarlet*, which first appeared in the 1887 edition of *Beeton's Christmas Annual*. Doctor Watson recounted Sherlock Holmes' unique detective skills in this, followed by a further three novels and 56 short stories, with all but *The Sign Of Four* making their initial appearance in *The Strand Magazine*.

Holmes became a phenomenon that not even Doyle could control. In fact, by 1893 he was so annoyed that his more serious literary endeavours were being neglected that he achieved what many criminals had failed to do. He killed Holmes. Following publication of *The Final Problem*, in which Holmes and his mortal foe, Professor Moriarty plunged over the Reichenbach Falls, there were public displays of grief and mourning. It was clear that the public were not going to let Holmes rest in peace, and eventually Doyle was forced to find an ingenious way of reviving the character. He penned his last Holmes story in 1927, a mere three years before his own death. Doyle's other famous character was Professor Challenger,who famously discovered the *Lost World*, which later inspired Steven Spielberg's *Jurassic Park*.

Other Scottish writers Doyle's personal favourites of these parodies were written by his 'older literary friend', **JM Barrie**. Born in Kirriemuir in 1860, James Matthew Barrie was the son of a weaver. Educated at Glasgow Academy and Edinburgh University, Barrie spent some years in Nottingham as a journalist before returning to Kirriemuir to write.

He moved to London in 1885, and it was there that he wrote his first novel, *Better Dead*. More novels and plays followed, best known of which is *Peter Pan and the Lost Boys*. First published in 1904, it was written for the children of a friend, Llewelyn Davis. Barrie returned to Kirriemuir. Before his death in 1937, he bequeathed the copyright for *Peter Pan* to Great Ormond Street Hospital in London.

The tradition of the adventure story has continued throughout the 20th century in the works of Perth-born **John Buchan,** author of *The Thirty-Nine Steps*. It was also the major theme in Glasgow-born **Alistair MacLean's** many novels, of which the most famous are *The Guns of Navarone*, *Ice Station Zebra* and *Where Eagles Dare*.

For its size, Orkney has produced a disproportionate number of well-loved and much-read authors. **Edwin Muir**, recognized as one of the most distinguished poets of the last century, received an MBE in 1953 for his significant contribution to Scottish poetry. He died in 1959. The poet, novelist and playwright, **George Mackay Brown**, gained even more popularity after the posthumous publication of his autobiography, following his death in 1996. **Eric Linklater** is another Orcadian whose copious output of books and poems gained him international recognition.

Other important Scottish books include: *The House with the Green Shutters* by **George Douglas Brown**, *Sunset Song* by **Lewis Grassic Gibbon**, *The Silver Darlings* by **Neil Gunn**, *The Prime of Miss Jean Brodie* by **Muriel Spark**, and **James Hogg's** *Confessions of a Justified Sinner*. One of the most important 20th century novelists is

Robin Jenkins, referred to as "the Scottish Thomas Hardy". He is recognised as the founder of new Scottish fiction and a precursor to Kelman and Welsh as portraying an unsentimental view of Scottish life. Among his novels are *The Cone Gatherers* (MacDonald 1955) and *Fergus Lamont* (Edinburgh Canongate 1979). His most recent work is *Childish Things* (Canongate 2001). Aside from Robert Burns, there are many fine **poets**, and the selected works of **Norman McCaig**, **Hugh McDiarmid** and **Ian Crichton-Smith** are all recommended. For an excellent overview, see The *New Penguin Book of Scottish Verse*, editied by Robert Crawford and Mick Imlah (2000).

Much contemporary fiction embodies a purely Scottish aesthetic, which challenges the linguistic othodoxy. Good examples are **James Kelman's** Booker prize-winning *How Late It Was, How Late*, and **Alan Warner's** cult classic, *Morvern Caller*. One of Scotland's most talented new brred is **Laura Hird**, whose debut novel, *Born Free* (Rebel Inc 1999), tells the tale of a dysfunctional family trying to cope with life in one of West Edinburgh's most notorious housing schemes. Many of the writers living and working in Scotland today use their environment for inspiration. **Iain Banks**, author of *The Wasp Factory*, *The Crow Road* and many others (as well as science fiction novels written under the name Iain M Banks), based his fantasy, *The Bridge*, on the structure of the Forth Railway Bridge. **Irvine Welsh** has explored the capital's drug culture in the likes of *Trainspotting*, while **Ian Rankin's** crime novels take place in the real streets and bars of Edinburgh. Another fine exponent of the so-called 'tartan noir' genre is **Christopher Brookmyre**, hailed as the Scottish Carl Hiaasen and a satirist of considerable standing. Other notable contemporary works of fiction include *Lanark* (Canongate, 1985) by **Alisdair Gray**, **William MacIlvanney's** *Docherty*, **Janice Galloway's** *The Trick is to Keep Breathing* (Vintage, 1990), which was short-listed for the Whitbread first novel award, and **A L Kennedy's** *Night Geometry and the Garscadden Trains*.

Contemporary Scottish fiction

Scottish music

It could easily be argued that, in its music, Scotland produces the finest and clearest expression of its culture. All tastes are currently catered for within its music scene, reflecting the cosmopolitan nature of a country standing at the threshold of a new era with its own parliament and a deep sense of love of its history and traditions, while keeping a weather eye on the future. Although the words 'Scottish music' often conjure up images of a tartan-clad piper on a mist-covered moor, that same piper is just as likely to be found supplying stirring melodies to the decidedly nineties edge of 'drums and bass' styles heard in clubs around the country. And that's not all – the sheer number of options available to those seeking any style of music, ranging from folk to funk, from 'Tattoo' to 'T In The Park', is truly remarkable.

Yet, despite the fact a new millennium has come and gone, bringing with it so many changes in music and technology, Scotland as a nation still responds, virtually as one, to the skirl of a full set of Highland **bagpipes**. Little wonder the pipes have been a dominant instrument for centuries – in celebration, in battle, in mourning – and are never far from the traveller's notion of all things Scottish. The pipes' unique sound is enjoyed the world over, not just in Scotland – witness the large numbers of pipe bands in the USA, Canada, across Europe, Australia and New Zealand. However, perhaps the best way to enjoy the pipes is to visit the country in summer when, accompanied by a full complement of drummers, many pipe bands can be seen taking part in competitions or playing at Highland Games in the open air. It would also be totally remiss not to mention the **Edinburgh Military Tattoo**, which takes place annually during August at the world-renowned Edinburgh Festival on the esplanade of Edinburgh Castle (see page 125).

Traditional Scottish music can be passionate or jocular, mournful or joyous. In the hands of a good player, few instruments compare to the violin, or 'fiddle'. For confirmation, simply seek out the work of **Ally Bain**. With **The Boys Of The Lough**, **Phil Cunningham** or solo, his handling of all traditional Scottish styles is superb. Delving a little deeper into Scotland's music, one may come across **Strathspey and Reel societies**. These are groups of fiddlers, large or small, which are well attended across the length and breadth of Scotland. Most welcome visitors to their meetings to enjoy the music and, as most of these take place in pubs and hotels, to enjoy the local brew, too! If this turns out to be impractical, a night spent at a ceilidh can be even more entertaining.

A **ceilidh** (pronounced 'kay-lee') is an evening of Scottish music and dancing, the music provided by a ceilidh band, which normally consists of a fiddler, an accordionist, a drummer and a singer. One can then spend the evening sampling the delights of Gay Gordons or Dashing White Sergeants. In case you're wondering, these aren't people who frequent these events – they are actually Scottish country dances which, along with eightsome reels, figure prominently in the ceilidh dance-band repertoire. Beware the well-meaning local lad or lassie bearing gifts of whisky, however – an excellent evening enjoying the music can often lead to a spectacular hangover the following morning!

In a similar vein (though with a slightly less frenetic style), folk music clubs still thrive in Scotland although, sadly, seem to be restricted to an 'early-in-the-week' slot of a Monday or Tuesday evening in bars, as landlords attempt to bring in customers on what are generally quieter nights for business. Even the Scots, with their fearsome (and well-earned) reputation for partying, can't do it *every* night of the week! Visiting the larger cities, look out for boards outside pubs which proclaim 'Live Music Tonight' or 'Folk Music Session – All Welcome', as the venues occasionally change from one week to the next, although the musicians tend to remain the same and are relatively easy to be found in both Edinburgh and Glasgow.

Folk festivals Thankfully, folk music is not just confined to pubs on Monday evenings. Folk festivals take place all over the country, from Arran to Shetland, and are great fun. Musicians from all over Scotland gather to play the tunes, sing the songs and maybe, just maybe, drink the odd beer or two. Amongst the best of the folk festivals are the **Celtic Connections**, held in Glasgow over three weeks in January, and the **Shetland Folk Festival**, held over a long weekend in mid-April. Also recommended are those held in **Edinburgh** before Easter, in **Inverness** in July and August, **Stonehaven** in mid-July, **Auchtermuchty** in mid-August, **Girvan** in early May, **Killin** at the end of June, **Islay** during the last two weeks in May, **Arran** in early June, **Skye** at the end of July and **Kirriemuir** on the first weekend in September. Details of these festivals, and many others, are available from the Scottish Area Tourist Boards (see page 23).

Scottish rock, pop & dance

The biggest annual music event in Britain (north of Glastonbury!) is T In The Park, held at Balado airfield near Kinross

The Scots may be stereotyped as a bunch of kilt-wearing, haggis-munching bagpipe players, but there's so much more to the country's musical heritage. This is the country that gave the world Lonnie Donegan and that perennial poor-man's Madonna, Lulu. Ex-Faces lead singer and sun-tanned bad-hair boy, Rod Stewart, still remembers his roots and wraps himself in tartan every time Scotland qualify for a World Cup. And speaking of tartan, there's the Bay City Rollers, who blazed a trail in the 1970s as the forefathers of the teeny-bop market. Glasgow-born Sheena Easton made it big stateside in the 1980s, while that decade was dominated by the Eurythmics, led by Aberdeen-born singer, Annie Lennox and Dave Stewart. Wet Wet Wet still hold the record for the number of weeks at number one (15) with 'Love is all around', and who could forget The Proclaimers who released the unashamedly

Clans and tartans

Before Culloden and the Clearances, Highland tradition decreed that a person's loyalty lay first and foremost with their own particular clan, or family group. There were two classes of clan: clansmen of the clan who were related by blood and shared the same family name, and individuals and groups who sought and obtained the protection of the clan. This resulted in a clan having septs, or sub-groups, of different surnames. Most Scottish surnames can be traced to a clan name, each with their own particular tartan.

Clan tartans are patterns for general use by clanspeople, but there are also variations of clan tartans which are used for specific purposes. Dress tartans were originally worn by the women of the clan who preferred light-coloured patterns, and were woven on a white background. Hunting tartans are worn for sport and outdoor activities, with brown or some other dark hue as the predominant colour, in order to give some form of camouflage. Rather confusingly, ancient clan tartan does not signify an older pattern, but is merely a term used to describe a tartan woven in lighter-coloured shades.

Those wishing to trace their Scottish ancestry should start at the Scots Ancestry Research Society, 20 York Place, Edinburgh.

---

sentimental 'Letter from America'. Other notable Scots names include Simple Minds, Edwin Collins, Aztec Camera, The Cocteau Twins, Love & Money, Altered Images, Texas, Del Amitri, Blue Nile, Lloyd Cold and the Commotions, the late, great Billy Mackenzie, Waterboys, Soup Dragons, Bronski Beat, KLF and The Shamen.

Behind the scenes, too, Scots have been influential, and none more so than Alan McGee, whose Creation label signed up the cream of talent north of the border in The Jesus and Mary Chain, Primal Scream and Teenage Fanclub (as well as a bunch of Mancunian upstarts by the name of Oasis). Scotland's fecund indie scene continues to produce a stream of contenders. As well as established favourites like Travis and Idlewild, there's Arab Strap, Belle and Sebastian and fringe groups like Mull Historical Society and Astrid.

Language

Though the vast majority of Scots speak English, one ancient Scottish language which survives is **Scottish Gaelic** *(Gaidhlig,* pronounced 'Gallic'). Preceded by the speech of the Celts, it is now Scotland's oldest surviving language. Often referred to as the national language, it has been spoken the longest. Introduced to the country by Irish immigrants in the third and fourth centuries, its use soon spread and became well established. The language is spoken by about 85,000 people in Scotland (about 2% of the population). This is in the *Gaidhealtachd,* the Gaelic-speaking areas of the Outer Hebrides, parts of Skye and a few of the smaller Hebridean islands. Gaelic is one of the Celtic languages, which has included Irish Gaelic, Manx, Welsh, Cornish and Breton. Today only Scottish and Irish Gaelic, Welsh and Breton survive.

Argyll takes its name from the Irish, Dal Rioda, and was the prime Gaelic-speaking area from the time Columba landed there in 563. Scottish Gaelic expanded greatly from the fifth century to around the 12th century and became the national language, spoken throughout most of the country with the exception of the Norse-speaking Orkney and Shetland isles. Galloway had a Gaelic community which was separated from the Highlands, but the language died out there about the 17th century.

From that point, Gaelic began a steady decline over the following centuries and, even before Union with England, was being usurped by English as more and more wealth and power passed into non-Gaelic hands. This transfer of power was given a major boost by the Reformation in the mid-16th century, as strong anti-Gaelic feeling was to the fore in the Church of Scotland.

Gaelic culture still flourished in the Highlands, but the failure of two successive Jacobite rebellions in the 18th century helped to seal its fate. In the wake of Culloden, all features of traditional Gaelic culture were proscribed and the clean sweep by government and landlords culminated in the Highland Clearances of the 19th century. The final nail in the coffin came in 1872, with the Education Act that gave no official recognition to Gaelic.

After two centuries of decline, Gaelic is now staging a comeback, thanks to financial help from government agencies and the EU which has enabled the introduction of bilingual primary and nursery schools and a massive increase in broadcasting time given to Gaelic language programmes. This renaissance can also be seen, and heard, in the fields of music and literature, and the recent return of the Scottish Parliament can surely only help to strengthen the position of Gaelic in Scottish society.

Land and environment

Geographically, Scotland can be divided into three areas: Southern Uplands, Central Lowlands and Highlands. The **Southern Uplands** is the area south from Edinburgh and Glasgow to the English border, and consists of a series of hill ranges sandwiched between fertile coastal plains. The **Central Lowlands**, the triangle formed by Edinburgh, Glasgow and Dundee to the north, contains most of the population, and is the country's industrial heartland. The Highland Boundary Fault is the geographical division running northeast from Helensburgh (west of Glasgow) to Stonehaven (south of Aberdeen). To the north of this line lie the **Highlands and Islands**, which comprise roughly two-thirds of the country. This is an area of high mountain ranges punctuated by steep-sided valleys, or glens, and deep lochs. The northwest coastline is indented by numerous steep, fjord-like sea lochs, and offshore are some 790 islands, 130 of which are inhabited. These are grouped into the Outer Hebrides, or Western Isles, the Inner Hebrides, and, to the north, the Orkney and Shetland Islands.

Much of Scotland was long ago covered by the **Caledonian forest**, which consisted mainly of the **Scots pine**, along with **oak**, **birch** and other hardwoods. Over the centuries, the trees were felled for timber and to accommodate livestock, and now only around 1% of this ancient forest still remains. Small pockets of native Scots pine can be found scattered around the Highlands, at Rothiemurchus, near Aviemore, at Glen Tanar, near Ballater in Deeside, around Braemar, at Strathyre near Callander and Achray Forest near Aberfoyle, at Rowardennan on Loch Lomond, in Glen Affric and on the shores of Loch Maree.

Several decades ago the **Forestry Commission**, a government body, set about fencing off large areas of moorland for reforestation. Now much of the landscape is dominated by regimented rows of fast-growing sitka spruce, which are not particularly attractive. There are also serious concerns over the damage coniferization causes to the unique habitats in many areas, in particular to large areas of bogland in the "Flow Country" of Caithness and Sutherland, a unique natural environment as precious as any tropical rainforest. This and other endangered habitats are registered as an SSSI – a Site of Special Scientific Interest – but this has proved less than adequate. The only real guarantee of protection is for such areas to be owned or managed by environmental organizations such as *Scottish Natural Heritage*, the *Scottish Wildlife Trust*, the *Royal Society for the Protection of Birds*, the *Woodland Trust* and *John Muir Trust* (see page 58).

In recognition of this, the new Scottish Parliament produced a draft bill to establish a series of National Parks, based on advice from Scottish National Heritage. This is aimed to reduce the conflict between social and economic development and long-term protection of the natural and cultural environment. There are currently two new parks proposed: one is the **Cairngorms National Park**, due to open in early 2003, and the other is **Loch Lomond and Trossachs National Park**, which is due to open in April 2002.

Scottish wildlife

The Scottish countryside plays host to some of Europe's rarest and most celebrated wildlife, though much of it has disappeared over the centuries. The ancient Caledonian forests were once home to wildlife that we now identify with other far-flung countries: the brown bear, lynx, wolf, reindeer and beaver to name but a few. Small numbers of beaver and reindeer have been reintroduced in recent years and there is the ongoing controversial debate regarding the reintroduction of the wolf.

Scotland boasts over 13,000 km of the British coastline. As a result seabirds and some **Coastal wildlife** sea mammals abound and both the resident and visitor list is impressive. Some of the more notable avian 'stars' include the **eider duck**, most famous for its feather 'down' which the birds use to keep their eggs warm and we use in quilts to keep us cosy. Both sexes are about the size of a small goose yet are quite different in appearance. The male, for courting purposes, looks very regal, being predominantly black and white with lime green cheeks and a pastel pink breast, while the female, for the purposes of camouflage, is a dull brown colour. During the breeding season on the coast fringes and off-shore islands it is not unusual to encounter the females at very close quarters while she is on the nest. They are very confident about their camouflage and will stay perfectly still even when you are within a few feet.

During the winter the firths (large coastal inlets) and estuaries play host to large numbers of predominantly arctic seaduck including the beautiful jet black common and velvet **scoter**, the **scaup** (very similar to the common tufted duck) and the spectacular and rare **king eider**. **Waders** too are present in large numbers around the coast and again, especially in winter. **Knot**, **dunlin** and **turnstones** are also common along the beaches and mudflats. During the summer perhaps the most commonly seen coastal wader is the **oystercatcher** which is black and white with a conspicuous orange beak. While around estuaries keep your ears open for the high pitched call of the **curlew**. The Firths of Forth, Tay, Moray and Dornoch on Scotland's east coast are prime wader and sea-duck watching areas along with excellent lesser known venues like St Andrews Bay and the Eden Estuary in Fife.

These firths and estuaries, along with many of the offshore islands also play host to Scotland's two resident seal species, the **common seal** and the **grey seal**. Although the two are at long range quite hard to distinguish, the common is generally lighter in colour and smaller with more delicate dog-like facial features. The common seal breeds in summer and generally independent of one another, while the grey breeds in mid-winter in rookeries predominantly on offshore islands. Both species can be seen throughout the year with the common most common on the west coast and the grey on the east. The Isle of May in the Firth of Forth is a well known breeding location for greys and an excellent place to see them in the wild.

Dolphins, **porpoises**, **basking sharks** and some species of **whale** can also been seen regularly around the Scottish coastline. The resident pod of bottlenose dolphins in the Moray Firth is best viewed between May and September, while minke whales, basking sharks and even orca (killer whales) are not entirely unusual off the west coast and Western Isles.

Background

Island wildlife The many offshore islands scattered around the Scottish coast provide sanctuary to a wide variety of seabirds, often in huge numbers. These islands are important both nationally and internationally for many breeding species and as such are designated National Nature Reserves (NNRs) and Sites of Special Scientific Interest (SSSIs). On the east coast the most noted are the **Bass Rock** and **The Isle of May** in the Firth of Forth, while to the north are the islands around **Orkney** and **Shetland** and on the west coast **Handa Island** near Cape Wrath

To visit these islands and the massive seabird colonies that inhabit their towering cliffs in the breeding season (April to September) is an unforgettable experience. Classic residents include members of the **auk** family, including the **guillemot**, **razorbill** and the **puffin**, without doubt the most colourful and charming seabird in Britain. Unlike the hardy guillemots and razorbills that nest precariously on the cliff ledges, the puffin nests in burrows, which they excavate with razor-sharp claws. After the eggs are incubated and the eggs hatch the chicks are raised in the burrow and this is the best time to view the birds.

The best places to see puffin and the seabird colonies are on a day trip to the Isle of May in the Firth of Forth, in Orkney and Shetland, or Handa Island in the far north west of the country, near Cape Wrath. Several other species inhabit other neighbourhoods within these seabird cities including the **Manx shearwater** and **fulmar**, which are both specialist pelagic petrels. The fulmar is worth special mention because it has the admirable habit of vomiting all over you should you stray too close. One of the most famous seabirds around Scotland is the large and very stern looking **gannet** which is black and white in colour with a 2 m wing span and an ochre coloured head. Its most famous international breeding site is the Bass Rock in the Firth of Forth where over 50,000 pairs breed annually. So famous is the Bass that it lends its name to the Northern or Atlantic gannet's official scientific name, *Morus bassanus*.

Other more unusual rare and resident species you might be very lucky to see on the coast is the **white-tailed sea eagle** around the Western Isles or the beautiful **snowy owl** on Fetlar in Shetland. The sea eagle used to be fairly common but was wiped out in Scotland by early last century. Now, after a successful reintroduction on the Isle of Rùm on the west coast, several pairs breed. The specific nesting locations are understandably keep secret but you may still see one on a fishing foray over its huge territorial range. Like the golden eagle its sheer size is an instant give away while the tail of course distinguishes it from its more common relative. The snowy owl is rarely seen outside Shetland and of course is instantly recognizable.

Some islands around the coast of Scotland are also well known internationally as migratory stopovers for vagrant species. The **Isle of May** in the Firth of Forth and **Fair Isle** between Shetland and Orkney are particularly important and well known often providing life saving shelter in spring and autumn storms for such exotically named species as the **jack snipe** or **black redstart**.

Rivers, lochs **Otters** are more commonly found along riverbanks in Europe but in Scotland are
& wetlands best observed on the tidal fringes searching for seafood. The Isle of Skye and Shetland are the best venues. The otter was for decades almost hunted to extinction in Britain but is now fully protected. It is often confused with the feral **mink** or **ferret**, which is far more commonly seen in the countryside throughout Britain.

Loch Garten in Speyside near Aviemore is the home to the **Osprey** and the venue of one of Scotland's most successful avian conservation stories. After being absent for many years the Loch Garten breeding site became a catalyst for what is now the successful national comeback of the species. You can view the birds nesting in summer at Loch Garten but if you are really lucky you will see one catching fish in a spectacular display of aerial acrobatics on the lochs and rivers of the region. The rivers **Tay** and **Spey** are world famous for their **salmon**. Some of the hydroelectric dams in Scotland have fish ladders where you can observe this archetype of inherent motivation as the fish struggle relentlessly upstream to breed. **Pitlochry** is one such venue.

Although not endemic to Scotland one of the most beautiful bird species you may encounter on the more remote lochs are **divers** (or loons as they are called in North America) – most commonly the red throated diver, the rarer black throated diver and occasionally the largest, the great northern diver. All three can be seen on the coast in winter. The best time to see these birds is in their superb summer breeding attire but it is perhaps their call that is most memorable. The haunting cry of the great northern or black throat that carries for miles across the moors and wide-open spaces is quite simply unforgettable. **Red throated divers** breed on lochs throughout the highlands while **black throated divers** can be found in the far north, especially round Lochinver and in Caithness. Also both rare and beautiful is the delicate **black neck grebe** which supports a headpiece in the breeding season to beat any human fashion label at the annual Royal Ascot horse races. **Loch Ruthven** near Inverness is an excellent place to observe this particular avian fashion parade.

For any Scot who is in tune with the countryside the first calls of greylag and pink footed **geese** are a sure sign that summer has ended. Huge numbers winter in Scotland especially in the central lowlands and parts of the west coast. Similarly, barnacle geese invade the Solway Firth in the south in their thousands. The V-shaped flying formations and constant honking of course make the type of bird if not the actual species instantly identifiable. Of course no mention of Scotland's waterways and wildlife would be complete without mention of Scotland's most famous aquatic creature – the **Loch Ness Monster**. Nessie does of course exist but like the wild haggis is very very shy and elusive.

Forests & lowlands

As opposed to its introduced North American cousin the native **red squirrel** is a delicate and shy creature. Their beautiful rustic colours can often herald their occasional public appearance in the forests of the Central Highlands, especially Speyside. If it were not for the grey squirrel pushing them out of former habitats and man destroying the habitat itself they could once again be classed as common. Even rarer is the elusive and rarely seen **wildcat** and **pine marten**. The wildcat is larger than the domestic 'moggy' and has a much courser, thicker fur coat, piercing, wild eyes and untamed attitude. Over the years the feral cat and wild variety have interbred and now it is very unusual to see the species in its rawest form. The pine marten is about the size of a mink and is occasionally seen in forested areas of more remote and unpopulated areas of the country.

The forests and lowlands are also home to some familiar bird species. The quite bizarre and wonderfully named **capercaille** (pronounced 'capper-kay-lee') is a member of the grouse family and the largest of the three species found in Scotland. It is the handsome black male that is most often seen deep in the forests, most commonly crossing forest paths and fire breaks while guarding his extensive territory. This is necessary not so much as protection from predators, but invasion by other highly sexed males intent on one thing and one thing only. An encounter and subsequent dispute results in audible threats and much puffing up of the plumage. Even more spectacular are the fights between the capercaillie's smaller relative the **black grouse**. Their version of a 'boxing ring' is called a 'lek' and can be the sight of spectacular displays of male hormonal overload.

Other unusual birds of the forest includes the **crossbill**, which is about the size of a overweight canary and has a beak that intersects, which it uses to expertly extract pine seeds from the cone. Crossbills can regularly be seen in the central highlands with National Nature Reserves like Loch Garten being a good bet. While in the Loch

Garten area you may also see the delicate little **crested tit**, which although not endemic, only breeds in this part of Scotland. In much of western Scotland the **hooded crow**, or 'hoodie' replaces the common crow found throughout Britain. The hooded crow can be distinguished by the diagnostic grey patches on its plumage.

Britain's only venomous snake the **adder** is relatively common throughout Scotland and is mainly found on open ground covered in bracken or heather. They are rarely seen and generally keep well out of your way, though you may be lucky enough to encounter one sunning itself on rocks early in the day.

Highlands   The **red deer** are as much an environmental problem as a feature of the Scottish landscape. They now number over 300,000 and in the absence of natural predators are essentially out of control in the central highlands. Extensive management through hunting and culling has so far failed to keep numbers in check. In summer they remain in herds on high ground and, despite their size, they are actually very hard to spot. In winter however you can often see them in large numbers on lower ground in the glens and beside the main roads. During the 'rut' in spring the males (stags) become highly aggressive and use their impressive antlers in fierce combat to win the females (hinds). This fighting is often accompanied by a loud roar that carries for miles. Other deer species seen commonly in Scotland in the Highlands, Central Lowlands and Borders are the roe, sitka and fallow deer.

Another famous Highlands inhabitant is the magnificent **golden eagle**. After periods of decline they are now present in relatively healthy numbers especially in the central and western highlands but are not exactly widespread or commonly seen. To the uninitiated the eagle is very often confused with the common **buzzard**, though the latter is actually much smaller. The golden eagle also dwarfs the large and menacing **raven** that is also a regular sight in central and western Scotland-usually accompanied by a raucous, 'throaty' call. Another regal and masterful lord of the highland skies is the **peregrine falcon**. In both flight and appearance they are the epitome of power. To watch a peregrine hunting other birds in flight is to witness one of the most spectacular acts in nature.

Two quite common masters of camouflage on the mountain slopes are the **mountain hare** and the **ptarmigan**, a bird similar in size and appearance to a red grouse. Both go through an incredible phase of moult from dark browns in summer to pure white in winter. They do this of course in order to blend in with their surroundings and avoid predators like the peregrine. Any time spent around the ski-fields in summer or winter should reveal one or both species.

Other rarer birds found breeding on the inhospitable high tops, especially in the **Cairngorms,** are the **dotterel,** a small attractive wading bird and the sparrow sized **snow bunting**. The snow bunting, like the mountain hare and ptarmigan, assumes a predominantly white plumage in summer. Few breed in Scotland as it is predominantly a winter visitor to the coast. On the lower slopes the **red grouse** is a common sight. Vast tracks of land are maintained to provide the ideal breeding habitat for this 'game bird' which are then hunted for sport.

Further reading

The best general overview of Scottish social history is given by **Professor Chris Smout** in his excellent *A History of the Scottish People (1560-1830)* and *A Century of the Scottish People (1830-1950)*. A worthy new contender is *Scotland A New History*, by **Michael Lynch** (Pimlico, 1999). Also *Scotland the Story of a Nation*, by **Magnus Manusson** (Harper Collins, 2000) is a mighty tome, and after reading it you're unlikely to pass on any questions on Scottish history. For a more emotive and subjective view of highland history, read any of **John** Prebble's books, including *1,000 years of Scotland's History*, *The Lion in the North*, *Glen Coe*, *Culloden* and *The Highland Clearances* (Penguin), or **Nigel Tranter**'s *The Story of Scotland*. Two excellent biographies of the most romantic figures in Scottish history are **Antonia Fraser**'s *Mary, Queen of Scots* (UK Mandarin) and **Fitzroy Maclean**'s *Bonnie Prince Charlie* (Canongate). An entertaining account of Scotland's often turbulent relationship with England is given by **Sir Ludovic Kennedy**'s *In Bed with an Elephant*. **Tom Nairn**'s *The Break-up of Britain* gives a radical perspective of Scottish independence and *Scotland's Story* (Fontana) is also insightful. A comprehensive guide to Scottish culture is **David Daiches**' *The New Companion to Scottish Culture* (Arnold). For an overview of Scottish, *Scottish Art*, by **Murdo Macdonald** (Thames & Hudson, 2000).

History, politics & culture

If you only read one, then make it **James Boswell** & **Samuel Johnson**'s *A Journey to the Western Islands of Scotland* (UK Penguin). Other notables include *In Search of Scotland* by **HV Morton** (Methuen), *A High and Lonely Place* and *Gulfs of Blue Air – A Highland Journey* (Mainstream) by **Jim Crumley** and **Elizabeth Grant** of Rothiemurchus, *Memoirs of a Highland Lady* (Canongate). One of the best known Highland memoirs is *A Ring of Bright Water* by **Gavin Maxwell**; a tale of otters and other wildlife set in Glenelg. *A Last Wild Place* by naturalist **Mike Tomkies** is a fascinating account of life in a remote West Highland croft. Also interesting is *Queen Victoria's Highland Journal*, edited by **David Duff** (UK Hamlyn). For a selection of the best, including Daniel Defoe, Edwin Muir and Jan Morris, there's *The Road North - 300 years of Classic Scottish Travel Writing*, Ed June Skinner Sawyers (The Inn Pinn, 2000).

Travelogues & memoirs

There are numerous **walking guides** available and this is only the briefest of selections. Two of the best are *Great Walks Scotland* by **Hamish Brown** and *100 Best Routes on Scottish Mountains* by **Ralph Storer**. Two helpful hill-walking guides published by the Scottish Mountaineering Trust are *The Munros* by **Donald Bennett** and *The Corbetts* by **Scott Johnstone** et al. The SMT also publishes a range of district guides listing mainly high level walks. Also useful are *The Munro Almanac* and *The Corbett Almanac* by **Cameron McNeish**. A healthy antidote to all those climbing anoraks is **Muriel Gray**'s entertaining and clean-shaven *The First Fifty: Munro Bagging without a Beard* (UK Corgi). Those wishing to attempt one of the long distance walks should read *The West Highland Way* or *The Southern Upland Way*, both highly informative guides by **Roger Smith** (HM Stationery Office). An excellent guide for both walkers and **mountain bikers** is Ralph Storer's *Exploring Scottish Hill Tracks*. Other recommended cycling guides include: *The Scottish Cycling Guide*, by **Brendan Walsh**; *101 Bike Routes in Scotland*, by **Henry Henniker** (Mainstream); *Cycling in Scotland* by **John Hancox** (Collins Pocket Reference, Harper Collins); and *Cycling in Great Britain: Bicycle Touring Adventures in England, Scotland and Wales*, by **Tim Hughes & Jo Cleary** (Bicycle Books, US). For a comprehensive guide to Scotland's **golf courses** try *Scotland – Home of Golf*, a Pastime publication produced by the Scottish Tourist Board and *The Scottish Golf Guide* by **David Hamilton** (Canongate Press). An outsider's view of golf in Scotland can be found in American **Michael Bamberger**'s highly

Outdoor activities

entertaining book *To the Linksland* (Mainstream Publishing), ideal if the Scottish weather keeps you from playing! A good **birdwatching** guide is *Where to Watch Birds in Scotland*, by **Michael Madders** and **Julia Welstead** (UK Christopher Helm).

Miscellaneous For a comprehensive history of Scottish clans and families, see *Scottish Family History*, by **Margaret Stuart and James Balfour Paul** (Edinburgh, 1930), or *The Surnames of Scotland: their origin, meaning and history* by **George Black** (New York, 1940). These books are available in most public libraries. For more detailed genealogical study, look at *Tracing your Ancestors* by Cecil Sinclair (HM Stationery Office). *Exploring Scotland's Heritage* is a beautifully-illustrated series of books on historic buildings and archaeological sites in different regions of Scotland (HM Stationery Office). Those wishing to bone up on their malt whiskies should refer to the *Malt Whisky Companion* by **Michael Jackson** (UK Dorling Kindersley). An excellent Scottish recipe book is the *Claire MacDonald Cookbook* by **Lady Claire MacDonald** (UK Bantam) who runs a hotel on Skye.

Footnotes

14

670

Footnotes

Index

Footnotes

Y

Map Index

Shorts

Will you help us?

We try as hard as we can to make each Footprint Handbook as up-to-date and accurate as possible but, of course, things always change. Many people email or write to us – with corrections, new information, or simply comments. If you want to let us know about your experiences and adventures – be they good, bad or ugly – then don't delay; we're dying to hear from you. And please try to include all the relevant details and juicy bits. Your help will be greatly appreciated, especially by other travellers. In return we will send you details about our special guidebook offer.

email Footprint at:
sco2_online@footprintbooks.com

or write to:
Elizabeth Taylor
Footprint Handbooks
6 Riverside Court
Lower Bristol Road
Bath   BA2 3DZ
UK

Scotland

Altitude in feet

	4,411
	1,828
	914
	457
	183
	0

Motorway

Primary Route, A Road

B Road

Other Road

A1 Road Number

Rail

Border

❼

Shetland Islands

Unst

Yell *Fetlar*

Mainland

Lerwick ○

❷

Orkney Islands

Pentland Firth

❶

North Sea

○ Wick

Lewis

Outer Hebrides

Harris

The Minch

○ Ullapool

North Uist

The Little Minch

Fraserburgh

Peterhead

Benbecula

Skye

○ Inverness

Moray Firth

❷

South Uist

○ Kyle of Lochalsh

Aviemore ○

Aberdeen

Barra

Rùm

○ Mallaig

Eigg

Fort William ○

Inner Hebrides

Coll

Pitlochry ○

Tiree

Mull

○ Oban

Crianlarich ○

Perth ○

Dundee ○

Atlantic Ocean

Colonsay

St Andrews ○

Stirling ○

Firth of Forth

❹

Jura

Greenock ○

Glasgow □

EDINBURGH □

❸

Islay

Bute

Arran

Prestwick ○

Ayr ○

Jedburgh ○

Campbeltown ○

❻

Dumfries ○

NORTHERN IRELAND

Stranraer ○

ENGLAND

Solway Firth

❺

N

0 km   40

0 miles   40

Map 1

A

N

0 km   10
0 miles   10

Flannan Islands or Seven Hunters

57° 50'

Boreray

Hirta

Soay

Dun

St Kilda

8° 30'

B

O u t e r   H e b r i d e s

Mealista Island

Scarp

Gasker

Mealisval (1,884ft) ▲

Loch Suainaval

Uig

Breanais

Timsgearraidh

Miabhig

Bearnaraigh

Bearnaraigh Beag

West Loch Roag

East Loch Roag

Gearrannan

Siabost

Carlabhagh

Tolastadh a'Chaolais

Breascleit

Calanais

Cruiabhig

Gearraidh na h-Aibhne

Einacleit

Achadh Mór

Crosbost

Baile Ailein

Loch Langavat

Loch Reasort

Loch Claidh

Cearsiadar

Grabhair

Leumrabhagh

Loch Shell

Airidh a'Bhruaich

Beinn Mhór (1,877ft) ▲

Loch Seaforth

North Harris (Ceann a Tuath na Hearadh)

Huisinis

Tirga Mór (2,228ft) ▲

Airidh a'Mhulaidh

Clishham (2,622ft) ▲

Abhainnsuidhe

Bun Abhainn Eadarra

Aird Asaig

Tarbert (An Tairbeart)

Urgha

Reinigeadal

Tarasaigh

A859

Caolas Scalpaigh

Scalpay (Eilean Scalpaigh)

Loch Bhrollum

Shiant Islands

Toe Head

South Harris (Ceann a Deas na Hearadh)

Shillay

Taobh Tuath

Pabbay

An t-Ob

Sound of Pabbay

Bearnaraigh

Boreray

Roghadal

Renish Point

Sound of Harris

C

Grimnis Point

Vallay

Baile Mhartainn

Solas

Otternish

Hogha Gearraidh

Cean a'Bhaigh

North Uist (Uibhist a'Tuath)

Lochamaddy (Loch na Madadh)

A865

A867

Claghan na Luib

Baile Seal

Saighdinis

Loch Euphoirt

Cairinis

Heisker or Monach Islands

Sound of Monach

Baile a'Mhanaich

Uachdar

A865

Benbecula (Beinn na Faoghla)

Creag Ghoraidh

Ardivachar Point

Loch Bee

Wiay

Bàgh nam Faoillean

Stadhlaigearraidh

Loch Sgioport

South Uist (Uibhist a'Deas)

Rubha Ardvuie

Isle of Lewis (Eilean Leòdhais)

Rubh' Robhanais

Eoropaidh

Tabost

Dail Bho Dheas

Sgiogarsta

Gabhsann Bho Dheas

Siadar

Baile an Truiseil

A857

Arnol

Barabhas

Bragar

Muirneag (814ft) ▲

Tolastadh Ùr

Griais

Rubha a'Tuath

Siabost

A858

Gearrannan

Beinn Mholach (958ft) ▲

Newmarket

Stornoway (Steòrnabhagh)

A857

Tunga

Port nan Giùran

Siulaisiadar

A866

An Rubha

A858

Loch Erisort

Loch a'Tuath

Rubha t-Siumpain

Little Minch

Vaternish Point

Rubha Hunish

Duntulm Castle

Kilmaluag

Kilmuir

A855

Staffin Bay

Staffin

Linicro

Culnaknock

Uig

Trotternish

A855

Trumpan

Ben Geary (932ft) ▲

Waternish

Loch Snizort

The Storr (2,360ft) ▲

Kensaleyre

Edinbane

Bernisdale

Borve

Dunvegan Head

Lusta

Boreraig

Loch Dunvegan

Milovaig

Dunvegan Castle

A850

Dunvegan

Carbost

Portree

Neist Point

Roskhill

Duirinish

Sound of Raasay

Healabhal Bheag (1,602ft) ▲

Skye

Bracadale

A87

Oskaig

Clachan

Feinchorran

A863

Portnalong

Talisker

Carbost

Sconser

Sligachan

A87

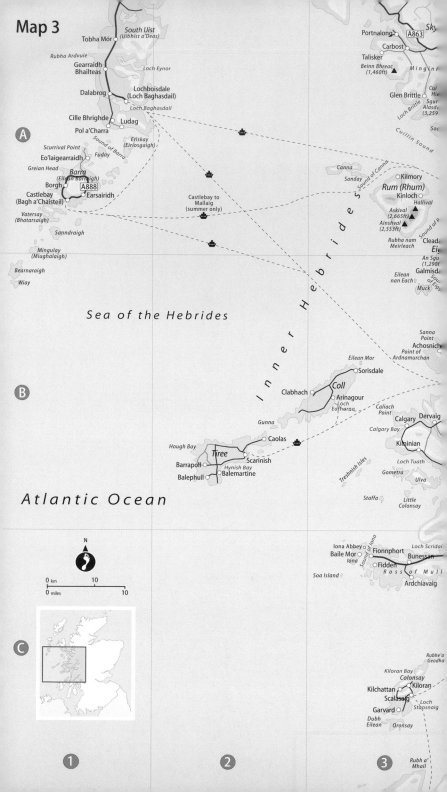

Map 3

South Uist (Uibhist a'Deas)
Tobha Mór
Rubha Ardvuie
Gearraidh Bhailteas
Loch Eynor
Dalabrog
Lochboisdale (Loch Baghasdail)
Loch Baghasdail
Cille Bhrighde
Ludag
Pol a'Charra
Eriskay (Eiriosgaigh)
A
Scurrival Point
Eo'laigearraidh
Fuday
Greian Head
Barra (Eilean Barraigh)
Borgh
A888
Earsairidh
Castlebay (Bagh a'Chaisteil)
Vatersay (Bhatarsaigh)
Sanndraigh

Castlebay to Mallaig (summer only)

Mingulay (Miughalaigh)
Bearnaraigh
Wiay

Sea of the Hebrides

Portnalong
A863
Sky
Carbost
Talisker
Beinn Bhreac (1,460ft)
Mingini
Cui Hi
Glen Brittle
Sgur Alasde (3,259
Loch Brittle
Cuillin Sound
Soc
Canna
Sanday
Sound of Canna
Kilmory
Rum (Rhum)
Kinloch
Hallival
Askival (2,665ft)
Ainshval (2,553ft)
Sound of R
Rubha nam Meirleach
Cleada
Ei
An Sgu (1,290f
Galmisda
Sou of Eisg
Eilean nan Each
Muck

I n n e r   H e b r i d e s

Eilean Mor
Sorisdale
Clabhach
Coll
Arinagour
Loch Eatharna
B
Gunna
Caliach Point
Calgary
Dervaig
Calgary Bay
Kilninian
Caolas
Loch Tuath
Hough Bay
Tiree
Scarinish
Treshnish Isles
Barrapoll
Hynish Bay
Balemartine
Gometra
Ulva
Balephuil
Staffa
Little Colonsay

Atlantic Ocean

Sanna Point
Achosnich
Point of Ardnamurchan

N
0 km   10
0 miles   10

Iona Abbey
Baile Mor
Iona
Fionnphort
Loch Scridai
Bunessan
Fidden
Sound of Iona
Ross of Mull
Soa Island
Ardchiavaig

C

Rubhe'a Geodha
Kiloran Bay
Colonsay
Kiloran
Kilchattan
Scalasaig
Loch Staosnaig
Garvard
Dubh Eilean
Oronsay
Rubh a' Mhail

1   **2**   **3**

Map 7 Shetland Isles

Acknowledgements

Alan Murphy would like to thank those who contributed to this book. Rebecca Ford is a full-time travel writer, who specialises in Britain and Italy. Her work has appeared in publications such as the Daily Telegraph, the Evening Standard and Scotland on Sunday. Rebecca researched and updated the Glasgow, Southern Scotland and Central Scotland chapters, as well as contributing to the Edinburgh chapter and History section.

Laura Dixon researched and updated the Inner Hebrides and Highlands and Skye chapters whilst braving the Scottish winter, and Norma Rowlerson updated Northeast Scotland as well as contributing to the History section and providing several new walks. Nigel Easton updated the Outer Hebrides chapter and also provided information on environmental issues. John Murphy updated the pubs and clubs of Edinburgh, Jane Hamilton updated the Glasgow entertainment section and John Binney researched Glasgow's gay clubs and bars.

Suzy Kennard wrote the History and Architecture sections, Duncan Lindsay wrote Music, Frank Nicholas wrote Literature and Darroch Donald wrote Wildlife.

Thanks also to those who helped with the research of the first edition: Suzy Kennard for the Northeast Highlands; William Clyde for Dundee; Duncan Lindsay for Perth; Norma Rowlerson for Aberdeen and Deeside; Sarah Thorowgood for Orkney and Shetland and John Murphy for Edinburgh.

Thanks go to the staff of the many local and regional tourist offices for their invaluable advice and assistance, to the staff at Caledonian McBrayne, the National Trust for Scotland and Historic Scotland.

A special thank you to Catherine Charles and all at Footprint, for their support and hard work and, as always, to Philippa, for her patience and support.

Alan Murphy

Born and raised in Fife, Alan Murphy then moved to Dundee where he embarked on a career in journalism. Ten years later he abandoned his freeloading playboy lifestyle and escaped to the relative obscurity of Bolivia, where he taught English, raised money for orphaned street children and helped establish an English language newspaper.

After brief stints as a performing condor in the Oruro Carnival and professional llama-wrestler in Potosí, Alan suffered a near-fatal accident and retired. Many months later, he turned up in London, where fate played her propitious hand and introduced him to the editor of the legendary South American Handbook.

The rest, as they say, is history. Alan now lives in Bath with his wife and family. As well as the Scotland Handbook, he has written Footprint guides to Bolivia, Ecuador, Peru, Venezuela, Edinburgh and Scotland Highlands and Islands.